DISCLOSURE

Third Edition

AUSTRALIA
Law Book Co.
Sydney

CANADA and USA
Carswell
Toronto

HONG KONG
Sweet & Maxwell Asia

NEW ZEALAND
Brookers
Wellington

SINGAPORE and MALAYSIA
Sweet & Maxwell Asia
Singapore and Kuala Lumpur

LITIGATION LIBRARY

DISCLOSURE

(being the third edition of DISCOVERY)

by

Paul Matthews, B.C.L. (Oxon.), LL.D. (Lond.)
Consultant Solicitor, Withers LLP
H.M. Coroner for the City of London
Visiting Professor, King's College, London

and

Hodge M. Malek Q.C., B.C.L., M.A. (Oxon.)
One of Her Majesty's Counsel,
A Bencher of Gray's Inn
A Recorder of the Crown Court

WITH A FOREWORD BY

The Rt. Hon. Lord Mance
A Lord of Appeal in Ordinary

LONDON
SWEET & MAXWELL
2007

Published in 2007 by
Sweet & Maxwell Limited of
100 Avenue Road,
London NW3 3PF
http://www.sweetandmaxwell.co.uk
Typeset by Interactive Sciences Ltd,
Gloucester
Printed and bound in Great Britain by
William Clowes Ltd, Beccles, Suffolk

A CIP catalogue record for
this book is available
from the British Library

ISBN 9780421922204

FOREWORD

Disclosure remains a key area in which English common law differs both from the more exhaustive procedures of American common law and from the less exhaustive rules of civil law jurisdictions. Most lawyers recall cases where disclosure assisted to get to the bottom of the facts. How frequently such assistance proves crucial may be open to question, as Lord Steyn observed in the foreword to the first edition. But differences between different countries in procedure and efficiency are probably more important to average litigants than differences in substantive law. Procedural delays and costs, for example, can make legal systems inaccessible or unattractive (except sometimes for those seeking to avoid justice). The speed of English law may be generally satisfactory, but cost is a real concern. Despite the practical relevance, procedural law has only quite recently begun to attract the academic treatment that it deserves. This work is in the vanguard.

Disclosure in English common law remains a central aspect of pre-trial preparation, capable of occupying time, incurring cost and giving rise to difficult issues of case management and law. The second edition of this work addressed the impact of the then recent Civil Procedure Rules on disclosure. This third edition provides a welcome update on both the law and practice, including a whole new chapter on electronic disclosure.

In this chapter, as elsewhere throughout the work, the authors include much useful foreign material. Not surprisingly American courts have been at the fore in grappling with the special problems arising from modern electronic communications. Paradoxically, the informality and ease of such communications vastly increases their potential for giving rise to disclosable documentation. As one American judge is quoted saying, "many informal messages that were previously relayed by telephone or at the water cooler are now sent by e-mail". Emails may be copied and responses sent, at a click and not always intentionally, to a multitude of others. And, lest it be thought that deletion, or saving a new version on top of an old, ends the trail, the authors explain the existence of embedded data, metadata, replicant data, back up data and residual data, as well as the revisions to CPR Pt 31 made (after the report of a working party chaired by Mr Justice Cresswell) with a view to constraining within reasonable bounds the disclosure requests of over-diligent or aggressive litigators.

This excellent work has had from its outset a clear and logical scheme upon which the authors have been able to continue to build. The exposition is lucid, perceptive and thorough. It is a great pleasure to commend it to practitioners and others interested in the area alike.

Jonathan Mance

House of Lords
2 March 2007

FOREWORD TO THE SECOND EDITION

It is sometimes asserted that in civil proceedings the task of a common law court is not to establish the truth but simply to resolve whether the claimant has discharged the burden of proof lying upon him. In a formal sense this is true. In reality it is not: the mills of adversarial litigation grind so exceeding small that by the end of a contested action the judge is usually in as good a position as anyone could be to decide exactly what happened and why.

In this process of establishing the truth, compulsory disclosure plays a crucial part. Letters, diary entries, memos and minutes made or written at the time often provide a surer guide to the truth than what the participants say years later when differences have arisen. So it is not surprising that a detailed code of rules has been developed to govern the disclosure of documents and information, nor that an ever-lengthening body of case law should have grown up around the subject.

This book provides a detailed, orderly and comprehensive summary of the law on disclosure in all its aspects. It is a treasure-house of learning, clearly and accurately distilled. And in this second edition the authors are able to present the law on disclosure in the new setting of the Civil Procedure Rules, with their timely recognition that while compulsory disclosure, properly conducted, can be a blessing it can also, improperly conducted, become an abuse.

A second edition of this book will prove invaluable to courts and practitioners as they seek to ensure that the process of compulsory disclosure is used to promote the ends of justice, by unearthing the truth, and not to wear down an opponent by subjecting him to disproportionate and unfruitful work and expense.

Tom Bingham

House of Lords
November 2, 2000

FOREWORD TO THE FIRST EDITION

A mastery of the rules of procedure is an essential qualification for a litigation lawyer. And there is probably no branch of the law of civil procedure governing trial actions which is of greater practical importance than discovery. But the published material on the subject was meagre and unsystematic. This book fills the gap. The authors are respectively a solicitor and barrister. That combination of authorship was a considerable advantage because not infrequently the perspectives of the two branches of the legal profession are slightly different. Both authors are highly experienced trial lawyers. A further advantage was the fact that one of the authors, Mr. Paul Matthews, is a former fulltime academic. That also shows. The subject has been intensively researched, and comparative sources have been extensively used. It is a carefully crafted work. Above all I applaud the fact that the authors have given a complicated and diffuse subject a logical and systematic framework.

Subject to a few limited criticisms of judicial decisions the authors have contented themselves with stating the law as it is. No doubt they were right to follow that course in a first edition. But I hope that in the next edition they will express criticism of precedents, which the authors regard as wrongly decided, more freely and trenchantly. In England we need more, not less, criticism of the decisions of courts. There is a tendency in England for some textbook writers to be too reverential towards aberrant judicial decisions which are often artificially fitted into the mosaic of the law by piling qualification upon qualification. That does not help students, the practising profession or judges.

Standing back from the minutiae of discovery, it seems to me appropriate to consider whether our system of discovery is satisfactory. Traditionally, English lawyers regard discovery as a great engine of truth in the civil justice system. Indeed, many think that without a mutual obligation imposed on parties to give discovery of documents which are damaging to their case, or of assistance to the opponents' case, a fair trial is not possible. A trial without discovery would be "trial by ambush." But there is another point of view. While it is not usually safe to generalise about a group of legal systems, it is tolerably clear that in civil law jurisdictions there is nothing like the English system of discovery. This fundamental difference in approach has been highlighted by the saying that "in England a lawyer is disbarred from practising for not giving discovery; in France he is disbarred for giving discovery."

While as English lawyers we understandably feel comfortable with our own system, I wonder whether it is really the case that the existing process of discovery significantly improves the prospect of a court arriving at the correct conclusion. Personally I would question any proposition that an English court is substantially more likely to arrive at the correct conclusion than a civilian court. But it is clear that the hearing of trial actions, and the hearing of arbitration proceedings, last markedly longer in England than comparable proceedings in continental countries. Sophisticated foreign users of the Commercial Court, and of London arbitration, frequently place the abuses of the discovery process at the top of the list of criticisms of London as a major centre of dispute resolution. There is a real problem. The discovery process often runs riot. It is the experience of Commercial judges that usually 95 per cent of the documents contained in the trial bundles are wholly irrelevant and never mentioned by either side. The discovery process adds greatly to the duration and cost of litigation, and helps a defendant (or plaintiff) to put off the day of financial reckoning. It contributes to the tyranny of modern civil litigation.

Unheroically, I must confess that I do not know what the solution is. I would not suggest that the existing system of discovery be abandoned but it seems to me that there should be a debate about ways of eliminating the abuses of the system. Tentatively, I would mention only three matters. First, in group actions and other complex litigation case management techniques, involving more interventionist judicial control than is presently usual, may assist. Secondly, we may have to move away from the attachment to one large scale hearing of an action to the continental system of hearing a case in logical phases, with discovery limited to the phase under consideration, for example, if the issue in a contractual dispute is whether there is a valid defence in reliance on an exception clause there is no reason to allow wide ranging discovery until that issue has been determined. Thirdly, it is possible that judges of first instance may be able to discipline the process of discovery more effectively by an appropriate order of costs where a party has made unnecessarily wide requests for discovery. I would hope that there are other and better ideas to achieve a much needed improvement of the system of discovery. In recent years our trial procedures have become markedly more open and efficient. It may be that the time has come also to focus attention on the abuses of pre-trial discovery.

In the meantime it is my great pleasure to commend to those who have to grapple with problems of discovery under existing law and practice this excellent new textbook.

Johan Steyn

Norfolk
September 1992

PREFACE
DISCLOSURE
THIRD EDITION 2007

It is now some 15 years since the first edition of this work was published. In that time the face of English civil litigation has completely changed. First, the procedural rules have been swept away and replaced by a new code, designed to reduce the delay and cost inherent up until now in litigation. Secondly, the advent of the internet and hence of email have both revolutionised everyday communications, and made it so much easier to obtain information about any subject under the sun. Thirdly, the enactment of the Human Rights Act 1998 has directed the attention of practitioners to internationally agreed standards of justice, against which our own rules may be measured.

That is not to say that any or all of these developments has necessarily been a good thing, or entirely successful even in its own terms. For example, much of the costs formerly involved in the early stages of litigation is now incurred beforehand, in compliance with the many "Protocols", and there is little or no reduction in overall cost in such cases. Again, huge amounts of court time have been and are currently spent on human rights issues, to the obvious detriment (since judicial resources are not infinitely expandable) of arguments on other, perhaps more substantive, matters. Yet so far the courts have for the most part found the English law Convention-compliant, so meaning that the beneficial return on the capital employed has been disproportionately small.

In this edition we have been able to look at how the Civil Procedure Rules really work in practice. This has necessitated a good deal of additional material and rewriting. We have also added a new chapter on Electronic Disclosure, and moved or rearranged other chapters so as to produce what we consider to be a more harmonious whole. In addition, there have been significant judicial developments in some areas of the law, such as privilege, which have been reflected in the new text. We have continued our practice of referring to significant Commonwealth and US cases, as we consider that the common law still has much to offer us all in the Anglophone legal world. It is our hope that our readers will think so too.

As usual, there are many people to thank for their assistance in the preparation of this edition. These include Jonathan Auburn, the Hon. Michael Beloff Q.C., Katie Bradford, Clive Freedman, Kay Georgiou, Dawn Goodman, Ann Kavanagh, Jonathan Maas, Ali Malek Q.C., Jeff Ourvan, Jeremy Scott, Kathy Stewart, Turlough Stone and Paula Stuart. We also thank our families for their forbearance during the time that we absented ourselves to work on the new edition.

We have attempted to state the law in the light of materials available to us as at December 2006, though we have managed to squeeze in a few references to subsequent developments. Finally, we invite our readers to let us have their comments and suggestions for future improvement. These are extremely useful to us.

Gray's Inn and   Hodge Malek Q.C.
City of London   Paul Matthews
9 March 2007

CONTENTS

PART 1
INTRODUCTION

Chapter 1
Introduction

PART 2
DOCUMENTARY DISCLOSURE

Chapter 2
Time of Discloure

Chapter 10
Production by non-parties

Chapter 11
Objections to inspection

Chapter 12
Loss of privilege

Chapter 13
Failure to Comply with Disclosure Obligation

Chapter 14
Solicitor's Obligations

Chapter 15
Collateral use of Documents

PART 3
NON-DOCUMENTARY DISCLOSURE

Chapter 16
Information Requests

Chapter 17
Other Disclosure of Facts

Chapter 18
Experts' Reports

Chapter 19
Real Evidence

PART 4
OTHER ASPECTS OF DISCLOSURE

Chapter 20
Disclosure in other Courts and Tribunals

Chapter 21
The impact of the Human Rights Act 1998

Appendices

Table of Cases

Table of Statutes

Table of Statutory Instruments

Table of Civil Procedure Rules

Table of Practice Directions and Pre-Action Protocols

CHAPTER 1

Introduction

CHAPTER 1

Introduction

A. NATURE AND PURPOSES OF DISCLOSURE

Historically, discovery was the name generally given to the procedure or **1.01** procedures by means of which one party to civil proceedings obtained compulsory disclosure of documents and other information relevant to those proceedings from another party or, exceptionally, from a non-party, *in advance of the trial*. The term "disclosure", which is now used in the Civil Procedure Rules 1998 ("CPR"), introduced in England and Wales with effect from April 26, 1999,[1] is in practice synonymous with "discovery". In this work the term disclosure is usually used in respect of the practice since the introduction of the CPR. Unlike in some legal systems, the "discovery" rules never applied as such in criminal proceedings in English law,[2] although there were (and are) certain analogous procedures.[3] Most civil proceedings in England are *accusatorial*, where one party alleges facts and another denies them, rather than *inquisitorial*, where there are no allegations and the tribunal is charged to find out the truth of the matter.[4] Whilst the latter system seeks to establish an absolute, the former system is relative, and seeks only to do justice as between the parties themselves.[5] Thus, instead of the judge taking it upon himself to investigate the matter, in the accusatorial system it is for the parties themselves to do so, and to present the facts found, if they think fit, in support of their respective allegations. Moreover,

---

[1] Having replaced "discovery" in the civil procedure of Queensland from May 1, 1994; see para.1.28 below.

[2] Bray, *Discovery* (1884) at p.3.

[3] See Ch.2, para.2.05, below.

[4] Rare examples of inquisitorial procedure in England include coroners' inquests, wardship proceedings, patent extensions and certain regulatory proceedings. Sir Richard Scott V.C. on March 22, 2000, at the 3rd Sir Michael Davies Lecture, expressed the view that the CPR mean that the new system in England cannot be regarded as an adversarial system "without a good deal of qualification".

[5] *cf.* the doctrine of "issue estoppel": *Carl Zeiss Stiftung v Rayner & Keeler Ltd* [1967] 1 A.C. 853, HL.

the importance in the common law system of the single, lengthy trial hearing means that all preparation must be completed in advance.[6]

1.02 Although much information can be obtained voluntarily, some cannot, and often the most relevant information is in the hands of the opposing party, who will certainly not disclose it willingly if it hurts his own case. Accordingly, compulsory procedures are needed to ensure that the parties are able successfully to extract all relevant documents and other information from others and thus to find evidence supporting their own case and undermining that of their opponents.[7] Further purposes of disclosure are to enable a party, on the one hand, to obtain the best possible evidence or admissions from his opponent and, on the other, to evaluate the strength of the opponent's case, in either case tending to shorten and thus lessen the cost of litigation. The perceived advantages of the disclosure process include fairness to both sides, playing "with all the cards face up on the table",[8] clarifying the issues between the parties, reducing surprise at trial and encouraging settlement.[9] Any system of disclosure should have as a broad rationale the just and efficient disposal of litigation.[10] It is against this broad rationale that any reforms should be considered.

1.03 Disclosure is not without its disadvantages. The principal one is that disclosure can be an expensive and burdensome process.[11] The courts are generally alert to the danger of oppressive disclosure and inappropriate requests for wide ranging disclosure are not infrequently dismissed for being not necessary for the fair disposal of litigation. The burden can not only fall on the party giving disclosure, but also on an opposing party presented with a mass of documentation of marginal relevance.[12] In such a case disclosure can, far from clarifying the issues, operate as a cloud. One of the reasons for the change in the disclosure rules in the CPR is to cut down the extent, and hence cost, of disclosure and for the disclosure to be proportionate to the case in hand.[13]

1.04 As will be seen later, disclosure in England is very much less extensive than in the United States,[14] and it is therefore sometimes criticised as not going far enough in support of the professed purposes and advantages.[15]

---

[6] See Zweigert and Kötz, *An Introduction to Comparative Law* (3rd edn, 1998), Ch.18, V.

[7] Where the proceedings are of an inquisitorial nature, powers to achieve this are usually conferred on the tribunal itself and not on the parties involved in the proceedings.

[8] *Naylor v Preston Area Health Authority* [1987] 1 W.L.R. 858 at 967, CA; *Davies v Eli Lilly & Co.* [1987] 1 W.L.R. 428 at 431, CA; *Black & Decker Inc v Flymo Ltd* [1991] 1 W.L.R. 753.

[9] In the nineteenth century a different view was taken: see, e.g. *Re Strachan* [1895] 1 Ch. 439 at 445–6, 447–8.

[10] See Lord Woolf's *Interim Report*, June 1995, Ch.21, paras 8–9, 18.

[11] *ibid.*, paras 3–4.

[12] *ibid.*, paras 5–6.

[13] *ibid.*, para.20.

[14] Paras 1.21 to 1.22, below.

[15] See, e.g. Levine, *Discovery* (1982), *passim*, and Cairns, *The Law of Discovery in Australia* (1984) at pp.2–3.

For example, it has been argued that, if disclosure was more far-reaching, more cases would be settled.[16] Whether this hypothesis would prove true for England if tested is unclear,[17] but there is no doubt that widened disclosure would be even more cumbersome and expensive than now,[18] and there is an undoubted "trade-off" to be obtained in buying comparative speed and cheapness (and hence accessibility to the courts) at the price of less perfect justice. This is one of the rationales behind Lord Woolf's reforms to the civil justice system, and the new CPR. Moreover, the almost invariable use of advance witness statements in modern civil proceedings[19] has gone some way to supply information previously lacking in English discovery of documents, and at much less cost than the witness deposition hearings which are such a feature of US pre-trial litigation procedure.[20]

B. MEANS OF DISCLOSURE

Disclosure under English law is given in a variety of ways and detailed   1.05
exposition of these is the main subject matter of this work. For present purposes they can be broken down into three general categories:

- (a) documents;
- (b) information;
- (c) real evidence.

(a) Disclosure of documents

Disclosure of the existence, past or present, of relevant documents is   1.06
usually given by list, known as a List of Documents.[21] This identifies the documents concerned, although, in the case of documents which are for some reason privileged from production,[22] the identification is very general, and need give no clue as to contents. Once notice of the existence of these documents has been given, those that are still in the party's control and not privileged from production must be produced for inspection and copying by

---

[16] *ibid.*

[17] See, e.g. The Justice Report, *Going to Law, A Critique of English Civil Procedure* (1974) where a number of recommendations for improving civil procedure were made, but none suggesting an extension of discovery; *cf. Re Strachan* [1895] 1 Ch. 439.

[18] See *Going to Law, A Critque of English Civil Procedure* (1974), Ch.5, paras 132–133.

[19] See Ch.17, paras 17.20–17.32, below.

[20] See, e.g. Levine, *op.cit.*, Ch.6; as to the Canadian experience, see Park and Cromie (eds.), *International Commercial Litigation* (2nd edn, 1997), pp.122–128.

[21] See Ch.6, below.

[22] See Ch.11, below.

other parties.[23] In terms of time and effort expended, this is the most important and time consuming part of the English disclosure process.

(b) Disclosure of information

1.07   Usually the information consists of facts, but sometimes of opinion. There are several ways in which this form of disclosure can be given:

(1) interrogatories, written questions relevant to the matters in issue which must be answered on oath, and designed to elicit evidence or even admissions from an opponent before the trial[24]; in England and Wales, interrogatories have now been replaced by information requests under CPR, Pt 18;

(2) witness statements, being unsworn written statements served before the trial of the evidence proposed to be given in chief by witnesses intended to be called at trial[25];

(3) experts' reports, which are similar to witness statements, except that they contain proposed expert opinion evidence rather than intended evidence of fact[26];

(4) depositions of witnesses, who for one reason or another give their evidence on oath before the trial, usually before an examiner of the court[27];

(5) letters of request, whether to foreign courts for the purposes of English proceedings or to the English courts for the purposes of foreign proceedings. These seek evidence on specified subjects, sometimes in the form of a written questionnaire, sometimes in the form of a deposition.[28]

Until comparatively recently, interrogatories and (to a lesser extent) depositions were the most important forms of this kind of discovery. Nowadays, witness statements and experts' reports are the most common, although prior to their replacement by information requests by CPR, Pt 18, the use of interrogatories had been encouraged by rule changes enabling them to be administered without the need for the leave of the court.[29]

---

[23] See Ch.9, below, and CPR, r.31.8 which defines "control" broadly. Formerly the requirement related to documents in a party's "possession, custody or power": see Ch.5, paras 5.39–5.54.

[24] See Ch.16, below.

[25] See Ch.17, paras 17.20–17.32, below.

[26] See Ch.18 below.

[27] See Ch.17, paras 17.01–17.09 below.

[28] See *ibid.*, paras 17.10–17.19, below.

[29] See Ch.16, para.16.03, below.

(c) Disclosure of real evidence

This refers mainly to the evidence that is derived from examining things, **1.08**
whether immovable property (e.g. land or buildings), or movable property
(e.g. machinery that is alleged to have caused an accident), or even people
(e.g. to ascertain the extent of injury or disability). This kind of disclosure
is usually given by a party's permitting his opponent to inspect property in
his possession or to which he has access,[30] or submitting to a personal
medical examination.[31] Exceptionally, it can also be given by the carrying
out of scientific experiments, as in patent proceedings.[32]

Although the above represent the main ways in which disclosure is given **1.09**
before trial or other final hearing, there are other procedures which have a
similar purpose, although it is not their *primary* purpose. These include
Mareva (freezing) injunctions,[33] *Anton Piller* (search) orders,[34] the Bankers'
Books Evidence Act 1879,[35] and witness summonses (formerly *subpoenas
duces tecum*),[36] and they are discussed at appropriate points later on in this
work.

C. HISTORY OF DISCOVERY

The origins of discovery in English law are obscure, but they appear to lie **1.10**
in the procedures of the civilian courts, such as the ecclesiastical courts.[37]
But from an early date[38] similar techniques were also developed and
employed in the various courts of equity, of which the most important was
the Court of Chancery.[39] By the late eighteenth century, the plaintiff's bill of
complaint in a Chancery suit invariably had three parts: allegations of fact
("stating part"), evidence ("charging part") and interrogatories to the defendant ("interrogating part"). Thus the bill included a discovery aspect from
the outset.[40] The plaintiff could also obtain discovery and production of
documents from the defendant by a separate "bill of discovery".[41] The
defendant could obtain similar discovery of facts and documents from the
plaintiff, by means of a "cross-bill". On the other hand, the common law

---

[30] See Ch.19, paras 19.02–19.13 below.
[31] *ibid.*, paras 19.20–19.22, below.
[32] *ibid.*, paras 19.14–19.19, below.
[33] See Ch.2, paras 2.11–2.19, below.
[34] *ibid.*, paras 2.20–2.30, below.
[35] See Ch.10, paras 10.37–10.53, below.
[36] *ibid.*, paras 10.02–10.36, below.
[37] Holdsworth, *A History of English Law*, Vol.XII, pp.678–680; see Gilbert, *History and Practice of the High Court of Chancery* (1757), Ch.2.
[38] *ibid.* Vol.V, pp.281–282, 332; see Vol.IV, pp.275–276.
[39] See, e.g. Jones, *The Elizabethan Court of Chancery* (1967), pp.455–457; Gilbert, *op.cit.*, Ch.3.
[40] Story, *Equity Jurisprudence* (2nd edn, 1839), para.689.
[41] *ibid.*, para.1483.

courts (except the Court of Exchequer in its equity jurisdiction) had prior to 1851 no general power to order discovery, though they did possess limited and somewhat technical methods of obtaining inspection of documents, including *profert and oyer* (deeds referred to in pleadings),[42] the so-called "equitable jurisdiction" (duty or trust to make documents available),[43] and *mandamus* (documents of a public character, e.g. court rolls, corporation documents).[44] Where the common law would not assist, a litigant had to go into Chancery to obtain discovery (including interrogatories) for his action.[45] The Evidence Act 1851 and the Common Law Procedure Act 1854 for the first time conferred powers on the common law courts to order general discovery and interrogatories, and although these were based on the practice in Chancery, they were exercised somewhat more narrowly than under that practice.[46] Nevertheless, it meant that a common law litigant no longer had to resort to the Court of Chancery for discovery.

1.11   The Supreme Court of Judicature Act 1873 wrought immense reforms in the English legal system as from 1875. The common law courts, the Court of Chancery, the Court of Exchequer Chamber and the Court of Appeal in Chancery were all abolished, and replaced by the unified Supreme Court of Judicature, comprising a single first instance court—the High Court of Justice—and a single appellate court—the Court of Appeal. The Supreme Court was "unified" in that it possessed unlimited legal *and* equitable jurisdiction. Although the judges of its trial level, the High Court, sat in "divisions" corresponding to the old independent courts, every High Court judge administered both law and equity. The Schedule to the 1873 Act (subsequently replaced by the Rules of the Supreme Court 1883) prescribed the procedure of the High Court, including that relating to discovery. The 1873 Act was first replaced by the Supreme Court of Judicature Act 1925, and subsequently by the Supreme Court Act 1981. Prior to the introduction of the CPR in 1999, the rules in the High Court were the Rules of the Supreme Court 1965, as amended.[47] In this work those rules are referred to simply as the RSC, and the current rules as the CPR. Some of the RSC have been retained with modifications after the introduction of the CPR, and are contained in Schedule 1 to those rules.

1.12   When the High Court was set up in 1875, its procedural rules on discovery were largely drawn from the practice of the Court of Chancery,

---

[42] See Bray, *op.cit.,* at p.264.

[43] *ibid.* at pp.264–269.

[44] *ibid.* at pp.281–290.

[45] The procedure of staying a common law action whilst proceeding by bill in equity for discovery is described in *McLean v Burns Philp Trustee Co. Pty Ltd* (1985) 2 N.S.W.L.R. 623 at 644; see also *Re Application of Cojuangco* (1986) 4 N.S.W.L.R. 513. The Chancery procedure by way of action for discovery is recognised in New South Wales by Pt I, r.14 of the N.S.W. Supreme Court Rules 1970, and in Tasmania by Ord.1, r.2(h) of the Civil Process Rules 1985.

[46] *Jones v Monte Video Gas Co.* (1879) 5 Q.B.D. 556 at 558.

[47] See *The Supreme Court Practice 1999* (the "White Book").

rather than from that of the common law courts.[48] To the extent that a specific provision was inconsistent with the previous discovery practice it necessarily prevailed over that practice,[49] but the new rules did not constitute an exhaustive code, and hence, if there was a gap in the discovery rules, it could be filled by referring to that previous practice.[50] Where the discovery practice in equity differed from that at common law, the court could adopt whichever practice it considered most suitable in the light of the procedural changes brought about by the 1873 Act.[51] However, if what was in question was whether a right of discovery existed in principle, then the court would look at the rules of equity alone.[52] Changes in the rules and also in general practice mean that caution must be exercised in using old discovery case law. In one case, prior to the new rules embodied in the CPR, the judge said that:

" . . . the citation of 19th century cases decided under different circumstances . . . and under different Rules of Court is not a correct approach to providing an answer to practical questions of procedure in the last decade of the 20th century under the present Rules of Court."[53]

The position of the county court must also be mentioned. The modern system of county courts, as a network of local courts with jurisdiction limited in territory and in claim value, dates from 1846.[54] From the outset the county court administered both law and equity. It had always had its own procedural rules, the rules prior to the CPR being the County Court Rules 1981,[55] referred to in this work as "CCR". They were based on, and to some extent incorporated, the Rules of the Supreme Court, but were frequently different, often in form and sometimes also in substance. The CPR now apply in both the High Court and the County Court. Some of the CCR have been retained—with modifications—and are now contained in Sch.2 to the CPR.

1.13

---

[48] *Jones v Monte Video Gas Co.* (1879) 5 Q.B.D. 556; *Lyell v Kennedy* (1883) 8 App.Cas. 217 at 223.

[49] *Bolckow, Vaughan & Co. v Fisher* (1883) 10 Q.B.D. 161 at 168.

[50] *Wilson v Church* (1878) 9 Ch.D. 552 at 554–556; *Att.Gen. v Gaskill* (1882) 20 Ch.D. 519 at 526, 528, 530.

[51] *Newbiggin-by-the-Sea Gas Co. v Armstrong* (1880) 13 Ch.D. 310, CA; *Jones v Monte Video Gas Co.* (1880) 5 Q.B.D. 556; *cf. Parker v Wells* (1881) 18 Ch.D. 477 at 485.

[52] *Kearsley v Phillips* (1883) 10 Q.B.D. 465 at 466; *Norwich Pharmacal Co. v Commissioners of Customs & Excise* [1974] A.C. 133, HL.

[53] *Sveriges Anfartygs Assurens Forening v The 1976 Eagle Assurance Co. S.A.,* March 28, 1990, unreported, Hobhouse J.

[54] County Courts Act 1846; see now the County Courts Act 1984; Polden, *A History of the County Court 1846–1971.*

[55] See *The Supreme Court Practice 1999* , Vol.1, pp.1829 ff; *The County Court Practice 1997* (the "Green Book").

1.14   Although the vast majority of civil disputes in England are dealt with by the High Court and the county court, it has to be borne in mind that a great many such disputes are resolved by specialist courts and tribunals, or by arbitrations. In some cases the discovery procedures are based on, or at least influenced by, those available in the High Court or county court; in other cases they are *sui generis*, or there are none at all. An overview of the position in these various courts and tribunals is given later.[56] Moreover, even before the reforms of 1875 the courts of common law and of equity had no monopoly of discovery techniques: the civilian courts (e.g. admiralty, ecclesiastical)[57] up to the middle of the nineteenth century employed a number of such procedures,[58] which are even today reflected in some of the civilian systems of continental Europe.[59]

D. COMPARATIVE DISCOVERY

1.15   Discovery procedures in the true sense are found in the legal systems of the so-called "common law" jurisdictions of the world, which derive their law originally from England. Discovery is less well known in the legal systems of the "civil law" jurisdictions deriving their law from Roman law. Although this work is concerned to set out the law of England and Wales, it will be helpful to explain the comparative position briefly.

British Isles

1.16   The position in Northern Ireland prior to the introduction of the CPR was practically identical to that in England.[60] That in the Republic of Ireland (politically independent since 1922) was very similar, the substantive principles of discovery being more or less the same.[61] The (Irish) Rules of the Superior Courts 1986 are strikingly similar to the (English) Rules of the Supreme Court 1883. Although English authorities are often cited in Eire,

---

[56] See Ch.20, below.
[57] Holdsworth, *A History of English Law*, Vol.XII, pp.678–680.
[58] See Ch.20, below.
[59] See para.1.24, below; and *cf. Arab Monetary Fund v Hashim (No.4)* [1992] 1 All E.R. 645 at 649.
[60] See, e.g. Valentine & Glass, *County Court Procedure in Northern Ireland* (1985), Ch.11, and the RSC (N.I.) (Revision) (SI 1980/346), esp. Ords 24, 26 and 39.
[61] See the Rules of the Superior Courts ("RSC") 1986; Cahill, *Discovery in Ireland* (1996); Byrne and McCutcheon, *The Irish Legal System* (3rd edn., 1996), at pp.204–205; and for the influence of English authority see, e.g. *Tromso Sparebank v Beirne (No.2)* [1989] I.L.R.M. 257.

the Irish Courts have departed from English practice in some areas. One important distinction between English and Irish disclosure law was that the Irish rules have since 1986 allowed general third party disclosure.[62] And the Supreme Court of Ireland, in what may be regarded as a controversial decision, a few years ago ruled that there is no ongoing obligation to provide disclosure of documents once a list of documents has been served.[63] Scotland is unusual, because it is a civil law jurisdiction, although heavily influenced by the English tradition, and much of the modern substantive law (e.g. taxation, employment, company law, social security) is of necessity identical (or at least very similar) to that in England. Nonetheless, the Scots system has its own distinctive procedural rules, including rules which perform a discovery function, although English authorities are referred to in appropriate cases.[64] In general, these rules are less comprehensive than the English discovery rules, although documents can be obtained from a non-party more easily than under the English system prior to the introduction of the CPR.[65]

In Jersey, originally a civil law jurisdiction whose common law is based   **1.17** on the *Coûtume de Normandie*, the current procedural rules are based on the RSC 1965 (though greatly simplified) and general discovery of documents by list, production for inspection, and interrogatories may all be ordered by the Royal Court.[66] There is even provision for a form of "automatic" discovery, without the need for the parties to apply,[67] and pre-action disclosure.[68] Because of the similarity of the local rules with the RSC, English authorities are often referred to on discovery questions.[69] The position in Guernsey, whose common law is also based on the *Coûtume de*

---

[62] See Ch.4, para.4.59, below. Third party disclosure was extended to all cases in England only as late as 1999, by virtue of the CPR.

[63] *Bula Ltd v Tara Mines (No.5)* [1994] 1 I.R. 487, Supreme Court of Ireland; *cf. Vernon v Bosley (No.2)* [1997] 1 All E.R. 614, CA, which reaffirmed the principle of ongoing discovery obligation in English law. CPR, r.31.11 expressly provides that there is a continuing duty; see Ch.6, para.6.31.

[64] *Conoco (UK) Ltd v The Commercial Law Practice*, 1997 S.L.T. 3, Outer House (solicitor ordered to disclose identity of client).

[65] *The Laws of Scotland*, Vol.17, 1989, paras 1144–1156; Macphail, *Sheriff Court Procedure* (1988), Ch.15; Maxwell, *The Practice of the Court of Session* (1980), Pt IX, Ch.6; Rules of Court 1965, Ch.II, s.7; MacSporran and Young, *Commission and Diligence*, 1995.

[66] Royal Court Rules 1992, rr.6/15, 6/16.

[67] See *Practice Direction (Discovery)* 1987–88 J.L.R. N–3.

[68] Law Reform (Disclosure and Conduct before Action) (Jersey) Law 1999, which came into force on December 1, 2001; r.6/16A of the Royal Court Rules.

[69] *Shirley v Channel Island Knitwear Company Ltd*, 1985–86 J.L.R. 404 at 410; *Mehra v Kilachand* 1987–88 J.L.R. 421; *Taylor v Taylor* 1990 J.L.R. 124, Jersey CA; *Victor Hanby Associates v Oliver* 1990 J.L.R. 337, Jersey CA; *Akinsete v South Pacific Investments Ltd* 1992 J.L.R.1; *Pacific Investments Ltd v Christensen*, 1996 J.L.R. N–6, Jersey CA, 1997 J.L.R. 170, Jersey CA; *Takilla Ltd v Olsen Backhurst & Dorey* [2003] J.R.C. 003 (specific discovery); *Broere v Mourant & Co. (Trustees) Ltd* [2004] J.C.A. 009 (discovery of documents in possession of party pursuant to separate fiduciary relationships). Under Practice Direction 92/2 it is not possible for application to be made for the trial or hearing of an action before all parties have completed discovery.

Normandie, appears now to be largely the same as Jersey.[70] The system in the Isle of Man is also similar to that in England prior to the introduction of the CPR.[71]

British Colonies and Dependent Territories

1.18   The remaining British colonies and dependencies, such as the Cayman Islands, Gibraltar, Bermuda and the Falkland Islands, all have legal systems based on that of England, including rules of court based on the RSC 1965. Subject to any exceptional local provision, discovery procedures will be similar to those described in this work. Traditionally in the former British colony of Hong Kong, English discovery case law has been heavily relied upon,[72] and this continues to be the case.[73]

Commonwealth

1.19   Most of the member states of the Commonwealth have legal systems derived from that of England, but some[74] have systems derived from civil law models. The legal systems of former colonies such as the Bahamas, Belize and Saint Christopher and Nevis, which gained their independence only recently, are almost as heavily based on English law as those of the remaining colonies and dependencies. Of the countries which have been independent for a long time, the legal systems of Australia and New Zealand today are the closest to the English system, in terms of both substantive and procedural law.[75] In Singapore English practice is closely followed,[76]

---

[70] Royal Court Civil Rules 1989, rr.38–42; see also *States Prison Board v Kirk* (1991) 11 G.L.J. 62, Guernsey, CA; *Van Leuven v Nielson* (1993) 15 G.L.J. 79, Guernsey CA; *Klabin v Technocom Ltd*, September 20, 2002, Guernsey, CA (discovery of documents referred to in affidavit applying *Dubai Bank Ltd v Galadari* [1990] 1 W.L.R. 731, CA); *cf. Birch v Islands' Insurance Company Ltd* (1993) 16 G.L.J. 47, commenting on the differences with the English rules, and *International Operations Ltd v Silver Falcon Enterprises Ltd* (1994) 17 G.L.J. 61, Guernsey CA, where, contrary to the English practice, it was held that the Guernsey court has no power to make a discovery order ancillary to a pre-action injunction.

[71] Rules of the High Court of Justice of the Isle of Man, Ord.23; see, e.g. *Potts v Mylchreest Motors Ltd* (1984–86) M.L.R. 93; *In re Asian Properties Limited* (1993–95) M.L.R. 404.

[72] *Choy v Nissei Sangyo America Ltd* [1992] H.K.L.R. 177, H.K.C.A.; *Parry v Bentley* [1993] H.K. Digest, F89, H.K.C.A.

[73] See, e.g. *Goldlion Properties Ltd v Regent National Enterprises Ltd* [2005] H.K.C.A. 331, [2005] H.K.C.F.I. 166 (waiver of legal privilege).

[74] e.g. Quebec (*Coûtume de Paris*), Sri Lanka (Roman-Dutch law); Mauritius is unusual, in that it substantive law is derived from the *Code Napoléon*, but its procedure is English-based; as to discovery, see *Lai Pat Fong v The Chinese Chamber of Commerce* 1973 M.C. 1. On English law in the Commonwealth, see, e.g. Matson (1993) 42 I.C.L.Q. 753.

[75] The Australian authorities do not always follow English practice and in some areas the distinctions are quite marked as with legal advice privilege and third parties or agents: *Pratt Holdings Pty Ltd v FCT* [2004] F.C.A. 122, (2004) 207 A.L.R. 217, Fed.Ct.Aus.

[76] *Reebok International Ltd v Royal Corporation* [1992] 2 S.L.R. 136; *Wright-Norman v Oversea-Chinese Banking Corporation Ltd* [1992] 2 S.L.R. 710, Singapore CA.

although the rules are not identical; for example in Singapore the rules provided for pre-action discovery in wider circumstances than in England prior to the introduction of the CPR[77] That of Canada (other than Quebec) is slightly further distant, being influenced to a greater degree by the legal systems of the United States.[78] For example the common law rules as to public interest immunity are no longer applicable in that there is now express statutory provision.[79] Despite both its long absence from the Commonwealth before it rejoined in 1994 and its Roman-Dutch substantive law, South Africa's legal system has discovery procedures heavily based on the English model.[80]

There are a large number of other Commonwealth countries, the **1.20** so-called "New Commonwealth", who in the years since independence have moved further away from what they may well perceive to be the attitudes and values of the Anglo-Saxon colonial administrators towards those of the majority of the indigenous population. In some (but not all) such cases, this has entailed considerable changes in the legal system since that time. The overall result is that the old English law of discovery remains authoritative in some of the smaller Commonwealth countries, is persuasive or influential in some of the larger ones, but probably is only of historical or passing interest in others. The reverse is also true, and accordingly, the reader will find reference in this work to a certain amount of Irish and Commonwealth authority, from Australia,[81] New Zealand and (to a lesser extent) Canada.[82]

United States of America

Ever since British settlors established the various American colonies on **1.21** the east coast of North America in the seventeenth century there has been debate over how much of English[83] law they took with them.[84] Blackstone, for example, thought they took none.[85] The fact, however, remains that the

---

[77] RSC, Ord.24, r.7A, not limited to where claims are likely to be made in respect of person injuries or death; *Kuah Kok Kim v Ernst & Young* [1996] 2 S.L.R. 364.

[78] See, e.g. Park and Cromie (eds.), *International Commercial Litigation* (2nd edn, 1997), pp.122–128.

[79] Sections 37–39 of the Canada Evidence Act 1985, c. C–5; see also *Canadian Association of Regulated Importers v Canada* (1992) 87 D.L.R. (4th) 730.

[80] See, e.g. Herbstein and Van Winsen, *The Civil Practice of the Superior Courts in South Africa* (3rd edn, 1979), Ch.29.

[81] See, generally, Cairns, *The Law of Discovery in Australia* (1984); McNicol, *The Law of Privilege* (1992); Cairns, *Australian Civil Procedure* (4th edn 1996); Bailey and Evans, *Discovery and Interrogatories* (1997).

[82] See, generally, Choate, *Discovery in Canada* (1977).

[83] Always English, note, and never Scots or Irish.

[84] See, e.g. Smith, *The English Criminal Law in Early America*, in *The English Legal System: Carryover to the Colonies* (1975).

[85] 1 Bl. Comm.105.

settlors *did* take with them the principles of the common law.[86] Equity, including the rules of equity relating to disclosure, apparently came later, although by the time that Story wrote in the 1830s, American equity practice could be said to be "founded upon, co-existence with, and, in most respects, conformable to, that of England."[87] Since that time disclosure procedures in America have been developed and expanded, so that the general ambit of discovery today is a great deal wider in the United States than it is in England.[88]

1.22 Thus in addition to production of documents by a party to his opponent[89] and the application of interrogatories,[90] there is general discovery of a party *and his witnesses*, and indeed of independent third parties, by means of pre-trial depositions of oral evidence.[91] The deposition has become a common but important, time consuming and hence expensive feature of modern United States civil procedure.[92] In an effort to cut costs, it is even conducted by telephone or video conference link in some cases.[93] The deposition can be used as a means of discovery of the existence of relevant documents, production of which can then be specifically sought. Another significant difference between England and the United States is that in the former jurisdiction all discovered material is automatically subjected to an obligation of confidentiality, whereas in the United States a "protective order" must be specifically obtained.[94] In recent times discovery procedures in the United States have been criticised as tending to inflate both the time taken to litigate disputes and the costs of doing so, to an extent where it has even been suggested that everyone would be better off with no disclosure at all.[95] The procedures for electronic disclosure have been recently revised and there is a significant body of case law in this area.[96]

---

[86] See Smith, *loc. cit.*

[87] *Equity Jurisprudence* (2nd edn, 1839), para.57. But it is to be noted that the US Supreme Court recently held (by 5–4) that it was not open to US Courts, in the absence of statutory authority, to grant asset-freezing ("*Mareva*") injunctions: *Grupo Mexicano de Desarrollo S.A v Alliance Bond Fund Inc.*, 527 US 308, 119 S. Ct. 1961 (1999).

[88] See, e.g. Black (1991) 40 I.C.L.Q. 901, and *South Carolina Insurance Co. v Assurantie Maatschapij "De Zeven Provincien" N.V.* [1987] A.C. 24 at 35–37; *cf.* also 28 United States Code, s.1782 (*ibid.* at 32–33), empowering the US courts to obtain evidence for use in foreign proceedings even outside the procedures laid down in the Hague Convention of 1970 (see Ch.2 para.2.62, below). On US law generally, see Dombroff, *Discovery* (1986); Simpson, *Civil Discovery and Depositions* (2nd edn, 1994).

[89] See, e.g. Federal Rules of Civil Procedure ("F.R.C.P."), r.34.

[90] See, e.g. *ibid.*, r.33; Berman (1993) 19 *Litigation*, No.4, p.42.

[91] See, e.g. *ibid.*, rr.30, 31, 45.

[92] See, e.g. Levine, *Discovery* (1982), Ch.6; Dombroff, *Discovery* (1986), Chs 8–11; Simpson, *Civil Discovery and Depositions* (2nd edn, 1994), Ch.4. Depositions may be videotaped; see Neuberger (1983) 19 *Litigation* No.4, p.60.

[93] See, e.g. F.R.C.P, r.30(b)(7), and Dombroff, *op.cit*, Ch.11, and Simpson, *op.cit.*, para.4.3.

[94] See, e.g. *Re Seattle Times Co.*,104 S.Ct. 2199 (1984); *The Brief* (1993) 22:2; Dombroff, *op.cit.*, paras 1.17–1.23; Simpson, *op.cit*, para.3.25.

[95] e.g. Kieve, *Discovery Reform*, ABA Journal, December 1991, at p.78.

[96] Ch.7, para.7.01.

Roman law

Before turning to consider the modern position in continental Europe, it **1.23** is useful to bear in mind the discovery procedures which existed in Roman law, since it is that law which has formed the foundation for most of the continental European legal systems. Four procedures are worthy of note. First, there were the *actiones interrogatoriae,* by which a plaintiff could ask a defendant to disclose facts relevant to the defendant's *personal* liability, but not liability generally.[97] Thus, if the main action were one in respect of a slave's alleged wrongdoing, the defendant could be asked about his ownership of the slave. Or if it were an action against an *heres*, the defendant could be asked if he were an *heres* and, if so, for what share. Secondly, there was the edict *de edendo*, under which a defendant could seek production from the plaintiff of all documents upon which the plaintiff proposed to rely and for his accounts (even though these were not to be relied on).[98] Neither of these procedures was available the other way round. Thirdly, a depositor in litigation with a banker could compel the banker to give disclosure of accounts pertaining to him, and this was so whatever the respective capacities of banker and depositor in the litigation, and despite the banker's death or giving up the business.[99] Fourthly, there was the *actio ad exhibendum,* by which a party could compel another to produce something (but here, a document) in which he claimed an interest, preparatory to beginning another, substantive action.[100] In addition to these methods of discovery, there appear also to have existed certain forms of proof by making a confession or taking an oath, which may have had discovery consequences, even though not necessarily so intended.[101]

Continental Europe[102]

The legal systems of Western Europe are, to a greater or lesser extent, **1.24** based on that of Rome, and typically their procedural rules have three "discovery" characteristics:

(a) an obligation on a party to produce to his opponent the documents on which he will rely in this case;

---

[97] Buckland, *A Textbook of Roman Law* (3rd edn, 1963), at pp.632–633; Buckland and McNair, *Roman Law & Common Law* (1936), at p.321; Story, *Equity Jurisprudence* (2nd edn, 1839), para.1487; Fortenberry (1988) 9 J. Leg. Hist. 214.

[98] Buckland and McNair, *op.cit.*, at pp.321–222.

[99] Fortenberry, *loc.cit.*, at pp.218–219.

[100] Buckland, *op.cit.* at pp.547–548; Story, *op.cit.*, para.1487.

[101] Story, *op.cit.*, para.1486.

[102] For general surveys, see O'Malley and Layton, *European Civil Practice* (1989), Chs 48–55; McIntosh and Holmes, *Civil Proceedings in EC Countries* (1991); see also Park and Cromie (eds.), *International Commercial Litigation* (2nd edn, 1997), 167–169 (France), 192–193 (Germany), 209–211 (Japan), 219–220, 223–224 (Switzerland).

(b) *no* obligation on a party to produce to his opponent documents in his possession which are *adverse* to his case or *helpful* to his opponent's; and

(c) a power in the court to order a party to produce to his opponent documents specifically shown to exist in his possession and whose importance to the opponent's case can be demonstrated.[103]

In addition, there are specific but limited powers for one party to obtain documents or information from another party in particular kinds of litigation or dispute.[104] Moreover, where administrative or public law is concerned, the individual may have considerably greater rights against the State to such documents or information—although not necessarily as part of the litigation process.

1.25　These characteristics represent a position significantly more discovery-oriented than that usually conceived by the Anglo-Saxon lawyer to exist in Europe, yet falling short of the norm in English common law systems. The continental european lawyer does not understand how an obligation to give general discovery can be made effective, or enforced (which is much the same thing). Indeed he may ask why his client should provide the opponent with material which is against his interest.[105] On the other hand, the Anglo-Saxon lawyer does not understand how it is possible to arrive at the truth without such an obligation. This position represents a curious kind of role reversal, in which the idealist civil lawyer worries about the pragmatic, and the pragmatic common lawyer worries about the ideal.

E. DISCOVERY LITERATURE

1.26　Discovery as a part of civil procedure does not possess a very large literature in England. It was originally dealt with as part of the general procedures of the Court of Chancery, in early works such as Mitford's *Pleadings* and Daniell's *Chancery Practice*.[106] It was also discussed in treatises on the law such as Fonblanque's *Treatise of Equity*, and Story's *Equity Jurisprudence*. In the nineteenth century Vice-Chancellor Wigram (1836) and his former pupil Vice-Chancellor Thomas Hare (1838) each produced a book devoted to the law of discovery as it existed in the Court of Chancery

---

[103] See, e.g. the *Nouveau Code de Procédure Civile*, Art.11 (France), and the *Codice di Procedura Civile*, Art.210 (Italy). Note that in some cases failure to comply with such an order attracts no greater sanction than the drawing of adverse inferences by the court.

[104] e.g. *saisie-contrefacon* in patent litigation: see Nelissen Grade, *International Business Lawyer*, July 1988, pp.315–317.

[105] A question answered by Donaldson M.R. in *Davies v Eli Lilly & Co.* [1987] 1 W.L.R. 858 at 967, CA: litigation is not a war or game, it is designed to do real justice between opposing parties, and, if the court does not have all the relevant information, it cannot achieve this object.

[106] See, e.g. the 8th edn, 1914, Ch.XIII.

before the Judicature Act. In 1884 Edward Bray (later a county court judge) produced his *Discovery*, a monumental survey of the entire law and practice of discovery in the unified High Court. He never produced a second edition, although two editions appeared (in 1904 and 1910) of a much shorter *Digest of the Law of Discovery with Practice Notes*, which contained the text of RSC 1883, Ord.31 (as it then was[107]) together with Bray's annotations upon the rules. The substance of these annotations is still to be found in *The Supreme Court Practice 1999* under RSC, Ord.24. In 1912 a Principal Clerk in the Criminal Appeal Office, R.E. Ross, published a new treatise on *The Law of Discovery*, but it did not achieve a second edition.

The most recent works solely devoted to English discovery law have been   **1.27**
two editions of Oyez' Practice Notes on the *Discovery and Inspection of Documents*[108] and *Pre-Action Discovery*.[109] Both of these are now very out of date and do not of course deal with disclosure under the CPR. *Documentary Evidence*[110] is a useful and practical work, but discovery is only one of several topics covered. There is also a comparative study of the English and United States discovery systems by Levine (1982), but this is more scholarly than practical. Privilege is dealt with as a separate topic in four useful works: Passmore, *Privilege*[111] Auburn, *Legal Professional Privilege: Law & Theory* (2000) and Thanki, *The Law of Privilege* (2006), all dealing primarily with English law, and McNichol, *The Law of Privilege* (1992), dealing primarily with Australian law. A summary of disclosure principles as well as forms are to be found in *Atkin's Court Forms*.[112] Finally the internet should not be omitted as it is an important resource, not only as an easy way of accessing decisions, but there are useful specialist websites such as that of the List Group (dealing with electronic disclosure).[113]

F. REFORM AND THE CIVIL PROCEDURE RULES 1998

In recent years, a number of common law jurisdictions have modified   **1.28**
their civil procedure systems, some significantly. In relation to discovery, one of the most radical has been that Queensland in Australia.[114] Among its reforms was the abolition of the "train of inquiry" (or *Peruvian Guano*) test of relevance, the introduction of power to relieve the discovery burden, the express confirmation of the continuing duty to disclose, and the removal of

---

[107] A happy coincidence, therefore, that under the new CPR disclosure is dealt with in Pt 31.
[108] 1967 and 1975 by Park W.D.
[109] Fletcher-Rogers (1991).
[110] Hollander (9th edn, 2006).
[111] 2nd edn, 2006.
[112] Vol.15 (2nd edn, 2007) by Malek and Auburn.
[113] *www.listgroup.org*
[114] Supreme Court Rules Amendment Order (No.1) 1994, replacing RSC 1900, Ord.35, as from May 1, 1994.

the requirement to disclose copies.[115] Following a wide ranging review of civil procedure in the High Court and County Court in England and Wales, in 1996 Lord Woolf published his final report recommending a new system and unified set of rules.[116] Curiously, of all the recent reforms to common law discovery systems, only those in Queensland were expressly referred to by Lord Woolf. Indeed, a number of his reforms—including the use of the term "disclosure"—follow those in Queensland. As regards the process of discovery of documents, the report concluded that it had become disproportionate, especially in larger cases where large numbers of documents may have to be searched for and disclosed, though only a small number turn out to be significant.

1.29   The recommended solution involved the identification of four categories of documents, which had to be disclosed on the basis of the then current rules, as follows:

> (1) the parties' own documents, which they relied upon in support of their contentions in the proceedings;
> (2) adverse documents of which a party was aware and which to a material extent adversely affected his own case or supported another party's case;
> (3) documents which did not fall within categories (1) or (2) but were part of the "story" or background, including documents which, though relevant, might not be necessary for the fair disposal of the case;
> (4) "train of inquiry" documents: these were documents which might lead to a train of inquiry enabling a party to advance his own case or damage that of his opponent.[117]

1.30   It was recommended that "standard disclosure" would cover only categories (1) and (2), with the power in the court to order extra disclosure covering categories (3) and (4) as well, if proportionate to do so.[118] It was also proposed that initial disclosure should only apply to relevant documents of which a party is aware at the time when the obligation to disclose arises.[119] Although these proposals were intended to cut down the scope and hence cost of disclosure in most cases, in respect of disclosure from

---

[115] Cairns, *New Discovery Regime for Queensland* (1994) 18 U.Q.L.J. 93
[116] Lord Woolf, *Access to Justice: Final Report* (July 1996). Ch.12, paras 37–52 deal with disclosure of documents. The report includes a proposed set of rules, which were revised and have (by and large) evolved into the CPR. In fact Lord Woolf's *Interim Report* (June 1995) contained more discussion of the basis and justification of discovery , together with a number of criticisms.
[117] *ibid.*, Ch.12, para.38.
[118] *ibid.*, Ch.12, paras 39–40.
[119] *ibid.*, Ch.12, para.41.

third parties and pre-action disclosure Lord Woolf recommended an *extension* of the court's powers.[120] The thrust of the recommendations have been incorporated into the Civil Procedure Rules 1998 ("CPR") which came into effect on April 26, 1999. These Rules introduce for the first time, in Pt 1, the concept of the "overriding objective", the light by which the new rules are to be interpreted and applied. This is to enable the court "to deal with cases justly".[121] The desired improvements in efficiency are subject to that objective.[122] So far as discovery is concerned, the CPR do not in fact follow the four-fold classification of documents recommended by Lord Woolf. Instead there is a three-fold classification: those documents *relied on* by a party and those which *adversely affect* his own or another party's case or *support* another's. The element of awareness[123] in Lord Woolf's category (2) and categories (3) and (4), have gone but there is additionally the power to add categories of document by practice direction.[124] The new rules not only make changes in substance, but there are also changes in terminology. Henceforward, for example, "discovery" is called "disclosure", and plaintiff called "claimant". Whether Lord Woolf's reforms has had the desired effect on civil procedure is perhaps debatable, though the problems are perhaps more complex than is often appreciated.[125] What can be said is that they have shown to be a significant improvement on the previous rules, although problems remain.

The new rules have now bedded down substantially. For a while the rules **1.31** were regularly amended, but now the pace of change has slowed down considerably. A new body of case law has built up, particularly in relation to pre-action disclosure (CPR, r.31.16) and non-party disclosure (CPR, r.31.17). The most significant recent developments are in relation to electronic disclosure, which now is specifically covered in the form of the list of documents.[126] The cost of disclosure is still a significant proportion of the costs of an action, particularly in multi-track cases. In small claims and fast track cases disclosure is generally kept within sensible bounds. The difficult area is the cases in the multi-track, particularly in large scale litigation, where disclosure has been allowed to become more extensive than before. Not only can you seek disclosure from a party to litigation, but you can seek it from him prior to proceedings, and also from non-parties during the proceedings. The CPR has sufficient control mechanisms in the overriding objective and CPR Pt 31 to keep disclosure under control. However, the courts are not consistent in how they apply the rules. It is often very difficult

---

[120] *ibid.*, paras 47–52.
[121] CPR, r.1.1(1).
[122] *Hannigan v Hannigan, The Independent,* May 23, 2000, CA.
[123] *Access to Justice: Final Report,* paras 41–45.
[124] CPR, r.31.6; see Ch.5, paras 5.08–5.18.
[125] See, e.g. Cairns, *Lord Woolf's Report on Access to Justice: an Australian Perspective* (1997) 16 C.J.Q. 98.
[126] See Ch.7 below.

to predict the result of a disclosure application, such is the broad discretion provided by the rules.[127]

1.32   Notwithstanding the reforms wrought by the CPR, it has been thought necessary to retain in this edition a good deal of the caselaw and other learning on the old rules.[128] The reasons for this are many and varied. First, in some areas of litigation (in particular some aspects of matrimonial causes) certain of the old rules on discovery are for the moment retained. Secondly, even where the rules are altered, they make use of concepts and practices found in the old system. Some areas of the subject, such as privilege, are unchanged in substance. Thirdly, the court's discretion may be exercised in some cases so as to impose disclosure obligations very similar, if not identical, to the old discovery obligations. Fourthly, the old cases will in many situations provide good examples, without constituting binding authority, and it is desirable that readers are reminded of the different principles on which the old system worked, as well as of the considerations which were considered intrinsically persuasive under that system, and which may still "be capable of contributing to a just result".[129] Lastly, but by no means least, England is but one of the common law jurisdictions in the world today, each of which can learn from the others. The old discovery law is a shared heritage, like a common point of departure, to which we can return to see where others have branched off. It is accordingly hoped that readers from other common law jurisdictions will find something of value in this new edition.

G. STRUCTURE OF THIS WORK

1.33   The bulk of this work is taken up with the detailed discussion of documentary disclosure: this comprises Pt 2, Chs 2 to 15, below. The general principles described in those chapters (e.g. the position of non-parties, privilege, solicitors' obligations) however apply also to the other kinds of disclosure. Part 3 (Chs 16 to 18) deals with non-documentary disclosure. Disclosure of facts and information is covered in Chs 16 and 17, the former

---

[127] Malek H.M., 'Disclosure and the CPR', *Graya News* 3 (2004), pp.40–43.

[128] *cf. Thorn Plc v Macdonald* [1999] C.P.L.R. 661, CA (setting aside default judgment); *UCB Bank Plc v Halifax (SW) Ltd, The Times,* December 23, 1999, CA (striking out as abuse of process); *Chapple v Williams* [1999] C.P.L.R. 731, CA (setting aside default judgment following "unless" order); *Purdy v Cambran* [1999] C.P.L.R. 843, CA (striking out for delay): in each case the court deprecated attempts to rely on pre-CPR caselaw. However, in *Omega Engineering Inc v Omega S.A.* [2003] EWHC 1482 (Ch), *The Times,* May 2003, a former rule under the RSC (Ord.3 r.5) was used as an aid to the construction of CPR, r.3.1(2)(a), and *Flynn v Scougall* [2004] EWCA Civ 873, [2005] C.P. Rep. 15, where references to earlier authorities was deemed appropriate in the context of CPR Pt 36 (payments into court).

[129] *Hickey v Marks*, unreported, July 6, 2000, CA; *Garratt v Saxby* [2004] 1 W.L.R. 2152 at [18], CA; *Phipson on Evidence* (16th edn, 2005), para.33–19.

dealing with information requests (and interrogatories) and the latter with depositions, witness statements and letters of request. Chapter 18 covers expert evidence. Chapter 19 deals with disclosure of "real evidence", which means inspection of property, medical examinations of persons, and also experiments. Throughout Pts 2 and 3 the procedure dealt with is that of the High Court and the county court, and references are given to the Civil Procedure Rules (CPR), and, where appropriate, the Rules of the Supreme Court (RSC) and the County Court Rules (CCR) respectively. Part 4 of the book consists of Ch.20, which gives an overview of the disclosure position in courts and tribunals having jurisdiction in England other than the High Court and county court, and Ch.21, which deals in overview with the impact of the Human Rights Act 1998 on disclosure law. There are three Appendices: the first containing statutory material dealing with disclosure, the second containing the text of the basic procedural rules of disclosure in the High Court and the county court and relevant practice directions and similar material, and the third comprising a selection of forms and precedents. Proceedings before professional and regulatory bodies are not covered in detail in this work. Typically, such disclosure is dealt with by reference to specific rules of the relevant body and, where applicable, a duty to act fairly.[130] Nevertheless, even before such bodies, disclosure may be amenable to the jurisdiction of the High Court on challenges as to the exercise of their powers.[131]

---

[130] See Harris, *Disciplinary and Regulatory Proceedings*, (4th edn, 2006), Ch.10.
[131] See, e.g. *R. (Rosen) v Solicitors Disciplinary Tribunal* [2002] EWHC 1323 (Admin), where decision of the SDT not to order disclosure of documents was quashed.

CHAPTER 2

Time of disclosure

CHAPTER 2

Time of disclosure

This chapter considers the point of time at which documentary disclosure **2.01** becomes available. Disclosure is usually given during the course of proceedings, at a point when the issues between the parties are known. Sometimes, however, disclosure is given before substantive proceedings have been commenced, or simultaneously with proceedings being commenced, and occasionally after judgment has been given. In a few cases, disclosure may be ordered although there are no English proceedings contemplated at all, such as for the purposes of a foreign legal action. Conversely, it is even possible to obtain disclosure from abroad for English proceedings. These categories of case are considered in order.

A. BEFORE PROCEEDINGS COMMENCED

There are a limited number of instances where disclosure is given before **2.02** substantive proceedings are commenced. Such cases involve the taking of preliminary legal action, the entire object of which is to obtain the disclosure needed for the separate, later proceedings. A logically prior question, however, is the use that may be made by a prospective litigant of documents already made available through other legal proceedings or public inquiries. In these situations the production of the documents or information concerned was for the purposes of those earlier proceedings, and it is coincidental that it is of assistance in the later proceedings. Such cases involve documents from previous litigation and arbitrations, and documents from inquests and public inquiries.

Documents from previous litigation and arbitrations

2.03   Civil court proceedings (whether interlocutory or at trial) are not secret,[1] and the general rule is that a hearing is to be in public.[2] Except in rare cases,[3] publication or other use of information heard by the public attending a hearing in public is not a contempt of court.[4] Official transcripts of evidence given orally, and of reasons for judgment given, can usually be obtained.[5] The public may normally inspect witness statements ordered to stand as evidence in chief,[6] and also written submissions and skeleton openings.[7] Even where, exceptionally, the public are lawfully excluded,[8] the order of the court may still normally be published.[9] But unauthorised invasion of lawyers' papers in court by others can amount to contempt of court.[10] Arbitration proceedings, on the other hand, are normally held in private, and the public has no right to attend or to use information given at the hearing, or to obtain transcripts or copies of the award without the consent of the parties or the permission of the court.[11] Publication or other use of such information may be a breach of contract, or of confidence, but it is not a contempt of court.

2.04   When documents are obtained by a party to English civil litigation on disclosure by another such party, they, and the information contained in them, are held subject to an obligation on the recipient not to use those documents or that information for any purpose other than that of the litigation in which they were disclosed without the permission of the court or the disclosing party and the owner of the document concerned being obtained. A similar implied obligation arises in relation to disclosure given in arbitrations. This subject (including the circumstances in which the undertaking or obligation is released) is more fully discussed in Ch.15 below. The different question of obtaining documents from the court file in

---

[1] *Scott v Scott* [1913] A.C. 417; *AG v Leveller* Magazine [1979] A.C. 440; *Forbes v Smith* [1998] 1 All E.R. 973; *Clibbery v Allan* [2002] EWCA Civ 45, [2002] Fam. 261, CA; *Phipson on Evidence* (16th edn, 2005) para.11–10.

[2] CPR, r.39.2(1).

[3] Administration of Justice Act 1960, s.12 (as amended).

[4] *Hodgson v Imperial Tobacco Ltd* [1998] 2 All E.R. 673, CA.

[5] See CPR Pt 39, Practice Direction, para.1.11; *cf. ibid.*, para.1.12; in family proceedings, see the Family Proceedings Rules 1991, r.10.15(6); *S. v S.* [1997] 1 W.L.R. 1621; *R. v R.* [1998] 1 F.L.R. 922.

[6] See Ch.17, para.17.28 below.

[7] *GIO Personal Investment Services Ltd v Liverpool and London Steamship Protection and Indemnity Association Ltd* [1999] 1 W.L.R. 984, CA.

[8] CPR, r.39.2(3).

[9] Administration of Justice Act 1960, s.12; see, e.g. *A v A, B v B* [2000] 1 F.L.R. 701 (ancillary relief proceedings).

[10] *Re Griffin, The Times*, November 6, 1996.

[11] *Dolling-Baker v Merrett* [1990] 1 W.L.R. 1205 at 1213; *Ali Shipping Corporation v Shipyard Trogir* [1998] 2 All E.R. 136, CA. Different considerations apply to court judgments relating to arbitrations: see *Department of Economic Policy and Development of the City of Moscow v Bankers Trust Co.* [2004] EWCA Civ 314; [2005] Q.B. 207, CA.

other litigation to which the person concerned is *not* a party is dealt with in Ch.3.[12]

Criminal cases

As in civil litigation, court hearings in criminal cases are generally[13] not secret. The Criminal Procedure Rules 2005 provide for the exercise of certain kinds of jurisdiction in chambers,[14] and a party may apply for a hearing to be held in camera.[15] Subject to limited exceptions,[16] information given publicly in open court in hearings in criminal cases can be published or otherwise used subsequently. Transcripts may be obtained.[17] The prosecuting authorities are not subject to any obligation to the court not to use material obtained in the course of a criminal investigation other than for the purpose of the criminal proceedings.[18] The disclosure of information between the parties at common law was a controversial subject, which developed very rapidly in recent times.[19] After some doubts, it was finally held that the disclosure of documents by the prosecution to the defence as unused material *did* generate an implied undertaking not to use them for any collateral purpose.[20] Doubts, however, remained in relation to used material and to material read out in open court.[21] The subject is now the subject of comprehensive statutory provision.[22] Where material is

2.05

---

[12] See Ch.3, paras 3.45 to 3.47 below.

[13] Though see the Children and Young Persons Act 1933, s.37(1) (as amended by the Youth Justice and Criminal Evidence Act 1999, s.67(1) and Sch.4, para.2(2)); Official Secrets Act 1920, s.8(4); Official Secrets Act 1989, s.11(4); Criminal Procedure Rules, Pt 16.

[14] Rule 16.11.

[15] Rule 16.10; *Re Guardian Newspapers Ltd* [1999] 1 Cr.App.R. 284.

[16] See, e.g. Contempt of Court Act 1981, s.4(2); Sexual Offences (Amendment) Act 1974, s.4; Children and Young Persons Act 1933, s.49 (as amended); Criminal Justice Act 1987, s.11 (as amended).

[17] Criminal Appeal Rules, r.68.13.

[18] *Preston Borough Council v McGrath, The Times*, May 19, 2000, CA. There are restrictions on the Serious Fraud Office in supplying material to third parties which has been obtained using their compulsory powers or warrant under the Criminal Justice Act 1987, s.2: see s.3 and *R. (Kent Pharmaceuticals) v Director of the Serious Fraud Office* [2004] EWCA Civ 1494, [2005] 1 W.L.R. 1302.

[19] See *R. v Maguire* [1992] Q.B. 936; *R. v Ward* [1993] 1 W.L.R. 619; *R. v Keene* [1994] 1 W.L.R. 746; *R. v Brown* [1994] 1 W.L.R. 1599; *R. v Bromley Justices, ex p. Smith* [1995] 1 W.L.R. 944, DC; *R. v Blackledge* [1996] 1 Cr.App.R. 326; *R. v Mills* [1998] A.C. 382, HL; *Taylor v Serious Fraud Office* [1999] 2 A.C. 177; *Rajan v General Medical Council* [2000] Lloyds Rep. Medical 153, PC; see also *Rowe and Davis v UK* (2000) 30 E.H.R.R. 1.

[20] *Taylor v Serious Fraud Office* [1999] 2 A.C. 177, HL.

[21] *Mahon v Rahn* [1998] Q.B. 424, CA (overruled in *Taylor* in relation to unused material).

[22] Criminal Procedure and Investigations Act 1996, Pt I, applying to disclosure in relation to proceedings where the investigation commenced on or after April 1, 1997. See Ch.15, paras 15.56–15.58, below. See also Protocol for the Control and Management of Unused Material in the Crown Court; *R. v K* [2006] EWCA Crim 724.

disclosed to the accused under the provisions of the legislation, he may use it for the purposes of his defence or in connected criminal proceedings (e.g. on appeal).[23] He may also use it elsewhere to the extent that it has become public in open court,[24] or to the extent that the court gives permission.[25] Other use is prohibited,[26] and is a contempt of court.[27]

Inquests and public inquiries

2.06   Inquests are inquiries, not litigation,[28] and they have no equivalent to the disclosure process.[29] However, the inquest procedure will result in the production of various documents, including post-mortem examination reports, notes of the evidence, the inquisition recording the results of the inquest, and various certificates which the coroner may have to give. Some or all of these documents may be of assistance in subsequent legal proceedings. It is unfortunately unclear whether there is any obligation not to use such documents in subsequent proceedings without the leave of the court.[30] As to documents obtained as a result of public inquiries, the position is perhaps clearer. Where documents are voluntarily submitted to an inquiry the submitter must be taken to waive confidence in them.[31] Even where compulsion has been used to require their submission, it seems that the better view is that there is no obligation to keep their contents confidential thereafter, and they may be used in subsequent litigation without leave.[32]

Probate cases

2.07   In probate cases, where there are any circumstances surrounding the making and execution of the will which give rise to suspicions of undue influence, want of knowledge and approval, or mental incapacity, the Law Society recommends that, on application by those attacking the will, the solicitor concerned in the making of the will should make a statement of the evidence which he could give in the matter, and should make it available to all concerned.[33] It should not be confined to narrow matters concerning execution, but should extend to all surrounding circumstances leading up to

---

[23] *ibid.*, s.17(2).
[24] *ibid.*, s.17(3).
[25] *ibid.*, s.17(4); Criminal Procedure Rules, rr.26.1 to 26.3.
[26] *ibid.*, s.17(1).
[27] *ibid.*, s.18; Criminal Procedure Rules, r.26.4.
[28] *R. v South London Coroner, ex p. Thompson, The Times,* July 9, 1982; *R. v Att. Gen. for Northern Ireland ex p. Devine* [1992] 1 W.L.R. 262, HL.
[29] See Ch.20, paras 20.16–20.19, below.
[30] See Ch.20, para.20.19, below.
[31] *cf. Derby & Co. Ltd v Weldon,* October 19, 1988, unreported.
[32] See Ch.20, para.20.19.
[33] See *The Guide to the Professional Conduct of Solicitors* (8th edn, 1999), at 450.

the preparation of the will.[34] If this recommendation is not followed it may have costs implications.[35]

The High Court has power to order a person believed on reasonable grounds to have "knowledge of any document which is or purports to be a testamentary document", to attend to be examined in open court, whether or not any proceedings are pending.[36] The court may not only order such person to bring the document with him (if appropriate), but may require him to answer any question in relation to it.[37] Similarly, where it appears that a person has in his possession, custody or power any document which is (or purports to be) a testamentary document, the High Court may issue a subpoena requiring him to produce the document as the court may direct, whether any proceedings are pending or not.[38] **2.08**

Cases involving preliminary legal action

Turning now to cases which involve taking some preliminary legal action, the sole purpose of which is to obtain the disclosure required, these are: **2.09**

    (a) *Norwich Pharmacal* orders;
    (b) Pre-action disclosure under the Supreme Court Act 1981, s.33;
    (c) corporate insolvency;
    (d) applications to inspect the court file in other litigation.

These are dealt with in Ch.3.

B. AT THE TIME THAT PROCEEDINGS ARE COMMENCED

In some cases disclosure orders are made simultaneously with proceedings being commenced. The main such cases are: **2.10**

    (a) disclosure orders ancillary to injunctions.
    (b) search orders (formerly known as *Anton Piller* orders).

(a) Orders ancillary to injunctions

These are orders which are ancillary, not just to "ordinary" interim injunctions to restrain a continuing or threatened wrong,[39] but also to **2.11**

---

[34] *Larke v Nugus* (1979) 123 Sol. Jo. 337, [2000] W.T.L.R. 1033, CA.
[35] *ibid.*
[36] Supreme Court Act 1981, s.122.
[37] *ibid.* As to procedure, see CPR PD57, para.7.
[38] Supreme Court Act 1981, s.123.
[39] CPR, r.25.1(1),(8).

"tracing" injunctions,[40] where the claimant makes a proprietary claim to the property in the defendant's hands and to freezing (formerly called *Mareva*) injunctions,[41] in which the claimant's claim is unrelated to the property, and the defendant is merely restrained from rendering himself "judgment-proof" before trial. Freezing injunctions are almost invariably granted by the High Court, as the county court's power to grant them is limited.[42]

2.12   In all these kinds of case, the court has jurisdiction at an interlocutory stage (indeed, even before proceedings are commenced)[43] to order disclosure of facts or documents which are important in ensuring the effectiveness of the injunction.[44] Thus, in the case of an injunction to restrain a breach of confidence, the court has power to order a defendant to disclose documents which concern the confidential information in question and which might reveal the "source" of the breach,[45] or to disclose the names and addresses of former business contacts.[46] However, the court will not order disclosure of information or documents which may be relevant in a remote sense to some future application for a freezing injunction.[47]

2.13   In tracing or "freezing" cases, the most important facts are often those concerning the defendant's assets. In the tracing case, this is because the claimant wants to know into what assets his tracing claim may now be made.[48] In the "freezing" case, the disclosure order[49] is usually made to enable the claimant to "police" his injunction by putting third parties in whose hands such assets may lie (typically banks) on notice of the court order.[50] A defendant making an application to vary the order (i.e. to permit increased or additional spending) will be required to give full disclosure of his means, liabilities and expenditure necessary to maintain his standard of living or, in the case of a corporate defendant, its ordinary way of busi-

---

[40] CPR, r.25.1(1)(c),(2).

[41] CPR, r.25.1(1)(f).

[42] County Courts (Remedies) Regulations 1991, reg.3. Instead a CPR Pt 23 application for such an injunction should be made in the High Court for the purposes of proceedings in the County Court: High Court and County Courts Jurisdiction Order 1991, Art.3; *Schmidt v Wong* [2005] EWCA Civ 1506.

[43] CPR, r.25.2 (1)(a), (2)(b), (3).

[44] CPR, r.25.1 (1)(g), (3); Supreme Court Act 1981, s.37(1).

[45] *X. Ltd v Morgan-Grampian (Publishers) Ltd* [1991] A.C. 1 at 38–40, HL.

[46] *Intelsec Systems Ltd v Grech-Cini* [2000] 1 W.L.R. 1190.

[47] *Parker v C.S. Structured Credit Fund Ltd* [2003] EWHC 391 (Ch), [2003] 1 W.L.R. 1680.

[48] See, e.g. *London & Counties Securities v Caplan*, May 26, 1978, unreported; *Mediterrania Raffineria v Mabanaft*, December 1, 1978, unreported, CA; *Bankers Trust Co. v Shapira* [1980] 1 W.L.R. 1274, CA; *Re D.P.R. Futures Ltd* [1989] 1 W.L.R. 778 at 787–788; *CIBC Mellon Trust Co. v Stolzenberg* [2003] EWHC 13 (Ch), *The Times*, March 3, 2003. Gee, *Commercial Injunctions* (5th edn, 2004).

[49] See CPR, Pt 25, Practice Direction—Interim Injunctions, Annex, Freezing Injunction, paras 9–10, and Search Order, paras 18–10; *Admiralty and Commercial Courts Guide* (7th edn 2006), Appendix 5.

[50] See, e.g. *A. v C.* [1981] Q.B. 956n; *A. J. Bekhor & Co. Ltd v Bilton* [1981] Q.B. 923, CA; *C.B.S. (UK) v Lambert* [1983] Ch. 37, CA; *Re a Company* [1985] B.C.L.C. 333, CA; *Motorola Credit Corporation v Uzan* [2002] EWCA Civ 989, [2002] 2 All E.R. (Comm) 945, *The Times*, July 10, 2002, CA.

ness.[51] Cross-examination can be ordered of the defendant on his statement of assets in an appropriate case.[52] But this is an exceptional measure, not to become a routine feature of freezing injunction proceedings,[53] and the court may make an order for cross-examination subject to an undertaking not to use the material without permission for the purpose of bringing contempt proceedings.[54] An order for cross-examination may also be made against a non-party pursuant to the *Norwich Pharmacal* jurisdiction, but again this is unusual.[55] The deposition arising from the examination may not be used by any person other than the examinee for any purpose other than that of the proceedings in question, except with the permission of the examinee or of the court.[56]

But a disclosure order may also be made, in exceptional cases, where the **2.14** defendant opposes the imposition of the injunction on a contested hearing, and it is desired to test his written evidence.[57] However, the court is not in such cases limited to information regarding assets. It is also open to the court to order, as ancillary to a freezing injunction, the disclosure or provision of other information designed to assist the injunction. For example, the court may order the defendant to sign letters instructing a Swiss bank to disclose to the claimant information concerning any account which the defendant maintained with that bank.[58] The court may also order a claimant who, in breach of the r.31.22 obligation or implied undertaking on disclosure,[59] has passed disclosed documents to a third party, to disclose on affidavit the circumstances and details of such passing.[60] But the information sought ought not to extend beyond the policing of the injunction.[61] The court is wary of allowing wide ranging disclosure as part of a freezing injunction. Thus a provision in a freezing order requiring a defendant to reveal whether he has obtained bribes other than those specifically alleged is objectionable.[62]

---

[51] *House of Spring Gardens Ltd v Waite* [1984] F.S.R. 277 at 284; *Bird v Hadkinson* [1999] B.P.I.R. 653 (duty to make full and accurate disclosure).

[52] *A.J. Bekhor & Co. v Bilton* [1981] Q.B. 923, CA; *House of Spring Gardens Ltd v Waite* [1985] F.S.R., 173, CA; *Bayer v Winter (No.2)* [1986] 1 W.L.R. 540; CPR, r.32.7 (*cf.* RSC, Ord.29, r.1A); *Pathways v West* [2004] N.S.W.S.C. 903, (2005) 212 A.L.R. 140 at [9] (possible for cross-examination even when no affidavit or statement).

[53] *Yukong Line Ltd of Korea v Rendsburg Investments Corporation of Liberia, The Times,* October 22, 1996, CA.

[54] *Motorola Credit Corporation v Uzan (No.2)* [2002] EWHC 2187 (Comm); order for cross-examination upheld on appeal, *Motorola Credit Corporation v Uzan (No.6)* [2003] EWCA Civ 752, [2004] 1 W.L.R. 113, CA.

[55] *Kensington International Limited v Republic of Congo* [2006] EWHC 1848 (Comm).

[56] CPR, r.34.12.

[57] *Bank of Crete S.A. v Koskotas* [1991] 2 Lloyd's Rep. 587, CA.

[58] *Bayer A.G. v Winter (No.2)* [1986] F.S.R. 357; *Bank of Crete S.A. v Koskotas* [1991] 2 Lloyd's Rep. 587, CA.

[59] See Ch.15 below.

[60] *Bhimji v Chatwani (No.2)* [1992] 1 W.L.R. 1158.

[61] *Armco Inc v Donohue,* unreported, October 25, 1999, R.Ct.Jersey.

[62] *International Fund for Agricultural Development v Jazayeri,* March 8, 2001, (Comm. Ct.); *Den Norske Bank v Antonatos* [1999] Q.B. 271.

2.15   It should be noted that disclosure orders in aid of freezing injunctions are made under s.37(1) of the Supreme Court Act 1981 or the court's inherent jurisdiction, and not under CPR, Pt 31, for the disclosure concerned is not likely to fall under "standard disclosure' in the action.[63] But it will probably be otherwise in tracing cases, and may be so in case of other interlocutory injunctions.[64] Whether disclosure is ordered under CPR, Pt 31, or under s.37(1) of the Supreme Court Act 1981 or the inherent jurisdiction, one thing that the court may not do is to order disclosure designed to reveal breaches of earlier orders.[65] The standard form of ancillary disclosure order requires the defendant to give the information "at once",[66] i.e. upon service of the order upon him. This has been described as draconian.[67] Usually, the court will refuse an application to stay the disclosure provision in a freezing order pending the determination of an application to set aside the order.[68] The failure to comply with the disclosure provision in a freezing injunction and search order may amount to a contempt of court.[69]

2.16   The extent of the territorial scope of injunctions (especially freezing injunctions) has been a live issue in recent years and, since ancillary discovery orders are generally tied to such orders, there has been similar debate about their scope. The basic principle is that the court has the power to grant an injunction against anyone who is amenable to its jurisdiction. This may be territorial, in the sense of persons being (even temporarily) within the territory of the jurisdiction (i.e. England and Wales). However, jurisdiction may also be extraterritorial, in the sense of persons who submit to the jurisdiction,[70] or are subject to it on some other basis.[71]

2.17   In tracing cases the court has never minded whether the assets concerned were within or without the territorial jurisdiction, so long as the defendant was personally amenable to the jurisdiction.[72] But in freezing cases the courts originally declined to impose injunctions in respect of assets outside the territorial jurisdiction, even though the defendant himself was subject to

---

[63] *A.J. Bekhor & Co. Ltd v Bilton* [1981] Q.B. 923 at 939.
[64] *A.J. Bekhor & Co. Ltd v Bilton* [1981] Q.B. 923 at 939; *R.H.M. Foods v Bovril Ltd* [1982] 1 W.L.R. 661 at 664–665; *Bayer A.G. v Winter (No.2)* [1986] 1 W.L.R. 540 at 544; *X Ltd v Morgan-Grampian (Publishers) Ltd* [1990] 2 All E.R. 1 at 5–6; *Bhimji v Chatwani (No.2)* [1992] 1 W.L.R. 1158 at 1166–1169; *Exagym Pty Ltd v Professional Gymnasium Equipment Pty Ltd (No.2)* [1994] 2 Qd. R. 129.
[65] *A. J. Bekhor & Co. Ltd v Bilton* [1981] Q.B. 923, CA.
[66] CPR, Pt 25, Practice Direction—Interim Injunctions, Annex, Freezing Injunction, paras 9–10.
[67] *S & T Bautrading v Nordling*, unreported, July 5, 1996, CA.
[68] *Raja v Van Hoogstraten* [2004] EWCA Civ 968; [2004] 4 All E.R. 793 at [101–105].
[69] *Daltel Europe Ltd v Makki* [2005] EWHC 749 (Ch), [2006] EWCA Civ 94.
[70] e.g. under pre-existing contract, or voluntarily on an *ad hoc* basis.
[71] e.g. pursuant to the Civil Jurisdiction and Judgments Act 1982, or under CPR, rr.6.17–6.35.
[72] *Penn v Lord Baltimore* (1750) 1 Ves. Sen. 444; *Cook Industries v Galliher* [1979] Ch. 489; cf. *Altertext Inc v Advanced Data Ltd* [1985] 1 W.L.R. 457, and see Ch.19, para.19.04, below.

such jurisdiction.[73] Disclosure orders ancillary to such injunctions were similarly limited.[74]

But the courts then found, in personal jurisdiction, the same freedom to impose extraterritorial injunctions in freezing cases as they had long enjoyed in tracing cases.[75] It is now not uncommon, in cases of worldwide freezing injunctions, to order disclosure of assets worldwide, even in cases in which the defendant is challenging the jurisdiction of the English Court.[76] Moreover the existence of worldwide asset discovery orders has persuaded the courts subsequently to order such worldwide discovery even in cases of injunctions limited to assets in England and Wales (though this is not, of course, inevitable). The main reason for this is to enable sensible decisions to be made about the need to use injuncted assets to pay existing debts, living and legal expenses and so on. **2.18**

In recent years, applications for freezing orders in aid of foreign proceedings have become a common feature in the High Court.[77] The court is usually cautious before making any such order[78] and will refuse to do so if it is inexpedient. The court will look at any connection with this jurisdiction of the defendant and his assets. Thus if the defendant neither has a presence nor assets within the jurisdiction it will refuse to make an order.[79] There are five particular considerations which should be borne in mind in considering whether it is inexpedient to make an order[80]: **2.19**

(1) Whether the making of the order will interfere with the management of the case in the primary court (e.g. where the order is inconsistent with an order in the primary court or overlaps with it).

(2) Whether it is the policy in the primary jurisdiction not itself to
  • make worldwide freezing/disclosure orders.

(3) Whether there is a danger that the orders made will give rise to disharmony or confusion and/or risk of inconsistent or overlapping orders in other jurisdictions, in particular the courts of the state where the person resides or where the assets affected are

---

[73] *Ashtiani v Kashi* [1987] Q.B. 888, CA; *Reilly v Fryer* (1988) 138 N.L.J. 134.

[74] *ibid.*

[75] *Babanaft International Co. S.A. v Bassantne* [1990] Q.B. 202, CA; *Republic of Haiti v Duvalier* [1990] Ch. 13, CA; *Derby & Co. Ltd v Weldon (No.1)* [1990] Ch. 48, CA; *Derby & Co. Ltd v Weldon (Nos 3 & 4)* [1990] Ch. 65, CA; *Baltic Shipping Co. v Traslink Shipping Ltd* [1995] 1 Lloyds Rep. 673; *Bank of China v NBM* [2002] 1 W.L.R. 844, CA; *Dadourian Group Int. Inc v Simms* [2006] EWCA Civ 399, [2006] 2 Lloyd's Rep. 354, CA.

[76] *Grupo Torras S.A. v Al-Sabah*, unreported, February 16, 1994, CA.

[77] Civil Jurisdiction and Judgments Act 1982, s.25.

[78] *Lewis v Eliades* [2002] EWHC 335 (Q.B.), *The Times*, February 28, 2002, Q.B.D.

[79] *Motorola Credit Corporation v Uzan (No.6)* [2003] EWCA Civ 752, [2004] 1 W.L.R. 113, CA.

[80] *Motorola Credit Corporation v Uzan (No.6)* [2003] EWCA Civ 752, [2004] 1 W.L.R. 113 at [115].

located. If so, then respect for the territorial jurisdiction of that state should discourage the English court from using its unusually wide powers against a foreign defendant.

(4) Whether at the time the order is sought there is likely to be a potential conflict as to jurisdiction rendering it inappropriate and inexpedient to make a worldwide order.

(5) Whether, in a case where jurisdiction is resisted and disobedience to be expected, the court will be making an order it cannot enforce.

(b) Search Orders (*Anton Piller* orders)

2.20   A "search order" (formerly known as an *Anton Piller* order[81]) is a particular form of mandatory interlocutory injunction, usually requiring the defendant (or a third party):

(a) to deliver up immediately to the plaintiff specific or categorised documents or other property; and/or

(b) to permit the plaintiff to search named premises and copy or take away all such specific or categorised documents or other property as may be found there.

Originally such orders were made under the inherent jurisdiction, but they now have a statutory basis.[82] Then,[83] as now,[84] the order directs the defendant (or other person to whom it is directed) to permit the claimant (or other person described in the order) to enter premises and search for and copy or take away specified material. Failure to permit entry may be a contempt of court,[85] so too a failure to comply with the disclosure obligations under a search order.[86] The detailed practice for the execution of search orders is regulated by Practice Direction.[87]

2.21   Although such orders began life in the intellectual property context, in order to prevent the destruction of evidence (e.g. infringing copies) in the defendant's hands, it is well established that such orders may be used for the

---

[81] From *Anton Piller K.G. v Manufacturing Processes Ltd* [1976] Ch. 55; see generally, Gee, *Commercial Injunctions* (5th edn, 2004). For the form of an order, see CPR, Pt.25, Practice Direction—Interim Injunctions, Annex; *Admiralty and Commercial Courts Guide* (7th edn, 2006) Appendix 5.

[82] Civil Procedure Act 1997, s.7; CPR, r.25.1(1)(h).

[83] See *Bhimji v Chatwani* [1991] 1 W.L.R. 989.

[84] Civil Procedure Act 1997, s.7(3).

[85] *Chanel Ltd v 3 Pears Wholesale Cash & Carry Co.* [1979] F.S.R. 393.

[86] *LTE Scientific Limited v Thomas* [2005] EWHC 7 (Q.B.); *Daltel Europe Ltd v Makki* [2005] EWHC 749 (Ch).

[87] CPR, Pt 25, Practice Direction—Interim Injunctions, paras 7–8; *Gadget Shop Ltd v Bug.com Ltd* [2001] F.S.R. 383, Ch.D (failure to follow standard form of order); *Elvee Ltd v Taylor* [2001] EWCA Civ 1943 at [65–69], *The Times*, December 18, 2001, CA (applications in intellectual property cases should be in Chancery division).

purpose of obtaining, in effect, advance disclosure from defendants or others in cases where there is, *inter alia*, evidence to show that documents tending to establish liability or other disclosable material are in the defendants' (or others') possession and a real possibility that they may be destroyed or suppressed if the defendants or others concerned are given the opportunity to do so.[88] In the *Anton Piller* case the Court of Appeal set out the three essential pre-conditions for the making of such an order as follows:

(1) An extremely strong prima facie case.
(2) The damage, potential or actual, must be very serious for the applicant.
(3) There must be clear evidence that the defendants have in their possession incriminating documents or things, and that there is a real possibility that they may destroy such material before any application inter partes can be made.[89]

These requirements are based on two factors. First, the court is being asked to make the order in the absence of, and without notice to, the person against whom it is to be made and without hearing his side of the case. Secondly, the order, if made, requires the defendant, if he is not to be at risk of being in contempt of court, to give access to his premises (which may be his home) and to permit those premises to be searched. The order thus permits, or at least provides the basis for, an invasion of the defendants property and his privacy. The applicant thus has a duty to ensure that there is full and frank disclosure on the without notice application for an order.[90]

The making of such an order in an appropriate case is not a violation of Art.8 of the European Convention on Human Rights.[91] The courts are, however, aware of the seriousness of such orders being made and enforced, particularly since they are made without notice and are enforced against defendants and third parties at a stage when they may not have access to legal advice. Thus, the courts now restrict the circumstances in which such orders will be made.[92] A search order is only justified where there is a paramount need to prevent a denial of justice and where an order for delivery up or preservation of documents would not suffice.[93] Moreover, search orders must not be used by claimants as a means of finding out what allegations can be made in the statement of case.[94] Nor will a search order

2.22

---

[88] See, e.g. *Rank Film Distributors v Video Information Centre* [1982] A.C. 380, HL; *Yousif v Salama* [1980] 1 W.L.R. 1540; *Emanuel v Emanuel* [1982] 1 W.L.R. 669.

[89] *Anton Piller AG v Manufacturing Processes Ltd* [1976] Ch. 55 at 62.

[90] *Elvee Ltd v Taylor* [2001] EWCA Civ 1943 at [49–53].

[91] *Chappell v United Kingdom* [1989] F.S.R. 617, ECHR; see also *Cantabrica Coach Holdings Ltd v Vehicle Inspectorate* (2000) 164 J.P. 593, DC.

[92] See, e.g. *Columbia Pictures v Robinson* [1987] Ch. 38, and *Universal Thermosensors Ltd v Hibben* [1992] 1 W.L.R. 840.

[93] *Lock International Plc v Beswick* [1989] 1 W.L.R. 1268 at 1281; *Expanded Metal Manufacturing Pte Ltd v Expanded Metal Co. Ltd* [1995] 1 S.L.R. 673, Singapore CA.

[94] *Hytrac Conveyors Ltd v Conveyors International Ltd* [1983] 1 W.L.R. 44 CA.

be made where the defendant is not personally amendable to the jurisdiction, whether by presence here or by voluntary submission.[95] Where the defendant is so amenable, it is not an objection at common law that the premises are outside England and Wales,[96] through the *statutory* basis for such orders does not extend so far.[97] The power of the county court to make a search order is very limited.[98] Particular care should be taken in the execution of a search order not to infringe a person's rights to legal professional privilege: *Celanese Canada Inc. v Murray Demolition Corp.*, 2006 SCC 36, Sup. Ct. of Canada (solicitor restrained from acting who had inspected privileged material).

The rule against self-incrimination

2.23   Disclosure orders, whether part of search orders or ancillary to freezing injunctions, are subject to the general common law principles in the absence of specific statutory provisions.[99] These principles include the rule that no one should be required to incriminate himself.[100]

2.24   In relation to freezing injunctions, the problem is the usual ancillary orders against defendants that they immediately inform the claimant of the value, location and details of their assets, and confirm this on affidavit.[101] To the extent that this information would be useful to a prosecuting authority in deciding whether or not to prosecute, or in so prosecuting, the order infringes the privilege and should not be made.[102] In relation to search orders, the problem is not only the usual order requiring the defendant to hand over to the claimant's solicitors the "listed items", but also the usual order requiring the defendant to allow the claimant's solicitors to search for, inspect, copy and take away such items.[103] To a similar extent, such orders infringe the privilege and should not be made.[104] The introduction of a statutory basis for search orders has not affected the general position.[105]

---

[95] See *Altertext Inc v Advanced Data Communications Ltd* [1986] F.S.R. 21, and Ch.19, para.19.04, below.

[96] *Cook Industries v Galliher* [1979] Ch.439; *cf. Protector Alarms v Maxim Alarms* [1978] F.S.R. 442.

[97] Civil Procedure Act 1997, s.7(3)(a).

[98] County Courts (Remedies) Regulations 1991, reg.3.

[99] As to which see Ch.11, paras 11.113–11.119 below.

[100] *Re Westinghouse Electric Corp.* [1978] A.C. 547, HL; *O Ltd v Z* [2005] EWHC 238 (Ch); *C Plc v P* [2006] EWHC 226 (Ch), [2006] 4 All E.R. 311, Ch.D.; and see Ch.11, paras 11.104–11.120 below.

[101] See CPR, Pt 25, Practice Direction—Interim Injunctions, Annex, Freezing Injunction, paras 9–10.

[102] *Sociedade Nacional de Combustiveis de Angola v Lundqvist* [1991] 2 Q.B. 310, CA; *Den Norske Bank A.S.A. v Antonatos* [1999] Q.B. 271.

[103] See CPR, Pt 25, Practice Direction—Interim Injunctions, Annex, Search Order, para.6.

[104] *Rank Film Distributors Ltd v Video Film Centre* [1982] A.C. 380, HL; *Tate Access Floors Inc v Boswell* [1991] Ch. 512; *cf. Twentieth Century Film Corporation v Tryrare Ltd* [1991] F.S.R. 58; *Den Norske Bank A.S.A. v Antonatos* [1999] Q.B. 271.

[105] Civil Procedure Act 1997, s.7(7); see *Hansard*, HL, Vol.576, col.902.

Statutory provisions apply to reduce or entirely remove the self-incrimi- **2.25**
nation problem in limited cases, e.g. where the only criminal charges that
might be brought are under the Theft Act 1968,[106] or where the civil
proceedings relate to the infringement of intellectual property rights and
passing off.[107] Typically they protect the defendant by making the information disclosed inadmissible in criminal proceedings. Where these do not
apply, the problem cannot be avoided by requiring the defendant to provide
the information concerned to an independent solicitor, holding it to the
order of the court.[108] Nor can the civil court make an order in effect
declaring certain evidence to be inadmissible in any subsequent criminal
proceedings.[109] On the other hand, it seems that sufficient protection
against incrimination is given, and hence an order otherwise infringing the
privilege can be made, if the prosecuting authorities undertake not to use the
resulting information in any criminal proceedings against the defendant.[110]
If the authorities will not so undertake, the privilege remains available.[111]

The courts at one time considered that the problem could be overcome by **2.26**
inserting a condition in the order to the effect that disclosure in compliance
with the order could not be used as evidence in criminal proceedings against
the defendant or his spouse.[112] But this was later rejected on the basis that
the condition could only be effective if the prosecuting authorities agree to
be bound by it, i.e. as if they had undertaken in those terms.[113] The position
is different when the Serious Fraud Office obtains transcripts of an examination under the Companies Act 1985, s.236, from the liquidators of an
insolvent company, to enable the SFO to investigate possible criminal
offences in relation to that company. In such a case (1) the liquidators could
not assure confidentiality to examinees, and (2) the SFO should not have to
give any undertaking as to the use, or non-use, of the transcripts concerned,
but (3) it should be left to the judge at any criminal trial to consider whether
to exclude the transcripts under s.78 of the Police and Criminal Evidence
Act 1984.[114] A similar situation arises where transcripts of interviews with
Department of Trade inspectors under the Companies Act 1985, s.434, are
passed to the prosecuting authorities. In both these statutory cases, the

---

[106] Theft Act 1968, s.31.
[107] Supreme Court Act 1981, s.72; *Cobra Golf Inc v Rata (No.2)* [1998] Ch. 109.
[108] *Den Norske Bank A.S.A. v Antonatos* [1999] Q.B. 271.
[109] *Rank Film Distributors Ltd v Video Film Centre* [1982] A.C. 380, HL; *A.T.&T. Istel Ltd v Tully* [1993] A.C. 45, HL; *Reid v Howard* (1995) 69 A.L.J.R. 863, H.Ct.Aus; *cf.* the "indemnity certificate" procedure in the Australian Capital Territory, New South Wales, Tasmania and Western Australia (statutory certificate by court protects witness); *Pathways Employment Services v West* [2004] NSWSC 903, (2005) 212 A.L.R. 140.
[110] *Re a Defendant, The Independent*, April 2, 1987.
[111] *United Norwest Corporation Ltd v Johnstone, The Times*, February 24, 1994, CA.
[112] *Re O (Restraint Order: Disclosure of Assets)* [1991] 2 Q.B. 520, CA; *Re T (Restraint Order: Disclosure of Assets)* [1992] 1 W.L.R. 949; *Re C, The Times*, April 21, 1995.
[113] *A.T.&T. Istel Ltd v Tully* [1993] A.C. 45, HL; *Reid v Howard* (1995) 69 A.L.J.R. 863, H. Ct. Aus.
[114] *Re Arrows Ltd (No.4)* [1995] 2 A.C. 75, HL; *cf. Re New Alliance Pty Ltd* (1993) 118 A.L.R. 699, Fed.Ct.Aus.

privilege against self-incrimination is overridden.[115] There is accordingly a risk of a violation of Art.6(1) of the European Convention on Human Rights.[116]

2.27 A person entitled to the privilege may of course waive it,[117] and therefore an order (whether or not it should have been made) once complied with by a defendant who has had his right to claim privilege brought to his attention but who has declined to do so and has complied with order will not be set aside.[118]

2.28 Where the risk of criminal proceedings is not in the English courts, but in some foreign jurisdiction, there is no privilege against self-incrimination. Nevertheless, the court retains a general and wide discretion whether or not to require disclosure in such circumstances.[119]

Use of documents obtained under freezing or search order

2.29 The standard form of order for a freezing order contains an undertaking that the applicant will not without the permission of the court use any information obtained as a result of the order for the purpose of any civil or criminal proceedings, either in England and Wales or in any other jurisdiction, other than the claim.[120] This standard undertaking may be modified in an appropriate case, such as where the proceedings within the jurisdiction are ancillary to proceedings abroad. The court may be willing to grant permission to use documents and information for the purposes of enforcing or policing the freezing order.[121] Where no such undertaking is contained in the order and it is silent as to the use of material, it may be that the court will find that there is an implied undertaking not to use the material for other proceedings in the case of information other than documents. In the case of documents there is a restriction on use imposed by virtue of CPR, r.31.22.[122]

2.30 The standard form of order for a search order contains an undertaking that the applicant will not, without permission of the court, use any information or documents obtained as a result of the carrying out of the order or inform anyone else of the proceedings except for the purpose of the proceedings (including adding further respondents) or commencing civil proceed-

---

[115] See Ch.11, para.11.113.
[116] *Saunders v United Kingdom* [1998] 1 B.C.L.C. 362, ECHR.
[117] *R. v Lincolnshire Coroner, ex p. Hay* [2000] Lloyd's Rep. Medical 264 at 273, DC; *Compagnie Noga D'importation et D'exportation S.A. v Australia and New Zealand Banking Group Ltd* [2007] EWHC 85 (Comm.) see Ch.12, para.12.37.
[118] *I.B.M. United Kingdom Ltd v Prima Data International Ltd* [1994] 1 W.L.R. 719.
[119] *Bank Geselleschaft Berlin International S.A. v Zihnali*, July 16, 2001, unreported (Com. Ct).
[120] CPR, Pt 25, Practice Direction, Annex, Freezing Injunction—undertaking (9); *Derby & Co. Ltd v Weldon (No.1)* [1990] Ch. 48 at 57.
[121] *Dadourian Group International Inc. v Simms* [2006] EWCA Civ 1745.
[122] See Ch.15 below; *Attorney General for Gibraltar v May* [1999] 1 W.L.R. 998 at 1005–1008 (implied undertaking).

ings in relation to the same or related subject matter until after the return date.[123]

C. AFTER PROCEEDINGS HAVE BEEN COMMENCED

Most forms of disclosure are only given after proceedings have been commenced. The most important forms of disclosure are: **2.31**

(1) Disclosure by List ordered under CPR, r.31.5,[124] and
(2) Applications for specific disclosure of documents under CPR, r.31.12.[125]

Each of these is discussed in the appropriate place later in this work. The purpose of mentioning them here is to note the point in time at which they take place.

Generally, there is no disclosure of documents in an ordinary action until   **2.32**
after the defence has been filed and the case has been allocated to one of the three tracks.[126] It is usual, in allocating a case, for the court to give directions for future management of the case, including for disclosure.[127] Although the court has jurisdiction to order that disclosure be given at an earlier stage, this will only happen "in the most exceptional circumstances".[128] An example occurred in a case[129] where the plaintiff was making a tracing claim, and the judge ordered discovery of the defendant's bank statements before service of the statement of claim in order to save the costs of the undoubtedly heavy amendments that would be needed once discovery was given. In a defamation action early disclosure was ordered of a journalist's notes where there was an issue as to what the claimant had said during an interview.[130] But just because the probable effect of an

---

[123] CPR, Pt 25, Practice Direction, Annex, Search Order—undertaking (4).

[124] Ch.4, para.4.01; Ch.6, paras 6.01–6.34, below.

[125] Ch.6, paras 6.45–6.56, below.

[126] CPR, rr.26.3, 26.5.

[127] CPR, rr.27.4 (1)(a) (small claims track), 28.3(1)(a), (2) (fast track), 29.2(1)(a) (multi-track); see Ch.6, paras 6.47–6.53.

[128] *Gale v Denman Picture-Houses Ltd* [1930] 1 K.B. 588, CA; *Disney v Longbourne* (1876) 2 Ch.D. 704 (application to interrogate plaintiff before defence served); *Intel Corp v General Instrument Corp* [1989] F.S.R. 640; *Dun & Bradstreet Ltd v Typesetting Facilities Ltd* [1992] F.S.R. 320; *Chater v Chater Productions Ltd v Rose* [1994] F.S.R. 491; *Union Carbide Corporation v BP Chemicals Ltd* [1995] F.S.R. 449, Ct. Sess.; *Visx Inc v Nidex Co.* [1999] F.S.R. 91, CA; *Turnstem Ltd v Bhanderi* [2004] EWHC 1318 (Ch) (usually inappropriate to order disclosure for purposes of defending summary judgment application). *Computershare Ltd v Perpetual Registrars Ltd* [2000] V.S.C. 139; *Parker v C.S. Structured Credit Fund* [2003] EWHC 391 (Ch), [2003] 1 W.L.R. 1680 (disclosure prior to CMC refused).

[129] *Speyside Estate and Trust Co. Ltd v Wraymond Freeman (Blenders) Ltd* [1950] Ch. 96; see also *Dun & Bradstreet Ltd v Typesetting Facilities Ltd* [1992] F.S.R. 640; *Lyndon v Yorkshire Regional Health Authority* (1991) 10 B.M.L.R. 49 at 61–62; *Law Society of Ireland v Rawlinson & Hunter* [1997] 3 I.R. 592, Irish High Ct.

[130] *Rigg v Associated Newspapers* [2003] EWHC 710 (Q.B.).

application for an interlocutory injunction (for the purposes of which discovery was sought) would be to conclude the whole action, this does not amount to such exceptional circumstances.[131]

2.33   Even when it comes to giving directions, the court may direct that there be no disclosure, or no disclosure yet,[132] or that it should only take place in stages,[133] as e.g. where there is to be a preliminary issue[134] or a split trial.[135] The old rule was that the court could postpone discovery, where it appeared to the court that any issue or question in the proceedings should be determined before any documents was made by the parties, until that issue or question of discovery had been determined.[136] In the late nineteenth century a number of cases were decided upon the then current versions of the rule in question,[137] but in the twentieth century the courts have been more hesitant to take steps which might involve a split trial,[138] and the use of the rule was rare in practice, at least until the early 1990s.[139] An order postponing disclosure by the claimant until after the exchange of witness statements, on the basis of preventing a defendant from manufacturing evidence, is inappropriate.[140] Generally, when orders have been made postponing disclosure, this has been on the basis that disclosure at that stage was unnecessary.

2.34   Apart from the general cases referred to above, there are a number of other cases which must be mentioned. Some, such as "ship's papers" cases,[141] apply only to particular kinds of litigation. Others, such as Bankers' Books Evidence Act cases,[142] apply only as against particular persons, whatever the nature of the case. Others again, such as witness summonses,[143] non-party disclosure,[144] and applications under CPR, r.31.14,[145] are general, and may apply to any kind of case and respondent.

---

[131] *RHM Foods Ltd v Bovril Ltd* [1982] 1 W.L.R. 661, CA; see also *Hytrac Conveyors Ltd v Conveyors International Ltd* [1983] 1 W.L.R. 44.

[132] CPR, r.31.5(2).

[133] CPR, r.31.13; see Rogers (1982) 56 A.L.J. 570 at 572; Cairns, *The Use of Discovery and Interrogatories in Civil Litigation*, 1990, at 28.

[134] *Hellenic Mutual War Risks Association (Bermuda) v Harrison* [1997] 1 Lloyd's Rep. 160.

[135] See, e.g. *Baldock v Addison* [1995] 1 W.L.R. 158; *Kapur v J.W. Francis & Co., The Times*, March 4, 1998, CA.

[136] RSC, Ord.24, r.4.

[137] Including *Wood v The Anglo-Italian Bank Ltd* (1876) 34 L.T. 255; *Re Leigh's Estate* (1877) 6 Ch.D. 256, CA; *The Tasmanian Main Life Railway Co. v Clark* (1879) 27 W.R. 677; *Whyte v Ahrens* (1884) 26 Ch.D. 717, CA; *Leitch v Abbott* (1866) 31 Ch.D. 374, CA; *Benno Jaffe and Darmstädter Lanolin Fabrik v Richardson & Co.* (1893) 62 L.J. Ch. 710; *Lever v Land Securities Co. Ltd* (1894) 70 L.T. 323, CA.

[138] See, e.g. *British Thomson-Houston Co. Ltd v Duram Ltd* [1915] 1 Ch. 823, CA.

[139] But see Ch.4, para.4.09, below.

[140] *Watford Petroleum Ltd v Interoil Trading SA* [2003] EWCA Civ 1417, [2003] All E.R. (D) 175 (Sep).

[141] Paras 2.35–2.37, below.

[142] Ch.10, paras 10.37–10.43, below.

[143] Ch.10, paras 10.02–10.36, below.

[144] Ch.4, paras 4.48–4.60, below.

[145] Ch.9, paras 9.04–9.10, below.

Ship's papers

One class of case which constitutes a general exception to the rule against   2.35
disclosure before pleadings is that relating to "ship's papers". For historical
reasons,[146] it had long been open to the insurer (usually defendant, but even
if plaintiff) in an action brought upon or concerning a marine insurance
policy, before delivering his pleadings, to apply for discovery of all relevant
documents ("ship's papers"), whether in the insured's hands or not and, if
the insurer was a defendant, to obtain a stay of the action in the meantime.

The practice in this area of the law was regulated for the first time by the   2.36
(High Court) Rules in 1936,[147] and subsequently in RSC, Ord.72, r.10. It is
now contained in CPR, r.58.14 (Commercial Court), which deals with
applications in proceedings relating to a marine insurance policy. In such
cases on an application under CPR, r.31.12 for specific disclosure by underwriters, the court may order a party to produce all the ships papers and
require that party to use his best endeavours to obtain and disclose documents which are not or have not been in his control. An order may be made
at any stage of the proceedings, and on such terms as the court thinks fit,
including a stay of proceedings.[148]

Much of the old case law remains of value today, however. Thus the   2.37
insured must prima facie produce all relevant documents even if they are not
in his possession, and is only excused by showing that he has used all
reasonable efforts to obtain them and has failed to do so.[149] Since the
Second World War, applications for orders for ship's papers have in effect
been confined to cases where the insurer intends to allege a deliberate loss
of the vessel (so-called "scuttling" cases). The modern practice is described
in *Probatina Shipping Co. Ltd v Sun Insurance Office Ltd.*[150]

Non-party disclosure

Section 34 of the Supreme Court Act 1981 confers power on the court to   2.38
order disclosure by a non-party to an action at any time after the commencement of proceedings. The court accordingly has power to order
disclosure against such a person before statements of case are served, but in
practice it is more likely to do so at the allocation hearing, or even
later.[151]

---

[146] As to which see *Leon v Casey* [1932] 2 K.B. 576.
[147] Then RSC (1883), Ord.31, r.12A.
[148] *Probatina Shipping Co. Ltd v Sun Insurance Office Ltd* [1974] Q.B. 635.
[149] *West of England Bank v Canton Insurance Co.* (1877) 2 Ex.D. 472; *Teneria Moderna Franco Espanola v New Zealand Insurance Co.* [1924] 1 K.B. 79, CA.
[150] [1974] Q.B. 635, CA.
[151] The procedure is fully set out in Ch.4, paras 4.48–4.59.

Disclosure in interlocutory proceedings

2.39 A further exception relates to disclosure ordered for the limited purpose of interlocutory proceedings. Under the old rules it was held that, in a dispute as to whether the court should set aside service of a writ for want of jurisdiction, the High Court had power to order discovery to be given going to that issue.[152] However, such discovery would be ordered sparingly and only of such documents as could be shown to be necessary for the fair disposal of the application.[153] Disclosure for the purposes of a defendant resisting a summary judgment application should only be ordered in exceptional circumstances.[154] Similarly it was also held that a district judge sitting as a taxing officer had jurisdiction to order discovery, though this power should not be over enthusiastically deployed.[155] Disclosure may be ordered in the context of other applications, such as for security for costs,[156] but it should be appreciated that disclosure for interlocutory proceedings is unusual in practice and is not routinely granted. Although the CPR are differently worded to the RSC, the position under the new rules is the same.[157] Indeed, if anything the argument for the court having such power is stronger, for disclosure is no longer tied to relevance to issues in the action, but depends on what is ordered.[158]

Disclosure of funding third party

2.40 Where the costs of a party who fails in litigation have been financed by a third party, the court has power to order costs against that third party,[159] even if he is out of the jurisdiction.[160] At that stage the court may also order disclosure of the existence of a third party funder.[161] But, prior to judgment and the making of costs orders, the court has power to stay an action because of the way in which the claimant's action is being financed, e.g. if the third party was not in good faith,[162] or the situation otherwise

---

[152] *Rome v Punjab National Bank* [1989] 2 All E.R. 136; *Nissho Iwai Corporation v Golf Fisheries Company*, unreported, July 12, 1988, Hirst J.; *Canada Trust Co. v Stolzenberg*[1997] 1 W.L.R. 1582, CA.

[153] *ibid.*

[154] *Customs & Excise v Turnstem Ltd*, May 19, 2004, Ch.D, (Unpreported).

[155] *Bailey v I.B.C. Vehicles Ltd* [1998] 3 All E.R. 570, CA.

[156] *Bailey v Beagle Management Pty Ltd* [2001] F.C.A. 60 (Fed.Ct.Aus.).

[157] *Fiona Trust Holding Corp. v Privalov* [2007] EWHC 39 (Comm.).

[158] CPR, rr.31.5, 31.12(2)(a); see paras 2.32–2.33, above.

[159] Supreme Court Act 1981, s.51; *Murphy v Young and Co.'s Brewery Ltd* [1997] 1 All E.R. 518, CA.

[160] *National Justice Compania Naviera S.A. v Prudential Life Assurance Co. Ltd*, unreported, July 30, 1999, Rix J.

[161] *Singh v Observer Ltd* [1989] 2 All E.R. 751; *Raiffeisen Zentralbank Österreich AG v Crosseas Shipping Ltd* [2003] EWHC 1381 (Comm) (defendant and solicitor ordered to disclose identity of funder(s) of defence).

[162] *Condliffe v Hislop* [1996] 1 W.L.R. 753, CA.

amounted to an abuse of process.[163] However, there is no power to stay proceedings merely because the third party would not or could not accept liability to pay the defendant's costs if the latter was successful.[164] When the court has power to grant a stay, it may, in aid of that jurisdiction, order disclosure of the identity of the third party funder, but normally the better course is to let the action proceed to trial and then seek an order for costs against the third party on the basis of the result of the trial.[165]

Inspection in intellectual property cases

In intellectual property cases a claimant often seeks an order for inspection of property being the subject matter of the infringement action at an early stage in the action. But it is only in exceptional cases, such as where the claimant genuinely cannot plead its case, that inspection will be ordered prior to the issues being identified by statement of case.[166]   **2.41**

Documents referred to in statements of case an other court documents

Another exception to the general rule is CPR, r.31.14,[167] which entitles a party to an action, at any time after proceedings have been commenced, to inspect documents referred to in the statements of case, witness statements, witness summaries, affidavits, and (in many cases) experts' reports of another party. The subject is dealt with in detail later.[168]   **2.42**

Witness summons (formerly *subpoena*)

This is a means of obtaining production of documents from third parties, usually for the purposes of the trial of an action itself, but also available for interlocutory hearings. The procedure applies generally to all kinds of action and to all kinds of evidence and is discussed in detail later.[169]   **2.43**

---

[163] *Abraham v Thompson* [1997] 4 All E.R. 362, CA.
[164] *ibid.*
[165] *ibid.*
[166] See, *Smith Myers Communications Ltd v Motorola Ltd* [1991] F.S.R. 262, where the earlier cases are reviewed, *Dun & Bradstreet Ltd v Typesetting Facilities Ltd* [1972] F.S.R. 320, and also Ch.19, paras 19.02–19.13, below, dealing with inspection of subject-matter generally.
[167] Formerly RSC, Ord.24, r.10, C.C.R., Ord.14, r.4.
[168] See Ch.9, paras 9.04–9.10, below.
[169] See Ch.10, paras 10.02–10.36, below.

Bankers' Books Evidence Act 1879

2.44   Another species of third party disclosure, available once an action has been started, relates, not to the kind of action, but to the evidence concerned. Where evidence from "bankers' books" is concerned, special rules apply.[170]

Discovery on taking depositions

2.45   CPR, r.34.8(4) enables the High Court to require the production of any document which the court considers is necessary for the purposes of the taking of a deposition under CPR, rr.34.8–34.10.[171] This procedure is also used (with modifications) where evidence is to be taken, under a letter of request, from a witness resident in a foreign jurisdiction, for use in English proceedings.[172]

D. DISCLOSURE AFTER JUDGMENT HAS BEEN GIVEN

2.46   There also exist means to obtain disclosure after judgment has been given, so as to facilitate the enforcement of that judgment. The primary method of so doing is by requiring the judgment debtor to attend court to provide information and documents about his means and to be orally examined under CPR, Part 71.[173] However, it is also possible for the court to order disclosure to be given by a judgment debtor who fails to pay the judgment debt, as relief ancillary to an injunction under s.37(1) of the Supreme Court Act 1981,[174] even where no injunction is in fact granted.[175] It may also order disclosure post-judgment where issues remain between the parties, such as where disclosure goes to an account between the parties.[176]

Oral examination

2.47   This is a procedure intended to reveal the existence and whereabouts of all the assets to which the judgment debtor is entitled by which the judgment may be satisfied.[177] The examination:

---

[170] See Ch.10, paras 10.37–10.53, below.
[171] See Ch.17, paras 17.01–17.09, below.
[172] CPR, r.34.13; see paras 2.59–2.61, below.
[173] Formerly CPR, Sch.1, RSC, Ord.48.
[174] *Gidrxsime Shipping Co. Ltd v Tantomar Transporters Maritimes Ltd* [1995] 1 W.L.R. 299 (arbitration award not yet converted into judgment).
[175] *Maclaine Watson & Co. Ltd v International Tin Council (No.2)* [1989] Ch. 286, CA.
[176] *Sogelease Australia Ltd v Griffin* [2003] NSWSC 178 (overturned on other grounds [2003] N.S.W.C.A. 158).
[177] *Watkins v Ross* (1893) 68 L.T. 423 at 424, 425.

" . . . is not only intended to be an examination, but to be a cross-examination, and that of the severest kind."[178]

It applies not only in cases of judgments for the payment of money, but also other judgments as well.

It may extend to assets outside, as well as within, the jurisdiction.[179] The **2.48** debtor may be ordered to produce relevant books or documents at the hearing.[180] However it should not extend to the seeking of information which may be useful in litigation between the judgment creditor and the third parties.[181] The persons who may be examined include the judgment debtor himself and officers of a corporate debtor (including past officers[182]). However an unincorporated association or body cannot be examined,[183] and neither, it appears, may a person outside the jurisdiction.[184]

An application for an order for examination is made without notice to the **2.49** master, registrar or district judge, as appropriate. The application by a judgment creditor must be made by filing an application notice in Practice Form N316 if the application is to question an individual judgment debtor, or N316A if the application is to question an officer of a company or other corporation.[185] The order once made must be served personally in cases.[186] Substituted service may be ordered in an appropriate case,[187] or even dispensed with altogether,[188] but a judgment debtor may be committed for failure to comply if it is shown that the order has come to his knowledge and he is evading service.[189] Where the examination is adjourned,[190] unless the court dispenses with personal service of notice of the new hearing, the judgment debtor must be served with an amended order indorsed with the new date of examination, otherwise failure to attend on the resumed hearing will not constitute contempt of court.[191] A person ordered to attend may require the judgment creditor to pay his reasonable travel expenses.[192]

At the hearing the questioning is carried out by a court officer, unless the **2.50** court has ordered that the hearing be before a judge.[193] The creditor may

---

[178] *Republic of Costa Rica v Strousberg* (1880) 16 Ch.D. 8 at 12–13.
[179] *Interpool Ltd v Galani* [1988] Q.B. 738, CA.
[180] CPR, Sch.1, RSC, Ord.48, r.1(1); C.C.R., Ord.25, r.3(1).
[181] *Watkins v Ross* (1893) 68 L.T. 423.
[182] CPR, r.71.2(1) *Société Générale v Johann Maria Farina & Co.* [1904] 1 K.B. 794, CA; *cf. Irwell v Eden* (1887) 18 Q.B.D. 588, and *Cowan v Carlill* (1885) 33 W.R. 583 (garnishee absolute).
[183] *Maclaine Watson & Co. Ltd v International Tin Council (No.2)* [1989] Ch. 286, CA.
[184] *Re Tucker* [1990] Ch. 148, CA.
[185] CPR, Pt 71, Practice Direction, para.1.1.
[186] CPR, r.71.3(1); CPR, Pt 71, Practice Direction, para.3.
[187] CPR, r.6.8.
[188] CPR, r.6.9.
[189] *Kistler v Tettmar* [1905] 1 K.B.39; *cf. Re Tuck* [1906] 1 Ch. 692, CA.
[190] CPR, r.71.7.
[191] *Beeston Shipping Ltd v Babanaft International S.A.* [1985] 1 All E.R. 923, CA.
[192] CPR, r.71.4.
[193] CPR, r.71.6(2).

also ask questions.[194] The court officer makes a written record of the evidence (unless the proceedings are tape recorded), which is read to the person being questioned, who is asked to sign it.[195] Where the hearing is before a judge, the questioning is by the creditor and the proceedings are tape recorded.[196] Failure to attend or comply with an order, or to answer questions may led to a committal order.[197] Whilst the current rules have no express restriction on repeat examinations, the court will use its case management powers to restrict unnecessary repeat examinations. Under the former rules it was held that after an examination is concluded, a further examination may only be held in special circumstances.[198]

Inherent jurisdiction

2.51   The court has an inherent power under what is now s.37(1) of the Supreme Court Act 1981 to make any ancillary order, including an order for disclosure, to ensure the effectiveness of any other order made by the court.[199] In an appropriate case (e.g. where the provisions of CPR, Pt 71), this will include making an appropriate order for disclosure, in order to render a judgment effective.[200] This may include disclosure of assets outside the jurisdiction.[201]

Banker's Books Evidence Act 1879

2.52   Finally, it should be recorded that an application under this Act may be made after judgment, as well as pre-trial.[202]

Disclosure before an appellate court

2.53   Although an appellate court has jurisdiction[203] to entertain an application for disclosure for the purposes of a pending appeal, such applications are rarely made and almost never granted. Under the RSC such applications

---

[194] CPR, r.71.6(3).
[195] CPR, Pt 71, Practice Direction, para.4.
[196] CPR, Pt 71, Practice Direction, para.5.
[197] CPR, r.71.8; CPR, Pt 71, Practice Direction, paras 6–8.
[198] *Sturges v Countess of Warwick* (1913) 30 T.L.R. 112, CA.
[199] *A.J. Bekhor & Co. Ltd v Bilton* [1981] Q.B. 923, CA.
[200] *Maclaine Watson & Co. Ltd v International Tin Council (No.2)* [1989] Ch. 286, CA. The court may of course grant post-judgment freezing orders, e.g. *C Inc Plc v L* [2001] 2 Lloyd's Rep. 459.
[201] *ibid., Gidrxsime Shipping Co. Ltd v Tantomar Transporters Maritime Ltd* [1995] 1 W.L.R. 299.
[202] See Ch.10, para.10.53, below.
[203] CPR, r.52.10(1).

usually failed on the ground that the requirements of *Ladd v Marshall*[204] for the use of fresh evidence[205] were not satisfied. In one case,[206] the Court of Appeal dismissed an application for discovery of documents for the purposes of an appeal pending before that court on the ground that the documents sought were not relevant to the issues on the appeal.[207] Under the CPR, unless it otherwise orders, the court will not receive evidence which was not before the lower court.[208] Unlike the position under RSC, it is not necessary to show "special grounds", but the principles in *Ladd v Marshall* remain relevant under the CPR, as matters which must necessarily be considered in the exercise of the court's discretion.[209] These principles apply to appeals and rehearings not only in the court of Appeal, but also in the High Court and the county court.[210]

E. DISCLOSURE WHERE NO ENGLISH PROCEEDINGS IN EXISTENCE OR CONTEMPLATED

There are two main situations where a form of disclosure can be obtained, although there are no English proceedings either in existence or contemplated. One is where there are legal proceedings in another jurisdiction, and disclosure is sought here as part of the evidence-gathering process. The other is where there is an arbitration, here or elsewhere. At common law the English courts had no power to order discovery (now disclosure) or issue a *subpoena* (now witness summons) in aid of foreign proceedings[211] or an arbitration, but the position in each case has now been altered by statute.   2.54

Evidence (Proceedings in Other Jurisdictions) Act 1975

This Act permits the court to order evidence (including documentary evidence) to be gathered for the purposes of legal proceedings in other   2.55

---

[204] [1954] 1 W.L.R. 1489, CA.
[205] Pursuant to RSC, Ord.59, r.10(2) ("no such further evidence . . . shall be admitted except on special grounds").
[206] *Whiteman v Whiteman*, unreported, March 9, 1994.
[207] See also *R. v Secretary of State for the Home Department, ex p. Gardian* [1996] Imm.A.R. 6, CA.
[208] CPR, r.52.11(2)(b).
[209] *Banks v Cox*, unreported, July 17, 2000, CA; *Hamilton v Al Fayed (No.2)* [2001] E.M.L.R. 394, CA; *Gillingham v Gillingham* [2001] EWCA Civ 906, CA; *Prentice v Hereward Housing Association* [2001] 2 All E.R. (Comm) 900, CA; *Saluja v Gill* [2004] EWHC 1435 (Ch); *Riyad Bank v Ahli Bank (UK) Plc* [2005] EWCA Civ 1419, CA.
[210] *Hertfordshire Investments Ltd v Bubb*, The Times, August 31, 2000, CA.
[211] *Dreyfus v Peruvian Guano Co.* (1889) 41 Ch.D. 151; but see Ch.3, para.3.8, below: a *Norwich Pharmacal* order may be made in aid of foreign proceedings.

jurisdictions.[212] Such an order shares many of the characteristics (including its effect on third parties) of a witness summons, whether to attend court and give oral evidence, or to produce documents.[213] This procedure is to be contrasted with two other methods where disclosure may be obtained in aid of foreign proceedings:

(1) *Norwich Pharmacal* relief in aid of foreign proceedings,[214]
(2) Disclosure as part of a freezing or search order made in aid of foreign proceedings pursuant to the Civil Jurisdiction and Judgments Act, s.25, where those proceedings are ongoing in another state party to the Brussels or Lugano Conventions.[215]

Arbitration Act 1996

2.56   This Act allows the court to issue a witness summons (whether for oral evidence or the production of documents) in aid of an arbitration[216] or to make an order for the issue of a commission of request for examination out of the jurisdiction.[217] The latter power is exercisable wherever the arbitration is being conducted,[218] whereas the former is only available if the witness is in the United Kingdom and the arbitration is being conducted in England and Wales, or Northern Ireland, as the case may be.[219] The court may decline to exercise its powers under s.44 of the Arbitration Act 1996 if it considers that the fact that the seat of the arbitration is abroad makes it appropriate to do so.[220] Under the Arbitration Act 1950, the court also had power to order discovery of documents and interrogatories,[221] but this was abrogated in 1990.[222] As a result, disclosure in arbitrations is now a matter for the arbitration agreement and therefore the arbitrators.[223] The court has no power under s.43 of the Arbitration Act 1996 to order disclosure of documents in the hands of a third party.[224]

---

[212] See Ch.10, paras 10.54–10.64, below.
[213] See Ch.10, paras 10.02–10.36, below.
[214] See Ch.3, para.3.8 below.
[215] See para.2.19 above.
[216] Arbitration Act 1996, s.43(1); Ch.20, para.20.05, below.
[217] *ibid.*, s.44(1), (2)(a).
[218] *ibid.*, s.2(3)(b).
[219] *ibid.*, s.43(3).
[220] *Commerce and Industry Co. of Canada v Certain Underwriters at Lloyd's of London* [2002] 1 W.L.R. 1323, Com. Ct., Moore-Bick J.
[221] Arbitration Act 1950, s.12(6)(b).
[222] Courts and Legal Services Act 1990, s.103.
[223] See Ch.20, para.20.04, below.
[224] *BNP Paribas v Deloitte & Touche* [2003] EWHC 2874 (Comm), [2004] 1 Lloyd's Rep. 233.

F. FOREIGN DISCLOSURE FOR ENGLISH PROCEEDINGS

Finally, it should not be forgotten that it may be possible to obtain disclosure abroad for use in English proceedings.   **2.57**

The English Court will not compel a non-party abroad to provide documentary or oral evidence.[225] However, in general it will not prevent a party to take steps abroad to obtain documents or evidence using the powers and remedies of the local court.[226]   **2.58**

Whilst the English Court cannot directly compel a person abroad to attend the English or any other court to give evidence or a non-party abroad to produce documents, it can request a foreign court or jurisdiction to exercise its own powers to assist. Any request can be made using one of a number of provisions or powers: **2.59**

(1) the Hague Convention on the Taking of Evidence Abroad in Civil or Commercial matters 1970[227];

(2) individual bilateral conventions with the United Kingdom which provide for the taking of evidence abroad[228];

(3) the Taking of Evidence Regulation on co-operation between the courts of the Member States of the European Union in the taking of evidence in civil or commercial matters[229];

(4) the court's inherent jurisdiction to issue a letter of request, even where no treaty or regulation applies.[230] In such a case the foreign court is under no treaty obligation to assist, but still may do so if it regards the request as proper. This jurisdiction is only rarely exercised.

The letter of request is issued by the English court and is directed to the foreign court.[231] The English court will request the foreign jurisdiction to act under its own procedures. Usually the evidence will be taken before a judge of the foreign court or a person appointed by that court. Where the   **2.60**

---

[225] *Mackinnon v Donaldson, Lufkin & Jenrette Securities Corp.* [1986] Ch. 482; *cf. Bankers Trust International Plc v P.T. Dharmala Sakti Sejahtera*, unreported, October 19, 1995, Mance J.

[226] *South Carolina Insurance Co. v Assurantie Maatschappij "De Zeven Provincien"* [1987] A.C. 24, HL.

[227] The list of parties to the Hague Convention, together with any reservations, may be found at *http://www.hcch.net/e/status*.

[228] See the list in the Supreme Court Practice 2005, para.34.13.7.

[229] Council Regulation (EC) No.1206/2001; CPR, r.34.23; CPR, Pt.34, Practice Direction, paras 7–10. Article 21 provides that the Regulation prevails over provisions contained in multilateral or bilateral agreements concluded by Member States, in particular the Hague Conventions of 1954 and 1970. See Ch.17, paras 17.14–17.19 below.

[230] This inherent jurisdiction may be exercised, even if all that is sought is the production of documents: *Panayiotou v Sony Music Entertainment (UK) Ltd* [1994] Ch. 142.

[231] CPR, r.34.13.

foreign court permits it, the English court may appoint a special examiner to take the evidence from the witness abroad.[232] In some cases it may be appropriate for the trial judge hearing a case within the jurisdiction to appoint himself as the special examiner to receive evidence abroad. This is appropriate where the evidence is significant and controversial and it is important for the judge himself to see the witnesses. The consent of the state in which the evidence is to be taken is required, but this procedure can be followed without the consent of the parties to the litigation.[233] In the Commercial Court it is the practice that it is only in a very exceptional case, and subject to necessary approvals being obtained and diplomatic requirements being satisfied, the court may be willing to conduct part of the proceedings abroad. However, if there is any reasonable opportunity for the witness to give evidence by video link, the court is unlikely to take that course.[234] In some circumstances, the special examiner may be the British Consul or Consul-General or his deputy in the country concerned.[235] Some jurisdictions do not permit examination pursuant to letters of request at all, others only permit for willing witnesses (or willing British witnesses). A letter of request cannot be directed to a company for the examination of a witness. A company cannot be required to attend, by its proper officer, to give oral evidence. An individual must be named.[236] In certain circumstances, a letter of request in respect of a special examiner taking oral evidence may be dispensed with. In one case it was observed that the letter of request procedure is to meet the position where it is quite unknown whether the government of the country would give its consent, where it is understood it might not indicate its consent to a special examiner examining a person in its country or where it may require time to fully consider the matter.[237] Despite this statement, in most cases a formal letter of request is both appropriate and necessary.

2.61   The letter of request must be put before the senior master for issue and must contain a statement of issues relevant to the proceedings and a list of questions or the subject matter of questions to be put before the proposed deponent.[238] The order of the English court may require the production of any document which the court considers is necessary for the purposes of the

---

[232] CPR, r.34.13(4); CPR, Pt.34, Practice Direction, para.5.8.

[233] *Peer International Corporation v Termidor Music Publishers Ltd* [2005] EWHC 1048 (Ch), *The Times*, June 2, 2005, Ch.D.

[234] *Admiralty and Commercial Courts Guide* (7th edn, 2006), para.H4.2.

[235] CPR, Pt.34, Practice Direction, para.5.8.

[236] *Penn-Texas Corporation v Murat Anstalt* [1964] 1 Q.B. 40; *Penn-Texas Corporation v Murat Anstalt (No.2)* [1964] 2 Q.B. 647, 662, 665; *Panayiotou v Sony Music Ltd* [1994] Ch. 142 at 147. However, where all that is sought is the production of documents the letter of request can be directed to a company by its proper officer.

[237] *Peer International Corporation v Termidor Music Publishers Ltd* [2005] EWHC 1048 (Ch), *The Times*, June 25, 2005, Lindsay J.

[238] CPR, r.34.13(6); CPR, Pt.34, Practice Direction, paras 5. The form of request under the Taking of Evidence Regulation is prescribed: CPR, r.34.23(3); CPR, Pt.34, Practice Direction, para.10.

examination.[239] The court does have jurisdiction to issue a letter of request concerned only with the production of documents. Nevertheless, a letter of request should not be used as a mechanism of getting general discovery from a non-party abroad. The purpose of a letter of request is to seek evidence, hence the jurisdiction in respect of documents is exercisable when the request is confined to particular documents which are admissible in evidence and directly material to an issue in the action. The court must be satisfied that the documents exist or did exist and is likely to be in the possession of the person from whom production is sought.[240] However, in a controversial decision, the Court of Appeal has held that limitation in ordinary litigation, that a request may only seek production of documents which can be proved to exist or have existed, does not apply to orders in financial proceedings following a divorce.[241] The master has a discretion to issue a letter of request[242] and in cases of uncertainty or difficulty he can direct that the application is notified to all the parties. In deciding whether to make an order the court may take into account a number of considerations such as[243]:

(1) Cost and whether there is a practical alternative such as another witness within the jurisdiction[244] or taking the evidence by some other means (e.g. videolink)[245];

(2) the willingness or ability of the witness to come to England to give evidence and whether his attendance within the jurisdiction cannot be procured[246];

---

[239] CPR, r.34.8(4).

[240] *Panayiotou v Sony Music Entertainment (UK) Ltd* [1994] Ch. 142: the degree of particularity in respect of documents is the same for witness summonses to produce documents, outgoing letters of request and incoming letters of request (at 152).

[241] *Charman v Charman* [2005] EWCA Civ 1606, [2006] 1 W.L.R. 1053, CA. Whether foreign courts would be willing to give effect to such a request is a different matter. In that case the Bermudian Court refused to give effect to the letter of request as being contrary to principle (Bell J., December 22, 2005, unreported).

[242] *Coch v Allcock* (1888) 21 Q.B.D. 178, CA.

[243] *Hardie Rubber Co. v General Tire & Rubber Co.* (1972) 46 A.J.L.R. 326 (1973) 47 A.J.L.R. 462; *Smith v Smith* (1975) 5 A.L.R. 444.

[244] *Armour v Walker* (1883) 25 Ch.D. 673, CA; *Lawson v Vacuum Brake Co.* (1884) 27 Ch.D. 137, CA; *Lewis v Kingsbury* (1888) 4 T.L.R. 629 at 639.

[245] *B. v Dentists Disciplinary Tribunal* [1994] 1 N.Z.L.R. 95 (video conference for expert abroad); *Bell Group Ltd v Westpac* [2004] WASC 162 (where the court decided to relocate to London from Perth to hear some witnesses and for others to give evidence by videolink).

[246] In *Willis v Trequair* (1906) 3 C.L.R. 912 at 919, it was held that where a party shows to the satisfaction of the court that a witness is out of the jurisdiction that the evidence to be proposed to be called is material, that the court has no power to enforce attendance and that party cannot procure his attendance, then prima facie the court is bound to exercise its discretion to make an order unless the other side can establish that he can and will attend. See also *Bell Group Ltd v Westpac* [2004] W.A.S.C. 162 at [154]. In order to prove that the attendance of material witnesses abroad can not be procured it is sufficient to show that they could not be reasonably expected to attend: *Smith v Smith* (1975) 5 A.L.R. 444 at 450.

(3) whether the application is made bona fide[247] or is an impermissible fishing exercise[248];

(4) the timing of the application (such that it will not cause delay)[249];

(5) whether the witness can give substantial and material evidence on a real question to be tried between the parties[250];

(6) whether the person whose evidence is sought is in fact a party to the proceedings[251];

(7) whether the order would be so oppressive on a non-party as to outweigh the likely value of the material in the determination of the proceedings[252];

(8) whether the execution letter of request in the foreign jurisdiction would cause injustice. In this context the court may take into account the procedure in the foreign state, including whether it would permit the evidence to be properly tested[253];

(9) whether having regard to the interests of the parties justice will be better served by granting or refusing an order for a letter of request.[254]

The court can refuse to authorise a letter of request which is designed to show that a friendly state in promulgating a particular law acted in a way such that the law is contrary to public policy and hence unenforceable in England.[255] The principles applicable to the issuing of an outgoing request are equated to those applicable to the giving effect to an incoming request.[256] Thus the court should refuse to issue an outgoing letter of request in circumstances in which had the request been incoming, it would not give effect to it.[257] The court can also impose terms on the order, including the provision of security and as to the use to which the evidence

---

[247] *Re Boyse* (1882) 20 Ch.D. 760.

[248] *Armour v Walker* (1883) 25 Ch.D. 673 at 677; *Hardie Rubber Co. v General Tire Co.* (1972) 46 A.J.L.R. 326 at 331, (1973) 47 A.J.L.R. 462 at 466. The court will not grant a roving commission.

[249] *Langen v Tate* (1883) 24 Ch.D. 522, CA; *Smith v Smith* (1975) 5 A.L.R. 444 at 451.

[250] *Ehrmann v Ehrmann* [1896] 2 Ch. 611.

[251] A party who has chosen an English forum is less likely to be able to give his evidence this way, than a defendant resident abroad: *Ross v Woodford* [1894] 1 Ch. 42; *New v Burns* (1894) 64 L.J.Q.B. 104, CA; *Cock v Allcock* (1888) 21 Q.B.D. 178; CA; *Emmanuel v Soltykoff* (1892) 8 T.L.R. 331.

[252] *Charman v Charman* [2005] EWCA Civ 1606, [2006] 1 W.L.R. 1053 at [53].

[253] *Hardie Rubber Co. v General Tire & Rubber Co.* (1972) 46 A.J.L.R. 326 at 328.

[254] *Smith v Smith* (1975) 5 A.L.R. 444 at 450. The interests of justice test is specifically provided for in s.8 Foreign Evidence Act 1994 (Cth) for the Australian federal jurisdiction, whilst at the state level there are specific provisions in the relevant Evidence Acts. For a detailed analysis see *Bell Group Ltd v Westpac* [2004] W.A.S.C. 162.

[255] *Settebello v Banco Totta and Acores* [1985] 1 W.L.R. 1050.

[256] *Panayiotou v Sony Music Entertainment (UK) Ltd* [1994] Ch. 142 at 152.

[257] *Charman v Charman* [2005] EWCA Civ 1606; [2006] 1 W.L.R. 1053 at [29].

may be put.[258] The procedure once the order has been made for the issue of a letter of request is governed by CPR, r.34.13 and the accompanying Practice Direction.

In respect of witnesses in the USA, rather than using the letter of request **2.62** procedure, it may be possible to apply direct to a US district court for evidence under US Code, Title 28, s.1782.[259] The following three requirements must be satisfied before an order can be made:

(1) that the person[260] from whom the discovery is sought resides or is found in the district of the US district court to which the application is made;
(2) that the discovery is for use in a proceeding[261] before a foreign tribunal[262];
(3) that the application is made by a foreign or international tribunal or any interested person.

The application to the US district court may be made without notice,[263] **2.63** but any order may be set aside on an inter partes application. The district court has a wide discretion to order, limit or refuse discovery.[264] There is no requirement that the evidence sought must be discoverable[265] or otherwise available under a similar procedure in the laws of the country concerned, although this may be a relevant factor.[266] It is no bar that the proceeding for which discovery is sought is of a criminal character, even one involving local exchange control legislation.[267] In the *South Carolina* case, the House of

---

[258] *Hardie Rubber Co. v General Tire & Rubber Co.* (1972) A.J.L.R. 326 at 335.

[259] *Malev Hungarian Airlines v United Technologies International Inc.* [1993] I.L. Pr. 422, US Ct. of Appeals, (1993) 42 I.C.L.Q. 356; *Re Euromepa S.A.*, 51F.3d. 1095 (2d. Cir., 1995); *In re Metallgesellschaft A.G.*, 121 F.3d 77 (2d. Cir., 1997).

[260] In this context "person" does not include the US Government *Al Fayed v Central Intelligence Agency*, 229 F.3d 272 (D.C. Cir. 2002).

[261] This means a proceeding in which an adjudicative function is being exercised: *Re Letters Rogatory*, 385 F.2d. 1017 (2d. Cir., 1967) at 1021. This includes a bankruptcy pending in court: *Lancaster Factoring Company Ltd v Mangone* [1998] I.L. Pr. 200, US Ct. of Appeals. The proceeding may be future, rather than pending: *Re Request from Ministry of Legal Affairs of Trinidad and Tobago*, 848 F.2d. 1151 (11th Cir., 1988). It does not include a proceeding such as an appeal before a tribunal that does not hear evidence: *Euromepa S.A. v R. Esmerian Inc* [1999] I.L. Pr. 694, US Ct. of Appeals (2nd Cir.).

[262] This includes an arbitration panel: *Re Application of Technostrogexport*, 853 F. Supp. 695 (S.D.N.Y., 1994). It does not include a superintendent of Exchange Control. *Fonseca v Blumenthal*, 620 F.2d. 322 (2nd Cir., 1980).

[263] *Re Letter Rogatory from Tokyo District*, 539 F.2d. 1216 (9th Cir., 1976).

[264] *Re Euromepa S.A.*, 51 F.3d. 1095 at 1097 (2nd. Cir., 1995).

[265] *Re Application by Bayer A.G.* [1999] I.L. Pr. 786, (US Ct. of Appeals, 3rd Cir.); *United Kingdom v US*, 238 F.3d 1312 (11th Cir. 2001).

[266] *Re Gianola*, 3 F.3d. 54 (2nd Cir., 1993); *Re Metallgesellschaft A.G.*, 121 F.3d. 77 (2d. Cir., 1997); *Intel Corp. v Advanced Micro Devices, Inc*, 542 US 241, 124 S.Ct. 2466 (2004) US Supreme Ct.; *In re Servico Pan Americano de Protection*, 354 F. Supp. 2d 269 (S.D.N.Y. 2004).

[267] *Re Request for Judicial Assistance from the Seoul District Criminal Court*, 555 F.2d. 720 (9th Cir., 1977).

Lords set aside an injunction restraining a party using the US pre-trial discovery procedure in aid of proceedings in England.[268] However, the English court retains a discretion to grant an injunction where it is unconscionable for a party to pursue a s.1782 application.[269]

---

[268] *South Carolina Insurance Co. v Assurantie Maatshappij De Zeven Provincien* [1987] A.C. 24.

[269] *Omega Group Holdings Ltd v Kozeny* [2002] C.L.C. 132, Com. Ct. (injunction granted).

CHAPTER 3

Norwich Pharmacal and other pre-action disclosure

CHAPTER 3

Norwich Pharmacal and other pre-action disclosure

This chapter deals with cases which involve taking some preliminary legal action, the sole purpose of which is to obtain the disclosure required. These are:

    3.01

  (a) *Norwich Pharmacal* orders.
  (b) Pre-action disclosure under the Supreme Court Act 1981, s.33 and CPR, r.31.16.
  (c) Corporate insolvency.
  (d) Applications to inspect the court file in other litigation.

In some litigation it may be appropriate to apply for both a *Norwich Pharmacal* order as well as pre-action disclosure under CPR r.31.16.

A. NORWICH PHARMACAL ORDERS

This is the modern manifestation of the old Chancery procedure, used in aid of common law actions, known as the "bill of discovery".[1] At the present day, other than in the context of tracing claims, such orders are largely directed, not so much to documents, as to disclosure of the identity (or address[2]) of a particular person, being either the person who has committed the wrong, or the person into whose hands property the subject of the action has passed. However, such orders could theoretically be made in respect of documents or other information, and in *Taylor v Anderton*,[3] Scott J. held that the old "bill of discovery" procedure of the Court of

    3.02

---

[1] *Gait v Osbaldeston* (1826) 1 Russ 158; *Mendizabal v Machado* (1826) 2 Russ. 540.
[2] *The Coca-Cola Company v British Telecommunications Plc* [1999] F.S.R. 518.
[3] *The Times*, October 21, 1986.

Chancery was still available for pre-action disclosure of documents from potential defendants. However, Scott J. found it difficult to construct circumstances where it might be proper to allow such an application to succeed, particularly given that today it is possible in special cases to issue proceedings and apply for disclosure *before* serving a statement of claim.[4]

3.03   After the nineteenth century, the bill of discovery procedure fell into disuse, until it was revived by the House of Lords in *Norwich Pharmacal Co. v Commissioners of Customs & Excise*.[5] In that case it was held that a person who was innocently caught up in the wrongdoing of another, so that he was more than a "mere witness" could be compelled to disclose the identity of the actual wrongdoer, in order that proceedings could be taken by the victim against the appropriate defendant. This *Norwich Pharmacal* jurisdiction has been developed by case law to become a useful mechanism to obtain information about wrongdoers and location of assets. The jurisdiction has been applied widely across the common law jurisdictions (albeit with varying scope): Australia,[6] Belize,[7] Canada,[8] Gibraltar,[9] Cayman Islands,[10]

---

[4] See para.2.32, above. This is all the more so, now that pre-action disclosure is available under CPR, r.31.16.

[5] [1974] A.C. 133.

[6] *Kirella Pty Ltd v Hooper* (1999) 161 A.L.R. 447, *Airservices v Transfield* (1999) 164 A.L.R. 330 and *Lifetime Investments Ltd v Commercial (Worldwide) Financial Services Pty Ltd* [2005] FCA 226 (Federal Court of Australia); *Re Pyne* [1997] 1 Qd.R. 326 (Queensland); *Idoport Pty Ltd v National Australia Bank Ltd* [2004] N.S.W.S.C. 695 (New South Wales); *Computershare Ltd v Perpetual Registrars Ltd* [2000] V.S.C. 139 (Victoria).

[7] *Securities and Exchange Commission v Banner Fund* (Action No.85 of 1994), February 2, 1996 (unreported), where *Bankers Trust Co. v Shipira* [1980] 1 W.L.R. 1274 recognised.

[8] *Glaxo Wellcome Plc v Minister of National Revenue* (1998) 172 D.L.R. (4th) 433, F.C.A. and *BMG Canada Inc v John Doe* (2005) 252 D.L.R. (4th) 342, F.C.A. (Federal decisions); *Re Johnston and Johnston Restaurants* (1980) 93 A.P.R. 341 (Prince Edward Island CA); *Leahy v Dr. A.B.* (1992) 113 N.S.R. (2d) 417 and *Re Comeau* (1986) 77 N.S.R. (2d) 47 (Nova Scotia Sup.Ct.); *Kenny v Loewen* (1999) 64 B.C.L.R. (3d) 346 (British Columbia Sup.Ct.); *National Bank of Canada v Mann* (1999) 37 C.P.C. (4th) 88 and *Straka v Humber River Regional Hospital* (2000) 193 D.L.R. (4th) 680 (Ontario CA); *Alberta Treasury Branches v Leahy*, 2000 A.B.Q.B. 575 and *Canadian Derivatives Clearing Corporation v EFA Software Services Ltd*, 2001 A.B.Q.B. 425 (Alberta Queen's Bench).

[9] *Secilpar SL v Fiduciary Trust Ltd*, September 24, 2004, Gibraltar CA (unreported).

[10] *Kilderkin Investments v Player*, 1980–83 C.I.L.R. 403; *Federal Savings v Molinaro*, 1988–89 C.I.L.R.6; *C Corporation v P.*, 1994–95 C.I.L.R. 189; *Grupo Torras v Butterfield Bank*, 2000 C.I.L.R. 442; *Deutsch-Südamerikanische Bank v Codelco*, 1996 C.I.L.R. 1; *Grupo Torras v Butterfield Bank*, 2000 C.I.L.R. 452. All these decisions of the Grand Court are in respect of fraud/tracing claims where *Bankers Trust Co. v Shapira* [1980] 1 W.L.R. 1274 was applied.

Guernsey,[11] Hong Kong,[12] Isle of Man,[13] Ireland,[14] Jersey,[15] Malaysia,[16] New Zealand,[17] and Northern Ireland.[18]

Requirements

In order to grant *Norwich Pharmacal* relief the following must be shown: **3.04**

(1) That a wrong has been carried out, or at least arguably carried out, by a wrongdoer.

(2) That the claimant intends to assert his legal rights against the wrongdoer.

(3) That there is the need for an order to enable action to be brought against the wrongdoer, usually to require the defendant to the application to identify the wrongdoer. In other words, that an order is necessary to assist the claimant in achieving justice and there is no other practical source of information, or that it is just and convenient to make the order sought.

(4) That the defendant or respondent is a person who was mixed up in, or facilitated the wrongdoing (even innocently) or has some relationship with the wrongdoer sought to be identified, and is able to provide the information necessary to enable the wrongdoer to be identified or sued.

The court has a residual discretion as to whether it is right that an order should be made in all the circumstances. In this respect, the court may

---

[11] *Novo Nordisk A/S v Banco Santandar (Guernsey) Ltd* (2000) 2 I.T.E.L.R. 557; *President of the State of Equatorial Guinea v Royal Bank of Scotland International* [2006] U.K.P.C. 7, Privy Council.
[12] *Computerland Corporaton v Yew Seng Computers Pte Ltd* [1985] H.K.C.A. 201; *Manufacturers Life Insurance Company of Canada v Harvest Hero International Ltd* [2002] H.K.C.A. 83; *Re Greater Beijing Region Expressway Ltd* [2000] H.K.C.F.I. 171; *Seacliff Ltd v Decca Ltd* [2002] H.K.C.F.I. 187; *A Co. v B Co.* [2002] H.K.C.F.I. 261; *Cinepoly Records Co. Ltd v Hong Kong Broadband Network Ltd* [2006] H.K.C.F.I. 84.
[13] *Secilpar SL v Burgundy Consultants Ltd*, August 3, 2004 unreported (Ch.D.), where the authorities were extensively reviewed; order made in aid of foreign proceedings.
[14] *Megaleasing UK v Barrett* [1993] I.R.L.M. 497; *Doyle v Commissioner of An Garda Siochana* [1999] 1 I.R. 147 (restrictive approach to the jurisdiction).
[15] *IBL v Planet* [1990] J.L.R. 294; *Grupo Torras S.A. v Royal Bank of Scotland* [1994] J.L.R. 42.
[16] *First Malaysia Finance Bbhd v Mohd Fathi Haji Ahmad* [1993] 2 A.M.R. 1293; *Teoh Pen Phe v Wan & Co.* [2001] 1 M.M.R. 358.
[17] *Fitzherbert v Faisandier* (1995) 8 P.R.N.Z. 592 (defendant required to disclose his assets worldwide).
[18] *Anderson v Halifax Plc* [2000] N.I.L.R. 1 (Ch.D.).

balance any interest in disclosure against any other public (e.g. freedom of the press) and private (e.g. confidentiality and privacy) interest in order to decide whether in all the circumstances it is appropriate to order disclosure.

3.05   As to the first requirement, the need to show a wrong, in *Norwich Pharmacal* itself the type of wrong was a tort. Subsequent cases have made clear that any type of wrong may be sufficient, whether civil or criminal. Thus the victim of a crime may seek the identity of the wrongdoer. An individual who has not suffered in consequence of a crime is not entitled to bring proceedings; such proceedings would need to be brought on behalf of the public by the Attorney General.[19] It is not necessary that the wrong complained of is criminal in character.[20] It may simply be a tort with no criminal counterpart.[21] Other examples are:

(1) breach of contract or confidence[22];
(2) a copyright[23] or trademark infringement[24];
(3) breach of trust or other equitable wrong[25];
(4) fraudulent payments[26];
(5) breaches of companies legislation as to shareholdings[27]

3.06   While the exercise of the jurisdiction does require that there should be some evidence of wrongdoing, the wrongdoing that is required is the wrongdoing of the person whose identity the claimant is seeking to establish and not that of the person against whom the proceedings are brought.[28] It is not necessary for the claimant to establish that there has in fact been a wrong, although there must be at least some reasonable basis for contending that a

---

[19] *Ashworth Security Hospital v MGN Ltd* [2002] UKHL 29, [2002] 1 W.L.R. 2033, HL, disapproving CA decision in *Interbrew S.A. v Financial Times* [2002] EWCA Civ 274, [2002] 1 Lloyd's Rep. 542 which had held that the detection of crime is not a proper object of the *Norwich Pharmacal* power.

[20] *P. v T. Ltd* [1997] 1 W.L.R. 1309.

[21] *P. v T. Ltd* [1997] 1 W.L.R. 1309; but *cf. Lyell v Kennedy* (1883) 8 App.Cas. 217 at 233, 234.

[22] *British Steel Corporation v Granada Television Ltd* [1981] A.C. 1096; *Computershare Ltd v Perpetual Registrars Ltd* [2000] V.S.C. 139; *China National Petroleum v Fenwick Elliott* [2002] EWHC 60 (Ch); *Hughes v Carratu International Plc* [2006] EWHC 1791 (Q.B.) (enquiry agent and unlawfully obtained data).

[23] *Michael O'Mara Books Ltd v Express Newspapers Plc* [1999] F.S.R. 518; *Microsoft Corporation v Plato Technology Ltd* [1999] F.S.R. 834; *Cinepoly Records Co. Ltd v Hong Kong Broadband Network Ltd* [2006] H.K.C.F.I. 84 (order against internet suppliers for identify of alleged online copyright infringers).

[24] *The Coca Cola Company v British Telecommunications Plc* [1999] F.S.R. 518; *Microsoft Corporation v Plato Technology Ltd* [1999] F.S.R. 834.

[25] *Bankers Trust v Shapira* [1980] 1 W.L.R. 1274, CA; *re Murphy's Settlements* [1998] 3 All E.R. 1.

[26] *Seacliff Ltd v Decca Ltd* [2001] H.K.C.F.I. 275.

[27] *Secilpar SL v Fiduciary Trust Ltd*, September 24, 2004, Gibraltar CA.

[28] *Ashworth Hospital v MGN Ltd* [2002] UKHL 29, [2002] 1 W.L.R. 29 at [26].

wrong may have been committed. In a number of cases the courts have made a *Norwich Pharmacal* order to enable claimants to discover whether or not a wrong has been committed,[29] and also to enable them to pursue other legitimate purposes connected with the action, even though the disclosure sought would not identify any wrongdoers.[30] In some cases the test applied has been whether the claimants can show a *bona fide* claim; it is not necessary to establish a *prima facie* case of wrongdoing.[31]

As to the second requirement, the purpose of the *Norwich Pharmacal* **3.07** action need not be for the purposes of bringing civil proceedings against a wrongdoer, although this is usually the case. It is enough that the claimant seeks to assert his legal rights.[32] The procedure is available when the claimant desires to obtain redress against the wrongdoer or to protect himself against further wrongdoing.[33] It has also been held to be available where the claimant requires the information to enable him to decide whether or not to support or oppose a winding up petition,[34] or to obtain information for the purpose of a prospective costs application against a non-party funder.[35] However, in one case it has been held that an order should not be made for the purpose of identifying a person against whom it was intended to bring proceedings for criminal contempt.[36]

In the nineteenth century it was ultimately held that a bill of discovery **3.08** was not available in aid of foreign proceedings contrary to some earlier authority to the effect that it was so available.[37] This restriction is no longer applicable and it has now been held that in appropriate cases a *Norwich Pharmacal* order may be made for discovery in aid of foreign proceedings.[38] It may also be possible to obtain *Norwich Pharmacal* relief in support of proceedings in another state, which is party to the Brussels or Lugano

---

[29] *P. v T.* [1997] 1 W.L.R. 1039 at 1318A–E; *Re Murphy's Settlements* [1998] 3 All E.R.1; *cf. Arab Monetary Fund v Hashim (No.5)* [1992] 2 All E.R. 911; *AXA Equity and Law Life Assurance Society Plc v National Westminster Bank Plc* [1998] P.N.L.R. 433.
[30] *CHC Software Care Ltd v Hopkins & Wood* [1993] F.S.R. 241; *Jade Engineering (Coventry) Ltd v Antiference Window Systems Ltd* [1996] F.S.R. 461; *cf. Norwich Pharmacal Co. v Customs & Excise Commissioners* [1974] A.C. 133 at 174, *per* Lord Reid.
[31] *BMG Canada Inc v John Doe* (2005) 252 D.L.R. (4th) 342, Fed. CA, Canada.
[32] *Ashworth Hospital v MGN* [2002] UKHL 29; [2002] 1 W.L.R. 29, HL.
[33] *British Steel Corp v Granada Television Ltd* [1981] A.C. 1096 at 1127 and 1132, HL.
[34] *Re Greater Beijing Region Expressway Ltd* [2000] H.K.C.F.I. 171.
[35] *Idoport Pty Ltd v National Australia Bank Ltd* [2004] N.S.W.C.S. 695.
[36] *Secretary for Justice v Apple Daily Ltd* [2000] H.K.C.F.I. 778 (decided before *Ashworth Hospital*).
[37] *Reiner v Salisbury* (1876) 2 Ch.D. 178 (related to land in India so the matter was for the courts in India); *Dreyfus v Peruvian Guano Co.* (1889) 41 Ch.D. 151 was based on the notion that the court would not grant an order in aid of proceedings before an inferior tribunal, and all foreign courts were then considered to be inferior.
[38] *Manufacturers Life Insurance Company of Canada v Harvest Hero* [2002] H.K.C.A. 83 (Hong Kong CA); *Secilpar SL v Fiduciary Trust Ltd*, September 24, 2004, Gibraltar CA; *Secilpar SL v Burgundy Consultants Ltd*, August 3, 2004, Isle of Man, Ch.D; *President of the State of Equatorial Guinea v Royal Bank of Scotland International*, April 5, 2005 (Guernsey CA), not challenged on appeal to Privy Council, [2006] U.K.P.C. 7 at [11]; *Davis v Turning Properties* [2005] N.S.W.S.C. 742, (2006) 222 A.L.R. 676 at [35].

Convention, pursuant to s.25 (as amended) of the Civil Jurisdiction and Judgments Act 1982 or to which Council Regulation (EC) 44 of 2001 applies. Whilst this provision expressly does not apply to applications for the provision of evidence, this exception has been restrictively applied.[39] Usually the subject matter of a *Norwich Pharmacal* application is information rather than evidence.[40] Thus in a number of cases it has been held appropriate to order discovery of information and documents under this provision in aid of foreign proceedings.[41] Where proceedings are to be brought within the jurisdiction, it does not matter that the alleged wrongdoer is outside it.[42]

3.09   As to the third requirement, it must be shown that the discovery sought is necessary to enable the claimant to take action, or that at least that it is just and convenient in the interests of justice to make the order sought.[43] This raises the following elements:

(1) whether the information sought can be shown to be necessary;
(2) the extent of information which may be ordered to be disclosed;
(3) whether there is an alternative and more appropriate method to obtain the information sought.

3.10   The information sought must be necessary for the purposes of the claimant asserting his legal rights. Thus a third party will not be ordered to disclose information which may lead to the preservation of assets to which the claimant is making a proprietary claim unless the claimant can show "a real prospect" that the information may so lead.[44] An order may be refused if the claimant is aware of the identity of the wrongdoer and has sufficient information to sue him.[45]

3.11   The extent of the information which needs to be disclosed varies. In many cases the disclosure of the identity of the wrongdoer may be enough. The

---

[39] Civil Jurisdiction and Judgments Act 1982, s.25(7). This exception does not extend to applications for disclosure ancillary to a freezing injunction: *Republic of Haiti v Duvalier*, June 7, 1988, CA, unreported (see [1989] Lloyd's Rep.111; [1990] 1 Q.B. 202 at 209).

[40] *Norwich Pharmacal Co. v Customs and Excise* [1974] A.C. 133 at 199, where Lord Cross stated "This case has nothing to do with the collection of evidence."

[41] *Secilpar SL v Fiduciary Trust Ltd*, September 24, 2004, Gibraltar CA; *Secilpar SL v Burgundy Consultants Ltd*, August 3, 2004, Isle of Man, Ch.D.

[42] *Smith Kline & French Laboratories Ltd v Global Pharmaceutics Ltd* [1986] R.P.C. 394; *Jade Engineering (Coventry) Ltd v Antiference Window Systems Ltd* [1996] F.S.R. 461.

[43] *President of the State of Equatorial Guinea v Royal Bank of Scotland International* [2006] U.K.P.C. 7 at [16], where it was observed that whether it is said it must be just and convenient in the interests of justice to grant relief, or that relief should only be granted if it is necessary in the interests of justice to grant it, makes little or no difference of substance.

[44] *Arab Monetary Fund v Hashim (No.5)* [1992] 2 All E.R. 911 at 918.

[45] *Nikitin v Butler LLP* [2007] EWHC 173 (Q.B.).

obligation may extend to giving full information,[46] and of course the order may expressly so provide. But "full information" does not mean general or standard disclosure of the kind obtainable under CPR, Pt 31. It means practical information to enable a claimant to make a commercial judgment as to the enforcement of its remedies against a wrongdoer.[47] In the context of a tracing claim where the claimant is seeking to follow the proceeds of a fraud or breach of trust, the disclosure order against banks and financial institutions can in practice be quite extensive.[48] In addition a person required to provide statement or affidavit as to his or someone else's assets and dealings, may also be required to attend for cross-examination on such statement or affidavit.[49] In any event, the information sought must be specific.[50] In one case where a defendant sold counterfeit copies of the claimant's software, *Norwich Pharmacal* relief was limited to counterfeit software from the same source.[51] The rule has also been extended to require the defendant to disclose the holding of the property in dispute (including the identity of any trustees),[52] or alternatively (if it be the case) the identity of a further "innocent" party mixed up in the wrongdoing, as being the party to whom the property in dispute (e.g. in a tracing action) has been transferred.[53] If the circumstances justify it, the new innocent party may be joined as a defendant, to disclose in turn whether the property is still held by it, or alternatively where the property may have been subsequently transferred.[54]

Where the person who could be required to give disclosure under the *Norwich Pharmacal* rule is a corporation, then an order can be obtained also to require the employees or agents of the corporation to give the necessary information.[55]   **3.12**

---

[46] *Norwich Pharmacal Co. v Customs & Excise Commissioners* [1974] A.C. 133 at 175; *Bankers Trust Co. v Shapira* [1980] 1 W.L.R. 1274 at 1281; *Société Romanaise de la Chaussure S.A. v British Shoe Corp. Ltd* [1991] F.S.R. 1 at 5; see also *Choy v Nissei Sangyo America Ltd* [1992] 2 H.K.L.R. 177, H.K.C.A.; *Aoot Kalmneft v Denton Wilde Sapte* [2002] 1 Lloyd's Rep. 417 at 423 (disclosure not limited to identity of wrongdoer, but also to information showing he has committed the wrong); *cf. Megaleasing UK, Ltd v Barrett* [1993] I.L.R.M. 497.

[47] *AXA Equity and Law Life Assurance Society Plc v National Westminster Bank Plc* [1998] P.N.L.R. 433.

[48] *Bankers Trust Co. v Shapira* [1980] 1 W.L.R. 1274, CA (tracing order against bank). *Alberta Treasury Branches v Leahy*, 2000 A.B.Q.B. 575 at [68–106], Q.B. of Alberta (tracing funds); *Seacliff ltd v Decca Ltd* [2001] H.K.C.F.I. 275 (order to uncover fraudulent payments); *Seacliff Ltd v Decca Ltd* [2002] H.K.C.F.I. 187 (tracing order against bank); see para.3.15 below; see also Cayman Island decisions referred to in para.3.3 above.

[49] *Kensington International Limited v Republic of Congo* [2006] EWHC 1848 (Comm)—non-party ordered to attend for cross-examination; see also Ch.2, para.2.13 above.

[50] *Arab Monetary Fund v Hashim (No.5)* [1992] 2 All E.R. 911 at 919.

[51] *Microsoft Corporation v Plato Technology Ltd* [1999] F.S.R. 834.

[52] *Re Murphy's Settlements* [1998] 3 All E.R.1.

[53] *A. v C.* [1981] Q.B. 956; *Bankers Trust Co. v Shapira* [1980] 1 W. L.R. 1274, CA; see also *Omar v Omar* [1995] 1 W.L.R. 1428.

[54] *Ibid.*

[55] See *Harrington v North London Polytechnic* [1984] 1 W.L.R. 1293, CA; *cf. Wilson v Church* (1878) 9 Ch.D. 552.

3.13   Where there is an alternative method of obtaining the information, relief may be refused. Thus if the claimant failed to make basic enquiries, which may have led to the identify of the wrongdoer, before making the application for a *Norwich Pharmacal* order, the court in its discretion may decline relief. Relief may be refused where the information will become available from a likely party to substantive proceedings,[56] but the fact that an intended defendant may have to produce the information in an action is generally not a valid ground of objection in a tracing claim.

3.14   As to the fourth requirement, it must be shown that the defendant is a person who was mixed up in, or facilitated the wrongdoing (even innocently). This requirement has been variously described in the authorities. In some cases it may be enough to show that the defendant has some relationship with the wrongdoing. Thus a telephone company may be required to provide information about a customer who has used a telephone as part of his wrongdoer, or a banker required to provide details of accounts where his customer has used the bank to transfer or deposit misappropriated funds. However, a person is not liable to disclose the identity of a wrongdoer if, although he knows that identity, he has not himself either committed or facilitated or otherwise become mixed up in the commission of that wrong.[57] There may be circumstances where the mere receipt of information wrongfully sent may be sufficient involvement for these purposes because that in itself facilitates the wrong.[58] In addition there is the "mere witness" rule.[59] This prevents a party from obtaining discovery against a person who will in due course be compellable to give that information either by oral testimony as a witness at trial or on a witness summons for the production of documents.[60] Originally the rule did not apply to cases where, without the disclosure sought, there would be no proceedings brought at all, in which the defendant would be a compellable witness.[61] But later cases have extended the *Norwich Pharmacal* jurisdiction to pre-trial cases where the defendant was *also* a wrongdoer, and proceedings in respect of the wrong

---

[56] *Mitsui & Co. Ltd v Nexen Petroleum UK Ltd* [2005] EWHC 625 (Ch), [2005] 3 All E.R. 511; *Nikitin v Butler LLP* [2007] EWHC 173 (Q.B.).

[57] See *Ricci v Chow* [1987] 1 W.L.R. 1658, CA; *Norwich Pharmacal Co. v Commissioners of Customs and Excise* [1974] A.C. 133 at 175, 188, 197, 203, 204: *Ashworth Health Authority v MGN Ltd* [2002] 1 W.L.R. 2033 at 2041, HL.

[58] *Campaign Against Arms Trade v BAE Systems Ltd* [2007] EWHC 330 (Q.B.) at [10–14].

[59] *Corporation of London v Levy* (1803) 8 Ves. Jun. 398 at 403; *Wilmot v Maccabe* (1831) 4 Sim. 263; *Darthez Brothers v Lee* (1836) 2 Y. & C. 5 at 13.

[60] This is the usual meaning of the "mere witness" rule. However some judges have used this phrase to denote the situation of a person who may have information, but who was not mixed up in the wrongdoing at all. In such a case the *Norwich Pharmacal* jurisdiction does not apply at all.

[61] *Frogmore Estates Ltd v Berish Berger*, cited [1993] B.C.L.C. 254–255, *per* Hoffmann J.; see also *The Coca-Cola Company v British Telecommunications Plc* [1999] F.S.R. 518 (plaintiffs knew identity of wrongdoer, but not address: order made).

could have been (and were being) brought against him.[62] However, the "mere witness" rule has never applied to prevent disclosure being sought in aid of the execution of a judgment.[63] The authorities are sometimes confused in their understanding of the mere witness rule, but in any event it is now narrowly confined. Thus it is well established that it does not apply in the following circumstances[64]:

(1) Where the identity of the wrongdoer is not known, as in such cases there will be no trial unless the order for discovery is made.

(2) Where there is a claim to trust property which may be dissipated, most commonly in tracing and fraud claims.[65]

(3) In respect of a post-judgment freezing injunction.[66]

(4) Where the defendant is himself a wrongdoer.

Bankers Trust

One of the most commonly encountered applications of the *Norwich*   **3.15**
Pharmacal jurisdiction are what are generally called *Bankers Trust* orders named after the Court of Appeal decision in *Bankers Trust Co. v Shapira*.[67] These orders are usually made against banks or other entities through whom stolen or misappropriated funds or their proceeds have passed. A claimant must show a *prima facie* case that his funds have been the subject of a fraud or some other misappropriation and that the funds or their proceeds have been paid into or through the bank from which discovery is sought. *Bankers Trust* orders are often made without notice and the order will usually specify the purposes for which the information may be used and contain an undertaking that the banks reasonable costs in complying with the order will be meet by the claimant.[68] A *Bankers* Trust order (or *Norwich Pharmacal* order) with an ancillary gagging order restraining the defendant from notifying anyone else (apart from his legal advisors) of the order may be granted on a without notice application. The purpose is to enable the

---

[62] *Loose v Williamson* [1978] 1 W.L.R. 639; *CHC Software Care Ltd v Hopkins & Wood* [1993] F.S.R. 241; *Jade Engineering (Coventry) Ltd v Antiference Window Systems Ltd* [1996] F.S.R. 461; *Michael O'Mara Books Ltd v Express Newspapers Plc* [1999] F.S.R. 49; *Microsoft Corporation v Plato Technology Ltd* [1999] F.S.R. 834 (summary judgment application); *Computershare Ltd v Perpetual Registrars Ltd* [2000] V.S.C. 139 (order made against existing defendants to substantive proceedings).

[63] *Mercantile Group (Europe) A.G. v Aiyela* [1994] Q.B. 366.

[64] *Axa Equity & Life Assurance Plc v National Westminster Bank Plc* [1998] P.N.L.R. 433, CA.

[65] *Arab Monetary Fund v Hashim (No.5)* [1992] 2 All E.R. 911.

[66] *Mercantile Group (Europe) AG v Aiyela* [1994] Q.B. 366.

[67] [1980] 1 W.L.R. 1274, CA; *Arab Monetary Fund v Hashim (No.5)* [1992] 2 All E.R. 911.

[68] For an example of a *Bankers Trust* order, see *Atkin's Court Forms* Vol.15 (2003), p.316.

claimant to commence further proceedings to preserve assets, whether within the jurisdiction or abroad. In considering whether to grant such an order, the court needs to balance the interests of the victim of the alleged wrongdoing and the innocent party caught up in the wrongdoing.[69] The fact that the information and documents may become available from the substantive defendant later in the course of disclosure is not usually a ground for refusing a *Bankers Trust* order. Where there is a fraud, although it may be too late and the money may have gone, the sooner that steps are taken to try and trace where it is the better.[70]

Defences

3.16 A *Norwich Pharmacal* order will not be made as of right: it is an equitable remedy, and the court has a discretion as to whether it should be granted.[71] But, assuming that the requirements for a *Norwich Pharmacal* order are otherwise satisfied, the following four defences may be put forward. First, the court will not require disclosure to be given under the *Norwich Pharmacal* rule if that disclosure would itself complete a cause of action.[72]

3.17 Secondly, a person will not be obliged to disclose the identity of another known to him that would tend to incriminate the disclosing party.[73] This is an application of the privilege against self-incrimination, discussed later.[74] However, there must be a real and appreciable risk of proceedings being taken against him, and moreover it must be disclosure of the identity which causes this risk, and not other circumstances which have come to light. Thus, in *British Steel Corporation v Granada Television Ltd*,[75] the House of Lords held that the "self-incrimination" rule could not help the defendants, because they had already stated in evidence all the matters which might disclose an offence, and disclosing the name would add nothing. In the case of a truly innocent person mixed up in another's wrongdoing, this defence will be of no application.

3.18 Thirdly, since the enactment of the Contempt of Court Act 1981, s.10, a person responsible for a "publication" will not be required to give discovery of the source of information contained in that publication, unless it is "necessary" in the interests of national security, the interests of justice, or for

---

[69] *A. Co. v B. Co.* [2002] H.K.C.F.I. 261; *Alberta Treasury Branches v Leahy*, 2000 A.B.Q.B. 575 at [267–269], Alberta Q.B.

[70] *Bankers Trust Co. v Shapira* [1980] 1 W.L.R. 1274 at 1283.

[71] *Norwich Pharmacal Co. v Customs & Excise Commissioners* [1974] A.C. 133; *British Steel Corporation v Granada Television Ltd* [1981] A.C. 1096.

[72] As used to be the case in, e.g. infringement of copyright: see *Roberts v Jump Knitwear* [1981] F.S.R. 527; *cf. Legenes Ltd v It's At (UK) Ltd* [1991] F.S.R. 492 at 505; *Jade Engineering (Coventry) Ltd v Antiference Window Systems Ltd* [1996] F.S.R. 461 at 465.

[73] *Re Westinghouse Electric Corp.* [1978] A.C. 547.

[74] See Ch.11, paras 11.104–11.120, below.

[75] [1981] A.C. 1096.

the prevention of disorder or crime. "Publication" is defined[76] to include "any speech, writing, broadcast, cable programme or other communication in whatever form, which is addressed to the public at large or any section of the public," and has been held, for example, to extend to photographs.[77] The *Norwich Pharmacal* jurisdiction is compatible with s.10 and Art.10 of the European Convention on Human Rights so long as it is only exercised to obtain the disclosure of the journalist's source when it is proportionate to do so.[78]

This provision has been widely construed. Firstly it covers the situation where information has been communicated and received for the purposes of publication, but in fact has not yet been published.[79] Secondly it covers the case where what is sought is not disclosure of the "source" itself, but disclosure of any other material which will indirectly identify the source, and this even though the application of the section may defeat the plaintiff's proprietary claim to the material in question.[80] **3.19**

In considering whether "necessity" has been established, the court must engage in a balancing exercise in which it is assumed that the protection of sources is itself a matter of high importance.[81] As to the *meaning* of "necessary", in one case[82] Lord Griffiths said: **3.20**

> "I doubt if it is possible to go further than to say that 'necessary' has a meaning that lies somewhere between 'indispensable' on the one hand and 'useful' or 'expedient' on the other, and to leave it to the judge to decide toward which end of the scale of meaning he will place it on the facts of any particular case. The nearest paraphrase I can suggest is 'really needed'."

The rest of the House agreed. In the same case it was also held that a wide construction should be given to the phrase "prevention of crime". It was not necessary that there be a particular future crime that would or might be prevented by disclosure.[83]

As to "interests of justice," it is not necessary that the disclosure be needed for the administration of justice in a court of law; it is in the interests **3.21**

---

[76] Contempt of Court Act 1981, ss.2(1), 19.
[77] *Handmade Films v Express Newspapers* [1986] F.S.R. 463; *cf.* CPR, r.53.3 (no requirement in defamation actions to provide details as to source, unless otherwise ordered).
[78] *Ashworth Hospital Authority v MGN Ltd* [2002] UKHL 29, [2002] 1 W.L.R. 2003, HL. See also *Interbrew S.A. v Financial Times* [2002] EWCA Civ 274, [2002] 1 Lloyd's Rep. 542, CA; *Mersey Care NHS Trust v Ackroyd* [2006] EWHC 107 (Q.B.).
[79] *X. Ltd v Morgan-Grampian (Publishers) Ltd* [1991] 1 A.C. 1 at 40; *cf. Francome v Mirror Group Newspapers Ltd* [1984] 1 W.L.R. 892 at 898.
[80] *Secretary of State for Defence v Guardian Newspapers Ltd* [1985] A.C. 339 at 349–350; *Trinity Mirror Plc v Punch Ltd*, unreported, July 19, 2000, Jacob J.
[81] *X. Ltd v Morgan-Grampian (Publishers) Ltd* [1991] 1 A.C. 1, HL.
[82] *Re an Inquiry under the Company Securities (Insider Dealing) Act 1985* [1988] A.C. 660, HL.
[83] The requirement of necessity was considered in some detail by the Court of Appeal in *Ashworth Hospital Authority v MGN Ltd* [2001] 1 W.L.R. 515 at 533–537.

of justice that persons should be in a position to exercise legal rights (e.g. by dismissing a disloyal employee) whether or not resort to courts of law is necessary.[84] The position is *a fortiori* where the plaintiff intends to bring legal proceedings to vindicate those legal rights.[85] The "interests of justice" in s.10 means interests that are justiciable[86] and the phrase is large enough to include the exercise of legal rights and self-protection from legal wrongs, whether or not by court action.[87] It is not necessary for the claimant to show that he intends to bring legal proceedings against the wrongdoer, thus it is sufficient that he intends to dismiss any employee identified as the wrong-doer.[88] On the other hand, disclosure must be *necessary*: relevance, importance and expediency are not enough.[89] Thus where an article was published relating to discussions between a client and his former solicitors, the court was not satisfied that the interests of justice made necessary the disclosure of the source.[90] In considering whether to make an order, the court can take into account any attempt (or lack) to obtain the information sought by other means,[91] and also any failure to show that there were no other means of obtaining it.[92] If journalists are to be ordered to depart from their normal professional standards, the merits of their doing so in the public interest must be clearly demonstrated.[93] In most cases where s.10 may be engaged, it may be inappropriate to grant an order against a journalist on a summary judgment application.[94]

3.22　　Fourthly, it should be noted also that the English courts will not normally make an order for disclosure where to do so would effectively amount to an infringement of the sovereignty of another country. Thus in one case the court discharged both a *subpoena duces tecum* and an order under the Bankers' Books Evidence Act 1879 directed to a third party, a United States

---

[84] *X. Ltd v Morgan-Grampian (Publishers) Ltd* [1991] 1 A.C. 1; *Camelot Group Plc v Centaur Communications Ltd* [1999] Q.B. 124, CA; *Michael O'Mara Books Ltd v Express Newspapers Plc*, [1999] F.S.R. 49; see also *Goodwin v UK* (1996) 22 E.H.R.R. 123, E.C.H.R. (protection of journalist's sources under Art.10 of the European Convention on Human Rights); see also Ch.21, para.21.15, below.

[85] *Secretary of State for Defence v Guardian Newspapers Ltd* [1984] Ch. 156, *per* Donaldson M.R. and Slade L.J., [1985] A.C. 339 at 350.

[86] *Ashworth Hospital Authority v MGN Ltd* [2001] 1 W.L.R. 515 at 533, CA; [2002] UKHL 29, [2002] 1 W.L.R. 2033, HL.

[87] *Interbrew S.A. v Financial Times* [2002] EWCA Civ 274, [2002] 1 Lloyd's Rep. 542, CA.

[88] *Ashworth Hospital Authority v MGN Ltd* [2002] UKHL 29, [2002] 1 W.L.R. 2033, HL.

[89] *Secretary of State for Defence v Guardian Newspapers Ltd* [1989] A.C. 339 at 350; *Maxwell v Pressdram Ltd* [1987] 1 W.L.R. 298, CA.

[90] *Saunders v Punch Ltd* [1998] 1 All E.R. 234.

[91] *Broadmoor Hospital v Hyde, The Independent*, March 4, 1994; *John v Express Newspapers* [2000] 1 W.L.R. 1931, CA.

[92] *Lonrho Plc v Fayed (No.2)* [1992] 1 W.L.R. 1; *Straka v River Regional Hospital* (2000) 193 D.L.R. (4th) 680, Ontario CA.

[93] *John v Express Newspapers* [2000] 1 W.L.R. 1931, CA; *Reavey v Century Newspapers* [2001] N.I.Q.B. 17 (no order requiring journalist to identify source; MP not required to identify source of allegations made in Parliament due to Art.9 of the Bill of Rights).

[94] *Mersey Care NHS Trust v Ackroyd* [2003] EWCA Civ 633, [2003] E.M.L.R. 36.

bank, relating to documents held at its head office in New York, as unjustifiably infringing the sovereignty of the United States.[95]

Procedure[96]

Turning to questions of procedure, proceedings for a *Norwich Pharmacal* order could be commenced under the old rules either by writ[97] or by originating summons,[98] as appropriate. There is nothing in the CPR to prevent a similar choice being made now between Pt 7 (ordinary) and Pt 8 (alternative) procedure. In each case the *Norwich Pharmacal* order may be the sole relief sought, or it may be ancillary to other relief.[99] If there are facts which need to be investigated at trial before any order can be made the court will not make the order until trial,[100] but in clear cases relief can be granted on interlocutory application with notice[101] or even, exceptionally, without notice.[102] A *Norwich Pharmacal* order may be made in the course of an existing action.[103] Once an innocent defendant has complied with any disclosure order made against him, that party should be released from the proceedings unless there is any reason for him to remain.[104] On any application the applicant must set out how the requirements set out above have been met[105] and specify:

(1) The wrongdoing about which he complains.
(2) What information is being sought.
(3) The purposes for which the information is being sought.

So far as the costs of such a disclosure action are concerned, if it is proper for the third party to resist the application at least until the court has adjudicated upon it, then the third party is entitled to his costs. Thus for

3.23

3.24

---

[95] See *McKinnon v Donaldson Lufkin and Jenrette Securities Corp.* [1986] Ch. 482; *cf. UJB Financial Corporation v Chilmark Offshore Capital Fund Ltd* 1992–93 C.I.L.R. 53; *Re Mid-East Trading Ltd (No.2)* [1998] 1 All E.R. 577, CA.

[96] For example of applications and orders, see *Atkin's Court Forms*, Vol.15 (2003), pp.311–316.

[97] As in *Orr v Diaper* (1876) 4 Ch.D. 92; *Dreyfus v Peruvian Guano. Co.* (1889) 41 Ch.D. 151.

[98] *Norwich Pharmacal* itself ([1974] A.C. 133).

[99] As in *Microsoft Corporation v Plato Technology Ltd* [1999] F.S.R. 834 (injunction, delivery-up order, inquiry as to damages).

[100] *Handmade Films v Express Newspapers* [1986] F.S.R. 463.

[101] *R.CA. Corp. v Reddingtons Rare Records* [1974] 1 W.L.R. 1445.

[102] *Loose v Williamson* [1978] 1 W.L.R. 639; *Bankers Trust Co. v Shapira* [1980] 1 W.L.R. 1274, CA.

[103] *Société Romanaise de Chaussure S.A. v British Shoe Corporation Ltd* [1991] F.S.R. 1; *The Coca-Cola Company Ltd v British Telecommunications Ltd* [1999] F.S.R. 518.

[104] *Australia and New Zealand Banking Group Ltd v National Westminster Bank Plc, The Times,* February 14, 2002, Ch.D.

[105] Paras 3.4 and following.

example in the *Norwich Pharmacal* case itself the respondents were entitled to their costs up to the end of the hearing at first instance, but were not entitled to their costs thereafter. The position may be different where a party supports or is implicated in a crime or tort or other wrongdoing and seeks to obstruct justice being done.[106] In appropriate cases the court may make the order conditional on costs being first paid.[107] The respondent who has to incur expense in complying with a disclosure order is normally entitled to recover this from the applicant,[108] and indeed may be entitled to security or a payment into court to cover it in an appropriate case.[109] If the applicant is thereby obliged to pay the costs of the respondent, then if he is successful at trial against a wrongdoer he should be in principle entitled to add those costs on to the other costs of the second action, as they are plainly foreseeable and not too remote.[110]

3.25   Finally, the question arises whether any implied undertaking as to collateral use is owed by an applicant who succeeds in getting, for example, documents from the respondent to an application for *Norwich Pharmacal* relief. In *Sybron v Barclays Bank*,[111] Scott J. seems to have accepted that there was an implied undertaking by the successful plaintiff in *Norwich Pharmacal* proceedings not to use any information so obtained, save for the purposes of the contemplated action.[112] On the other hand, in *Levi Strauss & Co. v Barclays Trading Corporation Inc*[113] it was held that where the was a dual purpose in the proceedings, i.e. to stop the defendants' activities *and also* to obtain information concerning third parties, there was no implied undertaking. But *Sybron* was not cited. However in *Alberta Treasury Branches v Leahy* the authorities were reviewed in detail and it was concluded that at least in Canada there is no implied undertaking.[114] In *Ashworth* the House of Lords stated that an order for disclosure should not be made unless the claimant has identified clearly the wrongdoing on which he relies in general terms and identifies the purpose for which the disclosure will be used when it is made. The use of the material will then be restricted expressly or implicitly to the disclosed purpose unless and until the court permits it to be used for another purpose.[115] In practice the *Norwich Pharmacal* order usually expressly provides for what uses the information may be put, whether in the body of the order or by way of an undertaking

---

[106] *Totalise Plc v The Motley Fool Ltd* [2002] 1 W.L.R. 1233, CA.

[107] *The Coca-Cola Company Ltd v British Telecommunications Ltd* [1999] F.S.R. 518 at 524.

[108] *Norwich Pharmacal Co. v Customs & Excise Commissioners* [1974] A.C. 133 at 199, *per* Lord Cross of Chelsea.

[109] ibid.; *Re Murphy's Settlements* [1998] 3 All E.R. 1.

[110] See *Morton-Norwich v Intercen (No.2)* [1981] F.S.R. 337.

[111] [1985] Ch. 299 at 320G.

[112] See further, Ch.15, para.15.11, below.

[113] [1993] F.S.R. 179, Judge Bromley Q.C.; see also *Omar v Omar* [1995] 1 W.L.R. 1428.

[114] 2000 A.B.Q.B. 575 at [207–288].

[115] *Ashworth Hospital Authority v MGN Ltd* [2002] UKHL 29 at [60], [2002] 1 W.L.R. 2033, HL.

by the claimant. Whilst it is arguable that the CPR, r.31.22 applies to any documents disclosed, this may not necessarily be the case, hence the need to deal with any restriction in the order. Often the wording of the order will follow the provisions of CPR, r.31.22 suitably modified to fit the circumstances as to the purposes for which the material may be used.

B. PRE-ACTION DISCLOSURE: CPR RULE 31.16

Whereas *Norwich Pharmacal* orders involve disclosure usually from third parties, orders under s.33 of the Supreme Court Act 1981 concern disclosure from the potential or intended defendant himself. This section is in two parts. Subsection (1) provides that, in any kind of case, the High Court has power to order the inspection, photographing, preservation, custody or detention of property which may become the subject matter of subsequent proceedings, or the taking of samples of such property.[116] (In its application to the Crown this provision is limited to proceedings involving a claim in respect of personal injuries or death.[117]) Subsection (2) provides that the High Court has power in preliminary proceedings to order a potential defendant to subsequent proceedings to disclose documents which he is likely to have or to have had in his possession, custody or power, relevant to an issue arising or likely to arise out of that claim. As originally enacted, subs.(2) was limited to cases where the subsequent proceedings would involve a claim in respect of personal injuries or death. This limitation was removed to coincide with the coming into force of the CPR on April 26, 1999, and so the subsection now applies generally.[118] Similar statutory provisions apply in the county court,[119] also amended at the same time.[120] The applicable rules of court, of course, apply in relation to both High Court and county courts.[121] But they do not limit any other power which the court has to order disclosure before substantive proceedings have started.[122]

3.26

Section 33(1), in dealing, *inter alia*, with inspection of "property which may become the subject matter of subsequent proceedings," is not in itself concerned with disclosure of documents, and it was held in cases under the old rules that the court has no power under that subsection to order such

3.27

---

[116] See Ch.19, paras 19.02–19.04, below.
[117] Supreme Court Act 1981, s.35(4).
[118] Civil Procedure (Modification of Enactments) Order 1998, SI 1998/2940, Art.5.
[119] County Courts Act 1984, s.52.
[120] Civil Procedure (Modification of Enactments) Order 1998, SI 1998/2940, Art.6; for an unsuccessful challenge to the Order, see *Burrell's Wharf Freeholds Ltd v Galliard Homes Ltd* [1999] 33 E.G. 82.
[121] CPR, rr.25.4, 31.16.
[122] CPR, r.31.18(a); *Mitsui & Co. Ltd v Nexen Petroleum UK Ltd* [2005] EWHC 625 (Ch), [2005] 3 All E.R. 511 at [36].

discovery.[123] Of course, if the property concerned is itself a document, then inspection may be obtained under this provision.[124]

3.28   Section 33(2) *does* deal expressly with pre-action disclosure against a potential defendant, but used to be limited to cases involving claims in respect of personal injury or death. This last phrase caused difficulties of interpretation, both in this context and in statutory provisions concerning limitation of actions.[125] A claim for damages for negligence causing personal injuries was obviously caught. So too were claims against solicitors for negligence in allowing a personal injury claim to become statute barred,[126] and against a supplier of machinery for breach of contract in supplying defective goods which injured their user (a partner in the proposed plaintiff).[127] But claims against insurance brokers for breach of contract in failing to obtain insurance cover which would have provided insurance against the plaintiff's personal injuries,[128] against a trade union for allowing a personal injury claim to become statute barred,[129] and against an insurer for indemnity under an insurance policy in respect of personal injuries[130] were held not to be caught. The distinction was said to be whether the breach of duty or contract on which the plaintiff founded also caused the personal injuries,[131] though this makes at least one of the cases wrongly decided.[132] However, as mentioned above, the limitation has been swept away and these cases are only of historical interest in this context.

Requirements for pre-action disclosure

3.29   Under CPR, r.31.16(3) the court may make an order for pre-action disclosure under that rule only where the following jurisdictional requirements are met:

---

[123] *Taylor v Anderton, The Times,* October 21, 1986; *Huddleston v Control Risks Information Services Ltd* [1987] 1 W.L.R. 701; *cf. Dun & Bradstreet Ltd v Typesetting Facilities* [1992] F.S.R. 320 at 322–323.

[124] e.g. *Re Saxton* [1962] 1 W.L.R. 589, varied [1962] 1 W.L.R. 968; *Vowell v Shire of Hastings* [1970] V.R. 764; *Snow v Hawthorn* [1969] N.Z.L.R. 776; *cf. Nicholls v McLevy* (1971) 1 S.A.S.R. 442; *Athlete's Foot Australia Pty. Ltd v Divergent Technologies Pty. Ltd* (1997) 78 F.C.R. 283, Fed.Ct.Aus.

[125] i.e. Limitation Act 1939, s.2(1); Limitation Act 1980, s.11; see on this *Burns v Shuttlehurst Ltd* [1999] 1 W.L.R. 1449, CA.

[126] *Paterson v Chadwick* [1974] 1 W.L.R. 890; *Oates v Harte Reede & Co.,* unreported, December 17, 1998, Singer J. (negligence in prosecuting action, causing stress); *Bennett v Greenlane* [1998] P.N.L.R. 458; *Phelps Hillingdon London Borough Council* [2000] 4 All E.R. 50, HL.

[127] *Howe v David Brown Tractors (Retail) Ltd* [1991] 4 All E.R. 30, CA.

[128] *Ackbar v C.F. Green & Co. Ltd,* [1975] 1 Q.B. 582.

[129] *McGahie v Union of Shop Distributive and Allied Workers,* 1966 S.L.T. 74.

[130] *Burns v Shuttlehurst Ltd* [1999] 1 W.L.R. 1449, CA.

[131] *Howe v David Brown Tractors (Retail) Ltd* [1991] 4 All E.R. 30 at 36, 41; *Burns v Shuttlehurst Ltd* [1999] 1 W.L.R. 1449, CA.

[132] i.e. *Paterson v Chadwick* [1974] 1 W.L.R. 890; *cf. Howe v David Brown Tractors (Retail) Ltd* [1991] 4 All E.R. 30 at 41, *per* Nicholls L.J.

(a) the respondent is likely to be a party to subsequent proceedings;

(b) the applicant is also likely to be a party to those proceedings;

(c) if proceedings had started, the respondent's duty by way of standard disclosure, set out in r.31.16, would extend to the documents or classes of documents which the applicant seeks disclosure; and

(d) disclosure before proceedings have started is desirable in order to—

    (i) dispose fairly of the anticipated proceedings;

    (ii) assist the dispute to be resolved without proceedings; or

    (iii) save costs.

These requirements have been considered in a number of cases,[133] but even so it is often difficult to predict the outcome of any application in view of the broad discretion given to the court in deciding whether to make disclosure. There is a degree of overlap between the requirements.   **3.30**

As to requirements (a) and (b), the application has to be made by a person likely to be a party to subsequent proceedings against a person likely to be a party to the proceedings. This means no more than that the persons concerned are likely to be parties in the proceedings if those proceedings are issued. Likely in this context means no more than "may well".[134] This has two aspects, one positive and one negative. First it must be shown that the applicant intends subsequently to make a claim, and there is a reasonable basis for making it.[135] But secondly, where the applicant does not yet have a cause of action,[136] or any such claim is bound to fail,[137] then the claim is not "likely", and the court will not make an order under s.33(2). However the mere fact that the proposed defendant has a strong argument on limitation is not enough to prevent the court making an order.[138] Where the substantive claim identified by the applicant would be bound to fail or not amount to a prima facie case,[139] then requirements (a) and (b) would not be satisfied. It is normally sufficient to found an application for the substantive   **3.31**

---

[133] Starting with *Black v Sumitomo Corporation* [2001] EWCA Civ 1818, [2002] 1 W.L.R. 1562 (see also *Bermuda International Securities Ltd v KPMG* [2001] EWCA Civ 263, [2001] 1 Lloyd's Rep. P.N. 392 in which the Court of Appeal refused to lay down guidelines).

[134] *Black v Sumitomo Corporation* [2001] EWCA Civ 1819, [2002] 1 W.L.R. 1562; *Moresfield v Banners* [2003] EWHC 1602 (Ch) at [32], which usefully summarises the relevant principles on a CPR, r.31.16 application.

[135] *Dunning v United Liverpool Hospitals Board of Governors* [1973] 1 W.L.R. 586, CA; *Burns v Shuttlehurst Ltd* [1999] 1 W.L.R. 1449, CA; *cf. Kuah Kok Kim v Ernst & Young* [1996] 2 S.L.R. 364, H.Ct.Singapore.

[136] *Burns Ltd v Shuttlehurst Ltd*, [1999] 1 W.L.R. 1449, CA.

[137] *Bradley v Eagle Star Insurance Co. Ltd* [1988] 2 Lloyd's Rep. 233, CA.

[138] *Harris v Newcastle Health Authority* [1989] 1 W.L.R. 96, CA.

[139] *Mars UK Ltd v Waitrose Ltd* [2004] EWHC 2264 (Ch.) (application failed as applicant could not show that its substantive claim amount to a *prima facie* case).

claim to be properly arguable and to have a real prospect of success.[140] The mere fact that the claim may be speculative does not necessarily mean that requirements (a) and (b) are not satisfied,[141] but the strength or weakness of the claim is a matter to be taken into consideration when deciding whether requirement (d) is satisfied.[142]

3.32   The provision does not expressly state that it must be contemplated that the proceedings may be brought within the jurisdiction, but it is implicit in requirement (c) that it is envisaged that the proceedings are to be brought within the jurisdiction as it refers to standard disclosure set out in CPR, r.31.6. Where there is more than one possible jurisdiction for the substantive proceedings, so long as it is contemplated that the proceedings may well be brought within the jurisdiction, then it may be said that this is sufficient. The fact that the defendant is a foreign corporation and the documents are held outside the jurisdiction, does not exclude the power in the court to order pre-action disclosure.[143] Even where a respondent claims that the substantive claim would not be justiciable in the English court or that England is not an appropriate forum, the court still may order pre-action disclosure.[144] A respondent would need to show a really strong prospect of success in the court declining jurisdiction in the potential claim, before the court may decline to make a disclosure order on that ground. The court may impose a requirement that the applicant undertake not to use the documents disclosed for any purpose other than the proceedings contemplated in the jurisdiction.[145]

3.33   As to requirement (c), disclosure will only be ordered in relation to documents which would be the subject of standard disclosure.[146] Section 33(2) requires that the respondent must be likely to have or have had in his "possession, custody or power" documents which are "relevant" to an issue arising or likely to arise out of the claim. As will be seen later, the tests of "possession, custody or power" and "relevance" found in the former Rules of the Supreme Court, have been replaced for the purposes of pre-*trial* disclosure under CPR Pt 31, but they remain relevant for the purposes of pre-*action* disclosure.[147] The court must be clear what the issues in the

---

[140] *Rose v Lynx Express Ltd* [2004] EWCA Civ 447, [2004] 1 B.C.L.C. 445 at [4], CA.

[141] *Jay v Wilder Coe* [2003] EWHC 1786 (Q.B.) Tugendhat J. held that pre-action disclosure could be appropriate even where the complaint might seem speculative.

[142] *Snowstar Shipping Co. Ltd v Graig Shipping Plc* [2003] EWHC 1367 (Comm) at [33].

[143] *Mitsui & Co. Ltd v Nexen Petroleum UK Ltd* [2005] EWHC 625 (Ch.), [2005] 3 All E.R. 511 at [32].

[144] *Total E&P S.A. v Edmonds* [2007] EWCA Civ 50.

[145] *Total E&P Sudan v Edmunds* [2006] EWHC 1136 (Comm.) on appeal [2007] EWCA Civ 50.

[146] *Mitsui & Co. Ltd v Nexen Petroleum UK Ltd* [2005] EWHC 625 (Ch.), [2005] 3 All E.R. 511 at [32]. In this context *would* means more likely than not on a balance of probabilities: *Findel Plc v White Arrow Express Ltd,* unreported, December 19, 2002 (Leeds Merchantile Court).

[147] See Ch.5, paras 5.39–5.54 ("possession, custody or power") and 5.08–5.18 ("relevance").

litigation are likely to be.[148] On any application the applicant should take care to specify in a focused manner exactly what documents or classes of documents are sought. The wider the disclosure sought the more cautious the court is in granting the application. The application should be limited to what is strictly necessary.[149] The narrower the disclosure requested and the more determinative it may be of the dispute in issue between the parties to the application, the easier it is for the court to find the request well founded.[150] In practice the court may reject too wide an application altogether or limit the scope of what is ordered to be disclosed.

As to requirement (d), CPR, r.31.16(3)(d) has both a jurisdictional threshold ("only where") and in terms of the exercise of a discretionary judgment ("desirable").[151] For jurisdictional purposes the court is only permitted to consider the granting of pre-action disclosure where there is a real prospect in principle of such an order being fair to the parties if litigation is commenced, or of assisting the parties to avoid litigation, or for saving costs in any event.[152] If there is such a real prospect, the court should go on to consider the question of discretion, which has to be considered on all the facts and not merely in principle, but in detail. The discretion is not confined and will depend upon all the facts of the case.[153] Among the important considerations are: **3.34**

(1) The relevance of any pre-action protocol or pre-action enquiries, including whether the applicant has followed any relevant pre-action protocol.[154]

---

[148] *Moresfield v Banners* [2003] EWHC 1602 (Ch.) at [32]; *Medisys Plc v Arthur Anderson (a firm)* [2002] Lloyd's Rep. PN 323, Q.B.D.

[149] *Snowstar Shipping Co. Ltd v Graig Shipping Plc* [2003] EWHC 1367 (Comm.) at [35].

[150] *Black v Sumitomo Corporation* [2001] EWCA Civ 1819, [2002] 1 W.L.R. 1562.

[151] In practice it may be artificial, if not difficult, to separate the two: *First Gulf Bank v Wachovia Bank National Association* [2005] EWHC 2827 (Comm.) at [23].

[152] *Shaw v Vauxhall Motors Ltd* [1974] 1 W.L.R. 1035, CA (burden on applicant); *K. v Secretary of State for the Home Office* [2001] 5 C.L. 17. In *Mitsui & Co. Ltd v Nexen Petroleum UK Ltd* [2005] EWHC 625 (Ch), [2005] 3 All E.R. 511 at [27], Lightman J. remarked that the jurisdictional threshold is low. See also *Total E&P Soudan S.A. v Edmonds* [2007] EWCA Civ 50.

[153] *Black v Sumitomo Corporation* [2001] EWCA Civ 1819, [2002] 1 W.L.R. 1562 at [88]; *Moresfield v Banners* [2003] EWHC 1602 (Ch.) at [32]. The list of considerations is derived from these two cases as well as the further cases referred to under each item. In Australia the courts have considered the interests of justice and the interests of both parties in deciding whether to exercise its discretion in favour of pre-action disclosure: *Central Exchange Ltd v Anaconda Nickel Ltd* [2001] WASC 128, Sup.Ct.W.A.; *CGU v Malaysia Corp.* [2001] F.C.A. 1223, (2001) 187 A.L.R. 279, Fed. Ct. of Aus. The principles applied on applications for preliminary disclosure under O.15A, r.6 of the Federal Court Rules are summarised in *St. George v Rabo* [2004] F.C.A. 1360, (2004) 211 A.L.R. 147 at [26]; *Benchmark v Standards Australia* [2004] F.C.A. 1489, (2005) 212 A.L.R. 464 at [2–7]; *Glencore v Selwyn Mines* [2005] F.C.A. 801, (2006) 223 A.L.R. 238 at [10–16]; *Australian Broadcasting Corporation v Seven Network Ltd* [2005] F.C.A. 1851 at [8].

[154] *Briggs & Forrester Electrical Ltd v Governors of Southfield School* [2005] EWHC 1734 (T.C.C.) at [18, 19, 47]; *Marshall (Executors of Marshall) v Alliotts (A Firm)* [2004] EWHC 1964 (Q.B.), [2005] P.N.L.R.11.

(2) What documents are already in the hands of the applicant and what has been provided or offered voluntarily by the respondent.

(3) Whether the parties at the pre-action stage have been acting reasonably as pre-action disclosure should not be ordered as a matter of course.

(4) The nature of the injury or loss complained of.[155] The jurisdiction used to be confined to personal injury cases. The expansion beyond personal injury cases means that there is a spectrum of cases in which the extent to which pre-action disclosure is likely to be appropriate varies. A personal injury case in which medical records are sought is at the top of the spectrum and a speculative commercial action, with broad disclosure being sought, is at the bottom.[156]

(5) The nature and strength of the claim. The more speculative or weak the claim the less inclined is the court to grant the application.[157] However, even in the case of speculative or weak claims the court still has a discretion whether or not to order disclosure.[158]

(6) The clarity and identification of the issues raised by the applicant.[159]

(7) The nature and importance of the documents requested. The more widely drawn the application, the less likely is the court to grant the request.[160] To seek highly confidential documents on the back of a speculative claim may be regarded as inappropriate.[161] If the documents are peripheral, a court is likely to refuse the application.[162]

---

[155] *Black v Sumitomo* [2002] 1 W.L.R. 1562 at [83].
[156] *Hands v Morrison Construction Services Ltd* [2006] EWHC 2018 (Ch.).
[157] *Snowstar Shipping Co. Ltd v Graig Shipping Plc* [2003] EWHC 1367 (Comm.) at [33]; *BSW Ltd v Balltec Ltd* [2006] EWHC 822 (Ch.).
[158] *Jay v Wilder Coe* [2003] EWHC 1786 (Q.B.) Tugendhat J. (pre-action disclosure could be appropriate even where the complaint may be speculative or application arguably constituted a "fishing expedition"); *Arsenal Football Club v Elite Sports Distribution* [2002] EWHC 3057 (Ch.), Lightman J. (pre-action disclosure ordered against defendant who applied to strike out claim with liberty to apply on strike out application following disclosure). See also *Total E&P Soudan S.A. v Edmonds* [2007] EWCA Civ 50.
[159] *Inland Revenue Commissioners v Blueslate Ltd* [2003] EWHC 2022 (Ch.).
[160] See para.3.33 above in context of requirement (c); *Snowstar Shipping Co. Ltd v Graig Shipping Plc* [2003] EWHC 1367 (Comm.) at [37] (application refused as claim speculative and application too widely drawn).
[161] *BSW Ltd v Balltec Ltd* [2006] EWHC 822 (Ch.) at [83].
[162] *Northumbrian Water Ltd v British Telecommunications Plc* [2005] EWHC 2408 (T.C.C.) at [32], where court was influenced by fact that peripheral documents were sought by a potential defendant in the hope that they will help set up a positive defence to a claim, rather than by a claimant.

(8) The opportunity the applicant has to make its case without pre-action disclosure.[163]

(9) The more focused the complaint and the more limited the disclosure sought, the easier it is for the court to exercise its discretion in favour of an order on the basis that transparency is what the interests of justice and proportionality must require.[164]

(10) The court must consider the discretionary question in detail and that will usually call for an examination of each of the categories of documents requested in any multiple requests. It need not be an all or nothing approach. It is open to the court to prune down requests.[165]

(11) The court may stand back at some point and look at the matter in the round. The question at that level may include the general question: does the request for pre-action disclosure further the overriding objective in the case, or not. The court may consider whether some lesser order would be desirable.[166]

(12) Pre-action disclosure should not be granted as a matter of course. It is for the applicant to satisfy the court that it is just to order that disclosure be given at a time other than the normal one, which is after proceedings have been commenced in the course of standard disclosure.[167]

Such disclosure or production may be ordered to be given to the applicant, **3.35** or alternatively may be limited to the applicant's legal or professional advisers.[168] The statute does not, however, permit disclosure to be limited to *medical* advisers alone.[169] The question arises as to the precise meaning of "legal adviser". No doubt solicitors and barristers qualify; but the position of notaries public, licenced conveyancers, legal executives and foreign lawyers must also be considered. Since all these persons may in certain circumstances

---

[163] *XL London Market Ltd v Zenith Syndicate Management Ltd* [2004] EWHC 1182 (Comm.) at [24], where it was observed that it is a powerful argument against an order that the applicant can well make a case without the disclosure sought; *First Gulf Bank v Wachovia Bank National Association* [2005] EWHC 2827 (Comm.).

[164] *Moresfield v Banners* [2003] EWHC 1602 (Ch.) at [32], item (g); *Snowstar Shipping Co. Ltd v Graig Shipping Plc* [2003] EWHC 1367 (Comm.) at [35].

[165] *Hands v Morrison Construction Services Ltd* [2006] EWHC 2018 (Ch.) at [29 and 70].

[166] *Hands v Morrison Construction Services Ltd* [2006] EWHC 2018 (Ch.).

[167] *Steamship Mutual v Baring Asset Management Ltd* [2004] EWHC 202 (Comm.); *First Gulf Bank v Wachovia Bank National Association* [2005] EWHC 2827 (Comm.); *cf. Phoenix Natural Gas Ltd v British Gas Trading Ltd* [2004] EWHC 451 (Q.B.), where Cooke J. stated that "exceptional circumstances" had to be shown.

[168] Supreme Court Act 1981, s.33(2)(b), County Courts Act 1984, s.52(2)(b), effectively reversing the effect of *McIvor v Southern Health and Social Services Board* [1978] 1 W.L.R. 757, HL and restoring *Dunning v United Liverpool Hospitals' Board of Governors* [1973] 1 W.L.R. 586, CA; *cf.* Ch.11, paras 11.18–11.25. See also *Re R. (a child)* [2004] EWHC 2085 (Fam), where disclosure was limited to R's legal and medical advisors.

[169] *Hipwood v Gloucester Health Authority* [1995] I.C.R. 999, CA; *Irvin v Donaghy* [1996] P.I.Q.R. 207, H. Ct. of N.I.

give legal advice, there seems no ground for excluding them from the scope of the phrase.[170] It should also be borne in mind that, where legal professional privilege is concerned in English litigation, the English courts have had no difficulty in recognising that communications with foreign lawyers may fall within the scope of that privilege.[171] In any event such advisers, if not "legal", are certainly "professional".

3.36   Although ss.33 to 35 bind the Crown,[172] but not the Monarch in Her private capacity, it is to be noted that s.35(1) contains a restriction on the court ordering disclosure on what may be called "public interest" grounds.[173] The same principles apply as in relation to disclosure after action commenced.[174]

Procedure

3.37   An application under s.33(2) is made by ordinary application, as if in an existing action,[175] supported by evidence.[176] The proposed claimant before taking out any application should ensure that any pre-action protocol to the extent that it deals with pre-action disclosure is complied with.[177] The proposed claimant before applying should set out in writing to the respondent the nature of his allegations and should state that information showed that the documents might be material to his claim.[178] Usually it will be necessary either in the application or in the evidence in support to show how the applicant contends that the requirements under CPR, r.31.16(3) have been satisfied.

3.38   Formerly the rules expressly provided that any discovery order made under this section might be conditional upon security being given for costs, or any other terms.[179] That has now gone, although the court under the CPR has the power to make any order subject to conditions.[180] But the order must specify the documents (or classes) to be disclosed, and require the respondent to specify those that he no longer has, and those that he

---

[170] *cf.* Ch.11, paras 11.18–11.25, below.
[171] See Ch.11, para.11.21, below.
[172] Supreme Court Act 1981, s.35(4).
[173] See, e.g. *Taylor v Anderton, The Times,* October 21, 1986, Scott J., and *cf.* RSC, Ord.77, r.12(2); Ch.4, para.4.39 and Ch.8, para.8.27, below.
[174] *Campbell v Tameside Metropolitan Borough Council* [1982] Q.B. 1065, CA; *Barrett v Ministry of Defence, The Times,* January 24, 1990; see Ch.11, paras 11.81–11.103 below.
[175] CPR, r.25.4(2); under the old rules it had to be made by originating summons (RSC, Ord.24, r.1 7A(1)).
[176] CPR, r.31.16(2).
[177] *Practice Directions—Protocols,* para.4; and the Pre-action Protocols dealing with specific types of proceedings.
[178] *Shaw v Vauxhall Motors Ltd* [1974] 1 W.L.R. 1035, CA.
[179] RSC, Ord.24, r.7A(5).
[180] CPR, r.3.1(3).

objects to produce.[181] It *may* also require him to say what has happened to documents which he no longer has, and specify time and place for disclosure and inspection.[182] Under the old rules the respondent could not have been compelled to disclose any document which he could not have been required to produce by a *subpoena duces tecum*.[183] This meant that legally privileged documents were excluded—even where the privilege was that of another person.[184] The position under the CPR is not made express, but it is submitted that it is the same.[185] There is no requirement, in giving pre-action disclosure under these provisions, to provide an itemised list of documents.[186]

Generally, a person ordered under s.33(2) to give disclosure is entitled to his costs (in relation to both the application and compliance with it),[187] but the court retains a discretion to order that he should be deprived of all or some part of his costs.[188] In exercising this discretion the court will take into account all the circumstances, including the reasonableness of opposition to the application and compliance with pre-action protocols. In so far as the application is concerned, if it has been unreasonably resisted, those are the very circumstances contemplated where the order for costs may be different.[189] "Costs in the case" is an inappropriate order, whether under s.33 (because there is no certainty that there would ever be a claim against the respondent[190]), or under s.34 (because it concerns a non-party who will not be further involved).   **3.39**

C. CORPORATE INSOLVENCY

Strictly, the procedures described here are not disclosure as such.[191] However, such applications produce a similar result, and often precede further litigation, so it is desirable to mention them at this point. The Insolvency Act 1986 confers power; (i) on the official receiver to apply to the court for the public examination of a present or former officer of a   **3.40**

---

[181] CPR, r.31.16(4).
[182] CPR, r.31.16(5).
[183] RSC, Ord.24, r.7A(6).
[184] See *Lee v South West Thames Regional Health Authority* [1985] 1 W.L.R. 845, CA.
[185] CPR, rr.31.16(3)(b)(ii), 31.19(3); see para.10.31, below.
[186] *M. v Plymouth Health Authority* [1993] 4 Med. L.R. 108.
[187] Supreme Court Act 1981, s.35(3); CPR, r.48.1(2).
[188] *cf. Hall v Wandsworth Health Authority, The Times*, February 16, 1985, where dilatoriness in responding to a proper request led to a party being denied its costs.
[189] *Bermuda International Securities Ltd v KPMG* [2001] EWCA Civ 269, [2001] Lloyd's Rep. P.N. 392, CA; *Re R. (a child)* [2004] EWHC 2085 (Fam), where each party ordered to pay own costs of application although resistance not unreasonable. See also *Total E&P Soudan S.A. v Edmonds* [2007] EWCA Civ 50.
[190] *Hall v Wandsworth Health Authority, ibid*; see also *Walker v Eli Lilly* (1986) 136 New L.J. 608.
[191] *Re B.C.C.I. S.A. (No.12)* [1997] 1 B.C.L.C. 526 at 538.

company being wound up[192]; and (ii) on the "office-holder" (the administrator, the administrative receiver, the liquidator or provisional liquidator of a company)[193] to apply to the court to obtain documents to which the company appears to be entitled.[194] In addition, the office-holder has additional powers under s.236 to apply to the court for documents. Section 236 provides, *inter alia*:

> "(2) The court may, on the application of the office-holder, summon to appear before it—
>
> (a) any officer of the company,
> (b) any person known or suspected to have in his possession any property of the company or supposed to be indebted to the company, or
> (c) any person whom the court thinks capable of giving information, concerning the promotion, formation, business, dealings, affairs or property of the company.[195]
>
> (3) The court may require any such person as is mentioned in subsection (2)(*a*) to (*c*) to submit an affidavit to the court containing an account of his dealings with the company or to produce any books, papers or other records in his possession or under his control relating to the company or the matters mentioned in paragraph (*c*) of the subsection."

3.41   The section confers a wide discretion, but it is not open textured. In re *British A Commonwealth Plc*[196] Ralph Gibson L.J. listed seven principles which are relevant to whether an order under s.236 should be made:

1. Section 236(2) confers a general discretion on the court.
2. The exercise of the discretion involves balancing the requirements of the office-holder to obtain information against the possible oppression to the person from whom the information is sought.
3. The power is an extraordinary power which the court may exercise on the application of the office-holder. It involves the power both to direct examination of a witness on oath and to require

---

[192] Insolvency Act 1986, s.133; see *Re Richbell Strategic Holdings Ltd (No.2)*, *The Times*, June 14, 2000.
[193] Insolvency Act 1986, s.234(1). No other party than an office holder has standing to apply for a person to be examined under s.236: *Re James McHale Automobiles Ltd* [1997] B.C.C. 202.
[194] Insolvency Act 1986, s.234(2).
[195] *Re Castle New Homes Ltd* [1979] 1 W.L.R. 1075; *Re Rhodes Ltd* (1986) 2 B.C.C. 99, 284.
[196] [1992] Ch. 342 at 370–372; decision upheld by HL, [1993] A.C. 426; see also *Joint Liquidators of Akai Holdings Ltd v The Grange Holdings Ltd* [2006] HKCFA 96, Hong Kong Court of Final Appeal.

production of documents. A reason for conferring that power is that the office-holder usually takes office as a stranger to the relevant events.

4. The purpose of the power is not confined to obtaining general information about the company's affairs, but may be used to discover facts and documents relating to specific claims against specific persons which the office-holder has in contemplation and it is in itself no bar that the office-holder may have commenced, or may be about to commence, proceedings against the proposed witness or someone connected with him.

5. The power is directed to enabling the court to help a liquidator to discover the truth of the circumstances connected with the affairs of the company in order that he may be able, as effectively as possible, to complete his function.

6. In determining what are the reasonable requirements of the office-holder and whether an order should be made, great weight is to be given to the views of the office-holder.

7. The matters which are relevant to the balancing of the require-ments of the office-holder against the risk of oppression to the person against whom the order is sought include the following:

A) the case for making an order against an officer, or former officer, of the company will usually be stronger than it would against a third party;

B) if, by giving the information sought, a third party risks exposing himself to liability that involves an element of oppres-sion;

C) an order for oral examination is more likely to be oppressive than an order for production of documents;

D) if someone is suspected of wrong doing, in particular fraud, it is oppressive to require him to prove the case against him on oath before any proceedings are brought.

The power may only be used for the purpose for which it was conferred, and the "common law supplements the omission of the legislature."[197] As stated in subs.(3), the court will not make a production order for documents unless they relate to the company in whose liquidation the application is made.[198] Because Parliament has expressly conferred on the High Court the power to wind up overseas companies, there is no territorial limitation on orders made under these provisions.[199] The power under this section is to order the production of original documents; it does not extend to ordering the supply of copies.[200] The office-holder or his solicitor or counsel may

---

[197] *Re Arrows Ltd (No.2)* [1994] 1 B.C.L.C. 355 at 361, *per* Steyn L.J.
[198] *Re Mid-East Trading Ltd* [1998] 1 All E.R. 577, CA.
[199] *ibid.*
[200] *Re Maxwell Communications Corporation Plc (No.2)* [1995] 1 B.C.L.C. 521 at 525.

examine a person summoned under subs.(2); but the court has no power to permit a foreign lawyer to do so.[201] An order may be made under this section on an application without notice, but good reason must be shown to justify that course.[202] The Crown is bound by the section, but the court will not order the Department of Trade and Industry to disclose transcripts of evidence furnished by an individual to inspectors appointed under s.432 of the Companies Act 1985 without first giving the individual the opportunity to be heard.[203] The court has no power under s.236 to order any disclosure prohibited by the Banking Act 1987, s.82.[204] Where material could not or should not be disclosed, the court can order disclosure of the documents concerned, redacted to exclude the objectionable material.[205] A factor tending to support the making of an order under s.236 is where a corporate failure is attended with secrecy and deception.[206]

3.42   Information obtained pursuant to this provision is only to be used for the purposes of the liquidation, and for no collateral purpose,[207] though the Serious Fraud Office has statutory power to require transcripts of evidence given under s.236 to be produced to it for its purposes.[208] In relation to information obtained by the Official Receiver using his powers under s.235, it has been held that he is free to disclose that material to the prosecuting authority where he is satisfied that it is required for the purpose of investigating crime.[209]

3.43   The former practice under this section was that the court would not normally make an order under s.236 against a person against whom the office-holder had taken or firmly intended to take proceedings (the so-called "Rubicon" test). This was on the basis that it would be unfair that a person who was or might be a defendant should be subjected to discovery or examination in advance of trial once the office-holder had commenced proceedings or when he had finally determined to commence proceedings.[210] This test has now been rejected as too inflexible.[211] So too has the

---

[201] *ibid.*, at 534.
[202] *ibid.*, at 528; *Re PFTZM Ltd (in liquidation)* [1995] B.C.C. 280.
[203] *Soden v Burns* [1996] 1 W.L.R. 1512; *British and Commonwealth Holdings Plc v Barclays de Zoete Wedd Ltd* [1998] B.C.C. 200.
[204] *Re Galileo Group Ltd* [1999] Ch. 100.
[205] *ibid.*
[206] *Re B.C.C.I. S.A. (No.12)* [1997] 1 B.C.L.C. 526.
[207] *Re Esal (Commodities) Ltd (No.2)* [1990] B.C.C. 708 at 723; *Re Barlow Clowes Gilt Managers Ltd* [1992] Ch. 208 at 217; *Macmillan Inc v Bishopsgate Investment Trust Plc (No.2)* [1993] I.C.R. 385; *Re a Company (No.005374 of 1993)* [1993] B.C.C. 734; *Re Polly Peck International Plc* [1994] B.C.C. 15, *cf. Morris v Director of Serious Fraud Office* [1993] Ch. 372 (liquidator cannot use s.236 against S.F.O. in respect of information obtained from officers of company unless the latter consent or are joined); *Carter v Gardner* [2003] F.C.A. 653, Fed.Ct.Aus. (use of documents by receiver obtained in response to an examination summons).
[208] Criminal Justice Act 1987, s.2(3); *Re Arrows Ltd (No.4)* [1995] 2 A.C. 75, HL.
[209] *R. v Brady* [2004] EWCA Crim 1763, [2004] 3 All E.R. 520, CA.
[210] *Re Castle New Homes Ltd* [1979] 1 W.L.R. 1075; *Re Rhodes Ltd* (1986) 2 B.C.C. 99, 284.
[211] *Re Cloverbay Ltd* [1991] Ch. 90.

suggestion[212] that the purpose of s.236 was to reconstitute the knowledge of the company in the person of the office-holder, and not to put the office-holder in a better position than if administration or liquidation had not supervened.[213] Instead the applicant must satisfy the court that, after balancing all the relevant factors, there is a proper case for an order to be made, i.e. one where the administrator reasonably requires to see the documents to carry out his functions, and the production does not impose an unnecessary and unreasonable burden on the respondent.[214] Oppression is a factor to be weighed against the making of a s.236 order not only against persons not involved in the running of the company, but also against insiders.[215] Section 236 contains no express limitation on the purpose for which it may be invoked apart from that it can only be a legitimate purpose in relation to the company which is being wound up. The only limitation which is implicit in the section is that it may be invoked only for the purpose of enabling the applicant to exercise his statutory functions in relation to the company which is being wound up. Thus, the court has the power to make an order, on the application of the Official Receiver, for the production of documents in circumstances where the sole or principal purpose of the application is to obtain documents for use as evidence in pending proceedings under the Company Directors Disqualification Act 1986.[216]

The court is not limited to ordering production of documents in respect of information to which the company was entitled, as a matter of contract or fiduciary duty; it can do so even in respect of information which would have been unavailable to the company other than in legal proceedings, if this is necessary to enable the office-holder to achieve the purposes for which he has been appointed. Section 236(3) is not limited to the records which formed part of the property of the company and can empass records which came into existence after the onset of insolvency or the appointment of an office holder upon an insolvency, including the working papers of a receiver.[217] Moreover, an application is not unreasonable merely because it would be inconvenient for the respondent, or would cause him considerable work, or make him vulnerable to future claims, or he is not an employee or officer of or contractor with the company in administration, though these are all relevant factors to take into account.[218] Nor can a respondent refuse to answer questions on the basis that the answer was already known, or that

3.44

---

[212] *Re Cloverbay Ltd* [1991] Ch. 90 at 102.
[213] See *Re British and Commonwealth Holdings Plc (Nos 1 & 2)* [1993] A.C. 426 at 437.
[214] *ibid.*, at 439; *Daltel Europe v Makki* [2004] EWHC 726 (Ch), [2005] 1 B.C.L.C. 594; *XL Communications Group Plc (in Liquidation), Green v BDO Stoy Hayward* [2005] EWHC 2413 (Ch), *The Times*, November 8, 2005, Ch.D.
[215] *Shierson v Rastogi* [2002] EWCA Civ 1624, [2003] 1 W.L.R. 586, CA; *Re Sasea Finance Ltd* [1998] 1 B.C.L.C. 559, Ch.D.
[216] *Re Pantmaenog Timber Co. Ltd; Official Receiver v Meade-King (a Firm)* [2003] UKHL 49, [2004] 1 A.C. 158, HL (overturning *Re Pantmaenog Timber Co. Ltd* [2001] EWCA Civ 1227, [2002] Ch. 239, CA).
[217] *Re Trading Partners; Akers v Lomas* [2002] 1 B.C.L.C. 655, Ch.D.
[218] *ibid.*, at 441.

he did not have the relevant documents.[219] Where the English Court is asked by a foreign court under s.426 of the Insolvency Act 1986 to assist in a foreign insolvency, the English Court will not normally make an order under s.236 in circumstances where an application under that section by an English liquidator would have been refused.[220] But if the order is being sought under the foreign law, an order can be made even though no order would be made under the equivalent English provision.[221] Section 236 overrides the privilege against self-incrimination,[222] but probably not legal professional privilege.[223] The effect of the section is to confer third party status on the office holder. Since a solicitor's lien only entitles him to retain documents at the instance of a client he cannot assert it against third parties entitled, in an application under s.236, to production as against the client.[224]

D. APPLICATIONS TO INSPECT COURT FILE

3.45 A party to proceedings in the High Court or county court (other than insolvency proceedings) may be supplied with copies of any specified types of documents in the records of the court relating to those proceedings, whether filed in the action or before its commencement but made with a view to that commencement, provided that he pays any prescribed fee and files a written request.[225] The categories of records which may be so obtained are specified in the relevant Practice Direction. A non-party is in a less privileged position: he may search for, inspect and take or bespeak copies of any claim form which has been served and any judgment or order given or made in public.[226] Furthermore, a non-party may obtain from the court records a copy of a statement of case, but not any documents filed

---

[219] *Re Richbell Strategic Holdings Ltd (No.2), The Times,* June 14, 2000.

[220] *England v Purves* [1999] 2 B.C.L.C. 256.

[221] *England v Smith* [2000] 2 W.L.R. 1141, CA.

[222] *Re Jeffrey S. Levitt Ltd* [1992] Ch. 457; *Bishopsgate Investment Management Ltd v Maxwell* [1993] 1 Ch. 1, CA; *Re Arrows Ltd (No.4)* [1995] 2 A.C. 75 at 93.

[223] *Re Highgrade Traders Ltd* [1984] B.C.L.C. 151, CA; *Re Brook Martin & Co. (Nominees) Ltd* [1993] B.C.L.C. 328 at 336–337; see Ch.11, para.11.78 below.

[224] *Re Aveline Barford Ltd* [1989] 1 W.L.R. 360.

[225] CPR, r.5.4(3); CPR, Pt 5, Practice Direction—Court Documents, para.4.2A; *cf. In re Guardian Newspapers Ltd (Court Records: Disclosure), The Times,* December 8, 2004, Ch.D.

[226] CPR, r.5.4(5); see *Milano Assicurazioni SpA v Walbrook Insurance Co. Ltd* [1994] 1 W.L.R. 977; *A.G. v Limbrick, The Times,* March 28, 1996; *Law Debenture Trust Corporation (Channel Islands) Ltd v Lexington* [2003] EWHC 2297 (Comm), (2003) 153 N.L.J. 1551; Family Proceedings Rules 1991, r.10.20(3) (Fam.D.; but not applying to originating process); *Re A (a Minor) (Disclosure of Medical Records to G.M.C.)* [1998] 2 F.L.R. 641; *Advance Engineering Ltd v Cleveland Engineering Ltd* [2000] 1 W.L.R. 558 (arbitration claim forms). An arbitration claim form may only be inspected with the permission of the court: CPR, Pt 62, Practice Direction—Arbitration, para.5.1

with or attached to it.[227] A party or a person identified in a statement of case may apply to the court for an order which restricts dissemination of the statement of case either wholly or in part.[228] In respect of all other documents, a non-party must obtain the permission of the court, which may be granted on application without notice,[229] although ordinarily evidence in support will be required. The application must be made under CPR, Pt 23. An applicant must identify the documents or classes of documents for which he wishes to search and explain why in the interests of justice he should be given access.[230] Whilst the court should generally incline in favour of access in accordance with the principles of open justice, it may be less prepared to grant permission to search for or copy affidavits or statements that had not been read by the court.[231] The court may be particularly reluctant to allow a non-party to inspect the court file in respect of documents relating to arbitral proceedings.[232] Not every document on the court file is accessible under this provision, as certain documents such as written submissions are not regarded as forming part of the court record.[233] The Attorney-General may search for, inspect and take a copy of any document within a court file for the purposes of an application to restrict vexatious proceedings under the Supreme Court Act 1981, s.42 and the Industrial Tribunals Act 1996, s.33.[234] The remedy of a person having the right of access who is denied that right is to seek an order of *mandamus*.[235] or perhaps an order under CPR, r.3.10. It is a contempt of court for a person who knows he has no right to do so to gain access to the documents on the court file by deception or mistake.[236] Publishing such information is *a fortiori*.[237]

The court's records of insolvency proceedings in general are open to **3.46** inspection by "any person".[238] But if the registrar is not satisfied as to the

---

[227] CPR, r.5.4C(3) introduced on October 2, 2006 pursuant to the Civil Procedure (Amendment) Rules 2006. Although this does not apply to statements of case filed before October 2, 2006: CPR, r.5.4C(1A), CPR, Pt 5, Practice Direction, para.4A.

[228] CPR, r.5.4C(4)–(5). In such a case the non-party will have to make an application on notice for permission: CPR, r.5.4C(6).

[229] CPR, r.5.4(9).

[230] CPR, Pt 5, Practice Direction—Court Documents, para.4.3.

[231] *Dian AO v Davis Frankel & Mead (A Firm)* [2004] EWHC 2662 (Comm), [2005] 1 W.L.R. 2951; *Cleveland Bridge UK Ltd v Multiplex Construction (UK) Ltd* [2006] EWHC 2101 (T.C.C.) (access to pleadings granted); *Seven Network v News (No.9)* [2005] F.C.A. 1394, (2006) 225 A.L.R. 256, Fed. Ct. of Aus.

[232] *Glidepath BV v Thompson* [2005] 2 Lloyd's Rep. 549.

[233] *Law Debenture Trust Corporation (Channel Islands) Ltd v Lexington* [2003] EWHC 2297 (Comm), (2003), 153 N.L.J. 1151; *Chan U Seek v Alvis Vehicles Ltd (Guardian Newspapers Ltd intervening)* [2005] 1 W.L.R. 2965, *The Times,* December 8, 2004, Ch.D. Where an applicant seeks a document which forms no part of the record of the court, this may be under the inherent jurisdiction of the court and not CPR, r.5.4.

[234] CPR, r.5.4A (inserted from June 1, 2004).

[235] *cf. Ex p. Associated Newspapers Ltd* [1959] 1 W.L.R. 993.

[236] *Dobson v Hastings* [1992] Ch. 394; see also *A v A, B v B* [2000] 1 F.L.R. 701 at 712–713.

[237] *ibid.*

[238] Insolvency Rules 1986, r.7.28(1).

propriety of the purpose for which inspection is required, he may refuse to allow it.[239] The person refused inspection may apply forthwith to the judge without notice, who may refuse inspection, or allow it on terms, but whose decision is final.[240] An "insolvency consultant" seeking records for names and addresses of potential clients is not inspecting for a proper purpose, and can be refused inspection.[241] Nor is it a proper purpose to seek to inspect the register in order to extract all the information and to make it available to third parties on commercial terms.[242]

3.47   In *particular* insolvency proceedings[243] the court file may be inspected at all reasonable times by the responsible insolvency practitioner, by any duly authorised officer of the Department of Trade and by any person stating himself in writing to be a creditor of the company or individual concerned.[244] A similar right is exercisable:

    (a) in company insolvency proceedings, by a past or present director or officer or a present member or contributory of the company;

    (b) in voluntary arrangement proceedings, by the debtor;

    (c) in bankruptcy proceedings, by the debtor or the petitioning creditor.[245]

    The Secretary of State, the Department of Trade and the official receiver additionally have the right to have the file sent to them.[246] A right of inspection may be restricted by the court in a particular case, on application made for the purpose.[247] Apart from the rights of inspection conferred by the rule, the court may give special leave to "any person" to inspect the file in an appropriate case.[248] It is an offence falsely to claim the status of creditor or member of a company or contributory in a winding up with the intention of obtaining sight of documents on the court file.[249]

---

[239] *ibid.*, r.7.28(2).
[240] *ibid.*, r.7.28(2), (3); *Re Austintel Ltd* [1997] B.C.C. 362, CA.
[241] *Re an Application pursuant to r.7.28* [1994] B.C.L.C. 104.
[242] *ex p. Creditnet Ltd* [1996] 1 W.L.R. 1291.
[243] i.e. proceedings under the Insolvency Act 1986 or the Insolvency Rules 1986: see the Insolvency Rules, rr.0.2(1), 13.7.
[244] Insolvency Rules 1986, r.7.31(1).
[245] *ibid.*, r.7.31(2).
[246] *ibid.*, r.7.31(6).
[247] *ibid.*, r.7.31(5); *Practice Statement (Administration Orders: Reports)* [2002] 1 W.L.R. 1358.
[248] *ibid.*, r.7.31(4).
[249] *ibid.*, r.12.18.

CHAPTER 4

Persons who must give disclosure

CHAPTER 4

Persons who must give disclosure

A. GENERAL POSITION OF SUBSTANTIVE PARTIES TO PROCEEDINGS

Claimants and defendants, petitioners and respondents

Ordinary claims procedure   Under the old discovery rules, in actions   **4.01**
brought in the High Court begun by writ of summons, discovery of documents by list between parties was generally automatic after close of pleadings.[1] In the county court it was automatic in all default or fixed date
actions, with certain exceptions.[2] Except in High Court patent proceedings,
where a rigorous timetable was laid down,[3] it was common for the parties
not to give discovery under the automatic discovery rules before the summons for directions was heard,[4] at which an order for discovery would be
made, pursuant to RSC, Ord.24, r.3.[5] Under the CPR, however, the position
is very different. There is no automatic disclosure. When the court gives
directions at a case management hearing for the future conduct of the
action, it will consider whether (and if so how far) disclosure should be
ordered.[6] Subject to the exceptional cases discussed later in this chapter,
disclosure is ordered to be given by one or more of the *parties* to the
action.[7]

---

[1] RSC, Ord.24, rr.1, 2; "close of pleadings" was defined by RSC, Ord.18, r.20, C.C.R.,
Ord.17, r.11(11).
[2] *i.e.* those set out in C.C.R., Ord.17, r.11.(1): see C.C.R., Ord.17, r.11(3)(a), (5).
[3] See RSC, Ord.104, rr.10–14.
[4] See RSC, Ord.25; C.C.R.—no equivalent, but *cf*. C.C.R., Ord.13; in High Court patent
proceedings, the summons for directions was heard later than in other proceedings: see
RSC, Ord.104, r.14.
[5] C.C.R., Ord.14, r.1; note that, in the county court, a request for discovery should have been
made before seeking an order: r.1(2).
[6] See Ch.2, paras 2.32–2.33, above.
[7] See CPR, rr.31.5, 31.6.

4.02 **Other actions**   Under the old rules, in High Court actions commenced by originating summons and in other court proceedings, discovery of documents was not automatic, and had to be specifically ordered under RSC, Ord.24, r.3,[8] or C.C.R., Ord.14, r.1, as appropriate.[9] Under the CPR, this is the general position anyway. So actions now under the Pt 8 (or "alternative") procedure will not in this respect be very different. Again, subject to exceptions, disclosure is ordered to be given by one or more of the *parties* to the action. Disclosure will normally be ordered if there are facts in issue,[10] and the order may be for all relevant documents or (more likely) specifically limited as appropriate.

4.03 **Matrimonial causes**   In the High Court and the county court the provisions of RSC, Ord.24 (including the automatic directions under r.2(1)) continue[11] to apply to *defended* matrimonial causes, albeit with certain important modifications.[12] This requires the *parties* to give discovery. Nevertheless the jurisdiction is paternal and, in some cases, inquisitorial.[13] In addition there was until 2000 a special procedure, for the purposes of applications for ancillary relief, under which *any party* to such an application might:

> "by letter require any other party to give further information concerning any matter contained in any affidavit filed or on behalf of any other party or any other relevant matter, or to furnish a list of relevant documents or to allow inspection of any such document . . . ".[14]

In practice the latter procedure was more usually relied on than conventional discovery. It has now been replaced[15] by a more proactive procedure under which the parties to an ancillary relief application must at least 35 days before the first court appointment exchange (and file with the court) a statement in a prescribed form[16] giving certain information and supplying copies of certain documents.[17] Thereafter, but at least 14 days before the

---

[8] See RSC, Ord.28, r.4(4).

[9] See Ch.6, para.6.35, below.

[10] *Coni v Robertson* [1969] 1 W.L.R. 1007; *Re Lifecare International* [1990] B.C.L.C. 225.

[11] Family Proceedings (Miscellaneous Amendments) Rules 1999, r.3.

[12] Family Proceedings Rules 1991, r.2.20; see *B. v B* [1978] Fam. 181; *cf. Hammond v Mitchell* [1991] 1 W.L.R. 1127 at 1139. Similarly in relation to interrogatories under which RSC, Ord.26 applies with modifications: Family Proceedings Rules 1991, r.2.21. Letters of request remain governed by RSC, Ord.39: *Charman v Charman* [2005] EWCA Civ 1606, [2006] 1 W.L.R. 1053, CA.

[13] *Hildebrand v Hildebrand* [1992] 1 F.L.R. 244 at 247.

[14] *ibid.*, r.2.63; *B v B.* [1978] Fam. 181; *G. v G.* [1992] 1 F.L.R. 40; see Cole [1988] L.S.Gaz., February, 26–27.

[15] Family Proceedings (Amendment No.2) Rules 1999, as from June 5, 2000.

[16] Form E.

[17] Family Proceedings Rules 1991, r.2.61B(1), (3).

first hearing, the parties must exchange (and file with the court) a statement of issues, a chronology and a questionnaire seeking any further information and documents.[18] At the first court appointment the district judge will determine whether such further disclosure should be given, and will give directions accordingly.[19] Thereafter a party is not entitled to production of further documents except in accordance with those directions or with the permission of the court.[20] In property disputes between unmarried cohabitants it is preferable that disclosure orders should be made early in the proceedings and enforced strictly.[21]

There is a specific power to require a non-party to attend the court to produce documents in the course of ancillary relief proceedings.[22]

Wardship and other children cases   In cases about the welfare of children,   4.04
such as wardship, care proceedings, adoption, and so on, the matter is very different. In the cases "disclosure" is used in at least three senses. Sometimes it refers to a pre-trial procedure for obtaining potential evidence; sometimes it refers to the process of revealing to (instead of withholding from) another of the parties evidence which the court will take into account in reaching a decision[23]; and sometimes it refers to revealing evidence given in, or the transcript of, these proceedings to non-parties for other purposes, e.g. some other legal proceedings.[24] Only the first of these is relevant here. In that sense, the inquisitorial nature of the wardship jurisdiction means that disclosure is practically unknown,[25] and general disclosure by lists "entirely inappropriate".[26] Wardship proceedings are commenced by originating summons.[27] The court has jurisdiction to order disclosure, and may for example direct one party to disclose specified documents to another party in rare cases.[28] The position is the same in child abduction cases.[29] In Children

---

[18] *ibid.*, r.2.61B(7).
[19] *ibid.*, r.2.61D(2).
[20] *ibid.*, r.2.61D(3).
[21] *Hammond v Mitchell* [1991] 1 W.L.R. 1127 at 1139.
[22] Family Proceedings Rules 1991, r.2.62(7); *Frary v Frary* [1993] 2 F.L.R. 696; *Charman v Charman* [2005] EWCA Civ 1606, [2006] 1 W.L.R. 1053, CA.
[23] See, e.g. *Re K. (Infants)* [1965] A.C. 201, HL (wardship); *Re B. (A Minor)* [1993] Fam. 142, CA; *Re D. (Minors)* [1996] A.C. 593 (adoption); *Re C.* [1996] 1 F.L.R. 797 and *Re BR and C (Care: Duty of Disclosure: Appeals)* [2002] EWCA Civ 1825, [2003] Fam. Law 305, CA (care proceedings).
[24] See, e.g. *Re R. (M.J.) (A Minor)* [1975] Fam.89 (wardship); *Re X(Minors)* [1992] Fam.124 (wardship); *Re Manda* [1993] Fam.183 CA; *Oxfordshire County Council v P.* [1995] Fam.161 (Children Act); *Re C. (A Minor)* [1997] Fam.76, CA (Children Act); *Re W. (Minors)* [1999] 1 W.L.R. 205, CA (Children Act); see also *R. v Local Authority in the Midlands, ex p. L.M.* [2000] 1 F.L.R. 612.
[25] *Re D. (Infants)* [1970] 1 W.L.R. 599, CA.
[26] *Re M. (A Minor)* (1989) 88 L.G.R. 841, CA.
[27] Family Proceedings Rules 1991, r.5.1(1).
[28] *Re M. (A Minor)* (1989) 88 L.G.R. 841 at 844, CA.
[29] Family Proceedings Rules 1991, r.6.2(1).

Act cases the relevant rules[30] make no express provision for disclosure, and there is no practice of general discovery,[31] although the court's power to give directions[32] is wide enough to permit an order for disclosure (when appropriate) to be made against another party.[33] The position appears to be the same in proceedings under the Human Fertilisation and Embryology Act 1990, s.30.[34] Court documents are confidential. The court's permission must be sought for disclosure to experts and others.[35] In relation to third parties, the court has no general power to order disclosure.[36] Specific documents can be obtained from third parties by the use of witness summonses, whether in wardship[37] or other cases.[38] In proceedings relating to a child's welfare there is specific statutory power to order third parties to disclose information to the court.[39] In care proceedings, photographs of medical evidence should be made available to all experts before they issue their reports.[40]

4.05 **Insolvency proceedings** Proceedings under the Insolvency Act 1986 or the Insolvency Rules 1986 were formerly governed by the RSC and are now governed by the CPR[41] except insofar as the CPR are inconsistent with the Insolvency Rules 1986. CPR Pt 31 is inconsistent and so does not apply to insolvency proceedings, because r.7.60 of the Insolvency Rules 1986 makes express power to order disclosure. Whether such an order will be made depends on the nature of the proceedings and matters in dispute. Orders for general disclosure are unheard of on winding up petitions.[42] Any party to such proceedings may apply to the court for an order that any other party clarify matters in dispute, provide additional information in relation to such

---

[30] Family Proceedings Rules 1991, Pt IV.

[31] *RC (Care Proceedings)* [2002] EWHC 1379 (Fam) [2002] 2 F.C.R. 673.

[32] *ibid.*, r.4.14.

[33] *cf. Re J.C.* [1995] 2 F.L.R. 77 at 82–83.

[34] Family Proceedings Rules 1991, r.4A.2.

[35] Family Proceedings Rules 1991, r.4.23; *Re A (A Minor), The Times*, August 21, 1998, CA. *Re A (Disclosure to Third Party)*[2002] N.I. Fam.5 (order permitting disclosure of medical reports filed in children proceedings to persons attending a review of a child protection conference); *Re R. (Children: disclosure)* [2003] EWCA Civ 19, [2003] 1 F.C.R. 193, CA (disclosure of court documents for other civil and other proceedings); *Kent County Council, Re B (A Child) v The Mother* [2004] EWHC 411 (Fam) (disclosure of care proceedings documents to GMC); *In re G (A Child) (Litigants in Person)* [2003] 2 F.L.R. 963, CA; *Re M (A Child) (Children and Family Reporter: Disclosure)* [2002] EWCA Civ 1199, [2003] Fam.26 (r.4.23 protects confidentiality of documents, not oral material).

[36] *D. v D.* [1993] 2 F.L.R. 802, CA.

[37] *Re S.L.* [1987] 2 F.L.R. 412.

[38] *Nottingham County Council v H.* [1995] 2 F.L.R. 571.

[39] Family Law Act 1986, s.33; *S. v S.* [1998] 1 W.L.R. 1716, CA.

[40] *Re T (Children) (Sexual Abuse Standard of Proof)* [2004] EWCA Civ 558, *The Independent*, May 27, 2004, CA.

[41] Insolvency Rules 1986, r.7.51 (as substituted by Insolvency (Amendment) (No.2) Rules 1999, r.5).

[42] *Highberry Ltd v Colt Telecom Group Plc* [2002] EWHC 2503 (Ch.), [2003] 1 B.C.L.C. 290.

matters or give disclosure,[43] Similarly, proceedings under the Company Directors Disqualification Act 1986 are now governed by the CPR instead of the RSC.[44]

Judicial review Under CPR, Pt 54, disclosure is in principle available, though not required unless the court so orders.[45] But compared with other proceedings, it is more circumscribed and it used to be said that it would only be ordered if it can be shown that it was necessary for disposing of the matter.[46] Under the CPR disclosure must be ordered by the court, and it is for the applicant to justify it. One starts from the proposition that there is no general disclosure in judicial review proceedings and is usually unnecessary. Orders for disclosure in judicial proceedings should not be automatic. The test is whether, in the given case, disclosure appears to be necessary in order to resolve the matter fairly and justly.[47] However, the court may be prepared to order disclosure to the extent that the justice of a particular case requires it.[48] What makes disclosure in judicial review more "circumscribed" is the fact that the issue is usually the lawfulness or otherwise of a subordinate body or tribunal's decision-making process and not the correctness of any substantive decision so produced.[49] Thus, for example, where a judge makes interlocutory decisions concerning the production of documents, the Administrative Court in reviewing those decisions looks at them on the basis of the material before the judge, and does not order the

4.06

---

[43] Insolvency Rules 1986, r.7.60 (as substituted); see also paras 3.40–3.44, above.

[44] Insolvent Companies (Disqualification of Unfit Directors) Proceedings Rules 1987, r.2(1) (as substituted by Insolvent Companies (Disqualification of Unfit Directors) Proceedings (Amendment) Rules 1999, r.3 and Sch., para.3).

[45] CPR, Pt 54, Practice Direction, para.12.1; *O'Reilly v Mackman* [1983] 2 A.C. 237 at 282; *R. v First Lord of the Treasury, ex p. Petch*, unreported, December 6, 1993, Laws J.

[46] *R. v Secretary of State for the Home Department, ex p. Harrison, The Independent*, December 21, 1987, CA; *R. v I.R.C., ex p. Rothschild Holdings Plc* [1986] S.T.C. 410, [1987] S.T.C. 410, [1987] S.T.C. 163; *R. v Secretary of State for the Home Department, ex p. Singh, The Independent*, April 1988; *R. v Secretary of State for the Home Department, ex p. Benson, The Times*, November 18, 1988; see Birkinshaw, *Freedom of Information* (2nd edn, 1996), at pp.320–324, and Lewis, *Judicial Remedies in Public Law* (3rd edn, 2004), paras 9.085–9.094. Fordham, *Judicial Review Handbook* (4th edn, 2004), para.17.4.

[47] *Tweed v Parades Commission for Northern Ireland* [2006] UKHL 53, [2007] 2 W.L.R. 1, at [2], *per* Lord Bingham.

[48] *JJ Gallagher Ltd v Secretary of State for Local Government Transport and the Regions* [2002] EWHC 1195 (Admin) at [14], Sullivan J.; *cf. G.S. v Minister for Justice* [2004] 2 I.R. 417 (discovery ordered for leave application for judicial review).

[49] *R. v Secretary of State for the Environment, ex p. Powis* [1981] 1 W.L.R. 584, CA; *R. v Secretary of State for the Home Department, ex p. Harrison, The Independent*, December 21, 1987, CA; *R. v Secretary of State for the Environment, ex p. Smith* [1988] C.O.D. 3; *R. v Secretary of State for the Environment, ex p. Doncaster Borough Council* [1990] C.O.D. 441; *Ex p. Islington London Borough Council* [1992] C.O.D. 67; *R. v Secretary of State for Transport, ex p. A.P.H. Road Safety Ltd* [1993] C.O.D. 150; *R. v Foreign Secretary, ex p. World Development Movement* [1995] 1 All E.R. 611; *Yu Chee Yin v Commissioner of the Independent Commission against Corruption* [2000] H.K.C.F.I. 838; *Clare v Health Insurance Commission* [2003] FCA 1279; *Tanner v Shergold* [2004] FCA 176.

disclosure of other material not before him on that occasion.[50] In the minority of judicial review applications in which the precise facts are significant, the court retains a discretion to order disclosure of specific documents, where such disclosure appears to be necessary in order to resolve the matter fairly and justly.[51]

4.07   All the evidence is given in writing, but the claimant is not entitled to disclosure in order to go behind an affidavit to ascertain its correctness, unless there is extrinsic material available suggesting its inaccuracy,[52] although if an affidavit deals inadequately with an issue it might be appropriate to order disclosure to supplement it, rather than to challenge its accuracy.[53] Thus, where the issue is whether the decision maker had power to make his decision, and there is no reason to doubt the bona fides or accuracy of the reasons given, usually there is no need to order disclosure relating to those reasons.[54] However in cases where proportionality is an issue in a judicial review, the courts may be more willing to order specific disclosure of documents referred to in the affidavits or witness statements.[55] As is the case in other kinds of legal proceedings,[56] disclosure will not be ordered on a "contingent" or "Micawber" basis, i.e. disclosure in the hope that something might turn up.[57] There may be cases where it is appropriate to order disclosure of material relevant to an allegation in a case before the allegation has been pleaded, but this is exceptional.[58] Nor will disclosure be ordered where the documents concerned are sought for the rehearing which would follow the quashing of the original decision, rather than for the

---

[50] *R. v Manchester Crown Court, ex p. Cunningham*, April 19, 1991, unreported, Q.B. Div. Ct.; see also *R. v Secretary of State for the Home Department, ex p. Guardian, The Times,* April 1, 1996, CA.

[51] *Tweed v Parades Commission for Northern Ireland* [2006] UKHL 53, [2007] 2 W.L.R. 1, at [3], *per* Lord Bingham; *London Regional Transport v Mayor of London* [2001] EWCA Civ 1491 (challenge to procurement decision, disclosure ordered of expert report on value for money; *R. (First Group Plc) v Strategic Rail Authority* [2003] EWHC 1611 (Admin) (disclosure ordered of scores in assessment of rival bids for franchise).

[52] *R. v Secretary of State for the Home Department, ex p. Harrison, The Independent,* December 21, 1987, CA; *R. v I.R.C., ex p. Taylor* [1989] 1 All E.R. 906, CA; *R. v Secretary of State for the Environment, ex p. Merton London Borough Council, The Times,* March 22, 1990; *R. v Parole Board, ex p. Bradley* [1990] C.O.D. 445; *R. v Arts Council of England, ex p. Women's Playhouse Trust, The Times,* August 20, 1997; *R. v Secretary of State for Education, ex p. J.* [1993] C.O.D. 146; *R. v Secretary of State for Transport, ex p. A.P.H. Road Safety Ltd* [1993] C.O.D. 150.

[53] *ex p. Islington London Borough Council* [1992] C.O.D.; *cf. R. v Secretary of State for the Home Department, ex p. Singh, The Times,* March 28, 1988.

[54] *R. v I.R.C., ex p. Taylor* [1989] 1 All E.R. 906, CA; *ex p. Islington London Borough Council* [1992] C.O.D. 67.

[55] *Tweed v Parades Commission for Northern Ireland* [2006] UKHL 53, [2007] 2 W.L.R. 1, at [32, 38–39], *per* Lord Carswell.

[56] See Ch.5, para.5.30, below.

[57] *Re Osman* [1990] C.O.D. 422; *ex p. Doncaster Borough Council* [1990] C.O.D. 441; *ex p. J.* [1993] C.O.D. 146; *R. v Secretary of State for Transport, ex p. A.P.H. Road Safety Ltd* [1993] C.O.D. 150.

[58] *R. (Ministry of Defence) v Wiltshire and Swindon Coroner* [2006] EWHC 889 (Admin), [2006] 1 W.L.R. 134, Q.B.D. (tape recording of Coroner's summing up and directions to jury).

application for judicial review itself.[59] It has been said in Australia that the court should be particularly cautious in ordering disclosure in relation to judicial review proceedings that are essentially collateral to the criminal process.[60] If there is no evidence or other material to support the allegations raised in judicial review proceedings, then as a general rule no disclosure order will be made. It is not open to an applicant to make a bare allegation that a decision was made without any basis and then use the process of disclosure to find out if the allegation has foundation.[61] The rules of disclosure in a civil action or a criminal trial do not apply to an extradition hearing, which is an inquisitorial process where the judge is not in a position to require the judicial authority or requesting state to provide information or evidence if it is not prepared to do so.[62]

Specific Disclosure   Whatever the form of proceedings, so long as the CPR apply, disclosure of particular documents or classes of documents (so-called "specific disclosure") may also be applied for under CPR, r.31.12. The matter is discussed in more detail later.[63]   **4.08**

Limits   Historically, discovery was only ordered as between those parties between whom some issue arose in the action.[64] This included preliminary issues (e.g. as to whether there had been good service of proceedings at all).[65] The position was straightforward as between plaintiffs and defendants (applicants/respondents) as they were clearly opposite parties. However in actions with more than one defendant the plaintiff would only be obliged to provide each particular defendant with such discovery as related to matters in issue between the plaintiff and the particular defendant, so the scope of a plaintiff's discovery might vary between co-defendants.[66] Discovery would not be ordered against a defendant in default of notice of intention to defend, as at that stage there was no issue between him and the plaintiff.[67] Before the introduction of the CPR this restricted approach was discarded, as inconsistent with the width of the express words of the relevant discovery rules.[68] The rules of the CPR are equally wide, but it seems unlikely that a similar approach will be taken by the Courts, as it   **4.09**

---

[59] *R. v Secretary of State for Education and Science, ex p. G.* [1990] C.O.D. 65.
[60] *Kizon v Palmer (No.2)* (1998) 82 F.C.R.310, Fed.Ct.Aus.
[61] *Jilani v Wilhelm* [2005] F.C.A.F.C. 269, (2006) 227 A.L.R. 93 at [108–112], Fed.Ct.Aus.
[62] *R. (USA) v Bow Street Magistrates' Court* [2006] EWHC 2256 (Admin), *The Times*, September 19, 2006.
[63] See Ch.6, paras 6.45–6.56, below.
[64] *Brown & Co. v Watkins & Co.* (1885) 16 Q.B.D. 125; *Shaw v Smith* (1886) 18 Q.B.D. 193, CA; *Grupo Torras S.A. v Al-Sabah*, unreported, June 5, 1997, Mance J.
[65] See Ch.2, para.2.33, above.
[66] *Pardy's Mozambique Syndicate v Alexander* [1903] 1 Ch. 191.
[67] *Gould v National Provincial Bank* [1960] 2 Ch. 337.
[68] *Manatee Towing Co. and Coastal Tug and Barge Inc. v Oceanbulk Maritime S.A.* [1999] 1 Lloyd's Rep. 876.

would be inconsistent with the reductivist principles behind the CPR[69] Accordingly, even though the rules confer a wide jurisdiction, that jurisdiction will normally only be exercised where there are issues to be resolved between the parties in question.[70]

4.10 **Group litigation** Although in principle the same rules apply where there are many actions by different claimants against a common defendant, in respect of similar causes of action (typically industrial diseases or pharmaceutical torts), the special problems caused by such "group litigation" demand particular attention. Where the courts are presented with large numbers of claims with special features in common they will devise new procedures specially adopted to such cases.[71] Whilst this will not alter the basic disclosure obligations of parties, it may well involve some restriction of the disclosure process pending the determination of common questions.[72] The Supreme Court Procedure Committee in 1991 produced a *Guide for Use in Group Actions*, which dealt, inter alia, with discovery procedures, and which suggested that such limitations might indeed be desirable.[73] Since the CPR were introduced, Pt 19, Pt III, the *Admiralty and Commercial Court Guide*[74] and a *Practice Direction*[75] have made special provision for such cases, but not in relation to disclosure.

Co-claimants and co-defendants

4.11 **General** For disclosure to be ordered as between parties other than claimants and defendants, it seems that there must be some issue between them for the determination of the court which arises out of their statements of case.[76] Under the old rules, it was held that, where there were no rights to be adjusted between co-defendants and no issue arose between them, discovery would be refused.[77] It was not enough that the relations between the co-defendants must be investigated in the action.[78] But where there was some right to be adjusted in the action between co-defendants, discovery might be ordered.[79]

---

[69] See paras 5.10–5.11, below.
[70] cf. *Manatee Towing Co. and Coastal Tug & Barge Inc. v Oceanbulk Maritime S.A.* [1999] 1 Lloyd's Rep. 876 at 881.
[71] *Horrocks v Ford Motor Co. Ltd, The Times*, February 15, 1990, CA.
[72] *Chrzanowska v Glaxo Laboratories Ltd, The Times*, March 16, 1990; see also Ch.2, para.2.33, above.
[73] May 1991, pp.37–39.
[74] (7th edn, 2006), s.L.
[75] CPR, Pt 19, Practice Direction—Group Litigation.
[76] *Birchal v Birch Crisp & Co.* [1913] 2 Ch.375.
[77] *Brown v Watkins* (1885) 16 Q.B.D. 125, as explained in *Shaw v Smith* (1886) 18 Q.B.D. 193; *Grupo Torras S.A. v Al-Sabah*, unreported, June 5, 1997, Mance J.; cf. *Manatee Towing Co. and Coastal Tug & Barge Inc. v Oceanbulk Maritime S.A.* [1999] 1 Lloyd's Rep. 876.
[78] *Birchal v Birch Crisp & Co.* [1913] 2 Ch. 375.
[79] *Alcoy and Gandia Rly. and Harbour Co. Ltd v Greenhill* (1896) 74 L.T. 345.

It might be thought the CPR would hardly be more generous in relation **4.12**
to same-side disclosure than the old rules in relation to discovery. But the
CPR do not deal expressly with such disclosure. On the contrary, where
"standard disclosure" is ordered,[80] *all* parties must serve lists of documents
on *all* the others,[81] listing (inter alia) documents which adversely affect, or
support, *any* other party's case.[82] Perhaps this situation is one in which the
court will, pursuant to its undoubted discretion, *not* order standard disclosure, but will restrict it to that necessary to deal with the actual issues
between the various parties. The cases under the old rules may afford useful
examples of the technique. Nevertheless, it must be recognised that CPR,
r.31.6 marks a change from the pre-CPR position that only documents
relevant to the issues between parties with a direct link in the litigation were
disclosable by those parties, and not documents which they might have
which, although irrelevant as between each other, might affect the strengths
and weaknesses of other parties cases in the litigation. It follows that
documents that Pt 20 defendants have which might go to the strength or
weakness of the claimants case against the defendant, or vice versa, are
disclosable in principle by the Pt 20 defendants, even if they are irrelevant
to the pleaded issues between the Pt 20 defendants and the defendant/Pt 20
claimant. [83]

Contribution or indemnity Where contribution or an indemnity was **4.13**
sought against a co-defendant, the court would not order discovery under
the old rules until a contribution notice had been served, thus putting the
issue on the record before the court.[84] The practice is the same under the
CPR in relation to documents solely relating to the position between the
co-defendants.

Co-defendant's List Under RSC, Ord.24, r.6[85] a defendant who had **4.14**
pleaded in an action was entitled to a copy free of charge of a co-defendant's
List of Documents and this rule applied also where a counterclaim was
made against a plaintiff.[86] There was no need for any issue to exist between
the two parties concerned.[87] The court could similarly order in actions
begun by originating summons, where the court had made an order under
RSC, Ord.24, r.3[88] requiring a defendant to serve a List of Documents on
the plaintiff. The rule did not—and does not—apply in matrimonial

---

[80] See para.4.01, above.
[81] CPR, r.31.10(2); see para.4.14, below.
[82] CPR, r.31.6(b)(ii), (iii).
[83] *Philip Donnelly v Weybridge Construction Ltd* [2006] EWHC 721 (T.C.C.), at [45–47].
[84] *Clayson v Rolls Royce Ltd* [1951] 1 K.B. 746.
[85] C.C.R.—no equivalent.
[86] See, e.g. *Manatee Towing Co. and Coastal Tug & Barge Inc. v Oceanbulk Maritime S.A.*
[1999] 1 Lloyd's Rep. 876.
[87] *ibid.*
[88] C.C.R., Ord.14, r.1.

causes,[89] but there was and is specific provision in such cases to even wider effect.[90] Under the CPR, the rule is equally wide: where standard disclosure is ordered, "each party" must make and serve a list of documents "on every other party".[91] But if standard disclosure is not ordered, the obligation to serve the list on every other party is not engaged.

Defendants to counterclaim

4.15   Disclosure is available in the normal way between claimants by counterclaim and defendants to counterclaim. In such actions under the old rules discovery would only be ordered to the extent that there was some issue between them and the defendant to the counterclaim. So in one case[92] interrogatories sought by defendants to counterclaim against plaintiffs in the original action were refused as no issue was joined between them. In another case,[93] discovery was ordered in favour of a co-defendant to counterclaim on the ground that there was some right between the co-defendants to counterclaim to be adjusted in the action. In a third case,[94] a defendant in the main action was held not entitled to see the list served by the plaintiff as co-defendant to the counterclaim made by another defendant in the main action.

Third and subsequent parties

4.16   In CPR Pt 20 proceedings (third party and subsequent proceedings), a person on whom such proceedings are served becomes (if not already) a party to the main action.[95] However, it seems likely that disclosure will only be ordered between those parties between whom an issue is raised and in relation to such issues. It is true that, in old cases under the former rules,[96] discovery was ordered between a plaintiff and third party where the third party disputed the plaintiff's claim and had put itself in a position of an opposing party. But more recently the judicial attitude has changed[97] and it is considered that under the CPR the position is as stated.

[89] Family Proceedings Rules 1991, r.2.20(1)(a).
[90] ibid. r.2.20(3).
[91] CPR, r.31.10(2).
[92] Molloy v Kilby (1880) 15 Ch.D. 162.
[93] Alcoy v Greenhill (1896) 74 L.T. 345.
[94] Grupo Torras S.A. v Al-Sabah, unreported, June 5, 1997, Mance J.
[95] CPR, r.20.10(1); this was so under the RSC: see Ord.15, r.3(2).
[96] MacAllister v Bishop of Rochester (1880) 5 C.P.D. 194; Eden v Weardale Iron and Coal Co. (1887) 34 Ch.D. 223.
[97] Gillespie Transport v Anglo Irish Beef Processors [1994] B.N.I.L., para.68.

Interpleader claimants

In the High Court the general provisions of CPR, Pt 31 apply, with **4.17** necessary modifications, in relation to interpleader issues.[98] Therefore in interpleader proceedings disclosure may be ordered between the parties to the extent that the court thinks fit. In the county court, there is no similar provision relating to disclosure.[99] Presumably disclosure can be ordered where necessary through the general rule applying High Court practice to the county court in the absence of specific provision.[100]

B. SPECIAL CASES

Certain cases require special consideration. These are as follows: **4.18**

- (a) Assignors and Assignees (including Bankruptcy).
- (b) Principal and Agent.
- (c) Trustees and Beneficiaries.
- (d) Personal Representatives.
- (e) Infants, Patients, Litigation Friends.
- (f) Representative Actions.
- (g) Relators.
- (h) Administrators and Receivers.
- (i) Liquidators.
- (j) Public Officers (including the Crown).
- (k) Attorney-General.
- (l) Foreign States or Sovereigns.

(a) Assignors and assignees (including bankruptcy)

As a general principle a person cannot be made a party to an action **4.19** merely for the purpose of disclosure; some existing interest in the action must be alleged.[101] Disclosure will not be ordered against a party who is not a proper party to an action.[102] Historically, the court had no power to order a non-party to provide disclosure, although the CPR have made inroads into this principle.[103] An assignor of an interest who no longer has an interest in the subject matter of proceedings cannot be joined in those proceedings

---

[98] RSC, Ord.17, r.10.
[99] See C.C.R., Ord.33.
[100] County Courts Act 1984, s.76; C.C.R., Ord.1, r.6.
[101] *Fenton v Hughes* (1802) 7 Vest. 287; *Queen of Portugal v Glyn* (1840) 7 Cl. & Fin. 466.
[102] *Gould v National Provincial Bank* [1960] 1 Ch. 337.
[103] See paras 4.48–4.59, below.

merely for the purposes of disclosure.[104] Therefore, a bankrupt cannot be joined as a party to an action brought against his trustee in bankruptcy merely for the purposes of obtaining disclosure.[105] On the other hand, an assignee who is a party to an action may be obliged to give disclosure of his assignor's documents to the extent that they are relevant and in his control.[106]

(b) Principal and agent

4.20   An agent's actions, within his authority, are those of his principal. And a principal's right of access to the agent's records is independent of contract.[107] So a party's obligation to disclose documents in his control naturally extends to documents which are or have been in the control of any agent for him.[108] Similarly, a party may be compelled to disclose information obtainable from his agent where the agent is in possession of information obtained in his capacity as such agent.[109] If the agent refuses to disclose such documents and information to his principal, the latter may have to take proceedings against the former for the purpose.[110] However documents belonging to the agent, which are not in the control of the principal, are not disclosable by the principal. Formerly, in an action involving a party who was merely holding relevant documents belonging to a principal as agent for the principal, the agent had to disclose their existence, but could not be compelled to produce such documents for inspection. However, since 1964 production has been a matter of discretion for the court.[111]

4.21   Where an agent was in effect a nominal plaintiff for a principal resident abroad, the court could stay the action until the agent had provided discovery of documents in the possession, custody or power of his principal.[112] On the other hand, where the agent had a real and substantial interest in the action, and was not merely a nominal plaintiff, the court would not order discovery of the documents in the possession custody or power of the

---

[104] *Bailie v Bloomfield Bakery* [1926] N.I. 53.

[105] *Whitworth v Davis* (1813) 1 Ves. & B. 545.

[106] *Whitbourne v Pettifer* (1834) 4 Moo. & B. 182.

[107] *Yasuda Fire & Marine Insurance v Orion Marine Insurance* [1995] Q.B., 174; *Hiscox Underwriting Ltd v Dixon Manchester & Co. Ltd* [2004] EWHC 479 (Comm).

[108] See, *Murray v Walter* (1839) Cr. & Ph. 114 at 125; *Swanston v Lishman* (1881) 45 L.T. *Mertens v Haigh* (1863) 3 De G.J. & S. 328; *Equiticorp Industries Group Ltd v Hawkins* [1994] 2 N.Z.L.R. 738.

[109] *Neate v Duke of Marlborough* (1836) 2 Y. & C. Ex. 3; *Bolckow, Vaughan & Co. v Fisher* (1882) 10 Q.B.D. 61. See Ch.5, para.5.43.

[110] *Equiticorp Industries Group Ltd v Hawkins* [1992] 2 N.Z L.R. 738 at 745.

[111] See Ch.11, para.11.145, below.

[112] *Willis & Co. v Baddeley* [1892] 2 Q.B. 324; *China Traders Insurance v Royal Exchange Assurance* [1898] 2 Q.B. 187; *Abu Dhabi National Tanker Co. v Product Star Shipping Ltd* [1991] 2 Lloyd's Rep. 508.

principal.[113] Similar principles applied to nominal defendants counterclaiming on behalf of principals.[114] It seems likely that the result under the CPR in these cases will be the same.

(c) Trustees and beneficiaries

In an action brought by or against a beneficiary, the beneficiary can only   **4.22**
be compelled to disclose documents which are in his own control. Where documents are held by a trustee, the beneficiary need only disclose those documents which he has a right to inspect.[115] This means that in the ordinary case a beneficiary is obliged to disclose otherwise relevant trust documents held by a trustee which he has the right to inspect in accordance with the principles in *Re Londonderry's Settlement*.[116] Although a beneficiary's right to seek inspection of trust documents has in the past been described as a proprietary right,[117] the Privy Council has held that it is best approached as one aspect of the court's inherent and fundamental jurisdiction to supervise and if appropriate intervene in the administration of a trust, including a discretionary trust. A proprietary right is neither sufficient nor necessary for the exercise of the court's jurisdiction.[118] In view of this reasoning, it will be difficult for the court considering making a disclosure order accurately to gauge the degree of "control" exercisable by the beneficiary in relation to documents in the hands of the trustee, at all events without first putting the question to the court concerned with the administration of the trust (which may be in a different country). This may well result in the beneficiary not being ordered to disclose such documents.

Where an action was brought by a trustee at the direction, and for the   **4.23**
benefit, of the beneficiaries, it was held that the trustee was obliged to provide discovery to the same extent as if he had not only the legal but also the beneficial interest.[119] The disclosure obligation under the CPR is presumably similar. Where the action is between the trustee and a beneficiary then, unless the question whether the beneficiary is such is an issue,[120] the beneficiary may inspect those documents in the trustee's control on the basis of his position as such beneficiary.[121]

The court will not necessarily distinguish between documents held in an   **4.24**
individual capacity and those held as trustee. Where a party is sued in a

---

[113] *James Nelson & Sons v Nelson Line* [1906] 2 K.B. 217.
[114] *Compania Naviera Vascongada v Hall (No.2)* (1906) 40 I.L.T. 246.
[115] CPR, r.31.8(2)(c).
[116] [1965] Ch. 918; *Jacobson v Dafna Nominees Pty Ltd* [1999] VSC 529, Sup.Ct.Victoria (potential beneficiary of a discretionary trust); see Ch.5, para.5.52, below.
[117] As in *O'Rourke v Darbishire* [1920] A.C. 581, HL.
[118] *Schmidt v Rosewood Trust* [2003] U.K.P.C. 26, [2003] 2 A.C. 709.
[119] *Few v Guppy* (1836) 13 Beav. 457.
[120] *A.T. & T. Istel Ltd v Tully* [1992] Q.B. 315, CA.
[121] *O'Rourke v Darbishire* [1920] A.C. 581, HL.

representative capacity and holds in an individual capacity documents which are relevant to the proceedings, the court may still order disclosure of such documents.[122] Thus a defendant, sued in his capacity as an executor of an estate, has been ordered to provide disclosure of documents he held in a personal capacity.[123] In another case a defendant, sued in his capacity as a beneficiary of a trust, has been ordered to provide disclosure of documents he held in his capacity as settlor of the trust and director of a company.[124] However, where a defendant is sued personally, who happens to be trustee for somebody else, he will not be compelled to provide disclosure of documents which he holds for his beneficiary.[125]

4.25   There are dicta to suggest that, under the old practice by bill in Chancery, where an action was brought by a trustee for the benefit and instigation of beneficiaries, and relevant documents were held by beneficiaries, a defendant could file a bill against both the trustee and the beneficiaries to produce the documents.[126] Such a course is contrary to current practice and principle and would not be followed today. (*Quaere* whether, in an appropriate case, the court may order a stay of proceedings brought by a trustee until the beneficiaries have given disclosure, as if a party, on the ground it would be unjust to the defendant if the real claimants did not provide disclosure.)[127]

(d) Personal Representatives

4.26   In an action brought by or against a personal representative disclosure is available in the ordinary way. A personal representative may be compelled to disclose documents in his own control. As with trustees, the court will not necessarily take a technical approach in distinguishing between documents held by a personal representative in his representative capacity and those held in his personal capacity. In one case[128] a defendant sued as a personal representative was ordered to provide discovery of documents which had been in her and the co-defendant's possession as personal representatives but transferred to her in her individual capacity. This decision was overturned on appeal, on the ground that discovery was premature, *without* considering the question whether a party sued in a personal capacity could

---

[122] *Buchanan-Michaelson v Rubinstein* [1965] Ch. 258.
[123] *Szental v Szental* [2001] VSC 42, Sup.Ct.Victoria.
[124] *Broere v Mourant & Co. (Trustees) Ltd* [2004] J.C.A. 009, Jersey CA.
[125] *Fenton Textile Association v Lodge* [1928] 1 K.B. 1 at 7.
[126] *Glyn v Sorres* (1836) 1 T. & C. 644 at 701.
[127] See, *Willis & Co. v Baddeley* [1892] 2 Q.B. 324; *Abu Dhabi National Tanker Co. v Product Star Shipping Ltd* [1991] 2 Lloyd's Rep. 508.; and see Ch.2, para.2.40, and Ch.19, para.[19.21], below; alternatively, non-party disclosure could be sought under CPR, r.31.17; see paras 4.48–4.61 below.
[128] *Buchanan-Michaelson v Rubenstein* [1965] Ch. 258; applied in *Szental v Szental* [2001] V.S.C. 42, Sup.Ct.Victoria.

be compelled to provide discovery of documents held in an individual capacity.[129] An application for an account may be brought against an executor of a will.[130]

(e) Children, patients, litigation friends

Children (i.e. persons under 18 years of age) and patients (being persons who by reason of mental disorder within the Mental Health Act 1983 are incapable of managing and administering their own affairs) can normally sue and be sued only through a litigation friend[131] (formerly next friend or guardian *ad litem*[132]). But the court has power to permit a child to conduct proceedings without a litigation friend.[133] There is no requirement under the CPR that a litigation friend must act by a solicitor.[134]

4.27

The former practice on discovery in this area was unsatisfactory. With rare exceptions,[135] a guardian *ad litem* to a person of unsound mind was not ordered to file a list of documents, as he was not a party to the action,[136] nor would he be compelled to answer interrogatories.[137] In the case of children, the courts also refused to order discovery by next friends.[138] A different practice prevailed in matrimonial proceedings where children and persons under a disability were subject to discovery.[139]

4.28

The anomalies of the previous practice were swept away by RSC, Ord.80, r.9, which applied Ords 24 (discovery) and 26 (interrogatories) both to a person under a disability *and* to his next friend and a guardian *ad litem*. The position in the county court was not made express, but appeared to be the same.[140] In practice, where the child was old enough or the patient was well enough, the list of documents or affidavit verifying the list would normally be made jointly by the child or patient and his next friend or guardian *ad litem*. In other cases, the list and any verifying affidavit would be made by the next friend or guardian *ad litem* on behalf of himself and the infant or patient.

4.29

All of this has changed again. CPR, Pt 21, has replaced RSC, Ord.80, and C.C.R., Ord.10. But Pt 21 does not deal with disclosure. Part 31, which

4.30

---

[129] [1965] 1 W.L.R. 390.
[130] Administration of Estates Act, 1925, s.25; Non-Contentious Probate Rules 1987, r.61; *C.I. v N.S.* [2004] EWHC 659 (Fam).
[131] CPR, rr.21.2(1),(2).
[132] RSC, Ord.80, r.2; C.C.R., Ord.10, r.1.
[133] CPR, r.21.2(3).
[134] *cf.* RSC, Ord.80, r.2(3).
[135] *Higginson v Hall* (1879) 10 Ch.D. 235.
[136] *Pink v Sharwood* [1913] 2 Ch. 286.
[137] *Ingram v Little* (1883) 11 Q.B.D. 251.
[138] *Dyke v Stephens* (1885) 30 Ch.D. 189; *Re Corsellis, Lawton v Elwes* (1883) 52 L.J. Ch.339.
[139] *Redfern v Redfern* [1891] P. 139; *Paspati v Paspati* [1914] P. 110.
[140] C.C.R. Ord.10, r.12; *cf.* County Courts Act 1984, s.76, and C.C.R., Ord.1, r.6.

does, imposes disclosure obligations only on *parties*. However the litigation friend is not a party[141] and accordingly is not personally obliged to give disclosure. Nonetheless, he has a duty to conduct the proceedings on behalf of the child or patient,[142] and this will include giving disclosure on their behalf.

4.31 Where the Official Solicitor, acting either pursuant to the authority of the Court of Protection within s.95 of the Mental Health Act 1983 or under CPR, Pt 21, as the litigation friend of a patient, has in his custody papers in an action which are the patient's property, a parent of the patient has no absolute right to see them. The proper course is for the parent to apply to the Court of Protection for an order for disclosure of such documents. The court will only order disclosure to the extent it considers it is necessary or expedient for the benefit of the patient; it will not order disclosure of the documents if it would be harmful to the patient.[143]

(f) Representative actions

4.32 In a representative action under CPR, Pt 19,[144] the court has no power to order *either* the representative party *or* the represented non-parties to give disclosure of the documents of the latter.[145] The reasoning is that the former cannot be ordered to give disclosure of documents which are not or have not been in his control and the latter are not parties to the action[146] and hence not within the scope of the bulk of CPR, Pt 31. But non-parties generally can now be ordered to give disclosure under CPR, r.31.17.[147] One of the benefits of a class action is that disclosure by the class representatives will usually suffice and make unnecessary disclosure by each individual class member. The necessity of individual disclosure may be a factor against allowing the action to proceed in representative form.[148]

(g) Relators

4.33 In relator proceedings brought to enforce some public right the Attorney-General is the nominal claimant. The relator is not joined as a separate co-claimant save in special circumstances or where he has an independent

---

[141] *cf. Pink v Sharwood* [1913] 2 Ch. 286.
[142] CPR, Pt 21, Practice Direction, para.2.1.
[143] *Re E* [1985] 1 W.L.R. 245; *Re Strachan* [1895] 1 Ch. 439.
[144] CPR, r.19.6, formerly RSC. Ord.15, r.12, C.C.R., Ord.5, r.5.
[145] *Ventouris v Mountain* [1991] 1 W.L.R. 607.
[146] See CPR, r.19.6(1).
[147] See paras.4.48–4.57, below.
[148] *Western Canadian Shopping Centres Inc. v Dutton* [2001] 2 S.C.R. 534 at [59], Sup.Ct.Canada.

cause of action arising out of the same facts.[149] Where the relator is a co-claimant he will be subject to disclosure in the ordinary way.[150] He cannot be required to provide disclosure where the relator holds relevant documents which if withheld from the defendant might cause an injustice, the Attorney-General will request him to make such documents available in the proceedings.[151] If the documents were not made available, the court could stay the action under its inherent jurisdiction,[152] or order non-party disclosure under CPR, r.31.17, of documents in the hands of the relator.[153]

(h) Administrators and receivers

Administrators and receivers will give disclosure in the ordinary way in actions brought by or against them.[154] But where they are sued personally, questions may arise as to whether they may be compelled to provide disclosure of documents held by them on behalf of the company or debenture holders. Ordinarily an administrator or receiver will not be compellable to provide disclosure of such documents, but will only be compellable in relation to their own documents. Working papers of an administrator or receiver belong to them and not to the company or debenture holder.[155] On the other hand, in one case[156] involving a claim based on an alleged fraudulent conspiracy between a receiver appointed by debenture holders and the company as co-defendants, it was held that as the company had a right to inspect relevant documents in the receiver's hands it was proper that the latter should be compellable to produce the documents at the instance of the plaintiff.   4.34

Disclosure in insolvency proceedings[157] will be ordered where it is necessary for the fair disposal of the issues in the proceedings and it would not be unduly burdensome or oppressive. So in one case[158] administrators were ordered to provide discovery by list in proceedings brought by a creditor to set aside a voluntary arrangement under s.6 of the Insolvency Act 1986.   4.35

---

[149] *Att.Gen. v Barker* (1900) 83 L.T. 245.
[150] *Att.Gen. v Castleford* (1872) 21 W.R. 117.
[151] *Att.Gen. v Clapham* (1853) 10 Hare Appx. lxviii.
[152] *cf. Edmeades v Thames Board Mills Ltd* [1969] 2 Q.B. 67 (medical examination); *S. v S.* [1972] A.C. 24, HL (blood test); *Dunn v British Coal Corporation* [1993] I.C.R. 591 (consent to medical disclosure); *Condliffe v Hislop* [1996] 1 W.L.R. 753, CA (funding action).
[153] See paras 4.48–4.59, below.
[154] As to pre-action disclosure in the corporate context, see Ch.3 paras 3.40–3.44, above.
[155] *Gomba Holdings v Minories Finance* [1988] 1 W.L.R. 1231 at 1234.
[156] *Fenton Textile Association v Lodge* [1928] 1 K.B. 1.
[157] See para.4.05, above.
[158] *Re Primlaks (U.K.) Ltd (No.2)* [1990] B.C.L.C. 234.

However, an order for disclosure or cross-examination in proceedings for an administration order is not normally made.[159]

(i) Liquidators

4.36   The obtaining of pre-action disclosure by liquidators has already been considered,[160] as has disclosure in insolvency proceedings themselves.[161] It should also be noted that, in a compulsory winding up, the Court has power to order such inspection of the company's "books and papers by creditors and contributories as [it] thinks just."[162] Good cause must be shown for such an order and inspection must be for the benefit of the liquidation,[163] not to enable the applicant to pursue personal claims against directors or promoters,[164] or to assist creditors to reconstruct the company.[165] Moreover, the court only has power to permit such inspection when the documents are in the company's possession.[166]

4.37   In actions brought by or against a company in liquidation which is being wound up, the liquidator may be obliged to give disclosure in the ordinary way on behalf of the company, so long as the proceedings are in substance brought by or against the company. The liquidator will not be compellable to provide disclosure in an action which does not concern the company.[167] The liquidator can of course seek disclosure against an opposing party.[168]

4.38   In one case[169] it was held that, in a winding up by the court, the liquidator being an officer of the court, and under its control, would not as a matter of practice be ordered to make an affidavit of documents before the opposite party had applied to him for inspection and it had been refused or not satisfactorily given. However, there is no reason in principle why a liquidator should not be obliged to disclose by list of documents in the ordinary way and in default be obliged to verify on affidavit. Where documents came into the hands of a party as a voluntary liquidator it was held that he might be compelled to disclose the documents in a subsequent action brought by

---

[159] *Highberry Ltd v Colt Telecom Group Plc* [2002] EWHC 2503 (Ch.), [2003] 1 B.C.L.C. 290.
[160] See Ch.3, paras 3.40–3.44, above.
[161] See para.4.05, above.
[162] Insolvency Act 1986, s.155(1).
[163] *Re Birmingham Banking Co., ex p. Brinsley* (1866) 36 L.J. Ch. 150.
[164] *Re Metropolitan and Provincial Bank, ex p. Davis* (1868) 16 W.R. 668; *Re North Brazilian Sugar Factories* (1887) 37 Ch.D. 83; *Re Pan Electric Industries* [1992] 2 S.L.R. 437, High Ct. Singapore.
[165] *Holden v Liquidator of Scottish Heritable Security Co. Ltd* (1887) 14 R.663.
[166] *Re D.P.R. Futures Ltd* [1989] 1 W.L.R. 778.
[167] *Re Barned's Banking Co., ex p. Contract Corp.* (1867) L.R. 2 Ch.App. 350; *Re Contract Corp., Gooch's Case* (1872) L.R. 7 Ch.App. 207.
[168] *Re Alexandra Palace Co.* (1883) 22 Ch.D. 58.
[169] *Re Mutual Society* (1883) 22 Ch.D. 714.

or against him personally, if the company was dissolved without there being any resolution of the company as to their disposal.[170]

(j) Public officers (including the Crown)[171]

Prior to the Crown Proceedings Act 1947, where the Crown was a party to an action it could not be compelled to provide discovery.[172] By virtue of s.28(1) of that Act this immunity from discovery was removed, and where the Crown is a party it is now compellable to provide disclosure.[173] Formerly, the Crown did not have to disclose the existence of documents protected by public interest immunity,[174] but under the CPR this is not automatic, and application must be made in each case to the Court for an appropriate order.[175] Where disclosure is ordered, any affidavit or witness statement verifying the list is made by such officer of the Crown as the Court may direct.[176] The impact of public interest immunity on the production and inspection of documents is considered later.[177]   **4.39**

One aspect of disclosure by the Crown relates to the concept of control.[178] Documents relating to a particular subject matter may be held by more than one government department. So if one government department is involved in litigation, documents in the hands of another department are not in separate control, for the Crown is indivisible. Hence, in appropriate circumstances, the Crown may have to give disclosure of documents from more than one department.[179]   **4.40**

(k) Attorney General

It is often the case that the Attorney-General takes proceedings in his own name, not in relator proceedings,[180] but under some statutory provision, e.g. an application to have a person declared a vexatious litigant under s.42 of the Supreme Court Act 1981. In such cases there is no reason in principle   **4.41**

---

[170] *London & Yorkshire Bank Limited v Cooper* (1885) 15 Q.B.D. 473, CA.
[171] See, generally, Birkinshaw, *Government & Information* (1990), Ch.7.
[172] *Att.Gen. v Newcastle-upon-Tyne Corp* [1997] 2 Q.B. 384; *Re La Société Affreteurs Réunis and the Shipping Controller* [1921] 3 K.B.1 at 14; 18, 21; *Cundan v Cammell Laird Co. Ltd* [1942] A.C. 624 at 632.
[173] In Australia, see *Re Commonwealth of Australia* (1991) 103 A.L.R. 267, Fed. Ct. Aus. (full Ct.).
[174] RSC, Ord.77, r.12(2); C.C.R., Ord.42, r.12(1).
[175] See Ch.8, para.8.27, below.
[176] RSC, Ord.77, r.12(3); C.C.R., Ord.42, 3.12(2).
[177] See Ch.11, paras 11.81–11.103, below.
[178] See Ch.5, paras 5.39–5.54, below.
[179] *R. v Blackledge* [1996] 1 Cr.App.R. 326 at 337, CA.
[180] See para.4.33, above.

why he should not give disclosure in the same way as any other litigant, if and to the extent that this is appropriate in the circumstances of the case.[181]

(1) Foreign states or sovereigns

4.42 Where a foreign sovereign or state brings an action, he or it is liable as any other party to provide disclosure.[182] Similarly once a foreign sovereign or state has submitted to the jurisdiction as a defendant, he or it is equally liable to give disclosure. The position of foreign diplomats is complicated by international conventions and is considered later.[183]

4.43 Where disclosure is required to be verified by witness statement or affidavit, a sovereign bringing an action must verify the discovery on his own oath and not on the oath of an agent on his behalf.[184] However foreign republics may give disclosure by their proper officers.[185] An action brought by a republic may be stayed until a proper person is named to provide disclosure.[186]

4.44 There is no head of "foreign state privilege" known to English law which prevents disclosure of documents solely on the ground that to do so would be contrary to the legitimate interests of a foreign sovereign or state.[187] On the other hand, it can sometimes be in the public interest of the United Kingdom to restrict disclosure.[188] Moreover, s.13(1) of the State Immunity Act 1978 provides that no penalty by way of committal or fine shall be imposed in respect of any failure or refusal by or on behalf of a foreign state to disclose or produce any document or other information for the purposes of proceedings to which it is a party. Accordingly, the only sanctions for failure to comply with a disclosure obligation in such a case are:

(1) staying or striking out a claim or debarring from defending a claim; and

(2) presuming the worst against the State concerned.[189]

---

[181] See, e.g. *Att.Gen. v Landau*, July 10, 1991, unreported (Div.Ct.) vexatious litigant).

[182] *Rothschild v Queen of Portugal* (1939) 3 Y. & C. Ex. 594; *King of Spain v Hullett* (1833) 7 Bli N.S. 359; *Prioleau v USA & Johnson* (1866) L.R. 2, Eq. 179 *South African Republic v Compagnie Franco-Belge* [1898] 1 Ch. 190.

[183] See Ch.11, paras 11.139–11.142, below.

[184] *Prioleau v USA & Johnson* (1866) L.R. 2 Eq. 659 at 633, 644.

[185] *Costa Rica v Erlanger* (1875) L.R. 2 Eq. 659 at 633, 644.

[186] *USA v Wagner* (1867) L.R. 2 Ch.App.852; *Costa Rica v Erlanger* (1875) L.R. 2 Eq. 659; *Peru Republic v Wequellin* (1875) L.R. 20 Eq. 140.

[187] *Buttes Gas and Oil Co. v Hammer (No.3)* [1981] Q.B. 223, CA.

[188] See Ch.11, para.11.97, below.

[189] See Lewis, *State and Diplomatic Immunity* (3rd edn, 1990), para.9.15, and see also Ch.13, para.13.34, below.

C. PARTIES JOINED TO AN EXISTING ACTION FOR THE PURPOSES OF DISCLOSURE

Although the old Chancery practice[190] permitted making a solicitor, agent **4.45** or arbitrator who was party to the fraud alleged in the bill a defendant for the purposes of obtaining discovery, the general rule now is that, with certain limited exceptions, a person cannot be joined to existing proceedings solely for the purpose of giving disclosure. This rule is put in various ways. In *Burstall v Beyfus*[191] Cotton L.J. said that:

> "to make a solicitor a party to an action without seeking any relief against him except to make him pay costs or give discovery is vexatious."

In *Gould v National Provincial Bank*[192] Russell J. said that, if the person concerned:

> "is not a proper party, I am clearly of opinion that discovery should not be ordered since it would mean this, that he would be being retained as a party for no purpose other than discovery . . . [I]t seems to me that, for a person to be a proper party to an action of this nature, it is essential that he should be legally or equitably interested in some part of the relief claimed . . . ."

More recently, in *Douihech v Findlay*,[193] Judge Dobry Q.C. reiterated and applied the rule that, as Lindley L.J. put it[194]:

> "the right to discovery or inspection must have some foundation and must depend on some other right . . . ."

Thus, in that case the judge held that a party could not be joined as a defendant solely for the purpose of obtaining inspection of the subject-matter of the action.

Accordingly, for a person to be joined as a party and liable to give **4.46** disclosure, some substantive relief must be sought against him in which he is legally or equitably interested or which affects his substantive rights. The main exception to this rule is the successor to the old bill of discovery

---

[190] See Bray, at pp.40–57.
[191] (1884) 26 Ch.D. 35 at 41.
[192] [1960] Ch. 337 at 341, 342.
[193] [1990] 1 W.L.R. 269.
[194] In *Shaw v Smith* (1886) 18 Q.B.D. 193.

procedure, the *Norwich Pharmacal* order.[195] But it appears to be permissible to join a person to an action for the sole purpose of giving disclosure where there is at least a good arguable case against that person for substantive relief, even though, were it not for the potential disclosure to be given, the claimant would not seek to join him.[196]

D. NON-PARTIES

4.47   Historically the court had no jurisdiction to order discovery against a person who was not a party to proceedings.[197] In this connection, it should be borne in mind that the solicitor to a party is not himself a party to any legal proceedings, but a stranger.[198] But there are a number of exceptions to the rule against obtaining disclosure from a non-party and there are also some other ways of obtaining information and document from third parties, which, whilst not constituting disclosure in the strict sense, nonetheless amount to much the same thing. These situations are as follows:

  (a) Supreme Court Act 1981, s.34 and CPR, r.31.17;
  (b) stay on proceedings;
  (c) *Norwich Pharmacal* orders;
  (d) employees and agents of a third party;
  (e) orders ancillary to injunctions;
  (f) inquests, public inquiries and previous proceedings;
  (g) witness summonses;
  (h) Bankers' Books Evidence Act 1879;
  (i) Evidence (Proceedings in Other Jurisdictions) Act 1975;
  (j) foreign disclosure for English proceedings;
  (k) depositions.

(a) Supreme Court Act 1981, s.34 and CPR, r.31.17

4.48   The first, and main, exception is to be found in the provisions of ss.34 and 35 of the Supreme Court Act 1981. These provisions were first introduced in the Administration of Justice Act 1969, s.21, and the Administration of

---

[195] Discussed in Ch.3, paras 3.02–3.25, above.
[196] *Molnlycke A.B. v Proctor & Gamble Ltd (No.4)* [1992] 1 W.L.R. 1112, CA; *Unilever plc v Chefaro Proprietaries Ltd* [1994] F.S.R. 135, CA; *Cordis Corporation v Pfizer Inc.* I.P.D. 18109, Jacob J.
[197] *Elder v Carter* (1890) 25 Q.B.D. 194, CA; *O'shea v Wood* [1891] P.286, CA; *Williams v Ingram* (1900) 16 T.L.R. 434; *Arab Monetary Fund v Hashim (No.5)* [1992] 2 ALL E.R. 911.
[198] *O'Shea v Wood* [1891] P. 286, CA.

Justice Act 1970, ss.32, 33 and 35 and were amended (to widen their scope) in 1999. Similar provision is made for county courts by the County Courts Act 1984, ss.53 and 54. The relevant CPR rules[199] apply to both the High Court and the County Court.

These provisions, which deal with the situation once the action has been commenced, may be compared with the provisions of ss.33 and 35 of the 1981 Act covering pre-action disclosure, which have already been dealt with above.[200] In each case there are two quite different kinds of power that may be exercised by the court, namely: **4.49**

    (1) a power to order the inspection, photographing, preservation, custody or detention of any property or the taking of samples of any property; and on the other hand

    (2) the power to order disclosure proper.

As to the first category, s.33(1) deals with the power to order inspection, photographing and so on of any property which may become the subject matter of proceedings, before the action has been commenced,[201] whereas s.34(3) confers similar power upon the court after the action has been commenced. Of course this power is unnecessary in relation to parties to the proceedings, for there the ordinary rules of court apply,[202] but s.34(3) extends to property belonging to, or in the possession of, a person who is not a party to the proceedings. Until 1999, this provision did not apply to all legal proceedings, but only to those where a claim was made in respect of personal injuries or death. However, it now applies in all kinds of proceedings.[203] It has already been noted[204] that s.33(1) has been held not to permit the court to order disclosure of documents.[205] For present purposes, these decisions must also limit the scope of s.34(3), which is in substantially the same terms as s.33(1). **4.50**

The second category of power, to order disclosure proper, is contained in s.33(2) (dealing with disclosure before action brought[206]) and in s.34(2), where disclosure may be ordered in an action, *once brought*, against a person who is not a party to that action. Like s.33(2), s.34(2) used to apply **4.51**

---

[199] CPR, rr.25.5, 31.17, replacing RSC, Ord.24, r.7A; Ord.29, r.7A; C.C.R., Ord.13, r.7(1)(g), (2A).

[200] See Ch.3, paras 3.26–3.39, above.

[201] See CPR, r.25.5.

[202] See CPR, r.25.1(1)(c), Ch.19, para.19.06, below.

[203] Civil Procedure (Modification of Enactment) Order 1998, SI 1998/2940, Art.5; see *Burrells Wharf Freeholds Ltd v Galliard Homes Ltd* [1999] 2 E.G.L.R. 81 (Art.5 not *ultra vires* Civil Procedure Act 1997).

[204] See Ch.3, para.3.27.

[205] *Taylor v Anderton, The Times*, October 21, 1986; *Huddleston v Control Risks Information Services Ltd* [1987] 1 W.L.R. 701.

[206] See Ch.3, paras 3.26–3.39, above.

only to claims in respect of personal injury and death,[207] but now applies in all kinds of proceedings.[208]

4.52   Disclosure can be ordered under these provisions restricted to legal advisers and/or medical advisers only,[209] though where the successful applicant in a personal injuries action for loss of earnings has legal advisers, he is entitled to have the records provided to both medical and legal advisers.[210] Who are the legal advisers for this purpose has already been discussed in the context of s.33 of the 1981 Act.[211] It is also possible for disclosure to be ordered only on certain express undertakings being given.[212] These provisions bind the Crown, but not the Monarch in Her private capacity, nor in right of the Duchy of Lancaster or the Duke of Cornwall.[213] The applicable rules of court[214] do not limit any other power of the Court to order disclosure against a person who is not a party to the proceedings.[215]

Requirements for non-party disclosure

4.53   The section gives power to the court to order disclosure against a person who is not a party to the proceedings: what if that non-party is outside the jurisdiction? Presumably in that case the normal territorial limitations will apply and unless the non-party submits to the jurisdiction, or proceedings can be served on him out of the jurisdiction under CPR, rr.6.17–6.31,[216] or pursuant to an international convention,[217] the disclosure cannot be ordered.

4.54   Under CPR, r.31.17(3) the court may make an order for non-party disclosure only where the following jurisdictional requirements are met:

(a)   the documents of which disclosure is sought are likely to support the case of the applicant or adversely affect the case of one of the other parties to the proceedings; and

(b)   disclosure is necessary in order to fairly of the claim or to save costs.

---

[207] As to the meaning of this phrase, see Ch.3, para.3.28, above.

[208] Civil Procedure (Modification of Enactments) Order 1998, SI 1998/2940, Art.5; see *Burrells Wharf Freeholds Ltd v Galliard Homes Ltd* [1999] 33 E.G. 82 (Art.5 not *ultra vires* Civil Procedure Act 1997).

[209] Supreme Court Act 1981, s.34(2)(b), reversing the effect of *McIvor v Southern Health and Social Services board* [1978] 1 W.L.R. 757, HL.

[210] *Hipwood v Gloucester Health Authority* [1995] I.C.R. 999, CA.

[211] See Ch.3, para.3.35, above.

[212] See, *Church of Scientology v D.H.S.S.* [1995] 1 W.L.R. 723.

[213] Supreme Court Act 1981, s.35(4).

[214] i.e. CPR, r.31.17.

[215] CPR, r.31.18(b).

[216] Formerly RSC, Ord.11, C.C.R., Ord.8. It is improbable that a court would permit service on a non-party outside the jurisdiction where the applicant simply seeks non-party disclosure.

[217] e.g. the Brussels Convention 1968 or the Lugano Convention 1988; see the Civil Jurisdiction and Judgments Act 1982, as amended.

These requirements have been considered in a number of cases,[218] but as **4.55** with pre-action disclosure under CPR, r.31.16 it is often difficult to predict the outcome of any application in view of the broad discretion given to the court in deciding whether to order disclosure from non-parties.

As to requirement (a), CPR, r.31.17(a) has not followed the wider test of **4.56** relevance to be found in s.34(2) of the Supreme Court Act 1981, which provided that disclosure may be ordered in respect of "documents which are relevant to an issue arising out of the said claim". Instead under CPR, r.31.17(a) the documents sought must be "likely to support the case of one of the other parties to the proceedings".[219] In this context "likely" means "might well". It is not necessary to show that the disclosure sought is more probable than not to support or adversely affect a party's case.[220] Where disclosure is sought of a class of documents, the threshold test must be applied to each document in the class. The test is not satisfied if there are documents within the class which are not relevant to any issue within the proceedings.[221] Whilst in general the applicant should be able to show how each and every document or class of documents of which disclosure is sought might well support its case or adversely affect that of an adversary, that is not necessary in every case.[222] The court must be satisfied that all the documents falling within the class are documents satisfying the requirements of CPR, r.31.17(3). It is not appropriate to leave the non-party with the duty of making its mind up whether they do or not. Equally the court must be satisfied that the documents do in fact exist, since it is not right to send the non-party off on a search before it can satisfy itself that no such documents do in fact exist.[223] In general it is neither necessary nor appropriate for the court to inspect the documents to ascertain actual relevance, as it is potential relevance which is the threshold.[224]

As to requirement (b), whether disclosure is necessary in order to dispose **4.57** fairly of the action or to save costs, this only falls for consideration when

---

[218] *Re Howglen Ltd* [2001] 1 All E.R. 376; *American Home Products Corp. v Novartis UK (No.2)* [2002] F.S.R. 784, CA; *Three Rivers District Council v Bank of England (No.4)* [2002] EWCA Civ 1182, [2003] 1 W.L.R. 210, CA; *Frankson v Home Office* [2003] EWCA Civ 655, [2003] 1 W.L.R. 1952, CA; *A. v X and B (Non-party)* [2004] EWHC 447 (Q.B.).

[219] *Three Rivers DC v Bank of England (No.4)* [2002] EWCA Civ 1182, [2003] 1 W.L.R. 210 at [28].

[220] *Three Rivers DC v Bank of England (No.4)* [2002] EWCA Civ. 1182, [2003] 1 W.L.R. 210 at [29, 32, 33].

[221] *Three Rivers DC v Bank of England (No.4)* [2002] EWCA Civ 1882, [2003] 1 W.L.R. 210 at [36, 38]; *American Home Products Corp. v Novartis Pharmaceuticals UK Ltd* [2001] F.S.R. 784, CA.

[222] *Three Rivers DC v Bank of England (No.4)* [2002] EWCA Civ 1182, [2003] 1 W.L.R. 210 at [17, 44]. However the circumstances in that case were exceptional.

[223] *Re Howglen Ltd* [2001] 1 All E.R. 376 at 382, 384 Pumfrey J.; *Three Rivers DC v Bank of England* [2002] EWHC 1118 (Comm) at [51].

[224] *Three Rivers DC v Bank of England* [2002] EWHC 2309 (Comm.) at [3]. However, it may be appropriate for the court to inspect where there are questions of public interest: *cf. Frankson v Home Office* [2003] EWCA Civ 655, [2003] 1 W.L.R. 1952 at [37].

requirement (a) as been satisfied. This requirement focuses on the *necessity* of disclosure because non-party disclosure ought not to be ordered by the court if it is not necessary to do so. The court also must consider whether the disclosure is needed to dispose fairly of the action or save costs. There may, for example, be another route to obtain the necessary information or documentation, such as where it is in the possession or control of another party to the proceedings. The disclosure sought may add to the costs rather than save them. The stage at which the proceedings have reached may be a relevant factor in this regard.[225] Only in a very exceptional factual situation would a court be justified in civil proceedings in ordering disclosure of a non-party's confidential medical data.[226]

4.58   Even where both requirements (a) and (b) are satisfied it does not necessarily follow that non-party disclosure will be ordered. The court retains a discretion. The word "only" in CPR r.31.17(3) emphasises that disclosure from non-parties is the exception rather than the rule.[227] The jurisdiction to make an order against a non-party must be exercised with some caution.[228] It is at this third and final stage that public interest considerations fall to be taken into account and if necessary balanced.[229] In many cases the applicant will need to consider what is the most appropriate route to obtain documents in the hands of a non-party, whether it be voluntarily, a witness summons, *Norwich Pharmacal* order, under the Bankers Books Evidence Act 1879, or non-party disclosure under CPR, r.31.17.[230]

4.59   An application under s.34(2) is made in the existing action, and is governed by the ordinary rules relating to interlocutory applications.[231] The application must be supported by evidence,[232] but it will be sufficient if the contents of the application notice (provided they cover all the material matters) have been verified by a statement of truth.[233] Any order made must specify the documents (or classes) to be disclosed and must require the respondent to identify any documents no longer in his control or of which he claims to withhold production.[234] In addition the order may require the respondent to state what has happened to documents no longer in his control, and to specify a time and place "for disclosure and inspection".[235] The final phrase is presumably an error for "production and inspection", as "disclosure" means disclosing the existence of documents,[236] and the

---

[225] *Frankson v Home Office* [2003] EWCA Civ 655, [2003] 1 W.L.R. 1952 at [12].
[226] *A v X* [2004] EWHC 447 (Q.B.).
[227] *Frankson v Home Office* [2003] EWCA Civ 655, [2003] 1 W.L.R. 1952 at [10].
[228] *Re Howglen Ltd* [2001] 1 All E.R. 376 at 381.
[229] *Frankson v Home Office* [2003] EWCA Civ 655, [2003] 1 W.L.R. 1952 at [13].
[230] *Re Howglen Ltd* [2001] 1 All E.R. 376 at 383.
[231] CPR, Pt 23.
[232] CPR, r.31.17(2); *Three Rivers DC v Bank of England (No.4)* [2002] EWCA Civ 1182, [2003] 1 W.L.R. 210 at [17].
[233] CPR, Pt 31, Practice Direction, para.9.7.
[234] CPR, r.31.17(4).
[235] CPR, r.31.17(5).
[236] CPR, r.31.2.

respondent will do this, and—if so ordered—specify the time and place for inspection, in his response to the order.[237] Although it may seem that there is a conflict between the statute (documents sought are those "likely to be" in the respondent's possession, custody or power[238]) and the rule (respondent must identify documents "no longer in his control"), this is not in fact the case. The applicant may seek documents which are "likely to be" in the respondent's possession, etc., but which are in fact not so. The rule then requires the respondent to state which of the documents *so sought* are no longer in his control. What it does *not* do (and perhaps should) is to require the respondent to state which of the sought documents he has *never had*. The respondent will normally be awarded his costs of the application, and of complying with the order,[239] but the court has power to make a different costs order, having regard to all the circumstances, including the reasonableness of any opposition to the application and compliance with pre-action protocols.[240] Where an application against a non-party has been due to the failure of a party to provide disclosure, that party may be ordered to pay the costs of the application.[241]

By extending the non-party discovery rules from personal injury and death actions to all cases, the English rules join those of many other common law jurisdictions, including those of some Australian jurisdictions,[242] Canada,[243] New Zealand,[244] Ireland[245] and Singapore.[246] Whilst the wording of the relevant rule varies from one jurisdiction to another, it is possible to make some general comments about the way in which these rules are construed. First, it is common to find that the local courts will not permit these rules to be used for "fishing" expeditions,[247] i.e. where the applicant does not know if there is anything to be had.[248] Secondly, in most cases[249] the rules do not require the respondent to give general disclosure, so

4.60

---

[237] See CPR, r.31(4)(b) ("when making disclosure").

[238] See para.4.54.

[239] CPR, r.48.1(2). This is in contrast with the costs position on witness summonses, which may be a factors in deciding that CPR, r.31.17 is more appropriate: *Re Howglen Ltd* [2001] 1 All E.R. 376 at 384; *Three Rivers DC v Bank of England* [2002] EWHC 1118 (Comm) at 59.

[240] CPR, r.48.1(3).

[241] *Environment Agency v Lewin Fryer & Partners* [2006] EWHC 1597 (T.C.C.).

[242] Fed. Ct. Rules, Ord.15A, r.8; Northern Territory, r.32.07; Queensland, RSC, Ord.40, r.5.38A; South Australia, Sup. Ct. Rules, r.60; Victoria, RSC, 1996, Ord.32, r.7; Western Australia, RSC, 1971, Ord.26A, r.5.

[243] Rules of Civil Procedure, R.R.O. 1990, Reg. 194, r.30.10(1); 75 *Care Canada v Canadian Broadcasting Corp.* (1999) 175 D.L.R. (4th) 743, Ont.Div.Ct.

[244] High Court Rules, r.301; *F. and L. Valks Ltd v B.N.Z. Offices Provident Association* [1996] N.Z.L.R. 735.

[245] RSC, 1986, Ord.31, r.29; *Irish Press Plc v Ingersoll Irish Publications Ltd* [1994] 1 I.R. 208, Sup. Ct.; *Chambers v Times Newspaper Ltd* [1999] 1 I.L.R.M. 504, High Ct.

[246] RSC, Ord.24, r.7A; *Kuah Kok Kim v Ernst & Young* [1996] 2 S.L.R. 364.

[247] See, e.g. *A.M.P. Society v Architectural Windows Ltd* [1986] 2 N.Z.L.R. 190, H.Ct.N.Z.; *Uthmann v Ipswich City Council* [1998] 1 Qd. R. 435, Sup.Ct.Queensland.

[248] See Ch.4, para.4.30.

[249] But perhaps not in Western Australia: RSC, Ord.26A, r.6(1).

that normally he does not need to form an opinion as to what documents relate to matters in issue in the action.[250] Even if they do, it may be possible to avoid the need for the respondent to form an opinion by permitting the documents produced by the respondent to be first inspected by the other party in the action, who can object if need be to the production of all such documents to the applicant.[251] Thirdly, the courts are astute to prevent oppressive orders being made.[252] Orders should only be made under these provisions when there is no realistic alternative.[253]

(b) Stay on proceedings

4.61   Although it does not constitute non-party disclosure as such, in limited circumstances the court may under its inherent jurisdiction stay proceedings until a claimant provides an authority for the defendant to inspect documents in the hands of a non-party, that non-party being unable or unwilling to disclose the documents without it.[254]

(c) Norwich Pharmacal orders

4.62   The substance of the rules relating to *Norwich Pharmacal* orders has already been dealt with above.[255] But it should be recorded here that such orders usually involve obtaining disclosure from non-parties, as such persons are not usually defendants (though of course they can be) in the substantive proceedings which may follow. The essence of such orders is that a non-party has become mixed up, even innocently, in the wrongdoing of a potential defendant towards a potential claimant.

(d) Employees and agents of a party

4.63   Although it is not strictly an exception to the general rule, it should be noted that the rule against obtaining disclosure from a non-party does not prevent the court from ordering discovery to be given by employees or

---

[250] cf. *Casley-Smith v District Council of Stirling* (1989) 51 S.A.S.R. 447 at 557, and *Uthmann v Ipswich City Council* [1998] 1 Qd.R. 435, and see also Lord Woolf's *Final Report*, July 1996, Ch.12, para.50.
[251] *McIvor v Southern Health and Social Servies Board* [1978] N.I.1, CA of N.I.; *Irvin v Donaghy* [1996] P.I.Q.R. 207 at 217, H.Ct. of N.I.
[252] *A.M.P. Society v Architectural Widows Ltd* [1986] 2 N.Z.L.R. 190, H. Ct. of N.Z.
[253] *Chambers v Times Newspapers Ltd* [1999] 1 I.L.R.M. 504, Eire H.Ct.; *Williams Aviation Pty Ltd v Santos Ltd* (1985) 40 S.A.S.R. 272.
[254] *Dunn v British Coal Corporation* [1993] I.C.R. 591, CA; *Elliott v M.E.M. Ltd*, unreported, March 11, 1993, CA. For other examples of the use of a stay see paras 4.25 and 4.33, above.
[255] See Ch.3, paras 3.02–3.25, above.

agents of a party to litigation, who are not to be regarded as "mere witnesses".[256] This is because the information in the possession of a party's employees as such is information in the possession of the party,[257] and where the party has been ordered to provide disclosure, the order can be enforced by a further order against his employees who have the necessary documents or information. Accordingly, in one case, where a polytechnic had been ordered to give discovery of the identities of persons depicted in certain photographs, the court had jurisdiction to order lecturers employed by the polytechnic to identify such of the persons as they were able.[258] However, although in exceptional circumstances such an order can be made without notice, ordinarily the employees or agents should be given an opportunity of being heard before an order is made against them.[259]

(e) Orders ancillary to injunctions

Disclosure orders ancillary to injunctions have already been discussed.[260] **4.64** Although such orders can be (and are) made or have effect against defendants in such cases, the concern here is more with orders being made against non-parties.[261] Typically, these non-parties are banks, but there is no reason in principle why such orders should be so limited.

Where the non-parties are within the jurisdiction, there are few problems. **4.65** It is now widely appreciated that a non-party who knows of the existence of an injunction against a defendant may be in contempt of court if he assists the defendant to breach the order,[262] for example if he considers it probable that, if he hands over an asset to the defendant, the defendant will dispose of it in breach of the order.[263] But suppose an injunction is granted with extra territorial effect against the assets of a defendant who is personally subject to the court's jurisdiction. What of foreign non-parties who, not being subject to the jurisdiction, hold such assets or have information which ought to be disclosed, or in some other way are affected by the order? First and foremost, this is a question of the exact scope and extent of the order concerned.

In *Babanaft International Co. S.A. v Bassatne*,[264] the Court of Appeal **4.66** qualified the extra territorial injunction by means of an express proviso

---

[256] *Dummer v Chippenham Corp.* (1807) 14 Ves. Jun. 245.
[257] *Anderson v Bank of British Columbia* (1876) 2 Ch.D. 644 at 659; see Ch.4, paras 4.20–4.21, above.
[258] *Harrington v North London Polytechnic* [1984] 1 W.L.R. 1293, CA.
[259] *ibid.*
[260] See Ch.2, paras 2.11–2.30, above.
[261] See, *A. v C.* [1981] Q.B. 956 at 959; *Bankers Trust Co. v Shapira* [1980] 1 W.L.R. 1274 (tracing claims); *A. v C.* [1981] Q.B. 956 at 961 (*Mareva* cases).
[262] See, *Z. Ltd v A.* [1982] Q.B. 558, CA.
[263] *Bank Mellat v Kazmi* [1989] Q.B. 541, CA.
[264] [1990] Ch. 13.

making clear that non-parties were not to be affected, in relation to extra territorial assets. So the order simply did not purport to do anything. However, the *Babanaft* proviso was modified in two major respects when it was considered in *Republic of Haiti v Duvalier*.[265] First, the protection given to *individual* third parties who were themselves subject to the jurisdiction was removed; thus, for example, an English-based third party with signing powers of a foreign bank account was not to be able to dispose of the foreign assets in breach of an order once he had notice of it. Secondly, the court added words limiting the operation of the proviso to cases where the order was *not* enforced by the local courts.

4.67   This "modified *Babanaft*" proviso was itself subsequently modified, in *Derby & Co. Ltd v Weldon (Nos 3 & 4)*,[266] and again in 1994,[267] and subsequently. The current version which is now to be found in the CPR provides[268]:

> **"19. Persons outside England and Wales**
>
> (1) Except as provided in paragraph (2) below, the terms of this Order do not affect or concern anyone outside the jurisdiction of this court.
>
> (2) The terms of this order will affect the following persons in a country or state outside the jurisdiction of this court—
>
>> (a) the Respondent or his officer or agent appointed by power of attorney;
>>
>> (b) any person who—
>>
>>> (i) is subject to the jurisdiction of this court;
>>>
>>> (ii) has been given written notice of this order at his residence or place of business within the jurisdiction of this court; and
>>>
>>> (iii) is able to prevent acts or omissions outside the jurisdiction of this court which constitute or assist in a breach of the terms of this order; and
>>
>> (c) any other person, only to the extent that this order is declared enforceable by or is enforced by a court in that country or state."

4.68   The disclosure aspects of search (*Anton Piller*) orders have already been discussed.[269] These may also have effect on non-parties and hence constitute

---

[265] [1990] Q.B. 202, CA.

[266] [1990] Ch. 65 at 87, CA.

[267] *Practice Direction* [1994] 1 W.L.R. 1233, Annex 2, Third Parties.

[268] CPR, Pt 25, Practice Direction—Interim Injunctions, Annex, Freezing Injunction, para.19; *Admiralty and Commercial Courts Guide* (7th edn, 2006), para.19.

[269] See Ch.2, paras 2.20–2.30, above. As to extra territoriality, and the problems it brings, see Ch.4, paras 4.64–4.67, above, dealing with *Mareva* injunctions.

a further exception to the rule that discovery is not available against non-parties.

As to limitations on such discovery orders, there can be no doubt that the **4.69** privilege against self-incrimination is as capable of being invoked, in an appropriate case, by a non-party against whom an ancillary discovery order operates, as by a defendant.[270] The only question will be whether, on the facts, there is a reasonable apprehension that a prosecution for an offence outside the scope of s.31 of the Theft Act 1968 and s.72 of the Supreme Court Act 1981 (e.g. conspiracy to defraud) might be brought in the United Kingdom and that, if the documents or information sought to be produced were produced, there is a real risk that that might incriminate the person on whom the order operates.

(f) Inquests, public inquiries and previous proceedings

The possibility of obtaining documents from non-parties by means of **4.70** inquests and public inquiries has been dealt with above,[271] and the problem of documents obtained from previous proceedings[272] has also been mentioned.

(g) Witness summons (formerly *subpoena*)

This is a means of obtaining production of documents from third parties, **4.71** usually for the purposes of the trial of an action itself, but also available for interlocutory hearings. The procedure applies generally to all kinds of action and to all kinds of evidence, and is discussed in detail later.[273]

(h) Bankers' Books Evidence Act 1879

Another species of third party disclosure, available once an action has **4.72** been started, relates, not to the kind of action, but to the evidence concerned. Where evidence from "bankers' books" is concerned, special rules apply.[274]

(i) Evidence (Proceedings in Other Jurisdictions) Act 1975

It is possible to obtain production of documents in England and Wales for **4.73** use in foreign proceedings. In many cases the person from whom the

---

[270] As to whom, see Ch.2, paras 2.23–2.28, above.
[271] See Ch.2, para.2.06.
[272] See Ch.2, para.2.03.
[273] See Ch.10, paras 10.02–10.36, below.
[274] See Ch.10 paras 10.37–10.53, below.

documents are sought is not a party to the foreign proceedings, and hence it is a form of non-party disclosure. The circumstances in which such production may be obtained are considered later.[275]

(j) Foreign disclosure for English proceedings

4.74   Conversely, it is possible to obtain disclosure abroad for use in English proceedings. Again, this will frequently result in a non-party producing documents or other information to one or other of the parties. The circumstances in which such disclosure can be obtained have already been considered.[276]

(k) Depositions

4.75   As will be seen later, depositions of evidence pre-trial are obtained much less frequently in England than the United States, and do not serve quite the same function.[277] For present purposes, dealing with the possibility of obtaining documentary disclosure from third parties, it is sufficient to mention that, where the court makes an order for the oral examination on oath of a witness before trial, the order may also require the production of any document which appears necessary for the purposes of the examination.[278] This provision is probably intended to apply only in relation to documents to be produced by the witness. Where documents are in the hands of another party or a third party, other than the witness, it is open for a person to apply for permission to issue a witness summons[279] requiring the production of documents.[280]

4.76   If the witness fails to attend before an examiner or refuses to produce any document at the examination or refuses to produce any document at the examination, a certificate to that effect by the examinee must be filed by the party requiring the deposition. On the certificate being filed, the party may apply for a court order requiring the person to attend and produce any document. The court may order the person to pay any costs resulting from his failure or refusal. Wilful failure to comply with an order is a contempt.[281]

---

[275] See Ch.10, paras 10.54–10.64 and Ch.17, paras 17.10–17.19 below.

[276] See Ch.2, paras 2.57–2.63.

[277] See Ch.17, para.17.10, below.

[278] CPR, r.34.8(4) (formerly RSC, Ord.39, r.1(2), applied in the county court by C.C.R., Ord.20, r.13(5)).

[279] As to which see Ch.10, paras 10.02–10.36 below.

[280] This is evident from the wording of the order provided in the practice from (N20): see p.579, below.

[281] CPR, r.34.10; Pt 34, Practice Direction, Depositions and Court attendance by witnesses, paras 4.8–4.11 (formerly RSC, Ord.39, r.5(1), (4); C.C.R., Ord.20, r.13(7)).

CHAPTER 5

What must be disclosed

CHAPTER 5

What must be disclosed

This chapter considers three elements of disclosure of documents. First, there must be a "document". Secondly, the document must be within the scope of the disclosure obligation (normally "standard disclosure") appropriate to the proceedings. Thirdly, the document must be or have been in the "control" of the party from whom the disclosure is sought. **5.01**

A. WHAT IS A DOCUMENT?

For disclosure to be fair and effective it should cover all records of information consistent with the concept of document. Formerly there was no statutory definition in the rules of the court, although for the purposes of the Civil Evidence Act 1968, "document" has been broadly defined in order to take account of modern technology.[1] Similarly, in the context of the Bankers Books Evidence Act 1879, the courts broadly construed the meaning of "bankers' books" within s.9 of that Act in order to take account of modern forms of holding information.[2] But now in the CPR "'document' means anything in which information of any description is recorded".[3] Even if information is displayed, without being recorded, so that there is no material object containing it, it seems that there is still a document.[4] **5.02**

Paper

Information written or printed on paper is generally the principal source of documents for disclosure in litigation. Discovery under the old rules was **5.03**

---

[1] See s.10(1).
[2] *Barker v Wilson* [1980] 1 W.L.R. 884: "microfilms" within definition.
[3] CPR, r.31.4.
[4] *Victor Chandler International Ltd v Commissioners of Customs and Excise* [2000] 2 All E.R. 315 ("document" for purposes of Betting and Gaming Duties Act 1981 included teletext advertisement).

not confined to paper, as was recognised by the often quoted definition of a document by Darling J. in *R v Daye*[5]:

> " . . . any written thing capable of being evidence is properly described as a document and . . . it is immaterial on what the writing may be inscribed. It might be inscribed on paper, as is the common case now; but the common case once was that it was not on paper but on parchment; and long before that it was on stone, marble, or clay, and it might be, and often was, on metal. So I should desire to guard myself against being supposed to assent to the argument that a thing is not a document unless it be a paper writing. I should say it is a document no matter upon what material it be, provided it is writing or printing and capable of being evidence."

5.04   A plan may be a document.[6] However not all pieces of paper are necessarily documents; in order to be a document information must be included. A blank piece of paper is therefore not a document.[7] In *Re Alderton and Barry's Application*[8] Morton J. doubted whether workmen's time cards, before they had been used, were documents because they contained no information. Where writing or other information appears on property this does not necessarily mean that the label or the property itself is a document. It is a question of degree in each case.[9] An exact copy of a disclosable document is not disclosable as such[10]; but it is otherwise if it contains a modification, obliteration or other marking or feature on which a party intends to rely, or which adversely affects his or another party's case or supports that of another party.[11]

Photographs, films and microfilms

5.05   It is well established that photographs may be documents. In *Lyell v Kennedy (No.3)*[12] the Court of Appeal held that photographs of tombstones and houses were documents for the purposes of discovery. It clearly follows from the photograph being a document that a moving film is also a document.[13] In the context of a *subpoena duces tecum* (now witness summons)

---

[5] [1908] 2 K.B. 333 at 440.
[6] *Hayes v Brown* [1920] 1 K.B. 250; see also para.3.27 and para.4.50, above.
[7] *Hill v The King* [1945] K.B. 3219 at 334.
[8] (1941) 59 R.P.C. 56.
[9] See *Smith v Harris* (1883) 48 L.T. 869 at 870: held, cask with brand name stamped on it not a document for the purposes of what became RSC, Ord.24, r.10.
[10] CPR, r.31.9(1); the old law was different: *Dubai Bank v Galadari (No.7)* [1992] 1 W.L.R. 106; see Ch.6, para.6.09, below.
[11] CPR, r.31.9(2).
[12] (1884) 50 L.T. 730.
[13] *Grant v Southwestern and County Properties Ltd* [1975] Ch. 185 at 191, 197; so held in Canada in *Spatafora v Wiebe* [1973] 1 Q.R. 93; *cf. Glyn v Western Feature Film Co.* [1916] 1 Ch. 36.

it has been held that a film is a document.[14] Likewise, it would seem that microfilms are documents.[15]

Video and audio tapes and discs

In principle there can be little doubt that video tapes containing informa-   **5.06** tion, like ordinary film, are documents.[16] The position in relation to audio tape recordings was clarified by Walton J. in *Grant v Southwestern and County Properties Ltd.*[17] In rejecting the argument that a tape recording is not a document because the information is not capable of being visually inspected, he made the following statement of principle[18]:

> " . . . the mere interposition of necessity of an instrument for decipher-
> ing the information cannot make any different in principle. A litigant
> who keeps all his documents in microdot form could not avoid discov-
> ery because in order to read the information extremely powerful micro-
> scopes or other sophisticated instruments would be required. Nor
> again, if he kept them by means of microfilm which could [not] be read
> without the aid of a projector."

He therefore held that tape recordings of evidence or information are documents.[19] As will be seen later,[20] inspection extends to examining such recordings or other documents with appropriate equipment. It should also be possible to obtain copies.[21] Given the position regarding audio tapes, there is no reason to doubt that video and audio discs are also documents for the purposes of disclosure.

---

[14] *Senior v Holdsworth* [1976] Q.B. 23.

[15] *Grant v Southwestern and County Property Ltd* [1975] Ch. 185 at 187; see also *Barker v Wilson.* [1980] 1 W.L.R. 884; *State Bank of South Australia v Heinrich* (1989) 52 S.A.S.R. 596 (microfiche).

[16] *Radio Ten Pty. Ltd v Brisbane T.V. Ltd* [1984] Qd.R. 113 at 123; *Bolton Borough v W,* April 3, 1987, unreported, Fam. D., Manchester; *Garcin v Amerindo Investment Advisors Ltd* [1991] 4 All E.R. 655 at 656; *J-Corp. Pty. Ltd v Australian Builders' Labourers Federated Union of Workers* (1992) 110 A.L.R. 520, Fed.Ct.Aus; *Chimera v Nguyen* (1993) 104 D.L.R. (4th) 244, Man CA; *Re M (Minors)* [1995] 2 F.L.R. 57; *Rall v Hume* [2001] 3 All E.R. 248 at 253, CA.

[17] [1975] Ch. 185; see also *Australian National Airlines Commission v Commonwealth* (1975) 49 A.L.J.R. 338 at 344.

[18] *ibid.* at 197.

[19] Following *Averill v Sunday Pictorial Newspapers Ltd*, *The Times.* April 22, 1959; *Cassidy v Engwirda Constructions Co.* [1976] Q.W.N. 16 and *De Mata v Menfred Properties (Pty) Ltd* 1969 (3) S.A.L.R. 332; not following *Beneficial Finance Corp. Co. Ltd v Conway* [1970] V.R. 321; cited with approval in *Australian National Airlines Commission v Commonwealth of Australia* [1975] 49 A.J.L.R. 338 at 344; in New Zealand also a tape recording has been held to be a document: *Snow v Hawthorn* [1969] N.Z.L.R. 776. As to admissibility, see *Ventouris v Mountain (No.2)* [1992] 1 W.L.R. 887, CA.

[20] See Ch.9, paras 9.23–9.29.

[21] See Ch.9 paras 9.19 and 9.21.

Computer discs and records

5.07   Records and information are increasingly held on computer, whether on disc, database, microchips or microcircuits. In principle the discs and other material holding the information should be regarded as documents, even though this may well pose difficulties when it comes to inspection.[22] Computer records are covered more fully in Ch.7.[23]

B. SCOPE OF THE OBLIGATION

Matters in question

5.08   The discovery obligation used to apply to documents "relating to matters in question in the action"[24] or "relating to any matter in question in the cause or matter."[25] The classic formulation of the test as to relevance was that of Brett L.J. in *Compagnie Financière du Pacifique v Peruvian Guano Co.*[26]:

> "It seems to me that every document relates to the matters in question in the action, which not only would be evidence upon any issue, but also which, it is reasonable to suppose, contains information which *may*—not which *must*—either directly or indirectly enable the party requiring the affidavit either to advance his own case or to damage the case of his adversary. I have put the words 'either directly or indirectly' because, as it seems to me, a document can properly be said to contain information which may enable the party requiring the affidavit either to advance his own case or to damage the case of his adversary, if it is a document which may fairly lead him to a train of enquiry, which may have either of these two consequences."

The *Peruvian Guano* test was applied and approved on many occasions and was regarded as the principal test as to relevance.[27] A somewhat

---

[22] *Format Communications v I.T.T. (UK) Ltd* [1983] F.S.R. 473, CA, computer software program; see also Ch.7, paras 7.02–7.05 and Ch.9, paras 9.23–9.29.
[23] As to the problems which arise in relation to inspection of a database, see Ch.7, para.7.14 and Ch.9, paras 9.23–9.29.
[24] RSC, Ord.24, r.1(1); C.C.R.—no equivalent.
[25] RSC, Ord.24, r.3(1); C.C.R. Ord.14, r.1(1); *cf.* Ord.24 r.2(1); "relating to any matter in question *between them* in the action" (emphasis supplied).
[26] (1882) 11 Q.B.D. 55 at 63.
[27] See, e.g. *The Consul Corfitzon* [1917] A.C. 559, P.C.; *Avory Ltd v Ashworth Son & Co. Ltd* (1915) 32 R.P.C. 463 at 469, aff. 32 R.P.C. 560. CA; *Martin & Miles Martin Pen Co. v Scrib* (1950) 67 R.P.C. 127 at 131, CA; *Mulley v Manifold* (1959) 103 C.L.R. 341, 345; *Wellcome Foundation Ltd v V.R. Laboratories (Austr.) Pty. Ltd* (1981) 148 C.L.R. 262; *Dolling-Baker v Merrett* [1990] 1 W.L.R. 1205, CA; *Commonwealth of Australia v Northern Land Council* (1993) 67 A.L.J.R. 405, H.Ct of Aus.; *Bank of Columbia v C.B.C.* (1995) 126 D.L.R. (4th) 644, CA of B.C.; *O. Co. v M. Co.* [1996] 2 Lloyd's Rep. 347; *Taylro v Clonmel Healthcare Ltd* [2004] 1 I.R. 169, Irish Sup. Ct.

broader test was adopted by Blackburn J. in *Hutchinson v Glover,*[28] where he stated that every document which would throw light on the case was prima facie subject to inspection.

"Matter in question" referred, not to the subject matter of an action but   5.09
to the questions in the action.[29] Thus in an action to recover land, the matter
in question did not mean the thing in dispute (i.e. the land itself), but the
alleged title of the plaintiff.[30] If an allegation of the plaintiff was admitted
then it was not a "matter in question" and there could be no discovery in
relation to it.[31] On the other hand matters could be "in question" even
though not raised on the pleadings.[32] As Bray noted,[33] "for the purpose of
testing the materiality of the discovery to a particular issue . . . it is the case
of the party seeking the discovery that must be assumed to be true, and not
that of the party from whom the discovery is sought.[34]"

Standard disclosure

The test of "relevance" to "matters in question" has been rejected by the   5.10
CPR as the usual criterion. Instead, CPR, r.31.5(1) provides that disclosure
will normally be limited to "standard disclosure".[35] CPR, r.31.6 defines
standard disclosure as requiring a party to disclose only:

(a) the documents on which he relies; and
(b) the documents which—

   (i) adversely affect his own case;
  (ii) adversely affect another party's case; and
 (iii) support another party's case; and

(c) the documents which he is required to disclose by a relevant
practice direction.

Although this formulation significantly reduces the obligation to disclose
from the *Peruvian Guano* test of relevance, it should be noted that the court

---

[28] (1875) 1 Q.B.D. 138 at 141 (explained in *Donaldson v Harris* (1973) 4 S.A.S.R. 299 at 304–305).
[29] *Thorpe v Chief Constable of Manchester* [1989] 1 W.L.R. 665 at 668.
[30] *Phillips v Phillips* (1879) 40 L.T. 815 at 821.
[31] cf. *Gould v National Provincial Bank Ltd* [1960] 1 Ch. 337; and see *M.G.N. Pension Trustees Ltd v Invesco Asset Management Ltd*, unreported, October 1993, Evans-Lombe J. However this is not necessarily the case and there may be circumstances where disclosure may be ordered in respect of an admitted allegation as admission of a fact is not necessarily an admission of an issue: *Premiere Agri Technologies Asia Inc. v Wong Siu Hung John* [2003] U.K.C.A. 273, [2003] H.K.C.F.I. 676.
[32] See para.5.12 below.
[33] Bray, at p.18.
[34] *Gresley v Mousley* (1856) 2 K. & J. 288 at 292; *Cannock v Jauncy* (1853) 1 Dr. 497 at 506–507; *Compagnie Financière du Pacifique v Peruvian Guano Co.* (1882) 11 Q.B.D. 55; *Format Communications Mfg. Ltd v ITT(United Kingdom) Ltd* [1983] F.S.R. 473, CA.
[35] CPR, r.31.5(1); *Chancery Guide*, para.4.2.

retains the power to order disclosure exceeding the "standard" level and to make an order for specific disclosure under CPR, r.31.12.[36] Indeed, it is conceivable that, in some commercial litigation, disclosure up to the *Peruvian Guano* level may be ordered.[37]

Limiting standard disclosure

5.11   "Standard disclosure" will in some cases be too much. CPR, r.31.5(2) provides that the ourt may dispense with or limit standard disclosure. Although cases on the CPR's "multi-track" will generally involve standard disclosure, or even greater, cases on the small claims track will not. Part 31 does not apply[38] and the court will give directions (*inter alia*) as to disclosure.[39] The standard directions[40] provide only for disclosure of documents on which the party intends to rely. And in relation to the fast track, the court may well direct less than "standard" disclosure.[41] The Technology and Construction Court Guide[42] expressly recognises that in many cases in the TCC standard disclosure may not be appropriate for one or more of the following reasons:

(a) The amount of documentation may be considerable, given the complexity of the dispute and the underlying contract or contracts, and the process of giving standard disclosure may consequently be disproportionate to the issues and the sums in dispute.

(b) The parties may have many of the documents in common from their previous dealings so that disclosure is not necessary or desirable.

(c) The parties may have provided informal disclosure and inspection of the majority of these documents, for example when complying with the pre-action Protocol.

(d) The cost of providing standard disclosure may be disproportionate.

Although this guidance is specifically tailored to the TCC, its rationale may be applicable to all types of proceedings. Thus where documents have already been disclosed whether by reason of pre-action disclosure under CPR, r.31.16 or under a pre-action protocol or otherwise, the order for standard disclosure may specifically exclude documents which have already been provided.

---

[36] CPR, r.31.12; *Chancery* Guide, para.4.3; see para.6.43 below.
[37] *Admiralty and Commercial Courts Guide*, (7th edn, 2006), para.E4.2.
[38] CPR, r.27.2(2)(b).
[39] CPR, r.27.4(1)(a)–(c).
[40] CPR, r.27.4(3)(a), Practice Direction, Appendix, Form A.
[41] CPR, Pt 28, Practice Direction, para.3.6(1)(c), (4).
[42] Para.11.2.1.

In cases such as in (a) to (d) above, the parties should seek to agree upon a more limited form of disclosure or to dispense with formal disclosure altogether. CPR, r.31.5(3) specifically provides that the parties may agree in writing to dispense with or limit standard disclosure. Such an agreement may limit disclosure to specified categories of documents or to such documents as may be specifically applied for. Even where an order for standard disclosure has been made, the obligations imposed by the order may be dispensed with or limited by the court or by written agreement between the parties. Any such written agreement should be lodged with the court.[43]

Statements of case

In the past relevance was primarily tested by reference to the pleadings[44] (now "statements of case"). However, "matters in question" covered a wider ground than the issues as disclosed in the pleadings.[45] On the other hand, discovery was not required of documents which related to irrelevant allegations in pleadings which even if substantiated could not affect the result of the action.[46] And, where a trial was split, so as to determine liability before considering quantum of damages, discovery as to quantum was not normally ordered until liability had been determined.[47] The practice under the CPR is the same. The pleadings are the crucial reference point in determining what are the respective cases of the parties for the purposes of standard disclosure.[48] Even so the pleadings are not necessarily decisive.[49]   **5.12**

Standard disclosure now involves three categories of document: one selected by the party himself (intended reliance), one by relevant practice directions, and only one by reference to its effect on the parties' cases (adversely affecting or supporting).[50] Accordingly it is only in this third category that the statements of case will normally be relevant.   **5.13**

---

[43] CPR, Pt 31, Practice Direction, para.1.4.

[44] See, e.g. *Donaldson v Harris* (1973) 4 S.A.S.R. 299 at 304–405, Sup.Ct.S.Aust.; *New Zealand Rail Ltd v Port Marlborough New Zealand Ltd* [1993] 2 N.Z.L.R. 641, CA of N.Z.

[45] *Thorpe v Chief Constable of Greater Manchester* [1989] 1 W.L.R. 665 at 672; *O. Co. v M. Co.* [1996] 2 Lloyds Rep. 347 at 349–501; see also *Phillips v Phillips* (1879) 40 L.T. 815 at 821.

[46] *Martin & Miles Martin Pen Co. Ltd* (1950) 67 R.P.C. 127 at 131, CA; followed in *Martin & Biro Swan Ltd v H. Millwood Ltd* (1954) 71 R.P.C. 361; *Deacons v White & Case* [2003] H.K.C.F.I. 227, applying *Allington Investments Corp. v First Pacific Bancshares Holdings Ltd* [1995] 2 H.K.C. 139, CA of Hong Kong.

[47] *Baldock v Addison* [1995] 1 W.L.R. 158; *Kapur v J.W. Francis & Co., The Times,* March 4, 1998, CA.

[48] *Paddick v Associated Newspaper* [2003] EWHC 2991 (Q.B.); *Harrods Ltd v Times Newspaper Ltd* [2006] EWCA Civ 294 at [12].

[49] *Chandler v Water Corporation* [2004] W.A.S.C. 95, Sup. Ct. of Western Australia.

[50] CPR, r.31.6; see paras 5.15–5.18 below.

Inadmissible evidence

5.14 Documents could relate to matters in question and be discoverable, even though they were inadmissible in evidence, so long as they might throw light on the case.[51] That a document would not be admissible in evidence was never in itself a ground for refusing discovery.[52] It is submitted that, under the CPR, it is equally not a ground for refusing disclosure. However, it should be borne in mind that, where a document is inadmissible evidence on an issue as being *irrelevant*, it is very unlikely to be disclosable, as it will not normally fall within any of the three categories set out in the rule.

Reliance

5.15 A party must disclose documents on which he relies.[53] The CPR contain no definition of "rely" or "reliance". It could mean "deploy in evidence", or "use in court" (i.e. including use for cross-examination) or it could mean "use in or out of court to advance the case". The first of these is too restrictive; the third too wide to police effectively. The second view appears preferable.

Adverse effect

5.16 A party must disclose documents which adversely affect his or another party's case.[54] The phrase "adversely affect" is not defined. Nor is it qualified by any adverb such as "substantially" or "materially". So a document having *any* negative effect on a party's case is disclosable. But a document, neutral in itself, though indicating lines of inquiry which may lead to other information having a negative effect, is not. Although the question of adverse effect will primarily be judged by considering statements of case, there is nothing in the CPR to restrict it to them alone. Indeed, a document casting doubt on the credibility of a party whose own evidence was important could be seen as one "adversely affecting" that party's case.[55]

---

[51] *Secretary of State for Trade and Industry v Baker* [1998] 2 W.L.R. 667.

[52] *Bustros v White* (1876) 1 Q.B.D. 423 at 425; *Compagnie Financière du Pacifique v Peruvian Guano Co.* (1882) 11 Q.B.D. 55 at 62; *O'Rourke v Derbyshire* [1920] A.C. 581 at 624, 630–631; also the practice in Australia: *Donaldson v Harris* (1973) 4 S.A.S.R. 299 at 305; *cf. Re Astra Holdings Plc* [1998] 2 B.C.L.C. 44.

[53] CPR, r.31.6(a).

[54] CPR, r.31.6(b)(i),(ii); *Re Cawgate Ltd* [2004] EWHC 1773 (Ch.) (disclosure of diaries ordered as capable of supporting or undermining petitioner's case).

[55] See further, paras 5.31–5.32.

Support

A party must disclose documents which support another party's case.[56]   **5.17**
The word "support" is not defined. Nor is it qualified, e.g. by "substantially" or "materially". Again, a neutral document which might lead to
supporting information is not disclosable.

Practice direction

It was intended to publish an Annex to the Practice Direction to CPR. Pt   **5.18**
31, specifying particular documents required to be disclosed in particular
kinds of claim. Even though the CPR came into effect in 1999, there is no
sign of any such Annex so far. However specific provision may be contained
in practice directions to other parts of the CPR. Once so specified, the
documents concerned will be required to be disclosed,[57] whether or not they
are relied on, or adversely affect or support any party's case.[58]

C. PARTICULAR INSTANCES

A number of factual situations require individual consideration: **5.19**

(a) documents for comparing handwriting;
(b) damages;
(c) construction of documents;
(d) insurance and legal aid;
(e) other transactions and incidents;
(f) hypothetical situations;
(g) fishing;
(h) credit.

(a) Documents for comparing handwriting

Documents required merely for the purpose of comparing handwriting   **5.20**
may sometimes be disclosable, particularly in cases where forgery is alleged.
This does not mean that a party will be required to produce all the documents he has signed over an extended period for the purposes of comparing
handwriting. In practice the production of a sufficient number of documents

---

[56] CPR, r.31.6(b) (iii).
[57] CPR, r.31.6(c).
[58] See also CPR r.63.8, CPR Pt 63 Practice Direction—Patents Etc., para.5.1. (paras
5.34–5.37, below).

for comparison in order to ascertain the genuineness of the document in dispute is all that will be required.[59]

(b) Damages

5.21   Documents shedding light on the amount of damages where quantum is in issue are normally disclosable. Thus in a personal injuries claim, where a claim for continuing loss is pleaded, documents relating to comparative earnings of other employees have been held relevant.[60] And where in an industrial injury case the plaintiff claimed damages for future loss of earnings, it was held that *all* his medical records were relevant to the question of loss of future earnings, whether they related to the particular injury or not.[61] In a libel action where no special damage was alleged, the defendant was not entitled to discovery as to the income of the plaintiff.[62] Discovery of documents relating to the defendant's state of mind was ordered in a case where they were relevant to the issue of mitigation of damages.[63] But in a shipping case where the plaintiffs sought to recover from the defendants the costs of legal actions intended to recoup losses and so mitigate damage, the judge refused to order discovery of correspondence between the plaintiffs English and foreign lawyers, on the basis that it was irrelevant.[64] In each case it is important to look at the statement of case to see what heads of damage are claimed in order to ascertain what documents on quantum ought to be disclosed. In a case where liability is to be determined before and separately from quantum of damage, there is normally no need for disclosure as to quantum until liability has been determined.[65]

(c) Construction of documents

5.22   The construction of an agreement or other legal document is a matter of law for the court,[66] and the opinion of any other person (however eminent) is irrelevant, and hence inadmissible.[67] Accordingly, in such a case under the

[59] *Wilson v Thornbury* (1874) L.R. 17 Eq. 517.
[60] *Rowley v Liverpool City Council, The Times*, October 26, 1989, CA.
[61] *Dunn v British Coal Corporation* [1993] I.C.R. 591, CA; see also *Hipwood v Gloucester Health Authority* [1995] I.C.R. 999, CA.
[62] *Calvet v Tomkies* [1963] 1 W.L.R. 1397, CA.
[63] *Hermon v Yorkshire Television Ltd* [1992] N.I. 27.
[64] *Oceanic Finance Corporation Ltd v Norton Rose*, unreported, March 26, 1997, Moore-Bick J.
[65] *Baldock v Addison* [1995] 1 W.L.R. 158; *Kapur v J.W. Francis & Co., The Times*, March 9, 1998, CA.
[66] *R. v Spens* [1991] 4 All E.R. 421 at 428.
[67] *Gleeson v J. Wippell & Co. Ltd* [1977] 1 W.L.R. 510 at 519; *Rabin v Gerson Berger Association Ltd* [1986] 1 W.L.R. 526, CA; *Glaverbel S.A. v British Coal Corporation* [1995] R.P.C. 255, CA.

old law there could be no discovery of documents on the grounds that they might show or tend to show what opinion a party, or his lawyers, or any other person held upon the very question of construction, since such opinion was not relevant to any matter in issue.[68] Similarly, under the CPR it would appear that such documents are not disclosable since, being inadmissible, they cannot adversely affect or support any party's case.

(d) Insurance and legal aid

Normally, the insurance position of a party is irrelevant to the issues in the action, and disclosure will not normally be ordered in respect of it.[69] However, it is:

> " ... possible to envisage a situation where in relation to reliance on [the Unfair Contract Terms Act 1977], discovery of a party's actual insurance arrangements becomes appropriate because of a factual dispute in the case as to the content of the contractual negotiations. Such arrangements might also be disclosable if a specific issue as to the availability of insurance or the terms on which it was available arose.[70]"

5.23

In limited circumstances an insured and insolvent party may be obliged by statute to provide details of insurance, once liability against him has been established.[71] It has been held that usually a third party claimant will be able to obtain disclosure of documentation as to insurance even before the establishment of the insured's liability to that third party.[72] Where legal aid is concerned, it might have been thought that it was irrelevant to the issues in the proceedings, and hence no disclosure would be ordered in respect of it. But in one case where the defendants had raised the question whether the

---

[68] *Schering Agrochemicals Ltd v A.B.M. Chemicals Ltd* [1987] R.P.C. 185; *Bay Milk Products Ltd v Earthquake and War Damage Commission* [1990] 1 N.Z.L.R. 139, CA of N.Z.; *Glaverbel S.A. v British Coal Corporation* [1995] R.P.C. 255, CA.

[69] *Gerald R. Smith & Partners v Wylie*, unreported, July 28, 1994, CA; *Cox v Bankside Members Agency Ltd* (1994) 145 N.L.J. 313; *Beneficial Finance Corporation Ltd v Price Waterhouse* (1996) 68 S.A.S.R. 19, South Australia Sup.Ct. (Full Ct.); there may be communications between a party and his insurers which are disclosable, but protected by privilege: *cf. Nauru v Allen, Allen and Hemsley* (1997) 13 P.N. 64, and see Ch.11, para.11.60, below.

[70] *Flamar Interocean Ltd v Denmac Ltd* [1990] 1 Lloyd's Rep. 434 at 440.

[71] Third Party (Rights Against Insurers) Act 1930, s.2.

[72] *First National Tricity Finance Ltd v OT Computers Ltd* (In Administration) [2004] EWCA Civ 653, [2004] 3 W.L.R. 886, CA; not following *Nigel Upchurch Associates v The Aldridge Estates Investments Co. Ltd* [1993] 1 Lloyd's Rep. 535; *Woolwich Building Society v Taylor* [1995] 1 B.C.L.C. 132.

legally-aided claimants were entitled to legal aid, the judge ordered limited disclosure of documents going to that.[73]

(e) Other transactions and incidents

5.24   Documents which relate to similar fact evidence, in cases where the evidence in one transaction is relevant to another which is the subject-matter of the proceedings, may well support or adversely affect a party's case and hence are prima facie disclosable.[74] But where documents relating to similar cases are not material to the issue raised, discovery has in the past been refused.[75] There is no reason to suppose that the courts will take a different view under the CPR. However, even where such documents are disclosable the court has power to,[76] and may, impose some limit, either as to the period covered, or the number of transactions. This will confine disclosure to reasonable proportions, so not to act oppressively to one of the parties to the litigation, and also to keep costs within reasonable bounds.[77] The court may refuse disclosure of material which would not be admissible in evidence, such as where the documents would merely show a disposition to commit the conduct alleged and was not required to rebut a defence of accident or coincidence or to prove a system of conduct.[78] However in one case under the old rules, involving allegations of dishonesty against a police officer, discovery was ordered of documents relating to the officer's conduct in other cases.[79]

5.25   Documents relating to complaints of subsequent users of a product alleged to be dangerous have been held to be relevant under the old rules and hence subject to discovery.[80] Where there was an issue as to whether a party was a moneylender, discovery could be ordered of documents relating

[73] *Harrison v Bloom Camillin*, unreported, May 19, 1999, Neuberger J.
[74] See, e.g. *Nyckeln Finance Co. Ltd v Edward Symmons & Partners* [1996] P.N.L.R. 245, CA; *Portman Building Society v Royal Insurance Plc* [1998] P.N.L.R. 672, CA; *Forum (Holdings) Ltd v Brook Street Computers Ltd*, unreported, May 5, 1998, CA (bespoke computer software).
[75] *Merchants & Manufacturers' Insurance Co. v Davies* [1938] 1 K.B. 196, CA; see also *Bay Milk Products Ltd v Earthquake and War Damage Commission* [1990] 1 N.Z.L.R. 139, CA of N.Z.
[76] CPR, r.31.5(2).
[77] *Drennan v Brooke Marine*, The Times, June 21, 1983; *Shaw v National Trust*, The Independent, February 13, 1989; *Forrester v British Railways Board*, The Times, April 18, 1996, CA.
[78] *Thorpe v Chief Constable of Manchester* [1989] 1 W.L.R. 665, CA; *N(K) v Alberta* (1999) 174 D.L.R. (4th) 366, Alberta Q.B.
[79] *Steel v Metropolitan Police Commissioner*, unreported, February 18, 1993, CA.
[80] *Board v Thomas Hedley & Co.* [1951] 2 All E.R. 431, CA; *Blakeborough v British Motor Corp. Ltd* (1969) 113 S.J. 366, CA; *Drennan v Brooke Marine*, The Times, June 21, 1983.

to loans later as well as earlier than the transaction in question, although the court in such a case was likely to impose a restriction on the time period involved.[81] In proceedings for infringement of a patent where the validity of the patent was in issue, the plaintiff might be liable to provide discovery of documents filed by him in applications for patent protection in foreign jurisdictions, notwithstanding that such documents might be inconclusive of the issues in the action, so long as such documents might assist the defendant by disclosing the line which might be taken by the plaintiff in resisting the attack on the validity of the patent.[82]

In an action for damages for negligence which has caused personal injury, evidence that to the defendant's knowledge there had been similar previous accidents in the same premises to other persons would be relevant to show the defendant's knowledge of the risk. Hence discovery of complaints of these previous injuries would in principle be ordered under the old rules.[83] However, wide-ranging requests in personal injury litigation which were not suitably confined to accidents occurring within a reasonable time of, and in an area reasonably proximate to the site of, the plaintiff's accident were often refused.[84] In an action for damages for professional negligence against a solicitor, evidence of other claims for negligence made or established against the defendant by other clients in respect of other matters would be irrelevant and inadmissible and discovery in respect of such other matters would be oppressive; it was said that a plaintiff charging a solicitor with negligence in one matter should not investigate other areas of his practice in an endeavour to establish that he had a propensity to be careless.[85] Finally, in unfair dismissal proceedings, where employees were selected for redundancy after a grading exercise, those dismissed were held not entitled to discovery of the assessment forms of those not made redundant.[86]

5.26

(f) Hypothetical situations

The court may be required to resolve an issue by assuming certain facts (which may or may not be true), such as:

5.27

---

[81] *Marshall v Goulston Discount (Northern) Ltd* [1967] Ch. 72, CA.

[82] *Vickers plc v Horsell Graphic Industries Ltd* [1988] R.P.C. 421; *cf. Avery Ltd v Ashworth, Son & Co. Ltd* (1915) 32 R.P.C. 560, CA and *Schering Agrochemicals Ltd v A.B.M. Chemicals Ltd* [1987] R.P.C. 185.

[83] *Thorpe v Chief Constable of Greater Manchester* [1989] 1 W.L.R. 665 at 669; see also *Gray v Malton Bacon Factory Ltd* [1995] P.I.Q.R. 175.

[84] As in *Edminston v British Transport Commission* [1955] 3 All E.R. 832, CA; see also *Moore v Woodman* [1970] V.R. 577.

[85] *Thorpe v Chief Constable of Greater Manchester* [1989] 1 W.L.R. 665; *cf. Cheung Kai Wing v Mak Sheum Shum* [1993] H.K. Digest, G134, H.K.C.A.

[86] *British Aerospace v Green* [1995] I.C.R. 1006. CA; *F.D.R. Ltd v Holloway* [1995] I.R.L.R. 400, E.A.T.

    (a) the amount of rent payable on review or following a lease renewal, when statutory and/or contracted assumptions and disregards will substitute assumed for real facts: or;

    (b) the consideration for a sale at arms' length in a hypothetical market.

In such cases, the question is almost always, "What would the market pay?" This in turn depends on the further question, "What would the market know?" In *Lynall v I.R.C.*[87] (an estate duty case) the House of Lords held that, for the purposes of the hypothetical sale in the open market required in that case, the market, including the hypothetical purchaser, could not be treated as having access to confidential information, so that such information was irrelevant to and inadmissible in arriving at the hypothetical market value.

5.28   This has important implications for disclosure: if the issue is "What does the market know?", information which the market does not know is irrelevant, cannot affect anyone's case, and is therefore not disclosable.[88] Thus it was held under the old rules that the confidential trading accounts and management information of a tenant operating a casino were not discoverable in a rent review arbitration, where the question was what was the hypothetical open market rent, to be judged (in part) by the information available to prospective lessees in that hypothetical market.[89] This can cut either way:

    (a) a party not having documents cannot get them from the other party (because irrelevant and so not disclosable);

    (b) a party having documents will not be able to put them in evidence (because irrelevant and so inadmissible).

5.29   The contract or lease between the parties,[90] or the statute governing their relationship,[91] may provide differently, such as expressly treating such confidential information as if it were available to the hypothetical market. The usual tests for disclosure will then apply.[92] Different considerations

---

[87] [1972] A.C. 680.

[88] See paras 5.15–5.18, above.

[89] *Cornwall Coast Country Club v Cardgrange Ltd* [1987] 1 E.G.L.R. 146, not following earlier cases as inconsistent with *Lynall v I.R.C.* [1972] A.C. 680; see also *ARC Ltd v Scholfield* [1990] 2 E.G.L R. 52; *cf. Urban Small Space Ltd v Burford Investment Co. Ltd* [1990] 2 E.G.L.R. 120.

[90] *Electricity Supply Nominees Ltd v London Clubs Ltd* [1988] 2 E.G.L.R. 152; *Re Dickinson* [1992] 2 N.Z.L.R., 43, CA of N.Z.

[91] e.g. Taxation of Chargeable Gains Act 1992, s.273(3).

[92] See also para.5.36, below, dealing with patent licences of right, and Ch.8, para.8.08, dealing with agreements to limit discovery.

may also apply where an action is being brought against a valuer for alleged negligence.[93]

(g) Fishing

The old law was clear, that discovery would not be ordered to enable a   5.30
party to frame a new case or to fish for evidence.[94] Nor would discovery be
ordered to enable "checks" to be made on opponents' statements on oath
regarding existing discovery. As Mustill L.J. said in *Berkeley Administration
Inc. v McClelland*[95]:

> "It is plain . . . that the plaintiffs just do not believe anything that the
> defendants have said in the course of this discovery, and would like to
> hunt around the documents in the hope that something useful would
> turn up enabling them to controvert what the defendants have said on
> oath. That is not what discovery is about at all."

Nor would the court order discovery designed to reveal whether the
defendant is in breach of a *Mareva* injunction (now asset freezing order).[96]
The CPR are even stricter than the old rules. Disclosure will not be ordered
for the purposes of "fishing". There must be a proper basis for seeking an
order for specific disclosure.[97] With pre-action disclosure under CPR,
r.31.16 there may be an element of speculation where the purpose of the
application is to determine whether there is a case worth pursuing.[98]

(h) Credit

Discovery was not ordered for material which would be used solely for   5.31
cross-examination of a witness as to credit, since it would be oppressive if
a party was obliged to disclose any document which might provide material

---

[93] *Mortgage Corporation v Halifax (SW) Ltd, The Times,* July 15, 1998.
[94] *Philipps v Philipps* (1870) 40 L.T. 815 at 819; *Radio Corp. of America v Rauland Corp.*
[1956] 1 Q.B. 618 at 649; *British Leyland Motor Corp. Ltd v Wyatt Interpart Co. Ltd*
[1979] F.S.R. 39; *Somerville v Australian Securities Commission* (1993) 118 A.L.R. 149;
British Aerospace v Green [1995] I.C.R. 1006; *Mortgage Express Ltd v S. Newman & Co*;
unreported, July 7, 1998, CA; *Bailey v Beagle Management Pty Ltd* [2004] FCA 60 Fed. Ct.
of Australia; *Framus Ltd v CRH Plc* [2004] 2 I.R. 20, Irish Sup. Ct.; *cf. F.D.R. v Holloway*
[1995] I.R.L.R. 400; *M. v L.*[1997] 3 N.Z.L.R. 424; *Re Astra Holdings Ltd* [1998] 2
B.C.L.C. 44.
[95] [1990] F.S.R. 381 at 383; *cf. Bank of Crete S.A. v Koskotas* [1991] 2 Lloyd's Rep. 587 at
588.
[96] *A. J. Bekhor & Co. Ltd v Bilton*[1981] Q.B. 923, CA; as to cross-examination on affidavit,
see Ch.6, para.6.44, below.
[97] See CPR, Pt 31 PD, para.5.
[98] See Ch.3 paras 3.31 and 3.34; *Jay v Wilder Coe* [2003] EWHC 1786 (Q.B.).

for cross-examination as to his credibility as a witness. Interrogatories were refused on the same ground.[99] Hence discovery was refused of documents relating to similar transactions in a passing off action as it related only to any attempt to impeach the credit of the opposite party,[100] and similarly in a copyright infringement action.[101] In an action against a Chief Constable, as being vicariously liable for torts committed by two officers, claiming damages for assault, unlawful arrest, false imprisonment and malicious prosecution, it was held that the Chief Constable was not required to provide discovery of documents relating to the "characters" of the two police officers.[102]

5.32   The position may not, however, be the same under the CPR. "Standard" disclosure includes documents adversely affecting, or supporting, a party's case.[103] Documents which (say) demonstrate that a party is a pathological liar, even though otherwise unrelated to the action, may well be thought to "adversely affect" his case, or "support" his opponent's, if his own evidence is important for success. In one case the court ordered disclosure of notes of a hearing, which might be put at a rehearing to show inconsistent statements by a key witness.[104] Of course the court would be astute to prevent abuse of this possibility, restricting it to cases where the party's own evidence was to be tendered and it was vital that he be believed. But the court may prefer to avoid the problem altogether, and to construe "case" in the narrow sense of what is set out in the statements of case (formerly pleadings). Moreover, since *Peruvian Guano* has in practice gone,[105] it will be necessary that the "adverse" or "supporting" effect of the document be apparent on its face, rather than merely form part of a chain of documents.

D. SPECIAL CASES

Libel[106]

5.33   In libel actions the scope of discovery was defined strictly by reference to the pleadings and especially any particulars provided. Hence a defendant

---

[99] *Kennedy v Dodson* [1895] Ch. 334, CA; *Rockwell International Corp. v Serck Industries Ltd* [1988] F.S.R. 187. See Ch.16, para.16.38, below.
[100] *George Ballantine & Son Ltd v F.E.R. Dixon & Son Ltd* [1974] 1 W.L.R. 1125.
[101] *E.F. Music v S. F. (Film) Distributors Ltd* [1978] F.S.R. 121.
[102] *Thorpe v Chief Constable of Greater Manchester* [1989] 1 W.L.R. 665, CA, followed in *G.E. Capital Group Ltd v Bankers Trust Co.* [1995] 1 W.L.R. 173 at 178, CA.
[103] See paras 5.16–5.17 above.
[104] *Comfort v Department of Constitutional Affairs* (2005) 102 (35) L.S.G. 42, E.A.T.
[105] See para.5.10, above.
[106] See also the discussion in Ch.16, paras 16.56–16.65.

seeking to justify a libel reference to specific instances could obtain discovery only in relation to those matters.[107] But in such a case the *plaintiff* was not so limited in obtaining discovery from the defendant.[108] In accordance with general principle, the court would not order discovery of the libel to allow the plaintiff to set it out in his pleading.[109] The CPR make no specific provision for disclosure in libel cases,[110] so that the ordinary rules apply. The claimant in the justification case would probably now be limited to disclosure in relation to the specific instances of justification, like the defendant. But the claimant who had not seen the alleged libel could probably obtain it by use of pre-action disclosure procedure.[111]

Patents

In patent actions where invalidity of the patent was pleaded and the defendant had given particulars of objections, discovery on that issue was confined to the matters relied upon in the particulars given.[112] The same was true where particulars of a patent infringement were given. Apart from that, in general, discovery in a patent action was no different in principle from discovery in any other action.[113] So, where there was a claim to see a class of documents, the class had not to be defined or described so widely as to include documents which were not relevant to the issue.[114] The extent of

5.34

---

[107] *Yorkshire Provident Life Assurance Co. v Gilbert & Rivington* [1895] 2 Q.B. 148, CA, followed in *Arnold & Butler v Bottomley* [1908] 2 Q.B. 151, CA, and considered in *Godman v Times Publishing Co.* [1926] 2 K.B. 273; also *Mulley v Manifold* (1959) 103 C.L.R. 341 at 345, H. Ct. of Aus; *Wright Norman v Oversea-Chinese Banking Corp. Ltd* [1992] 2 S.L.R. 710 Singapore CA; *Kent v Kehoe* (2000) 1 D.L.R. (4th) 50 Nova Scotia, CA; *Cooper Flynn v RTE* [2001] 1 I.L.R.M. 208, Irish High Ct (provided a plea of justification is properly particularised, a defendant is entitled to seek support for his case from documents revealed on disclosure); *I.B.E.W. Local 213 v Pacific Newspaper Group Inc* (2005) 249 D.L.R. (4th) 647, British Columbia CA.

[108] *Evans v Granada Television Ltd*, unreported, February 19, 1993, CA; *Hodkin v Caven Atack*, unreported, March 9, 1995, Sir Haydn Tudor Evans.

[109] *Shah v Standard Chartered Bank*, unreported, February 2, 1996, Sachs J.; *British Data Management Plc v Boxer Commercial Rewards Plc* [1996] 3 All E.R. 707, CA; *cf. Rigg v Associated Newspapers* [2004] EWHC 710 (Q.B.) (early disclosure of journalist's notes ordered in defamation action where issue as to what claimant said in interview).

[110] *cf.* CPR r.53.3 (party not required to provide further information about identity of defendant's sources of information, unless court so orders).

[111] See Ch.3, paras 3.26–3.39, above.

[112] *Avery Ltd v Ashworth* (1915) 32 R.P.C. 463, aff. 32 R.P.C. 560, CA; see also *Edison & Swan Electric Light Co. v Holland* (1888) 5 R.P.C. 213; *AG Für Autogene Aluminium Schweissung v London Aluminium Co. Ltd* (1919) 36 R.P.C. 199, CA; *Intalite International N.V. v Celluar Ceilings Ltd (No.1)* [1987] R.P.C. 532; *Intel Corp v General Instrument Corp.* [1989] F.S.R. 640 at 646–647.

[113] *SKM S.A. v Wagner Spraytech* [1982] R.P.C. 497 at 499.

[114] *Molnlycke A.B. v Procter & Gamble Ltd (No.3)* [1990] R.P.C. 498 at 502; *Fuji Photo Film Co. Ltd* [1989] R.P.C. 713; *Poseidon Industri A/B v Cerosa Ltd* [1975] F.S.R. 122 (correspondence between patentee and patent office not relevant).

disclosure is generally circumscribed by the pleadings. Thus for a defendant to an infringement action, disclosure obligation is confined to the issues raised in the particulars of infringements (and his own pleadings); he is not normally required to give disclosure of all his sales.[115]

5.35 In a patent action where obviousness was raised as an issue, the test for discovery on that issue was whether there was any way in which the documents of which discovery was sought could assist the defendant's case on obviousness, either offensively or defensively.[116] Where the issue of commercial success is raised, discovery relating to processes used in the manufacture of the commercial article might be ordered.[117] On the other hand, where the only issue was invalidity of the patent in suit on the ground of lack of fair basis, under s.32 of the Patents Act 1949,[118] specific discovery of documents tending to show what the patentees or their advisers thought about the extent of the disclosure in the specification or the width of the claim was not ordered.[119] In principle, and assuming relevance, the issue of the sufficiency of the description of a patent invention may attract disclosure,[120] so may the issue of utility.[121]

5.36 Where patent licences of right or compulsory licences are concerned, if the parties cannot agree on terms then they must be fixed by the Patent Office (or the court).[122] The test for the royalty or other payment is not (as in, e.g. rent review) a hypothetical purchaser in the open market,[123] but a purely objective standard, i.e. "reasonable remuneration having regard to the nature of the invention."[124] This means that all comparable voluntary

[115] *Belegging v Witten* [1979] F.S.R. 59, CA.
[116] *Halcon International Inc. v Shell Transport and Trading Co. Ltd* [1979] R.P.C. 459; *Wellcome Foundation v V.R. Laboratories (Australia) Pty Ltd* [1981] R.P.C. 35, [1982] R.P.C. 343. *SKM S.A. v Wagner Spraytech (U.K.) Ltd* [1982] R.P.C. 497, CA; *Molnlycke A.B. v Proctor & Gamble Ltd (No.3)* [1990] R.P.C. 498 at 502; *cf. Fuji Photo Film Co. Ltd v Carr's Paper Ltd* [1989] R.P.C. 713. See also *Unilever Plc v Chefaro Properties Ltd* [1994] F.S.R. 135, CA; *Glaverbel S.A.'s Patent,* I.P.D 18043; *Cordis Corporation v Pfizer Inc,* I.P.D. 18109; *Hoechst Celanese Corporation v B.P. Chemicals Ltd* [1997] F.S.R. 547; *Norton Healthcare Ltd v Minnesota Mining & Manufacturing Co.* [1999] F.S.R 636; *F. Hoffmann-La Roche A.G. v Chiron Corp.* (2000) 171 A.L.R. 295, Fed. Ct. Aus.; *Gambro Pty Ltd v Fresenius Medical Care Australia Pty Ltd* [2001] F.C.A. 235, Fed. Ct. Aus.
[117] *American Cyanamid Co. v Ethicon Ltd (Discovery and Experiments)* [1978] R.P.C. 667, CA; *John Guest (Southern) Ltd's Patent* [1987] R.P.C. 259; *Molnlycke A.B. v Proctor & Gamble Ltd (No.3)* [1990] R.P.C. 498.
[118] Replaced by s.72 of the Patents Act 1977 (specification does not disclose invention clearly and completely enough for it to be performed by a person skilled in the art).
[119] *Schering Agrochemicals Ltd v ABM Chemicals Ltd* [1987] R.P.C. 185; *cf. Vickers Plc v Horsell Graphic Industries Ltd* [1988] R.P.C. 421; and see also *Wenham Co. Ltd v Champion Gas Lamp Co. Ltd* (1890) 8 R.P.C. 22; *Delta Metal Co. Ltd v Maxim Nordenfeldt Guns and Ammunition Co. Ltd* (1891) 8 R.P.C. 169; *Bibby & Baron Ltd v Duerden* (1910) 27 R.P.C. 283; *Glaverbel S.A. v British Coal Corporation (No.2)* [1993] R.P.C. 90.
[120] *F. Hoffman-La Roche A.G. v Chiron Corp.* (2000) 171 A.L.R. 295, Fed.Ct.Aus.
[121] *Alphapharm Pty Ltd v Merck & Co. Inc* [2006] FCA 1227, Fed.Ct.Aus.
[122] Patents Act 1977, ss.46–54.
[123] See para.5.27, above.
[124] Patents Act 1977, s.59(1)(b).

licence agreements which are available are potentially discoverable, and not merely those known to the market.[125]

Under the CPR, the ordinary rules regarding disclosure apply in patent validity, infringement or non-infringement actions, with two main exceptions.[126] Firstly, three classes of documents are omitted from "standard disclosure": (1) documents relating to infringement where the alleged infringer has already served full particulars of the allegedly infringing product or process; (2) documents relating to the issue of validity which fall outside the period of two years either side of the earliest claimed priority date; (3) documents relating to the issue of commercial success.[127] Secondly, where the issue of commercial success arises in patent validity, infringement or non-infringement actions, the patentee must serve a schedule containing certain sales and financial information relating to commercial success.[128] In view of the commercial sensitivity of information in such actions, the court may in practice order disclosure limited to certain persons or subject to specific restrictions as to use.[129]

5.37

Actions for the recovery of land

There was never a rule that a plaintiff seeking to recover land from a defendant could not obtain discovery from that defendant, whether by reason of the rule that a plaintiff must succeed by virtue of the strength of his own title and not by the weakness of the defendant's, or otherwise.[130] The "matter in question" in such an action was the plaintiff's title to recover the land, and not the land itself. Hence discovery was directed to the former and not to the latter.[131] The CPR make no change to this and disclosure may be ordered in relation to the claimant's title in an appropriate case.

5.38

E. "POSSESSION, CUSTODY OR POWER"/"CONTROL"

The third element of the disclosure of documents is the question of "control" by the party giving disclosure. Until 1964 the rules referred merely to "possession or power", although the old Chancery practice also required discovery (but not inspection) to be given of relevant documents in

5.39

---

[125] *Smith Kline & French Laboratories Ltd (Cimetidine) Patents* [1990] R.P.C. 203, CA; *Merrell Dow Pharmaceuticals Inc.'s (Terfenadine) Patent* [1991] R.P.C. 221.

[126] CPR, r.63.8; CPR, Pt 63, Practice Direction—Patents Etc., para.5.1.

[127] *ibid.*, para.5.1; *Nokia Corp. v Interdigital Technology Corp.* [2004] EWHC 2920 (Pat).

[128] *ibid.*, para.5.2.

[129] *Warner-Lambert & Co. v Glaxo Laboratories* [1975] R.P.C. 354, CA; *Roussel Uclaf v ICI (No.2)* [1990] R.P.C. 45; *Helitune Ltd v Stewart Hughes Ltd* [1994] F.S.R. 422; *cf. Dyson Ltd v Hoover Ltd (No.3)* [2002] R.P.C. 42.

[130] *Lyell v Kennedy* (1883) 8 App.Cas. 217, HL.

[131] *Phillips v Phillips* (1879) 40 L.T. 815 at 821.

a person's custody as well.[132] After 1964 the revised RSC, Ord.24, rr.1(1), 2(1) 3(1) and 7(1)[133] referred to "possession, custody, or power". The old distinction persists in the Australian Capital Territory, where the rules refer only to possession or power,[134] and in Queensland, where the rules refer to possession or control.[135] In the other Australian States,[136] and in the Federal Courts,[137] the formulation is as in the revised RSC[138] This compares with the United States Federal Rules of Civil Procedure, r.34(a), which refers to "possession, custody, or control".[139] Note that the requirements of the rules were "disjunctive in their operation so far as possession, custody and power are concerned",[140] i.e. only one limb needed to be satisfied for the obligation to attach.

5.40   The CPR make fresh provision, requiring disclosure of documents which are or have been in a party's "control".[141] But "control" is defined to cover physical possession, the right to possession, and the right to inspect or take copies.[142] Each of these will be considered in more detail later. The definition does not state that "control" *includes* these cases, but instead says that these *are* the cases of "control". It therefore appears that the definition is exclusive, and there can be no other cases of control than those set out. The test is not one of ownership. Thus whilst usually the right to possession and the right to inspect follow ownership, this may not always be the case.[143]

5.41   It must be borne in mind that the requirements of the CPR, like those of the RSC and the C.C.R. before them, are not limited back in time: disclosure documents are those "which are *or have been*" in the party's control. Moreover, the only forward cut-off point is the conclusion of proceedings, and therefore documents coming into a party's control at any stage after proceedings commenced, even during trial, are potentially disclosable. This was finally established by case law under the old rules[144] and is now made

---

[132] Bray, pp.224–225; Digest 7, 49; *B. v B.* [1978] Fam. 181 at 186–187; *Alfred Crompton Amusement Machines Ltd v Commissioners of Customs & Excise (No.2)* [1974] A.C. 405 at 429.

[133] C.C.R., Ord.14, rr.1(1), 2(1), (3).

[134] Supreme Court Rules 1933 (ACT), Ord.34, r.13.

[135] Uniform Civil Procedure Rules 1999 (Q.L.D.), r.211(1)(a).

[136] Supreme Court Rules 1970 (N.S.W.), Pt 23, r.6(2); Supreme Court Rules 1970 (S.A.), r.58(1); Rules of the Supreme Court 1965 (T.A.S.), Ord.33, r.12(1); Rules of the Supreme Court 1996 (V.I.C.), Ord.29, rr.1(2), 2(1); Rules of the Supreme Court 1971 (W.A.), Ord.26, r.1(1).

[137] Federal Court Rules 1979, Ord.15, r.6(2).

[138] See, e.g. *Turner v Davies* [1981] 2 N.S.W.L.R. 324 at 325.

[139] See also Ch.1, para.1.21, above.

[140] *B. v B.* [1978] Fam. 181 at 186.

[141] CPR, r.31.8(1).

[142] CPR, r.31.8(2).

[143] *Three Rivers DC v Bank of England* [2002] EWHC 1118 (Comm.) at [54]; *Three Rivers DC v Bank of England (No.4)* [2002] EWCA Civ 1182, [2003] 1 W.L.R. 210 at [49–51].

[144] *Vernon v Bosley (No.2)* [1999] Q.B. 18, CA; *Scott v Commissioners of Inland Revenue* [2004] EWCA Civ 400, at [11–22]; *cf. Bula Ltd v Tara Mines (No.5)* [1994] 1 I.R. 487 (Eire); *T.N.T. Management Pty. Ltd v Trade Practice Commission* (1983) 47 A.L.R. 693

express by the CPR.[145] Indeed, once a party has notice that disclosable documents have come into his control, he is bound immediately to notify every other party.[146] The Admiralty and Commercial Courts Guide specifically provides that if, after a list of documents has been prepared and served, the existence (present or past) of further documents to which the order applies comes to the attention of the disclosing party, that party must prepare and serve a supplemental list.[147] However, documents are not disclosable until they do come into a party's control, even though they may or will do so in future.[148] Under the old rules it was clear that the courts had no power to require a party to create particular documents for the purposes of the proceedings, where those documents did not already exist.[149] Nor did they have the power to require a party to do all that can reasonably be done to obtain material from third parties.[150]

The CPR have made inroads on those principles. Under CPR, Pt 18, **5.42** which (broadly speaking) covers both further and better particulars of pleadings and interrogatories under the old system, the court has power to order a party to "give additional information in relation to" any matter in dispute in the proceedings.[151] Moreover, there is a rule in Pt 35 (otherwise dealing with experts and assessors) which empowers the court to direct a party having access to information not reasonably available to the other party to "prepare and file a document recording the information" and to "serve a copy of that document on the other party".[152] Nothing in the rule itself limits its application to information needed for instructing an expert, although given its place in Pt 35 it is possible that the court may so confine it. Subject to that point, these two rules confer wide power on the court to require a party to *create* a document, which must then be disclosed. However, it seems that the information contained in the document must either already be in the party's possession, or at least be available to him. The rule in Pt 35 could not be used to require a party to go out and search for information, record it, and then disclose it. As for Pt 18, it may be that, by analogy with the old case law on interrogatories, a party can in effect be

---

(South Australia); *Lanzon v State Transport Authority* (1985) 38 S.A.S.R. 321 (South Australia); *Cooke v Australia National Railways Commission* [1985] 39 S.A.S.R. 146 (South Australia).

[145] CPR, r.31.11(1). In the Federal Court of Australia, Queensland, South Australia and Western Australia, the rules likewise impose a continuing obligation.

[146] CPR, r.31.11(2).

[147] (7th edn, 2006), para.E2.2.

[148] *Lonrho Ltd v Shell Petroleum Co Ltd* [1980] 1 W.L.R. 627 at 635 (position under RSC).

[149] See, e.g. *Carrington v Helix Lighting Ltd* [1990] I.C.R. 125, E.A.T. (schedule of ethnic origins or workers); *Derby & Co. Ltd v Weldon*, *The Times*, November 9, 1990, CA (expert's report); cf. *Ash v Buxted Poultry Ltd*, *The Times*, May 17, 1990 (one party ordered to permit other party to enter his premises and make video film of industrial purposes); *Twentieth Century Film Corp. v Tryare Ltd* [1991] F.S.R. 58 (defendant ordered to allow plaintiff to enter premises and make list of articles found there).

[150] *Dubai Bank Ltd v Galadari (No.6)*, *The Times*, October 14, 1992, CA.

[151] CPR, r.18.1(1)(b).

[152] CPR, r.35.9.

obliged to make *reasonable* inquiries, e.g. of servants or agents, or former servants or agents.[153]

Possession

5.43   In *B. v B.*[154] Dunn J. said:

> "Before 1964 the word 'possession' was held to mean 'corporeal possession pursuant to legal possession,' but 'corporeal possession' is now embraced by the word 'custody'."

Thus, under the revised RSC "'possession' mean[t] 'the right to the possession of a document'."[155] It did not require actual physical possession. The CPR distinguish between "physical possession"[156] (equivalent to the former "custody") and the "right to possession"[157] (equivalent to the former "possession"). So it appears that the old law on possession continues to apply, albeit under a new name. If A's own documents are in the hands of his agent or servant B, A has "the right to possession" within the Rules, just as A had "possession" under the pre-1996 Rules.[158] Of course, where the agent B holds the documents concerned for a different principal, or for himself in his own right, A had no right to possession.[159] If B is a professional man and A his client, then a distinction may be drawn between B's own working papers, which belong to him and documents (e.g. correspondence with third parties) in B's hands, which belong to A.[160] It appears that, in appropriate circumstances, documents in the possession of any government department can be regarded as in the possession of the Crown as an indivisible entity.[161]

5.44   A question arises where a party has a right to possession of documents jointly with another or others. Under the RSC it was settled that he had to

---

[153] See Ch.16 below, paras 16.95–16.104.

[154] [1978] Fam. 181 at 186.

[155] *B. v B.* [1978] Fam. 181 at 186.

[156] CPR, r.31.8(2)(a).

[157] CPR, r.31.8(2)(b).

[158] *Murray v Walter* (1839) Cr. & Ph. 114 at 125; Ross, p.195; Bray. p.225.

[159] *Swanston v Lishman* (1881) 45 L.T. 360, CA; *Grupo Torras S.A. v Al-Sabah*, unreported, June 5, 1997, Mance J. (solicitor acting for two clients: one had no right in relation to the documents of the other).

[160] *Chantrey Martin v Martin* [1953] 2 Q.B. 286, CA; *Gomba Holdings UK Ltd v Minories Finance Ltd* [1989] B.C.L.C. 115, CA; *Bula Ltd v Tara Mines Ltd* [1994] I.L.R.M. 111, Irish Sup. Ct.; *Equiticorp Industries Group Ltd v Hawkins* [1994] 2 N.Z.L.R. 738, H. Ct. N.Z.; *R. v Mid-Glamorgan Family Health Services, ex p. Martin* [1995] 1 W.L.R. 110, CA; *Formica Ltd v Export Credit Guarantees Department* [1995] 1 Lloyds Rep. 692; *Johnson v Church of Scientology* [2004] 2 I.L.R.M. 110, Irish Sup. Ct.

[161] *R. v Blackledge* [1996] 1 Cr.App.R. 326 at 337, CA.

give discovery,[162] although before 1964 he could not be compelled to produce the documents,[163] and under the revised RSC production was a matter of discretion in the court.[164] Moreover, the fact that a person in possession of documents might be obliged to return them, as a matter of property law, to their true owner, did not prevent their being in the meantime in that person's possession or custody, and hence discoverable by him. The CPR do not make clear what is to happen in cases of joint rights to possession.[165] It seems unlikely that it was intended to remove disclosability altogether in such a case, and hence the better view is that a party with a right of possession held jointly with others must still disclose the document's existence, with the question of inspection being considered separately.[166]

"Custody" and "physical possession"

In *B. v B.*,[167] Dunn J. said: 5.45

> "'custody' means 'the actual physical or corporeal holding of a document regardless of the right to possession, for example a holding of a document by a party as servant or agent of the true owner'."

Thus a company director who had the company's documents in his physical custody was obliged to give discovery of them if relevant, although such custody was only in his capacity as an officer of the company.[168] The CPR now refer to "physical possession", which appears to be the same concept. However, there is nothing in the Rules to limit disclosure to cases where the physical possession is lawful. Accordingly, it is submitted that even a thief would have to give disclosure of stolen documents if appropriate to litigation to which he was a party.[169]

By analogy with the cases on joint possession (most of which were decided on the old wider meaning of possession anyway), a party must give disclosure of documents even if he only has a physical possession of them jointly with another person.[170]

---

[162] *Alfred Crompton Amusement Machines Ltd v Commissioners of Customs & Excise (No.2)* [1974] A.C. 405 at 429.
[163] *Kearsley v Phillips* (1882) 10 Q.B.D. 36.
[164] See Ch.11, para.11.144, below.
[165] See, e.g. *Arab Monetary Fund v Hashim (No.5)* [1992] 2 All E.R. 911 at 917.
[166] See para.5.45, below.
[167] [1978] Fam. 181 at 186 referring to Halsbury's *Laws of England*, 4th edn, Vol.13, para.39.
[168] *ibid.*; *Roux v Australian Broadcasting Commission* [1992] 2 V.R. 577.
[169] A question of the privilege against self-incrimination (Ch.11, paras 11.104–11.120, below) may arise in relation to the *production* of such documents, but not in relation to their *disclosure*: see Ch.8, para.8.12, below.
[170] *cf. B. v B.* [1978] Fam. 181 at 187.

"Power" and "right to inspect/take copies"

5.46   In *B. v B.*,[171] Dunn J. said:

> "'power' means 'an enforceable right to inspect the document or to
> obtain possession or control of the document from the person who
> ordinarily has it in fact'."

This view was adopted from *Halsbury's Laws of England*,[172] itself based
on nineteenth century case law.

In *Lonrho Ltd v Shell Petroleum Ltd*, Lord Diplock put it this way:

> " . . . the expression 'power' must, in my view, mean a presently
> enforceable legal right to obtain from whoever actually holds the
> document inspection of it without the need to obtain the consent of
> anyone else. Provided that the right is presently enforceable, the fact
> that for physical reasons it may not be possible for the person entitled
> to it to obtain immediate inspection would not prevent the document
> from being within his power. . . . ".[173]

It would appear, however, that the "power" concerned had to be one
vested in the person concerned in his personal capacity, and not for example
as a company director or other fiduciary.[174] On the other hand, mere
physical ability to inspect documents, but involving a breach of confidence
or other private law right, was held not to amount to "power" under the
RSC[175] Liens on documents are dealt with later.[176]

5.47   The CPR do not refer to "power", but to having "a right to inspect or take
copies".[177] To judge from Lord Diplock's statement above, this covers the
cases which would have amounted to "power" under the old rules. So
examples of situations where "power" was held to exist will still be useful.
But the question is whether the CPR go further, and require disclosure of

---

[171] [1978] Fam. 181 at 186.

[172] 4th edn, Vol.13, para.39.

[173] [1980] 1 W.L.R. 627 at 635; see also *Turner v Davies* [1981] 2 N.S.W.L.R. 324; *Douglas-Hill v Parke-Davis Pty. Ltd* (1990) 54 S.A.S.R. 346; *Roux v Australian Broadcasting Commission* [1992] 2 V.R. 577, at 589–591. In Ireland there are a series of decisions on the meaning of "power", which requires an enforceable legal right to obtain documents from whoever actually holds the documents: *Bula Ltd v Tara Mines Ltd* [1994] 1 I.L.R.M. 111; *Quinlivan v Conroy* [1999] 1 I.R. 271; *Johnson v Church of Scientology* [2001] 1 I.L.R.M. 110, Irish Sup. Ct.

[174] See also *Macmillan Inv. v Bishopsgate Investment Trust Plc* [1993] I.C.R.385; *Bula Ltd v Tara Mines Ltd* [1994] I.L.R.M. 111, Irish Sup. Ct.; *Equiticorp Industries Group Ltd v Hawkins* [1994] 2 N.Z.L.R. 738; *cf. Henly Cosmosair* [1995] C.L.Y. 449; *Horgan v Murray* [1999] 1 I.R.L.M. 257, Irish High Ct.

[175] *Grupo Torras S.A. v Al-Sabah*, unreported, June 5, 1997, Mance J.

[176] See Ch.11, paras 11.148–11.149.

[177] CPR, r.31.8(2)(c).

documents which would not have been discoverable. This is considered later.[178]

In the *Lonrho* case, the House of Lords held that documents in the possession of subsidiary companies were not in the "power" of their parent companies for the purposes of the RSC, since the parents had no presently enforceable legal right (failing alteration of the subsidiaries' Articles of Association) to obtain the subsidiaries' documents without their consent.[179] The opposite conclusion was reached in an Australian case where parent and subsidiaries were staffed by the same people, and the subsidiaries were operating on behalf of the parent.[180] In *Lonrho*, the House of Lords specifically declined, however, to deal with "one man companies in which a natural person and/or his nominees are the sole shareholders and directors."[181]

5.48

The situation of the "one man company" arose in the Canadian case of *Dallas v Dallas*,[182] where the court held on the facts of that case that the company was the alter ego of the controlling director and shareholder, and therefore the companies' documents were within his power. On the other hand, there are cases where the company has been held, on the facts of the case, *not* to be the alter ego of the controlling director and shareholder.[183]

5.49

The converse situation, where it is sought to make the subsidiary company give discovery of the *parent's* documents, arose in *Procter & Gamble Ltd v Peaudouce (UK) Ltd*.[184] Evidence was given that the subsidiary company had no right, legal or moral (the parent was a French company, and it was therefore a question partly of French law) to call for documents or information from the parent company. The applicants argued that the degree of involvement of the parent in the action on behalf of the subsidiary, including the fact that the parent exercised effective control over the litigation on behalf of the subsidiary, resulted in an obligation to disclose relevant documents to the subsidiary. Falconer J. held that that was not so, and that the parent's documents were not in the subsidiary's "power".[185]

5.50

Plainly, a right of inspection of documents, pursuant to a contract, satisfies the test in the CPR. But a "right" which is in fact discretionary and

5.51

---

[178] See para.5.53.
[179] See also *Taylor v Santos Ltd* (1998) 71 S.A.S.R. 434, South Australia Sup.Ct. (Full Ct.).
[180] *Linfa Pty. Ltd v Citibank Ltd* [1995] 1 V.R. 643.
[181] See also Shaw L.J. in the Court of Appeal: [1980] Q.B. 358 at 376.
[182] (1960) 24 D.L.R. 2d. 746
[183] *B. v B.* [1978] Fam.181; *Re Technican Investments Ltd* [1985] B.C.L.C. 434, CA; *Innovisions Ltd v Chan Sing-Chuck* [1992] 2 H.K.L.R. 306, H.Ct. of H.K.
[184] November 23, 1984, unreported, Falconer J. (disapproved on another point in *Visx Ltd v Nidex Co.* [1999] F.S.R. 91, CA).
[185] See also *Unilever Plc v Chefaro Proprietaries Ltd* [1994] F.S.R. 135, CA (two companies in same group); *Catt v Church of Scientology Religious Education College Inc.* (2001) 5 C.L.17 (documents held by Mother Church a separate legal entity, not in control of UK entities who had no right to possession or inspection).

not absolute, probably does not.[186] Moreover, under the old rules, it was held that such a right would not make such documents within the "power" of a party for discovery purposes if the contract expressly or impliedly required the documents or their contents to be kept confidential.[187] It is submitted that the same is true under the CPR.

5.52   Other rights to obtain such inspection or production may flow, not from contract, but from status such as the right of a beneficiary to see documents relating to a deceased estate[188] or trust documents,[189] the right of a principal to see his agent's records,[190] and the right of a company director to inspect the company's books.[191] Or they may be based on statute, such as the right of a partner to inspect partnership books,[192] the right of patients to see medical records and reports,[193] the right of subjects of computer or other files to see those files,[194] the right of a local government elector to inspect minutes of proceedings, orders for the payment of money and accounts for local authority,[195] and the right of a union member to inspect the union's accounting records.[196] Another example is the right of a party to litigation to be supplied with copies of court documents relating to the proceedings.[197] Non-parties (i.e. the general public) may inspect claim forms which have been served, and judgments and orders made in public, but require the permission of the court to inspect any other documents on the court file.[198] There are also rights to inspect the register of insolvency proceedings.[199]

5.53   In some cases, however, the terms or circumstances under which such rights arise may impose a duty of confidentiality upon the information thus acquired and this may prevent the rights satisfying the test in the CPR[200]

---

[186] cf. Re Lombard Shipping and Forwarding Ltd [1993] B.C.L.C. 238.

[187] Unilever Plc v Gillette (UK) Ltd [1988] R.P.C. 416.

[188] C.I. v N.S. [2004] EWHC 659 (Fam).

[189] Re Londonderry Settlement [1965] Ch. 918, CA; O'Rouke v Darbishire [1920] A.C. 581, HL; Schmidt v Rosewood Trust Ltd [2003] U.K.P.C. 26, [2003] 2 A.C. 709, PC; see Ch.4, para.4.22.

[190] Yasuda Fire & Marine Insurance v Orion Marine Insurance [1995] Q.B.174. However the mere fact that a person is an agent is not determinative of whether his documents are in the control of his principal: Nova Scotia v Royal & Sun Alliance (2005) 251 D.L.R. (4th) 483, Nova Scotia CA.

[191] Conway v Petronius Clothing Co. [1978] 1 W.L.R. 72 at 89; State of South Australia v Barrett (1995) 64 S.A.S.R. 73 (right persists only whilst director holds office); Berlei Hestia (N.Z.) Ltd v Fernyhough [1980] 2 N.Z.L.R. 150 (same point).

[192] Partnership Act 1890, s.24(9), though this might also be contractual.

[193] Access to Medical Reports Act 1988; Access to Health Records Act 1990; Cowley, Access to Medical Records and Reports, 1994; cf. R. v Mid-Glamorgan Family Health Services, ex p. Martin [1995] 1 W.L.R. 110, CA; Breen v Williams (1996) 70 A.L.J.R. 772, H. Ct. Aus. (no right at common law).

[194] Data Protection Act 1984, Access to Personal Files Act 1987, Data Protection Act 1998.

[195] Local Government Act 1982, s.6; see also Birmingham City Council v O [1983] 1 A.C. 578 (councillor's right to see council documents).

[196] Trade Union and Labour Relations (Consolidation) Act 1992, s.30.

[197] See CPR, r.5.4(1).

[198] CPR, r.5.4(2). See Ch.3, para.3.45, above.

[199] See Ch.3, paras 3.46−3.47, above.

[200] See, e.g. Bevan v Webb [1901] 2 Ch. 59 at 81.

This would be so, for example, in relation to documents disclosed in other proceedings and therefore subject to the restriction on collateral use (formerly implied undertaking of confidentiality).[201] Of course, if the party is supplied with *copies*, they will belong to him,[202] and will be in his physical possession. They will therefore be disclosable on that basis, though still covered by the implied restriction on collateral use (or undertaking). This raises a number of difficulties which are discussed elsewhere.[203] Or the "right" concerned may be subject to the discretion of the possessor of the document concerned to refuse inspection. So where documents of an insolvent company are in the physical possession of an administrative receiver, they are subject to a right which is not an "indefeasible right" of the Secretary of State to inspect. Hence they were held not to be within the latter's "power" for discovery purposes.[204] Similarly documents from the Bingham Inquiry (B.C.C.I.) have been held not to have been disclosable by the Bank of England as it had no right to inspect and take copies, such documents being held in the Public Record Office.[205]

The problem with basing disclosure on a right to inspect is that this may   **5.54**
go too far. Just because anyone could make a search of documents filed at Companies House or the Land Registry does not mean that all such documents are potentially disclosable by every litigant. Perhaps a distinction is to be drawn between cases where a party is the only person, or one of a restricted class of persons, having the right to inspect documents in the possession of a third party and cases where anyone, or almost anyone, may do so. However, in an Australian case,[206] the court held that, whilst the plaintiff was obliged to give discovery of documents sent by him to a third party (a public official), the plaintiff did not have to give discovery of documents held on the same file by that public official coming from other sources, even though the plaintiff had the right to inspect and take copies of such documents. A *fortiori*, such documents were not within the plaintiff's power by virtue of the possible access given to them conferred by the (Australian) Freedom of Information Act 1982.[207]

---

[201] See Ch.15.
[202] *Brue Ltd v Solly, The Times*, February 9, 1988.
[203] See Ch.8, para.8.16, and Ch.11, para.11.147, below.
[204] *Re Lombard Shipping and Forwarding Ltd* [1993] B.C.L.C. 238.
[205] *Three Rivers DC v Bank of England (No.4)* [2002] EWCA Civ 1182, [2003] 1 W.L.R. 210, CA.
[206] *Theodore v Australian Postal Commission* [1988] V.R. 272.
[207] See also *Rogers v Hougland* (1991) Tas. R. 372.

CHAPTER 6

Means of disclosure

CHAPTER 6

Means of disclosure

A. LISTS OF DOCUMENTS

Form and contents of list

CPR, r.31.10 provides that a party giving standard disclosure must make **6.01** and serve on every other party, a list of documents in the relevant practice form, N265.[1] In practice, although the List need not precisely follow the wording in N265, the form must be substantively followed.[2] The List must also include a disclosure statement.[3] The parties may agree to a less formal mode of disclosure in appropriate cases, such as where there are only a few documents to be disclosed. Thus, the parties may agree in writing to disclose documents without making a list or without the disclosing party making a disclosure statement.[4] The court itself may order that no list is to be served, but that disclosure be by way of supplying copy documents.[5] Where there are a very large number of documents to be disclosed, the parties may agree or the court may order disclosure in a form which does not involve the individual listing of each document or class of document. Thus it may be directed that a party can list by file or box. This can lead to practical difficulties: it may lead to a vast amount of irrelevant material being disclosed; privileged documents may be disclosed by mistake; key documents may be hidden away in a disclosed box or file; it may impose a burden on

---

[1] Appendix 3, para.B03]; see formerly RSC, Ord.24, r.5 (1) and Form 26 in RSC, Appendix 1; Court Form N265, Appendix 3, para.C.04, below. There is an adopted form for use in the Commercial Court, Form N265 (CC): *Admiralty and Commercial Courts Guide* (7th edn, 2006) para.E3.9.

[2] CPR, Pt 4, Practice Direction, para.1.2.

[3] CPR, r.31.10(5) and (6).

[4] CPR, r.31.10(8); *Admiralty and Commercial Courts Guide* (7th edn, 2006), para.E2.1(v); *Technology and Construction Court Guide* (2nd edn, 2005), para.11.2.2. Such written agreement must be lodged with the court; CPR, Pt 31, Practice Direction, Disclosure and Inspection, para.1.4.

[5] CPR, Pt 28, Practice Direction, The Multi-Track, para.4.7(3)(b).

the opposing party to sift through material which ordinarily ought to be done by the disclosing party; there may be an inadequate audit trail of what has in fact been disclosed. In one case where disclosure was by file and box, the opposing party found that one box only contained a broken chair leg.[6] However, subject to such agreement or order permitting a less formal mode of disclosure, the obligation to give disclosure must be discharged properly. In one case under the old rules where there were up to a million documents to be sorted out, the judge said:

> "It does not seem to me to a proper solution simply to give the [inspecting party] the task of rummaging through the documents and giving them the key of the warehouse in order to do so. The onus to make discovery is on the party whose documents they are."[7]

6.02 Standard disclosure requires a party to disclose only—

(a) the documents on which he relies;
(b) the documents which—

  (i) adversely affect his own case;
  (ii) adversely affect another party's case; or
  (iii) support another party's case; and

(c) the documents which he is required to disclose by a relevant practice direction.[8]

6.03 When giving standard disclosure, a party is required to make a reasonable search for documents falling within CPR, r.31.6(b) or (c). The factors relevant in deciding the reasonableness of a search include the following—

(a) the number of documents involved;
(b) the nature and complexity of the proceedings;
(c) the ease and expense of retrieval of any particular document; and
(d) the significance of any document which is likely to be located during the search.

Where a party has not searched for a category or class of document on the grounds that to do so would be unreasonable, he must state this in his disclosure statement and identify the category or class of document.[9]

---

[6] *Three Rivers DC v Bank of England* [2006] EWHC 816 (Comm.), at [133].
[7] *Minories Finance Ltd v Arthur Young*, March 31, 1988, unreported, *per* Henry J.; see also *Sveriges Angrartygs Assurans Forening v The 1976 Eagle Insurance Co. SA*, March 28, 1990, unreported, *per* Hobhouse J.
[8] CPR, r.31.6; see Ch.5, paras 5.8–5.18, above.
[9] CPR, r.31.7; CPR, Pt 31, Practice Direction, Disclosure and Inspection, para.2.

Using the prescribed form the party providing disclosure is required to **6.04** state the following in the List of Documents:

(a) what documents falling within standard disclosure are now in his control;

(b) what documents falling within standard disclosure are now in his control, he objects to produce, stating his grounds of objection;

(c) what documents falling within standard disclosure were once in his control, but are no longer, stating when they were last in his control and where they are now.

Disclosure statement

The list must also include a disclosure statement by the party disclosing **6.05** the documents[10]:

(a) setting out the extent of the search that has been made to locate the documents which he is required to disclose. In particular the practice form provides that he must state that he has carried out a reasonable and proportionate search for such documents and draw attention to any particular limitations on the extent of the search which were adopted for proportionality reasons, giving the reasons why the limitations were adopted;

(b) certifying that he understands the duty of disclosure and that he must inform the Court and the other parties immediately if any further document required to be disclosed by CPR, r.31.6 comes into his control at any time before the conclusion of the case;

(c) certifying that to the best of his knowledge he has carried out that duty;

(d) certifying that the list is a complete list of all documents which are or have been in his control and which he is obliged to disclose;

(e) asserting any right to or duty to withhold production of a document or part of a document and stating the grounds on which he claims that right or duty;

(f) dealing specifically with electronic documents.[11]

Where the party making the disclosure statement is a company, firm, **6.06** association or other organisation, the statement must also —

---

[10] CPR, rr.31.10(5), (6), and 31.7(3); Form N265, Appendix 3, para.C.04, below; CPR, Pt 31, Practice Direction, Disclosure and Inspection, para.4 and Annex A. In the Commercial Court the disclosure statement must comply with CPR, rr.31.7(3) and 31.10(6), and also (a) identify any respects in which the search has been limited; (b) set out in detail the facts considered in arriving at the decision that it was reasonable to limit the search in those respects; and (c) specify by whom the search has been conducted: *Admiralty and Commercial Courts Guide* (7th edn, 2006), paras E3.6–9.

[11] See Ch.7, para.7.14, below.

(a) identify the person making the statement; and

(b) explain why he is considered an appropriate person to make the statement.[12]

The disclosure statement may be made by a person who is not a party where this is permitted by a relevant practice direction.[13] The legal representative of the disclosing party must endeavour to ensure that the person making the disclosure statement understands the duty of disclosure under CPR, Pt 31.[14] The court may direct that a disclosure statement be verified by affidavit.[15] An insurer or the Motor Insurers' Bureau having a financial interest in proceedings brought by or against a party may sign a disclosure statement on behalf of that other party.[16] The Admiralty and Commercial Courts Guide expands on the question of who may give the disclosure statement[17]:

(a) The court will normally regard as an appropriate person any person who is in a position responsibly and authoritatively to search for the documents required to be disclosed by that party and to make statements contained in the disclosure statement concerning the documents which must be disclosed by that party.

(b) A legal representative may in certain circumstances be an appropriate person.[18]

(c) An explanation why the person is considered an appropriate person must still be given in the disclosure statement.

(d) The court may of its own initiative or on application require that a disclosure statement also be signed by another appropriate person.

In one case it has been held that a disclosure statement by one shareholder on behalf of himself and other defendants failed to comply with CPR, r.31.10. The purpose of the rule is to bring home to each party his responsibility for giving disclosure. It is not a mere technicality and except to the extent permitted by the rules, it requires the party himself to make the disclosure statement.[19]

---

[12] CPR, r.31.10(7); CPR, Pt 31, Practice Direction, Disclosure and Inspection, para.4.3; *Carlco Ltd v Chief Constable of Dyfed-Powys Police* [2002] EWCA Civ 1754, CA.

[13] CPR, r.31.10(9).

[14] CPR, Pt 31, Practice Direction, Disclosure and Inspection, para.4.4; see also Ch.14 for solicitors' duties.

[15] *Admiralty and Commercial Courts Guide* (7th edn, 2006), para.E3.9.

[16] CPR, Pt 31, Practice Direction, Disclosure and Inspection para.4.7.

[17] Para.E3.10.

[18] In practice it is not uncommon for a corporate party's solicitor or in house legal officer to sign the disclosure statement.

[19] *Arrow Trading v Edwardian Group Ltd* [2004] EWHC 1319 (Ch) at [45]; *cf. Rio Tinto Ltd v Commissioner of Taxation* [2005] F.C.A. 1335, Fed. Ct. of Aus. (disclosure statement by company secretary of parent company in a composite list for a number of group companies).

Failure to follow practice form

Where the practice form as to List has not been followed, the court may **6.07** make an order requiring the party to comply with his obligations properly, or for specific disclosure,[20] including an order that the party in default do produce a further or amended List in correct form.[21] Under the old rules, the omission of the words "and never has had" from an affidavit of documents was held in itself to be a sufficient reason for ordering a further and better affidavit.[22]

List

Form N265 requires that the documents being disclosed must be put into **6.08** a list, divided into three parts. The first part lists documents that the party has in his control, in respect of which no objection to inspection is raised. The second part lists documents that the party has in his control, but to which objection is made to inspection. It must include a statement of the objections.[23] The third part lists documents which the party has had, but has not now, in his control. In this case, the party must state when the documents were last in his control and what has happened to them.[24] Form N265 additionally requires the party to state where they now are.[25] The court can require specific itemisation of documents no longer in a party's control.[26]

Under the RSC a copy of a discoverable document (whether carbon, **6.09** photocopy or otherwise) was as much discoverable as the original, and accordingly, had to be listed.[27] This was regarded as unnecessary by those formulating the CPR and hence it is now provided that a party need not disclose more than one copy of a document. However a copy of a document that contains a modification, obliteration or other marking or feature:

(a) on which a party intends to rely; or

(b) which adversely affects his own case or another party's case or supports another party's case;

should be treated as a separate document.[28]

---

[20] CPR, r.31.12; see para.6.37, below; *Anon* [1876] W.N. 39, Lindley J.
[21] *Arrow Trading v Edwardian Group Ltd* [2004] EHWC 1319 (Ch.), where a new list and disclosure statement was ordered.
[22] *Wagstaffe v Anderson, Moss & Michell* (1878) 39 L.T. 322; see also *Gardner v Irwin* (1878) 4 Ex. D. 49 at 53, CA and *Ledwidge v Mayne* (1878) I.R. 11 Eq. 463.
[23] CPR, r.31.10 (4)(a).
[24] CPR, r.31.10 (4)(b)(ii).
[25] See also *Buchanan-Michaelson v Rubenstein* [1965] Ch. 258; [1965] 1 W.L.R. 390, CA.
[26] *Punjab National Bank v Jain* [2004] EWCA Civ 589, CA.
[27] *Dubai Bank Ltd v Galadari (No.7)* [1992] 1 W.L.R. 106; *cf. Ventouris v Mountain* [1991] 3 All E.R. 472, CA, where the point was assumed.
[28] CPR, r.31.9; see Ch.5, para.5.04.

6.10   The list must identify the documents in a convenient order and manner and as concisely as possible.[29] Each individual document should be listed, save in the case of categories of documents and bundles[30] in which case each category or bundle should be described sufficiently to enable it to be identified. Where a party's disclosure includes a large number of documents all falling within a particular category (e.g. invoices or bank statements) consideration should be given to listing such documents in bundles rather than individually. To list large numbers of documents individually where bundles would have been appropriate may be regarded as wasteful from a costs perspective and may lead to a prolix and oppressively long list.[31]

Enumeration and description

6.11   The principal reasons for the provisions as to enumeration and description are fourfold. First, it is intended to ensure that all disclosure has been given. Secondly, it enables the opposite party to identify the documents of which disclosure is being made and to request particular documents to be produced for inspection or for copying.[32] Thirdly, it will enable the court, if necessary, to make an effective order for the production of particular documents.[33] Fourthly, it enables the provisions contained in CPR, r.32.19[34] (deemed admissions of authenticity of documents disclosed under CPR, Pt 31) to operate effectively.[35] It is not the purpose of the provisions that a party is required to give such a detailed description of the documents so as to enable the opposing party to ascertain the content of the documents from the description provided.[36]

6.12   Accordingly, a List of Documents in respect of individual documents should normally:

   (a) list the documents in date order, numbering them consecutively;
   (b) provide a concise description of each document (e.g. letter from A to B); and
   (c) state the date borne by each document, or to be attributed to it.[37]

---

[29] CPR, r.31.10(3); CPR, Pt 31, Practice Direction, Disclosure and Inspection, para.3.2 (formerly RSC, Ord.24, r.5(1)).

[30] As to what constitutes a bundle, see para.6.13, below.

[31] *Hill v Hart-Davis* (1884) 26 Ch.D. 470, CA.

[32] *Cooke v Smith* [1891] 1 Ch. 509 at 522; *Guinness Peat Properties Ltd v Fitzroy Robinson Partnership* [1987] 1 W.L.R. 1027 at 1039.

[33] *Taylor v Batten* (1878) 4 Q.B.D. 85; *Mayor and Corporation of Bristol v Cox* (1884) 26 Ch.D. 678; *Budden v Wilkinson* [1893] 2 Q.B. 431.

[34] Formerly RSC, Ord.27, r.4; C.C.R.—no equivalent.

[35] *Sveriges Angrartygs Assurans Forening v The 1976 Eagle Insurance Co. SA*, March 28, 1990, unreported, *per* Hobhouse J.

[36] See para.6.15, below.

[37] CPR, r.31.10(3); CPR, Pt 31, Practice Direction, Disclosure and Inspection, para.3.2; *Admiralty and Commercial Courts Guide* (7th edn, 2006), para.E3.4.

However, in some cases the original order of documents may be of importance at trial, such as whether a particular document was in a file at a particular time. In insurance cases it may be important to have the underwriting file intact. In such cases, it may be appropriate to keep the file in the original order. Alternatively, the solicitor when he receives the file from the client should copy the file in the original order, before taking any documents out or re-ordering it for disclosure purposes.[38]

Bundles

In so far as the List refers to bundles, the List should accord with the following:

6.13

(a) the bundles must be of documents of the same nature (e.g. invoices);

(b) the documents within each bundle must be numbered and the total number stated in the List;

(c) the nature of the documents within each bundle must be stated (e.g. invoices from A to B in respect of goods supplied); and

(d) the date or date range of the documents within each bundle must be stated.[39]

Thus, in one case[40] decided under the former rules, the inclusion in a List of Documents of five items, each described as a file having a certain number of pages, being a copy of a broker's file concerning a single transaction, but containing documents of very different kinds, was held not to comply with the rules. The judge held that the disclosing party was attempting to transfer part of its responsibilities under the rules to the other party, which (except by agreement) it might not do. He also held that:

" . . . the citation of 19th century cases decided under different circumstances . . . and under different Rules of Court is not a correct

---

[38] As suggested in *Admiralty and Commercial Courts Guide* (7th edn, 2006), para.E3.5.

[39] CPR, Pt 31, Practice Direction, Disclosure and Inspection, para.3.2. *Taylor v Batten* (1878) 4 Q.B.D. 85; *Mayor and Corporation of Bristol v Cox* (1884) 26 Ch.D. 678; *Morris v Edwards* (1890) 15 App.Cas. 309; *Cooke v Smith* [1891] 1 Ch. 509; *Budden v Wilkinson* [1893] 2 Q.B. 432; *Milbank v Milbank* [1900] 1 Ch. 376 at 383–384; *Sveriges Angrartygs Assurans Forening v The 1976 Eagle Insurance Co. SA*, March 28, 1990, unreported, *per* Hobhouse J.; *cf. O'Brien v McKenzie* (1900) 21 L.R. (N.S.W.) (Eq.) 117 where the New South Wales Court held that where the documents had been described by bundle, it was unnecessary to order a further description by referring to the class or classes of documents in the bundle.

[40] *Sveriges Angrartygs Assurans Forening v The 1976 Eagle Insurance Co. SA*, March 28, 1990, unreported, *per* Hobhouse J.; *cf. Lonrho Ltd v Shell Petroleum Co. Ltd*, January 25, 1980, unreported, *per* Goff J. See also *Kumar v United Air Travel (Services) Ltd*, unreported, January 14, 1993, CA, where Dillon L.J. described a List of Documents setting out "a number of what are called litigation files, including [various names of files as] a hopeless and wholly improper way of seeking to disclose documents."

approach to providing an answer to practical questions of procedure in the last decade of the 20th century under the present Rules of Court."

Claims to withhold disclosure and inspection

6.14   If it is desired to claim that in respect of any documents a party has a right or a duty to withhold inspection of a document, or part of a document he must state in writing:

  (a) that he has such a right or duty;
  (b) the grounds on which he claims that right or duty.[41]

The claim must be in the List, where there is one, or in writing to the person wishing to inspect the document.[42] This procedure applies in relation to claims to legal professional privilege, which is the claim most frequently encountered in practice, although it equally applies in relation to other privileges such as the privilege against self-incrimination. It also applies in relation to public interest immunity, save that, where the public interest may be damaged by the mere fact of disclosure in a list, then a person may apply, without notice, for an order permitting him to withhold disclosure of a document on the ground that disclosure would damage the public interest.[43] Such an application must be supported by evidence.[44] Unless the court orders otherwise, an order of the court in favour of the application must not be served on any other person and must not be open for inspection by any person.[45]

6.15   There are three main requirements in relation to documents in respect of which it is claimed that they are privileged from production. First, the documents for which privilege is claimed must be listed in part two of the list. However, this is to identify the documents: it is not necessary to specify the provenance, makers or the date of such documents.[46] Form N265 provides that the documents should be listed and numbered. It is not the

---

[41] CPR, r.31.19(3); CPR, Pt 31, Practice Direction, Disclosure and Inspection, paras 4.5 and 4.6. Formerly RSC, Ord.24, r.5(2) provided that the claim must be made in the List of Documents with a sufficient statement of the grounds of privilege. See *Desborough v Rawlins* (1838) 3 My. & Cr. 515; *Bovill v Cowan* (1870) L.R.5 Ch.App. 495; *Taylor v Batten* (1878) 4 Q.B.D. 85 at 87, CA; *Gardner v Irvin* (1878) 4 Ex.D.49, CA; *Bulman and Dixon v Young, Ehlers and Co.* (1884) 49 L.T. 736, CA; *Budden v Wilkinson* [1893] 2 Q.B. 432, CA; *Derby & Co. Ltd v Weldon (No.7)* [1990] 1 W.L.R. 1156 at 1175–1180, where the earlier authorities are considered.
[42] CPR, r.31.19(4).
[43] CPR, r.31.19(1).
[44] CPR, r.31.19(8).
[45] CPR, r.31.19(2).
[46] *Gardner v Irvin* (1878) 4 Ex.D. 49 at 53; *Ventouris v Mountain* [1990] 1 W.L.R. 1370 at 1373 (reversed on other grounds [1991] 3 All E.R. 472).

usual practice to individually number every document covered by legal professional privilege,[47] although in certain cases this may be the appropriate course.[48] Secondly, the nature of the documents must be stated and, in the case of classes of documents, the class must be clearly defined so that it is possible to identify documents which fall within the class.[49] Thirdly, the ground of privilege and the grounds giving rise to the claim for privilege must be clearly stated.[50] In particular, the wording must not be so wide that it is impossible to be sure it contains no description of documents which came into existence in circumstances not attracting privilege.[51] It is not enough to state that the documents are privileged; the factual basis of the grounds giving rise to that claim must be set out.[52] It is not necessary to describe the documents so fully as to enable the opposing party to discover the contents of the privileged documents.[53]

Where a party considers that it would be disproportionate to the issues in the case to permit inspection of documents within a category or class of document disclosed under r.31.6(b)[54]: **6.16**

(a) he is not required to permit inspection of documents within that category or class; but

(b) he must state in his disclosure statement that inspection of those documents will not be permitted on the grounds to do so would be disproportionate.[55]

Sealed up documents[56]

Where part only of a document is relevant, and the remainder deals with a separate and confidential subject matter,[57] the relevant part alone need be **6.17**

---

[47] *Derby & Co. Ltd v Weldon (No.7)* [1990] 1 W.L.R. 1156 at 1179.

[48] *Braegrove Pty Ltd v Benedeich* [1993] 2 Qd.R. 239, Sup.Ct. of Queensland.

[49] *Woodhouse & Co. Ltd v Woodhouse* (1914) 30 T.L.R. 559 at 560, CA.

[50] *The City of Baroda* (1926) 134 L.T. 576.

[51] *Alfred Crompton Amusement Machines Ltd v Commissioners of Customs & Excise* [1971] 2 All E.R. 843.

[52] *Gardner v Irvin* (1878) 4 Ex.D. 49; *Webb v East* (1880) 5 Ex.D. 108 at 112–113, CA.

[53] *Gardner v Irvin* (1878) 4 Ex.D. 49, at 53, CA; *Taylor v Oliver* (1876) 45 L.J. Ch. 774; *Kain v Farrer* (1887) 37 L.T. 469 at 479–471; *Lazenby v Zammit* [1987] Tas. R. 54, Sup. Ct. Tasmania (Full Ct.); *Interchase Corporation Ltd v Grosvenor Hill (Queensland) Pty Ltd (No.2)* [1999] 1 Qd. R. 163, Queensland CA; *cf. Kadlunga v Electricity Trust of South Australia* (1986) 39 S.A.S.R. 410, South Australia Sup. Ct.; *Dubai Bank Ltd v Galadari (No.7)* [1992] 1 W.L.R. 106.

[54] Documents which (i) adversely affect his own case; (ii) adversely affect another party's case; or (iii) support another party's case: see Ch.4, para.4.10.

[55] CPR, r.31.3(2). Although this provision only refers to documents disclosed under CPR, r.31.6 (b), the practice from N265 (p.[533], below) permits a claim in respect of documents disclosed under r.31.6(c) (documents required to be disclosed under a relevant practice direction) as well.

[56] As to sealing-up for the purposes of production for inspection, see Ch.9, paras 9.37–9.38, below.

[57] As to which see Ch.12, para.12.34, below.

disclosed in the List of Documents.[58] In the List itself, the grounds for sealing-up, what has been done to examine the whole document and by whom, and a statement that no relevant and unprivileged parts have been sealed up, must be set out.[59] The court has power to unseal documents to assess the plea of irrelevancy[60] and to require the party to verify and explain the sealing-up on affidavit.[61]

6.18   Where sealing-up on the grounds of privilege is claimed it is the duty of the party's solicitor to inspect the whole document and to satisfy himself that the sealing-up is carried out properly and appropriately.[62] In the List of Documents itself, the grounds of privilege and the facts giving rise to the claim for privilege must be stated, and it must be apparent from the List of Documents which documents are sealed up. Where only part of a document is privileged, the party providing disclosure should seal up that part and make available for inspection the remainder.[63]

Prolixity

6.19   Where a party has filed a List of Documents which contains a prolix description of the documents or numerous irrelevant documents the party upon whom it is served may apply for an order that a new List of Documents be prepared. The appropriate order will depend on the circumstances. In a particularly bad case, the court may order the List to be taken off the file and an entirely new List be prepared and served at the cost of the defaulting party.[64] Alternatively the court may order that the List be amended and re-served. Where unnecessary delay and expense would be incurred in ordering a new or amended List of Documents, the court may in its discretion permit the oppressive or prolix List to remain on file, but order that the party filing it bear the costs of its preparation in any event.[65]

Notice to inspect

6.20   Under the former rules every List of Documents had to be accompanied by "a notice stating a time within seven days thereof at which the said

---

[58] *Kettlewell v Barstow* (1872) L.R. 7 Ch.App. 686; *Re Pickering, Pickering v Pickering* (1883) 25 Ch.D. 247, CA; *Jones v Andrews* (1888) 58 L.T. 601, CA; *Graham v Sutton, Carden & Co.* [1897] 1 Ch. 761, CA.

[59] *Jones v Andrews* (1888) 58 L.T. 601 at 605, CA.

[60] *Ehrmann v Ehrmann* [1896] 2 Ch. 826.

[61] This paragraph in the 1st edition of this work was quoted with approval by Girvan J. in *Irvin v Donaghy* [1996] P.I.Q.R. 207 at 216–217, H.Ct. of N.I.

[62] *Myers v Elman* [1940] A.C. 282 at 339, HL.

[63] *The Good Luck* [1992] 2 Lloyd's Rep. 540 at 541.

[64] *Walker v Poole* (1882) 21 Ch.D. 835.

[65] *Hill v Hart-Davis* (1884) 26 Ch.D. 470, CA; see also *Bolton v Natal Land and Colonization Co.* [1887] W.N. 143 and 178.

documents may be inspected at a place specified in the notice".[66] The procedure is different under the CPR, where there is no requirement to include a notice to inspect with or in a List of Documents. Instead, where a party has a right[67] to inspect a document, he may give the other written notice of his wish to inspect it and the other must permit inspection not more than seven days after the date on which he received the notice.[68]

Service/exchange of lists

Usually the order for disclosure will specify the date by which the List is to be served.[69] Sometimes orders will provide that Lists are to be exchanged.[70] But unless a party's disclosure obligation can be said to be conditional upon performance by his opponent of the same obligation, he should serve his List whether or not his opponent is ready. Sometimes a List is served but it is attempted to postpone inspection by the opponent until the latter has served his List. In principle this is wrong, and the attempt may not be effective, unless it can be shown that there is a real risk that the opponent may tailor his own disclosure and List in the light of that provided by another party.

It should be noted that a party shall be deemed to admit the authenticity of a document disclosed to him under CPR, Pt 31, unless he serves notice that he wishes the document proved at trial. A notice to prove a document must be served by the latest date for serving witness statements or within seven days of disclosure of the document,[71] whichever is the later.[72] Where a party has failed to serve a notice, the court will probably have a discretion to permit him to challenge authenticity at trial, particularly where a good reason can be given for not having served a notice at the appropriate time. The court will no doubt look at all the circumstances, including when and how the document was disclosed and inspected, when the party ought first have appreciated that the document may not be authentic, and when the

6.21

6.22

---

[66] RSC, Ord.24, r.9; CCR, Ord.14, r.3. Notice was not required by a party complying with an order to give specific discovery under RSC, Ord.24, r.7, or CCR, Ord.14, r.2.
[67] As to which, see Ch.9, paras 9.03, 9.04.
[68] See Ch.9, paras 9.03, 9.04.
[69] The Fast Track Standard Directions provide for the latest date for delivery of the Lists: CPR, Pt 28, Practice Direction, The Fast Track, Appendix.
[70] Formerly RSC, Ord.24, r.2 (1) provided that for automatic discovery Lists were to be exchanged.
[71] Where the List is defective it may be that the seven day period will not start until the defects in the List are remedied or the court has decided that no remedy is to be ordered: see *Arab Monetary Fund v Hashim*, unreported, January 21, 1993, where Chadwick J. so ordered in the context of RSC, Ord.27, r.4(2).
[72] CPR, r.32.19: formerly RSC, Ord.27, r.4. The parties may agree an extension of time pursuant to CPR, r.2.11. In default of agreement the court may grant an extension of time in the exercise of its powers under CPR, r.3.1(2)(a).

objection was first raised. The failure to serve a notice does not constitute an admission as to the admissibility in evidence of any such documents.

6.23   In the High Court, a defendant who had pleaded in an action was entitled to have a copy of any List of Documents (including any verifying affidavit) served under RSC, Ord.24, rr.1–5 on the plaintiff by any other defendant to the action; similarly a plaintiff against whom a counterclaim had been made in an action begun by writ was entitled to have a copy of any List of Documents (including any verifying affidavit) served under any of those rules on the party making the counterclaim by any other defendant to the counterclaim.[73] This copy had to be supplied free of charge on request.[74] Where in an action begun by originating summons the court made an order under RSC, Ord.24, r.3 requiring a defendant to the action to serve a List of Documents on the plaintiff, it might also order the defendant to supply any other defendant to the action with a copy of that list, together with any verifying affidavit.[75]

6.24   Under the CPR; it is specifically provided that each party must serve on every other party a List of Documents when giving standard disclosure.[76] Any party to whom a document has been disclosed has a right to inspect that document except where[77]:

(a)   the document is no longer in the control of the party who disclosed it;

(b)   the party disclosing the document has a right or duty to withhold inspection of it; or

(c)   where the disclosing party seeks to withhold production on the grounds that it would be disproportionate to the issues to permit inspection.[78]

Correction of errors

6.25   There is no provision in the CPR for the amendment of a List of Documents without permission. However, until inspection has taken place the party providing the List may correct it by notifying the other side of the error.[79] Thus where privileged documents have been erroneously listed in

---

[73] RSC, Ord.24, r.6(1); see Ch.4, para.4.14.
[74] *ibid.* r.6(2).
[75] *ibid.* r.6(3).
[76] CPR, r.31.10(2).
[77] CPR, r.31.3(1).
[78] CPR, r.31.3(2); see para.6.16, above. This does not apply in relation to documents disclosed under r.31.6(a) (documents on which the party relies).
[79] *Re Briamore Ltd* [1986] 1 W.L.R. 1429 at 1431.

the first part instead of the second part of the List, the party may notify the other side of the mistake prior to inspection giving grounds why production is objected to. If necessary, the court will give leave to amend the List.[80]

Where privileged documents have been erroneously listed in the first part **6.26** and are subsequently inspected, it is, as a general rule, too late to correct the error, because the inspecting party may be able to give secondary evidence of their contents and it would illogical for the court to be precluded from relying on the documents themselves as the best evidence.[81] But in certain circumstances the error may in effect be rectified even after inspection, by invoking the equitable jurisdiction of the court to grant an injection preventing use of privileged documents and information in cases of fraud and obvious mistake. As Slade L.J. put it in *Guinness Peat Properties Ltd v Fitzroy Robinson Partnership*[82]:

> "If, however, the other party or his solicitor either (a) has procured inspection of the relevant document by fraud, or (b) on inspection, realises that he has been permitted to see a document only by a reason of an obvious mistake, the court has the power to intervene for the protection of the mistaken party by the grant of an injunction in exercise of the equitable jurisdiction illustrated by the *Ashburton*,[83] *Goddard*[84] and *Herbert Smith*[85] cases. Furthermore in my view it should ordinarily intervene in such cases, unless the case is one where the injunction can properly be refused on the general principles affecting the grant of a discretionary remedy, for example, on the ground of inordinate delay... "[86]

The court in deciding whether to intervene in favour of a party who has **6.27** disclosed privileged material by a mistake applies a two stage test:

(1) Was it evident to the solicitor receiving the privileged documents that a mistake had been made? If so, the solicitor should return the documents.

---

[80] Formerly under RSC, Ord.20, r.8; *C.H Beazer (Commercial & Industrial) v Smith* (1984) 1 Const. L.J. 196; *Guinness Peat Properties Ltd v Fitzroy Robinson Partnership* [1987] 1 W.L.R. 1027 at 1045.

[81] *Re Briamore Ltd* [1986] 1 W.L.R. 1429. Permission is needed under CPR, r.31.20. In the context of criminal proceedings where documents covered by public interest immunity had been disclosed by mistake to defence counsel, see *R. v G* [2004] EWCA Crim. 1368, [2004] 1 W.L.R. 2932.

[82] [1987] 1 W.L.R. 1027 at 1045–1046; see Ch.12, para.12.16.

[83] *Ashburton v Pape* [1913] 2 Ch. 469.

[84] *Goddard v Nationwide Building Society* [1987] Q.B. 670.

[85] *English and American Insurance Company v Herbert Smith* [1988] F.S.R. 232.

[86] Followed in *Derby & Co. Ltd Weldon (No.8)* [1991] 1 W.L.R. 73, CA; *Pizzey v Ford Motor Co. Ltd, The Times*, March 8, 1993. See also *Canadian Bearings Ltd v Celanese Canada Inc.* 2006 S.C.C. 36.

   (2) If it was not obvious, would it have been obvious to the hypothet-
       ical reasonable solicitor that disclosure had occurred as a result of
       a mistake?[87]

6.28   The authorities were analysed by the Court of Appeal in *Al-Fayed v
Commissioner of Police for the Metropolis, which set out the following
principles[88]:

   (1) A party giving inspection of documents must decide before doing
       so what privileged documents he wishes to allow the other party
       to see and what he does not.
   (2) Although the privilege is that of the client and not the solicitor, a
       party clothes his solicitor with ostensible authority (if not implied
       or express authority) to waive privilege in respect of relevant
       documents.
   (3) A solicitor considering documents made available by the other
       party to litigation owes no duty of care to that party and is in
       general entitled to assume that any privilege which might other-
       wise have been claimed for such documents has been waived.
   (4) In these circumstances, where a party has given inspection of
       documents, including privileged documents which he has allowed
       the other party to inspect by mistake, it will in general be too late
       for him to claim privilege in order to attempt to correct the
       mistake by obtaining injunctive relief.
   (5) However the court has jurisdiction to intervene to prevent the use
       of documents made available for inspection by mistake where
       justice requires, as for example, in the case of inspection procured
       by fraud.
   (6) In the absence of fraud, all will depend on the circumstances, by
       the court may grant an injunction if the documents have been
       made available for inspection as a result of an obvious mistake.
   (7) A mistake is likely to be held to be obvious and an injunction
       granted where the documents are received by a solicitor and:

       (a) the solicitor appreciates that a mistake has been made before
           making some use of the documents; or

---

[87] *IBM Corporation v Phoenix International (Computers) Ltd* [1995] 1 All E.R. 412 at 421,
    423; *Breeze v John Stacey and Sons Ltd, The Times,* July 8, 1999, CA. There are practical
    difficulties in applying this test where the person receiving the privileged documents is a
    litigant in person, who in many situations may not be in a position to appreciate that the
    documents were privileged in the first place: see *News International Plc v Clinger,* unre-
    ported, April 6, 1998, Lindsay J.
[88] [2002] EWCA Civ 780 at [16], *The Times,* June 17, 2002.

(b) it would be obvious to a reasonable solicitor in his position that a mistake has been made;

and, in either case, there are no other circumstances which would make it unjust or inequitable to grant relief.

(8) Where a solicitor gives detailed consideration to the question whether the documents have been made available for inspection by mistake and honestly concludes that they have not, that fact will be a relevant (and in many cases an important) pointer to the conclusion that it would not be obvious to the reasonable solicitor that a mistake had been made, but is not conclusive, the decision remains with the court.

(9) In both cases identified in (7)(a) and (b) above, there may be many circumstances in which it may nevertheless be held to be inequitable or unjust to grant relief, but all will depend upon the particular circumstances.

(10) Since the court is exercising an equitable jurisdiction, there are no rigid rules.

Where a solicitor reads documents disclosed as a result of an obvious mistake, therefore he may be at risk from a successful application for an order for the following relief: **6.29**

(1) Delivery up of the privileged material and destruction of any notes made from such materials, together with a prohibition on him and his client from using the privileged material or information derived from it.[89]

(2) Restraining the solicitor from continuing to act in the litigation in extreme cases, where that is necessary for the protection for the claim to privilege.[90]

CPR, r.31.20 now specifically provides that where a party inadvertently allows a privileged document to be inspected, the party who has inspected the document may use it or its contents only with the permission of the court. Accordingly the onus is now on the inspecting party to take the initiative and apply to the court. In practice, inadvertent listing of privileged documents rarely creates a problem, as in general when a solicitor is unsure whether a privileged document has been deliberately listed as not privileged, he confirms the position with the disclosing party. **6.30**

---

[89] Even where an opposing party has obtained privileged communications, the court may in its discretion refuse an injunction restraining use: *ISTIL Group Inc. v Zahoor* [2003] EWHC 165 (Ch), [2003] 2 All E.R. 252.

[90] *Ablitt v Mills & Reeve, The Times,* October 25, 1995. *Celanese Canada Inc. v Murray Demolition Corp.* 2006 S.C.C. 36, Sup. Ct. of Canada (solicitor restrained from acting who had inspected privileged electronic material taken during *Anton Piller* search).

Supplementary lists

6.31   It is not uncommon for further relevant documents to come to light after the service of the original List of Documents by a party.[91] The proper course is to notify every other party at the earliest opportunity of the existence of such documents and to serve a supplementary List of Documents.[92] CPR, r.31.11 provides that any duty of disclosure continues until the proceedings are concluded and if documents to which that duty extend, come to a party's notice at any time during the proceedings, he must immediately notify every other party. If there are only a few additional documents, the other party may agree to the additional discovery being listed by letter rather than by way of a supplementary List of Documents. If a solicitor is aware or becomes aware that the List served on behalf of his client is inadequate and omits relevant documents, he is under a duty to put the matter the right at the earliest opportunity and should not wait until a further order of the court.[93]

Duty of search

6.32   When giving standard disclosure, a party is required to make a reasonable search for documents falling within CPR, r.31.6(b) or (c), that is documents which adversely affect his own case, adversely affect another party's case or support another party's case, and the documents which he is required to disclose by a relevant practice direction.[94] This is a major change from the former practice under the RSC, whereby a party was required to disclose all relevant documents in his list and there was no limitation merely requiring a party to conduct a reasonable search for documents. The thinking behind this change was set out in the following terms in the report which preceded the introduction of the CPR:

> "It is no use, however, limiting the categories of a document which a party has to disclose if he still has to search through all his documents to identify those in categories (1) and (2) [the parties' own documents, which they rely upon in support of their contentions in the proceedings, and adverse documents of which a party is aware and which to a material extent adversely affect his own case or support another party's case]. I therefore recommended that an initial disclosure should apply

---

[91] See Ch.5, para.5.41, above.

[92] *Mitchell v Darley Main Colliery Co.* (1884) 1 Cab. & El. 215. *Admiralty and Commercial Courts* Guide (7th edn, 2006), para.E2.2 provides that a supplemental list must be served.

[93] *Myers v Elman* [1940] A.C. 282 at 294; see Ch.14, para.14.10, below.

[94] CPR, r.31.7(1). See also *McCabe v British American Tobacco Australia Services Ltd* [2002] V.S.C. 73 at [182], Victoria Sup. Ct. (reversed on other grounds) [2002] V.S.C.A. 197.

only to relevant documents of which a party is aware at the time when the obligation to disclose arises. I recognise that this is the most difficult aspect of my proposals in practice. The test of awareness is particularly problematic where the disclosing party is not an individual; in a company, firm or other organisation, it is likely that a number of people will have known about relevant documents. My proposal here is that there should be an obligation for the organisation to nominate a supervising officer whose task would be to identify individuals within the organisation who were likely to recollect relevant documents. On the basis of their combined recollections, documents would be extracted and disclosed (subject to any claim of privilege). When it made its lists of documents in accordance with rules of Court, the company, etc, would also include a statement of the identity and status of the supervising officer and those whose recollections he had canvassed. This would assist the other party to make an appropriate application for specific discovery if he thought that enquiries should reasonably have been made of some additional person or department in the organisation".[95]

What constitutes a reasonable search may be regarded as being to a certain extent subjective and thus the disclosing party is given a degree of latitude in making standard disclosure. The factors relevant in deciding the reasonableness of a search include the following: **6.33**

    (a) The number of documents involved.
    (b) The nature and complexity of the proceedings.
    (c) The ease and expense of retrieval of any particular document.
    (d) The significance of any document which is likely to be located during the search.[96]

In considering the extent of the search, the parties should bear in mind the overriding principle of proportionality. It may, for example, be reasonable to decide not to search for documents coming into existence before some particular date, or to limit the search to documents in some particular place or places, or to documents falling into particular categories.[97] Where the disclosing party is not an individual, it is likely that a number of people will have known about relevant documents and enquiries should be made of key individuals in this regard. It will be often prudent to send out a memorandum to those individuals explaining the disclosure obligation and asking them to make available documents falling within that obligation. In practical terms the person making the disclosure statement and his solicitor

---

[95] Lord Woolf, *Access to Justice: Final Report* (1996), Ch.12, para.41.
[96] CPR, r.31.7(2). In respect of electronic disclosure, these factors have been elaborated upon; see Ch.7, paras 7.06–7.12 below.
[97] CPR, Pt 31, Practice Direction, Disclosure and Inspection, paras 2 and 2A.4.

should be working together to make the decision as to which documents ought and need to be disclosed and hence the individuals enquired of should not be put in the position of making the final decision as to what needs to be disclosed and hence they should be encouraged to make available the documents they know of which may possibly fall within the disclosure obligation. In most cases the person making the disclosure statement will not need to pursue his enquiries with former employees of the organisation who have had knowledge of relevant documents.

6.34   In order that the other parties to an action may know the extent of the search and, if appropriate, make an application for specific disclosure under CPR, r.31.12, where a party has not searched for a category or class of document on the grounds that to do so would be unreasonable, he must state this in his disclosure statement and identify the category or class of document.[98] In the Commercial Court a party who considers that to search for a category or class of document under CPR, r.31.6(b) would be unreasonable must, where practicable, also indicate this in advance in his case management information sheet. The judge hearing the case management conference may direct that, notwithstanding that the party considers that to search for a category or class of document under CPR, r.31.6(b) would be unreasonable, there is to be a search for all documents falling within CPR, r.31.6(b). Documents held in electronic form raise particular considerations and are covered in Ch.7.

B. CHALLENGING ADEQUACY OF DISCLOSURE

6.35   A party not satisfied with the adequacy of a List of Documents under the former rules had a number of courses of action open to him to seek proper disclosure or otherwise satisfy himself that full disclosure had been given. In particular the old Rules of Court provided the following avenues which were available depending upon the circumstances:

(1) RSC, Ord.24, r.2(7): requiring a List of Documents provided under the automatic provisions for discovery under r.2 to be verified on affidavit.
(2) RSC, Ord.24, r.3(2): where a party was in default of the automatic provisions of discovery under r.2, application for a first or further and better List of Documents, with or without verifying affidavit.
(3) RSC, Ord.24, r.3(2): application for affidavit verifying List of Documents required under r.2 where party had failed to comply with any provision of r.2.

---

[98] CPR, r.31.7(3). As to the disclosure statement see paras 6.05–6.06, above.

(4) RSC, Ord.24, r.3(1): application for a further and better List of Documents, with or without verifying affidavit.[99]

(5) RSC, Ord.24, r.3(1): application for affidavit verifying List of Documents ordered under r.3(1).[100]

(6) RSC, Ord.24, r.7(1): application supported by affidavit for an affidavit as to the specific documents or classes of documents.

(7) Application for interrogatories as to particular documents (in exceptional circumstances).

In addition there were the sanctions for failure to give proper discovery, such as striking out a statement of claim or defence and contempt.[101]

The procedures under the CPR would appear to be simpler. Various options under the former rules are no longer available, primarily on the basis they are not necessary or appropriate. Under the CPR there are the following options available to ensure compliance with the obligation to provide proper disclosure: **6.36**

(1) Application for an affidavit verifying disclosure statement in list of documents, specific disclosure.[102]

(2) CPR, r.3.10(b): application for an order that a party comply with a rule or practice direction breached.[103]

(3) CPR, r.3.4(2): application for an order that a statement of case be struck out for failure to comply with a rule, practice direction or court order.[104]

(4) CPR, r.31.12: application for specific disclosure.[105]

(5) CPR, r.31.12: application for an order for specific inspection.[106]

(6) Information Request under CPR, Pt 18, or cross-examination in exceptional circumstances.[107]

C. VERIFICATION ON AFFIDAVIT

There is no specific power in CPR, Pt 31 to require a party to provide his disclosure on affidavit or to verify on affidavit his disclosure. The purpose of the provisions under the former rules in relation to affidavits was to   **6.37**

---

[99] CCR, Ord.14, r.1(1).
[100] CCR, Ord.14, r.2.
[101] See Ch.13, paras 13.07–13.18, 13.27–13.29, below.
[102] Paras 6.37–6.38, below.
[103] Paras 6.41–6.42, below.
[104] Paras 6.39–6.40, below.
[105] Paras 6.45–6.56, below.
[106] See Ch.9, para.9.33–9.34.
[107] Paras 6.43–6.44, below.

encourage a party to comply fully with his obligations. Under the CPR the role of the affidavit is largely covered by the requirement to provide a disclosure statement. A party or other person providing the disclosure statement opens himself up to the various sanctions for perjury if he knowingly has omitted documents subject to the disclosure obligation from the list. The requirement of a disclosure statement is a useful and important incentive for proper disclosure as well as giving the opposing party an opportunity to challenge that disclosure if the enquiries made appear to be unreasonable or otherwise inadequate.

6.38   Although there is no express power in CPR, Pt 31 and accompanying Practice Direction for a court to order that a party file an affidavit or witness statement, the court does have the jurisdiction to order a party to make and file an affidavit or witness statement as to disclosure.[108] In view of the provisions as to disclosure statements in most cases it will not be necessary to order an affidavit or witness statement. A false disclosure statement may be a contempt of court.[109] Where the court considers it necessary or appropriate to reinforce the disclosure obligation and ensure compliance, it may order a party to verify his disclosure statement in the List of Documents or specific disclosure on affidavit or by witness statement.[110] A party filing an affidavit or witness statement knowing that it is untrue will be liable to contempt proceedings as well as the usual sanctions for perjury.[111]

D. ORDER THAT PARTY COMPLY

6.39   Where it appears that a party has given inadequate disclosure, whether it be that the search was too limited or that relevant documents have been omitted, normally the appropriate route is to apply for an order for specific disclosure under CPR, r.31.12. However where no list has been served, or the list is defective and is not in proper form, normally the appropriate means of ensuring compliance is to apply to the court under CPR, rr.3.10(b) and 3.4(2)(c). These powers are not mutually exclusive, so that even where a defective list has been served a party may still apply in an appropriate case for an order under CPR, r.31.12.

6.40   Under the CPR, if a party fails to comply with any part of Pt 31, such as not providing a list of documents or failing to provide a list of documents in proper form, then it is open for another party to make an application to

---

[108] CPR, rr.3.1(1)(m), 32.1(1).

[109] CPR, r.31.23; see Ch.13, para.13.27.

[110] See *Admiralty and Commercial Courts Guide* (7th edn, 2006), para.E3.9, which specifically provides that the court may at any stage order that a disclosure statement be verified by affidavit.

[111] Where the party is not an individual, consideration should be given as to who is the appropriate person to provide the affidavit or witness statement: *cf. Claus v Pir* [1988] Ch. 287.

the court for an order under CPR, r.3.10(b), thus ordering the party to comply with the rule or practice direction breached. In addition a party may apply for the statement of case to be struck out under CPR, r.3.4(2)(c) where there has been a failure to comply with a rule, practice direction or court order.[112]

E. CONCLUSIVENESS OF LIST OR AFFIDAVIT

Subject to applications for a further and better list or an affidavit as to **6.41** specific documents or classes of documents under RSC, Ord.24, rr.3 and 7, a List of Documents, whether or not verified by affidavit, or an affidavit of documents served under the former rules was normally regarded as conclusive as to its contents.[113] In particular the List or affidavit served under the old rules was regarded as being normally conclusive as to the following:

(a) Whether not the party has or has had any relevant documents other than those disclosed in his custody, possession or power.[114]

(b) The grounds stated in support of a claim of privilege from inspection.[115] However, the court had power to inspect a document for which privilege had been claimed in order to consider and rule on the validity of the claim.[116]

(c) The relevance, for the purposes of discovery, of the documents disclosed, including blanked out documents.[117]

---

[112] See Ch.13.

[113] *Walker v Ost* [1970] R.P.C. 151, CA; *G.E. Capital Corporate Finance Group v Bankers Trust Co.* [1995] 1 W.L.R. 172, CA; *Proctor & Gamble v Medical Research* [2001] N.S.W.S.C. 183, N.S.W. Sup. Ct.

[114] *Gardner v Irvin* (1878) 4 Ex.D. 49, CA; *Jones v Monte Video Co.* (1880) 5 Q.B.D. 556, CA; *Compagnie Financière du Pacifique v Peruvian Guano Co.* (1882) 11 Q.B.D. 55, CA; *Hall v Truman, Hanbury & Co.* (1885) 29 Ch.D. 307 at 319; *Lonrho Plc v Fayed (No.3), The Times,* June 24, 1993, CA.

[115] *Bewicke v Graham* (1881) 7 Q.B.D. 400, CA; *Att.Gen. v Emerson* (1882) 10 Q.B.D. 191; *Bulman v Young, Ehlers & Co.* (1883) 49 L.T. 736, CA; *Lyell v Kennedy (No.3)* (1884) 27 Ch.D. 1 at 19; *Budden v Wilkinson* [1893] 2 Q.B. 432, CA; *Frankenstein v Gavin House-to-House Cycle Cleaning and Insurance Co.* [1897] 2 Q.B. 62, CA; *Chowood v Lyall* [1929] 2 Ch. 406; *Brookes v Prescott* [1948] 2 K.B. 133; *Westminster Airways v Kuwait Oil* [1951] 1 K.B. 174, CA.

[116] See Ch.11, para.11.02, below.

[117] *Budden v Wilkinson* [1893] 2 Q.B. 432 at 433, CA; *Mogul S.S. Co. v McGregor* (1886) 2 T.L.R. 2; *Hastings Corp v Ivall* (1873) L.R. 8 Ch.App. 1017; *Victor Hanby Associates Ltd v Oliver* (1990) J.L.R. 337, Jersey CA; *G.E. Capital Corporation Finance Group v BankersTrust Co.* [1995] 1 W.L.R. 172, CA (oath of party that blanked out parts of documents as irrelevant was conclusive, as the court was not satisfied from the documents produced or anything in the affidavit that it did not truly state what it ought to state). In *Svenska Handelsbanken v Sun Alliance and London Insurance Plc* [1995] 2 Lloyd's Rep. 84, Rix J. held that, for an affidavit of irrelevance to be conclusive, he had to be satisfied that the deponent (and those advising her) had considered each document for the purpose of identifying whether there was any relevant material in it.

Whilst the affidavit of discovery was normally regarded as exclusive, it would not be so where it could be shown that there had been an insufficiency of discovery. This insufficiency could be established from:

(a) the pleadings, the list and affidavit of documents themselves, or documents referred to therein;

(b) any other source that constitutes an admission of the existence of a discoverable document not so far discovered;

(c) an apparent exclusion of documents from discovery by a party under a misconception of the case.[118]

6.42   In respect of lists of documents and affidavits served under the CPR, they will be regarded as conclusive in comparable circumstances, save in relation to an application for specific disclosure under CPR, r.31.12. As with a list of documents served under the old rules, it is generally not sufficient to adduce evidence to show that the List is untrue in order to challenge it, save in the context of a specific disclosure application.[119]

6.43   In the context of the old rules it was held that a party could not serve interrogatories for the purposes of showing that a list of documents is insufficient, although in special circumstances interrogatories were allowed as to the existence of particular documents.[120] Similarly the court will not allow the mechanism of Information Request under CPR, Pt 18 to be used as a means of challenging a list of documents.

6.44   Under the RSC, the court did not generally permit that a deponent be cross-examined on his affidavit for the purposes of obtaining further disclosure.[121] Indeed, the weight of authority was to the effect that an opposing party could not cross-examine the deponent on his verifying affidavit at all. This was on the basis that the affidavit did not go to any of the issues in the action.[122] The position is the same under the CPR. The only circumstances where cross-examination as to documents and disclosure may be appropriate at an interlocutory stage is in the context of freezing and search orders, where it may be crucial to establish what has happened to and the

---

[118] *British Association of Glass Bottle Manufacturers v Nettlefield* [1912] A.C. 709 at 712; *Mulley v Manifold* (1959) 103 C.L.R. 341; *Moran v Erstream (Australia) Pty Ltd* [2006] N.S.W.S.C. 79.

[119] See *Edmiston v British Transport Commission* [1956] 1 Q.B. 191, CA.

[120] *Jones v Monte Video Co.* (1880) 5 Q.B.D. 556 at 558; *Hall v Truman* (1885) 29 Ch.D. 307 at 320; *Nicholl v Wheeler* (1886) 17 Q.B.D. 101; *Morris v Edward* (1890) 15 App.Cas. 309 at 313 to 315; *Bray*, at pp.213 to 214. See Ch.14, paras 14.039–14.040, below.

[121] *Lyell v Kennedy (No.3)* (1884) 27 Ch.D. 1, CA; *Birmingham & Midland Omnibus v London and North Western Rly* [1913] 3 K.B. 850, CA; *Fruehauf Finance v Zurich Australian Insurance Ltd* (1990) 20 N.S.W.L.R. 359.

[122] *Bray*, at p.211; *Birmingham and Midland Omnibus v London and North Western Ry.* [1913] 3 K.B. 850 at 855; *Re Grosvenor Hotel, London* [1964] 1 Ch. 464 at 481; *Lonrho Plc v Fayed (No.3)*, *The Times*, June 24, 1993, CA, disproving a dictum to the contrary effect in *Berkeley Administration Inc. v McClelland* [1990] F.S.R. 381; *cf. Re Pickering, Pickering v Pickering* (1883) 25 Ch.D. 247 at 274, 248.

location of assets prior to trial.[123] In Ireland, however, the position is less strict, and cross-examination on a discovery affidavit is possible in rare circumstances, where other remedies are inadequate.[124] Where a *final* injunction requires delivery up of a document and the disclosure of information by affidavit, however, cross-examination of the deponent can be ordered, and disproportionality is not a defence to non-compliance with the order.[125]

F. APPLICATION FOR SPECIFIC DISCLOSURE

A List of Documents is not conclusive in the context of an application for   **6.45** specific disclosure under CPR, r.31.12. An application under this rule is for an order that a party must do one or more of the following things:

  (a) disclose documents or classes of documents specified in the order;
  (b) carry out a search to the extent stated in the order;
  (c) disclose any documents located as a result of that search.

In cases on the Small Claims Track, after allocation the court will usually   **6.46** give standard directions and fix a date for the final hearing.[126] The standard directions provide for each party serving on the other copies of all documents on which he intends to rely at the hearing. Where a party wishes further disclosure, the appropriate course is to make an application for special directions and the court may direct a preliminary hearing to determine such an application.[127] The application will not be under CPR, r.31.12 as Pt 31 does not apply to cases on the Small Claims Track.[128]

In relation to cases on the Fast Track, the general approach of the court   **6.47** is to direct on allocation standard disclosure between the parties.[129] Where a party wants wider disclosure or to challenge the disclosure given under standard disclosure, the appropriate course is to make an application under CPR, r.31.12. The timing of the application will depend on the circumstances, and often it will be appropriate to apply at the stages where directions are usually given, namely at the allocation to the track and on the filing of listing questionnaires.[130] In relation to cases on the Multi-Track, the

---

[123] *House of Spring Gardens Ltd v Waite* [1985] F.S.R. 173, CA; *Motorola Credit Corp. v Uzan* [2002] EWHC 2187 (Comm); Ch.2, para.2.13, above; Ch.16, para.16.114, below.
[124] *Duncan v Governor of Portlaiose Prison* [1997] 1 I.R. 558, High Ct. Eire.
[125] *Warner Brothers Productions Ltd v The Telegraph Group Ltd*, unreported, November 19, 1999 (Eady J.).
[126] CPR, r.27.4 (1)(a).
[127] CPR, r.27.6.
[128] CPR, r.27.2(1)(b).
[129] CPR, Pt 28, Practice Direction, The Fast Track, para.3.9 (2).
[130] CPR, Pt 28, Practice Direction, The Fast Track, para.2.

direction on allocation will generally provide for standard disclosure.[131] Applications for specific disclosure can be made at the case management conference (though the *Queen's Bench Guide* discourages this),[132] and in appropriate cases at a later stage as part of the listing questionnaire.[133] In the Commercial Court disclosure is usually dealt with at the case management conference, including applications for specific disclosure.[134] The court has jurisdiction to make an order for specific disclosure at any time, whether or not standard disclosure under CPR, r.31.5 has taken place.[135]

Mode of application

6.48   A party seeking specific disclosure under CPR, r.31.12 should file an application notice specifying the order that he intends to ask the court to make and this must be supported by evidence. The grounds on which the order is sought may be set out in the application notice itself, but if not, they must be set out in the evidence filed in support of the application.[136] The most common situations in practice are:

(1) where it is contended that the extent of the search carried out by the party has been unreasonably limited;

(2) where the party believes that there are relevant documents which ought to be disclosed and it is appropriate to require the disclosing party to disclose them.

6.49   The application should specify the documents or classes of documents sought, and this may be done by way of schedule to the application notice. It is important that the application notice should not define the class of documents too broadly or otherwise the court in its discretion may refuse disclosure of the whole class of documents altogether, or in appropriate cases it may re-draw the wording into proper limits.[137] Similarly the application should be specific about the extent of the search sought.

6.50   The evidence in support of the application should describe the document or classes of documents and the extent of the search sought, and should

---

[131] CPR, Pt 29, Practice Direction, The Multi-Track, paras 4.7(1)(c) and 4.10(1).

[132] Para.7.85, suggesting a separate application under CPR, Pt 23; see para.6.51, below.

[133] As to timing of applications generally, see para.6.51, below.

[134] *Admiralty and Commercial Courts Guide* (7th edn, 2006), para.E2.1.

[135] *Dayman v Canyon Holdings Ltd*, January 11, 2006, Ch D (unreported).

[136] CPR, Pt 31, Practice Direction, Disclosure and Inspection, paras 5.2 and 5.3.

[137] *David Khan Inc. v Conway Stewart & Co.* [1972] F.S.R. 174; *R. v First Lord of the Treasury, ex p. Petch*, unreported, January 31, 1994, Harrison J. (application refused as it was far too wide in ambit and failed to be specific); *City of Gotha v Sotheby's* [1998] 1 W.L.R. 114 at 123; *Portman Building Society v Royal Insurance Plc* [1998] P.N.L.R. 672, CA; *Australian Competition & Consumer Commission v Advanced Medical Institute Pty Ltd* [2005] F.C.A. 366 (class too wide) see also *Multigroup Bulgaria Holdings A.D. v Oxford Analytica Ltd*, unreported, June 30, 1999, Eady J. (failure to define term in original order).

explain in relation to each class or category of documents why it is reasonable and proportionate for those items to be disclosed. Ordinarily the evidence should explain why the documents sought are relevant to the issues in the action.[138] The evidence must also state the source (if necessary) and grounds of the belief that such documents exist.[139]

An application under CPR, r.31.12 may be made at any stage, and may be made notwithstanding that the party has already made a List of Documents. In every case the party should consider when is an appropriate time to make the application and much will depend on what track the proceedings are and whether it is convenient to make the application at a stage when the court usually gives directions, such as allocation, case management conference, with the listing questionnaire, pre-trial review or other hearing.[140] In theory an application may be made even before the service of the claimant's statement of case, although such an application would be rarely acceded to, as a statement of case is generally required in order to define the issues properly.[141] Exceptionally an order may be made for specific disclosure before the service of the defendant's defence.[142] In rare cases a party who is contesting the jurisdiction of proceedings under CPR, Pt 11, may make an application for specific disclosure where that is necessary in order to deal with his application to contest jurisdiction.[143] Rarely will the court grant specific disclosure for the purposes of an interlocutory application.[144] Where the disclosure is material, disclosure may be allowed even at a late stage in the proceedings; where that is in the disclosing party's capabilities.[145] **6.51**

Before the court will order specific disclosure it will need to be satisfied, at least prima facie, that the documents are (or have been) in the control of the party and the documents sought are relevant.[146] Whilst a court may inspect documents for determining relevance, this is not the normal course **6.52**

---

[138] *City of Gotha v Sotheby's* [1998] 1 W.L.R. 114 at 123; *Portman Building Society v Royal Insurance Plc* [1998] P.N.L.R. 672, CA.

[139] Under the former rules this was a specific requirement: RSC, Ord.24, r.7(3).

[140] See paras 6.46–6.47, above; *Parker v C.S. Structured Credit Fund Ltd* [2003] EWHC 391 (Ch.), (disclosure prior to CMC refused).

[141] *R.H.M. Foods v Bovril Freeman (Blenders) Ltd* [1982] 1 W.L.R. 661; *Speyside Estate v Wraymond Ltd* [1950] Ch. 96, where such an order was made for the purpose of saving costs; see Ch.2, para.2.32.

[142] *Shippam v Princes-Buitoni* [1983] F.S.R. 427; *Edelston v Russell* (1888) 57 L.T. 927; *Rigg v Associated* Newspapers [2003] EWHC 710 (Q.B.) see Ch.2, para.2.32.

[143] See Ch.2, para.2.33, above.

[144] *Chater & Chater Productions Ltd v Rose* [1994] F.S.R. 491, Jacob J. (held that the court should be slow to order discovery of document in support of a motion for an interlocutory injunction to restrain infringement of copyright); *Bailey v Beagle Management Pty Ltd* [2001] F.C.A. 60, Fed. Ct. of Aus. (production for purposes of security for costs application).

[145] *Legal & General Assurance Society Ltd v Taulke-Johnson* [2002] EWHC 120 (Q.B.).

[146] *Portman Building Society v Royal Insurance Plc* [1998] P.N.L.R. 672, CA; *cf. Astra National Production v Neo-Art Productions* [1928] W.N. 218, approved in *Format Communications Manufacturing Ltd v I.T.T. (United Kingdom) Ltd* [1983] F.S.R. 473 and 483–4, CA. See also *Deacons v White & Case* [2003] H.K.C.F.I. 227.

and is rarely done in practice.[147] The courts are more willing to inspect where there is a disputed claim to privilege.

6.53   The application may be based merely on probability arising from the surrounding circumstances or in part on specific facts deposed to. Once this test has been satisfied, the court has a discretion whether or not to order disclosure.[148] In deciding whether or not to make an order for this specific disclosure, the court will take into account all the circumstances of the case and in particular, the overriding objective. Thus the court will take into account the importance of the documents sought, the nature and complexity of the issues, the amount at stake in the litigation, the cost and burden to the disclosing party of complying with the order, the financial position of the parties, the importance of the case and general considerations of proportionality.[149] On an application for specific disclosure, it is essential to first identify the factual issues that arise for determination at the trial as disclosure should be limited to documents relevant to those issues. For this purpose it is necessary to analyse the pleadings as the purpose of pleadings is to identify those factual issues which are in dispute and in relation to which evidence can properly be adduced.[150]

6.54   If the court concludes that the party from whom specific disclosure is sought has failed adequately to comply with the obligations imposed by an order for disclosure (whether by failing to make a sufficient search for documents or otherwise) the court will usually make such order as is necessary to ensure that those obligations are properly complied with.[151] Thus once an order for standard disclosure has been made, the court will make such order to ensure that the original standard disclosure obligation is complied with. This may take the form of an "unless order" striking out the statement of case of the party in default if proper disclosure is not forthcoming within a specified period of time.[152]

6.55   Whether the respondent to an application needs to file evidence for the purposes of resisting an order for specific disclosure depends on the circumstances. It will be generally prudent to file evidence in opposition to such an order, as generally the order will provide that the party should disclose any documents located as a result of the search required by the order. It is not usually open to the court, in the absence of clear evidence to the contrary,

---

[147] *Patrick v Capital Finance Pty Ltd (No.3)* [2003] F.C.A. 385, (2003) 198 A.L.R. 323, Fed. Ct. of Aus.

[148] *Berkeley Administration Inc. v MacClelland* 1990] F.S.R. 381, CA.

[149] CPR, Pt 31, Practice Direction, Disclosure and Inspection, para.5.4; Chancery Guide (2005), paras 4.3 to 4.5; *Queen's Bench Guide*, paras 7.8.3 to 7.8.5; *Admiralty and Commercial Courts Guide* (7th edn, 2006), paras E3.11 and E4.3. It may also bear in mind other considerations such as confidentiality. *De Molestina v Ponto* [2002] EWHC 366 (Comm) (specific disclosure limited to what was necessary to enable a valuation of the shares in question).

[150] *Harrods Ltd v Times Newspaper Ltd* [2006] EWCA Civ 294 at [12]; see also para.5.12 above.

[151] CPR, Pt 31, Practice Direction, Disclosure and Inspection, para.5.4.

[152] CPR, rr.3.4(2)(c) and 3.10(b). See Ch.13, paras 13.07–13.17 below (unless orders)

to reject the evidence of a party's solicitor after due enquiry that the requested documents did not exist.[153] However, once an order has been made for specific disclosure, that does not preclude the respondent stating in his specific disclosure that he has no such documents or, unless this has been determined against him at the hearing of the application, from claiming privilege or sealing up in part. Whether or not the party who is ordered to disclose documents under CPR, r.31.12 may assert in his response that the documents he has are irrelevant will depend on whether the court has ruled that the documents he holds are relevant. It would not be desirable to allow a party to reopen any question of relevance already decided against him when responding to the order.[154]

An order for specific disclosure should identify with precision the document or documents or categories of documents which are required to be disclosed so that there can be no doubt as to the obligations of the disclosing party.[155] In an appropriate case the order may direct a party to carry out a search for any documents which it is reasonable to suppose may contain information which may (a) enable the party applying for disclosure either to advance his own case or to damage that of the party giving disclosure; (b) lead to a train of enquiry which has either of these circumstances.[156] The formulation in (b) is the *Peruvian Guano* test and may be appropriate in cases where fraud is involved or other factually contentious cases. The form of the order will depend on the circumstances and the court may direct that the specific disclosure be by way of list together with disclosure statement, affidavit, witness statement or some less formal mode, such as by letter. The court may direct that any List or other form of specific disclosure be verified by affidavit or witness statement.

6.56

G. APPEALS

An appeal against the decision of a Master or district judge in a disclosure matter lies to the (High Court or circuit) judge.[157] Under the RSC this was on the basis that, although the appellant began, it was a complete rehearing of the matter. Under CPR appeals are now normally limited to a *review* of the lower court's decision.[158] The grounds for such review are that the decision was wrong, or that it was unfair because of a serious irregularity in the proceedings.[159] There is provision for a "leap-frog"appeal direct to the

6.57

---

[153] *Henderson v Overall*, December 13, 2001, Q.B.D. (Unreported).
[154] cf. *Thornet v Barclays Bank (France) Ltd* [1939] 1 K.B. 675.
[155] *Berkeley Administration v McClelland* [1990] F.S.R. 381, CA.
[156] CPR, Pt.31, Practice Direction—Disclosure and Inspection, para.5.5; *Admiralty and Commercial Courts Guide* (7th edn, 2006), para.E4.2.
[157] CPR, Pt 52.
[158] CPR, r.52.11(1); *Tanfern Ltd v Macdonald*, *The Times*, May 17, 2000, CA.
[159] CPR, r.52.11(3).

Court of Appeal in certain, rare, cases.[160] A further appeal (or, in the case of the Commercial Court or the Technology and Construction Court, an appeal) lies to the Court of Appeal.[161] A first appeal requires the permission of either the court which made the original order or of the court to which the appeal is made.[162] Permission to appeal is only to be given where the court considers that the appeal has a real prospect of success, or there is some other compelling reason why it should be heard.[163] Similarly, the grant of permission will only be reconsidered where there is a compelling reason to do so.[164] A further appeal requires the permission of the Court of Appeal, which will be given only where it considers that the appeal raises an important point of principle or practice or there is some other compelling reason.[165] The Court of Appeal will not interfere with the exercise of the judge's discretion, unless he has misdirected himself in law,[166] has taken into account irrelevant considerations,[167] has failed to exercise his discretion,[168] or has reached a conclusion on the question of discretion that no reasonably-minded judge properly directed could do. Only once the judge's exercise of discretion has been set aside on such a basis made can the Court of Appeal exercise the discretion itself.[169] In principle there can be a further appeal to the House of Lords, with the leave of the Court of Appeal or the House of Lords itself, but in interlocutory matters, such as disclosure is, leave (permission) will only be given in rare cases.[170]

H. PUBLICITY

6.58   The general principle is that all hearings, both of original applications and of any appeals, are to be in public.[171] There is no general exception for

---

[160] CPR, r.52.14.

[161] Also under CPR, Pt 52.

[162] CPR, r.52.3.

[163] CPR, r.52.3(6); see CPR, Pt 52, Practice Direction, paras 4.4 and 4.5; *Clark v Perks*, unreported, September 1, 2000, CA.

[164] CPR, r.52.9; *Hunt v Presgood, The Times,* October 20, 2000, CA; *Athletic Union of Constantinople v National Basketball Association (No.2)* [2002] EWCA Civ 830, [2002] 1 W.L.R. 2863, CA; *Nathan v Smilovitch* [2002] EWCA Civ 759, CA.

[165] CPR, r.52.13; CPR, Pt 52, Practice Direction, paras 4.9 and 4.10; *Uphill v BRB (Residuary) Ltd* [2005] EWCA Civ 60, [2005] 3 All E.R. 269, CA; *Cramp v Hastings BC* [2005] 3 All E.R. 1014, CA.

[166] *Evans v Bartlam* [1937] A.C. 473, HL.

[167] *Egerton v Jones* [1939] 3 All E.R. 889 at 892, CA.

[168] *Crowther v Elgood* (1887) 34 Ch.D. 691 at 697.

[169] *Hadmor Productions Ltd v Hamilton* [1983] 1 A.C. 191, HL.

[170] *Garden Cottage Foods Ltd v Milk Marketing Board* [1984] A.C. 130 at 138. See also *Al-Sabah v Grupo Torras S.A.*, unreported, October 10, 2000, P.C. In practice, it is only cases where important principles (such as privilege) are involved that reach the House of Lords.

[171] CPR, r.39.2(1); *Clibbery v Allan* [2002] EWCA Civ 45, [2002] Fam 261, CA. As to the meaning of "public", see *Storer v British Gas Plc* [2000] 2 All E.R. 440, CA.

interlocutory hearings before the master or district judge.[172] But there are a number of specific exceptions,[173] and one general exception for the case where the court considers that a private hearing would be in the interests of justice.[174] The most likely of the specific exceptions to apply in the context of disclosure applications is that where the hearing "involves confidential information (including information relating to personal financial matters) and publicity would damage that confidentiality".[175] This exception is exemplified (though not exhaustively) by the 10 specific instances given in the Practice Direction.[176] But none of these relates to disclosure as such. In deciding whether to sit in public or in private, the judge must also have regard to Art.6(1) of the European Convention on Human Rights.[177] Where the hearing takes place in public any member of the public may obtain a transcript of any judgment given or a copy of any order made, subject to paying the appropriate fee.[178] But, where a judgment is given or an order is made in private, a member of the public who is not a party to the proceedings needs the permission of the judge to obtain such transcript or copy order.[179]

---

[172] *cf. Forbes v Smith* [1998] 1 All E.R. 973 at 974 and *Hodgson v Imperial Tobacco Ltd* [1998] 2 All E.R. 673 at 684–687, in relation to the former RSC.

[173] CPR, r.39.2(3)((a)–(f).

[174] CPR, r.39.2(3)(g).

[175] CPR, r.39.2(3) (c); *H. v Associated Newspapers* [2002] E.M.L.R. 425, CA.

[176] CPR, Pt 39, Practice Direction, para.1.5.

[177] CPR, Pt 39, Practice Direction, para.1.4A, see Ch.21, para.21.05, below.

[178] *ibid.*, para.1.11.

[179] *ibid.*, para.1.12.

CHAPTER 7

Electronic disclosure

CHAPTER 7

Electronic disclosure

CHAPTER 7

Electronic disclosure

This chapter considers the issue of electronic disclosure, which until 2005 **7.01** was not specifically covered in any detail in CPR Pt 31, but is now expressly dealt with in the Practice Direction and in the standard form of disclosure statement.[1] A substantial body of case law has developed in the USA where many of the problems with electronic disclosure have been considered.[2] The Federal Rules of Civil Procedure have been revised to take account of electronic disclosure and the modifications confirm that electronically stored information stands on an equal footing with discovery of paper documents.[3] In addition the issues arising from electronic disclosure, but not inspection, are the subject of a report of a committee chaired by Mr Justice Cresswell.[4]

---

[1] CPR, Pt 31, Practice Direction—Disclosure and Inspection, para.2A and Annex, Disclosure Statement; *Admiralty and Commercial Courts Guide* (7th edn, 2006), para.3.11.

[2] *Laura Zubulake v UBS Warburg LLC*, 220 F.R.D. 212, 02 Civ 1243, (2003) 217 F.R.D. 209; *Byers v Illinois State Police*, 53 Fed. R. Serv. 3d 740 (N.D.III, May 31, 2002); *Antioch Co. v Scrapbook Borders Inc*, 210 F.R.D. 645 (D.Minn.2002); *Simon Property Group LP v My Simon Inc*, 194 F.R.D. 639 (S.D. Ind. 2000); *Rowe Entertainment, Inc v The William Morris Agency, Inc*, 205 F.R.D. 421 (S.D.N.Y. 2002); *India Brewing, Inc v Miller Brewing Co.*, 237 F.R.D. 190 (E.D. Wis. 2006). Also useful is the *Sedona Principles: Best Practices, Recommendations & Principles for Addressing Electronic Document Production (Sedona Conference, January 2004)*; cf. Scheindlin S. and Rabin J., "Electronic discovery in Federal Civil Litigation: Is Rule 34 up to the task?" 41 B.C.L. Rev. 327 (1999–2000).

[3] Federal Rules of Civil Procedure, Rule 34, amended as of December 1, 2006; Paul G.L., *The Discovery Revolution: E-Discovery Amendments to the Federal Rules of Civil Procedure* (American Bar Association, 2006).

[4] *Electronic Disclosure: A report of a working party chaired by Mr Justice Cresswell dated 6 October 2004*. Much of this chapter is derived from this report. Clive Freedman, Jonathan Mass and Jeff Ourvan have made valuable contributions to this chapter.

A. WHAT ARE ELECTRONIC DOCUMENTS?

7.02   As has been seen CPR r.31.4 defines "documents" widely as meaning anything in which information of any description is recorded.[5] In *Derby & Co. Ltd v Weldon (No.9)*[6] it was held that a computer database so far as it contained information capable of being retrieved and converted into readable form is a document. Thus the document so far as electronic disclosure is concerned is the database on which the information is stored, whether it be a computer, the hard disk, the CD-ROM etc. The definition of document is a very wide one and clearly covers computer databases[7] and e-mail,[8] word processed documents, imaged documents and metadata held on computer databases and even includes electronic documents that have been "deleted".[9] Also included are electronically recorded communications and activities such as instant messaging, voice-mail, on-line systems and multimedia files.[10] The Australian Courts have also taken the view that document is to be approached generally to encompass the electronic storage media, rather than at a more specific level by reference to where each item of information is recorded. The latter will constitute in itself part of an electronic record, which in turn is a discrete document. Thus the Australian Courts have ordered disclosure of electronic records, such as computer files and CD-ROMs and this has been the case even where the CD-ROM, tapes or other electronic devices include a wide range of other information not relevant to the case.[11]

7.03   The various types of electronically held data can be categorised in a number of ways, and they include the following[12]:

   (1) *Active or online data*: This is data which is directly accessible on the desktop computer. Online storage is used in the very active

---

[5] See Ch.5, paras 5.01 to 5.07; *Admiralty and Commercial Courts Guide* (7th edn, 2006) para.E3.11(a).

[6] [1992] 2 All E.R. 901, Vinelott J.

[7] *Molton v Tectronix UK Holdings* [2003] EWHC 383 (Ch).

[8] *Chantrey Vellacott v The Convergence Group Plc*, February 3, 2006, Ch.D. (unreported).

[9] CPR, Pt.31, Practice Direction, para.2A.1.

[10] Categories of "document" available for e-discovery in the US, include voicemail, computer security logs (including firewall router/access logs, server access and login records, print queue logs) and physical security logs (including door access logs, garage access logs, and security video camera recordings).

[11] *London Electronics (Aus) Pty Ltd v Frontier Economics Pty Ltd* [1999] F.C.A. 932; *Wimmera Industrial Minerals Pty Ltd v RGC Mineral Sands Ltd* [1998] F.C.A. 299; *Sony Music Entertainment (Australia) Ltd v University of Tasmania* [2003] F.C.A. 532 at [49–54].

[12] These are not exhaustive, and are not mutually exclusive. *Zubulake v UBS Warburg LLC* (2003) 217 F.R.D. 219 splits data into five categories: 1. active, online data; 2. near-line data; 3. offline storage/archives; 4. back-up tapes; and 5. erased, fragmented or damaged data.

steps of an electronic record's life, when it is being created or received and processed, as well as when the access frequency is high and the required speed of access is fast. Examples of such data include material held on hard drives, filed documents and inbox and sent items in an email system.

(2) *Embedded data*: This includes data which is not normally visible when a document is printed although it can be viewed on the screen. Examples are formulae for spreadsheets and calculations which are programmed into a system, but are not usually visible on print-outs. Some types of data may not be retrievable when using a software program in the usual way, such as hidden data revealing the identity of persons who have edited a word-processing file.

(3) *Metadata*: Metadata is data about data, such as details of the date and time when data files are created, edited or printed and by whom these steps were taken. Metadata is also not normally visible when a document is printed, although it can be viewed on the screen.

(4) *Replicant data* (also referred to as "temporary files"): This is data which has been automatically created by the computer. Many programs have an automatic backup feature which creates and periodically saves copies of a file as the user works on it. These are intended to assist recovery of data caused by computer malfunction, power failure or when the computer is turned off without the user saving the data. Examples of such data include automatic saves of draft documents, temporary copies of open email attachments, recovered files automatically available following a computer malfunction, and the temporary cache of visited web pages created by internet browser software.

(5) *Back-up data*: This is data held in a storage system. On the most basic level, it can consist of offline storage in the form of a removable optical disk or magnetic tape media, which can be labelled and stored on a shelf (in contrast with near line data which is directly accessible from the computer and is readily accessible). Most organisations use back-up data to preserve information in case of a disaster. This can take various forms ranging from copying information stored on the system to a back-up system in the form of magnetic tapes or by sending files over the internet to a third party's computer (some companies even offer computer users free storage space on their websites). The disadvantage with back-up systems is that usually the data is compressed and can be difficult and costly to retrieve.

(6) *Residual data*: This is material deleted from the user's active data and then stored elsewhere on the hard disk drive. Deleting a file

or email removes it from the user's active data; instead the data is stored elsewhere and can become fragmented. The data may still be retrievable with sufficient expertise and time, although there are programs and methods which are designed to make the data impossible (or very much harder) to retrieve.[13]

7.04   Computer-based disclosure is in some respects very different from paper-based disclosure. In one US case the court noted some of the differences[14]:

> "Computer files, including emails, are discoverable . . . However the Court is not persuaded by the plaintiffs' attempt to equate traditional paper-based discovery with the discovery of email files . . . Chief among these differences it the sheer volume of electronic information. Emails have replaced other forms of communication besides just paper-based communications. Many informal messages that were previously relayed by telephone or at the water cooler are now sent by email. Additionally, computers have the ability to capture several copies (or drafts) of the same email, thus multiplying the volume of documents. All of these emails must be scanned for both relevance and privilege. Also, unlike most paper-based discovery, archived emails typically lack a coherent filing system. Moreover, dated archival systems commonly store information on magnetic tapes which have become obsolete. Thus, parties incur additional costs in translating the data from the tapes into usable form."

7.05   In considering electronic disclosure, it is important to recognise and take account of the substantial differences between disclosure of such documents compared with paper documents. The differences arise from the following:

(1) The huge volume of documents which are created and stored electronically. Businesses can generate literally hundreds of thousands of emails. Computers have the ability to capture many copies and drafts of the same electronic documents and create large databases. A single computer tape or disc can hold up to 100 million pages. Even Blackberrys and other PDAs are able to hold a very large number of files of data. Searching for relevant documents amongst electronically held documents and then

---

[13] *Prest v Marc Rich & Co. Investment AG* [2006] EWHC 927 (Comm.), where steps were taken to wipe the hard disk of a laptop computer.
[14] *Byers v Illinois State Police*, 53 Fed. R. Serv. 3d 740 (N.D. III May 31, 2002), Magistrate Judge Nolan.

reviewing all the documents produced by a search may be extremely time consuming and costly.[15]

(2) Electronic documents are more easily duplicated than paper documents. Email users frequently send the same email to a large number of recipients who then reply, copying in other recipients, or forward the message onto others. Spreadsheets and databases held electronically can also be more easily modified than paper documents, and the computer stores in its memory details of all the modifications. This increases the amount of data held and adds to the complexity of disclosure.

(3) The lack of order in which electronic documents are stored.

(4) The differing retention policies of the parties. Many businesses have policies of destroying documents as part of a routine document retention policy, and policies for electronic documents may be different from policies for paper documents.[16]

(5) Electronic documents, unlike paper documents, contain metadata, which is information about the document or file which is recorded in the computer, such as the dates of creation and modification of the document, and the authorship history and details of the route an email has followed. Not only will it often be necessary to review the metadata, but the documents themselves and the metadata must be reviewed with care to avoid alteration of the metadata.

(6) Electronic documents are more difficult to dispose of than paper documents. Deleting an email or an electronic file (whether deliberately or accidentally) does not automatically erase the data from the computer's storage system. The deletion of an electronic document may be a contempt of court once an order for disclosure has been made.[17] Moreover electronic documents may be manipulated (again, either deliberately or accidentally). In addition there is the risk of unauthorised hacking into computers and interception of messages.[18]

(7) Inspection and provision of copies creates its own difficulties. The relevant electronic document may contain privileged or irrelevant

---

[15] See e.g. *Hands v Morrison Construction Services Ltd* [2006] EWHC 2018 (Ch.), where Briggs J. declined to order pre-action disclosure of electronic documents (despite an offer by the applicant to meet the cost) on the ground that it would be excessively burdensome (but making a limited order for disclosure of hard copy documents instead).

[16] However "a corporation cannot blindly destroy documents and expect to be shielded by a seemingly innocuous document retention policy": *Lewy v Remington Arms Co.*, 836 F. 2d 1104 at 1112.

[17] *Alliance & Leicester Building Society v Ghahremani* (1992) 32 R.V.R. 198 (deletion of document stored on computer disk contempt of court); see also *Prest v Marc Rich & Co. Investment AG* [2006] EWHC 927 (Comm.). In respect of destruction of documents pre-litigation see Ch.13, para.13.18, below.

[18] *Ashton Investments v Rusal* [2006] EWHC 2545 (Comm.), where alleged defendants hacked into claimant's computer system.

material.[19] Further, the parties may use differing computer programs, proprietary software or outdated software. Data may become corrupted when used on another party's system, or may not be usable on another party's system.

B. DUTY OF SEARCH

7.06 The recognition of the differences between electronic disclosure and paper based disclosure and the substantial growth in electronically held information and computer use, has led to revisions to the Practice Direction accompanying CPR Pt.31. The changes followed the *Report on Electronic Disclosure of the working party chaired by Mr Justice Cresswell* in 2004. The Practice Direction focuses on the duty of search and form of disclosure statement.[20]

7.07 When giving standard disclosure, a party is required to make a reasonable search for documents as provided by CPR r.31.7.[21] Further, when a court makes an order for specific disclosure or inspection under CPR r.31.12, the order may require that a party must carry out a search to the extent stated in the order. The relevant Practice Direction provides that the factors that may be relevant in deciding the reasonableness of a search for electronic documents include the following[22]:

(a) The number of documents involved.
(b) The nature and complexity of the proceedings.
(c) The ease and expense of retrieval of any particular document. This includes:

(i) The accessibility of electronic documents or data including email communications on computer systems, servers, back-up systems and other electronic devices or media that may contain such documents taking into account alterations or developments in hardware or software systems used by the disclosing party and/or available to enable access to such documents.
(ii) The location of relevant electronic documents, data, computer systems, servers, back-up systems and other electronic devices or media that may contain such documents.

---

[19] *Nucleus Information Systems v Palmer* [2003] EWHC 2013 (Ch.). This problem can be particularly acute in the context of search orders: *Celanese Canada Inc. v Murray Demolition Corp.*, 2006 S.C.C. 36, Sup. Ct. of Canada (solicitors who inspected privileged data from electronic records restrained from continuing to act).
[20] CPR, Pt 31, Practice Direction—Disclosure and Inspection, para.2A and Annex, Disclosure Statement; *Admiralty and Commercial Courts Guide* (7th edn, 2006), para.E3.11.
[21] Ch.6, paras 6.28 to 6.30.
[22] CPR, Pt.31, Practice Direction, para.2A.4; *Admiralty and Commercial Courts Guide* (7th edn, 2006), para.E3.11(d).

  (iii) The likelihood of locating relevant data.
  (iv) The cost of recovering any electronic documents.
   (v) The cost of disclosing and providing inspection of any rele-
       vant electronic documents.
  (vi) The likelihood that electronic documents will be materially
       altered in the course of recovery, disclosure or inspection.

 (d) The significance of any document which is likely to be located
     during the search.

It may be reasonable to search some or all of the party's electronic storage   **7.08**
systems. In some circumstances, it may be reasonable to search for electronic documents by means of key word searches (agreed as far as possible
between the parties) even where a full review of each document and every
document would be unreasonable.[23] There may be other forms of electronic
search that may be appropriate in particular circumstances.[24]

The extent to which a party should be expected to search in respect of   **7.09**
information held in electronic form very much depends on the nature of the
case, the issues involved, the relevance of the information and the cost and
practicality of the search as reflected in the overriding objective, CPR r.31.7
and the Practice Direction. It will be rarely appropriate to require a party to
obtain deleted emails or other documents or to have go to the expense of
engaging an IT specialist to recover such material as part of an order for
standard disclosure. On the other hand, there may be circumstances where
it is necessary and appropriate to do so where a key document is involved
and there is an issue as to whether or not a party received it. Nevertheless,
the Practice Direction makes clear that a document which has been apparently "deleted" remains a document within the meaning of the rules.[25]
Metadata, which includes additional information stored and associated
with electronic documents, may also be disclosable as it may show who has
opened or altered a particular document at any particular time and it may
be possible to display tracked changes in a document; where metadata may
have to be disclosed, care must be taken to avoid inadvertent alteration of
metadata while accessing electronic documents. Further, there are types of
documents such as spreadsheets which may be incomplete without the
embedded formulae.

The approach in the USA in relation to documents which are expensive to   **7.10**
retrieve, such as deleted computer files, has been to adopt a practice of cost-
shifting where the cost burden of conducting discovery is shifted onto the

---

[23] See paras 7.11–7.12 below.
[24] CPR, Pt.31, Practice Direction, para.2A.5; *Admiralty and Commercial Courts* Guide (7th
 edn, 2006), para.E3.11(e); see also *Sony Music Entertainment (Australia) Ltd v University
 of Tasmania* [2003] F.C.A. 532 (defined electronic search involving specified words).
[25] CPR, Pt.31, Practice Direction, para.2A.1.

applicant for the discovery.[26] This is an approach that has not yet been followed in England which so far has taken the approach that if a disclosure exercise is going to be unduly burdensome and costly to the respondent to an application, then the application for disclosure should be refused, rather than making an order that the applicant pay for the costs of the exercise.[27]

7.11 In practice disputes arise between the parties as to the extent of the searches to be undertaken for relevant documents. Many parties limit their searches for electronic documents to active data, rather than a more costly exercise of searching back-up data. In cases where there is a large amount of electronic documents, parties will often make use of key word searches for the purposes of identifying relevant documents to be reviewed. Simply handing over to the other side or providing access to the computer hard drive is usually not a viable option, particularly as the hard drive will often contain a mass of irrelevant material, some of which may be confidential or privileged. Moreover, the use of key word searches alone will rarely be sufficient to ensure that disclosure is given of all documents which fall within standard disclosure; it will usually be necessary for the email accounts of the persons most closely involved to be searched visually by a member of the legal team.

7.12 The volume of information stored electronically can be overwhelming and thus parties are expected to be sensible both in the searches that they undertake and the demands being made on the opposing party. The parties should, prior to the first Case Management Conference, discuss any issues that may arise regarding searches for and the preservation of electronic documents. This may involve the parties providing information about the categories of electronic documents within their control, their computer systems and software, electronic devices and media in and on which any relevant documents may be held, the storage systems maintained by the parties and their document retention policies.[28] Where key word searches are to be used, it is likely to be important for the parties to discuss not only the key words to be used, but also which types of data should be searched (such as whether back-up data and deleted data should be searched, or whether documents created by certain types of software should be included or excluded), which email accounts or document holders' folders should be searched and the time periods within which the search should be made—the benefits of a key word search may be reduced if the search is carried out

---

[26] *Rowe Entertainment Inc v William Morris Agency Inc*, 205 F.R.D. 421, 431 (S.D.N.Y. 2002) and *Zubulake v UBS Warburg LLC* (2003) 217 F.R.D. 309 (discovery ordered of relevant emails that had been deleted and resided only on back-up discs).

[27] e.g. *Hands v Morrison Construction Services Ltd* [2006] EWHC 2018 (Ch.), referred to above.

[28] Questionnaires which may assist when exchanging this information have been prepared by the LiST Group (*http://www.listgroup.org/publications.htm*) and the Commercial Litigators' Forum (*http://www.sjberwin.com/clf/pdf/electronicdisclosure1004.pdf*).

across too many categories of documents, as the search will identify quantities of irrelevant documents as well as relevant documents. In some cases it may be cost-effective to adopt a staged approach, modifying the search terms and dateranges after the initial results have been reviewed. In the case of difficulty or disagreement, the matter should be referred to a judge for directions at the earliest practical date, if possible at the first Case Management Conference.[29]

C. FORM OF DISCLOSURE

Special consideration needs to be given as to how electronic documents **7.13** are to be listed, the form of disclosure statement and inspection. Whilst in theory, the electronic document is the device on which the data is stored, in practice parties tend to individually list or list by category (where appropriate) the individual items. For example, where a computer holds a number of emails, the list can simply list the relevant emails or list the computer database as including the relevant emails, the remainder on the database being referred to as falling outside the disclosure obligation. In cases involving large numbers of documents it is helpful to prepare the list in a manner which enables the list to be imported into a documents database.[30]

The Disclosure Statement itself specifically provides for electronic docu- **7.14** ments.[31] A party is required to state whether or not he carried out a search for electronic documents and if so, provide a list of what was searched and the extent of search. The standard form requires a party to state what he did not search for. This form of disclosure statement for electronic documents is very helpful as it provides the opposing party and the court information as to what searches had been carried out and what searches could have been carried out but were not.

Inspection of electronically held documents, databases and other types of **7.15** data has its own problems. The parties should co-operate at an early stage as to the format in which electronic copy documents and other data are to be provided on inspection. In the case of difficulty or disagreement, the matter should be referred to a judge for directions at the earliest practical date, if possible at the first Case Management Conference.[32] Inspection of electronic documents and data is dealt with in more detail in Ch.9.[33]

---

[29] CPR, Pt.31, Practice Direction, para.2A.2. There have been cases where judges have had to give specific directions in relation to key words to be used, which email accounts should be searched, and within which time periods.
[30] The LiST Group have prepared guidance on preparing a List of Documents in this form: *http://www.listgroup.org/publications.htm.*
[31] CPR, Pt.31, Practice Direction, Annex—Disclosure Statement.
[32] CPR, Pt.31, Practice Direction, para.2A.3; *Admiralty and Commercial Courts Guide* (7th edn, 2006), para.E3.11(b).
[33] Ch.9, paras 9.23–9.29 below.

CHAPTER 8

Objections to disclosure

CHAPTER 8

Objections to Disclosure

A. INTRODUCTION

The old rules of court distinguished the process of disclosing the existence **8.01** of certain documents ("disclosure")[1] from that of producing them for inspection ("production", or "inspection").[2] Different considerations applied to each stage.[3] The distinction between "discovery" (now "disclosure") and "inspection" is carried over into CPR.[4] In this chapter consideration is given to the grounds upon which a party may properly object, not to producing documents for inspection, but to revealing their existence at all. For ease of reference, these objections are listed here, and then discussed in the succeeding paragraphs:

    (a) actions for penalties[5];
    (b) consent of parties[6];
    (c) Bank of England Act 1998, s.37 and Sch.7[7];
    (d) former objections:

            (i) common informers[8];

---

[1] RSC, Ord.24, rr.1–8.
[2] RSC, Ord.24, rr.9–14; the scheme in the county court (C.C.R., Ord.14) was slightly different.
[3] *Swanston v Lishman* (1881) 45 L.T. 360; *Alfred Crompton Amusement Machines Ltd v Commissioners of Customers & Excise* [1974] A.C. 405 at 429; *Dolling-Baker v Merrett* [1990] 1 W.L.R. 1205, CA; *Ventouris v Mountain* [1991] 1 W.L.R. 607; *cf. Format Communications Mfg. Ltd v I.T.T. (U.K.) Ltd* [1983] F.S.R. 473, CA.
[4] See CPR, rr.31.2, 31.3. But see *Smithkline Beecham Plc v Generics (UK) Ltd* [2003] EWCA Civ 1109 (disclosure in r.31.2 includes voluntary disclosure by a party, e.g. by referring to a document in a witness statement; *sed quaere*).
[5] See para.8.06, below.
[6] See para.8.08, below.
[7] See para.8.09, below.
[8] See para.8.10, below.

(ii) forfeiture[9];

(e) injunctions[10];
(f) documents from previous cases[11];
(g) discretionary objections:

  (i) unlikelihood or absence of relevant documents[12];
  (ii) expense, inconvenience, trouble[13];
  (iii) alternative sources[14];
  (iv) confidentiality of third parties[15];
  (v) exposure of party's trade secrets or other confidential information[16];
  (vi) compliance with foreign legal obligations[17];
  (vii) public interest immunity.[18]

8.02   Unlike the former discovery rules, the CPR do not require disclosure to be given automatically. It has to be ordered by the court. And, except in claims on the small claims track,[19] the disclosure ordered is to be "standard disclosure" unless the court otherwise orders.[20] At first sight, therefore, there is no room for any objection to be taken to disclosing the existence of all "standard disclosure" documents in the List. But it must be noted that:

(a) the court in any event possesses the power to dispense with or limit standard disclosure[21];
(b) the ultimate test of whether disclosure should be done is whether it furthers the "overriding objective",[22] and in particular whether it is proportionate to the value, importance and complexity of the cost and to the parties' resources[23]; and
(c) the disclosing party may state in his List that he has not searched for a category or class of document on the grounds that to do so would be unreasonable.[24]

---

[9] See para.8.10, below.
[10] See para.8.13, below.
[11] See para.8.16, below.
[12] See para.8.19, below.
[13] See para.8.20, below.
[14] See para.8.22, below.
[15] See para.8.23, below.
[16] See para.8.25, below.
[17] See para.8.26, below.
[18] See para.8.27, below.
[19] Where CPR, Pt 31 does not apply: see Ch.5, para.5.11, and Ch.6, para.6.42.
[20] CPR, r.31.5(1); see Ch.5, para.5.10.
[21] CPR, r.31.5(2); see para.5.11.
[22] CPR, rr.1.1, 1.2.
[23] CPR, r.1.1(2)(c).
[24] CPR, r.31.7; see Ch.6, paras 6.03, 6.16, 6.30.

The machinery of disclosure must also be borne in mind. A List of **8.03** Documents may be prepared and served pursuant to CPR, r.31.10.[25] The court may also order "specific disclosure", i.e. to disclose specified documents or classes, or to search for specified documents or classes and then disclose the result.[26] The prescribed form of a List of Documents requires that documents be divided into three classes:

(1) Documents still in the party's control, where inspection is not objected to.
(2) Documents still in the party's control, but where inspection *is* objected to.
(3) Documents no longer in the party's control.[27]

It will be apparent that there is no place, in this scheme of things, for an **8.04** objection to putting the documents concerned into the List at all. Thus it may be thought that the simple position is reached, subject to the minor exceptions and limitations already mentioned,[28] that all relevant documents must be "disclosed", and hence no objection to disclosure can prevail. However, in practice fewer details are given of documents in the second and third classes set out above, than of those in the first class. Details of documents in the third class may be lacking because, *ex hypothesi*, the party no longer has them to refer to. Documents in the second class are usually not listed individually (despite the wording in the prescribed form[29]), but are normally reduced to a series of *classes* of documents, each giving sufficient details of the type as to make clear the nature of the claim made for privilege, but not giving sufficient information to enable the identity, much less the contents, of any particular document to be known. In this way, the existence of such documents in the hands of the party is "disclosed", but nothing more.[30]

Accordingly, although the technical position is that, once a party has been **8.05** ordered to disclose the existence of documents, there can generally be no valid objection to doing so, the practical consequence of a claim to withhold inspection of a document is that the List is unlikely to reveal its *individual* existence. It is therefore necessary to be aware of the circumstances in which a claim to withhold inspection may properly be made. In addition, reasons which may or may not justify a privilege from production may in any event justify the court in limiting the disclosure to be given in the first place.[31]

---

[25] See Ch.6, para.6.01.
[26] CPR, r.31.12(2); see Ch.6, para.6.41.
[27] See Ch.6, para.6.04, above.
[28] See para.8.02, above.
[29] See para.8.03, above.
[30] See Ch.6, para.6.11, above.
[31] See para.8.02, above.

B. OBJECTIONS AS OF RIGHT

8.06   Notwithstanding the general position stated above, if a party has been ordered to give disclosure,[32] and has searched for and found documents,[33] there are three valid objections to giving disclosure that he may put forward. The first objection may be made by a defendant to an action for the recovery of any statutory penalty. It was settled under the old rules that the court would not order discovery in such a case,[34] and there is nothing in the CPR to suggest that the position is now different. The penalty concerned must be penal rather than compensatory in nature.[35] Thus a fine which the EU Commission might impose as a result of a breach of the competition provisions of the Treaty of Rome *is* such a "penalty",[36] but claims for conversion damages pursuant to s.18 of the Copyright Act 1956,[37] or for "additional damages" pursuant to s.17(3) of that Act[38] are *not* (although even if they had been, s.72 of the Supreme Court Act 1981 would now have altered the position). The fact that a penalty may have a "protective" function does not mean that it is not penal as well.[39]

8.07   The question is whether the issue raised by the action relates to the recovery of a penalty and not as to the remedy sought. Thus, where a penalty, damages and an injunction were sought in respect of a cause of action arising under the statute for which a penalty was prescribed, it was held that discovery would not be ordered in relation to the claims for damages and an injunction any more than it would be in relation to the claim for recovery of a penalty.[40]

8.08   The second objection is where the parties have agreed in writing to limit or exclude standard disclosure.[41] Such an agreement may be contained in a larger agreement,[42] or may conceivably be implied, as long as the agreement

---

[32] The disclosure ordered may be less than "standard", or indeed none at all: see Ch.2, para.2.34, and Ch.5, para.5.11.

[33] Bearing in mind the objection to searching to an unreasonable extent: see para.8.02, above and Ch.6, para.6.03.

[34] *Hunnings v Williamson* (1883) 10 Q.B.D. 459; *Martin v Treacher* (1886) 16 Q.B.D. 507, CA.

[35] *Adams v Batley, Cole v Francis* (1887) 18 Q.B.D. 625; *Jones v Jones* (1889) 22 Q.B.D. 425; *Hobbs v Hudson* (1890) 25 Q.B.D. 232; *Sanders v Wiel* [1892] 2 Q.B. 321, CA; *Colne Valley Water Co. v Waterford & St Albans Gas Co.* [1948] 1 K.B. 500, CA.

[36] *Rio Tinto Zinc Corp. v Westinghouse Electric Corp.* [1978] A.C. 547, HL.

[37] *Richmark Camera Services Inc. v Neilson-Hordell Ltd* [1981] F.S.R. 413.

[38] *Overseas Programming Co. Ltd v Cinematographische Comets-Anstalt & Induna Film GmbH, The Times,* May 16, 1984.

[39] *Rich v Australian Securities and Investments Commission* (2004) 220 C.L.R. 129, H.Ct. Aus.

[40] *Colne Valley Water Co. v Watford & St Albans Gas Co.* [1948] 1 K.B. 500, CA.

[41] CPR, r.31.5(2); RSC, Ord.24, r.1(2), specifically disapplied to matrimonial causes: Family Proceedings Rules 1991, r.2.20(1)(a); see also *Whiffen v Hartwright* (1848) 11 Beav. 111; *Turner v Bayley* (1864) 4 De G.J. & Sm. 332.

[42] e.g. one of the Articles of Association of a company: *Berry and Stewart v Tottenham Hotspur Football and Athletic Co. Ltd* [1935] Ch. 718.

in which it is implied is in writing.[43] Strictly speaking, the agreement of the parties cannot oust the jurisdiction of the court to order disclosure, but it is a strong factor to take into account.[44] Any such written agreement should be lodged with the court.[45] The position is even stronger in an arbitration, for the court's former power under s.12(6)(b) of the Arbitration Act 1950 to order discovery has been abrogated[46] and the power of the arbitrator to do so derives solely from the arbitration agreement.[47]

A third objection arises under the Bank of England Act 1998, s.37 and   **8.09** Sch.7, and the Financial Services and Markets Act 2000, s.348, containing provisions which in substance were formerly contained in the Banking Act 1987, s.82. It was held under the former legislation that s.82, by rendering criminal disclosure of information received under the Act relating to the affairs of "any person", prevented disclosure in lists of documents of documents containing such information.[48] However, the judge in that case based his view on authority[49] relating to a statutory prohibition on the production of documents to the court by a third party pursuant to a witness summons, and the distinction between disclosure of the existence of documents, and objection to producing them, was not adverted to. In a more recent case under s.348 of the 2000 Act, it appears to have been agreed that the statutory rule did not forbid disclosure of the *existence* of such documents, nor did it forbid *inspection* of documents to the extent that they contained information not obtained directly or indirectly by the statutory body under its legal powers.[50] The judge moreover held[51] that the statute did not forbid inspection of documents so far as containing information which the statutory body had so obtained where that information was independently

---

[43] *cf. Rabin v Mendoza & Co.* [1954] 1 W.L.R. 271, CA (a case of production rather than discovery).

[44] *cf. Bank of Baroda v Panesar* [1987] Ch. 335, concerning an agreement to pay indemnity costs.

[45] CPR, Pt 31, Practice Direction, Disclosure and Inspection, para.1.4; *cf. Admiralty and Commercial Court Guide* (7th edn, 2006), s.E.

[46] Courts and Legal Services Act 1990, s.103.

[47] *cf. Bank Mellat v Helliniki S.A.* [1984] Q.B. 291, an application for security for costs, and see Ch.20, para.20.04, below.

[48] *Bank of Credit and Commerce International (Overseas) Ltd v Price Waterhouse* [1998] Ch. 84; see also *Re Galileo Group Ltd* [1999] Ch. 100, and *cf. Barings Plc v Coopers & Lybrand* [2000] 3 All E.R. 910, CA. In *A v B* (2002) 4 I.T.E.L.R. 877, the High Court of the Cook Islands rejected the view that s.23 of the International Trusts Act 1984 (creating an offence of communicating information about an international trust to another person) prevented discovery from being given in a trust action.

[49] *Rowell v Pratt* [1938] A.C. 101, HL.

[50] *Real Estate Opportunities Ltd v Aberdeen Asset Managers Jersey Ltd* [2006] 2006] EWHC 3249 (Ch.); indeed, the judge said that the documents "should have been separately listed, except where the description of the document would itself disclose confidential information contrary to" the statute: para.58.

[51] Following *Arbuthnott v Fagan* [1996] 1 L.R.L.R. 143, CA, decided under a byelaw made by virtue of the Lloyd's Acts 1871 to 1982, and *Re Galileo Group Ltd* [1999] Ch. 100.

known to the disclosing party. This will usually mean that information not so known must be redacted out of the documents.[52]

8.10   Two classes of case where discovery could not be ordered under the old rules should be specifically mentioned, because although they no longer represent English law there are many references to them in the older cases[53] and they continue in effect in at least some common law jurisdictions.[54] The first is the case of the action for penalties brought by a "common informer", a procedure by which any person could sue a doer of certain prohibited acts for penalties, and which was abolished by the Common Informers Act 1951. In such cases discovery could not be ordered at all.[55] The second is the case of an action to forfeit a property interest, e.g. a lease. In this case too, no discovery could be ordered.[56] The "forfeiture" privilege was abolished by s.16(1)(a) of the Civil Evidence Act 1968, for non-criminal cases. It should be noted that, in all remaining non-statutory penalty cases, the privilege against self-incrimination may prevent production of documents for inspection, but does not prevent disclosure of their existence.[57] Finally, it should be noted that the former objection as of right to the Crown disclosing documents protected by public interest immunity has been replaced by a discretionary objection extending to all who have such documents in their control. This is dealt with later.[58]

C. PRIVILEGE FROM PRODUCTION FOR INSPECTION

8.11   There are a number of classes of document which may be withheld from inspection in the disclosure process. They are dealt with more fully in Ch.11, but for completeness they are also listed here:

> (1) documents covered by legal professional privilege, which is either legal advice privilege or litigation privilege;
>
> (2) documents covered by public interest immunity;
>
> (3) documents tending to criminate the party or his spouse or expose him (her) to a penalty;

---

[52] As to redaction, see Ch.9, paras 9.37–9.38 below.

[53] In "running-down" actions, discovery was not automatic, but could in theory be ordered by the court: RSC, Ord.24, r.2(2).

[54] e.g. Australia: *Daniels Corporation International Pty Ltd v Australian Compensation and Consumer Commission* (2002) 213 C.L.R. 543, at para.13; *Rich v Australian Securities and Investments Commission* (2004) 220 C.L.R. 129, H.Ct.Aus.

[55] *Martin v Treacher* (1886) 16 Q.B.D. 507, CA; *Mexborough v Whitwood U.D.C.* [1897] 2 Q.B. 111 at 115.

[56] *Mexborough v Whitwood U.D.C.* [1897] 2 Q.B. 111; *Seddon v Commercial Salt Co. Ltd* [1925] Ch. 198, CA; cf. *Mascherpa v Direck Ltd* [1960] 1 W.L.R. 447, CA.

[57] See Ch.11, para.11.109, below.

[58] See para.8.27, below.

(4) "without prejudice" communications;
(5) witness statement privilege;
(6) diplomatic privilege;
(7) documents privileged by virtue of specific statutory provisions, such as the Legal Aid Act 1988, s.38, the Bank of England Act 1998, s.37 and Sch.7, or the Financial Services and Markets Act 2000, s.348.

With three exceptions, the *existence* of documents falling within these classes of case must still be disclosed by the litigant by including them in his List.[59] One of the exceptions relates to cases of penalties made recoverable by virtue of any enactment, where neither discovery nor production will be ordered.[60] The second relates to s.82 of the Banking Act 1987. As already mentioned, this was held to prohibit disclosure in a list of documents, as well as production for inspection.[61] The third exception is the case of documents covered by public interest immunity, where the court orders that their existence should not be disclosed.[62]   **8.12**

D. INJUNCTIONS

A rather different problem arises where a party to litigation is already subject, in prior proceedings, to an injunction or other order of the court restraining him from disclosing documents the existence of which in the ordinary course he would have to disclose in subsequent proceedings. The first question to be addressed is one of scope: does the prior injunction on its true construction seek to restrain the party from disclosing the *existence* of documents, or merely from disclosing their *contents*? If only the latter, then the party faces no difficulties at this stage—he may disclose the existence of the documents without a breach of the order in the first proceedings. As to the question of construction, there is little authority and, in the nature of things, there can be no general guidance, for each case is different. However, in one case it was held that an injunction to restrain a bank from disclosing the contents of certain documents to any third party was no answer to a notice under s.39 of the Banking Act 1987 requiring the bank   **8.13**

---

[59] See, e.g. *Spokes v Grosvenor and West End Railway Terminus Hotel Co. Ltd* [1897] 2 Q.B. 124, CA; *National Association of Operative Plasterers v Smithies* [1906] A.C. 434, HL; *British Leyland Motor Corp Ltd v T. I. Silencers Ltd* [1979] F.S.R. 591 at 602; *A J Bekhor & Co. Ltd v Bilton* [1981] Q.B. 923, CA.
[60] See para.8.06, above.
[61] See para.8.09, above.
[62] See para.8.27, below.

to produce some of those documents for inspection by the Bank of England.[63] In another case,[64] guidance was given on the procedure to be adopted where a financial institution considered that, were it to comply with a disclosure order, it would or might thereby commit a criminal offence under the "tipping-off" provisions in the Criminal Justice Act 1988, s.93D.[65]

8.14   If, on its true construction, the injunction is wide enough to forbid the party even to disclose the existence of certain documents in its List of Documents, and assuming that the injunction has not been granted by a foreign court,[66] the party finds himself in an impossible position. Either he discloses the existence of the documents, and thus breaches the injunction, or he does not mention the documents, and thus deliberately fails to comply with the disclosure order. He could of course have applied to the court in the second proceedings, when disclosure was being considered, for a limitation on the disclosure to be given,[67] but that might have revealed the very existence of documents to his opponent that the injunction forbids. Moreover, the claimant in the first proceedings, whose interest is in preventing such disclosure, would have no right to notice of, or to appear on, that application (though if he knew about it he could presumably apply to be joined in the second proceedings).

8.15   It would seem that the preferable course is for the party to apply to the court in the first proceedings for directions or a variation of the injunction to permit compliance with his disclosure obligations in the second proceedings.[68] If necessary or appropriate, the other party in the second proceedings can be invited to intervene in those proceedings, so that all parties are before the same court.[69] It might be thought that it should matter whether the party is claimant or defendant in the second proceedings, i.e. whether he had any choice as to getting involved in the discovery process, but it is submitted that it would be unjust to distinguish the two cases. These days it is often accidental which of two parties is claimant and which is defendant, often depending on which party is bold enough to take the law into his own hands, leaving the other to go to court. Besides, it is harsh in effect to punish someone for attempting to vindicate his rights.

---

[63] *A v B Bank* [1993] Q.B. 311.

[64] *C v S* [1999] 2 All E.R. 343, CA.

[65] Now replaced by the Proceeds of Crime Act 2002, s.333, but subject to a defence for "professional legal advisers" who make a disclosure "to any person in connection with legal proceedings" (s.333(3)), which is wide enough to cover *their* compliance with litigation disclosure procedures, though not their clients'.

[66] When different considerations apply: *cf. X. A.G. v A Bank* [1983] 2 All E.R. 464, and see Ch.11, para.11.146, below.

[67] CPR, r.31.5(2); see para.8.02, above.

[68] See, e.g. *Adham v B.C.C.I.* [1995] 2 B.C.L.C. 581; *El Jawhary v B.C.C.I.* [1993] B.C.L.C. 396.

[69] As happened in *Adham v B.C.C.I.* [1995] 2 B.C.L.C. 581, and see also *A v B Bank* [1993] Q.B. 311.

E. DOCUMENTS FROM PREVIOUS CASES

A similar problem arises when a party obtains copy documents[70] from his **8.16** opponent by disclosure in one set of proceedings and subsequently find that they are relevant to a second set of proceedings in which he is now involved. The r.31.22 obligation (formerly the implied undertaking on discovery)[71] while it lasts certainly means that he cannot make use of those documents in the second proceedings without the permission of his erstwhile opponent and the owner of the documents, or of the court. However, it seems doubtful that the obligation prevents the party from at least disclosing that the documents exist, by listing them in the second of the three classes in the List of Documents. To that extent the problem is less than where injunctions are concerned, where there will also be the preliminary question of construction involved. In Australia it has been held that the implied obligation on discovery in one action must yield to inconsistent statutory provisions and to the requirements of curial process in other litigation, such as discovery and inspection.[72] Thus it has also been held that in a subsequent action the court could order discovery of a document which had been disclosed in an earlier one without an application needing to be made to the court in the earlier action for a release or modification of the undertaking.[73]

A similar question arises in relation to arbitrations, although the obliga- **8.17** tion of confidentiality in relation to the (first) arbitration proceedings is (in English law, at least) founded on contract, not the general law.[74] But the obligation is subject to exceptions, such as where it is subsequently neces- sary to protect the legitimate interests of an arbitrating party,[75] and also to any order of the court.[76] The latter exception would normally cover the case of an action in court following an arbitration.[77]

F. OTHER OBJECTIONS

A number of other objections to giving disclosure may sometimes be put **8.18** forward. These include:

---

[70] Documents still in the possession of the other party, which the party may inspect, are not within the party's power at all: Ch.5, para.5.53, above.
[71] See Ch.15, para.15.03, below.
[72] *Esso Australia Resources Ltd v Plowman* (1995) 183 C.L.R. 10 at 33, H.Ct.Aus.; *Austra- lian Securities Commission v Ampolex Ltd* (1995) 38 N.S.W.L.R. 504.
[73] *Patrick v Capital Finance Pty Ltd (No.4)* [2003] F.C.A. 436, Fed.Ct.Aus.
[74] *Dolling-Baker v Merrett* [1990] 1 W.L.R. 1205; *Hassneh Insurance Co. of Israel v Mew* [1993] 2 Lloyd's Rep. 243; *Insurance Co. v Lloyd's Syndicate* [1995] 1 Lloyd's Rep. 272; *Ali Shipping Corporation v Shipyard Trogir* [1999] 1 W.L.R 314, CA; see generally Ch.15, paras 15.47–14.48.
[75] *Hassneh Insurance Co. of Israel v Mew* [1993] 2 Lloyd's Rep. 243; *cf. El Jawhary v B.C.C.I.* [1993] B.C.L.C. 396.
[76] *Ali Shipping Corporation v Shipyard Trogir* [1999] 1 W.L.R. 314 at 327, CA.
[77] *ibid.*

(1) unlikelihood of relevant documents being in existence;
(2) expense, inconvenience or trouble in complying;
(3) existence of alternative sources of same information;
(4) threat to confidentiality of third parties;
(5) threat to trade secrets or other confidential information belonging to the party;
(6) compliance with foreign legal obligations;
(7) public interest immunity.

In general none of these is an objection *as of right* to giving disclosure. But they may be factors tending to influence the court in the exercise of its discretion to limit disclosure.[78] In the past, the "cards on the table" approach to litigation[79] meant that the court rarely exercised its discretion to limit or not to order discovery. But the culture is now different under the CPR Disclosure is not longer automatic but must always be ordered, and that which is regularly ordered is narrower than before. The court will consider what is needed in each case.

(a) Unlikelihood or absence of relevant documents

8.19   The court may dispense with disclosure in the exercise of its discretion where no issue arises in the action in relation to which relevant documents are likely to exist.[80] Even if the respondent says he has no documents of the category requested, this is not in itself an answer to an otherwise proper request, though a statement to that effect on oath (or verified by a statement of truth) may be a reason why, in the exercise of the court's discretion, it should not make the order.[81] If the court makes the order, but does not rule on the extent of the search required, the party concerned may still respond that he has not searched to an extent he considers unreasonable.[82]

(b) Expense, inconvenience, trouble

8.20   Even under the old rules it was held that the court would exercise a proper control over any attempt to press for vexatious or oppressive discovery.[83] However, the mere fact that discovery was expensive, inconvenient or

---

[78] In the case of public interest immunity, the discretion has a has a special statutory basis: see para.8.26, below.
[79] *Khan v Armaguard Ltd* [1994] 1 W.L.R. 1204, CA.
[80] See, e.g. *Downing v Falmouth United Sewerage Board* (1887) 37 Ch.D. 234, CA; *Edelston v Russell* (1888) 57 L.T. 927.
[81] *Berkeley Administration Inc. v McClelland* [1990] F.S.R. 381 at 382–383; *Glaverbel S.A. v British Coal Corp.* [1992] F.S.R. 642.
[82] See para.8.02, above, and Ch.6, paras 6.03, 6.16, 6.30.
[83] *Elmer v Creasy* (1873) L.R. 9 Ch.App. 69 at 73 to 74; *Saull v Browne* (1874) L.R. 9 Ch.App. 364 at 367.

troublesome to give was no objection in itself, but went to discretion.[84] Thus, in one case where it was speculatively alleged that the defendant was the plaintiff's agent, the court refused to allow discovery of the accounts of the defendant's private business, as vexatious or unreasonable.[85] And in another[86] the judge said that:

"An order may be refused on the ground that it is unduly oppressive to the party giving discovery. The court takes account of such considerations as the value of the discovery to the person seeking it and the burden imposed on the party giving it, with a view to restricting the volume of documents and the labour and expense involved to that which is necessary for fairly disposing of the issues in the case."

So, where an insured sought discovery (in an action to avoid the policy for non-disclosure) from the insurer of documents relating to other policies where disclosure of the same kind had been made, the Court of Appeal refused to make the order, Greene M.R. saying that the oppressive nature of the order outweighed the negligible probative value the discovery might have.[87]

These objections may be thought to have become much more important **8.21** under the CPR. Indeed, the present rules are narrower than the former *because* they have taken those objections into account. Disclosure is normally limited to standard disclosure,[88] and only a "reasonable" search for documents has to be made.[89] Pure copies need not be disclosed.[90] Any disclosure order made must satisfy the "overriding objective" test,[91] and it is now an objection to permitting inspection that it would be disproportionate to the issues to do so.[92] Moreover the court has power to make appropriate costs orders where a party has behaved unreasonably or improperly.[93] Indeed it can require security to be given as a condition of

---

[84] *Berkeley Administration Inc. v McClelland* [1990] F.S.R. 381 at 384; and see *Minories Finance Ltd v Arthur Young*, March 31, 1988, unreported, Henry J.
[85] *Great Western Colliery Co. v Tucker* (1874) L.R. 9 Ch.App. 376 at 378; see also *Att.Gen. v North Metropolitan Tramways Co.* [1892] 3 Ch. 70, CA; *Petre v Sutherland* (1887) 3 T.L.R. 275, CA; *cf. Hall v L.N.W.R. Co.* (1879) 35 L.T. 848.
[86] *Molnlycke AB v Procter & Gamble Ltd (No.3)* [1990] R.P.C. 498 at 503; see also *West Midland Passenger Executive v Singh* [1988] 2 All E.R. 873 at 878; *Vickers v Horsell Graphic Industries* [1988] R.P.C. 421; *Berkeley Administration Ltd v McClelland*, May 1, 1991, unreported, CA.
[87] *Merchants' and Manufacturers' Insurance Co. Ltd v Davies* [1938] 1 K.B. 196 at 208; see also *David Kahn Inc. v Conway Stewart & Co. Ltd* [1972] F.S.R. 169 at 175; *Baldock v Addison* [1995] 1 W.L.R. 158; *cf. Equiticorp Industries Group v Hawkins* [1994] 2 N.Z.L.R. 738, H.Ct. of N.Z. (principal might have to take proceedings to obtain documents held by agent).
[88] See para.8.02, above.
[89] See para.8.02, above, and Ch.5, para.5.03, 5.16, 5.30.
[90] See Ch.5, para.5.09.
[91] See para.8.02, above.
[92] See Ch.11, para.11.156, below.
[93] See Ch.13, para.13.37, below.

making an order.[94] But paradoxically these changes—and particularly the objection to inspection—may make it less likely that these objections will prevent a disclosure order being made in the first place. The order will be narrower, and sanctions for abuse are available. But an order of some sort will generally still be made.

(c) Alternative sources

8.22　Similarly, the fact that the party seeking the disclosure can obtain the information elsewhere is not in itself an objection.[95] However, it is a factor to be taken into account by the court in deciding whether the disclosure sought would operate oppressively,[96] or whether confidential reports containing sensitive information should be disclosed.[97]

(d) Confidentiality of third parties

8.23　The objection being considered here is confidentiality pure and simple, not amounting to public interest immunity.[98] As Lord Wilberforce said in *Science Research Council v Nasse*[99]:

> "There is no principle in English law by which documents are protected from discovery by reason of confidentiality alone. But there is no reason why, in the exercise of its discretion to order discovery, the [court] should not have regard to the fact that the documents are confidential, and that to order disclosure would involve a breach of confidence."[100]

8.24　In that case it was held that, in order for the court to decide whether the discovery concerned was necessary, the court "should inspect the documents", considering whether special measures (e.g. covering up certain material, or hearing *in camera*) should be adopted, and following procedures which would avoid delay and unnecessary applications.[101] Thus in

---

[94] See Ch.13, para.13.05, below (the county court already enjoyed this power: C.C.R., Ord.13, r.1(1)(a)).
[95] *Hodsoll v Taylor* (1873) L.R. 9 Q.B. 79 at 83; *Rew v Hutchins* (1861) 10 C.B. (N.S.) 829 at 837; *Lyell v Kennedy* (1883) 8 App.Cas. 217 at 228; *cf. Bird v Malzy* (1856) 1 C.B. (N.S.) 308.
[96] *Att.Gen. v North Metropolitan Tramways Co.* [1892] 3 Ch.70.
[97] *Science Research Council v Nassé* [1980] A.C. 1028 at 1085; *Air Canada v Secretary of State for Trade (No.2)* [1983] 2 A.C. 394.
[98] As to which see Ch.11, paras 11.81–11.103.
[99] [1980] A.C. 1028 at 1065.
[100] See also *Wheeler v Le Marchant* (1991) 17 Ch.D. 675; *D. v N.S.P.C.C.* [1978] A.C. 171, HL; *Arab Monetary Fund v Hashim (No.5)* [1992] 2 All E.R. 911 at 915; *Douglas v Pindling* [1996] A.C. 890, P.C.; *Cooper Flynn v RTE* [2001] 1 I.L.R.M. 208.
[101] *Science Research Council v Nassé* [1980] A.C. 1028, at 1066; *quaere* whether "should inspect" ought not to read "may inspect."

one case an education authority was ordered to disclose reports of teachers, psychologists and psychiatrists upon a pupil who had assaulted the plaintiff teacher, after inspection by the court, and notwithstanding their confidential nature.[102] Considerations where inspection is being sought rather than disclosure are not quite the same.[103] The non-disclosure provisions of the Data Protection Act 1984 did not prevent disclosure being given of relevant computer data.[104] Similarly, there is nothing to stop an individual who has been refused access to data under the Data Protection Act 1998 seeking access to the same data in a specific disclosure application in the course of proceedings alleging a breach of the Act itself.[105] In cases under the CPR the court must now take into account the "overriding objective",[106] so that applications for disclosure which invade the confidence of others for a disproportionately small benefit may be refused.[107]

(e) Exposure of the party's trade secrets or other confidential information

As with third party confidentiality, the fact that giving disclosure would 8.25 involve the loss of the party's own trade secrets or confidences is no answer in itself. Indeed, since it is the party's and not even a third party's confidence which is threatened, the position is *a fortiori*. But the court will more closely scrutinise the disclosure sought, to ensure that it truly is material and not oppressive.[108] Although disclosure will normally have to be given, protective limitations may be (and often are) introduced at the stage of inspection.[109]

(f) Compliance with foreign legal obligations

The court may take into account, in deciding whether to order disclosure, 8.26 the fact that compliance with the order would or might entail a breach of foreign law. But to make the objection good, it must be shown that the

---

[102] *Campbell v Tameside Metropolitan Borough Council* [1982] Q.B. 1065, CA.
[103] See Ch.11, paras 11.01–11.02, below.
[104] *Rowley v Liverpool City Council, The Times,* October 26, 1989, CA; and see Ch.11, para.11.152, below. Presumably the same will apply to the Data Protection Act 1998, when it comes into force.
[105] *Johnson v Medical Defence Union Ltd* [2005] F.S.R. 657, Ch.D.
[106] See Ch.1, para.1.30 above.
[107] *Simba-Tola (Abena) v Elizabeth Fry Hostel (Trustees)* [2001] E.W.C.A. Civ. 1371; see also Ch.11, para.11.156 below.
[108] *Great Western Colliery Co. v Tucker* (1874) L.R. 9 Ch.App. 376, CA; *Moore v Craven* (1870) L.R. 7 Ch.App. 94n; *Carver v Pinto Leite* (1871) L.R. 7 Ch.App. 90; *Janson v Solarte* (1836) 2 Y. & Co. 127 at 136; see also *Aktiebolaget Hassle v Pacific Pharmaceuticals Ltd* [1991] 3 N.Z.L.R. 186.
[109] See Ch.9, paras 9.142–9.148, below.

foreign law concerned forbids, not merely disclosing the *contents* of the relevant documents, but their very existence. If it is only the former, the objection is left to the stage of inspection.[110] It will also need to be shown that the foreign law concerned contains no exception for legal proceedings, and that it is not just a text, or an empty vessel, but is regularly enforced, so that the threat to the party is real.[111] Even so, the court has a discretion and, on the basis that English litigation is to be played according to English and not foreign rules, it will rarely be persuaded not to make a disclosure order on this ground.[112]

(g) Public interest immunity

8.27   Under the old rules a discovery order against the Crown did not require the Crown to give discovery (i.e. disclose the *existence*) of documents protected by public interest immunity.[113] That has now gone. Instead, there is a more general provision in the CPR, that a person may apply, without notice, for an order permitting him to withhold disclosure of a document on the ground that disclosure would damage the public interest.[114] The application must be supported by evidence.[115] The court may require the document concerned to be produced to the court, and may invite any other person to make representatives.[116] There is no rule *requiring* the court to make such an order, so it is a matter of discretion. But unless the court otherwise orders, any such order that it does make must not be served on, or open to inspection by any other person.[117]

(h) RSC, Order 24, r.8: the "necessity" test

8.28   Under the old discovery rules, the power of the court to make discovery orders was expressly circumscribed by the so-called "necessity" test. Under the CPR there is no equivalent limit set on disclosure orders in Pt 31. But the making of court orders generally is subject to the "overriding objective" in Pt 1, previously considered. For comparative purposes and also so that the

---

[110] See Ch.9, para.9.139.
[111] *Partenreederei M/S "Heidberg" v Grosvenor Grain and Feed Company Ltd* [1993] 2 Lloyd's Rep 324 at 332.
[112] *The Consul Corfitzon* [1917] A.C. 550 at 550–556; *Banque Keyser Ullmann S.A. v Skandia (UK) Insurance Co. Ltd*, July 2, 1985, unreported, Staughton J.; *Bank of Crete S.A. v Koskotas* [1991] 2 Lloyd's Rep. 587 at 590; *Partenreederei M/S "Heidberg" v Grosvenor Grain and Feed Company Ltd* [1993] 2 Lloyd's Rep. 324 at 332–333; see also *Morris v Banque Arabe et Internationale d'Investissement S.A.* (1999) 2 I.T.E.L.R. 492.
[113] RSC, Ord.77, r.12(2); C.C.R., Ord.42, r.12(1).
[114] CPR, r.31.19(1).
[115] CPR, r.31.19(7).
[116] CPR, r.31.19(6).
[117] CPR, r.31.19(2).

old cases may be properly understood, it is desirable to say a few words about the "necessity" test. This rule applied only to cases falling outside the automatic discovery provisions,[118] for which there was a separate rule.[119] It broke down into two sub-rules:

(1) If the court was satisfied that discovery was not necessary, *either* at that stage,[120] *or* at all,[121] it might dismiss or adjourn the application.
(2) If and so far as the court was of opinion that discovery was not necessary, *either* for disposing fairly of the cause or matter *or* for saving costs, it had to refuse to make the order sought.

Thus, the burden of showing that discovery was not necessary (and thus bringing the rule into play) lay on the party objecting to the order.[122] Accordingly, where the burden was not discharged, a discovery order would be made. Under the CPR, of course, the burden must be on the party seeking a disclosure order, or (where the court is minded to make the order) on the party seeking an order other than for standard disclosure.[123]

It will also be observed that, whereas sub-rule (1) above was put in discretionary terms (*"may* dismiss"), sub-rule (2) was put in mandatory terms (*"shall* refuse"). However, it is clear that the courts have always treated the rule (and its equivalents in the rules governing other courts and tribunals) as conferring a discretion as to whether discovery be ordered.[124] Although the rule referred to "disposing fairly of the cause or matter", it was not necessary to test the discovery application by reference to the *whole* case or action; the fair disposal of a cause or matter involved the fair disposal of all stages of that cause or matter as it progressed through the courts and consequently the discovery application might be tested against a particular part of the action, or even against the specific application.[125] It was open to the court to consider what stage the disclosure should relate to.[126]

8.29

---

[118] See Ch.4, para.4.01, above.
[119] See para.8.30 below.
[120] See *Buchanan-Michaelson v Rubenstein* [1965] 1 W.L.R. 390; *R.H.M. Foods Ltd v Bovril Ltd* [1982] 1 W.L.R. 661.
[121] See *David Kahn Inc. v Conway Stewart & Co. Ltd* [1972] F.S.R. 169.
[122] *Dolling-Baker v Merrett* [1990] 1 W.L.R. 1205 at 1209.
[123] See paras 5.11, 6.43, above.
[124] *Downing v Falmouth United Sewerage Board* (1887) 37 Ch.D. 235, CA; *Science Research Council v Nassé* [1980] A.C. 1028, HL; *Berkeley Administration Inc. v McClelland* [1990] F.S.R. 381 at 382, CA. This discretion was exercised, in part, by taking into account the various factors referred to in paras 8.18–8.25, above.
[125] *Dubai Bank Ltd v Galadari (No.2)* [1990] 1 W.L.R. 731 at 737.
[126] *Baldock v Addison* [1995] 1 W.L.R. 158; *Kapur v J.W. Francis & Co.*, The Times, March 4, 1998, CA (discovery limited to quantum where split trial ordered as to liability and quantum); *Hellenic Mutual War Risks Association (Bermuda) Ltd v Harrison* [1997] 1 Lloyd's Rep. 160 (discovery limited to preliminary issue).

(i) RSC, Order 24, r.2(5)[127]: limit on automatic discovery

8.30   This rule contained the "necessity" test applicable where the automatic discovery provisions[128] applied, and the party concerned wished to limit it.[129] Since discovery in such cases was automatic, there was no application by a party seeking it; the burden was on the party who would otherwise give discovery to apply to have it cut down or exercised completely. The bulk of Ord.24, r.2(5) dealt with such applications, but concluded that:

> " . . . the Court shall make such an order [i.e. cutting down or excising discovery] if and so far[130] as it is of opinion that discovery is not necessary for disposing fairly of the action or for saving costs."

These words (with an appropriate shift from the negative "refuse to make" to the positive "make") tracked the relevant words of RSC, Ord.24, r.8,[131] and hence the burden was on the party objecting to give discovery to show why he should not do so.

---

[127] CCR, Ord.18, r.11(5).
[128] See Ch.4, para.4.01, above.
[129] See, e.g. *Baldock v Addison* [1995] 1 W.L.R. 158.
[130] In the county court, "if and only so far . . . "
[131] CCR, Ord.14, r.8.

CHAPTER 9

Inspection of documents

CHAPTER 9

Inspection of documents

A. INTRODUCTION

Inspection of documents by another party may take place in a number of   **9.01**
different circumstances, including cases where (1) freezing (*Mareva*), (2)
search (*Anton Piller*) or (3) *Norwich Pharmacal* orders have been made. In
such cases it is the court's order that will regulate such inspection. But the
more usual case is that of inspection following a notice under CPR, r.31.5,
informing a party of his opponent's wish to inspect documents. These may
be (4) documents disclosed in the List of Documents, or they may be (5)
documents mentioned in a statement of case, a witness statement, a witness
summary, an affidavit or an expert's report. This chapter deals expressly
with cases (4) and (5), although some of the following discussion will also
be relevant even in cases of (1), (2) and (3) referred to above.

B. NOTICE TO INSPECT

Under the old rules a party serving a List of Documents had also to give   **9.02**
notice of the documents' availability for inspection.[1] This had to state a time
within seven days after service at which the documents might be inspected
at a specified place.[2] The production for inspection of documents disclosed
on discovery usually took place in accordance with that Notice, although
the court might order alternative arrangements in some cases.[3] The party

---

[1] RSC, Ord.24, r.9; C.C.R., Ord.14, r.3.
[2] Although sometimes it was attempted to defer inspection until a particular condition was
satisfied, e.g. that the other party had served his List: *Football League Ltd v Football
Association Ltd*, unreported, September 20, 1991, CA.
[3] See paras 9.12 and 9.15 below, and see also para.9.36 in relation to "business books".

serving a list was deemed to have been served by the party on whom the List was served with a notice requiring the production at the trial of such documents specified in the List or affidavit as were in his possession, custody or power.[4]

9.03   Both of these rules have now gone.[5] Under the CPR, a party has a right to inspect documents whose existence is disclosed to him under Pt 31,[6] except where the document is no longer in the disclosing party's control,[7] where the disclosing party has a right or duty to withhold inspection,[8] or where he considers it would be disproportionate to the issues in the case to permit inspection[9] (and so states in his disclosure statement).[10] CPR, r.31.2 provides that a party discloses a document by stating that the document exists or has existed. It also includes voluntary disclosure as where it is mentioned in a witness statement.[11] A party also has also a right to inspect documents mentioned in certain documents prepared by his opponent for use in court and served on him.[12] But, in order to exercise those rights, he must give written notice to the disclosing party of his wish to inspect.[13] The disclosing party then has seven days to permit inspection.[14] The place[15] and the time[16] of inspection, the redaction of the original documents,[17] and the supply of copies,[18] are all dealt with later in this chapter. It should however be borne in mind that the parties may agree in writing, or the court may direct, that inspection should take place in stages.[19]

C. DOCUMENTS MENTIONED IN STATEMENTS OF CASE ETC.

9.04   This is quite different from inspection of documents disclosed in Lists of Documents. It was said of the equivalent rule under the old RSC[20] that,

---

[4] RSC, Ord.27, r.4(3).
[5] Though cf. CPR, r.32.19, which has a misleading heading.
[6] CPR, r.31.3(1).
[7] CPR, r.31.3 (1)(a); as to "control", see Ch.5, paras 5.39–5.54.
[8] CPR, r.31.3 (1)(b); see generally Ch.11.
[9] CPR, r.31.3(1)(c), (2)(a); see Ch.11, paras 11.156.
[10] CPR, r.31.3 (2)(d); as to the "disclosure statement", see Ch.6, para.6.05.
[11] *Smithkline Beecham Plc v Generics (UK) Ltd* [2003] EWCA Civ 1109; [2004] 1 W.L.R. 1479, CA.
[12] CPR, r.31.14; see paras 9.04–9.10, below.
[13] CPR, r.31.15(a).
[14] CPR, r.31.3 (1)(c), (2)(a).
[15] See para.9.11, below.
[16] See para.9.15, below.
[17] See para.9.37, below.
[18] See para.9.17, below.
[19] CPR, r.31.13. The same is true of disclosure: see Ch.2, para.2.33.
[20] From 1965 to 1999, it was RSC, Ord.24, r.10 (C.C.R., Ord.14, r.4).

instead of bring "intended to give a party discovery of all documents relating to the case which are in his adversary's possession", the rule applicable here was "intended to give the opposite party the same advantage as if the document referred to had been fully set out in the pleadings".[21] There was no need for a List of Documents to have been served, or even for pleadings to be closed.[22] The same is true today under the current rule.[23] Under this rule, a party "may inspect a document mentioned in" a statement of case, a witness statement, a witness summary, an affidavit,[24] or (with certain exceptions)[25] an expert's report.[26] As with documents disclosed in a list of documents, however, the party with the right must give written notice to his opponent of his wish to inspect,[27] and inspection must be permitted within seven days.[28] Under the old rules the producing party had to serve a counter-notice setting time and place for inspection, together with a statement of any objection to production of any of them.[29] It was an objection that the document was irrelevant,[30] or that it was privileged.[31] A failure to give such a counter-notice, or an objection to production of any document, enabled the court to make an order for production at such time and place and in such manner as it thought fit.[32]

But there is no requirement for counter-notices under the CPR, nor for   **9.05** any statement of objection to inspection; nor indeed is there express power for the court to order inspection which is wrongly refused. There *is* express power for the court to order "specific inspection",[33] but in terms this power only applies to documents referred to in r.31.3(2) (inspection refused on proportionality grounds).[34] Presumably the court may make an order for inspection in such a case under its general power to rectify errors of procedure,[35] on the basis of the failure to comply with r.31.15(b). Once it is shown or admitted that a document is mentioned in a statement of case, a witness statement, a witness summons, a witness summary, an affidavit or

---

[21] *Quilter v Heatly* (1883) 23 Ch.D. 42 at 50; *Rafadain Bank v Agom Universal Sugar Trading Co. Ltd* [1987] 1 W.L.R. 1606 at 1610–11; *Mantaray Pty. Ltd v Brookfield Breeding Co. Pty. Ltd* [1992] 1 Qd.R. 91 at 96.
[22] *Quilter v Heatly* (1883) 23 Ch.D. 42, CA; *Smith v Harris* (1883) 48 L.T. 869 at 870; *Mantaray Pty. Ltd v Brookfield Breeding Co. Pty. Ltd* [1992] 1 Qd. R. 91 at 96; *Robinson v Adskead (No.1)* (1995) 12 W.A.R. 574.
[23] CPR, r.31.14.
[24] CPR, r.31.14(1).
[25] See CPR, r.35.10(4).
[26] CPR, r.31.14(2).
[27] CPR, r.31.15(a).
[28] CPR, r.31.15(b).
[29] RSC, Ord.24, r.10(2); CCR, Ord.14, r.4(2).
[30] *Siddeley-Deary Motor Car Co. v Thompson* (1916) 140 L.T. Jo. 3374.
[31] *Roberts v Oppenheim* (1884) 26 Ch.D. 734; *Bristol Corporation v Cox* (1884) 26 Ch.D. 678; *Atikin v Ettershank* (1885) 7 A.L.T. 21.
[32] RSC, Ord.24, r.11(1); CCR, Ord.14, r.5(1).
[33] CPR, r.31.12(1); as to the mode of application, see para.9.33, below.
[34] CPR, r.13.12(3).
[35] CPR, r.3.10.

an expert's report, the onus is on the party against whom the application is made to produce it unless he can show good cause why he should not.[36] However, the court's power to order production is subject to the overriding objective in CPR, r.1.1, which the court must seek to give effect to in exercising any power given to it by the Rules.[37] This may be compared with the former rule, under RSC, Ord.24, r.13,[38] that production should be necessary either for disposing fairly of the cause or matter or for saving costs.[39]

9.06   In the case of experts' reports, a party may apply for an order for inspection of any document mentioned in an expert's report which has not already been disclosed in the proceedings.[40] However, before issuing an application the party should request inspection of the document informally, and inspection should be provided by agreement unless the request is unreasonable.[41] Where an expert report refers to a large number of documents and it would be burdensome to copy or collate them, the court will only order inspection if it is satisfied that it is necessary for the just disposal of the proceedings and the party cannot reasonably obtain the document from another source.[42] Where a party already has documents and it would be expensive or burdensome on the requesting party to obtain copies elsewhere, then it may not be reasonable to expect him to obtain the documents by himself rather than from the party who has disclosed or served the expert report referring to them. An expert report must state the substance of all material instructions, whether oral or written, on the basis of which the report was written.[43] Such instructions are not privileged against disclosure (and inspection)[44] and hence any privileged is in effect waived once the report has been served. The court will not order disclosure of those instructions or permit any questioning in court (other than by the party who instructed the expert) in relation to those instructions unless it is satisfied that there are reasonable grounds to consider that the statement of instructions given in the report to be inaccurate or incomplete.[45] The reference in CPR r.31.10 is to the actual expert's report served in the

---

[36] *Quilter v Heatly* (1883) 23 Ch.D. 42 at 51; *Hunter v Dublin, Wicklow and Wexford Railway Co.* (1891) 28 Ir. R. 489 at 495.

[37] CPR, r.1.2.

[38] C.C.R., Ord.14, r.8.

[39] *Hydro-Dynamic Products Ltd v A H Products Ltd*, August 21, 1986, unreported, Hoffmann J.; *Oystercatcher Commodities Ltd v J M Harwood & Co. Ltd*, October 29, 1986, unreported, Hoffmann J.; *Union Insurance Ltd v Incorporated General Assurance Ltd*, July 2, 1991, unreported, CA; see Ch.11, para.11.01, below.

[40] CPR, r.31.14(2).

[41] CPR, Pt.31, Practice Direction, para.7.1.

[42] CPR, Pt.31, Practice Direction, para.7.2; *Admiralty and Commercial Courts Guide* (7th edn, 2006), para.H2.21.

[43] CPR, r.35.10(3); CPR, Pt.35, Practice Direction, para.2.28(8).

[44] CPR, r.35.10(4); CPR Pt.35, Practice Direction, para.4. See Ch.18, para.18.16 (privilege).

[45] CPR, r.31.10(4).

proceedings and hence does not override privilege in any earlier draft reports that may exist.[46] Material supplied by the instructing party to the expert on the basis on which the expert is asked to advise should be considered part of the instructions.[47]

"Document" is defined for the purposes of CPR, Pt 31, and this has **9.07** already been discussed.[48] "Statement of case" for this purpose not only includes a claim form, particulars of claim, a defence, a Pt 20 claim, and a reply to defence, but also includes further information given in relation to them voluntarily or by court order under CPR, r.18.1.[49] "Affidavit" has been held to include an affidavit verifying a List of Documents,[50] an affidavit responding to interrogatories,[51] and an affidavit sworn and served on an opposing party though not filed in court.[52] It would seem that the rule covers not only any affidavit sworn by a party to the action, but also any affidavit sworn by an unconnected third party and filed or used on behalf of a party.[53] It has also been held to include an exhibit to an affidavit,[54] as the effect of an exhibit is the same as if the contents of that exhibit were set out in the body of the affidavit.[55] Logically, this may lead, in modern litigation with large exhibits, to very wide potential production under CPR, r.31.14, limited only by the "overriding objective" in CPR, Pt 1.[56]

Under the old rules, it was held that, for the court to have jurisdiction **9.08** under RSC, Ord.24, r.11[57] to order production, there was no requirement that the document concerned should actually be in the possession custody or power of the respondent; the question was one of discretion to be exercised on the facts of each case[58] and there was no rule that production of documents not in the possession, custody or power of the respondent should be only be ordered in rare cases.[59] The question of the court's power to

---

[46] *Jackson v Marley Davenport Ltd* [2004] EWCA Civ 1225; [2004] 1 W.L.R. 2926, CA.
[47] *Lucas v Barking, Havering & Redbridge Hospitals NHS Trust* [2003] EWCA Civ 1102; [2004] 1 W.L.R. 220, CA.
[48] See Ch.5, paras 5.02 to 5.07 and Ch.7, paras 7.02 to 7.05.
[49] CPR, r.2.3(1); under the old rules, see *Cass v Fitzgerald* [1884] W.N. 18; *Milbank v Milbank* [1900] 1 Ch. 376 at 385.
[50] *Pardy's Mozambique Syndicate Ltd v Alexander* [1903] 1 Ch. 191.
[51] *Moore v Peachey* [1891] 2 Q.B. 707.
[52] *Re Fenner and Lord* [1897] 1 Q.B. 667, CA.
[53] *Dubai Bank Ltd v Galadari (No.2)*, *The Times*, December 11, 1989, *per* Morritt J.; on appeal [1990] 1 W.L.R. 731 at 737.
[54] *Hunter v Dublin, Wicklow and Wexford Railway Co.* (1891) 28 Ir.R. 489; *Re Hinchcliffe* [1895] 1 Ch. 117, CA (not a case under Ord.24, r.10) followed in *Nissho Iwai Corp. v Gulf Fisheries Company*, July 12, 1988, unreported, Hirst J. (an Ord.24, r.10 case); *cf. Sloane v British Steamship Co.* [1897] 1 Q.B. 185.
[55] *Re Hinchcliffe* [1895] 1 Ch. 117, at 120.
[56] See *Nissho Iwai Corp. v Gulf Fisheries Company,* July 12, 1988, unreported, Hirst J. (RSC, Ord.24 r.10).
[57] CCR, Ord.14, r.5.
[58] *Rafadain Bank v Agom Universal Sugar Trading Co. Ltd* [1978] 1 W.L.R. 1606, CA; *cf. Quilter v Heatly* (1883) 23 Ch.D. 42 at 49; *Robinson v Adshead (No.1)* (1995) 12 W.A.R. 574.
[59] *Dubai Bank Ltd v Galadari (No.2)* [1990] 1 W.L.R. 731 at 741.

order inspection under the CPR has already been considered,[60] but there is
nothing in the new rules to suggest that the position as regards control of the
document concerned is any different. The court will not generally order
production under this rule of a document privileged from production, unless
privilege is waived by the reference to it in the affidavit, statement of case or
witness statement.[61] In an appropriate case, the court will order production
subject to sealing up irrelevant material.[62] But, if a party fails to permit
inspection of a document which under the Rules he should, he may not rely
on it without the court's permission.[63]

9.09   The more difficult question under RSC, Ord.24, r.10[64] was what constituted a "reference" in the pleadings or affidavit to the "document" concerned. First, it was clear that a general or compendious reference to a class
of documents, as opposed to a reference to individual documents, fell within
the rule. Thus in one case[65] the plaintiff referred generally to all his business
invoices, letters and bill heads, and these were held within the rule. On the
other hand it was clear that the mere fact that a particular transaction,
referred to in an affidavit or pleading, would be likely to be *evidenced* by a
document, did not in itself import a reference to that document.[66] Nor was
it enough that a particular transaction, so referred to, was likely to have
been effected by a document, as that would involve "reference by inference"; what was required was the making of a direct allusion to a document
or documents.[67] However where there was an insufficient allusion for the
purposes of the production requirement, a more definite reference could
often be obtained by seeking further and better particulars of the particular
pleading or objecting to the affidavit concerned as an insufficient statement
of sources of information.[68]

9.10   Under the CPR, the rule is no longer whether "reference is made" to the
document. What now matters is whether it is "mentioned" in the larger
document.[69] The deliberate change in wording, coupled with the reductivist

[60] See para.9.05, above.
[61] *Roberts v Oppenheim* (1884) 26 Ch.D. 724 at 733; the question of waiver appears not to
have been considered: *cf. R. v I.R.C., exp. Taylor* [1989] 1 All E.R. 906, CA; as to waiver
of privilege by reference in a statement of case, in an affidavit or a witness statement, see
Ch.12, paras 12.11–12.15, 12.19–12.20 below.
[62] *Quilter v Heatly* (1883) 23 Ch.D.42; see para.9.37, below.
[63] CPR, r.31.21; see also *Webster v Whewall* (1880) 15 Ch.D. 120; *Roberts v Oppenheim*
(1884) 26 Ch.D. 734; *Bristol Corporation v Cox* (1884) 26 Ch.D. 678 at 685.
[64] CCR, Ord.14, r.4.
[65] *Smith v Harris* (1883) 48 L.T. 869.
[66] *Dubai Bank Ltd v Galadari (No.2)* [1990] 1 W.L.R. 731 at 738.
[67] *ibid.,* at 739; *Eagle Star Insurance Co. Ltd v Arab Bank Plc,* February 25, 1991, unreported, Hobhouse J.; *Overseas Union Insurance Ltd v Incorporated General Insurance
Ltd,* July 2, 1991, unreported, CA; *Continental Bank N.A. v Aeakos Compania Naviera
S.A.,* unreported, January 20, 1993, CA (reference in affidavit to "transfer" of interest in a
loan was sufficient reference to the document by which the transfer was made); *Klabin v
Technocom Ltd,* September 20, 2002, Guernsey CA (compendious reference to documents
in affidavit is sufficient).
[68] *ibid.*
[69] CPR, r.31.14.

philosophy behind the Woolf reforms, suggest that is the intention significantly to reduce the scope of this rule. It is therefore submitted that a document is not "mentioned" in another unless the reference to it is specific and direct. Thus mere reference to a *transaction* which (to be effective in law) must have been carried out by a document in writing would not be sufficient: the document itself would not be mentioned. In one case a defence contained quotes from the notes of an interview without mentioning the fact that the quotes had been taken from the notes. It was held that this did not fall within CPR, r.31.14 on the basis that quoting from a document does not amount to mentioning or quoting from it.[70] In another case a defence only referred to the defendant's experts provisional advice, and made no reference to any documents so fell outside CPR, r.31.14.[71]

D. PLACE OF INSPECTION

Discovery was, as has already been mentioned, originally a procedure of the Court of Chancery.[72] Under the old Chancery practice documents produced for inspection by a party pursuant to an Affidavit of Documents were deposited in court and inspected there by his opponent.[73] Subsequently a practice grew up, as a matter of indulgence to the disclosing party, that, unless there was some special reason, the documents could be produced at the party's own solicitor's offices.[74] When discovery was introduced in the common law courts in the mid-nineteenth century, the procedure had to be different because the common law courts had no facilities for accepting such deposits and enabling inspection to take place. Accordingly, production was ordered at the offices of the solicitor of the owner of the documents.[75]   **9.11**

Under the RSC, the court did not normally concern itself with where the inspection should take place. It was for the disclosing party to state where he proposed to produce the documents for inspection,[76] and for the other party to object. If the court considered on application by an aggrieved party that inspection was being offered unreasonably, in terms of time or place,   **9.12**

---

[70] *Rigg v Associated Newspapers* [2003] EWHC 710 (Q.B.), [2003] All E.R. (D) 97 (Apr); however disclosure was ordered under CPR r.31.12.

[71] *Cherrywood Restaurants Ltd v Gamma Investments Ltd* [2004] EWHC 3227 (Ch.), [2004] All E.R. (D) 260 (Dec).

[72] See Ch.1, para.1.10, above.

[73] *Bonnardet v Taylor* (1861) 1 John. & H. 383; *A.G. v Whitwood Local Board* (1871) 40 L.J. Ch. 592; *Brown v Sewell* (1880) 16 Ch.D. 517; *Prestney v Mayor of Colchester* (1883) 24 Ch.D. 376, CA.

[74] See Bray, p.165, citing *Prentice v Phillips* (1843) 2 Hare. 152; *Groves v Groves* (1853) 2 W.R. 86; *Brown v Sewell* (1880) 16 Ch.D. 517 at 518; and *Prestney v Mayor of Colchester* (1883) 24 Ch.D. 376, CA, amongst other cases.

[75] Bray, at p.166.

[76] RSC, Ord.24, r.9; CCR, Ord.14, r.3.

then it might make an order for production at such time and place and in such manner as it thought fit.[77]

9.13   Thus in appropriate cases the court might order production in the place where the documents were in constant business use,[78] partly in one place and partly in another,[79] or even abroad.[80] The court might even order deposit in court as under the former practice,[81] for example where there were grounds for suspicion that the documents might be tampered with.[82] At the end of the day it was a matter for the discretion of the court, with the exercise of which the Court of Appeal would not readily interfere.[83]

9.14   Under the CPR there is no longer an obligation on the disclosing party to state where the documents may be inspected.[84] The burden is on the party wishing to inspect to give written notice of his wish to do so.[85] Then the disclosing party has seven days in which to provide inspection.[86] In practice this will normally occur at his solicitor's office, as before, but the matter is at large. If circumstances properly call for different arrangements, the disclosing party can make them, and it will be for the inspecting party to object. If the disclosing party does not permit inspection or will only permit it at an unreasonable place or time, the matter will have to be resolved by application to the court.[87]

E. TIME OF INSPECTION

9.15   The old Chancery practice is set out by Bray,[88] who also points out that the common law practice was to provide expressly for time of inspection in the order. Under the RSC, the Notice to Inspect served by the disclosing party[89] had to state the time or times at which inspection would be available. Under the CPR, there is no requirement on the disclosing party to do anything of this kind. The burden is on the inspecting party to give written

---

[77] RSC, Ord.24, r.11(1); C.C.R., Ord.14, r.5(1).

[78] *Mertens v Haigh* (1860) Johns. 735; *Crane v Cooper* (1838) 4 Myl. & Cr. 263; *Gerard v Penswick* (1818) 1 Wils. Ch. Ca. 222, 1 Swan. 534.

[79] *Bustros v Bustros* (1882) 30 W.R. 374, CA; *Prestney v Colchester Corp.* (1883) 24 Ch.D. 376, CA.

[80] *Whyte & Co. v Ahrens & Co.* (1884) 50 L.T. 344; *Bustros v Bustros* (1882) 30 W.R. 374; cf. *Lindsay v Gladstone* (1869) L.R. 9 Eq. 132 at 133 (defendant's documents brought from India at plaintiff's expense).

[81] *Leslie v Cave* [1886] W.N. 162.

[82] *Mertons v Haigh* (1860) Johns. 735 at 738. As to the practice in such a case, see Bray, pp.166–170.

[83] *Bustros v Bustros* (1882) 30 W.R. 374, CA; *Prestney v Colchester Corp.* (1883) 24 Ch.D. 376 at 382, 383, 385.

[84] But Form 265, in part one of the list, requires a statement as to whether documents are kept elsewhere: see Appendix [3, p.533].

[85] CPR, r.31.15(a).

[86] CPR, r.31.15(b); see para.9.03, above.

[87] See para.9.33, below.

[88] Bray, at p.171.

[89] See Ch.6, para.6.20, above.

notice of his wish to inspect,[90] and then the disclosing party has seven days to permit it.[91] In practice, the parties will agree on the time for inspection.[92] As with the place of inspection, if the disclosing party offers inspection at unreasonable times, the matter will have to be resolved by application to the court.[93]

In modern times, with the quality, speed and cheapness of photocopying, **9.16** an inspecting party looks at the originals either in order to decide which are important enough to have copied[94] or sometimes, with copies already obtained, in order to check particular documents for markings or writing which have not copied well. Where documents are numerous, it may not be possible to inspect all of them on one occasion, so that several attendances may be needed, and this was so even in the nineteenth century.[95] But this does not mean that a party may inspect the same document(s) as many times as he pleases. Strictly, the disclosing party is only obliged to produce each document for inspection once, although parties are expected to co-operate with each other and behave reasonably in these matters.

F. COPIES

The rule has long been that a party entitled to inspect original documents **9.17** is entitled to take copies (i.e. in the sense of copying out their contents)[96] of those documents at his own expense. With the advent of photocopying the practice grew up whereby the producing party's solicitor would provide photocopies of documents as requested, for an appropriate fee. However, although in practice it was in the solicitor's financial interest to supply the copies, he could not be compelled to do so, and neither was the inspecting party entitled to remove the original documents so as to be able to use his own or his solicitor's photocopying equipment.

But in 1987 the old rules of court were amended to provide machinery for **9.18** the inspecting party to require the disclosing party to supply copies.[97] Now, CPR, r.31.15 (c) serves a similar function. The inspecting party may (even without having seen the original) request a copy of a document[98] and, if he undertakes to pay reasonable copying costs, the disclosing party has seven

---

[90] CPR, r.31.15(a); see paras 9.03, 9.14, above.
[91] CPR, r.31.15(b); see paras 9.03, 9.14, above.
[92] cf. *Prentice v Phillips* (1843) 2 Hare. 152.
[93] See para.9.33 , below.
[94] As to which see para.9.17, below.
[95] cf. *Mertens v Haigh* (1860) Johns. 735 at 749, where production was limited to three weeks.
[96] See Bray, pp.174–175, and *Ormerod, Grierson & Co. v St. George's Ironworks Ltd* [1905] 1 Ch. 505, CA; such copies do not infringe any copyright, as being made for a judicial purpose: Copyright, Designs and Patents Act 1988, s.45.
[97] RSC, Ord.24, r.11A; CCR, Ord.14, r.5A.
[98] cf. *The American Endeavour Fund Ltd v Trueger*, unreported, January 23, 1998, R. Ct. of Jersey (order for "inspection of documents to be given by CD-ROM").

days to supply that copy. There is no requirement that the request be in writing. The previous rule included a number of limitations on the right. The document had to be capable of being copied by photographic or other process. The request had to be made "at or before the time when inspection takes place." There are no similar provisions in the CPR. Under the previous rule, where there was a failure to supply the copy, there was express provision for application to the court.[99] That too has gone, and so application must now be made under the general provision to that effect.[100]

9.19 It is likely that these provisions apply to pre-action or non-party disclosure under ss.33–35 of the Supreme Court Act 1981.[101] It is true that such disclosure, and the right of inspection, is ordered under the Act, not under the CPR. The new Rules merely regulate the procedure,[102] and indeed the relevant rules[103] refer to "an application . . . under any Act." But CPR, r.31.15, refers to "a right to inspect a document", and r.31.3 confers such a right on a party to whom a document has been "disclosed". Presumably a document is "disclosed" for this purpose even though disclosed under quite separate statutory provisions.

9.20 The reference in the old rule to "photographic or similar process," and its absence from r.31.15(c), raise the question how far the rule applies to "documents" in other than the conventional sense, i.e. tape recordings, microfiches and computer programs and databases.[104] Now that the rule omits the restrictive words "capable of being copied by photographic or similar process", and given the wide definition of document for the purposes of Pt 31,[105] all these cases must now be covered.[106] In one case, under the old rules, 50,000 documents were scanned into electronic form, from which compact discs could be made.[107] It was held that since the plaintiffs had scanned the documents for their own purposes, they could not charge any part of the scanning costs to other parties, but only the costs of cutting and supplying the compact discs. The costs of the scanning would form part of the plaintiffs' reasonable costs of the action. It is doubtful that where a party discloses a tape of poor quality, that he can be required to provide a transcript.[108]

9.21 The r.31.22 obligation (formerly implied undertaking) on disclosure[109] applies just as much to copies of original documents, and to the information

---

[99] RSC, Ord.24, r.11A(3); CCR, Ord.14, r.5A(3).
[100] CPR, r.3.10; see para.9.33, below.
[101] County Courts Act 1984, ss.52–54.
[102] *O'Sullivan v Herdmans Ltd* [1987] 1 W.L.R. 1047, HL.
[103] CPR, rr.31.16, 31.17.
[104] *cf.* O'Hare and Hill, *Civil Litigation* (9th edn, 2000), p.535.
[105] CPR, r.31.4; see Ch.5, para.5.02, above.
[106] *cf. The American Endeavour Fund Ltd v Trueger*, unreported, January 23, 1998, R.Ct. of Jersey (order for "inspection of documents to be given by CD-ROM").
[107] *Grupo Torras S.A. v Al-Sabah, The Times*, October 13, 1997.
[108] *cf. Paddick v Associated Newspapers Ltd* [2003] EWHC 2991 (Q.B.); [2003] All E.R. (D) 179 (Dec), where the point was left open.
[109] See Ch.15, para.15.03, below.

contained in those copies, as to the originals themselves. However, property in the copies, paid for by the inspecting party, will belong to the inspecting party, and the court will not order their return to the disclosing party, or their destruction at the end of the case, unless there is real cause to believe that the inspecting party will breach the obligation.[110]

G. TRANSLATIONS

It frequently happens in modern practice that disclosure is given of documents wholly or partly in foreign languages. The disclosing party will obviously have had to consider the relevance of the documents before disclosing them. If they are important they will need to form part of the trial bundle and almost certainly will need to be translated into English, each such document preferably in a single, agreed translation. This is both time consuming to arrange, and expensive to pay for. But as a matter of law a disclosing party is under no obligation to provide a translation of any document at or before the time of inspection (or indeed thereafter).[111] If the party disclosing the documents is successful in the action, the cost of the translations will probably form part of the reasonable costs of the action.[112] However, if a party already has in his control translations of documents, these translations will be disclosable and should be made available in the normal way.[113]

9.22

H. ELECTRONICALLY HELD DOCUMENTS AND EQUIPMENT

Electronic disclosure has already been covered in Ch.7. However, the problems and issues are no less potentially complex when it comes to inspection of electronically held data. Whilst the document is not the information, but the media on which the data is stored, in practice it is often inappropriate or impractical to allow an opposing party access to a data-base. A computer database may contain all sorts of confidential, personal, irrelevant or privileged material.

9.23

Inspection of such material raises a number of issues:

9.24

    (1) Should inspection be confined to the provision of printouts of the relevant material.

---

[110] *Brue Ltd v Solly, The Times*, February 9, 1988.
[111] *Bayer A.G. v Harris Pharmaceuticals Ltd* [1991] F.S.R. 170.
[112] *cf. Grupo Torras S.A. v Al-Sabah* [1998] Masons C.L.R. 90 at 97.
[113] *Sumitomo v Credit Lyonnais Rouse* [2001] EWCA Civ 1152, [2002] 1 W.L.R. 479, CA (translations of non-privileged documents are in same position as copies).

(2) Should the documents be disclosed in electronic form, such as by the provision of data on a CD-ROM.

(3) In what format should the data be provided.

(4) Can the material be easily read by the other party and are the systems used by the parties compatible.

(5) What facilities or equipment should the disclosing party make available.

(6) If there is to be inspection of the disclosing parties computer or database, what conditions or restrictions should be imposed?

9.25   In *Derby & Co. Ltd v Weldon (No.9)*[114] Vinelott J. pointed out a number of the difficulties that might arise in the context of computer databases:

(a) the need to screen out from the database irrelevant or privileged material;

(b) the retrieval of information by reprogramming the computer;

(c) the problems of access and reprogramming without interrupting other daily use of the computer;

(d) the need for safeguards:

(i) to protect old tapes or discs against damage through being read, and

(ii) to protect the computer reader against damage from old tapes or discs;

(e) the possibility of copying the database onto a disc or a tape, or directly onto another computer, giving rise to the further possibility of analysis in ways not originally contemplated.

9.26   Vinelott J. added that:

" . . . these problems arise not at the initial stage of discovery when disclosure must be made of the extent of relevant information recorded in a computer database, but when application is made for production for inspection and copying of a document. It is clear . . . that the court has a discretion whether to order production and inspection and that the burden is on the party seeking inspection to satisfy the court that it is necessary for the disposing fairly of the case or cause or matter or for saving costs. At that point the court will have to consider, if necessary in the light of expert evidence, what information is or can be made available, how far it is necessary for there to be inspection or copying of the original document (the database) or whether the provision of print-outs or hard copy is sufficient, and what safeguards should be

---

[114] [1991] 2 All E.R. 901.

incorporated to avoid damage to the database and to minimise interference with everyday use if inspection is ordered".[115]

Parties are now expected to co-operate at an early stage as to the format **9.27** in which electronic copy documents are to be provided on inspection. In the case of difficulty or disagreement, the matter should be referred to the judge for directions at the earliest practical date, if possible at the first case management conference.[116] In practice, particularly where there is a limited amount of material, inspection can be by the provision of printouts of the relevant material.[117] This may not be appropriate where there is a large volume of material or where a printout will not capture all the relevant data or be in a form difficult to read such as in the case of spreadsheets or some calculations. In such a case, inspection may be by the provision of the data in electronic form, such as by the provision of a CD-ROM or even as an attachment to an email or a posting on an internet site.[118] More and more frequently parties are scanning documents and then providing the scanned material in electronic form. Whether it be the provision of scanned material or of material already held in electronic form, it is important that the parties co-operate as to the format in which the electronic data is to be provided. In some cases the provision of documents in electronic format may be more appropriate for specific categories of documents identified by the requesting party than for all categories of documents disclosed. In large scale litigation parties will often agree a protocol for inspection and ensure that their systems are compatible. The LiST Group has produced a very helpful Data Exchange Protocol, which is updated from time to time as practices in this area change.[119]

Documents held in electronic form cannot be read without the aid of **9.28** equipment, which may be specialised equipment. The court has an inherent jurisdiction to order the disclosing party to provide facilities for the "documents" to be read: these may be microfiche readers, tape and video recorders, or computers, as the case may be.[120] Obviously, however, there will be

---

[115] *ibid.* at 907.

[116] CPR, Pt.31, Practice Direction, para.2A.3.

[117] Where printouts are provided, in certain circumstances it may be appropriate to provide some additional information, e.g. creation date, edits and author. There may also be issues as to whether hidden database fields should also be disclosed.

[118] Considerable cost may be incurred in putting the documents into a manageable electronic form. Parties should discuss in advance how this cost should be shared, and if necessary obtain directions from the court. In *Grupo Torras S.A. v Al-Sabah* [1998] Masons C.L.R. 90, Mance J. held that the cost of providing copies to the other parties should be related to the cost of providing individual CD-ROMs (approximately £20 each), and not to the amount usually charged for each photocopied page or the cost of putting the documents into an electronic database. The costs of creating the database might however be recoverable as part of the costs recoverable following the conclusion of the case.

[119] *http://www.listgroup.org/publications.htm.*

[120] *Grant v Southwestern and County Properties Ltd* [1975] Ch. 185 at 198; *Athlete's Foot Australia Pty. Ltd v Divergent Technologies Pty. Ltd* (1997) 78 F.C.R. 283, Fed.Ct.Aus.; *cf. Senior v Holdsworth* [1976] Q.B. 23 at 32, 36, 41, CA.

special circumstances in each case requiring the court to tailor the order to the specific needs of the case.

9.29 The court does have power to order inspection of the database itself and give access to a party's computer or direct the provision of an imaged version of a database (e.g. copy of the hard drive). Both situations may pose practical difficulties as usually the database will hold something more than the relevant and disclosable material. The masking or editing of irrelevant and privileged material can be impractical and costly where documents are to be disclosed in electronic form. The court will usually not make an order for access to a party's computer or for the provision of a copy of a hard drive[121] and will only do so if it can be shown to be necessary and proportionate. Where there are technical issues or where it is appropriate not to allow a party to have access to other material, the court may permit inspection and interrogation of a computer system by an independent expert, who will be subject to undertakings necessary to protect the interests of the disclosing party. It is generally where there are issues as to whether documents have been concealed or deleted or an issue as to whether material has been distorted, retained or created or received on a computer or particular database, that an expert inspection has been ordered.[122]

I. WHO MAY INSPECT?

9.30 In ordinary cases, it is obviously open to the inspecting party himself to inspect, but this is rare in cases where he has legal representation. The usual course is for his solicitor to inspect, although this latter may do so by means of admitted or unadmitted staff, at any rate as long as he is not a "mere office-boy".[123] In large cases, solicitors may be accompanied by barristers. There may be special cases where the court is justified in preventing the party himself from inspecting or in making other arrangements,[124] but such cases will be rare. In the nineteenth century, the courts were much exercised by the question whether a person who had the right to inspect could bring with him, or even send in his place, a non-lawyer professional expert.[125]

9.31 Prima facie a party may inspect by his solicitor or other agent, but the party's "agent" must be general, and not appointed specially for this purpose.[126] The court has power, upon application being made for the purpose, to permit inspection by a "special" agent, e.g. one qualified in accounting,

---

[121] e.g. *Nucleus Information Systems v Palmer* [2003] EWHC 2013 (Ch.).
[122] *Molton v Tectronix UK Holdings* [2003] EWHC 383 (Ch.).
[123] *Lindsay v Gladstone* (1869) L.R. 9 Eq. 132 at 136.
[124] e.g. *Church of Scientology v D.H.S.S.* [1979] 1 W.L.R. 723, and see also Ch.11, para.11.159, below.
[125] See Bray, pp.177–180.
[126] *Draper v Manchester, Sheffield & Lincolnshire Railway Co.* (1861) 3 De G.F. & J. 23 at 27; *Bonnardet v Taylor* (1861) 1 J. & H. 383.

scientific or other expertise where this is necessary, but the burden of satisfying the court of this lies on the inspecting party.[127] It is of course open to the disclosing party to object to the particular agent put forward, but the burden lies on him to show that the agent is not to be accepted.[128] The court may impose terms upon inspection by such expert agents, and these are dealt with later.[129]

J. THE EFFECT OF INSPECTION

The effect of inspection of documents upon privilege and other rights of confidence in those documents is dealt with later.[130]   **9.32**

K. APPLICATIONS TO THE COURT

An application for an order for inspection is made to the master or district   **9.33**
judge.[131] The former rules conferred express power on the court to make orders for inspection of documents.[132] The CPR only do so expressly where inspection has been refused on grounds of lack of proportionality.[133] In all other cases, the application is founded on the general power of the court to make orders putting right failures to comply with the rules.[134] Generally speaking, the CPR do not expressly require that such applications be supported by evidence. But in practice the court will need to be satisfied that the factual premises for the making of the Order are satisfied,[135] and so it will be sensible at least to verify the application notice with a statement of truth,[136] so that its contents may be relied on as evidence.[137] As already mentioned, the court in making an inspection order must seek to give effect to the overriding objective.[138] Sanctions for failure to comply with an order for inspection are discussed later.[139]

CPR, rr.31.3 and 31.14 confer a right to inspect. The effect of CPR,   **9.34**
r.31.12(3), even though on its face it appears to refer to documents referred

---

[127] *Davies v Eli Lilly & Co.* [1987] 1 W.L.R. 428, CA.
[128] *ibid.*
[129] Ch.11, paras 11.157–11.163.
[130] See Ch.12, paras 12.16–12.18, below.
[131] To the judge in the Commercial Court. Technology and Construction Court and the Patents County Court. Appeals are dealt with in Ch.6, para.6.53, above.
[132] RSC, Ord.24, r.11; CCR, Ord.14, r.5.
[133] CPR, r.31.12(1), (3).
[134] CPR, r.3.10.
[135] CPR, Pt 23, Practice Direction, para.9.1.
[136] CPR, r.22.1(3).
[137] CPR, Pt 23, Practice Direction, para.9.7.
[138] CPR, r.1.2(2).
[139] See Ch.13, below.

to in CPR, r.31.3(2) and of CPR, r.3.1(2)(m), is to give the court power to order a party to permit another party to inspect any document which he has a right to inspect. Ordinarily, the appropriate order will be to order the party concerned to permit inspection (or provide copies as appropriate). However, there may be cases in which the appropriate order will be to require a party to give specific authority to solicitors (or experts) for another party to inspect records in the hands of a non-party. Such an order must be drafted with particular care where it provides that the party authorise a non-party to permit an opposing party to inspect medical records.[140]

L. RSC, ORDER 24, RULE 12[141]: PRODUCTION TO THE COURT

9.35   This rule formerly allowed the court, at any stage of proceedings, to order any party to produce to the court any document in his possession, custody or power relating to any matter in question in the proceedings, and to deal with the document when produced in such manner as it thought fit.[142] The rule was rarely used in practice, and there is no equivalent in the CPR. A similar result may now be obtained by the use of a witness summons.[143]

M. BUSINESS BOOKS

9.36   Again formerly, where production of any "business books" for inspection was applied for, the court might, instead of ordering production of the original books, order a copy of entries in the books to be supplied, to be verified on affidavit by a person who had examined the copy with the originals.[144] Again this rule was rarely used in practice, and there is no equivalent in the CPR.

N. SEALING-UP

9.37   Sealing-up for the purposes of disclosure by List was considered earlier.[145] So far as inspection is concerned, the old Chancery practice was to order

---

[140] *Bennett v Compass Group* [2002] EWCA Civ 612, CA.

[141] C.C.R., Ord.14, r.7.

[142] *Lewis v Londesborough* [1893] 2 Q.B. 191; *Pardy's Mozambique Syndicate Ltd v Alexander* [1903] 1 Ch. 191; *Ron West Motors Ltd v Broadcasting Corp of New Zealand* [1989] 2 N.Z.L.R. 433.

[143] See Ch.10, paras 10.02–10.36, below.

[144] RSC, Ord.24, r.14(1); CCR—no equivalent, but *cf.* the County Courts Act 1984, s.76, and CCR, Ord.1, r.6.

[145] See Ch.6, paras 6.17–6.18, above.

production for inspection, but to give the producing party leave to seal up such parts of books or similar documents as were sworn by him not to relate to the matters in question in the proceedings.[146] The inspecting party had no right to inspect the sealed-up parts, even if he suspected that they were relevant and the affidavit was untrue,[147] and even if the sealing-up had been done carelessly.[148] The leave given was to seal up, not to remove or mutilate parts of documents, and hence documents had to be produced in their integrity.[149] The old practice was applied generally to the High Court after 1875,[150] and although by the time the CPR were introduced, in 1999, the "common form" order for production, including liberty to seal up irrelevant material, was no longer made, there was nothing to prevent application being made for an appropriate variation in the order for production. Where covering-up would be more appropriate or less burdensome than sealing-up then the court might permit that.[151] In practice, what often happened was that the parties agreed that irrelevant material might be covered up, or the producing party covered it up anyway and left it to the inspecting party to complain. The test was whether the part covered up was irrelevant and there was no requirement that such part constituted or related to separate subject matter. The producing party's oath of irrelevance was conclusive unless the court could be satisfied from the documents produced or from anything in the affidavit that it did not truly state what it sought.[152] Thus, in one case where the terms, but not the financial limits, of the insurance cover of one party were relevant, the policies in question could be produced with the financial limit on cover blanked out.[153] Under the CPR, the test of "relevance" is abandoned in favour of the tests of reliance, adverse effect and support.[154] But there is nothing in the CPR to prevent the same technique being used and it is routinely adopted in practice. The producing party will cover up the material not required to be disclosed and will permit the inspecting party to inspect only the redacted text. Or (more usually) he will photocopy the sealed-up text and permit inspection only of the copy. In either case it will be for the inspecting party thereafter to complain. It is also

---

[146] *Campbell v French* (1792) 1 Anst. 58; 2 Cox Eq. Cas. 286; *Sheffield Canal Co. v Sheffield & Rotherham Railway Co.* (1843) 1 Ph. 484; *Curd v Curd* (1842) 1 Hare. 274; *Bull v Clarke* (1864) 15 C.B. (N.S.) 851.

[147] *Sheffield Canal Co. v Sheffield & Rotherham Railway Co.* (1843) 1 Ph. 484; *Crow v Columbine* (1843) 2 L.T. (O.S.) 454; cf. *Eaton v Lewis* (1853) 20 L.T. (O.S.) 243.

[148] *Jones v Andrews* (1888) 58 L.T. 601, CA.

[149] *Ayres v Levy* (1868) 19 L.T. 8.

[150] *Re Pickering* (1833) 25 Ch.D. 247, CA; *Jones v Andrews* (1888) 58 L.T. 601, CA; *Graham v Sutton, Carden & Co.* [1897] 1 Ch. 761, CA; and see also Ch.1, para.1.12, above.

[151] *Graham v Sutton, Carden & Co.* [1897] 1 Ch. 761, CA.

[152] *G.E. Capital Corporate Finance Group v Bankers Trust Co.* [1995] 1 W.L.R. 172, CA; *Paddick v Associated Newspapers* Ltd [2003] EWHC 2991 (Q.B.), [2003] All E.R. (D) 179 (Dec); see also *Curlex Manufacturing Pty Ltd v Carlingford Australia General Insurance Ltd* [1987] 2 Qd. R. 335.

[153] *Cox .v Bankside Members Agency Ltd* (1994), noted 145 N.L.J. 313, CA; see also *Pacific Investments Ltd v Christensen*, 1997 J.L.R. 170 at 175–6, Jersey CA.

[154] See Ch.5, para.5.10, above.

possible to mask passages where documents have been produced electronically, although where large numbers of documents are being disclosed, it is almost inevitable that mistakes may be made.[155] As the Practice Direction accompanying CPR Pt 31 makes clear,[156] a claim to withhold inspection of a document or part of a document, disclosed in a list of documents does not require an application to the court. Where such a claim has been made, a party who wishes to challenge it must apply to the court. Even so, it is should be made clear in the list itself what documents have been redacted or sealed up and on what grounds.[157] In Australia there are two lines of authority. The first follows *G.E. Capital* in permitting a party to provide inspection on the basis of the production of redacted copies or masked documents, with the confidential and irrelevant portions blanked out.[158] The second states that a party should not be allowed to provide disclosure and inspection on this basis unilaterally, but should only do so if the parties agree or with the sanction of the court.[159]

9.38   As indicated above, the practice related to material sworn to be irrelevant. Where privileged material was concerned the producing party could not assert its irrelevance.[160] However, in two cases at first instance the High Court permitted a producing party to cover up privileged material contained in documents being produced.[161] These decisions were criticised as inconsistent with authorities on waiver of privilege[162] but were subsequently approved by the Court of Appeal,[163] and followed subsequently.[164] So a producing party may redact a document on grounds of privilege, whether that document deals with one subject matter or several. But if he then introduces in evidence the document so redacted and *in fact* it relates entirely to one subject matter, he may be held to have waived the privilege in the whole document, and (if that were to be the case) the redaction would have to be reversed.[165]

---

[155] *Seven Network Ltd v News Ltd (No.13)* [2006] F.C.A. 354, Fed.Ct.Aus.

[156] CPR, Pt.31, Practice Direction, para.6.1.

[157] Ch.6, paras 6.17–6.18.

[158] *Optus Communications Pty Ltd v Telstra Corporation Ltd* [1995] F.C.A. 254.

[159] *Gray v Associated Book Publishers (Aust) Pty Ltd* [2002] F.C.A. 1045; *Rio Tinto Ltd v Commissioner of Taxation* [2005] F.C.A. 1335.

[160] Though *cf. Carew v White* (1842) 5 Beav. 172 and *Churton v Frewen* (1865) 2 Dr. & Sm. 390.

[161] *Bank of Nova Scotia v Hellenic Mutual War Risk Association (Bermuda) Ltd* [1992] 2 Lloyds Rep. 540; *British & Commonwealth Holdings v Quadrex Holdings Inc.*, July 4, 1990, unreported, Gatehouse J.

[162] Style & Hollander, *Documentary Evidence* (4th edn, 1993) at pp.139–140; see now (9th edn, 2006) paras 12–07 and 12–08; Ch.12. para.12.34, below.

[163] *G.E. Capital Corporate Finance Group v Bankers Trust Co.* [1995] 1 W.L.R. 172, CA; see also *Re Galileo Group Ltd* [1999] Ch. 100.

[164] *Hellenic Mutual War Risks Association (Bermuda) Ltd v Harrison* [1997] 1 Lloyd's Rep. 160; see also *Somervile v Australian Securities Commission* (1993) 118 A.L.R. 149 at 155, Fed. Ct. Aus.

[165] See Ch.12, paras 12.33–12.34, below.

CHAPTER 10

Production by non-parties

CHAPTER 10

Production by non-parties

A. GENERAL

There are a number of procedures by which persons who are not parties **10.01**
to legal proceedings can be required by court order to produce documents
for inspection, whether by the court or by the parties. In this chapter a
number of these procedures are dealt with, namely the witness summons,
the Bankers Books Evidence Act 1879 and the Evidence (Proceedings in
other Jurisdictions) Act 1975. These three procedures are dealt with in
order. Other procedures, such as Norwich Pharmacal orders,[1] the Supreme
Court Act 1981, s.34,[2] foreign disclosure for English proceedings,[3] and
production orders in connection with the taking of depositions[4] have been
considered elsewhere.

B. WITNESS SUMMONS

Introduction

A most important means of obtaining documents from non-parties during **10.02**
the currency of litigation is the witness summons, already known by that
name in the county court, but formerly known in the High Court in relation
to documents as the *subpoena duces tecum*. There are two forms of witness
summons, although the relevant practice form combines both elements.
First there is the summons to attend court to provide oral evidence on behalf
of the party issuing the summons (in the High Court formerly known as a

---

[1] See Ch.3, paras 3.02–3.25 above.
[2] See Ch.4, paras 4.48–4.60 above.
[3] See Ch.2, paras 2.57–2.63 above.
[4] See Ch.4, paras 4.75–4.76 above.

subpoena ad testificandum). Secondly, there is the summons to attend court to produce specified documents (in the High Court formerly known as a *subpoena duces tecum*). It is this second type of witness summons which is the subject of this section. Witness summonses in the High Court and county court are governed by CPR, rr.34.1–34.7.[5] However, it should be noted that similar principles apply in relation to criminal proceedings, where witnesses summonses for the production of documents may be issued under ss.2–2E of the Criminal Procedure (Attendance of Witnesses) Act 1965.[6]

10.03   In principle, a witness summons for the production of documents differs from inter partes disclosure of documents in a number of important ways:

> (a) it requires the *production* of documents; it does not require the recipient to disclose the existence of documents, or to list them;
>
> (b) it requires production of documents *identified* by the summons itself;
>
> (c) it requires production *at the trial* or other hearing in the action, not at the disclosure stage[7];
>
> (d) it requires production *to the court*, not to either or both parties; if the non-party does not wish to co-operate (and, indeed, in some cases, such as where professional confidence is involved, he may be unable to) the parties will often not know what the specific documents contain until the documents are produced at the trial.

10.04   For the above reasons, the use of a witness summons is normally regarded as very much a last resort, usually confined to cases where the party seeking production of documents (a) is confident of their content, and (b) needs the documents concerned in order to succeed in his case, or at least significantly to improve his prospects. In exceptional circumstances, such as for the purposes of committal proceedings, the court may issue a witness summons of its own motion.[8]

10.05   Non-party disclosure under CPR, r.31.17 will often be available as an alternative to a witness summons, albeit their functions are different. Non-party disclosure under CPR, r.31.17 is a form of disclosure of documents which may or may not constitute evidence. A witness summons is part of the

---

[5] Formerly RSC, Ord.38, rr.14–19.

[6] Substituted by the Criminal Procedure and Investigations Act 1996, s.66; see also *R. v Clowes* (1992) 95 Cr.App.R. 440; *R. v P.J. O'N and M. O'N* [2001] N.I.C.C. 5; *R. v Alibhai* [2004] EWCA Crim 681 at [34], noting that the procedure is not altogether satisfactory; *Phipson on Evidence* (16th edn, 2005), paras 8.23–8.24. *R.(B) v Stafford Combined Court* [2006] EWHC 1645 (Admin) [2007] 1 All E.R. 102.

[7] Permission is required for a witness summons to be issued for a witness to attend court to produce documents on any date except for the date fixed for trial: CPR r.34.3(2); para.10.22 below.

[8] *Yianni v Yianni* [1966] 1 W.L.R. 120; see also para.10.19 below.

process of the production of evidence. It is important in practice to apply for documents from non-parties by way of the most appropriate route. One factor is costs.[9] Ordinarily a recipient of a witness summons is entitled to very limited costs of compliance (conduct money),[10] whereas under CPR, r.31.17 the non-party is usually entitled to his costs of searching, listing and providing copies of documents.[11]

Requirements

The witness summons must comply with the following requirements: **10.06**

(a) the summons must be addressed to a specific individual;
(b) the documents must be in the actual possession or custody of the recipient;
(c) the witness summons may only be served on a person within the United Kingdom;
(d) the documents sought must be identified;
(e) the documents must be relevant to the issues in the action and admissible;
(f) the request must not be too wide and must be confined to what is reasonably necessary;
(g) production must be necessary for fairly disposing of the issues in the action.

As has been succinctly summarised by the Court of Appeal:

"As the law now stands in light of the authorities, including the decision of this Court in *Burchard v MacFarlane*,[12] it is necessary in order to justify the issue of a *subpoena duces tecum* that the particular document or documents must be identified either individually or compendiously, and that each document must be shown to be likely to exist, to be relevant to some issue in the proceedings, and to be admissible as evidence in respect of that issue, as well as to be necessary for fairly disposing of the action".[13]

(a) Addressed to a specific individual

In the High Court and the county court, CPR, r.34.2(2) provides that the   **10.07**
witness summons must be in the relevant practice form. The practice form

---

[9] *Re Howglen Ltd* [2001] 1 All E.R. 376 at 384; *Three Rivers DC v Bank of England* [2002] EWHC 1118 (Comm) at 59; see also *Individual Homes Ltd v MacBreem Investment Ltd*, *The Times*, November 14, 2002, Ch.D; see also paras 10.13 and 10.35 below.
[10] Ch.4, para.4.59 above.
[11] Para.10.34 below.
[12] [1891] 2 Q.B. 241.
[13] *Omar v Omar*, unreported, October 11, 1996, *per* Peter Gibson L.J.

(N20)[14] requires the actual production of documents by the person named in the witness summons. Therefore, prior to issuing a witness summons consideration should always be given as to who is the most appropriate person to be required to produce the documents. Where documents are held by a corporate entity or partnership, it is usually appropriate to ask the organisation in advance as to who is the appropriate person in a position to produce the documents. Although witness summonses are generally used in relation to non-parties, they are not so restricted as a matter of principle, and it is not of itself oppressive or an abuse of the process for a party to issue and serve a witness summons upon his opponent.[15] In most cases, the appropriate method of obtaining documents from an opponent is of course by way of disclosure under CPR, Pt 31. However, there are situations where a witness summons is more appropriate, and there are many cases where CPR, Pt 31 does not apply, such as claims on the small claims track[16] or arbitrations.[17] The court may decline to issue a witness summons directed to a minor if it would be oppressive.[18]

(b) Actual possession or custody

10.08
Actual possession or custody of the documents by the recipient is necessary.[19] Actual custody on behalf of another person, e.g. an employer or other principal, is not enough, at least when the other refuses the documents to be produced.[20] Ordinarily a corporation will not object to an employee producing a document held by him merely on the ground that he holds it in the capacity of an employee. Where the employer or other principal has not refused authority to produce the documents (e.g. because he has not been asked) the employee must produce the documents.[21] Though it appears that the documents are confidential and the principal has not been consulted, it

---

[14] See Appendix 3, para.C.02, below.

[15] *Halford v Brookes, The Independent*, September 12, 1991; see also *Scott v Sampson* (1882) 8 Q.B.D. 491; *Price v Manning* (1884) 42 Ch.D. 373; *Bradshaw v Widdington* (1902) 86 L.T. 726; *Tedeschi v Singh* [1948] Ch. 319; cf. *Australian Competition and Consumer Commission v Shell Co. of Australia Ltd* (1999) 161 A.L.R. 686, Fed.Ct.Aus; *Bengalla Mining Co. Pty Ltd v Barclay Mowlem Construction* [2001] N.S.W.S.C. 93, N.S.W. Supreme Ct.; *Azzi v Volvo* [2006] N.S.W.S.C. 283 (witness summons seeking documents from a party which could have been sought by disclosure may be an abuse of process); see also para.10.13 below.

[16] CPR, Pt 31, does not apply to cases in the small claims track: CPR, r.27.2(1)(b).

[17] *Assimina Maritime Ltd v Pakistan Shipping Corp* [2004] EWHC 3005 (Comm), [2005] 1 Lloyd's Rep. 525 (non-party disclosure under CPR, r.31.17 not available pursuant to s.44 Arbitration Act 1996, but witness summons available under s.43).

[18] *Re P (a Minor) (Witness Summons)* [1997] 2 F.L.R. 447, CA.

[19] *Amery v Long* (1808) 9 East 472 at 482; *R. v Stuart* (1886) 2 T.L.R.144 at 146.

[20] *Falmouth v Moss* (1822) 11 Price 455 (employee); *Crowther v Appleby* (1873) L.R. 9 C.P. 23 (company secretary and solicitor); *Eccles & Co. v Louisville and Nashville Railroad Co.* [1912] 1 K.B. 135, CA.

[21] *Rochfort v Trade Practices Commission* (1982) 153 C.L.R.134, H.Ct.Aus.

is open to the court to direct that the principal be notified of the summons, so that he or it can raise any objection he or it may have. Custody by one of two joint possessors is insufficient.[22] In such a case a witness summons should be served on all the persons having joint custody, unless such persons agree not to take the point.

(c) Witness within the United Kingdom

A witness summons may be directed to a person anywhere in the United Kingdom (which does not include the Channel Islands or the Isle of Man),[23] even in Scotland or Northern Ireland.[24] The court cannot compel the attendance of a witness outside the United Kingdom by this means.[25] The court will take into account the location of the documents and the place of residence of the witness in deciding whether to uphold a witness summons. The witness summons may be served on a person during a temporary visit to the United Kingdom and it may be unduly burdensome to require him to return to give evidence at a trial. Other than in exceptional circumstances, the court should not require a non-resident, who is not a party to the proceedings, but who happens to be within the jurisdiction, to produce documents situated outside the jurisdiction relating to business transacted outside the jurisdiction, because the summons would be an infringement of local sovereignty.[26]

10.09

(d) Identification

The witness summons must identify the documents required, by means of a particular description and not a general description.[27] The documents

10.10

---

[22] *Att.Gen. v Wilson* (1829) 9 Sim. 526; *Fookes v Samuel* [1913] 3 K.B. 706 at 722.

[23] *Davison v Farmer* (1851) 6 Exch. Rep. 242; *Re Brown* (1864) 33 L.J.Q.B. 193; *Navigation and General Insurance Co. Ltd v Ringrose* [1962] 1 W.L.R. 173, CA; *Rover International Ltd v Cannon Films Sales Ltd* [1987] 1 W.L.R. 1597 at 1603.

[24] Supreme Court Act 1981, s.36 (which does not allow a subpoena or witness summons to be issued in aid of an inferior tribunal or arbitration, where the witness is in Scotland or Northern Ireland); *Cheshire County Council v C* [1995] 2 F.L.R. 862 (held, on the facts, it was inappropriate to issue a *subpoena duces tecum* for service in Scotland, where criminal proceedings were pending).

[25] *Re Tucker* [1990] Ch. 148 at 158; *Re Seagull Manufacturing Co. Ltd* [1991] 4 All E.R. 257 at 262; *Rover International Ltd v Cannon Films Sales Ltd* [1987] 1 W.L.R. 1597 at 1603.

[26] *R. v Grossman* (1981) 73 Cr.App.R. 302, CA; *Mackinnon v Donaldson, Lufkin & Jenrette Securities Corp.* [1986] Ch. 482; *Arhill Pty. Ltd v General Terminal Company Pty. Ltd* (1991) 23 N.S.W.L.R. 545; *cf. UJB Financial Corporation v Chilmark Offshore Fund Ltd* 1992–93 C.I.L.R. 53, Cayman Grand Ct.

[27] *Att.Gen. v Watson* (1839) 9 Sim. 526; *Panayiotou v Sony Music Ltd* [1994] Ch. 142 at 151–5; *Hunt v Judge Russell* (1995) 63 S.A.S.R. 402; *Uthmann v Ipswich City Council* [1998] 1 Qd.R.435; *Australian Competition and Consumer Commission v Shell Co. of Australia Ltd* (1999) 161 A.L.R.686, Fed.Ct. Aus; *Re Global Info Ltd* [1999] 1 B.C.L.C. 74. *South Tyneside BC v Wickes Building Supplies Ltd* [2004] EWHC 2428 (Q.B.); *Tajik Aluminium Plant v Hydro Aluminium* [2005] EWCA Civ 1218, [2006] 1 W.L.R. 767, CA.

must either be individually identified, or identified by reference to a class of documents or things by which criterion the recipient can know what is the obligation which the court places on him. This requirement is particularly important, as failure to comply with a witness summons without sufficient excuse is a contempt of court. Thus the recipient should be able to determine from the description of the documents required precisely what documents are covered. A summons calling on a witness to go through his files and search for documents "relating to" specified matters "is too wide, being in effect a bill of discovery against a witness".[28] To put it another way, it is wrong in a summons to describe the documents required merely by reference to their relevance to the issues in the action.[29] A witness summons in this form will be set aside.[30] On the other hand, a compendious description of several documents may be sufficient, provided that the exact documents are thereby indicated.[31] In most cases a request for a file is too wide, and is liable to be set aside.[32] The requirement that the documents must be specified in one of the major limiting factors in practice, as often the party will not be in a position to specify the documents sought with sufficient precision.[33]

(e) Relevance and admissibility

10.11   The documents sought must be relevant to one or more of the issues in the proceedings, and admissible in the proceedings.[34] The stronger the claim to relevance, the more likely the court will uphold the summons. The court is

---

[28] *Lee v Angas* (1866) L.R.2 Eq.59; *Arhill Pty. Ltd v General Terminal Company Pty. Ltd* (1991) 23 N.S.W.L.R. 545; *Re Global Info Ltd* [1999] 1 B.C.L.C. 74 ("in relation to").

[29] *Derby & Co. Ltd v Weldon*, unreported, July 24, 1990, Vinelott J.

[30] *Williams & Glyn's Bank Ltd v Barnes*, January 16, 1979, unreported; *Sunderland Steamship P&I. Association v Gatoil International Inc.* [1988] 1 Lloyd's Rep. 180; *Wakefield v Outhwaite* [1990]2 Lloyd's Rep. 157; *Arhill Pty. Ltd v General Terminal Company Pty. Ltd* (1991) 23 N.S.W.L.R. 545

[31] *Re Asbestos Insurance Litigation* [1985] 1 W.L.R. 331 at 337.

[32] *Panayiotou v Sony Music Ltd* [1994] Ch. 142 at 154; *Omar v Omar*, unreported, October 11, 1996, CA; *cf. Wakefield v Outhwaite* [1990] 2 Lloyds Rep. 157 at 164.

[33] See *Omar v Omar*, unreported, October 11, 1996, CA.

[34] *R. v Cheltenham Justices, ex p. Secretary of State* [1977] 1 W.L.R. 95; *Sphere Drake Insurance Plc v Denby*, The Times, December 20, 1991; *R. v Skegness Magistrates Court, exp. Cardy* [1985] R.T.R. 49; *R. v Coventry Magistrates Court, ex p. Perks* [1985] R.T.R. 74; *Continental Reinsurance Corp. (UK) Ltd v Pine Top Insurance Ltd* [1986] 1 Lloyd's Rep. 8 at 10; *Multi-Guarantee Co. Ltd v Cavalier Insurance Co. Ltd (No.1)*, The Times, June 24, 1986; *R. v Peterborough Magistrates' Court, ex p. Willis* (1987) 151 J.P. 785, D.C.; *R. v Clowes* [1992] 3 All E.R. 440; *Macmillan Inc. v Bishopsgate Investment Trust Plc* [1993]1 W.L.R. 1372, CA; *Re Inquests into the deaths of Toman, Mckerr and others*, unreported, July 11, 1994, Nicholson J., H.Ct. of N.I. (*subpoena duces tecum* set aside as documents sought went beyond scope of inquest and hence were irrelevant); *London & Leeds Estates Ltd v Paribas Ltd (No.2)* [1995] 1 E.G.L.R. 102, Mance J.; *Evans v Granada Television Ltd*, unreported, April 2, 1993, Drake J. (excluded documents from *subpoena* on grounds of inadmissibility in evidence); *R. v Reading Justices, ex p. Berkshire County Council* [1996] 1 F.L.R. 149, D.C.; *cf. Re Dickinson* [1992] 2 N.Z.L.R. 43 (where the parties in effect agreed that any evidence was admissible), and *Dunn v British Coal Corporation* [1993] I.C.R. 591, CA; *Butler v Police Ombudsman for Northern Ireland* [2003] N.I.Q.B. 64.

unlikely to uphold a summons in respect of documents of marginal relevance, as in such a case it is difficult to justify the inconvenience to the third party, and the costs involved.[35] In one criminal case, the court held that the judge could accept the assertion of the possessor of the documents as to their irrelevance, or (if that were implausible or suspect) that of an independent competent lawyer.[36] The question of relevance is one for the first instance court and an appeal court will only interfere on limited grounds.[37] The requirement of admissibility is founded upon the fact that the witness summons is designed to bring evidence directly to the court. However in one Australian case a subpoena was upheld even though its purpose was to support an application for discovery against a party to the action and did not go to any of the substantive or final issues in the action.[38]

(f) Request must not be too wide

The courts are astute to ensure that witness summonses are kept within sensible bounds. Thus a summons which is in effect a request for discovery from a third party and lacks precision will be set aside as being an improper use of the procedure.[39] The summons must not be a fishing or speculative exercise. The request must be based on some reason to believe that the recipient actually has the documents sought, i.e. it is not simply fishing.[40] A summons issued on the basis of a hope that it may turn up some documents of assistance to the applicant's case is likely to be set aside on this ground.[41] A *subpoena duces tecum* has been set aside on the ground that the documents were not necessary, in that the applicant wanted the documents on a speculative basis to see if they contained material inconsistent with what a witness was saying in evidence.[42] Even where there is some basis for supposing that the respondent has the documents, he ought not to be required to undertake a search of an excessively large number of such documents.[43]

10.12

---

[35] *Xstrata Queensland Ltd v Santos Ltd* [2005] QSC 323 (no requirement documents sought must be directly relevant, but must be apparently relevant).

[36] *R. v W*, *The Times*, July 12, 1996, CA.

[37] *Noorani v Merseyside Tec Ltd* [1999] I.R.L.R. 184, CA.

[38] *ASIC v Rich* [2003] N.S.W.S.C. 257. This runs contrary to the practice in England.

[39] *Bürchard v MacFarlane* [1891] 2 Q.B.241; *Macmillan Inc. v Bishopsgate Investment Trust Plc* [1993] 1 W.L.R. 1372 at 1376–7; *Sunderland v Gatoil* [1988]1 Lloyd's Rep. 181 at 184–6; *Re Global Info. Ltd* [1999] 1 B.C.L.C. 74.

[40] *Senior v Holdsworth* [1976] Q.B. 23, CA; *Babanaft International Co. S.A. v Bassatne (No.2)*, unreported, May 23, 1989, CA; *Wakefield v Outhwaite* [1990] 2 Lloyd's Rep. 157; *Sphere Drake Insurance Plc v M. E. Denby*, *The Times*, December 20, 1991; *Macmillan Inc. v Bishopsgate Investment Trust Plc* [1993]1 W.L.R. 1372, CA; *Uthmann v Ipswich City Council* [1998] 1 Qd.R.435; *Re Global Info. Ltd* [1999] 1 B.C.L.C. 74; *Trade Practices Commission v Kimberley Homes Pty Ltd* (2005) 217 A.L.R. 110, Fed.Ct.Aus; *Mandic v Phillis* [2005] F.C.A. 1279, (2006) 225 A.L.R. 760, Fed.Ct.Aus.

[41] *Wasted Costs Order (No.5 of 1997)*, *The Times*, September 7, 1999, CA.

[42] *Macmillan Inc. v Bishopsgate Investment Trust Plc* [1993] 1 W.L.R. 1372; *cf. London & Leeds Estates plc v Paribas Ltd (No.2)* [1995] 02 E.G. 134.

[43] *Australian Competition and Consumer Commission v Shell Co. of Australia Ltd* (1999) 161 A.L.R.686, Fed.Ct.Aus.

(g) Necessity

10.13   The court must be satisfied that production of the documents sought is necessary for fairly disposing of the issues in the action,[44] or for saving costs, and is consistent with the overriding objective in CPR, r.1.1. The court will taken into account the requirements set out above and whether inter-partes disclosure has already been refused. A witness summons should not be used against an opposing party as a substitute for a disclosure application where that would be appropriate.[45] Even if the documents are sufficiently described, or by reference to a category, the summons may be set aside if it would operate oppressively on the third party.[46] The court will take into account the value of the documents of the case, and balance this against the hardship to the third party.

10.14   In deciding whether to uphold a witness summons the court may take into account whether the documents or copies of them are already in the hands of a party to the action. If they are, the court may consider that, rather than compelling a third party to produce them, the appropriate course is for a specific disclosure application to be made. If specific disclosure of documents as between the parties has been refused by the court, that is a cogent factor against treating such documents as the proper subject of a witness summons.[47]

10.15   The fact that a person has been compelled by a properly formulated witness summons to produce documents is a defence to an allegation of breach of confidentiality.[48] Confidentiality[49] and privacy are also relevant discretionary factors for the consideration of the court in deciding whether to uphold a witness summons. The third party's privacy should not be invaded unless that is counterbalanced by the interests of justice in the

---

[44] *Marcel v Metropolitan Police Commissioner* [1992] Ch. 225, CA; *Bookbinder v Tebbit (No.2)* [1992] 1 W.L.R. 217; *Arhill Pty Ltd v General Terminal Company Pty. Ltd* (1991) 23 N.S.W.L.R. 545; *Re Global Info. Ltd* [1999] 1 B.C.L.C. 74.

[45] *McIlwain v Ramsay Food Packaging Pty Ltd* [2005] F.C.A. 1233, (2006) 221 A.L.R. 785; *Azzi v Volvo* [2006] N.S.W.S.C. 283; see also para.10.07 above.

[46] *Derby & Co. Ltd v Weldon*, unreported, July 24, 1990, Vinelott J.; *Warren v Richard Costain Ltd*, unreported, May 15, 1991; *Marcel v Metropolitan Police Commissioner* [1992] Ch. 225, CA; *Frary v Frary* [1993] 2 F.L.R. 696, CA (production summons under Family Proceedings Rules, r.2.62); *Banque Bruxelles Lambert S.A. v Eagle Star Insurance Co. Ltd*, unreported, February 26, 1993, Phillips J.; *Re P (a Minor)(Witness summons)* [2000] 2 F.L.R. 447, CA (witness summons directed to minor aged 12); *Australian Competition and Consumer Commission v Shell Co. of Australia Ltd* (1999) 161 A.L.R. 686, Fed.Ct.Aus.

[47] *Steele v Savour* (1891) 8 T.L.R. 94; *cf. Australian Rugby Union Ltd v Hospitality Group Pty. Ltd* (2000) 173 A.L.R. 702 at 749–750; *ASIC v Rich* [2003] N.S.W.S.C. 257 (subpoena designed to support case that claimant should be ordered to provide proper discovery).

[48] *Barclays Bank Plc v Taylor* [1989] 1 W.L.R. 1066, CA; *Robertson v Canadian Imperial Bank of Commerce* [1994] 1 W.L.R. 1493, P.C.

[49] *Hassneh Insurance Co. of Israel v Mew* [1993] 2 Lloyd's Rep. 243 at 250–1; *London & Leeds Estates Ltd v Paribas Ltd (No.2)* [1995] 2 E.G. 134 at 137; *Mandic v Phillis* [2005] F.C.A. 1279, Fed.Ct.Aus.

individual case.[50] Thus witness summonses have been set aside where they have amounted to unwarranted intrusions into the private affairs of the recipients of the summonses.[51] Often a witness summons will require a third party to produce documents in respect of which he owes a duty of confidence to another. Prima facie, the fact that a third party owes a duty to another not to release a document without his consent, not being privileged,[52] is not an absolute objection to a witness summons, any more than a duty of confidence owed by a witness to another (not amounting to legal privilege or public interest immunity) justifies a refusal to answer a question asked in evidence,[53] or such a duty owed by a litigant to a third party justifies failing to give disclosure.[54] Thus, apart from cases of privilege, the court will not grant an injunction to restrain a breach of confidence in the use of documents in legal proceedings[55] and it is even open to a party to serve a witness summons upon the police, requiring them to produce documents seized under powers contained the Police and Criminal Evidence Act 1984.[56] In the case of particularly confidential or sensitive documents, it is open to the court to direct that the document should be produced but that disclosure should be confined to legal advisers and experts, with the sanction of contempt if the documents are disseminated further.[57]

Procedure

Issuing witness summons

A witness summons in the High Court and county court is obtained by filing two copies of the relevant practice form (N20)[58] with the court for sealing, one of which is retained on the court file.[59] A witness summons is   **10.16**

---

[50] See the European Convention on Human Rights, Art.8(1) (right to private life), Ch.21, paras 21.08–21.13, below, and cf. Z. v Finland (1997) 25 E.H.R.R. 371, 45 B.M.L.R. 107, E.Ct.H.R. (invasion justified for prevention of crime, and protection of rights of others), and Cantabrica Coach Holdings Ltd v Vehicle Inspectorate, The Times, April 13, 2000 (invasion justified for public safety).

[51] Morgan v Morgan [1977] Fam.122 (subpoena oppressive where it sought to force a non-party to reveal his private information); Parnell v Wood [1892] P.137 at 141; Harrison v Bloom Camillin, unreported, May 12, 1999, Neuberger J.; Australian Rugby Union Ltd v Hospitality Group Pty. Ltd (2000) 173 A.L.R. 702.

[52] R. v Daye [1908] 2 K.B. 333 at 338; Re Dickinson [1992] 2 N.Z.L.R. 43.

[53] Att.Gen. v Clough [1963] 1 Q.B. 733; Att.Gen. v Mulholland [1963] 2 Q.B. 477.

[54] See Ch.8, paras 8.23–8.24 above.

[55] Beer v Ward (1821) Jac. 77; Lewis v Smith (1849) 1 Mac. & G. 417; Goddard v Nationwide Building Society [1987] Q.B. 670 at 685.

[56] Marcel v Metropolitan Police Commissioner [1992] Ch. 225, CA; cf. Nottinghamshire County Council v H. [1995] 1 F.L.R. 115; Re M (Minors) [1995] 2 F.L.R. 57.

[57] Welfare v Birdon Sands Pty. Ltd (1997) 79 F.C.R. 220, Fed.Ct.Aus.; Re a Solicitor (Disclosure of Confidential Records) [1997] 1 F.L.R. 101 (contempt).

[58] See Appendix 3, para.C.02, below.

[59] CPR, Pt 34, Practice Direction, Depositions and Court Attendance by Witnesses, para.1.2.

issued on the date entered on the summons by the court.[60] The witness summons must be issued by the court where the case is proceeding or where the hearing in question will be held.[61] The witness summons is served by the court unless the party indicates in writing, when he asks the court to issue the summons, that he wishes to serve it himself.[62] Where the court is to serve the summons, the party must deposit in court conduct money to be paid to the witness.[63] Only one witnesses name may be included in the summons.[64]

10.17 In most situations, permission of the court is not required to issue a witness summons. It was held under the old rules that there was no need for pleadings to be closed or a summons for directions issued.[65] In principle, a witness summons under the CPR may be issued at any time. Permission is required however where the party seeking the witness summons wishes:

(a) to have a summons issued less than seven days before the date of the trial;

(b) to have a summons for a witness to attend court to give evidence or to produce documents on any date except the date fixed for the trial;

(c) to have a summons issued for a witness to attend court to give evidence or to produce evidence at any hearing except the trial.[66]

10.18 In considering whether or not to grant permission, the court will take into account, albeit on a preliminary basis, whether the requirements for a witness summons are met. This will usually be in the absence of argument on the part of the witness, and hence the fact that permission to issue has been granted does not preclude the court from setting aside or varying the summons on a subsequent occasion.[67]

10.19 Whether the court can issue a witness summons of its own volition is an open question. It had been a long established rule of practice prior to the CPR that a judge may not summon a witness on his own volition without the assent of the parties.[68] However the Court of Appeal has held that an

---

[60] CPR, r.34.3(1), formerly CCR, Ord.20, r.12(1), (2). The practice in the High Court was different, whereby a *subpoena duces tecum* was obtained by filing a *praecipe* in the court office and the writ was sealed at the same time: RSC, Ord.38, r.14.

[61] CPR, r.34.3(3).

[62] CPR, r.34.6(1).

[63] CPR, r.34.6(2).

[64] CPR, r.34.3(2), formerly CCR, Ord.20, r.12(3). In the High Court more than one person's name could be inserted in a writ of *subpoena ad testificandum*: RSC, Ord.38, r.15.

[65] *MacBryan v Brooke* [1946] 2 All E.R. 688, CA.

[66] CPR, r.34.3(2); *cf.* the former practice where leave was only required when proceedings were in chambers (RSC, Ord.32, r.7; CCR, Ord.20, r.12(8)) or in the Court of Appeal.

[67] CPR, r.34(4); *Harrison v Bloom Camillin*, unreported, May 12, 1999, Neuberger J.

[68] *Re Enoch and Zaretsky, Bock & Co.'s Arbitration* [1910] 1 K.B. 327, CA; *Jones v NCB* [1957] 2 All E.R. 157 at 159, CA.

Immigration Appeal Tribunal has the power to summon a witness against the wishes of both parties under r.27(1) of the Immigration Appeals (Procedure) Rules.[69] The court left open the question whether a judge in civil proceedings has, since the introduction of the CPR, power to call a witness in circumstances where neither party wishes to call him. Whilst it may be possible to conceive of circumstances where such a course of action may be appropriate, the power should be regarded as one only to be exercised in exceptional circumstances. The system is adversarial, rather than inquisitorial, and there may be good reasons (not necessarily known to the judge) why neither party desires to call a particular witness. The judge may face the situation of having to examine in chief a witness, without knowing what the witness may say. The court does have the power to order a party to attend a hearing.[70]

Service

The summons must normally be issued and served on the witness at least **10.20** seven days before the date on which the witness is required to attend before the court or tribunal.[71] The court may direct that a witness summons shall be binding, although it may be served less than seven days before that date.[72] It is not appropriate to serve short, and then apply to the court for permission. Travelling expenses and compensation for loss of time must be tendered at the time of service.[73] Service is by the court, unless the party elects to carry it out himself.[74] Where the witness summons is served by the court, it will usually do so by first class post.[75] Where the party elects to carry out service himself, he still has the option of using first class post, but often it will be safer to effect personal service, particularly where there is the possibility that the witness may be reluctant to attend court. The court has power to direct service by an alternative method (formerly called substituted service).[76]

Duration

Once served, the witness summons continues to be binding until the **10.21** conclusion of the hearing at which the attendance of the witness is

---

[69] *Kesse v Secretary of State for the Home Department* [2001] EWCA Civ 177; [2001] Imm.A.R. 366, *The Times*, March 21, 2001, CA.

[70] CPR, r.3.1(2)(c); *Tarajan Overseas Ltd v Kaye* [2001] EWCA Civ 1859, *The Times*, January 22, 2002, CA.

[71] CPR, r.34.5(1).

[72] CPR, r.34.5(2).

[73] CPR, r.34.7; Pt 34, Practice Direction, Depositions and Court Attendance by Witnesses, para.3; Supreme Court Act 1981, s.36(4).

[74] CPR, r.34.6; *cf.* RSC, Ord.38, r.17 (personal service was normal rule).

[75] See Form N20 standard wording for certificate of service to be signed by court officer (Appendix 3, para.C.02, below).

[76] CPR, r.6.8; *Dyson v Foster*, unreported, February 7, 1908, Jeff J.

required.[77] It is open to the court to release the witness once he has given evidence, or produced the documents required and that is the usual practice.[78]

Amendment

10.22   A mistake in the name or address of a person named in a witness summons may be corrected if the summons has not been served. The corrected summons must be resealed by the court and marked "amended and resealed".[79] If other amendments are required before service, presumably the permission of the court may be obtained, but often it will be cheaper and simpler to issue a fresh witness summons. Once a summons has been served, it may be amended with the permission of the court or by its own motion if it considers that the wording of the documents sought is too wide or otherwise inappropriate.[80]

Return Day

10.23   Prior to the introduction of the CPR in April 1999, the standard forms of subpoena[81] (in the High Court) and witness summons[82] (in the County Court) required the recipient to bring the documents concerned to the court on the first day of the trial of the action (which was stated). This was far too late for the usual purposes of disclosure. Accordingly, a practice grew up whereby a subpoena was made returnable on a day artificially fixed by the court as the first day of the trial, although in fact the trial proper would not begin until later.[83] In this way the party seeking production of documents had the opportunity of seeing them in advance of the trial, so preventing adjournments and saving costs. This practice stretched the traditional role of the subpoena, in which it had no pre-trial function at all and was not

---

[77] CPR, r.34.5(3); formerly RSC, Ord.38 r.18.
[78] cf. Wakefield v Outhwaite [1990] 2 Lloyd's Rep. 157 at 165 (requirement that witness attend throughout arbitration deleted from subpoena by court).
[79] CPR, Pt 34, Practice Direction, Depositions and Court Attendance by Witnesses, paras 1.3, 1.4; formerly RSC, Ord.38 r.17.
[80] CPR, r.34.3(4).
[81] RSC, App.A, Form 28.
[82] County Court Forms, N20.
[83] Suggested in Williams v Williams [1988] Q.B. 161 at 169, CA, and put on a formal footing in Khanna v Lovell White Durrant [1995] 1 W.L.R. 121; see also Southern Pacific Hotel Services Inc v Southern Pacific Hotel Corp [1984] 1 N.S.W.L.R. 710 at 716; Re B.S.B. Holdings Ltd [1993] B.C.L.C. 246 at 255; Nottingham County Council v H. [1995] 1 F.L.R. 115; cf. O'Sullivan v Herdmans Ltd [1987] 1 W.L.R. 1047, HL. The Australian authorities are exhaustively examined in J. Boag & Son Brewing Ltd v Cascade Brewery Co. Pty. Ltd (1997) 7 Tas.R.119, where the subpoena was set aside.

permitted to become a "bill of discovery against a witness".[84] Under the CPR, the rules expressly provide that a witness summons may be issued for a return date other than the date fixed for trial. However, in such a case the permission of the court is required prior to the issue of the summons.[85] In this way, the court can prevent inappropriate witness summonses being issued for hearings prior to trial. Such a procedure will usually be appropriate where the witness has no material oral evidence to give and all that is sought is that he produce specified documents and prove their authenticity. Under the old rules, there was a limited power to apply to the court to require a person to attend any proceedings in the cause or matter and produce specified or describe documents, where their production appeared to be necessary for the purposes of that proceeding. Whilst this could require attendance at a proceeding in a cause or matter prior to trial, this power was rarely exercised and narrowly construed.[86]

Inferior courts and tribunals

Special provisions apply in relation to witness summonses issued by the court in aid of an inferior court or of a tribunal.[87] An "inferior court or tribunal" means any court or tribunal[88] that does not have power to issue a witness summons in relation to proceedings before it.[89] Similarly, a witness summons may be issued by the court in aid of an arbitration.[90] Such a witness summons may be set aside by the court which issued it, and in particular by a master or district judge in the High court, or a district judge in the county court.[91] Unless the court otherwise directs, the applicant for an order to set aside must give at least two days' notice of the application to the party who issued the witness summons, and the application is

10.24

---

[84] *Lee v Angas* (1866) L.R. 2 Eq. 59 at 63; see also *R. v Skegness Magistrates' Court, exp. Cardy* [1985] R.T.R. 49 at 58, 61; *R. v Clowes* [1992] 3 All E.R. 440 at 449; *Macmillan Inc v Bishopsgate Investment Trust Plc* [1993] 1 W.L.R. 1372, CA.
[85] CPR, r.34.3(2).
[86] RSC, Ord.38, r.13; *Elder v Carter* (1890) 25 Q.B.D. 194, CA; *Straker Brothers & Co. v Reynolds* (1889) 22 Q.B.D. 262; *Khanna v Lovell White Durrant* [1995] 1 W.L.R. 121.
[87] CPR, r.34.4(1); Pt 34, Practice Direction, Depositions and Court Attendance by Witnesses, para.2.1; formerly RSC, Ord.38, r.19; *Soul v Inland Revenue Commissioners* [1963] 1 W.L.R. 112, CA.
[88] See *Currie v Chief Constable of Surrey* [1982] 1 W.L.R. 215 (an inferior tribunal must be recognised by law, be acting judicially or quasi-judicially and upon evidence).
[89] CPR, r.34.4(3); Pt 34, Practice Direction, Depositions and Court Attendance by Witnesses, para.2.2; some tribunals have statutory powers to issue witness summonses: see Ch.20, passim.
[90] Arbitration Act 1996, s.43; *Assimina Maritime Ltd v Pakistan Shipping Corp.* [2004] EWHC 3005 (Comm), [2005] Lloyd's Rep. 525; *BNP Paribas v Deloitte & Touche LLP* [2003] EWHC 2874 (Comm); *Xstrata Queensland Ltd v Santos Ltd* [2005] QSC 323.
[91] CPR, Pt 34, Practice Direction, Depositions and Court Attendance by Witnesses, para.2.3.

normally dealt with at a hearing.[92] There are various statutory powers for the court to issue witness summonses in aid of specific tribunals or for specific purposes.[93] In the context of a hearing before the Parole Board it is open to the panel to require the Secretary of State to arrange the attendance of a witness, if necessary by obtaining a witness summons pursuant to CPR, r.34.4.[94]

Production

10.25   Production of the documents is to *the court*, not to either party, or both parties, in the action. If he does otherwise, the third party producing the documents may be guilty of a breach of confidence, as he would have voluntarily produced the documents without compulsion of law. In one case[95] the third party recipient of a *subpoena duces tecum*, an area health authority, sought to comply with it by supplying the documents concerned (the confidential medical records of a non-party) to the solicitor for the party issuing the writ. Booth J. said[96]:

> "A further matter of grave concern is the fact that on receipt of the *subpoena duces tecum* the area health authority sought to comply with it by sending the file containing Mr A's records to the solicitors responsible for the issue of the writ. I have not thought it necessary to request the attendance of an officer of the area health authority concerned to give me an explanation as to how this came about, but, for whatever reason that procedure was adopted, it was clearly incorrect. Not only are the documents concerned of a highly confidential nature, and as such are entitled to protection from unauthorised disclosure, but it amounts to a fundamental misunderstanding of the writ of *subpoena duces tecum*. That writ 'commands' the attendance at Court of the person to whom it is addressed with the further requirement that he should bring with him and produce the specified documents. This makes it clear that it is to the Court that the documents are to be produced and, pending the direction of the Court, to no one else. It was, therefore, quite incorrect on the part of the area health authority to send the records to the mother's solicitors and it amounted to a

---

[92] CPR, Pt 34, Practice Direction, Depositions and Court Attendance by Witnesses, para.2.4.

[93] Dentists Act 1984, Sch.3. para.4 (General Dental Council); Professions Supplementary to Medicine Act 1960, Sch.2, Pt 2, para.2 (Disciplinary Committee); Nurses Amendment Act 1961, s.9; Solicitors Act 1974, s.46(11); Lloyd's Act 1982, s.7; Financial Services and Markets Tribunal Rules 2001, r.12 (FSMT).

[94] *R. (on the application of Brooks) v Parole Board* [2004] EWCA Civ 80, (2004) 148 S.J.L.B. 233, by way of a direction under r.9 of the Parole Board Rules 1997.

[95] *Re S.L. (A Minor)* [1987] 2 F.L.R. 412.

[96] *ibid.* at 414; see also *Marcel v Metropolitan Police Commissioner* [1992] Ch. 225, CA.

wholly unauthorised disclosure by them of confidential documents relating to Mr A. If in any case where a *subpoena duces tecum* has been issued and served and there are difficulties for the person to whom it is addressed or his authorised representative in attending court to produce the documents, or other problems impede compliance with its terms, then it is essential that the guidance of the Court should be sought".

10.26 There may be exceptional cases where a different course is justified. Thus in one case[97] *subpoenas duces tecum* directed to a certain bank required the production of a considerable number of documents relating to another non-party, who was understandably concerned that some of such documents might not be relevant to the action, and others might be privileged. The Court of Appeal devised a system of submission by the banks of the documents to the court, for onward transmission to solicitors acting for the non-party concerned, sifting, listing of documents, and giving an opportunity for debate before the court of the list by the party at whose instance the *subpoenas* were issued. A similar procedure was subsequently employed in another case[98] in relation to documents in the hands of a non-party, in respect of which documents the defendants themselves claimed privilege or irrelevance, but the defendants did not seek in that case to argue that the *subpoenas* (which were couched in terms of very wide categories of documents sought) should be set aside as oppressive or as an abuse of process.[99]

10.27 There is no set procedure as to how the documents should be produced to the court.[100] Much may depend on the circumstances, such as the number of documents and whether the summons is being challenged. Ordinarily the witness will be called and will produce the documents by reference to the summons. The list in the summons can be gone through and the witness can confirm whether or not he has documents within each category. The judge may permit brief questions of the witness as to what searches he has carried out and whether he knows the whereabouts of documents he is unable to produce. Normally the court will not permit a witness to be cross examined on a normal witness summons to produce documents. The witness may be called to authenticate the documents he produces. Once the documents have been produced to the court, the judge may release the documents into the custody of one of the parties (or his solicitor), on appropriate undertakings,

---

[97] *Babanaft International Co. S.A. v Bassatne (No.2)*, unreported, May 23, 1989, CA.
[98] *Derby & Co. Ltd v Weldon*, unreported, July 25, 1990, Vinelott J.
[99] A non-party who did so argue succeeded in having a *subpoena* against him set aside.
[100] *Waind v Hill and National Employers' Mutual General Association Ltd* [1987] 1 N.S.W.L.R. 376, CA of N.S.W., describes a three-stage procedure: (1) compliance with the witness summons by the recipient producing the documents to the court; (2) decision of the court as to whether to allow either or all of the parties to inspect them before the trial; (3) if a party tenders them in evidence, court decides whether they are admissible (or, if not put in evidence, court decides what use may be made of them, e.g. in cross-examination).

such as to hold the documents to the order of the court, to permit access to the other parties and for copying, and to return the originals to the person who produced them. Once the witness has produced the documents and answered any questions about them, the judge will usually release the witness.

Responding to and challenging witness summonses

10.28   A recipient of a witness summons should always consider whether the documents relate to the confidential affairs of another, particularly a person other than the one who issued the summons.[101] Where the documents sought are confidential, then the person whose affairs they relate to will have the right to appear before the court and object to the summons.[102] It is doubtful that the recipient of a witness summons is under a legal obligation to another to contest a properly formulated witness summons,[103] although he may be expected to point out to the court if the documents are covered by the legal professional privilege of a third party.[104] On the other hand, a recipient may be under an obligation at least to use reasonable endeavours to inform the person whose confidential affairs the documents relate to of the existence of the witness summons, so that that person has the opportunity of objecting.[105] It is therefore usually prudent to inform the person whose confidential affairs are covered by the document sought under the witness summons of the existence of the summons, or at the very least to inform the court when complying with the summons that such persons have not been informed. In appropriate cases it may be sensible to ask the person issuing the witness summons whether or not the person whose affairs are covered by that summons has been informed of the application.

10.29   As the issue of a witness summons is an administrative rather than a judicial function, there is no effective check on the propriety of issue at that stage, save in those cases where permission of the court is required. Accordingly, it not infrequently occurs that inappropriate witness summonses are served. An application may be made to the master or district judge, as appropriate, of the court that issued the summons, to set aside or vary it upon notice in writing to the party who issued the witness summons[106]; usually an application on notice should be taken out.[107] In the case of

---

[101] *London & Leeds Estates Ltd v Paribas Ltd (No.2)* [1995] 1 E.G.L.R. 102; see also para.10.15 above.
[102] *Mandic v Phillis* [2005] F.C.A. 1279, (2006) 225 A.L.R. 760, Fed.Ct.Aus; *Trade Practices Commission v Kimberley Homes Pty Ltd* (2005) 217 A.L.R. 110, Fed. Ct. of Aus.; see also the cases cited in footnotes to this paragraph.
[103] *Barclays Bank Plc v Taylor* [1989] 1 W.L.R. 1066.
[104] *Robertson v Canadian Imperial Bank of Commerce* [1994] 1 W.L.R. 1493 at 1499.
[105] *Robertson v Canadian Imperial Bank of Commerce* [1994] 1 W.L.R. 1493, P.C.
[106] CPR, r.34.3(4).
[107] Applications should generally be served at least three days before the court is to deal with the application: CPR, r.23.7(1)(b); the court may abridge this period: r.23.7(4).

inferior courts and tribunals, usually two days' notice should be given, although the court may vary or dispense with this period of notice.[108] In appropriate cases, such as where the matter is being tried before a judge, the application should be referred to the trial judge.[109] In the Commercial Court and the Technology and Construction Court, the application is in any event to the judge. An application to set aside or limit the scope of a witness summons may be made, not only by the persons by or on whom it is served, but also by "any person whose legal rights will be interfered with by [its] execution".[110] Examples are the person who owns the documents which are the subject of the witness summons[111] and a person entitled to the confidentiality or privacy in the documents concerned.[112] Ordinarily the other parties to the action lack standing to make an application to set aside the witness summons,[113] unless of course they have an interest in the documents concerned. If a general right were recognised in an opposite party to raise objections to the witness summons, it would encourage ancillary litigation.[114] In Australia it has been recognised that an opposing party in litigation may have a limited interest in setting aside a subpoena, namely an interest that the hearing should not be allowed to expand beyond a trial of the issues raised by the pleadings and matters necessarily ancillary thereto.[115] An opposing party may object to the production and admissibility of the documents when the witness summons is complied with in court.[116]

Where a recipient of a witness summons considers that he may wish to challenge its terms, the sensible course is to write to the party who issued it, and ask him to:

10.30

(a) supply a copy of the statements of case in the action;

(b) explain the relevance of each category of documents sought;

(c) confirm whether or not any person whose affairs the documents relate to has been notified of the witness summons; and, where appropriate;

---

[108] CPR, Pt 34, Practice Direction, Depositions and Court Attendance by Witnesses, paras 2.2–2.4 (witness summons in aid of an inferior court or tribunal).

[109] As in *Harrison v Bloom Camillin*, unreported, May 12, 1999 Neuberger J.

[110] *Marcel v Metropolitan Police Commissioner* [1992] Ch. 225 at 239, upheld by CA on this point; *cf. Boeing Co. v P.P.G. Industries Inc.* [1988] 3 All E.R. 839, CA (similar decision under the Evidence (Proceedings in Other Jurisdictions) Act 1975).

[111] *Marcel v Metropolitan Police Commissioner* [1992] Ch. 225 at 253.

[112] *London & Leeds Estates Ltd v Paribas Ltd (No.2)* [1995] 2 E.G. 134 at 137; *Hunt v Judge Russell* (1995) 63 S.A.S.R. 402; see also *Nationwide Mutual Insurance Co. v Home Insurance Co.*, unreported, October 20, 1998, Sachs J. *R.(B) v Stafford Combined Court* [2006] EWHC 1645 (Admin), [2007] 1 All E.R. 102.

[113] *Jonal Properties Pty Ltd v Ms McLeod Holdings Ltd* [1994] S.A.S.C. 4380, Sup.Ct.South Australia.

[114] *ibid.; cf. Botany Bay Instrumentation & Control Pty. Ltd v Stewart* [1984] 3 N.S.W.L.R. 98.

[115] *Bengalla Mining Co. Pty Ltd v Barclay Mowlem Construction* [2001] N.S.W.S.C. 93, N.S.W. Sup. Ct.

[116] *Boeing Co. v P.P.G. Industries Inc.* [1988] 3 All E.R. 839 at 842.

> (d) state whether any of the documents sought are already in the hands of any of the parties to the action.

In the light of any response, the recipient will be in a better position to decide whether or not it is appropriate to make an application to the court.[117]

10.31 On an application to set aside or vary a witness summons, the burden is on the party who issued it to justify the summons, and the categories of documents sought.[118] Potentially there are numerous grounds of objection which may be raised. CPR, r.34.2(5) expressly provides that the only documents that a witness summons can require a person to produce before a hearing are documents which that person could be required to produce at the hearing. The principal objections are as follows:

> (a) the witness summons is not addressed to a specific individual, or is addressed to an inappropriate individual[119];
>
> (b) the witness does not have custody of the documents, or has custody jointly with another, or on behalf of another[120];
>
> (c) the witness has not been properly served, or was not served within the United Kingdom[121];
>
> (d) the description of the documents is not sufficiently specific[122];
>
> (e) the documents sought are not relevant, or are inadmissible[123];
>
> (f) the request for documents is fishing, or a speculative exercise, or is too wide, or oppressive, or is not confined to what is reasonably necessary[124];
>
> (g) production is not reasonably necessary for fairly disposing of the issues in the action or for saving costs, or is not consistent with the overriding objective in CPR, r.1.1[125]; in this regard the court may take into account:
>
>> (i) the costs involved;
>>
>> (ii) the burden on the recipient[126];
>>
>> (iii) the importance of the documents concerned in determining the issues in the case;

---

[117] See also *R. v M* [1996] 1 F.L.R. 750 at 752 (local authority files).

[118] *Sunderland Steamship P. & I. Association v Gatoil International Inc.* [1988] 1 Lloyds Rep. 180 at 185; *Macmillan Inc. v Bishopsgate Investment Trust Plc* [1993] 1 W.L.R. 1372 at 1375, 1378; *Arhill Pty. Ltd v General Terminal Company Pty. Ltd* (1991) 23 N.S.W.L.R. 545 at 555–6.

[119] See para.10.07 above.

[120] See para.10.08 above.

[121] See para.10.09 above.

[122] See para.10.10 above.

[123] See para.10.11 above.

[124] See para.10.12 above.

[125] See para.10.13 above.

[126] See para.10.13 above.

    (iv) confidentiality and privacy[127];

    (v) whether the documents are already in the hands of a party or inter partes disclosure has already been refused[128];

(h) the documents sought are covered by legal professional privilege or other recognised privilege[129] and the person in whom the privilege is vested is not prepared to waive it[130];

(i) the documents sought are covered by public interest immunity; in this situation the court will normally expect to have evidence filed by the person asserting public interest immunity, and will engage in the same balancing exercise as with disclosure of documents under CPR, r.31.19, in order to decide whether production should be ordered; just because the documents are in the hands of the police or regulatory body is not conclusive in deciding whether public interest immunity applies at all or, if it does apply, whether the documents should be ordered to be produced in the interests of justice in any event[131];

(j) production of the documents would expose the witness to a criminal charge or penalty[132];

(k) production of the documents would constitute a criminal offence under English law[133];

(l) the witness is an unwilling expert witness.[134]

The court will not necessarily set aside a witness summons merely on the basis of an assertion in a witness statement or affidavit that the witness can give no relevant evidence.[135] However, on an application to set aside, the recipient should always consider whether evidence is required. At the hearing of an application to set aside, or when the witness attends court to comply with the summons, the court may, instead of setting aside the whole

10.32

---

[127] See para.10.15 above.

[128] See para.10.14 above.

[129] *Ainsworth Lumber Co. v Canada (Attorney-General)* (2003) 326 D.L.R. (4th) 93, British Columbia CA; *Telezone Inc. v Manley* (2004) 235 D.L.R. (4th) 719, Ontario CA (parliamentary privilege raised by Member of Parliament whilst Parliament in session).

[130] See Ch.12, paras 12.03–12.10; *Roux v Australian Broadcasting Commission* [1992] 2 V.R. 577 at 595–6.

[131] See Ch.11, paras 11.88–11.90; *Marcel v Metropolitan Police Commissioner* [1992] Ch. 225; *R. v Clowes* (1992) 95 Cr.App.R. 440; *Nottingham County Council v H.* [1995] 1 F.L.R. 115; *Re M (Minors)* [1995] 2 F.L.R. 57; see also *Auten v Rayner (No.2)* [1960] 1 Q.B. 669, and *Bookbinder v Tebbit (No.2)* [1992] 1 W.L.R. 217; *Re A Subpoena issued by the Commissioner for Local Administration* [1996] 2 F.L.R. 629.

[132] See Ch.11, para.11.105; *Whitaker v Izod* (1809) 2 Taunt. 115; *Roe v Harvey* (1769) 4 Burr. 2484.

[133] *cf.* Banking Act 1987, s.42; *Bank of Credit and Commerce International (Overseas) Ltd v Price Waterhouse (No.2)* [1998] Ch. 84; Financial Services Act 1986, s.179; as to taking into account exposure to prosecution under foreign law, see para.11.150.

[134] *Brown v Bennett, The Times,* November 2, 2000.

[135] *R. v Baines* [1909] 1 K.B. 258 at 262; *cf. R. v Lewis Justices, exp. Home Secretary* [1972] 1 Q.B. 232; *R. v W, The Times,* July 12, 1996, CA.

summons, amend or redraw it as necessary.[136] But variation can only take place where, as a result, specific relevant documents can be identified, the disclosure of which is necessary for the fair trial of the action or to save costs.[137] Normally the court will only consider a variation to save the summons where a considered draft has been put before the court.[138] Where the witness summons is too wide, the court may simply set aside the whole summons, rather than permitting it to be varied. Once the recipient has collated the documents and admitted that they are in his possession, the court may reject any application to set aside on the basis that the request for documents is too wide.[139]

10.33   Similar principles apply in relation to applications to set aside witness summonses in aid of criminal proceedings issued under s.2 of the Criminal Procedure (Attendance of Witnesses) Act 1965. Section 2C of the Act provides that, if a person in respect of whom a witness summons has been issued applies to the Crown Court and satisfies the court (inter alia) that he cannot give any material evidence, or, as the case may be, produce any document or thing likely to be material evidence, the court may direct that the summons shall be of no effect.[140]

Failure to comply with witness summons

10.34   Failure to comply with a properly served witness summons constitutes a contempt of court, and opens up the recipient to the possibility of a fine, imprisonment and/or an adverse costs order. The practice form (N20)[141] includes a warning to the recipient not to ignore the summons. It states that, if the recipient was offered money for travel expenses and compensation for loss of time at the time of service, and fails to attend or produce documents as required by the summons, or refuses to take an oath or affirm for the purposes of answering questions about his evidence or the documents he has been asked to produce, he may be liable to a fine or imprisonment and may be ordered to pay costs. Even where it is believed that the witness summons is misconceived, the correct course is to apply to set it aside, and not simply

---

[136] CPR, r.34.3(4); *Sunderland Steamship P. & I. Association v Gatoil International Inc.* [1988] 1 Lloyd's Rep. 180 at 185.

[137] *Re Global Info. Ltd* [1999] 1 B.C.L.C. 74 at 83.

[138] *Wakefield v Outhwaite* [1990] 2 Lloyd's Rep. 157 at 165; *Re Global Info. Ltd* [1999] 1 B.C.L.C. 74 at 84.

[139] *Lee v Angas* (1866) L.R. 2 Eq. 59.

[140] Crown Court Rules 1982, r.23; *R. v Hove Justices, exp. Donne* [1967] 2 All E.R. 1253n.; the relevant principles for setting aside were considered in *R. v Lewes Justices, exp. Secretary of State for Home Department* [1972] 1 Q.B. 232; *R. v Cheltenham Justices, exp. Secretary of State for Trade* [1977] 1 W.L.R. 95, D.C.; *R. v Clowes* (1992) 95 Cr.App.R. 440, CCC; *R. v Reading Justices, exp. Berkshire County Council* [1996] 1 F.L.R. 149, D.C.

[141] See Appendix 3, para.C.02.

to ignore it. An order for committal will not be made unless it is established that the witness summons has been served in accordance with the rules, that the travelling expenses and compensation for loss of time was tendered and the witness was otherwise liable to obey the summons. It has been held in the context of a *subpoena duces tecum* that it must also be shown that the documents sought existed at the relevant time and were in possession of the witness.[142] However, this should not be taken as a licence for a recipient simply to ignore the summons if he has no documents covered by the summons. Where he has no documents, he should notify the person who issued the summons and invite him to withdraw it. In default of withdrawal, he should either apply to set it aside if appropriate, or simply attend court on the return day and give evidence to the court that he has no such documents. The court may enforce obedience to a witness summons by committal even in cases where the disobedience is not wilful.[143] The court will not countenance steps by a recipient to remove documents out of his possession after service of a summons on him, though he will not be committed for contempt if the documents are taken out of his possession by a third party.[144]

Costs

The recipient of a witness summons is entitled to travelling expenses and compensation for loss of time, and this must be tendered at the time of service.[145] The travelling expenses must be in a sum sufficient to pay for the witness's expenses in travelling to the court and in returning to his home or place of work. Often it will be prudent to check with the witness in advance of service what this sum will be. The sum for loss of earnings or benefit is based on the sums payable to witnesses attending the Crown Court,[146] which may be less than his actual earnings, particularly in the case of executives and senior employees. It seems that the recipient is not entitled to

10.35

---

[142] *O'Born v Commissioner for Government Transport* (1960) 77 W.N. (N.S.W.) 81.

[143] *R. v Daye* [1908] 2 K.B. 333; the Criminal Procedure (Attendance of Witnesses) Act 1965, s.3, provides that a person "who without just excuse disobeys a witness order or witness summons" is guilty of contempt and liable to imprisonment for up to three months; the Crown Court may also issue an arrest warrant to compel attendance under s.4, as amended by the Criminal Procedure and Investigations Act 1996, s.67.

[144] *R. v Stuart* (1886) 2 T.L.R. 244 (no contempt by company secretary served with *subpoena* to produce company's books, when books taken out of his possession by directors' resolution); *quaere* whether a third party, removing documents from the recipient's possession in order to avoid production, is himself liable for contempt of court.

[145] CPR, Pt 34, Practice Direction, Depositions and Court Attendance by Witnesses, para.3; Supreme Court Act 1981, s.36(4).

[146] Fixed pursuant to the Prosecution of Offences Act 1985, s.19(3), and the Costs in Criminal Cases (General) Regulations 1986, regs 18, 19, 20 and 25. The rates are not generous.

his costs for searching for the documents,[147] although the court may take into consideration the extent of these costs in deciding whether to uphold the witness summons. The fact that a witness attending under CPR r.34.2 is likely only to obtain conduct money and his expenses in contrast to non-party disclosure under CPR r.31.17 may be a material factor in deciding which procedure should be adopted.[148] In one case where a witness summons was served on a bank where it would have been more appropriate to have sought non-party disclosure under CPR r.31.17, after the party decided not to proceed with the summons at the last moment, the court joined the bank as a party and awarded it costs of complying with the witness summons (in locating the documents).[149] In practice, where there are likely to be a large number of documents to be collated, the party issuing the witness summons may offer to pay the reasonable costs of the witness. A recipient who successfully challenges a witness summons will normally be awarded his costs in doing so.[150] In practice, even where the challenge is unsuccessful, the recipient is often awarded his costs, so long as he acted reasonably in making the challenge in the first place. Where the challenge is unreasonable, the recipient may be ordered to pay the costs of the application. Where a witness summons is set aside as having been applied for without reasonable cause, the lawyers concerned are at risk of having a wasted costs order made against them.[151] In some jurisdictions (notably Australia) there are specific provisions enabling the court to compensate a recipient for expenses and costs incurred in complying with a subpoena.[152]

Restriction on collateral use

10.36   A document produced pursuant to a witness summons is subject to an implied undertaking against use for a purpose other than the proceedings in

---

[147] *Bank of New South Wales v Withers* (1981) 35 A.L.R. 21; *Re Marriage of Kennedy and Evans* (1994) 18 Fam. L.R. 472 ("conduct money" does not include the cost of searching for the documents sought).

[148] *Re Howglen Ltd* [2001] 1 All E.R. 376 at 384, Ch.D; para.10.05 above.

[149] *Individual Homes Ltd v Macbream Investments Ltd* (2002) 99 (46) L.S.G. 32, *The Times,* November 14, 2002, Ch.D.

[150] *Warren v Richard Costain Ltd,* unreported, May 15, 1991; *Shannon v Country Casuals Holdings Plc, The Times,* June 16, 1997; *Danieletto v Khera* (1995) 35 N.S.W.L.R. 684; *Pyramid Building Society v Farrow Finance Corp.* [1995] 1 V.R. 464; *Harrison v Bloom Camillin,* unreported, May 12, 1999, Neuberger J.

[151] *R. v M.* [1996] 1 F.L.R. 750; *Re Ronald A. Prior & Co. (Solicitors)* [1996] 1 Cr.App.R. 248; *Wasted Costs Order (No.5 of 1997), The Times,* September 7, 1999, CA.

[152] e.g. Federal Court Rules 0.27 r.4A, considered in *Chapman v Luminis Pty Ltd (No.3)* (2000) 179 A.L.R. 702, Fed.Ct.Aus. (recipient awarded costs of obtaining legal advice, but not of unsuccessful challenge to subpoena); Supreme Court Rules Pt 37 r.9 considered in *Fuel Express Ltd. v L.M. Ericsson Pty Ltd* (1987) 75 A.L.R. 284 and *Marsden v Amalgamated Television Services Pty Ltd* [2001] N.S.W.S.C. 77 (recipient awarded costs of obtaining legal advice and preparing production).

which they were produced.[153] The provisions in respect of subsequent use of disclosed documents in CPR, r.31.22 probably do not apply, as it appears that those provisions are confined to documents produced pursuant to CPR, Pt 31.[154]

C. BANKER'S BOOKS EVIDENCE ACT 1879

Sections 1–6

The Act was first passed in 1876, and re-enacted in modified form in 1879, in order to get over the difficulty and hardship relating to the production of banker's books. If such books contained anything which would be evidence for either of the parties, the banker or his clerk had to produce them at the trial under a *subpoena duces tecum*, which was an inconvenience when the books were in regular use. The leading object of this Act was to relieve bankers from that inconvenience. This is accomplished by the first six sections of the Act, which enable bankers to send attested copies of entries in their books, instead of producing the originals.[155] Although the Act is concerned to make the proof at trial of banking transactions easier—and therefore it amends the substantive law of evidence—it also has an impact on the law and practice of disclosure, by enabling orders to be made for pre-trial disclosure of documentary evidence in the hands of non-parties (i.e. banks) relating to accounts held by the parties to the litigation and, indeed, sometimes by non-parties as well. It also enables such disclosure to take place after the trial.[156] **10.37**

The general principle of the Act is that a copy of an entry in a banker's book is in all legal proceedings to be received as prima facie (not conclusive) evidence of such entry, and of the facts recorded by such entry.[157] Thus, not only are copies admissible where the original is admissible, but they are admissible evidence even where the original would not be (e.g. because the original is only hearsay evidence of the facts stated in it).[158] Evidence under the Act is prima facie evidence against all the world.[159] For this purpose, legal proceedings means any civil or criminal proceeding or enquiry in **10.38**

---

[153] See Ch.15, para.15.11. *Sybron Corp v Barclays Bank Plc* [1985] 1 Ch. 299 at 318; *Dendron GmbH v University of California* [2004] EWHC 589 (Patents), [2004] F.S.R. 42, [2005] 1 W.L.R. 200 (letter of request).

[154] See Ch.15, para.15.15.

[155] *Pollock v Garle* [1898] 1 Ch. 1 at 4, CA.

[156] See para.10.53 below.

[157] Bankers' Books Evidence Act 1879, s.3.

[158] *Harding v Williams* (1880) 14 Ch.D. 197.

[159] *London and Westminster Bank v Button* (1907) 51 Sol.Jo. 466; *quaere* whether the non-existence of any entry in a banker's book constitutes prima facie evidence of the non-existence of an alleged account: *cf. Douglas v Lloyds Bank Ltd* (1929) 34 Com. Cas. 263.

which evidence is or may be given, and includes an arbitration and an application to, or enquiry or other proceeding before, the Solicitors' Disciplinary Tribunal.[160]

10.39   For the purposes of the Act, "bank" and "banker" mean a deposit taker and the National Savings Bank.[161] The court does not need a certificate as to authorisation from the Financial Services Authority; it is sufficient if an inference can be drawn, as where the application concerns one of the major United Kingdom clearing banks.[162]

10.40   "Banker's books" include ledgers, day books, cash books, account books and other records used in the ordinary business of the bank, whether those records are in written form or are kept on microfilm, magnetic tape or any other form of mechanical or electronic data retrieval mechanism.[163] They include a microfilmed record of a customer's transactions and of his cheques,[164] but not letters in a bank correspondence file,[165] notes of interviews or conversations or other internal memoranda,[166] nor individual returned cheques and credit slips in the bank's possession.[167] The phrase "used in the ordinary business of the bank" does not require daily use.[168] In one case it was very broadly defined as "any form of permanent record maintained by a bank in relation to the transactions of a customer."[169] The Act applies equally to the successors to the bank by whom the entries were made.[170]

10.41   In order for an entry to be admissible, ss.4 and 5 of the Act require that it must be proved (either orally or on affidavit):

(a)   that the book was at the time of the making of the entry one of the ordinary books of the bank;

(b)   that the entry was made in the usual and ordinary course of business;

(c)   that the book is in the custody or control of the bank; and

(d)   that the copy has been examined with the original entry and is correct, such proof to be given by the person who has examined both copy and original entry.

---

[160] Bankers' Books Evidence Act 1879, s.10, as amended by Solicitors Act 1974, s.86.
[161] *ibid.* s.9(1), as amended; Financial Services and Markets Act 2000, s.22 and Sch.2.
[162] *Jessop v Rae* 1991 S.L.T. 267.
[163] Bankers' Books Evidence Act 1879, s.9(2), as amended.
[164] *Barker v Wilson* [1980] 1 W.L.R. 884.
[165] *R. v Dadson* (1983) 77 Cr.App.R. 291.
[166] *Re Howglen Ltd* [2001] 1 All E.R. 376, Ch.D.
[167] *Williams v Williams* [1988] Q.B. 161, CA.
[168] *Asylum for Idiots v Handyside* (1906) 22 T.L.R. 573, CA.
[169] *Wee Soon Kim Authority v UBS AG* [2003] S.G.C.A. 5 at [36]. A bank's video surveillance footage has been held to be a "copy of any entry in any book or record in any financial institution" within ss.29 and 30 of the Canadian Evidence Act, RSC 1985; *R. v Moison* (2001) 141 CCC (3d) 213, Alberta Q.B.D.
[170] *Asylum for Idiots v Handyside* (1906) 22 T.L.R. 573, CA.

The evidence of (a), (b), and (c) must be by a partner or officer of the bank. However, the evidence of (d) need not be.[171]

The corollary of admissibility of the entry is that, where the contents of **10.42** a banker's book can be proved under the Act, no banker or bank officer is compellable to produce any such banker's book, or otherwise to prove their contents, in any action to which the bank is not a party, unless the judge otherwise orders "for special cause".[172] But if the bank or bank officer has not furnished verified copies of the required entries, the books may still be obtained by witness summons.[173]

Section 7

For the purposes of the present discussion, the main interest lies, not in **10.43** the ultimate admissibility of the entries, but in the fact that the banker may be ordered to disclose them, *before trial*, under s.7. That section allows the court to order that a party be at liberty to inspect and take copies of any entries in a banker's book for the purposes of the proceedings. For this purpose "court" means "the court, judge, arbitrator, persons or person before whom a legal proceedings is held or taken,"[174] and includes a stipendiary magistrate in criminal proceedings.[175] In the High Court an application before trial will be made to the master or district judge, as appropriate. In the county court, it will be made to the district judge. An order must be served on the bank at least three clear days (excluding both the day of service and the day of compliance)[176] before it is to be obeyed, unless the court otherwise directs.

Normally such orders are applied for and made without notice,[177] leaving **10.44** it to the court to direct service of the application, or, if an order is made, for the bank (if it wishes) to apply to the court to vary or set aside the order. Orders concerned with documents outside the jurisdiction are so unusual that they should ordinarily be made on notice to the bank.[178] Similarly, although orders may be made without notice in relation to the account of a

---

[171] *R. v Albutt* (1910) 6 Cr.App.R. 55, C.CA.
[172] Bankers' Books Evidence Act 1879, s.6; *Douglas v Pindling* [1996] A.C. 890 at 901, P.C.; *R. v Moison* (2001) 141 C.C.C. (3d) 213, Alberta Q.B.D. ("special cause" includes use as exculpatory evidence in a criminal trial).
[173] *Emmott v Star Newspaper Co.* (1892) 62 L.J.Q.B. 77; 67 L.T. 718.
[174] Banker's Books Evidence Act 1879, s.10
[175] *R. v Kinghorn* [1908] 2 K.B. 949; for the considerations which apply in a criminal case, see *Williams v Summerfield* [1972] 2 Q.B. 512, and see also *R. v Grossman* (1981) 73 Cr.App.R. 302, CA.
[176] *R. v Herefordshire Justices* (1820) 3 B. & Ald. 581; *R. v Long* [1960] 1 Q.B. 687.
[177] *Arnott v Hayes* (1887) 36 Ch.D. 7331, CA; s.7 provides that an order may be made without notice; in practice, if the master or district judge is not sure as to the appropriateness of the application, he may direct that notice be given to the bank and/or its customer and/or other parties and direct a hearing: *cf. Parnell v Wood* [1892] P. 137.
[178] *MacKinnon v Donaldson Lufkin and Jenrette Securities Corporation* [1986] Ch. 482.

party to the litigation, where the account is in the name of a non-party, notice should be given to the non-party concerned.[179] Application may be made early on in the proceedings, particularly where a claim is made to trace into the bank account concerned.[180]

10.45 An affidavit or witness statement in support of the application is not strictly necessary, unless the materiality of the entry sought does not appear from the pleadings or application notice itself, or unless a question arises as to bona fides,[181] but in practice an affidavit or witness statement is usually made. Where an affidavit or witness statement is made, it should show:

(1) the nature of the proceedings;
(2) the materiality of and necessity for the inspection; and
(3) the period over which it should extend.

At the hearing it will be for the court to satisfy itself that the entries of which inspection is sought will be admissible in evidence at the trial of the action.[182]

10.46 The court has a discretion as to whether to make an order, and if so in what terms.[183] The court may refuse the application altogether if not satisfied as to relevance, or if it considers that to make an order would act oppressively.[184] Fishing applications are discouraged, and there must be evidence that there are material entries or documents.[185] Applications that are too wide may be dismissed altogether or cut down by the court.

10.47 In general, orders under s.7 should be in respect of a limited and reasonable period of time.[186] In line with the overriding objective embodied in CPR, r.1.1, the court may take into account:

(1) whether the information sought is already available to the party, or has been deposed to as being irrelevant by the party whose account it relates to, or has already been refused on disclosure between the parties[187];

---

[179] *South Staffordshire Tramways Co. v Ebbsmith* [1895] 2 Q.B. 669; *Ironmonger & Co. v Dyne* (1928) 44 T.L.R. 579; *R. v Grossman* (1981) 73 Cr.App.R. 302, CA.
[180] *Bankers Trust Co. v Shapira* [1980] 1 W.L.R. 1274, CA.
[181] *Arnott v Hayes* (1887) 36 Ch.D. 731, CA.
[182] *Howard v Beall* (1889) 23 Q.B.D. 1.
[183] *R. v Bono* (1913) 29 T.L.R. 635.
[184] *R. v Bono* (1913) 29 T.L.R. 635; *Williams v Summerfield* [1972] 2 Q.B. 512.
[185] *D.B. Deniz Nakliyati Tas v Yugopetrol* [1992] 1 W.L.R. 437, CA; *South Staffordshire Tramways Co. v Ebbsmith* [1895] 2 Q.B. 669.
[186] *R. v Marlborough Street Magistrates' Court Metropolitan Stipendiary Magistrate, exp. Simpson* (1980) 70 Cr.App.R. 291; *Owen v Sambrook* [1981] Crim.L.R. 329; *R. v Nottingham Justices, exp. Lynn* (1984) 79 Cr.App.R. 238.
[187] *Parnell v Wood* [1892] P. 137, CA; *South Staffordshire Tramways Co. v Ebbsmith* [1895] 2 Q.B. 669, CA.

(2) whether there is a more convenient method of obtaining the information, such as an application for specific disclosure under CPR, r.31.12;

(3) the relevance to the issues and how important to the resolution of those issues the information is;

(4) confidentiality (particularly that of non-parties)[188] and whether that is outweighed in the interests of justice[189]; and

(5) the need for proportionality and the costs involved.

As set out below, the court is particularly careful in relation to accounts   **10.48**
of non-parties or where it is sought to obtain documents in relation to business conducted outside the United Kingdom. It is clear that the court has jurisdiction under the Act to make an order, not only in relation to the account of a party to the action, but also in relation to that of a non-party.[190] However, it is settled that the court will only exercise the power to make such an order with caution, and will do so where the account "is in form or substance the account of a party to the litigation",[191] or where "the public interest in helping the prosecution outweighs the private interest in keeping a customer's bank account confidential".[192]

The court's powers under s.7 extend to banker's books in any part of the   **10.49**
United Kingdom, so a judge in England and Wales may make an order in respect of banker's books held in Scotland or Northern Ireland.[193] Save in exceptional circumstances, the court should not require a foreign bank within the United Kingdom to produce documents outside the United Kingdom in relation to business transacted outside the United Kingdom.[194] For this purpose, a foreign branch or subsidiary of a United Kingdom bank should be considered as a foreign bank, because it is subject to local laws.[195]

In exercising its powers under s.7, the court should exercise care in   **10.50**
framing its order, putting it in clear words so that the bank knows exactly

---

[188] *Pollock v Garle* [1898]1 Ch. 1, CA.
[189] *R. v Marlborough Street Magistrates' Court Stipendiary Magistrate, exp. Simpson* (1980) 70 Cr.App.R. 291; *Owen v Sambrook* [1981] Crim.L.R. 329; *R. v Nottingham Justices, exp. Lynn* (1984) 79 Cr.App.R. 238; *R. v Grossman* (1981) 73 Cr.App.R. 302 at 307; *Douglas v Pindling* [1996] A.C. 890 at 902, P.C.
[190] *Howard v Beall* (1889) 23 Q.B.D. 1 (where alleged that accounts in non-parties'names were kept for defendant); *South Staffordshire Tramways Co. v Ebbsmith* [1895] 2 Q.B. 669, CA; *Waterhouse v Barker* [1924] 2 K.B. 759 at 771–2; *Williams v Summerfield* [1972] 2 Q.B. 512; *R. v Andover Justices, exp. Rhodes* [1980] Crim.L.R. 644; *cf. Pollock v Garle* [1897] 1 Ch. 1, CA.
[191] *Pollock v Garle* [1897] 1 Ch. 1, at 5, CA; *R. v Andover Justices, exp. Rhodes* [1980] Crim.L.R. 644.
[192] *R. v Grossman* (1981) 73 Cr.App.R. 302, CA.
[193] *Kissman v Link* [1896] 1 Q.B. 574, CA.
[194] *Mackinnon v Donaldson Lufkin and Jenrette Securities Corp.* [1986] Ch. 482.
[195] *R. v Grossman* (1981) 73 Cr.App.R. 302, CA.

what should be done.[196] The court will not order inspection of banker's books entries relating to the account of a party to a greater extent than it would order production of the same material from the party on disclosure. Thus, where a party swore that only certain entries in a banker's book were relevant to the matters in issue, only those entries were to be inspected.[197] Often a bank will blank out irrelevant entries and depose to the irrelevance of the parts blanked out in response to an order. Again, where a party swore that entries would tend to incriminate him, inspection of them was refused.[198] In other words, the Act does not remove any privilege from, or extend disclosure against, a party, but permits inspection of entries in the hands of certain third parties.[199]

10.51 Where the order is made without notice, it may be challenged on notice rather than appealed, and indeed the former is the proper course.[200] Not only the party whose account is affected, but also the bank on whom the order is served may apply on notice for an order made without notice to be discharged.[201] A bank served with an order should consider whether it is appropriate to notify its customer before complying. If the customer is not a party, or has not been served with the order, he will not normally be in a position to know of the order. Generally, the safest course for a bank to adopt is to ask the party serving the order to state whether the customer has been informed of the order and whether the party has any objection to the customer being notified prior to compliance. It may also request a copy of the application and any supporting affidavit or witness statement. Where the order is in the nature of a tracing order, it may be sometimes be inappropriate for the banker to notify its customer, as it may lead to a further dissipation of assets. If the bank is in doubt, it should apply to the court for guidance or directions.

Implied undertaking

10.52 Material disclosed pursuant to an application made under the Act is subject to an implied undertaking that it will not be used for a collateral purpose.[202] But exceptionally the court may in making the order expressly permit the material to be used in other specified proceedings as well.[203]

---

[196] R. v Marlborough Street Magistrates' Court Metropolitan Stipendiary Magistrate, exp. Simpson (1980) 70 Cr.App.R. 291.

[197] South Staffordshire Tramways Co. v Ebbsmith [1895] 2 Q.B. 669, CA.

[198] Waterhouse v Barker [1924] 2 K.B. 759, CA.

[199] Perry v Phosphor Bronze Co. (1895) 71 L.T. 854.

[200] CPR, r.23.10; formerly RSC, Ord.32, r.6; WEA Ltd v Visions Channel 4 Ltd [1983] 1 W.L.R. 721 at 727.

[201] Mackinnon v Donaldson Lufkin and Jenrette Securities Corp. [1986] Ch. 483 at 492; cf. R. v Grossman (1981) 73 Cr.App. R. 302.

[202] Bhimji v Chatwani (No.2) [1992] 1 W.L.R. 1158; see Ch.15, para.15.11.

[203] e.g. The Russell-Cooke Trust Company v Richard Prentis & Co., unreported, August 24, 2000, Jonathan Parker L.J.

Post judgment applications

Although the main importance of the Act is in permitting pre-trial dis- **10.53**
closure of third party banking information, it should be noted that it is not
limited in time, and applications may be made even after judgment has been
obtained, provided the same requirements are met.[204] In the case of post
judgment applications under s.7, the following requirements must be met
before the court will permit inspection of entries in the bank account of a
third party:

(1) that the bank account of the third party is in substance the
account of the judgment debtor, or one with which he is so
connected that items in it will be evidence material to the question
of the whereabouts of his assets;

(2) that there is firm evidence amounting to almost certainty that
there are material items in the account;

(3) that the purpose of the application is not merely to provide
material for the cross- examination of the judgment debtor;
and

(4) that there are no other reasons for refusing inspection.

D. EVIDENCE (PROCEEDINGS IN OTHER JURISDICTIONS) ACT 1975

Introduction

Foreign disclosure for English proceedings is dealt with in Ch.2.[205] This **10.54**
section deals with English disclosure for foreign proceedings where many of
the principles are the same.[206] At common law the English courts had no
power to order discovery in aid of foreign legal proceedings.[207] This Act was
passed in order to give effect in the United Kingdom to the Hague Convention on the Taking of Evidence Abroad in Civil or Commercial Matters of
1970,[208] and it replaced earlier statutes, including the Foreign Tribunals
Evidence Act 1856, as amended. It confers power on the High Court to

---

[204] *Ironmonger & Co. v Dyne* (1928) 44 T.L.R. 579; *D.B. Deniz Nakliyati Tas v Yugopetrol*
[1992] 1 W.L.R. 437, CA.
[205] Ch.2, paras 2.57–2.63.
[206] *Panayiotou v Sony Music Entertainment (UK) Ltd* [1994] Ch. 142 at 152; *Charman v
Charman* [2005] EWCA Civ 1606, [2006] 1 W.L.R. 1050.
[207] *Dreyfus v Peruvian Guano Co.* (1889) 41 Ch.D. 151.
[208] Cmnd. 3991, 6737 (1970); see Black (1991) 40 I.C.L.Q. 901.

assist non-English courts in foreign civil[209] proceedings, actual or contemplated, by enabling evidence to be obtained from witnesses in England and Wales for the purposes of those foreign proceedings. For the purposes of the Act, foreign proceedings include those in other parts of the United Kingdom and the European Court of Justice, as well as those in jurisdictions outside the United Kingdom. It does not apply in respect of requests in aid of a private arbitral tribunal.[210] The Act applies both to oral and to documentary evidence, although it is the latter which is presently important. The procedure is governed by CPR, Pt 34,[211] although the Act itself contains a number of important limitations on the assistance which the High Court may render. There are specific provisions in relation to the taking of evidence for the purposes of proceedings in Member States of the European Union.[212] Orders under the Act have much in common with witness summonses, but ultimately they are quite different, as they are entirely the creatures of statute.[213] In general the duty of the court is to give all assistance as it can to the requesting court within the limits prescribed by the 1975 Act.[214] Nevertheless the court retains a discretion whether or not to accept a letter of request. In one Canadian case, it was held that the court must consider whether to accept the request would be contrary to public policy or otherwise contrary to the nation's sovereignty or otherwise prejudicial to the private interests of its citizens.[215]

Limitations imposed by the Act

10.55   First of all, the evidence sought from the witness in England has to be "evidence . . . for the purposes of civil proceedings" instituted or contem-

---

[209] As to criminal proceedings, see the Crime (International Co-Operation) Act 2003, ss.13 to 15. *R. v Secretary of State for the Home Department, ex p. Finivest SpA* [1997] 1 W.L.R. 743, D.C.; *BOC v Instrument Technology Ltd* [2002] Q.B. 537, CA; *Abacha v Secretary of State for the Home Department* [2001] EWHC Admin 787, Admin. Ct; *R. (Evans) v Director of the Serious Fraud Office* [2002] EWHC 2304 (Admin), [2002] 1 W.L.R. 299, D.C.; *Marlwood Commercial Inc. v Kozeny* [2004] EWCA Civ 798, [2005] 1 W.L.R. 104, CA; *Energy Financing Team Ltd v Director of the Serious Fraud* Office [2005] EWHC 1626 (Admin); *Durrant International Corporation v HM Attorney* General [2006] J.C.A. 039, Jersey CA; see also *Phipson on Evidence* (16th edn, 2005), paras 8.45–8.46.

[210] *Commerce and Industry Co. of Canada v Certain Underwriters of Lloyd's of London* [2002] 1 W.L.R. 1323.

[211] See also CPR, Pt 34, Practice Direction, Depositions and Court Attendance of Witnesses, para.6.

[212] Council Regulation (EC) 1206/2001; CPR, rr.34.22–34; *Dendron GmbH v Regents of the University of California* [2004] EWHC 589 (Patents), [2004] F.S.R. 42; para.10.64 below.

[213] *Boeing Co. v P.P.G. Industries Inc.* [1988] 3 All E.R. 839 at 842.

[214] *USA v Philip Morris Inc.* [2004] EWCA Civ 330, [2004] 1 C.L.C. 811 at [16], CA.

[215] *Presbyterian Church of Sudan v Taylor* (2005) 256 D.L.R. (4th) 750, Ontario CA Superior Ct.

plated before the foreign courts.[216] Under the 1856 Act (where the word "testimony") was used, it was clear that this evidence had to be for the *trial* itself of the matter, rather than any interlocutory proceedings.[217] There is no clear authority on the position under the 1975 Act, but a majority[218] of the House of Lords in *Rio Tinto Zinc Corporation v Westinghouse Electric Corporation*[219] took the view that "evidence" in s.1 of the 1975 Act meant the same as "testimony" in the 1865 Act and that, accordingly, the evidence sought had to be for the trial. Thus, where the foreign proceedings are in the nature of bankruptcy or liquidation proceedings, and there will never be a "trial" in the English sense, the 1975 Act is inapplicable.[220] The relevant proceedings must be proceedings in a civil or commercial matter in both the United Kingdom and the requesting state.[221] The court will not simply accept the assertion of the letter of request as to whether its purpose is to obtain evidence for use at trial, but will go behind it, and judge the reality of the situation.[222]

Secondly, the High Court may not order steps to be taken under the Act unless they are steps which can be required to be taken by way of obtaining evidence for the purposes of civil proceedings in the High Court.[223] There was no equivalent provision in the 1856 Act.[224] Thus an attempt to obtain general discovery against a mere witness (being impermissible in English law at that time) failed for this reason, as well as for others.[225] And a request for oral evidence to be taken from a company was held impermissible under the earlier law.[226] It is open to the court to add safeguards in the order so as to ensure that the restrictions imposed by s.2(3) of the Act can be observed and enforced.[227] The court may "edit" a request, but not substitute another

10.56

---

[216] Evidence (Proceedings in Other Jurisdictions) Act 1975, s.1(b).
[217] *Burchard v Macfarlane, exp. Tindall* [1891] 2 Q.B. 241, CA; *Radio Corp. of America v Rouland Corp.* [1956] 1 Q.B. 618.
[218] Lords Wilberforce, Dilhorne, Fraser.
[219] [1978] A.C. 547.
[220] *Re International Power Industries N.V.* [1985] B.C.L.C. 128.
[221] *Re State of Norway's Application (Nos 1&2)* [1990] 1 A.C. 723, HL.
[222] *Rio Tinto Zinc Corp. v Westinghouse Electric Corp.* [1978] A.C. 547 at 610, 624, 643, 652; *Re Westinghouse Corporation and Duquesne Light Company* (1977) 16 O.R. (2d) 273 at 286, Ontario H. Ct.; *Fecht v Deloitte & Touche* [2000] I.L.Pr. 398 at 403–404; *Application of Nicholas Basil Cannar, re Sharon Y Eubanks* [2003] N.S.W.S.C. 802, NSW Sup. Ct. (court declined to draw inference from timing of request, that application was seeking pre-trial discovery).
[223] Evidence (Proceedings in Other Jurisdictions) Act 1975, s.2(3).
[224] *cf. Desilla v Fells & Co.* (1879) 40 L.T. 423; *Eccles & Co v Louisville and Nashville Railroad Co.* [1912] 1 K.B. 135 at 144.
[225] *Rio Tinto Zinc Corp. v Westinghouse Electric Corp.* [1978] A.C. 547 at 634, 652; whilst it may be suggested that the position may now be different, in that disclosure is available against non-parties under CPR, r.31.17: (see Ch.4, paras 4.48–4.60), in practice this limitation has continued; C.R. para.10.10 above.
[226] *Penn-Tas Corporation v Murat Anstalt* [1964] 1 Q.B. 40 at 57.
[227] *Golden Eagle Refinery Company v The Associated International Insurance Company* [1998] EWCA Civ 428; *Securities and Exchange Commission v Credit Bancorp Ltd* February 20, 2001, Q.B.D. (unreported).

one.[228] Thus, although a request which goes too far might be saved by restricting it, the court will not rewrite it, but instead will refuse it.[229] Whilst the courts are generally unwilling to revise requests for documents save in the limited respects indicated here, in the context of requests for oral evidence the court may, if appropriate, be prepared to give the request an amended effect where the request requires revision.[230]

10.57   Thirdly, the High Court may not order a person to give general disclosure (i.e. disclosure of the existence) of relevant documents, or to produce documents for inspection other than "particular documents specified in the order", being documents appearing to the High Court to be or to be likely to be in his possession, custody or power.[231] It will be noted that the 1975 Act uses the old discovery test of "possession, custody or power", rather than the new test of "control" under the CPR.[232] The phrase "particular documents specified in the order" is to be given a strict construction, so as not to permit mere "fishing expeditions".[233] The documents must be exactly indicated as individual documents rather than as a class.[234] This requirement that particular documents must be specified has been strictly construed so as not to allow an order to be made which would involve altering the letter of request other than striking out words with a blue pencil.[235] The court must also be satisfied that such documents exist and that they are likely to be in the respondent's possession.[236] Merely inferring from the existence of document A that documents B, C and D probably exist is not enough.[237] Moreover, requests which are oppressive to the witness are likely to be set aside.[238]

10.58   Fourthly, the court may not order a respondent to give evidence (including producing documents)[239] which he could not be compelled to give in

---

[228] Rio Tinto Zinc Corp. v Westinghouse Electric Corp. [1978] A.C. 547 at 611, 635, 654.

[229] Re State of Norway's Application [1987] 1 Q.B.433; State of Minnesota v Philip Morris Inc. [1997] I.L.Pr. 170; First American Corporation v Al-Nahyan [1999] 1 W.L.R.1154.

[230] Genira Trade & Finance Inc. v CS First Boston and Standard Bank (London) Ltd [2001] EWCA Civ 1733, The Times, December 7, 2001, [2002] C.P. Rep. 15, CA.

[231] Evidence (Proceedings in Other Jurisdictions) Act 1975, s.2(4); on a drafting error in s.2(4)(b), see Re Asbestos Insurance Coverage Cases [1985] 1 W.L.R. 331 at 336; on US recognition of this restriction, see First American Corporation v Price Waterhouse L.L.P. [1999] I.L.Pr.745 at 755.

[232] See above, Ch.4, paras 4.39–4.54.

[233] Rio Tinto Zinc Corp. v Westinghouse Electric Corp. [1978] A.C. 547 at 609, 635, 644; UJB Financial Corporation v Chilmark Offshore Capital Fund Ltd 1992–93 C.I.L.R. 53 (Cayman Grand Court); Nationwide Mutual Insurance Co. v Home Insurance Co., unreported, October 20, 1998, Sachs J.

[234] cf. The Lorenzo Halcoussi [1988] 1 Lloyd's Rep. 180; Wakefield v Outhwaite [1990] 2 Lloyd's Rep. 157; Panayiotou v Sony Music [1994] Ch. 142; Conopco v Ernst & Young, unreported, September 1, 1993, CA.

[235] Genira Trade & Finance Inc v CS First Boston and Standard Bank (London) Limited [2001] EWCA Civ. 1733, The Times, December 7, 2001, [2002] C.P. Rep. 15, CA.

[236] Re Asbestos Insurance Coverage Cases [1985] 1 W.L.R. 331 at 337–338.

[237] Rio Tinto Zinc, above, at 610.

[238] Atlanta Gas Light Co. v Aetna Casualty & Surety, unreported, February 7, 1993, David Steel Q.C.

[239] Evidence (Proceedings in Other Jurisdictions) Act 1975, s.3(4).

English civil proceedings or in such proceedings in a foreign court,[240] or which would be prejudicial to the security of the United Kingdom.[241] A certificate of the Secretary of State to that effect is conclusive evidence of that latter fact.[242] The first limb covers the various heads of privilege, as well as public interest immunity, discussed in Ch.9. Nor may an order be made under the Act against the Crown or requiring evidence to be given by "any person in his capacity as an officer or servant of the Crown".[243]

Fifthly, the jurisdiction to order oral testimony, like documentary evidence, is subject to various objections which may be raised in practice. The principal two objections are fishing[244] and oppression, although a request may be rejected as having both attributes, as to a certain extent the objections may overlap. Where the intention is to obtain information rather than to obtain evidence for use at trial, that amounts to fishing. Whether the objection as to fishing goes any further in the context of oral testimony has been doubted.[245] The court will not generally make an order for the examination of a witness under the 1975 Act where the request is mainly of an investigatory nature.[246] A request which is not relevant is objectionable, and this may be a ground of objection in its own right, or merely a type of fishing. However, the English courts will rarely intervene on grounds of irrelevance, as relevance is regarded primarily as a matter for the foreign court to determine. A request may be rejected on grounds of irrelevance where there is insufficient ground for believing that an intended witness might have relevant evidence to give on topics which are relevant to the issues in the action.[247] A recipient cannot be compelled to comply with an oppressive request. In deciding whether to disallow a request on the ground of oppression the court balances the legitimate requirements of the foreign court and the burden those requirements may place on the intended recipient.[248] The width, uncertainty or vagueness of a request may render it oppressive—a witness is entitled to know within reasonable limits the

10.59

---

[240] *ibid.*, s.3(1), (2); see *Securities and Exchange Commission v Stockholders of Santa Fe International*, unreported, February 23, 1984, and *Overseas Programming v Cinematolographische Commerz-Anstalt and Iduna Film, The Times*, May 16, 1984.

[241] Evidence (Proceedings in Other Jurisdictions) Act 1975, s.3(3).

[242] *ibid.*

[243] *ibid.*, s.9(4); this does not include evidence in respect of matters not coming to the notice of the witness in his capacity as a Crown Officer or servant, but does include evidence in respect of matters which come to his notice in such capacity even though he is now retired: *Re Pan American World Airways Inc's Application* [1992] 1 Q.B. 854, CA.

[244] *Re State of Norway's Application* [1987] Q.B. 433, CA; see also *Re State of Norway's Application (No.2)* [1990] 1 A.C. 723 at 781–2 (*per* Woolf L.J., CA) and 810 (*per* Lord Goff, HL).

[245] *First American Corpn. v Zayed* [1999] 1 W.L.R. 1154 at 1166, CA. See also *Application of Nicholas Basil Cannar; re Sharon Y. Eubanks* [2003] NSWSC 802, N.S.W. Sup. Ct.

[246] *Smith v Phillip Morris Companies Inc* [2006] EWHC 916 (Q.B.), letter of request for oral evidence for USA proceedings disallowed as sought an impermissible investigation; *Land Rover North America Inc. v Windh* [2005] EWHC 432 (Q.B.), not fishing.

[247] *ibid.* at 1165.

[248] *ibid.* at 1165–6.

matters about which he is to be examined.[249] On an application for oral testimony, the court must hold a fair balance between the interests of the requesting court and the interests of the witness.[250] It is only in the clearest case that the court will refuse to make an order for the examination where the witness could and would refuse to answer any questions of substance.[251]

Procedure

10.60   An application under the 1975 Act where the Taking of Evidence Regulation does not apply is normally made without notice, supported by a witness statement or an affidavit.[252] In some cases the Treasury Solicitor may make the application.[253] The application must be made to the High Court and should be made by the issue of a claim form under the Pt 8, alternative claims, procedure, and should be supported by evidence containing the following:

    (1) the draft letter of request;
    (2) a statement of the issues relevant to the proceedings;
    (3) a list of questions or the subject matter of questions to be put to the proposed deponent;
    (4) a translation of the documents in (1), (2) and (3) if necessary;
    (5) a draft order.[254]

Although in appropriate circumstances the matter can be dealt with by a judge, the application is normally made to a Queen's Bench Division master[255] and the Queen's Bench Masters' Secretary's Department[256] deals with the paperwork. The court may order the examination of the witness to be taken before a person nominated by the applicant (who will do so in the supporting witness statement or affidavit) or before a person selected by the court, e.g. one of the examiners of the court.[257] An applicant usually contacts the Masters' Secretary's department for the name of a suitable person to conduct the examination, and then checks his availability for

---

[249] *ibid.* at 1167, citing Lord Woolf M.R. in *State of Minnesota v Philip Morris Inc.* [1997] I.L.Pr. 170, CA.

[250] *USA v Philip Morris Inc* [2004] EWCA Civ 330 at [17], *The Times*, April 16, 2004, CA.

[251] *ibid.* at [88].

[252] CPR, r.34.17.

[253] CPR, Pt 34, Practice Direction, Depositions and Court Attendance by Witnesses, para.6.4(2).

[254] CPR, Pt 34, Practice Direction, Depositions and Court Attendances by Witnesses, para.6.3; if the letter of request is in a foreign language a translation should be provided.

[255] *cf.* CPR, Pt 34, Practice Direction, para.5.5.

[256] R.C.J., Room E214.

[257] CPR, Pt 34, Practice Direction, para.6.7.

particular dates (making an informal "reservation") *before* making the application. The court may also order the payment of fees and expenses due to the examiner under CPR, r.34.14.

If a without notice application is in any way unusual, or there is any **10.61** doubt whether it falls properly within the scope of the applicable rules, such matters should be drawn specifically to the court's attention.[258] As any order obtained is without notice, it may be set aside by the court upon an application with notice being made for that purpose by application under CPR, r.23.10.[259] It is usually wrong to appeal an order made without notice without first having applied on notice to set it aside.[260] Unless the order is patently defective, an affidavit or witness statement should be made, stating the grounds of the application to discharge. These may include failure by the claimant to make full and frank disclosure.[261] It is usually the witness himself who applies to set aside the order, but a party in the foreign proceedings has standing (*locus standi*) to do so as well[262] and also the person to whom the documents belong or who has rights of confidentiality in them.[263] Again, the application is normally made to a Queen's Bench Division master, but the judge may also hear it in appropriate circumstances.[264]

The examination

Subject to any special directions contained in the order for examination, **10.62** the examination is taken in the manner provided for by CPR, rr.34.9–34.10 for the taking of depositions.[265] Thus, the examiner will appoint the date, time and place, unless that is already specified in the order,[266] but the other arrangements (provision of shorthand writer, interpreter and so on) will be made by the solicitor having conduct of the matter. He will also supply the examiner with all necessary documents.[267] The examination will usually follow the practice in English proceedings, but if a foreign court requests a particular manner for taking depositions then, subject to the exercise of judicial discretion in any particular case, and unless it is so contrary to

---

[258] *Nationwide Mutual Insurance Co. v Home Insurance Co.*, unreported, October 20, 1998, Sachs J.

[259] CPR, Pt 34, Practice Direction, para.6.6. Provision formerly was RSC, Ord.32, r.6.

[260] *WEA Ltd v Visions Channel 4 Ltd* [1988] 1 W.L.R. 721 at 727.

[261] *Overseas Programming v Cinematographische Commerz-Anstalt and Iduna Film, The Times*, May 16, 1984.

[262] *Boeing Co. v P.P.G. Industries Ltd* [1988] 3 All E.R. 839, CA.

[263] *Nationwide Mutual Insurance Co. v Home Insurance Co.*, unreported, October 20, 1998, Sachs J.

[264] See, e.g., *Boeing Co. v P.P.G. Industries Inc.* [1988] 3 All E.R. 839, CA.

[265] CPR, r.34.18(2); formerly RSC, Ord.39, rr.5–10, 11(1)–(3).

[266] *cf.* CPR, r.34.8(5).

[267] CPR, Pt 34, Practice Direction, Depositions and Court Attendances by Witnesses, para.4.2(2).

English procedures that it ought not to be adopted, the English court will employ it.[268] As to the rules of evidence, the examination will follow those of the foreign court, if they are known.[269] A company may be required by its proper officer to produce specified documents.[270]

10.63   The evidence of the witness is recorded in a deposition,[271] which is subsequently transmitted by the examiner to the senior master.[272] The witness must give his answers without the intervention of legal advice and is not entitled to receive such advice whilst being examined.[273] The examiner himself may put any question to the witness as to the meaning of his answers or any matter arising in the course of the examination.[274] There are procedures for the court to adjudicate on a witness's refusal[275] or objection[276] to answering a question or producing a document. The examiner has no power to do more than record the dispute and express an opinion on it.[277] Accordingly, the examiner may not give directions as to the witness being treated as hostile.[278] There is a special procedure for dealing with claims to privilege.[279]

Taking of Evidence Regulation[280]

10.64   The procedure is similar where the Taking of Evidence Regulation applies, which deals with requests between EU member states. The procedure is governed by CPR, rr.34.22–34.24 and CPR, Pt 34, Practice Direction, Depositions and Court Attendance by Witnesses, paras 7–11. Particular courts in England and Wales have been designated to deal with such requests[281] and the Central Body responsible for supplying information to courts, seeking solutions to any difficulties and forwarding a request to a competent court is the Senior Master, Queen's Bench Division.[282] The procedure is dealt with more fully in Ch.17 below.[283]

---

[268] *J. Barker & Sons v Lloyds Underwriters* [1987] Q.B. 103; *R. v Horseferry Road Magistrates Court, exp. Bennett (No.3), The Times,* January 14, 1994: videotaping permitted.
[269] *Desilla v Fells* (1879) 40 L.T. 423 at 423–424.
[270] *Penn-Tas Corp. v Murat Anstalt* [1964] 1 Q.B. 40; *Panthalu v Ramnord Research Laboratories* [1966] 2 Q.B. 173.
[271] CPR, r.34.9.
[272] CPR, r.34.19.
[273] *R. v Rathbone, exp. Dikko* [1985] Q.B. 630.
[274] CPR, Pt 34, Practice Direction, Depositions and Court Attendance by Witnesses, para.4.7.
[275] *ibid.,* para.4.8; CPR, r.34.10.
[276] *ibid.,* para.4.5.
[277] *R. v Rathbone, exp. Dikko* [1985] Q.B. 630.
[278] *ibid.*
[279] CPR, r.34.20.
[280] Council Regulation (EC) No.1206/2001 of May 28 2001 on co-operation between the courts of the Member States in the taking of evidence in civil or commercial matters.
[281] CPR, Pt 34, Practice Direction, para.8.3 and Annex C.
[282] CPR, Pt 34, Practice Direction, para.9.1.
[283] Paras 17.14–17.19 below.

CHAPTER 11

Objections to inspection

CHAPTER 11

Objections to inspection

A. THE GENERAL RULE

In Ch.8 *disclosure* of documents was distinguished from their *inspection* **11.01** and objections to the former were discussed. This chapter considers in what cases, disclosure of documents having been given, objection may be made to their inspection. Under the former rules, as has been seen, at the stage of disclosure, the burden was on the disclosing party to show why disclosure was not necessary, either for disposing fairly of the cause or matter, or for saving costs.[1] In relation to inspection, the general rule involved the same test, but (in the High Court)[2] it reversed the burden of proof, i.e. that no order for production, or for the supply of a copy, of any document is to be made unless the court was satisfied that the order was necessary either for disposing fairly of the cause or matter or for saving costs.[3] Thus the burden was on the inspecting party to show why he should have inspection or supply, and not on the disclosing party to show why he should not. These rules have now gone. A person to whom disclosure of a document has been given now has, subject to exceptions, an automatic right to inspect it.[4] But the court will only make an order for inspection after taking into account,

---

[1] See Ch.8, paras 8.28–8.29.
[2] For the county court, see CCR, Ord.14, r.8.
[3] RSC, Ord.24, r.13(1); *Dolling-Baker v Merrett* [1990] 1 W.L.R. 1205 at 1209; *Khan v Armaguard Ltd* [1994] 1 W.L.R. 1204, CA; *Arbuthnott v Fagan* [1994] 3 W.L.R. 761, CA; *Svenska Handelsbanken v Sun Alliance and London Insurance Plc* [1995] 2 Lloyd's Rep. 84; *Wallace Smith Trust Co. Ltd v Deloitte, Haskins & Sells* [1997] 1 W.L.R. 257, CA; *Mortgage Express Ltd v S. Newman & Co.*, unreported, July 7, 1998, CA; *Goodridge v Chief Constable of Hampshire* [1999] 1 All E.R. 896; *British and Commonwealth Holdings Plc v Barclays de Zoete Wedd Ltd* [1999] 1 B.C.L.C. 86; in Hong Kong, see *Au Shui-yuen v Ford* [1991] 1 H.K.L.R. 525; *Innovisions Ltd v Chan Sing-Chuk* [1992] 2 H.K.L.R. 306, CA of H.K.
[4] CPR, r.31.3; see Ch.9, para.9.03.

and seeking to further, the overriding objective in CPR, Pt 1, which also applies at the stage of making an order for disclosure.[5]

11.02 In addition, on an application for production for inspection, the court may require production of a document to itself in order to decide whether a claim to privilege or other objection is valid.[6] The question whether to inspect is for the court's discretion, and primarily for that of the judge at first instance. Under the old rules it was said that the Court of Appeal would generally accept a formally correct claim to privilege and decline to inspect the documents.[7] Indeed, in *Burmah Oil v Bank of England*[8] Lord Wilberforce (dissenting in the result) said it was not desirable for the court to inspect "except in rare instances where a strong positive case is made out . . . ". In public interest immunity cases, however, the position may be different. Formerly it was held that a judge should not himself inspect documents for which public interest immunity is claimed unless he was satisfied by the party urging such inspection that the documents were likely to support his own case.[9] More recently, however, it was held that, where a party seeking inspection had satisfied a threshold test of showing that production might be necessary for the fair disposal of the action, then in ordinary circumstances the court should not refuse to make an order for production without itself examining the document(s) concerned.[10]

B. OBJECTIONS TO INSPECTION GENERALLY

11.03 A number of objections to inspection are grouped under the heading "privilege".[11] Where any of these is established, then as a matter of law[12] production cannot be ordered: that is the "privilege". But other objections are less powerful, and go instead to the exercise of the court's discretion under CPR, r.3.10.[13] They include injunctions, liens, expense and inconven-

---

[5] See Ch.6, paras 6.41–6.52.

[6] CPR, r.31.19(6)(a); formerly RSC, Ord.24, r.13(2); CCR, Ord.14, r.6.

[7] *Westminster Airways Ltd v Kuwait Oil Co. Ltd* [1951] 1 K.B. 134 at 146.

[8] [1980] A.C. 1090 at 1117.

[9] *Air Canada v Secretary of State for Trade (No.2)* [1983] 2 A.C. 394. See also para.11.84, below.

[10] *Wallace Smith Trust Co. Ltd v Deloitte, Haskins & Sells* [1997] 1 W. L.R. 257, CA; *Goodridge v Chief Constable of Hampshire Constabulary* [1999] 1 All E.R. 896; *cf. British and Commonwealth Holdings Plc v Barclays de Zoete Wedd Ltd* [1999] 1 B.C.L.C. 86 (production ordered without the court first inspecting); in New Zealand, see *Kupe Group Ltd v Seamar Holdings Ltd* [1993] 3 N.Z.L.R. 209. In *Alcoota v CLC* [2001] N.T.S.C. 30 (Supreme Court of Northern Territory) the judge inspected cabinet documents as he was not satisfied as to claim of public interest immunity; *The Commonwealth v Northern Land Council* (1992–93) 176 C.L.R. 604 at 619 followed. The judge also inspected documents for which legal professional privilege was claimed.

[11] See generally McNicol, *Privilege*, 1992; Passmore, *Privilege*, 2nd edn, 2006; Thanki (ed.), *The Law of Privilege*, 2006.

[12] Public interest immunity may be an exception: see below, paras 11.81–11.94.

[13] See paras 11.144–11.156.

ience, alternative sources, foreign legal obligations and confidentiality (both of the party concerned and in relation to other professionals, such as doctors, priests and journalists). By and large, such considerations carry more weight at the stage of inspection than they do at the stage of disclosure.[14] Under the CPR, there is now also an intermediate case, namely "disproportionality". A party may claim to withhold inspection on the grounds that to permit it would be disproportionate to the issues in the case.[15] This is not so absolute as privilege, but stronger than the other discretionary objections.

First to be considered, however, are the absolute objections, for conven-   **11.04**
ience collectively called "privilege". Chief amongst these is legal professional privilege, with public interest immunity and the privilege against self-incrimination also being of practical importance. Other heads of privilege include "without prejudice" communications, diplomatic privilege and finally a number of specific statutory provisions conferring privilege in particular circumstances. As already mentioned,[16] a party will normally[17] have had to disclose the *existence* of documents subject to these privileges, in the second part of his List of Documents[18]; the "privilege" is a privilege not to produce such documents for inspection. Each head is dealt with in turn.

C. LEGAL PROFESSIONAL PRIVILEGE[19]

Lawyers owe their clients obligations of confidentiality in their relations.   **11.05**
But it is important to be clear that not everything that they have a duty to keep confidential is privileged. There are two heads—or sub-heads[20]—of legal privilege. One applies whether or not litigation is contemplated or pending, but covers a narrow range of communications: it is often called "advice" privilege for short. The other applies only where litigation is contemplated or pending, but extends over a wider range of documents: this is often referred to as "litigation" privilege. Whether they are two distinct kinds of privilege, or (more likely) integral parts of a single privilege,[21] the

---

[14] *cf.* Ch.8, paras 8.18–8.30.
[15] CPR, r.31.3(2); see para.11.156, below.
[16] See Ch.6, paras 6.14–6.16, above.
[17] There is a potential exception in the case of public interest immunity: see Ch.6, para.6.14, above.
[18] See Ch.6, para.6.15, above.
[19] See generally, Auburn, *Legal Professional Privilege: Law & Theory*, 2000; Thanki (ed.), *The Law of Privilege*, 2006, Ch.1; Passmore, *Privilege*, 2nd edn 2006, Ch.1.
[20] *Three Rivers District Council v Bank of England (No.6)* [2005] 1 A.C. 610, at para.105; *cf.* at para.10.
[21] *Re L (A Minor)* [1997] A.C. 16 at 33; see also *Three Rivers District Council v Bank of England (No.6)* [2005] 1 A.C. 610, HL; *Lamey v Rice* (2000) 190 D.L.R. (4th) 486, New Brunswick CA and *Morrissey v Morrissey* (2000) 196 D.L.R. (4th) 94, Newfoundland CA.

rationale of both has been said to be the same,[22] and was explained by Lord Brougham as follows:

> "It is founded on a regard to the interests of justice which cannot be upholden and to the administration of justice which cannot go on without the aid of men skilled in jurisprudence, in the practice of the courts and in those matters affecting rights and obligations which form the subject of all judicial proceedings. If the privilege did not exist at all every one would be thrown upon his own legal resources: deprived of all professional assistance a man would not venture to consult any skilful person or would only dare to tell his counsel half his case."[23]

More recent authority suggests that the rationales are slightly different. Legal advice privilege advances the rule of law, by enabling clients to obtain appropriate legal advice more easily.[24] Litigation privilege supports access to justice and a fair trial with equality of arms.[25] It has been suggested that these rationales are unconvincing and may need to be reviewed.[26]

11.06   However that may be, from these explanations it follows that the privilege is that of the client and not of the lawyer,[27] of the client rather than the witness who provides a statement or report,[28] and of the principal rather than the agent.[29] Sometimes it may be difficult to identify which of several parties is the client for this purpose. Thus, where would-be personal injury claimants sought "after the event" insurance at a time when personal injury

---

[22] See *Re Barings Plc* [1998] 1 All E.R. 673 at 687; *Clements, Dunne & Bell v Commissioner of Australian Federal Police* (2001) 188 A.L.R. 515, Fed.Ct.Aus.

[23] *Greenough v Gaskell* (1833) 1 Myl. & K. 98 at 103; see also *Anderson v Bank of British Columbia* (1876) 2 Ch.D. 644, CA; *Southwark Water Co. v Quick* (1873) 3 Q.B.D. 315, CA; *Jones v Great Central Railway Co. v Quick* [1910] A.C. 4 at 5; *Grant v Downs* (1976) 135 C.L.R. 674 at 685; *Baker v Campbell* (1983) C.L.R. 52 at 66; *A.G. v Maurice* (1986) 161 C.L.R. 475 at 480, 487, 490; *Balabel v Air India* [1988] Ch. 317 at 329–330; *Ventouris v Mountain* [1991] 3 All E.R. 472, CA; *R. v Derby Magistrates Court, ex p. B.* [1996] A.C. 487, HL; *R. v Crown Court at Manchester, ex p. Rogers* [1999] 1 W.L.R. 832, D.C.; *General Manager, WorkCover Authority of New South Wales v Law Society of New South Wales* [2006] N.S.W.C.A. 84, at para.67, CA of N.S.W.

[24] *Three Rivers District Council v Bank of England (No.6)* [2005] 1 A.C. 610, at para.34; *Winterthur Swiss Insurance v A.G. (Manchester) Ltd* [2006] EWHC 839 (Comm.).

[25] *Three Rivers District Council v Bank of England (No.6)* [2005] 1 A.C. 610, at para.27; *Winterthur Swiss Insurance v A.G. (Manchester) Ltd* [2006] EWHC 839 (Comm.).

[26] Tapper (2005) 121 L.Q.R. 181, cited in *Candacal Pty Ltd v Industry Research & Development Board* [2005] F.C.A. 649, Fed.Ct.Aus. See also *Minister of Justice v Blank*, 2006 S.C.C. 39, paras 26–30.

[27] *Anderson v Bank of British Columbia* (1876) 2 Ch.D. 644 at 649; *Procter v Smiles* (1886) 55 L.J.Q.B. 467 at 527, 528; *Re International Power Industries N.V.* [1985] B.C.L.C. 128; *Randolph M.Fields v Watts*, January 22, 1986, unreported, CA; *Ventouris v Mountain* [1991] 3 All E.R. 472 at 475; *CHC Software Care Ltd v Hopkins & Wood*, unreported, February 18, 1994, Millett J.; *Abbey National Plc v Clive Travers & Co.* [1999] P.N.L.R. 753 at 755, CA.

[28] *Schneider v Leigh* [1955] 2 Q.B. 195, CA; *M. v Ryan* (1994) 119 D.L.R. (4th) 18, CA of B.C.; *cf.* CPR, r.32.12(2)(a), and see Ch.17, para.17.26, below.

[29] *cf. Chantrey Martin v Martin* [1953] 2 Q.B. 286, CA.

litigation was contemplated, and the insurers made and received commu-nications from lawyers in order to decide whether or not to underwrite such policies, the client was the prospective insurer rather than the would-be claimant.[30] Where a client company is in liquidation, it is the liquidator who asserts privilege.[31] As will be seen, these distinctions are important when it comes to considering the question of waiver of privilege.[32] It also means that where questions of privilege arise between two different clients who have instructed the same lawyer,[33] communications between the lawyer and one may be privileged as against the other.[34] The privilege is not lost by the death of the client,[35] and indeed inures for the benefit of the client's succes-sor in title in the relevant sense.[36] Presumably, in the absence of any other relevant transfer, the Crown will succeed to the rights of privilege relating to the property of a dissolved company as *bona vacantia*,[37] although subject to a revesting in the company if it is revived.[38] In general, the rule is "once privileged, always privileged,"[39] so that, provided the privilege is available to the original holder or his relevant successor, it will apply even in sub-sequent proceedings having no similarity of subject matter with the first,[40] and even though the original holder or his successor no longer has any interest to protect.[41]

Subject to certain exceptions, the professional relationship of lawyer and client (not necessarily a formal retainer[42]) must exist before the privilege can apply.[43] Before that relationship exists, or after it has ceased, no privilege

11.07

---

[30] *Winterthur Swiss Insurance v A.G. (Manchester) Ltd* [2006] EWHC 839 (Comm).

[31] *Mercantile Credit Ltd v Dallhold Investments Pty Ltd* (1994) 130 A.L.R. 287; *Winterthur Swiss Insurance v A.G. (Manchester) Ltd* [2006] EWHC 839 (Comm).

[32] See Ch.12, para.12.41, below.

[33] Not being *joint* clients: see para.11.074, below.

[34] *Eadie v Addison* (1882) 52 L.J. Ch. 80; *Goddard v Nationwide Building Society* [1987] Q.B. 670, CA; *Nationwide Building Society v Various Solicitors* [1999] P.N.L.R. 52.

[35] *Chant v Brown* (1849) 7 Hare 84; *Russell v Jackson* (1851) 9 Hare 387; *Bullivant v Att.Gen. for Victoria* [1901] A.C. 196, HL; see also *Swider & Berlin and Hamilton, Petitioners v United States*, 118 S.Ct. 2081 (1998), US Sup. Ct.; Ho, (1999) 115 L.Q.R. 27.

[36] *Minet v Morgan* (1873) L.R. 8 Ch.App. 361; *Calcraft v Guest* [1898] 1 Q.B. 759, CA; *Crescent Farm (Sidcup) Sports Ltd v Sterling Offices Ltd* [1972] Ch.553; *Re Konigsberg* [1989] 1 W.L.R. 1257 (trustee in bankruptcy); *Surface Technology v Young* [2002] F.S.R. 387; cf. *Reeves Bros Inc. v Lewis Reed & Co. Ltd* [1971] F.S.R.17 (patent licensee is not successor in title for this purpose); *Worrell v Woods* (1999) 163 A.L.R. 195, Fed.Ct.Aus. (trustee in bankruptcy is not successor for this purpose in Australian law).

[37] Companies Act 1985, s.654 ("all property *and rights* whatsoever").

[38] *ibid.*, s.655.

[39] *Calcraft v Guest* [1898] 1 Q.B. 759 at 761; *Goldstone v Williams* [1899] 1 Ch. 47 at 52; *R. v Derby Magistrates Court, ex p. B* [1996] 1 A.C. 487, HL; *S County Council v B* [2000] Fam.76; *B. v Auckland District Law Society* [2003] 2 A.C., at para.44; *Winterthur Swiss Insurance v A.G. (Manchester) Ltd* [2006] EWHC 839 (Comm.). Cf. *Minister of Justice v Blank*, 2006, S.C.C. 39, para.37.

[40] *The Aegis Blaze* [1986] 1 Lloyd's Rep. 203, CA; *S County Council v B* [2000] Fam. 76.

[41] *Nationwide Building Society v Various Solicitors* [1999] P.N.L.R. 52 at 65–69.

[42] *Minter v Priest* [1930] A.C. 558, HL.

[43] *Smith v Daniell* (1874) L.R. 18 Eq. 649 (lawyer consulted as friend—no privilege); *Kelly v Denman*, unreported, February 21, 1996, Rimer J.

can apply.[44] One exception is that privilege will apply to documents brought into existence for the purpose of obtaining legal advice, even before the lawyer is retained, and even if, in the event, he never is.[45] A second, less clear exception arises where the "client" reasonably believes that the lawyer is acting for him, though this is not in fact the case. In Australia, it is accepted that the privilege can arise in this case also.[46] A third exception may be where a person imparts information to another whom he wrongly believes to be a lawyer.[47]

11.08 The importance of the privilege can hardly be overestimated. It is "much more than an ordinary rule of evidence, limited in its application to the facts of a particular case."[48] It is instead a substantive legal principle.[49] So, for example, a rule of court overriding legal privilege, made under statutory power to "modify the rules of evidence", has been held *ultra vires*.[50] Four further general points may be made. The first is that there is nothing improper in the client standing on his privilege where it is made out, and accordingly he is not to be subject to the rule that the keeping back of evidence is to be taken against the person who does so.[51] The second is that the policy of the English law is to conduct litigation "cards face up on the table."[52] The privilege is therefore a restriction on relevant material available to the parties and to the court to enable justice to be done, and it must

---

[44] *Greenough v Gaskell* (1833) 1 Myl. & K. 98.

[45] See para.11.39, below.

[46] *Global Funds Management (N.S.W.) Ltd v Rooney* (1994) 36 N.S.W.L.R. 122, Sup.Ct.N.S.W.; see also *Grofam Pty Ltd v Australia and New Zealand Banking Group Ltd* (1993) 117 A.L.R. 669, Fed.Ct.Aus. (Full Ct.).

[47] *Calley v Richards* (1854) 19 Beav. 401.

[48] *R. v Derby Magistrates Court, ex p.B.* [1996] 1 A.C. 487 at 507; *Re L (A Minor)* [1997] A.C. 16 at 24, 30; see Auburn, *op.cit.*, 31–32.

[49] *R. v Colvin* [1970] 3 O.R. 612 at 617, Ont.H.Ct.; *Solosky v R.* (1979) 105 D.L.R. (3rd) 745, S.C.C.; *Baker v Campbell* (1983) 153 C.L.R. 52, H.Ct.Aus.; *Att.Gen. (N.T.) v Maurice* (1986) 161 C.L.R. 475 at 480, 490–91; *R. v Gray* (1992) 74 CCC (3d.) 267 at 273, B.C.Sup.Ct.; *Goldberg v Ng* (1995) 185 C.L.R. 83 at 93–9; *Carter v The Managing Partner, Northmore Hale Davy & Leake* (1995) 183 C.L.R. 121 at 132–33, 161; *Esso Australia Resources Ltd v Commissioner of Taxation* (1999) 201 C.L.R. 49, H.Ct.Aus.; *Daniels Corp. International Pty Ltd v Australian Competition and Consumer Commission* (2002) 213 C.L.R. 543, at para.9, H.Ct.Aus.; *R. v I.R.C., ex p. Morgan Grenfell* [2003] 1 A.C. 563, at para.7; *Three Rivers District Council v Bank of England (No.6)* [2005] 1 A.C. 610, at para.26, HL; *General Manager, WorkCover Authority of New South Wales v Law Society of New South Wales* [2006] N.S.W.C.A. 84, CA of N.S.W.; *cf. R. v Bell, ex. p. Lees* (1980) 146 C.L.R. 141, H.Ct.Aus.; *Lavallee, Rackel & Heintz v Attorney General of Canada* (2002) 216 D.L.R. (4th) 257, S.C.C.

[50] *General Mediterranean Holdings S.A. v Patel* [1999] 3 All E.R. 673; see also *State Bank of South Australia v Ferguson* (1995) 64 S.A.S.R. 232, Sup.Ct.S.Aus.; *Festing v Canada (Attorney General)* (2002) 206 D.L.R. (4th) 98, British Columbia CA; *cf. Re L (A Minor)* [1997] A.C. 16, HL; and see also *Morrissey v Morrissey* (2000) 196 D.L.R. (4th) 94, Newfoundland CA (r.30.04(2) of the Rules of the Supreme Court of Newfoundland held to have overridden litigation privilege in context of orders for medical examinations).

[51] *Wentworth v Lloyd* (1864) 10 H.L.C. 589, HL.

[52] *Davies v Eli Lilly & Co.* [1987] 1 W.L.R. 428 at 431, CA; *Naylor v Preston Area Health Authority* [1987] 1 W.L.R. 858 at 967; *Black & Decker Inc. v Flymo Ltd* [1991] 1 W.L.R. 753; *Khan v Armaguard Ltd* [1994] 1 W.L.R. 1204, CA.

not be extended beyond its proper purpose,[53] but rather must be kept "within justifiable bounds."[54] Although the policy of the CPR is to reduce the extent and cost of modern litigation,[55] and those rules have introduced a new objection to disclosure and inspection, based on disproportionality,[56] there is nothing to indicate that "cards on the table" as a policy has been abandoned, and accordingly it still has a role to play in controlling the operation of the doctrines of privilege. Thirdly, a lawyer who is sued by a third party may—indeed, normally has a duty to—assert the privilege which belongs to his client.[57] But, where application is made for disclosure of privileged communications, lawyer-defendants ought ordinarily to consult their clients to see whether they wish the privilege to be asserted.[58] If the client is happy to waive privilege, the lawyer cannot object.[59] The fourth point is that the privilege is not violated merely by seizing or even copying privileged material, but only by reading it.[60]

D. LEGAL ADVICE PRIVILEGE[61]

The basic rule

Legal advice privilege is both a procedural and a substantive right,[62] not tied to the conduct of litigation.[63] Communications[64] between (i) a lawyer in his professional capacity[65] and (ii) his client are privileged from production if they are confidential[66] and for the purposes of seeking or giving legal

11.09

---

[53] *Wheeler v Le Marchant* (1881) 17 Ch.D. 675 at 682; see also *Grant v Downs* (1976) 135 C.L.R. 674 at 685–688.

[54] *Balabel v Air India* [1988] Ch. 317 at 332; see also *Re Barings Plc* [1998] 1 All E.R. 673 at 687.

[55] See Ch.1, paras 1.28–1.30.

[56] See para.11.156, below.

[57] *Nationwide Building Society v Various Solicitors* [1999] P.N.L.R. 52 at 69; *Winterthur Swiss Insurance v A.G. (Manchester) Ltd* [2006] EWHC 839 (Comm).

[58] *R. v Central Criminal Court, ex p. Francis and Francis* [1989] 1 A.C. 347 at 385, 386; *Abbey National Plc v Clive Travers & Co.* [1999] Lloyd's Rep. P.N. 753 at 755, CA.

[59] *Re International Power Industries N.V.* [1985] B.C.L.C. 128.

[60] *Solosky v R.* (1979) 105 D.L.R. (3rd) 745, at 758; *Allitt v Sullivan* [1988] V.L.R. 621, at 640; *JMA Accounting Pty Ltd v Commissioner of Taxation* (2004) 211 A.L.R. 380, at paras 13–14, Fed.Ct.Aus.

[61] Thanki (ed.), *The Law of Privilege*, 2006, Ch.2; Passmore, *Privilege*, 2nd edn, 2006, Ch.2.

[62] *Three Rivers District Council v Bank of England (No.6)* [2005] 1 A.C. 610, at para.26, HL.

[63] *Three Rivers District Council v Bank of England (No.6)* [2005] 1 A.C. 610, at para.34, HL.

[64] *Three Rivers District Council v Bank of England (No.5)* [2003] Q.B. 1556, at para.21; *National Westminster Bank Plc v Rabobank Nederland* [2006] EWHC 2332 (Comm.), at paras 26–29.

[65] See *Smith v Daniell* (1874) L.R. 18 Eq. 649; *Kelly v Denman*, unreported, February 21, 1996, Rimer J. (solicitor consulted as friend).

[66] *Three Rivers District Council v Bank of England (No.6)* [2005] 1 A.C. 610, at para.24, HL.

advice for the client.[67] However, those purposes have to be construed broadly and will include communications in "the continuum aimed at keeping [solicitor and client] informed," and "must include advice as to what should prudently and sensibly be done in the relevant legal context".[68] The "relevant legal context" is not confined to advice relating to the legal rights and obligations of the client. It may thus include advice on presentation of evidence to an inquiry (not litigation) by someone whose conduct might be criticised by it.[69] It appears also to cover advice to an objector at a planning inquiry,[70] advice to an interested person at a coroner's inquest,[71] advice and assistance given to promoters of private bills,[72] and advice to the Government in relation to the drafting and preparation of public bills.[73] Cases in England,[74] Australia,[75] and Canada,[76] but not New Zealand,[77]

---

[67] *Wheeler v Le Marchant* (1881) 17 Ch.D. 675, CA; *Kennedy v Lyell* (1883) 23 Ch.D. 387, CA; *O'Shea v Wood* [1891] P. 286, CA; *Minter v Priest* [1930] A.C. 558, HL; *R. v Uljee* [1982] 1 N.Z.L.R. 561, CA of N.Z.; *Balabel v Air India* [1988] Ch. 317, CA; *Broadcasting Corp. of New Zealand & Horton Ltd* [1991] 1 N.Z.L.R. 335; *Nationwide Building Society v Various Solicitors* [1999] P.N.L.R. 52; *Visx Inc. v Nidex Co.* [1999] F.S.R. 91, CA; *R. v Manchester Crown Court, ex p. Rogers* [1999] 1 W.L.R. 832, D.C.; *Commissioner of Taxation v Pratt Holdings Pty Ltd* (2005) 225 A.L.R. 266, Fed.Ct.Aus.

[68] *Balabel v Air India* [1988] Ch. 317 at 330; *Internationa; Minerals & Chemical Corpoation (Canada) v Commonwealth Insurance Co.* (1991) 47 C.C.C.I. 196; *Nederlandse Reassurantie Groep Holdings N.V. v Bacon & Woodrow* [1995] 1 All E.R. 976; *Nationwide Building Society v Various Solicitors* [1999] P.N.L.R. 52 at 63; *Komarek v Ramco Energy Plc,* unreported, November 21, 2002, Eady J.; *Wah v Gold Chief Investment Ltd* [2003] H.K.C.F.I. 468; *DSE Holdings Ltd v Intertan* (2003) 135 F.C.R. 151, 203 A.L.R. 348, Fed.Ct.Aus; *Three Rivers District Council v Bank of England (No.6)* [2005] 1 A.C. 610, HL; *General Manager, WorkCover Authority of New South Wales v Law Society of New South Wales* [2006] N.S.W.C.A. 84, CA of N.S.W.; see also *Re Konigsberg (a bankrupt)* [1989] 3 All E.R. 289 at 294; *cf. Smurfit Paribas Bank v A.A.B. Export Finance* [1990] I.R.L.M. 588, Irish Sup.Ct. (correspondence with solicitors not privileged).

[69] *Three Rivers District Council v Bank of England (No.6)* [2005] 1 A.C. 610, HL; *AWB Ltd v Cole* [2006] F.C.A. 1234, Fed.Ct.Aus.

[70] *Three Rivers District Council v Bank of England (No.6)* [2005] 1 A.C. 610, at para.39, 56, HL.

[71] *Three Rivers District Council v Bank of England (No.6)* [2005] 1 A.C. 610, at para.115, HL.

[72] *Three Rivers District Council v Bank of England (No.6)* [2005] 1 A.C. 610, at para.40, HL.

[73] *Three Rivers District Council v Bank of England (No.6)* [2005] 1 A.C. 610, at para.41, HL; see also *General Manager, WorkCover Authority of New South Wales v Law Society of New South Wales* [2006] N.S.W.C.A. 84, at para.74, CA of N.S.W.

[74] *Chant v Brown* (1852) 9 Hare 790; *Turton v Barber* (1874) 17 Eq. 329; *Ainsworth v Wilding* [1900] 2 Ch. 315; *Daily Express (1908) Ltd v Mountain* (1916) 32 T.L.R. 592; *International Business Machines Corp. v Phoenix International (Computers) Ltd* [1995] 1 All E.R. 412, at 419, 424; *Dickenson v Rushmer,* unreported, December 21, 2001, Rimer J., at paras 12–13; *cf. Burton v Dodd* (1890) S.J. 39, Stirling J. (some entries relevant; others sealed up).

[75] *Packer v Deputy Commissioner of Taxation* (1984) 33 A.L.R. 243, Sup.Ct.Queensland; *Lake Cumberline Pty Ltd v Effem Foods Pty Ltd* (1994) 126 A.L.R. 58; *cf. Alcoota v C.L.C.* [2001] N.T.S.C. 30, Sup.Ct.N.T. (bills of costs not privileged per se, but privileged to extent they contain or refer directly to confidential matters so as to disclose the subject of the communication).

[76] *Maranda v Richer* (2004) 232 D.L.R. (4th) 14, S.C.C.

[77] *Re Merit Finance and Investment Group Ltd* [1993] 1 N.Z.L.R. 152.

have held that solicitors' bills of costs and statements of account are privileged.

But the scope of the privilege is not without limit. The "range of assistance given by solicitors to their clients" and the range "of activities carried out on their behalf" having "greatly broadened in recent times," it is necessary "to re-examine the scope of legal professional privilege and keep it within justifiable bounds."[78] Thus, by itself, "the mere fact that a person speaking is a solicitor, and the person to whom he speaks is his client affords no protection."[79] To put the matter more precisely, the advice given must be directly related to the lawyer's performance of his professional duty *as the client's legal adviser*, rather than just as (say) his man of business.[80] So a "communication in furtherance of a criminal purpose does not 'come into the ordinary scope of professional employment'," and is not privileged.[81] Again, in one case, a client's letter to his solicitor telling him, in answer to an inquiry, of a *fait accompli*, was held not privileged,[82] in another a client's letters to his solicitor authorising him to offer terms of settlement were likewise held not privileged,[83] and in yet another a client care letter, setting out the terms of the retainer, was not privileged.[84] An Australian case has also held that instructions given to prepare a will are not privileged,[85] and an English one that communications about a conveyancing transaction were not privileged,[86] though neither now probably represents English law.[87] More recently there has been said to be force in the submission that "advice or assistance in collecting or collating, listing, spring-cleaning, storing, transporting and warehousing documents" is not privileged under this head.[88]

11.10

---

[78] *Balabel v Air India* [1988] Ch. 317 at 332; *Three Rivers District Council v Bank of England (No.6)* [2005] 1 A.C. 610, at paras 111–12, HL.

[79] *Minter v Priest* [1930] A.C. 558 at 568.

[80] *Three Rivers District Council v Bank of England (No.6)* [2005] 1 A.C. 610, at paras 38, 58, 111, HL; see also *Balabel v Air India* [1988] Ch. 317 at 331; *Dalleagles Pty Ltd v Ausralian Securities Commission* (1991) 4 W.A.R. 325 at 332–33; *Nederlandse Reassurantie Groep Holdings N.V. v Bacon & Woodrow* [1995] 1 All E.R. 976; *AWB Ltd v Cole* [2006] F.C.A. 1234, at para.47, Fed.Ct.Aus.

[81] *R. v Cox and Railton* (1884) 14 Q.B.D. 153 at 167, and see *Minter v Priest* [1930] A.C. 558, HL, and paras 11.67–11.70, below.

[82] *Smith Bird v Blower* [1939] 2 All E.R. 406; *cf.University of Southampton v Kelly*, unreported, November 14, 2005, E.A.T. (legal advice sought to back up existing decision to terminate employment contract held privileged).

[83] *Conlon v Conlons Ltd* [1952] 2 All E.R. 462, CA; though in that case the scope of the solicitor's authority was a material fact: see para.11.64, below.

[84] *Dickenson v Rushmer* [2001] EWHC 9018 (Costs), Rimer J., at para.13.

[85] *Tickell v Trifleska* (1990) 24 N.S.W.L.R. 548; see also *Three Rivers District Council v Bank of England (No.6)* [2004] Q.B. 916, at para.39, CA.

[86] *C. v C. (Privilege: Criminal Communications)* [2002] Fam. 42, at para.11, *per* Thorpe L.J.

[87] *Three Rivers District Council v Bank of England (No.6)* [2005] 1 A.C. 610, at paras 55, 62, 106, HL.

[88] *United States of America v Philip Morris Inc.* [2004] EWCA Civ. 330, para.80 (but this case must now be seen in the light of *Three Rivers District Council v Bank of England (No.6)* [2005] 1 A.C. 610, HL).

11.11   But it must be borne in mind that it does not follow that non-privileged material must invariably be produced. Although there may be some documents which could not be said to enjoy privilege, such documents will often be irrelevant, and hence not disclosable, let alone liable to production.[89]

11.12   However, the rule relates to *communications*,[90] and does not therefore cover all documents relating to a client's affairs. For example, it does not protect the conveyancing documents by which immovable property is transferred from one person to another,[91] or the client account ledger which a solicitor maintains in relation to his client's money,[92] or any appointment diary or record of time on an attendance note, time sheet or fee record, relating to the client.[93] Nor does it extend to all information which a lawyer knows about his client. In one case[94] it was said that:

> "The privilege does not extend to matters of fact which the attorney knows by any other means than confidential communication with his client, though if he had not been employed as attorney, he probably would not have known them."

11.13   So the privilege does not apply to asking a lawyer whether he had a particular document with him in court,[95] or about the contents of a book he saw during trial,[96] or as to whether he saw his client in court on a previous occasion be disqualified from driving.[97] In another case a solicitor was required to reveal the names and addresses of his clients, trustees of a settlement and to produce the deed of settlement, which was in his custody as the trustee's solicitor.[98] However, there may be rare cases where revealing the client's identity will also reveal the substance of the advice given, and in

---

[89] *Balabel v Air India* [1988] Ch. 317 at 330; *Nationwide Building Society v Various Solicitors* [1999] P.N.L.R. 52 at 63.

[90] *Brown v Foster* (1857) 1 H. & N. 736 at 740; *Grant v Downs* (1976) 135 C.L.R. 674 at 690; *O'Reilly v State Bank of Victoria Commissioners* (1983) 153 C.L.R. 1 at 22–23; *Baker v Campbell* (1983) 153 C.L.R. 52 at 122; *Commissioner, Australian Federal Police v Propend Finance Pty Ltd* (1997) 71 A.L.J.R. 327 at 330–331, 334–335, 351, 355–356; *Three Rivers District Council v Bank of England (No.5)* [2003] Q.B. 1556, at para.21; *National Westiminster Bank Plc v Rabobank Nederland* [2006] EWHC 2332 (Comm), at paras 26–29.

[91] *R. v Inner London Crown Court, ex p. Baines & Baines* [1988] Q.B. 579 at 587; *Tickell v Trifleska* (1990) 24 N.S.W.L.R. 548 (will); *Geffen v Goodman Estate* (1991) 81 D.L.R. (4th) 211; *J-Corp. v Australian Builders' Labourers' Federated Union of Workers (W.A. Branch)* (1992) 110 A.L.R. 510.

[92] *Nationwide Building Society v Various solicitors* [1999] P.N.L.R. 53 at 76.

[93] *R. v Manchester Crown Court, ex p. Rogers* [1999] 1 W.L.R. 832, D.C; *R. v Minshull Street Crown Court, ex p. Miller Gardner* [2002] EWHC 3077 (Admin.) (telephone contact details and entries in solicitors' office diary); *R. (Howe) v South Durham Magistrates Court* [2004] EWHC 36, D.C. (attendance note of hearing).

[94] *Dwyer v Collins* (1852) 7 Exch. 639 at 648; see also *R. v Horsham District Council, exp. Wenman* [1992] C.O.D. 427, *The Times*, October 21, 1993.

[95] *ibid.*

[96] *Brown v Foster* (1857) 1 H. & N. 736 at 740.

[97] *R. (Howe) v South Durham Magistrates' Court* [2004] EWHC 361, D.C.

[98] *Bursill v Tanner* (1885) 16 Q.B.D. 1; see also *Pascall v Galinski* [1970] Q.B. 38, CA; *Police*

such cases the identity of the client will be protected.[99] Again, legal privilege will not prevent the court ordering the lawyer (in an appropriate case[100]) to reveal his client's whereabouts.[101] Nor does privilege attach to a solicitor's attendance note of what happens in court or at a meeting between the parties,[102] or to depositions taken in the presence of the opposing party,[103] or the recording of a non-privileged conversation.[104] On a wasted costs application it is permissible for the respondent barristers to be asked whether they saw or knew of non-privileged documents, provided that the purpose of the question is not to discover what was in the barristers' brief or instructions.[105]

Third parties

In principle it should make no difference if the confidential communica-   **11.14**
tions concerned between lawyer and client are effected via third parties, whether they are the agent of the lawyer[106] or the client.[107] It also applies to an interpreter.[108] However, the third party must be, not merely an agent of the solicitor or client in a general sense, but an agent for the purpose of communicating with the other party to give or obtain legal advice.[109] This test can be satisfied by the circulation (within the client-organisation) of internal memoranda for the purpose of transmitting such advice, which

---

  v Mills [1993] 2 N.Z.L.R. 592 (barrister obliged to provide client's name); *Conoco (UK) Ltd v The Commercial Law Practice, The Times*, February 13, 1996, C.S. (O.H.); *International Credit and Investment Co. (Overseas) Ltd v Adham, The Times*, February 10, 1997; *Miley v Flood* [2001] I.E.H.C. 9, Irish High Ct. (where the authorities are extensively reviewed); *CIBC Mellon v Stolzenberg*, unreported, November 15, 2000, Ch.D. (affd. [2001] EWCA Civ 1222, CA); *cf.* Financial Services and Markets Act 2000, s.175(4).

[99] *Federal Commissioner of Taxation v Coombes (No.2)* (1998) 160 A.L.R. 456, Fed.Ct.Aus., reversed by the Full Court, (1999) 92 F.C.R. 240, on the facts.

[100] See *Heath v Crealock* (1873) L.R. 15 Eq. 257 (no power to require answer at all).

[101] *ex p. Campbell, re Cathcart* (1870) L.R. 5 Ch.App. 703; *Re Arnott* (1888) 60 L.T.N.S. 109; see also *Ramsbotham v Senior* (1869) L.R. 8 Eq. 575; *cf. R. v Bell, exp. Lees* (1980) 146 C.L.R. 141, H.Ct.Aus.; *Hamdan v MIMIA* (2004) 211 A.L.R. 642, Fed.Ct.Aus. (client's telephone number not protected by privilege).

[102] *Parry v News Group Newspapers Ltd* (1990) 140 New L.J. 1719, CA; *Nederlandse Reassurantie Groep Holdings N.V. v Bacon & Woodrow* [1995] 1 All E.R. 976; *Hayes v Dowding* [1996] P.N.L.R. 578; as to "without prejudice" privilege, see paras 11.121–11.135, below.

[103] *Visx Inc. v Nidex Co.* [1999] F.S.R.73, CA.

[104] *Crisford v Hazard* [2000] 2 N.Z.L.R. 729, N.Z.C.A.

[105] *Brown v Bennett (No.3), The Times*, January 4, 2002, Ch.D.

[106] *Wheeler v Le Marchant* (1881) 17 Ch.D. 675 at 682; *cf. National Westiminster Bank Plc v Rabobank Nederland* [2006] EWHC 2332 (Comm.), at paras 14, 20 (bank's audit department not agents of lawyers).

[107] *Anderson v Bank of British Columbia* (1876) 2 Ch.D. 644 at 649; *Wheeler v Le Marchant* (1881) 17 Ch.D. 675 at 682, 684; *Lamey v Rice* (2000) 190 D.L.R. (4th) 486, New Brunswick CA.

[108] *Du Barré v Livette* (1791) Peake 108; *Bozkurt v Thames Magistrates Court* (2001) EWHC Admin 400.

[109] *Wheeler v Le Marchant* (1881) 17 Ch.D. 675 at 684; *C-C Bottlers Ltd v Lion Nathan Ltd* [1993] 2 N.Z.L.R. 445; *Australian Rugby Union Ltd v Hospitality Group Pty Ltd* (1999)

memoranda will also be privileged.[110] Similarly, communications between lawyers in the same firm may be protected,[111] and the same applies to two "in-house" lawyers[112] of the same client as well.[113]

11.15 Generally, in England and New Zealand, where the third party is *not* the lawyer's or the client's agent for the purpose of communicating between them, but is, say, simply someone with information bearing on the question to be submitted to the lawyer, a communication between the lawyer and the third party cannot attract advice privilege, because it simply cannot be one between lawyer and client for the purposes of seeking or giving legal advice.[114] This is so even as between co-plaintiffs[115] or co-defendants,[116] unless one of them is the lawyer.[117] It may in appropriate cases attract litigation privilege, but that is another matter.[118] On the other hand, communications between a *lawyer* and third party from whom he obtains information which he passes on to his client in privileged communications are also privileged, not because the third party is his or the client's agent, but because there is no basis for separating the parts of the lawyer/client communications dealing with that information from the parts not so dealing.[119] Another, more recent, exception to the general rule relates to so-called "common interest" privilege, which protects communications between a client (or his lawyer) and a third party with a common interest. This grew up in the context of litigation privilege, and hence is discussed later.[120] But it should be noted that it has been extended also to cases of advice only, where no litigation is in contemplation.[121]

165 A.L.R. 253; *Mitsubushi Electric Australia Pty Ltd v Victorian Work Cover Authority* [2002] 4 V.R. 332; *DSE Holdings Ltd v Intertan* (2003) A.L.R. 348, Fed.Ct.Aus.; *cf. Pratt Holdings Pty Ltd v Commissioners of Taxation* (2004) 207 A.L.R. 217, Fed.Ct.Aus. (F.C.)., taking the opposite view, followed in *Commissioner of Taxation v Pratt Holdings Pty Ltd* (2005) 225 A.L.R. 266, Fed.Ct.Aus.

[110] *Bank of Nova Scotia v Hellenic War Risk Association (Bermuda) Ltd* [1992] 2 Lloyd's Rep. 540; *British & Commonwealth Holdings v Quadrex Holdings Inc.,* July 4, 1990, unreported, Gatehouse J.; *Kennedy v Wallace* (2004) 213 A.L.R. 108, Full Fed.Ct.Aus.
[111] *Mostyn v West Mostyn Coal Co.* (1876) 34 L.T. 531.
[112] See para.11.19, below.
[113] *R. v Law Society, ex p. Rosen, The Independent,* February 19, 1990.
[114] *Anderson v Bank of British Columbia* (1876) 2 Ch.D. 644, CA; *Wheeler v Le Marchant* (1881) 17 Ch.D. 675, CA; *Re Highgrade Traders Ltd* [1984] B.C.L.C. 151 at 164; *Guardian Royal exchange Assurance of New Zealand v Stuart* [1985] 1 N.Z.L.R. 596, at 602; *Price Waterhouse v B.C.C.I.Holdings (Luxembourg) S.A.* [1992] B.C.L.C. 583; *Three Rivers District Council v Bank of England (No.5)* [2003] Q.B. 1556, CA; para.11.24, below; but a different approach has been taken in Australia: *PricewaterhouseCoopers v Commissioner of Taxation of the Commonwealth of Australia* [2004] F.C.A. 122, Fed. Ct.Aus. (Full Ct.).
[115] *Hutt v Haileybury College* (1888) 4 T.L.R. 277, CA.
[116] *Jenkyns v.Busby* (1866) L.R. 2 Eq. 547; *Hamilton v Nott* (1873) L.R.16 Eq. 112.
[117] *cf. O'Rourke v Darbishire* [1920] A.C. 581, HL.
[118] See paras 11.47–11.51, below.
[119] *Re Sarah C. Getty Trust* [1985] Q.B. 956; *cf.* the cases cited in paras 11.29–11.30, below, dealing with copy documents.
[120] See paras 11.59–11.62, below.
[121] *Unilateral Investments Ltd v VNZ Acquisitions Ltd* [1993] 1 N.Z.L.R. 468; *Svenska Handelsbanken v Sun Alliance & London Insurance Plc* [1995] 2 Lloyd's Rep. 84.

The corporate client has no physical *persona* and can only act through **11.16** others as agents, whether directors or other officers, employees, or independent contractors. The question therefore arises as to whether communications with such agents (whatever their contractual status vis-à-vis the company) are communications with *the client* or with *third parties*.[122] In *Three Rivers District Council v Bank of England (No.5)*[123] the Court of Appeal, reversing the decision of the judge, held that communications between the bank's solicitors and the bank's employees and ex-employees as to facts and matters that had occurred in the bank's business, for the purpose of advising the bank on presentation of evidence to a non-statutory (non-litigation) inquiry were not privileged. In the course of that decision the Court of Appeal rather surprisingly held "that information from an employee stands in the same position as information from an independent agent",[124] and that the solicitors' "client" in this case was a group of three named bank officials (not including, for example, the Governor) who had been internally designated as the conduit through which all communications with the solicitors should pass. It therefore seems that the Court of Appeal's decision on the privilege point was in part determined by the decision to treat the bank's employees (and ex-employees) as mere third party witnesses, rather than as emanations of the client.[125] The bank was refused leave to appeal from this decision. When the bank successfully appealed a subsequent decision building upon the earlier one,[126] it invited the House of Lords to comment on the correctness of the earlier Court of Appeal decision, in particular as to who was "the client". However, despite the fact that the House had given leave to the Law Society and the Bar Council to argue the "client" point, it ultimately declined the invitation to revisit the earlier decision,[127] as it strictly did not arise in the later case.

That leaves the decision of the Court of Appeal technically intact.[128] But **11.17** it is to be noted that in the House of Lords Lord Carswell considered *obiter* that there was "considerable force" in the view of the judge (reversed by the Court of Appeal) that the communications with the employees, "not being a communication with a third party", were privileged.[129] This suggests that

---

[122] In Australia, the point is settled by statute: Evidence Act 1995, s.117(1)(b), including within the definition of "client" "an employee or agent of a client".

[123] [2003] Q.B. 1556, CA.

[124] *Three Rivers District Council v Bank of England (No.5)* [2003] Q.B. 1556, at para.18, apparently relying on *Anderson v Bank of British Columbia* (1876) 2 Ch.D. 644; but see [2005] 1 A.C. 610, at 630–31.

[125] *cf. Dummer v Chippenham Corp.* (1807) 14 Ves. Jun. 245 (bill of discovery could be maintained against members of defendant corporation who were most likely to have relevant infoemation, as they were not "mere witnesses").

[126] *Three Rivers District Council v Bank of England (No.6)* [2005] 1 A.C. 610, HL.

[127] *Three Rivers District Council v Bank of England (No.6)* [2005] 1 A.C. 610, at paras 20–22, 46–48, 49, 63, 118.

[128] It was followed by Simon J. in *National Westiminster Bank Plc v Rabobank Nederland* [2006] EWHC 2332 (Comm), at paras 26–29.

[129] *Three Rivers District Council v Bank of England (No.6)* [2005] 1 A.C. 610, at para.70; see also at para.118.

the employees should have been treated as emanations of the client, after all.[130] On principle, the Court of Appeal's view is at the least too sweeping.[131] There may well be cases where employees (and, more likely, ex-employees) should be treated as mere third parties rather than as the client. On the other hand, in cases where they in essence are authorised by the company to (and do) prepare, contribute to or make requests for legal advice, or receive and disseminate or discuss and implement such advice appropriately, then, for the purposes of legal privilege, they should be treated as the client and the client's privilege upheld accordingly.[132] After all, in the context of waiver,[133]

> "Where a corporate client has received legal advice, any disclosure of the terms of that advice or the substance thereof from one officer to another within the corporation will not constitute a 'disclosure to another person' and thereby result in a loss by the client of the relevant privilege".[134]

What kind of lawyer?

11.18   Plainly the solicitor in private practice is within the scope of the rule, whether he holds a practising certificate or not,[135] as are the solicitor's employees and trainees acting on his behalf.[136] Similarly included is the barrister, so that instructions and briefs to counsel, and counsel's opinions, advices, drafts and notes thereon are within the scope of the privilege.[137] It is submitted that the position remains the same for the barrister, vis-à-vis the lay client, notwithstanding the introduction of "direct access" from certain non-legal professions (e.g. accountants, surveyors) to counsel.[138] It seems probable that notaries public (whether members of the Scriveners' Com-

---

[130] As were the members of the defendant corporation in *Dummer v Chippenham Corp.* (1807) 14 Ves. Jun. 245.

[131] See Thanki (ed.), *The Law of Privilege*, 2006, paras 2.17–2.45, for a detailed analysis (and criticism) of the decision.

[132] See, in the context of US law, *Upjohn Co. v United States*, 449 US 383 (1981), US Sup.Ct. (communications from foreign managers to general counsel at request of chairman about possible bribes paid abroad, for the purpose of obtaining advice, held privileged).

[133] As to which, see generally Ch.12.

[134] *Seven Network Limited v News Limited* [2005] F.C.A. 864, Fed.Ct.Aus.

[135] *Australian Hospital Care (Pindara) Pty Ltd v Duggan* [1999] V.S.C. 131, Sup.Ct.Vic.; *McKinnon and Secretary, Department of Foreign Affairs and Trade* [2004] A.A.T.A. 1365; see also *Commonwealth of Australia v Vance* (2005) 158 A.C.T.R. 47, CA of Aus.Cap. Terr.

[136] *Wheeler v Le Marchant* (1881) 17 Ch.D. 675 at 682.

[137] *Mostyn v West Mostyn Coal and Iron Co.* (1876) 34 L.T. 531; *Bristol Corp. v Cox* (1884) 26 Ch.D. 678; *Lowden v Blakey* (1889) 23 Q.B.D. 332; *Curtis v Beaney* [1911] P. 181.

[138] But see para.11.21, below, for other anomalies resulting from this change.

pany or not) and proctors, i.e. practitioners in the few Civil Law Courts now remaining, acting as such are also within the scope of the privilege.

With one exception, the rule applies to employed ("in-house") solicitors **11.19** and barristers as it does to those in private practice,[139] although obviously the communications must qualify in the usual way as involving the giving or seeking of legal advice and with a sufficient degree of independence, rather than administrative matters.[140] The single exception relates to the European Commission's power to require production of documents in the course of an investigation into infringements of Arts 85 and 86 of the Treaty of Rome. That power is limited by lawyer/client privilege where the lawyer is independent of the client, but not where the lawyer is an employee of the client.[141]

The position of non-solicitors employed by solicitors has already been **11.20** considered.[142] What of non-solicitors *supervised* by solicitors, e.g. in an in-house legal department, where solicitor and non-solicitor alike are employees of a common employer? If the reality is that the non-solicitor is acting as the agent or delegate of the employed solicitor, the advice of and communications with the non-solicitor may be privileged. But if the structure of the department is such that the non-solicitor works independently of the solicitor, even though subject to his guidance, they will not be.

The rule also applies to lawyers qualified in foreign law, advising on that **11.21** law,[143] and also, it appears, when advising on English law.[144] However,

---

[139] *Alfred Crompton Amusement Machines Ltd v Commissioners of Customs & Excise (No.2)* [1972] 2 Q.B. 102 at 129 (the point was not raised in the House of Lords); *Geraghty v Minister for Local Government* [1975] I.R. 300, Sup.Ct.; *Re Director of Investigation & Research and Shell Canada Ltd* (1975) 55 D.L.R. (3d) 713 at 721; *Att.Gen. for the Northern Territory v Kearney* (1985) 158 C.L.R. 500, H.Ct. of Aus.; *Waterford v Commonwealth of Australia* (1986–87) 163 C.L.R. 54, H.Ct. Of Aus.; *Grofam Pty Ltd v Australia and New Zealand Banking Group Ltd* (1993) 117 A.L.R. 669, Fed.Ct.Aus (Full Ct.) (legal privilege applied to advice given by DPP to government department even if no power for DPP to do so); *Pritchard v Ontario (Human Rights Commission)* (2004) 238 D.L.R. (4th) 1, Sup.Ct.Canada; *Commonwealth of Australia v.Vance* (2005) 158 A.C.T.R. 47, CA of Aus.Cap.Terr.
[140] *Arrow Pharmaceuticals Ltd v Merck & Co. Inc.* (2004) 210 A.L.R. 593, Fed.Ct.Aus.; *Commonwealth of Australia v Vance* (2005) 158 A.C.T.R. 47, CA of Aus.Cap.Terr.; *Seven Network Ltd v News Ltd* (2005) 225 A.L.R.671, Fed.Ct.Aus.; *cf. Blackpool Corp. v Locker* [1948] 1 All E.R. 85, CA, where the employed solicitor was also town clerk and the communications in question were made in the latter capacity.
[141] *A. M. & S. Ltd v EC Commission* [1983] Q.B. 878, E.C.J.
[142] See para.11.18, above.
[143] *Bunbury v Bunbury* (1839) 2 Beav. 173; *Lawrence v Campbell* (1859) 4 Drew. 485; *MacFarlan v Rolt* (1872) L.R. 14 Eq. 580; *Wheeler v Le Marchant* (1881) 17 Ch.D. 675 at 679; *Re Duncan* [1968] p.306 at 311; *Great Atlantic Insurance Co. v Home Insurance Co.* [1981] 1 W.L.R. 529, CA; *Minnesota Mining & Manufacturing Co. v Rennicks (UK) Ltd* [1991] F.S.R. 97; *Visx Inc. v Nidex Co.* [1999] F.S.R. 91 at 110. But see *Kennedy v Wallace* (2005) 213 A.L.R. 108, Fed.Ct.Aus.
[144] *International Business Machines Corporation v Phoenix International (Computers) Ltd* [1995] 1 All E.R. 413; *Gower v Tolko Manibota Inc.* (2001) 196 D.L.R. (4th) 716, Manitoba CA; see also *R. (Van Hoogstraten) v Governor of Belmarsh Prison* [2003] 1 W.L.R. 263 (Italian lawyer is "legal adviser" within r.2 of the Prison Rules 1999); see also *Kennedy v Wallace* (2005) 213 A.L.R. 108, Fed.Ct.Aus.

subject to one exception, the rule does not apply to non-lawyer professionals who may advise on law, such as accountants, surveyors or architects.[145] This position sits uneasily with the change in Bar practice to permit "direct access" by certain professions (notably those mentioned above) to counsel, without the need of a solicitor. To the extent that the non-lawyer professional seeks or receives counsel's advice or drafts and transmits instructions from and advice to the lay client, he can be said to be acting as the lay client's agent and the communications may be privileged within the rule.[146] But to the extent that the non-lawyer professional takes it upon himself to advise on the law, then communications between himself and his client will not be privileged. The one exception referred to above concerns auditors and tax advisers (usually accountants), who have a very limited statutory privilege in relation to documents belonging to them and created for the purposes of the auditing function or the giving of tax advice respectively.[147] The privilege only applies to statutory notices by the Inland Revenue seeking relevant documents for tax purposes.[148]

11.22 Patent and trade mark agents are in a special position. The clients of patent agents have enjoyed a kind of "litigation" privilege since 1968,[149] but both they and the clients of trade mark agents (who had never previously enjoyed any such privilege[150]) have been accorded a wider privilege by the Copyright, Designs and Patents Act 1988. By s.280[151] of that Act patent agents and by s.284[152] trade mark agents, are placed in the same position as solicitors so far as concerns communications as to any matter relating to the protection of any design or trade mark, or as to any matter involving passing off, or (in relation to patent agents only) the protection of any invention or technical information:

(a) between the client and his patent or trade mark agent; or
(b) for the purpose of obtaining, or in response to a request for, information which the client is seeking for the purpose of instructing his patent or trade mark agent.

These provisions create a kind of "advice" privilege for clients of patent and trade mark agents in relation to communications (on certain matters

---

[145] *Slade v Tucker* (1880) 14 Ch.D. 824; *Chantrey Martin v Martin* [1953] 2 Q.B. 286; *Wilden Pump Engineering Co. v Fusfeld* [1985] F.S.R. 159; *New Victoria Hospital v Ryan* [1993] I.C.R. 201; *cf. M.W. Glazebrook Ltd v Wallens* [1973] I.C.R. 256.
[146] See para.11.14, above.
[147] Taxes Management Act 1970, s.20B(9).
[148] *ibid.*, ss.20, 20A. See Ch.20, paras 20.73–20.82, below.
[149] See para.11.41, below.
[150] Though *cf. McGregor Clothing Company Ltd's Trade Mark* [1978] F.S.R. 353.
[151] See **Appendix 3, p.481.**
[152] Now the Trade Marks Act 1994, s.87.

only) between them or third parties which would be privileged if the agent were a solicitor.[153]

Finally what of the legal executive or licensed conveyancer who advises **11.23** on English law not in the course of employment by a solicitor? They do not possess a full English legal qualification, and yet often give advice on English law, either as private practitioners or as employed lawyers. There is no express authority,[154] but legal executives and licensed conveyancers at least have training and (often) a formal qualification in English law, and one might have thought that the principle of *Greenough v Gaskell* and the other seminal cases was large enough to cover them.[155] As to legal executives and licensed conveyancers employed by solicitors, the rule will apply to them as agents of their principals. The problem arises when they act as principals in their own right.

However, and significantly,[156] the draftsmen of s.33 of the Administration **11.24** of Justice Act 1985 and of s.63 of the Courts and Legal Services Act 1990 seem to have assumed that legal professional privilege does not apply to the advice of legal executives and licensed conveyancers. The former provision extends privilege to any communication made to or by a licensed convey-ancer in the course of acting as such for a client "in like manner as if the licensed conveyancer had at all material times been acting as the client's solicitor." The latter provision applies the same privilege as enjoyed by solicitors and barristers to communications to or by unqualified persons in the provision by them of:

(a) advocacy or litigation services as an authorised advocate or liti-gator under the Act;

(b) conveyancing services as an authorised conveyancing practitio-ner;

(c) probate services as a probate practitioner.

Of these three categories, only that part of s.63 relating to category (a) has so far been brought into force, on April 1, 1991.[157]

Client acting in person

The rule is expressed in terms of a lawyer advising his client. What if a **11.25** lawyer acts for himself: has he, in the words of the old adage, a fool for a

---

[153] In Australia see *Sepa Waste Water Treatment Pty Ltd v J.M.T. Welding Pty Ltd* [1986] 6 N.S.W.L.R. 41; in New Zealand see *Frucor Beverages Ltd v Rio Beverages Ltd* [2001] 2 N.Z.L.R. 604.

[154] Though see the 16th Report of the Law Reform Committee on Privilege in Civil Proceed-ings, Cmnd. 3472, para.24 (against).

[155] See, e.g. *Anderson v Bank of British Columbia* (1876) 2 Ch.D. 644 at 651, referring to "members of the legal profession."

[156] cf. *Wilden Pump Engineering Co. v Fusfeld* [1985] F.S.R. 159 at 168.

[157] Courts and Legal Services Act 1990 (Commencement No.3) Order 1991 (S.I. 1991/608).

client? In one case,[158] a solicitor-trustee's legal advice to his co-trustees was held privileged, but this was not really a case of the solicitor advising himself. And in another,[159] the Director of Public Prosecutions appears to have been treated as both client and his own solicitor for the purposes of claiming legal professional privilege. Suppose, however, that the client carries out research into his own legal problem. Are his notes and work papers privileged from production? Does it matter if he is not himself a lawyer? The rationale of the rule in the past has always been put in terms of enabling the client to unburden himself to his legal adviser,[160] which cannot happen in such a case. And in *Lyell v Kennedy (No.3)*,[161] Cotton L.J. said that:

> "If a man does not employ a solicitor, he cannot protect that which, if he had employed a solicitor, would be protected."

So there is no advice privilege. Notwithstanding that the rationale of litigation privilege is the same as that of advice privilege, the authorities concerning litigation privilege are, as will be seen,[162] more sympathetic when it comes to a litigant in person.

Lawyer advising a third party

11.26   The privilege only extends to the lawyer advising his own client, and a communication between the lawyer and the third party (not being the agent of either lawyer or client for the purposes of such communication) should not be not privileged under this head.[163] Thus, if the lawyer writes to the client's auditors to inform them of the state of the client's legal affairs (debts, titles, claims made, actual or prospective litigation), then even if the letter should amount to advice, it may not be advice to the client (because the auditor is independent of the company), and hence, the original in the auditors' hands ought not to be privileged under this head.[164] On this view, as the auditor is not the company's agent, the document is not discloseable

---

[158] *O'Rourke v Darbishire* [1920] A.C. 581, HL.

[159] *Auten v Rayner (No.2)* [1960] 1 Q.B. 669.

[160] See para.11.05, above.

[161] (1884) 27 Ch.D. 1 at 18.

[162] Paras 11.43, below.

[163] *Wheeler v Le Marchant* (1881) 17 Ch.D. 675, CA; *Price Waterhouse v B.C.C.I. Holdings (Luxembourg) S.A.* [1992] B.C.L.C. 583. *Mitsubishi Electric Australia Pty Ltd v Victorian Work Cover Authority* [2002] 4 V.R. 332; *Commissioner of Taxation v Pratt Holdings Ltd* (2004) 207 A.L.R. 217, Fed.Ct.Aus. (F.C.); *Three Rivers District Council v Bank of England (No.6)* [2005] 1 A.C. 610, HL.

[164] *789Ten Pty Ltd v Westpac* (2005) 215 A.L.R. 131, N.S.W. Sup.Ct.; *cf. McGregor Clothing Company Ltd's Trade Mark* [1978] F.S.R. 353, which seems wrong on principle; *Pratt Holdings Pty Ltd v Commissioners of Taxation* (2004) 207 A.L.R. 217, Fed.Ct.Aus. (F.C.). As to whether it might fall under "litigation" privilege, see para.11.043, below.

by the company as in its "control",[165] but would have to be produced to the court if sought by witness summons,[166] or under the third party disclosure procedure.[167] Any copy of that letter retained by the lawyer would, depending on the precise facts, either be retained on behalf of the client (when it would be in the client's control)[168] or as part of the lawyer's working papers (when it would not).[169] But, as a copy of a non-privileged document, almost certainly made for a non-privileged purpose, it would not itself be privileged.[170] On this view, in order to maintain privilege, the lawyer must write to the client with advice on the position. The client may then permit the auditor to inspect the advice (on a confidential basis, so as not to waive the privilege).[171] But this may not be acceptable to the auditor. The client must then choose.

However, the recent decision of Mann J. in *USP Strategies Ltd v London General Holdings Ltd*[172] cuts across this analysis, and, indeed, makes the whole of "common interest privilege"[173] unnecessary. There a client who had received legal advice supplied a copy of that advice, for commercial reasons but in confidence, without intending to waive privilege, to a third party who could not have been within the scope of "common interest privilege". The judge held that, not only was there no waiver in the *original* of the advice (still in the client's hands), but the new *copy* in the hands of the third party was also privileged from production. Reliance was placed on authorities not strictly in point,[174] but also on the recent statement of Longmore L.J. in *Three Rivers (No.5)* in the Court of Appeal,[175] where he concluded that the nineteenth century authorities allowed privilege to "documents . . . passing between the client and his legal advisers and *evidence of the contents* of such communications . . . ".[176] The judge considered that the copy supplied of the legal advice was merely evidence of the original advice. Yet in context Longmore L.J. in referring to evidence of privileged communications was surely referring to records made of advice to be retained by

11.27

---

[165] See Ch.5, paras 5.39–5.54, above.
[166] See Ch.10, paras 10.02–10.36, above.
[167] See Ch.4, paras 4.48–4.60, above.
[168] See Ch.5, para.5.43, above.
[169] See Ch.5, para.5.43, above.
[170] See paras 11.32–11.33, below.
[171] See Ch.12, para.12.07, below.
[172] [2004] EWHC 373 (Ch.), *The Times*, April 30, 2004.
[173] See paras 11.59–11.62 below.
[174] *The Good Luck* [1992] 2 Lloyd's Rep. 540 (dissemination of privileged advice *inside* corporate client); *City of Gotha v Sotheby's* [1998] 1 W.L.R. 114 (case about waiver; privileged status assumed).
[175] *Three Rivers District Council v Bank of England (No.5)* [2003] Q.B. 1556. The House of Lords in *Three Rivers District Council v Bank of England (No.6)* [2005] 1 A.C. 610 declined to rule on the correctness of the decision in *Three Rivers (No.5)*, but it is notable that the statements of principle of their lordships about legal advice privilege nowhere refer to any such idea as "evidence of the contents of such communications".
[176] At para.19 (emphasis supplied).

the lawyer or his client. He could not have been referring to the case where a *fresh* copy of the advice was made for the purpose of supply to a third party, informing him of its contents. The communication to the third party was, *ex hypothesi*, not made for a privileged purpose, and is hence not privileged. This is so, even though (as is seen later)[177] the act of informing the third party in confidence does not normally waive privilege in the original. If the judge in *USP* is right, either judges since the nineteenth century have seriously misunderstood the old authorities on this point, or Longmore L.J. drew too wide a principle from those authorities. It is submitted that neither is correct, and the judge was wrong to rely on the dictum of Longmore L.J. for the proposition which he did. It is further submitted that the true position remains as stated in the previous paragraph, though it must be accepted that, until an appellate court rules on the point, some uncertainty will persist.

Confidentiality

11.28   It is crucial for the existence of the privilege that the contents of the communication should be confidential. Thus endorsements on counsel's brief as to the order of the court,[178] depositions taken in the presence of the other party in the course of an action (whether filed in court[179] or not[180]), shorthand or other notes of proceedings in open court,[181] or of proceedings at an arbitration between the same parties,[182] and correspondence [183] or notes of meetings or conversations[184] between opposing lawyers are not capable of being covered by privilege, because their contents are not confidential. In Australia both video[185] and audio[186] tapes of non-confidential views and conversations have been held not privileged, even though made for the purpose of obtaining legal advice. But a lawyer's "work product", or other results of the exercise of professional skill and judgment, (e.g. notes of

---

[177] See Ch.12, paras 12.7–12.8 below.

[178] *Nicholl v Jones* (1865) 2 H. & M. 588.

[179] *Goldstone v Williams* [1899] 1 Ch. 47; *Trade Practices Commission v Ampol Petroleum Victoria Pty Ltd* (1994) 127 A.L.R. 533, Fed.Ct.Aus.

[180] *Visc Inc. v Nidex Co.* [1999] F.S.R. 91, CA.

[181] *Re Worswick* (1888) 38 Ch.D. 370; *Ainsworth v Wilding* [1900] 2 Ch. 315 at 320; *Lambert v Home* [1914] 3 K.B. 86, CA; *Parry v News Group Newspapers Ltd* (1990) 140 New L.J. 1719, CA; *Comfort v Department for Constitutional Affairs*, unreported, July 4, 2005, E.A.T. (Burton J.).

[182] *Rawstone v Preston Corp.* (1885) 30 Ch.D. 116.

[183] *Gore v Harris* (1851) 21 L.J. Ch. 10; *Ford v Tennant* (1863) 32 Beav. 162.

[184] *Parry v News Group Newspapers Ltd* (1990) 140 New L.J. 1719, CA; *Hayes v Dowding* [1996] P.N.L.R. 578.

[185] *J. Corp. Pty Ltd v Australian Builders Labourers Federation Union of Workers* (1992) 110 A.L.R. 510, Fed.Ct.Aus.; as to litigation privilege, see para.11.31, below.

[186] *Telebooth Pty Ltd v Telstra Corporation Ltd* [1994] 1 V.R. 337, Sup.Ct.Vic.

research into or collections of extracts from public documents) can nonetheless be sufficiently confidential as to attract privilege.[187] Where a lawyer has acted for two parties[188] between whom the question of privilege arises, communications between the lawyer and one are still capable of being privileged from the other.[189] Even where legal and non-legal advisers together formed a "team", sharing information, lawyer-client communications not shared with non-legal advisers were still confidential, and hence privileged.[190] Finally, where a director enjoyed confidential access to his company's otherwise legally privileged documents, but ceased to have such access on resigning, the documents continued to be confidential, and thus preserved that privilege, even as against that director in subsequent litigation between director and company.[191]

Copy documents

The cases concerning copy documents mostly relate to litigation privilege and are accordingly dealt with below.[192] But, with the possible exception of the recent decision of Mann J. in *USP Strategies Ltd v London General Holdings Ltd*[193] there is no reason to suppose that the rule is any different where legal advice privilege is concerned.

11.29

Parts of documents

Unless a document deals with two or more different subject matters, so that it can in effect be divided into two or more separate documents, a document must satisfy the applicable test (i.e. here confidential and brought into existence for the purposes of seeking or giving legal advice) as a whole.[194] It cannot be partly privileged and partly not. However, as discussed elsewhere,[195] it is possible to redact a document for inspection so that privileged material is not seen on inspection. This does not seem

11.30

---

[187] *Lyell v Kennedy (No.3)* (1884) 27 Ch.D. 1 at 25–27, 31, CA; *Lambert v Home* [1914] 3 K.B. 86 at 90, 92; *R. v Board of Inland Revenue, exp. Goldberg* [1989] Q.B. 267; *Kupe Group Ltd v Seamar Holdings Ltd* [1993] 3 N.S.L.R. 209.

[188] Not being *joint* clients: see para.11.74, below.

[189] *Eadie v Addison* (1881) 52 L.J. Ch. 80 at 81; *Goddard v Nationwide Building Society* [1987] Q.B. 670, CA.

[190] *Nederlandse Reassurantie Groep Holdings N.V. v Bacon & Woodrow* [1995] 1 All E.R. 976.

[191] *State of South Australia v Barrett* (1995) 64 S.A.S.R. 73, Sup.Ct.S.Aus. (Full Ct.); *Cf. GE Capital Commercial Finance Ltd v Sutton*, unreported, July 4, 2003, McCombe J.

[192] Paras 11.32–11.33, below. Original documents are dealt with in para.11.34, below.

[193] [2004] EWHC 373, *The Times*, April 30, 2004; see the discussion in para.11.27 above.

[194] *Great Atlantic Insurance Co. v Home Insurance Co.* [1981] 1 W.L.R. 529, CA; *Hongkong Bank of Australia Ltd v Murphy* [1993] 2 V.R. 419, Sup.Ct.Vic.; *Arab Monetary Fund v Hashim*, unreported, March 2, 1993, Chadwick J. (affirmed, CA, September 30, 1993).

[195] See Ch.9, para.9.38.

altogether consistent[196] and may create difficulties where waiver is concerned,[197] but is nonetheless convenient.

E. LITIGATION PRIVILEGE[198]

The basic rule

11.31   Confidential communications made, after litigation is commenced or even contemplated, between (a) a lawyer and his client, (b) a lawyer and his non-professional agent, or (c) a lawyer and a third party,[199] for the sole or dominant purpose of such litigation (whether for seeking or giving advice in relation to it, or for obtaining evidence to be used in it, or for obtaining information leading to such obtaining) are privileged from production.[200] As with "advice" privilege, it is necessary that the communication in question be confidential and the considerations relevant in the context of "advice" privilege will be relevant here also.[201] Thus no communication made by the opposite party can be confidential.[202] Accordingly, no privilege will attach to video[203] and audio[204] tapes made by one party of the other party, nor to depositions[205] or transcripts of compulsory examinations of

---

[196] cf. *Hellenic Mutual War Risks Association (Bermuda) Ltd v Harrison* [1997] 1 Lloyd's Rep. 160.

[197] See Ch.12, para.12.35.

[198] Thanki (ed.), *The Law of Privilege*, 2006, Ch.3; Passmore, *Privilege*, 2nd edn 2006, Ch.3.

[199] See paras 11.47–11.51, below.

[200] *Anderson v Bank of British Columbia* (1876) 2 Ch.D. 644 at 649; *Wheeler v Le Marchant* (1881) 17 Ch.D. 675 at 681; *Guardian Royal Exchange Assurance of New Zealand Ltd v Stuart* [1985] 1 N.Z.L.R. 596, CA of N.Z.; *Lee v South West Thames Regional Health Authority* [1985] 1 W.L.R. 845; *Ventouris v Mountain* [1991] 3 All E.R. 472 at 475–476; *Broadcasting Corp. of New Zealand v Wilson & Horton Ltd* [1991] 1 N.Z.L.R. 335; *Re Barings Plc* [1998] 1 All E.R. 673; *Three Rivers District Council v Bank of England (No.6)* [2005] 1 A.C. 610, at para.102; *Comfort v Department for Constitutional Affairs*, unreported, July 4, 2005, E.A.T. (Burton J.); *AWB Ltd v Cole* [2006] F.C.A. 571, Fed. Ct.Aus.

[201] Para.11.28, above.

[202] *Kennedy v Lyell* (1883) 23 Ch.D. 387 at 403, 405–406; *Ainsworth v Wilding* [1900] 2 Ch. 315 at 320; *Grant v Southwestern and Country Properties Ltd* [1975] Ch. 185 at 199; *McKay v McKay* [1988] N.I. 79 at 92–93; cf. *Feuerheerd v London General Omnibus Co.* [1918] 2 K.B. 565, CA, where the first two of the above cases were not cited, followed in *Reitler v N.Z.I. Insurance Australia* (1992) 1 Tas.R. 173; *Health & Life Care Ltd v Price Waterhouse* (1997) 69 S.A.S.R. 362, Sup.Ct.S.Aus. (Full Ct.). See also *Lubrizol Corp. v Esso Petroleum Ltd* [1992] 1 W.L.R. 957.

[203] *J-Corp. Pty Ltd v Australian Builders Labourers Federation Union of Workers* (1992) 110 A.L.R. 510, Fed.Ct.Aus.; cf. *Chmara v Nguyen* (1993) 104 D.L.R. (4th) 244, Manitoba CA (litigation privilege attached); in *Khan v Armaguard Ltd* [1994] 1 W.L.R. 1204, CA, no question of privilege was raised.

[204] *Telebooth Pty Ltd v Telstra Corporation Ltd* [1994] 1 V.R. 337, Sup.Ct.Vic.

[205] *Visx Inc. v Nidex Co.* [1999] F.S.R. 73, CA.

third parties.[206] The basis of such privilege originally was not simply that they are documents brought into existence for the purposes of litigation,[207] but "because of the light they might cast on the client's instructions to the solicitor or the solicitor's advice to the client regarding the conduct of the case or on the client's prospects".[208] Hence, if "documents for which privilege was sought did not relate in some fashion to communications between client and legal adviser, there was no element of public interest that could override the ordinary rights of discovery and no privilege."[209] But other authorities[210] appear to dispense with the connection between the privilege and the inviolacy of lawyer/client communications and support the wider proposition that litigation privilege arises where a document has been brought into existence for the dominant purpose of *use* for the purposes of litigation.[211] The test is the purpose at the time of creation; it is not necessary that the document should actually be so used.[212] Whether a conditional fee agreement between solicitor and client is privileged has been considered, but the point left open.[213]

Copies

The law of privilege relating to copy documents has for some years been in a state of flux, and subject to some debate. But it is submitted that the following propositions are warranted by the weight of the authorities. Where a copy is made of an original document and transmitted to another, this is a "communication" within the rule.[214] If the original was privileged and the copy was made for a privileged purpose (e.g. submission to a lawyer for his opinion), the copy will also be privileged.[215] But if the copy was

11.32

---

[206] *Trade Practices Commission v Ampol Petroleum (Victoria) Pty* Ltd (1994) 127 A.L.R. 533, Fed.Ct.Aus.; *cf. Dubai Bank Ltd v Galadari* [1990] B.C.L.C. 90 (examination under Companies Act 1985, s.561).

[207] *cf. Australian Competition and Consumer Commission v Australian Safeway Stores Pty Ltd* (1998) 81 F.C.R. 526, Fed.Ct.Aus.

[208] *Re Barings Plc* [1998] 1 All E.R. 673 at 687, approved in *Visx Inc. v Nidex Co.* [1999] F.S.R. 90, CA; *ISTIL Group Inc. v Zahoor* [2003] 2 All E.R. 252.

[209] *ibid.*, see also *R. v Manchester Crown Court, ex p. Rogers* [1999] 1 W.L.R. 832, D.C. (solicitor's time records not privileged).

[210] *Re Highgrade Traders Ltd* [1984] B.C.L.C. 151, CA; *Guinness Peat Properties Ltd v Fitzroy Robinson Partnership* [1987] 1 W.L.R. 1027, CA; *Robert Hitchins Ltd v International Computers Ltd*, unreported, December 10, 1996, CA (draft witness statements).

[211] *Re Barings Plc* [1998] 1 All E.R. 673 at 687; *cf. R. v Minshull Street Crown Court, ex p. Miller Gardner* [2002] EWHC 3077 (Admin.) (telephone contact details and entries in solicitors' office diary not privileged).

[212] See para.11.44, below.

[213] *Hollins v Russell* [2003] 1 W.L.R. 2487, CA.

[214] *Commissioner, Australian Federal Police v Propend Finance Pty Ltd* (1997) 71 AL.J.R. 327, at 336, 340, 350, 356; *cf. USP Strategies Ltd v London General Holdings Ltd* [2004] EWHC 373, *The Times*, April 30, 2004, discussed in para.11.27 above.

[215] *Re Fuld (No.2)* [1965] p.405 at 409; *Cole v Elders Finance & Investment Co. Ltd* [1993] 2 V.R. 356, Sup.Ct.Vic.; *AWB Ltd v Cole* [2006] F.C.A. 1234, at para.247, Fed.Ct.Aus.

made for a non-privileged purpose (e.g. to show an auditor the likely result of litigation), then on principle it should not be a privileged document.[216] A copy made of a document already privileged in the hands of one party (e.g. a draft witness statement) for handing over to another party with no intention of waiving privilege as against other parties is privileged in that second party's hands and that second party may himself assert the privilege.[217]

11.33   Where an original document now or formerly in the control of a party or his lawyers (so that he must disclose its existence) came into existence for a *non-privileged* purpose, then in English law, and subject to one exception, a copy made by the party or his lawyers of that document even for a privileged purpose (e.g. submission to a lawyer for his advice) is not itself privileged.[218] The one exception is that, where a collection or abstract of various non-privileged documents is made for a privileged purpose (e.g. in the course of legal research for particular litigation) that collection or abstract will be privileged even though the originals would not be.[219] But if the original, non-privileged document has never been in the party's (or his lawyers') control, but is in the control of a third party, then a copy made by the party or his lawyers for a privileged purpose is covered by privilege,[220] at all events as long as the opposite party does not have a copy of the same document.[221] Thus, for example, if a third party has a file of documents

---

[216] *Vardas v South British Insurance Co. Ltd* [1984] 2 N.S.W.L.R. 652; *cf. C-C Bottlers Ltd v Lion Nathan Ltd* [1993] 2 N.Z.L.R. 445 at 449; and *USP Strategies Ltd v London General Holdings Ltd* [2004] EWHC 373, *The Times*, April 30, 2004, discussed in para.11.27 above.

[217] *Cole v Elders Finance & Investment Co. Ltd* [1993] 2 V.R. 356; *Robert Hitchins Ltd v International Computers Ltd*, unreported, December 10, 1996, CA.

[218] *Chadwick v Bowman* (1886)16 Q.B.D. 561; *Lambert v Home* [1914] 3 K.B. 86; *Buttes Gas & Oil Co. v Hammer (No.3)* [1981] Q.B. 223 at 244; *Dubai Bank Ltd v Galadari* [1990] Ch. 98, CA, *Moser v Cotton,* July 31, 1990, unreported, CA; *Ventouris v Mountain* [1991] 1 W.L.R. 607 at 619; *cf. R. v Board of Inland Revenue, exp. Goldberg* [1989] Q.B. 267; *Sumitomo Corporation v Credit Lyonnais Rouse Ltd* [2002] 1 W.L.R. 479. Despite earlier cases taking the same view, the law in Australia is now different and a copy of a non-privileged document made for a privileged purpose is itself privileged: *Commissioner, Australian Federal Police v Propend Finance Pty Ltd* (1997) 188 C.L.R. 501, H.Ct.Aus.

[219] *Lyell v Kennedy (No.3)* (1884) 27 Ch.D. 1, CA; *Dubai Bank v Galadari (No.7)* [1992] 1 W.L.R. 106; *Sumitomo Corporation v Credit Lyonnais Rouse Ltd* [2002] 1 W.L.R. 479.

[220] *The Palermo* (1883) 9 P.D. 6, CA; *Watson v Cammell Laid & Co.* [1959] 1 W.L.R. 702, CA; *Wallace Smith Trust Co. Ltd v Deloitte Haskins & Sells* [1995] C.L.C. 223 at 229, affd. [1997] 1 W.L.R. 25(no evidence that copies made for privileged purpose; claim to privilege failed); *Grupo Torras S.A. v Al-Sabah,* unreported, June 5, 1997, Mance J.; *cf. Buttes Gas & Oil Co. v Hammer (No.3)* [1981] Q.B. 223 at 244; *Lubrizol Corp. v Esso Petroleum Ltd* [1992] 1 W.L.R. 957; *Crown Prosecution Service v Holman, Fenwick & Willan,* unreported, December 13, 1993, D.C.; *Robert Hitchins Ltd v International Computers Ltd,* unreported, December 10, 1996, CA (doubting distinction between original and copy documents). *Dubai Bank v Galadari (No.7)* [1992] 1 W.L.R. 106 at 110 was disapproved in *Sumitomo Corpn v Credit Lyonnais Rouse Ltd* [2002] 1 W.L.R. 497 in so far as it rejected a submission that the *Lyell v Kennedy* principle could not apply to a selection made from own client documents.

[221] See *Lubrizol Corp v Esso Petroleum Ltd* [1992] 1 W.L.R. 957 (but then the document may not be "confidential" under para.11.28 anyway).

which he sends to a party to litigation, who copies it for the purposes of the litigation and returns the file, the copies cannot be privileged. On the other hand, if the party inspected the file whilst in the third party's control and obtained copies of it there, those copies could be privileged. Finally, there is no relevant distinction for this purpose between the *copying* and the *translation* of an unprivileged document in the control of the party claiming privilege.[222]

Original documents

The same rule as already stated applies: where an original document is not brought into existence for a privileged purpose under the foregoing rules, and hence is not already privileged, it does not become so by being submitted to a lawyer for advice or otherwise for a privileged purpose.[223] If the original in the hands of a party has been subsequently lost, and there is no unprivileged copy available, then any privileged copies that have been made and are in the hands of that party simply replace it, and must be produced.[224] On the other hand, in principle, it seems that a non-privileged original document can become a new document, and capable of being privileged, if annotated or otherwise worked on by a lawyer to whom it has been submitted.[225]   **11.34**

What is "litigation"?

For the purposes of the rule, litigation clearly includes all adversarial proceedings, civil and criminal, in the High Court, the Crown Court, county courts, magistrates courts and industrial tribunals. It also includes similar proceedings in foreign courts[226] and this is so even if the foreign law   **11.35**

---

[222] *Sumitomo Corporation v Credit Lyonnais Rouse Ltd* [2002] 1 W.L.R. 479.
[223] *Pearce v Foster* (1885) 15 Q.B.D. 114 at 118–119; *Bursill v Tanner* (1885) 16 Q.B.D. 1, CA; *Graham v Bogle* [1924] 1 I.R. 68; *Hodgkinson v Simms* (1988) 55 D.L.R. (4th) 577 at 594; *R. v Board of Inland Revenue, exp. Goldberg* [1989] Q.B. 267 at 278; *Dubai Bank Ltd v Galadari* [1990] Ch. 98, CA; *Ventouris v Mountain* [1991] 1 W.L.R. 607, CA; *Commissioner, Australian Federal Police v Propend Finance Pty Ltd* (1997) 71 A.L.J.R. 327 at 335; *Brooks v Medical Defence Association of Western Australia* (1999) 94 F.C.R. 164, Fed.Ct.Aus.
[224] *Chadwick v Bowman* (1886) 16 Q.B.D. 561; *Land Corp. of Canada v Puleston* [1884] W.N. 1; *Lambert v Home* [1914] 3 K.B. 86; *Watson v Cammell Laird & Co.* [1959] 1 W.L.R. 702 at 704; *Dubai Bank Ltd v Galadari* [1990] Ch. 98, CA; *Commissioner, Australian Federal Police v Propend Finance Pty Ltd* (1997) 71 A.L.J.R. 327 at 331–332.
[225] *McCaskell v Mirror Newspapers Ltd* [1984] 1 N.S.W.L.R. 66, Sup.Ct.N.S.W.; *Water Authority of Western Australia v AIL Holdings Pty Ltd* (1992) 7 W.A.R. 135, Sup.Ct. W.Aus.
[226] *Re Duncan* [1968] p.306 at 313; *Société Française Hoechst v Allied Colloids Ltd* [1992] F.S.R. 66.

concerned knows no such privilege.[227] It extends to proceedings before a "tribunal exercising judicial functions"[228] and to arbitrations.[229]

11.36   However, there are several kinds of inquisitorial or non-adversarial proceeding before English courts[230] and other quasi-judicial or non-judicial statutory inquiries.[231] These do not so much amount to a contest between two or more parties, but rather to a fact-finding inquiry with a view to a "public interest" decision being made. Moreover, such proceedings usually do not apply the strict rules of evidence, of which legal privilege was considered to form merely a part.[232] Thus, for example, it has been held that litigation privilege cannot be claimed in order to protect from disclosure a report prepared for use in non-adversarial proceedings.[233] Changes in procedure may alter the fundamental nature of proceedings. Lord Scott has recently said that "[c]ivil litigation conducted pursuant to the current Civil Procedure Rules is in many respects no longer adversarial".[234]

11.37   There are suggestions that legal privilege first arose in the context of adversarial proceedings,[235] and it is a fact that in inquisitorial proceedings such as inquests there is usually no pre-inquest disclosure at all.[236] In wardship it is practically unknown and usually "entirely inappropriate."[237] The only questions of privilege which seem to arise in such cases relate to public interest immunity.[238] In the context of care proceedings it has been held that "litigation" privilege is simply inapplicable, having been impliedly excluded by the Children Act 1989,[239] though that does not mean that the court in such proceedings can override privilege for communications

---

[227] *Re Duncan* [1968] p.306 at 311.

[228] *Parry-Jones v The Law Society* [1969] 1 Ch. 1 at 9, *per* Diplock L.J.

[229] As in *Alfred Crompton Amusement Machines Ltd v Customs & Excise Commissioners (No.2)* [1974] A.C. 405, HL; and see *Sunderland Steamship P. & I. Association v Gatoil International Inc.* [1988] 1 Lloyd's Rep. 180, where a *subpoena* was used.

[230] e.g. inquests, wardships, Children Act cases (see *Re L (a minor)* [1997] A.C. 16, HL), patent extensions (*cf. Aktiebolaget Hassle v Pacific Pharmaceuticals Ltd* [1991] 3 N.Z.L.R. 186).

[231] e.g. under the Companies Act 1985, the Financial Services Act 1986, and the Financial Services and Markets Act 2000; see *Re Pergamon Press* [1970] 3 All E.R. 535 at 539; *Three Rivers District Council v Bank of England (No.6)* [2005] 1 A.C. 610, HL.

[232] *O'Reilly v State Bank of Victoria Commissioners* (1983) 153 C.L.R.I, H.Ct.Aus.; *Commissioner, Australian Federal Police v Propend Finance Pty Ltd* (1997) 71 A.L.J.R. 327 at 363.

[233] *Re L. (a minor)* [1997] A.C. 16, HL.

[234] *Three Rivers District Council v Bank of England (No.6)* [2005] 1 A.C. 610, at para.29.

[235] *Causton v Mann Egerton (Johnsons) Ltd* [1974] 1 W.L.R. 162 at 170; *D. v N.S.P.C.C.* [1978] A.C. 171 at 231–232; *Waugh v British Railways Board* [1980] A.C. 521 at 535–536; *cf. ibid.* at 531; *Three Rivers District Council v Bank of England (No.6)* [2005] 1 A.C. 610, at paras 90–91; *cf.* at para.92.

[236] See Ch.20, paras 20.17–20.20.

[237] See Ch.4, para.4.04, above.

[238] *Re D. (Infants)* [1970] 1 W.L.R. 599; *Re M (A Minor)* [1990] 2 F.L.R. 36; see also *R. v Bell, exp. Lees* (1980) 146 C.L.R. 141, H.Ct.Aus. (legal privilege gives way to higher public interest in child's welfare).

[239] *Re L. (A Minor)* [1997] A.C. 16, HL; *cf. R. v Bell, exp. Lees* (1980) 146 C.L.R. 141, H.Ct.Aus.

obtained in the context of other, adversarial proceedings.[240] Legal privilege has also been treated as irrelevant in the context of a Law Society inquiry into a solicitor's accounts.[241] On the other hand, in recent times the fundamental nature of legal privilege has been reasserted, as more than just a rule of evidence.[242] Apart from cases where statute has abrogated the privilege,[243] the courts may apply litigation privilege even to non-adversarial proceedings.[244]

When is litigation contemplated?

First of all, the test is not when litigation commences.[245] Nor is it even **11.38** when the cause of action arises,[246] nor when a decision is taken to obtain legal advice.[247] Bray put the test in this way:

> "There must be some definite prospect of litigation and not a mere vague anticipation of it."[248]

The modern test is simply when litigation is "reasonably in prospect"[249] which may precede in time all of the above. It is not necessary to show that litigation is more likely than not.[250] The test appears to be an objective one.[251] It should be noted that the "contemplated" litigation need not be the particular litigation in which the disclosure is being sought, but may be

---

[240] *S County Council v B* [2000] Fam. 76.

[241] *Parry-Jones v Law Society* [1969] 1 Ch. 1, CA; *Re Robertson Stromberg* (1995) 119 D.L.R. (4th) 551, Sask. Q.B.; see also *Simms v Law Society* [2005] EWCA Civ 749, CA.

[242] See para.11.08, above.

[243] See para.11.77, below.

[244] See, e.g. *Newcastle Wallsend Coal Co. Pty Ltd v Court Coal Miners Regulation* (1997) 42 N.S.W.L.R. 351; *cf. Re L. (A Minor)* [1997] A.C. 16 at 31–31.

[245] Though see *R. v Law Society, exp. Rosen, The Independent,* February 19, 1990.

[246] *Bristol Corp. v Cox* (1884) 26 Ch.D. 678.

[247] *Guinness Peat Properties v Fitzroy Robinson Partnership* [1987] 1 W.L.R. 1027 at 1037, CA.

[248] Bray, at p.408; approved by Lord Denning M.R. in *Alfred Crompton Amusement Machines Ltd v Customs & Excise Commissioners* [1972] 2 Q.B. 102 at 130; see also *Collins v London General Omnibus Co.* (1893) 68 L.T. 831.

[249] *Grant v Downs* (1976) 135 C.L.R. 674 at 677; *Waugh v British Railways Board* [1980] A.C. 521, HL; *Re Highgrade Traders Ltd* [1984] B.C.L.C. 151 at 172; *Plummers Ltd v Debenhams Plc* [1986] B.C.L.C. 447 at 457; *Guinness Peat Properties v Fitzroy Robinson Partnership* [1987] 1 W.L.R. 1027, CA; *Three Rivers District Council v Bank of England (No.6)* [2005] 1 A.C. 610, at para.83; *Donnelly v Weybridge Construction Ltd* [2006] EWHC 721, at para.25 (T.C.C.).

[250] See the surveys of caselaw in *Mitsubishi Electric Australia Pty Ltd v Victorian Work Cover Authority* [2002] V.S.C.A. 59, at paras 16–19, and in *United States of America v Philip Morris Inc.* [2004] EWCA Civ 330, at paras 59–66.

[251] *Singapore Airlines v Sydney Airports Corporation* [2004] N.S.W.S.C. 380.

other litigation, involving different parties and subject matter.[252] Thus it was held that, where intending personal injury claimants sought "after the event" insurance for legal costs and expenses in pursuing their claims, communications between the would-be claimants and the insurers and brokers were made at a time when litigation was contemplated and could in principle be privileged, even though the litigation in which the privilege issue arose was between the insurers and their agents and the lawyers involved, rather than the personal injury litigation itself.[253] Of course, the fact that legal proceedings are contemplated does not mean that all subsequent documents are privileged[254]; the question of purpose must also be considered.[255]

Directly or indirectly

11.39   As with advice privilege,[256] communications may be covered by litigation privilege if they otherwise qualify, but are made through the medium of agents.[257] It may even happen, for the purposes of litigation privilege (which extends to certain communications between a lawyer and third parties), that the client himself becomes a kind of agent of the lawyer for the purposes of third party communications[258] and they may be protected. This is so in English law[259] even if the client obtains the documents with a view to submitting them to a lawyer, but intends to try to settle the case without doing so,[260] or indeed never actually does so.[261] Even an unsolicited communication from a third party to a party's lawyer may be privileged.[262] But

---

[252] Bray, at p.409, citing *Bullock & Co. v Corry & Co.* (1878) 3 Q.B.D. 356; *Nordon v Defries* (1882) 8 Q.B.D. 508 at 510; *Kennedy v Lyell* (1883) 23 Ch.D. 387, CA; cf. *Taylor v Taylor*, 1990 J.L.R. 124, Jersey CA.

[253] *Winterthur Swiss Insurance v A.G. (Manchester) Ltd* [2006] EWHC 839 (Comm.).

[254] *Australian Competition and Consumer Commission v Australian Safeway Stores Pty Ltd* (1998) 81 F.C.R. 526, Fed.Ct.Aus.

[255] See paras 11.44–11.46, below.

[256] See para.11.14, above.

[257] *Anderson v Bank of British Columbia* (1876) 2 Ch.D. 644 at 650; *Wheeler v Le Marchant* (1881) 17 Ch.D. 675 at 681.

[258] *Anderson v Bank of British Columbia* (1876) 2 Ch.D. 644; *The Adam Steamship Company Ltd v The London Assurance Corporation* [1914] 3 K.B. 1256, CA.

[259] But perhaps not now in Australian law: *National Employers' Mutual General Insurance Association Ltd v Waind* (1979) 141 C.L.R. 648 at 654.

[260] *Birmingham and Midland Motor Omnibus Co. Ltd v London and North Western Railway Co.* [1913] 3 K.B. 850 at 856.

[261] *Southwark and Vauxhall Water Co. v Quick* (1878) 3 Q.B.D. 315, CA; *Mummery v Victorian Railway Commissioners* (1887) 9 A.L.T.21; *Bartram & Son v E. A. Clark & Son Pty Ltd* [1905] V.R. 442; *Trade Practices Commission v Sterling* (1979) 36 F.L.R. 244 at 245; *Re Murray Consultants Ltd* [1999] 1 I.L.R.M. 257, Irish H. Ct.; see also *Anderson v Bank of British Columbia* (1876) 2 Ch.D. 644; cf. *Société Française Hoechst v Allied Colloids Ltd* [1992] F.S.R. 66 at 68, and *Minister of Justice v Blank*, 2006, S.C.C. 39, para.32.

[262] *Re Holloway* (1887) 12 P.D. 167, CA; cf. *Caper v Commissioner of Police* (1994) 34 N.S.W.L.R. 715; *Re Barings Plc* [1998] 1 All E.R. 673 at 687.

client-third party communications, even after litigation is contemplated, in which the client is not effectively the lawyer's agent, are not within this privilege.[263]

What kind of lawyer?

This question was discussed above in relation to advice privilege,[264] and the position is that anyone who counts as a "lawyer" for the purposes of that head of privilege will also be treated as one for the purposes of litigation privilege. Needless to say, the limited privilege for auditors and tax advisers in respect of Inland Revenue notices to produce documents[265] has no application to litigation generally. However, the "notice" procedure may be employed by the Revenue even after the tax appeal has been commenced.[266] In addition to that, there are three further cases to deal with. First, in industrial tribunal proceedings, the privilege was originally held to extend to legally unqualified advisers, albeit "only in relation to communications with an actual view to the litigation in hand and the mode of conduct of it."[267] But subsequently the Employment Appeal Tribunal held that litigation privilege in such proceedings should be confined to professionally qualified legal advisers, members of professional bodies, subject to the rules and etiquette of their professions, and owing a duty to the court.[268]

11.40–11.41

The second case relates to patent agents. Originally no privilege attached to communications with a patent agent who gave legal advice, even in relation to pending proceedings.[269] Following the recommendation of the Law Reform Committee's 16th Report,[270] s.15 of the Civil Evidence Act 1968 for the first time introduced a kind of "litigation privilege" for patent agents, and this was repeated in s.104 of the Patents Act 1977. Those provisions were limited to communications "made for the purpose of pending or contemplated patent proceedings."[271] "Contemplated patent proceedings" include a contemplated application for a patent.[272] As already

11.42

---

[263] *Anderson v Bank of British Columbia* (1876) 2 Ch.D. 644; *Jones v Great Central Railway Co.* [1910] A.C. 4, HL. As to whether such communications may be protected on other grounds, see paras 11.52–11.57, below.

[264] Paras 11.18–11.24, above.

[265] See para.11.21, above.

[266] *R. v I.R.C., exp. Taylor (No.2)* [1989] 3 All E.R. 353, D.C.; *affd.* [1990] 2 All E.R. 409, CA.

[267] *M. W. Grazebrook Ltd v Wallens* [1973] I.C.R. 256, N.I.R.C.

[268] *New Victoria Hospital v Ryan* [1993] I.C.R. 201 (personnel consultants).

[269] *Moseley v The Victoria Rubber Co.* (1886) 3 R.P.C. 351.

[270] Paras 24 to 26.

[271] See *Wilden Pump Engineering Co. v Fusfeld* [1985] F.S.R. 159, CA; *Sony Tape Plc's Patent* [1987] R.P.C. 251 (proceedings had to be in UK), and *Société Française Hoechst v Allied Colloids Ltd* [1992] F.S.R. 66 (common law privilege wider than s.104).

[272] *Rockwell International Corp. v Serck Industries Ltd* [1987] R.P.C. 89.

noted above, those provisions have been superseded by s.280 of the Copyright, Designs and Patents Act 1988,[273] which is in broadly wider terms.[274] The section is not limited to "pending or contemplated proceedings" at all, nor is it limited purely to patent business, but extends to "communications as to any matter relating to the protection of any invention, design, technical information, trade mark or service mark, or as to any matter involving passing off."[275] It also extends to both civil and criminal proceedings, whereas the predecessor provisions did not apply to criminal proceedings. On the other hand, it does not extend to copyright pure and simple. Nor does it extend to communications between the patent agent and a third party (which were covered under the previous law), unless for the purpose of obtaining or giving information which a person is seeking for the purpose of instructing his patent agent. To that limited extent, the new law is more restrictive than the old.

The third case is that of the trade mark agent. Like patent agents, trade mark agents were not treated at common law as in any way equivalent to solicitors, even in relation to their conduct of those legal proceedings which they could and did conduct.[276] Unlike patent agents, who received recognition in relation to patent litigation as early as 1968, trade mark agents obtained no equivalent treatment until 1988, in s.284 of the Copyright, Designs and Patents Act.[277] This provision is similar to that for patent agents in s.280,[278] save that its scope is slightly narrower, in extending to "communications as to any matter relating to the protection of any design, trade mark, or as to any matter involving passing off."[279] As with s.280, it extends to both civil and criminal proceedings.

Client acting in person

11.43   Once more the question arises of the client acting for himself, without retaining a lawyer.[280] Notwithstanding the remarks of Cotton L.J. quoted above,[281] there are a number of statements to the effect that a litigant in person ought to be entitled to privilege in his communications with third parties and in his preparation for trial, just as if he were a lawyer. But in view of the many judicial statements limiting legal professional privilege to cases where a lawyer is involved, it is conceived that such a privilege cannot

---

[273] Which came into force on August 13, 1990.
[274] See para.11.22, above.
[275] Copyright, Designs and Patents Act 1988, s.280(1).
[276] *Dormeuil Trade Mark* [1983] R.P.C. 131; *cf. McGregor Clothing Company Ltd's Trade Mark* [1978] F.S.R. 353.
[277] Now the Trade Marks Act 1994, s.87 (see **Appendix 3, p.493**).
[278] Para.11.41, above.
[279] Trade Marks Act 1994, s.87(1).
[280] *cf.* para.11.25, above.
[281] Para.11.25, above.

exist as part of that privilege. Bray[282] suggests that such communications should be protected as being "materials for evidence." This is on the basis, not so much of freedom of communication with lawyers, but rather of freedom to assemble evidence and other materials for one's case. The whole matter is discussed later.[283]

The question of purpose

A document may be brought into existence for a number of purposes and **11.44** it will be necessary to analyse these purposes in considering whether it attracts litigation privilege. In such cases, it may sometimes be possible to locate all these various purposes within a "single wider purpose" which is itself privileged.[284] But if this is not possible, then in English law the document will only be covered by litigation privilege if the *dominant purpose* for which it came into existence was that of submitting it to a lawyer for advice (or for obtaining it for that purpose) or use in litigation, actual or anticipated.[285] In this context "use in litigation" excludes documents created to try to settle the litigation and intended to be shown to the other side.[286] Thus claims to litigation privilege failed:

(a) where an internal enquiry report concerning an accident was prepared for safety reasons, and for submission to lawyers in anticipation of litigation[287];

(b) where statements from witnesses were taken in relation to a complaint against the police under s.49 of the Police Act 1964, but also with litigation in prospect[288];

---

[282] Bray, at pp.392, 410.
[283] Paras 11.52–11.57, below.
[284] See, e.g. *Re Highgrade Traders Ltd* [1984] B.C.L.C. 151, CA; *cf. Winterthur Swiss Insurance v A.G. (Manchester) Ltd* [2006] EWHC 839 (Comm.).
[285] *Waugh v British Railways Board* [1980] A.C. 521, HL; *Guardian Royal Assurance v Stuart* [1985] 1 N.Z.L.R. 596; *W (J) (Guardian ad litem) v Yukon Territory (Comr)* (1992) 85 D.L.R. (4th) 533, Yukon CA; *Esso Australia Resources Ltd v The Commissioner of Taxation* (1999) 201 C.L.R. 49, 168 A.L.R. 123, H.Ct.Aus. (overruling the decision in *Grant v Downs* (1976) 135 C.L.R. 674, which established a narrower, "sole purpose" test); but for Australian Federal Court proceedings after April 17, 1995 the Evidence Act 1995 (Cth), ss.118 and 119, in any event applies the "dominant purpose" test in relation to admissibility in evidence; there is debate as to its effect on discovery: see, e.g. *Esso Australia Resources Ltd v Federal Commissioner of Taxation* (1998) 159 A.L.R. 664, Fed.Ct.Aus. (Full Ct.); *Telstra Corp. Ltd v B.T. Australasia Pty Ltd* (1998) 156 A.L.R. 634, Fed.Ct.Aus. (Full Ct.).
[286] *Bailey v Beagle Management Pty Ltd* (2001) 182 A.L.R. 264, at para.11.
[287] *Waugh v British Railways Board* [1980] A.C. 521, HL; *Lask v Gloucester Health Authority, The Times*, December 13, 1985; [1991] 2 Med.L.R. 379, CA.
[288] *Neilson v Laugharne* [1981] Q.B. 736, CA.

(c) where a report was made by a trade union member on an accident with a view to allowing the union to consider whether to give financial assistance to the member to bring an action, such litigation being then contemplated[289];

(d) where documents were procured from third parties for the dominant purpose of valuing the other party's goods for purchase tax, although litigation was then in prospect[290];

(e) where reports were made to a bank's lawyers on problem loans but contemplated litigation was not the dominant purpose[291];

(f) where a party to litigation procured a third party to swear an affidavit in that litigation, but then did not deploy it, or indeed disclose its existence to his opponent[292];

(g) where reports made by police investigating a murder and allegations that other police had been involved in it, were sent to the DPP in accordance with their statutory duties[293];

(h) where administrators of an insolvent bank submitted a report to the Secretary of State pursuant to their statutory duty[294];

(i) where a party commissioned a surveyor's report to verify his liability under an existing court order rather than to prepare for a future dispute[295];

(j) where a government officer prepared a report on suspected breaches of competition law to inform his superiors of the results of his inquiries[296]; and

(k) where would-be personal injury claimants sought "after the event" insurance at a time when personal injury litigation was contemplated, and the insurers made and received communications in order to decide whether or not to underwrite such policies.[297]

11.45   On the other hand, claims to privilege have succeeded:

(a) where reports were made by an employee to employers, or by an

---

[289] *Jones v Great Central Railway Co.* [1910] A.C. 4, H.L; see also *National Employers' Mutual General Insurance Association Ltd v Waind* (1979) 141 C.L.R. 648, H.Ct.Aus.

[290] *Alfred Crompton Amusement Machines Ltd v Commissioners of Customs & Excise (No.2)* [1974] A.C. 405, HL.

[291] *Price Waterhouse v BCCI Holdings (Luxembourg) S.A.* [1992] B.C.L.C. 583.

[292] *Sanger v Punjab National Bank*, unreported, July 19, 1994 (Rattee J.); *cf. Southern Equities Corporation Ltd v West Australian Government Holdings Ltd* (1993) 10 W.A.R.1, Sup.Ct. W.Aus. (Full Ct.) (litigation privilege could attach).

[293] *Goodridge v Chief Constable of Hampshire Constabulary* [1999] 1 All E.R. 896.

[294] *Re Barings Plc* [1991] 1 All E.R. 673.

[295] *Taylor v Taylor*, 1990 J.L.R.124, Jersey CA; *Lamey v Rice* (2000) 190 D.L.R. (4th) 486, New Brunswick CA.

[296] *Australian Competition and Consumer Commission v.Australian Safeway Stores Pty Ltd* (1998) 81 F.C.R. 326, Fed.Ct.Aus.

[297] *Winterthur Swiss Insurance v A.G. (Manchester) Ltd* [2006] EWHC 839 (Comm.).

insured to insurers, the dominant purpose of which was the obtaining of legal advice (even by the recipient rather than the maker)[298] whether to resist a claim for damages[299];

(b) where transcripts were prepared of the examination of a person under s.236 of the Insolvency Act 1986, such examination being made in order that the liquidator may obtain legal advice as to whether to institute proceedings[300];

(c) where a valuation report of a property the subject of proceedings was sought by a party following a without prejudice offer by the opposing party to settle[301]; and

(d) where an accountant's report was commissioned by a seller of department stores on the financial position of the buyer in order to obtain legal advice on taking certain legal steps,[302]; and

(e) where an application was made to the Law Society for legal aid[303];

(f) where loss adjustors prepared reports at the request of the lawyer[304];

(g) where a standard form report of an invention was sent to an in-house patents department for assessment as to patentability.[305]

The burden is on the party claiming privilege to establish it. In practice this is more difficult where the document predates the litigation concerned.[306] In considering the question of the dominant purpose, it is not right to look merely at the purpose of the creator of the document in question.[307] Often it is the intention of the employer of the creator that will **11.46**

---

[298] *Guinness Peat Properties Ltd v Fitzroy Robinson Partnership* [1987] 1 W.L.R. 1027, CA; in Canada, see *Davies v American Home Assurance Co.* (2002) 217 D.L.R. (4th) 157, Ont.Div.Ct.

[299] *Ogden v London Electric Railway Co.* (1933) 49 T.L.R. 542; *Westminster Airways v Kuwait Oil Co.* [1951] 1 K.B. 134; *Seabrook v British Transport Commission* [1959] 1 W.L.R. 509; *Re Highgrade Traders Ltd* [1984] B.C.L.C. 151, CA; *Guinness Peat Properties Ltd v Fitzroy Robinson Partnership* [1987] 1 W.L.R. 1027, CA; *cf. Guardian Royal Assurance of New Zealand Ltd v Stuart* [1985] 1 N.Z.L.R. 596, CA of N.Z.; *Carlton Cranes Ltd v Consolidated Hotels Ltd* [1988] 2 N.Z.L.R. 555; *Broadcasting Corp. of New Zealand v Wilson & Horton Ltd* [1991] 1 N.Z.L.R. 335.

[300] *Dubai Bank Ltd v Galadari* [1990] B.C.L.C. 90; *cf. Parry v News Group Newspapers Ltd* (1990) 140 New L.J. 1719, CA.

[301] *State Bank of South Australia v Ferguson* (1995) 64 S.A.S.R. 232, Sup.Ct.S.Aus.; *cf. Taylor v Taylor*, 1990 J.L.R. 124, Jersey CA (litigation purpose not established; claim failed).

[302] *Plummers Ltd v Debenhams Plc* [1986] B.C.L.C. 447.

[303] *R. v Snaresbrook Crown Court, exp. Director of Public Prosecutions* [1988] 1 Q.B. 532, D.C.

[304] *Lamey v Rice* (2000) 190 D.L.R. (4th) 486, New Brunswick CA.

[305] *Arrow Pharmaceuticals Ltd v Merck & Co. Inc.* (2004) 210 A.L.R. 593, Fed.Ct.Aus.

[306] See, e.g. *Taylor v Taylor*, 1990 J.L.R. 124, Jersey CA.

[307] *Guinness Peat Properties Ltd v Fitzroy Robinson Partnership* [1987] 1 W.L.R. 1027, CA.

be the relevant one.[308] Where a document is created for submission to insurers, the purpose of insurers in having the document created must be taken into account.[309] On the other hand, although it is necessary for litigation to be contemplated by the party seeking advice, the other prospective party to the litigation need not know that this is contemplated.[310] For the purpose of deciding what was the dominant purpose in creating a particular document, the court will not go behind an unchallenged statement in an affidavit unless there is something obviously wrong on the face of it.[311] But where the affidavit evidence is clearly wrong, the court is entitled to go behind it.[312]

Communications with third parties

11.47   In considering how far communications between lawyers and third parties are protected, there is first of all the question as to whether the usual agents (officers, employees, and so on) of a corporate client count simply as "the client", or on the other hand whether they are properly to be treated as third parties. This has been discussed already in the context of advice privilege[313] and, since the principle is the same even in the context of litigation privilege, nothing further need be said here. As to cases where the communication is with a person who cannot be treated as the client, there are two cases to consider: first, where the lawyer himself communicates with third parties and second, where the client does so. Each case itself can be subdivided into two, agency or no agency.

11.48   The case of the lawyer communicating with third parties is considered first. The third party may be the lawyer's own agent for communicating with his client, or he may be the client's own agent for communicating with

---

[308] *Waugh v British Railways Board* [1980] A.C. 521; *McAvan v London Transport Executive* (1983) 133 New L.J. 1101, CA; *Price Waterhouse v B.C.C.I. Holdings (Luxembourg) S.A.* [1992] B.C.L.C. 583; *Singapore Airlines v Sydney Airports Corporation* [2004] N.S.W.S.C. 380.

[309] *Re Highgrade Traders Ltd* [1984] B.C.L.C. 151, CA; *Guinness Peat Properties Ltd v Fitzroy Robinson Partnership* [1987] 1 W.L.R. 1027, CA; *General Accident Assurance Co. v Chrusz* (2000) 180 D.L.R. (4th) 241, Ont. CA; *Harding v Royal Canadian Legion* (1999) 166 D.L.R. (4th) 570, Newfoundland Sup.Ct. (statements taken by adjusters; not privileged); *Hill v Arcola School Division No.72* (2000) 179 D.L.R. (4th) 539, Sask, CA (statements taken by adjusters in preparation for litigation; privileged); *Winterthur Swiss Insurance v A.G. (Manchester) Ltd* [2006] EWHC 839 (Comm).

[310] *Plummers Ltd v Debenhams Ltd* [1986] B.C.L.C. 447.

[311] *Birmingham and Midland Motor Omnibus Co. Ltd v London and North Western Railway* [1913] 3 K.B. 850 at 858; *Re Highgrade Traders Ltd* [1984] B.C.L.C. 151 at 166.

[312] *Neilson v Laugharne* [1981] 1 Q.B. 736, CA; *cf. Lask v Gloucester Health Authority, The Times,* December 13, 1985; [1991] 2 Med.L.R. 379, CA; *Australian Competition and Consumer Commission v Australian Safeway Stores Pty Ltd* (1998) 81 F.C.R. 326, Fed.Ct.Aus.

[313] See paras 11.16 above.

his lawyer; in either case, the other conditions being satisfied, the communications in question will be protected.[314] Alternatively, the third party may be no one's agent, and the lawyer may be communicating with him as a principal, e.g. as an expert or as a witness.[315] In that case, where the communication is made for the dominant purpose of existing or contemplated (adversarial) litigation, it is protected,[316] as where a surveyor's or other expert's report is obtained by the lawyer so as to be able to advise his client,[317] or where a lawyer obtains documents coming into existence with a view to enabling him to carry on, or advise with reference to, actual or contemplated litigation,[318] even if the documents are sent to him anonymously.[319] Where the third party is also a lawyer (e.g. a barrister or a foreign lawyer asked for an opinion), the communication may be protected either way, i.e. the lawyer is the client's agent for dealing with the third party,[320] or he is obtaining documents to advise his client. It should be noted that, where a third party prepares a document (e.g. a report) which is privileged, the privilege is normally[321] that of the client, not of the third party. If the client waives his privilege, the witness has none.[322] Note also that although communications with an expert may be privileged,[323] his opinion is not and he can, for example, be served with a witness summons requiring him to testify as to his opinion and also reveal on what original materials he based that opinion,[324] except to the extent that those materials were themselves privileged.[325]

---

[314] See para.11.14, above.

[315] In the normal course of proceedings a solicitor will interview and obtain proofs of evidence from potential witnesses. Both the information given and the identity of the person supplying it are confidential and privileged unless and until the privilege is waived: *China National Petroleum Corporation v Fenwick Elliott* [2002] EWHC 60, Ch.D.

[316] *Three Rivers District Council v Bank of England (No.6)* [2005] 1 A.C. 610, at para.102, *per* Lord Carswell.

[317] *Wheeler v Le Marchant* (1881) 17 Ch.D. 675 at 683; *Taylor v Taylor*, 1990 J.L.R. 124, Jersey CA (claim failed on facts); *Trade Practices Commission v Ampol Petroleum (Victoria) Pty Ltd* (1994) 127 A.L.R. 533, Fed.Ct.Aus.; *The Patraikos 2* [2001] 4 S.L.R. 308, H.Ct. Singapore (no privilege for communications between lawyer and third party) following *Secretary of State for Trade and Industry v Baker* [1998] Ch. 356 at 366; *Jackson v Marley Davenport Ltd* [2004] 1 W.L.R. 2926, CA; *cf. Price Waterhouse v BCCI Holdings (Luxembourg) S.A.* [1992] B.C.L.C. 583 (litigation not dominant purpose: no privilege).

[318] *Learoyd v Halifax Banking Co.* [1892] 1 Ch. 686; although the problems with copies must be borne in mind: para.11.33, above.

[319] *Re Holloway* (1887) 12 P.D. 167, CA; *cf. Capar v Commissioner of Police* (1994) 34 N.S.W.L.R. 715; *Re Barings Plc* [1998] 1 All E.R. 673 at 687.

[320] *Hughes v Biddulph* (1827) 4 Russ. 190; *Hobbs v Hobbs* [1960] p.112.

[321] Though *cf.* CPR, r.32.12(2)(a), and see para.11.136, below ("witness statement" privilege).

[322] *Schneider v Leigh* [1955] 2 Q.B.195, CA; see Ch.10, para.10.02, below.

[323] *Jones v Smith* [1999] 1 S.C.R. 455, Sup.Ct.Can.

[324] *Harmony Shipping S.A. v Saudi-Europe Line Ltd* [1979] 1 W.L.R. 1380, CA; *R. v King* [1983] 1 W.L.R. 411, CA; *Re L (A Minor)* [1997] A.C. 16 at 25, 29, 34; *Interchase Corporation Ltd v Grosvenor Hill (Queensland) Pty Ltd (No.1)* [1999] 1 Qd. R. 141, Queensland CA; *cf. R. v R.* [1994] 4 All E.R. 260, CA (privileged item under Police and Criminal Evidence Act 1984).

[325] *R. v Davies* [2002] EWCA Crim. 85.

11.49   Where the client deals with the third party there are again two sub-cases. The first is where there is agency, i.e. where either the client is really acting as the agent of his lawyer in carrying out the lawyer's protected functions[326] or the third party is the lawyer's agent for the purpose of lawyer/client protected communications.[327] In either case privilege attaches. The second is more difficult and involves direct communication between client and third party, each acting as principal. The problem here is that no lawyer is involved. As Lord Loreburn L.C. put it in one case[328]:

> "Both client and solicitor may act through an agent, and therefore communications to or through the agent are within the privilege. But if communications are made to him as a person who has himself to consider and act upon them, then the privilege is gone; and this is because the principle which protects communications only between solicitor and client no longer applies. Here documents are in existence relating to the matter in dispute which were communicated to some one who is not a solicitor, nor the mere alter ego of a solicitor."

Thus, as mentioned above,[329] communications between co-plaintiffs or co-defendants are not privileged, unless they fall within what is called "common interest" privilege.[330] There is one anomalous situation, where a client obtains documents for the purpose of submitting them to a lawyer for advice on contemplated or actual litigation, in circumstances where they would be privileged if so submitted. These also are privileged, even if they are never so submitted.[331]

11.50   At the same time it is plain that there should be some means by which a client's own preparations for litigation (not intended for submission to a lawyer, especially if he has no lawyer) should be protected from production like those of his richer opponent who has had a lawyer from the beginning. In one case,[332] Bingham L.J. said:

> "the expression 'legal professional privilege' . . . also suggests, surely wrongly, that a litigant in person is denied, in preparing his litigation, the protection of secrecy which is enjoyed by a litigant who instructs a lawyer."

11.51   Until 1968 a separate head of privilege for documents existed which might have covered many—even most—such communications between a

---

[326] Para.11.39, above.
[327] ibid.
[328] Jones v Great Central Railway Co. [1910] A.C. 4 at 6.
[329] Para.11.15, above.
[330] Paras 11.59–11.61, below.
[331] See para.11.39, above.
[332] Ventouris v Mountain [1991] 3 All E.R. 472 at 475.

client and a third party. This was the privilege against giving discovery relating solely to your own case and not tending to impeach that case nor to support the case of any opposing party.[333] It covered both discovery of documents or facts which themselves constituted evidence in a party's favour (such as title deeds) and also documents which contained such evidence. Except in criminal cases, this privilege was abolished in England, so far as production of documents was concerned, by s.16(2) of the Civil Evidence Act 1968,[334] and the state of the case law immediately before abolition is indicated in the then current *Supreme Court Practice*.[335] But the privilege lived on, so far as discovery by interrogatories was concerned and even today a party generally may not make an information request of another for his evidence, such as the names of his witnesses or how he intends to conduct his case.[336] Moreover, in some other common law jurisdictions, it continues to subsist even for documents.[337]

"Materials for evidence"?

Given that the privilege under s.16(2) of the Civil Evidence Act 1968 is no longer available, the question arises whether there is any other privilege for documents. As mentioned above,[338] Bray supports the existence of a head of privilege covering "materials for evidence."[339] He distinguishes this from legal professional privilege in this way[340]:   **11.52**

> "Professional privilege rests on the impossibility of conducting litigation without professional advice, whereas the ground on which a party is protected from disclosing his evidence is that the adversary may not be thus enabled so to shape his case as to defeat the ends of justice."

There are dicta in support of this view in *Anderson v Bank of British Columbia*,[341] and also in *Kennedy v Lyell*,[342] where Cotton L. J. says: **11.53**

---

[333] *Bewicke v Graham* (1881) 7 Q.B.D. 400, CA; *Att.Gen. v Emerson* (1882) 10 Q.B.D. 191, CA; *Morris v Edwards* (1890) 15 App.Cas. 309, HL; *Brooks v Prescott* [1948] 1 All E.R. 907, CA.
[334] Following a recommendation in the Law Reform Committee's 16th Report, 1967, para.30.
[335] 1967 edn, para.24/5/12.
[336] See Ch.14 para.14.36, below.
[337] See *National Employers' Mutual General Insurance Association Ltd v Waind* (1979) 141 C.L.R. 648 at 654, H.Ct.Aus.
[338] Para.11.43, above.
[339] See Bray, pp.392, 406–408, 410.
[340] Bray, at p.407.
[341] (1876) 2 Ch.D. 644 at 656 (James L.J.) and at 658–659 (Mellish L.J.).
[342] (1883) 23 Ch.D. 387 at 404; *cf.* the views of the same judge in *Lyell v Kennedy (No.3)* (1884) 27 Ch.D. 1 at 18, in relation to advice privilege (para.11.25, above).

"There is also another principle, that no one is to be fettered in obtaining materials for his defence, and if he for the purpose of his defence obtains evidence, the adverse party cannot ask to see it before the trial. I do not think that this principle applies here, but I mention it that I may not be supposed to limit protection to the simple professional privilege which arises where information has been obtained through a solicitor."

It is also supported by the judgment of Smith J. in *Kyshe v Holt*,[343] the other judge, Cave J., taking the opposite view. And in its 16th Report[344] the Law Reform Committee, which then included six current and three future judges, said that a litigant in person in principle:

" . . . would appear to be entitled to privilege for communications between himself and third parties, if made for the purpose of obtaining factual information for the preparation of his case in pending or contemplated litigation."[345]

11.54 It might at first sight be supposed that this "privilege" was nothing more than a manifestation of the privilege against disclosing documents relating solely to your own case, abolished in England in 1968. Yet it is not so. In the first place, Bray treated them as distinct, dealing with them in different chapters in his book.[346] Secondly, the rule that was abolished in England in 1968 went both wider than protecting materials for evidence, because it covered documents a party had no intention of relying on at trial but which did not help his opponent, and narrower, in that it would not cover, for example, a witness statement which mostly supported the party's own case but partly supported his opponent's.

11.55 Thirdly, in addition to copious notes on the privilege under s.16(2) of the Civil Evidence Act 1968, a separate note, originally prepared by Bray himself (who contributed the notes to RSC, Ord.31—as it then was—in the *Annual Practice*),[347] appeared in the Annual Practice for many years down at least to 1962 in the following terms:

"Materials for evidence. It is conceived that on principle documents come into existence or communications made for the purpose of getting evidence ought to be protected independently of its having been done under the direction of or for communication to the solicitor so as to come within the above conditions [i.e. those for legal professional

---

[343] [1888] W.N. 128.
[344] On Privilege in Civil Proceedings, 1967.
[345] Law Reform Committee's 16th Report, 1967, para.17.
[346] Bk.II, Ch.II, for material for evidence, and Bk.II, Ch.III for discovery of a party's case; so did the Law Reform Committee, in their 16th Report, paras 17 and 30 respectively.
[347] See his *Digest of the Law of Discovery* (2nd edn, 1910) at pp.31–32.

privilege], for instance, where a party is conducting his own case: but the weight of authority is against it . . . "[348]

Plainly, this note reflected Bray's view that the "materials for evidence" privilege was different from the s.16(2) privilege, first because it was given a separate note and secondly, because it said that the principle was doubtful because the weight of authority was against it, which (whether right or wrong) was plainly not the s.16(2) privilege, then clearly in existence. Curiously, although the s.16(2) privilege continued to be separately noted until 1967, the separate note on materials for evidence had vanished before then. Fourthly and lastly, there have been judicial dicta supporting the existence of this head of privilege even after 1968.[349] **11.56**

More difficult is the question whether the "materials for evidence" privilege can be said to exist at all today. The authorities are certainly meagre, although the dicta of Bingham L.J. in *Ventouris v Mountain*[350] and of Murphy J. in *Baker v Campbell*[351] are in favour of there being some sort of privilege. On the other hand, the Court of Appeal has held that a litigant receiving anonymous letters relevant to the action, which would have been privileged if received by her lawyer, were not privileged in her hands[352] and the High Court of Australia has doubted the existence of the "materials for evidence" privilege.[353] The Irish High Court has considered the issue but not reached any conclusion on the principle, as the claim failed on the facts in any event.[354] In Canada, ordinary litigation privilege applies.[355] **11.57**

Until 1968 the existence of the overlapping privilege for documents solely supporting a party's own case reduced, if it did not obviate, the need for this separate head of privilege and it is hardly surprising that the point has been so little discussed. In its favour is the public policy in favour of enabling free preparation of a party's case, because no one should be inhibited from doing the best he can to find evidence to support his case.[356] There is also the consumerist argument against disadvantaging even further the litigant who chooses to fight without engaging a lawyer.[357] And it would be odd if a party **11.58**

---

[348] Three cases are cited: *Jones v Great Central Railway Co.* [1910] A.C. 4, and *Re Holloway, Young v Holloway* (1887) 12 P.D. 167, both *sub silentio* authorities on this point and *Kyske v Holt* [1888] W.N. 128, where the judges differed.

[349] *Waugh v British Railways Board* [1980] A.C. 521 at 531, 537; *Buttes Gas & Oil Co. v Hammer (No.3)* [1981] Q.B. 223 at 243–244; *Baker v Campbell* (1983) 49 A.L.R. 385 at 412; *Ventouris v Mountain* (1991) 3 All E.R. 472 at 475 (see para.11.45, above); *Société Française Hoechst v Allied Colloids Ltd* [1992] F.S.R. 66 at 68.

[350] [1991] 3 All E.R. 472 at 475; see para.11.50, above.

[351] (1983) 49 A.L.R. 385 at 439.

[352] *Re Holloway* (1887) 12 P.D. 167 at 171, 172.

[353] *National Employers' Mutual General Insurance Association Ltd v Waind* (1979) 141 C.L.R. 648 at 654.

[354] *Woori Bank v KDB Ireland Ltd* [2005] I.E.H.C. 451.

[355] *Minister of Justice v Blank*, 2006 S.C.C. 39, para.32.

[356] *Kennedy v Lyell* (1883) 23 Ch.D. 387 at 404; Law Reform Committee, 16th Report, 1967, para.17.

[357] cf. *Bevan v Hastings-Jones* [1978] 1 W.L.R. 294 at 296.

without a lawyer could exchange information with another party, protected by "common interest" privilege,[358] but could not protect his own materials, prepared without contact with anyone else. On the other hand, against the privilege is the principle of litigation being conducted "cards face up on the table,"[359] in which the disclosure rules play so important a role. Every privilege against production is a restriction on information which must be adequately justified.[360] In the absence of binding authority, it is submitted that the "materials for evidence" privilege is justified, but that its limits must be clearly defined, not least so as to enable litigants in person to understand it and to be able to operate within it. It is suggested that it be confined to communications made or solicited[361] by or to, or materials prepared by or on behalf of, a litigant for the dominant purpose of either:

(a) deciding whether to prosecute or defend legal proceedings; or
(b) prosecuting or defending such proceedings.

Communications between persons with a "common interest"[362]

11.59 Some communications with third parties which do not properly fall within the scope of the preceding discussion may still be privileged, because they take place between persons having a common interest.[363] In *Buttes Gas and Oil Co. v Hammer (No.3)*[364] Brightman L.J. said:

> " . . . if two parties with a common interest and a common solicitor exchange information for the dominant purpose of informing each other of the facts, or the issues, or advice received, or of obtaining legal advice in respect of contemplated or pending litigation, the documents or copies containing that information are privileged from production in the hands of each."[365]

This has been variously described as "no more than a variety of legal professional privilege"[366] and as "different in nature from litigation privi-

---

[358] See paras 11.59–11.61, below.

[359] Para.11.08, above.

[360] *Re Barings Plc* [1999] 1 All E.R. 673.

[361] See *Re Holloway* (1887) 12 P.D. 167 in relation to *unsolicited* communications.

[362] See generally, Thanki (ed.), *The Law of Privilege*, 2006, Ch.6; Passmore, *Privilege*, 2nd edn 2006, Ch.6.

[363] *Jenkyns v Bushby* (1866) L.R.2 Eq. 547; *Winterthur Swiss Insurance v A.G. (Manchester) Ltd* [2006] EWHC 839 (Comm.).

[364] [1981] Q.B. 223 at 267.

[365] Approved in *Guinness Peat Properties Ltd v Fitzroy Robinson Partnership* [1987] 1 W.L.R. 1027, CA; see also *per* Lord Denning M.R. at 243 and *per* Donaldson L.J. at 251, to the same effect.

[366] *Leif Hoegh & Co. A/S v Petrolsea Inc.* [1993] 1 Lloyd's Rep. 363; *Naura Phosphate Royalties Trust v Allen, Allen & Hemsley*, (1997) 13 P.N. 64.

lege or legal privilege".[367] Indeed, a recent decision at first instance threatens to eclipse it altogether.[368] Although it usually arises in the same context as litigation privilege, i.e. where litigation exists or is contemplated,[369] this is not a requirement.[370]

At first sight it resembles the case of joint privilege, i.e. where two or more **11.60** persons jointly instruct a lawyer, so that communications between them and the lawyer are privileged against third parties, though not as between the joint clients.[371] Where joint privilege exists, it is normally unnecessary to rely on common interest privilege.[372] But common interest privilege is different, both formally and in substance. And the rules on waiver are different.[373] It does not matter whether both parties are in the same litigation, or only one is, or whether they are both plaintiffs or both defendants,[374] as long as they have a genuine common interest.[375] Nor is it necessary for them to be represented by the same solicitor, as long as their interests are close enough to be able to do so.[376] And, although they must have a common interest, i.e. an area of interest which is common to both, they need not have exactly the same interests. The insurers of a party in litigation will usually have a "common interest" with that party sufficient to attract the privilege,[377] as will reinsurers of insurers,[378] at least so long as

---

[367] Style & Hollander, *Documentary Evidence*, 6th edn 1997, at 209.
[368] *USP Strategies Ltd v London General Holdings Ltd* [2004] EWHC 373 (Ch.), *The Times*, April 30, 2004; see para.11–27 above.
[369] *Buttes Gas & Oil Co. v Hammer (No.3)* [1981] Q.B. 223 at 243.
[370] *Unilateral Investments Ltd v VNZ Acquisitions Ltd* [1993] 1 N.Z.L.R. 468; *Svenska Handlesbank v Sun Alliance and London Assurance Plc* [1995] 2 Lloyd's Rep. 84; *Farrow Mortgage Services Pty Ltd v Webb* (1995) 13 A.C.L.C. 1329, *affd*. July 5, 1996, CA of N.S.W.
[371] See para.11.74, below.
[372] *Hellenic Mutual War Risk Association (Bermuda) Ltd v Harrison* [1997] 1 Lloyd's Rep. 160 at 167.
[373] See Ch.12, para.12.02, below.
[374] *Buttes Gas & Oil Co. v Hammer (No.3)* [1981] Q.B. 223 at 243.
[375] *Lee v South West Thames Regional Health Authority* [1985] 1 W.L.R. 845, CA: defendant and third party's interests diametrically opposed, so no "common interest" privilege; *Robert Hitchins Ltd v International Computers Ltd,* unreported, December 12, 1996, CA, *per* Peter Gibson L.J. (same point); *cf. Sanger v Punjab National Bank,* unreported, June 29, 1994, Rattee J. (where two parties pleaded the same case against a third, although they might have pleaded cases opposed to each other, they had a sufficient common interest).
[376] *Bulk Materials (Coal Handling) Services Pty Ltd v Coal and Allied Operations Pty Ltd* (1988) 13 N.S.W.L.R., 68 at 695; *Bank of Nova Scotia v Hellenic Mutual War Risk Association (Bermuda) Ltd* [1992] 2 Lloyd's Rep. 540, not following Brightman L.J. in *Buttes* [1981] Q.B. 223 at 267 ("a common interest and a common solicitor"); *Lee Lighting v Central Properties,* unreported, September 27, 1994, Morison J.; *Rank Film Distributors Ltd v ENT Ltd* (1994) 4 Tas. R. 281 at 294; *Network Ten Ltd v Capital Television Holdings Ltd* (1995) 36 N.S.W.L.R. 275 at 279–280, Sup.Ct.N.S.W.; *USP Strategies Ltd v London General Holdings Ltd* [2004] EWHC 373, *The Times*, April 30, 2004.
[377] *Westminster Airways v Kuwait* [1951] 1 K.B. 134; *Guinness Peat Properties Ltd v Fitzroy Robinson Partnership* [1987] 1 W.L.R. 1027, CA; *Leach v Chilton Transport (Bow) Ltd,* unreported, April 29, 1987, CA; *Nauru Phosphates Royalties Trust v Allen Allen & Hemsley* (1997) 13 P.N. 64, Robert Walker J.; *Winterthur Swiss Insurance v A.G. (Manchester) Ltd* [2006] EWHC 839 (Comm.).
[378] *Formica Ltd v Export Credit Guarantors Department* [1951] Lloyd's Rep. 692; *Svenska*

the contract of insurance or reinsurance is not avoided.[379] Where A and B have a profit-sharing agreement, and C claims a share of those profits as against A, A and B have a common interest against C.[380]

11.61   It is not clear whether the common interest needs to exist at the time of the creation of the document,[381] at the time of disclosure,[382] or indeed either.[383] But it is clear that common interest will survive a dispute as to which party should litigate against the third party,[384] or some other falling-out between them,[385] but in that case documents thereafter brought into existence will not be covered by common interest privilege against the third party.[386] This suggests that the critical date is that of *creation* rather than of disclosure, which is consistent with rules elsewhere in the law of disclosure.[387] In the converse situation, where there is no common interest at the time of disclosure, but later on the parties settle and their differences and make common cause (e.g. on costs), common interest privilege will not apply.[388]

11.62   Merely because a party is interested, as creditor, in the outcome of previous litigation between his opponent and a third party is not a sufficient "common interest" within the rule.[389] Indeed, in Canada it has been held that there is no common interest privilege between a bankrupt and his trustee in pursuing a third party.[390] Nor does a potential purchaser of shares have a sufficient common interest in the outcome of litigation between the vendor and a third party.[391] And neither is it sufficient that two or more persons are interested in the same legal question, which will affect their own

---

Handelsbanken v Sun Alliance and London Assurance Plc [1995] 2 Lloyd's Rep. 84; *Commercial Union Assurance Co Plc v Mander* [1996] 2 Lloyd's Rep. 640; *Hellenic Mutual War Risk Association (Bermuda) Ltd v Harrison* [1997] 1 Lloyd's Rep. 160 at 167.

[379] *Commercial Union Assurance Co. Plc v Mander* [1996] 2 Lloyd's Rep. 640.

[380] *United Capital Corporation v Bender* [2005] J.R.C. 144, R.Ct.Jersey.

[381] *Cia Barca de Panama S.A. v Geo Wimpey & Co. Ltd* [1980] 1 Lloyd's Rep. 598, at 615; *Formica Ltd v Export Credits Guarantee Dept* [1995] 1 Lloyd's Rep. 692; *Robert Hitchins Ltd v International Computers Ltd*, unreported, December 12, 1996, CA, per Peter Gibson L.J.; *R. v Trutch* [2001] EWCA Crim. 1750.

[382] Suggested by Hollander, *Documentary Evidence*, 9th edn, para.15–12.

[383] *Commercial Assurance Co. Plc v Mander* [1996] 2 Lloyd's Rep. 640, at 648.

[384] *Leif Hoegh & Co. A./S. v Petrolsea Inc.* [1993] 1 Lloyd's Rep. 363.

[385] *Cia Barca de Panama S.A. v Geo Wimpey & Co. Ltd* [1980] 1 Lloyd's Rep. 598, CA; *Winterthur Swiss Insurance v A.G. (Manchester) Ltd* [2006] EWHC 839 (Comm); see also *Commercial Assurance Co. Plc v Mander* [1996] 2 Lloyd's Rep. 640.

[386] *ibid.*

[387] E.g. the rules on copies: see para.11.32–11.33.

[388] *Patrick v Capital Finance Corporation (Australasia) Pty Ltd* (2004) 211 A.L.R. 272, Fed.Ct.Aus.

[389] *Bank of Nova Scotia v Hellenic Mutual War Risk Association (Bermuda) Ltd* [1992] 2 Lloyd's Rep. 540; *cf. Brown v Guardian Royal Insurance Plc* [1994] 2 Lloyd's Rep. 325, CA.

[390] *Anderson v John Zivanovic Holdings Ltd* (2000) 195 D.L.R. (4th) 713, Ont.Sup.Ct. (Div.Ct.), though public policy was held to justify non-disclosure in that case.

[391] *Network Ten Ltd v Capital Television Holdings Ltd* (1995) 36 N.S.W.L.R. 275, Sup.Ct.N.S.W.

individual actions and circumstances.[392] There is no common interest privilege in an affidavit sent by a defendant to a claimant as part of settlement of proceedings between them.[393] The effect of common interest privilege is usually to provide protection against inspection by third parties (use "as a shield").[394] But it does not apply as between the parties entitled to it, so (absent other considerations) one party can obtain disclosure of documents from the other ("as a sword").[395] Dicta[396] apparently suggesting that common interest privilege gives rise to an independent right to obtain disclosure even of documents which would otherwise be privileged in favour of one party against the other have been explained[397] as not going so far.[398]

F. EXCEPTIONS TO LEGAL PROFESSIONAL PRIVILEGE

There are numerous exceptions to or restrictions on legal privilege in both forms. In summary these are as follows: **11.63**

(a) where the communication concerned is a material fact in itself;
(b) where the documents will help prove innocence in a criminal trial;
(c) where the legal advice was sought or given to assist in a fraud or illegality;
(d) as between trustee and beneficiary;
(e) as between company and shareholder;
(f) as between joint clients;
(g) where the other party has a better right to the document in question;
(h) where secondary evidence can be given of the privileged material;
(i) certain statutory exceptions;

---

[392] *Ampolex Ltd v Perpetual Trustee Co. (Canberra) Ltd* (1995) 37 N.S.W.L.R. 405, Sup.Ct.N.S.W.
[393] *R. v Trutch* [2001] EWCA Crim. 1750.
[394] See the cases cited in notes 368–373, above, and also *Phipson on Evidence*, 16th edn, 2005, at paras 24–04 – 24–05.
[395] *Cia Barca de Panama S.A. v Geo Wimpey & Co. Ltd* [1980] 1 Lloyd's Rep. 598, CA; *Svenska Handelsbanken v Sun Alliance and London Insurance Plc* [1995] 2 Lloyd's Rep. 84 at 88; *Commercial Assurance Co. Plc v Mander* [1996] 2 Lloyd's Rep. 640; *Winterthur Swiss Insurance v A.G. (Manchester) Ltd* [2006] EWHC 839 (Comm.); *cf. Brown v Guardian Royal Assurance Plc* [1994] 2 Lloyd's Rep. 325, CA.
[396] *Formica Ltd v Export Credits Guarantee Dept.* [1995] 1 Lloyd's Rep. 692 at 699–700.
[397] *Commercial Assurance Co. Plc v Mander* [1996] 2 Lloyd's Rep. 640 at 647–648.
[398] See also *Brown v Guardian Royal Assurance Plc* [1994] 2 Lloyd's Rep. 325, CA (insurer's express contractual right to see privileged material).

(j)   (in Australia) where a legislative body requires access to legal advice given to the executive;

(k)   (in Canada) where the privilege must yield to the interests of public safety; and

(l)   where the privilege has been waived or otherwise lost.

With the exception of the last category, which is dealt with in Ch.12, these categories are discussed below.

11.64   **(a) Material fact in itself**   Where information which is otherwise privileged itself constitutes a material fact in the proceedings, it is not privileged from disclosure. Thus the names of a party's witnesses, being the persons in whose presence a slander was alleged to have been uttered, are not privileged.[399] Again, in a case where the authority of a solicitor to settle a claim was in dispute, letters from the client to the solicitor which were alleged to constitute such authority were held not privileged.[400] The position would probably be the same if the authority of the solicitor to commence proceedings at all were in issue. However, where judicial review of a public law decision is sought, privilege is not lost in any otherwise privileged material on which the respondent relied, by reason only that that it constitutes in part the subject matter of the action.[401] Where in litigation allegations are made by a party concerning his state of mind (e.g. in entering an agreement) to which legal advice contributed, that party cannot withhold the advice on grounds of privilege, but this is because of implied waiver, rather than because no privilege attached in the first place.[402]

11.65   **(b) Documents to prove innocence in a criminal trial**[403]   It had been said that legal privilege would not justify withholding documents which, if produced: " . . . would perhaps enable a man either to establish his innocence or to resist an allegation made by the Crown" in a criminal trial.[404] More recently in both England and Australia this exception to legal privilege has been held not to exist, as being inconsistent with the fundamental

---

[399] *Roselle v Buchanan* (1886) 16 Q.B.D. 656; *Marriot v Chamberlain* (1886) Q.B.D. 154; *Dalgleish v Lowther* [1899] 2 Q.B., 590, CA.

[400] *Conlon v Conlons Ltd* [1952] 2 All E.R. 462, CA; *cf. Benecke v National Australia Bank Ltd* (1993) 35 N.S.W.L.R. 110, CA of N.S.W.; *Moreay Nominees Pty Ltd v McCarthy* (1994) 10 W.A.R. 293, Sup.Ct.W.Aus (implied waiver).

[401] *Re Fritz* [1995] 2 Qd.R.580, Queensland CA.

[402] *Wardrope v Dunn* [1996] 1 Qd.R. 224, Queensland Sup. Ct.; *Ampolex Ltd v Perpetual Trustee Co. (Canberra) Ltd* (1995) 37 N.S.W.L.R. 405; *Hayes v Dowding* [1996] P.N.L.R. 578 (overruled on another point in *Paragon Finance Plc v Freshfields* [1999] 1 W.L.R. 1183, CA).

[403] See Auburn, *op.cit.*, Ch.9.

[404] *R. v Barton* [1973] 1 W.L.R. 115 at 118; *R. v Ataou* [1988] Q.B. 798, CA; see also *R. v Craig* [1975] 1 N.Z.L.R. 597; *R. v Dunbar and Logan* (1983) 138 D.L.R. 21, Ontario CA; *S. v Safatsa* 1988(1) S.A. 868, A.D.; *R. v Gray* (1992) 74 CCC (3d) 267, B.C. Sup.Ct.

nature of the privilege.[405] But it continues to apply in Canada[406] and, it would seem,[407] in New Zealand.[408]

However, if the document is produced in criminal proceedings, privilege is not lost and can still be claimed in any subsequent civil proceedings.[409] This may be compared with the rule that the court will not restrain use by the Crown in a public prosecution of a privileged but otherwise relevant document, even if it had been obtained in circumstances ordinarily giving rise to an actionable breach of confidence where an injunction would otherwise have been granted.[410] The criminal court does however have a discretion to exclude evidence, depending, in part, on how it was obtained.[411] In one case the criminal court was prepared by witness summons to order a third party to disclose to the defendant's counsel material in which the third party had privilege, but only on the basis of an express undertaking by the defendant not to use the information in any civil proceedings with the third party.[412] This would probably not now be followed.[413]

11.66

(c) **Fraud or illegality**[414] Privilege may be claimed for communications with or from lawyers on how to stay on the right side of the law[415] or constituting warnings against the results of contemplated acts.[416] However:

11.67

> "Legal professional privilege does not exist in respect of documents which are in themselves part of a criminal or fraudulent proceeding or, if it be different, communications made in order to get advice for the

---

[405] *R. v Derby Magistrates Court, exp. B* [1996] 1 A.C. 487, HL; *Carter v Northmore, Hale, Dary & Leake* (1995) 183 C.L.R. 121, H.Ct.Aus. (reversed by the Evidence Act 1995 (Cth.), s.123); *Three Rivers District Council v Bank of England (No.6)* [2005] 1 A.C. 610, at para.25; see also *S. v Jija* 1991 (2) S.A. 52, Eastern Cape Div.

[406] *Smith v Jones* (1999) 132 CCC (Sd.) 225 at 242–3, Sup.Ct.Can., approving *R. v Dunbar and Logan* (1982) 138 D.L.R. (3d.) 221; *R. v Brown* (2002) 210 D.L.R. (4th) 341, S.C.C.

[407] See the New Zealand Law Commission, Report 55, 1999, ii, 184, draft Evidence Code, s.71(2).

[408] *R. v Craig* [1975] 1 N.Z.L.R. 597.

[409] *British Coal Corp. v Dennis Rye Ltd* [1988] 1 W.L.R. 1113, CA; and see Ch.10, para.10.30, below.

[410] *Butler v Board of Trade* [1971] Ch. 680; *R. v.Tompkins* (1977) 67 Cr.App.R. 181, CA; *cf. R. v Uljee* [1982] 1 N.Z.L.R. 561.

[411] Police and Criminal Evidence Act 1984, s.78.

[412] *R. v Saunders*, January 10, 1990, unreported, Central Criminal Court (Henry J.).

[413] See *R. v Derby Magistrates Court, ex p. B* [1996] 1 A.C. 487, HL.

[414] See generally Auburn, *op. cit.*, Ch.8, Thanki (ed.), *The Law of Privilege*, 2006, paras 4.33–4.63; Passmore, *Privilege*, 2nd edn 2006, Ch.8.

[415] *Bullivant v Att.Gen. for Victoria* [1901] A.C. 196 at 207; *cf. Barclays Bank Plc v Eustice* [1995] 1 W.L.R. 1238 at 1250; see also *E. v A.* (2003) 5 I.T.E.L.R. 760, CA of Cook Islands (creation of asset protection trust alleged fraud on creditors).

[416] *Butler v Board of Trade* [1971] Ch. 680.

purpose of carrying out fraud, and . . . this is so whether or not the solicitor was or was not ignorant of the fact that he was being used for that purpose."[417]

The rule also covers communications which are criminal in themselves.[418] Despite earlier doubts,[419] it is now clear that the exception applies equally to litigation privilege as to legal advice privilege.[420]

Where the principle applies, it does not deprive the client of all legal professional privilege, but only that in respect of documents which are part or in furtherance of the fraud; all other legal privilege (e.g. in the conduct of subsequent litigation) remains unaffected.[421]

11.68   The relevant intention (i.e. to further the fraud) need not be held by the client either; it is enough if a third party intends the lawyer/client communications to be made with that purpose (e.g. where the client is an intermediary or innocent tool), and this is so both at common law[422] and under s.10(2) of the Police and Criminal Evidence Act 1984.[423] On the other hand, where the only "fraud" alleged is that of the lawyer, the client's privilege is unaffected.[424] To fall within the scope of this rule, the lawyer must have been instructed before the commission of the fraud or illegality, not afterwards for the purpose of being defended.[425] The rule applies to those who further the fraud, not those who are victims of it.[426] A lawyer who realises or comes to suspect that he has been unwittingly involved in a fraud is entitled to raise the question with the court and seek an order that he be at liberty to disclose the facts to the victim.[427]

---

[417] *Banque Keyser Ullman S.A. v Skandia (UK) Insurance Co. Ltd* [1986] 1 Lloyd's Rep. 336 at 337; *Chandler v Church* (1987) 137 New L.J. 451; *Re Moage Ltd* (1998) 82 F.C.R. 10, Fed.Ct.Aus; *Abbey National Plc v Clive Travers & Co* [1999] Lloyd's Rep. P.N. 753, CA; *Clements, Dunne & Bell Pty Ltd v Commissioner of Australian Federal Police* (2001) 188 A.L.R. 515, Fed.Ct.Aus.
[418] *C. v C. (Privilege: Criminal Communications)* [2002] Fam 45, CA, applying *R. v Cox and Railton* (1884) 14 Q.B.D. 157 at 167.
[419] *Dubai Bank Ltd v Galadari (No.6), The Times,* April 22, 1991, leave to appeal refused, May 7, 1991 (Dillon L.J.), but appealed on another point, *The Times,* October 14, 1992, CA.
[420] *Kuwait Airways Corporation v Iraqi Airways Company* [2005] 1 W.L.R. 2734, CA.
[421] *Derby & Co. Ltd v Weldon (No.7)* [1990] 1 W.L.R. 1156.
[422] *R. v Cox and Railton* (1884) 14 Q.B.D. 153; *Capar v Commissioner of Police* (1994) 34 N.S.W.L.R. 715; *Abbey National Plc v Clive Travers & Co.* [1999] Lloyd's Rep. P.N. 753, CA; *Clements, Dunne & Bell Pty Ltd v Commissioner of Australian Federal Police* (2001) 188 A.L.R. 515, Fed.Ct.Aus.
[423] *R. v Central Criminal Court, ex p. Francis & Francis* [1989] 1 A.C. 346, HL, applied in *R. v Guildhall Magistrates' Court, ex p. Primlaks Holding Co. (Panama) Inc.* [1990] 1 Q.B. 261; *R (Hallinan Blackburn Gittings & Nott (A Firm)) v Middlesex Guildhall Crown Court* [2005] 1 W.L.R. 766, CA.
[424] *Randolph M. Fields v Watts,* January 22, 1986, unreported, CA.
[425] *R. v Cox and Railton* (1884) 14 Q.B.D. 153 at 175.
[426] *Banque Keyser Ullman S.A. v Skandia (UK) Insurance Co. Ltd* [1986] 1 Lloyd's Rep. 336, CA.
[427] *Finers v Miro* [1991] 1 W.L.R. 35, CA.

There must be a definite charge of fraud or illegality, supported by prima **11.69** facie evidence, and not a mere allegation.[428] There must also be a prima facie case that the document came into existence as part of the fraud.[429] Indeed, it may be that there needs to be a "strong prima facie case."[430] In Australia the evidence to show fraud must be admissible evidence.[431] The court will be astute to prevent such allegations being made in order to enable discovery "fishing" applications to be mounted[432] and "very slow" to deprive a defendant of legal privilege on an interlocutory application.[433] It is not however necessary that the word "fraud" be used, if the facts alleged enable the court to recognise it.[434] The "fraud" need not amount to a criminal offence: civil fraud (such as deliberate misrepresentation by a borrower to obtain a loan[435]) is sufficient.[436] Nor need it be the foundation of the plaintiff's claim; relevance to an issue in the action is enough.[437] Indeed, the court is more likely to apply the rule if the (alleged) fraud said to justify applying the rule is "free-standing and independent".[438] To put it

---

[428] *O'Rourke v Darbishire* [1920] A.C. 581 at 604; *Bankers' Trust Co. v Shapira* [1980] 1 W.L.R. 1274 at 1283; *Buttes Gas and Oil Co. v Hammer (No.3)* [1981] Q.B. 223 at 246, 252; *Derby & Co. Ltd v Weldon (No.7)* [1990] 1 W.L.R. 1156.; *Dubai Bank Ltd v Galadari (No.6), The Times,* April 22, 1991, leave to appeal refused, May 7, 1991 (Dillon L.J.), but appealed on another point, *The Times,* October 14, 1992, CA; *Commissioner, Australian Federal Police v Proposed Finance Pty Ltd* (1997) 188 C.L.R. 501, H.Ct.Aus.; *AWB Ltd v Cole (No.5)* [2006] F.C.A. 134, at para.218, Fed.Ct.Aus.

[429] *R. v Gibbins* [2004] EWCA Crim. 311, CA.

[430] *Barclays Bank Plc v Eustice* [1995] 1 W.L.R. 1238, CA; *Matua Finance Ltd v Equiticorp Industries Group Ltd* [1993] 3 N.Z.L.R. 650 at 654, CA of N.Z.; *Seamar Holdings Ltd v Kupe Group Ltd* [1995] 2 N.Z.L.R. 274, CA of N.Z.; *Nationwide Building Society v Various Solicitors* [1999] P.N.L.R. 52 at 74; *Dubai Aluminium Ltd v Al-Alawi* [1999] 1 All E.R. 703; see also *Walsh Automation (Europe) Ltd v Bridgeman* [2002] EWHC 1344 (Q.B.) ("an obvious fraud") and *E. v A.* (2003) 5 I.T.E.L.R. 760, CA of Cook Islands.

[431] *Commissioner, Australian Federal Police v Proposed Finance Pty Ltd* (1997) 188 C.L.R. 501, H.Ct.Aus.

[432] *Buttes Gas and Oil Co. v Hammer (No.3)* [1981] Q.B. 223 at 252.

[433] *Derby & Co. Ltd v Weldon (No.7)* [1990] 1 W.L.R. 1156; see also *Chandler v Church* (1987) 137 New L.J. 451; *AOOT Kalmneft v Denton Wilde Sapte* [2002] 1 Lloyd's Rep. 417 at 423, Q.B.

[434] *Gamlen Chemical Co. (UK) Ltd v. Rochem Ltd* [1983] R.P.C. 1; see also *Abbey National Plc v Clive Travers & Co.* [1999] Lloyd's Rep. P.N. 753 at 756, CA.

[435] *Nationwide Building Society v Various Solicitors* [1999] P.N.L.R. 52 at 73; *cf. Birmingham Midshires Mortgage Services Ltd v Ansell* [1998] P.N.L.R. 237.

[436] *Williams v Quebrada Railway, Land & Copper Co.* [1895] 2 Ch. 751; *Bullivant v Att.Gen. for Victoria* [1901] A.C. 196, P.C.; *Gamlen Chemical Co. (UK) Ltd v Rochem Ltd* [1983] R.P.C. 1; *Royscot Spa Leasing Ltd v Lovett,* unreported, November 16, 1994, CA; *Barclays Bank Plc v Eustice* [1995] 1 W.L.R. 1238, CA; *R. v Wijesinha* (1995) 127 D.L.R. (4th), S.C.C.; *Gemini Personnel Ltd v Morgan Banks Ltd* [2001] 1 N.Z.L.R. 14 and 672, CA of N.Z.

[437] *Dubai Bank Ltd v Galadari (No.6), The Times,* April 22, 1991, leave to appeal refused, May 7, 1991 (Dillon L.J.), but appealed on another point, *The Times,* October 14, 1992, CA.

[438] *R. (Hallinan Blackburn Gittings & Nott (A Firm)) v Middlesex Guildhall Crown Court* [2005] 1 W.L.R. 766, CA; *Kuwait Airways Corporation v Iraqi Airways Company* [2005] 1 W.L.R. 2734, CA.

another way, the evidence will need to be stronger in a case where the fraud relied on is itself part of the substantive case.[439]

11.70 For the purposes of the rule, fraud includes "all forms of fraud and dishonesty such as fraudulent breach of trust, fraudulent conspiracy, trickery[440] and sham contrivances,[441]" but not mere inducement to breach of contract.[442] Nor does it include entering into an improper contingency fee agreement,[443] or interference with goods.[444] On the other hand it includes fraud on creditors within s.423 of the Insolvency Act 1986[445] and this is so even if all parties wrongly believe the actions concerned to fall outside the scope of the section.[446] In Ireland the principle has been extended to malicious prosecution and abuse of process.[447] In Australia the principle has been held to extend to a case of deliberate[448] (though not inadvertent[449]) abuse by a governmental authority of statutory power intended to prevent others from exercising their rights under the law, to making false claims for tax deductions,[450] and to "fraud on justice".[451]

11.71 Steps taken subsequently to the alleged fraud can be "in furtherance of" that fraud, for example, if taken to conceal and render profits irrecoverable to which the plaintiff asserts a proprietary claim.[452] They can also amount to a fraud in themselves, if, for example, a bogus defence is put forward,[453]

---

[439] *Kuwait Airways Corporation v Iraqi Airways Company* [2005] 1 W.L.R. 2734, at para.42, CA.

[440] See, e.g. *AWB Ltd v Cole (No.5)* [2006] F.C.A. 134, Fed.Ct.Aus.

[441] See, e.g. *Australian Securities & Investments Commission (No.3)* [2006] F.C.A. 772, Fed.Ct.Aus.

[442] *Crescent Farm (Sidcup) Sports Ltd v Sterling Offices Ltd* [1972] Ch. 553 at 565; *Royscot Spa Leasing Ltd v Lovett,* unreported, November 16, 1994, CA; *Gemini Personnel Ltd v Morgan Banks Ltd* [2001] 1 N.Z.L.R. 14 and 672, CA of N.Z.; see also *University of Southampton v Kelly,* unreported, November 14, 2005, E.A.T. (legal advice sought to back up existing decision to terminate employment contract held privileged).

[443] *Skuse v Granada Television Ltd* [1994] 1 W.L.R. 1156.

[444] *Dubai Aluminium Ltd v Al-Alawi* [1999] 1 W.L.R. 1964.

[445] *Barclays Bank Plc v Eustice* [1995] 1 W.L.R. 1238, CA, applied in *The David Agmashenebeli* [2001] C.L.C. 942, Colman J.; see also *Gartner v Carter* [2004] F.C.A. 258, Fed.Ct.Aus.

[446] *ibid.*

[447] *Murphy v Kirwan* [1993] 3 I.R. 501, Sup.Ct.Ireland.

[448] *Att.Gen. for the Northern Territory v Kearney* (1985) 158 C.L.R.500, H.Ct. of Aus.; *cf. Idoport Pty Ltd v National Australia Bank Ltd* [2001] N.S.W.S.C. 22 (Sup.Ct. of N.S.W.): abuse of process is not now "fraud" excluding privilege within the meaning of Evidence Act 1995, s.125 (even though it may have excluded privilege at common law).

[449] *Freeman v Health Insurance Commission* (1997) 78 F.C.R. 91, Fed.Ct.Aus.

[450] *Clements, Dunne & Bell Pty Ltd v Commissioner of Australian Federal Police* (2001) 188 A.L.R. 515, Fed.Ct.Aus.

[451] *Gartner v Carter* [2004] F.C.A. 258, Fed.Ct.Aus.

[452] *Derby & Co. Ltd v Weldon (No.7)* [1990] 1 W.L.R. 1156; *Finers v Miro* [1991] 1 W.L.R. 35, CA; *Gartner v Carter* [2004] F.C.A. 258, Fed.Ct.Aus.

[453] *Chandler v Church* (1987) 137 New L.J. 451; see also *Hawick Jersey International Ltd v Caplan, The Times,* March 11, 1988; *cf. R. v Snaresbrook Crown Court, ex p. Director of Public Prosecutions* [1988] 1 Q.B. 532, at 537–38, D.C. (application for legal aid), and *R. v Central Criminal Court, ex p. Francis & Francis* [1989] 1 A.C. 346, at 397, *per* Lord Goff (mere fact that pursuing false defence would involve commission of perjury not enough to engage rule).

false evidence is created,[454] criminal acts are used to obtain evidence,[455] or other steps are taken to cover up the original fraud.[456] However:

> " . . . disclosure at an interlocutory stage based upon prima facie evidence of fraud in the conduct of the proceedings carries, as it seems to me, a far greater risk of injustice to the defendant if he should turn out to have been innocent than disclosure of advice concerning an earlier non-contentious transaction . . . ."[457]

Accordingly, the court may hold that the risk of injustice to the defendant outweighs the risk of injustice to the plaintiff and refuse to order disclosure.[458] The court is entitled to look at the document concerned in order to determine whether it came into existence in furtherance of an illegal purpose.[459]

(d) As between trustee and beneficiary It is necessary to distinguish clearly **11.72** two situations. One is where the trustee communicates with a lawyer (or third party, where this is protected) for the benefit of the trust. For example, he may seek or obtain advice with reference to the trust's relations with others, or as to the trustee's powers under the settlement. The other is where the trustee does so for his own personal benefit, vis-à-vis the beneficiaries, as to whether he has committed a breach of trust. Although there can be litigation privilege as against the beneficiary in the latter case, there can be no privilege, as against the beneficiary, in the former case.[460]

(e) As between company and shareholders A similar situation obtains in **11.73** relation to a company and its shareholders. The company may have litigation privilege in respect of communications having reference to a dispute between the company on the one hand and a shareholder or shareholders on

---

[454] *The David Agmashenebeli* [2001] C.L.C. 942, [2000] All E.R. (D.) 2324, Colman J.

[455] *Dubai Aluminium Ltd v Al-Alawi* [1999] 1 W.L.R. 1964; see also *ISTIL Group Inc. v Zahoor* [2003] 2 All E.R. 252.

[456] *Dubai Bank Ltd v Galadari (No.6), The Times,* April 22, 1991, leave to appeal refused, May 7, 1991 (Dillon L.J.), but appealed on another point, *The Times,* October 14, 1992, CA.

[457] *Chandler v Church* (1987) 137 New L.J. 451; see also *Re Omar(a bankrupt)* [1999] B.P.I.R. 1001, at 1007.

[458] See also *Derby & Co. Ltd v Weldon (No.7)* [1990] 1 W.L.R. 1156; *cf. AOOT Kalmneft v Denton Wilde Sapte* [2002] 1 Lloyd's Rep. 417, Q.B.

[459] *R. v Cox and Railton* (1884) 14 Q.B.D. 153 at 175; *R. v Governor of Pentonville Prison, exp. Osman (No.2)* [1989] 3 All E.R. 701 at 729–730; *Seamar Holdings Ltd v Kupe Group Ltd* [1995] 2 N.Z.L.R. 274, CA of N.Z.

[460] *Re Mason* (1883) 22 Ch.D. 609; *Postlewaite v Richman* (1887) 35 Ch.D. 722; see also *Gourard v Edison Co.* (1988) 57 L.J. Ch. 498; *Re Whitworth* [1919] 1 Ch. 320, aff. [1920] A.C. 581 *sub nom. O'Rourke v Darbishire; cf. Bristol Corp. v Cox* (1884) 26 Ch.D. 678 at 683.

the other, but otherwise the company's communications with lawyers are not privileged as against the shareholder(s).[461]

11.74   (f) **Joint clients**   Where two or more clients jointly instruct a lawyer (as opposed to two or more clients separately doing so) the rule is that there is no privilege for the communications of one with the lawyer against the other,[462] unless outside the joint retainer and in an exclusive capacity.[463] As will be seen, the privilege of the joint clients can only be waived by them acting together; a waiver by one is insufficient.[464] Even if the parties did not, strictly speaking, jointly instruct the lawyer, but merely had a joint interest in the subject matter of the communications, there will be no privilege for one as against the other if they later fall out and litigation ensues.[465] But where one party instructs a lawyer entirely on behalf of another, the first party is merely an agent, and there is no lawyer-client relationship between him and the lawyer.[466] In such a case the only client is the other party.

11.75   (g) **Other party having a better right**   As a general principle, legal professional privilege is a restriction on what the client, his lawyer or his witness can be required by their opponent to do (e.g. to produce a document for inspection). But if the document is already available to the opponent, or he can lawfully obtain it (e.g. because he has a better right to it than whoever has it) then he needs no assistance from the original client, and privilege is irrelevant.[467] The only exception to this is where the opponent has obtained the document in circumstances, or there is otherwise an agreement, giving rise to a right in the original client to restrain use of it.[468]

---

[461] *W. Dennis & Sons Ltd v West Norfolk Farmers' Manure and Chemical Co-Operative Ltd* [1943] Ch. 220; *Re Hydrosan Ltd* [1991] B.C.L.C. 418; *Woodhouse & Co. v Woodhouse* (1914) 30 T.L.R. 559; *CAS Nominees Ltd v Nottingham Forest Plc* [2001] 1 All E.R. 954, applied in *Arrow Trading & Investments Est. 1920 v Edwardian Group Ltd* [2005] 1 B.C.L.C. 696.

[462] *Shore v Bedford* (1843) 5 Man. &. G. 271; *Re Konigsberg (a bankrupt)* [1989] 3 All E.R. 289; *Re Brook Martin & Co. (Nominees) Ltd* [1993] B.C.L.C. 328 at 332–333; *The Sagheera* [1997] 1 Lloyd's Rep. 160 at 165; *Gemini Personnel Ltd v Morgan & Banks Ltd* [2001] 1 N.Z.L.R. 672, N.Z.C.A.; *Long v Farrer & Co.* [2004] EWHC 1774 (Ch.).

[463] *Perry v Smith* (1842) 9 M. & W. 681; *cf. T.S.B. Bank Plc v Robert Irving & Burns* [2000] 2 All E.R. 826, CA (implied waiver of privilege excludes communications after actual conflict of interest arises); *Re Doran Constructions Pty Ltd* (2002) 194 A.L.R. 101, Sup.Ct.N.S.W.

[464] *Rochefoucauld v Boustead* (1896) 65 L.J. Ch. 794, and see Ch.12, para.12.02, below.

[465] *Cia Barca de Panama S.A. v George Wimpey & Co. Ltd* [1980] 1 Lloyd's Rep. 598 at 614–615, CA; *Formica Ltd v Export Credits Guarantee Department* [1995] 1 Lloyd's Rep. 692; as to "common interest" privilege, see paras 11.59–11.61, above.

[466] *Re E.G.* [1914] 1 Ch. 927, CA.

[467] *Re Whitworth* [1919] 1 Ch. 320, affd. *sub nom. O'Rourke v Darbishire* [1920] A.C. 581; or course, privilege may still be claimed by the party in possession.

[468] e.g. an actionable breach of confidence; *cf.* para.11.76, below.

(h) Secondary evidence available   Again, if in principle an opponent has **11.76** secondary evidence available to him of a privileged original document, then privilege has nothing to do with the matter, for the client, his lawyer or his witness is not being asked to disclose anything, and the question is simply one of the admissibility of the secondary evidence.[469] However, if the circumstances in which the evidence was obtained give rise to an actionable breach of confidence, then the opponent may be restrained from using that evidence and may be ordered to deliver up all copies and notes of it (on the basis of breach of confidence rather than privilege).[470] Indeed, in such cases the court has no discretion on the basis of materiality or "justice", but should normally intervene.[471] This was accordingly the case:

(a) where a party by a trick had obtained privileged documents from the other party's former[472] or present[473] solicitors;

(b) where a solicitor who had acted for both parties let one client have a document privileged in favour of the other[474];

(c) where counsel's clerk inadvertently returned counsel's papers to the solicitors for the other side, who read them and advised their clients of the contents[475];

(d) where a plaintiff disclosed privileged documents to the police for the purposes of an investigation into, and ultimately prosecution of, the defendants, which documents were disclosed by the police to the defendants pursuant to the *Attorney-General's Guidelines on Unused Material*[476]; and

(e) where solicitors, who must have realised that their opponents had probably mistakenly allowed privileged documents to be inspected, said nothing but asked for copies to be supplied[477]; (in

---

[469] *Calcraft v Guest* [1898] 1 Q.B. 759, CA.

[470] *Goddard v Nationwide Building Society* [1987] Q.B. 670, at 684–85; *Sutton v G.E. Capital Finance Ltd* [2004] EWCA Civ 315, at para.23.

[471] *Goddard v Nationwide Building Society* [1987] Q.B. 670, at 685; *B v Auckland District Law Society* [2003] 2 A.C. 736, at para.71, P.C.; *ISTIL Group Inc. v Zahoor* [2003] 2 All E.R. 252, at para.91; *USP Strategies Ltd v London General Holdings Ltd* [2004] EWHC 373 (Ch.), at para.25, *The Times*, April 30, 2004; *Sutton v G.E. Capital Finance Ltd* [2004] EWCA Civ 315, at para.25.

[472] *Lord Ashburton v Pape* [1913] 2 Ch. 469, CA.

[473] *I.T.C. Film Distributors Ltd v Video Exchange* [1982] Ch. 431.

[474] *Goddard v Nationwide Building Society* [1987] Q.B. 670, CA.

[475] *English and American Insurance Co. v Herbert Smith* [1988] F.S.R. 232; *Ablitt v Mills & Reeve, The Times*, October 25, 1995; *cf. Professional Conduct of Solicitors*, 1990, para.12.07, commentary (4), (5); *The Guide to Professional Conduct of Solicitors*, 8th edn, 1999, para.16.06.

[476] *British Coal Corp. v Dennis Rye (No.2)* [1988] 1 W.L.R. 113, CA; the *Guidelines* are set out at [1982] 1 All E.R. 734.

[477] *Derby & Co. Ltd v Weldon (No.8)* [1991] 1 W.L.R. 73, CA; *Thames Housing Association Ltd v Bishop*, September 2, 1991, unreported, CA; *National Insurance Co Ltd v Whirly-bird Holdings Ltd* [1994] 2 N.Z.L.R. 513, CA of N.Z.; *Lee Lighting v Central Properties*, unreported, September 27, 1994, Morison J.; *International Business Machines Corporation v Phoenix International (Computers) Ltd* [1995] 1 All E.R. 413; *Ablitt v Mills & Reeve,*

this last case, the rules now require that the court's permission be obtained before use may be made of the privilege material[478]);

(f) where a defendant, in confidence and without intending to waive privilege, disclosed legal advice to a third party who disclosed it to the claimant, who then sought to rely on it in evidence.[479]

On the other hand, where a copy of an expert's report was sent by mistake by the plaintiff's solicitors to the defendant's solicitors (who did not know, but suspected, that disclosure was "accidental"), the court entered upon a balancing exercise, and refused an injunction.[480] In a later case, however, the court refused to enter on a balancing exercise, because that task was done by the rules of privilege themselves.[481] Instead, an injunction was refused because the disputed evidence suggested that there was forgery involved and the court might otherwise be misled. The interaction between this principle and that of waiver of privilege (when no injunction will be granted) is discussed later in this work.[482]

11.77 (i) **Statutory exceptions** There are a limited number of cases where legal privilege is restricted by statute. But, because privilege is a fundamental right, in the absence of an express exclusion of legal professional privilege in a statute, the courts should be slow to find that it has been impliedly excluded. Thus the House of Lords held that legal professional privilege (in respect of documents in the hands of the client) was not excluded by the provisions of s.20[483] of the Taxes Management Act 1970,[484] overturning the decision of the Court of Appeal to the effect that it had been impliedly excluded by the express preservation of privilege for documents in the possession of a barrister, advocate or tax adviser. Similarly, the House disapproved a decision that s.39 of the Banking Act 1987 allows the Bank of England to require a person to produce privileged material for its purposes.[485] On the other hand, a bankrupt cannot withhold privileged docu-

---

The Times, October 25, 1995; *Breeze v John Stacey and Sons Ltd, The Times*, July 8, 1999, CA.

[478] CPR, r.31.20; see Ch.6, para.6.26, above.

[479] *USP Strategies Ltd v London General Holdings Ltd* [2004] EWHC 373 (Ch.), at para.25, *The Times*, April 30, 2004.

[480] *Webster v James Chapman & Co.* [1989] 3 All E.R. 939, followed in *Burkle Holdings Ltd v Laing (No.2)* [2005] EWHC 2022 (T.C.C.); the Court of Appeal in *Derby & Co. Ltd v Weldon (No.8)* [1991] 1 W.L.R. 73 declined to do this.

[481] *ISTIL Group Inc. v Zahoor* [2003] 2 All E.R. 252, at para.93.

[482] Ch.12, paras 12.17–12.18, below.

[483] *cf.* ss.20B(8) and 20C(3).

[484] *R. v. I.R.C., ex parte Morgan Grenfell* [2003] 1 A.C. 563, HL; see also *Pritchard v Ontario (Human Rights Commission)* (2004) 238 D.L.R. (4th) 1, Sup.Ct.Canada.

[485] *R. v I.R.C., ex parte Morgan Grenfell* [2003] 1 A.C. 563, HL, disapproving *Price Waterhouse v B.C.C.I. Holdings (Luxembourg) S.A.* [1992] B.C.L.C. 583.

ments from the Official Receiver.[486] However the court's statutory power[487] to summon and examine a bankrupt or those connected with him does not override legal professional privilege otherwise attaching.[488] It seems to be the same with the equivalent power[489] in relation to an insolvent company.[490] In England,[491] Australia[492] and Canada[493] the relevant statutory rules enabling the lawyers' professional body to investigate a law firm have been held to override client legal privilege, although there is also authority for the view that the true basis of the decisions is that the clients' privilege is not being infringed, as the professional body could only use the information for the purposes of the investigation.[494] In Australia, privilege was held not to be overridden by a notice to produce under the Trade Practice Act 1974, s.155.[495]

Where children are concerned, it has been held that the Children Act **11.78** 1989 has impliedly excluded litigation privilege (though not advice privilege) from care proceedings.[496] Although in non-adversarial proceedings concerning children when their welfare is paramount, legal professional privilege does not arise in respect of an expert's report based on papers disclosed in those proceedings, the duty of disclosure which arises in such proceedings does not override the right of a party to such proceedings to claim privilege arising or in connection with other proceedings (e.g. expert reports prepared for criminal proceedings).[497] A rule in the CPR[498] expressly removing the legal privilege otherwise attaching to documents and information in a solicitor's hands in the context of an application for a

---

[486] Insolvency Act 1986, s.291; *cf. Foxley v UK, The Times,* July 24, 2000, E.Ct.H.R. (retention of bankrupt's mail including privileged items to trustee in bankrupt held in breach of Art.8).

[487] Insolvency Act 1986, s.366.

[488] *Re Ouvaroff* [1997] B.P.I.R. 1712; *Worrell v Woods* (1999) 163 A.L.R. 195, Fed.Ct.Aus.; *R. v Dunwoody* (2005) 212 A.L.R. 103, Sup.Ct.Queensland; see also *Re Murjani* [1996] 1 All E.R. 65; *cf. Re Konigsberg* [1989]1 W.L.R. 1257 at 1266–1267

[489] Insolvency Act 1986, s.236; see Ch.3, paras 3.40–3.44, above.

[490] *Sutton v G.E. Capital Finance Ltd* [2004] EWCA Civ. 315; in Australia, see *Meteyard v Love* (2005) 224 A.L.R. 588, CA of N.S.W.

[491] *Parry-Jones v Law Society* [1969] 1 Ch. 1, CA; *Simms v Law Society* [2005] EWCA Civ 749, CA.

[492] *Rogerson v Law Society of the Northern Territory* (1993) 88 N.T.R. 1; *Re Steele, exp. Official Trustee in Bankruptcy v Clayton Utz* (1994) 48 F.C.R. 236; *Worrell v Woods* (1999) 163 A.L.R. 195, Fed.Ct.Aus,; see also *Esso Australia Resources Ltd v Dawson* (1999) 162 A.L.R. 79, Fed.Ct.Aus. (Full Ct.).

[493] *Re Robertson Stromberg* (1994) 119 D.L.R. (4th) 551, Sask. Q.B.

[494] *R. v I.R.C., ex parte Morgan Grenfell* [2003] 1 A.C. 563, *per* Lord Hoffmann; see also *Simms v Law Society* [2005] EWCA Civ. 749, CA; for the position in New Zealand, see *B. v Auckland District Law Society* [2003] 2 A.C. 736, P.C.

[495] *Daniels Corporation International Pty Ltd v Australian Competition and Consumer Commission* (2002) 194 A.L.R. 561, H.Ct.Aus.; *Woolworths Ltd v F.E.L.S.* (2002) 193 A.L.R. 1, H.Ct.Aus.

[496] *Re L (A Minor)* [1997] A.C. 16, HL; *cf. R. v Bell, ex p. Lees* (1980) 146 C.L.R. 141, H.Ct.Aus.

[497] *S. County Council v B* [2000] Fam. 76, Fam. D.

[498] CPR, r.48.7(3).

wasted costs order was held *ultra vires* and void.[499] It is unclear whether this also applies to other rules in the CPR purporting to remove privilege.[500] A procedural rule in Newfoundland dealing with medical examinations has been held to override privilege.[501] An oblique abrogation of privilege occurs in the Limitation Act 1980, s.33(3)(f), where the court, in deciding whether to override a time limit for certain kinds of action, is obliged to take into account any legal or expert advice received by the claimant. Whilst this has been held to enable a defendant to administer interrogatories to the plaintiff on the subject of advice received,[502] it does not require a claimant to give discovery of documents containing such advice, even though at trial he might need to waive privilege in order to make good his Limitation Act plea.[503]

11.79   **(j) Parliament and the executive**   In Australia it has been held that, as the Legislative Council of New South Wales[504] has "such powers as are reasonably necessary for the proper exercise of its functions",[505] its power to call for documents extends to compel the Executive to produce documents to the Council in respect of which a claim of legal professional privilege (or public interest immunity) is made.[506]

11.80   **(k) Public safety**   In Canada it has been held that the privilege may be set aside when the safety of the public is at risk, i.e. where there is an imminent risk of serious bodily harm or death to an identifiable person or group. So communications with an expert from a prisoner convicted of aggravated sexual assault, detailing plans for murdering prostitutes, were held not privileged.[507]

---

[499] *General Mediterranean Holdings S.A. v Patel* [1999] 3 All E.R. 673.

[500] e.g. CPR, r.35.10(4) (instructions to expert), and *cf.* r.32.12 (2) (a) (privilege of *party* may be waived by *witness*).

[501] *Morrissey v Morrissey* (2000) 196 D.L.R. (4th) 94, Newfoundland CA (r.30.04(2) of the Rules of the Supreme Court of Newfoundland.

[502] *Jones v G.D. Searle & Co.* [1979] 1 W.L.R. 101; *R. v First Lord of the Treasury, ex p. Petch*, unreported January 31, 1994, Harrison J.; *cf. Arab Monetary Fund v Hashim*, unreported, September 30, 1993, CA (*Jones v Searle* does not apply by analogy under the Foreign Limitation Periods Act 1984).

[503] *Tatlock v G. P. Worsley & Co. Ltd*, unreported, June 22, 1989, CA.

[504] The upper house of the State Parliament.

[505] *Egan v Willis* (1998) 158 A.L.R. 527, H.Ct.Aus.

[506] *Egan v Chadwick*, unreported, June 10, 1999, CA of N.S.W.

[507] *Jones v Smith* [1999] 1 S.C.R. 455, Sup.Ct. of Can.; *cf. Woolgar v Chief Constable of Sussex Police, The Times*, May 28, 1999, CA (public health and safety may justify breach of confidence).

G. PUBLIC INTEREST IMMUNITY[508]

This objection to production is simply that the production of the docu- **11.81**
ment(s) concerned would so harm the public interest generally (as opposed
to the particular public interest in the administration of justice) as to justify
withholding it or them, even at the cost of justice in the particular case. As
such, it differs markedly from the other kinds of "privilege" discussed in this
chapter. In the first place it is not only an objection to production, but often
also to the disclosure of the existence of documents as well.[509] Secondly, it
is not a privilege of either litigant as such, but the necessary protection of the
public interest (whether at national or other level). It is "public law, not
private right."[510] Accordingly, if the immunity applies it is the duty of the
court to take the point, even if neither party does so.[511] As will be seen
later,[512] this difference has important implications when it comes to the
question of waiver.

The objection has long existed at common law,[513] although today it is **11.82**
also recognised by statute[514] and rules of court.[515] It was originally called
"Crown privilege"—although it was not a "privilege" like the others[516]—
and extended beyond the interests of the Crown as such (e.g. national
security, central government) to other areas of public life (e.g. the Monopolies Commission, the police, cases involving informants). What it involves is
the balancing of two competing interests; the public interest in the proper
administration of justice by making all relevant material available to the
litigants, and the public interest in not harming society as a whole by
releasing highly confidential state information.[517] Each case must be taken
on its own merits, and the balancing exercise carried out anew, because it is

---

[508] See also Birkinshaw, *Government and Information*, 1990, at pp.323–328. In Canada this
area of the law is governed by express statutory provision, in ss.37–39 of the Canada
Evidence Act, R.S.C. 1985, C.C.–5; see also *Canadian Association of Regulated Importers
v Canada* (1992) 87 D.L.R. (4th) 730.

[509] See Ch.8, para.8.27, above.

[510] *Science Research Council v Nasse* [1980] A.C. 1028 at 1087.

[511] *Duncan v Cammell Laird & Co.* [1942] A.C. 624 at 641; *MGN Pension Trustees Ltd v
Invesco Asset Management Ltd*, unreported, October 14, 1993, Evans-Lombe J. (at p.23);
but either party may raise it (*Sankey v Whitlam* (1978) 142 C.L.R. 1, H.Ct. of Aus), and
there was authority for saying that it is the duty of the party in possession of the documents
to do so: *Makanjuola v Metropolitan Police Commissioner* [1992] 3 All E.R. 617, CA;
Halford v Sharples [1991] 1 W.L.R. 736, CA. It is now recognised that the immunity can
in effect be waived, if it is considered by the relevant body that the immunity is outweighed
by the interests of justice: see para.11.85, below.

[512] See Ch.12, para.12.42, below.

[513] See Bray, pp.547–549. But as to Ireland, see *Ambiorix Ltd v Minister for the Environment*
[1992] 1 I.R. 277, Irish Sup.Ct.

[514] e.g. Crown Proceedings Act 1947, s.28.

[515] e.g. CPR, r.31.19; formerly RSC, Ord.24, r.15; CCR, Ord.14, r.9.

[516] *Duncan v Cammell Laird & Co.* [1942] A.C. 624; *Rogers v Secretary of State for the Home
Department* [1973] A.C. 388 at 400.

[517] See, e.g. *Ellis v Home Office* [1953] 2 Q.B. 135, CA; *Conway v Rimmer* [1968] A.C. 910
at 940, 952.

not only the circumstances in which the document in question came to be produced that may vary from case to case, and the facts of each case to which that document is relevant, but also the need in a given case for the particular document will depend on the other evidence potentially available from other sources. Although this work is not concerned with criminal proceedings, it may be noted in passing that the same question may arise, and a similar balancing exercise be performed, in criminal cases, as well as civil.[518]

"Class" claims and "contents" claims

11.83   Traditionally claims to public interest immunity have been divided into two categories: class claims and contents claims. The former is a claim that the document ought not to be disclosed because of the class of documents to which it belongs, and the latter is a similar claim because of its contents. The distinction is that:

> " . . . with a class claim it is immaterial whether the disclosure of the particular contents of particular documents would be injurious to the public interest—the point being that it is the maintenance of the immunity of the class from disclosure in litigation that is important; whereas in a contents claim the protection is claimed for particular contents in a particular document."[519]

In view of this distinction it might be thought that the balancing exercise referred to above could only apply to "contents" claims, but this is not so, and it applies just as much to "class" claims,[520] although, will be seen, there are procedural and other differences between them.

---

[518] *R. v Governor of Brixton Prison, exp. Osman (No.1)* [1991] 1 W.L.R. 281 at 288–289; *R. v Clowes* [1992] 3 All E.R. 440 at 450–455; *R. v Davis* [1993] 1 W.L.R. 613; *R. v Ward* [1993] 1 W.L.R. 619, CA; *R. v Keane* [1994] 1 W.L.R.746, CA, *R. v K* (1992) 97 Cr.App.R. 342, CA; *R. v Horseferry Road Magistrates Court, ex p. Bennett (No.2)* [1994] 1 All E.R. 289, D.C. (voluntary disclosure of documents by C.P.S. with Treasury consent); *R. v Chief Constable, ex p. Wiley* [1995] 1 A.C. 274, HL; Criminal Procedure and Investigations Act 1996, s.16; *R. v Botmeh* [2002] 1 W.L.R. 531, CA (Court of Appeal consideration of public interest immunity application, when none was made before a trial judge, was not a breach of Art.6 of ECHR); *Altan v United Kingdom* (2002) 34 H.R.R. 33, E.Ct.H.R. (breach of Art.6 where non-disclosure of PII evidence to judge at trial; breach not remedied by ex parte procedure before the Court of Appeal); *Edwards v UK* (2003) 15 B.H.R.C. 189, Grand Chamber (breach found); see also *R. v McDonald* [2004] EWCA Crim. 2617, *The Times,* November 8, 2004 (Court of Appeal should review all material on appeal); *R. v H.* [2004] 2 A.C. 134, at para.42 (review of general principles in criminal cases). It may be desirable that the same judge who has ruled on the public immunity application should conduct the trial: *R. (D.P.P.) v Acton Youth Court* [2001] 1 W.L.R. 1828, D.C.

[519] *Burmah Oil Co. Ltd v Bank of England* [1980] A.C. 1090 at 1111; see also *Conway v Rimmer* [1968] A.C. 910 at 993; *R.v. Robertson, ex p. McAuley* (1983) 71 Fed.L.R. 429.

[520] *Air Canada v Secretary of State for Trade* [1983] 2 A.C. 394 at 432; *Continental Reinsurance Corp. (UK) Ltd v Pine Top Insurance Ltd* [1986] 1 Lloyd's Rep. 8, CA.

Where a document's disclosure would be harmful to the public interest on **11.84** a contents basis, a class claim is not necessary, nor has such a claim generally been made in practice. Class claims in recent years have been the subject matter of a great deal of judicial and extra judicial criticism. Such claims are difficult to justify merely on the basis of candour and the need to speak openly between departments. Indeed in the context of criminal cases Sir Richard Scott V.C. has disapproved of class claims and concluded:

> "Where class claims are concerned, the 'balance' between, on the one hand, the public interest in withholding the documents and, on the other hand, the interests of justice would, in a criminal trial, unlike in civil litigation, be bound always to come down on the side of the interests of justice."[521]

For claims by Government departments, the distinction between class and contents claims has been eradicated in effect by the Government's announcement of December 18, 1996 and publication of a report, which sets out the Government's new approach to public interest immunity.[522] The new approach heralded by the December 1996 paper is:

> "based on the principle that PII can only ever apply where disclosure of material would cause real damage to the public interest. This criterion of damage has always been central to PII law, but it has become obscured in some cases by the identification and maintenance of classes of protected documents. Ministers will no longer apply the former division into class and contents claims, but will focus on the damage which disclosure would cause".[523]

The distinction between class and contents claims is not wholly dead. This is partly because the December 1996 report does not apply to bodies other than Government departments. Indeed since the December 1996 report class claims have been made and upheld.[524]

---

[521] *Report of the Inquiry into the Export of Defence Equipment and Dual—Use Goods to Iraq and Related Prosecutions* (1996), para.G.18.83; see also his article "The Acceptable and Unacceptable Use of Public Interest Immunity", [1996] P. L. 427.

[522] On July 11, 1997 the Attorney General and Lord Chancellor made statements in both Houses confirming that the December 1996 report can be regarded as representing current Government policy. For a critique of the December 1996 paper, see, M. Supperstone Q.C. and J. Coppel, "A New Approach to Public Interest Immunity?" [1997] P.L. 211.

[523] December 1996 report, para.4.1.

[524] *Kelly v Commissioner of Police of the Metropolis, The Times*, August 20, 1997, CA (forms used by police forces sent to the C.P.S); *Goodridge v Chief Constable* [1999] 1 W.L.R. 1558 (correspondence and reports passing between police and DPP and report to Police Complaints Authority).

The three stage approach in considering to claim

11.85 The current Government practice requires a three stage approach in considering whether to make a public interest immunity claim for a document or piece of information. The December 1996 report sets out a three step approach for both criminal and civil proceedings[525]:

> "**First:** A decision must be taken on whether there is a duty to disclose the document at all. Broadly speaking, the question in civil and criminal cases will be whether the document is relevant or potentially relevant to an issue in the case. If there is no duty to disclose the document, questions of PII do not arise.
>
> Sir Richard Scott recommended that if a disclosure point involving documents which are the subject of a PII claim is referred to the judge, the judge should be invited to decide first whether the documents are disclosable. In the Government's view, this is a correct and useful approach.
>
> **Second:** If there is a duty to disclose, a decision must be taken on whether the document attracts PII. Existing practice has been to determine this question by asking whether the document attracts PII because of its 'contents' or because it falls into a 'class' of documents which attracts PII. The Government regards this distinction as no longer helpful. It proposes to abandon it and adopt a new approach which applies the fundamental test of whether the maker of the certificate believes that disclosure would cause real damage.
>
> **Third:** This step applies to some claims, including those made by Ministers. If the document attracts PII, the decision maker will consider (so far as he can judge it) the strength of the public interest in disclosing the document. This will require an assessment of the issues in the case. The decision maker performs what is described in this report as the *Wiley* balancing exercise, usually after taking advice from counsel in the case or Treasury Counsel. If the balance appears to him to favour disclosure, he is entitled to disclose the document. If the balance appear to go the other way, or if the decision maker is uncertain, he will put a certificate to the court explaining clearly his reasons for asserting PII; and the court will then be invited to determine whether disclosure should be made."

The threshold test

11.86 The threshold test as to when public interest immunity may be asserted has been expressed in various ways in the authorities and changed over time. There has been a tightening of circumstances in which public interest

---

[525] Para.2.3.

immunity may be asserted. The House of Lords has adopted the test of whether disclosure will cause "substantial harm" to the public interest.[526] The Government's approach in the December 1996 report uses the criterion of whether disclosure would cause "real damage" to the public interest. When the December 1996 report was announced the Government confirmed that "real damage" meant the same as "substantial harm".[527]

The balancing exercise

The balancing exercise consists of the court balancing competing public interests. There is the public interest that substantial harm or real damage should not be done to the state or public service by the disclosure of certain documents, and there is the public interest that the administration of justice should not be frustrated by the withholding of documents necessary for the fair determination of proceedings.[528] Although the December 1996 report applies equally to civil and criminal proceedings there are crucial distinctions in practice,[529] both as to how public immunity claims are asserted, but also in the application of the balancing exercise as between the public interest in withholding a particular document and the administration of justice in the individual case. This distinction arises as a result of the different nature of proceedings. As stated by Sir Richard Scott V.C. in his report in the context of class claims:

11.87

> "It is of the essence of the 'balancing exercise' to be carried out in a civil case in which a PII claim has been made, that the public interest factors prayed in aid as justifying the withholding of documents must be weighed against the public interest in the administration of justice and the extent to which the withholding of the documents might prevent a just result being reached in the case. In this 'balancing exercise' the greater the weight of the public interest reasons for withholding the documents, the more likely will be that the scale will come down against disclosure. But, in criminal cases, the only question is (or at least should be) whether the documents sought to be withheld might be of assistance to the defendant in defending himself. If they are, they must be disclosed . . . There is, I believe, no reported criminal case in which the judge has concluded that the documents would be of assistance to the defendant but has nonetheless declined, on, PII grounds, to order them to be disclosed. The firm conclusion is, in my opinion,

---

[526] R. v Chief Constable, ex p. Wiley [1995] 1 A.C. 274 at 281.
[527] H.C.Deb., Vol.287, cols. 950–1 (December 18, 1996).
[528] Sankey v Whitlam (1978) 142 C.L.R. 1.
[529] cf. R. v Governor of Brixton Prison, exp. Osman [1991] 1 W.L.R. 281, which in effect equated the PII principles in civil and criminal proceedings.

justified that in criminal cases the only question should be whether the documents might be of assistance to the defendant. This is not a 'balancing exercise'. The issue does not depend on the weight of the PII factors that are being invoked".[530]

Procedure

11.88 CPR, r.31.19 sets out the procedure for claiming public interest immunity as a ground for withholding disclosure of the existence of documents as well as withholding inspection. The application in support of a claim to withhold disclosure may be made without notice[531] and must be supported by evidence.[532] If the claim is upheld the order must not be served on any other person or be open to inspection by any other person unless the court otherwise orders.[533] A claim that inspection should be withheld should be set out in the list of documents or, if there is no list, to the person wishing to inspect the document.[534] The person making the claim that he has a right or duty to withhold a document or part of a document must state that he has such a right or duty and give the grounds on which he claims that right or duty.[535] A party may apply to the court to decide whether a claim to withhold inspection should be upheld.[536] Such an application should be supported by evidence.[537] For the purpose of deciding an application to withhold disclosure or inspection the court may require the person seeking to withhold disclosure or inspection to produce the document to the court and invite any person to make representations.[538] Some aspects of this procedure require some elaboration as set out below.

11.89 There are two different situations that may arise. First, there may be litigation between two private litigants, and one already has documents, potentially subject to public interest immunity, which would ordinarily be disclosed on disclosure. The other case is where the litigation is with a public authority which wishes, as litigant, to assert the claim to public interest immunity in respect of some (or all) of its documents. In the former case one of the parties may notify the relevant public authority of the fact that the documents concerned may be produced for inspection, and then the Attorney-General may seek to intervene in order to assert the claim to

---

[530] G.18.79.
[531] CPR, r.31.19(1).
[532] CPR, r.31.19(7).
[533] CPR, r.31.19(2).
[534] CPR, r.31.19(4).
[535] CPR, r.31.19(3).
[536] CPR, r.31.19(5).
[537] CPR, r.31.19(7).
[538] CPR, r.31.19(6).

public interest immunity,[539] though of course he is not obliged to do so.[540] In the latter case this is usually not necessary, as the public authority concerned is already involved.[541] In each case, however, an official view will be put forward, usually by certificate or affidavit or witness statement, by the Minister or other appropriate official such as the head of the organisation concerned,[542] as to why the documents concerned ought not to be disclosed or produced. In accordance with the three stage approach set out above,[543] the official must consider whether disclosure would cause real damage or substantial harm. If he is satisfied that the damage test is met he should consider (so far as he can judge it) the strength of the public interest in disclosing the document and carry out the balancing exercise. There is no obligation to claim public interest immunity, if the decision maker is satisfied that the public interest is in favour of disclosure.[544] This view as expressed is not conclusive; it is for the court to decide.[545]

This judicial control is critical to ensure a fair trial within Art.6 of the European Convention on Human Rights.[546] The certificate, affidavit or witness statement should describe the documents concerned and the nature of the objection(s) to their disclosure, and, if different objections apply to different document or classes of documents, should set out the various categories and the considerations that apply to each. Both the nature of the documents concerned and the class to which they are said to belong must be described with sufficient particularity to allow the court to check both that the documents belong to the class and that the class is one which ought to

11.90

---

[539] *Adams v Adams* [1971] P. 188 at 198; *Rio Tinto Zinc Corp. v Westinghouse Corp.* [1978] A.C. 547, HL. See also *Lonhro Plc v Fayed (No.4)* [1994] Q.B. 749, CA, where the Inland Revenue declined to object to production of tax documents in the hands of a litigant; *Wallace Smith Trust Co. Ltd v Deloitte Haskins & Sells* [1995] C.L.C. 223, *affd.* [1997] 1 W.L.R. 257, CA (copy transcripts of interviews with S.F.O in defendant's hands, S.F.O not objecting; held, not covered by PII); *Kaufmann v Credit Lyonnais Bank* [1995] C.L.C. 300 at 313.

[540] *cf.*, e.g. *Buttes Gas and Oil Co. v Hammer (No.3)* [1981] Q.B. 223, CA; [1982] A.C. 888, HL.

[541] But *cf. Evans v Chief Constable of Surrey* [1988] Q.B. 588, where the Attorney-General intervened in a case in which the Chief Constable was defendant.

[542] Normally the Minister, or other political head, but the permanent head if this is inconvenient or impractical: see, e.g. *Alfred Crompton Amusement Machines Ltd v Commissioners of Customs and Excise* [1971] 2 All E.R. 843. In *O'Sullivan v Commissioner of Police for the Metropolis, The Times,* July 3, 1995, Butterfield J. held that it was not necessary for the claim to immunity to be raised by a minister or other permanent head of the department concerned. It was sufficient for the claim to be raised by a responsible official within the organisation.

[543] Para.11.85, above.

[544] *R. v Chief Constable, ex. p. Wiley* [1995] 1 A.C. 274, HL; *Bennett v Metropolitan Commissioner* [1995] 1 W.L.R. 488; December 1996 report, para.2.3.

[545] *Conway v Rimmer* [1968] A.C. 910, HL, overruling *Duncan v Cammell Laird & Co.* [1942] A.C. 624 on this point; *Robinson v State of South Australia* [1931] A.C. 704, P.C; see also *Sethia v Stern, The Times,* November 4, 1987, CA.

[546] *Rowe and Davis v United Kingdom* (2000) 30 E.H.R.R.; see also *R. v Davis, The Times,* April 24, 2000, CA.

be protected.[547] In some cases it will not be necessary to claim public interest immunity for a whole document; redacting the sensitive parts of a document should usually be considered. Where the claim is only as to inspection as opposed to disclosure, the claim to public interest immunity should be set out in the list of documents or, if there is no list, in writing to the party seeking inspection. In such a case the party claiming public interest immunity should produce evidence in support of his claim in the event an application is made seeking inspection.

11.91 Where a document is potentially covered by public interest immunity, but also the document itself is of questionable relevance or it is arguable that production is in any event not necessary, the court will usually consider relevance first and, only once it is decided that prima facie the document should be disclosed produced, will it then go on to consider public interest immunity.[548] If the document is privileged on the basis of legal professional privilege it will not usually be necessary to consider public interest immunity as well.[549]

11.92 In considering whether public interest applies the judge will carry out a three-stage process:

(a) satisfying himself from the certificate/affidavit/witness that:

    (i) the class of documents concerned is capable of attracting the immunity;

    (ii) there is no reason to believe that the actual documents do not fall within the class aimed; and

    (iii) both the documents and the claim have been properly considered by an appropriate person;

(b) determining whether there is a public interest in production of the documents, by reason of both:

    (i) relevance to matters in question, and

    (ii) necessity for disposing fairly of the case;

(c) balancing the public interest in withholding the documents against the public interest in producing them.[550]

11.93 Once public interest immunity has been properly raised, the burden is on the applicant for production to show that the documents should be pro-

---

[547] *Re Grosvenor Hotel London* [1964] Ch. 464; *Merricks v Nott-Bowers* [1965] 1 Q.B. 57, CA.

[548] December 1996 report, para.2.3; *R. v Chief Constable, exp. Wiley* [1995] 1 A.C. 274 at 280–1, HL.

[549] *R. v Derby Magistrates Court, exp. B* [1996] 1 A.C. 487, HL: with legal professional privilege there is no balancing exercise.

[550] See *Air Canada v Secretary of State for Trade (No.2)* [1983] 1 All E.R. 161 at 165–166, *per* Bingham J.; later reversed on another point: [1983] 2 A.C. 394, HL.

duced.[551] It should incidentally be noted that the court does not apply a more stringent test of public interest immunity in an application for disclosure before pleading[552] than in an application by a litigant who has already pleaded his case.[553] Once the balancing exercise has been carried out, and it has come down in favour of preserving the immunity from disclosure, the court has no further discretion: it is then a rule of law that the material has to be excluded from the case.[554]

A difficult question is whether, and in what circumstances, the court **11.94** should inspect the documents in question in order to help decide on the applicability of the immunity to these documents.[555] It is not enough that the documents are considered likely to assist in the resolution of the litigation one way or another, i.e. that they will either help or hinder the applicant for disclosure/production. On the contrary, before the court can inspect, it must satisfied that the documents are "very likely to contain material which would give substantial support" to some part of the applicant's own case in the litigation.[556] Even then, it is only if there is a real doubt whether the claim to immunity outweighs the claim to production that the court should inspect.[557] On the other hand, and not altogether consistently, it is said that in class claims, where the grounds for immunity of the class appear weak, so that the balance is in favour of production, the court *should* nevertheless inspect, in case the class claim ought to be a contents claim, and immune on that basis.[558] In one case of a class claim, the judge decided to inspect on the basis that, although the (relevant) material was not likely, in itself, to decide any major issue, nonetheless the partial disclosures of the material by the government department concerned, coupled with the consents to disclosure

---

[551] *Air Canada*, n.549, above, at 433. *MGN Pension Trustees Ltd v Invesco Asset Management Ltd*, unreported, October 14, 1993, Evans-Lombe J. (at pp.20–22); *Kaufmann v Credit Lyonnais Bank* [1995] C.L.C.500; *Mercer v St. Helen's and Knowsley Hospitals* [1995] C.L.Y. 626. Contrast the position in Ireland: *Ambiorix Ltd v Minister for the Environment* [1992] 1 I.R. 277, Irish Sup.Ct.

[552] As to which see Ch.2, para.2.33, above.

[553] *Barrett v Ministry of Defence, The Independent*, January 23, 1990; *The Times*, January 24, 1990.

[554] *Marks v Beyfus* (1890) 25 Q.B.D. 494 at 498–99; *Powell v Chief Constable of North Wales Constabulary, The Times*, February 11, 2000, CA.

[555] CPR, 31.19(6)(a). In Australia, see *Alcoota v CLC* [2001] N.T.S.C. 30 (Supreme Court of Northern Territory), following *The Commonwealth v Northern Land Council* (1992–93) 176 C.L.R. 604 at 619. In Ireland, see *Ambiorix Ltd v Minister for the Environment* [1992] 1 I.R. 277, Irish Sup.Ct.. In criminal cases a proper balancing exercise can only be carried out by the judge if he looks at the documents concerned: *R. v K* (1992) 97 Cr.App.R. 342, CA.

[556] *Air Canada*, n.549, above, at 435; *Re HIV Haemophiliac Litigation* [1996] P.N.L.R. 290, CA; *cf.* in Australia, *Australian National Airlines Corp. v Commonwealth of Australia* (1975) 49 A.L.J.R. 338; *Sankey v Whitlam* (1978) 142 C.L.R. 1; and in Ireland, *Duncan v Govenor of Portlaoise Prison* [1997] 1 I.R. 559, H.Ct.Eire.

[557] *Continental Reinsurance Corp. (UK) Ltd v Pine Top Insurance Ltd* [1986] 1 Lloyd's Rep. 8, CA.

[558] *ibid.* See also *MGN Pension Trustees Ltd v Invesco Asset Management Ltd*, unreported, October 14, 1993, Evans Lombe J. (at p.22); *cf. Kaufmann v Credit Lyonnais Bank* [1995] C.L.C. 300, 313.

by some of those who had supplied the information in confidence, so weakened the claim to immunity as to justify inspection.[559] It also appears that, where class claims are concerned, it may exceptionally be necessary to inspect the document to verify the fact that a class claim is validly made.[560] The correct approach, both in respect of class and contents claims, is that once the court is satisfied that the documents might be necessary for the fair disposal of the action, the court should examine them with a view to considering whether they are capable of giving substantial support to the applicant's case and if so, whether, bearing in mind not only their importance to the applicant in furthering his case but also any real and significant damage their disclosure might cause to the public interest, they ought to be released to him.[561] Where national security considerations are concerned, once there is an actual or potential risk to national security demonstrated by an appropriate certificate the court will generally decline to exercise its right to inspect.[562] Where the court does inspect, this may mean the judge deciding a case by reference to documents not seen by one side.[563]

Categories of immunity

11.95   The difficulty with attempting any summary of the case law is the infinite variety of fact situations in which the question of immunity arises. In addition to the three factors referred to in para.11.82, above, which make it difficult to apply any decided case directly to the facts of a new one, there is the additional factor of changes in judicial attitude over the years, so that a case that might be decided one way some years ago would now be decided differently. Although cases decided in the context of criminal proceedings may sometimes be cited by analogy in civil cases, it should be recognised that there are differences both in the balancing exercise and procedure. Within very broad limits, however, it is possible to group together cases on the immunity to show the way in which it operates, and also to demonstrate its limits. Thus cases where immunity has been held to exist can be summarised as: national security, international relations, workings of central government and allied branches of the public service, the police and armed forces and informants.

---

[559] *Multi-Guarantee Co. Ltd v Cavalier Insurance Co. Ltd, The Times,* June 24, 1986.
[560] *Burmah Oil Co. Ltd v Bank of England* [1980] A.C. 1090 at 1111.
[561] *Goodridge v Chief Constable of Hampshire* [1999] 1 W.L.R. 1558; *cf. Camden London Borough Council v Dempster,* unreported, January 16, 1998, E.A.T. (disclosure ordered without tribunal inspecting the documents).
[562] *Balfour v Foreign and Commonwealth Office* [1994] 1 W.L.R. 681, CA.
[563] See *R. v Doubtfire* [2001] 2 Cr.App.R. 209, CA (appeal against conviction was allowed on basis of material covered by PII without detailed reasons or referring to material); *R. v Smith (Joe)* [2001] 1 W.L.R. 1031, CA (judge in criminal trial entitled to rely on PII material not disclosed to the defence in deciding whether or not reasonable grounds for suspicion)(disapproved in *R. v H.* [2004] 2 A.C. 134, at para.42).

National Security   Plainly, cases can occur where the documents sought   **11.96**
contain secret information potentially useful to an enemy, and the risk of
harm is greater when there is a war or a threat of war. Thus documents
relating to the government's plans for future war campaigns[564] and to the
design of a submarine[565] have been withheld, both being wartime cases.
Such issues can also arise in peacetime.[566] Even in peacetime, however, it
seems that the executive is to be treated as the sole judge of what national
security requires, and accordingly evidence that national security requires
particular non-disclosure will in effect be irrebuttable.[567] Reasoning based
on general damage to the workings of the security and intelligence services
has been used to justify claims to public interest immunity. A document may
attract public interest immunity where it contains information relating to a
method or technique in current or future operations, or the identity or
appearance of current or former members of the security and intelligence
services, so that disclosure could put the individual in danger or impair his
ability to operate effectively.[568]

International Relations   The "public interest" in public interest immunity   **11.97**
is that of the United Kingdom, and there is no equivalent immunity for
documents which injure the interests of foreign states, a kind of "foreign
state privilege."[569] But there is nonetheless a public interest of the United
Kingdom to be protected in its relations with other states. Thus:

> " . . . it is in the public interest of the United Kingdom that the contents
> of confidential documents addressed to or emanating from sovereign
> states, or concerning the interests of sovereign states arising in connec-
> tion with an international territorial dispute between sovereign states,
> shall not be ordered by the courts of this country to be disclosed by a
> private litigant without the consent of the sovereign states con-
> cerned . . . ."[570]

---

[564] *Asiatic Petroleum Co. Ltd v Anglo-Persian Oil Co. Ltd* [1916] 1 K.B. 822.

[565] *Duncan v Cammell Laird & Co. Ltd* [1942] A.C. 624, HL.

[566] *Conway v Rimmer* [1968] A.C. 910 at 993.

[567] *Thorburn v Hermon, The Times*, May 14, 1992; *Balfour v Foreign and Commonwealth Office* [1993] I.C.R. 663, E.A.T. and [1994] 1 W.L.R. 681, CA *cf. Council of Civil Service Unions v Minister for the Civil Service* [1985] A.C. 375, HL see also *Re Ministry of Defence's Application*, unreported, June 17, 1994, N.I.CA; *Re Inquests into the deaths of Toman, McKerr and Others*, unreported, July 11, 1994, H.Ct. of N.I.

[568] December 1996 report, para.5.3; note also categories of sensitive information in the Intelligence Services Act 1994; *R. v Jack*, April 7, 1998, (CA unreported) (tracking device).

[569] *Buttes Gas and Oil Co. v Hammer (No.3)* [1981] Q.B. 223, CA, reversed on other grounds: [1982] A.C. 888, HL.

[570] [1981] Q.B. 223 at 265; see also at 256; *cf. M. Isaacs & Sons Ltd v Cook* [1925] 2 K.B. 391 (diplomatic dispatches). See also *Zaiwalla & Co. v Union of India*, unreported, November 27, 1992, Tuckey J.

Public interest immunity may be asserted where real damage is anticipated to British interests in the area of international relations. Thus a
document may be the subject of a claim because it reveals the Government's
policies towards other states or exposes a negotiating position. Another
example is where by disclosing information given in confidence by another
state, it would jeopardise future communications or relations with that
stage.[571]

11.98   **Workings of central government**   The main reason for withholding these
documents is said to be the avoidance of ill-informed criticism[572]; the need
for frank and uninhibited advice from advisers and organs of government,
sometimes urged,[573] has not found much support.[574] Thus ministerial
papers relating to the formulation of policy have been withheld in cases
where a hotel company sought a new lease of a hotel owned by the British
Railways Board, who were bound to follow the directions of the Minister of
Transport,[575] where the plaintiff claimed to set aside a purchase of its shares
in a nationalised company by the Bank of England as unconscionable[576] and
where airlines sought judicial review of decisions relating to charges made
by the British Airports Authority for aircraft landing at Heathrow Airport.[577] At a lower level documents have been withheld where they were
given to the Department of Trade and Industry in confidence to enable it to
perform its functions under the Insurance Acts,[578] and where they were
produced by the Bank of England for submission to a committee set up to
consider banking supervision under the Banking Act 1979, and where those
documents related to the formulation and development of government
policy at a high level.[579] On the other hand, documents relating to the
formulation of ministerial policy were ordered to be produced in a case
where a prisoner sued for false imprisonment in connection with the experimental special control unit at Wakefield Prison.[580] In Australian and Canadian cases submissions by ministers to Cabinet, correspondence between
ministers and civil servants, and Cabinet decisions have been held not

---

[571] December 1996 report, para.5.15. See also Code of Practice on Access to Government
Information; Official Secrets Act 1989, s.3.
[572] *Conway v Rimmer* [1968] A.C. 910 at 952; *Sankey v Whitlam* (1978) 142 C.L.R. 1 at 40,
63, 97.
[573] *Burmah Oil Co. Ltd v Bank of England* [1980] A.C. 1090 at 1112.
[574] cf. *Conway v Rimmer*, n.571, above, at 993; *Burmah Oil Co. Ltd v Bank of England*, n.572
above at 1112, 1132, 1145; *Williams v Home Office* [1981] 1 All E.R. 1151; *Sankey v
Whitlam* (1978) 148 C.L.R. 1 at 40, 63, 96.
[575] *Re Grosvenor Hotel, London (No.2)* [1965] Ch. 1210.
[576] *Burmah Oil Co. Ltd v Bank of England* [1980] A.C. 1090.
[577] *Air Canada v Secretary of State for Trade* [1983] 2 A.C. 394, HL; *Ambiorix Ltd v Minister
for the Environment* [1992] 1 I.R. 277, Irish Sup.Ct.
[578] *Continental Reinsurance Corp. (UK) Ltd v Pine Top Insurance Ltd* [1986] 1 Lloyd's Rep.
8, CA; cf. *Multi-Guarantee Co. Ltd v Cavalier Insurance Co. Ltd*, The Times, June 24,
1986, Knox J.
[579] *Johnson Matthey Bankers Ltd v Arthur Young Ltd*, The Independent, May 6, 1988.
[580] *Williams v Home Office* [1981] 1 All E.R. 1151; these documents were later the basis of the

protected by public interest immunity when the competing interests were balanced against each other.[581] In a New Zealand case production of documents by the Inland Revenue was ordered despite an argument that their production might reveal confidential investigative techniques and might make easier the discharge of the onus of proof on the taxpayer in objection proceedings.[582] Returns to government departments pursuant to statutory obligation are dealt with later.[583]

Other branches of public service   Bodies by means of which government   **11.99** policy is implemented may be treated, for the purposes of public interest immunity, as if they formed part of central government. Thus confidential letters to the Gaming Board, commenting on applicants for certain certificates, have been withheld,[584] as have information obtained by Customs & Excise under statutory powers from third parties,[585] internal memoranda within the Monopolies Commission in the course of preparation of a report,[586] and information obtained by the Audit Commission in the course of an investigation.[587] Similarly, immunity was held to apply to transcripts of evidence given to an enquiry under the Southern Rhodesia (United Nations Sanctions) (No.2) Ord.1968.[588] In the context of regulation of the financial services industry, documents of IMRO in relation to its regulatory

---

contempt application against the plaintiff's solicitor, Harriet Harman: *Home Office v Harman* [1983] 1 A.C. 280, HL; *R. v Home Secretary, ex p. Duggan, The Independent,* January 28, 1994, prisoner seeking security status reports: PII on "contents" basis properly attached to information leading to identification of informants, or impinging on escape risk.

[581] *Sankey v Whitlam* (1978) 142 C.L.R. 1, H.Ct. of Aus.; *Gloucester v R.* (1981) 129 D.L.R. (3d) 275, CA of B.C; *Koowarta v Bjelke-Petersen* (1989) 92 F.L.R. 104, Sup.Ct.Qld.; *cf. Att.Gen. v Jonathan Cape Ltd* [1976] Q.B. 752 at 764; *Lanyon Pty Ltd v Commonwealth of Australia* (1973) 129 C.L.R.. 650, H.Ct.Aus.; *Commonwealth of Australia v Northern Land Council* (1993) 67 A.L.J.R. 405, H.Ct.Aus. (refusal to order inspection of documents relating to cabinet meetings); *Commonwealth v C.F.M.E.U.* (2000) 98 F.C.R. 31 (refusal to order production of letter from Minister to Prime Minister); *Alcoota v CLC* [2001] N.T.S.C. 30, Sup.Ct. of Northern Territory (refusal to order inspection of cabinet documents etc.); *National Tertiary Education Industry Union v Commonwealth of Australia* (2001) 188 A.L.R. 614, Fed.Ct.Aus. (Ministerial submission to Cabinet protected by immunity); *Babcock v Attorney-General of Canada* (2002) 214 D.L.R. (4th) 193, S.C.C.; see also *Egan v Chadwick* (1999) 46 N.S.W.L.R. 563, CA of N.S.W.

[582] *Green v Commissioner of Inland Revenue* [1991] 3 N.Z.L.R. 88; *cf. Lonhro v Fayed (No.4)* [1994] Q.B. 749, CA (no immunity in respect of tax documents in hands of taxpayer, Inland Revenue not objecting); *R. v Inland Revenue Commissioners, ex p. National Federation of Self-Employed and Small Businesses Ltd* [1982] A.C. 617 at 654, HL (possibility of Inland Revenue raising immunity); *Mount Murray Country Club Ltd v McLeod* [2003] U.K.P.C. 53.

[583] See para.11.143, below.

[584] *Rogers v Home Secretary* [1973] A.C. 388, HL.

[585] *Alfred Crompton Amusement Machines Ltd v Customs & Excise Commissioners (No.2)* [1974] A.C. 405, HL.

[586] *Hoffman-La Roche & Co. A.G. v Secretary of State for Trade and Industry, The Times,* April 18, 1975.

[587] *Bookbinder v Tebbit (No.2)* [1992] 1 W.L.R 217.

[588] *Lonrho Ltd v Shell Petroleum Co. Ltd* [1980] 1 W.L.R. 627, HL; *cf. Att.Gen. v Birss* [1991] 1 N.Z.L.R. 669, where *Lonrho* was not cited.

functions have been held to be covered by public interest immunity,[589] whilst confidential reports disclosed voluntarily by a bank to its regulatory body were held not to be covered at least as a class in the hands of the bank.[590] Transcripts of evidence given to a Lloyd's loss review committee[591] and answers provided by a solicitor to the Law Society investigating a client complaint[592] have been ordered to disclosed in the context of civil proceedings. Public interest immunity has been held not to apply to copies of interviews conducted by the SFO.[593] It appears that immunity will attach to communications between a prisoner and a legal aid officer about the substance of a legal aid application,[594] but not (as a class, at least) to prisoners' medical reports in proceedings for review of parole boards' decisions.[595] Reports on categorisation of prisoners are not protected on the basis of a *class* claim, although *contents* claims may be justified. In many cases it may be sufficient to provide a prisoner with a document setting out the gist of those reports; however in some cases it may be appropriate and fair to disclose the reports in full (with PII redactions).[596] Although it is perhaps less of an emanation of government policy, and more based on the Crown's duties as *parens patriae,* documents produced by the child care service have been held immune in both wardship[597] and personal injuries[598] proceedings. On the other hand, absolute immunity has been refused to local authority social work records,[599] adoption agency records,[600] local education author-

---

[589] *MGN Pension Trustees Ltd v Invesco Asset Management Ltd*, unreported, October 14, 1993.

[590] *Kaufmann v Credit Lyonnais Bank* [1995] C.L.C. 300.

[591] *Arbuthnott v Fagan* [1996] L.R.L.R. 143, CA.

[592] *Goldberg v Ng* (1994) 33 N.S.W.L.R. 639, CA of N.S.W.; *Sayer v National Mutual Life Association of Australia Ltd* (1994) 34 N.S.W.L.R. 132, CA of N.S.W.

[593] *Wallace Smith Trust Co. Ltd v Deloitte Haskins & Sells* [1997] 1 W.L.R. 257, CA (S.F.O. did not object to production of copies in hands of defendants).

[594] *R. v Umoh* (1987) 84 Cr.App.R.138, CA.

[595] *R. v Home Secretary, ex p. Benson, The Times*, November 8, 1988.

[596] *R. v Secretary of State for the Home Department ex p. Doody* [1993] 1 A.C. 531; *R. v Secretary of State for the Home Department, ex p. Duggan* [1994] 3 All E.R. 277 (class claim failed); *R. v Secretary of State for the Home Department ex p. McAvoy* [1998] 1 W.L.R. 790; *R. (Lord) v Secretary of State for the Home Department* [2003] EWHC 2073 (Admin); *Williams v Secretary of State for the Home Department* [2002] EWCA Civ 498.

[597] *Re D. (Infants)* [1970] 1 W.L.R. 599, CA; *cf. Re M (Minors: Disclosure of Welfare Report)* [1994] 1 F.L.R. 760, CA For children cases see *Re C* [1995] 1 F.L.R. 204.

[598] *Gaskin v Liverpool City Council* [1980] 1 W.L.R. 1549, CA.

[599] *Re M. (a Minor)* (1989) 88 L.G.R. 841, [1990] 2 F.L.R. 36, CA; *R. v Brushett* [2001] Crim.L.R. 471, CA (social services files); see J. Temkin, "Digging the dirt: disclosure of records in sexual assault cases" (2002) 61 C.L.J. 126.

[600] *R. v Bournemouth Justices, ex p. Grey* [1987] 1 F.L.R. 36; *Re T (A Minor)* [1994] 1 F.L.R. 632 (right of guardian *ad litem* under s.42(1) of the Children Act 1989 to examine and copy certain local authority records—here an adoption agency—not subject to any potential claim to public interest immunity); *Re H* [1995] 1 F.L.R. 964 (disclosure of adoption records for purposes of a criminal trial: procedure to be used); *Re a Subpoena (Adoption: Commissioner for Local Administration)* [1996] 2 F.L.R. 629 (*subpoena* to obtain local authority adoption records for purposes of ombudsman's inquiries); *Gunn-Russo v Nugent Care Society*, July 20, 2001 (unreported), Admin.Ct. (disclosure of adoption records by

ity records[601] and reports,[602] and, in Australia, to documents in the hands of the Protective Commissioner[603] (similar to the Master of the Court of Protection in England). Hospital records relating to a patient have been held not to be covered by public interest immunity in a personal injuries action by that patient,[604] whilst public interest immunity has been held to apply to documents of an abortion clinic relating to abortions carried out there.[605] Public interest immunity attaches to the deliberations in private of the professional conduct committee of the General Medical Council.[606] Documents relating to a court or tribunal's deliberative process may be subject to public interest immunity, such as drafts of a decision.[607] Covert sound recordings of the private deliberations of school governors sitting as a disciplinary body in relation to employment issues were held not protected from admissibility in evidence before the employment tribunal by public interest immunity, yet were to be excluded on "public policy" grounds, to encourage full discussion during private deliberations.[608]

The police and armed forces   The position of the police is complex. Public   **11.100** interest immunity has been held formerly to attach to statements taken in an investigation, under the Police Act 1964, into a complaint,[609] even where the makers of the statements consent to disclosure,[610] to the transcripts of disciplinary hearings,[611] and also to a letter from the Police Complaints Authority to a complainant stating the authority's findings.[612] It was recognised that there was no general public immunity in respect of documents coming into existence during an investigation into a complaint against the

---

voluntary adoption agency); *Re J. (a Child) (Care proceedings: Disclosure)*, *The Times*, May 16, 2003 (no PII for report prepared by local authority concerning handling of care proceedings, as child's guardian entitled to see report under s.42 of Children Act 1989).

[601] *Thompson v I.L.E.A.* (1977) 74 L.S. Gaz. 66; *West Midlands Police Authority v Walsall Metropolitan Borough Council*, *The Independent*, February 26, 1992.

[602] *Campbell v Tameside Metropolitan Borough Council* [1982] Q.B. 1065, CA; see also *Brown v Matthews* [1990] Ch. 662, CA (court welfare officer's report).

[603] *B v N* (1994) 35 N.S.W.L.R. 140, N.S.W.Sup.Ct. In that case the court ordered disclosure after balancing the competing aspects of the public interest.

[604] *Flett v North Tyneside Health Authority* [1989] C.L.Y. 2968.

[605] *DPP v Morrow* (1993) 14 B.M.L.R. 54, D.C.

[606] *Roylance v General Medical Council*, *The Times*, January 27, 1999, P.C.

[607] *Comalco New Zealand Ltd v Broadcasting Standards Authority* [1995] 3 N.Z.L.R. 469; *Tau v Duvrie* [1996] 2 N.Z.L.R. 193.

[608] *Chairman & Governors of Amwell View School v Dogherty*, unreported, September 15, 2006, E.A.T.

[609] *Neilson v Laugharne* [1981] Q.B. 736, CA; *Hehir v Metropolitan Police Commissioner* [1982] 1 W.L.R. 715, CA; *Halford v Sharples* [1992] 1 W.L.R. 736, CA; *ex p. Coventry Newspapers Ltd* [1993] Q.B. 278, CA; *Evans v Granada Television Ltd*, unreported, April 2, 1993, Drake J. (documents created during investigation of complaint against police officers).

[610] *Makanjuola v Metropolitan Police Commissioner* [1992] 3 All E.R. 617, CA.

[611] *ibid.*

[612] *Police Complaints Authority v Greater Manchester Police Authority*, *The Times*, December 3, 1990; (1990) 3 Admin L.R. 757.

police under Pt IX of the Police and Criminal Evidence Act 1984.[613] Nevertheless it was held that reports prepared by investigating officers under Pt IX formed a class entitled to public interest immunity, and thus their production would be ordered only where the balance came down in that direction.[614] It did not attach to the written complaint on which the investigation is founded,[615] and neither did it apply where the purpose of the statement was for a dominant purpose other than the investigation itself.[616] The current system for investigating complaints against the police is found in Pt IV of the Police Act 1996. Information received in the course of an investigation is subject to a restriction on disclosure by s.80(1).[617] But in a recent case,[618] it was held that there was no automatic immunity attaching to interviews under caution taken in the course of investigating ordinary allegations of criminal conduct, and the interviews were ordered to be disclosed under CPR, r.31.17.[619]

11.101 Police grievance procedure documents have been held to be not covered by public interest immunity.[620] Statements made by the Lord Chancellor in the House of Lords on two occasions have been to the effect that immunity will not be claimed in proceedings for malicious prosecution, wrongful arrest and similar proceedings where the justification for the police action is in issue, unless production of the document would reveal the identity of a police informer.[621] Documents arising from police disciplinary proceedings have been held immune from disclosure,[622] although reports on a probationary police constable suspected of theft have been held not so immune.[623] Immunity has also been held to attach to a police report (with witness statements) sent to the DPP seeking his advice,[624] as also to documents relating to the private lives of chief police officers and to positive vetting in files of the Association of Chief Police Officers (in a sex discrimination

---

[613] *R. v Chief Constable of West Midlands Police, exp. Wiley* [1995] 1 A.C. 274, HL; *Skeffington v Rooney* [1997] 1 I.R. 22.

[614] *Taylor v Chief Constable of Greater Manchester* [1995] 1 W.L.R. 447, CA; *O'Sullivan v Commissioner of Police of the Metropolis, The Times,* July 3, 1995; *Kelly v Metropolitan Police Commissioner, The Times,* August 20, 1997, CA.

[615] *Conerney v Jacklin* (1985) 129 S.J. 285, CA.

[616] *Peach v Metropolitan Police Commissioner* [1986] Q.B. 1064, CA.

[617] See *Butler v Police Ombudsman for Northern Ireland* [2003] N.I.Q.B. 64; *R. (Green) v Police Complaints Authority* [2004] 1 W.L.R. 725, HL.

[618] *Rowe v Fryers* [2003] 1 W.L.R. 1952, CA.

[619] See paras 4.48–4.60 above.

[620] *Metropolitan Police Commissioner v Locker* [1993] 3 All E.R. 584; [1993] I.C.R. 440, E.A.T.

[621] See *The Times,* June 1956, and March 9, 1962, and also *Conway v Rimmer* [1968] A.C. 910, HL.

[622] *R. v Metropolitan Police Commissioner, ex p. Hart-Leverton, The Times,* February 8, 1990; *Halford v Sharples* [1992] 1 W.L.R. 736, CA.

[623] *Conway v Rimmer* [1968] A.C. 910, HL.

[624] *Evans v Chief Constable of Surrey* [1988] Q.B. 588; *Goodridge v Chief Constable of Hampshire* [1999] 1 W.L.R. 1558; see also *Kelly v Metropolitan Police Commissioner, The Times,* August 20, 1997, CA; *Re McCaughey's Application for Judicial Review* [2004] N.I.Q.B. 2; but *cf. Ellis v Home Office* [1953] 2 Q.B. 135, CA.

case).[625] Public interest immunity has been held to cover a police public order manual.[626] But documents seized by the police in the course of an investigation do not thereby become immune from production,[627] nor are photographs of the defendant in a criminal case once arrested and relevant crime reports,[628] nor (apparently) witness statements and police video recordings of interviews with child witnesses in criminal proceedings.[629] In certain cases it may be appropriate to keep the names of individual officers confidential and from being disclosed to any party by reason of the nature of the officer's work, such as covert activity or as a tactical firearms officer.[630] As for the armed services, the report of a naval board of inquiry into a death on station abroad has been held not subject to immunity.[631] This is inconsistent with an old case where evidence to an army court of inquiry was held immune from production.[632] It is submitted that the modern view is better, as, in any case where national security is threatened, there is a quite different basis for claiming to withhold the documents concerned.[633]

Confidentiality   It is often argued, in support of a claim to public interest immunity, that the free flow of accurate information to a public authority, whether from employees, advisers, or members of the public, would be inhibited if that information (or the identity of the supplier) were to be disclosed on discovery in subsequent litigation. Usually such arguments fail, and thus Customs and Excise were held not entitled to refuse to produce documents identifying patent-infringing importers,[634] employers in discrimination cases were not entitled to withhold confidential personal reports on other candidates,[635] journalists were not permitted to withhold the name of a source who might have committed an actionable wrong against the plaintiff,[636] and (in New Zealand) non-party disclosure of confidential blood donor forms was ordered in order to prove the adequacy of blood-   **11.102**

---

[625] *Halford v Sharples* [1992] 1 W.L.R. 736, CA.

[626] *Goodwin v Chief Constable of Lancashire*, *The Times*, November 3, 1992, CA.

[627] *Marcel v Metropolitan Police Commissioner* [1992] Ch. 225, CA.

[628] *R. v Fergus* (1993) 98 Cr.App.R. 313, 324.

[629] *Nottinghamshire County Council v H.* [1995] 1 F.L.R. 115; *Re M (Minors)* [1995] 2 F.L.R. 57.

[630] *R. v Crown Prosecution Service, ex p. J.*, *The Times*, July 8, 1999, D.C.; *R. v Bedfordshire Coroner, ex p. Local Sunday Newspapers Limited* (2000) 164 J.P. 283, Burton J.; *R. (Bennett) v Inner South London Coroner* [2004] EWCA Civ 1439, CA.

[631] *Barrett v Ministry of Defence*, *The Times*, January 24, 1990; *cf. R. v Secretary of State for Defence, ex p. Sancto*, *The Guardian*, July 29, 1992 (no litigation between parties: no right to see report).

[632] *Dawkins v Rokesby* (1873) L.R. 8 Q.B. 255.

[633] See para.11.96, above.

[634] *Norwich Pharmacal Co. Ltd v Customs & Excise Commissioners* [1974] A.C. 133, HL.

[635] *Science Research Council v Nassé* [1980] A.C. 1028, HL.

[636] *British Steel Corp. v Granada Television Ltd* [1981] A.C. 1096, HL; *cf. European Pacific Banking Corporation v Television New Zealand Ltd* [1994] 3 N.Z.L.R. 43, CA; see now the Contempt of Court Act 1981, s.10, and Ch.3, para.3.18, above.

screening procedures.[637] There is no public interest immunity (based on confidentiality) excluding transcripts of an examination made under s.236 of the Companies Act 1985,[638] from being admitted in evidence in subsequent proceedings, or from being disclosed to prosecution or regulatory authorities.[639] But traditionally there is one area where such arguments succeed, and that relates to informants.

11.103 **Informants** It is said that the police and other enforcement agencies depend to a considerable extent, in carrying out their duties, on informants. Here the courts, exceptionally, recognise a public interest sufficient to outweigh the public interest in giving disclosure.[640] Thus the DPP was held not obliged to reveal the informant(s) on the basis of whose evidence he had decided to prosecute,[641] the N.S.P.C.C. were able to withhold discovery of documents identifying an informant who had wrongly suggested that a mother was beating her child,[642] the Law Society were entitled to immunity in respect of the identity of informants leading them to suspect dishonesty by a solicitor,[643] immunity attached to documents on the strength of which the police obtained a search warrant,[644] and the police were not obliged to identify places from which they observed the commission of offences, where this would reveal the identity of members of the public who had assisted them.[645] In all these cases the authority concerned was that whose responsibility it was to investigate breaches of the relevant law.[646] But the principle

---

[637] *Long v Attorney-General* [2001] 2 N.Z.L.R. 529, N.Z.H.Ct.; *cf. Straka v Humber River Regional Hospital* (2000) 193 D.L.R. (4th) 680, Ontario CA (references given in confidence to a hospital on a candidate held privileged).

[638] *Re Arrows Ltd (No.4)* [1995] 2 A.C. 75, HL; *cf. Re Barlow Clowes Gilt Managers Ltd* [1992] Ch.208 (transcripts of interviews taken on behalf of liquidators in compulsory winding up held to be prima facie protected); *Soden v Burns* [1996] 1 W.L.R. 1512 (notice should be given to witnesses concerned before disclosure).

[639] *Re Headington Investments Ltd* [1993] Ch. 452, CA.

[640] For the justification for the immunity see *R. v Gordon* (1999) 136 C.C.C. (3d) 64 at 76–77, Ontario Ct. In Canada informer privilege is regarded as fundamental and is subject only to the innocence at stake exception: *Standen's Land v Pinkerton's of Canada Ltd* (2001) 203 D.L.R. (4th) 744, Alberta Ct; see also *Hawley v Fearn-Stewart* (2004) 233 D.L.R. (4th) 160, Ont.Sup.Ct.; *Royal Canadian Mounted Police Public Complaints Commission v A.G. of Canada* (2005) 256 D.L.R. (4th) 579, Fed.CA. (refusal to supply information to complaints commission as to sworn evidence on which search warrant obtained: upheld).

[641] *Marks v Beyfus* (1890) 25 Q.B.D. 494, CA; see also *R. v Hennessey* (1978) 68 Cr.App.R. 419, CA; *R. v Hallett* [1986] Crim.L.R. 463, CA; *R. v Agar* [1991] 1 All E.R. 442, CA.

[642] *D v N.S.P.C.C.* [1978] A.C. 171, HL; see also *Director of Consumer Affairs and Fair Trading v Sugar Distributors* [1991] 1 I.R. 225 (Sup.Ct.Eire).

[643] *Buckley v The Law Society (No.2)* [1984] 1 W.L.R. 1101; *cf. Sayer v National Mutual Life Association of Australia Ltd* (1994) 34 N.S.W.L.R. 132 (production ordered of reports produced by receiver appointed by N.S.W. Law Society).

[644] *Taylor v Anderton, The Times,* October 21, 1986.

[645] *R. v Rankine* [1986] Q.B. 224, CA; *R. v Johnson* [1988] 1 W.L.R. 1377, CA; *R. v Hewitt, The Times,* January 1, 1992, CA; *Austin v DPP, The Times,* November 26, 1992, D.C.; *R. v Keane* [1994] 1 W.L.R. 746, CA; *R. v Turner* [1995] 1 W.L.R. 264, CA.

[646] See also *Continental Reinsurance Corp. (UK) Ltd v Pine Top Insurance Ltd* [1986] 1 Lloyd's Rep. 8, CA.

also applies where the informant tells a journalist, who then resists disclosure of the informant's identity.[647] Where an informer is willing for his identity to be disclosed then the primary justification for anonymity is no longer applicable and the immunity will generally not apply in such a case.[648] And in one exceptional case the Court of Appeal even ordered the disclosure of details of a police informer in a civil action against the police on the basis that the public interest in keeping the informer's identity secret was outweighed by the claimant's interest in a fair trial.[649] Where disclosure is ordered of such information the court may impose express restrictions on use and access to the material.[650] In New Zealand it has been held that, where the informant's communication is an element of an offence (e.g. because it was deliberately false, in order to harass someone), the communication is outside the scope of the immunity.[651] An argument analogous to those applicable in informer cases in respect of records of blood donors was held not sufficient to compel a court to refuse disclosure of such records.[652]

H. PRIVILEGE AGAINST INCRIMINATION[653]

The old law

At common law the rule was that a person (party or witness) could not be **11.104** obliged to provide evidence which might expose him, or even increase existing exposure, to the risk of criminal conviction, the imposition of a penalty or liability to forfeiture.[654] The rule extended to punishment by ecclesiastical courts,[655] and to charges of adultery,[656] but it was unclear

---

[647] *R. v Shannon, The Times*, October 11, 2000, CA.

[648] *Savage v Chief Constable of Hampshire* [1997] 2 All E.R. 631, CA, distinguished in *Carnduff v Rock* [2001] 1 W.L.R. 1786, CA (informers claim for payment for information struck out in the public interest).

[649] *Chief Constable of Manchester v McNally* [2002] 2 Cr.App.R. 37; *cf. Whitmarsh v Chief Constable of Avon & Somerset*, unreported, March 31, 2000, CA; *Powell v Chief Constable of North Wales, The Times*, February 11, 2000, CA (not usually appropriate to override privilege for informants in civil proceedings).

[650] *J(P) v Canada (Attorney General)* (2002) 198 D.L.R. (4th) 733, B.C. Sup.Ct.

[651] *R. v Strawbridge* [2003] 1 N.Z.L.R. 683, CA of N.Z.

[652] *D v Australian Red Cross Society* (1993) 30 N.S.W.L.R. 376, CA of N.S.W.; see also *A.B. v Scottish National Blood Transfusion Service* [1990] S.C.L.R. 263, and *Long v Attorney-General* [2001] 2 N.Z.L.R. 529, N.Z.H.Ct

[653] See generally, Thanki (ed.), *The Law of Privilege*, 2006, Ch.8. The privilege has been criticised in the context of civil proceedings: *Istel Ltd v Tully* [1993] A.C. 45 at 53, *per* Lord Templeman. See also Consultation Paper, *The Privilege Against Self-Incrimination in Civil Proceedings* (Lord Chancellor's Department, 1992).

[654] See *Blunt v Park Lane Hotel Ltd* [1942] 2 K.B. 253, CA; Law Reform Committee, 16th Report, paras 8–18; *Rio Tinto Zinc Corp. v Westinghouse Electric Corp.* [1978] A.C. 547, HL.

[655] *Redfern v Redfern* [1891] P.139, CA.

[656] *ibid.*

whether it covered criminal liability under foreign law,[657] and it did not include incrimination of a spouse.[658] The rule was not confined to judicial proceedings, but applied generally, e.g. to public inquiries,[659] inquests,[660] and to professional disciplinary proceedings.[661]

The modern law

11.105 The law is now in certain important respects different. The rule no longer extends to censure of lay persons by ecclesiastical courts,[662] though presumably clerks in holy orders remain covered. Nor (in the UK) does it now extend to charges of adultery,[663] or to non-criminal cases involving a mere liability to forfeiture.[664] It has also been held not to apply to the risk of liability to be committed to prison for non-payment of the community charge.[665] The territorial scope of the rule is now clearer, in that the Civil Evidence Act 1968, s.14(1)(a), has restricted it in non-criminal proceedings to criminal offences under the law of "any part of the United Kingdom."[666] Since the European Communities Act 1972, this law includes E.U. law[667]; the privilege applies in the European Court of Justice as in English courts.[668] But criminal offences and penalties under any other foreign law may still be taken into account as a factor in cases where the court has a discretion as to whether a disclosure order is made.[669] The Civil Evidence Act, by s.14(1)(b), has also extended the rule (again, in non-criminal cases) to

---

[657] *King of the Two Sicilies v Willcox* (1851) 1 Sim. (N.S.) 301 (against); *USA v McRae* (1868) L.R. 3 Ch.App. 79 (for); *Re Atherton* [1912] 2 K.B. 251 at 253 (against); *Brannigan v Davison* [1997] A.C. 238, P.C., held no privilege where incrimination under foreign law, but may be a factor in court's discretion in deciding whether to compel answer; followed in *Morris v Banque Arabe et Internationale d'Investissement S.A.* (1999) 2 I.T.E.L.R. 492; see also *X v Australian Crime Commission* (2005) 212 A.L.R. 596, Fed.Ct.Aus.

[658] *Rio Tinto Zinc Corp.* [1978] A.C. 547, at 637, HL.

[659] *Sorby v The Commonwealth* (1983) 152 C.L.R. 281, H.Ct.Aus.

[660] *R. v Lincoln Coroner, exp. Hay* [2000] Lloyd's Rep. Medical 264, D.C.

[661] *R. v The Institute of Chartered Accountants of England and Wales, ex p. Taher Nawaz* [1997] P.N.L.R. 433, affd. CA, April 25, 1997 (CA assuming but not deciding the point).

[662] *Blunt v Park Lane Hotel Ltd* [1942] 2 K.B. 253, CA.

[663] Civil Evidence Act 1968, s.16(5), as explained in *Nast v Nast* [1972] Fam. 142, CA.

[664] *ibid.* s.16(1)(a); but it still so extends elsewhere in the common law world: see, e.g. *Re Warden Burton S.M., ex p. Roberts* (1997) 18 W.A.R. 379, Sup.Ct.W.Aus. (Full Ct.).

[665] *R. v Highbury Corner Justices, exp. Watkins, The Times*, October 22, 1992, Q.B.D.

[666] i.e. including Scotland and Northern Ireland, but not the Channel Islands or the Isle of Man; *cf. Davison v Farmer* (1851) 6 Exch.Rep. 242; *Re Brown* (1864) 33 L.J.Q.B. 193; *Navigators and General Insurance Co. Ltd v Ringrose* [1962] 1 W.L.R. 173, CA.

[667] *Rio Tinto Zinc Corp. v Westinghouse Electric Corp.* [1978] A.C. 547 at 564.

[668] *Orkem v European Commission* [1989] E.C.R. 3283, E.C.J.

[669] *Arab Monetary Fund v Hashim* [1989] 1 W.L.R. 565; *Bank Geselleschaft Berlin International S.A. v Zihnali*, July 16, 2001 (Comm. Ct, unreported); and see para.11.135, below; *cf. A.G. for Gibraltar v May* [1999] 1 W.L.R. 998, CA and *Compagnie Noga d'Importation et d'Exportation S.A. v Australia and New Zealand Banking Group Ltd* [2007] EWHC 85 (Comm.).

include incrimination of a person's spouse. It should be noted, however, that the rule is a rule against self-incrimination, not against incrimination itself.[670] In purported pursuance of this principle, it has been held that the privilege is no objection to an order that the defendant permit the plaintiff to enter the former's premises and list infringing articles to be seen there,[671] but this must be regarded as doubtful. The right not to incriminate oneself lies at the heart of the notion of a fair trial under Art.6 of the European Convention on Human Rights,[672] incorporated into English law by the Human Rights Act 1998. Although the English courts must take into account caselaw of the European Court of Human Rights, the lower courts are bound by the reasoning of the superior courts which have examined and expressed a view on that caselaw.[673]

Where the rule applies,[674] a person need not answer questions, and can object to answering requests for information under CPR, Pt 18, which have now replaced interrogatories[675] and letters rogatory,[676] and to producing documents for inspection.[677] With two exceptions, the privilege does not prevent a question being asked, disclosure order being made, or an order being made for further information under CPR, Pt 18: the objection has to be taken to production or answering, as appropriate.[678] The objection

11.106

[670] *Controlled Consultants Pty Ltd v Commissioner for Corporate Affairs* (1984–1986) 156 C.L.R. 385 at 393.
[671] *Twentieth Century Film Corporation v Tryrare Ltd* [1991] F.S.R. 58; see Ch.2, para.2.55, above.
[672] *Saunders v United Kingdom* (1996) 23 E.H.R.R. 313, E.Ct.H.R. (statements made under compulsion to DTI used in criminal trial, held to infringe Art.6); *R. v Secretary of State for Trade and Industry, exp. McCormick* [1998] B.C.C. 379 (held not applicable to director's disqualification proceedings); *Re Westminster Property Management Ltd* [2000] U.K.H.R.R. 332, CA (use of information obtained under compulsion under s.235 of the Insolvency Act 1986 admissible in director's disqualification proceedings); *cf. Brown v Stott (Procurator Fiscal, Dunfermline)* [2003] 1 A.C. 681, P.C. (s.172 Road Traffic Act not inconsistent with Art.6 insofar as it requires a suspect to admit he was driver of suspect vehicle); *C. Plc v P (Home Secretary intervening)* [2006] 4 All E.R. 311, Ch.D. (court may cut down privilege in relation to freestanding evidence not created under compulsion); see generally Ch.21, below.
[673] *Kaya v Haringey London Borough Council* [2001] EWCA Civ 677, at paras 35–38; *R. (Bright) v Central Criminal Court* [2001] 1 W.L.R. 662, at 682, CA, referring to *R. v Hertfordshire City Council, ex p. Green Environmental Industries Ltd* [2000] A.C. 412, HL; *Kay v Lambeth London Borough Council* [2006] 4 All E.R. 128, HL.
[674] As to the form of the objection, see *Griffin v Sogalease Australia Ltd* (2003) 57 N.S.W.L.R. 257, CA of N.S.W.
[675] *Triplex Safety Glass Co. Ltd v Lancegaye Safety Glass (1934) Ltd* [1939] 2 K.B. 395, CA.
[676] *Rio Tinto Zinc Corp.* [1978] A.C. 547, HL.
[677] *Spokes v Grosvenor Hotel* [1897] 2 Q.B. 124; Civil Evidence Act 1968, s.14(1); *cf.* contrary proposition in error, *Accident Insurance Mutual Holdings Ltd v Fadden* (1993) 31 N.S.W.L.R. 412 at 438.
[678] *Spokes v Grosvenor Hotel* [1897] 2 Q.B. 124; *National Association of Operative Plasterers v Smithies* [1906] A.C. 434, HL; *A.J. Bekhor & Co. Ltd v Bilton* [1981] Q.B. 923, CA; *R. v The Institute of Chartered Accountants of England and Wales, ex p. Taher Nawaz* [1999] P.N.L.R. 433, affd., CA, April 25, 1997; *cf. R. v D.C.T., ex p. Briggs* (1987) 71 A.L.R. 86.

should be claimed on oath.[679] Of the two exceptions, the first is that if a disclosure order is made to be complied with peremptorily, without any real opportunity for legal advice on reflection, as where a freezing (*Mareva*) or search (*Anton Piller*) order contains ancillary discovery provisions, then formerly a disclosure order should not be made at all if it infringes the rule,[680] save in exceptional circumstances where there could be incorporated effective safeguards for the defendant.[681] Nowadays, the use of the independent Supervising Solicitor, explicit statements of the privilege in the order, and provision for temporary suspension if the defendant wishes to obtain legal advice mean that more such orders are made without notice, and it is left to the defendant to object if he wishes.[682] The second exception relates to actions to recover a statutory penalty, where disclosure is not ordered at all.[683] In Australia, on the other hand, there has been a tendency,[684] in cases not themselves concerned with the imposition of penalties, to make disclosure orders nonetheless and reserve the objection on grounds of privilege to the stage of inspection, and also reserving liberty to apply in relation to the degree of specificity with which a document is to be described in the individual's list of documents.[685] But this trend is not universally shared.[686]

11.107   Although it has been held in England and Wales that the privilege against self-incrimination extends beyond individuals to corporate bodies,[687] this view is not universally shared. In Australia it has been held that an incorporated company is not entitled to the benefit of the privilege,[688] and this is

---

[679] *Downie v Coe, The Times,* November 28, 1997, CA.

[680] *Rank Film Distribution Ltd v Video Information Centre* [1982] A.C. 380 HL; *Sociedade Nacional de Combustiveis de Angola V.E.E v Lundquist* [1991] 2 Q.B. 310, CA; *Tate Access Floors Ltd v Boswell* [1991] Ch.512 at 530; *Griffin v Sogelease Australia Ltd* (2003) 57 N.S.W.L.R. 257, CA of N.S.W.; *cf. Waterhouse v Barker* [1924] 2 K.B. 759, CA.

[681] As in drug trafficking and similar cases: see Ch.2, paras 2.25–2.26, above. See also discussion in *Refrigerated Express Lines (Alasia) Pty v Australian Meat and Livestock Corp.* (1979) 42 F.L.R. 204 at 207–8, and *Re New World Alliance Pty Ltd* (1993) 118 A.L.R. 699, Fed.Ct.Aus.

[682] See *O Ltd v Z.* [2005] EWHC 238 (Ch.), at paras 35–36; *C. plc v P (Home Secretary intervening)* [2006] 4 All E.R. 311, at paras 5–9, Ch.D.; but in Australia the "sealed envelope" prodecure has been judicially disapproved: *Reid v Howard* (1995) 184 C.L.R. 1, at 7–8, H.Ct.Aus.; *Ross v Internet Wines Ltd* [2004] N.S.W.C.A. 195, at paras 101–04, CA of N.S.W.

[683] *Hunnings v Williamson* (1883) 10 Q.B.D. 459; see Ch.8, para.8.07, above.

[684] Since *Refrigerated Express Lines (Australasia) Pty Ltd v Australian Meat & Livestock Corporation* (1979) 42 F.L.R. 204.

[685] *Microsoft Corporation v CX Computer Pty Ltd* (2002) 187 A.L.R. 326, Fed.Ct.Aus.

[686] *Griffin v Sogelease Australia Ltd* (2003) 57 N.S.W.L.R. 257, CA of N.S.W.

[687] *Triplex Safety Glass Co. Ltd v Lancegaye Safety Glass (1934) Ltd* [1939] 2 K.B. 395, CA.

[688] *Environment Protection Authority v Caltex Refining Co. Pty Ltd* (1992–3) 178 C.L.R. 477, H.Ct. of Aus., noted by Tapper (1994) 110 L.Q.R. 350; *Trade Practices Commission v Abbco Ice Works Pty Ltd* (1994) 123 A.L.R. 503, Fed.Ct.Aus. (F.C.); *Bridal Fashions Pty Ltd v Comptroller-General of Customs* (1997) 17 W.A.R. 499, Sup.Ct.W.Aus. (F.C.) (exposure to a penalty); *Re Warden Burton S.M., ex. p. Roberts* (1997) 18 W.A.R. 379, Sup.Ct.W.Aus. (F.C.) (forfeiture); *Australian Securities and Investments Commission v Michalik* (2003) 211 A.L.R. 285, Sup.Ct.N.S.W.

also the position in the USA.[689] The privilege remains available to corporations in New Zealand[690] and was available in Canada until restricted to witnesses.[691]

The privilege against self-incrimination does not of course give rise to a **11.108** defence in civil proceedings, nor to a right not to plead a defence.[692] The rule is one against *obliging* the party to disclose information. If the party discloses entirely voluntarily, then (subject to any other rules relating to duplicating, disclosing or making use of information) a subsequent disclosure of the information to others does not infringe the privilege.[693] And a litigant is not *obliged* to supply information merely because if he fails to do so he may incur civil liability, as, e.g. where an application for summary judgment is pending against him.[694] More recently, it has been held that the court may under the Human Rights Act 1998 modify the application of the privilege, so as to extend only to testimonial evidence, and so as to exclude "freestanding" or "self-standing" evidence, not produced under compulsion.[695] The court relied on cases where statutes cutting down the privilege have been held Human Rights Convention compliant.[696] But, with respect, that is a far cry from the court taking upon itself to cut down the privilege at common law simply because a party to civil proceedings has asked it to.

Before 1968 the rule in the UK applied to cases where there was a risk of **11.109** committal for civil contempt of court,[697] where there was a risk of penalties for pound-breach,[698] fraudulent removal of goods by a tenant[699] and indeed the statutory penalty cases referred to in Ch.6, para.6.06, above, where not only might there be no production of documents for inspection, but also no

---

[689] *Hale v Henkel,* 201 US 43 (1906); *Bellis v US,* 417 US 85 (1974); *Braswell v US,* 487 US 99 (1988).

[690] *New Zealand Apple and Pear Marketing Board v Master & Sons Ltd* [1986] 1 N.Z.L.R. 191.

[691] *Webster v Salloway* [1931] 1 D.L.R. 831. It was restricted by s.11(c) of the Canadian Charter of Rights and Freedoms: *R. v Amray Corp.* (1989) 56 D.L.R. (3d.) 309, Sup.Ct. Can.

[692] *V v C* [2001] EWCA Civ 1509, [2002] CPR 8, *sub nom. Re Versailles Trade Finance Ltd (in administrative receivership), The Times,* November 1, 2001.

[693] *Re L (Minors) (Police Investigation: Privilege)* [1995] 1 F.L.R. 999, CA; [1997] A.C. 16, HL (disclosure to police of a report obtained without compulsion and filed without objection); *cf. Oxford County Council v P.* [1995] Fam. 161, *Cleveland County Council v F* [1995] 1 W.L.R. 785, *Re G (A Minor), The Times,* November 14, 1995, CA; see also *Allan v United Kingdom* (2003) 36 E.H.R.R. 12 (use of police informant who shared accused's cell to extract confession held violation of ECHR, Art.6); *Dadourian Group International Inc. v Simms* [2006] EWCA 1745.

[694] *V v C* [2001] EWCA Civ 1509, [2002] CPR 8, *sub nom. Re Versailles Trade Finance Ltd (in administrative receivership), The Times,* November 1, 2001.

[695] *C. Plc v P (Home Secretary intervening)* [2006] 4 All E.R. 311, Ch.D.

[696] *A-G's Reference (No.7 of 2000)* [2001] 1 W.L.R. 1879, CA; *R. v Kearns* [2002] 1 W.L.R. 2815, CA; *R. v Hundal* [2004] 2 Cr.App.R. 307, CA.

[697] *Yianni v Yianni* [1966] 1 W.L.R. 120, *Re Bramblevale Ltd* [1970] Ch. 128, CA; *Comet Products UK Ltd v Hawkex Plastics Ltd* [1971] 2 Q.B. 67, CA.

[698] *Jones v Jones* (1889) 22 Q.B.D. 425.

[699] *T.W. Hobbs & Co. Ltd v Hudson* (1890) 25 Q.B.D. 233, CA.

discovery of their very existence either. As noted above,[700] however, s.14(1) of the Civil Evidence Act 1968 has now restricted the privilege to cases of criminal offences and actions to recover penalties under United Kingdom law.[701] But the privilege still applies to the risk of committal for civil contempt,[702] even in the same action,[703] on the basis that they are proceedings for the recovery of a penalty. There is authority that there is no privilege against self-incrimination for perjury committed in the same proceedings in which the privilege is sought to be asserted.[704] Despite this, it probably still applies to pound-breach and fraudulent removal of goods, and it certainly applies to cases involving fines for breaches of the anti-competition provisions of the Treaty of Rome.[705] But the rule does not cover disqualification proceedings under the Company Directors Disqualification Act 1986,[706] or claims for conversion damages under s.18 of the Copyright Act 1956,[707] or for "additional damages" under s.17(3) of that Act.[708] The remedies position is now different under the Copyright, Designs and Patents Act 1988.[709]

The degree of risk

11.110   The mere fact that the party concerned believes, even swears, that his supplying information would tend to incriminate him is not conclusive.[710]

---

[700] See para.11.105, above.

[701] As to Australia, where no statutory abrogation has taken place, see *Rich v Australian Securities and Investments Commission* (2004) 220 C.L.R. 129, H.Ct.Aus.

[702] *Cobra Golf Inc v Rata* [1998] Ch. 109; *Bhimji v Chatwani (No.2)* [1992] 1 W.L.R. 1158, declining to follow the contrary view in *Garvin v Domus Publishing Ltd* [1989] Ch. 335; cf. *Donovan v Deputy Commissioner of Taxation* (1992) 105 A.L.R. 661, Fed.Ct.Aus. (s.264 of the Income Tax Assessment Act 1936 (Cth) held to abrogate privilege against self-incrimination and to authorise action constituting contempt of court). In committal proceedings the court cannot compel a respondent to give evidence: *Comet Products UK Ltd v Hawkex Plastics Ltd* [1971] 2 Q.B. 67 at 74, CA; *Re B (Contempt of Court: Affidavit Evidence)* [1996] 1 W.L.R. 627.

[703] *Memory Corporation Plc v Sidhu* [2000] 1 All E.R. 434.

[704] *Cobra Golf Inc. v Rata* [1998] Ch. 109 at 158.

[705] *Rio Tinto Zinc Corp. v Westinghouse Electric Corp.* [1978] A.C. 547; *British Leyland Motor Corp. Ltd v T.I. Silencers Ltd* [1979] F.S.R. 591.

[706] *Re Westminster Property Management Ltd* [2000] U.K.H.R.R. 332, CA; *Rich v Australian Securities Exchange Commission* (2003) 203 A.L.R. 671, CA of N.S.W.

[707] *Richmark Camera Services Inc. v Neilson-Hordell Ltd* [1981] F.S.R. 413. Damages for infringement are now covered by ss.96–97 of the Copyright, Designs and Patents Act 1988.

[708] *Overseas Programming Co. Ltd v Cinematographische Comets-Anstalt, Induna Film GmbH, The Times,* May 16, 1984. Section 17(3) of the 1956 Act is now replaced by s.97 of the 1988 Act.

[709] See *Lagenes Ltd v It's At (UK) Ltd* [1991] F.S.R. 492.

[710] *Triplex Safety Glass Co. Ltd v Lancegaye Safety Glass (1934) Ltd* [1939] 2 K.B. 395 at 403, CA.

Instead, what matters is that the risk should be apparent to the court.[711] Whilst it is not for the court to try to assess the probability of the risk of proceedings being taken,[712] the court must be satisfied that "there is reasonable ground to apprehend danger" to the party claiming privilege,[713] or that the risk is "reasonably likely"[714] or that "there must be grounds to apprehend danger to the witness, and those grounds must be reasonable, rather than fanciful,"[715] or that there is a "real and appreciable" risk of prosecution if the documents are produced for inspection.[716] A "mere possibility" of grounds for charge being disclosed is insufficient.[717]

The privilege can be invoked, not merely in relation to actually incriminating evidence, but also to "steps in the chain", i.e. evidence which, though not itself incriminating, may or does lead to such evidence,[718] and even where there is already a considerable amount of evidence tending to incriminate the party,[719] including an admission in a signed statement by the defendant of having admitted the crime.[720] The privilege will apply where production of documents and information might render a party liable to additional charges in respect of past acts of infringement.[721] Where a disclosure order has been made against a person who is subsequently involved in criminal proceedings (e.g. by being arrested and charged), the court may discharge the order if to give the discovery would incriminate him.[722]

11.111

---

[711] *Lamb v Munster* (1882) 10 Q.B.D. 110. See also *Tarasov v Nassif*, unreported, February 11, 1994, CA (objection overridden on basis that no evidence that the defendant had conspired with third party to defraud plaintiff).

[712] *Rio Tinto Zinc Corp. v Westinghouse Electric Corp.* [1978] A.C. 547 at 579.

[713] *R. v Boyes* (1861) 1 B. & S.311 at 330; *ex p.Reynolds, re Reynolds* (1882) 20 Ch.D. 294 at 299; *Triplex Safety Glass Co. Ltd v Lancegaye Safety Glass (1934) Ltd* [1939] 2 K.B. 395 at 404; *Accident Insurance Mutual Holdings v McFadden* (1993) 31 N.S.W.L.R. 412 at 424, CA of N.S.W.

[714] *Blunt v Park Lane Hotel Ltd* [1942] 2 K.B. 253 at 257; but see *Rio Tinto Zinc* [1978] A.C. 547 at 574, 579, 581.

[715] *Sociedade Nacional de Combustiveis de Angola VEE v Lundquist* [1991] 2 Q.B. 310 at 324, where the cases are reviewed.

[716] *Re New World Alliance Pty Ltd* (1993) 118 A.L.R. 699, Fed.Ct.Aus.; *Microsoft Corporation v CX Computer Pty Ltd* (2002) 187 A.L.R. 362, Fed.Ct.Aus; *Compagnie Noga d'Importation et d'Exportation S.A. v Australia and New Zealand Banking Group Ltd* [2007] EWHC 85 (Comm.).

[717] *Tarasov v Nassif*, unreported, February 11, 1994, CA.

[718] *Re Genese* (1885) 34 W.R. 79; *Rio Tinto Zinc Corp. v Westinghouse Electric Corp.* [1978] A.C. 547, at 612; *Rank Film Distributors Ltd v Video Information Centre* [1982] A.C. 380 at 443; *Sorby v Commonwealth* (1983) 152 C.L.R. 281, at 312, H.Ct.Aus.; *Reid v Howard* (1995) 184 C.L.R. 1, H.Ct.Aus.; *Griffin v Sogalease Australia Ltd* (2003) 57 N.S.W.L.R. 257, CA of N.S.W.; *Australian Securities and Investments Commission v Michalik* (2004) 211 A.L.R.. 285, N.S.W. Sup.Ct.

[719] *Tate Access Floors Ltd v Boswell* [1991] Ch. 512 at 529; *cf. Brebner v Perry* [1961] S.A.S.R. 177; *Sociedade Nacional de Combustiveis de Angola VEE v Lundquist* [1991] 2 Q.B. 310, at 323–325.

[720] *Accident Insurance Mutual Holdings Ltd v McFadden* (1993) 31 N.S.W.L.R. 412, CA of N.S.W.; *Den Norske Bank A.S.A. v Antonatos* [1999] Q.B. 271 at 289, CA.

[721] *Expanded Metal Manufacturing Pte Ltd v Expanded Metal Co. Ltd* [1995] 1 S.L.R. 673, Singapore CA.

[722] *John Cochrane & Sons v Shipton, The Times*, October 5, 1966.

Other requirements

11.112 It used to be considered that it was a requirement that the claim to the
privilege must be put forward in good faith; if it is not, there was authority
that it could not be insisted on.[723] The requirement of good faith has now
been rejected on the basis that the issue is not the subjective fears of the
witness or party, but the objective tendency of the disclosure to expose the
person to criminal prosecution.[724] Moreover, it is a privilege only for the
benefit of the party concerned (and, since 1968, his/her spouse). It therefore
does not apply for the benefit of co-defendants,[725] a journalist's source,[726]
or the corporate creatures of the party concerned.[727] However, it is inappropriate to order the person who might be incriminated to give the documents to another party who is then ordered to give discovery.[728] More
problematic is the case of employees of a corporate body entitled to claim
the privilege. The issue arises as to whether the privilege can be put at
naught by asking the employees to give evidence.[729] The matter was raised,
but left open, in *Rio Tinto Zinc Corporation v Westinghouse Electric
Corporation*,[730] but three of their Lordships commented, not unfavourably,
on the claim to privilege in such circumstances.[731] The claim is supported by
text-writers[732] and authorities from other common law systems,[733] and it is
submitted that it is correct. Just as the employees are the agents for *knowing*
the information, and thus not true third parties,[734] so too they should be
their employer's agents for the purpose of claiming privilege. However, if the
relevant documents are in the hands of a genuine third party (e.g. the police)
who are otherwise bound to produce them (e.g. by witness summons), the

[723] *ex p. Reynolds, re Reynolds* (1882) 20 Ch.D. 294 at 300; *R. v Armagh* (1883) 18 Ir.L.T. 2;
Société Immobilière St Honoré Monceau v Financial General Trust Ltd, unreported, cited
[1939] 2 K.B. 395 at 406, CA; *British Steel Corp. v Granada Television Ltd* [1981] A.C.
1096 at 1106.
[724] *Accident Insurance Mutual Holdings v McFadden* (1993) 31 N.S.W.L.R. 412 at 424–5, CA
of N.S.W., *per* Kirby P.; *Den Norske Bank A.S.A. v Antonatos* [1999] Q.B. 271 at 289,
CA.
[725] *Kelly v Colhoun* [1899] 2 I.R. 199; *Microsoft Corporation v CX Computer Pty Ltd* (2002)
187 A.L.R. 362, Fed.Ct.Aus.
[726] *British Streel Corp. v Granada Television Ltd* [1981] A.C. 1096.
[727] *Tate Access Floors Ltd v Boswell* [1991] Ch. 512 at 530–532.
[728] *Griffin v Sogalease Australia Ltd* (2003) 57 N.S.W.L.R. 257, CA of N.S.W.
[729] *Cf. Three Rivers District Council v Bank of England (No.5)* [2003] Q.B. 1556, CA,
discussed above at paras 11.16–11.17.
[730] [1978] A.C. 547, HL.
[731] At pp.617, 632, 652; see also *Garvin v Domus Publishing Ltd* [1989] Ch. 335 at 342–343,
and *Sociedade Nacional de Combustiveis de Angola V.E.E v Lundquist* [1991] 2 Q.B. 310,
CA.
[732] *Phipson on Evidence* (16th edn, 2005), para.24–50; Hollander, *Documentary Evidence,*
9th edn 2006, para.17–16.
[733] See *Upjohn & Co. v United States,* 449 US 383 (1981), US.Sup.Ct.; *R. v Nova Scotia
Pharmaceutical Society* (1990) 73 D.L.R. (4th) 184; *Environment Protection Agency v
Caltex refining Co. Pty Ltd* (1993) 178 C.L.R. 477, H.Ct.Aus.
[734] See Ch.4, para.4.20, above.

original party can no longer claim the privilege in respect of such documents.[735]

Exceptions to the privilege[736]

There are a number of statutory exceptions to the privilege against self-incrimination. These fall into two categories. One takes away the privilege and puts nothing in its place.[737] The other removes it in exchange for protection against criminal prosecution. Thus self-incriminating answers obtained as a result of exceptions in the first category may thereafter be used without limit, as whatever is not validly prohibited is inferentially permitted.[738] In that first category are provisions concerning insolvency, both personal and corporate, banking and taxation. For example, in a public examination under s.290 of the Insolvency Act 1986 (replacing earlier legislation), the bankrupt in answering questions has no privilege against self-incrimination.[739] Under s.291(1) of that Act, a bankrupt must deliver up all relevant documents to the official receiver without regard to privilege.[740] In the corporate context, it has been held that the privilege against self-incrimination is no answer to an otherwise proper demand to a corporate officer under ss.235 and 236 of the Insolvency Act 1986,[741] even after the officer concerned has been charged with a criminal offence.[742] Again, a person cannot rely on the privilege to refuse to answer questions put to him by inspectors appointed by the Secretary of State under s.432 of the Companies Act 1985[743] and his answers are admissible evidence against him in subsequent criminal proceedings.[744] After the European Court of Human

11.113

---

[735] *Marcel v Metropolitan Police Commissioner* [1992] Ch. 225, CA.

[736] See, generally, Heydon [1971] Crim.L.R. 13; 87 L.Q.R. 214; *R. v Hertfordshire County Council, ex p. Green Environmental Industries Ltd* [2002] 2 A.C. 412, HL.

[737] Though the Human Rights Act 1998 may in rare cases now do so: *cf. Brown v Stott (Procurator Fiscal)* [2003] 1 A.C. 681, P.C. (where however the claim to protection failed).

[738] *Hong Kong Special Administrative Region v Lee Ming Tee* [2001] 4 H.K.C.F.A.R. 133, Ct.Final App. of H.K.

[739] *Re Atherton* [1912] 2 K.B. 251; *Re Jawett* [1929] 1 Ch. 108; however, the examination may be postponed until after any criminal proceedings have taken place: *Re Butterfield* (1890) 7 Morr. 293. See also *R. v Kansal (No.2)* [2002] 2 A.C. 69, HL, leading (ultimately) to *Kansal v United Kingdom* (2004) 39 E.H.R.R. 31, E.Ct.H.R. (use at criminal trial of answers given under compulsion at examination by Official Receiver breached Art.6 of the Convention).

[740] In Australia, however, *cf. Griffin v Pantzer* (2004) 207 A.L.R. 169, Fed.Ct.Aus.

[741] *Re Jeffrey S. Levitt Ltd* [1992] Ch. 457; *Re A.E. Farr Ltd* [1992] B.C.L.C. 333; *Bishopsgate Investment Management Ltd v Maxwell* [1993] Ch.1, CA; Re Arrows Ltd (No.4) [1995] 2 A.C. 75, HL; see Ch.3, paras 3.40–3.44, above.

[742] *Re Arrows Ltd* [1992] B.C.L.C. 1176.

[743] *Re London United Investments Ltd* [1992] Ch. 578, CA.

[744] *R. v Seelig* [1992] 1 W.L.R. 148 (dealing with s.434); *R. v Lyons* [2003] 1 A.C. 976, HL; *cf. McClelland, Pope & Langley v Howard* [1968] 1 All E.R. 569 (Note), as to the position under earlier legislation. The trial judge may exclude the evidence in the exercise of his discretion, see para.11.106 below.

Rights gave its decision in *Saunders v United Kingdom*,[745] Parliament amended s.434(5) of the Companies Act 1985 so that evidence obtained by DTI inspectors may not be used in prosecutions for certain offences.[746] But this did not make unsafe convictions under the previous law.[747] On the other hand, s.354(3)(a) of the Companies Act 1985 (as amended) does not infringe Art.6.[748]

11.114   A similar situation arises in s.2 of the Criminal Justice Act 1987 and it has been held that the Serious Fraud Office's investigatory and inquisitorial powers override the privilege, again even after the time that the person concerned is charged with an offence.[749] However s.2(8) provides a limited form of protection in that a statement under s.2 may only be used against the maker in proceedings for making a false or misleading statement or in proceedings for some other offence where in giving evidence he makes an inconsistent statement.[750] Section 9 of the Police and Criminal Evidence Act 1984 by necessary implication includes the power for the Crown Court to make production orders which actually or potentially infringe a person's right against self-incrimination.[751] So far as banking is concerned, the Banking Act 1987, s.42, excludes the privilege in relation to interrogatories or the production of documents in proceedings under that Act.[752] As to taxation, this has been dealt with above.[753]

11.115   The second category of exception provides in addition for a measure of protection. There are statutory powers to compel the disclosure of printers, publishers and proprietors of newspapers containing libels,[754] which powers override the privilege, though the information given may only be used in the proceedings in which it was obtained. Protection is often conferred by an Act specifically against criminal prosecution for offences under that Act. Examples include the Land Registration Act 1925, s.119(2), the Theft Act 1968, s.31(1), and the Criminal Damage Act 1971, s.9.[755] The difficulty with this approach is that, where the privilege is removed, it is removed for

---

[745] (1996) 23 E.H.R.R. 313.

[746] Similar provisions in other statutes have also been amended to the same effect: s.59 and sch.3 of the Youth and Criminal Justice Act 1999.

[747] *R. v Lyons* [2003] 1 A.C. 976, HL.

[748] *R. v Kearns* [2002] EWCA Crim 748, *The Times*, April 4, 2002, CA.

[749] *R. v Director of the Serious Fraud Office, exp. Smith* [1993] A.C. 1, HL; *Re Bishopsgate Management Ltd, The Times*, April 27, 1993, CA; *A v Boulton* (2004) 204 A.L.R. 598, Fed.Ct.Aus.

[750] In practice statements under s.2 are not used in evidence save for proceedings against the maker for making a false or misleading statement: see para.11.119, below.

[751] *R. v (Bright) v Central Criminal Court* [2001] 1 W.L.R. 662, Div.Ct.

[752] *Bank of England v Riley* [1992] Ch. 475

[753] See para.11.113; *cf. R. v Harz and Power* [1967] 1 A.C. 760, HL; see also *Donovan v D.C.T.* (1992) 105 A.L.R. 661.

[754] See the Stamp Duties on Newspapers Act 1836, Newspapers Printers and Reading Rooms Repeal Act 1869, and the Inland Revenue Repeal Act 1870.

[755] In Australia, see *Controlled Consultants Proprietary Ltd v Commissioner for Corporate Affairs* (1984) 156 C.L.R. 385, H.Ct.Aus.

all purposes,[756] but in many cases the protection conferred is only in relation to offences under the particular Act. Thus where the evidence (in respect of which privilege has gone) proves an offence at common law or under a different statute, there is no restriction on its use for prosecuting that other offence.[757] On this basis the privilege may be asserted if there is a real threat of criminal proceedings for an offence other than one provided by the particular Act. The privilege does not apply, for example, where there is only a remote threat of criminal proceedings on a charge other than that covered by s.31 of the Theft Act 1968.[758]

A similar, but not identical, approach is taken by the Supreme Court Act 1981, s.72. This was enacted after the decision of the House of Lords in *Rank Film Distributors Ltd v Video Information Centre*,[759] to the effect that the discovery parts of an *Anton Piller* order[760] could not be included if they infringed (as they did there) the privilege against self-incrimination. *Rank* was an intellectual property case, and, it being considered that the bulk of *Anton Piller* orders were made in such cases, an ad hoc solution was found in enacting s.72.[761] Although based on s.31 of the 1968 Act, s.72 is both wider and narrower than that provision. It is narrower because it relates only to intellectual property proceedings (including passing off). It is wider because, in relation to proceedings to prevent future torts, it applies to any offence of any nature revealed by the facts on which the claimant relies, and is not restricted (as it is in proceedings in respect of present or past torts) merely to offences committed by or in the course of the infringement or passing off concerned or to offences of fraud or dishonestly committed in connection with that infringement or passing off.[762] In addition, the section is not restricted to cases where criminal proceedings have not yet been commenced, but includes cases where they are already on foot.[763] Finally, it should be noted that the House of Lords has held that a defendant is sufficiently protected against self-incrimination if the Crown Prosecution Service (although not a party) agree to a condition in a discovery order

11.116

---

[756] *Hong Kong Special Administrative Region v Lee Ming Tee* [2001] 4 H.K.C.F.A.R. 133, Ct.Final App. of H.K.

[757] *Khan v Khan* [1982] 1 W.L.R. 513, CA; see now, under the Human Rights Act 1998, *Brown v Stott (Procurator Fiscal)* [2003] 1 A.C. 681, P.C.

[758] *Renworth v Stephansen* [1996] 3 All E.R. 244, CA.

[759] [1982] A.C. 380.

[760] See Ch.2, para.2.24, above.

[761] *Crest Homes Plc v Marks* [1987] A.C. 829, HL; *Cobra Golf Inc. v Rata* [1998] Ch. 109; *Coca-Cola v Gilbey* [1995] 4 All E.R. 711; in Australia, no equivalent to s.72 has been enacted: *BPA Industries Ltd v Black* (1987) 11 N.S.W.L.R. 609, N.S.W. Sup.Ct.; *Pathways Employment Services v West* (2004) 212 A.L.R. 140, N.S.W.Sup.Ct. For the problems that have arisen in non-intellectual property cases, see Ch.2, paras 2.23–2.28, above.

[762] *Universal City Studios Inc. v Hubbard* [1984] Ch. 225, CA.

[763] *Charles of the Ritz Group Ltd v Jory* [1986] F.S.R. 14. Similar examples are contained in the Children Act 1989, ss.48(2) and 98, rendering statements inadmissible in proceedings for "an offence other than perjury".

preventing the information compulsory obtained thereby from being used in a criminal prosecution against him.[764]

11.117   There are some provisions which override the privilege against self-incrimination, but which specifically provide that the information provided shall not be admissible in evidence in proceedings for any offence other than perjury. Examples of such a provision are contained in the Children Act 1989.[765] In New South Wales and in some other Australian states, statute provides that a witness who chooses to give evidence covered by the privilege is usually protected from that evidence being given in other New South Wales proceedings.[766]

11.118   The privilege against self-incrimination is not absolute, and is not expressly guaranteed by Art.6 of the European Convention on Human Rights.[767] However, the right to silence and the right not to incriminate oneself are generally recognised international standards which lie at the heart of the nation of a fair procedure under Art.6.[768] Accordingly, such a right must be implied.[769] But Art.6 is concerned with the fairness of a judicial trial where there is an "adjudication". It is not concerned with extra-judicial enquiries as such.[770] A distinction is to be drawn between the compulsory production of documents or other material which had an existence independent of the will of the suspect (where there will be no infringement of Art.6) and statements he has had to make under compulsion (where they may be).[771]

11.119   Because the deployment in criminal proceedings of evidence obtained by compulsory process from a defendant may contravene Art.6 of the European Convention on Human Rights,[772] the Attorney-General's guidance to prosecutors is that such material should not be used as part of the

---

[764] *A.T. & T. Istel Ltd v Tully* [1993] A.C. 45, HL; *cf. Reid v Howard* (1995) 184 C.L.R. 1, H.Ct. of Aus.; see Ch.2, paras 2.25–2.26.

[765] s.48(1)–(2), order requiring a person to disclose whereabouts of a child by a court making an emergency protection order; s.50(3)(c) and (11), similar provision in context of a recovery order; s.98, proceedings under Pts IV and v See also *Re L (A Minor)* [1997] A.C. 16, HL.

[766] Evidence Act 1995 (N.S.W), s.128; *Pathways Employment Services v West* (2004) 212 A.L.R. 140, N.S.W.Sup.Ct.

[767] *R. v Central Criminal Court, ex parte Bright* [2001] 1 W.L.R. 662, Div.Ct.; *R. v Kearns* [2002] 1 W.L.R. 2815, CA.

[768] *Murray v United Kingdom* (1996) 22 E.H.R.R. 29 at 60–61; *Saunders v United Kingdom* (1996) 23 E.H.R.R. 313 at 337–340; see also *Allen v United Kingdom, The Times,* November 12, 2002, E.Ct.H.R.

[769] *R. v Kearns* [2002] 1 W.L.R. 2815, CA; *Brown v Stott (Procurator Fiscal, Dunfermline)* [2003] 1 A.C. 681, P.C.

[770] *R. v Kearns* [2002] 1 W.L.R. 2815, CA; *R. v Hertfordshire County Council ex p. Green Environmental Industries Ltd* [2002] 2 A.C. 412, HL.

[771] *Attorney General's Reference (No.7 of 2000)* [2001] 1 W.L.R. 1879, CA (no infringement of art.6 in using documents delivered by bankrupt under compulsion pursuant to s.291 of the Insolvency Act 1986); *R. v Kearns* [2002] 1 W.L.R. 2815, CA; see also *C. Plc v P (Home Secretary intervening)* [2006] 4 All E.R. 311, Ch.D.

[772] *Saunders v UK* (1996) 23 E.H.R.R. 313, [1998] 1 B.C.L.C. 362, ECHR; *cf. R. v Staines and Morrisey* [1997] 2 Cr.App.R. 426, CA In criminal proceedings court may exercise its discretion under s.78 of PACE to exclude evidence obtained under compulsion; *cf. R. v*

prosecution evidence or for the purpose of cross-examination.[773] This policy does not preclude the use of compulsorily acquired answers in a prosecution for failing or refusing to answer, or an omission to disclose a material fact which ought to be disclosed, or giving an untruthful answer. But the statute requiring an answer may be "read down" under the Human Rights Act 1998 so as to exclude the admissibility of that answer in subsequent proceedings.[774]

Although in the course of an investigation or proceedings a person may **11.120** specifically waive the privilege, the Court of Appeal has left open the question whether the law will permit or give effect to a contract whereby a contracting party agrees not to rely on the privilege against the other in relation to dealings covered by the contract.[775] It may well be that the courts will be wary of allowing such a derogation from the privilege, if they do then there will no doubt grow up a practice of excluding the privilege in employment contracts. In the context of the membership of the Institute of Chartered Accountants the court has been willing to give effect to a provision in the rules binding as a condition of membership which overrides the privilege in the context of an investigation into a complaint by the Investigation Committee.[776] The proposition that any person who agrees to act as a fiduciary impliedly contracts not to raise any claim to the privilege against self-incrimination has been rejected.[777] The Court of Appeal has also rejected the contention that the privilege is not available to a defendant if, immediately before the relevant time, the defendant was a fiduciary, servant or agent of the plaintiffs in the action and the plaintiff by the action are seeking to recover from the defendant monies or property of the plaintiffs, or an account of or information about, such monies or property, for which the defendant as such fiduciary, servant or agent is accountable to the plaintiff in equity.[778] Similarly, a trustee or other fiduciary may invoke the

---

Hertfordshire County Council ex p. Green Environmental Industries Ltd [2002] 2 A.C. 412, HL.

[773] Guidance issued on February 3, 1998: 148 N.L.J. 208; Hansard, H.C., Vol.305, cols. 639–640; see also R. v Secretary of State for Trade and Industry, ex p. McCormick [1998] B.C.C. 379, CA (held entitled to use compulsorily obtained evidence in director's disqualification proceedings).

[774] cf. Brown v Stott (Procurator Fiscal, Dunfermline) [2003] 1 A.C. 681, P.C. (use of admission under Road Traffic Act 1988, s.172(2)(a) not incompatible with Art.6); D.P.P. v Wilson [2002] R.T.R. 37, Div. Ct. (similarly under s.172(2)(b)).

[775] Bishopsgate Investment Ltd v Maxwell [1993] Ch.1, CA.

[776] R. v Institute of Chartered Accountants of England and Wales, ex p. Taher Nawaz, [1997] P.N.L.R. 433, Q.B.D.; affd. CA, April 25, 1997 (unreported). Under para.8(a) of Sch.2 of the Institute's bye laws the Investigation Committee has the power to call for and it is the duty of every member to provide, such information as the Committee may consider necessary to enable it to discharge its functions.

[777] Tate Access Floors Inc. v Boswell [1991] Ch. 512 at 518.

[778] Bishopsgate Investment Management Ltd v Maxwell [1993] Ch. 1, CA.

privilege in answer to disclosure in civil proceedings brought by a beneficiary.[779]

I. "WITHOUT PREJUDICE" PRIVILEGE[780]

11.121   Most forms of privilege depend on the fact that certain information is
known to one side in litigation but not to the other. But "without prejudice"
privilege is different, in that it largely concerns information known to
opposing parties. It is also unusual in that the "privilege" in the law of
disclosure is based on a separate rule of the law of evidence governing
admissibility, notwithstanding that, as has been seen,[781] admissibility and
disclosability are concepts generally independent of each other. Not all that
is admissible is disclosable; not all that is disclosable is admissible.

Rule of evidence

11.122   The basic rule of evidence is that evidence to prove admissions made by
a party in the course of genuine negotiations to settle actual or contemplated
litigation is inadmissible in the same or any subsequent litigation connected
with the same subject matter,[782] whether a settlement is reached in those
negotiations or not, and whether with the party to whom the admissions
were made or not.[783] The rationale of this rule is:

> " . . . that parties should be encouraged so far as possible to settle their
> disputes without resort to litigation and should not be discouraged by
> the knowledge that anything that is said in the course of such negotia-
> tions (and that includes, of course, as much the failure to reply to an

---

[779] *Reid v Howard* (1993) 31 N.S.W.L.R. 298 at 303–4, CA of N.S.W; (1995) 184 C.L.R. 1,
H.Ct.Aus.
[780] See generally, Thanki (ed.), *The Law of Privilege*, 2006, Ch.7; Passmore, *Privilege*, 2nd edn,
2006, Ch.10.
[781] See Ch.5, para.5.14, above.
[782] *Instance v Denny Bros. Printing Ltd* [2000] F.S.R. 869, Ch.D. (rule not limited to things
relevant to original dispute).
[783] *Rush & Tompkins Ltd v Greater London Council* [1989] 1 A.C. 1280, HL; *Alizadeh v
Nikbin*, The Times, March 19, 1992, CA; *UYB Ltd v British Railways Board* [2000] 43
L.S.G. 602, *The Times*, November 15, 2000, CA (draft report submitted in without
prejudice negotiations not admissible at stage when court, having ruled on liability, was
considering question of interest); the position is not quite the same in considering the
privilege itself: see para.11.124, below.

offer as an actual reply) may be used to their prejudice in the course of the proceedings . . . "[784]

This may be referred to as the "public policy" basis. It is normally the only explanation for cases where the seeker and the holder of "without prejudice" documents were not the parties to the negotiations or settlement agreement concerned (sometimes called "three-party" cases). There is an alternative juridical basis for the rule in so-called "two-party" cases, where the seeker and the holder *were* the parties to the negotiations or settlement agreement. This is (express or) implied agreement that the communication should not be admitted in evidence (or, at any rate, disclosed) by either party.[785] Of course, an express agreement may extend to communications which would or might not otherwise be within the scope of the privilege.[786]

As will be seen below, the "without prejudice" rule is not unlimited. For **11.123** example, it does not apply to exclude evidence of admissions where improper threats are made.[787] Moreover, the without prejudice rule is generally expressed as one concerning the admissibility of material *in court*. It is clear that sometimes material subject to the privilege may still be disclosed to another person under relevant disclosure rules.[788] But it is an open question whether it extends beyond that, so as to preclude an administrative decision maker taking into account admissions that may be made in the course of without prejudice negotiations.[789] In Australia the evidential rule is now governed by statute.[790]

Impact on disclosure

There is no *a priori* reason why the rule of evidence should also be the rule **11.124** relating to disclosure.[791] Or, indeed, vice versa.[792] So the question arises as

---

[784] *Cutts v Head* [1984] Ch. 290 at 306; see also *Rush & Tompkins*, above, at 1291; *Prudential Insurance Co. of America v Prudential Assurance Co. Ltd* [2003] EWCA Civ 1154, [2004] E.T.M.R. 29, CA; *Bradford & Bingley Plc v Rashid* [2006] 1 W.L.R. 2066, HL. As to whether a judge should recuse himself on the grounds that he had seen without prejudice correspondence, see *Berg v IML London Ltd* [2002] 1 W.L.R. 3271, Stanley Burnton J..
[785] *Rabin v Mendoza & Co.* [1954] 1 W.L.R. 271, CA; see also *Schwartz (Litigation Guardian of) v Schwartz Estate* (2000) 189 D.L.R. (4th) 79, Nova Scotia CA.
[786] *Compagnie Noga D'Importation et D'Exportation SA v Australia & New Zealand Banking Group Ltd*, unreported, December 10, 1999, CA.
[787] See para.11.129, below.
[788] See para.11.125, below.
[789] *cf. White v Overland* [2001] F.C.A. 1835; *Brown v Commissioner of Taxation* [2002] F.C.A. 318, Fed.Ct.Aus.
[790] Evidence Act 1995 (Cwlth.); see, e.g. *Seven Network Ltd v News Ltd* [2006] F.C.A. 343, Fed.Ct.Aus.
[791] *B.C. Children's Hospital v Air Products Canada* (2003) 224 D.L.R. (4th) 47, CA of B.C.
[792] *Smiths Group Plc v Weiss*, March 22, 2002 (Ch.D. unreported).

to how this rule of evidence impacts upon the law of disclosure. Where two parties are in litigation, admissions in negotiations between them to settle that litigation may be inadmissible, but they are known to both parties, and no disclosure question is likely to arise,[793] although even as between the parties to without prejudice correspondence they are not entitled to disclosure (in the sense of being required to make them available for production) as against each other.[794] But if the litigation has three or more parties, negotiations between two or more may not be known to the rest, and the rules of disclosure, not admissibility, will govern their access to the communications in question. Until *Rush & Tompkins Ltd v Greater London Council*,[795] admissibility and discoverability in this part of the law were often confused,[796] and, although it was thought that "negotiations" communications were not to be disclosed to third parties if no settlement resulted, it was far from clear what was the position if a settlement did result. In *Rush v Tompkins*, the House of Lords made clear the essential difference between admissibility and discoverability, but went on to hold (for the first time expressly in English law) that, where communications were inadmissible on the basis of the rule of evidence above described, they were also protected "from production to other parties in the same litigation."[797] It appears that, as with other kinds of privilege, the rule is "once privileged, always privileged"[798] and the privilege endures even after the litigation is over.[799] Similarly, there is no privilege in "without prejudice" communications made in furtherance of crime or fraud.[800]

11.125   There are exceptional cases where without prejudice communications may be liable to be produced on disclosure to a person who was not party to the communications, as pointed out by Hoffmann L.J.:

> "Although in general, as *Rush & Tomkins* shows, without prejudice communications will not be liable to be produced on discovery at the instance of a third party, there may well be cases in which the document

---

[793] Although see *Rabin v Mendoza & Co. (ibid.)* and *Somatra Ltd v Sinclair Roche* [2000] 1 Lloyd's Rep. 311 (revsd. CA, [2000] 1 W.L.R. 2453) for examples of cases where it did. See also *R. v First Lord of the Treasury, ex p. Petch*, unreported, January 31, 1994, Harrison J.; *Sampson v John Boddy Timber Ltd* (1995) 145 N.L.J. 851, CA; *Smiths Group Plc v Weiss*, March 22, 2002 (Ch.D unreported), (inclusion of without prejudice communications between the parties in a disclosure list did not make them admissible).

[794] *Rush & Tompkins Ltd v G.L.C.* [1989] 1 A.C. 1280 at 1304A.

[795] [1989] 1 A.C. 1280, HL.

[796] See *The Supreme Court Practice 1989*, para.24/5/45, and *Chocoladefabriken Lindt & Sprunghi A.G. v Nestlé Co. Ltd* [1978] R.P.C. 287.

[797] [1989] 1 A.C. 1280 at 1305; followed in Canada: *Middlekamp v Fraser Valley Real Estate Board* (1992) 96 D.L.R. (4th) 227, CA of B.C. (not following *Derco Industries Ltd v A.R. Grimwood Ltd* (1984) 47 C.P.C. 82); *Bailey v Beagle Management Pty Ltd* (2001) 182 A.L.R. 264, Fed.Ct.Aus.

[798] *cf.* para.11.06, above.

[799] *Rush & Tompkins* [1989] 1 A.C. 1280 at 1301, 1304; *I. Waxman & Sons Ltd v Texaco Canada Ltd* [1968] 2 O.R. 452, Ont. CA.

[800] *Hawick International Jersey Ltd v Caplan, The Times*, March 11, 1988.

is relevant within the terms of the discovery rules, for purposes which do not necessarily involve its admissibility in evidence."[801]

The Court of Appeal has held that a series of "without prejudice" communications between the plaintiff and a third party, on a compromised action brought against the third party to mitigate the plaintiff's loss caused by the defendant's alleged negligence, was not protected from production because it went to the reasonableness of the compromise (which was in issue) rather than to its admissibility to establish the truth of the statements in it.[802]

It will be noted that the privilege is stated by the House of Lords to be one **11.126** against production rather than one against disclosure. *Rush & Tompkins* was the case of an application by the second defendants for production of documents listed in Sch.1, Pt II of the plaintiffs' List of Documents, "being correspondence between the plaintiffs and the first defendant brought into existence for the purpose of reaching settlement with the first defendant, which preceded and culminated in the compromise agreement made between those parties."[803] This is consistent with the other privileges, such as legal privilege, self-incrimination and public interest immunity,[804] and also with previous authority,[805] and indeed subsequent cases.[806] Accordingly, where communications are protected by this privilege, their existence must be disclosed in the parties' Lists of Documents.[807]

Extent of the evidential rule

Although the phrase "without prejudice" is often used at the head of **11.127** communications intended to attract the benefit of the rule of evidence governing admissibility, it is important to note that the use of this, or any

---

[801] *Forster v Friedland*, unreported, November 10, 1992, CA; but see *Bradford & Bingley Plc v Rashid* [2006] 1 W.L.R. 2066, HL, where Lord Hoffmann's approach to the privilege was a minority view.

[802] *Muller v Linsley and Mortimer* [1996] 1 P.N.L.R. 74, CA, applied in *Dora v Simper, The Times*, May 26, 1999; *Murrell v Healy* [2001] 4 All E.R. 345, CA (without prejudice material from insurers file in relation to an earlier accident admissible in subsequent proceedings).; *Unilever Plc v Procter & Gamble* [2000] 1 W.L.R. 2436, CA; see also *Gnitrow Ltd v Cape Plc* [2000] 3 All E.R. 763, CA (claimant's agreement with third party not privileged as against defendant, who needed disclosure in order to make realistic Pt 36 offer). It was (wrongly) conceded in similar cases that the privilege applied to prevent production in *DSL Group Ltd v Unisys International Services Ltd* (1994) 67 B.L.R. 117 and *Lloyd's v Kitsons Environmental Services Ltd* (1994) 64 B.L.R. 102.

[803] [1989] 1 A.C. 1280 at 1282.

[804] See Ch.8, para.8.26, above.

[805] *Rabin v Mendoza & Co.* [1954] 1 W.L.R. 271, CA.

[806] *Parry v News Group Newspapers Ltd* (1999) 140 New L.J. 1719, CA.

[807] See Ch.8, para.8.12, above.

similar, phrase does not of itself confer such benefit,[808] and neither is it necessary for the purpose.[809] If the status of the communication is challenged, the court must examine it to establish its real status.[810] Where negotiations have been carried on "without prejudice", the burden will be on a party seeking to show that the basis of communication has changed to an "open" one.[811] The evidential rule renders inadmissible admissions in the course of negotiations to settle disputes. The test is objective, in the context of the factual matrix.[812] If there is as yet no dispute, the rule cannot apply,[813] nor does it apply to a letter merely asserting rights or arguing a party's case.[814] However, it can apply to a letter reinitiating or offering negotiations in relation to an existing dispute.[815] But the document does not have to be "unequivocally" a negotiating document.[816] The rule is not limited to negotiations aimed at resolving legal issues between the parties.[817]

11.128   Whilst the rule applies to a letter written in reply to a letter written "without prejudice" or which is part of a continuing sequence of negotiations, it does not apply to a letter written as an open letter[818] and not part of continuing without prejudice negotiations.[819] Thus it seems that the privilege cannot apply to materials prepared before any dispute arises, as for example a paper prepared for a corporate tenant's or landlord's board by the company's surveyor in relation to a forthcoming rent review which has not yet been the subject of negotiations between the parties. On the other hand, if a written agreement results from a dispute, the rule applies to the preceding negotiations, but does not (it would seem) apply to the settlement agreement itself, since this is not a "without prejudice" communication.

---

[808] *Buckinghamshire County Council v Moran* [1990] Ch. 623, CA; *B.N.P. Paribas v Mezzotoro* [2004] I.R.L.R. 508, E.A.T. (meeting stated to be "without prejudice" not aimed at compromise, and therefore contents admissible).

[809] *Rush & Tompkins* [1989] 1 A.C. 1280 at 1299; *Sampson v John Boddy Timber Ltd* (1995) 145 N.L.J. 851, CA; *Pearson Education Ltd v Prentice Hall India Pte Ltd* [2006] F.S.R. 111, Q.B.D.; *cf. Cheddar Valley Engineering Ltd v Chaddlewood Homes Ltd* [1992] 1 W.L.R. 820.

[810] *South Shropshire District Council v Amos* [1986] 1 W.L.R 1271, CA; *B.N.P. Paribas v Mezzotoro* [2004] I.R.L.R. 508, E.A.T.; though see *Prudential Insurance Co. of America v Prudential Assurance Co. Ltd* [2003] EWCA Civ 1154, [2004] E.T.M.R. 29, CA; *Bolt v Basildon & Thurrock N.H.S. Trust* [2004] EWHC 738 (Q.B.).

[811] *Cheddar Valley Engineering Ltd v Chaddlewood Homes Ltd* [1992] 1 W.L.R. 820.

[812] *Pearson Education Ltd v Prentice Hall India Pte Ltd* [2006] F.S.R. 111, Q.B.D.

[813] *Standrin v Yenton Minister Homes Ltd, The Times,* July 22, 1991, CA (letters asserting insurance claim).

[814] *Buckinghamshire County Council v Moran* [1990] Ch. 623.

[815] *South Shropshire District Council v Amos* [1986] 1 W.L.R. 1271; *Schering Corporation v Cipla Ltd, The Times,* December 2, 2004, Ch.D; *Pearson Education Ltd v Prentice Hall India Pte Ltd* [2006] F.S.R. 111, Q.B.D.

[816] *Pearson Education Ltd v Prentice Hall India Pte Ltd* [2006] F.S.R. 111, Q.B.D.

[817] *Forster v Friedland,* unreported, November 10, 1992, CA; but see *B.N.P. Paribas v Mezzotoro* [2004] I.R.L.R. 508, E.A.T.

[818] *Bradford & Bingley Plc v Rashid* [2006] 1 W.L.R. 2066, HL.

[819] *Dixon Stores Group Ltd v Thames Television Plc* [1993] 1 All E.R. 349, Q.B.D.

However, in a Canadian case it was held that a party was not entitled to refer in his statement of claim to a settlement agreement where he was not seeking to enforce that agreement.[820] An action based on statements made in the course of without prejudice negotiations may be struck out as an abuse of process.[821]

In any event, it does not prevent the communications concerned from being admitted in subsequent litigation for certain other purposes, in particular[822]:   **11.129**

(a) constituting an act of bankruptcy[823];

(b) where there is an unlawful threat [824] or substantial wrongdoing,[825] or "unambiguous impropriety"[826];

(c) a severance of a joint tenancy[827];

(d) a trigger for a rent review clause[828];

(e) for the purposes of explaining delay when resisting a defence of laches or an attempt to strike out for want of prosecution[829];

---

[820] *Sun Life Trust Co. v Dewshi* (1993) D.L.R. (4th) 232, Ont. CA; see also *B.C. Children's Hospital v Air Products Canada* (2003) 224 D.L.R. (4th) 47, CA of B.C.

[821] *Unilever Plc v Procter & Gamble* [1999] 1 W.L.R. 1630, affd. CA [2000] 1 W.L.R. 2436, CA; *C.I.B.C. Mellon Trust Co. v Stolzenberg* [2001] EWCA Civ 1222, CA; *Schering Corporation v Cipla Ltd, The Times,* December 2, 2004, Ch.D.

[822] See generally, *Cedenco Foods Ltd v State Insurance Ltd* [1996] 3 N.Z.L.R. 205, H.Ct. of N.Z.

[823] *Re Daintrey, ex p. Holt* [1893] 2 Q.B.116; *Re Connor (Debtors), ex p. Carter Holt Harvey Ltd* [1996] 1 N.Z.L.R. 244; see also *Bradford & Bingley Plc v Rashid* [2006] 1 W.L.R. 2066, HL, *per* Lord Hoffmann (admission in evidence in order to prove an acknowledgment of a debt within s.29(5) of the Limitation Act 1980).

[824] This exception is to be narrowly construed: *Kitcat v Sharp* (1882) 48 L.T. 64; *Kurtz v Spence* (1887) 58 L.T. 438; *Watts v Watts* [1905] A.C. 115; *Forster v Friedland*, unreported, November 10, 1992; *Alizadeh v Nikbin, The Times*, March 19, 1993, CA; *Unilever Plc v Proctor & Gamble* [2000] 1 W.L.R. 2436, CA; *Hall v Pertemps Group Ltd, The Times*, December 23, 2005, Lewison J. (threats made during a mediation covered by privilege, unless waived by other action).

[825] *Unilever Plc v Proctor & Gamble* [1999] 1 W.L.R. 1630, affd. CA, [2000] 1 W.L.R. 2436; *Hodgkinson & Corby Ltd v Wards Mobility Services Ltd* [1997] F.S.R. 178; *W.H. Smith Ltd v Colman* [2001] F.S.R. 91, CA; *Kooltrade Ltd v XTS Ltd* [2001] F.S.R. 158, Pumfrey J.; *Hawick International Jersey Ltd v Caplan, The Times*, March 11, 1988 (furtherance of a fraud).

[826] *Berry Trade Ltd v Moussavi* [2003] EWCA Civ 715, *The Times*, June 3, 2003, CA; *Savings & Investment Bank Ltd v Fincken* [2003] 3 All E.R. 1091, Patten J. (unambiguous admission of facts in "without prejudice" meeting, followed by equally unambiguous denial of such facts by same person amounted to abuse and constituted "unambiguous impropriety"); *Wilkinson v West Coast Capital* [2005] EWHC 1606 (Ch.), at para.14 (negotiating in bad faith); *cf. Aird v Prime Meridian Ltd* [2006] EWHC 2338 (T.C.C.) (no sufficient unambiguous impropriety to justify losing privilege).

[827] *McDowall v Hirschfield Lipson & Rumney, The Times*, February 13, 1992.

[828] *Norwich Union Life Insurance Society v Tony Waller* (1984) 270 E.G. 42, disapproved on another point in *South Shropshire District Council v Amos* [1986] 1 W.L.R. 1271.

[829] *Walker v Wilsher* (1889) 23 Q.B.D. 335 at 338; *Simaan General Contracting Co. Ltd v Pilkington Glass Co. Ltd* [1987] 1 W.L.R. 516 at 520; *Rediffusion Simulation v Link Miles* [1992] F.S.R.195; *Family Housing Association (Manchester) Ltd v Michael Hyde and Partners* [1993] 1 W.L.R. 354, CA.

(f) proving a party's signature on a bill of exchange when this question was not part of the negotiations (but this is more doubtful)[830];

(g) seeing whether the negotiations gave rise to an estoppel[831];

(h) where there is in issue the reasonableness of steps taken to reach settlement of claims[832];

(i) for the purpose of construing an order made by consent.[833]

11.130   The above are all examples where the justice of the case requires that resort may be had to without prejudice material.[834] Indeed, in some cases of without notice applications, there may even be a duty to refer the court to (or to the existence of) a without prejudice offer made by the other side.[835] The rule also does not prevent admissibility of the communications for the purpose of establishing whether an agreement has been come to as a result of the negotiations[836] and even (in Canada) whether the agreement so entered into should be set aside as procured by misrepresentation, fraud or undue influence.[837] It was also suggested, in a comparatively early case, that the rule did not apply to interlocutory applications,[838] as opposed to trial, but that distinction seems (rightly) to have gone.[839] On the other hand, it should be noted that the rule *does* apply to prevent the fact of a "without prejudice" offer being admitted in order to resist an application for security for costs.[840] In Australia it has also been held to prevent reference to

---

[830] *Waldridge v Kennison* (1794) 1 Esp. 142.

[831] *Hodgkinson Corby Ltd v Wards Mobility Services Ltd* [1997] F.S.R. 178.

[832] *Zanen Dredging and Contracting Co. Ltd v Costain* (1996) 12 Const. L.J. 129; *Muller v Linsley and Mortimer* [1996] 1 P.N.L.R. 74, CA.

[833] *Admiral Management Services Ltd v Para-Protect Europe Ltd* [2002] 1 W.L.R. 2722, Stanley Burnton J.

[834] *Rush & Tompkins v G.L.C.* [1989] 1 A.C. 1280 at 1300; *Somatra Ltd v Sinclair Roche &Temperley* [2000] 1 W.L.R. 2453, CA; *Smiths Group Plc v Weiss*, March 22, 2002 (Ch.D. unreported); see also *Independent Research Services v Catterall* [1993] I.C.R. 1, E.A.T. (without prejudice statements admitted to prevent dishonest case being pursued) and *Knightstone Housing Association v Crawford*, unreported, October 27, 1999, E.A.T. (without prejudice correspondence admitted to show that employee was wrong to assert that employers had "set their minds against" part-time working; *sed quaere*).

[835] *The Giovanna* [1999] 1 Lloyd's Rep. 867; *Pearson Education Ltd v Prentice Hall India Pte Ltd* [2006] F.S.R. 111, Q.B.D.; see also *Somatra Ltd v Sinclair Roche &Temperley* [2000] 1 W.L.R. 2453, CA; *Harmony Precious Metals Service SAS v BCPMS (Europe)* [2002] EWHC 1687, T.C.C.

[836] *Walker v Wilsher* (1889) 23 Q.B.D. 335 at 337, CA; *Tomlin v Standard Telephones & Cables Ltd* [1969] 1 W.L.R. 1378, CA; *Rush & Tompkins v G.L.C.* [1989] 1 A.C. 1280 at 1300; *Cedenco Foods v State Insurance* [1996] 3 N.Z.L.R. 205 at 211, H.Ct. of N.Z.; *Gnitrow Ltd v Cape Plc* [2000] 1 W.L.R. 2327, CA; *Admiral Management Services v Para-Protect Europe* [2002] F.S.R. 914.

[837] *Underwood v Cox* [1912] 4 D.L.R. 66.

[838] *Family Housing Association (Manchester) Ltd v Michael Hyde and Partners* [1993] 1 W.L.R. 354, CA.

[839] See *The Giovanna* [1999] 1 Lloyd's Rep. 867; *Somatra Ltd v Sinclair Roche &Temperley* [2000] 1 W.L.R. 2453, CA.

[840] *Simaan General Contracting Co. Ltd v Pilkington Glass Co. Ltd* [1987] 1 W.L.R. 516; *Redifusion Simulation Ltd v Link Miles Ltd* [1992] F.S.R. 195 at 200; but see CPR,

without prejudice communications even for the purpose of proving the existence of documents,[841] and in Canada to documents enabling a party to know how much damages recovered related to a particular head of loss.[842]

Although the disclosure rule is brought in on the back of the evidential rule, and so cannot apply where the evidential rule does not, the disclosure rule is wider in that it does not merely cover admissions, but protects the communications themselves from production.[843] This means that, so far as a third party not yet in possession of the documents is concerned, questions of admissibility for other purposes[844] will probably never arise. The communication being privileged at all, that is an end of the matter. Unlike other privileges, the "without prejudice" privilege belongs to both parties of the communication concerned and, as will be seen,[845] this has implications when it comes to waiver or other loss of the privilege.

11.131

Where the privilege operates and nothing has been said or agreed to cut down its scope, its operation is absolute, so that an offer to compromise is not only not admissible one way, to prove admissions, but it is not admissible the other, on questions of costs.[846] However, a variant of the "without prejudice" evidential rule allows a restriction to be put on the "without prejudice" limitation itself, so that in the excepted circumstances the otherwise privileged document is regarded as "open" and may be admitted in evidence. Thus a practice has grown up of expressing offers of compromise (in all kinds of cases, including damages claims) to be "without prejudice, save as to costs." This allows the court, in considering what order to make on costs, to have regard to any offers of settlement made by either party. The practice originated in the Family Division,[847] but now extends across all divisions and courts. The practice is now embodied in the rules themselves, which provide that a CPR, Pt 36 offer is to be treated as "without prejudice" except as to costs.[848] The court will not take into account any without prejudice communications on the question of the reasonableness of a refusal to mediate a dispute (which may sound in costs), unless the communications fall within this category, i.e. are "without prejudice, save as to costs."[849]

11.132

---

r.36.19(2). In certain interlocutory proceedings it may be appropriate for the court to be told of a Pt 36 payment: *cf. Williams v Bogg* (1941) 57 T.L.R. 70 at 71, *per* Goddard L.J.

[841] *Chandler v Water Corporation* [2004] W.A.S.C. 95, Sup.Ct.W.A.

[842] *Dos Santos v Sun Life Assurance Co. of Canada* (2005) 249 D.L.R. (4th) 416, CA of B.C.

[843] *Rush & Tompkins* [1989] 1 A.C. 1280 at 1305.

[844] As in para.11.129, above.

[845] See Ch.12, para.12.39, below.

[846] *Walker v Wilsher* (1889) 23 Q.B.D. 335; *Reed Executive Plc v Reed Business Information Ltd* [2004] 1 W.L.R. 3026, CA.

[847] *Calderbank v Calderbank* [1976] Fam. 93 at 196.

[848] CPR, r.36.19.

[849] *Reed Executive Plc v Reed Business Information Ltd* [2004] 1 W.L.R. 3026, CA.

Third parties

11.133   Sometimes there are communications which are "without prejudice" in the sense described above, but which take place between the parties via a third party, or indeed between each party and the third party, who acts in a rule of conciliator or mediator between the parties. In sex discrimination, industrial and race relations cases, communications between a party and a conciliation officer in relation to certain functions enjoy the status of inadmissibility in industrial tribunal proceedings.[850] It is to be inferred that inadmissibility carries with it the like privilege from production as other "without prejudice" communications, described above. In ordinary litigation, mediation is encouraged and facilitated by the Civil Procedure Rules[851] and it is clear that "without prejudice" privilege can apply to communications made and other materials produced during the mediation process for the purpose of exploring the possibilities of settlement, even if such attempts fail.[852] It is less clear that privilege attaches to materials prepared by the mediator for his own use, but his position is often the subject of express agreement between the parties that no attempt will be made by either party to obtain information or documents from him for the purpose of legal proceedings.

11.134   In matrimonial cases, the common law has long applied a similar rule of inadmissibility and privilege from production, where matrimonial reconciliation is being attempted.[853] This is so, whether the communication be made to the other spouse,[854] a probation officer,[855] a clergyman,[856] a marriage guidance councillor,[857] or indeed anyone to whom either or both parties resorted "with a view to reconciliation."[858] The privilege is that of the parties jointly, not of the conciliator,[859] and the conciliator may not make admissions for either party.[860] It should be noted that, in matrimonial cases,

---

[850] Sex Discrimination Act 1975, s.64(4); Race Relations Act 1976, s.55(4); Employment Protection (Consolidation) Act 1978, ss.133(s), 134(5).

[851] CPR, rr.1.4(2)(f), 26.4, 56.3(4)(a); see generally on mediation **Ch.[ ], paras. [ ] below.**

[852] *Smiths Group Plc v Weiss*, March 22, 2002 (Ch.D. unreported); *Halsey v Milton Keynes N.H.S. Trust* [2004] 1 W.L.R. 3002, CA; *Hall v Pertemps Group Ltd, The Times*, December 23, 2005, Lewison J. (threats made during a mediation covered by privilege, unless waived by other action); *cf. Aird v Prime Meridian Ltd* [2006] EWCA Civ 1866 (joint statement by parties' experts under CPR r.35.12, used for purposes of mediation held not privileged).

[853] See the Law Reform Committee's 16th Report (1967), paras 36040.

[854] *Theodoropoulos v Theodoropoulos* [1964] p.311.

[855] *McTaggart v McTaggart* [1949] p.94.

[856] *Henley v Henley* [1955] p.202.

[857] *Pais v Pais* [1971] p.119.

[858] *Mole v Mole* [1951] p.21 at 24; *cf. Broome v Broome* [1955] p.190 and *Whitehall v Whitehall* 1957 S.L.T. 196, dealing with "Crown" privilege and communications between the parties and the Soldiers, Sailors and Airmans Families Association.

[859] *McTaggart v McTaggart*, n.854, above, *Theodoropoulos v Theodoropoulos*, n.853, above, *Pais v Pais*, n.856, above.

[860] *Smith v Smith* [1957] 1 W.L.R. 802.

there is no need for any legal proceedings to be on foot, or even contemplated.[861] Given the policy of the law to encourage the settlement of disputes, the same principles should apply even to non-matrimonial cases.

In wardship and Children Act 1989 proceedings the welfare of the child **11.135** is paramount. Thus, although in general evidence may not be given in Children Act 1989 cases of statements made by one or other of the parties in the course of meetings held or communications made for the purposes of matrimonial conciliation, the rule does not apply where a statement has been made which clearly indicates that the maker had in the past caused or was likely to cause serious harm to the well-being of the child.[862]

J. WITNESS STATEMENTS

As will be seen later,[863] service of a hitherto privileged witness statement **11.136** upon an opponent, pursuant to the rules, will result in the loss of legal professional privilege. But, just as there is a public interest in not allowing use of documents disclosed under CPR, Pt 31 for purposes collateral to those of the action, so too there is a public interest in not allowing collateral use to be made of such witness statements. Accordingly, when a privileged witness statement is served on the opposite party pursuant to the former rules it was held that legal professional privilege was waived, but that a separate obligation, similar to, but different from, "without prejudice" privilege arose.[864] Changes even to the old rules altered this, to make it analogous to the implied undertaking on discovery.[865] The substance of these changes has been carried forward into the CPR. Thus where a party serves a witness statement under the rules, it may be used only for the purpose of the proceedings in which it was served, unless the witness[866] consents, the court gives permission or it has been put in evidence at a hearing held in public.[867] This does not merely mean that it is inadmissible in evidence in any other legal proceedings, but also means that it remains confidential and any unauthorised use may be restrained.[868] The privilege does not, however, prevent use of the statement by the opposing party in

---

[861] *cf. D v N.S.P.C.C.* [1978] A.C. 171 at 236.
[862] *Re D (Minors)* [1993] Fam.231, CA; Ingman (1995) 111 L.Q.R. 68.
[863] See Ch.12, para.12.21, below.
[864] *Prudential Assurance Co. Ltd v Fountain Page Ltd* [1991] 1 W.L.R. 756.
[865] RSC, Ord.38, r.2A (11); C.C.R., Ord.20, r.12A (11); *cf. Springfield Nominees Pty Ltd v Bridgelands Securities Ltd* (1992) 110 A.L.R. 685, Fed.Ct.Aus; *Complete Technology Pty Ltd v Toshiba (Australia) Pty Ltd* (1994) 124 A.L.R. 493, Fed.Ct.Aus.
[866] The old rule however referred to the consent of the party serving the statement (who might well not be the witness). *Quaere* whether this change can survive the decision in *General Mediterranean Holdings S.A. v Patel* [1991] 3 All E.R. 673; see Ch.12, para.10.41.
[867] CPR, r.32.12.
[868] *Prudential Assurance Co. Ltd v Fountain Page Ltd* [1991] 1 W.L.R. 756.

and for the purposes of the litigation in which it was served, such as an application for specific disclosure.[869]

K. DOCUMENTS PRIVILEGED BY THE LAW OF DEFAMATION

11.137   Certain statements or communications are regarded as "privileged" for the purposes of the law of defamation. Some have "absolute" privilege: others have "qualified" privilege.[870] It is important to recognise that this is a quite different privilege from that now under consideration, and its function is completely different. Privilege in the context of disclosure deals with the availability of information to the opposing party; privilege in the context of defamation is concerned with whether the communication concerned can itself found a cause of action.[871]

11.138   It had been suggested in the old *Supreme Court Practice* that:

> "In an action of slander a defendant interrogated as to whether he spoke the words may object to answer on the ground that, if spoken, they were spoken on an occasion absolutely privileged."[872]

But this wide proposition was not supported by the authority cited,[873] a case of a witness giving evidence to a private ecclesiastical commission. In its turn, this case itself misinterpreted earlier authority[874] in which it was held that evidence given to a military court of inquiry was not only "privileged" in the defamation sense, but also, by reason of the peculiar nature of the tribunal, was confidential, protected from production by public interest immunity, and inadmissible in evidence.[875] No equivalent proposition appears in the current *Civil Procedure*. The general rule is that, merely because a communication is "privileged" for defamation purposes does not render it also privileged for the purposes of discovery.[876] It is of course

---

[869] *Black & Decker Inc. v Flymo Ltd* [1991] 1 W.L.R. 753; *Prudential Assurance Co. Ltd v Fountain Page Ltd* [1991] 1 W.L.R. 756 at 775.

[870] See, e.g. *Clerk and Lindsell on Torts* (19th edn, 2006) paras 23.91–23.166; *Gatley on Libel and Slander* (10th edn, 2005) Chs 13–15; Price and Duodu, *Defamation Law, Procedure & Practice*, 3rd edn, 2004, Chs 10–14; *Reynolds v Times Newspapers Ltd* [1999] 3 W.L.R. 1010, HL; *Turkington v Times Newspapers Ltd* [2000] UKHL 57, *The Times*, November 3, 2000, HL; *Jameel v Wall Street Journal Europe Sprl* [2006] UKHL 44, *The Times*, October 10, 2006, HL.

[871] *Minter v Priest* [1930] A.C. 558 at 579–580; cf. *M. Isaacs & Sons Ltd v Cook* [1925] 2 K.B. 391 at 399.

[872] *The Supreme Court Practice*, 1999, para.24/5/39.

[873] *Barratt v Kearns* [1905] 1 K.B. 504, CA.

[874] *Dawkins v Rokesby* (1873) L.R. 8 Q.B. 255.

[875] *ibid.* at 269–270, and cf. Bray, at p.548.

[876] *Webb v East* (1880) 5 Ex.D. 108, CA; *Minter v Priest* [1930] A.C. 558 at 579.

possible for the same communication to attract both privileges simultaneously, but only by satisfying the conditions for each privilege separately. The best example is that of solicitor/client communications.[877]

L. DIPLOMATIC PRIVILEGE[878]

Under the Vienna Convention on Diplomatic Relations, 1961, Art.24, "... the archives[879] and documents of the [diplomatic] mission shall be inviolable at any time and wherever they may be." Similarly, Art.30.2 of the Convention provides that a diplomatic agent's "papers, correspondence ... shall likewise enjoy inviolability." These provisions are incorporated into United Kingdom law by the Diplomatic Privileges Act 1961, Sch.1. Their effect on the law of disclosure is not clear. It is necessary to distinguish the case where the diplomatic mission or agent concerned is a party to the litigation in which the disclosure question arises, from the case where it or he is not. In the latter case there is no doubt that the diplomatic mission or agent is entitled to resist attempts to make it or him produce documents, although once a document has been given to a third party then (save in exceptional circumstances) it will cease to be a part of the archive within Art.24 and hence will no longer be protected by it.[880] Sending a document to the government that a mission represents is not giving it to a third party for this purpose.[881] But Art.24 is not confined to protection against executive or judicial action by the host State and extends therefore to cases where a document is stolen or obtained by improper means from the mission or agent, and is sought subsequently to be used by third parties in legal proceedings.[882]

11.139

Diplomatic mission as claimant

Different considerations apply where the diplomatic mission or agent is a party to the litigation. If the mission or agent is a claimant, it or he has voluntarily submitted the dispute to the jurisdiction of the English courts, and it may be argued that accordingly it or he should abide by the same

11.140

---

[877] *Minter v Priest* [1930] A.C. 558; see also *M. Isaacs & Sons Ltd v Cook* [1925] 2 K.B. 391 (diplomatic dispatches).

[878] See, generally, Lewis, *State and Diplomatic Immunity* (3rd edn, 1990).

[879] As to this word, see the discussion in *Shearson Lehman Brothers Inc. v MacLaine Watson & Co. Ltd* [1988] 1 W.L.R. 16 at 24.

[880] *Shearson Lehman Brothers Inc. v MacLaine Watson & Co. Ltd* [1988] 1 W.L.R. 16, HL.

[881] *Zaiwalla & Co. v Union of India*, unreported, November 27, 1992, Tuckey J.

[882] *Shearson Lehman Brothers Inc. v MacLaine Watson & Co. Ltd* [1988] 1 W.L.R. 16 at 27.

rules as all other litigants, the submission to the jurisdiction operating as an implied waiver of the immunity. As Hoffmann J. once said,[883] " . . . if you join the game you must play according to the local rules." And, as already noted,[884] a sovereign state bringing proceedings in England must comply with the rules of disclosure. It would be strange if its diplomatic missions or agents did not have to do so.[885] Indeed, were it otherwise, a diplomatic mission or agent would enjoy a very significant litigation advantage over its or his opponent. This view of Art.24 is supported by the decision in *Zaiwalla & Co. v Union of India*,[886] that a diplomatic mission is merely an agent of the sending State and that accordingly a mission may invoke diplomatic privilege on behalf of that State.

Diplomatic mission as defendant

11.141 The position where the diplomatic mission or agent is a defendant is more difficult. At least where the mission or agent is liable to be sued as of right,[887] there is no conduct amounting to voluntary submission to the jurisdiction, or implying the consent of the sovereign to the disclosure of the relevant documents. On the other hand, it is often a matter of chance as to which of two parties to a dispute is claimant and which defendant, and where there is a genuine dispute which the general law permits to be dealt with by the courts (i.e. because the mission cannot claim state immunity) it seems hard to apply Art.24 of the Convention so as to disadvantage one party to the litigation. One resolution of the problem would be to hold that Art.24 does not necessarily prevent production of documents by a mission or agent which or who is party to litigation, though the court may, in the exercise of its discretion, restrict such production where appropriate, one factor to take into account being whether the mission or agent is a claimant or a defendant.[888] But this approach has not been adopted by the court.[889]

11.142 The protection of Art.24 is in any event confined to diplomatic missions and agents, i.e. embassies, High Commissions, and some international bodies given similar status under international law,[890] together with certain

---

[883] *McKinnon v Donaldson Lufkin and Jenrette Securities Corporation* [1986] Ch. 482 at 494.

[884] See Ch.3, para.3.42, above.

[885] *cf. Buttes Gas and Oil Co. v Hammer (No.3)* [1981] Q.B. 223 at 225.

[886] Unreported, November 27, 1992, Tuckey J.; see also *Fayed v Al-Tajir* [1988] Q.B. 712.

[887] See, e.g. commercial activity: see Art.31.1(c) of the Vienna Convention, and *cf.* the State Immunity Act 1978, s.3.

[888] *cf. Banque Keyser Ullmann S.A. v Skandia (UK) Insurance Co. Ltd*, para.11.154, below.

[889] *Zaiwalla & Co. v Union of India*, unreported, November 27, 1992, Tuckey J.

[890] See the International Organisations Act 1968, Sch.1, para.2.

of their staff and their families. Consulates and consular agents are governed by the 1963 Vienna Convention on Consular Relations,[891] Art.33 of which is similar to Art.24 of the 1961 Convention. There is, however, no equivalent to Art.30.2 of the 1961 Convention for consular agents.

M. OTHER STATUTORY OBJECTIONS TO INSPECTION

There are a number of statutory provisions expressly forbidding dis-   **11.143**
closure of information obtained under statutory powers. Most of these
provisions deal with matters such as census forms, farmers' agricultural
returns, trade and export returns, and so on, and are unlikely to be relevant
to a disclosure dispute.[892] One such provision that is more likely to be
relevant is the Legal Aid Act 1988, s.38, which forbids information supplied
for the purposes of the Act to be disclosed otherwise than for those purposes
(which do not include the purposes of the action in connection with which
legal aid was sought). Thus the Legal Aid Board, the Law Society and
similar bodies holding such information cannot disclose it in the action.[893]
Another statutory provision was s.82 of the Banking Act 1987,[894] which
was held to prevent both discovery[895] and production[896] of "information
relating to the business or other affairs of any person" received for the
purposes of the Act,[897] and documents would be capable of production once
material caught by s.82 had been redacted.[898] Indeed a Scots case has gone
further and held that, unless there is something in the statutory provision to
the contrary, documents kept by a government department pursuant to a
statutory obligation to report information for a statutory purpose are

---

[891] Incorporated into UK law by the Consular Relations Act 1968.
[892] *Rowell v Pratt* [1938] A.C. 101; through see *Bookbinder v Tebbit (No.2)* [1992] 1 W.L.R. 217 (information obtained by the Audit Commission and protected under the Local Government Finance Act 1982, s.30) and *Arbuthnott v Fagan* [1996] L.R.L.R. 143, CA (byelaw made under Lloyd's Act 1982 did not protect transcripts of evidence to a loss review committee from being disclosed in subsequent legal proceedings).
[893] *Whipman v Whipman* [1951] 2 All E.R. 228 (*subpoena duces tecum); R. v Stubbs* (1982) 74 Cr.App.R. 246 at 249 (application for criminal legal aid); see also *R. v Umoh* (1987) 84 Cr.App.R. 138, CA, and *Stein v Blake*, unreported, October 24, 2000, Neuberger J.
[894] See now Bank of England Act 1998, s.37 and Sch.7, and the Financial Services and Markets Act 2000, s.348.
[895] *Bank of Credit and Commerce International (Overseas) Ltd v Price Waterhouse* [1998] Ch. 84; but see *Barings Plc v Coopers & Lybrand* [2000] 3 All E.R. 910, CA, and *Real Estate Opportunities Ltd v Aberdeen Asset Managers Jersey Ltd* [2006] 2006] EWHC 3249 (Ch.).
[896] *Re Galileo Group Ltd* [1998] 1 B.C.L.C. 318 (Insolvency Act 1986, s.236).
[897] Although it is now clear that this does not cover material known to the disclosing party independently of the Act: *Arbuthnott v Fagan* [1996] 1 LRLR 143, CA, *Real Estate Opportunities Ltd v Aberdeen Asset Managers Jersey Ltd* [2006] 2006] EWHC 3249 (Ch.).
[898] *ibid.; Real Estate Opportunities Ltd v Aberdeen Asset Managers Jersey Ltd* [2006] 2006] EWHC 3249 (Ch.).

simply not disclosable.[899] In England such cases are likely to be governed by principles of public interest immunity.[900]

N. DISCRETIONARY OBJECTIONS TO INSPECTION

Joint possession

11.144   Until 1964 it was a conclusive answer to a claim for *production for inspection* that the document concerned, though properly disclosed on discovery,[901] was in fact in the joint possession of the party and another, non-party.[902] In 1964,[903] it became a matter of discretion in the court as to whether production was ordered in such a case.[904] The position is the same in at least some of the Australian states.[905] The CPR do not deal expressly with the problem of joint rights to possession. It seems likely that the court will continue to assert jurisdiction to order inspection, but exercise discretion as to when it should be ordered.

Possession as agent for another

11.145   In like fashion, before 1964 it was a valid objection to a claim for production that the party having custody of the document concerned had it only as agent for a non-party, the non-party having some proprietary interest in the document, and the party himself having none. Examples included documents held by an official in an official capacity,[906] a company's documents held by a director[907] or a receiver or liquidator,[908] and a client's documents held by his professional adviser.[909] In 1964 "custody"

---

[899] *Johnstone v National Coal Board*, 1968 S.L.T. 233, a decision of the Inner House of the Court of Session, equivalent to the Court of Appeal.

[900] See, e.g. *Lonrho Plc v Fayed (No.4)* [1994] Q.B. 749, CA (tax documents in hands of Inland Revenue protected; in hands of taxpayer not protected); *cf. Pooraka Holdings v Participation Nominees* (1990) 52 S.A.S.R. 148, Sup.Ct.S.Aus.; see also *Mount Murray Country Club Ltd v McLeod* [2003] U.K.P.C. 53

[901] See Ch.5, para.5.44, above.

[902] *Kearsley v Phillips* (1882) 10 Q.B.D. 36; *Chantrey Martin & Co. v Martin* [1953] 2 Q.B. 286, CA.

[903] See *Alfred Crompton Amusement Machines Ltd v Commissioners of Customs & Excise (No.2)* [1974] A.C. 405 at 429.

[904] RSC, Ord.24, r.11; CCR, Ord.14 r.5.

[905] See *Turner v Davies* [1981] 2 N.S.W.L.R. 324; *Langford v Cleary* [1993] 2 Tas. R. 1; *cf. Biala Pty Ltd v Mallina Holdings Ltd* [1990] W.A.R., 174.

[906] *Wright & Co. v Mills* (1890) 62 L.T. 558.

[907] *Williams v Ingram* (1990) 16 T.L.R. 451, CA.

[908] *Fenton Textile Association v Lodge* [1928] 1 K.B. 1, CA.

[909] *Few v Guppy* (1836) 13 Beav. 457 (solicitors); *Chantrey Martin & Co. v Martin* [1953] 2 Q.B. 286, CA (accountants); *Gomba Holdings UK Ltd v Minories Finance Ltd* [1989] B.C.L.C. 115, CA (receivers).

was added to the phrase "possession or power,"[910] and production of such documents became a matter of discretion for the court.[911] The position under the CPR is effectively the same, as there is a duty to disclose documents in a party's physical possession,[912] from which the right to inspect follows,[913] with the court ordering such inspection on a discretionary basis.[914]

Injunctions

Consideration was previously[915] given to the problems arising in the rare case where a party is injuncted in one set of proceedings from disclosing documents, and on its true construction the injunction prevents the disclosure of documents in a second set of proceedings. Where an injunction on its true construction restrains *inspection* of documents in subsequent proceedings, rather than mere disclosure, the same principles will undoubtedly apply. Where both sets of proceedings are in the same court, or even in the same jurisdiction, it seems inconceivable that the court or courts will not provide assistance to the injuncted party to prevent his being caught between two inconsistent orders.[916] Where one set of proceedings is here and the other out of the jurisdiction the matter is less certain.[917]   **11.146**

Documents from previous cases

A similar problem arises where documents obtained in one action, subject to the r.31.22 obligation or the implied undertaking,[918] are liable to be inspected in another action. This has also been discussed previously, in the context of disclosure rather than inspection, but the principle is the same.[919] In the context of documents produced in a previous arbitration, it has been held that an implied (contractual) obligation not to use the documents for any collateral purpose arises,[920] but of course this is not a r.31.22 obligation   **11.147**

---

[910] See Ch.5, para.5.36, above.

[911] RSC, Ord.24, r.11; CCR, Ord.14, r.5.

[912] CPR, r.31.8(2)(a); see Ch.5, para.5.45.

[913] CPR, r.31.3; see Ch.9, para.9.03.

[914] See Ch.9, paras.9.33.

[915] See Ch.8, paras 8.13–8.15, above.

[916] *cf. C. v S.* [1999] 2 All E.R. 343 (guidelines where financial institution ordered to give disclosure which might constitute "tipping-off" in relation to money-laundering).

[917] *cf.* para.8.14, above, and also *Lubrizol Corp. v Esso Petroleum Ltd* [1992] 1 W.L.R. 957.

[918] See Ch.15, below.

[919] See Ch.8, para.8.16, above.

[920] *Dolling-Baker v. Merrett* [1990] 1 W.L.R. 1205, CA; *Hassieh Insurance Co. of Israel v Mew* [1993] 2 Lloyd's Rep. 243; *Insurance Co. v Lloyd's Syndicate* [1995] 1 Lloyd's Rep. 272; *Ali Shipping Corporation v Shipyard Trogir* [1999] 1 W.L.R. 314, CA.

or an undertaking to the court. So there will be no conflict between two court orders. If the court orders disclosure, the implied obligation must give way.[921] Nonetheless:

> "When a question arises [i.e. in subsequent proceedings] as to production of documents or indeed discovery by list or affidavit, the court must, it appears to me, have regard to the existence of the implied obligation, whatever its precise limits may be. If it is satisfied that despite the implied obligation, disclosure and inspection is necessary for the fair disposal of the action, that consideration must prevail. But in reaching a conclusion, the court should consider, amongst other things, whether there are other and possibly less costly ways of obtaining the information which is sought which do not involve any breach of the implied undertaking."[922]

Liens

11.148   Where a lien is claimed by a party on documents which he wishes to withhold from the other party until his bill is paid, the court will not order inspection unless there is an issue or issues in the action which cannot be tried without reference to the contents of those documents so that inspection is needed in order to dispose fairly of the matter. This is so even if the court suspects that issues have been raised as tactical moves to enable a successful application for inspection to be made, thus (in effect) defeating the lien.[923] However, the court may order inspection of such documents by the party claiming the lien *conditionally* on the other party providing other security for the sums claimed.[924]

11.149   A related question arises where a party has disclosed documents as being, for example, in his control, when they are in fact in the control of a third party adviser who claims a lien over them. Of course the inspecting party may seek an order for inspection,[925] and the court may ultimately have to determine whether (in effect) to order the producing party to discharge the lien or to sue the third party to obtain the documents. It is submitted that the court will only do this in very clear cases.[926] In the first instance, however, the court will make an order for inspection, with liberty for the producing party to apply if he can show a genuine difficulty in obtaining

---

[921] *Ali Shipping Corporation v Shipyard Trogir* [1999] 1 W.L.R. 314 at 327.

[922] *Dolling-Baker v Merrett* [1990] 1 W.L.R. 1205 at 1213–1214: "implied undertaking" is plainly an error for "implied obligation".

[923] *Woodworth v Conroy* [1976] Q.B. 885, CA.

[924] *Hammerstone Pty Ltd v Lewis* [1994] 2 Qd. R.267, Sup.Ct.Queensland; *Ismail v Richards Butler* [1996] Q.B. 711.

[925] See Ch.9, para.9.33.

[926] e.g. *Equiticorp Industries Group Ltd v Hawkins* [1994] 2 N.2.L.R. 738; *cf. ex p. Shaw* (1821) Jac. 270.

them: a mere statement that he has applied for them and been refused,[927] or is unwilling to discharge the lien on the grounds of an alleged claim for negligence[928] will not necessarily persuade the court to relieve him of his obligation to permit inspection. An alternative for the inspecting party, is to serve a witness summons on the third party or to apply for third party disclosure.[929] Indeed the court will undoubtedly take into account the possibility of obtaining the documents in another way, in exercising its discretion under the rules.[930]

Self-incrimination not within the privilege

Not all self-incrimination falls within the scope of the privilege against self-incrimination.[931] Where the privilege applies, there is a right not to answer, or not to permit inspection of documents, as the case may be. But it is clear that, where the privilege does not apply, but there is nonetheless a risk of self-incrimination, the court has a discretion as to whether to order an answer or production for inspection, or whether to postpone such order or production for inspection. This is so, whether the reason that the privilege does not apply is that statute has taken the privilege away,[932] or whether it is that the risk is one of prosecution under non-United Kingdom law.[933]   **11.150**

Expense and inconvenience, alternative sources, third party confidentiality and trade secrets

These headings have already been considered in relation to disclosure,[934] and the same points arise,[935] albeit with greater weight.[936] However, in general, the court will consider, amongst other things, whether there are other ways of obtaining the information which is sought, particularly where   **11.151**

---

[927] *Vale v Oppert* (1875) L.R. 10 Ch.App. 340.

[928] *Lewis v Powell* [1897] 1 Ch. 678.

[929] See Ch.4, paras 4.48–4.60, and Ch.10, paras 10.02–10.36, above; and see *Hope v Liddell* (1855) 7 De G.M. & G. 331.

[930] See para.11.151, below.

[931] See paras 11.105–11.109, above.

[932] *Charles of the Ritz Group Ltd v Jory* [1986] F.S.R. 14.

[933] *Arab Monetary Fund v Hashim* [1989] 1 W.L.R. 565; *Levi Strauss & Co. v Barclays Trading Corporation Inc.* [1993] F.S.R. 179; *Canada Trust Co. v Stolzenberg* (1997) 1 O.F.L.R. 606, Ch.D.; *Crédit Suisse Fides Trust S.A. v Cuoghi* [1998] Q.B. 818, CA; *Bank Gesellschaft Berlin International S.A. v Zihnali*, July 16, 2001 (Comm Ct, unreported).

[934] See Ch.8, paras 8.8–8.25, above.

[935] As to inconvenience, see *Commercial Union Assurance Co. Plc v Mander* [1996] 2 Lloyd's Rep. 640 at 648.

[936] See Ch.8, para.8.21, above.

the production in question would infringe third party confidentiality.[937] However, if the court concludes that inspection is more important than third-party confidence, then it has power so to order.[938] There are three further aspects of confidentiality which should be mentioned, and these relate to data protection, non-legal professional confidences and foreign legal obligations.

Data protection

11.152   Computer data falling within the data protection legislation[939] is protected and restricted in various ways. However, there are also specific provisions[940] exempting from the statutory protection any disclosure "required by or under any enactment, by any rule of law or by the order of a court". The consequence that permitting inspection, in the disclosure process, of such data pursuant to rules of court (being subordinate legislation) or pursuant to an order of the court does not contravene the legislation.[941] This may lead to an individual who has been refused access to data under the Act seeking access to the same data in a specific disclosure application in the course of proceedings alleging a breach of the Act itself.[942] Considerations of public interest immunity limiting disclosure under the Data Protection Act 1998 come into play by virtue of s.29(1) of that Act.[943]

Non-legal professional confidences

11.153   Statute apart, confidential communications to and from professionals

---

[937] See, e.g. *Dolling-Baker v Merrett* [1990] 1 W.L.R. 1205 at 1214; *CHC Software Care Ltd v Hopkins & Wood* [1993] F.S.R. 241; *Wallace Smith Trust Co. Ltd v Deloitte Haskins & Sells* [1995] C.L.C. 223, [1997] 1 W.L.R. 257; *Mackay Sugar Co-operative Association Ltd v CSR Ltd* (1996) 137 A.L.R. 183, Fed.Ct.Aus.; *Douglas v Pindling* [1996] A.C. 890, P.C.; *Mortgage Corporation v Halifax (SW) Ltd*, The Times, July 15, 1998, H.H.J. Hutton.
[938] [1990] 1 W.L.R. 1205 at 1214.
[939] Data Protection Act 1984; Data Protection Act 1998 (replacing the 1984 Act).
[940] 1984 Act, s.34(5); 1998 Act, s.35(1).
[941] See *Rowley v Liverpool City Council*, The Times, October 26, 1989, CA.
[942] *Johnson v Medical Defence Union Ltd* [2005] F.S.R. 657, Ch.D.
[943] *R. (Lord) v Secretary of State for the Home Department* [2003] EWHC 2073 (Admin) (reports on categorisation of high risk prisoners).

such as doctors,[944] probation officers,[945] prison officers,[946] priests[947] and other counsellors[948] enjoy no privilege as such.[949] But the courts are particularly astute to prevent such confidences being broken unless it is absolutely necessary.[950] It goes almost without saying that it is the court, and not the professional concerned, who must judge the necessity of breaking the confidence.[951] Journalists are in a slightly improved position since the enactment of the Contempt of Court Act 1981, s.10,[952] but, whilst there is perhaps more weight given today than formerly to the protection of a journalist's sources,[953] it remains the fact that he has no absolute privilege, and a balancing exercise must be carried out by the court.[954]

Foreign legal obligations

It has already been observed that the risk of prosecution under non-United Kingdom law does not fall within the privilege against self-incrimination,[955] but that the court nonetheless has a discretion not to order disclosure of information.[956] Likewise, the court has not been deterred under the RSC from making an appropriate order for disclosure or inspection merely because such disclosure or inspection would be contrary

11.154

---

[944] *Duchess of Kingston's Case* (1776) 20 St.Tr. 355; *Anderson v Bank of British Columbia* (1876) 2 Ch.D. 644 at 651, 656; *Wheeler v Le Marchant* (1881) 17 Ch.D. 675 at 681; *Garner v Garner* (1920) 36 T.L.R. 196; *Hunter v Mann* [1974] Q.B. 767; *cf.* Evidence Act 1958, s.28(2) (Vic.); Evidence Amendment Act (No.2) 1980, s.32 (N.Z.); Evidence Act 1995, s.127 (Cth.); but in Canada medical records have in certain circumstances been found to be privileged: *M(A) v Ryan* (1997) 143 D.L.R. (4th) 1, Sup.Ct; *cf. F(K) v White* (2001) 198 D.L.R. 541, Ontario CA;.see also *Frenette v Metropolitan Life Insurance* [1992] 1 S.C.R. 647, S.C.C., and *M(N) v Drew Estate* (2003) 230 D.L.R. ($th) 697, Alberta CA.

[945] *McTaggart v McTaggart* [1949] p.94 at 97.

[946] *R. v Umoh* (1987) 84 Cr.App.R. 138, CA; though see **para.**[ ] as to public interest immunity.

[947] *R. v Hay* (1860 2 F. & F. 4; *Anderson v Bank of British Columbia* (1876) 2 Ch.D. 644; *Wheeler v Le Marchant* (1881) 17 Ch.D. 675 at 681; *Normanshaw v Normanshaw* (1893) 69 L.T. 468; *Pais v Pais* [1971] p.119; *cf. Cook v Carroll* [1945] I.R. 515; Evidence Act 1970, s.6 (Newfoundland); Evidence Amendment Act (No.2) 1980, s.31 (N.Z.); Evidence (Religious Confessions) Amendment Act 1989, s.3 (N.S.W.); Charter of Rights and Freedoms 1990, Art.9, para.2 (Quebec); Evidence Act 1995, s.127 (Cth.).

[948] *M v L* [1999] 1 N.Z.L.R. 747, CA of N.Z.; but in Canada see *B (L.M.) v B (I.J.)* (2005) 251 D.L.R. (4th), Alberta CA (marriage counselling records privileged).

[949] Though see para.11.119, above, in relation to "without prejudice" privilege.

[950] *Hunter v Mann* [1974] Q.B. 767; *Att.Gen. v Lundin* (1982) 75 Cr.App.R. 90; *Re C (A Minor)* [1991] 2 F.L.R. 478, CA; *Dunn v British Coal Corporation* [1993] I.C.R. 591, CA; *European Pacific Banking Corporation v Television New Zealand Ltd* [1994] 3 N.Z.L.R. 43, CA of N.Z.; *Cooper Flynn v R.T.E.* [2001] 1 I.L.R.M., Irish H.Ct.

[951] *X. Ltd v Morgan-Grampian (Publishers) Ltd* [1991] 1 A.C. 1, HL.

[952] Discussed in Ch.3, paras 3.18–3.21, above.

[953] *cf. Att.Gen. v Mulholland* [1963] 2 Q.B. 477, CA.

[954] *X Ltd v Morgan-Grampian (Publishers) Ltd* [1991] 1 A.C. 1, HL; *Goodwin v United Kingdom* (1996) 22 E.H.R.R. 123, E.Ct.H.R.

[955] See para.11.105, above.

[956] See para.11.150, above.

to some foreign law to which one of the litigants was subject.[957] The position is the same under the CPR.[958] But the court does have power, in cases where foreign law obligations of confidentiality are involved, to limit or even dispense with disclosure or production of documents, for example, where the banking secrecy of third parties will be breached by giving discovery. The court will take into account various factors, such as whether the party seeking the restriction is claimant or defendant, and the identities of the third parties whose confidentiality is at stake, but in general, this being part of English legal procedure, English notions will predominate.[959] The question of restrictions on inspection of documents is dealt with in more detail later.[960]

Contracting out of inspection

11.155   As with the right to disclosure itself,[961] it is possible for a party to contract out of the right to inspection, and in such a case inspection will usually not be ordered. The principles are the same as apply to agreements to limit disclosure.

O. DISPROPORTIONALITY

11.156   The CPR have introduced a new ground of objection to inspection of documents, namely that it would be disproportionate to the issues in the case to permit inspection of them. Where a party who would otherwise produce documents within a category or class of document already disclosed for inspection by his opponent considers that it would be disproportionate so to do, he is not required to permit inspection of documents within that category or class.[962] But he must state in his disclosure statement that inspection of those documents will not be permitted on those grounds.[963]

---

[957] *The Consul Corfitzon* [1917] A.C. 550 at 555–556; see also *Bank of Crete S.A. v Koskotas* [1991] 2 Lloyd's Rep. 587 at 590; *Partenreederei M/S "Heidberg" v Grosvenor Grain and Feed Company Ltd* [1993] 2 Lloyd's Rep. 324; *Comaplex Resources International Ltd v Schaffhauser Kantonalbank* (1992) 84 D.L.R. (4th) 343; *The Canada Trust Company v Stolzenberg* (1997) 1 O.F.L.R. 606, Ch.D.
[958] *Morris v Banque Arabe et Internationale d'Investissement S.A.* (1999) 2 I.T.E.L.R. 492.
[959] *Banque Keyser Ullman S.A. v Skandia (UK) Insurance Co. Ltd*, July 2, 1985, unreported, Staughton J.; *cf. Comaplex Resources International Ltd v Schaffhauser Kantonalbank* [1990] I.L.Pr. 319 (Sup.Ct.Ont.); see also (1991) 84 D.L.R. (4th) 343; *Partenreederei M/S "Heidberg" v Grosvenor Grain and Food Company Ltd* [1993] 2 Lloyd's Rep. 234; *The Canada Trust Company v Stolzenberg* (1997) 1 O.F.L.R. 606, Ch.D.; *Morris v Banque Arabe et Internationale d'Investissement* (1999) 2 I.T.E.L.R. 492.
[960] Para.11.157.
[961] See Ch.8, para.8.08, above.
[962] CPR, r.31.3(2)(a).
[963] CPR, r.31.3(2)(b).

The opponent may then apply to the court for an order for specific inspection, i.e. that the first party permits the opponent to inspect one or more such documents.[964] The application will be made in accordance with the ordinary rules governing interlocutory applications.[965] There is no definition of "disproportionate" for the purposes of this rule,[966] but it is plainly related to the concept of proportionality used in the overriding objective contained in CPR, Pt 1.[967] However, the overriding objective uses proportionality in relation to the value, importance, and complexity of the case, and the financial positions of the parties, whereas the disclosure rule requires disproportionality only to *the issues in the case*. Nonetheless, the court will take account of all the circumstances, and indeed is bound in exercising its powers under the rules seek to give effect to the overriding objective.[968]

P. CONDITIONAL OR RESTRICTED INSPECTION

The court's discretion to order inspection is not exercisable merely in an "all or nothing" fashion, but includes power to order such inspection subject to conditions or restrictions. These might include specific undertakings to be given in relation to the documents produced,[969] or restrictions on where any copy documents may be kept or read, on who in the other party's camp may inspect them, and on the making of further copies or extracts. The court will not order such additional protection lightly, but only where the risk of damage or loss to the producing party (or, exceptionally, to others) is so significant that some additional restriction on the usual position can be justified. Such cases are usually cases of trade secrets which, if disclosed at all, may be irretrievably lost[970] and they usually arise in intellectual property litigation. But the question can also arise in other types of action, such as breach of confidence or concerning a contested takeover bid.[971]

11.157

---

[964] CPR, r.31.12(1),(3).

[965] CPR, Pt 23.

[966] See *Real Estate Opportunities Ltd v Aberdeen Asset Managers Jersey Ltd* [2006] EWHC 3249 (Ch.), at paras 50–56.

[967] CPR, r.1.1(2)(c).

[968] CPR, r.1.2; see *Simba-Tola (Abena) v Elizabeth Fry Hostel (Trustees)* [2001] EWCA Civ 1371.

[969] *cf.* the automatic obligation under which disclosure and inspection are given anyway: Ch.15.

[970] See, e.g. *Mackay Sugar Co-operative Association Ltd v C.S.R. Ltd* (1996) 137 A.L.R. 183, Fed.Ct.Aus.

[971] *Magellan Petroleum Australia Ltd v Sagasco Amadeus Pty Ltd* [1994] 2 Qd. R. 37, Sup.Ct.Qld.

Basic principles

11.158   The additional protection that may be ordered by the court must depend on the facts of the particular case. The principles upon which the court acts have been stated as follows:

> "Each case has to be decided on its own facts and the broad principle must be that the court has the task of deciding how justice can be achieved taking account the rights and needs of the parties. The object to be achieved is that the applicant [i.e. *for inspection*] should have as full a degree of disclosure as will be consistent with adequate protection of the secret. In so doing, the court will be careful not to expose a party to any unnecessary risk of its trade secrets leaking to or being used by competitors. What is necessary or unnecessary will depend upon the nature of the secret, the position of the parties and the extent of the disclosure ordered. However, it would be exceptional to prevent a party from access to information which would play a substantial part in the case, as such would mean that the party would be unable to hear a substantial part of the case, would be unable to understand the reasons for the advice given to him and, in some cases, the reasons for the judgment. Thus what disclosure is necessary entails not only practical matters arising in the conduct of a case but also the general position that a party should know the case he has to meet, should hear matters given in evidence and understand the reasons for this judgment."[972]

This case concerned trade secrets, but it is conceived that the principles stated are of general application.

Examples

11.159   Thus, orders have in the past been made for inspection by an independent solicitor reporting directly to the court,[973] for inspection by the plaintiff's (claimant's) experts but not the plaintiff,[974] and for inspection by the plaintiff's lawyers' patent agent and expert but not the plaintiff.[975] Where

---

[972] *per* Aldous J. in *Roussel Uclaf v I.C.I. Plc* [1990] F.S.R. 25 at 29–30; see also *per* Buckley L.J. in *Warner-Lambert Co. v Glaxo Laboratories Ltd* [1975] R.P.C. 354 at 358, 360; and *per* Hoffmann J. in *Molynlycke A.B. v Proctor & Gamble Ltd*, April 15, 1991, unreported; *cf. Chiron Corporation v Organon Teknika Ltd* (1994) I.P.D. 10832. See also *Mackay Sugar Co-operative Association Ltd v C.S.R. Ltd* (1996) 137 A.L.R. 183, Fed.Ct.Aus.

[973] *Colley v Hart* (1890) 7 R.P.C. 101.

[974] *Swain v Edlin-Sinclair Tyre Co.* (1903) 20 R.P.C. 435; *Dunn v British Coal Corporation* [1993] I.C.R. 591, CA; *Elliott v MEM Ltd*, unreported, March 11, 1993, CA; *Hipwood v Gloucester Health Authority* [1995] I.C.R. 999, CA.

[975] *British Xylonite Co. Ltd v Fibrenyle Ltd* [1959] R.P.C. 252, CA; *Cooper Flynn v R.T.E.* [2001] 1 I.L.R.M., Irish H.Ct.; *Premier Profiles Ltd v Tioxide Europe Ltd* [2002] B.L.R. 467, [2003] F.S.R. 20, Comm.Ct.

the plaintiff has not been allowed inspection the order has sometimes nonetheless permitted a report in general terms to him of what has been found,[976] and more occasionally has permitted transmission to him of all information considered relevant by those inspecting.[977] In modern times, however, it is rare that the claimant himself (or, where the claimant is a corporate body, a named officer) is excluded from knowledge, because decisions whether to continue or abandon the action, for example, should be made by the claimant, and not by his advisers.[978] But exceptional cases do occur from time to time.[979]

Personnel abroad

Where the relevant personnel are out of the jurisdiction other considera- **11.160** tions are involved. Thus the court has declined to allow inspection by the United States general counsel or United States patent counsel of a United States plaintiff in an English patent action where only English law was involved[980] and has declined to allow inspection by nominated experts in the field, being scientists based in Italy[981] and France,[982] on the basis that if the secret leaked out there was no effective remedy, that it had not been shown that no independent expert of the appropriate calibre was available within the jurisdiction, and that there was accordingly no need for the additional risk to be taken that would be entailed by sending documents

---

[976] *Coloured Asphalt Co. Ltd v British Asphalt & Bitumen Ltd* (1936) 53 R.P.C. 89.

[977] *British Xylonite Co. Ltd v Fibrenlye Ltd* [1959] R.P.C. 252, CA.

[978] *Warner-Lambert Co. v Glaxo Laboratories Ltd* [1975] R.P.C. 354, CA; and see *McIvor v Southern Health and Social Services Board* [1978] 1 W.L.R. 757, HL; *Kirin-Amgen Inc. v Boehringer Mannheim GmbH*, unreported, March 3, 1995, D.E.M. Young Q.C.; *Magellan Petroleum Australia Ltd v Sagesco Amadeus Pty Ltd* [1994] 2 Qd. R. 37, Sup.Ct.Qld.; *Decor Corporation Pty Ltd v Australian Housewares Pty Ltd*, unreported, November 25, 1998, Fed.Ct.Aus. (in-house experts excluded); *SmithKline Beecham Plc v Alphapharm Pty Ltd* [2001] F.CA. 271, Fed.Ct.Aus. (pre-action disclosure of documents containing trade secrets restricted to solicitors, counsel, patent attorney, independent expert and one director of applicant company who can decide whether to commence infringement proceedings); *Macquarie Generation v Coal & Allied Industries Ltd* [2001] F.C.A. 1349, Fed.Ct.Aus. (access to non-independent expert).

[979] See, e.g. *Church of Scientology of California v D.H.S.S.* [1979] 1 W.L.R. 723, CA (protecting informers from harrassment); *Arab Monetary Fund v Hashim* [1989] 1 W.L.R. 564 (concealing identities of persons implicated in currency offences punishable under foreign law by death); *Helitune Ltd v Stewart Hughes Ltd* [1994] F.S.R. 422 at 431; *M. v Ryan* (1995) 119 D.L.R. (4th) 19, CA of B.C.; *Popwich v Saskatchewan* (1998) 159 D.L.R. (4th) 756, Sask. Ct. of Q.B. (discovery of medical records from non-party restricted to defendant's solicitors); *R. v Secretary of State for Health, ex p. Association of Pharmaceutical Importers*, November 15, 2000 (Admin. Ct unreported), applied *Helitune v Stewart Hughes (No.2)* [1994] F.S.R. 442, and the cases referred to in note 974 above.

[980] *Warner-Lambert Co. v Glaxo Laboratories Ltd* [1975] R.P.C. 354, CA; see also *Dendron GmbH v Regents of University of California* [2004] F.S.R. 842, Pat. Ct.

[981] *Warner-Lambert Co. v Glaxo Laboratories Ltd* [1975] R.P.C. 354, CA.

[982] *Roussel Uclaf v I.C.I. Plc* [1989] R.P.C. 59, CA.

abroad.[983] On the other hand, the court has permitted inspection by the French in-house patent agent of a French plaintiff,[984] and by a United States-based expert employed by a third party who was also a competitor of the defendant.[985] It must depend on the facts of the case.

Choice of expert

11.161   The next question to be considered is the choice of expert. In one case the judge commented on the defendants' suggestion that there might be other independent witnesses by saying:

> "In my view, the plaintiffs, unless there is some suggestion of bad faith, are entitled to choose their own team. It is not for the defendants to choose who should be the witnesses to give evidence against them".[986]

The same principle applies even where the expert is not intended to be an expert witness as such, but an expert co-ordinator or assistant in the "team" of one party and that party desires to be able to give access to the disclosure documents to that expert.[987] However, the burden of showing the need for an order permitting such access lies on the party who seeks it and it is open to his opponent to establish a reasonable objection to such an order by showing a real risk that information thus communicated would be used for a collateral purpose.[988] Although, as has already been seen,[989] a party may by contract exclude his right to disclosure, in whole or in part, it should be noted that, even where a party has contracted to allow access to disclosure documents to a particular person, he is still entitled to seek to establish an objection to that person, he is still entitled to seek to establish an objection to that person and the court may decline to make the appropriate order for access.[990]

---

[983] See also *Aktiebolaget Hassle v Pacific Pharmaceuticals Ltd* [1991] 3 N.Z.L.R. 186.

[984] *Roussel Uclaf v I.C.I. Plc* [1989] R.P.C. 59, CA.

[985] *Molnlycke A.B. v Proctor & Gamble Ltd*, April 15, 1991, unreported, Hoffmann J.

[986] *ibid.*; see also *P.L.G. Research Ltd v Ardon International Ltd* (1992) I.P.D. 15081; *cf. Decor Corporation Pty Ltd v Australian Housewares Pty Ltd*, unreported, November 25, 1998, Fed.Ct.Aus. (inspection restricted to lawyers and *independent* experts); *Macquarie Generation v Coal & Allied Industries Ltd* [2001] F.C.A. 1349, Fed.Ct.Aus. (access to non-independent expert).

[987] *Davies v Eli Lilly & Co.* [1987] 1 W.L.R. 428, CA.

[988] *ibid.*, see also *P.L.G. Research Ltd v Ardon International Ltd* (1992) I.P.D. 15081.

[989] See Ch.8, para.8.08; and para.11.155, above.

[990] *Molnlycke A.B. v Proctor & Gamble Ltd*, unreported, April 15, 1991, Hoffmann J.; *cf. Chiron Corporation v Organon Teknika Ltd* (1994) I.P.D. 18032.

Where to keep documents

As to where documents should be kept and inspected, this is commonly a **11.162** matter of agreement, but the courts have on occasion made orders regulating this aspect of inspection as well. Thus, in one case the documents had to be retained in the plaintiffs' solicitors' offices, even for counsel[991] and, in another case, the United States-based expert employed by the defendants' competitor was ordered to keep them at his own home.[992]

Specific undertakings

Notwithstanding the automatic obligation imposed on (formerly, implied **11.163** undertaking given by) every party to litigation in relation to disclosure,[993] the court may sometimes exact an express undertaking, either duplicating the obligation or undertaking, or even going further. The express duplication of the obligation or undertaking is usually required where the person concerned is not a party but, for example, an officer of a corporate party,[994] an employee expert,[995] or a third party expert.[996] An express undertaking may also be required where there is a risk of misuse of documents.[997] This has the advantage of bringing home to such persons (who are not usually lawyers) the terms of the obligations by which they are bound and warning third parties who might otherwise be tempted to try to obtain information from them of the dangers of their doing so. Where the express undertakings go further than the automatic obligation, then this must be justified by reference to the circumstances of each case.[998] In one case an injunction was imposed to restrain collateral use of affidavit evidence referring to disclosed documents.[999] In another case,[1000] it was held that the court could and should vary express (but one-sided) undertakings which had been given by the claimant to the defendant in order to obtain samples from the defendant for testing, so as to bring the results of the tests within CPR, r.31.22, with the result that neither party was free on its own to use them outside the proceedings.

---

[991] *Format Communications Mfg. Ltd v I.T.T. (United Kingdom) Ltd* [1983] F.S.R. 473, CA; *Atari Inc v Philips Electronics and Associated Industries Ltd* [1988] F.S.R. 416 at 421.
[992] *Molnycke A.B. v Proctor & Gamble Ltd*, unreported April 15, 1991, Hoffmann J.
[993] See, Ch.15, below.
[994] See, e.g. *Warner-Lambert Co. v Glaxo Laboratories Ltd* [1975] R.P.C. 354, CA.
[995] *Format Communications Mfg. Ltd v I.T.T. (United Kingdom) Ltd* [1983] F.S.R. 473, CA.
[996] *Davies v Eli Lilly & Co.* [1987] 1 W.L.R. 428, CA; *Decor Corporation Pty Ltd v Australian Housewares Pty Ltd*, unreported, October 26, 1998, Fed.Ct.Aus.
[997] *Church of Scientology v D.H.S.S.* [1979] 1 W.L.R. 723 at 735.
[998] See, e.g. *Davies v Eli Lilly & Co.* [1987] 1 W.L.R. 428, CA; *cf. Chiron Corporation v Organon Teknika Ltd* (1994) I.P.D. 18032.
[999] *Lubrizol Corporation v Esso Petroleum Company Ltd (No.2)* [1993] F.S.R. 53.
[1000] *Smithkline Beecham Plc v Apotex Europe Ltd* [2003] E.W.H.C. 127 (Pat.) Laddie J.

CHAPTER 12

Loss of privilege

CHAPTER 12

Loss of privilege[1]

A. INTRODUCTION

It has been seen that there are a number of objections to production of documents (conveniently called "privilege") which will prevail as of right.[2] In some circumstances this privilege may be lost, as where a party expressly makes open use in the proceedings of the contents of a document in which he has privilege. In most (though not all) cases, privilege can be deliberately abrogated by the party entitled to it, and this is called "waiver". But there are other ways in which privilege can be lost, and special rules apply to that species of privilege more properly known as "public interest immunity."[3] The rules concerning waiver of privilege are the first to be considered. It should be noted that the rules on waiver at present are entirely the product of domestic law, although there are relevant decisions of the Strasbourg institutions bearing on the compatibility of domestic rules from other systems with the ECHR,[4] and these may become relevant in future English cases too.

B. WHO CAN WAIVE?

Legal professional privilege is the privilege of the *client* and not of the *lawyer*[5] or the *witness* who gives a statement or report.[6] Accordingly, it may

12.01

12.02

---

[1] See generally Thanki (ed.), *The Law of Privilege*, 2006, Ch.5; Passmore, *Privilege*, 2nd edn 2006, Ch.7.
[2] See Ch.11, above.
[3] See Ch.11, paras 11.81–11.103, above.
[4] See Ch.21, para.21.13, below.
[5] *Anderson v Bank of British Columbia* (1876) 2 Ch.D. 644 at 649; *Procter v Smiles* (1886) 55 L.J.Q.B. 467 at 527; *Randolph M. Fields v Watts*, unreported, January 22, 1986, CA; *Ventouris v Mountain* [1991] 3 All E.R. 472 at 475; *Abbey National Plc v Clive Travers & Co.* [1999] Lloyd's Rep. P.N. 753, CA.
[6] *Schneider v Leigh* [1955] 2 Q.B. 195, CA; *R. v R.* [1994] 1 W.L.R. 758, CA.

be waived by the client[7] (even against the lawyer's or witness's wishes[8]), but not by the lawyer[9] or the witness.[10] The privilege against incrimination belongs to the person who (or whose spouse) is at risk of incrimination, and can only be waived by such person, and not by the party (if this is different). In principle, "without prejudice" privilege can be waived bilaterally, but not unilaterally.[11] However, a party unilaterally deploying evidence of what was said in "without prejudice" communications in support of its case on the merits loses the right to object to the admissibility of any admissions made in such communications.[12] Diplomatic privilege can only be waived by the state to which it relates, or the ambassador on behalf of that state[13]; it cannot be waived by the individual concerned.[14] However, a lawyer acting on behalf of his client can waive the client's privilege on his behalf. It is clear that solicitors and counsel have their client's authority to waive privilege.[15] Where two or more parties are jointly entitled to a privilege, and there is no agreement between them governing the matter,[16] all must join in a waiver to be effective.[17] But where they are severally entitled to a privilege (e.g.

---

[7] *Calcraft v Guest* [1898] 1 Q.B. 759 at 761; where the client is a company, now in liquidation, the liquidator may assert and waive such privilege (*Mercantile Credit Ltd v Dallhold Investments Pty Ltd* (1994) 130 A.L.R. 287; see also 69 A.L.J. 252); in Canada, however, the trustee in bankruptcy of a corporation may not waive privilege (*Re Bre-X Minerals Ltd* (2002) 206 D.L.R. (4th) 280, Alberta CA; *Re Chilcott and Clarkson Co. Ltd* (1985) 13 D.L.R. (4th) 481, Ont. CA); where the client is an individual, now bankrupt, under English law the privilege vests in the trustee in bankruptcy, in relation to "examinable affairs", and hence the trustee may waive it (*Re Konigsberg* [1989] 1 W.L.R. 1257 at 1266–1267), but not under Australian law (*Worrell v Woods* (1999) 163 A.L.R. 195).

[8] *Re International Power Industries N.V.* [1985] B.C.L.C. 128.

[9] *Procter v Smiles* (1886) 55 L.J.Q.B. 467; *CHC Software Care v Hopkins & Wood*, unreported, February 18, 1994, Millett J.; *Ridehalgh v Horsefield* [1994] Ch. 205, CA; *Federal Commissioner of Taxation v Coombes (No.2)* (1998) 160 A.L.R. 456 at 468, reversed on facts (1999) 92 F.C.R. 240, Fed.Ct.Aus. (Full Ct.). Indeed, it is the lawyer's duty to assert the privilege so long as the client has not waived it: *Nationwide Building Society v Various solicitors* [1999] P.N.L.R. 52 at 69.

[10] *Schneider v Leigh* [1955] 2 Q.B. 195, CA; *Donnelly v Weybridge Construction Ltd* [2006] EWHC 721, at para.50 (T.C.C.); as to "witness statement" privilege, see para.12.41, below.

[11] *Walker v Wilshire* (1889) 23 Q.B.D. 335, CA; see 12.39, below.

[12] *Somatra Ltd v Sinclair, Roche & Temperley* [2000] 1 W.L.R. 2453, CA; see para.12.37, below.

[13] *R. v A.B.* [1941] 1 K.B. 454.

[14] *R. v Madan* [1961] 2 Q.B. 1, CA.

[15] *Causton v Mann Egerton (Johnsons) Ltd* [1974] 1 W.L.R. 162; *Great Atlantic Insurance Co. v Home Insurance Co.* [1981] 1 W.L.R. 529 at 539; *Pozzi v Eli Lilly & Co.*, The Times, December 3, 1986, Hirst J.

[16] cf. *TSB Bank Plc v Robert Irving & Burns* [2000] 2 All E.R. 826, CA; see para.12.03, below.

[17] Bray, at p.427; *Rochefoucauld v Boustead* (1896) 65 L.J. Ch. 794; *Ampolex Ltd v Perpetual Trustee Co. (Canberra) Ltd* (1995) 37 N.S.W.L.R. 405 at 412; *Farrow Mortgage Services Pty Ltd v Webb*, unreported, July 5, 1996, CA of N.S.W.; *Helenic Mutual War Risks Association (Bermuda) Ltd v Harrison* [1997] 1 Lloyd's Rep. 160; *Thysson-Bornemisza v Thysson-Bornemisza* (1999) 2 I.T.E.L.R. 467 at 471–472, Bermuda CA; *Patrick v Capital Finance Corporation (Australiasia) Pty Ltd* (2004) 211 A.L.R. 272, Fed.Ct.Aus.; cf. *Newcrest Mining (W.A.) Ltd v Commonwealth of Australia* (1993) 113 A.L.R. 370, Fed.Ct.Aus. As for "common interest" privilege, see para.12.08, below.

common interest privilege[18]), and there is no relevant agreement, then any of them may waive privilege without the concurrence of the others.[19]

C. WHAT IS A WAIVER?[20]

Legal professional privilege can be waived: **12.03**

(a) by express or implied agreement;
(b) by conduct in the course of litigation making a fair adjudication impossible without such waiver; or
(c) by destroying the confidentiality of the privileged material.[21]

(a) Consent

As to (a), an express consent to the opposing party's inspecting material known to be privileged is a waiver, although it can be withdrawn at any time before the inspection takes place.[22] An insured claiming under an insurance policy involving legal advice or action on his behalf paid for by the insurer may find that the terms of the policy operate to waive his privilege as against the insurer.[23] Publication of privileged documents with implied consent of the party amounts to a waiver.[24] Where a lawyer has two or more clients in respect of the same matter, it is necessary to distinguish a joint retainer (each client sharing the same interest) from a several one (each having a different interest). In the absence of express agreement between joint clients, there is an implied waiver of privilege in respect of the communications of either with the lawyer, *until* the point is reached that an actual conflict of interest

---

[18] As to which, see Ch.11, paras 11.59–11.62, above.
[19] *Lee v South West Thames Regional Health Authority* [1985] 1 W.L.R. 845, CA; *Ampolex Ltd v Perpetual Trustee Co. (Canberra) Ltd* (1995) 37 N.S.W.L.R. 405 at 413; *Farrow Mortgage Services Pty Ltd v Webb*, unreported, July 5, 1996, CA of N.S.W.
[20] See generally, Auburn, *Legal Professional Privilege: Law and Theory*, 2000, Chs 10–12.
[21] *CHC Software Care v Hopkins & Wood*, unreported, February 18, 1994, Millett J.; Auburn, *op. cit.*, 195–196.
[22] *Goldman v Hesper* [1988] 1 W.L.R. 529 at 539; *Birrell v A.N.A. Commission* (1994) 55 A.L.R. 211 at 217.
[23] *Brown v Guardian Royal Exchange Assurance Plc* [1994] 2 Lloyd's Rep. 325, CA; *Winterthur Swiss Insurance Compnay v AG (Manchester) Ltd* [2006] EWHC 839 (Comm.); *cf. TSB Bank Plc v Robert Irving & Burns* [2000] 2 All E.R. 826, CA.
[24] *Cannar, re Application of, re Eubanks* [2003] N.S.W.S.C. 802, Sup. Ct. N.S.W.; *cf. Britsh American Tobacco (Investments) Ltd v United States* [2004] EWCA Civ 1064 (on similar facts, the English CA held that there had been no implied consent to publication, hence no waiver: see para.10.06 below).

emerges between them.[25] In the case of a several retainer (e.g. borrower and lender in a conveyancing transaction) there is no implied waiver of confidentiality or privilege by one in favour of the other, nor any implied authorisation for the solicitor to make disclosure to one of documents passing between the solicitor and the other.[26]

(b) Conduct[27]

12.04   As to (b), the conduct concerned may relate to the making of the claim itself, or it may relate to acts in the course of the proceedings.[28] As to the former, where a client sues his former solicitor, he impliedly waives his claim to privilege and confidence in relation to all matters relevant to an issue in the proceedings.[29] This is because he cannot both open up the confidential relationship between himself and his solicitor (in order to prove his case) and at the same time seek to enforce against the solicitor his duty of confidence (to prevent the solicitor adducing evidence of matters relevant to the issues in the proceedings).[30] It is a principle of fairness,[31] and goes beyond the particular matter in dispute to other matters dealt with by the same solicitor, if they are relevant.[32] Despite a number of decisions to the contrary,[33] the weight of English authority is now that the waiver applies only to communications between the client and the solicitor whom he is

---

[25] *TSB Bank Plc v Robert Irving & Burns* [2000] 2 All E.R. 826, CA.

[26] *Nationwide Building Society v Various solicitors* [1999] P.N.L.R. 52 at 69–72.

[27] See generally Mathieson Q.C. and Page, *Implied Waiver of Privilege* [2000] N.Z.L.R. 355.

[28] *cf. General Accident Corporation v Tanter* [1984] 1 W.L.R. 100 at 114 (referring to unfairness *at trial*), reversed [1985] 2 Lloyds Rep. 529, CA; *R. v Shirose* (1999) 171 D.L.R. (4th) 193, S.C.C.

[29] *Lillicrap v Nalder & Son* [1996] 1 W.L.R. 94, CA; *cf. B v John Wyeth & Brother Ltd* [1996] 7 Med.L.R. 300, Kennedy J.; *Shaw v Skeet* [1996] 7 Med.L.R. 371, Buckley J. (patient suing doctor, putting medical condition in issue, waives right of confidence in medical records and communications).

[30] *Muller v Linsley and Mortimer* [1996] 1 P.N.L.R. 74, CA, *per* Leggatt L.J.; *Nederlandse Reassurantie Groep Holding N.V. v Bacon & Woodrow* [1995] 1 All E.R. 976; *Oceanic Finance Corporation Ltd v Norton Rose*, unreported, March 26, 1997, Moore-Bick J.; *Paragon Finance Plc v Freshfields* [1999] 1 W.L.R. 1183, CA, pet. dis. [1999] 1 W.L.R. 1463, HL.

[31] *Lillicrap v Nalder & Son* [1996] 1 W.L.R. 94 at 99; *Paragon Finance Plc v Freshfields* [1999] 1 W.L.R. 1183 at 1192; *Testra Corporation Ltd v BT Australasia Pty Ltd* (1998) 85 F.C.R. 152, at 164, Fed.Ct.Aus. (F.C.).

[32] *Lillicrap v Nalder & Son* [1996] 1 W.L.R. 94 at 99, 101, 102–103; *Paragon Finance Plc v Freshfields* [1999] 1 W.L.R. 1183 at 1190.

[33] *Kershaw v Whelan* [1996] 1 W.L.R. 358; *Hayes v Dowding* [1996] P.N.L.R. 578; *Oceanic Finance Corporation Ltd v Norton Rose*, unreported, March 26, 1997, Moore-Bick J.; see also *Lloyd's v Kitsons Environmental Services Ltd* (1994) 67 B.L.R. 102; *B v John Wyeth & Brother Ltd* [1996] 7 Med.L.R. 300, Kennedy J.; *Shaw v Skeet* [1996] 7 Med.L.R. 371.

suing,[34] and not to privileged communications between the client and some other solicitor. This seems wrong in principle. Either the action of suing a solicitor can operate to waive privilege, because of *unfairness* to the defendant,[35] or it cannot.[36] If it can, and the implied waiver can go further than the particular matter in dispute,[37] it should not matter whether the earlier (relevant) transactions were carried out by the same solicitor or not.[38] That would be a matter of pure coincidence, and not a proper basis for such an important legal consequence.[39]

As a result of all this, where a client seeks a wasted costs order against his own lawyer, a waiver of privilege in relation to all relevant matters will be implied by law.[40] But there will be no implied waiver of privilege where the client's *opponent* applies for a wasted costs order against the client's lawyer and, although the client could choose to waive privilege, he may be expected usually refuse to do so.[41] Hence the court must make allowance on such an application for the lawyer's being unable to tell the whole story.[42] Nor is a patentee who, in infringement proceedings, seeks to amend the patent pursuant to s.75 of the Patents Act 1997 obliged to waive privilege in any document relevant to the court's exercise of discretion to permit or refuse the amendment.[43]   **12.05**

The principle of waiver through "fairness" exists in other common law jurisdictions, but has developed differently. It is often referred to as the "putting in issue" or the "inconsistency" exception.[44] Thus, for example, allegations of poor legal services have long led to waiver of privilege in   **12.06**

---

[34] *Nederlandse Reassurantie Groep Holding N.V. v Bacon & Woodrow* [1995] 1 All E.R. 976; *Banque Bruxelles Lambert S.A. v Simmons & Simmons*, unreported, November 24, 1995; *Paragon Finance Plc v Freshfields* [1999] 1 W.L.R. 1183, CA, pet. dis. [1999] 1 W.L.R. 1463, HL; see also *D.S.L. Group Ltd v Unisys International Services Ltd* (1994) 67 B.L.R. 117.

[35] *Lillicrap v Nalder & Son* [1996] 1 W.L.R. 94 at 99; *Paragon Finance Plc v Freshfields* [1999] 1 W.L.R. 1183 at 1192.

[36] *cf. R. v Derby Magistrates' Court, ex p. B* [1996] A.C. 487, HL (privilege is absolute, and no "fairness" balancing excerice is to be undertaken); note also the possible effect of Art.8 of the Convention of Human Rights (right to respect for private life), and *cf. MS v Sweden* (1997) 3 B.H.R.C. 248 (no breach of Art.8 where medical records of claimant under state compensation scheme disclosed).

[37] *Lillicrap v Nalder & Son* [1996] 1 W.L.R. 94 at 99, 101, 102–103; *Paragon Finance Plc v Freshfields* [1999] 1 W.L.R. 1183 at 1190.

[38] As Buckley J. held at first instance: see [1999] 1 W.L.R. 1183 at 1187.

[39] See further Auburn (2000) 63 M.L.R. 104.

[40] *Medcalf v Mardell* (also known as *Medcalf v Weatherill*) [2003] 1 A.C. 120, HL.

[41] *Medcalf v Mardell* (also known as *Medcalf v Weatherill*) [2003] 1 A.C. 120, at para.31; see also *Drums & Packaging Ltd v Freeman*, unreported, August 6, 1999, George Laurence Q.C. ("wasted costs" jurisdiction to be cautiously exercised in case clients are pressured into waiving privilege).

[42] *Ridehalgh v Horsefield* [1994] Ch. 205, CA; *Medcalf v Mardell* (also known as *Medcalf v Weatherill*) [2003] 1 A.C. 120, HL; *Brown v Bennett* [2002] 1 W.L.R. 713, Ch.D.

[43] *Oxford Gene Technology Ltd v Affymetrix Inc.* [2001] R.P.C. 18, CA, disapproving *dicta* in *Kimberley-Clark Worldwide Inc. v Proctor and Gamble Ltd* [2000] F.S.R. 235 at 237.

[44] See *Mann v, Carnell* (1999) 201 C.L.R. 1, at paras 28–29.

relation to the subject matter of the allegations, in both the United States[45] and Canada,[46] but the principle undoubtedly goes wider than this.[47] In Australia,[48] at least four categories of case can be identified where "fairness", "putting in issue" or "inconsistency" waiver applies[49]:

(i) where professional negligence is alleged against a legal practitioner, and the entirety of the professional advice given by him to the plaintiff would be admissible[50];

(ii) where the state of mind of a plaintiff is in issue, and legal advice given to him is relevant to this issue,[51] though relevance is said not to be conclusive[52];

---

[45] *Hunter v Blackburn*, 128 US 464, 9 S.Ct. 125 (1888); *United States v Woodall*, 438 F. 2d. 1317 at 1324 (1970); *Sedco International S.A. v Cory*, 683 F.2d. 1201 at 1206 (1982); *cf. People v Lines*, 531 P.2d. 793 (1975). See also Harman (1988) Univ.Ill.L.Rev. 999; Porter (1990) 39 Cath.Univ.L.Rev. 1007, at 1029–52; Pinto (2004) 106 W.Virg.L.Rev. 359 at 372.

[46] *Nowak v Sanyshyn* (1979) 23 O.R. (2d.) 797, Ont. H.Ct.; *Harich v Stamp* (1979) 27 O.R. (2d.) 395, Ont. CA; *S & K Processors Ltd v Campbell Ave Herring Producers Ltd* (1983) C.P.C. 146, Sup.Ct. B.C.; *Lev v Lev (No.2)* (1990) 64 Man.R. (2d.) 306, Man.Ct. Q.B.; *Professional Institute of the Public Service of Canada v Canada (Director of the Canadian Museum of Nature)* [1995] 3 F.C. 643; *Souter v 375561 B.C. Ltd* (1995) 130 D.L.R. (4th) 81 at 85–86, CA of B.C.; *British Columbia (Securities Commission) v B.D.S.* (2003) 226 D.L.R. (4th) 393, CA of B.C.

[47] See, e.g. *Hearn v Rhay*, 68 F.R.D. 574 (1975) (affirmative defence of acting in good faith); *United States v Exxon Corporation*, 94 F.R.D. 246 (1981) (defence of reliance on government interpretation of regulations), criticised, (1985) 98 Harv.L.R. 1450 at 1642; *Byers v Burleson*, 100 F.R.D. 436 at 440 (1983) (application to extend limitation period).

[48] It should be noted that the position in Australia is complicated by the enactment of the Evidence Act 1995 (Cth.), ss.118 and 122, which are concerned with privilege in the context of adducing evidence, but the effect of these provisions is beyond the scope of this work. Many of the authorities cited deal with the position both at common law and under the statute. See also *Mann v Carnell* (1999) 201 C.L.R 1, 168 A.L.R. 86; *Re Doran Constructions Pty Ltd* (2002) 194 A.L.R. 101, Sup.Ct. N.S.W.; *Cannar, re Application of, re Eubanks* [2003] N.S.W.S.C. 802, Sup.Ct.N.S.W.

[49] *Telstra Corp. Ltd v B.T. Australasia Pty Ltd* (1998) 156 A.L.R. 634, 85 F.C.R. 152, Fed.Ct.Aus. (Full Ct.); *Transport Industries Insurance Co. Ltd v Masel*, unreported, October 19, 1998, Sup.Ct.Vic.

[50] *Transport Industries Insurance Co. Ltd v Masel*, unreported, October 19, 1998, Sup.Ct .Vic. (privilege waived for legal advice given by other lawyers); *cf. Pickering v Edmunds* (1994) 63 S.A.S.R. 357 at 363.

[51] *Thomason v Campbelltown Municpal Council* (1939) 39 S.R.(N.S.W.) 347 at 358–359; *Commercial Bank of Australia Ltd v Amadio* (1983) 151 C.L.R. 447 at 474; *Pickering v Edmunds* (1994) 63 S.A.S.R. 357; *Data Access Corp. v Powerflex Services* [1994] A.I.P.C. 91; *Ampolex Ltd v Perpetual Trustee Co. (Canberra) Ltd* (1995) 37 N.S.W.L.R. 405 at 411; *Wardope v Dunne* [1996] 1 Qd.R.224; *Telstra Corp. Ltd v B.T. Australasia Pty Ltd* (1998) 156 A.L.R. 634, 85 F.C.R. 152, Fed. Ct. Aus. (Full Ct.); *cf. Southern Equities Corporation Ltd v Arthur Andersen & Co.* (1997) 70 S.A.S.R. 166, Sup.Ct.S.Aus. (Full Ct.); *Hammer v Sunman*, unreported, October 2, 1998, Fed.Ct.Aus.; *John Tanner Holdings v Mortgage Management* [2001] F.C.A. 194, Fed.Ct.Aus. (disapproving *Telstra Corporation Ltd* in part); *Garratt's Ltd v Thanga Thangathurai* [2002] N.S.W.S.C. 39, Sup.Ct.N.S.W.; and see also *Goldlion Properties Ltd v Regent Enterprises Ltd* [2005] H.K.C.A. 331.

[52] *Seven Network Ltd v News Ltd* (2005) 227 A.L.R. 704, at para.44, Fed.Ct.Aus.

(iii) where a party's use of privileged material makes it unfair to deny his opponent the opportunity to refer to such material[53];

(iv) where the fact finding role of the court would be seriously compromised, or the court might be misled, if privileged material could not be referred to.[54]

In New Zealand, the Court of Appeal has declined to introduce the "putting in issue" exception, at any rate in the broad terms found in Australia, on the ground that it would involve too great an inroad into legal professional privilege.[55]

(c) Loss of confidentiality

As to (c), deliberate[56] supply of a privileged document to the opposing party in litigation[57] or his agent or representative[58] would normally amount to a waiver, by depriving the document of that confidentiality which is an essential element of privilege.[59] But this is not always the case.[60] Similarly, where evidence is given (whether at trial or in interlocutory proceedings) by a party or his lawyer of privileged material, the privilege goes, even if the

12.07

---

[53] *Attorney General (N.T.) v Maurice* (1986) 161 C.L.R. 475, H.Ct.Aus.; *Goldberg v Ng* (1995) 185 C.L.R. 83 at 96; *Mgica (1992) Ltd v Kenny & Good Pty Ltd (No.2)* (1996) 135 A.L.R. 743; *Rio Tinto Ltd v Commissioner of Taxation* (2005) 224 A.L.R. 299, Fed.Ct.Aus.; *AWB Ltd v Cole* [2006] F.C.A. 1234, Fed.Ct.Aus.; *cf. Candacal Pty Ltd v Industry Research & Development Board* [2005] F.C.A. 649, Fed.Ct.Aus. (public law decision minuted as based on legal advice; no waiver); *Commissioner of Taxation v Rio Tinto Ltd* (2006) 229 A.L.R. 304, Fed.Ct.Aus. (F.C.) (particulars of plrading referring to legal advice: privilege waived).

[54] *Benecke v National Australia Bank Ltd* (1993) 35 N.S.W.L.R. 110, CA of N.S.W. (lawyer's authority to settle claim in issue); *Hong Kong Bank of Australia Ltd v Murphy* [1993] 2 V.R. 419; *Moreay Nominees Pty Ltd v McCarthy* (1994) 10 W.A.R. 293; *Pickering v Edmunds* (1994) 63 S.A.S.R. 357.

[55] *Shannon v Shannon* [2005] N.Z.C.A. 91, following *B. v Auckland District Law Society* [2003] 2 A.C. 736, P.C.; see also *The Ophthalmological Society of New Zealand v Boulton* [2003] N.Z.C.A. 26.

[56] Supply under compulsion of law will not amount to waiver: *Goldman v Hesper* [1988] 1 W.L.R. 1238; *AWB Ltd v Cole* [2006] F.C.A. 1234, at para.138, Fed.Ct.Aus.

[57] See Bray at p.432; *Government Trading Corp. v Tate & Lyle, The Times*, October 24, 1984, CA.

[58] *Harbour Inn Seafoods Ltd v Switzerland General Insurance Co. Ltd* [1990] 2 N.Z.L.R. 381.

[59] See Ch.11, paras 11.28 and 11.31 above, and also *City of Gotha v Sotheby's* [1998] 1 W.L.R. 114, CA; *USP Strategies Ltd v London General Holdings Ltd* [2004] EWHC 373, *The Times*, April 30, 2004; *Burkle Holdings Ltd v Laing (No.2)* [2005] EHWC 2022 (T.C.C.). In *British American Tobacco (Investments) Ltd v United States of America* [2004] EWCA Civ 1064, the CA held that, once the US court released privileged material into the public domain, against the objections of the litigant, confidentiality had gone, and so had privilege.

[60] See *Bourns Inc. v Raychem Corporation* [1999] F.S.R. 641, CA (supply of documents for the purposes of taxation); *Arrow Pharmaceuticals Ltd v Merck & Co. Inc.* (2004) 210 A.L.R. 593, at para.12, Fed.Ct.Aus.; and see para.12.30, below.

evidence was being adduced to try to maintain privilege.[61] However, where administrative receivers of a company involved in litigation obtained the delivery up of privileged files from the company's solicitors and then at the request of the other party to the litigation handed over the files to the opponent's solicitors, this was held to be outside their powers, and was held not to waive the company's privilege.[62]

12.08   The position is less clear where there is a deliberate supply of a privileged document to a third party.[63] One aspect of the question is the intention with which it was supplied. Was it supplied in confidence, without prejudice to the privilege, e.g. to the directors of the client company,[64] another professional adviser of the client, such as his accountant,[65] a person otherwise with a "common interest",[66] non-clients attending a meeting where privileged communications took place,[67] a witness of fact,[68] an expert witness, an opponent in other litigation in compliance with a court order,[69] the court in private in other proceedings,[70] to a regulator,[71] to a commercial partner

---

[61] *Dubai Bank v Galadari, The Times,* April 22, 1991.

[62] *G.E. Capital Commercial Finance Ltd v Sutton* [2004] EWCA Civ 315, *The Times,* April 8, 2004, CA.

[63] See Bray at p.366; *Mann v Carnell* (1999) 201 C.L.R 1, 168 A.L.R. 86, H.Ct.Aus. (supply by minister to member of legislature held not disclosure to third party); where copies of disclosed documents are supplied, see paras 12.17–12.18, below.

[64] *Farrow Mortgage Services Pty Ltd v Webb,* unreported, July 5, 1996, CA of N.S.W.; see also *Arrow Pharmaceuticals Ltd v Merck & Co. Inc.* (2004) 210 A.L.R. 593 at 597 (disclosure by one corporate officer to another of legal advice to corporation is not disclosure to third party); *Seven Network Ltd v News Ltd* [2005] F.C.A. 864, at para.56, Fed.Ct.Aus.

[65] *C-C Bottlers Ltd v Lion Nathan Ltd* [1993] 2 N.Z.L.R. 445.

[66] *Rank Film Distributors Ltd v ENT Ltd* (1994) 4 Tas. R. 281 at 294; *Svenska Handelsbanken v Sun Alliance & London* [1995] 2 Lloyd's Rep. 84 (defendant insurer supplies legal advice to reinsurer); *Robert Hitchins Ltd v International Computers Ltd,* unreported, December 10, 1996, CA (third party supplies draft witness statements to defendant); *City of Gotha v Sotheby's* [1998] 1 W.L.R. 114, CA (second defendant copies legal advice to first defendant); *Southern Cross Airlines Holdings Ltd v Arthur Andersen & Co.* (1998) 84 F.C.R. 472, Fed. Ct. Aus. (report by liquidator to creditors); *Nationwide Building Society v Various solicitors* [1999] P.N.L.R. 52 at 72 (borrower authorises disclosure of privileged information to lender in conveyancing transaction); *Mann v Carnell* (1999) 201 C.L.R. 1, 168 A.L.R. 86, H.Ct. Aus. (Chief Minister of A.C.T. Executive supplied member of A.C.T. legislature with privileged documents in course of duty), applied in *GEC Marconi Systems Pty Ltd v BHP Information Technology Pty Ltd* [2000] F.C.A. 593, *Atkinson v T&P Fabrications* [2001] TAS.S.C. 38, Sup.Ct.Tas., and *Commissioner of Taxation v Pratt Holdings Pty Ltd* [2003] F.C.A. 6, Fed.Ct.Aus.; *Singapore Airlines v Sydney Airport Corporation* [2004] N.S.W.S.C. 380; *United Capital Corporation v Bender* [2005] J.R.C. 144, at para.24, R.Ct. Jersey; *cf. Patrick v Capital Finance Corporation (Australiasia) Pty Ltd* (2004) 211 A.L.R. 272, at para.23, Fed.Ct.Aus.

[67] *Australian Rugby Union Ltd v Hospitality Group Pty Ltd* (1999) 165 A.L.R. 253.

[68] *Newcastle Wallsend Coal Co. Pty Ltd v Court of Coal Mines Regulation* (1997) 42 N.S.W.L.R. 351 at 354, 389 (record of interview supplied for checking and return).

[69] *State Bank of South Australia v Smoothdale (No.2) Ltd* (1995) 63 S.A.S.R. 224, Sup. Ct.S. Aus. (Full Ct.).

[70] *Leif Hoegh & Co. A/S v Petrolsea Inc.* [1993] 1 Lloyd's Rep. 363; but see *Baxter v RMC Group Plc* [2003] 1 N.Z.L.R. 304.

[71] *Fyffes Plc v DCC Plc* [2005] I.E.S.C. 3, Irish Sup.Ct. (stock exchange).

under an express confidentiality agreement,[72] or to the police for the purposes of a criminal investigation?[73] In such cases the privilege is generally not lost. Or was it supplied with the intention of abandoning the privilege, e.g. to the court to be released to parties and non-parties in the exercise of the court's discretion,[74] to the media, in the hope of publication,[75] or to the public generally?[76] In these cases it is normally lost.

But this is not conclusive, because, as English[77] Australian[78] and New Zealand[79] authorities show, beyond a certain point it is a question of fairness whether a person who discloses material may be permitted to continue to assert that it is privileged from production.[80] In Australia, where the unsuccessful plaintiff in proceedings, faced with an application for costs against himself or his solicitors, filed an affidavit (exhibiting privileged documents) supporting the defendant's application against his own solicitors,[81] where a broadcaster in order to advance its own commercial interest disclosed legal advice it had received to a competition regulator, under an expectation that it would be kept confidential,[82] and where for its own commercial reasons a company voluntarily disclosed the substance of legal advice to official inquiries set up to look at possible infringements of export restrictions to Iraq,[83] it was held (in each case) that privilege had been waived. On the other hand, where a litigant in US proceedings agreed to a consent judgment which left it open to the US court later to decide to release documents to the public, and the court later did so, against the litigant's objection the litigant was held by the English court not to have consented to the release, and there was no waiver for the purposes of English proceedings.[84]

12.09

---

[72] *USP Strategies Ltd v London General Holdings Ltd* [2004] EWHC 373, *The Times*, April 30, 2004.

[73] *British Coal Corporation v Dennis Rye Ltd (No.2)* [1988] 1 W.L.R. 1113, CA. See also *Equiticorp Industries Group Ltd v Hawkins* [1990] 2 N.Z.L.R. 175 at 183, and *R. v Skingley*, unreported, December 17, 1999, CA (heavy burden on ultimate prosecutor to make even privileged documents available to prosecuting authority). See also *B. v Auckland Law Society* [2003] 2 A.C. 736, P.C.

[74] *Re L (A Minor)(Police Investigation: Privilege)* [1997] A.C. 16 at 29, HL (privilege against self-incrimination).; see also *Restom v Battenberg* [2006] F.C.A. 781, Fed.Ct.Aus.

[75] *Harbour Inn Seafoods Ltd v Switzerland General Insurance Co. Ltd* [1990] 2 N.Z.L.R. 381, at 384.

[76] *Chandris Lines Ltd v Wilson & Horton Ltd* [1981] 2 N.Z.L.R. 600.

[77] See para.12.04, above.

[78] See para.12.06, above.

[79] *The Ophthalmological Society of New Zealand v Boulton* [2003] N.Z.C.A. 26.

[80] See also *Re Robertson Stromberg* (1994) 119 D.L.R. (4th) 551, Sask.Q.B.

[81] *Patrick v Capital Finance Corporation (Australiasia) Pty Ltd* (2004) 211 A.L.R. 272, Fed.Ct.Aus.

[82] *Seven Network Ltd v News Ltd* [2005] F.C.A. 864, at paras 56–62.

[83] *AWB Ltd v Cole* [2006] F.C.A. 1234, Fed.Ct.Aus.

[84] *British American Tobacco (Investments) Ltd v United States of America* [2004] EWCA Civ 1064, CA (but confidentiality having gone, so had privilege).

12.10   One important area of deliberate supply to the opposing party concerns witness statements[85] and experts' reports[86] exchanged by the parties pursuant to an order of the court. Where witness statements are concerned, it is clear that any legal privilege which they formerly had is waived once they are served on the other side.[87] However, an obligation of confidence akin to "without prejudice" privilege arises on exchange and endures until either the witness statement becomes evidence at the trial or the party for whom it was prepared waives his right of confidence.[88] Moreover, the original privilege is retained for connected documents until the witness statement is deployed in court.[89] The position is the same so far as experts' reports are concerned, i.e. legal privilege[90] is waived when they are served on the other side,[91] although because the wording of the applicable rules is different no equivalent obligation of confidence arises thereafter.[92] In some cases the document itself is not disclosed or supplied to the opposing party, but some reference to it or other use of it in the litigation is made by the party whose privilege it is. The question is whether this amounts to a waiver.

D. REFERENCE IN PLEADINGS

12.11   There is a preliminary point to notice here. The CPR have made a significant change to the status of pleadings (statements of case) compared with the old rules. They must now be verified by a "statement of truth",[93] with the consequence that they may also be used, instead of an affidavit or witness statement, as evidence of the facts pleaded, in interlocutory proceedings.[94] In practice, it will not often be the case that reliance is placed on the statement of case as evidence, but in theory it is possible. So there is less

---

[85] See Ch.17, paras 17.20–17.32, below.

[86] See Ch.18, paras 18.02–18.23, below.

[87] *Comfort Holtels Ltd v Wembley Stadium Ltd* [1988] 1 W.L.R. 872; *Youell v Bland, Welch & Co. Ltd* [1991] 1 W.L.R. 122; *Black and Decksr Inc. v Flymo Ltd* [1991] 1 W.L.R. 753; *Bourns Inc. v Raychem Corporation* [1999] 3 All E.R. 154, [1999] F.S.R. 641, CA; cf. *Fairfield-Mabey Ltd v Shell UK Ltd* [1989] 1 All E.R. 576; *Akins v Abigroup Ltd* (1998) 43 N.S.W.L.R. 539, CA of N.S.W. (disclosure of statement under rules of court is pursuant to "compulsion of law", and hence privilege not lost, by virtue of Evidence Act 1995, s.122).

[88] See Ch.11, para.11.136 above; as to waiver of this obligation of confidence, see para.12.41, below.

[89] *Balkanbank v Taher, The Times*, February 19, 1994.

[90] See *Causton v Mann Egerton (Johnsons) Ltd* [194] 1 W.L.R. 162; cf. *Re L (A Minor)(Police Investigation: Privilege)* [1997] A.C. 16, HL (no litigation privilege under Children Act 1989).

[91] *Derby & Co. Ltd v Weldon, The Times*, November 9, 1990, CA; *Prudential Assurance Co. Ltd v Fountain Page Ltd* [1991] 1 W.L.R. 756; *Hajigeorgiou v Vasiliou* [2005] EWCA Civ 236, CA.

[92] See Ch.15, para.15.34, below.

[93] CPR, r.22.1(1)(a).

[94] CPR, r.32.6(2)(a).

difference than formerly between pleadings and affidavits, for example, and the old authorities must be read in that light.

First of all, there is the case of a privileged document referred to expressly   **12.12** in the pleadings of that party. *Roberts v Oppenheim*[95] is sometimes cited for the proposition that a mere reference in the pleadings does not amount to an implied waiver of privilege. However, that is not what that case decided. The plaintiffs referred to certain title deeds in their statement of claim, although these were privileged from production to the defendants on the basis that they related only to the plaintiffs' case and supported their own title.[96] The defendants did not seek to argue that the reference to these documents in the pleadings amounted to a waiver of privilege; instead they argued that RSC (1883) Ord.31, r.15,[97] which had just been introduced into the Rules, had changed the pre-existing law on the production of documents, and allowed an opposing party to obtain production of documents even where privilege was claimed. Fry L.J. said[98]:

> "We are invited to say that Order 31, Rule 15 has introduced a new practice, namely, that where a document is referred to in the pleadings, all privilege with regard to it is gone. The Rule does not say any such thing."

It was never suggested by the defendants in that case (who were the party   **12.13** seeking discovery) that the plaintiff had in effect waived his privilege, but only that a change in the Rules had meant that privilege could no longer be claimed in the case where the pleading referred to a document. Nonetheless, this mistaken view of *Roberts v Oppenheim* was taken by Sir Wilfred Greene M.R. in *Infields Ltd v P. Rosen & Son*.[99] However, in any event it should be noted that the Rules are no longer in the same form as they were in the time of *Roberts v Oppenheim*. At that time, RSC, Ord.31, r.15 concluded by saying:

> "And any party not complying with such notice shall not afterwards be at liberty to put any such document in evidence on his behalf on such case or matter, . . . "

In other words, the sanction for non-compliance with the notice under r.15 was that a party could not put the privileged document in evidence at trial.[100] But the words cited above from r.15 do not appear in its modern

---

[95] (1884) 26 Ch.D. 724.
[96] A ground of privilege abolished by the Civil Evidence Act 1968, s.16.
[97] Later RSC (1965), Ord.24, r.10, and now CPR, r.31.14.
[98] (1884) 26 Ch.D. 724 at 735.
[99] [1938] 3 All E.R. 591 at 597E.
[100] See (1884) 26 Ch.D. 724 at 734–735, *per* Cotton L.J.

equivalent[101] or elsewhere, and this is an additional reason why reliance should not be placed on *Roberts v Oppenheim* today.

12.14   In *Buttes Gas & Oil Co. v Hammer (No.3)*[102] two members of the Court of Appeal expressed a broadly similar view to that of the Court of Appeal in *Roberts v Oppenheim* (which was cited to them, although not referred to in the judgments). Lord Denning M.R. said)[103]:

> "Buttes in their amended reply and defence to counterclaim referred to a number of documents. By pleading them, Buttes show that they intend to rely on them. They should make them available for production. If and so far as they contend that those documents are the subject of a privilege, they should amend their pleading by striking out all reference to them."

And Brightman L.J. said[104]:

> "It is to my mind . . . clear that a party cannot rely on a privileged document so pleaded without thereby waiving the privilege. Therefore sooner or later Buttes will have to decide whether to forego privilege in respect of a privileged document which is pleaded, or to abandon reliance on it."

12.15   On the central question of whether reference to a privileged document in a pleading of itself constituted an implied waiver of that privilege, Donaldson L.J.[105] and Brightman L.J.[106] were clear that mere reference to a document in a pleading does not waive any professional privilege attached to it.[107] On the other hand, both judges were clear that reliance on the document would amount to a waiver of privilege. Similar views have been expressed in Australia[108] and New Zealand.[109] Indeed, in *Buttes* Brightman L.J. considered[110] that there was much to be said for the view that the other party could force Buttes to make up their minds before the trial, whether they were going to rely on the document or not by making an application to

---

[101] CPR, r.31.14.

[102] [1981] Q.B. 223; reversed [1982] A.C. 888, HL, though on different grounds, leaving the question of waiver of privilege untouched.

[103] *ibid.* at 246F.

[104] *ibid.* at 268C.

[105] *ibid.* at 252E.

[106] *ibid.* at 268B.

[107] *cf. Jobson v Johnson*, unreported, December 12, 1986, CA, where Ralph Gibson L.J. said: "If a party has in his pleading referred to a privileged document, he must produce it. The other side can make use of it." But it may be that this was simply a reference to the former RSC, Ord.24, r.10, now CPR, r.31.14 (right to inspect document referred to in pleading).

[108] *A.G. (N.T.) v Maurice* (1986) 161 C.L.R. 475, H.Ct.Aus.; *Somerville v Australian Securities Commission* (1993) 118 A.L.R. 149, Fed.Ct.Aus.

[109] *Tau v Durie* [1996] 2 N.Z.L.R. 190.

[110] *ibid.* at 268D.

strike out references to it in the pleading, although he did not decide this point, and Lord Denning may well have been thinking along the same lines.[111] But where a party goes further than simple reliance and puts in issue on the pleadings the contents of privileged documents, he may well be treated as having impliedly waived the privilege in any event.[112]

E. INCLUSION IN LIST OF DOCUMENTS

Where a List of Documents is concerned, there are three stages at which the question of waiver can be tested: **12.16**

(a) When the List is served on the opposing party, disclosing the existence of a particular document and making no claim to withhold production.[113]

(b) When the opposing party is permitted to inspect the original document concerned,[114] so no attempt is made to withhold production.

(c) When a copy of the document in question is supplied to the opposing party.[115]

It is clear that mere inclusion of a privileged document in the first part of the List of Documents[116] will not be treated as a waiver of privilege; if the document was mistakenly so included, the court will ordinarily permit the party whose document it is to amend the List[117] at any time before inspection has taken place.[118] But once inspection has taken place,[119] the general rule is that the privilege has gone, and it is too late to correct the mistake,   **12.17**

---

[111] *ibid.* at 246F. See also *CHC Software Care v Hopkins & Wood*, unreported, February 18 1994, Millett J.; *University of Southampton v Kelly*, unreported, November 14, 2005, E.A.T.

[112] As has been held in Australia and Canada: *Hong Kong Bank of Australia Ltd v Murphy* [1993] 2 V.R. 419, Sup.Ct. Vic.; *Samoila v Prudential of Australia General Insurance Co. (Canada)* (2000) 50 O.R. (3d) 64, Ont. Sup.Ct.; *S.Q.M.B. v M.I.M.I.A.* (2004) 205 A.L.R. 392, Fed.Ct.Aus.; *cf. Gower v Tolko Manitoba Inc.* (2001) 196 D.L.R. (4th) 716, Man. CA.

[113] See Ch.6, paras 6.01–6.30, above.

[114] See Ch.9, paras 9.02–9.16, above.

[115] See Ch.9, paras 9.17–9.38, above.

[116] As to the List and its three parts, see Ch.6, para.6.08, above.

[117] There is no specific power in the CPR, but the terms of rr.3.1(2)(m) and 3.10 seem to be wide enough for the purpose.

[118] *Re Briamore Manufacturing Ltd* [1986] 1 W.L.R. 1429; *Guinness Peat Properties Ltd v Fitzroy Robinson Partnership* [1987] 1 W.L.R. 1027 at 1045; *R. v First Lord of the Treasury, ex p. Petch*, unreported, January 31, 1994, Harrison J.

[119] As to which see Ch.9, paras 9.02–9.16, above.

the substance of the document having been communicated to the other side, who (with the court's permission[120]) may give secondary evidence of those contents or otherwise make use of them.[121] The position is *a fortiori* if copies have been supplied.

12.18   But permission is needed. As has been seen,[122] there are circumstances in which the court will not allow the opposing party to give secondary evidence or make use of privileged information which he has obtained. Thus where such circumstances occur in the context of an inspection of documents, such as procuring inspection of the relevant document by fraud, or realising the mistake on inspection but saying nothing, the court will in effect allow the mistake to be corrected, and refuse to permit the opposing party to use the privileged document. The test is in two stages: (1) Was it evident to the solicitor seeing privileged documents that a mistake had been made? (2) If not, would it have been obvious to the hypothetical reasonable solicitor that disclosure had occurred as the result of a mistake?[123] A relevant factor under (2) will be if the solicitor gave detailed consideration to the question and honestly concludes that there was no mistake. This will tend to show that it would not be obvious to the reasonable solicitor that a mistake had been made.[124] But if the answer to either question is "Yes", then under the old rules the court would normally restrain the solicitor if he did not give the documents back,[125] and might restrain him from acting further if he had read the documents and it was impossible for the advantage to be removed in any other way.[126] The CPR have not changed this position.[127] The test appears to be the same for a litigant in person who inspects the documents.[128] Where there are multiple parties, and the test is satisfied for

---

[120] See Ch.6, para.6.26, above.

[121] *Re Briamore Manufacturing Ltd* [1986] 1 W.L.R. 1429; *Guinness Peat Properties Ltd v Fitzroy Robinson Partnership* [1987] 1 W.L.R. 1027; *Pizzey v Ford Motor Co. Ltd, The Times*, March 8, 1993; *Breeze v John Stacey and Sons Ltd, The Times*, July 8, 1999, CA; *News International Plc v Clinger*, unreported, April 6, 1998, Lindsay J.; *Hoad v Nationwide News Pty Ltd* (1998) 19 W.A.R. 468, Sup.Ct.W.Aus.; *Al Fayed v Commissioner of Police for the Metropolis* [2002] EWCA Civ 780, *The Times*, June 17, 2002, CA.

[122] See Ch.11, para.11.76.

[123] *Breeze v John Stacey and Sons Ltd, The Times*, July 8, 1999, CA; *Al Fayed v Commissioner of Police for the Metropolis* [2002] EWCA Civ 780, *The Times*, June 17, 2002, CA.

[124] *Al Fayed v Commissioner of Police for the Metropolis* [2002] EWCA Civ 780, *The Times*, June 17, 2002, CA.

[125] *Guinness Peat Properties Ltd v Fitzroy Robinson Partnership* [1987] 1 W.L.R. 1027, CA; *Derby & Co. Ltd v Weldon (No.8)* [1991] 1 W.L.R. 73, CA; *Thames Housing Association Ltd v Bishop*, unreported, September 2, 1991, CA; *National Insurance Co. Ltd v Whirlybird Holdings Ltd* [1994] 2 N.Z.L.R. 513, CA of N.Z.; *Lee Lighting v Central Properties*, unreported, September 27, 1994, Morison J.; *I.B.M. Corporation v Phoenix International (Computers) Ltd* [1995] 1 All E.R. 412; *Spicers Paper (N.Z.) Ltd v Whitcoulls Group Ltd* [1996] 1 N.Z.L.R. 72; *Hayes v Dowding* [1996] P.N.L.R. 578.

[126] *English & American Insurance Co. v Herbert Smith & Co.* [1988] F.S.R. 232; *Ablitt v Mills & Reeve, The Times*, October 25, 1995. *Canadian Bearings Ltd v Celanese Canada Inc.*, 2006 S.C.C. 36.

[127] *Al Fayed v Commissioner of Police for the Metropolis* [2002] EWCA Civ 780, *The Times*, June 17, 2002, CA.

[128] *News International Plc v Clinger*, unreported, April 6, 1998, Lindsay J.

some but not for others, it may be that all of them will be permitted to use the documents.[129]

F. REFERENCE IN AFFIDAVIT OR WITNESS STATEMENT

Under the CPR, written evidence to be put before the court, particularly in respect of interlocutory applications, may sometimes be in the form of an affidavit,[130] but more usually will be in the form of a witness statement,[131] containing a "statement of truth",[132] rendering the maker liable for perjury if it contains false statements without an honest belief in their truth.[133] The general rule is that:

12.19

> "Where a person is deploying in court material which would otherwise be privileged, the opposite party and the court must have the opportunity of satisfying themselves that what the party has chosen to release from privilege represents the whole of the material relevant to the issue in question. To allow an individual item to be plucked out of context would be to risk injustice through its real weight or meaning being misunderstood."[134]

The key word here is "deploying". A mere reference to a privileged document in an affidavit does not of itself amount to a waiver of privilege[135] and this is so even if the document referred to is being relied on for some purpose, for reliance in itself is said not to be the test.[136] Instead, the test is whether the *contents* of the document are being relied on, rather than its *effect*.[137] The problem is acute in cases where the maker of an affidavit or witness statement has to give details of the source of his information and

---

[129] *ibid.*

[130] CPR, r.32.15.

[131] CPR, r.32.6.

[132] CPR, r.22.1; CPR, Pt 32 Practice Direction, para.20.

[133] CPR, r.32.14.

[134] *Nea Karteria Maritime Co. Ltd v Atlantic and Great Lakes Steamship Corporation* [1981] Com.L.R. 138 at 139, *per* Mustill J., based on *Burnell v British Transport Commission* [1956] 1 Q.B. 187; *Great Atlantic Insurance Co. v Home Insurance Co.* [1981] 1 W.L.R. 529 at 538; *Derby & Co. Ltd v Weldon (No.10)* [1991] 2 All E.R. 908; *Re Robertson Stromberg* (1994) 119 D.L.R.(4) 551, Sask. Q.B.; *Somatra Ltd v Sinclair, Roche & Temperley* [2000] 1 W.L.R. 2453, CA; *Dunlop Slazenger International Ltd v Joe Bloggs Sports Ltd* [2003] EWCA Civ 901, CA (where this quotation and the remainder of the paragraph were cited with approval); *Mayne Pharma Pty Ltd v Debiopharm S.A.* [2006] EWHC 164 (Pat.); see also *Hannigan v D.P.P.* [2002] I.E.S.C. 92, Irish Sup.Ct.

[135] *King v AG Australia Holdings Ltd* (2002) 191 A.L.R. 697, Fed.Ct.Aus.

[136] *Marubeni Corporation v Alafouzos*, unreported, November 6, 1986, CA, *per* Lloyd L.J.

[137] *ibid.*, *cf. Equiticorp Industries Group Ltd v Hawkins* [1990] 2 N.Z.L.R. 175; *Burkle Holdings Ltd v Laing (No.2)* [2005] EWHC 2022 (T.C.C.); *cf. United Capital Corporation v Bender* [2005] J.R.C. 144, R.Ct. Jersey.

belief, in order to comply with the rules of admissibility of such affidavit or witness statement.[138] Provided that the maker does not quote the contents, or summarise them, but simply refers to the document's effect, there is apparently no waiver of privilege.[139] This benevolent view has not been extended to the case where the maker refers to the document in order to comply with the party's need to give full and frank disclosure, e.g. on a without notice (*ex parte*) application.[140]

12.20   This test, distinguishing contents and effect, is difficult to draw in practice. It may be that a better way of dealing with the question (and one more in keeping with the notion of "deploying" material in court) is to treat written evidence in the same way as pleadings, just as the Rules do for some purposes.[141] It has already been seen that a party can probably require his opponent to elect either to produce a document referred to in a pleading or to delete the reference.[142] Similarly the test of waiver for written evidence would be whether, when the paragraph of the document containing the reference came to be adduced in evidence, and the opposing party challenged the adducing party either to produce the document or to delete the reference, the adducing party chose to produce it, thus waiving privilege. This was the approach adopted by Sir Wilfred Greene M.R. in *Infields Ltd v P. Rosen & Son*,[143] where he held that, no such challenge having been made at the time of reading the affidavit in evidence, and therefore the document not having been produced, the mere fact of so reading the affidavit (and thus relying on it) did not amount to a waiver of privilege.[144] It is true that this might cause a difficulty in drafting evidence for interlocutory applications, but it may be that the disclosure of certain (limited) legal advice is the price that must be paid for being permitted to put in hearsay evidence in order to obtain certain valuable procedural advantages.

---

[138] CPR, Pt 32, Practice Direction, paras 4.2(2), 18.2A(2); the former rules also required a statement of grounds of belief, but that does not appear in the CPR.

[139] *Government Trading Corporation v Tate & Lyle, The Times*, October 24, 1984, CA; *Marubeni Corporation v Alafouzos*, unreported, November 6, 1986, CA; *R. v I.R.C., ex p. Taylor* [1989] 1 All E.R., CA, where the question of waiver does not appear to have been argued and privilege was upheld. This part of the paragraph was quoted with apparent approval by the Court of Appeal of Hong Kong in *Goldlion Properties Ltd v Regent Enterprises Ltd* [2005] H.K.C.A. 331 (references to legal advice to show state of mind waived privilege).

[140] *Derby & Co. Ltd v Weldon (No.10)* [1991] 2 All E.R. 908.

[141] CPR, rr.22.1 (need for statement of truth), 31.14 (right to inspect documents referred to).

[142] See para.12.15, above.

[143] [1938] 3 All E.R. 591, approved in *Marubeni Corporation v Alafouzos*, unreported, November 6, 1986, CA, *Government Trading Corporation v Tate & Lyle, The Times*, October 24, 1984, CA, and *Bourns Inc. v Raychem Corporation* [1999] 3 All E.R. 154 at 164, [1999] F.S.R. 641 at 673–676, CA.

[144] See also *Goldstone v Williams, Deacon & Co.* [1899] 1 Ch. 47 (privileged documents produced, admitted by witness to be correct, and exhibited to deposition, but contents not on record, and no other use made; *held*, privilege not waived), followed in *United Capital Corporation v Bender* [2005] J.R.C. 144, R.Ct. Jersey.

G. REFERENCE IN EXPERT'S REPORT OR WITNESS STATEMENT

These are documents served in compliance with orders made under rules of court,[145] intended to convey to the opposing party, before the trial, the substance of the evidence of a witness (whether of fact or expert) that will be given at the trial.[146] They are voluntary in the sense that a party need not call any witness at trial, and hence need not serve any such statement or report, but the price of calling a particular witness in such a case is advance disclosure of his evidence.[147] Privilege in the statements and reports themselves is waived by serving them on the opposite side.[148] Here we are concerned with documents *referred to* in such statements and reports.

12.21

On principle it seems that the same rule should apply as with written evidence, i.e. that references to privileged material in a witness statement or expert's report will amount to a waiver of that privilege *if* they amount to a "deployment" of such material.[149] It seems that there cannot be such a deployment in a witness statement or expert's report without at least reference to the contents of the privileged material and reliance placed on them.[150] The link with the rules for written evidence is reinforced by the fact that, under the CPR, witness statements prepared for the purpose of giving advance notice of evidence at trial can also be used, in place of affidavits, as evidence in interlocutory proceedings.[151] The rule as to statement of sources[152] applies to witness statements, but not to experts' reports, and therefore in the latter case the contents/effect distinction[153] is unnecessary. There seems no reason why a party seeking to adduce a statement or report should not be challenged on the one hand to produce the privileged material referred to,[154] or, on the other, either suffer the deletion of the reference[155] or at any rate disclaim any intention to rely on such material referred to.[156]

12.22

---

[145] CPR, rr.32.4 (witness statements), 35.4 (experts' reports).

[146] See Ch.17, paras 17.20–17.32 (witness statements) and Ch.18, paras 18.02–18.23 (experts' reports).

[147] *cf.* Ch.11, para.11.136, above.

[148] See para.12.10, above.

[149] See para.12.19, above; see also *R. v Davies* [2002] EWCA Crim 85, paras 35–38.

[150] *Bourns Inc. v Raychem Corporation* [1999] 3 All E.R. 154 at 167, [1999] F.S.R. 641 at 676, CA; *Atkinson v T&P Fabrications* [2001] Tas.S.C. 38, Sup.Ct.Tas. (no waiver of privilege in statement referred to in expert report as not relied upon by expert for the purpose of his report).

[151] CPR, r.32.6; see para.12.19, above.

[152] See para.17.22, above.

[153] See para.12.19, above.

[154] Under CPR, r.31.14; see Ch.9, paras 9.04–7.10, above.

[155] See para.12.18, above.

[156] See *R. v Secretary of State for Transport, ex p. Factortame Ltd (No.5)* (1997) 9 Admin.L.R. 591, D.C.; *Vista Maritime Inc. v Sesa Goa*, unreported, October 24, 1997, Mance J. (note the suggestion in the latter case to redacting the statements to excise the references to privileged material).

12.23   It should be borne in mind that a witness statement (not being used in an interlocutory hearing) or expert report is not evidence, to be taken into account on the merits of the case, until the trial takes place. Under the old rules, a party retained the right not to call the witness at trial, so that the statement or report was inadmissible in evidence.[157] In these circumstances the party did not need to elect whether to give up the privileged material until the last moment. Under the CPR, where a witness of fact whose statement has been provided to other parties is not called to give oral evidence, any party may put in the statement as hearsay evidence.[158] Where an expert's report has been disclosed, similarly any party may use that report as evidence at the trial.[159] But either way (except where the party has deployed a witness statement at an interlocutory stage) witness statements and experts' reports have no evidential significance *until* the trial. Hence deployment, strictly speaking, does not take place till then.[160] However, there are recent cases suggesting that waiver can occur at an earlier stage, where a party refers to privileged material in a statement or report (thereby prima facie[161] indicating his intention to rely on it at trial[162]) and does not in correspondence or otherwise disclaim any such intention.[163] This is not consistent with the earlier authorities,[164] nor with the former rules of court, which treated witness statements and experts' reports as purely facultative for the party serving them. But the position under the CPR is different, and the recent cases may fit better with that.

12.24   There are two additional points relating to experts' reports. First, an expert witness gives opinion evidence, and his report will be based, on assumed facts supplied to him, often in privileged material. Since there is no property in a witness, whether expert or of fact,[165] the court may require the

---

[157] See Ch.11, para.11.136, above.

[158] CPR, r.32.5(1), (5); see Ch.17, para.17.26, below.

[159] CPR, r.35.11; note that it is not necessary that the expert be not called to give evidence.

[160] *Booth v Warrington Health Authority* [1992] P.I.Q.R. 137; *Balkanbank v Taher, The Times*, February 19, 1994, Clarke J.; *cf. Clough v Tameside & Glossop Health Authority* [1998] 1 W.L.R. 1478 (privilege waived in document referred to in expert's report once report disclosed), disapproved in *Bourns Inc. v Raychem Corporation* [1999] 3 All E.R. 154 at 164, [1999] F.S.R. 641 at 672–673, CA.

[161] In *Vista Maritime Inc. v Sesa Goa*, unreported, October 24, 1997, Mance J. pointed out that witness statements and experts' reports may be served, not with the fixed intention to adduce such evidence at trial, but to preserve the right to do so, and any such possibility should be taken into account in considering whether disclosure of privileged material should be ordered.

[162] See para.12.21, above.

[163] *R. v Secretary of State for Transport, ex p. Factortame Ltd (No.5)*, (1997) 9 Admin.L.R. 591, D.C.; *Vista Maritime Inc. v Sesa Goa*, unreported, October 24, 1997, Mance J.; *cf. Bourns Inc. v Raychem Corporation* [1999] 3 All E.R. 154, [1999] F.S.R. 641, CA, where these cases were not cited. See also *State of New South Wales v B.T. Australasia Pty Ltd*, unreported, July 24, 1998, Fed.Ct.Aus. (Full Ct.), *per* Beaumont J. (witness statement referred to privileged material to corroborate own evidence on central issue; *held*, privilege waived).

[164] See the cases cited at n.160, above.

[165] *Harmony Shipping Co. S.A. v Saudi Europe Line S.A.* [1979] 1 W.L.R. 1380, CA; *R. v R.*

expert witness to state both his opinion and the facts upon which it is based, only excluding communications covered by legal professional privilege.[166] Moreover, the rules now expressly provide that the instructions to an expert are not to be privileged.[167] Accordingly, any documents referred to by the expert forming part of his instructions will be caught by this provision and privilege in effect waived by serving the report.[168] Secondly, where a medical report was served in a personal injuries action under the old rules,[169] the defendant might seek limited disclosure of documents identified in that report, the plaintiff to give effect to that request in a manner in his discretion, such identification not being taken to waive privilege in such documents.[170] The CPR do not indicate that a different approach should now be taken.

H. REFERENCE IN CORRESPONDENCE AND DISCLOSED DOCUMENTS

Statements of case (pleadings), written evidence, experts' reports and witness statements are all relied on in proceedings, and it is comparatively easy to produce a principle covering waiver of privilege in such documents. Correspondence is different, since it is not by itself admissible in, nor otherwise forms part of, proceedings. There is no "deployment" of privileged material. But it is common for parties and their solicitors to write to the other side referring to privileged material in terms such as: "We have been advised by our solicitors that . . . ", "Counsel has advised that . . . " or "Upon counsel's advice . . . ". Certainly the setting out of privileged material is *extenso* is to be avoided, for (unless done "without prejudice") it plainly waives privilege in the disclosed material, if only by depriving it of confidentiality,[171] and raises the vexed question of waiver of the whole by waiver of part.[172] **12.25**

So far as short references are concerned, there are broadly two views. One is that, since the correspondence does not form part of the proceedings, the **12.26**

[1994] 1 W.L.R. 758, CA; *Connolly v Dale* [1995] 3 W.L.R. 786, D.C.; *Shaw v Skeet* [1996] 7 Med.L.R. 371.
[166] *Harmony Shipping Co. S.A. v Saudi Europe Line S.A.* [1979] 1 W.L.R. 1380, CA; *R. v Davies* [2002] EWCA Crim 85.
[167] CPR, r.35.10(4); see Ch.18, para.18.16, below. *cf. Tirango Nominees Pty Ltd v Dairy Vale Foods Ltd (No.2)* (1998) 83 F.C.R. 397, Fed. Ct. Aus. (calling expert does not involve disclosure of substance of instructions).
[168] See Ch.18, para.18.16, below.
[169] RSC, Ord.18, r.12(1A).
[170] *B v John Wyeth & Brother Ltd* [1992] 1 W.L.R. 168, CA.
[171] *Buttes Gas and Oil Co. v Hammer (No.3)* [1981] Q.B. 223 at 252; *Marubeni Corporation v Alafouzos*, unreported, November 6, 1986, CA; see Ch.11, paras 11.28 and 11.31, above.
[172] See para.12.34, below.

referor cannot be put to his election whether to produce the document or delete the reference and therefore the question does not arise. The other is that even debates in correspondence are a part of the legal process, and in any event letters may become relevant (e.g. as exhibits to an affidavit or at trial), so that the same rule ought to apply. This is supported by the argument from fairness, that you ought not to be allowed to select points without opening up the source to permit verification of the accuracy and fairness of the summary or extract.[173] A relevant factor may be the degree of detail which has been given.[174] The arguments are finely balanced, but in England the second view appears preferable, as it is consistent with the spirit of the reforms wrought by the CPR,[175] i.e. to ensure that the parties have all the necessary information to enable them to decide whether to fight or to settle[176] and also with the "cards on the table" principle which is said to underlie the rules of disclosure in English law.[177] In other jurisdictions, a different approach may be taken.[178] In any event, it would be unwise to expose oneself to the risk of waiver being held to have occurred by making short references.

I. INCLUSION IN TRIAL BUNDLE

12.27   Where privileged material has been introduced into the trial bundle by one party and made available to the other, privilege is waived by the introducing party, even if he did so by mistake, unless the other party knew of the mistake at the time and said nothing.[179] In effect the position is *a fortiori* that where inspection of privileged material takes place accidentally.[180] However, even if there is a waiver, use of privileged material may not be permitted where both sides acted in the mistaken belief that it was possible to include documents in the bundle in a redacted form, so as to exclude privileged material, without thereby waiving privilege.[181]

---

[173] See para.12.34, below.

[174] See, e.g. *Bennett v Chief Executive Officer, Australian Customs Service* (2004) 210 A.L.R. 220, Fed.Ct.Aus. (disclosure in letter of gist or conclusions of legal advice may amount to implied waiver of privilege for whole of it)

[175] See Ch.1, para.1.30, above.

[176] See *Visx Inc. v Nidex Co.* [1999] F.S.R. 91 at 110–111.

[177] See Ch.11, para.11.08, above.

[178] See, e.g. *Hammer v Sunman*, unreported, October 2, 1998, Fed.Ct.Aus. (references to discussions with counsel, disclosure of questions for counsel; *held*, no waiver of privilege in counsel's advice).

[179] *Derby & Co. Ltd v Weldon (No.10)* [1991] 2 All E.R. 908. As this is not *inspection* of the document, CPR, r.31.20 does not apply.

[180] See paras 12.17–12.18, above.

[181] *Arab Monetary Fund v Hashim*, unreported, September 30, 1993, CA, affirming the refusal of Chadwick J. to order production of full copies of the redacted documents.

J. WAIVER AT TRIAL

It is clear that an advocate at trial has authority to waive his client's **12.28** privilege on his behalf.[182] He may do so in the course of his speeches to the court, for example, by reading out the privileged document, and even if he is unaware that it is privileged and has no intention of waiving privilege.[183] But this does not apply where the document is introduced at an interlocutory hearing and the opposite party has already seen it.[184] He may also do so by calling certain evidence, such as calling a party's solicitor to give evidence of a conversation with that party,[185] or to give evidence referring to having taken counsel's advice,[186] asking an opposing witness to give evidence of a statement made to him by that solicitor[187] or asking his own witness whether a part of his evidence featured in the (privileged) proof taken by his solicitors.[188] In Australia it has been held that simply calling an expert witness who happens to have read privileged material to refresh his memory before entering the witness box amounts to a waiver of privilege in that material.[189] Again, an advocate may waive privilege by his cross-examination of the other side's witnesses, e.g. if he asks an opposing witness if he said certain things in a (privileged) statement previously given to the cross-examiner's own solicitors.[190]

But use of privileged material will not amount to waiver of privilege in **12.29** relation to other proceedings (whether in the same or some other jurisdiction) where the waiver was limited to the first proceedings,[191] or (in the case of foreign proceedings) an order has been made beforehand expressly preserving privilege.[192] Nor can a witness (not being the party or an agent of such a party) by his own actions waive the party's legal privilege,[193] though

---

[182] See para.12.02, above.

[183] *Great Atlantic Insurance Co. v Home Insurance Co.* [1981] 1 W.L.R. 529, CA.

[184] *Def American Inc. v Phonogram Ltd, The Times,* August 16, 1994, Lindsay J. (counsel read to motions judge 2–3 lines out of 300 to indicate relevance, reserving right to complain of breach of confidence by other side; *held,* no waiver).

[185] *George Doland Ltd v Blackburn Robson Coates & Co.* [1972] 1 W.L.R. 1338; see also *Nea Karteria Maritime Co. Ltd v Atlantic and Great Lakes Steamship Corporation* [1981] Com.L.R. 138, Mustill J.; as to how far the waiver extends in that case, see para.12.36, below.

[186] *Tanap Investments (UK) Ltd v Tozer,* unreported, October 11, 1991, CA.

[187] *R. v Bowden* [1999] 1 W.L.R. 823, CA, criticised by Auburn, (1999) 115 L.Q.R. 590.

[188] *Banque Keyser Ullmann S.A. v Skandia (U.K.) Insurance Co. Ltd,* unreported, July 11, 1986, CA.

[189] *Mgica (1992) Ltd v Kenny & Good Pty Ltd (No.2)* (1996) 135 A.L.R. 743, Fed.Ct.Aus.

[190] *Burnell v British Transport Commission* [1956] 1 Q.B. 187, CA; *cf. Goldstone v Willams, Deacon & Co.* [1899] 1 Ch. 47 (privileged document put to witness and admitted correct; *held,* privilege not waived).

[191] *Bourns Inc. v Raychem Corporation* [1999] 3 All E.R. 154 at 167–168, [1999] F.S.R. 641 at 671, CA.

[192] See para.12.33, below.

[193] See para.12.02, above. As to "witness statement" privilege, see para.12.41, below.

he may waive his own in other material.[194] In criminal cases, however, it seems that a defendant at trial, who in order to rebut an accusation of recent fabrication of facts gives evidence that he mentioned them to his lawyer at an earlier stage, and even calls other evidence to prove that fact, does not thereby waive privilege in that communication (or, *a fortiori* any further).[195] This is a generous approach, and contrary to principle.

K. WAIVER ON ASSESSMENT OF COSTS

12.30   On summary assessment (formerly taxation) of a bill of costs a party is obliged to lodge with (and hence disclose to) the court a considerable amount of material relating to the case, including privileged documents.[196] This is not a process of disclosure in the compulsory sense, since the receiving party can withdraw the item rather than disclose the privileged material. It is more a case of election. If the claim is maintained, then whilst the district judge, "costs judge" (formerly taxing master), or "authorised court officer" (formerly taxing officer) conducting the assessment must maintain privilege so far as possible, and thus not disclose the contents of a privileged document unnecessarily, he has a duty to see that the paying party is treated fairly and given a proper opportunity to raise a bona fide challenge.[197] In cases where the content of a privileged document is relevant to the detailed assessment, natural justice may require him to elect whether to disclose part or all of that document to the paying party, or to withdraw reliance on it (proving the point another way, if he can).[198] Any such disclosure would be made solely for the purposes of the taxation, and hence privilege would be preserved for all other purposes.[199] The same applies where one party supplies privileged documents to the other outside the rules but nonetheless solely for the purposes of the detailed assessment.[200] The Court of Appeal has applied a similar procedure in relation to a conditional

---

[194] See *Sanger v Punjab National Bank*, unreported, July 19, 1994, Rattee J. (where witness in giving sworn oral evidence refers to affidavit made by him in past, court and parties entitled to see it as part of credibility assessment).

[195] *R. v Wishart and Boutcher* [2005] EWCA Crim 1337, CA.

[196] CPR, Costs Practice Direction, directions relating to Pt 47, paras 4.3, 4.13 (formerly RSC, Ord.62, r.29(7); CCR, Ord.38, r.20(1)).

[197] *Goldman v Hesper* [1988] 1 W.L.R. 1238 at 1244; *cf. Pamplin v Express Nespapers Ltd* [1985] 1 W.L.R. 689.

[198] *Pamplin v Express Newspapers Ltd* [1985] 1 W.L.R. 689; *Goldman v Hesper* [1988] 1 W.L.R. 1238, CA; *Bourns Inc. v Raychem Corporation* [1999] 3 All E.R. 154, [1999] F.S.R. 641, CA; *Dickinson v Rushmer* (2002) 152 New L.J. 58, Ch.D.; *South Coast Shipping Co. Ltd v Havant B.C.* [2002] 3 All E.R. 779, Ch.D.; *Giambrone v JMC Holdings Ltd* [2002] 4 C.P.L.R. 440, Q.B.D.; CPR Pt 47 Practice Direction—Procedure for Detailed Assessment of Costs and Default Provisions, para.40.14.

[199] *Goldman v Hesper* [1988] 1 W.L.R. 1238, CA; *Bourns Inc. v Raychem Corporation* [1999] 3 All E.R. 154, [1999] F.S.R. 641, CA; and see para.12.32, below.

[200] *Bourns Inc. v Raychem Corporation* [1999] 3 All E.R. 154, [1999] F.S.R. 641, CA.

fee agreement, i.e. the receiving party is put to an election either to produce the agreement or rely on other evidence.[201]

L. EXTENT OF WAIVER

In considering the extent to which a waiver goes, there are three distinct questions that must be addressed:　　　　　　　　　　　　　　　　**12.31**

(a) Is the waiver limited to the purposes of certain proceedings only?

(b) What is the effect of waiver of privilege in part of a document?

(c) How far does a waiver extend beyond the document in question, for example, to other documents dealing with the same transaction, or to material dealing with other transactions?

Each is considered in turn.

(a) Purposes of waiver

A waiver of privilege made for the purposes of particular, limited proceedings has effect only in relation to those proceedings, and privilege may be asserted in any other, separate proceedings thereafter. Thus, for example, where privileged documents were handed (by the future plaintiffs) to the police to assist with their investigations, and subsequently supplied to the defendants in criminal proceedings pursuant to the *Attorney-General's Guidelines*,[202] privilege was not waived for subsequent civil proceedings brought by the plaintiffs against the defendants.[203] There is now a statutory regime for disclosure to the defendants in criminal cases,[204] but there is no reason to suppose that the position on waiver would be different if disclosure took place under it.[205] Again, where privileged documents are lodged with the court for a taxation of costs, privilege is waived only in relation to the taxation itself, and may be reasserted in relation to subsequent proceedings.[206]　　　　　　　　　　　　　　　　　　**12.32**

---

[201] *Hollins v Russell* [2003] 1 W.L.R. 2487, CA (whether it was privileged or not was left open).

[202] [1982] 1 All E.R. 734.

[203] *British Coal Corporation v Dennis Rye Ltd (No.2)* [1988] 1 W.L.R. 1113, CA; see also *R. v Saunders*, unreported, January 10, 1990, Central Criminal Court, Henry J.

[204] Criminal Procedure and Investigations Act 1996, s.17, discussed in Ch.15, para.15.57, below.

[205] *cf. R. v Skingley*, unreported, December 17, 1999, CA (heavy burden on ultimate prosecutor to supply relevant documents, including privileged, to C.P.S., for onward disclosure to defendants).

[206] *Goldman v Hesper* [1988] 1 W.L.R. 1238, CA; *Bourns Inc. v Raychem Corporation* [1999] 3 All E.R. 154, [1999] F.S.R. 641, CA; *cf. Visx Inc. v Nidex Co.* [1999] F.S.R. 92 at 106.

12.33   Although this may work satisfactorily where all the proceedings concerned take place in England and Wales, there is a potential difficulty where the subsequent proceedings between the parties take place in another jurisdiction, whose courts may not reach the same conclusion as the English court. So the (English) court, in an appropriate case, where a party wishes, or is required, to disclose privileged documents only in relation to particular proceedings, may grant an injunction restraining use of the privileged documents outside the jurisdiction, or may hear that part of the evidence derived from such documents in private (*in camera*).[207] The same result may be achieved in the opposite direction, i.e. where use is made in foreign proceedings subject to an order of the court preserving privilege.[208]

(b) Waiver of privilege in part

12.34   If a party waives privilege in part of a document or conversation, does he waive privilege in the whole? The principle of fairness which was discussed above[209] in relation to written evidence also operates here: a party cannot be allowed to "cherry-pick" from privileged material without giving the court and the other parties the opportunity to check on what was left.[210] Accordingly, in principle, privilege relating to a document which deals with one subject matter cannot be waived as to part and asserted as to the remainder.[211] If the document deals with entirely separate subject matters, and is in effect two (or more) documents in one, then waiver of privilege as to the part dealing with one such subject-matter will not amount to waiver of privilege as to others.[212] However, it is not enough to show that the different parts of the document deal with different categories of information.[213] The

---

[207] *Bonzel Ltd v Intervention Ltd (No.2)* [1991] R.P.C. 231.

[208] *Minnesota Mining & Manufacturing Co. v Rennicks (UK) Ltd* [1991] F.S.R. 97, disapproved on another point in *Visx Inc. v Nidex Co.* [1999] F.S.R. 91, CA.

[209] See para.12.04, above.

[210] *Nea Karteria Maritime Co. Ltd v Atlantic and Great Lakes Steamship Corporation* [1981] Com.L.R. 138 at 139, *per* Mustill J., based on *Burnell v British Transport Commission* [1956] 1 Q.B. 187; *Great Atlantic Insurance Co. v Home Insurance Co.* [1981] 1 W.L.R. 529 at 538; *Derby & Co. Ltd v Weldon (No.10)* [1991] 2 All E.R. 908; *C-C Bottlers Ltd v Lion Nathan Ltd* [1993] 2 N.Z.L.R. 445; *Re Robertson Stromberg* (1994) 119 D.L.R.(4th) 551, Sask. Q.B.; *Tau v Durie* [1996] 2 N.Z.L.R. 190 at 193–194; *Hoad v Nationwide News Pty Ltd* (1998) 19 W.A.R. 468, Sup.Ct. W.Aus.; *Somatra Ltd v Sinclair, Roche & Temperley* [2000] 1 W.L.R. 2453, CA; *Fulham Leisure Holdings Ltd v Nicholson Graham & Jones* [2006] EWHC 158 (Ch.); *cf. United Capital Corporation v Bender* [2005] J.R.C. 144, R.Ct. Jersey.

[211] *Lyell v Kennedy* (1884) 27 Ch.D. 1; *Burnell v British Transport Commission* [1956] 1 Q.B. 187, CA; *Great Atlantic Insurance Co. v Home Insurance Co.* [1981] 1 W.L.R. 529, CA; *General Accident Fire and Life Assurance Corporation Ltd v Tanter* [1984] 1 W.L.R. 100 at 114; *A.G. (N.T.) v Maurice* (1986) 161 C.L.R. 475, H.Ct.Aus.

[212] *Great Atlantic Insurance Co. v Home Insurance Co.* [1981] 1 W.L.R. 529, CA; *Pozzi v Eli Lilly & Co., The Times*, December 3, 1986.

[213] *Pozzi v Eli Lilly & Co., The Times*, December 3, 1986.

court will not normally inspect the disputed document in order to decide,[214] unless the other side has also seen it and can argue from knowledge of the contents.[215]

The case of attempted partial waiver of privilege must be distinguished **12.35** from that of redaction of a document to remove privileged matter altogether. Where a document contains both privileged and non-privileged material, the privileged material (e.g. legal advice) may be "blanked-out," thus allowing an "edited" document to be produced.[216] Disclosure of the unprivileged remainder of the document does not waive the privilege in the privileged part, even though both parts deal with the same subject matter.[217]

(c) Effect of waiver on other material

Where privilege in a document or documents is waived, the question **12.36** arises as to the effect of this waiver upon other privileged material. There are broadly four possibilities:

(1) No effect (i.e. waiver only for the document(s) concerned).
(2) Waiver of privilege for all material dealing with the transaction[218] the subject of the document(s) concerned.
(3) Waiver of privilege for all material covered by the same class or privilege.
(4) Waiver of privilege for all material covered by any class of privilege.

---

[214] *Great Atlantic Insurance Co. v Home Insurance Co.* [1981] 1 W.L.R. 529, CA; *Pozzi v Eli Lilly & Co., The Times*, December 3, 1986.
[215] As happened in *Derby & Co. Ltd v Weldon (No.10)* [1991] 2 All E.R. 908.
[216] *Bank of Nova Scotia v Hellenic Mutual War Risk Association (Bermuda) Ltd* [1992] 2 Lloyd's Rep. 540; *British & Commonwealth Holdings v Quadrex Holdings Inc.*, unreported, July 4, 1990, Gatehouse J. (both approved in *G.E. Capital Corporate Finance Group v Bankers Trust Co.* [1995] 1 W.L.R. 172, CA); *R. v First Lord of the Treasury, ex p. Petch*, unreported, January 31, 1994, Harrison J.; *Somerville v Australian Securities Commission* (1993) 118 A.L.R. 149 at 155, Fed.Ct.Aus.; see also *Curlex Manufacturing Pty v Carlingford Australia General Insurance* [1987] 2 Qd.R 335; *Stevens v Canada* (1998) 161 D.L.R. (4th) 85, Fed. CA (narrative portions of lawyers' bill blanked out).
[217] *G.E. Capital Corporate Finance Group v Bankers Trust Co.* [1995] 1 W.L.R. 172, CA; *cf. Arab Monetary Fund v Hashim*, unreported, September 30, 1993, CA (affirming Chadwick J., who had refused to order production of full copies of redacted documents, as redacted on basis of mistake common to both sides that privilege would thereby be preserved).
[218] In *R. v Secretary of State for Transport, ex p. Factortame Ltd (No.5)*, (1997) 9 Admin.L.R. 591, D.C., Auld L.J. said that, where the issue was broad, or there were several issues, or there was a long or complicated history, "it is not . . . apt terminology to ask whether a series of connected events or matters is a single 'transaction' or series of separate 'transactions' for this purpose. Where a party's conduct over time is in issue the effect of partial disclosure of documents must depend on the facts of the case." See also *Vista Maritime Inc. v Sesa Goa*, unreported, October 24, 1997, Mance J., *Ramac Holdings Ltd v Brachers*, unreported, August 30, 2002, Etherton J., and *Fulham Leisure Holdings Ltd v Nicholson Graham & Jones* [2006] EWHC 158 (Ch.), at paras 12–20.

The authorities are not consistent, but the last possibility seems wrong on principle and there is authority against it.[219] In cases where the waiver takes place pre-trial, rather than at trial, there is a conflict of authority as to whether waiver is confined to the document or documents concerned (the first possibility above),[220] or goes wider (the second possibility above).[221] Where the waiver takes place at trial, there is again a conflict of authority, this time as to whether the second[222] or the third[223] possibility is correct. In each case the second view seems more consistent with the "fairness" principle referred to above,[224] and this view is to be preferred.[225] There is, however, room for argument in any given case as to what constitutes the "transaction" in question.[226] Once that "has been identified, and proper disclosure made of that, then the additional principles of fairness may come into play if it is apparent from the disclosure that has been made that it is in fact part of some bigger picture . . . and fairness, and the need not to mislead, requires further disclosure."[227]

M. PRIVILEGE AGAINST SELF-INCRIMINATION

12.37   This privilege can be waived, expressly or impliedly, in the same way as legal professional privilege.[228] The rule is one against obliging the party to disclose information. Hence if the party does so entirely voluntarily, then a subsequent disclosure of the information to others does not infringe the

---

[219] *General Accident Fire and Life Assurance Corporation Ltd v Tanter* [1984] 1 W.L.R. 100.

[220] *General Accident Fire and Life Assurance Corporation Ltd v Tanter* [1984] 1 W.L.R. 100; *Balkanbank v Taher, The Times*, February 19, 1994, Clarke J.

[221] *Re Konigsberg* [1989] 1 W.L.R. 1257 at 1264–65; *Hayes v Dowding* [1996] P.N.L.R. 578; *Oceanic Finance Corporation Ltd v Norton Rose*, unreported, March 26 , 1997, Moore-Bick J.; *R. v Secretary of State for Transport, ex p. Factortame Ltd (No.5)* (1997) 9 Admin.L.R. 591, D.C.; *cf. Derby & Co. Ltd v Weldon (No.10)* [1991] 2 All E.R. 908, and *Parry v News Group Newspapers Ltd* (1990) 140 New L.J. 1719, CA.

[222] *Re Konigsberg* [1989] 1 W.L.R. 1257; *Tanap Investments (UK) Ltd v Tozer*, October 11, 1991, CA; *R. v Bowden* [1999] 1 W.L.R. 823, CA.

[223] *George Doland Ltd v Blackburn Robson Coates & Co.* [1972] 1 W.L.R. 1338.

[224] See para.12.04, above.

[225] *Fulham Leisure Holdings Ltd v Nicholson Graham & Jones* [2006] EWHC 158 (Ch.); see also the survey in *AWB Ltd v Cole (No.5)* [2006] F.C.A. 1234, at paras 164–76, Fed.Ct.Aus.

[226] See, e.g. *Tanap Investments (UK) Ltd v Tozer*, October 11, 1991, CA; *R. v Secretary of State for Transport, ex p. Factortame Ltd (No.5)* (1997) 9 Admin.L.R. 591, D.C.; *Ramac Holdings Ltd v Brachers*, unreported, August 30, 2002, Etherton J.; *Fulham Leisure Holdings Ltd v Nicholson Graham & Jones* [2006] EWHC 158 (Ch.).

[227] *Fulham Leisure Holdings Ltd v Nicholson Graham & Jones* [2006] EWHC 158 (Ch.), at para.19.

[228] See para.12.02, above. Similarly the privilege against the production of documents on the ground of self-exposure to a penalty may also be waived: *Birrell v A.N.A. Commission* (1984) 55 A.L.R. 221.

privilege.[229] The same consequence follows when a party to litigation complies with an order to file or serve a document subject to the privilege without complaint or reservation,[230] or answers questions in court when those answers would be protected by the privilege.[231] The privilege is lost not only in the substantive proceedings but also for any committal proceedings arising out of them.[232] The privilege will also be lost where the privileged material comes into the hands of a third party who comes under an obligation to produce it (e.g. by means of a witness summons or non-party disclosure under CPR, r.31.17).[233] Another example would be where a search order is executed, material incriminating the defendant in an unrelated matter is found and the defendant allows it to be taken by the Supervising Solicitor without first claiming the privilege.[234]

Whilst it is clear that a party may waive the privilege during the course of proceedings,[235] the extent to which a person may waive the privilege in advance of proceedings will depend on the circumstances. Thus: **12.38**

(1) The Court of Appeal has left open the question whether the law will give effect to a contract whereby a contracting party agrees not to rely on the privilege against the other in relation to dealings covered by the contract.[236]

(2) A party may be bound to supply information to a regulatory body, where one of the rules of that body requires members to provide information in the context of an investigation.[237]

(3) It has been held in Australia that merely making an out-of-court statement does not waive the privilege.[238]

(4) There is no waiver by a person merely through the fact that he was a trustee or fiduciary with a duty to account to the claimant in proceedings.[239]

---

[229] See Ch.11, para.11.108, above.

[230] *Re L (A Minor)(Police Investigation: Privilege)* [1997] A.C. 16, HL; *Compagnie Noga d'Importation et d'Exportation S.A. v Australia and New Zealand Banking Group Ltd* [2007] EWHC 85 (Comm.).

[231] *R. v Lincoln Coroner, ex p. Hay* [2000] Lloyd's Rep. Medical 264 at 273, D.C.; *Dadourian Group International Inc. v Simms* [2006] EWCA 1745, at para.14.

[232] *Dadourian Group International Inc. v Simms* [2006] EWCA 1745.

[233] *Marcel v Metropolitan Police Commissioner* [1992] Ch. 225, CA; see Ch.11, para.11.112, above.

[234] *O Ltd v Z* [2005] EWHC 238 (Ch.); *cf. C Plc v P* [2006] 4 All E.R. 311, at para.23 (privilege claimed in time).

[235] e.g. *R. v Lincoln Coroner, ex p. Hay* [2000] Lloyd's Rep. Med. 264 at 273, D.C.

[236] *Bishopsgate Investment Ltd v Maxwell* [1993] Ch.1, CA; see Ch.11, para.11.120, above.

[237] *R. v Institute of Chartered Accountants of England and Wales, ex p. Taher Nawaz, The Times*, November 7, 1996, Q.B.D.; upheld on appeal to CA, April 25, 1997 (unreported); see para.11.107, above.

[238] *Accident Insurance Mutual Holdings Ltd v McFadden* (1993) 31 N.S.W. L.R. 412, CA of N.S.W.; see also *Reid v Howard* (1993) 31 N.S.W.L.R. 298 at 302, CA of N.S.W.

[239] *Tate Access Floors Inc. v Boswell* [1991] Ch. 512 at 518; *Bishopsgate Investment Management Ltd v Maxwell* [1993] Ch. 1, CA; *Reid v Howard* (1993) 31 N.S.W.L.R. 298 at 303–4 (CA of N.S.W.) and (1995) 184 C.L.R. 1 (H.Ct.Aus.).

N. "WITHOUT PREJUDICE" PRIVILEGE

12.39   "Without prejudice" privilege is effectively a joint privilege and may not be waived by one party unilaterally, but only by both parties together.[240] Thus there may be waiver if both parties to the communications agree or if one party is deemed to have waived the privilege and that waiver is accepted by the other party.[241] However, a party deploying evidence of what was said in "without prejudice" communications in support of its case on the merits loses the right to object to the admissibility of any admissions made in such communications.[242] However, where parties have engaged in without prejudice mediation and correspondence, the inclusion of without prejudice documents in a list of documents (without claiming privilege in the list) does not amount to a waiver for the purposes of admissibility in evidence.[243]

12.40   It was once thought that any privilege came to an end if a settlement resulted from the negotiations,[244] but this is not so. If there is an alleged settlement, then "without prejudice" communications will be admissible evidence as between the parties concerned,[245] to prove it,[246] but the privilege of either (and obligation of both) not to produce the material to any third or other party continues even after the litigation is over.[247] Although there is some Australian authority to the effect that the mere disclosure of[248] or reliance upon without prejudice communications at an interlocutory stage[249] results in a waiver of the privilege for all purposes, in England the correct test has been held to be whether the justice of the case requires on the facts that the other party should be permitted to use their without prejudice documents at trial (and in turn the party who has relied upon without prejudice communications should be forced to disclose his documents). Where there has only been limited deployment (not on the merits)

---

[240] *Walker v Wisher* (1889) 23 Q.B.D. 335 at 337; *Somatra Ltd v Sinclair Roche & Temperley* [2000] 1 Lloyd's Rep. 311 at 314, reversed, [2000] 1 W.L.R. 2453, CA, on other grounds.

[241] *Stotesbury v Turner* [1943] 1 K.B. 370 at 373; *cf. Burg Design Pty Ltd v Wolki* (1999) 162 A.L.R. 639, Fed.Ct.Aus.; *Instance v Denny Bros. Printing Ltd, The Times,* February 28, 2000 (request for discovery in other proceedings is not offer to waive privilege).

[242] *Somatra Ltd v Sinclair Roche & Temperley* [2000] 1 W.L.R. 2453, CA; *cf. Forster v Friedland,* unreported, November 10, 1992, CA, *per* Hoffmann L.J. (production or supply of a privileged document did not itself constitute a waiver; the question was whether in so doing the objection to admissibility had been waived); see also *Sampson v John Boddy Timber Ltd* (1995) 145 New L.J. 851, CA.

[243] *Smiths Group Plc v Weiss,* unreported , March 22, 2002, Ch.D.

[244] *Rush & Tompkins Ltd v Greater London Council* [1988] 1 All ER 549 at 552, CA.

[245] Both of whom will have access to such communications already as regards correspondence passing between them, but not necessarily of each other's notes or records of meetings and other conversations: *cf. Somatra Ltd v Sinclair Roche & Temperley* [2000] 1 Lloyd's Rep. 311, reversed [2000] 1 W.L.R. 2453, CA.

[246] See Ch.11, para.11.127, above.

[247] *Rush & Tompkins Ltd v Greater London Council* [1989] 1 A.C. 1280, HL.

[248] *Johnston v Jackson* (1860) 6 V.L.R. 1.

[249] *Trade Practices Commission v Arnotts Ltd* (1989) 88 A.L.R. 69, Fed.Ct.Aus.

of without prejudice material at an interlocutory stage and not before the trial judge, this is unlikely to constitute good grounds for opening up without prejudice communications for all purposes.[250] In another case, where threats were allegedly made during a mediation (which failed to result in a settlement), evidence of the allegations could be given after trial on the issue of costs, but only because the parties had been involved in satellite litigation where the same allegations were made and denied, thus amounting to a mutual waiver of the privilege covering whether or not such threats were indeed made during the mediation.[251]

O. WITNESS STATEMENTS

The obligation that arises on service of witness statements not to use them save for the purposes of the proceedings has already been discussed.[252] The obligation will come to an end, either completely, or *pro tanto*, if the witness consents, the court gives permission or it has been put in evidence at a hearing held in public.[253] The former rules referred to the consent of the party serving the statement, who might well not be the witness.[254] In principle the privilege should be that of the party who has served the statement and it remains to be seen whether the courts will uphold this rule change, which has the effect of undermining the party's privilege.[255] This change perhaps can be justified on the basis that, once a witness statement has been served, there has already been some waiver of legal professional privilege, and because the party would have served the statement in the knowledge that it might be used with the consent of the person making the statement.

12.41

P. PUBLIC INTEREST IMMUNITY

This "privilege" is different from those previously discussed, being "public law not private right",[256] and the objection must be taken by the court if neither party does so.[257] Accordingly it has often been said that it is not

12.42

---

[250] *Somatra Ltd v Sinclair Roche & Temperley* [2000] 1 Lloyd's Rep. 311 at 314, reversed on other grounds [2000] 1 W.L.R. 2453, CA.
[251] *Hall v Pertemps Group Ltd, The Times,* December 23, 2005, Ch.D.
[252] See Ch.11, para.11.36 above.
[253] CPR, r.32.12.
[254] RSC, Ord.38, r.2A(11); CCR, Ord.20, r.12A(11).
[255] *cf. General Mediterranean Holdings S.A. v Patel* [1999] 3 All E.R. 673, Toulson J.
[256] *Science Research Council v Nassé* [1980] A.C. 1028 at 1087.
[257] *Duncan v Cammell Laird & Co.* [1942] A.C. 624 at 641; see Ch.9, para.11.072.

capable of waiver by a party, even if the party concerned is the Crown.[258] The width of this proposition has been challenged, and it is now the practice that the immunity may be waived by the Crown or other body prima facie entitled to the immunity,[259] although even in such a case the court presumably has the jurisdiction to override the waiver if it considers that the public interest so requires. As stated elsewhere,[260] both under the December 1996 paper, and as a matter of case law, there is no longer an obligation to claim public interest immunity if the relevant decision maker is satisfied that the public interest is in favour of disclosure, ie the immunity is outweighed by the interests of justice. The maker of a statement which is subject to public interest immunity may produce a situation in which the immunity ceases to exist.[261] Thus where an informer is willing for his identity to be disclosed, then the primary justification for his anonymity is no longer applicable and the immunity will generally not apply in such a case.[262] Where the material has come into the public domain,[263] the courts will generally find no point in maintaining the immunity: "if the cat has already four legs out of the bag, there is little point in holding on to his tail".[264]

12.43   There may be circumstances in which considerations of fairness mean that some measure of access must be given to material covered by public interest immunity. Thus if there is a risk that the material presented to the other party and the court might be misleading or create an unfair situation without the disclosure and production of other material covered by public interest immunity, then the court may order disclosure and production of such other material,[265] but usually only after having inspected that other material itself.

---

[258] *Air Canada v Secretary of State for Trade (No.2)* [1983] 2 A.C. 394 at 436; *Australian Securities Commission v Zorro* [1992] A.C.L. Rep. 195 F.C. 3; *Babcock v Attorney-General of Canada* (2002) 214 D.L.R. (4th) 193, at 207.

[259] In *McDonald v Radio Telefís Eireann* [2001] 1 I.E.S.C. 91, the Irish Supreme Court held that, where police officers, summoned to give evidence in a civil action by subpoena, consulted with the defendants and their lawyers at court, "even if some reference to the files was made by the [police], does not amount to a waiver by the notice parties of any public interest privilege [sic] which may attach to the documents in question."

[260] Ch.11, para.11.085; *R. v Chief Constable, ex p. Wiley* [1995] 1 A.C. 274, HL; *Bennett v Metropolitan Commissioner* [1995] 1 W.L.R. 488; December 1996 paper, para.2.3.

[261] *Hehir v Metropolitan Police Commissioner* [1982] 1 W.L.R. 723.

[262] *Savage v Chief Constable of Hampshire* [1997] 2 All E.R. 631, CA; *Multi-Guarantee Co. Ltd v Cavalier Insurance Co. Ltd, The Times,* June 24, 1986; *cf. Thorburn v Hermon, The Times,* May 14, 1992; *A v Hayden (No.2)* (1984) 56 A.L.R. 82 at 90–91. See also *Carnduff v Rock* [2001] 1 W.L.R. 1786, CA (informers claim for information struck out in the public interest).

[263] e.g. being read out in open court: *Barings Plc v Coopers & Lybrand* [2000] 3 All E.R. 910, CA (Banking Act 1982, s.82(1)).

[264] *Multi-Guarantee Co. Ltd v Cavalier Insurance Co. Ltd, The Times,* June 24, 1986; *cf. Halford v Sharples* [1992] 1 W.L.R. 736, CA; see also *R. v G and B* [2004] 2 Cr.App.R. 37, CA (inappropriate to restrain counsel in criminal trial from making use of PII material accidentally disclosed to them).

[265] *B v N* (1994) 35 N.S.W.L.R. 140.

CHAPTER 13

Failure to comply with disclosure obligation

CHAPTER 13

Failure to comply with disclosure obligation

Formerly there was an express provision in the rules for striking out **13.01** where there had been a failure to provide disclosure.[1] Now, where a party who is required by any of the CPR (including Pt 31) or any order made thereunder, to give disclosure of documents or to produce any documents for the purposes of inspection or any other purpose or to supply copies thereof, fails to comply with any provision of that rule or that order, then it is open to the court to make an order requiring the party to comply with express consequences set out for failure to comply[2] or an order that the statement of case of the party in default be struck out and judgment be entered accordingly.[3] There is an exception for matrimonial causes, where the sanction of dismissal or striking out is not available.[4]

A. APPLICATION

Where there has been no response to a court order under CPR, Pt 31, any **13.02** sanctions stipulated in the order will take effect unless and until the party who has failed to comply has sought and obtained relief by way of separate application.[5] Where the order itself does not provide any sanction and, in breach of the order, no response has been provided, then the opposing party may apply to the court for the statement of case to be struck out or for an

---

[1] RSC, Ord.24, r.16(1); CCR, Ord.14, r.10(1).
[2] CPR, r.3.1(3).
[3] CPR, r.3.4(2)(c), (3).
[4] Family Proceedings Rules 1991, r.2.20(1)(b), applying a modified version of RSC, Ord.24, r.16(1).
[5] CPR, rr.3.8, 3.9.

order that unless the original order is complied with within a period of time the statement of case will be struck out.[6]

13.03   Where there is some form of response, it is more difficult to say that a sanction stipulated in the order should automatically apply as there may be some debate as to whether the response complies with the order or is a bona fide attempt to comply with the order.[7] In such a case it will be often for the opposing party to make the application for a strike out order, rather than the party arguably in default making an application for relief from the consequences of the original order. Where the opposing party makes an application for a strike out, alleging that there has been breach of an order, then in appropriate cases the prudent course may be for the party arguably in default to make a cross application for relief from the consequences stipulated in the original order that it is alleged he has failed to comply with.[8]

13.04   In relation to applications arising out of a failure to comply with an order, practice direction or rule relating to disclosure, it will depend on the circumstances, including the nature of the default, as to whether or not evidence needs to be filed. Thus, if there has been a failure to provide a list of documents, an affidavit (or witness statement) from the applicant will generally be unnecessary. If it is contended that the discovery provided is inadequate, then evidence will usually be appropriate; such evidence should set out the history of the matter, identify the inadequacies in the disclosure provided and the defaults relied upon. The party alleged to be in default will often need to file evidence.

B. PURPOSE

13.05   CPR, rr.3.1(3) and 3.4(2)(c) and (3) are designed to secure compliance with the rules, practice directions and court orders, and not to punish a party for not having complied with them in time. The object of the powers vested in the courts to ensure compliance in relation to disclosure is not to punish the defaulting party for his conduct, but to secure a fair trial of the action in accordance with the due process of the court.[9] Although the court has an express power to make an order subject to conditions, including a condition to pay a sum of money into court,[10] in principle a condition requiring a defendant to pay the balance of the claim into court and in default being debarred from defending the action will often usually be

---

[6] CPR, r.3.4(2)(c).
[7] *Realkredit Danmark A/S v York Montague Ltd, The Times*, February 1, 1999, CA.
[8] CPR, r.3.9.
[9] *Cropper v Smith* (1884) 26 Ch.D. 700 at 710; *The World Protector* [1985] 1 Lloyd's Rep.227; *Logicrose Ltd v Southend United Football Club Ltd, The Times*, March 5, 1988; *Star News Shops Ltd v Stafford Refrigeration Ltd* [1998] 1 W.L.R. 536, CA (old rules).
[10] CPR, r.3.1(3)(a) and (5).

regarded as inappropriate as a means of enforcing compliance with an order for disclosure.[11]

In accordance with its purpose, the court has a broad range of orders it may make in its discretion pursuant to an application to enforce a party's obligations on disclosure. The appropriate order in each case will depend on the circumstances. The principal options are as follows:

    13.06

(1) An extension of time within which the defaulting party must comply with the relevant order or rule.[12] Where there has been more than a technical default, the court is likely to make such an order a "final" one. This does not in fact mean that the order is the last one that will be made: an "unless" order may follow.

(2) An extension of time under an "unless" or conditional order, spelling out the consequences of the failure to comply.[13] The condition may be to strike out the statement of case of the defaulting party unless the order is complied with within a specified period of time. Such an order is appropriate where the party is substantially in default of his disclosure obligations. But it must be made "in the clearest and most precise language".[14]

(3) An immediate order striking out the statement of case of the defaulting party.[15] This power will only be exercised in the most exceptional circumstances, such as where it is clear that the defaulting party has no intention of complying with his obligations as to disclosure.[16] It cannot be used in matrimonial causes.[17]

C. STRIKING OUT

Although the court has the express power to strike out a statement of case of a defaulting party for the breach of any rule, practice direction or court order,[18] such an order will generally be made only where there has been a deliberate and continuing refusal to provide disclosure or where the default

    13.07

---

[11] *Husband's of Marchwood Ltd v Drummond Walker Developments Ltd* [1975] 1 W.L.R. 603, CA.

[12] CPR, r.3.1(2)(a); *Ropac Ltd v Inntrepreneur Pub Co, The Times,* June 21, 2000 ("unless" order made by consent: extension refused); *Keith v CPM Field Marketing Ltd, The Times,* August 29, 2000, CA (interrelationship with relief from sanctions under CPR, r.3.9(1)).

[13] CPR, r.3.1(3).

[14] *Abalian v Innous* [1936] 2 All E.R. 833, *per* Greene L.J.; *Morgans v Needham,* unreported, October 28, 1999, CA.

[15] CPR, r.3(2)(c).

[16] *Star News Shops Ltd v Stafford Refrigeration Ltd* [1998] 1 W.L.R. 536, CA (held wrong in principle and a wrong exercise of discretion to strike out a defence for breach of a non-peremptory order); *Johnson v Valks* [2000] 1 W.L.R. 1502, CA.

[17] Family Proceedings Rules 1991, r.2.20(1)(b), applying a modified version of RSC, Ord.24, r.16(1).

[18] CPR, r.3.4(2)(c); *cf. Biguzzi v Rank Leisure Plc* [1999] 1 W.L.R. 1926, CA.

has made the fair trial of an action impossible.[19] Such an order may be made where the default relied upon is giving no disclosure, and also giving insufficient disclosure.[20] A statement of case will not be struck out merely because the party is in contempt of court.[21] Under the CPR the court may make "unless" orders for striking out statements of case for failure to comply with disclosure obligations. But in principle, it will often grant relief from sanctions in appropriate cases on the application of the defaulting party where that party is able to show that it bona fide intends to comply with its disclosure obligations and that, despite the default so far, a fair trial of the action is still possible.[22] However, where a party was guilty of conduct which put the fairness of the trial in jeopardy , or which rendered further proceedings unsatisfactory and to prevent the court from doing justice, the court is bound to refuse to allow the party to take further part in the proceedings and (where appropriate) to determine the proceedings against him.[23]

13.08   Thus, where a claimant has continued to keep back documents which he ought to disclose, the action may be dismissed. In *Danvillier v Myers*,[24] the effect of such an order was to defeat the plaintiff's claim in its entirety, even though the missing disclosure only related to part of the plaintiff's action. Such an order was justified as being the consequences of having combined the other part of his action with claims he attempted to support by suppression of information he was bound to give. Although in an appropriate case it is open to the court to dismiss only that part of a party's claim as relates to the inadequate disclosure, the Court of Appeal has held that[25]:

> "The ordinary practice is not to strike out part of the claim, that is the claim for damages, leaving the claim for an injunction alive, but to dismiss the whole action if default in discovery is made."

13.09   Similarly, where a defendant has failed to provide disclosure, despite adjournments to enable him to do so, the court is justified in striking out the

---

[19] *Danvillier v Myers* [1883] W.N. 58, CA; *Republic of Liberia v Roye* (1876) 1 App.Cas. 139; *James Nelson v Nelson* [1906] 2 K.B. 217; *Logicrose Ltd v Southend United Football Club*, *The Times*, March 5, 1988; *Canter v Stone, Odell & Frankson*, April 19, 1991, unreported, CA; *Grand Metropolitan Nominee (No.2) Co. Ltd v Evans* [1992] 1 W.L.R. 1191, CA (further and better particulars); *Re Jokai Tea Holdings Ltd* [1992] 1 W.L.R. 1196, CA; *Mercantile Credit Company of Ireland Ltd v Heelan* [1998] 1 I.R. 81, Sup.Ct. Ireland.
[20] *Kennedy v Lyell* [1882] W.N. 137, CA (interrogatories).
[21] *Re Swaptronics Ltd, The Times*, August 17, 1998.
[22] *Keith v CPM Field Marketing Ltd, The Times*, August 29, 2000, CA; *Cank v Broadyard Associates Ltd*, unreported, July 11, 2000, CA.
[23] *Arrow Nominees Inc. v Blackledge* [2000] All E.R. (D) 854, *The Times*, July 7, 2000, CA; *Commission for the New Towns v Edwards*, unreported, July 10, 2000, Smith J.; *Raja v Van Hoogstraten (No.8)* [2006] EWHC 1315 (Ch). See also Tronson (2006) 25 C.I.R. 451.
[24] [1883] W.N. 58, CA.
[25] *Caven-Atack v Church of Scientology Religious Education College Inc.*, October 31, 1994, unreported, CA.

defence on the ground that the default is deliberate and continuing.[26] But in general it is wrong in principle, and a wrong exercise of discretion, to strike out a statement of case for breach of a non-peremptory order,[27] unless perhaps the default has already made a fair trial impossible as it is apparent that the defaulting party has no intention of complying. In one case the Court of Appeal allowed an appeal from a striking out order, on the basis that the failure to comply with earlier disclosure orders, because the failures were not "gross" enough to justify striking out.[28]

In modern times, the party ordered to give disclosure will be given every **13.10** opportunity to comply with his disclosure obligations, but if he fails to comply with an "unless" order, usually made after serious failure to comply with earlier orders, striking out a party's statement of case is automatic, and applications for relief against the consequences are generally unsympathetically received.[29] However, where failure to comply with an "unless" order has not been deliberate, particularly where the defaulting party can provide a reasonable excuse, the court may in its discretion be willing to grant him relief against the consequences of such an "unless" order. Thus where the failure to comply is due to a party's solicitors' incompetence, rather than an intentional failure by the defendant himself, the court has been willing to grant relief from the consequences of an "unless" order, albeit on the strictest terms as to compliance with the original disclosure order.[30] It has also been held that, where the court has to decide the consequences of a failure to comply with an "unless" order, the relevant question is whether such failure is intentional and contumelious.[31] However, it will not be a good excuse in all cases for a party simply to blame his legal advisers.[32] The general rule is that the court does not distinguish between the litigant and his advisers[33] and even where the litigant's chosen intermediary for giving instructions was outside England and Wales.[34]

---

[26] *Fisher v Hughes* (1887) 25 W.R. 528; *Haigh v Haigh* (1885) 31 Ch.D. 478; *Gibson v Sykes* (1884) 28 S.J. 533 (interrogatories); *Farden v Richter* (1889) 23 Q.B.D. 124 (interrogatories).

[27] *Star News Shop Ltd v Stafford Refrigeration Ltd* [1998] 1 W.L.R. 536, CA; *Johnson v Valks* [2000] 1 W.L.R. 1502, CA.

[28] *Carlco Ltd v Chief Constable of Dyfed-Powys Police* [2002] EWCA Civ 1754.

[29] *Owen v Sepro Building Services Ltd*, April 16, 1991, unreported, CA (failure to comply with Order); *CIBC Mellon Trust Co v Stolzenberg* [2004] EWCA Civ 827, (2004) S.J.L.B. 824, CA (refused to set aside judgment in default of compliance with unless order to provide disclosure required by freezing order); *cf. Raja v Van Hoogstraten* [2004] EWCA Civ 968, [2004] 4 All E.R. 793 at [112–113] (CA held inappropriate to strike out defence for failure to comply with disclosure provision in freezing order where no risk that this failure put in jeopardy the fairness of the trial).

[30] *Beeforth v Beeforth, The Times*, September 17, 1998, CA; *Pereira v Beamlands, The Times*, March 7, 1996, Ch.D; *Western Trust & Savings Ltd v Acland & Lensam*, unreported, May 23, 2000.

[31] *Re Jokai Tea Holdings Ltd* [1992] 1 W.L.R. 1196 at 1203.

[32] *Hytec Ltd v Coventry City Council* [1997] 1 W.L.R. 1666, CA (failure to comply with an "unless" order for Further and Better Particulars of Defence and Counterclaim).

[33] *ibid.*, 1675–6; *cf. Murphy v J. Donohoe Ltd* [1996] 1 I.R.123, Sup.Ct. Ireland.

[34] *Downes Manor Properties Ltd v Bank of Namibia, The Times,* March 18, 1999, CA.

13.11   Often, there may be a dispute between the parties as to whether or not there has been compliance with the "unless" order. Thus, where it appears that a party has endeavoured to comply with the order and believes on reasonable grounds that he has complied with the order, then the court may be willing to relieve that party from the consequences of a failure to comply or, indeed, to hold that it had not been proven that the "unless" order has not been complied with.[35] Where there has been complete non-compliance with an "unless" order it will follow that the statement of case of the defaulting party is struck out without more, and it will be unnecessary for the opposing party to apply to the court for a further order.[36] Where there has been some attempt at compliance, it may be more debatable as to whether or not the "unless" order takes effect,[37] and, in such circumstances, it may be necessary for the opposing party to apply to the court for an order that the statement of case be or has been struck out,[38] and it has been doubted that the opposing party is *not* required to apply for an order that the claim be struck out.[39]

13.12   In every case where the court has to consider whether to make an order striking out a statement of case without more or to give effect to an "unless" order, the court will look at the circumstances, including whether or not the failure was deliberate or contumelious, the reasons given for non-compliance, the extent of non-compliance and the prejudice caused to the other party.[40] Even in cases short of a deliberate and contumelious failure, it is open to the court to justify the striking out of a statement of case in appropriate cases.[41]

13.13   In the event that the disclosure sought is provided prior to the hearing of an application to strike out a statement of case or an application for relief against the consequences of such an order, the court will generally decline to

---

[35] *Realkredit Danmark AS v York Montague Ltd, The Times*, February 1, 1999, CA; *Morgans v Needham*, unreported, October 28, 1999, CA.

[36] *Lonrho Plc v Fayed (No.3), The Times*, June 24, 1993, CA; *cf. Kumar v United Air Travel (Services) Ltd*, unreported, January 14, 1993, CA (a case of plaintiff's failure to comply with an "unless" disclosure order), and *Artisan Scaffolding Co. v The Antique Hypermarket Ltd*, February 10, 1993, unreported, CA (defendant's non-compliance with an "unless" order for disclosure was not sufficient in itself to justify striking out the defence).

[37] *Realkredit Danmark A/S v York Montague Ltd, The Times*, February 1, 1999, CA; *Scottish & Newcastle Plc v Raguz* [2004] EWHC 1835 (Ch.).

[38] See, e.g. *QPS Consultants Ltd v Kruger Tissue (Manufacturing) Ltd*, unreported, September 10, 1999, CA (f.b.p.—struck out).

[39] *Langtree Group Plc v Richardson* [2004] EWCA Civ 1447.

[40] *Caribbean General Insurance Ltd v Frizzell Insurance Brokers Ltd* [1994] 1 Lloyd's Rep 32, CA; *Hogg v Aggarwal, The Times*, August 1, 1995 ("unless" order to set down not complied with); *Keith v CPM Field Marketing Ltd, The Times*, August 29, 2000, CA; *Cank v Broadyard Associates Ltd*, unreported, July 11, 2000, Smith J.

[41] *Manilal & Sons (PTE) Ltd v Bhupendra F K J Shan* [1990] 2 M.L.J. 282, Singapore High Court (claim struck out for failing to make full disclosure of documents in circumstances where the omission, if not deliberate, had arisen out of gross negligence amounting to wilfulness); *cf. QPS Consultants Ltd v Kruger Tissue (Manufacturing) Ltd*, unreported September 10, 1999, CA (f.b.p.—struck out).

strike out the statement of case or will grant relief again a striking out as the object of the application would have been achieved. An action ought to be dismissed or the defence struck out only in the most exceptional circumstances once the missing disclosure has been provided, and then only if, despite its production, there remains a real risk that justice cannot be done.[42] However, it is open to the court to refuse to grant relief against the consequences of an "unless" order, even when the documents have been produced, if the original default was intentional or contumelious. In an extreme case, the court may dismiss a claim or strike out a defence where the failure to provide the disclosure has not been wilful or deliberate, where the failure has the result of making a fair trial of the action impossible.[43] In an appropriate case the court may adjourn to trial an application to strike out on the ground that the destruction of documents has made a fair trial impossible.[44]

Where no prejudice can be shown to the opposing party, the court may take that into consideration in deciding not to strike out a party's statement of case for non-compliance. So in one case,[45] the judge faced with an application at trial to dismiss the plaintiff's claim for failure to give proper disclosure, held that as the defendants were able to establish their factual case on the basis of documentary and other case available to them (and succeeded on the merits), the absence of other documentation "could not be said ultimately to have prejudiced the defendants" and dismissed an application to strike out the plaintiff's claim.

13.14

Where a party is in default through no fault of his own, the court generally will not exercise its powers to strike out, although in an appropriate case, it may stay the proceedings.[46] But, as already stated, the court will not ordinarily distinguish the litigant from his advisers for that purpose of deciding whether the default arises through any fault of his.[47]

13.15

---

[42] *Logicrose Ltd v Southend United Football Club Ltd, The Times*, March 5, 1988. This approach was doubted by Rose L.J. in *Artisan Scaffolding Co. v The Antique Hypermarket Ltd*, February 10, 1993, unreported, CA, but it was referred to without criticism by Stuart-Smith L.J. in *Lonhro Plc v Fayed (No.3), The Times,* June 24, 1993, CA. See also *Murphy v J. Donohoe Ltd* [1996] 1 I.R. 123, Sup.Ct. Ireland; *Mercantile Credit Company of Ireland Ltd v Heelan* [1998] 1 I.R.81, Sup.Ct. Ireland; *Gates v Pirate's Lure Beverage Room* (2004) 237 D.L.R. (4th), Nova Scotia CA (relief granted against dismissal where a failure to provide disclosure pursuant to a consent order).

[43] *Landauer Ltd v Comins & Co., The Times*, August 7, 1991, CA: action struck out where the claimant introduced a policy of destruction and documents after commencing the proceedings. This case was distinguished in *GMTC Tools v Yuasa Warwick Machinery* (1994) 73 B.L.R. 102, CA (destruction of customer orders caused no prejudice, hence leave to amend given). See also *Coleman v Dunlop Ltd*, unreported, October 20, 1999, CA.

[44] *Prest v Marc Rich & Co Investment AG* [2006] EWHC 927 (Comm).

[45] *Cepheus Shipping Corporation v Guardian Royal Exchange Assurance Plc* [1995] 1 Lloyd's Rep. 622.

[46] *Wilson v Raffalofitch* (1881) 7 Q.B.D. 553, CA; *Cardwell v Tomlinson* (1885) 52 L.T. 746.

[47] *Hytec Information Systems Ltd v Coventry City Council* [1997] 1 W.L.R. 1666, 1675–6, CA; *Downes Manor Properties Ltd v Bank of Namibia, The Times*, March 18, 1999, CA.

13.16   In approaching an application to dismiss an application on the basis of non-compliance for an order for specific disclosure, a court may give the benefit of any doubt in the construction of the order to the claimant whose action is facing the prospect of being dismissed.[48]

13.17   In deciding whether or not to strike out a statement of case for a failure to make proper disclosure, the court may be required to consider whether a strike out order is a proportionate step to take in that it may have the result of depriving the defaulting party from pursuing or defending a claim in court. Such a requirement may be derived both from the overriding objective[49] and Art.6.1 of the European Convention on Human Rights. First, the new procedural code embodied in the CPR is subject to the overriding objective of enabling the court to deal with cases justly, including dealing with cases in ways which are proportionate. Secondly, Art.6.1 of the European Convention on Human Rights embodies the "right to a court" of which the right of access, that is, the right to institute proceedings before a court, constitutes one aspect. This is not an absolute right and restrictions on this right are permissible where there is a reasonable relationship of proportionality between the means employed and a legitimate aim sought to be achieved. Legitimate aims no doubt include ensuring court orders are obeyed and that proper disclosure is made to ensure a fair trial.[50]

Destruction of documents pre-litigation

13.18   Many businesses have document retention policies. This may lead to relevant documents being destroyed either before or during litigation. Once litigation has started it is clear that there is an obligation to preserve relevant documents, more so once an order for disclosure of documents has been made. The position is not so straight forward in respect of the preservation of documents prior to litigation. Absence an agreement between the parties or a special relationship requiring the retention of documents (such as principal and agent, broker and underwriter), in general a party owes no duty to another to preserve documents so that they may be available to be produced in litigation at a time where no litigation is contemplated. However, once litigation is contemplated it is the general practice of solicitors to advise their clients of the need to preserve relevant documents so that they can be available on disclosure.[51] What if relevant documents are destroyed

---

[48] *Triolacan Ltd v Medway Power Drives Ltd, The Times,* October 21, 1991, CA; *Murphy v J. Donohoe Ltd* [1996] 1 I.R. 123, Sup.Ct. Ireland.

[49] *Keith v CPM Field Marketing Ltd, The Times,* August 29, 2000, CA.

[50] *Osman v United Kingdom* (1998) 5 B.H.R.C. 293, E.Ct.H.R.; *Arrow Nominees Inc. v Blackledge, The Times,* July 7, 2000, CA.

[51] Ch.14, para.14.03 below. In the USA it is recognised that an obligation to preserve evidence arises when a party is on notice that the evidence is relevant to litigation or when a party should have known that the evidence is relevant to future litigation: *Zubulake v UBS Warburg* (2003) 220 F.R.D. 212.

by a party prior to the commencement of litigation? In principle, there is much to be said for a test based on whether the destruction of documents has made a fair trial impossible.[52] However, the test that has been adopted in Victoria, is that in cases of pre-litigation of destruction of documents the criteria for sanctions (including strike out, but not including drawing of adverse inferences) is whether the conduct amounted to an attempt to pervert the course of justice.[53] This has been followed at first instance in England.[54] It would be more satisfactory to have the test based on whether a fair trial is still possible (if not the action or statement of case should be struck out) and whether there has been a deliberate attempt to pervert the course of justice.[55]

D. CONDITIONS

Short of striking out an action or a defence, the court may impose conditions on the defaulting party, so long as such conditions are consistent with the purposes of the Rules in relation to disclosure.[56] So for example where, on an application to dismiss the action for the plaintiff's failure to serve a list of documents, the list of documents was provided shortly before the hearing of the application, the court required that an undertaking that the summons for directions be restored within 28 days as a term of not dismissing the action.[57] A condition requiring a defendant to pay the balance of the claimant's claim into court or be debarred from defending the action was held under the old rules to be inappropriate.[58] Under the CPR the court is expressly given power to make an order subject to conditions, including a condition to pay money into court,[59] and to order a party to pay money into court where that party has, without good reason, failed to comply with a rule, a practice direction or a relevant pre-action protocol.[60]

13.19

---

[52] Cameron C. and Liberman J. "Destruction of documents before proceedings commence: what is a court to do", (2003) 27 Melbourne University Law Review 273.
[53] *British American Tobacco Australia Services Ltd v McCabe* [2002] V.S.C.A. 197 at [175], where the Court of Appeal of Victoria reversed a decision to strike out a defence on the ground that a fair trial was not possible due to a policy of destruction of documents being implemented at a time when litigation was contemplated. The purpose of the policy had the intention of ensuring the destruction of documents which might be harmful to the defence of such litigation.
[54] *Douglas v Hello! Ltd* [2003] 1 All E.R. 1087, Ch.D.
[55] *Electronic Disclosure: A report of a working party chaired by Mr Justice Cresswell*, para.2.35.
[56] CPR, r.3.1(3).
[57] *Chiprose v Rosemand* [1965] 1 W.L.R. 153.
[58] *Husband's of Marchwood Ltd v Drummond Walker Developments Ltd* [1975] 1 W.L.R.603, CA.
[59] CPR, r.3.1(3)(a).
[60] CPR, r.3.1(5); *Grundy v Naqvi* [2001] EWCA Civ 139, CA (no strike out for failure of exchange of witness statement in breach of unless order; instead payment into account ordered).

So the position may well now be different particularly where a party has repeatedly breached timetables or court orders, or has behaved in bad faith.[61] It would certainly seem that it is open to the court to make an order that unless the disclosure is provided by a certain date, the party in default will be precluded from producing documents later and relying upon them at trial.[62]

13.20   Where a claimant is in default, as an alternative to striking out his claim, the court may in an appropriate case, stay the proceedings until the disclosure is provided.[63]

13.21   Generally, the party in default will be ordered to pay the costs of any application. The court may exercise its powers to order that the costs to be assessed summarily by the court and give the party a limited amount of time to pay the costs to the opposing party.[64] As a condition, the court may impose the stipulation that the statement of case of the defaulting party be struck out unless the costs are paid within the stipulated period or in the case of a claimant that the claim is stayed until payment is made. Where an immediate assessment by the court is not practicable, then it is open to the court to direct a party to pay a sum of money into court, thus providing the opposing party some security for his costs.[65]

E. REVOCATION AND VARIATION OF ORDERS

13.22   Any order made under CPR, Pt 31 may, on sufficient cause being shown, be revoked or varied by a subsequent order or direction of the court made or given at or before the trial of the cause or matter in the action in which the original order was made.[66]

13.23   Except where the Rules provide otherwise, the court may extend or shorten the time for compliance with any rule, practice direction or court order (even if an application for extension is made after the time for compliance has expired).[67] It was held under the old rules that[68] the court has power to extend time even after the expiry of an "unless" order, but the that jurisdiction would be exercised sparingly and where appropriate, only on stringent terms.[69] The position appears to be same under the CPR.

---

[61] *Mealey Horgan Plc v Horgan, The Times,* July 6, 1999.

[62] See CPR, r.3.1(3)(b) (specifying the consequence of failure to comply with a condition).

[63] *Republic of Liberia v Roye* (1876) 1 App.Cas. 139 at 143.

[64] *Keith v CPM Field Marketing Ltd, The Times,* August 29, 2000, CA.

[65] CPR, r.3.1(3)(a), (5); *Grundy v Naqvi* [2001] EWCA 139, CA (no strike out for failure to exchange witness statement in breach of unless order; instead payment into court ordered).

[66] CPR, r.3.1(7). Formerly, there was an express provision in relation to disclosure: RSC, Ord.24, r.17; CCR, Ord.14, r.12.

[67] CPR, r.3.1(2)(a).

[68] RSC, Ord.3, r.5; CCR, Ord.13, r.4.

[69] *Samuels v Linzi Dresses Ltd* [1981] Q.B. 115, CA, not following the former practice to the effect that where an action is at an end, the court cannot entertain an application a result

Where a party has failed to comply with a rule, practice direction or court **13.24**
order, any sanction for failure to comply imposed by the rule, practice
direction or order has effect unless the party in default applied for and
obtains relief from the sanction.[70] Furthermore, where a rule, practice
direction or court requires a party to do something within the specified time
and specifies the consequences of failure to comply, the time for doing the
act in question may not be extended by agreement between the parties.[71] A
party seeking relief from a sanction provided by court order may apply to
that court and the court will consider all the circumstances including[72]:

(a) the interests of the administration of justice;

(b) whether the application for relief has been made promptly;

(c) whether the failure to comply was intentional[73];

(d) whether there is a good explanation for the failure[74];

(e) the extent to which the party in default has complied with other
rules, practice directions and court orders and any relevant pre-
action protocol[75];

(f) whether the failure to comply was caused by the party or his legal
representative[76];

---

of which would be set it on foot again: *The Script Photography Co. v Gregg* (1890) 59 L.J.
Ch. 406; *Whistler v Hancock* (1878) 3 Q.B.D. 83; and *King v Davenport* (1879) 4 Q.B.D.
402, overruled.

[70] CPR, r.3.8(1).

[71] CPR, r.3.8(3).

[72] CPR, r.3.9(1); *Keith v CPM Field Marketing Ltd, The Times*, August 29, 2000, CA;
Whittaker v Soper [2001] EWCA Civ 1462, CA; *R.C. Residuals Ltd v Linton Fuel Oils Ltd*
[2002] 1 W.L.R. 2782, CA.

[73] In considering whether or not to grant a party relief from an "unless" order, the courts have
in the past placed a great deal of emphasis on whether or not the failure was intentional:
Re Jokai Tea Holdings Ltd [1992] 1 W.L.R. 1196, CA. Where the court has found the
failure to comply was intentional or contumelious, it has not hesitated to exercise its powers
to strike out: *Caven-Atack v Church of Scientology & Religious Education College*,
unreported, October 31, 1994, CA (deliberate failure to disclose documents in relation to
claim for damages); *Kumar v United Air Travel (Services) Ltd*, unreported, January 14,
1993, CA (a case of claimant's deliberate and contumelious failure to comply with an
"unless" disclosure order); *Caribbean General Insurance v Frizzell* [1994] 2 Lloyd's Rep.
32, CA (contumacious failure to comply with peremptory order). Where the failure has not
been intentional and has been the fault of a litigant's lawyer, the court has been more willing
to give relief from the consequences of an "unless" order: *Pereira v Beanlands, The Times*,
March 7, 1996 Ch.D.; *Beeforth v Beeforth, The Times*, September 17, 1998; *cf. Hytec Ltd
v Coventry City Council* [1997] 1 W.L.R. 1666, CA.

[74] The courts have given great weight to the explanation given for the failure, although where
there has been failure to comply with an "unless" order, the courts have been willing to
examine the adequacy and credibility of the reasons given for the failure: *Caribbean
General Insurance Ltd v Frizzell* [1994] 2 Lloyd's Rep. 32, CA.

[75] By looking at the extent of compliance with earlier orders, rules and practice directions, the
court may be able to ascertain whether or not the party in default is guilty of a pattern of
default. In finding that a failure to comply was not deliberate, the court on one occasion
took into account that there had been no history of repetition: *Hogg v Aggarwal, The
Times*, August 1, 1995 (failure to comply with "unless" order to set action down).

[76] *Hytec v Coventry City Council* [1997] 1 W.L.R. 1666, CA; *Downes Manor Properties Ltd
v Bank of Namibia, The Times*, March 18, 1999, CA.

    (g) whether the trial date or the likely date can still be met if relief is granted[77];

    (h) the effect which the failure to comply had on each party[78]; and

    (i) the effect which the granting of relief would have on each party.

An application for relief must be supported by evidence, which should set out all the circumstances, and give reasons why the previous order, practice direction or rule was not complied with, and set out the extent to which the order has now been complied with. A party who has failed to comply with the order, who by the time his application is heard has still not provided the disclosure required by the order, is unlikely to be sympathetically received by the court.

13.25   The court is not confined to the specific circumstances set out in CPR, r.3.9 in deciding whether or not to grant relief from any sanction. For example, where there has been an order striking out a defence for failure to provide disclosure and judgment has been entered in default, the court may refuse to set aside the judgment in the absence of the defendant's being able to show a good defence on the merits.[79] The court will, of course, not permit the parties go into the merits in any detail on an application in relation to disclosure; but where it can be demonstrated relatively shortly that the defence or claim is manifestly weak, that the merits are all one way, or that there is no realistic possibility of a good claim or defence, as the case may be, that may be a relevant factor.

13.26   The court may impose conditions as a term of restoring an action or a defence. In one case[80] the Court of Appeal held, in relation to an action where a defence had been struck out for failure to provide a list of documents, that as a condition of restoration some responsible officer of the defendant should make an affidavit stating whether or not the defendants have or ever had in their possession documents within a specified category.

F. CONTEMPT

13.27   The former rules in relation to disclosure of documents specifically provided that, where a party failed to comply to an order for discovery or

---

[77] *Caribbean General Insurance v Frizzell* [1994] 2 Lloyd's Rep. 32, CA (action struck out where defendants prejudiced because they had in the course of the claimant's continuing default lost two dates for trial and the trial itself had therefore been delayed).

[78] Where prejudice is shown by the opposing party, the court is less likely to be willing to grant an application for relief from any sanction: *Caribbean General Insurance v Frizzell* [1994]1 Lloyd's Rep. 32, CA (loss of trial dates).

[79] *Farden v Richter* (1889) 23 Q.B.D. 124.

[80] *John Walker & Son Ltd v Henry Ost & Co. Ltd* [1970] R.P.C. 151.

production of documents, that party was liable to committal.[81] In practice, contempt applications in relation to failure to provide disclosure of documents were rare and continue to be so under the CPR. Except in relation to false disclosure statements,[82] there is no express provision as to contempt in CPR, Pt 31, but it is open to the court to find a party in contempt who has deliberately failed to provide disclosure. Thus, a continuing failure to comply with an order for disclosure would justify an application for contempt.[83] At the hearing of such an application, unless it is clear that the defaulter has no intention of complying with the order, the court will often give the defaulter a short period in which to comply.[84] In practice most contempt applications are in relation to failures to comply with disclosure provisions in freezing and search orders. In such cases the courts are willing to make findings of contempt and punish non-compliance accordingly.[85] In exceptional circumstances the court may even issue a bench warrant to ensure compliance with its orders.[86] The court will not use its contempt powers to punish a party where failure to comply with the order for disclosure is not deliberate. Thus, if the party is unable to obtain access to the documents through no fault of his own, this penal power will not be exercised.[87] On the other hand, a deliberate suppression or removal of documents by a party may lead to the court exercising its powers of attachment.[88] Deliberate disobedience of a peremptory order for disclosure is a contempt and, if proved, in accordance with the criminal standard, might be visited with a fine or imprisonment.[89] However, the appropriate sanction for contempt will depend on the nature and seriousness of the breach. It is open to the court to adjourn a contempt application to trial, rather than deal with a contempt application at an interlocutory stage.[90]

---

[81] RSC, Ord.24, r.16(2); CCR, Ord.14, r.10(2).

[82] CPR, r.31.23 (making false disclosure statement without honest belief in its truth); proceedings may only be brought by the Attorney General or with the court's permission. See CPR, Pt 31, Practice Direction, para.8; CPR, Pt 32, Practice Direction, para.28.

[83] *Thomas v Palin* (1882) 24 Ch.D. 360.

[84] *Litchfield v Jones* [1883] W.N. 164; *Geary v Buxton* (1860) 29 L.J. Ex. 280, where a defendant in default of an order for interrogatories was given seven days to answer and the order for attachment was directed to lie in the office for that period; *Coston v Blackburn* (1872) L.R. 8 Q.B.D. 54, order for attachment made against claimant who had failed to provide interrogatories, writ directed to lie in the office for a fortnight.

[85] *Daltel Europe Ltd v Makki* [2005] EWHC 749 (Ch.), [2006] EWCA Civ 94, [2006] 1 W.L.R. 2704, CA; *LTE Scientific Ltd v Thomas* [2005] EWHC 7 (Q.B.), contempt in deleting files from computer and not complying with disclosure obligations under search order; *IC Mutual Ltd v Raven* [2005] EWHC 2680 (Ch.), contempt in failing to comply with disclosure order as to assets, part of a freezing injunction.

[86] *Zakharov v White* [2003] EWHC 2463 (Ch.).

[87] *Wilson v Raffalovich* (1881) 7 Q.B.D. 553 at 561.

[88] *Mornington v Keene* (1856) 4 W.R. 793.

[89] *Logicrose Ltd v Southend United Football Club Ltd*, *The Times*, March 5, 1988; *Tate v Tate* [2003] Fam. CA. 112, Fam.Ct. of Aus. (three months' imprisonment for deliberate and contumacious contempt in failing to give discovery).

[90] *Prest v Marc & Co. Investment AG* [2006] EWHC 927 (Comm.).

13.28   Where there is more than one claimant, it is open to a claimant to apply for attachment against a co-claimant who has failed to provide disclosure, in order to prevent the action from being dismissed.[91]

13.29   Ordinarily, the appropriate sanction for a failure to comply with a disclosure order will be to strike out a statement of case together with an adverse costs order. Hence contempt applications rarely will be appropriate or necessary. However, in certain cases a contempt application may be the appropriate route. These may include cases where a party has failed to provide information in response to an order in aid of a freezing injunction, search order or tracing relief,[92] or where there has been a deliberate destruction of documents.

G. OTHER CONSEQUENCES

13.30   The usual consequence of a continuing failure to comply with a disclosure order is that the statement of case of the defaulting party will be struck out, in most cases for failure to comply with an "unless" order. The defaulting party will also be penalised in costs. As set out above, contempt applications are most rare and should be reserved for the most serious of circumstances. However, there are also the following orders which may be made or inferences drawn in appropriate circumstances:

(1) that the party in default is cross-examined on his disclosure[93];

(2) that the party in default is precluded from relying upon any documents at trial which he has not disclosed in his disclosure[94];

(3) a party who has destroyed documents may not be allowed to adduce secondary evidence as to their contents[95];

(4) that adverse inferences are drawn at trial in relation to a failure to disclose or produce documents for inspection[96];

(5) that the action is dismissed at trial[97];

(6) that a re-trial is ordered where it transpires after judgment that proper disclosure had not been given prior to or at trial[98];

---

[91] *Seal v Kingston* [1908] 1 K.B. 579, CA.
[92] *Bird v Hadkinson, The Times,* April 7, 1999; *Daltel Europe Ltd v Makki* [2005] EWHC 749 (Ch.); *LTE Scientific Ltd v Thames* [2005] EWHC 7 (Q.B.).
[93] Para.13.31, below.
[94] Para.13.32, below.
[95] Para.13.33, below.
[96] Para.13.34, below.
[97] Para.13.35, below.
[98] Para.13.36, below.

(7) that the party in default bears the costs, or a greater proportion of the costs, of the action than might otherwise have been the case.[99]

Cross-examination

Cross-examination at trial on a party's disclosure will generally be appro-   **13.31**
priate where that is relevant for the determination of the issues at that stage. It would be rarely appropriate for a party to be cross-examined on his disclosure or his response to an order for disclosure at an interlocutory stage. The typical situation where it may be appropriate is where there was been no or no adequate disclosure in the context of an order in aid of a freezing injunction, search order or tracing relief.[100]

Restriction on use of documents at trial

CPR, r.31.21 expressly provides that a party may not rely on any docu-   **13.32**
ment which he fails to disclose or in respect which he fails to permit inspection, unless the court gives permission. Where the documents may contain material which is contentious, it is all the more important that proper disclosure is given well before trial. To produce documents for the first time only at trial may prejudice the opposing party, who may contend that he would have handled the case differently, or called other witnesses, or covered the matter in the witness statements, or made investigations as to the authenticity of the documents, had the documents been disclosed at the proper time. Where no prejudice can be shown on the part of the opposing party,[101] the court is likely to allow the documents to be admitted in evidence.

---

[99] Para.13.37, below.
[100] *Yukong Line of Korea v Rendsberg Investment Corp of Liberia Ltd, The Times,* October 22, 1996, CA (cross-examination on affidavit of assets of defendant subject to freezing injunction); Ch.2, para.2.13 above.
[101] *Koh Tech Hee v Leow Swee Lim* [1992] 1 S.L.R. 905, Singapore H.Ct. (court refused to admit in evidence an invoice which had not been disclosed prior to trial, but formed part of the bundle the defendant lodged for the trial); *Shipbuilders Ltd v Benson* [1992] 3 N.Z.L.R. 549, N.Z.C.A. (documentary evidence excluded which had not been disclosed on discovery in breach of the relevant rules, in a case where the opposite party had since died, so that the documents could not be put to him and he could not give any evidence in relation to them); *Abelene Ltd v Cranbrook Finance Inc.,* unreported, July 24, 2000, Rimer J. (relevant documents produced for first time in response to application for summary judgment, without explanation of circumstances of execution, or why not disclosed earlier; court suspicions of genuiness and declined to rely on them).

Restriction on use of secondary evidence

13.33   In general where a document is missing, it is open to the court to receive secondary evidence of its contents.[102] However, where a party has destroyed relevant documents, the court may refuse to allow that party to rely on secondary evidence of the original documents which it has destroyed.[103]

Adverse inferences at trial

13.34   Where a party has failed to provide proper disclosure or has destroyed documents, without there necessarily being any breach of an order or disclosure obligations, it is open to the court to draw adverse inferences at trial in relation to the absence of documents.[104] If the court considers that the absence of documents is deliberate, then the court may take that into consideration in assessing the credibility generally of the person in default. Thus the inference may be drawn that the deliberate destruction demonstrates a consciousness of the weakness of the party's cause in general, and from that consciousness may be inferred the fact itself of the cause's lack of truth and merit. The second main inference is that the specific document is unfavourable to the cause of the party who has destroyed it. It has been held that for the latter inference to be drawn there must be some evidence of the contents of the destroyed document,[105] although this may be too stringent and inflexible a test. Furthermore, negative inferences can be drawn in relation to those issues which specifically relate to the categories of documents a party has failed to disclose in breach of his disclosure obligations.[106] In one case,[107] adverse inferences were drawn against a defendant who had not preserved documents affecting the quantum of damage after proceedings had been commenced.[108] In contrast, in an Australian case where documents (relating to volume of business) were deliberately not disclosed, the court held that it was not entitled to simply guess as to their contents and therefore it was unable to award damages on the basis of what they might have contained.[109]

---

[102] *Springsteen v Masquerade Music Ltd* [2001] E.M.L.R. 654, CA.

[103] *Post Office Counters v Mahida* [2003] EWCA Civ 1583, *The Times*, October 31, 2003, CA.

[104] *Gray v Haig & Son* (1855) 20 Beav. 219; *The Ophelia* [1916] 2 A.C. 206; *Malhotra v Dhawan* [1997] 8 Med.L.R. 319, CA. See also Tronson (2006) 25 C.J.Q. 451.

[105] *McCabe v British American Tobacco Australia Services Ltd* [2002] V.S.C. 73 at [368], Sup.Ct.Victoria (reversed on other grounds [2002] V.S.C.A. 197).

[106] *Cevel Alimontos v Agrimpex Trading Co. Ltd* [1995] 2 Lloyd's Rep. 380 (arbitration). In *I.N.A. v Iran* (1985) 8 IRAN–US C.T.R 373, negative inferences were drawn in an international arbitration from a party's failure to submit documents it had been ordered to produce.

[107] *Infabrics Ltd v Jaytex Ltd* [1985] F.S.R. 75.

[108] See also *Mahon v Air New Zealand* [1984] A.C. 808, P.C.

[109] *Buchanan Turf Supplies Pty Ltd v Premier Turf Supplies Pty Ltd* [2003] FCA 230, Fed.Ct.Aus.

Dismissal of action at a trial

In extreme cases, the court may dismiss the action at trial, where there is **13.35** a real risk that a fair trial of the issues is not possible in view of the failure to provide proper disclosure or destruction of the relevant documents.[110] Where the absence of documentation does not prejudice the opposing party, the court will not dismiss an action at trial on this ground.[111]

Retrial

Where it transpires, after judgment has been given at trial, that the **13.36** successful party failed to give proper disclosure, then consideration needs to be given as to whether or not, had disclosure been given, this might have affected the result. In one case,[112] the Court of Appeal ordered a new trial where the defendant's failure to give proper disclosure had resulted in the claimant's claim being dismissed. In determining whether to order any new trial, the court may take account of a variety of factors, in addition to the general considerations relating to the administration of justice, including the degree of culpability of the successful party,[113] any lack of diligence by the unsuccessful party, and the extent of any likelihood that the result would have been different if the order had been complied with and the undisclosed material had been made available.[114] The appellate court will not order a retrial unless it can be persuaded that there is a real possibility that an opposite result would have been produced had proper disclosure been given.[115] It is open to a court to find that an arbitration award has been obtained by fraud, if it can be shown that a party has deliberately concealed a document ordered to be discussed and as a consequence of that conceal-ment has obtained an award in his favor.[116]

---

[110] *Landauer Ltd v Comins & Co., The Times,* August 7, 1991, CA.

[111] *Cepheus Shipping Corporation v Guardian Royal Exchange* [1995] 1 Lloyd's Rep. 622.

[112] *Cunningham v North Manchester Health Authority, The Independent,* February 15, 1994, CA; see also *Vernon v Bosley (No.2)* [1999] Q.B. 18, CA (fresh appeal after original appeal dismissed) *cf. Gray v Malton Bacon Factory Ltd* [1995] P.I.Q.R. 1 (documents not disclosed at trial admitted on appeal).

[113] *Profilati v Paine Webber* [2001] 1 Lloyd's Rep. 715: an innocent failure to disclose documents (as opposed to a deliberate withholding) in an arbitration is not a ground to interfere with an arbitration award under s.68 of the Arbitration Act 1996.

[114] *Commonwealth Bank of Australia v Quade* (1991) 178 C.L.R. 134, *Londish v Gulf Pacify Pty Ltd* (1993) 117 A.L.R. 361; *Gillingham v Gillingham* [2001] EWCA Civ 906, [2001] C.P.L.R. 355, CA (retrial ordered where both sides had failed to disclose an important document); *Brookfield v Yevad Products Pty Ltd* [2004] F.C.A.F.C. 117 (retrial ordered where unexplained but not fraudulent failure to disclose documents which may have affected trial).

[115] *Commonwealth Bank of Australia v Quade* (1991) 178 C.L.R. 134, H.Ct.Aus.

[116] *Elektrim S.A. v Vivendi Universal S.A.* [2007] EWHC 1 (Comm.).

Costs

13.37   In relation to applications arising out of a failure to comply with an order, practice direction or rule relating to disclosure, the party in default will usually be ordered to pay the costs.[117] When considering what costs order to make, the court is entitled to take into account non-disclosure which prevented a party from properly assessing whether or not to accept a CPR, Pt 36 offer to settle. So, in one case, the defendants paid money into court which in fact exceeded the damages ultimately awarded, but covertly filmed the claimant, disclosing this evidence during the trial. The judge awarded the claimant his costs, a decision upheld by the Court of Appeal, on the basis that the claimant had been deprived of the information needed to decide whether to settle under Pt 36.[118] The court may also, in cases of unreasonable or improper conduct, disallow costs or order the party at fault or his legal representative to pay costs incurred by other parties.[119]

Other remedies

13.38   In the USA a tort of spoliation is recognised in some jurisdictions under which a person may be sued for the deliberate or negligent destruction of evidence at the behest of the party whose case has been destroyed or injured by the lack of the evidence.[120] Such a tort has not been recognised in England and has been rejected in other common law jurisdictions.[121] However, in one case in Australia it was held that where a non-party procures a party to proceedings to breach his duty to give proper disclosure, and the opposing party suffers loss as a result, an action by the opposing party against the non-party is not demurrable.[122]

---

[117] See para.13.21 above.

[118] *Ford v G.K.R. Construction Ltd*, unreported, October 22, 1999, CA; see also *Factortame v Secretary of State for Transport* [2002] EWCA Civ 22, [2002] 1 W.L.R. 2438, CA.

[119] CPR, r.44.14; *Palmeira Square v Van Hoogstraten*, March 28, 2001, Q.B.D. (inadequate disclosure taken into account in deciding to order non-party to pay costs).

[120] *Smith v Howard Johnson Company*, 615 NE 2d 1037, 1038 (1993), *Ohio Supreme Court* (elements of claim for intentional spoliation); *Holmes v Amerex Rent-a-Car*, 710A 2d 846, 854 (1998) District of Columbia CA (negligent or reckless spoliation). There is no consensus even in the USA as to whether an independent tort of spoliation should be recognised.

[121] *Burns v National Bank of New Zealand* [2003] N.Z.C.A. 232, [2004] 3 N.Z.L.R. 289, New Zealand CA; *British American Tobacco Australia Services v McCabe* [2002] V.S.C.A. 197, Sup.Ct.Victoria; *Endean v Canadian Red Cross Society* (1998) 157 D.L.R. (4th) 465, British Columbia; c.f. *Spastic Estate v Imperial Tobacco Ltd* (2000) 49 O.R. (3d) 699, Ontario CA (claim allowed to proceed to trial).

[122] *Brookfield v McPherson's Ltd* [2003] F.C.A. 1237, Fed.Ct.Aus.

CHAPTER 14

Solicitor's obligations

CHAPTER 14

Solicitor's obligations

A. CLIENTS' OBLIGATIONS

Under the old law of discovery a party was under an obligation to carry **14.01**
out a careful search for all relevant documents in his possession custody or
power and to make proper inquiries and efforts with regard to those which
once were but are not now.[1] In respect of the obligation of disclosure under
CPR, Pt 31, the duty of the party is to carry out a reasonable (and proportionate) search for documents which are or have been in his control and
which either adversely affect or support a party's case or fall within the
scope of a relevant practice direction.[2] Moreover, the disclosure obligation
is a continuing one, extending to documents coming into a party's control
in the future.[3] However, a litigant cannot be expected to realise the whole
scope of his obligations on disclosure without the aid and advice of his
solicitor,[4] and accordingly it is crucial that the solicitor should properly
explain to his client what those obligations are.[5]

B. SOLICITOR'S DUTIES

General

A solicitor's duty is to investigate the position carefully and to ensure so **14.02**
far as is possible that full and proper disclosure of all relevant documents is

---

[1] *Mertens v Haigh* (1863) 1 De.G.J. & Sm. 528; *Re McGorm* (1989) 86 A.L.R. 275.
[2] CPR, r.31.7; see Ch.6, paras 6.33–6.34, above.
[3] See Ch.5, para.5.41 above.
[4] *Myers v Elman* [1940] A.C. 282 at 322.
[5] *Rockwell Machine v Barrus* [1968] 1 W.L.R. 693 at 694; CPR, Pt 31, Practice Direction—
Disclosure and Inspection, para.4.4.

made.[6] This duty owed to the court, is "one on which the administration of justice very greatly [depends], and there [is] no question on which solicitors, in the exercise of their duty to assist the court, ought to search their consciences more."[7]

Explanation to client

14.03   The solicitor's duty extends to explaining to his client the existence and precise scope of the disclosure obligation and the need to preserve documents. In a case decided under the old discovery rules[8] Megarry J. outlined this aspect of the solicitor's duty as follows:

> "It seems to me necessary for solicitors to take positive steps to ensure that their clients appreciate at an early stage of the litigation, promptly after writ issued, not only the duty of discovery and its width, but also the importance of not destroying documents which might by possibility have to be disclosed. This burden extends, in my judgment, to taking steps to ensure that in any corporate organisation knowledge of this burden is passed on to any who may be affected by it."

Indeed, a solicitor should not wait until proceedings have been commenced before explaining the obligation of disclosure to his client: once litigation is contemplated, the solicitor should advise his client as to his obligations on disclosure, and in addition take reasonable steps to ensure that those obligations are fulfilled.[9] In addition, from the client's point of view the very width, and potential cost, of the disclosure obligation may be a significant factor in the decision whether to become involved in proceedings at all.[10]

Preservation of documents

14.04   In relation to preservation of documents duties are owed both to the client and to the court. First, the solicitor's explanation to his client must include advice on the preservation of documents, as destruction of relevant documents may lead to adverse inferences being drawn against the client at

---

[6] *Myers v Elman* [1940] A.C. 282, HL; *Practice Note* [1944] W.N. 49; *Woods v Martins Bank* [1959] 1 Q.B. 55.

[7] *Practice Note* [1944] W.N. 49; see also the Solicitors' Practice Rules 1990, r.1(f).

[8] *Rockwell Machine v Barrus* [1968] 1 W.L.R. 693 at 694; see also *Koh Teck Hee v Leow Swee Lim* [1992] 1 S.L.R. 905, H.Ct. of Singapore.

[9] *Yu v Chiu Wah v Gold Chief Investment Ltd* [2003] H.K.C.F.I. 468 (Hong Kong).

[10] Where a claim may be brought in more than one jurisdiction, the comparative extent of disclosure may be a consideration in deciding which forum to select.

trial[11] and, particularly with organisations which routinely destroy documents after a time, the client ought to be warned to preserve documents as soon as the dispute has arisen, irrespective of whether proceedings have been issued or not. In extreme cases where documents have been destroyed after proceedings have been commenced with the result that a fair trial of the issues would not be possible, the court may exercise its powers under CPR, r.3.4[12] to strike out the proceedings,[13] and there may also be criminal liability for perverting the course of justice, where destruction is a deliberate attempt to suppress evidence.[14] However where documents have been destroyed prior to the commencement of proceedings or even after proceedings have been launched but before a disclosure order has been made, the position is not so clear. Instead of applying as a test for striking out purposes whether a fair trial of the issues is not possible where there has been a deliberate destruction of documents, a test of whether the conduct amounts to an attempt to pervert he course of justice has been applied.[15]

Secondly, if a solicitor *knows* (and the emphasis is important) that his **14.05** client, against advice, either has destroyed or proposes to destroy relevant documents, he must be extremely careful how he conducts the case thereafter, if he continues to act at all. He cannot thereafter conduct the case in any way which suggests to the court, or to his opponent, that full disclosure has been or will be given.[16] He must also (with his client's consent) include full details of any documents destroyed in the List of Documents,[17] or otherwise inform his opponent. If he cannot do this, he must cease to act.[18] It is doubtful that he is obliged to go further and, without his client's consent, specifically inform the court or the other side of what he knows, although it may well be that no legal professional privilege attaches to that knowledge,[19] and therefore he can be required by court order or other legal authority to divulge it without committing a breach of his duty to his client. In one case[20] where a solicitor's clients admitted to him that their affidavit

---

[11] *Infabrics Ltd v Jaytex Ltd* [1985] F.S.R. 75; see Ch.13, para.13.34, above.

[12] Formerly RSC, Ord.24, r.16 and CCR, Ord.14, r.10, which specifically applied in relation to failures to comply with orders for disclosure of documents.

[13] See, *Logicrose Ltd v Southend United Football Club Ltd, The Times,* March 5, 1988; *Landauer Ltd v Comins & Co., The Times,* August 7, 1991, CA; see also, Ch.13, paras 13.07–13.17, above.

[14] *R. v Vreones* [1891] 1 Q.B. 360; *R. v Rowell* [1978] 1 W.L.R. 132. It may also be a contempt where documents are deliberately destroyed once a disclosure order has been made. See Ch.13, para.13.27.

[15] See Ch.13, para.13.18 above; *British American Tobacco Australia Services v McCabe* [2002] V.S.C.A. 197 at [175], Victoria CA; *Douglas v Hello! Ltd* [2003] 1 All E.R. 1087, Ch.D.

[16] *The Guide to the Professional Conduct of Solicitors* (8th edn, 1999), para.21.01 and Annex 21I, para.10. This paragraph in the 2nd edn, para.12.05, was cited with approval in *McCabe v British American Tobacco Australia Services Ltd* [2002] V.S.C. 74 at [235 and 360], Sup.Ct.Victoria

[17] See Ch.6, para.6.08.

[18] See *Myers v Elman* [1940] A.C. 282, at 293–4, 322.

[19] See Ch.11, paras 11.09–11.13, above.

[20] *R. v Liverpool City Council, exp. Horn* [1997] P.N.L.R. 95.

evidence was false, he continued to act for some time before coming off the record, the falsehood not having been mentioned. The opponents were held entitled to a wasted costs order against the solicitor, though it is not clear whether the judge considered that it was the failure to inform the opponents (or the court) or the failure to come off the record sooner which justified the order.

New documents

14.06   Although it is not a duty owed to the court, the solicitor should undoubtedly warn his client, once litigation is in prospect, as to the consequences of creating any new documents (e.g. internal memoranda), which it would be embarrassing or even damaging to disclose in the proceedings. Depending on the circumstances, some such documents may be privileged from production,[21] but later difficulties will be avoided if unnecessary or damaging documents are not created thereafter.

Obtaining the documents

14.07   The solicitor has an overall responsibility of careful investigation and supervision in the disclosure process and he cannot simply leave this task to his client.[22] The best way for the solicitor to fulfil his own duty and to ensure that his client's duty is fulfilled too is to take possession of all the original documents as early as possible. The client should not be allowed to decide relevance—or even potential relevance—for himself, so either the client musts send all the files to the solicitor, or the solicitor must visit the client to review the files and take the relevant documents into his possession. It is then for the solicitor to decide which documents are relevant and disclosable.[23] It is sometimes very difficult to remove original documents from the place where they are kept (particularly accounting documents, but also computer records and programs stored in the computer),[24] so the solicitor may have to be satisfied in some cases with copies in the first instance, but he must satisfy himself of the accuracy and completeness of these copies. It must be borne in mind that the relevant issues in dispute may not be clear until statements of case have been filed and it is wise to err on the side of caution, to avoid criticism or adverse consequences later. Again, where the solicitor *knows* that his client has concealed relevant documents with a view to their not being disclosed, the solicitor must not act so as to

---

[21] As to which see Ch.11, para.11.31, above.
[22] *Myers v Elman* [1940] A.C. 282, at 322, 325, 338.
[23] *Koh Teck Hee v Leow Swee Lim* [1992] 1 S.L.R. 905, at 909.
[24] See Ch.9, paras 9.23–9.29, above.

suggest that full disclosure has been or will be given, and this may lead to his ceasing to act.[25]

Where the client is a business organisation, a visit to his premises will be useful also to gain an insight into the way the business is administered, how and when documents are generated, and the personalities of the people involved. All of this knowledge will assist the solicitor, both in locating documents which may be subject to the disclosure obligation, and in dealing with any queries on, or criticisms of, the client's disclosure once given. This will save time and costs later. There is an additional reason for obtaining the documents as early as possible. A feature of modern business life is the turnover of employees. Once the documents have been reviewed by the solicitor, the need for witnesses to explain such documents or to fill in gaps in them will be apparent, and statements can be taken before the employees concerned move on, and their evidence becomes more difficult, or even impossible, to obtain. In some cases it may be a good idea to circulate all relevant employees giving general information about the disclosure process, and enquiring whether any relevant files or documents are or have been held by them. It may be necessary later to depose to the enquiries made, and to circulate enquiries of this kind may go some considerable way towards showing that the disclosure obligation has been properly performed. **14.08**

Checking the documents

Once the documents have been produced by the client, the solicitor should carefully go through the documents disclosed to make sure, so far as is possible, that no documents subject to the disclosure obligation are omitted from the List.[26] In a business organisation, documents are often copied to more than one person or department. Under the CPR it is no longer the case that all copies of a document are separately disclosable, although copies with relevant annotations are disclosable.[27] A solicitor should be astute to follow up the "copy trail" and obtain the files of the persons concerned, because experience shows that such files often contain other relevant documents. A solicitor must not necessarily be satisfied by the statement of his client that he has no documents or no more than he chooses to disclose. If he has reasonable grounds for suspecting that there are others, then he must investigate the matter further, but he need not go beyond taking reasonable steps to ascertain the truth. He is not the ultimate judge and if he has decided on reasonable grounds to believe his client, criticism **14.09**

---

[25] See para.14.05, above.

[26] *Woods v Martins Bank* [1959] 1 Q.B. 55 at 60. This paragraph in the 2nd edn, para.12.09, was cited with approval in *McCabe v British American Tobacco Australia Services Ltd* [2002] V.S.C. 73 at [237], Sup.Ct.Victoria (reversed on other grounds, [2002] V.S.C.A. 197).

[27] CPR, r.31.9; see Ch.5, para.5.04, and Ch.6, para.6.09, above.

cannot be directed at him.[28] A solicitor should be particularly vigilant and searching where there is a charge of dishonesty or fraud or where the bona fides of his client is in issue.

14.10   If a solicitor is or becomes aware that the List of Documents or any verifying affidavit or statement of truth is inadequate and omits relevant documents, or is wrong or misleading, he is under a duty to put the matter right at the earliest opportunity and should not wait until a further order of the court. His duty is to notify his client that he must inform the other side of the omitted documents, and if this course is not assented to he must cease to act for the client.[29] If the client is not prepared to give full disclosure, the solicitor's duty to the court is to withdraw from the case. The client must be told that the disclosure obligation is a continuing one, and applies to documents coming into existence or located for the first time after disclosure has first been given.[30]

Disclosure statement

14.11   Every list of documents served under CPR, Pt 31 must include a disclosure statement by the party serving the list. It is now expressly provided that if the disclosing party has a legal representative acting for him, the legal representative must endeavour to ensure that the party making the disclosure statement understands the duty of disclosure under r.31.[31]

Preparation for inspection

14.12   It is a common phenomenon today, especially in large scale litigation, for clerks or paralegals to sort out disclosure documents into those which fall within the disclosure obligation, and those that do not, and then the former class into the "privileged" (which will be withheld from inspection) and the "non-privileged" (which will be produced). If this is to be done there must be:

(1) clear guidance for the paralegals at the outset; and
(2) procedures for reviewing this sorting out, both at the time (e.g. for the sorter to seek guidance on a borderline document) and afterwards, when a solicitor who is familiar with all the issues

---

[28] *Myers v Elman* [1940] A.C. 282, at 304.
[29] *Myers v Elman* [1940] A.C. 282 at 293–4, 323; *cf. The Guide to the Professional Conduct of Solicitors* (8th edn, 1999), paras 12.12 (circumstances where solicitor may terminate his retainer) and 21.13 (client's perjury or misleading court).
[30] CPR, r.31.11; see Ch.5, para.5.41, above.
[31] CPR, Pt 31, Practice Direction—Disclosure and Inspection, para.4.4.

should check the disclosure, both as to what will be produced and what will be withheld, and also as to what was discarded as outside the disclosure obligation altogether (this last category is particularly important, because in most cases it is never looked at again).

If proper procedures are not employed then there is the real risk that disclosable documents are never disclosed non-privileged documents are withheld from inspection and privileged documents are produced by mistake. The last mentioned problem has been partially solved by CPR, r.31.20,[32] but it constitutes an imperfect solution, and in the nature of things the first two problems mentioned rarely come to light, whatever suspicions an opponent might harbour. Where it is obvious that the other side has disclosed privileged documents by mistake, the solicitor should cease reading the documents, inform the other side and return the documents concerned.[33]

In some cases it is possible, either by agreement or by an appropriate court order, to produce for inspection only parts of certain documents, the remainder being masked or sealed up in some way.[34] This should not be left to clerks or paralegals. In such cases, where documents are masked or sealed up, it is the duty of the solicitor to inspect the whole document to ensure that the sealing up is appropriately carried out.[35]   **14.13**

Explaining orders

A solicitor also has a duty to inform his client of any orders for interrogatories or CPR, Pt 18 information (which has replaced interrogatories in England and Wales since April 1999), disclosure of documents or inspection. Prior to the introduction of the CPR the rules expressly provided that a solicitor was guilty of procedural contempt and was liable to committal if he neglected, without reasonable excuse, to inform his client of any order made against him for interrogatories, disclosure of documents or inspection.[36] Although the CPR does not expressly provide that a solicitor is guilty of procedural contempt, it seems that even under the CPR a solicitor will be liable for procedural contempt, or at the very least at risk of a personal costs order, in similar circumstances.   **14.14**

---

[32] See Ch.6, para. 6.26, above.
[33] *The Guide to the Professional Conduct of Solicitors* (8th edn, 1999), para.16.06, n.6.
[34] See Ch.9, paras 9.37–9.38, above.
[35] *Myers v Elman* [1940] A.C. 282, at 338.
[36] RSC, Ord.24, r.16(4); Ord.26, r.6(4); CCR, Ord.14, rr.10(4), 11(5); *Cordery on Solicitors* (9th edn, 1995) at para.F469.

Restriction on collateral use of documents or information

14.15   It is the duty of a solicitor of one party to civil litigation, who in the course of disclosure in that litigation has obtained possession of copies of documents from the other party to the litigation, to refrain from using the advantage enjoyed by virtue of such possession for some collateral or ulterior purpose of his own or of his client not reasonably necessary for the proper conduct of the action on his client's behalf; breach of such duty is a contempt of court.[37] His client is under a similar duty.[38] It is particularly important that a solicitor should comply with his duty to advise his client as to the nature and import of any obligation not to use documents or information for any purposes outside the proceedings in which the documents have been disclosed.[39] In modern times, where the client may be a large business organisation, it is not enough just to inform one person in the organisation and rely on that person to pass the advice on. Everyone with whom there is contact, or who will have any contact with the discovery documents of the other side, should be told:

(1) of the restrictions on the use and dissemination of the information contained in the documents; and
(2) that if the information is lawfully passed on to another person (i.e. within the client organisation), that person must be told of the restrictions as well.

Liability of costs and contempt by solicitor

14.16   A personal liability for costs may arise through a failure by a solicitor to comply fully with his duties regarding disclosure of documents.[40] The failure to comply with his obligations on disclosure may amount to professional misconduct on the part of a solicitor. In *Myers v Elman*[41] a solicitor was found guilty of professional misconduct in not insisting on his clients disclosing the relevant documents as soon as he knew that they were or had been in their possession, custody or power, in preparing and putting on the file affidavits of documents which he knew to be very inadequate, and in resisting further discovery which had the result of obstructing the interests of justice and causing delay. The solicitor was ordered to pay part of the

---

[37] *Home Office v Harman* [1983] A.C. 280; see now CPR, r.31.22.
[38] See Ch.15, paras 15.03, 15.09, below.
[39] *Watkins v A.J. Wright (Electrical) Ltd* [1996] 3 All E.R. 31 (solicitor in breach of duty in not informing client of implied obligation on discovery).
[40] CPR, r.48.7; formerly RSC, Ord.62, r.11; CCR, Ord.38, r.1(3); *Cordery*, at para.F462. See, e.g. *Wilkinson v Kenny*, unreported, February 9, 1993, CA (solicitors' failure to answer interrogatories within 28 days and to pay money into court even though serving two notices of payment in).
[41] [1940] A.C. 282.

costs of the successful plaintiffs. A solicitor cannot avoid the consequences of breach of this duty by showing that the performance of the particular duty as to disclosure was delegated to a clerk.[42] The appropriate order as to costs were breach of duty is found is to order the solicitor to pay those costs thrown away or lost because of the conduct complained of.[43] Whether or not a breach of duty was committed by the solicitor, a wasted costs order can also be made against him in favour of his client's opponent if his conduct was "improper, unreasonable or negligent."[44] So where a solicitor discovered that his clients' affidavit evidence was false but continued for some time to remain on the record without informing either the court or the opponents, a wasted costs order was made against him.[45] An application for a witness summons without reasonable cause gives rise to a risk of a wasted costs order.[46] So a solicitor acting for a defendant in a rape case, who sought disclosure from a local authority of social services files gong more widely than "could possibly be reasonable", was open to a wasted costs order.[47]

Where documents have been disclosed subject to a restriction that copies **14.17** may only be seen by the lawyers and experts for a party, it is a contempt of court for the solicitor to supply copies to his client, even if the documents are passed on by mistake.[48] Where a solicitor himself breaches the implied obligation against collateral use, or CPR, r.31.22 obligation, that too is a contempt of court and it is no defence that the solicitor himself is unaware of his legal duties.[49]

---

[42] *Myers v Elman* [1940] A.C. 282 at 302; Solicitors' Practice Rules 1990, r.13.

[43] *ibid.*, at 319.

[44] Supreme Court Act 1981, s.51(6), (7).

[45] *R. v Liverpool City Council, ex p. Horn* [1997] P.N.L.R. 95.

[46] *Re Ronald A. Prior & Co. (Solicitors)* [1996] 1 Cr.App.R. 248

[47] *R. v M (Wasted Costs Order)* [1996] 1 F.L.R. 750; *Wasted Costs Order (No.5 of 1997)*, *The Times*, September 7, 1999, CA.

[48] *Re A Solicitor (Disclosure of Confidential Records)* [1997] 1 F.L.R. 101 (solicitor held to be in contempt, firm fined and ordered to pay costs on an indemnity basis).

[49] *Watkins v A.J. Wright (Electrical) Ltd* [1996] 3 All E.R. 31 (solicitor held in contempt in passing documents disclosed on discovery to the Revenue and ordered to pay costs of contempt application on an indemnity basis).

CHAPTER 15

Collateral use of documents

CHAPTER 15

Collateral use of documents

A. THE UNDERTAKING

The courts have long since recognised that any party on whom a list of **15.01** documents is served or to whom documents are produced on discovery or pursuant to an order of the court impliedly undertakes to the court that he will not use them or any information derived from them for a collateral or ulterior purpose, without the leave of the court or consent of the party providing such discovery.[1] This is part of the wider principle that:

" . . . private information obtained under compulsory powers cannot be used for purposes other than those for which the powers were conferred."[2]

In the nineteenth century often an express undertaking was required by **15.02** the court before production was ordered of documents of a particularly

---

[1] *Alterskye v Scott* [1948] 1 All E.R. 469; *Distiller Co. v Times Newspapers* [1975] Q.B. 613; *Halcon International Inc. v The Shell Transport and Trading Co.* [1979] R.P.C. 97, CA; *Home Office v Harman* [1983] A.C. 180, HL; *Sybron Corp. v Barclays Bank Plc* [1985] 1 Ch. 299; *Crest Homes Plc v Marks* [1987] 1 A.C. 829, HL; *Taylor v Serious Fraud Office* [1999] 2 A.C. 177, HL. The principle has been adopted in other common law jurisdictions, e.g. Australia, *Kimberley Mineral Holdings Ltd v McEwan* [1980] 1 N.S.W.L.R. 210, New South Wales CA; Canada: *Lac Minerals Ltd v New Cinch Uranium Ltd* (1985) 17 D.L.R. (4th) 745, Ont. H.C., *Lac Minerals Ltd v Vancouver Stock Exchange* (1985) 17 D.L.R. (4th) 687, B.C. Sup.Ct.; Ireland: e.g. *Ambiorex Ltd v Minister for Environment (No.1)* [1992] 1 I.R. 277 at 286 *per* Finlay C.J.; *Greencore Group Plc v Murphy* [1995] 3 I.R. 520. In Quebec there is an implied rule of confidentiality at an examination on discovery: *Lac d'Amiante du Québec Ltée v 2858–0702 Québec Inc.* [2001] 2 S.C.R. 743, (2000) 204 D.L.R. (4th) 331, Sup.Ct. Canada.

[2] *Marcel v Metropolitan Police Commissioner* [1992] Ch. 225 at 237; *R. v I.R.C., ex p. Taylor (No.2)* [1989] 3 All E.R. 353 at 360; *Re Esal (Commodities) Ltd (No.2)* [1990] B.C.C. 708 at 723; *Re Barlow Clowes Gilt Managers Ltd* [1992] Ch. 208 at 217; *Wallace Smith Trust Co. Ltd v Deloitte Haskins & Sells* [1995] C.L.C. 223; *Graphia Holdings A.G. v Quebocor Printing (UK) Plc* [1996] F.S.R. 71. As to criminal cases, see Ch.2, para.2.03, above, and paras 15.56–15.57, below.

confidential or sensitive nature.[3] However, since the clear recognition of the implied undertaking in *Alterskye v Scott*[4] by Jenkins J., the courts generally relied upon the implied undertaking without imposing an express one.[5]

B. CPR, RULE 31.22

15.03   In England and Wales the implied undertaking at least in relation to documents disclosed on discovery has been replaced with effect from April 26, 1999 by the express provisions of CPR, r.31.22.[6] The Rule is intended to provide a self-contained provision which deals with documents disclosed under Pt 31 and sweeps away some of the fine distinctions in practice, but produces some uncertainties of its own. The general rule is that a party to whom a document has been disclosed may use the document only for the purpose of the proceedings in which it is disclosed, except in three cases. These are where:

(a)   the document has been read to or by the court, or referred to, at a hearing which has been held in public;

(b)   the court gives permission; or

(c)   the party who disclosed the document and the person to whom the document belongs agree.[7]

But the first exception is not conclusive. A party, or a person to whom the document belongs,[8] may apply to the court for an order restricting or prohibiting the use of a document which has been disclosed, even where the document has been read to or by the court, or referred to, at a hearing which has been held in public.[9]

15.04   It is still important to bear in mind the principles which developed in relation to this implied undertaking. It continues to apply in England and

---

[3] See Bray, at pp.238–239; *Richardson v Hastings* (1844) 7 Beav. 354; *Williams v Prince of Wales* (1857) 23 Beav. 336; *Re Birmingham Banking Co., ex p. Brinsley* (1866) 36 L.J. Ch. 150; *Hopkinson v Lord Burghley* (1867) L.R. 2 Ch.App. 447; *cf. Tagg v South Devon Railway Co.* (1849) 12 Beav. 151, where Lord Langdale M.R. refused to make discovery conditional upon such an undertaking, on the ground he could see no necessity for it.

[4] [1948] 1 All E.R. 469.

[5] See para.15.24, below.

[6] But in *Smithkline Beecham Plc v Generics (UK) Ltd* [2004] 1 W.L.R. 1479, CA, the court (it is submitted, erroneously) held that "no limitation is placed on the way that a statement [that a document exists, within r.31.2] is made," and hence "a reference by a party to a document in a witness statement is a statement that the document exists." If that were correct, r.31.14 would be otiose, as r.31.3 would have already provided for inspection of such a document.

[7] CPR, r.31.22(1).

[8] As to this concept, see para.15.08, below.

[9] CPR, r.31.22(2); *Lilly Icos v Pfizer* [2002] 1 W.L.R. 2253, CA.

Wales in relation to documents disclosed prior to April 26, 1999, it applies in other common law jurisdictions, it gives an indication as to how the discretion contained in CPR, r.31.22 may be exercised in practice, and provides an aid as to how the rule should be construed. Further the implied undertaking may continue to apply in relation to situations where documents or information are produced under compulsion in circumstances falling outside CPR, Pt 31 disclosure.[10] Such circumstances are considered elsewhere in this work:

(1) freezing and search orders[11];
(2) witness summonses[12];
(3) bankers' books[13];
(4) *Norwich Pharmacal* orders[14];
(5) letters of request[15];
(6) further information.[16]

Therefore, this chapter sets out the practice in relation to both the undertaking and the provisions of CPR, r.31.22.

C. RATIONALE

The primary rationale for the imposition of the implied undertaking is the protection of privacy. Discovery is an invasion of the right of the individual to keep his own documents to himself.[17] It is a matter of public interest to safeguard that right.[18] The purpose of the undertaking has been to protect, so far as is consistent with the proper conduct of the action, the confidentiality of a party's documents.[19] It is in general wrong that one who is compelled by law to produce documents for the purpose of particular   **15.05**

---

[10] See para.[15.11] below. CPR, r.25.1 provides several circumstances where documents or information may be sought or ordered under compulsion: e.g. ancillary to a freezing order or as part of a search order. "Disclosed" in r.31.22 *prima facie* refers to "disclosure" under Pt 31, not production under other rules; see para.15.15, below.
[11] CPR, r.25.1; see Ch.2, paras 2.30–2.31 above.
[12] See Ch.10, para.[10.36] above.
[13] See Ch.10, para.[10.52] above.
[14] See Ch.3, para.[3.25] above.
[15] See Ch.17, para.[17.13] below.
[16] See Ch.16, paras [16.117–16.118], and para.[15.17], below.
[17] *Home Office v Harman* [1983] A.C. 280 at 300, 312, 321, HL.
[18] *Distillers Co. v Times Newspapers* [1975] 1 Q.B. 613 at 621; *Riddick v Thames Board Mills* [1977] 1 Q.B. 881 at 896.
[19] *Sybron Corp. v Barclays Bank Plc* [1985] 1 Ch. 299 at 322.

proceedings should be in peril of having those documents used by the other party for some purpose other than the purpose of the particular legal proceedings and, in particular, that they should be made available to third parties who might use them to the detriment of the party who has produced them on discovery.[20] So it has been said that the implied undertaking is more a matter of justice and fairness, to ensure that a person's privacy and confidentiality are not invaded more than is absolutely necessary for the purposes of justice.[21] A further rationale is the promotion of full discovery, as without such an undertaking the fear of collateral use may in some cases operate as a disincentive to proper discovery.[22] The interests of proper administration of justice require that there should be no disincentive to full and frank discovery.[23]

15.06   The same rationale applies in relation to the CPR, r.31.22 obligation, but arguably it goes further than that, as it protects the rights, not only of a party to proceedings, but also of the person to whom the documents belong.[24]

D. TO WHOM OWED

15.07   In *Home Office v Harman*[25] Lord Keith stated that the implied obligation not to make improper use of discovered documents is owed not to the owner of the documents but to the court. Nevertheless, from the standpoint of principle the obligation ought to be regarded as being in effect owed both to the party providing discovery and to the court.[26] The undertaking is imposed for the benefit of the party providing discovery and it is recognised that he can release his opponent from the undertaking by giving his consent to collateral use.[27] However, the possibility of a wider private duty of

---

[20] *Halcon International Inc. v The Shell Transport and Trading Co.* [1979] R.P.C. 97 at 121.

[21] *Taylor v Serious Fraud Office* [1999] 2 A.C. 177 at 210; *A v A, B v B* [2000] 1 F.L.R. 701 at 715–716.

[22] *Riddick v Thames Board Mills* [1977] 1 Q.B. 881 at 986, 912, CA; *Crest Homes Plc v Marks* [1987] 1 A.C. 829 at 857.

[23] *Halcon International Inc. v The Shell Transport and Trading Co.* [1979] R.P.C. 97, at 121; *Home Office v Harman* [1983] A.C. 280 at 326. This paragraph in the first edition of this book was quoted in *Goodman v Ross* (1995) 125 D.L.R. (4th) 613, Ontario CA, as setting out the rationale for the implied undertaking on discovery. See also *Reimer v Christmas* (2003) 224 D.L.R. (4th) 635, Ont. CA.

[24] As to this concept, see para.15.8, below.

[25] [1983] A.C. 280 at 308; *Bourns Inc. v Raychem Corp.* [1999] 3 All E.R. 154 at 168, CA.

[26] *Riddick v Thames Board Mills* [1971] 1 Q.B. 881 at 901.

[27] *EMI Records Ltd v Spillane* [1986] 1 W.L.R. 967 at 976; *Hemmersley Iron Pty Ltd v Lovell* (1998) 19 W.A.R. 316, Sup.Ct. W.Aus. (Full Ct.). If the litigant has since become bankrupt, his trustee in bankruptcy can do so: *Lombe v Pollak* [2004] F.C.A. 593, Fed.Ct.Aus.

confidence owed to the party giving discovery subsisting alongside the independent of the implied undertaking has been rejected.[28]

The CPR, r.31.22 obligation is owed to the court. In effect, it is also owed to the party providing the disclosure and to the person to whom the document belongs. This arises from the wording of the rule, which provides that disclosure is permitted where both the party who disclosed the document *and* the person to whom the document belongs agree. The rule does not specify what is meant by the person to whom the document belongs, but it must extend beyond the owner of the physical piece of paper, and probably extends to the owner of the information contained in the document.[29]

15.08

E. ON WHOM BINDING

The undertaking is not only binding upon the party to whom the documents have been disclosed, but also extends to his solicitor[30] and to anyone into whose hands the document may come.[31] In the latter situation no doubt the undertaking will bind the third party once he is aware that the documents have been obtained by way of discovery.

15.09

CPR, r.31.22 only imposes an express obligation on the person to whom the document has been disclosed. However the correct view is probably that the restriction also extends to third parties aware that the documents have been disclosed in the course of proceedings. It could not have been intended that the rule could simply be circumvented by simply transferring the documents to third parties.

15.10

F. DOCUMENTS OR INFORMATION

At common law the undertaking covers not only documents disclosed on discovery, but also any other documents disclosed by a party under compulsion of court process.[32] Thus the undertaking has been held to apply to

15.11

---

[28] *Derby & Co. Ltd v Weldon, The Times,* October 20, 1988; *Apple Corp. Ltd v Apple Computer Inc.* [1992] 1 C.M.L.R. 969.

[29] *cf.* the law relating to breach of confidence, e.g. *Coco v A. N. Clark Engineers Ltd* [1969] R.P.C. 41; *Fraser v Thames Television Ltd* [1983] 2 All E.R. 101; *Att.Gen. v Guardian Newspapers Ltd (No.2)* [1990] 1 A.C. 109, HL.

[30] *Home Office v Harman* [1983] A.C. 280, HL.

[31] *Distillers Co. v Times Newspapers Ltd* [1975] 1 Q.B. 613 (expert witness); *Solifas v Cable Sands (W.A.) Pty Ltd* (1993) 9 W.A.R. 196 (expert witness).

[32] *Sybron Corp. v Barclays Bank Plc* [1985] 1 Ch. 299 at 315; *Marcel v Metropolitan Police Commissioner* [1992] Ch. 225 at 237; see Ch.2, paras 2.30–2.31, above.

documents produced under a *subpoena duces tecum*,[33] or under the *Norwich Pharmacal* procedure,[34] or under an order made pursuant to s.7 of the Bankers' Books Evidence Act 1879,[35] or for the purposes of detailed assessment of costs,[36] or under the procedure for giving effect to letters of request,[37] as well as affidavits and exhibits produced only because the court has ordered them to be provided by way of discovery of assets pursuant to the asset-freezing (*Mareva*) jurisdiction[38] or a search (formerly *Anton Piller*) order,[39] or in matrimonial proceedings.[40] The undertaking also extends to information in Lists of Documents given on discovery as well as to the documents themselves.[41] It has even been held to apply beyond documents, but where an equivalent process of compulsory disclosure has been used by the court to order inspection of a machine[42] or tests on samples,[43] and, in Canada, to transcripts of oral discovery examinations.[44] Particulars of alleged infringement given in a patent action in substitution for providing discovery on the topic, have been held to be subject to the implied undertaking.[45]

15.12 The undertaking does not apply to documents voluntarily disclosed, such as affidavits and exhibits put in voluntarily and not by any order of the court in opposition to an application for asset freezing (*Mareva*) relief,[46] or in support of a strike out application.[47] This is consistent with the rationale of the implied undertaking. In relation to documents voluntarily disclosed, the court has not invaded the privacy of the party; it is the party himself who has destroyed the privacy of the documents. Nor does the undertaking apply

---

[33] *Sybron Corp. v Barclays Bank Plc* [1985] 1 Ch. 299 at 318; *Welfare v Birdon Sands Pty Ltd* (1997) 79 F.C.R. 220, Fed.Ct.Aus.; *Cunningham v Essex County Council, The Times,* March 31, 1997 (summons in criminal case); *cf. Dunn v British Coal Corporation* [1993] I.C.R. 591 at 598, CA (where *Sybron* does not appear to have been cited).

[34] See Ch.3, para.3.25, above; *cf. Grapha Holding A.G. v Quebecor Printing (UK) Plc* [1996] F.S.R. 711 at 715.

[35] *Bhimiji v Chatwani (No.2)* [1992] 1 W.L.R. 1158, Ch.D.

[36] *Bourns Inc. v Raychem Corp.* [1999] 3 All E.R. 154 at 169–171, CA.

[37] *Dendron GmbH v Regents of University of California* [2004] F.S.R. 842, Pat.Ct.; see Ch.17, para.17.13, below.

[38] *Derby & Co. Ltd v Weldon, The Times,* October 20, 1988; *A.G. for Gibraltar v May* [1999] 1 W.L.R. 998, CA; see Ch.2, paras 2.30–2.31, above.

[39] *EMI Records Ltd v Spillane* [1986] 1 W.L.R. 967; *Process Development Ltd v Hogg* [1996] F.S.R. 45; *O Ltd v Z* [2005] EWHC 238 (Ch.); *C Ltd v P* [2006] 4 All E.R. 311.

[40] *Medway v Doublelock Ltd* [1978] 1 W.L.R. 710; *A v A, B v B* [2000] 1 F.L.R. 701 at 717; *Clibbery v Allan* [2002] Fam. 261, CA (implied undertaking extends to voluntary disclosure in ancillary relief proceedings, to the information contained in the documents and to affidavits and statements of truth and witness statements).

[41] *Dory v Wolf GmbH* [1990] 1 F.S.R. 266.

[42] *Grapha Holding AG v Quebecor Printing (UK) Plc* [1996] F.S.R 711; *cf.* CPR, r.25.1(1)(c).

[43] *Smithkline Beecham Plc v Apotex Europe Ltd* [2003] EWHC 127 (Pat.).

[44] *Sterling v Sullivan* (2004) 231 D.L.R. (4th) 344, Sask. Q.B.

[45] *Chiron Corp. v Evans Medical Ltd* [1997] F.S.R. 268, Pat.Ct.

[46] *Derby & Co. Ltd v Weldon, The Times,* October 20, 1988; *Schwartz (Litigation Guardian of) v Schwartz Estate* (2000) 189 D.L.R. (4th) 79, Nova Scotia CA (accountant's report voluntarily produced not subject to undertaking).

[47] *Esterhuysen v Lonrho Plc, The Times,* May 29, 1989, CA.

to documents or information which belong to the claimant who recovers them as a result of the execution of a "search and seize" (*Anton Piller*) order.[48] More curiously, it seems that is does not apply to information disclosed pursuant to an interim receiving order under the Proceeds of Crime Act 2002.[49]

Documents which have been produced pursuant to the former provisions of RSC, Ord.24, r.10[50] or pursuant to an order of the court under RSC, Ord.24, r.11[51] enforcing the obligation under the previous rule, occupy a middle position. On the one hand, they have been produced because the rules of the court so required, which looks like compulsion. On the other, they are only within the rules at all because they have been voluntarily referred to in pleadings or affidavits, and the rules are designed to prevent litigants from benefiting from references to documents without disclosing their entire contents. Accordingly, it has been held[52] that the implied undertaking does not apply to such documents.[53]   **15.13**

The undertaking is not confined to the distribution or use of the documents themselves, but applies to information derived from discovered documents whether it be information embodied in a copy or stored in the mind.[54] Hence the undertaking that binds the party on whom it is imposed prevents use by him of the information contained in a discovered document unless he has obtained the information from a source which is independent of and is not derived from, the discovery.[55]   **15.14**

CPR, r.31.22 appears to apply to all documents disclosed under Pt 31, including documents disclosed pursuant to r.31.14, being documents referred to in a statement of case, witness statement, a witness summary, an affidavit or an expert's report. This extends further than was formerly the case with the implied undertaking. However, unless r.31.22 is extended to circumstances where documents are produced pursuant to powers or provisions falling outside Pt 31, then this rule provides less protection than the implied undertaking, which was not limited to documents disclosed on discovery, but extended to any other documents or information disclosed by a party under compulsion of court process. The courts can deal with this   **15.15**

---

[48] *Process Development Ltd v Hogg* [1996] F.S.R. 45, CA.
[49] *Director of Assets Recovery Agency v Szepietowski, The Times*, October 25, 2006, Silber J.
[50] CCR Ord.14, r.4.
[51] *ibid.*, r.5.
[52] *Eagle Star Insurance Co. Ltd v Arab Bank Plc*, unreported, February 25, 1991, Hobhouse J.; *Cassidy v Hawcroft*, unreported, July 27, 2000, CA; *Shun Kai Finance Co. Ltd v Japan Leasing (Hong Kong) Ltd* [2001] H.K.C.A. 481. *Cf. Bhimji v Chatwani (No.2)* [1992] 1 W.L.R. 1158, Ch.D., where the parties and (it would seem) the judge accepted that documents obtained under R.S.C Ord.24, r.10 *were* subject to be implied undertaking, but *Eagle Star* was not cited.
[53] The position is different for documents disclosed under the equivalent provision in the CPR, r.31.14; see para.15.15, below.
[54] *Sybron Corp. v Barclays Bank Plc* [1985] 1 Ch. 299 at 318; approved in *Crest Homes Plc v Marks* [1987] 1 A.C. 829 at 854.
[55] *Sybron Corp.* [1985] 1 Ch. 299 at 322.

possible lacuna *either* by holding that r.31.22 is not confined to documents produced under Pt 31, *or* by holding that there continues to be an implied undertaking in circumstances where documents or information are produced under compulsion not by way of Pt 31 disclosure, or by imposing restrictions as conditions of relief, such as where a disclosure order is part of a freezing or search order.[56]

15.16   CPR, r.31.22 only refers to the subsequent use of a disclosed document, whereas the implied undertaking applies to information derived from a disclosed document. To limit the obligation to the document itself and not extent it to the information would be to negate the impact of the rule. Such a far reaching change in practice could not have been intended. The better view is that the obligation extends to information contained in disclosed documents.

15.17   The rules provide for other circumstances where documents may not be used for a collateral purpose. Thus in respect of information provided voluntarily or pursuant to a r.18.1 order (formerly interrogatories, and further and better particulars), the court may direct that that information must not be used for any purpose except in the action in which it was given.[57] The court is likely to make such an order where the information is confidential and is not akin to particulars of a pleading. Where the court orders a party to be examined about his or any assets for the purpose of any hearing except the trial, the deposition may be used only for the purpose of the proceedings in which the order was made. However it may be used for some other purpose by the party who was examined, if the party who was examined agrees, or if the court gives permission.[58] A witness statement may be used only for the purpose of the proceedings in which it is served, save to the extent that the witness gives consent in writing to some other use of it, the court gives permission for some other use, or the witness statement has been put in evidence at a hearing held in public.[59]

---

[56] CPR, r.25(1)(g) and (h). *The Practice Direction—Interim Injunctions*, which supplements CPR, Pt 25 has examples of such orders at para.25PD.13. The freezing injunction order to restrain assets in Sch.B, para.(9), contains an undertaking against collateral use of information obtained as a result of the order in any civil or criminal proceedings, in this jurisdiction or elsewhere, without the court's permission. The search order in Sch.C, para.(4) contains an undertaking against collateral use of information or documents obtained as a result of the order except for the purpose of the proceedings or commencing civil proceedings in relation to the same or related subject matter until after the return date, without the court's permission.

[57] CPR, r.18.2. Answers to interrogatories being provided under compulsion were subject to the implied undertaking; see Ch.16, paras [16.117–16.118].

[58] CPR, r.34.12; *cf.* RSC, Ord.29, r.1A(3).

[59] C.P.R, r.32.12; *cf.* RSC, Ord.38, r.2A(11) and CCR Ord.20, r.12A(11); see Ch.17, para.[17.28], below.

G. COLLATERAL OR ULTERIOR PURPOSE

In *Alterskye v Scott*[60] Jenkins J. described the undertaking in terms of use **15.18** of documents "for any collateral or ulterior purpose" or "improper use." Although the authorities have described the nature of the undertaking in various ways,[61] the basic test may fairly be described as the use of documents for any collateral or ulterior use not reasonably necessary for the proper conduct of the action.[62]

Usually, if not invariably, the use of documents disclosed in one action for **15.19** the purposes of another action will be a collateral or ulterior purpose,[63] even where the parties to both actions are identical[64] and where the causes of action are identical.[65] If a party begins an action based on documents disclosed in other proceedings, the action is liable to be struck out as an abuse of the process of the court.[66]

An exceptional case may be where documents disclosed in one action are **15.20** used in separate proceedings, the sole purpose of the separate proceedings being the furtherance of the party's case in the original action. In such a case it has been held that there is no breach of the implied undertaking.[67] It is submitted, that in any case where it is intended to use documents disclosed in one action for the purposes of bringing another action, even in such an exceptional case, the prudent and proper course is to seek leave of the court do so.

Proceedings for contempt of court in breaching an order or an under- **15.21** taking are not collateral to the action in which they are launched.[68] On the other hand, it is a collateral or ulterior use of documents disclosed to use them as a basis for the harassment of individuals[69] or to leak them to the press in order to expose alleged wrongdoing.[70] It would appear that the exposure of wrongdoing revealed by documents disclosed on discovery to the appropriate law enforcement authorities amounts to a breach of the undertaking, and accordingly leave of the court is required before so doing.[71] That it is for the court and not the party to the litigation that

---

[60] [1948] 1 All E.R. 297.
[61] *Sybron Corp. v Barclays Bank Plc* [1985] 1 Ch. 299 at 319.
[62] *Home Office v Harman* [1983] A.C. 280 at 302, 312, 319.
[63] *Crest Homes Plc v Marks* [1987] 1 A.C. 829, at 837, HL.
[64] *Riddick v Thames Board Mills* [1977] Q.B. 881, CA, where documents disclosed in one action were improperly used as the basis for a separate libel action between the same parties; *Miller v Scorey* [1996] 1 W.L.R. 1122.
[65] *Sybron Corp v Barclays Bank Plc* [1985] 1 Ch. 299, at 320.
[66] *Church of Scientology v D.H.S.S.* [1979] 1 W.L.R. 723 at 746; *Miller v Scorey* [1996] 1 W.L.R. 1122 (action struck out as based on documents disclosed in an earlier action used without permission of court).
[67] *Wilden Pump v Fusfield* [1985] F.S.R. 581.
[68] *Dadourian Group International Inc. v Simms* [2006] EWCA 1745, at para.13.
[69] *Church of Scientology v D.H.S.S.* [1979] 1 W.L.R. 723, CA.
[70] *Distillers Co. v Times Newspapers* [1975] 1 Q.B. 613.
[71] *EMI Records Ltd v Spillane* [1986] 1 W.L.R. 969; *Rowlands v Al-Fayed, The Times*, July 20, 1998; cf. *Alterskye v Scott* [1948] 1 All E.R. 469. In *Process Development Ltd v Hogg*

should be the final arbiter as to what should be provided to the authorities is indicated by three factors. First, the purpose of such a disclosure is not to further a party's case in the action in which the documents are disclosed. Secondly, the fear that documents disclosed on discovery might then be provided to the police by the opposing party may operate as a disincentive to full and frank discovery. Thirdly, there is a risk that an opposing party may use the threat of him providing copies of documents to the authorities as an improper bargaining tool in the litigation. It is not entirely clear what approach the court will adopt on such applications for leave; simply because documents may reveal that a criminal offence has been committed is not conclusive,[72] and in relation to breaches of fiscal laws the court has been reluctant to grant leave.[73] It would be a collateral or improper use to read a disclosed document out in open court, if the purpose in so doing was ulterior to the litigation in hand. Similarly, it may be improper to issue a specially endorsed writ or claim form with particulars of claim referring to information obtained on disclosure or to amend a writ or claim form so as to refer to disclosed documents, if the intention is to provide information to third parties so that they can bring proceedings.[74]

15.22   It is not a collateral or ulterior use to use documents disclosed on discovery for the purposes of adding new causes of action or parties to the action in which the documents have been disclosed. Joinder of additional parties as a consequence of discovery is a common procedural occurrence.[75] In a case such as *Norwich Pharmacal Co. v Commissioners of Customs & Excise*,[76] where the object of the proceedings is to identify a wrongdoer, there is no breach of the undertaking in bringing subsequent proceedings

---

[1996] F.S.R. 45, the Court of Appeal held that a claimant who on executing an *Anton Piller* order recovered his own property from the defendant was entitled to inform the police of this, as the collateral purpose rule did not apply to the claimant's own property.

[72] *cf. General Nutrition v Pradip Pattni* [1984] F.S.R. 403 where Walton J. refused leave to provide copies to the police, and *Bank of Crete S.A. v. Koskotas (No.2)* [1992] 1 W.L.R. 919, where Millett J. gave leave to a plaintiff bank to use disclosed material in the production of an audit report for submission to the authorities of a foreign state. As to criminal offences committed against children, see *Oxfordshire County Council v P* [1995] Fam.161 and *Cleveland County Council v F* [1995] 1 W.L.R. 785; *cf. Re L (A Minor) (Police Investigation: Privilege)* [1997] A.C. 16, HL.

[73] *cf. EMI Records Ltd v Spillane* [1986] 1 W.L.R. 969 not following *Customs and Excise Commissioners v A.E. Hamlin & Co.* [1984] 1 W.L.R. 509.

[74] *Milano Assicurazioni SpA v Walbrook Insurance Co. Ltd* [1994] 1 W.L.R. 977. Any person may inspect and take copies of claim forms and statements of case which have been served: CPR, rr.5.4(2)(a) and 5.4C. Permission is needed to inspect and take copies of other documents from court records (other than judgments and court orders given or made in public): CPR, r.5.4(2); see Ch.2, para.[3.45].

[75] *Sybron Corp. v Barclays Bank Plc* [1985] 1 Ch. 299 at 328. However, in *Parry v Bentley* [1993] H.K. Digest, F89, the Hong Kong CA held that a defendant to a libel action could not use documents disclosed on discovery in support of a counterclaim without leave of the court (which, in the event, was refused).

[76] [1974] A.C. 133.

against the wrongdoer once identified.[77] Similarly, information received as a result of the execution of an *Anton Piller* order may be used to bring proceedings against other parties shown by that material to be involved in misuse of the claimant's name or commercial property. However, in practice the court may require an express undertaking not to use the material against third parties without the leave of the court as a condition of granting an *Anton Piller* order.[78] In *Sony Corporation v Anand*[79] Browne-Wilkinson J. held that information obtained under an *Anton Piller* (search) order, on the basis that the defendants were implicated in a tortious wrongdoing, can be used for the purposes of pursuing claims against third parties implicated in the same wrongful handling of the same infringing goods. The learned judge also held that the undertaking did not prevent the claimants from using the same material for the purposes of criminal proceedings against third parties for infringements of copyright and trade marks. In *Omar v Omar* Jacob J. held that information obtained from a third party bank under a *Bankers Trust v Shapira* order in what was essentially a tracing claim could be used without leave to amend the pleadings in the existing claim, up to and including trial in foreign proceedings having the same object, in proposed personal claims (in England and abroad) against the same defendants arising out of the same facts, and to assist inquiries as to the whereabouts of the property which had allegedly been wrongfully converted.[80]

CPR, r.31.22 sweeps away some of the finer distinctions which arose in relation to the implied undertaking. Documents produced under Pt 31 may only be used for the purpose of the proceedings in which they are disclosed. **15.23**

H. EXPRESS UNDERTAKING

It is only in exceptional circumstances that the court has required an express undertaking as a condition of providing discovery. Usually the implied undertaking was regarded as sufficient to protect the position of the party giving discovery.[81] These circumstances have already been discussed.[82] Similarly where a document is protected by CPR, r.31.22 there will **15.24**

---

[77] *Wilden Pump v Fusfield* [1985] F.S.R. 581, at 590; *Alberta Treasury Branches v Leahy*, 2000 A.B.Q.B. 575, Alb. Q.B.; Ch.3, para.[3.25], above.
[78] *Sony Corp. v Anand* [1981] F.S.R. 398; *Cobra Golf Inc. v Rata* [1998] Ch. 109 at 166; *cf.* sample Search Order in *Practice Direction—Interim Injunctions* (see p.551), below.
[79] [1981] F.S.R. 398. See also *Reebok International Ltd v Royal Corp* [1992] 2 S.L.R 137, H.Ct. of Singapore, on use of materials seized pursuant to *Anton Piller* order for foreign and civil and criminal proceedings against the same defendant and third parties.
[80] [1995] 1 W.L.R. 1428.
[81] *Alterskye v Scott* [1948] 1 All E.R. 469; *Church of Scientology v D.H.S.S.* [1979] 1 W.L.R. 723 at 735; *The Lubrizol Corporation v Esso Petroleum (No.2)* [1993] F.S.R. 53, Pat. Ct.; see also para.15.02, above.
[82] See Ch.11, para.11.163, above.

generally be no need for an express undertaking. In other circumstances an express undertaking or condition may be appropriate. Thus where information on documents are produced pursuant to a freezing or *Anton Piller* (search) order there may be an express undertaking or direction restricting collateral use.[83] Information produced under Pt 18, or voluntarily, may also be subject to an express direction against collateral use.[84] Similarly with transcripts of cross-examination on unsatisfactory affidavits made in compliance with a freezing order.[85] Where a court makes a direction for a party to provide information in respect of expert evidence, it may make it subject to a condition limiting the use of any information provided.[86]

I. DURATION OF OBLIGATION

15.25   In *Home Office v Harman*[87] the House of Lords held by a majority that the undertaking did not end once the documents had been read out in open court. Thus a solicitor was held to be in contempt of court in giving access to a newspaper journalist to documents discovered by the Home Office in an action[88] brought by her client. Even documents referred to or set out in a judge's judgment have been held to be subject to the undertakings.[89] This continues to be the position in nearly every common law jurisdiction which has not introduced a specific rule to deal with the point.[90]

15.26   Miss Harman applied to the European Commission of Human Rights contending that the House of Lords' ruling was contrary to the right of freedom of expression enshrined in the European Convention of Human Rights.[91] The application was compromised upon an undertaking by the United Kingdom Government in the following terms:

> "The Government are prepared to undertake to seek to change the law so that it will no longer be a contempt of court to make public material

---

[83] *Cobra Golf Inc. v Rata* [1998] Ch.109 at 166.

[84] CPR, r.18.2; see Ch.14, para.[16.118], below.

[85] *Dadourian Group International Inc. v Simms* [2006] EWCA 1745, at para.13.

[86] CPR, r.35.9; r.3.1(3).

[87] [1983] A.C. 280; *Hammersley Iron Pty Ltd v Lovell* (1998) 19 W.A.R. 316, Sup.Ct. W.Aus. (Full Ct.).

[88] *Williams v Home Office* [1981] 1 All E.R. 1151; *Williams v Home Office (No.2)* [1982] 2 All E.R. 564, CA.

[89] *Sybron Corp. v Barclays Bank Plc* [1985] 1 Ch. 299 at 321–323.

[90] e.g. *Mayo Associates S.A. v Anagram (Bermuda) Ltd* 1998 J.L.R. N-4, R.Ct. Jersey; *E.H. v Information Commissioner* [2001] 2 I.R. 463, at para.46, Irish H.Ct.; *Spalla v St. George Motor Finance* (2004) 209 A.L.R. 703, Fed. Ct. Aus.; but in New Zealand the minority view in *Harman* has prevailed, and the undertaking goes once the document is read out or referred to in open court: *Wilson v White* [2005] 3 N.Z.L.R. 619, CA of N.Z.

[91] Art.10(1).

contained in documents compulsorily disclosed in civil proceedings, once those documents have been read out in open court. The substance of the change would be that where a document or part of a document is disclosed to a party in civil proceedings has been read out in open court, the implied undertaking given by the person to whom such disclosure has been made not to use the document for any purpose other than the property conduct of his own case should not prevent him using that document for the purpose of his making the contents of the document, or that part of it, as the case may be, known to any person. This change would not apply in the case of a document, or part of a document, which was the subject of an order of the court preventing its disclosure otherwise than to the parties to the action."

On October 1, 1987, RSC, Ord.24, r.14A came into force in order to give effect to the undertaking.[92] The new rule had no retrospective effect, and hence did not apply to documents disclosed subject to the undertaking prior to October 1, 1987.[93] As will be seen, the terms of the change in the law effected by r.14A went beyond the facts of the *Harman* case, and could have done substantial damage to the integrity of the confidentiality principle which had hitherto been the *quid pro quo* of the requirement to give full discovery of private documents. It will be noted that the problem of confidential documents being read out publicly at trial is a peculiarly British (and Irish) one: none of the other countries adhering to the European Convention on Human Rights has such an extensive process for litigants being obliged to disclose relevant private documents which can then be used at trial by the other side. Thus the problem simply could not have arisen elsewhere in Europe. The British Government's undertaking at one fell swoop simply gave away a large measure of the protection afforded to British litigants (who have no choice but to give disclosure if they wish to litigate), whilst at the same time leaving untouched the complete confidentiality which litigants in other European countries have continued to enjoy. It is notable that no such rule change has ever been made in the Republic of Ireland,[94] and in that jurisdiction therefore the implied undertaking still continues beyond the reading out in open court of the documents.[95] **15.27**

Under RSC, Ord.24, r.14A[96] the undertaking ceased in respect of documents once they had been read to or by the court, or referred to, in open court, unless the court for special reasons had otherwise so ordered on the **15.28**

---

[92] In the county court, CCR Ord.14, r.8A.

[93] *Bibby Bulk Carriers Ltd v Cansulex Ltd* [1989] Q.B. 155.

[94] See the Rules of the Superior Courts 1986, Ord.31, as amended by the Rules of the Superior Courts (No.2) (Discovery) 1999.

[95] *cf. E.H. v Information Commissioner* [2001] 2 I.R. 463, Irish H.Ct., at paras 42 (where the *Harman* decision is cited with approval) and 46.

[96] CCR, Ord.14, r.8A.

application of a party or of the person to whom the document belonged.[97] This was a very significant change, not just in court practice, but in the substantive law. Indeed, it may be doubted how far it was within the powers of the relevant Rules Committees to make these changes. The new rule was made under s.84 of the Supreme Court Act 1981,[98] which enabled rules to be made "for the purpose of regulating and prescribing the practice and procedure to be followed" in the Supreme Court.[99] The predecessor of s.84[100] as held not to enable rules to be made altering the law on public interest immunity,[101] because that related to substantive law rather than practice and procedure, and it is difficult to see why rules dealing with the confidentiality obligation should be different.[102]

15.29   RSC, Ord.24, r.14A was replaced in 1999 by CPR, r.31.22(1)(a), (2) and (3). As with the former rule, under CPR, r.31.22(1)(a) the restriction against collateral use ceases to apply once the document has been read to or by the court, or referred to, at a hearing which has been held in public. However, unlike the former rule,[103] any party, or any person to whom the document belongs,[104] may apply under CPR, r.31.22(2) for an order restricting or prohibiting the use of a document which has been disclosed, even after the document has been read to or by the court, or referred to, at a hearing which has been held in public. It is of course sensible to make any application either before the document is referred to or at least at the same hearing.[105] This is more likely to ensure that the document does not get into the public domain. An application at a subsequent hearing may be liable to be refused particularly if the contents of the documents have been disseminated in the intervening period.[106] But the formulation of the new rule at least deals with the potential injustice to persons not parties to the action who may have their confidential documents referred to at a hearing where they are unrepresented.[107] Thus, for example, in *Smithkline Beecham Plc v Generics*

---

[97] In *Singh v Christie* [1995] E.M.L.R. 579, a very narrow construction was placed on this rule in order to get round the potential injustice to persons not party to the action in view of the fact that the rule did not permit an order continuing the undertaking once it had been read out in open court. This was disapproved in *Mahon v Rahn* [1998] Q.B. 424, CA, and was not to be followed: *Colbeck v Ferguson*, unreported, January 1, 2002, Q.B.D.

[98] County Courts Act 1984, s.75.

[99] In the County Court, "all matters of procedure or practice, or matters relating to or concerning the effect or operation in law of any procedure or practice."

[100] Supreme Court (Consolidation) Act 1925, s.99.

[101] *Re Grosvenor Hotel, London (No.2)* [1965] 1 Ch. 1210, CA.

[102] *Mayo Associates S.A. v Anagram (Bermuda) Ltd*, 1998 J.L.R. N-4, R.Ct. of Jersey; see also *General Mediterranean Holdings S.A. v Patel* [1999] 3 All E.R. 673, Toulson J. (CPR, r.48.7(3) *ultra vires* Civil Procedure Act 1997, s.1).

[103] *Derby & Co. Ltd v Weldon*, *The Times*, October 20, 1988, Browne-Wilkinson V.C.

[104] As to this expression, see para.15.08, above.

[105] See *Plant v Plant* [1998] 1 B.C.L.C. 38.

[106] cf. *Plant v Plant* [1998] 1 B.C.L.C. 38 (some use of documents before motions judge who decided that the application should be heard as a motion by order; judge hearing motion by order ordered that any such use should not cause undertaking to cease to apply).

[107] See *Lilly Icos v Pfizer* [2002] 1 W.L.R. 2253, CA.

(UK) Ltd,[108] the application under CPR r.31.22(2) was made by separate application after the original hearing (and the application was successful both at first instance and on appeal).

Although in practice it will usually be clear whether or not a particular **15.30** document has been read or referred to in open court, there will sometimes be room for argument as to whether a document has been read by the court, particularly where it has not been specifically referred to or read during argument. For example, the court will frequently read or peruse documents in private prior to a hearing in order to save court time. Under the old rule it was held that documents in a bundle lodged with the court and referred to in a skeleton argument,[109] or confidential material referred to in skeleton arguments read by the court in private before a hearing, when there was no contested hearing,[110] were no longer covered by the implied undertaking. However, on the face of it, without more such a situation does not appear to fall within CPR, r.31.22(1)(a), as the document has not been read to or by the court, or referred to, *at a public hearing*. It is submitted that where a document, although included in a bundle lodged with the court, has not been referred to in open court, whether orally or in a skeleton argument, it should not be assumed that the document falls within CPR, r.31.22(1)(a) simply because the court may have read the document in private. But it is obviously prudent to seek the guidance of the court whenever there is any doubt as to whether a document falls within CPR, r.31.22(1)(a) before making use of the document for any purpose other than the proceedings in which it had been disclosed. However, a written opening is not part of the court records, and access should only be provided where there is an effective hearing (and *a fortiori* where there is a judgment).[111]

CPR, r.31.22(2) does not expressly provide that the power to make or **15.31** continue a restriction may only be exercised in special circumstances, but provides a general discretion.[112] However, as stated above, RSC, Ord.24, r.14A was brought into force in order to reverse the effect of *Home Office v Harman*.[113] Therefore the court will only rarely exercise its discretion to continue the undertaking after a document has been referred to in open court.[114] Thus the fact that documents had been disclosed under court order, and only used in open court in interlocutory proceedings, did not constitute a special reason why the undertaking should continue.[115] Nor did the fact that the documents might be used by third parties for purposes uncongenial to the defendants, particularly as it was open to those third

---

[108] [2003] EWCA Civ 1109, *The Times*, August 25, 2003, CA.

[109] *Derby & Co. Ltd v Weldon*, *The Times*, October 20, 1988.

[110] *Smithkline Beecham v Connaught Laboratories Inc.* [1999] 4 All E.R. 498, CA.

[111] *Law Debenture Trust Corporation (Channel Islands) Ltd v Lexington* [2003] EWHC 2297 (Comm.).

[112] For relevant considerations, see *Lilly Icos v Pfizer* [2002] 1 W.L.R. 2253, CA.

[113] [1983] A.C. 280.

[114] *Derby & Co. Ltd v Weldon*, unreported, November 4, 1988, Browne-Wilkinson V.C.

[115] *Derby & Co. Ltd v Weldon*, unreported, November 4, 1988, Browne-Wilkinson V.C.

parties to take steps to obtain an account of what occurred in court when the documents were originally referred to.[116] On the other hand, in another case the undertaking was continued, on the ground that the very purpose of the application before him had been to decide whether or not a document ought to be released under the old law or not constituted a special reason.[117] In yet another case,[118] the judge by consent made a "blanket" order at the start of the trial of a patent action continuing the undertaking in respect of all documents disclosed on discovery and dated after a certain date. It is however fair to add that the earlier authorities[119] were not cited to him. In another patent action, it was held that where the matter was still at an interlocutory stage and the parties themselves had considered the documents as so potentially sensitive as to justify the creation of a "confidentiality" club, there were special reasons to continue the undertaking.[120]

15.32   It is considered that the court will not countenance tactical references to documents in open court, whether during argument or as part of a bundle or exhibit, where the real purpose of the reference is to take advantage of CPR, r.31.22(1)(a). It is submitted that in such a case the court would be more willing to find good reason for continuing the undertaking or requiring an express undertaking at a subsequent hearing.

J. RELEASE FROM OR MODIFICATION OF OBLIGATION

15.33   The implied undertaking under the old rules will cease to have effect or may be modified in the following circumstances:

(1) It ceases to have effect once the document has been read to or by the court, or referred to, in open court, unless the court has otherwise so ordered under RSC, Ord.24, r.14A.[121]

(2) Where the party who disclosed the document has given his consent for the undertaking to be released or modified.[122]

(3) Where the court has given permission for the undertaking to be released or modified. It may do so if special circumstances can be shown.[123]

---

[116] *Derby & Co. Ltd v Weldon,* unreported, November 4, 1988, Browne-Wilkinson V.C.
[117] *Bibby Bulk Carriers Ltd v Cansulex Ltd* [1989] Q.B. 155; *Apple Corps v Apple Computer Inc.* [1992] 1 C.M.L.R. 969 at 974.
[118] *Molnlycke AB v Proctor & Gamble Ltd,* unreported, November 20, 1991, Morritt J.
[119] Particularly *Derby & Co. Ltd v Weldon* and *Bibby.*
[120] *The Lubrizol Corporation v Esso Petroleum (No.2)* [1993] F.S.R. 53.
[121] See para.15.28–32, above.
[122] See para.15.35, below.
[123] See para.15.35–43, below.

Under CPR, r.31.22 there are three exceptions to the prohibition against   **15.34**
using a disclosed document for any purpose other than for the proceedings
in which it has been disclosed:

   (1) Where the document has been read to or by the court, or referred
       to, at a hearing which has been held in public.[124]

   (2) Where the court has given permission.[125]

   (3) Where the party who disclosed the document *and* the party to
       whom the document belongs agree.[126]

Additionally, in rare cases, the court may of its own motion order disclosure of such documents to third parties, such as to prosecuting[127] or
regulatory bodies, or revenue authorities.[128]

The implied undertaking is only an undertaking not to use for any   **15.35**
collateral or ulterior purpose without the consent of the party who gave
discovery.[129] Hence the undertaking may be released or modified by the
party giving discovery, and this was so at common law.[130] CPR, r.31.22 goes
further and provides that, not only must the party who provided the
document must give his consent, but also consent must be obtained from the
person to whom the document belongs.[131] Where it is intended to use
discovered documents in a manner adverse to the interests of the party
giving discovery consent will often be refused, and it will be necessary to
obtain the permission of the court. It was clear that the court had power to
give such permission at common law,[132] even before the introduction of
specific rules[133] to regulate the problem. If the refusal to provide consent is
deemed by the court to be unreasonable, it is open to the court to take that
into consideration in making a costs order.

The application for permission should generally be by an application   **15.36**
notice[134] in the action in which the documents were disclosed, and supported by evidence setting out the grounds relied upon. The application
ought to specify clearly the documents in respect of which permission is
sought and similar care should be taken in drawing up any order, listing the
documents by way of schedule in appropriate cases so there can be no doubt

---

[124] CPR, r.31.22(1)(a); see paras 15.28–32, above.
[125] CPR, r.31.22(1)(b); see paras 15.35–43, below.
[126] CPR, r.31.22(1)(c) (emphasis supplied); see para.15.35, below.
[127] *O Ltd v Z* [2005] EWHC 238 (Ch.); *C Plc v P* [2006] 4 All E.R. 311.
[128] *A v A, B v B* [2000] 1 F.L.R. 701.
[129] *EMI Records Ltd v Spillane* [1986] 1 W.L.R. 969 at 977.
[130] *E.H. v Information Commissioner* [2001] 2 I.R. 463, Irish H.Ct., at para.43.
[131] As to this expression, see para.15.8, above.
[132] e.g. *Crest Homes Plc v Marks* [1987] A.C. 829, HL; *Roussel v Farchepro Ltd* [1999] 3 I.R.
567, Irish H.Ct.
[133] i.e. R.S.C, Ord.24, r.14A, CPR, r.31.22.
[134] CPR, Pt 23.

which documents are covered.[135] Where the application for permission is made at trial, a formal application may not be strictly necessary, but sufficient notice of the application should be given to the party who provided the discovery to enable him to consider his position adequately and, if thought fit, defend his interests accordingly.

15.37 In *Crest Homes Plc v Marks*,[136] Lord Oliver formulated the general principle that the court will not release or modify the implied undertaking given on discovery save in special circumstances, and where the release or modification will not occasion injustice to the person giving discovery.[137] Thus special circumstances based upon persuasive and cogent reasons for modification or release need to be shown to the satisfaction of the court before leave will be granted to permit collateral use of disclosed documents subject to the undertaking. In one Australian case, where one party alleged that the other had failed to disclose a relevant document on discovery, but the former party knew of its existence only because it had been disclosed in other proceedings in a different court (so that the implied undertaking applied), the court held that it was appropriate in the circumstances to inspect the document in question so as to be able to adjudicate fairly on an application for further and better discovery.[138]

15.38 Most applications for permission have been cases where a party to the original action in which the documents have been disclosed has sought permission to use the documents for the purpose of other proceedings in which he is involved. In *Halcon International Inc. v The Shell Transport and Trading Co.*,[139] a plaintiff in patent proceedings was refused permission, both at first instance and on appeal, to use documents disclosed by the defendant for the purpose of Dutch proceedings in the patent office between

---

[135] *cf. Sybron Corp. v Barclays Bank Plc* [1985] 1 Ch. 299 at 315–317, where there was a dispute as to which documents were covered by the permission originally granted and no order had been drawn up.

[136] [1987] A.C. 829 at 860.

[137] Followed by *Bibby Bulk Carriers Ltd v Cansulex Ltd* [1989] Q.B. 155; *Apple Corp. Ltd v Apple Computer Inc.* [1992] 1 C.M.L.R. 969; see also *O'Connor v Mirror Group Newspapers (1986) Ltd*, unreported, February 1, 1993, CA; *Sofilas v Cable Sands (W.A.) Pty Ltd* (1993) 9 W.A.R. 196, Sup.Ct. of W.A.; *A v A, B v B* [2000] 1 F.L.R. 701 at 718–720; *Chase v News Group Newspapers Ltd* [2002] EWHC 1101 (Q.B.) (libel claimant granted permission to refer to disclosed documents so as to put record straight with regard to television programme); *Dadourian Group International Inc. v Simms* [2006] EWCA 1745 (court should enable party who has obtained freezing order to use information thereby obtained in contempt proceedings in order to protect its position).

[138] *Patrick v Capital Finance Pty Ltd (No.3)* [2003] F.C.A. 385, Fed.Ct.Aus. In a further decision ([2003] F.C.A. 436), the same judge held that the document was not discoverable.

[139] [1979] R.P.C. 97; *cf. Connolly v Taylor*, unreported, May 11, 2001 (permission pursuant to CPR, r.31.22(1)(b) to use documents disclosed by solicitor to former client in action over fees, so client can use them for purposes of a detailed assessment in proceedings between him and a third party in which the solicitor had acted for him); *Dendron GmbH v Regents of University of California* [2004] F.S.R. 842, Pat.Ct. (permission given to use evidence obtained under letters of request in German and Dutch proceedings).

the same parties. Permission was refused by the Court of Appeal primarily on the ground that it considered that such use would be unfair to the defendant in that:

(a) in the Netherlands the use of the documents would result in them being put upon a public file;
(b) it might well be necessary for the defendant to disclose further many more confidential documents in the light of the claimant's use of the documents; and
(c) the facts in the two proceedings were sufficiently different for there to be a lack of mutuality.[140]

However, it is submitted that the test adopted by Walton J. at first instance was too narrow, in suggesting that the furtherance of a private interest could not justify the grant of leave to use discovered documents for the purpose of other proceedings and that some overriding public interest would normally be required.[141] In *Sybron Corporation v Barclays Bank Plc*,[142] this approach was not followed.[143] Scott J. rightly emphasised that whether leave ought to be granted should depend on the nature of the original action, the circumstances in which discovery was given and the nature of the proposed new action; in most cases the court will not attempt an assessment of the strength of the case, unless the proposed action is shown to be an abuse of process or is obviously unsustainable. In that case Scott J. granted leave in view of the fact that the causes of action in both proceedings were the same, particularly as where there is joinder instead of a new action the position is not substantially different.[144] In one case in the House of Lords[145] permission was granted to use documents obtained in subsequent *Anton Piller* proceedings in an earlier action between the same parties for the purposes of a contempt application.[146] In granting and upholding leave it was stressed that in the circumstances it was purely adventitious that there were two actions and in substance they were a single set of proceedings. Similarly, permission has been given where there are two

15.39

---

[140] *per* Waller L.J. at 124–125.
[141] *Halcon International Inc. v The Shell Transport Trading Co.* [1979] R.P.C. 97 at 109–110.
[142] [1985] Ch. 299 at 326.
[143] [1985] Ch. 299 at 327–328.
[144] *ibid.* at 327–328; see also *Bates v Microstar Ltd*, *The Times*, April 15, 2003.
[145] *Crest Homes Plc v Marks* [1987] 1 A.C. 829, HL.
[146] See also *Gavin v Domus Publishing Ltd* [1989] 1 Ch. 335 (claimants given permission to use documents obtained under *Anton Piller* order for purposes of contempt proceedings against managing director/owner of defendant companies). In *Cobra Golf Inc v Rata* [1998] Ch. 109, the court refused an application by a claimant for permission to use materials disclosed by a defendant under an *Anton Piller* (search) order for the purpose of a proposed committal application in another action by the same claimants against the same defendants.

sets of proceedings in different legal systems, but between the same parties and concerning related issues.[147]

15.40 However, permission can also be granted where the two sets of proceedings involve different parties. In one case,[148] the Court of Appeal released the defendants from their implied undertaking in respect of the claimant's discovery in a libel action brought by him against the defendants but subsequently compromised, to the extent necessary to enable the defendants to use such documents to defend on unrelated libel claim made against them by a third party. The two actions were sufficiently related to enable the third party to have been a co-claimant in the first action. In another case it was held that, where there is only a collateral connection between the disclosure and the intended action, the court may also find that is a special reason for granting permission.[149] More recently, an application to allow documents covered by the r.31.22 obligation in other litigation against other parties succeeded, on the basis that the interests of the owners could be protected by an order under r.31.22, there was "a real argument" that they would be discloseable under CPR r.31.17, and refusal of use could reflect adversely on the administration of justice.[150]

15.41 Where permission is sought by or for the benefit of a person who is not a party to the action in which the documents were disclosed, the burden on the applicant is a particularly heavy one. In *Bibby Bulk Carriers Ltd v Cansulex Ltd*[151] such an application was refused by Hirst J., who weighed up the amount of publicity hitherto given to the document, the value of the document to the applicant and the risk of prejudice to the party who disclosed the document, and held that there was an absence of cogent and persuasive reasons which would be required to justify release of the undertaking. The learned judge also rejected the submission that the introduction of RSC, Ord.24, r.14A had worked a fundamental change in the law on applications to modify or release the undertaking.[152] But in another, crimi-

---

[147] *Dory v Wolf GmbH* [1990] F.S.R. 226; *Apple Corporation Ltd v Apple Computer Inc.* [1992] 1 C.M.L.R. 969; *Synstar Ltd v ICL (Sorbus) Ltd* [2002] I.C.R. 112 at [19] (in principle court likely to give permission for disclosed documents to be used in parallel proceedings before the Appeal Tribunal of the Competition Commission); see also *Lac Minerals Ltd v New Cinch Uranium Ltd* (1985) 17 D.L.R. (4th) 745, Ont. H.C.; *Lac Minerals Ltd v Vancouver Stock Exchange* (1985) 17 D.L.R. (4th) 687, B.C. Sup.Ct.; *Roussel v Farchepro Ltd* [1999] 3 I.R. 567, Irish H.Ct.
[148] *O'Connor v Mirror Group Newspapers (1986) Ltd*, unreported, February 1, 1993; *cf. Parry v Bentley* [1993] H.K. Digest F89, where the Hong Kong CA refused to allow a defendant in a defamation action to use material disclosed by the claimant on discovery as the basis for a counterclaim (also defamation) against the claimant.
[149] *Sony Corp. v Time Electronics* [1981] 1 W.L.R. 1293.
[150] *Smithkline Beecham Plc v Generics (UK) Ltd* [2003] EWCA Civ 1109, at para.43, *The Times*, August 25, 2003.
[151] [1989] Q.B. 155; see also *Milano Assicurazioni SpA v Walbrook Insurance Co. Ltd* [1994] 1 W.L.R. 977.
[152] [1989] Q.B. 155 at 161–162; see also *Apple Corp. Ltd v Apple Computer Inc.* [1992] C.M.L.R. 969.

nal case[153] the Court of Appeal varied the implied undertaking of the defendant in relation to documents provided to him by the prosecution in the course of a criminal appeal, so as to permit a newspaper proprietor to use them for the purposes of a libel action brought by two policemen against the newspaper. Similarly, an Australian court allowed a trustee in bankruptcy to have access to, and leave to use, documents obtained by subpoena from a third party for the purposes of the administration of the bankrupts' estates.[154]

Where permission is sought to use documents for the purpose of disclosing breaches of the criminal law to the authorities or for the purpose of criminal proceedings, the court may in special circumstances grant permission for such use.[155] In deciding whether or not to grant permission it is submitted that the correct approach is for the court to look at all the circumstances including the circumstances of the original disclosure, the nature and strength of the evidence, the type of criminality involved and the interests of both the applicant and the party providing discovery as well as any public interest involved. However permission will not be readily given, particularly where the criminality relied upon is breach of fiscal laws having no connection with the original cause of action.[156] Simply because the documents may disclose a breach of the criminal law is far from conclusive in favour of granting permission.[157] **15.42**

The court may be more willing to grant permission, if necessary, to enable a claimant to institute or support criminal proceedings against third parties for infringement of copyright or trade marks in respect of documents disclosed in civil enforcement proceedings.[158] The court has also given permission to a litigant served with a notice under the Criminal Justice Act 1987, s.2, to disclose to the S.F.O. documents disclosed to it by its opponents in the litigation, when the S.F.O. was acting in response to a request from foreign prosecutors for assistance, and intended to pass the documents **15.43**

---

[153] *Ex p. Coventry Newspapers Ltd* [1993] Q.B. 278; see also *Springfield Nominees Pty Ltd v Bridgelands Securities* (1992) 110 A.L.R. 685, Fed.Ct.Aus. (permission for witness statement served but not read in open court in one action to be used for purposes of second action between different parties). In Canada, see *Consolidated NBS Inc. v Price Waterhouse* (1992) 94 D.L.R. (4th) 176, Ont.Ct. (no implied undertaking on party receiving documents pursuant to Crown's obligation to make disclosure in criminal proceedings).

[154] *Edge Technology v Wang* [2001] F.C.A. 247, Fed.Ct.Aus.

[155] See para.15.21, above; see also *Bank of Crete S.A. v Koskotas (No.2)* [1992] 1 W.L.R. 919; cf. *Derby & Co. Ltd v Weldon, The Times,* October 20, 1988; *A.G. for Gibraltar v May* [1999] 1 W.L.R. 998, CA; *Bank of China v Xu Chao Fan* [2003] B.C.S.C. 1672, Sup.Ct.B.C.; cf. *Bourns Inc. v Raychem Corp.* [1999] 3 All E.R. 154 at 171, CA; *Eronat v Tabbah* [2002] EWCA Civ 950 (no release of implied obligations so as to permit respondent to give evidence—as he wished—to US Grand Jury, as likely to be used to damage appellant's interests). As to disclosure to police for prosecution purposes see *Oxford County Council v P* [1995] Fam. 161 and *Cleveland County Council v F* [1995] 1 W.L.R. 785; cf. *Re L (A Minor) (police investigation: privilege)* [1997] A.C. 16, HL.

[156] *EMI Records v Spillane* [1986] 1 W.L.R. 969 at 977.

[157] *General Nutrition v Pradip Pattni* [1984] F.S.R. 403.

[158] cf. *Sony Corp. v Anand* [1981] F.S.R. 398 at 402–403.

on to those prosecutors.[159] Indeed, the court on occasion has even directed that papers in the case held by the court or on its behalf but subject to the implied obligation be passed directly to the prosecution authorities.[160] Where a defendant to criminal proceedings seeks leave to use in those proceedings documents disclosed in civil proceedings, the court will generally grant the defendant permission to use those documents which are necessary for the proper conduct of his defence.[161] But the implied undertaking does not prevent the use of material by a prosecuting authority not itself bound by it.[162]

K. ENFORCEMENT OF OBLIGATION

15.44 A solicitor is under a duty to explain to his client the nature and import of the undertaking on discovery and restriction under CPR, r.31.22.[163] This duty is owed both to his client and to the court. A solicitor is personally bound by the undertaking and CPR, r.31.22 obligation and should ensure that there is no breach. In *Home Office v Harman*[164] Lord Diplock defined the undertaking in the following terms:

> " . . . the implied undertaking given by the solicitor personally to the court (of which he is an officer) that he himself will not use or allow the documents or copies of them to be used for any collateral or ulterior purpose of his own, his client or anyone else; and any breach of that implied undertaking is a contempt of court by the solicitor himself."

15.45 An improper use of disclosed documents amounts to a contempt of court and may be restrained by injunction.[165] An action based on a misused

---

[159] *Marlwood Commercial Inc. v Kozeny* [2005] 1 W.L.R. 104, C.A; see also *Jyske Bank Ltd v Spjeldnaes* 1993 J.L.R. 99, R.Ct. Jersey.

[160] *A v A, B v B* [2000] 1 F.L.R. 701 (court in some circumstances may disclose to revenue authorities of own motion); *O Ltd v Z* [2005] EWHC 238 (Ch.); *C Plc v P* [2006] 4 All E.R. 311.

[161] *Cleveland County Council v F* [1995] 1 W.L.R. 785 at 789–790; *Re D (Minors)* [1994] 1 F.L.R 346 (wardship); *Re K (Minors)* [1994] 1 W.L.R. 912 (Children Act proceedings).

[162] *A.G. for Gibraltar v May* [1999] 1 W.L.R. 998 at 1007, CA.

[163] See Ch.14, para.14.15, above; *Watkins v A.J. Wright (Electrical) Ltd* [1996] 3 All E.R. 31.

[164] [1983] 1 A.C. 280 at 284.

[165] *Alterskye v Scott* [1948] 1 All E.R. 469; *Distillers Co. v Times Newspapers* [1975] Q.B. 613 (injunction granted against expert); *Home Office v Harman* [1983] A.C. 280, HL (solicitor found to be in contempt in giving access to journalist); *Sentry Corp. v Peat Marwick Mitchell (1990)* 95 A.L.R. 11 (injunction granted against party to prevent use of documents in US proceedings); *Watkins v A.J. Wright (Electrical) Ltd* [1996] 3 All E.R. 31 (contempt found for breach of undertaking with costs implications for the party's solicitor); *Attorney-General v Punch* [2003] 1 A.C. 1046, HL (issue of contempt in third party publishing information already subject to an order preventing its use); Lowe N. and Sufrin B., *The Law of Contempt* (3rd edn, 1996), pp.592–6; Miller, *Contempt of Court*, 3rd edn, 2000, paras 10.145–10.153; Arlidge, Eady and Smith, *Contempt*, 3rd edn, 2005, paras 11.76–11.77; *cf. A-G v Newspaper Publishing* [1997] 1 W.L.R. 926, CA (no contempt

document will ordinarily be dismissed as an abuse of the process of the court.[166] It is unlikely that criminal proceedings will be stopped merely because they are based on documents disclosed in civil proceedings where evidence obtained in breach of the undertaking or CPR, r.31.22 is sought to be used.[167] It is a contempt to provide documents produced under the disclosure rules to the Revenue.[168] Where documents have been provided to a *third party* in breach of the undertaking or CPR, r.31.22, the court may order delivery up of any copies of the documents in the third party's hands in addition to an injunction restraining misuse of the documents.[169] Although the court will not ordinarily order a *litigant* to return copy documents provided to him on discovery, it appears that the court has a discretion to do so under its inherent jurisdiction to prevent an abuse of its process, where there is real cause to believe that the party would breach the undertaking or CPR, r.31.22.[170] Such a power will only be exercised in exceptional circumstances.

Restraining the use of pure (confidential) information is not so easy. It is **15.46** sometimes possible to insist on the erection of a "Chinese wall" inside a corporate entity or law firm.[171] In rare cases lawyers may even be restrained from acting,[172] where there is a risk of breach of confidence that cannot be dealt with any other way. But the courts will not always take such drastic steps. Where an engineer on leaving the plaintiff's employment undertook not to make use of or disclose its confidential information, and then went to work for the defendant, who was a subcontractor to the plaintiff on a government contract, and an arbitration arose between plaintiff and defendant on that subcontract, in which the plaintiff learned that the engineer had worked on the defendant's claim, the plaintiff bought an action for breach of contract and an injunction restraining the engineer from involvement in the arbitration. Since the plaintiff was represented by the same lawyers in both arbitration and action, the defendant was concerned that, on discovery in the action, the plaintiff might obtain information held privileged in the arbitration and sought an order that the plaintiff construct a "Chinese wall" within itself and for the plaintiff's lawyers to cease to act

---

found where newspaper published extracts from documents subject to an order restricting use).

[166] *Riddick v Thames Board Mills Ltd* [1977] Q.B. 881, CA; *Halcon International Inc. v The Shell Transport and Trading Co. Ltd* [1979] R.P.C. 97 at 109; *Miller v Scorey* [1996] 1 W.L.R. 1122, Ch.D; *Goodman v Rossi* (1995) 125 D.L.R. (4th) 613, Ontario CA.

[167] *Rank Film Ltd v Video Information Centre* [1982] A.C. 380, HL; *cf. S v S* [1997] 1 W.L.R. 1621.

[168] *Watkins v A.J. Wright (Electrical) Ltd* [1996] 3 All E.R. 31.

[169] *Medway v Doublelock Ltd* [1978] 1 W.L.R. 710; *Proposed Finance Pty Ltd v Sing, The Times*, 1997, CA.

[170] *Brue Ltd v Solly, The Times*, February 9, 1988.

[171] *Prince Jefri Bolkiah v K.P.M.G.* [1999] 2 A.C. 222; *Koch v Richards Butler* [2002] EWCA Civ 1280; *Gus Consulting GmbH v Leboeuf, Lamb, Greene & Macrae* [2006] P.N.L.R. 587, CA.

[172] *Marks & Spencer Group Plc v Freshfields Bruckhaus Deringer* [2005] P.N.L.R. 69, CA.

in the action. The judge refused the relief sought, holding that solicitors engaged in separate serial actions against the same defendant cannot be removed simply because confidential information has been obtained in an earlier action.[173]

L. ARBITRATION

15.47   CPR, r.31.22 does not apply to arbitrations. However, a practice has grown up which is analogous to the implied undertaking on discovery. Arising out of the fact that arbitrations are intended to be private and confidential, the principle has developed that there is an implied obligation on both parties not to disclose or use for any other purpose any documents prepared for and used in the arbitration, or disclosed or produced in the course of the arbitration, or transcripts or notes of the evidence in the arbitration or the award, and indeed not to disclose in any other way what evidence has been given by any witness in the arbitration.[174] As set out below this is not an absolute obligation and is subject to various exceptions, some of which are yet to be developed in full.

15.48   The obligation of confidentiality is regarded in England as a term implied by law, which arises as an essential corollary of the privacy of arbitration proceedings.[175] However this view has been rejected by the High Court of Australia, which has held that confidentiality is not an essential attribute of a private arbitration,[176] and also doubted by the Privy Council.[177]

15.49   In England and Wales five exceptions to the implied obligation are recognised.[178] These are:

    (1) Consent: where disclosure is made with the express or implied consent of the party who originally produced the material.

    (2) Court Order: for example, when an order for disclosure of documents is made in an action in respect of documents generated in an earlier arbitration.

    (3) Leave of Court.

    (4) When disclosure is reasonably necessary for the protection of the legitimate interests of an arbitrating party.

---

[173] McKinnon J., in the Ontario Superior Court, followed *Merck & Co. v Interpharm Inc.* (1992) 44 CPR (3d) 440; (1993) 46 CPR (3d) 513.

[174] *Dolling-Baker v Merrett* [1990] 1 W.L.R. 1025, 1213–4, CA.

[175] *Ali Shipping v Shipyard Trogir* [1999] 1 W.L.R. 314 at 326.

[176] *Esso Australia Resources v Plowman* (1995) 183 C.L.R. 10.

[177] *Associated Electric and Gas Insurance Services Ltd v European Reinsurance Co. of Zurich* [2003] U.K.P.C. 11, at para.20.

[178] *Ali Shipping v Shipyard Trogir* [1999] 1 W.L.R. 314 at 326–7.

(5) When disclosure is in the public interest or in the interests of justice.

The fourth and fifth exceptions are generally aspects of the third and occasionally the second exceptions.

Consent can be given by the party who originally produced the material, **15.50** or in the context of the arbitration award, by the opposing party to the arbitration. Implied consent may arise where, for example, the opposing party in the arbitration subsequently commences fresh proceedings against the same party to the arbitration, he may be taken as having impliedly given consent to disclosure.

The court may order disclosure of documents in the context of sub- **15.51** sequent proceedings in respect of documents generated in an earlier arbitration. But if disclosure of documents has taken place in an arbitration, and one of the parties to the arbitration is party to subsequent proceedings, he will be under an obligation to list those documents if relevant in the subsequent proceedings. He should not permit inspection of those documents until either the party who produced those documents in the arbitration has given his consent or the court has given permission to allow inspection taking into account the confidential nature of the documents and the fact that they were produced in the context of a private arbitration. The party disclosing the documents in the subsequent proceedings should in any event notify the party who disclosed those documents in the arbitration of his intention to list the documents and should invite that party to state whether he: (i) consents to the documents being inspected and used in the proceedings; and (ii) wishes to be represented at any hearing where the question of inspection is raised. The matter can come before the court either by the issue being raised by the party listing the documents, or on an application by the opposing party for inspection of the documents listed. The court must then consider the evidential significance of the documents in the context of the pending proceedings and investigate whether it is appropriate to preserve the confidentiality of the documents by leaving it to the parties to the action to prove their case on the basis of alternative evidence, or to override the duty of confidentiality in the interests of fairness. The court will not do so if it would be disproportionate to order inspection.[179]

The court will grant permission if it is satisfied that, despite the implied **15.52** obligation, disclosure and inspection is necessary for the fair disposal of the action, and is not disproportionate. In reaching its conclusion the court should consider whether there are other ways of obtaining the information which is sought, and which do not involve any breach of the implied

---

[179] *Hassneh Insurance v Mew* [1993] 2 Lloyd's Rep. 243 at 252; CPR, r.31.2.

undertaking.[180] The courts have formulated a test of "reasonable necessity" in deciding whether to grant permission. If disclosure is reasonably necessary for the establishment or protection of an arbitrating party's legal right *vis-à-vis* a third party in order to found a cause of action against that third party or to defend a claim, or counterclaim, brought by the third party, then permission may be given.[181] In reaching its decision on reasonable necessity, the court should approach the manner in the round, taking account of the nature and purpose of the proceedings for which the material is required, the powers and procedures of the tribunal in which the proceedings are being conducted, the issues to which the evidence or information sought is directed and the practicality and expense of obtaining such evidence or information elsewhere.[182]

15.53   One party to an arbitration may enforce the arbitration award against the other, whether by proceedings in court or in a subsequent arbitration (and whether by issue estoppel or otherwise) without the need for any permission, as it would be fundamentally inconsistent with the purpose of arbitration to require otherwise.[183] So far as concerns other documents in the arbitration, the view is expressed in one authority[184] that, if it is reasonably necessary for the establishment by a party of his causes of action or defence against another party that he should disclose or in his pleadings quote from the arbitration award, including the reasons, he should be entitled to do so, without editing either the award or the reasons and without having to apply to the court for leave to do so. But the prudent course is to seek permission of the opposing party in the arbitration and if this is refused to apply to the court for leave to do so.

15.54   The interests of justice exception has been recognised, albeit not fully developed. In one case it was held that a party to court proceedings was entitled to call for the proof of an expert witness in a previous arbitration in a situation where it appeared that the views expressed by him in that arbitration was at odds with his views as expressed in the court proceedings. It was held that the disclosure was in the interests of the individual litigants involved and in the public interest.[185] The Court of Appeal has expressed the view that this exception should perhaps be categorised as disclosure in the interests of justice as opposed to the public interest, and has left open the possibility of a public interest exception to be developed in subsequent cases.[186]

---

[180] *Dolling-Baker v Merrett* [1990] 1 W.L.R. 1205 at 1213–4.
[181] *Ali Shipping v Shipyard Trogir* [1999] 1 W.L.R. 314 at 327, overruling the narrow construction of the "reasonable necessity" test of "unavoidably necessary" in *Insurance Co. v Lloyds Syndicate* [1995] 1 Lloyd's Rep. 272 at 275.
[182] *Ali Shipping v Shipyard Trogir* [1999] 1 W.L.R. 314 at 327.
[183] *Associated Electric and Gas Insurance Services Ltd v European Reinsurance Co. of Zurich* [2003] U.K.P.C. 11.
[184] *Hassneh Insurance v Mew* [1993] 2 Lloyd's Rep. 243 at 250.
[185] *London & Leeds Estates Ltd v Paribas (No.2)* [1995] 1 E.G.L.R 102.
[186] *Ali Shipping v Shipyard Trogir* [1999] 1 W.L.R. 314 at 327–8.

M. ASSESSMENT (TAXATION) OF COSTS

When documents are produced for the purpose of an assessment (for- **15.55** merly "taxation") of costs, there is an implied undertaking not to make collateral use of documents so produced. As with the implied undertaking on discovery, this undertaking may be released either by the party providing the documents or by the court. The court will not release or modify the implied undertaking, save in special circumstances and where the release or modification will not occasion injustice to the person providing the documents.[187]

N. CRIMINAL PROCEEDINGS

Compliance by the prosecution with its obligation to disclose material to **15.56** the defence generates an implied undertaking at common law not to use unused (and probably also used) material for any purpose other than the conduct of the defence.[188] Similarly, there is an undertaking when the Court of Appeal orders disclosure by the prosecution for the purposes of a criminal appeal.[189] This undertaking continues even after the document has been read out in open court in criminal proceedings.[190] There is no reciprocal implied undertaking binding the prosecution authority.[191] In Canada, it has been held that material disclosed to the defence in criminal proceedings should be disclosed,[192] and even produced for inspection,[193] as part of discovery in civil proceedings to which the defendant was party.

In relation to criminal proceedings where the criminal investigation began **15.57** after March 1997, disclosure is governed by the Criminal Procedure and Investigations Act 1996. Section 17 provides for confidentiality of documents and information provided by the Crown to the defence and sets out the circumstances in which information may be used. The general rule[194] is that, where an accused person is given or allowed to inspect a document or other object under various provisions of the Act, then, with certain exceptions,[195] he must not use or disclose it or any information recorded in it. But

---

[187] *Bourns Inc v Raychem Corp.* [1999] 3 All E.R. 154 at 169–171, CA.

[188] *Taylor v S.F.O.* [1999] 2 A.C. 177, HL. In Canada it has been held that no undertaking exists in relation to documents provided by the Crown: *Consolidated NBS Inc. v Price Waterhouse* (1992) 94 D.L.R. (4th) 176, Ont. Ct.; though see also *P (D) v Wagg* (2004) 239 D.L.R. (4th) 501, Ont. CA.

[189] *ex p. Coventry Newspapers Ltd* [1993] Q.B. 278, CA.

[190] *Cunningham v Essex County Council, The Times*, March 31, 1997; *cf. Taylor v S.F.O.* [1999] 2 A.C. 177 at 212, HL.

[191] *Preston Borough Council v McGrath, The Times*, February 18, 1999.

[192] *P(D) v Wagg* (2004) 239 D.L.R. (4th) 501, Ont. CA.

[193] *Consolidated NBS Inc. v Price Waterhouse* (1994) 111 D.L.R. (4th) 656; *Lang v Crowe* (2000) 131 O.A.C. 26.

[194] s.17(1).

[195] ss.17(2)–(4).

he may use or disclose the information or object in conjunction with the same proceedings or with a view to the taking of, or in connection with, further criminal proceedings with regard to the same matter.[196] Moreover the prohibition does not apply to the extent that the object has been displayed to the public in open court, or that the information to the extent that it has been communicated to the public in open court (unless those proceedings were to deal with a contempt of court),[197] or where the court so orders as an application made by the accused (when the prosecutor or a person claiming to have an interest may be heard).[198] But these provisions do not affect any other restriction or prohibition on the use or disclosure of an object or information, however the restriction or prohibition arises.[199] And s.17 does not apply to documents produced pursuant to a witness summons. Hence the implied undertaking at common law will continue to apply in respect of such documents.[200] Section 18 provides that is is a contempt of court for a person knowingly to use or disclose an object or information recorded in it if the use or disclosure contravenes s.17.

15.58   Where material has been inadvertently disclosed by the prosecution, such as material covered by public interest immunity, the court may grant an injunction restraining use even in the proceedings in which they have been disclosed. But before making such an order, the court must have regard to the potential consequences.[201]

---

[196] s.17(2).
[197] s.17(3).
[198] s.17(4), (6); see The Crown Court (Criminal Procedure and Investigations Act 1996) (Confidentiality) Rules 1997, SI 1997/699; The Magistrates' Courts (Criminal Procedure and Investigations Act 1996 (Confidentiality) Rules 1997, SI 1997/704.
[199] s.17(8).
[200] See para.15.56, above; *Cunningham v Essex County Council, The Times,* March 31, 1997.
[201] *R. v G.* [2004] 2 Cr.App.R. 37, CA.

CHAPTER 16

Information requests

CHAPTER 16

Information requests

A. BACKGROUND

CPR, Pt 18, introduced the concept of the information request. This **16.01** encompasses and replaces two established methods of obtaining information from a party, namely:

(1) Interrogatories,[1] the purpose of which is to seek information about an opposing party's case, which is to be verified on affidavit.
(2) Requests for Further and Better Particulars,[2] the purpose of which is to obtain details or clarification of a party's pleadings.

Whilst interrogatories have now been replaced in England and Wales, **16.02** much of the learning relating to interrogatories is still relevant. Interrogatories are still used in other common law jurisdictions. The courts in England and Wales continue to follow many of the principles which have applied to interrogatories in dealing with information requests, particularly in relation to privilege and objections to requests.[3]

The practice of obtaining interrogatories and the extent of their use varied **16.03** considerably over time up until their replacement in April 1999 by information requests. Most of the reported authorities relating to interrogatories were decided in the period 1885 to 1926. The small number of reported decisions on interrogatories between 1926 and 1990 was a reflection of how little interrogatories were being used during that period, despite judicial encouragement to do so.[4] The use of interrogatories may well have been

---

[1] Formerly governed by RSC, Ord.26.
[2] Formerly governed by RSC, Ord.12, r.12.
[3] Similar considerations apply in relation to the practice of Requests for Further and Better Particulars, although many of the authorities are no longer relevant.
[4] *Duke of Sutherland v British Dominions Land Settlement Corp.* [1926] Ch. 746 at 753.

limited because between 1893 and 1990 leave of the court was necessary to serve interrogatories, thus increasing the cost of litigation, and the success of an application for leave could rarely be guaranteed. Indeed, interrogatories were often refused on various grounds such as prolixity, oppressiveness, fishing or as being unnecessary. The Civil Justice Review of 1988[5] recognised that interrogatories do have a useful purpose and that the necessity to apply to the court for an order may well have been a limiting factor in practice. In 1990 a new procedure was introduced, whereby a party might serve interrogatories without court order, and this placed the burden on the party served to apply to the court for an order varying or withdrawing the interrogatories.[6] The new procedure led to a discernible increase in this form of discovery in the 1990s as reflected in the level of reported decisions.

16.04 Part 18 of the CPR, Pt 18, and the Practice Direction supplementing it represented a major change from the former practice of serving interrogatories without leave and leaving it to the party opposing the interrogatories to apply to the court to set aside or vary the request. The CPR introduced a twofold approach whereby a party may serve a preliminary request for further information or clarification and only if that is not responded to satisfactorily or at all, then an application for an order under Pt 18 can be made in order to require the party to provide information or clarification. Part 18 does not apply to cases proceeding on the small claims track,[7] although in such proceedings the court may on its own initiative require a party to provide further information.[8]

16.05 Since the introduction of information requests in 1999 certain trends can be observed in practice which may be summarised as follows:

(1) Information requests have shown themselves to be a useful and practical source of obtaining clarification and information from an opposing party. In most cases, on the multi-track they are deployed.

(2) There are extremely few reported cases dealing with information requests. This is not through any lack of use, but in practice most requests are answered or their scope reduced between the parties without any court order.

(3) Decisions at first instance on an information request are rarely appealed. These are case management decisions best left to the discretion of the first instance judge, rather than interfered with on an appeal.

---

[5] Cm.392 (1988).
[6] RSC, Ord.26, r.1(1).
[7] CPR, r.27.2(1)(f).
[8] CPR, r.27.2(3).

(4) Generally requests are being made and answered within the spirit of the overriding objective, where costs, necessity and proportionality are paramount. The courts have been vigilant to discourage costly and oppressive requests.

(5) In practice it is often difficult to predict how the court will deal with a request for further information. Rather than risk the costs of an adverse ruling, parties tend to use an element of give and take in dealing with requests.

B. OBJECTIVES OF REQUEST

The purpose of information requests is to seek information about a party's case. Information requests may be used to fulfil the following objectives: **16.06**

(1) To obtain admissions.
(2) To reveal weaknesses in the other party's case.
(3) To obtain information as to material facts which the applicant needs to prove in support of his case.
(4) To ascertain details of aspects of the other party's case so as to reduce surprise at the exchange of witness statement stage or at trial.
(5) To obtain clarification of the other party's case and to limit the other party's ability to depart from his case as clarified.
(6) To narrow the issues between the parties and thus reduce the expense and length of trial, including the expense of earlier stages in litigation such as disclosure of documents and witness statements.

The above objectives are reflected in para.1.2 of the Practice Direction, which provides that a request should be concise and strictly confined to matters which are reasonably necessary and proportionate to enable the requesting party to prepare his own case or to understand the case he has to meet. **16.07**

C. THE PRELIMINARY REQUEST

Form of request

The Practice Direction provides that before making an application to the court for an order under Pt 18, the party seeking clarification or information should first serve on the party from whom it is sought a written Request for **16.08** that clarification or information stating a date by which the response to the Request should be served. The date must allow the second party a reasonable time to respond.[9] The Practice Direction sensibly does not specify the period as what is reasonable depends on the circumstances, including the length of the Request and the nature of the enquiries necessary in order to respond.

16.09   A Request must comply with para.1.2 of the Practice Direction which stipulates the following requirements:

(1) The Request should be concise. This probably goes further than the practice of the court in relation to interrogatories, whereby prolix interrogatories were disallowed.

(2) The Request should be strictly confined to matters which are reasonably necessary and proportionate. This requirement in essence means that the Request should relate to matters in issue, and be kept within sensible bounds and appropriate in all the circumstances.

(3) The Request must be directed enabling the requesting party to prepare his own case or to understand the case he has to meet. In essence the Request must be to fulfil one of the proper objectives identified above.

16.10   The form of the Request depends on what is appropriate in the circumstances. A Request may be made by letter if the text of the Request is brief and the reply is likely to be brief, otherwise the Request should be made in a separate document.[10] This is a sensible approach as Requests by letter are likely to be cheaper for all concerned.[11] A Request by letter should state that it contains a Request under Pt 18 and deal with no matters other than the Request.[12] Thus for trial bundles the Request and any response can conveniently be placed amongst the statements of case.

16.11   A Request (whether made by letter or in a separate document) must[13]:

(1) be headed with the name of the court and the title and number of the claim;

(2) in its heading state that it is a Request made under Pt 18, identify the first party (party making the Request) and the second party (party from whom a response is sought) and state the date on which it is made;

---

[9] CPR, Pt 18, Practice Direction, para.1.1. References in this chapter to the Practice Direction are to the Practice Direction issued in relation to CPR, Pt 18 unless otherwise stated.

[10] CPR, Pt 18, Practice Direction, para.1.4.

[11] Prior to the introduction of the CPR a practice grew up in the Commercial Court whereby requests for information were often dealt with in correspondence rather than formal interrogatories with responses verified on affidavit.

[12] CPR, Pt 18, Practice Direction, para.1.5.

[13] CPR, Pt 18, Practice Direction, para.1.6.

(3) set out in a separate numbered paragraph each request for information or clarification;

(4) where a Request relates to a document, identify that document and (if relevant) the paragraph or words to which it relates;

(5) state the date by which the first party expects a response to the Request.

A Request which is not in the form of a letter may, if convenient, be prepared in such a way that the response may be given on the same document. To do this the numbered paragraphs of the Request should appear on the left hand half of each sheet so that the paragraphs of the response then may appear on the right. Where a Request is prepared in this form an extra copy should be served for the use of the second party.[14] If reasonably practicable a request should be served by email.[15] **16.12**

The Practice Direction provides that Requests must be made as far as possible in a single comprehensive document and not piecemeal.[16] There should be no objection in principle to a party serving separate Requests for each statement of case (or other pleading). This will often be the most convenient course. The Request and response can then be placed behind the relevant statement of case for bundle purposes. It is often sensible to make a Request relatively soon after a statement of case has been served, rather than waiting for pleadings to be closed and serving a global request relating to more than one such statement. Even so it is open to a party to make all his requests in one composite document seeking information and clarification of statements of case and matters which in the past would have been the subject of interrogatories. **16.13**

The Practice Direction makes no distinction between parties who are individuals and other parties such as partnerships or corporations. This follows the practice in relation to Requests for Further and Better Particulars of a pleading where the Request was directed to a party and no named individual. The practice in relation to interrogatories was that where they were to be served on two or more parties or were required to be answered by an agent or servant of a party, a note at the end of the interrogatory should have specified which of the interrogatories each party or, as the case may be, an agent or servant was required to answer, and which agent or servant.[17] However, where the party to be interrogated was a body corporate or unincorporated, which was empowered by law to sue or be sued whether in its own name or in the name of an officer of other person, the officer or member on whom the interrogatories were to be served had to be specified in a note at the end of the interrogatories.[18] Where a party is **16.14**

---

[14] CPR, Pt 18, Practice Direction, para.1.6(2).
[15] CPR, Pt 18, Practice Direction, para.1.7.
[16] CPR, Pt 18, Practice Direction, para.1.3.
[17] RSC, Ord.26, r.2(1)(c).
[18] RSC, Ord.26, r.2(1)(b).

serving a Request under Pt 18, there seems to be no objection in principle to specifying in the Request which officer, servant or agent of a party should provide the information for a response. Indeed in appropriate cases there is no objection to asking questions about individuals; the responding party would no doubt look to that individual, where appropriate and practicable, to provide the information for the response.

Form of response to a Request

16.15   A response to a Request must be in writing, dated and signed by the second party or his legal representative.[19] Where the Request is made in a letter the second party may give his response in a letter or in a formal reply. Such a letter should identify itself as a response to the Request and deal with no other matters than the response.[20]

16.16   Unless the Request is in the format which permits the response to be provided on the same sheet, a response must[21]:

(1) be headed with the name of the court and the title and number of the claim;

(2) in its heading identify itself as a response to that Request;

(3) repeat the text of each separate paragraph of the Request and set out under each paragraph the response to it;

(4) refer and have attached to it a copy of any document not already in the possession of the first party which forms part of the response.

A second or supplementary response to a Request must identify itself as such in the heading. The second party must when he serves his response on the first party serve on every other party and file with the court a copy of the Request and of his response.[22] The parties may use Practice Form PF56 for a combined request and reply.[23]

Statement of truth

16.17   The response to a Request, whether given voluntarily or by court order under r.18.1 becomes part of a party's statement of case to the extent the response includes any further information given in relation to the statement

---

[19] CPR, Pt 18, Practice Direction, para.2.1.
[20] CPR, Pt 18, Practice Direction, para.2.2.
[21] CPR, Pt 18, Practice Direction, para.2.3.
[22] CPR, Pt 18, Practice Direction, para.2.4.
[23] Queen's Bench Guide, para.7.7.1.

of case.[24] A voluntary response to a Request without court order should be verified by a statement of truth, if the response includes any further information given in relation to a claim form, particulars of claim where these are not included in a claim form, defence, Pt 20 claim, or reply to defence. This is because these documents fall within the definition of a statement of case, which must be verified by a statement of truth.[25] CPR, r.22.1 does not expressly stipulate that a response which is neither part of a statement of case nor one which is made in compliance with an order under r.18.1 to provide further information is required to be verified by a statement of truth. However, the Practice Direction suggests that all responses should be verified by a statement of truth.[26] CPR, r.22.1(1)(a) provides that a response complying with an order made under CPR, r.18.1 to provide further information, must be verified by a statement of truth.

Form of objection

The nature of objections is considered separately below. The formal requirements are that, if a second party objects to complying with the Request or part of it, or is unable to do so at all or within the time stated in the Request, he must inform the first party promptly and in any event within that time. He may do so in a letter or in a separate document by way of a formal response, but in either case he must give reasons and, where relevant, give a date by which he expects to be able to comply.[27] Where a second party considers that a Request can only be complied with at disproportionate expense, and objects to comply for that reason, he should say so in his reply and explain briefly why he has taken that view.[28] This is a considerable improvement on the former practice in relation to interrogatories and Requests for Further and Better Particular of a pleading, where often the objecting party's reasons for objection were not spelt out in the response and the nature of the objection often was only clarified at a court hearing. **16.18**

Unlike the former practice in relation to interrogatories, where it was for the party opposing the interrogatories to apply to the court to set aside the interrogatories,[29] in relation to a Request under Pt 18, there is no need for a second party to apply to the court if he objects to a request or is unable **16.19**

---

[24] CPR, r.2.3(1), which defines a "statement of case" as a claim form, particulars of claim where these are not included in a claim form, defence, Pt 20 claim, or reply to defence and includes any further information given in relation to them voluntarily or by court under r.18.1.

[25] CPR, r.22.1.

[26] CPR, Pt 18, Practice Direction, para.3.

[27] CPR, Pt 18, Practice Direction, para.4.1.

[28] CPR, Pt 18, Practice Direction, para.4.2(2).

[29] RSC, Ord.26, r.3(2).

to comply with it at all or within the stated time. It is then for the requesting party to apply to the court for an order under Pt 18.[30]

D. APPLICATIONS FOR ORDERS UNDER PART 18

Rule 18.1(1)

16.20   The court may at any time order a party to:

(1) clarify any matter which is in dispute in the proceedings; or
(2) give additional information in relation to any such matter, whether or not the matter is contained or referred to in a statement of case.

16.21   The power to make an order is subject to any rule of law to the contrary.[31] It is not entirely clear what is meant by this restriction, but it undoubtedly covers situations where a person is prohibited by statute from providing information. It probably also covers privilege in the sense that, where privilege is taken, the court should not override that privilege unless the case falls within a recognised exception.[32]

Court's own initiative

16.22   The court may make an order under Pt 18 of its own initiative,[33] even in cases on the small claims track.[34] The procedure provided by the rules is that where the court proposes to make an order of its own initiative it may (not must) give any person likely to be affected by the order an opportunity to make representations and specify the time by and manner in which the representations must be made.[35] Where the court proposes to hold a hearing to decide whether to make the order it must give each party likely to be affected at least three days' notice of the hearing.[36] However, the court may make an order without hearing the parties or giving them an opportunity to make representations.[37] In such a case the party affected may apply to set aside or vary the order.[38] Where a defence appears to disclose no reasonable

---

[30] CPR, Pt 18, Practice Direction, para.4.2(1).
[31] CPR, r.18.1(2).
[32] See Ch.11, paras 11.04–11.143.
[33] CPR, r.3.3(1).
[34] CPR, r.27.2(3).
[35] CPR, r.3.3(2).
[36] CPR, r.3.3(3).
[37] CPR, r.3.3(4).
[38] CPR, r.3.3(5), (6).

grounds for defending a claim, or to be an abuse of the process, of the court's process or otherwise likely to obstruct the just disposal of the proceedings, then the court may make an order under CPR, r.18.1, requiring the defendant within a stated time to clarify his defence or to give additional information about it.[39] Before deciding the track to which to allocate proceedings or deciding whether to give directions for an allocation hearing to be fixed, the court may order a party to provide information about his case.[40]

The application

The application notice for an order under Pt 18 should set out or have attached to it the text of the order sought. It should specify the matter or matters in respect of which the clarification or information is sought.[41] The format of the order sought should cover the formal requirements for a Request.[42] If a Request for further information or clarification has not been made, the application notice should explain why not. If a Request has been made, the application notice or the evidence in support should describe the response, if any.[43] Applicants may use Practice Form PF57 for their application notice.[44] Both the first party and the second party should consider whether evidence in support of or in opposition to the application is required.[45] In view of the overriding objective of the new procedural code of enabling the court to deal with cases justly, which includes saving expense and dealing with the case in ways which are proportionate,[46] in most cases it will not be necessary or appropriate to file evidence in relation to an application. Parties are expected to act sensibly in relation to requests, and generally only take out an application after attempting to reach agreement. The Admiralty and Commercial Courts Guide, expressly provides that if a party declines to provide further information, the solicitors or counsel for the parties must communicate directly with each other before any application is made to the court.[47] **16.23**

Where the second party has made no response to a Request served on him, the first party need not serve the application notice on the second party and the court may deal with the application without a hearing. This applies only if at least 14 days have passed since the Request was served and the **16.24**

---

[39] CPR, r.3.4(2)(a) and (b); Practice Direction—striking out a statement of case, para.3.4.
[40] CPR, r.26.5(3).
[41] CPR, Pt 18, Practice Direction, para.5.2.
[42] CPR, Pt 18, Practice Direction, para.1.6.
[43] CPR, Pt 18, Practice Direction, para.5.3.
[44] Queen's Bench Guide, para.7.7.3.
[45] CPR, Pt 18, Practice Direction, para.5.4.
[46] CPR, r.1.1(2)(b), (c).
[47] (7th edn, 2006), para.D15.1. To similar effect is the Chancery Guide, para.3.10.

time stated in it for a response has expired.[48] The court in such a situation will not necessarily be in the best position to ascertain whether any objections to the information or clarification sought apply. Unless the court otherwise orders, the order will be served on the second party with a copy of the application notice and any supporting evidence.[49] The second party may apply to the court within seven days of service to set aside the order.[50] In addition, or alternatively, he may state the grounds of his objection in his response to the order. It is open to the court in cases where the application is dealt with without a hearing[51] specifically to include a liberty to apply to set aside or vary the order within a specified period, even where the application notice has been served.

16.25 Unless there has been no response to a Request, then the application notice must be served on the second party and all other parties to the claim.[52] An order made under Pt 18 must be served on all parties to the claim.[53] The order will specify the time within which the response should be provided; the length of time will of course depend on the circumstances. The court may specify the consequences of non-compliance with the order. Thus in appropriate cases it may order that non-compliance will lead to the statement of case being struck out. Where the order requires particulars to be given of a particular pleaded allegation, it may specify that allegation be struck out from the statement of case if there is non-compliance. The response to an order made under Pt 18 must be verified by a statement of truth.[54]

Timing

16.26 CPR, Pt 18 does not specify when an application for an order should be made. Generally the Case Management Conference, where there is one, is a convenient time.[55] When an application should be made will of course depend on all the circumstances and the court's powers are subject to the overriding objective in CPR, Pt 1.[56] Where the application is in relation to a statement of case and it is necessary for a question to be answered for the opposing party to understand the case he has to meet, the application may follow relatively soon after the statement of case has been served and a

---

[48] CPR, Pt 18, Practice Direction, para.5.5.
[49] CPR, r.23.9(2).
[50] CPR, r.23.10; the order must contain a statement of this right: r.23.9(3).
[51] CPR, r.23.8.
[52] CPR, Pt 18, Practice Direction, para.5.6.
[53] CPR, Pt 18, Practice Direction, para.5.7; CPR, r.18.1(3).
[54] CPR, r.22.1(1)(b).
[55] The Technology and Construction Court Guide para.5.5.2 provides that if the defendant wants to request further information of the Particulars of Claim, the request should if possible, be formulated prior to the first CMC, so it can be considered on that occasion. In practice this course is usually followed in all divisions.
[56] *Toussaint v Mattis*, unreported, May 22, 2000, CA.

preliminary Request has been made and not answered or not answered satisfactorily. Where further information is sought of a matter not contained in a statement of case, consideration should be given as to whether it is more appropriate to wait until after disclosure of documents or exchange of witness statements.[57] There can be no hard and fast rule as to whether an application should be made before or after disclosure of documents or exchange of witness statements, as sometimes a response may narrow the issues between the parties and hence narrow the issues for which disclosure or witness statements are necessary.[58] It would only rarely be appropriate to make an application prior to the service of the defence, as until then it is not normally known what matters are in dispute.[59] Similarly, it will rarely be appropriate to make an application against a claimant prior to the service of the defence[60]; making an application prior to the defence may only delay the claimant in proceeding with his claim.[61] In exceptional circumstances it may be appropriate to make an application under CPR, Pt 18 even prior to the service of particulars of claim by a claimant, although there will be a heavy burden on any party making an application to establish that a response is necessary at that stage. In the context of interrogatories, they have been allowed before service of the claim as to the circumstances of a collision in Admiralty,[62] and in defamation proceedings as to the exact words spoken in order to enable a claimant to plead a particulars of claim, where he was able to adduce evidence that he had been defamed but was unable to set out the words used as there were no witnesses willing to provide him with such information.[63] But in another case the Court of Appeal refused an order under Pt 18 (for disclosure of a third party's identity) where the judge had not yet considered various case management issues, and the relevance of the

---

[57] *Thrombosis Research Institute v Demoliou-Mason* [1996] F.S.R. 785 (interrogatories inappropriate before disclosure and exchange of witness statements); *Det Danske Hedeselskabet v KDM International Plc* [1994] 2 Lloyd's Rep. 534 at 537 (interrogatories prior to exchange of witness statements almost always premature); see also *Hall v Sevalco Ltd*, [1996] P.I.Q.R. 344, CA.

[58] Where a clear litigious purpose would be served, interrogatories have been allowed prior to disclosure of documents: *UCB Bank Plc v Halifax (SW) Ltd, The Times*, July 15, 1996; *Corporacion Nacional del Cobre de Chile v Metallgesellschaft AG, The Times*, January 6, 1999 (interrogatories exceptionally allowed for purposes of summary judgment application, prior to disclosure of documents); *Hall v Sevalco* [1996] P.I.Q.R. 344, CA.

[59] *Mercier v Cotton* (1876) 1 Q.B.D. 442, CA; *Re a debtor* [1910] 1 K.B. 59, CA (bankruptcy petition); *Fenwick v Johnston* (1876) Bitt.Prac.Cas. 120; *cf. Beal v Pilling* (1878) 38 L.T. 846 (interrogatories ordered after defence filed by co-defendant).

[60] *Re Sutton Glassworks Ltd* [1997] 1 B.C.L.C. 26 (interrogatories prior to service of respondent's evidence in directors disqualification proceedings inappropriate and premature). It may be appropriate to seek further information of the claimant's particulars of claim prior to the service of the defence, where a response is necessary to enable the defendant to plead properly to the claim.

[61] *Disney v Longbourne* (1876) 2 Ch.D. 704; *cf. Hawley v Reade* [1876] W.N. 64, where the answer of the claimant to interrogatories would affect whether or not any defence was to be filed at all.

[62] *The Isle of Cyprus* (1890) 15 P.D. 134.

[63] *Atkinson v Fosbroke* (1866) L.R. 1 Q.B. 628.

disclosure to the pleaded cases.[64] It is not appropriate to couple an application for the summary dismissal of a claim or a strike out of a pleading, with an application for further information. In principle, a request for further information implies that further information may exist. It should, therefore, be made before there is an application for summary determination, unless that application for summary determination is already justified. Combining the two is likely to lead to wasteful satellite litigation.[65]

E. BETWEEN WHOM AVAILABLE

16.27   A Request may be served and an order under Pt 18 may be made, against any party to proceedings.[66] The rules and Practice Direction do not expressly provide that there must be some issue between the requesting party and the other party for the determination of the court; whereas with interrogatories the rules expressly provided that they had to relate to "any matter in question between the applicant and that other party in the cause".[67] The practice developed in relation to interrogatories was that, as between parties other than claimants and defendants, there had to be some right to adjust between them in the action or proceedings.[68] Thus a claimant was not obliged to respond to interrogatories from a co-claimant unless there was some issue between them and interrogatories were confined to such issues. The same principles applied to co-defendants.[69] Where there were no rights to be adjusted between defendants and no issue arose between them, interrogatories were refused.[70]

16.28   Requests are available between claimants to counterclaim and defendants to counterclaim. A Pt 18 order sought by defendants to counterclaim against claimants in the original action may be sought, but in the usual case an application will be refused unless there is an issue joined between them.[71]

16.29   A Pt 18 order may be sought by a co-defendant to a counterclaim, but again the court is unlikely to make an order unless there is some right between the co-defendants to counterclaim to be adjusted in the action.[72]

---

[64] *Toussaint v Mattis*, unreported, May 22, 2000, CA.
[65] *Watson v Ian Snipe & Co.* [2002] EWCA Civ 293 at [35], CA.
[66] CPR, r.18.1(1).
[67] RSC, Ord.26, r.1(1). *Birchal v Birch Crisp & Co.* [1913] 2 Ch. 375, CA.
[68] *Shaw v Smith* (1886) 18 Q.B.D. 193, 198, 200, CA; *Molloy v Kilby* (1880) 15 Ch.D 162, CA; *cf. Brown v Watkins* (1885) 16 Q.B.D. 125.
[69] *cf. Clayson v Rolls Royce* [1951] 1 K.B. 746, CA; *Marshall v Langley* [1889] W.N. 222.
[70] *Brown v Watkins* (1885) 16 Q.B.D. 125, as explained in *Shaw v Smith* (1886) 18 Q.B.D. 193; *cf. Manatee Towing Co. and Coastal Tug & Barge Inc. v Oceanbulk Maritime S.A.* [1999] 1 Lloyd's Rep. 876.
[71] *Molloy v Kilby* (1880) 15 Ch.D 162, CA (interrogatories).
[72] *Alcoy v Greenhill* [1896] 1 Ch. 19, CA.

A Request may be made and a Pt 18 order may be sought in Pt 20 **16.30** proceedings; generally the court is only likely to make an order where an issue is raised between the party seeking the order and the respondent.[73]

The Pt 18 procedure applies in relation to "litigation friends"[74] as fully as **16.31** against a person under no disability. The same principles apply in relation to Requests and Pt 18 applications in proceedings involving foreign states or sovereigns as with disclosure of documents.

An order may be made against the Crown as against any other party. The **16.32** order must direct by what officer of the Crown the further information is to be provided. Care should be taken to select the officer in the best position to supply the information.[75]

F. RELEVANCE

A Request must relate to a matter which is in dispute in the proceedings.[76] **16.33** Thus for a Request to be permissible and a Pt 18 order available, the Request must be relevant to the issues in the proceedings. There is probably no real difference between this and the test for interrogatories which was that the interrogatories must relate to a "matter in question". However the test for interrogatories was that the "matter in question" had to be between the applicant and the other party in the cause or matter, whereas Pt 18 does not specifically state that the matter in dispute must be between the applicant and the party from whom information is sought. In view of the change in wording, the court would appear to have jurisdiction to permit requests where there is no issue between the applicant and the other party, at least where the request relates to a matter in issue between the applicant and some other party.[77] Despite this, it is most unlikely that the court will allow a general practice to arise whereby parties are permitted to make Requests of other parties on matters which are not in issue as between them.[78]

---

[73] CPR, Pt 20 encompasses what were called third party proceedings in the RSC. With interrogatories the practice was that they could be sought as between a defendant and the third party and as between the plaintiff and the third party where some issue on the pleadings was raised between them: *Bates v Burchell* [1884] W.N. 108; *Eden v Weardale Iron Co.* (1887) 34 Ch.D. 223, 35 Ch.D. 287, CA. Interrogatories were available in interpleader proceedings: *White v Watts* (1862) 12 C.B.(N.S.) 267. Interrogatories were available as between claimants to a limitation fund: *The Nedenes* [1925] W.N. 23. They were also available in adverse proceedings in the winding of a company: *Re Barned's Banking Co., exp. Contract Corp.* (1867) L.R. 2 Ch.App. 350; *Re Contract Corp. (Cooch Case)* (1872) L.R. 7 Ch.App. 207; *London and Yorkshire Bank v Cooper* (1885) 15 Q.B.D. 473, CA.

[74] See CPR, Pt 21.

[75] *Re Sutton Glassworks* [1997] 1 B.C.L.C. 26 at 30 (interrogatories directed to Secretary of State inappropriate in directors' disqualification proceedings).

[76] CPR, r.18.1(1).

[77] *Manatee Towing Co. and Coastal Tug & Barge Inc. v Oceanbulk Martime S.A.* [1991] 1 Lloyd's Rep. 876.

[78] *cf.* RSC, Ord.26, r.1(1).

16.34   Matter in question is a fairly broad concept, and the right to make Requests is not confined to facts directly in issue, but will extend to any facts the existence of which is relevant to the existence or non-existence of facts directly in issue.[79] However, the relevancy test must not be extended too far and the court will be astute to prevent Requests from becoming an instrument of oppression and from straying away from the real issues between the parties in the action. For the purposes of ascertaining what matters are in dispute, it is the statements of case which should be primarily referred to. Incidental matters not related to matters raised in the statement of case should not ordinarily form part of Requests. Even where Requests may (to a limited extent) extend beyond facts directly in issue, the court will generally not permit Requests as to what line of facts the applicant's opponent is going to rely on as relevant to the existence or non-existence of the facts directly in issue.[80] In the usual case, it is unlikely that the court will compel a party by means of a Pt 18 order to disclose the evidence which he intends to adduce at trial.[81]

16.35   It is not necessary that the response to a Request should be conclusive on the matter in dispute. It is enough that the Request should have some bearing on the question and the response might form a step in establishing liability.[82] A Request will generally be permissible if it is directed to matters which would tend either to support the applicant's case or destroy the other party's case.[83] It is quite proper for a Request to seek information from a party as to material facts as well as for the purpose of obtaining admissions which will narrow the issues at trial.[84] The fact that the party making the Request is aware of or is able to prove the facts sought to be admitted is of course no ground for objecting to the Request.[85]

---

[79] This was the approach by the courts in relation to interrogatories: *Mariott v Chamberlain* (1886) 17 Q.B.D. 154 at 163, CA; approved in *Nash v Layton* [1911] 2 Ch.71, CA, *Osram Lamp Works v Gabriel Lamp* [1914] 2 Ch. 129, CA; see also the Australian decisions: *Potter's Sulphide Ore Treatment v Sulphide Corp.* (1911) 13 C.L.R. 101; *Australian Blue Metal v Hughes* [1960] N.S.W.R. 673; *Cumming v Matheson* (1970) 92 W.N.(N.S.W.) 339; *Fischer v City Hotels Pty* (1970) 92 W.N.(N.S.W.) 322; *Sharpe v Smail* (1975) 49 A.L.J.R. 130. A narrower test formulated by Smith L.J. in *Kennedy v Dodson* [1895] 1 Ch. 334 at 341 was held to be not good law insofar as it conflicted with the test of Lord Esher (*Rockwell Corp. v Serck Industries* [1988] F.S.R. 187 at 203); however it has been followed in some Australian cases: see *Osborne v Sparke* (1907) 7 S.R.(N.S.W.) 460, *Green v Green* (1913) 13 S.R.(N.S.W.) 126 and in particular *Tiver v Tiver* [1969] S.A.S.R. 40 where the full Court of South Australia tried to reconcile the two lines of authorities.

[80] *Hooton v Dalby* [1907] 2 K.B. 18 at 21 (interrogatories).

[81] In the case of interrogatories the practice of the court was to refuse them in such cases: *Eade v Jacobs* (1877) 3 Ex. D.335 at 337; *Att.Gen. v Gaskill* (1882) 20 Ch.D. 519, CA.

[82] cf. *Blair v Haycock Cadle Co.* (1917) 34 T.L.R. 39 at 40, HL (interrogatories).

[83] This was the approach taken in relation to interrogatories: *Hennessy v Wright* [1897] 2 Q.B. 188, CA; *Plymouth Mutual Co-op v Traders Publishing Association* [1906] 1 KB 403 at 416–417, CA; see also *Goodman v Holroyd* (1864) 15 CB(NS) 839 at 844. It is also consistent with CPR, r.31.6(b), dealing with documentary disclosure.

[84] *Att.Gen. v Gaskill* (1882) 20 Ch.D. 519, CA.

[85] *Lyell v Kennedy (No.1)* (1883) 8 App.Cas. 217 at 228 (objection not founded in relation to interrogatories).

In the context of interrogatories, the practice grew up that they might not **16.36** extend to the evidence which the other party sought to rely upon in support of his case at trial. Hence interrogatories were not permitted to be used as a method of obtaining the names of the witnesses of the opposing party, save where the name of the witness itself was a relevant fact.[86] In principle the court is likely to follow a similar stance in relation to Requests and applications under Pt 18. The court will probably refuse to make a Pt 18 order in respect of a request for information which merely aims to provide material for the cross-examination of a witness. This is because the request would not fulfil the requirement that the information sought must relate to matters in dispute.[87]

The court will generally look at the statements of case in order to **16.37** determine what matters are in dispute as between the parties. However Requests are not necessarily confined to the issues as disclosed on the pleadings.[88] All requests for further information should be kept within reasonable limits.[89]

G. PARTICULAR INSTANCES

Credit

The court will generally refuse Requests and applications under Pt 18 in **16.38** respect of questions which go solely as to credit, not least because the request must relate to a matter in dispute in the proceedings. In relation to interrogatories the court applied the principle that interrogatories which go solely as to credit are not permissible, even though the information if obtained could be used for cross-examination of a witness at trial, since it may be oppressive if a party is obliged to disclose any information which might provide material for cross-examination as to his credibility as a witness.[90]

Damages

There is no reason in principle why a Request should not ask questions as **16.39** to the nature and extent of damages. This will assist a defendant who may

---

[86] *Marriott v Chamberlain* (1886) 17 Q.B.D. 154, CA.
[87] In the context of interrogatories the rules expressly excluded such interrogatories: RSC, Ord.26, r.1(3).
[88] *Marriott v Chamberlain* (1886) 17 Q.B.D. 154, CA (interrogatories).
[89] Technology and Construction Court Guide, para.5.5.2, which also provides that requests should concentrate on the important parts of the case.
[90] *Kennedy v Dodson* [1895] 1 Ch. 334, CA; *Rockwell Corp. v Serck Industries* [1988] F.S.R. 187; see also *Baker v Newton* (1875) Bitt.Prac.Cas. 80; *Allusen v Labouchere* (1878) 3 Q.B.D. 654, CA; *Sheward v Lonsdale* (1879) 5 C.P.D. 47; *Thorpe v Chief Constable of Manchester* [1989] 1 W.L.R. 655, CA.

wish to make a payment into court[91] or where a defendant has already paid money into court.[92] A Request may be appropriate as to matters which affect the level of damages[93] including matters relating to mitigation where that has been put in issue.[94] Interrogatories as to the quantum of a claim were generally not permitted, save where a defendant could show that the claim in damages was prima facie extortionate[95] or where it was sought to show that no damage had in fact been suffered.[96] There is no reason in principle why such a restrictive approach should be taken in relation to Requests. Even in relation to interrogatories it is doubtful that there was ever any general rule in principle against interrogatories as to damages. In relation to requests for particulars of a pleading it has been the practice that full particulars should be provided of any special damages.[97] The rules provide that, in respect of the particulars of claim, if the claimant is seeking aggravated or exemplary damages, this must be pleaded with the grounds for claiming them; similarly with provisional damages.[98] As regards Requests and Pt 18 applications, the court will examine each case on its merits as to whether questions on this subject are really appropriate and necessary.[99]

Documents

16.40   The court generally will not permit Requests and Pt 18 applications to be used as a means of challenging the accuracy and completeness of an opposing party's disclosure of documents. Where disclosure of documents is believed to be inadequate, the appropriate route is to apply for specific disclosure under CPR, r.31.12. In relation to interrogatories, it was held that interrogatories asking generally what documents the party had or had had in his possession, custody or power,[100] or as to whether the opposing party

---

[91] *Horne v Hough* (1874) L.R. 9 C.P.135; *Frost v Brooke* (1875) 32 L.T. 312; *Wright v Goodlake* (1865) 13 L.T. 120 (interrogatories).

[92] *Dobson v Richardson* (1868) L.R. 3 Q.B. 778; *cf. Jourdain v Palmer* (1866) L.R. 1 Exch. 102; see also *Clarke v Bennett* (1884) 32 W.R. 550 (interrogatories).

[93] *Marriott v Chamberlain* (1886) 17 Q.B.D. 154 at 162, 164; *Cocks v Royskill Steel Erection Ltd* November 20, 1991, unreported, CA, (interrogatories ordered of defendant employer as to claimant's prospects of promotion if accident had not happened).

[94] *Scaife v Kemp* [1892] 2 Q.B. 319 (interrogatories).

[95] *Clarke v Bennett* (1884) 32 W.R. 550.

[96] *Wilks & Berks Canal Navigation v Swindon Waterworks* (1872) 2 W.R. 353; *Dobson v Richardson* (1868) L.R. 3 Q.B. 778.

[97] *Supreme Court Practice 1999*, para.18/12/12; *Perestrello Companhia Limitada v United Paint* [1969] 1 W.L.R. 570; *Domsalla v Barr* [1969] 1 W.L.R. 630. Similarly, facts in support of a claim for aggravated damages should be pleaded: *Rookes v Barnard* [1964] A.C. 1129, HL.

[98] CPR, r.16.4(1)(c) and (d).

[99] *Heaton v Goldney* [1910] 1 K.B. 754 at 758; *Clarke v Bennett* (1884) 32 W.R. 550 (interrogatories).

[100] *Jacobs v G.W. Ry. Co.* [1884] W.N. 33; *Hall v Truman* (1885) 28 Ch.D. 307, CA.

had or had had documents other than those disclosed in a list or affidavit of documents[101] would generally be refused. Only in special circumstances have interrogatories been allowed as to the existence of particular documents.[102]

Where a Request is not used as a method of obtaining or challenging any **16.41** disclosure of documents, a Request as to documents is permissible so far as it relates to matters in dispute. In relation to interrogatories the practice grew up whereby whilst interrogatories as to the contents of an *existing* document would not usually be permitted,[103] they would be permitted as to the contents of a *lost* document.[104] A party may be asked as to whether he wrote a particular document. Before answering the party is entitled to see a copy of it; thus in practice it will often be convenient to exhibit a copy of the document to the Request, if a copy is not already in the hands of the other party.[105] There can be no objection in principle to a party being asked whether a document is in the hand of a particular person.[106] Similarly a party may be asked whether a particular document was prepared or sent with his consent, or whether it is in his handwriting[107] or whether a particular document had been received.[108]

Fishing

Requests designed to prove a cause of action or defence not yet pleaded **16.42** are fishing, and are not permissible. Interrogatories were often refused on this ground.[109] Thus interrogatories designed to assist a party in formulating a case not yet pleaded and those designed to find a cause of action against a party not yet a party to the action have been refused.[110] In libel actions generally, interrogatories designed to establish whether the defendant published words to other persons not identified in the statement of

---

[101] *Robinson v Budgett* [1884] W.N. 94.
[102] *Jones v Monte Video Co.* (1880) 5 Q.B.D. 556 at 558; *Hall v Truman* (1885) 29 Ch.D. 307, esp. at 320; *Nicholl v Wheeler* (1886) 17 Q.B.D. 101; *Morris v Edwards* (1890) 15 App.Cas. 309 at 313–315; Bray, at pp.213–214; *CTC Resources NL v Australian Stock Exchange* [2001] W.A.S.C. 40.
[103] *Hershfield v Clarke* (1856) 11 Exch. 712, which was not followed by Simon Brown J. in *Butler v GKN Foundations Ltd*, unreported, May 22, 1992.
[104] *Wolverhampton New Water Works v Hawksford* (1859) 5 C.B.(N.S.) 703; *cf. Ramsey v Ramsey* [1956] 1 W.L.R. 542.
[105] This has been the practice in relation to interrogatories: *Dalrymple v Leslie* (1881) 8 Q.B.D. 5; *Lyell v Kennedy (No.4)* (1883) 33 W.R. 44.
[106] *Lovell v Lovell* [1970] 1 W.L.R. 1451, CA (interrogatories).
[107] *Jones v Richards* (1885) 15 Q.B.D. 439 for the purposes of proving the handwriting in another document (interrogatories).
[108] *King v Commercial Bank of Australia* [1920] V.L.R. 218; *Jordan v Sanders* [1934] S.A.S.R. 424 (interrogatories).
[109] *Hennessy v Wright (No.2)* (1888) 24 Q.B.D. 445n; see also *EDS v South Pacific Aluminium* [1981] 1 N.Z.L.R. 146 at 150, CA of N.Z.
[110] *Sebright v Hanbury* [1916] 2 Ch. 245.

claim were refused.[111] Interrogatories sought with a view so as to enable a plaintiff to decide whether or not to abandon part of his claim have also been refused on the grounds of fishing.[112] Interrogatories intended to ascertain the names of witnesses of the opposing party, where those names are not material facts in themselves, have been rejected as being fishing.[113] Interrogatories have also been refused where they have been directed to no part of the claimant's case and which do not tend to disprove the case of the defendant, sought in the hope that they may furnish the claimant with proof of a cause of action not at present alleged, or with information as to the defendant's knowledge on matters not required by the rules to be pleaded by him.[114] In summary, Requests and applications under Pt 18 which are fishing will be rejected, and the authorities on interrogatories provide useful illustrations of the application of the general principle that fishing is not allowed.

Futile Request

16.43   Where a party has already pleaded to a fact to the best of his recollection, a Request may be inappropriate and a Pt 18 application may be refused on the grounds that it would be futile to require an answer. Where it is clear that that party has no knowledge of the facts sought to be admitted a Request and Pt 18 application may be held to be inappropriate.[115] Similarly a party will not be required to provide a response to a Request where the purpose of the Request is to secure an admission of fact solely within the knowledge of the party applying. However, the fact that the party making the Request has the means of ascertaining the information as to the facts is not of itself a ground of refusing a response to a Request, as an admission may well lead to the saving of costs at trial.[116]

Insurance

16.44   Save in insurance disputes, the insurance position of a party is usually irrelevant to the issues in the action, and a party will normally not be required to answer Requests in respect of it unless that party has himself

---

[111] *Barham v Lord Huntingfield* [1913] 2 K.B. 193; *cf. Dalgleish v Lowther* [1899] 2 Q.B. 590; *Russell v Stubbs* [1913] 2 K.B. 200n; *CHC Software Ltd v Hopkins & Wood* [1993] F.S.R. 241, Ch.D.

[112] *Rockwell Corp. v Serck Industries* [1988] F.S.R. 187 at 206.

[113] *Hooton v Dalby* [1907] 2 K.B. 18 at 20–21, CA; *Rockwell Corp. v Serck Industries* [1988] F.S.R. 187 at 206.

[114] *The Shropshire* (1922) 127 L.T. 487 at 488, CA.

[115] *Rofe v Kevorkian* [1936] 2 All E.R. 1334, CA (interrogatories).

[116] *Lyell v Kennedy (No.1)* (1883) App.Cas. 217 at 228, HL (interrogatories).

referred to insurance in his own pleading.[117] It is conceivable that in actions involving the Unfair Contract Terms Act 1977 the insurance position of a party may be relevant and Requests permissible on the subject.[118]

Law

There is no overriding objection in principle to a Request extending to **16.45** matters of law or mixed fact and law,[119] particularly where propositions of law are contained in the statements of case. A party may refer in his statement of case to any point of law on which his claim or defence is based.[120] Where matters of law are pleaded it may be open to the opposing party to require further information or clarification to be provided. The court will be astute to refuse Pt 18 applications which merely seek to compel a lay person with no knowledge of the law to set out legal propositions. The practice in relation to interrogatories was that it was regarded as inappropriate for a party to be interrogated on a matter of law, as this would often be one of the very questions for the court's determination.[121]

Opinion/Expert evidence

There is no express rule that Requests and Pt 18 applications may not be **16.46** directed to matters of opinion and matters which the other party can only learn from an expert, even though that has been the case generally in respect of interrogatories.[122] However the interrelationship with CPR, Pt 35 should be borne in mind, and generally matters of expert evidence should be dealt with either by written questions to experts under CPR, r.35.6,[123] or by way of a r.35.9 application for an order directing a party to provide information which is not reasonably available to the other party.[124]

---

[117] *Bolckow, Vaughan & Co. v Young* (1880) 42 L.T. 690.
[118] *Flamar Interocean Ltd v Denmac Ltd* [1990] 1 Lloyd's Rep. 434 at 440.
[119] *Corporation of Trustees of Roman Catholic Archdiocese of Brisbane v Discovery Bay Developments Pty Ltd* [1995] 2 Qd.R. 121 (interrogatories).
[120] CPR, Pt 16, Practice Direction, para.13.1(1).
[121] *Att.Gen. v Wang NZ* [1990] 3 N.Z.L.R. 148, CA of N.Z.; see also Renwick v Renwick [1918] N.Z.L.R 615 at 616; *Hope v McLoughlin* [1976] 1 N.Z.L.R. 715 at 719; and the Australian decisions of *Looker v Murphy* (1889) 15 V.L.R. 348 at 351, *McBride v Sandland* (1917) S.A.L.R. 249 at 253; *King v Commercial Bank* [1920] V.L.R. 218 at 224; and *Coal Cliff Collieries v CE Heath Insurance* (1988) 5 N.S.W.L.R 703 at 707–708.
[122] *Rofe v Kevorkian* [1936] 2 All E.R. 1334, CA. Similarly where the party sought to be interrogated was not an expert in foreign law, interrogatories as to foreign law were generally not permissible: *Phillips v Barron* [1876] W.N. 54; *Perlak Petroleum v Deen* [1924] 1 K.B. 111.
[123] See Ch.18, para.18.17, below.
[124] See Ch.18, para.18.18, below.

Other transactions and incidents

16.47 Requests which relate to similar fact evidence, in cases where the evidence on one transaction is relevant to another which is the subject matter of proceedings, are prima facie permissible so long as they sufficiently relate to matters in question. The principles are similar to those which apply in relation to disclosure of documents. The court will be astute to confine Requests relating to other transactions to reasonable bounds, as it has done in the past with interrogatories. Thus interrogatories have also been permitted in respect of previous transactions to prove money lending[125] and dealings with other policies in a dispute as to the rate of premium for an insurance policy.[126] They have been permitted in respect of other claims made by a claimant where such claims were relevant to the issues in the action between the parties.[127]

Pleadings

16.48 In relation to Requests for Further and Better Particulars of a pleading, special rules and practices grew up which provided a framework for deciding which requests were permissible and impermissible. Many of the distinctions which grew up in practice will have little application under the new Rules, particularly as the new Rules were introduced as a new procedural code, and interrogatories have been merged with Request for Particulars to form CPR, Pt 18. In dealing with Pt 18 applications, the court will bear in mind the overriding objective and the desirability of properly formulated and particularised statements of case. Where a statement of case is inadequately particularised, then the other party can serve a Request and make a Pt 18 application if necessary or appropriate.

16.49 Examples of the court's practice in relation to particulars prior to the introduction of the CPR are as follows:

(1) Admission: particulars of an admission have been held to be not permissible.[128] It is unlikely that the court will regard this as an absolute objection in relation to Pt 18 applications, particularly if the nature and extent of the admission is unclear.

(2) Burden of proof: generally, particulars were not ordered of allegations in relation to which the burden of proof lay on the applicant.[129] The court will not regard itself as constrained by this

[125] *Nash v Layton* [1911] 2 Ch. 71.
[126] *Girdlestone v North British Mercantile Insurance* (1870) LR 11 Eq. 197; *cf. Merchants & Manufacturers Insurance v Davies* [1938] 1 K.B. 96, CA.
[127] *McKenna v Cammell Laird Ship Repairers Ltd, The Times*, May 11, 1989, CA.
[128] *Fox v H. Wood (Harrow) Ltd* [1963] 2 Q.B. 601, CA.
[129] *Cheeseman v Bowaters United Kingdom Paper Mills Ltd* [1971] 1 W.L.R. 1773, CA.

former practice in dealing with Pt 18 applications. Simply because the burden of proof lies on a party does not necessarily mean he should not be required to provide clarification or information in relation to such an allegation.

(3) Contributory negligence: the practice has been that particulars should be given or will be ordered where necessary.[130] The court will of course in appropriate cases require information or clarification to be provided in relation to a pleaded case of contributory negligence.[131]

Witness at trial

The mere fact that the object of a Request is to obtain an admission of fact which can be proved by a witness, who will in any case be called at trial, is not necessarily a valid ground of objection.[132] Where it is clear that answering the Request will not save, but add to, costs, then in principle a party may be entitled to refuse to respond and the court may refuse to make an order on a Pt 18 application. The mere fact that a witness can or will in any case be called at trial is therefore not a ground in itself for refusing to respond to a Request.[133] In any event, prior to the exchange of any witness evidence, it will often be uncertain as to precisely which witnesses will be called by the other side at trial and what the content of their evidence will be. Further, admissions of fact can be useful in narrowing the issues prior to trial and can assist the applicant to decide which witnesses he needs to call at trial.[134] Where a party is unlikely to be in a position to call any witnesses at trial, this may be a factor indicating that a response to a Request is reasonably necessary and proportionate.[135]

16.50

H. NECESSITY AND PROPORTIONALITY

In line with the overriding objective, a Request should be strictly confined to matters which are reasonably necessary and proportionate to enable the requesting party to prepare his own case or to understand the case he has to

16.51

---

[130] *Atkinson v Stewart and Partners Ltd* [1954] N.I.L.R 146, CA; *Savage v Kirk* (1907) 40 Ir. L.R. 82.

[131] Other examples are set out in the *Supreme Court Practice 1999*, paras 18/12/4–51.

[132] This has been the practice in relation to particulars: *Supreme Court Practice 1999*, para.18/12/50.

[133] *Cox v Royskill Steel Erection Ltd*, November 20, 1991, unreported, CA (interrogatories); *Parfums Yves Saint Laurent v The Ritz Hotel Ltd* [1990] F.S.R 36, H.K.C.A.

[134] *Lyell v Kennedy (No.1)* (1883) 8 App.Cas. 217 at 228, HL.

[135] The practice in relation to interrogatories was that this was a factor indicating that they were necessary for fairly disposing of the action: *Griebart v Morris* [1920] 1 K.B. 659, CA; see also *Lang v Australian Coastal Shipping Corp.* [1974] 2 N.S.W.L.R 70.

meet.[136] The emphasis is on confining this part of any litigation strictly to what is necessary and proportionate and to the avoidance of disproportionate expense.[137] This requirement may well be stricter than the principle that applied in relation to interrogatories, namely that the interrogatories sought must be necessary for disposing fairly of the cause or matter or for saving costs.[138] Typical situations in which a Request may be justified on the grounds of being reasonably necessary and proportionate are as follows:

(1) Where an admission of fact is sought which if admitted would result in the saving costs or the narrowing of issues in the action.
(2) Where it would enable the applicant to decide whether some of his witnesses need to be called at trial.
(3) Where the response may assist the parties to settle the litigation.[139]

The Request must be reasonably necessary at the stage in the action at which the response is sought.[140]

I. OPPRESSIVE, PROLIX, SCANDALOUS, VAGUE AND IRRELEVANT REQUESTS

16.52   Oppressive Requests and Pt 18 applications will not be allowed as this would conflict with the requirement that a Request should be concise and strictly confined to matters which are reasonably necessary and proportionate.[141] In the past the courts were astute to oppressive interrogatories.[142] Similarly prolix Requests are not permissible as Requests should be concise.[143] For example, a Request requiring verification of facts by extensive search through records spanning many years will generally be regarded as inappropriate.[144] It is likely that the individual authorities on oppressive and prolix interrogatories will not be of much assistance to the court in

---

[136] CPR, Pt 18, Practice Direction, para.1.2; see *Coflexip S.A. v Stolt Comex Seaways M.S. Ltd* [1999] F.S.R. 911 at 916–917.
[137] *King v Telegraph Group Plc* [2004] EWCA Civ 613, [2005] 1 W.L.R. 2282 at [63]; *McPhilemy v Times Newspapers* [1999] 3 All E.R. 775 at 792–4.
[138] RSC, Ord.26, r.1(1); *Coflexip S.A. v Stolt Comex Seaways M.S. Ltd* [1999] F.S.R. 911.
[139] *Sutherland v British Dominions Land Settlement Corp.* [1926] Ch. 746 at 753 (interrogatories).
[140] See para.16.026, above; also *Hall v Selvaco Ltd* [1996] P.I.Q.R. 344, *The Times*, March 27, 1996, CA, *The Thrombosis Research Institute v Demoliou-Mason* [1996] F.S.R. 785.
[141] CPR, Pt 18, Practice Direction, para.1.2.
[142] *White & Co. v Credit Reform Association* [1905] 1 K.B. 653 at 659, CA; *Lovell v Lovell* [1970] 1 W.L.R. 1451; *Rockwell Corp. v Serck Industries* [1988] F.S.R 187; Bray at pp.106–108.
[143] *Oppenheim v Sheffield* [1893] 1 Q.B. 5, CA (prolix interrogatories not allowed).
[144] *Parker v Wells* (1881) 18 Ch.D 477, CA (interrogatories).

relation to Requests and Pt 18 applications as everything depends on the particular circumstances. However, even in the case of interrogatories, the courts were often reluctant to allow lengthy and complex interrogatories, even in substantial actions. This is because challenges to voluminous requests may take a considerable amount of court time, and in some cases judges have rejected interrogatories in their entirety as being oppressive. This was of course appropriate in particularly abusive situations. However, in other cases, judges have been prepared to go through the interrogatories one by one to decide which should be allowed and which disallowed.[145] Oppressive interrogatories were strongly discouraged in the Commercial Court, and a similar approach will be taken in respect of Requests and Pt 18 application, as reflected in the Commercial Court Guide.[146]

Vaguely framed questions may be rejected on the grounds of oppression **16.53** or as being embarrassing.[147] Requests which are scandalous are similarly impermissible[148]; however a relevant question should not be categorised as scandalous.[149] A Request made other than for the bona fide purposes of the action is not permissible[150] as Pt 18 only relates to matters which are in dispute in the proceedings.[151] Under the old rules it was held not unfair to serve interrogatories seeking information from a foreign defendant which could not be obtained in his home jurisdiction.[152] It is doubtful that a different result would obtain under the CPR.[153]

J. SPECIAL CASES

Admiralty

Requests may be made in Admiralty actions in the usual way. The **16.54** practice of the Commercial Court and the Admiralty Courts are set out in the Admiralty and Commercial Courts Guide.[154] Requests may be particularly helpful in collision actions or where vessels have sunk in situations where a party has no available witnesses to the incident in question. Interrogatories were sometimes permitted in collision actions as to the information contained in the preliminary acts, and in special cases a plaintiff was

---

[145] *Fisher v Owen* (1878) 8 Ch.D. 645; *Allhusen v Labuchere* (1878) 3 Q.B.D. 654.
[146] See para.15.54, below; *Det Danske Hedeselskabet v KDM International Plc* [1994] 2 Lloyd's Rep. 534 at 536–7 (interrogatories).
[147] *The Radnorshire* (1880) 5 P.D. 172 (interrogatories).
[148] *Kemble v Hope* (1894) 10 T.L.R. 371, CA; *Oppenheim & Co. v Sheffield* [1893] 1 Q.B. 5.
[149] *Fisher v Owen* (1878) 8 Ch.D. 645 at 653, CA (interrogatories); Bray, at pp.105–106.
[150] CPR, r.18.1 (1).
[151] Interrogatories were refused on these grounds: *Allhusen v Labuchere* (1878) 3 Q.B.D. 654 at 664, CA; *Sebright v Hanbury* [1916] 2 Ch. 245.
[152] *B.C.C.I. S.A. v Al-Kaylani*, unreported, July 7, 1999, Evans-Lombe J.
[153] *B.C.C.I. S.A. v Al-Kaylani*, unreported, December 13, 1999, Jules Sher Q.C.
[154] (7th edn, 2006), para.D15.

allowed to administer interrogatories to the owners of a vessel as to the circumstances of a collision even before the delivery of a statement or particulars of claim.[155] Interrogatories were permitted between claimants to a limitation fund.[156] Interrogatories framed with the object of compelling the defendants to set up an affirmative case, on matters which form no part of the claimant's case and do not go to disprove the case of the defendant, were held to be inadmissible.[157] Just as interrogatories proved to be a useful tool in Admiralty actions, Requests and Pt 18 applications will be able to serve a useful purpose in such actions.

Commercial court

16.55   Part 18 of the CPR applies to Commercial Court and Admiralty proceedings.[158] The Admiralty and Commercial Court Guide gives specific guidance as to how Requests and Pt 18 applications are to be dealt with.[159] But before seeking an Order from the court for further information the parties must first attempt, by direct communication, to reach agreement on the point, and a proposed applicant must certify that this has occurred before the matter will be listed.[160] Any response providing further information must of course be verified by a statement of truth.[161]

Defamation

16.56   Requests and Pt 18 applications have an important function in defamation actions. By virtue of their special nature, particular rules grew up in relation to the circumstances in which interrogatories would be allowed.[162] The court will no doubt take into account the particular nature of a defamation action, including what matters are required to be particularised

---

[155] *The Isle of Cyprus* (1890) 15 P.D. 134; see also other collision actions: *The Biola* (1876) 34 L.T. (N.S.) 185 (interrogatories seeking to obtain information given in the preliminary acts of the party interrogated held to be inadmissible); *The Radnorshire* (1880) 5 P.D. 172 (interrogatories permitted as to the circumstances of the collision even though the information sought would to a great extent be afforded by the claimant's preliminary act); *The Bernard* [1905] W.N. 73, CA; see also *The Lowdock v Edwards* (1941) 70 Ll. Rep. 133 at 134.
[156] *The Nedenes* [1925] W.N. 23; (1925) 91 T.L.R 243.
[157] *The Shropshire* (1922) 127 L.T. 487, CA.
[158] CPR, Practice Directions, Pts 58 and 61 respectively.
[159] (6th edn, 2002), para.D15.
[160] Para.D15.1.
[161] Para.D15.2.
[162] *Gatley on Libel and Slander* (9th edn, 1998), paras 30.96–30.124; see now in relation nto information requests, *Gatley on Libel and Slander* (10th edn, 2004), para.26.43.

under the rules, in deciding which Requests and applications under Pt 18 are appropriate.

Where a Request is designed to obtain information or clarification in relation to a pleading, this is against the background of the specific requirements in the rules which require parties to give specific particulars of various matters. In particular:

16.57

(1) The claim form must, in a claim for libel, identify the publication the subject of the claim, and, in a claim for slander, so far as possible contain the words complained of, and identify the person to whom they were spoken and when.[163]

(2) In a claim for slander the precise words used and the names of the persons to whom they were spoken and when must be set out (so far as possible) in the particulars of claim, if not already contained in the claim form.[164]

(3) The claimant must specify in the particulars of claim the defamatory meaning which he alleges that the words or matters complained of conveyed, both (a) as to their natural and ordinary meaning, and (b) as to any innuendo meaning; in the latter case, the claimant must also identify the relevant extraneous facts.[165]

(4) Where the defendant alleges that the words complained of are true, he must specify the defamatory meanings he seeks to justify, and give details of the matters on which he relies in support of that allegation.[166]

(5) Where the defendant alleges that the words complained of are fair comment on a matter of public interest, he must specify the defamatory meaning he seeks to defend as such and give details of the matters on which he relies in support of that allegation.[167]

(6) Where the defendant alleges that the words complained of were published on a privileged occasion he must specify the circumstances he relies on in support of that contention.[168]

(7) Where the defendant alleges that the words complained of are true, or are fair comment on a matter of public interest, the claimant must serve a reply specifically admitting or denying the

---

[163] CPR, Pt 53, Practice Direction, para.2.2; formerly RSC Ord.82, r.2 (libel).
[164] CPR, Pt 53, Practice Direction, para.2.4; as to libel, see *Harris v Warre* (1879) 4 C.P.D. 125; *Collins v Jones* [1955] 1 Q.B. 564.
[165] CPR, Pt 53, Practice Direction, para.2.3; formerly RSC Ord.82, r.3(1); see also *Lewis v Daily Telegraph* [1964] A.C. 234; *Grubb v Bristol United Press* [1963] 1 Q.B. 309; *Fullam v Newcastle Chronicle* [1977] 1 W.L.R. 651; *Grappelli v Derek Block* [1981] 1 W.L.R. 822; *Lucas-Box v News Group Newspapers* [1986] 1 W.L.R. 147.
[166] CPR, Pt 53, Practice Direction, para.2.5.
[167] CPR, Pt 53, Practice Direction, para.2.6; formerly RSC Ord.82, r.3(1); *Peter Walker & Son Ltd v Hodgson* [1909] 1 K.B. 239 at 243, CA.
[168] CPR, Pt 53, Practice Direction, para.2.7.

allegation or denying the allegation and giving the facts on which he relies.[169]

(8) If the defendant pleads fair comment or privilege and the claimant intends to allege malice, the claimant must serve a reply giving details of the facts and matters relied upon.[170]

(9) A claimant must give full details of the facts and matters on which he relies in support of his claim for damages, and, if he claims aggravated or exemplary damages, he must provide the information specified in CPR, r.16(1)(c).b.[171]

16.58 In a claim for libel or slander where the defendant states in his statement of case that the words or matters complained of are fair comment on a matter of public interest or published on a privileged occasion, the old rules provided that no further information as to the defendant's sources of information or grounds of belief should be allowed.[172] The CPR provide that, unless the court otherwise orders, a party will not be required to provide further information about the identity of the defendant's sources of information.[173] Thus a Request or Pt 18 application seeking such information is usually inappropriate.

16.59 There can be no objection in principle to a party seeking information or clarification of matters pleaded in defamation actions, particularly in relation to those matters which under the rules ought to be particularised. As regards Requests and Pt 18 applications for information or clarification of matters not specifically pleaded, the practice in relation to interrogatories may be instructive as to the circumstances where questions may or may not be appropriate, but it is unlikely that the court will rigidly apply the authorities dealing with interrogatories.

16.60 In an action for slander it has been held that a defendant may be interrogated as to whether he did on or about a given date, or when, speak the words complained of or words to that effect.[174] Interrogatories directed to a defendant as to whether the words were spoken in the presence of named persons have been allowed.[175] In exceptional circumstances a plaintiff was allowed to interrogate as to the exact words spoken in order to enable him to plead a statement or particulars of claim, where he could

---

[169] CPR, Pt 53, Practice Direction, para.2.8.
[170] CPR, Pt 53, Practice Direction, para.2.9.
[171] CPR, Pt 53, Practice Direction, para.2.10.
[172] RSC, Ord.82, r.6.
[173] CPR, r.53.3.
[174] *Dalgleish v Lowther* [1899] 2 Q.B. 590, CA; *Barham v Huntingfield* [1913] 2 K.B. 193, CA; *Tournier v National Bank* [1924] 1 K.B. 461 at 478, CA; see also *Stern v Sevastopulo* (1863) 14 C.B. (N.S.) 737; *Saunderson v Von Radeck* (1905) 119 L.T.J. 33, HL; *Phelps v Kemsley* (1943) 168 L.T. 20; *Garnaut v Bennett* (No.1) (1909) 29 N.Z.L.R. 378.
[175] *Dalgleish v Lowther* [1899] 2 Q.B. 590, CA; see also *Bradbury v Cooper* (1883) 12 Q.B.D 94.

adduce evidence that he had been defamed but was unable to set out the words used as there were no witnesses willing to provide him with such information.[176] Interrogatories as to publication on occasions other than those specifically alleged in the statement or particulars of claim have been held to be generally not permissible in the absence of clear affidavit evidence but there has been in fact publication to other persons unknown, although even in such cases interrogatories which are no more than fishing have been disallowed.[177]

In a libel action it has been held that a defendant may be interrogated as to whether he wrote or published the words complained of,[178] although in appropriate cases it has been open to a defendant to meet such a request with a refusal to answer on the grounds of self-incrimination.[179] Interrogatories have been permitted of a defendant as to whether he was the printer and/or publisher of the newspaper which contained the words complained of.[180] Where a defendant has denied that he wrote the libellous letter complained of, interrogatories have been allowed as to whether he was the author of another letter so that handwriting may be compared.[181] Where a defendant denied that he spoke the words complained of, but pleaded in the alternative that if he did so it was at the claimant's invitation, interrogatories have been allowed as to how and where such invitation was given by the claimant.[182] **16.61**

The court will be astute to prevent oppressive or irrelevant Requests being used. In relation to interrogatories this has been the approach followed by the court. Thus an interrogatory as to the name of persons to whom a book has been published has been held to be oppressive.[183] Interrogatories as to the circulation figures for a newspaper containing allegedly defamatory matter were generally not allowed, although it appears that, where the newspaper was obscure and not widely known, such interrogatories had been permitted.[184] In an action involving libel contained in newspapers, interrogatories have been allowed of a defendant as to whether he was the proprietor at the relevant time,[185] the printer or publisher at the relevant **16.62**

---

[176] *Atkinson v Fosbroke* (1866) L.R. 1 Q.B. 628.
[177] *Barham v Huntingfield* [1913] 2 K.B. 193, CA; *Russell v Stubbs* [1913] 2 K.B. 200n; see also *Chertkow v Retail Credit* [1932] 1 W.W.R. 905; *CHC Software Ltd v Hopkins & Wood* [1993] F.S.R. 241, Ch.D.
[178] *Greenfield v Reay* (1875) L.R. 10 Q.B. 217, *McLoughlin v Dwyer* (1895) Ir.R.9 C.L. 170; *Jones v Richards* (1885) 15 Q.B.D. 439.
[179] *Lamb v Munster* (1882) 10 Q.B.D. 110.
[180] *Ramsden v Brealey* (1875) 33 L.T. 322.
[181] *Jones v Richards* (1885) 15 Q.B.D. 349.
[182] *Barratt v Kearns* [1905] 1 K.B. 504, CA.
[183] *White v Credit Reform Association* [1905] 1 K.B. 653, CA.
[184] *Whitaker v Scarborough Post Newspaper* [1896] 2 Q.B. 148, CA, overruling *Parnell v Walter* (1890) 24 Q.B.D. 441; see also *Rumney v Walter* (1891) 61 L.J.Q.B. 149 and *James v Carr* (1890) 7 T.L.R. 4.
[185] Stamp Duties on Newspapers Act 1836, s.19, re-enacted as the Newspapers, Printers and Reading Rooms Repeal Act 1869, s.1; *LeFroy v Burnside (No.1)* (1879) 4 L.R. Ir. 340.

time[186] and whether a co-defendant was proprietor at the relevant time[187]; but interrogatories have not been allowed as to whether he was the author of the alleged libel[188] or the editor of the newspaper.[189]

16.63   A plaintiff was allowed to interrogate a proprietor of a newspaper as to the name of the printer, and where the defendant was the printer as to the name of the proprietor, even though the information was sought to enable the claimant to bring an action against the printer or proprietor respectively.[190] A rule of practice grew up in relation to actions against newspapers, whereby interrogatories were not permitted as to the name of the person who supplied the information[191]; however interrogatories were allowed in general as to the name of the writer of the alleged libel.[192] There was no such special rule applying to defendants who were not proprietors of the newspaper,[193] although in such an action it was still necessary to show that the interrogatories were relevant to an issue in the action, and in any event such interrogatories must have been for the bona fide purposes of the action.[194] Where fair comment or privilege was pleaded, interrogatories as to the defendant's sources of information or grounds of belief were not allowed, and the current rules in relation to Requests and Pt 18 applications do not encourage such requests.[195]

16.64   An interrogatory requiring the defendant to state whether the words published by him referred to the claimant has been held to be not permissible.[196] It is clearly open to the court on a Pt 18 application to take a different approach and require a defendant to provide this type of information as a response to this type of question will enable the parties to focus on the true issues in the action. An interrogatory requesting the defendant to state whether he intended the words in the meaning attributed by the pleaded innuendo has been held to be not permissible as it is immaterial whether the defendant intended the words to bear such meaning.[197] In

---

[186] *Ramsden v Brealey* (1875) 33 L.T. 322.

[187] *Dickson v Enoch* (1871) L.R. 13 Eq. 394.

[188] *Walton v Brignell* [1875] W.N. 239.

[189] *Carter v Leeds Daily News* [1876] W.N. 11; *Palmer v Fraser* (1888) 7 V.L.R. 77; *Murray v Northern Whig* (1912) 46 Ir. LT 77, CA.

[190] *Hillman's Airways v Société Anonyme* [1934] 2 K.B. 356; Stamp Duties on Newspapers Act 1836, s.19.

[191] *Plymouth Mutual Society v Traders Association* [1906] 1 K.B. 403; *Lyle Samuel v Odhams* [1920] 1 K.B. 135, CA; *South Suburban Co-op v Orum* [1937] 2 K.B. 690; *Lawson v Odhams Press* [1949] 1 K.B. 129, CA; see CPR, r.53.3, and para.16.058, above.

[192] *Hennessy v Wright* (1888) 24 Q.B.D. 445n; *Gibson v Evans* (1889) 23 Q.B.D. 384.

[193] *Georgius v Oxford University Press* [1949] 1 K.B. 729.

[194] *Marriott v Chamberlain* (1886) 17 Q.B.D. 154; *Edmondson v Birch* [1905] 2 K.B. 523, CA.

[195] CPR, r.53.3; formerly RSC, Ord.82, r.6, introduced in 1949; *Adams v Sunday Pictorial Newspapers* [1951] 1 K.B. 354; see para.16.058, above.

[196] *Spiers & Pond v John Bull* (1916) 85 L.J.K.B. 992; see also *Bridgmont v Associated Newspapers* [1951] 2 All E.R. 285 and *Franklin v Daily Mirror Newspapers* (1933) 149 L.T. 443.

[197] *Heaton v Goldney* [1910] 1 Q.B. 754, CA, not following *Foster v Perryman* (1891) 8 T.L.R. 115.

principle the court will refuse a Request or Pt 18 application seeking such information on the grounds of irrelevance.

Where fair comment has been pleaded and particulars provided, a defendant has been allowed to interrogate as to the truth of the matters relied upon even though there has been no plea of justification.[198] Whether the court will permit a Request or Pt 18 application depends on the circumstances, as it is far from clear that it is appropriate that a defendant should be entitled to seek further information as to the truth of matters relied upon where there is no plea of justification. Where justification is pleaded, it has been held that the defendant can only seek interrogatories as to such matters of justification as are referred to in the particulars.[199] This approach is appropriate in relation to Requests and Pt 18 applications. Similarly the court will not permit Requests and Pt 18 applications which fish for evidence in support of a plea of justification.[200] Requests as to whether the claimant has had similar libels published of him and whether he has taken any steps to contradict these are inappropriate as they do not relate to matters in dispute.[201] On the other hand a defendant will be entitled to make a Request of the claimant as to the damages received or that he is due to receive in respect of the same or similar libels, as this may be relevant on the question of quantum of damages.[202] Requests are permissible on questions affecting the level of damages such as where the defendant has given particulars of matters on which he relies on the question of mitigation[203] or where the defendant intends to make or has made a payment into court. **16.65**

Insolvency

Where a liquidator represents a company in proceedings, a Request may be served and a Pt 18 order applied for on the same basis as in proceedings where the company is an ordinary solvent litigant.[204] The same is true in the winding-up itself, if the proceeding in relation to which a Request is to be served is in substance an action by or against the Company.[205] Furthermore, in a winding-up the liquidator may serve a Request on a person claiming to **16.66**

---

[198] *Peter Walker v Hodgson* [1909] 1 K.B. 239, CA; see also *Wright Norman v Oversea-Chinese Banking Corp. Ltd* [1992] 2 S.L.R. 710, CA of Singapore.

[199] *Yorkshire Provident Life Assurance v Gilbert* [1895] 2 Q.B. 148, CA; *Arnold & Butler v Bottomley* [1908] 2 K.B. 1512, CA.

[200] Interrogatories were refused on these grounds: *Gourley v Plimsoll* (1893) L.R. 8 C.P. 362; *Buchanan v Taylor* [1896] W.N. 73; *Zierenberg v Labouchire* [1893] 2 Q.B. 183, CA.

[201] Interrogatories were refused on this ground: *Pankhurst v Hamilton* (1886) 2 T.L.R. 862; *Hindlip v Mudford* (1890) 6 T.L.R. 367.

[202] Defamation Act 1952, s.12.

[203] *Scaife v Kemp* [1892] 2 Q.B. 319.

[204] This was the case in relation to interrogatories: *Re Barned's Banking Co.* (1868) L.R. 2 Ch.App. 350; *Re Contract Corp. (Gooch's Case)* (1872) L.R. 7, Ch.App. 207.

[205] *Re Barned's Banking Co., exp. The Contract Corporation* (1867) L.R. 2 Ch.App. 350; *Re Contract Corporation (Gooch's Case)* (1872) L.R. 7, Ch.App. 207.

prove in the liquidation.[206] In directors' disqualification proceedings, it was held inappropriate for the respondent to seek to use interrogatories against the Secretary of State where it was alleged that his evidence was unclear; if the clarification sought was not obtained by correspondence, the right course was to seek to strike out the unclear evidence as embarassing.[207]

16.67   An "office-holder" (administrator, administrative receiver, liquidator or provisional liquidator) of a company additionally has various powers to obtain information from officers of the company and from others having the company's property, owing money to the company or being otherwise considered by the court to be capable of giving information relating to the company.[208] So far as these powers relate to the obtaining of documents they have already been considered,[209] but it is common for them to be exercised by asking questions in the form of a written questionnaire. The principles on which these powers may be exercised are the same as for documents. The powers are exercisable either informally, as between the office-holder and the person concerned,[210] or formally, by the court.[211]

Injunctions and Anton Piller Orders

16.68   The principles governing disclosure orders ancillary to *Mareva* (freezing) and tracing injunctions and *Anton Piller* orders, have also been discussed in the context of disclosure of documents.[212] Such disclosure may be, and commonly is, ordered in the form of answers to questions.[213] This is particularly so in seeking information about the defendant's assets,[214] or the assets being traced by way of a specific order under CPR, r.25.1(1)(g).[215]

Norwich Pharmacal Orders

16.69   The principle of law known as the *Norwich Pharmacal* rule, requiring a person mixed up in the wrongful acts of others to disclose to the intended claimant the identity of the wrongdoers, and other information, is discussed in the context of disclosure of documents.[216] However it should be borne in

---

[206] *Re Alexandra Palace Co.* (1880) 16 Ch.D. 58 (interrogatories).
[207] *Re Sutton Glassworks Ltd* [1997] 1 B.C.L.C. 26.
[208] Insolvency Act 1986, ss.235, 236.
[209] See Ch.3, paras 3.40–3.44, above.
[210] Insolvency Act 1986, s.235.
[211] Insolvency Act 1986, s.236.
[212] See Ch.2, paras 2.10–2.30, above.
[213] *A v C* [1981] Q.B. 956n; *AJ Bekhor & Co. Ltd v Bilton* [1981] Q.B. 923, CA.
[214] e.g. *AJ Bekhor & Co. Ltd v Bilton* [1981] Q.B. 923, CA; *CBS United Kingdom Ltd v Lambert* [1983] 1 Ch. 37, CA; *Re a Company* [1985] B.C.L.C. 333, CA; *Ashtiani v Kashi* [1987] Q.B. 888, CA.
[215] *cf. A v C* [1981] Q.B. 956n.
[216] See Ch.3, paras 3.02–3.25, above.

mind that disclosure given in accordance with this rule is more often given in the form of responses to Pt 18 orders rather than the production of documents.[217] In such cases, the practice relating to Requests set out in this chapter is applicable.

Patent and Copyright Actions

Pt 18 and its associated Practice Direction applies to the business of the **16.70** Patent Court and proceedings under the Copyright, Designs and Patents Act 1988, the Trade Marks Acts 1938 and 1994 and the Olympic Symbol, etc., Protection Act 1995 and Olympic Association Right (Infringement Proceedings) Regulations 1995.[218] The court will ensure that Requests and Pt 18 applications do not become burdensome in copyright and patent actions. The practice in relation to interrogatories, although not binding on the court in a Pt 18 application, is illustrative of the circumstances in which Requests or Pt 18 applications may or may not be appropriate.

In a copyright action interrogatories have been refused as to the develop- **16.71** ment and design of the defendant's product where infringement has been denied.[219] It will be open to the court to allow Requests and Pt 18 applications in such circumstances in appropriate cases. Interrogatories have been allowed as to the sources from which a defendant has compiled his work.[220] A defendant has been permitted to interrogate the claimant as to the number of copies sold by the claimant where the defendant intended to make a payment into court.[221] These are both examples where a Pt 18 application may be appropriate.

In general, interrogatories in patent actions have been permitted as in any **16.72** other action.[222] However, a claimant was not permitted to require answers to interrogatories seeking to establish infringement not forming part of the breaches particularised in the statement or particulars of claim. Such interrogatories going beyond the particulars have been found to be in the nature of fishing.[223] In an infringement action the practice as to interrogatories was

---

[217] Interrogatories have often been sought in this context; see for example, *R.C.A. Corp. v Reddingtons Rare Records* [1974] 1 W.L.R. 1445; *Loose v Williamson* [1978] 1 W.L.R. 739; *Ricci v Chow* [1987] 1 W.L.R. 1658.

[218] CPR, r.63.2.

[219] *Rockwell Corp. v Serck Industries* [1988] F.S.R. 187.

[220] *Kelly v Wyman* (1869) 17 W.R. 399.

[221] *Wright v Goodlake* (1865) 13 L.T. 120.

[222] *Birch v Mather* (1883) 22 Ch.D. 629; *Re Haddon's Patent* (1885) 54 L.J. Ch. 126; *Ashworth v Roberts* (1890) 45 Ch.D. 623; *Sharpe v Boots Co.* (1927) 44 R.P.C. 69; *Henrikson v Tallon* [1963] RPC 308; see also *The Digest* at pp.218–221.

[223] *Aktiengesellschaft Für Autogene Aluminium v London Aluminium Co.* [1919] 2 Ch. 67; see also *Benno Jaffe v John Richardson* (1893) 62 L.J. Ch. 710 and *Saccharin Corp. v Haines* (1898) 15 R.P.C. 344, CA.

that a plaintiff might interrogate as to the chemical composition and constitution of the alleged infringing substance.[224] In appropriate cases a plaintiff was entitled to interrogate as to the identity as to the manufacturer and supplier of infringing items.[225] In a dispute as to inventorship, it was held that an interrogatory as to that nature and extent of a contribution which would entitle a person to be named as inventor was hypothetical, and one as to which parts of which documents were confidential were unnecessary; both were refused.[226]

16.73   The Practice Direction relating to Patent and Copyright actions[227] specifies in many respects the particulars which are required to be provided by a claimant and defendant respectively. Requests seeking such particulars and Pt 18 applications are appropriate in most cases. The CPR, Pt 63 and the Practice Direction requires a party to provide particulars in the following circumstances:

(1) In an application in proceedings before the court for permission to amend a patent specification under s.75 of the Patents Act 1977, the applicant must give particulars of the amendment sought, the grounds on which the amendment is sought, and state whether the applicant will contend that the claims prior to amendment are valid.[228]

(2) The claimant in a claim for infringement must serve with his claim form particulars of the infringement relied upon, showing which of the claims in the specification of the patent are alleged to be infringed and giving at least one instance of each type of infringement alleged.[229] The Practice Direction sets out the matters which must be pleaded by a defendant challenging the validity of a patent or registered design.[230]

Recovery of land

16.74   It is submitted that there are no special principles which apply which would restrict the use of Requests and Pt 18 applications in actions relating to the recovery of land. The particulars of claim must include all the matters required by the rules, and Requests as to those matters are in general

---

[224] *Sharpe & Dohme v Boots Pure Drug* (1927) 44 R.P.C. 69.

[225] *Osram Lamp Works v Gabriel Lamp* [1914] 2 Ch. 129, CA; see also *Saccharin Corp. v Haines, Ward & Co.* (1898) 15 R.P.C. 344 and *Alliance Flooring v Winsoflor* [1961] R.P.C. 375.

[226] *The Thrombosis Research Institute v Demoliou-Mason* [1996] F.S.R. 785.

[227] CPR, Pt 63.

[228] CPR, r.63.10(2).

[229] CPR, Pt 63, Practice Direction, para.11.1.

[230] CPR, Pt 63, Practice Direction, paras 11.2–11.5.

appropriate.[231] Although many of the authorities on interrogatories treated such proceedings as if they were a distinct class, there is no need for this in principle. However, for completeness the principles which were applied in relation to interrogatories are set out in the following paragraph.

A claimant seeking to recover land from a defendant was entitled to **16.75** interrogate on all matters relevant to intending support his own case.[232] In past a practice grew up whereby a claimant was not entitled to interrogate as to a defendant's title on the grounds that it was not relevant to show that the defendant was without title.[233] In view of the fact that a defendant is required to plead his title specifically, it is likely that a defendant could have been required to answer interrogatories as to his title. A claimant has been able to interrogate a defendant as to the nature of the claimant's own title[234] and as to whether the defendant was merely a nominal defendant and if so who the real defendant was in an action for ejectment.[235] Formerly there was a privilege against answering questions which might expose the party interrogated to a forfeiture, but this was repealed.[236]

K. OBJECTIONS TO REQUESTS

A party on whom a Request is served may object to answering on various **16.76** grounds. Similarly, an application for an order under Pt 18 may be resisted on the same grounds. The grounds may be categorised as falling under the following categories, although there is often an overlap in practice:

(1) The Request does not relate to any matter in dispute. This objection encompasses the following grounds:

(a) the Requests are not relevant to the issues between the parties[237];

(b) the Request amounts to fishing[238];

(c) the Request solely goes to the credit of the party.[239]

(2) A response to the Request is not reasonably necessary and proportionate to enable the requesting party to prepare his own case

---

[231] CPR, Pt 16, Practice Direction—Statements of Case, para.7.

[232] *Lyell v Kennedy (No.1)* (1883) 8 App.Cas. 217, HL; *Miller v Kirwan* [1903] 2 I.R. 118; *Eyre v Rodgers* (1891) 40 W.R. 137; *Leeke v Portsmouth Corp.* (1912) 106 L.T. 627.

[233] *Horton v Donnington* (1886) T.L.R. 73; *Lyell v Kennedy (No.1)* (1883) 8 App.Cas. 217, HL; *Nicholl v Wheeler* (1886) 17 Q.B.D. 101, CA; *Morris v Edwards* (1890) 15 App.Cas. 309, HL.

[234] *Cayley v Sandycroft Brick* (1885) 33 W.R 557.

[235] *Sketchley v Connolly* (1863) 11 W.R. 573.

[236] Civil Evidence Act 1968, s.16(1)(a); see Ch.8, para.8.10, above.

[237] See paras 16.027–16.037, above.

[238] See para.16.042, above.

[239] See para.16.038, above.

or to understand the case he has to meet, either at all, or at the stage in the action at which the Request is served.[240] This objection includes, but is not limited to, the following grounds:

(a) the Request is futile[241];
(b) the Request relates to matters of opinion/expert evidence/law[242];
(c) the Request is oppressive, and this includes the objection that the questions posed are vague or unclear[243];
(d) the Request is scandalous[244];
(e) the Request is prolix and not concise[245];
(f) the Request is not made bona fide for the purposes of the action[246];
(g) the Request is inappropriate in the circumstances, including considerations such as the ability to seek the information by some other way (e.g. as under Pt 35 in respect of expert evidence).[247]

(3) The party on whom the Request has been served is privileged from answering the questions sought on various grounds, including:

(a) legal professional privilege[248];
(b) public interest immunity[249];
(c) self incrimination/exposure to penalty[250];
(d) "without prejudice" and witness statement privilege[251];
(e) diplomatic privilege[252];
(f) statutory prohibition.[253]

16.77 Where a Request has been served, it is incumbent upon the respondent to identify any objections and give reasons.[254] Where the party considers that a Request can only be complied with at disproportionate expense and objects to comply for that reason, he should say so in his reply and explain briefly why he has taken that view.[255] In the case of an application for an

---

[240] CPR, Pt 18, Practice Direction, para.1.2; see para.16.026, above.
[241] See para.16.043, above.
[242] See paras 16.045–16.046, above.
[243] See paras 16.045–16.046, above.
[244] See para.16.053, above.
[245] See para.16.052, above.
[246] See para.16.053, above.
[247] See para.16.056, above.
[248] See paras 16.080–16.083, below.
[249] See para.16.084, below.
[250] See paras 16.088–16.089, below.
[251] See para.16.090, below.
[252] See paras 16.088–16.089, below.
[253] See para.16.090, below.
[254] CPR, Pt 18, Practice Direction, para.4.1.
[255] CPR, Pt 18, Practice Direction, para.4.2(2).

order under Pt 18, in the ordinary case a Request would already have been served and the responding party would have set out the grounds of his objection. Where privilege has been sufficiently raised and has been considered to be appropriate by the court, the court will ordinarily not make an order under Pt 18 in respect of that. In appropriate cases, the court may consider that the convenient route is to make an order under Pt 18, leaving it to the respondent to set out his claim to privilege in his response to the order. The prudent course for a respondent is to clarify the situation at the time of the making of the order as to whether he may raise privilege in his response to the Order. Ordinarily it should be open for him to do so, unless the court has already ruled against him on the question of privilege at the time of making the original order. Objections other than privilege and statutory prohibition should not be made in response to an order under Pt 18, as such objections are discretionary and should have been raised and dealt with at the time of the making of the order in the first place, or on an application to vary or set aside on order made without notice.

L. PRIVILEGE AND STATUTORY PROHIBITION

In certain circumstances a party sought to be questioned by way of a 16.78 Request for Pt 18 application is entitled to object to answering some or all of the questions, and the ground of objection is usually described as "privilege". The heads of privilege and prohibition include:

(1) legal professional privilege[256];
(2) public interest immunity[257];
(3) privilege against (self) incrimination[258];
(4) "without prejudice" and witness statement privilege[259];
(5) diplomatic privilege[260];
(6) statutory prohibition.[261]

As stated above, although objections may be taken in response to a 16.79 Request, or on an application under Pt 18 for an order, the objection may also be taken in the response to a Pt 18 order, unless the court has already ruled against the objection at the Pt 18 application hearing. Where such an objection is appropriate, it must be taken separately for each question in response to the Pt 18 order, and must state the ground of privilege relied

---

[256] See paras 16.080–16.083, below.
[257] See para.16.084, below.
[258] See paras 16.085–16.086, below.
[259] See para.16.087, below.
[260] See paras 116.088–16.089, below.
[261] See para.16.090, below.

on.[262] The subject of privilege has been dealt with in detail above in connection with disclosure of documents,[263] and generally the rules concerning the Requests are the same.[264] Thus, in principle, if a party is entitled to withhold production of a document in his control on any of the above grounds, he is equally entitled to object to answer a Request seeking the same information. The following paragraphs set out aspects of the various kinds of privilege that are or may be particularly relevant for requests and Pt 18 applications.

(1) Legal Professional Privilege[265]

16.80   The objection that the Request and Pt 18 application relates to matters covered by legal professional privilege is generally as with discovery of documents. Thus a party cannot be compelled to answer a Request asking as to his knowledge, information and belief with regard to matters of fact, if his response is that he has no knowledge or information with regard to those matters except that derived from privileged communications made to him by his solicitors.[266] Where the Request relates to non-confidential communications between a party and his solicitor, a party may be required to answer even though his knowledge is derived from such communications.[267] The answers that a party gives to a Request generally cannot be privileged.[268]

16.81   In two respects special rules developed in relation to legal privilege as applied in interrogatories. In fact, neither of these is applicable to Requests and Pt 18 applications under the CPR. Hence, those special rules are principally only of historical interest in England and Wales, but they may apply in jurisdictions where interrogatories are still used.

16.82   Where leave had been given to interrogate a corporate party through the medium of an officer who was also its legal adviser, that party might have been able to claim legal privilege in respect of confidential information in the officer's possession as such legal adviser.[269] The special rule which

---

[262] This has been the practice in relation to interrogatories: *Dalgleish v Lowther* [1899] 2 Q.B. 590; *Church v Perry* (1877) 36 L.T. 573; *Smith v Berg* (1877) 36 L.T. 471.

[263] See Ch.11.

[264] Bray, for example, dealt with privilege for both documents and interrogatories in a single section of his book, and many of the leading cases in this area of law are in fact cases concerning interrogatories rather than documents: e.g. *Kennedy v Lyell* (1883) 23 Ch.D. 387, CA; (1883) 9 App.Cas. 81, HL.

[265] See generally Chap.11, paras 11.05–11.80, above.

[266] *Kennedy v Lyell* (1883) 23 Ch.D. 387, CA; (1883) 9 App.Cas. 81, HL. (interrogatories); however, in some cases a party may be called upon to answer a simple question of fact, even though he obtained the information from his solicitor.

[267] *Foakes v Webb* (1884) 28 Ch.D. 287 (interrogatories).

[268] *Visx Inc. v Nidex Co.* [1999] F.S.R. 91, CA (interrogatories).

[269] *Salford Corp. v Lever* (1890) 24 Q.B.D. 695.

developed in the context of interrogatories was that if the corporation itself elected that the officer/lawyer should give answers to interrogatories on its behalf, the privilege was regarded as having been waived.[270]

The second special rule was that a party could properly object to interrog- **16.83** atories seeking disclosure of matters as solely supporting his own case and not damaging that case or supporting his opponent's.[271] This privilege formerly applied to both documentary disclosure as well as interrogatories, but was abolished in civil cases so far as *documentary* disclosure was concerned in 1968.[272]

(2) Public Interest Immunity[273]

The occasions on which public interest immunity will be an objection will **16.84** not in practice be many, but there can be no doubt that it is a valid objection. There is no rule that Requests cannot be served on the Crown if they seek information covered by the immunity. The proper course is for the Crown to make its objection either in its response to the Request, and/or at the hearing of an application under Pt 18, or in the response to an order, as appropriate.[274] Where the Crown, or other body in whom a right (and duty) to claim public interest immunity is vested, is not the party to or against whom the Request is made or Pt 18 application order is sought, then steps should be taken to preserve such immunity and for it to be considered by the appropriate persons and the court.[275] Thus where the party to or against on whom a Request is served believes that to answer may infringe an interest which is the subject of a potential public interest immunity claim by another body, he should refer the Request to that body and if appropriate state in his response to the Request that public interest immunity may be applicable. It is open to the court on a Pt 18 application to give a person who may have a public interest immunity claim leave to appear on the application to argue public interest immunity.[276] Or the judge may direct that any draft response to a Pt 18 order should be sent to that person, to give him the opportunity to assert that any particular answer or answers should not be given. Such an approach would be consistent with the practical approach adopted by the

---

[270] *Mayor of Swansea v Quirk* (1879) 5 C.P.D. 106.
[271] *Commissioners of the Sewers of the City of London v Glasse* (1873) L.R. 15 Eq. 302 at 304; *Bidder v Bridges* (1885) 29 Ch.D. 29 at 34–35, 44 (though *cf.* at 46); *Lyell v Kennedy* (1883) 8 App.Cas. 217 at 225; *Morris v Edwards* (1890) 15 App.Cas. 309.
[272] Civil Evidence Act 1968, s.16(2).
[273] See generally, Ch.11, paras 11.81–11.103.
[274] *cf. Continental Reinsurance Corp. (UK) Ltd v Pine Top Insurance Ltd* [1986] 1 Lloyd's Rep. 8 at 27 (*subpoena ad testificandum*).
[275] *cf.* the procedure under CPR, r.31.19, for *documents*: see Ch.11, paras 11.88–11.94.
[276] See by analogy CPR, r.31.19 (6)(b).

court in one case[277] where, on an application to set aside interrogatories, the judge ordered that none of the interrogatories should be answered to the extent that the answers would travel into those categories of information objected to by the Crown (which was not a party to the proceedings), and the Crown, should have an opportunity to see draft answers in order to be allowed to assert that any particular answer or answers should not be given.

(3) Privilege Against (Self) Incrimination[278]

16.85   This privilege applies to Requests and Pt 18 applications as to documents. The objection must be taken by the respondent in response to the Request and in appropriate cases where the court has not already ruled against the privilege, it may be taken in the response to a Pt 18 order.[279] Thus where a substantive response to a Request or Pt 18 order might tend to incriminate the person, he may refuse to answer,[280] but he may be compelled to answer if it would not justify the institution of criminal proceedings.[281] In his response, the party wishing to rely on the privilege must state his belief that answering the Request or complying with the Pt 18 order would tend to incriminate him.[282] An order under Pt 18 may not be made against a respondent to a committal application.[283]

16.86   In an action brought only to recover a penalty, it has been held that interrogatories are not available, and interrogatories put by a claimant solely for the purposes of proving his claim for penalties was not permissible.[284] The rationale for the rule is that in an action brought only to recover an penalty is in the nature of a criminal proceeding and it would be contrary to policy to compel the defendant before trial to make admissions

---

[277] *Thorburn v Herman, The Times,* May 14, 1992. Also the approach set out CPR, r.31.9 in relation to documents may be followed by analogy to the extent appropriate.

[278] See generally, Ch.11, paras 11.104–11.120.

[279] With interrogatories the practice was that the objection must be taken in the answer and that interrogatories would not be set aside or disallowed beforehand: *Fisher v Owen* (1878) 8 Ch.D. 645, CA; *Allhusen v Labouchere* (1878) 3 Q.B.D. 654, CA; *Harvey v Lovekin* (1884) 10 PD 122, CA; *Spokes v The Grosvenor and West End Railway Terminus Hotel Company* [1897] 2 Q.B. 124 (disclosure of documents) as applied in *Corporacion Nacional del Cobre de Chile v Metallgesellchaft, The Times,* January 6, 1999; *National Association of Operative Plasterers v Smithies* [1906] A.C. 434 at 437; *cf. R. v D.T.T., exp. Briggs* (1987) 71 A.L.R. 86.

[280] *Allhusen v Labouchere* (1878) 3 Q.B.D. 654.

[281] *McLoughlin v Dwyer* (1875) Ir. R. 9 C.L. 170; *cf. Greenfield v Reay* (1875) L.R. 10 Q.B. 217 (interrogatories).

[282] *Webb v East* (1880) 5 Ex. Ch. 108 at 114 (interrogatories). In the context of interrogatories, it was held in *Lamb v Munster* (1882) 10 Q.B.D. 110 that it was a sufficient answer to state.

[283] CPR, Sch.1, RSC, Ord.52, Practice Direction—Committal Applications, para.7.

[284] See Ch.11, para.11.109, above, and also Ch.9, paras 9.06–9.07, above.

which would incriminate himself.[285] Given this rationale, a court is likely to refuse a Pt 18 application in similar circumstances. It has been held by analogy that a petitioning creditor in a bankruptcy petition was not entitled to an order for interrogatories to prove the allegations in the petition.[286] It is unlikely that the court will regard this as binding for the purpose of the current rules.

(4) "Without Prejudice" and Witness Statement Privilege[287]

There is no reason to suppose that the operation of these privileges (which are very similar) is any different in dealing with Requests and Pt 18 applications than in dealing with disclosure of documents.   **16.87**

(5) Diplomatic Privilege[288]

The provisions of the Vienna Convention 1961 previously considered concerned documents, and therefore do not directly apply to Requests and Pt 18 applications. A diplomatic agent does, however, enjoy immunity from the "civil and administrative jurisdiction" of the receiving State, except in limited circumstances[289] and he is "not obliged to give evidence as a witness".[290] Neither provision is apt to cover requests for further information; the second in particular because only a party to proceedings need respond to a Request or Pt 18 order, and, although the responses may be admissible at trial, the process constitutes giving disclosure of facts to the other party, not giving evidence to the court. The better view must be that where a diplomatic agent is party to legal proceedings, the court properly having jurisdiction (whether by submission or otherwise) to deal with the matter, he has no privilege by reason only of his status to object to answering a Request or complying with a Pt 18 order. It should, however, be noted that, where a State is party to proceedings, no penalty by way of committal or fine may be imposed in respect of its failure or refusal to disclose any information for the purposes of those proceedings.[291]   **16.88**

---

[285] *Martin v Treacher* (1886) 16 Q.B.D. 507; action by common informer for penalty; a claim for statutory compensation not penal in nature does not fall within this principle: see *Adams v. Batley* (1887) 18 Q.B.D. 625; an action under statute for double value of goods fraudulently removed by a tenant is a penal action: *Hobbs & Co. v Hudson* (1890) 25 Q.B.D. 232; action under Patents, Designs and Trade Marks Act 1883 for forfeiture of a sum held to be penal: in *Saunders v Wiel* [1892] 2 Q.B. 321, CA; see also *Colne Valley Water Co. v Watford* [1948] 1 K.B. 500, CA.
[286] *Re A Debtor* [1910] 2 K.B. 59, CA.
[287] See generally, Ch.11, paras 11.121–11.136, above.
[288] See generally, Ch.11 paras 11.139–11.142, above.
[289] Vienna Convention 1961, Art.31(1).
[290] Art.31(2).
[291] State Immunity Act 1978, s.13(1).

16.89   Consular agents are in a weaker position still. Their immunity from the "jurisdiction of the judicial or administrative authorities of the receiving State" only applies "in respect of acts performed in the exercise of consular functions"[292] (and even then is subject to exceptions[293]). Moreover, "members of a consular post may be called upon to attend as witnesses in the course of judicial or administrative proceedings", although they "are under no obligation to give evidence concerning matters connected with the exercise of their functions . . . ".[294] Accordingly, it seems that there is no question of their having a privilege to refuse to answer in proceedings to which they are a party, save in relation to consular acts.

(6) Statutory Prohibition[295]

16.90   Under certain statutes a person is prohibited from providing information to a third party either not at all, or only in specific circumstances. Where a statutory prohibition applies, then a party cannot be compelled to provide the answer by way of a response to a Request or pursuant to a Pt 18 application. CPR, r.18.1(2) specifically provides that the power of the court to make an order is subject to any rule of law to the contrary. An example of such a provision is the Banking Act 1987, s.82.[296]

M. RESPONSE

16.91   The formal requirements for a response to a Request are considered above.[297] The Practice Direction does not specifically deal with the form of a response to an order under Pt 18, but essentially it should be more or less in the same format as a response to a Request without court order. Each question must be dealt with and answered specifically and substantially.[298] The answer must be direct and not be evasive.[299] Aside from directly answering the question posed, there is no objection in principle to the party responding where appropriate to provide a reasonable explanation or qualification to his answer. Thus if an answer is such as would be unfair or unjust without qualification, the party may add any reasonable explanation

---

[292] Vienna Convention 1963, Art.43(1).

[293] Art.43(2).

[294] Art.44(1), 44(3).

[295] See generally, Ch.8, para.8.09, and Ch.11, para.11.143, above.

[296] *Bank of Credit and Commercial International (Overseas) Ltd v Price Waterhouse (No.12)* [1998] Ch. 84; *cf. Rowell v Pratt* [1938] A.C. 101 in the context of disclosure of documents.

[297] See paras 16.015–16.016, above; CPR, Pt 18, Practice Direction, paras 2 and 4.

[298] *Easey v Webber* (1870) 18 W.R. 1064; *Gray v Bateman* (1872) 21 W.R. 137 (interrogatories).

[299] *Turner v Jack* (1871) 23 L.T. 800 (interrogatories).

or qualification, but should not add in irrelevant material so as to obscure the actual answer to the question posed.[300] Where a prolix or scandalous answer is given this may be liable to challenge as being an insufficient answer. The answer should be divided into consecutively numbered paragraphs with each question being dealt with in a separate paragraph.[301]

Timing

The timing of a response to an order under CPR, Pt 18 is governed by the period of time provided in the order itself. CPR, r.18.1(3) provides that, where the court makes an order, the party against whom it is made must file a response and serve it on the other parties within the time specified by the court. The length of time specified by the court will depend on the circumstances, but ordinarily 14 days should be sufficient, particularly as, before an application is made, the party seeking a response usually has to go through the procedure of a preliminary Request. The court will take into account the circumstances in fixing the time for an answer in the order. Thus if detailed inquiries are necessary which may take some time, the court will no doubt be sympathetic to submissions on behalf of the other party for longer than 14 days to respond. If the party is unable to respond within the time stipulated by the court, he should notify the other party before the time period has expired and explain the reasons why more time is needed. Parties are expected to be sensible, and if there are good reasons for needing more time, the opposing party should give an extension of time. Where the order provides for a sanction for failure to comply, then it is incumbent upon the party to apply to the court to seek relief from the sanction.[302] Where the order requires a party to respond within a specified time, and specifies the consequence of failure to comply, the time for doing the act in question may not be extended by agreement between the parties[303]; in such circumstances an application must be made to the court if more time is needed.[304] **16.92**

Objections

Where a Request is objected to on the grounds of privilege this objection should be taken in the response.[305] In appropriate cases the objection as to **16.93**

---

[300] *Lyell v Kennedy* [1884] 33 W.R. 44; *Lyell v Kennedy* (1884) 27 Ch.D. 1, CA (interrogatories).
[301] *cf.* CPR, Pt 18, Practice Direction, para.2.3; *Dalgleish v Lowther* [1899] 2 Q.B. 590 at 594, CA (interrogatories).
[302] CPR, r.3.8(1).
[303] CPR, r.3.8(3).
[304] In cases not covered by r.3.8(3), the parties are able to agree an extension of time under CPR, r.2.11.
[305] See paras 16.018–16.019, above.

privilege may be taken in the response to a Pt 18 order, unless privilege has already been dealt with and the plea overruled on the hearing of the application.[306] The grounds of objection must be clearly stated with a sufficient statement of the grounds on which the objection is based.[307]

Response to best of knowledge, information and belief

16.94 The rules do not specifically provide that the party responding to a Request or Pt 18 order, must answer to the best of his knowledge, information and belief. This was the practice in relation to interrogatories.[308] However the requirement that responses must be verified by a Pt 22 statement of truth means that the party putting forward the response must believe the facts stated in the document to be true.[309] In answering, a party is not bound to speculate.[310] Thus where he is asked as to the contents of a lost document, it is a sufficient reply to state that the party has no recollection as to the contents.[311]

Enquiries

16.95 It is incumbent upon a party responding to a Request to a Pt 18 order to exercise reasonable diligence in formulating a response.[312] Where matters enquired of are such as relate to matters carried out by or known to the employees or agents of the party in the ordinary course of employment, the party should make reasonable enquiries of them[313] and respond in the light of such enquiries.[314] An agent for this purpose may include bankers as well

---

[306] See para.16.077, above.

[307] This has been the practice in relation to interrogatories: *Church v Perry* (1877) 36 L.T. 513; *Smith v Berg* (1877) 36 L.T. 471; see in particular Grove J., dissenting.

[308] *Lyell v Kennedy (No.2)* (1883) 9 App.Cas. 81 at 85, HL; *Foakes v Webb* (1884) 28 Ch.D. 287 and 289; *Wealsbach Incandescent Gas Lighting v New Sunlight* [1900] 2 Ch. 1, CA; *Douglas v Morning Post* (1923) 39 T.L.R. 404, CA.

[309] The practice in relation to interrogatories was that if a party merely deposed to his belief, or to his knowledge, a further answer or supplementary affidavit might have been required: see *Douglas v Morning Post* (1923) 39 T.L.R. 402, CA; *Bank of Russian Trade v British Screen Productions* [1930] 2 K.B. 90, CA.

[310] In the context of interrogatories see *Lyell v Kennedy (No.2)* (1883) 9 App.Cas. 81 at 91; *Gilchrist v Wallace* [1972] V.R. 481; *cf. Sharpe v Smail* (1975) 5 A.L.R. 377.

[311] *Dalrymple v Leslie* (1881) 8 Q.B.D. 5 (interrogatories).

[312] *Bird v Hadkinson* [1999] B.P.I.R. 653, *The Times*, April 7, 1999: person responding to a disclosure order contained in a *Mareva* injunction must take reasonable steps to investigate the truth or otherwise of the answer.

[313] *cf.* Ch.5, para.5.43, above.

[314] This is the practice which has grown up in the context of interrogatories: *Anderson v Bank of Columbia* (1876) 2 Ch.D.644 at 657, 659, 661–662, CA; *Bolckow v Fisher* (1882) 10 Q.B.D. 161; *Alliott v Smith* [1895] 2 Ch.111; *Welsbach Incandescent Gas Lighting v New Sunlight* [1900] 2 Ch. 1, CA.

as solicitors[315]; but a solicitor is not bound to provide information covered by legal privilege.[316]

The responding party cannot avoid answering a Request by saying he has **16.96** no personal knowledge, when he has the means of ascertaining the answer to the Request from his servants or agents.[317]

The practice in relation to interrogatories was that a party was regarded **16.97** as being under a duty to undertake reasonable enquiries of persons who were his servants or agents at the relevant time, although they were no longer employed by him.[318] In respect of Requests and Pt 18 orders the court is likely to regard a party being under a duty to undertake reasonable enquiries, but what constitutes reasonable enquiries will depend on the circumstances. Thus, where the servant or agent has long ceased to be in the party's employ, and especially where his whereabouts are unknown, enquiries may be unnecessary,[319] and in the context of interrogatories an executor has been held not bound to inquire of solicitors and bankers to a testator as to matters occurring 20 years before death.[320] In short a party is not bound to make enquiries to the extent that such enquiries place an unfair or oppressive burden on him.[321]

Although it has been held in the context of interrogatories that a party is **16.98** not bound to obtain and disclose information acquired by his servants or agents otherwise than in the course of their employment, it is doubtful that this principle would be applied in the context of Pt 18, at least to the extent that once a party has obtained such information he should not hold it back.[322] It has been held that a party interrogated is not bound to state in his answer that he has made enquiries of persons in his employment when there is nothing to indicate that the acts referred to were done in the presence, or within the knowledge of, persons employed by him.[323] There is no such obligation in the context of Pt 18.

Where a party has no knowledge and has been unable to obtain the **16.99** information requested, despite enquiries of his servants or agents, it may be prudent to indicate in the response in general terms that reasonable enquiries have been made. In the case of a company it may be in the form of stating that diligent enquiries have been made of all officers, servants and agents of the company who might reasonably be expected to have some knowledge

---

[315] *Alliott v Smith* [1895] 2 Ch. 111; *Foakes v Webb* (1884) 28 Ch.D. 287 (interrogatories).

[316] *Kennedy v Lyell* (1883) 23 Ch.D. 387, CA; (1883) 9 App.Cas. 81, HL (interrogatories).

[317] *Southwark Water Co. v Quick* (1878) 3 Q.B.D. 315 at 321, CA (interrogatories).

[318] *Stanfield Properties v National Westminster Bank* [1983] 1 W.L.R. 568 at 570; cf. *Bolckow Vaughan & Co. v Fisher* (1882) 10 Q.B.D. 161 at 169. See Ch.5, para.5.43, above.

[319] *Stanfield Properties v National Westminster Bank* [1983] 1 W.L.R. 568 at 570; *Bolchow Vaughan & Co. v Fisher* (1882) 10 Q.B.D. 161 at 169–170.

[320] *Alliott v Smith* [1895] 2 Ch. 111.

[321] *Alliott v Smith* [1895] 2 Ch. 111 at 115; see also *Derham v Anev* (1978) 20 A.C.T.R. 23; *Sharpe v Smail* (1975) 49 A.L.J.R. 130; *Sroka v Gorbal* (1980) 25 S.A.S.R. 356.

[322] *Bolchow Vaughan & Co. v Fisher* (1882) 10 Q.B.D. 161 at 169; *Wealsbach Incandescent Gas Lighting Co. v New Sunlight* [1900] 2 Ch.1, CA.

[323] *Rasbotham v Shropshire Union Railways* (1883) 24 Ch.D. 111.

relevant to the questions, but in most cases such a response will probably not be necessary.[324] In the context of interrogatories it has been held that a publisher need not make enquiries from the author of work where the author is not the servant or agent of the publisher.[325]

Examining documents

16.100   If it is necessary for the purposes of responding to a Request, the party must examine the documents in his control[326] (formerly possession, custody or power) or that of his servants or agents held in that capacity. If a such search would be unduly burdensome, then that may be a ground for objecting to the Request. In the context of interrogatories, it has been held that in this context "power" means an enforceable right to the document and the party interrogated should take all reasonable steps to obtain such documents.[327] It has been held that it is not an excuse for providing the information requested merely on the ground that the information is contained in documents accessible to the other party. However, where the interrogatory can be answered only by reference to documents available to the other party and it would be burdensome to extract the information, then the party has been held entitled to object to the interrogatory.[328]

Companies and corporations

16.101   Where a party is a company or corporation, the practice in relation to interrogatories was that the person required to answer the interrogatories was generally named in the Request. There is a great deal of learning in relation to what inquiries an individual member or officer answering an interrogatory was expected to carry out. Requests under CPR, Pt 18 are addressed to a party and not to individual members or officers of corporate parties, although there is nothing objectionable for a Request in seeking information which in the ordinary course of events would be known by only one particular individual within that company. It will then be necessary upon the party to make inquiries of that individual in formulating the response. Set out in the following paragraphs is the practice which has grown up in the context of interrogatories.

---

[324] *Stanfield Properties v National Westminster Bank* [1983] 1 W.L.R. 568 at 571; see also *Bank of Russian Trade v British Green Productions* [1930] 2 K.B. 90 at 96, CA (interrogatories).
[325] *Crozier v Wishart Books* [1936] 1 K.B. 471, CA.
[326] On this, see Ch.5, paras 5.39–5.54.
[327] *Taylor v Rundell* (1843) 1 Ph.222; *Emmott & Co. v Walters* [1891] W.N. 79; Bray, at pp.135–138.
[328] *Lockett v Lockett* (1869) L.R. 4 Ch.App. 366.

It was incumbent upon the member or officer answering the interrogatory **16.102** to give such information as the corporation or company, if an individual, would have been bound to give.[329] The person answering the interrogatories was bound to answer to his own individual knowledge, and to obtain the information sought from other servants or agents of the company who personally conducted the transaction or acquired the knowledge in their capacity as servants or agents.[330] An answer confined to his own knowledge was insufficient where there were other officials and servants of the company who may have the knowledge.[331]

The inquiries to be made need not have extended to the knowledge of the **16.103** directors or other officers, servants or agents about matters which did not come to their knowledge in such capacity.[332] The inquiries were expected to extend not only to persons currently the servants or agents of the company, but also to former officers, servants or agents where it was reasonable to do so; the lack of any power to compel and answer was no reason why the question should not have been asked. But if the departure or retirement was a long while ago, it might well have been unreasonable to expect inquiries to be made, especially if the company was unaware where the officer or servant now was.[333] The person answering the interrogatories was bound to make all reasonable inquiries which were likely to reveal, or might reveal, what was known to the company. In order to show that this had been done, it was desirable that the answers included a statement indicating that the person swearing the answers had applied his mind to his duty and had attempted to discharge it. There was no duty to go further and set out the details of the inquiries made, giving the names and addresses of persons questioned, specifying what questions were asked, and so on. If the answers did not at least state in general terms that the persons swearing to them had made diligent inquiries from all officers, servants and agents/company who might reasonably be expected to have some knowledge relevant to the interrogatories, the party administrating the interrogatories might have justifiably questioned whether the company had discharged its obligations in answering the questions.[334]

Often the interrogatory requested an answer by "the secretary or other **16.104** proper officer of the company". In such case the party interrogated had to exercise care in selecting the person who was the most appropriate person

[329] *Berkeley v Standard Discount Co.* (1879) 13 Ch.D. 97 at 101, CA; *Welsbach Incandescent Gas Lighting Co. v New Sunlight* [1900] 2 Ch. 1 at 13, CA; *Stanfield Properties v National Westminster Bank* [1983] 1 W.L.R. 568 at 571.
[330] *Southwark Water Co. v Quick* (1878) 3 Q.B.D. 315 at 321.
[331] *Bank of Russian Trade v British Screen Production* [1930] 2 K.B. 90.
[332] *Welsbach Incandescent Gas Light Co. v New Sunlight* [1900] 2 Ch. 1, CA; *Bolckow Vaughan & Co. v Fisher* (1882) 10 Q.B.D. 161 at 169, CA.
[333] *Bolckow, Vaughan & Co. v Fisher* (1882) 10 Q.B.D. 161 at 169; *Little v Bennet* (1900) 25 V.L.R. 645 at 647; *Stanfield Properties v National Westminster Bank* [1983] 1 W.L.R. 568 at 570; *The Corporation of the Trustees of the Roman Catholic Archdiocese of Brisbane v Discovery Bay Developments Pty Ltd* [1995] 2 Qd.R. 121 at 126–127.
[334] *Stanfield Properties v National Westminster Bank* [1983] 1 W.L.R. 568 at 571.

to answer the interrogatory. If the officer selected by the interrogated party was also the solicitor for that party, then there was a risk that the officer might be compelled to answer with information which would otherwise be covered by legal professional privilege.[335] The answer of the member or officer was binding on the company and could be used against the company at trial, although it may well have been that the company was permitted to show that the answer was mistaken.[336] The usual course was for the solicitor of the company to prepare the answer of the officer or member, and for the officer or member to be indemnified as to his costs by the company; it was generally regarded as inappropriate for the officer or member to instruct a separate solicitor for this purpose.[337]

Correction of answer

16.105   After a party has filed his response in answer to a Request or Pt 18 order, he may amend or correct the response with the leave of the court, and at the court's discretion. In general, the appropriate course is to file a corrective affidavit or witness statement which should include an explanation for the correction. In relation to interrogatories, corrective affidavits were permitted with the consent of the parties concerned.[338] Where a party or his solicitor realises that the response provided is untrue or misleading, the appropriate course is, to bring that fact to the attention of the opposing party, and, if the client's consent to doing so is refused, the solicitor must cease to act for the client.[339]

N. INADEQUATE RESPONSE

Preliminary request

16.106   The remedy for a party faced with no or an inadequate response to an preliminary Request is to make a CPR, Pt 18 application. Where some form of response has been provided and all that is needed is clarification of that response, it may be simpler and more cost efficient to ask a party to clarify the response either informally or by way of a further Request.

---

[335] *Swansea Court v Quirke* (1879) 5 C.P.D. 106, *quaere* whether this was correct; the position was different where the interrogatory is addressed to be answered by a specific officer who was also the solicitor; *Salford Corp. v Lever* (1890) 24 Q.B.D. 695.

[336] *Chaddock v British South Africa Co.* [1896] 2 Q.B. 153 at 158, CA; *Welsbach Incandescent Gas Lighting v New Sunlight* [1900] 2 Ch. 1, CA; *cf.* Bray, at pp.83–84.

[337] *Berkeley v Standard Discount* (1879) 13 Ch.D 97 at 99, CA.

[338] *Compagnie Financière du Pacifique v The Peruvian Guano Co.* (1882) 28 S.J. 410; see also Bray, at p.150.

[339] *Myers v Elman* [1940] A.C. 282 at 293–4; *cf. R. v Liverpool City Council, ex. p. Horn* [1997] P.N.L.R. 95.

O. ORDERED RESPONSE

Request for clarification or court application for further response

Where further clarification of a response to a court order for information **16.107** is necessary or appropriate, the party need not apply to the court straight away for a further order. In some circumstances it may be more appropriate to ask the opposing party first to clarify his response and only if no such clarification is forthcoming an application to the court may be made. There are of course degrees of inadequacy in a response, and a party should consider which is the most convenient and cost effective way of obtaining the information he needs. Where there is some form of response, the court will assess whether there has been a bona fide attempt to provide an answer and the sufficiency of the response. It will not usually look into the truth of a response at an interlocutory stage, unless where the response is so clearly in bad faith or demonstrably untruthful. Generally, the court at the interlocutory stage will be prepared to assume that the party has made an honest and true answer to the questions which are put to him.[340] However where tracing claims are concerned, it is not necessarily an answer to an application for an order requiring a further response that the issue sought to be raised at the interlocutory stage would also overlap with the issues that would have to be determined at trial. In such claims the court may be more willing to look into the truth of a response and order a further response, if it will assist a party to trace assets.[341]

Strike out

Where there has been no response to a court order under CPR, Pt 18 any **16.108** sanction stipulated in the order will take effect unless and until the party who has failed to comply has sought and obtained relief by way of a separate application.[342] Where the order itself does not provide for any sanction and no response has been provided in breach of the order, then the opposing party may apply to the court for the statement of case to be struck out or for an order that unless the original order is complied with the statement of case be struck out.

Where there is some form of response, it is more difficult to say that a **16.109** sanction stipulated in the order should automatically apply as there may be

---

[340] This was the practice in relation to interrogatories: *Kennedy v Lyell* (1883) 23 Ch.D. 387 at 399, CA; *Lyell v Kennedy* (1884) 27 Ch.D. 1 at 19, 21, CA; see also *Field v Bennett* (1885) 2 T.L.R. 122.
[341] *Derby & Co. Ltd v Weldon*, November 2, 1988, unreported, Browne-Wilkinson V.C.; *Dubai Bank v Galadari*, February 26, 1992, unreported, Morritt J.
[342] CPR, rr.3.8, 3.9.

some debate as to whether the response complies with the order or is a bona fide attempt to comply with the order. Where the response is so insufficient as to show a want of bona fides then the court may strike out a statement of case for failure to provide an adequate response.[343] At the hearing of an application to enforce the original order, it is open to the court to give the party one final chance to provide a response by making an unless or conditional order, spelling out the consequences of the failure to comply.[344]

16.110 The court has power to strike out a statement of case if it appears that the statement of case discloses no reasonable grounds for bringing or defending the claim or that it is an abuse of the court's process or is otherwise likely to obstruct the just disposal of the proceedings.[345] If the judge decides that the statement of case falls within either of these categories, it is open to him to make an order under r.18.1 requiring the defendant within a stated time to clarify his defence or give additional information about it. The order may provide that the defence will be struck out if the defendant does not comply.[346]

16.111 A party seeking relief from a sanction provided by court order may apply to that court and the court will consider all the circumstances including[347]:

(a) the interest of the administration of justice;

(b) whether the application for relief has been made promptly;

(c) whether the failure to comply was intentional;

(d) whether there is a good explanation for the failure;

(e) the extent to which the party in default has complied with other rules, practice directions and court orders and any relevant pre-action protocol;

(f) whether the failure to comply was caused by the party or his legal representative;

(g) whether the trial date or likely date can still be met if relief is granted;

(h) the effect which the failure to comply had on each party; and

(i) the effect which the granting of relief would have on each party.

Any application for relief must be supported by evidence.[348]

---

[343] *Kennedy v Lyell (No.5)* [1882] W.N. 137, CA (interrogatories).

[344] The court has an express power to strike out a statement of case for a failure to comply with a rule, practice direction or court order: CPR, r.3.4.

[345] CPR, r.3.4(2)(a), (b).

[346] Practice Direction—Striking out a statement of claim (supplementing CPR, r.3.4), para.3.4.

[347] CPR, r.3.9(1); see also Ch.13, paras 13.24–13.26.

[348] CPR, r.3.9(2).

Costs

A party who has failed to adequately respond to an order under Pt 18 will   **16.112**
be liable to a costs sanction when the matter comes back before the
court.[349]

Committal

The rules in relation to interrogatories specifically provided that, where a   **16.113**
party failed to answer ordered interrogatories or to comply with an order
requiring a further answer, he was liable to committal.[350] In practice contempt applications in relation to failure to provide interrogatories were rare.
There is no such express provision in CPR, Pt 18, but it is open to the court
to find a party in contempt who has deliberately failed to provide a proper
response or has deliberately provided an untruthful response.[351] Ordinarily
the sanction will be to strike out a statement of case,[352] or in costs.[353]
However, in certain cases a contempt application may be the appropriate
route, such as where a party has failed to provide information in response
to an order in aid of *Mareva* (freezing), *Anton Piller* (search) or tracing
relief.[354] An order under Pt 18 may not be made against a respondent to a
committal application.[355]

Cross-examination

Cross-examination at trial on a party's response will generally be appro-   **16.114**
priate. But it will rarely be appropriate for a party to be cross-examined on
a response to an order for further information at an interlocutory stage. The
exceptional case where it may be appropriate is where an inadequate
response has been filed in the context of an order in aid of *Mareva* (freezing), *Anton Piller* (search) or tracing relief.[356]

---

[349] CPR, Pt 18 Practice Direction, para.5.8; CPR, rr.44.3(4)(2), (5), 44.14(1)(b).
[350] RSC, Ord.26, r.6(2).
[351] CPR, Sch.1, RSC, Ord.45, r.5(1)(a).
[352] CPR, r.3.4(2)(c).
[353] See para.16.112, above.
[354] *Bird v Hadkinson* [1999] B.P.I.R. 653, *The Times*, April 7, 1999: inaccurate answer in
response to disclosure order contained in *Mareva* injunction.
[355] CPR, Sch.1, RSC, Ord.52, Practice Direction Committal Applications para.7.
[356] *Yukong Line of Korea v Rendsberg Investment Corp. of Liberia, The Times*, October 22,
1996, CA (cross-examination on affidavit of assets of defendant subject to *Mareva*
injunction).

P. USE OF RESPONSE AT TRIAL

16.115   A response, whether provided voluntarily or pursuant to a court order, may be used at trial by the opposing party. Indeed, unless otherwise ordered, the trial bundle should include copies of all information requests and responses.[357] All responses to CPR, Pt 18 orders must be verified by a statement of truth.[358] Where this has occurred, it will be difficult for a party to resile from his response.

16.116   The learning in relation to interrogatories may be relevant in relation to information provided in response to a Request for court order. The practice in relation to interrogatories was that a party was allowed to put in evidence at the trial of an action only some of the answers to interrogatories or only part of such an answer, without having to put in evidence the other answers or the whole of that answer. However, the court was able to look at the whole of the answer or answers, and, if it was of the opinion that any other answer or other part of the answer was so connected with an answer or part thereof used in evidence that one ought not to be so used without the order, the court was able to direct that the other answer or part of the answer should be put in evidence.[359] It was open to the party interrogated to adduce evidence at trial to show that the answer given was incorrect, although the court would look at the entirety of the evidence including the interrogatories in forming its own assessment of the matters in issue.[360] It was open to the party tending the interrogatories evidence to adduce evidence contrary to the interrogatories; he was not bound to accept their accuracy or truthfulness.[361]

Q. COLLATERAL USE OF RESPONSE

16.117   In relation to interrogatories it has been held that the implied undertaking extends to information provided in response to interrogatories. [362] But in view of the express provisions in CPR, r.18.2, it does not appear that there is any implied undertaking not to use a response or information contained in a response for any collateral purpose.

---

[357] CPR, Pt 39, Practice Direction, para.3.2(3).

[358] CPR, r.22.1(1)(b).

[359] RSC, Ord.26, r.7; *Lyell v Kennedy (No.3)* (1882) 27 Ch.D. 1 at 15, 29, CA; *cf. Pleat v Perrins* (1868) L.R. 3 Q.B. 658 (interrogatories filed in separate action).

[360] *Gannon v Gannon* (1971) 125 C.L.R. 629; *Kabadains v Panagiotou* (1970) 47 F.L.R. 221, *Stateline Pty v Legal & General Assurance Society* (1982) 29 S.A.S.R. 16 at 46.

[361] *Endeavour Wines v Martin* (1948) 92 S.J. 574.

[362] *Ainsworth v Hanrahan* (1991) 25 N.S.W.L.R. 155, CA of N.S.W.; see also *Springfield Nominees Pty Ltd v Bridgelands Securities Ltd* (1992) 110 A.L.R. 685, Fed.Ct.Aus., and *Sofilas v Cable Sands (WA) Pty Ltd* (1993) 9 W.A.R. 196 at 201, W.A.Sup.Ct.. The same probably applies in Ontario: see *Goodman v Rossi* (1995) 25 D.L.R. (4th) 613, 629–630.

Under CPR, r.18.2, the court may direct that information provided by a **16.118** party to another party (whether given voluntarily or following an order under r.18.1) must not be used for any purpose except for that of the proceedings in which it is given. Whether or not it will be appropriate for the court to give a direction restricting use will of course depend on the circumstances, including the nature of the further information ordered. If the information ordered is merely seeking particulars of a pleading, then normally no restriction will be imposed.

CHAPTER 17

Other disclosure of facts

CHAPTER 17

Other disclosure of facts

A. DEPOSITIONS

A deposition is a written record of the oral evidence, given on oath, of a **17.01** witness before the trial. This more or less compulsory procedure has been discussed above, in the context of obtaining documentary disclosure pursuant to letters of request.[1] It may also be employed in appropriate circumstances to obtain factual disclosure from witnesses and indeed from parties. It is well known that the American discovery process makes extensive use of the pre-trial deposition, whereby the oral evidence and documents of a witness are obtained in advance of the trial at which that witness will give evidence.[2] In Canada witnesses may be examined before the hearing of a pending motion or application[3] and the court may grant leave to examine for discovery any person who there is reason to believe has information relevant to an issue in an action.[4] In England the position is very different. Under the former rules there was a limited power to require a person giving inadequate answers to interrogatories to attend for oral examination,[5] but it was rarely used. The court does have power to order depositions to be made of oral evidence before trial or some other hearing,[6] but the purpose

---

[1] See Ch.2, para.2.57–2.63 (letters of request to foreign courts) and Ch.10, paras 10.54–10.64 (letters of request to English courts).

[2] See, e.g. Drombroff, *Discovery* (1986), Chs 8–11; Simpson, *Civil Discovery and Depositions*, 2nd edn, 1994, Ch.4. As to video-taping depositions in the USA, see Neubauer (1993) 19 *Litigation*, Pt 4, 10.

[3] Rules of Civil Procedure, r.39.04 (Ontario); *Ontario Federation of Anglers & Hunters v Ontario* (2001) 196 D.L.R. (4th) 367, Ontario Div.Ct. In Quebec there is an implied rule of confidentiality at an examination on discovery: *Lac d'Amiante du Québec Ltée v 2858—0702 Québec Inc* [2001] 2 S.C.R. 743, (2000) 204 D.L.R. (4th) 331, Sup.Ct. Canada.

[4] Rules of Civil Procedure, r.31.10, R.R.O. 1990, reg.194; *Lana International Ltd v Menasco Aerospace* (2000) 195 D.L.R. (4th) 497, Ontario Div.Ct.

[5] RSC, Ord.26, r.5; CCR, Ord.14, r.11(1).

[6] CPR, r.34.8, formerly RSC, Ord.38, r.1; CCR, Ord.20, r.13(1).

of this rule is to enable evidence to be given at trial or some other substantive hearing which would not otherwise be available, rather than to give advance notice of evidence to other parties. This position has occasionally been criticised[7]; but any pressure to change the English system in this respect has been removed by the introduction of the process of exchange of witness statements.[8] Although not intended as a means of disclosure, depositions do nonetheless have that effect, and it is appropriate to deal briefly with them here.

The making of the order

17.02   There is no express restriction on the power to order a deposition to be taken in CPR, r.34.8. The court will exercise its discretion to make an order for evidence by deposition taking into account the overriding objective.[9] Thus the court may refuse an order if it considers that it is not necessary or would be disproportionate to require a witness to attend. The usual grounds for the exercise of the discretion in favour of an order are that the witness is too old or too ill to attend the trial or might die or intends to leave the country before the trial. Exceptionally an order for examination may be made where the witness has refused to make an affidavit[10] or a witness statement. In considering whether to make an order, the court will also take into account whether there is a more appropriate alternative. Where the witness cannot attend the court through age or illness, it may also possible for the trial of the action to be adjourned to the place where the witness is. In some cases evidence by video link, which can be before the trial judge, may be preferable.[11] Where a witness has refused to make an affidavit or witness statement, but would be available to attend the trial, usually it would be more appropriate to leave it to the party to proceed by way of a witness summons for the person to attend the trial, rather than by way of a pre-trial examination.

17.03   The order for evidence by deposition is an order that the deponent be examined on oath before:

(a) a judge;
(b) an examiner of the court; or
(c) such other person as the court appoints.[12]

---

[7] See, e.g. Levine, *Discovery* (1982), Ch.6.
[8] See paras 17.20 to 17.30, below.
[9] CPR, r.34.8(1); CPR rr.1.1, 1.2; *Warner v Moses* (1880) 16 Ch.D. 100, CA.
[10] *Warner v Moses* (1880) 16 Ch.D. 100, CA; *Re Springall* [1875] W.N.225.
[11] CPR, r.32.3; *The Admiralty and Commercial Courts Guide* (7th edn, 2006), para.H3 and Appendix 15 (Video conferencing Protocol); *Polanski v Condé Nast Publications Ltd* [2005] UKHL 10, [2005] 1 W.L.R. 637 (claimant giving evidence from abroad by video-link where fear of arrest if came to UK).
[12] CPR, r.34.8(3); *BCCI v Rahim*, November 11, 2005, Ch.D (Unreported) (witness who was ill and feared arrest, permitted to give evidence by video-link).

Usually the examination is before an examiner of the court appointed as such by the Lord Chancellor.[13] Where there is no suitable examiner in the locality where the examination is to take place, a suitable person will be appointed on an ad hoc basis. The party who obtains an order for the examination of a deponent before an examiner of the court must: (i) apply to the Foreign Process Section of the Masters' Secretary's Department at the Royal Courts of Justice for the allocation of an examiner; (ii) when allocated, provide the examiner with copies of all documents in the proceedings necessary to inform the examiner of the issues; and (iii) pay the deponent a sum to cover his travelling expenses to and from the examination and compensation for his loss of time.[14] It is only in rare cases that an examination will be ordered before a judge and generally such an order will only be made with the consent of a High Court or county court judge. The exceptional circumstances where the examination will be before a judge are such as where the greater authority of the judge is required as the witness is known to be difficult to control[15] or where it is important that the trial judge actually sees the witness giving evidence such as in a case where the witness is one of the main witnesses in the case and the truthfulness of his evidence is in question. Where the court makes an order for a deposition to be taken, it may also order the party who obtains the order to serve a witness statement or witness summary in relation to the evidence to be given by the person to be examined.[16] The court may also require the production of any document which it considers necessary for the purposes of the application.[17]

Arranging the hearing

The order for a person to be examined by deposition should state the date, time and place of the examination.[18] As regards the timing of the examination, it is usually prudent to check with the witness and the person before whom the evidence is to be taken as to a convenient time. If it subsequently transpires that the time is inconvenient, the parties or the witness may of course apply to the examiner or other person before whom the evidence is to be taken to alter the time. As regards the place of the examination, anywhere convenient may be used and can even be the residence of a witness who is too ill to attend elsewhere.[19] It is the duty of the

17.04

---

[13] *cf.* CPR, r.34.15.

[14] CPR, Pt 34, Practice Direction—Depositions and Court Attendance by Witnesses, para.4.2; CPR, r.34.8(6).

[15] *Re Brickman's Settlement, Brickman v Goddard Trustees (Jersey) Ltd* (Note) [1982] 1 All E.R.336; *Practice Direction (Chancery: Deposition)* [1981] 1 W.L.R. 1560.

[16] CPR, r.34.8(7).

[17] CPR, r.34.8(4), which does not expressly limit against whom the production order may be made, whether it be a party or the witness.

[18] CPR, r.34.8(5).

[19] *Re Bradbrook* (1889) 23 Q.B.D. 226, CA.

applicant party to supply the examiner with all necessary documents so that the examiner will be informed as to the issues.[20]

Securing the attendance of witnesses

17.05   Once for the order for an examination has been obtained, it should be served as soon as practicable on the witness. At the time of service of the order the deponent must be offered or paid a sum reasonably sufficient to cover his expenses in travelling to and from the place of examination, and such sum by way of compensation for loss of time as specified in the relevant practice direction.[21] An order of the court under CPR, r.34.8 for examination of a witness before an examiner is not an order on the witness directing him to attend.[22] If the person duly served fails to attend or refuses to be sworn for the purpose of the examination or to answer any lawful question or produce any documents at the examination, a certificate of his failure or refusal, signed by the examiner,[23] must be filed by the party requiring the deposition. On the certificate being filed, the party requiring the deposition may apply to the court for an order requiring that person to attend, or to be sworn or to answer any question or to produce any document, as the case may be. An application for an order enforcing the attendance of a witness may be made without notice and the court may order the person against whom an order is made to pay any costs resulting from his failure or refusal.[24] Once the court has made an order requiring the attendance of a witness, disobedience to such an order would be a contempt of court[25] and an order for committal may be sought.

Conduct of the examination

17.06   The examiner may conduct the examination in private if he considers it appropriate to do so.[26] In such a case the examiner may therefore exclude persons other than the parties, their lawyers and agents, and the witnesses.[27] Although such examinations are commonly conducted by counsel, it is open

---

[20] CPR, Pt 34, Practice Direction—Depositions and Court Attendance by Witnesses, para.4.2(2).
[21] CPR, r.34.8(6).
[22] *Stuart v Balkis* (1884) 50 L.T. 479.
[23] CPR, Pt 34, Practice Direction—Depositions and Court Attendance by Witnesses, para.4.8.
[24] CPR, r.34.10; CPR, Pt 34, Practice Direction—Depositions and Court Attendance by Witnesses, paras 4.9, 4.10.
[25] CPR, Pt 34, Practice Direction—Depositions and Court Attendance by Witnesses, para.4.11.
[26] CPR, r.34.9(3).
[27] *Wright v Wilkin* (1858) 6 W.R. 643.

to a solicitor to do so.[28] Subject to any directions contained in the order for examination, the examination is conducted in the same way as at a trial, with the witness being sworn, examined, cross-examined and re-examined.[29] The examiner has the power to put his own questions to a witness about the meaning of any of his answers or any matter arising in the course of the examination,[30] to allow a hostile witness to be treated as such by the party calling him,[31] to obtain the assistance of an interpreter,[32] and to adjourn the examination from time to time.[33]

The examiner must ensure that the evidence given by the witness is recorded in full.[34] In ensuring that the deponent's evidence is recorded in full, the court or the examiner may permit it to be recorded on audio tape or video tape, but the deposition must always be recorded in writing by him or by a competent shorthand writer or stenographer.[35] In practice, usually a shorthand writer is employed to take the evidence down and the deposition takes the form of a verbatim transcript of the evidence.[36] If the deposition is not recorded word for word, it must contain, as nearly as may be, the statement of the deponent; the examiner may record word for word any particular questions and answers which appear to him to have special importance.[37] Where the evidence given by a deponent is likely to be contentious and his demeanour may be a relevant factor in the assessment of his credibility, it may be appropriate to have the evidence video recorded. If a deponent objects to answering any question or where any objection is taken to the question, the examiner must record in the deposition or a document attached to it the question, the nature of and the grounds for the objection, and any answer given, and give his opinion as to the validity of the objection and record it in the deposition or a document attached to it. The court will decide as to the validity of the objection and of any question of costs arising from it.[38] As already observed, where a deponent refuses to be sworn, or answer any lawful question or produce any document, the examiner will sign a certificate of such failure or refusal and may include in his certificate any comment as to the conduct of the deponent or any person

17.07

---

[28] *Vimbos v Meadowcroft* (1901) 46 S.J. 2: it appears from this case that the examination may also be conducted by a solicitor's clerk, but this is not to be recommended.

[29] CPR, r.34.9(1).

[30] CPR, Pt 34, Practice Direction—Depositions and Court Attendance by Witnesses, para.4.7.

[31] *Ohlsen v Terreo* (1875) L.R. 10 Ch. 127.

[32] *Marquis of Bute v James* (1886) 33 Ch.D. 157.

[33] Not specifically provided in the Rules or the Practice Direction, but no doubt implicit; it was specifically provided for in the former rules: RSC, Ord.39, r.8(3).

[34] CPR, r.34.9(4).

[35] CPR, Pt 34, Practice Direction—Depositions and Court Attendance by Witnesses, para.4.3.

[36] *Lloyds Bank Ltd v Marcan* [1973] 1 W.L.R. 339 at 348–9.

[37] CPR, Pt 34, Practice Direction—Depositions and Court Attendance by Witnesses, para.4.4.

[38] CPR, Pt 34, Practice Direction—Depositions and Court Attendance by Witnesses, para.4.5.

attending the examination. The party who obtained the order for the examination must file the certificate with the court and may apply without notice for an appropriate order. The court will make such order on the application as it thinks fit, including an order for the deponent to pay any costs resulting from his failure or refusal. A deponent who wilfully refuses to obey an order made against him under CPR, r.34.10 may be proceeded against for contempt of court.[39]

17.08 A deposition must be signed by the examiner, have any amendments to it initialled by the examiner and the deponent, and be endorsed by the examiner with a statement of the time occupied by the examination and a record of any refusal by the deponent to sign the deposition and of his reasons for not doing so.[40] Even if the examiner fails to sign the deposition, this does not prevent it from being filed and admitted in evidence.[41] The former rules specifically provided that an examiner might make a special report to the court with regard to the examination,[42] for example, concerning a witness's conduct, but this did not entitle him to give his opinion on the credibility of the witness.[43] Finally, the examiner should send the deposition to the court where the proceedings are taking place for filing on the court file and to the person who obtained the order for the examination of the witness.[44] The party who obtained the order must send each of the other parties a copy of the deposition which he receives from the examiner.[45] It should be noted that if all parties are present, the examiner may conduct the examination of a person not named in the order for examination if all the parties and the person to be examined consent.[46]

Use of deposition

17.09 A deposition ordered under CPR, r.34.8 may be given in evidence at a hearing unless the court orders otherwise.[47] It is not subject to legal professional privilege.[48] A party intending to put in evidence a deposition at a hearing must serve notice of his intention to do so on every other party, at least 21 days before the day fixed for the hearing.[49] The court may require

---

[39] CPR, Pt 34, Practice Direction—Depositions and Court Attendance by Witnesses, paras 4.8–4.11.

[40] CPR, Pt 34, Practice Direction—Depositions and Court Attendance by Witnesses, para.4.12.

[41] *Stephens v Wanklin* (1854) 19 Beav. 585 (filing directed on terms); *Felthouse v Bailey* (1866) 14 W.R. 827 (death of the examiner before signing).

[42] RSC, Ord.39, r.13.

[43] *Re Wipperman* [1955] P. 59.

[44] CPR, r.34.9(5); CPR, Pt 34, Practice Direction—Depositions and Court Attendance by Witnesses, para.4.12(4).

[45] CPR, r.34.9(6).

[46] CPR, r.34.9(2).

[47] CPR, r.34.11(1).

[48] *Visx Inc. v Nidex* [1999] F.S.R. 91, CA.

[49] CPR, r.34.11(2)–(3).

a deponent to attend the hearing and give evidence orally.[50] Where a deposition is given in evidence at trial, it should be treated as if it were a witness statement for the purposes of CPR, r.32.13 relating to the availability of witness statements for inspection.[51] Where the court orders a party to be examined about his or any other assets for the purpose of any hearing except the trial, the deposition may be used only for the purpose and for the proceedings in which the order was made. However, it may be used for some other purpose by the party who was examined, if the party who was examined agrees or if the court gives permission.[52]

B. LETTERS OF REQUEST

Depositions are most frequently encountered in the context of letters of request. The rules differ depending on whether the other state involved is or is not an EU member state. There are various types of situation where letters of request may be deployed, most of which are covered elsewhere in the relevant parts of this work: **17.10**

(1) Letter of request to England and Wales for the obtaining of evidence for foreign proceedings, whether for documents or witness evidence.[53]

(2) Letter of request from England and Wales for the obtaining of evidence abroad, whether for documents or witness evidence.[54] The procedure for examinations abroad is considered in the next section.[55]

(3) Letter of request to England and Wales for the obtaining of evidence for proceedings in an EU member state under Council Regulation (EC) No.1206/2001 on co-operation between the courts of member states in the taking of evidence in civil or commercial matters, whether for documents or witness evidence.[56] The procedure is considered below.[57]

(4) Letter of request from England and Wales for the obtaining of evidence from another EU member state under Council Regulation No.1206/2001, whether for documents or witness evidence.[58] The procedure is considered below.[59]

---

[50] CPR, r.34.11(4).
[51] CPR, r.34.11(5).
[52] CPR, r.34.12.
[53] Ch.10, para.10.54–10.63 above; CPR, r.34.13 (depositions).
[54] Ch.2, paras 2.58–2.61 above; CPR, rr.34.16–21.
[55] Paras 17.11–17.13 below.
[56] Ch.2, para.2.59(2) above; CPR, r.34.23.
[57] Para.17.19 below.
[58] Ch.10, para.10.64 above, CPR, r.34.24.
[59] Paras 17.14–17.18 below.

(1) Witness out of jurisdiction (non-EU)

17.11   Where the person to be examined is out of the jurisdiction the application is either for the issue of a letter of request to the appropriate foreign court, or (if the foreign government concerned so permits) for the appointment of a special examiner to take the evidence of the witness in the foreign country.[60] This procedure has already been briefly discussed in the context of documentary disclosure, and in particular details were given of the various conventions in existence under which a letter of request may be entertained by foreign courts.[61] The application for the issue of a letter of request or for the appointment of a special examiner is to be made to the Senior Master in the Queen's Bench Division of the High Court by way of a CPR, Pt 23 application.[62] The party applying for an order for the issue of a letter of request must file with his application notice the following:

(1) A draft letter of request in the prescribed form at Annex B to the relevant practice direction.

(2) A statement of the issues relevant to the proceedings.

(3) A list of questions or the subject matter of questions to be put to the proposed deponent.

(4) A translation of the documents in (1), (2) and (3) above unless the proposed opponent is in a country:

   (a) of which English is one of the official languages, or
   (b) listed at Annex B to the relevant practice direction, unless the particular circumstances of the case require a translation.

(5) An undertaking to be responsible for the expenses of the Secretary of State.

(6) A draft order.[63]

17.12   Where evidence is to be obtained by means of written questions, the applicants' questions should be submitted to the other side in advance to enable questions in cross-examination to be framed, and the latter should equally be submitted to the applicant in advance to enable questions in re-examination to be proposed. The court will not consider objections to such answers at this stage: the admissibility of questions (and any answers) will be considered at trial. The application is dealt with by the Senior Master of the Queen's Bench Division who will, if appropriate, sign the letter of request.[64] Whether the court will in fact make an order for the issue of a

---

[60] CPR, r.34.13(1)–(4).
[61] Ch.2, paras 2.59–2.63, above.
[62] CPR, Pt 34, Practice Direction: Depositions and Court Attendance by Witnesses, paras 5.1, 5.2, 5.4 and 5.5.
[63] *ibid.*, para.5.3.
[64] *ibid.*, para.5.5.

letter of request or for the appointment of a special examiner is a matter of discretion.[65] If the evidence can be obtained in other ways it may not.[66] In a number of cases, the trial judge has travelled abroad to take the evidence, but this is a course which will be followed only in the most exceptional circumstances.[67] In some cases evidence by video conference link will be cheaper and more convenient, and will have the advantage that it can be conducted in the presence of the trial judge.[68] An order is often made where a witness abroad who can give substantial evidence material to the issue[69] refuses or is unable to attend the trial and the application is made bona fide[70] and with such promptness as not to cause unreasonable delay.[71] It may also be made to allow a defendant resident abroad to give his evidence there,[72] but it is less likely in the case of a claimant, who has after all chosen an English forum.[73] An order will not be made if it is shown to be necessary for the purposes of justice that the witness should be examined in England,[74] for example, because the circumstances are such that cross-examination is needed to test his evidence and the local procedure will not include it[75]; or because his demeanour should be seen by the trial judge.[76] The court is also unlikely to accede to an application designed to obtain evidence from a foreign friendly state to support the contention that a law of that state is unenforceable in the United Kingdom as contrary to public policy.[77] The High Court may make an order for examination in relation to county court proceedings.[78]

Once an order has been made for the issue of a letter of request, the obtaining party must file with the court the draft letter of request, a statement of the issues relevant to the proceedings, a list of questions or the subject matter of questions to be put to the person to be examined, and an

17.13

---

[65] *Coch v Allcock* (1888) 21 Q.B.D. 178, CA.

[66] *Lewis v Kingsbury* (1888) 4 T.L.R. 629 at 639.

[67] *Admiralty and Commercial Courts Guide* (7th edn, 2006), para.H4.2. *Peer International Corporation v Termidor Music Publishers Ltd* [2005] EWHC 1048 (Ch.); see para.2.60 above.

[68] *ibid.*, para.H.3, H4.2, Appendix 15 (Videoconferencing Protocol); CPR, r.32.3; *Bell Group Ltd v Westpac* [2004] W.A.S.C. 162, (2004) 208 A.L.R. 491, Sup.Ct. W.Aus.; *Polanski v Condé Nast Publications Ltd* [2005] UKHL 10, [2005] 1 W.L.R. 637; *BCCI v Rahim*, November 11, 2005, Ch.D. (Unreported).

[69] *Langen v Tate* (1883) 24 Ch.D. 522, CA; *Ehrmann v Ehrmann* [1896] 2 Ch. 611.

[70] *Re Boyse* (1882) 20 Ch.D. 760; *Ross v Woodford* [1894] 1 Ch. 38.

[71] *Langen v Tate* (1883) 24 Ch.D. 522, CA.

[72] *Ross v Woodford* [1894] 1 Ch. 38; *New v Burns* (1894) 64 L.J.Q.B. 104, CA.

[73] *Ross v Woodford* [1894] 1 Ch. 38; *Coch v Allcock* (1888) 21 Q.B.D. 178, CA; *Emanuel v Soltykoff* (1892) 8 T.L.R. 331.

[74] *Armour v Walker* (1883) 25 Ch.D. 673, CA.

[75] *Re Boyse* (1882) 20 Ch.D. 760.

[76] *Lawson v Vacuum Brake Co.* (1884) 27 Ch.D. 137, CA; although in such a case the availability of video conference should be considered as an alternative, or in exceptional cases, the trial judge travelling abroad to take the evidence.

[77] *Settebello Ltd v Banco Totta & Acores* [1985] 1 W.L.R. 1050, CA.

[78] CPR, r.34.13(3).

undertaking to be responsible for the Secretary of State's expenses. The document should be accompanied by translations unless English is one of the official languages of the country where the examination is to take place, or a practice direction has specified that country is a country where no translation is necessary.[79] Where the order has been made without notice, then of course any party may apply to set aside the order[80] and no doubt in an appropriate case the witness may apply to set aside the order. A person may be examined pursuant to a letter of request on oath or affirmation or in accordance with any procedure permitted in the country in which the examination is to take place.[81] As to the taking of the deposition, the principles in relation to taking depositions in England are generally applicable.[82] A special examiner appointed under CPR, r.34.13(4) may be the British Consul or the Consul-General or his deputy in the country where the evidence is to be taken if there is in respect of that country a Civil Procedure Convention providing for the taking of evidence in that country for the assistance of proceedings in the High Court or another court in England or with the consent of the Secretary of State.[83] There is an implied restriction on collateral use of evidence obtained pursuant to a letter of request.[84]

(2) Witness in another EU Member State

17.14   CPR, rr.34.22–34.24 were added with effect from January 1, 2004 to give effect to Council Regulation (EC) 1206/2001 for the taking of evidence in Member States of the European Union. Under the regulation, the request must be made by a requesting court to a requested court and directed to the examination of and production of documents by an individual. The provisions of the regulation govern the procedure for making and responding to letters of request amongst Member States of the European Union,[85] save for those who have opted out. The Regulation does not cover Denmark.[86] The regulation has the limited purpose of obtaining evidence for civil or commercial judicial proceedings and as a matter of construction any use of evidence obtained outside that limited purpose is prohibited save with the permission of the requesting court or the person or parties from whom the

---

[79] CPR, r.34.13(6) and (7).
[80] CPR, Pt 34, Practice Direction—Depositions and Court Attendance by Witnesses, para.5.6; CPR, r.23.10.
[81] CPR, r.34.13(5).
[82] CPR, Pt 34, Practice Direction—Depositions and Court Attendance by Witnesses, para.5.9 which provides that the provisions of paras 4.1 to 4.12 apply.
[83] *ibid.*, para.5.8.
[84] *Dendron GmbH v The Regents of the University of California* [2004] EWHC 589 (Pat), [2005] 1 W.L.R. 200.
[85] Taking of Evidence Regulation, Art.21(1); CPR, Pt 34, Practice Direction, para.7.4
[86] CPR, r.34.22(b); CPR, Pt 34, Practice Direction, para.7.3.

evidence was sought. In any event, there is a common law restriction on collateral use.[87]

Each Regulation State has a list of courts competent to take evidence. In **17.15** England and Wales each circuit has its own designated court.[88] For London and the South Eastern Circuit the designated court is the Queen's Bench Division at the Royal Courts of Justice. Each Regulation State has nominated a Central Body for supplying information to courts. The Senior Master has been nominated as the Central Body for England and Wales.[89] Within seven days of receipt the requested court must acknowledge receipt.[90] If a request cannot be executed before there is incomplete information, the requested court must within 30 days make a request for the missing information.[91] The request must be executed within 90 days of receipt of a satisfactory request, but if this is not practicable the requesting court should be informed.[92] The requesting court may ask for a special procedure to be adopted and this will be followed unless it is incompatible with the law of the Regulation State of the requested stae or there are practical difficulties.[93] At the hearing the parties and their lawyers may attend and seek to participate.[94] The judges and representatives (including experts) of the requesting state may attend and participate (subject to conditions).[95] A witness summons may be used to enforce the attendance of a witness.[96] There are particular provisions which deal with the situation where a witness asserts a right to refuse to give evidence or claims that he is prohibited from giving evidence.[97] Whilst a requesting court may seek to come to another jurisdiction to take evidence itself, no witness summons may be used in such circumstances and the witness must consent to giving evidence.[98] A request to take evidence directly in England and Wales is made to the Senior Master as the Central Body.

An application for an order for the issuance of a letter of request to a **17.16** designated court in another Regulation State should be by way of a CPR Pt 23 application notice.[99] The letter of request is issued to a designated court in the Regulation State in which the proposed deponent is. The application

---

[87] *Dendron GmbH v Regents of the University of California* [2004] EWHC 589 (Patents), [2005] 1 W.L.R. 200.
[88] CPR, Pt 34, Practice Direction, para.8 and Annex C.
[89] Taking of Evidence Regulation, Art.3; CPR, Pt 34, Practice Direction, para.9.
[90] Taking of Evidence Regulation, Form B.
[91] Taking of Evidence Regulation, Form C.
[92] Taking of Evidence Regulation, Arts 9, 10 and 15, Form G.
[93] Taking of Evidence Regulation, Art.10. If the requested court does not comply it should inform the requesting court using Form E.
[94] Taking of Evidence Regulation, Art.11.
[95] Taking of Evidence Regulation, Art.12.
[96] Taking of Evidence Regulation, Art.13.
[97] Taking of Evidence Regulation, Art.14.
[98] Taking of Evidence Regulation, Art.17; CPR, r.34.23(5); CPR, Pt 34, Practice Direction, paras 9.3 and 10.6.
[99] CPR, Pt 34, Practice Direction, para.10.4.

should include a draft Form A, any relevant translations and costs under-takings.[100]

17.17   The Regulation provides that requests should follow Form A and must contain the following details (in practice appended to the application notice for an order)[101]:

    (a) the requesting and, where appropriate, the requested court;

    (b) the names and addresses of the parties to the proceedings, and their representatives if any;

    (c) a description of the taking of evidence to be performed;

    (d) where the request is for the examination of a person:

      — the name(s) and address(es) of the person(s) to be examined;

      — the questions to be put to the person(s) to be examined or a statement of the facts about which he is (they are) to be examined;

      — where appropriate a reference to a right to refuse to testify under the laws of the Member State of the requesting court;

      — any requirement that the examination is to be carried out under oath or affirmation in lieu thereof, and any special form to be used;

      — where appropriate, any other information that the requesting court deems necessary;

    (e) where the request is for any other form of taking of evidence, the documents or other objects to be inspected;

    (f) where appropriate, any request pursuant to Art.10(3) and (4), and Arts 11 and 12 and any information necessary for the application thereof.

17.18   If the court grants the order it will send the form of request directly to the designated court.[102] Where the taking of evidence requires the use of an expert, the designated court may require a deposit in advance towards the costs of the expert. The party who obtained the order is responsible for the payment of such deposit.[103]

(3) Request from another EU Member State

17.19   Where a requesting court in another Regulation State issues a request for evidence to be taken from a person within the jurisdiction, the application

---

[100] CPR, r.34.23(3); CPR, Pt 34, Practice Direction, para.10.3.
[101] Taking of Evidence Regulation, Art.4.
[102] CPR, Pt 34, Practice Direction, para.10.4.
[103] CPR, Pt 34, Practice Direction, para.10.5.

for an order to be taken must be made to a designated court and accompanied by the form of request and where appropriate a translation.[104] Such an application may be made without notice.[105] Where a designated court in England and Wales receives a request, the designated court sends it to the Treasury Solicitor.[106] On receipt the Treasury Solicitor may, with the consent of the Treasury, may apply for an order to give effect to the request.[107] The order for the deponent to attend and be examined, together with the evidence on which the order was made, must be served on the deponent.[108] An examiner of the court or other suitable or nominated person may be appointed to take the evidence.[109] Upon completion of the examination, the examiner must send the deposition to the court for transmission to the requesting court and a copy to the person who obtained the order for the evidence to be taken.[110]

C. WITNESS STATEMENTS

General

In proceedings begun by originating summons, it had long been usual for all the evidence to be given on affidavit, in advance of the trial, and for the deponents to attend at the hearing for a cross-examination. Until 1988, the court had no power to adopt a similar procedure in relation to writ actions: a witness could be "proofed" in secret and sprung upon the other side at trial at absolutely the last moment. As part of the increasing trend towards litigation played with "cards face up on the table," power was successively[111] conferred on the several divisions of the High Court, and the county court to direct the service and exchange of witness statements.[112] Under the CPR, the general position is that the court will order a party to serve on the other parties any witness statement of the oral evidence which the party serving the statement intends to rely on in relation to any issues to be decided at the trial.[113] Advance disclosure of this evidence is in effect the "price" to be paid for leave to call the witness. Although, unlike depositions

17.20

---

[104] CPR, r.34.24(2). The United Kingdom has indicated that it will accept requests in French as well as English. Where it is in French, the documents will be translated into English by the Treasury Solicitor (which may lead to delay): CPR Pt 34, Practice Direction, para.11.4
[105] CPR, r.34.24(2)(c).
[106] CPR, Pt 34, Practice Direction, para.11.1.
[107] CPR, Pt 34, Practice Direction, para.11.2.
[108] CPR, Pt 34, Practice Direction, para.11.5.
[109] CPR, rr.34.24(3) and 34.18.
[110] CPR, r.34.24(4).
[111] See RSC (Amendment) 1988.
[112] RSC, Ord.38, r.2A(2); C.C.R., Ord.20, r.12A. Witness statements were introduced in the Commercial Court in 1986 and well before that in the Restrictive Practices Court.
[113] CPR, r.32.4(2).

and letters of request, it is not a compulsory procedure, it is, as the Court of Appeal has said, "a process of discovery and not of pleading,"[114] and hence is discussed here. The purposes of the exchange of factual witness statements prior to trial are: (i) to save trial time by making examination in chief largely unnecessary; (ii) to enable the parties to know in advance what the remaining factual issues are; (iii) to enable opposing parties to prepare cross-examination in advance of trial; and (iv) to encourage early settlement of actions.[115]

Direction of the court

17.21   The standard direction is that the court will order a party to serve on the other parties a witness statement of the oral evidence which the party serving the statement intends to rely on in relation to any issues of fact to be decided at the trial. The court retains a discretion not to order the service of witness statements where to do so would conflict with the overriding objective, such as where it would be oppressive.[116] In Australia the Federal Court has refused to order the service of witness statements by defendants in an action for a civil penalty where this would infringe the privilege against self incrimination.[117] When a case is allocated to the fast track the court will give directions under CPR, r.28.3 and it is specifically provided in the rules that the matters to be dealt with will include the service of witness statements.[118] Normally, in fast track cases, directions are confined to the service of witness summaries, at least in the first instance. When a case is allocated to the multi-track, the court will give directions for the management of the case and this includes directions as to witness statements.[119] In making an order as to the service of witness statements, the court may give directions as to the order in which witness statements are to be served and whether or not the witness statements are to be filed.[120] Usually the court will direct that witness statements are to be simultaneously exchanged.[121] However, the court does have the express power to order sequential exchange. In some cases it may be appropriate and more effective to order sequential exchange of witness statements, particularly where one party's

---

[114] *Mercer v Chief Constable of Lancashire* [1991] 2 All E.R. 504 at 511.

[115] *Nederlandse v Bacon & Woodrow* [1995] 2 Lloyd's Rep. 404 at 408.

[116] *cf. Richard Saunders & Partners v Eastglen Ltd* [1990] 3 All E.R. 946; *Rowlands v Al-Fayed, The Times,* July 20, 1998.

[117] *Australian Competition and Consumer Commission v Amcor Printing Papers Group Ltd* (1999) 163 A.L.R. 465.

[118] CPR, r.28.3(1)(b); CPR, Pt 28, Appendix to Practice Direction (The Fast Track).

[119] CPR, r.29.2(1); CPR, r.34.4(2); CPR, Pt 29, Practice Direction (The Multi-Track), para.4.7(1)(d).

[120] CPR, r.32.4(3).

[121] *Mercer v Chief Constable of Lancashire* [1991] 2 All E.R. 504 at 511, CA; *Rowlands v Al-Fayed, The Times,* July 20, 1998.

evidence is largely to be responsive to that to be served by the other side.[122] If a witness statement or witness summary for use at trial is not served in respect of an intended witness within the time specified by the court, then the witness may not be called to give oral evidence unless the court gives permission.[123] In practice, a small failure to comply (e.g. service a little late) will never be a bar to adducing the evidence, especially if the result of a mistake,[124] unless it results in serious prejudice to the other side which cannot be cured.[125] Even where there has been substantial default in providing a witness statement late, it would usually be unjust to exclude a party from adducing evidence at trial, save in very extreme circumstances, for example where there has been a deliberate flouting of court orders, or inexcusable delay such that the only way the court could fairly entertain the evidence would be by adjourning the trial.[126]

Form and contents of witness statements

In general the witness statement will stand as part or all of the evidence in chief of the witness in question. Hence it should resemble that oral evidence as far as possible. Rather than being a legalistic document, the witness statement should be in the witness' own words.[127] The witness statement must indicate which of the statements in it are made from the witness' own knowledge and which are matters of information and belief and the source for any matters of information or belief.[128]   **17.22**

The witness statement must comply with the format required by the relevant practice direction,[129] which sets out how the witness statement should be headed, what should be contained in the body of the witness statement, its format, its verification by a statement of truth, a certificate by an authorised person if the witness cannot read or sign the witness statement, any alterations and the requirements for filing.[130] Inadmissible and   **17.23**

---

[122] cf. *Rayment v Ministry of Defence, The Times,* July 6, 1998 (experts reports).
[123] CPR, r.32.10; see, e.g. *Stroh v Haringey London Borough Council,* unreported, July 13, 1999, CA (judge's refusal to allow further four witnesses upheld).
[124] *Jenkins v Grocott,* unreprted, July 30, 1999, Hale J.
[125] cf. *Cowland v District Judges of West London County Court,* unreported, July 20, 1999, CA (no prejudice suffered: appeal against judge's refusal to permit extra witness allowed).
[126] *Letpak Ltd v Harris* [1997] P.N.L.R. 239, CA (C.C.R.); *Mealey Horgan Plc v Horgan, The Times,* July 6, 1999; cf. *Beachley Property Ltd v Edgar* [1997] P.N.L.R. 197, CA (leave refused in case under C.C.R.); *Grundy v Naqvi* [2001] EWCA Civ 139, CA (breach of unless order to exchange witness statements, defence not struck out as not proportionate to do so).
[127] *Chancery Guide,* Appendix 9, para.1; *The Admiralty and Commercial Courts Guide* (7th edn, 2006), para.H1.1(1); CPR, Pt 32, Practice Direction—Written Evidence, para.18.1; *Assi v Dina Foods Ltd* [2005] EWHC 1099 (Q.B.).
[128] ibid., para.18.2.
[129] CPR, r.32.8.
[130] CPR, Pt 32, Practice Direction—Written Evidence, paras 17–23; see also *Queen's Bench Guide,* para.7.10.4; *Chancery Guide,* Appendix 9.

irrelevant matters should not be included in a witness statement.[131] The court has the power to strike out irrelevant matters collateral to the issues to be tried from witness statements.[132]

Amendment and supplementary statements

17.24   The court has power to permit the amendment of any document used in proceedings, which includes the witness statement. If there is an error in the witness statement or further matters have arisen since the witness statement, these may be dealt with by way of a supplemental witness statement. The most common circumstances where supplemental witness statements are used are where it is appropriate to set out in advance of trial a response to matters which have arisen upon the service of the other side's witness statements or to deal with events since service of the original witness statement. In these cases, a supplementary witness statement should if practicable be served as soon as possible. Permission to adduce the evidence contained in the supplemental witness statement will be needed unless the other party consents. However, this need not be sought prior to service.[133] In the Commercial Court, a supplemental witness statement should normally be served where the witness proposes materially to add to, alter, correct or retract from what is in his original witness statement. Again, permission will be required in the absence of consent from the opposing party for the service of a supplemental statement.[134]

Procedure at trial

17.25   If a party has served a witness statement and it wishes to rely at trial on the evidence of the witness who made the statement, he must call the witness to give oral evidence unless the court otherwise orders or he puts in the statement as hearsay evidence.[135] Where the witness is called to give oral evidence, his evidence shall stand as evidence in chief unless the court orders otherwise.[136] In an appropriate case, the trial judge may require the whole or any part of the witnesses evidence in chief to be given orally.[137] Where there is a conflict of fact, particularly where the witness's credibility may be in issue and his evidence is contentious, it may be appropriate for the trial

---

[131] *Chancery Guide*, Appendix 9, para.3.
[132] CPR, r.32.1; *Akhtar v Kushi* [2002] EWHC 673 (Ch.) (strike out of evidence likely to lead to proliferation of issues).
[133] *Chancery Guide*, para.8.11.
[134] *The Admiralty and Commercial Courts Guide* (7th edn, 2006), para.H1.6(b).
[135] CPR, r.32.5(1).
[136] CPR, r.32.5(2).
[137] *The Admiralty and Commercial Courts Guide* (7th edn, 2006), para.H1.5(b).

judge to direct at least certain parts of the evidence to be given in chief.[138] Where the matter is tried by a jury it is usually preferable for the evidence in chief to be given orally, since a jury may be more able to absorb evidence in that form.[139] A witness giving oral evidence at trial may with the permission of the court amplify his witness statement and give evidence in relation to new matters which have arisen since the witness statement was served on other parties. The court will give such permission only if it considers there is good reason not to confine the evidence of the witness to the contents of his witness statement.[140] Where the additional evidence is likely to be substantial or may lead to surprise at trial, the prudent course is not to rely on this provision by seeking leave at trial, but instead to serve a supplemental witness statement and seek leave to adduce it prior to trial.

If a party, having duly served a witness statement, decides not to call the witness to give evidence at trial, it is good practice that prompt notice of this decision should be given to all other parties. The party should make plain when he gives this notice whether he proposes to put, or seek to put, the witness statement in as hearsay evidence. If he does not put the witness statement in as hearsay evidence, any other party may put it in as hearsay evidence.[141] This does not preclude an application by the party who originally served the statement for an order that the witness be called to be cross-examined.[142] Further, this change from the former practice does not mean that the other party can put the evidence in and seek to invite the court to disbelieve as untrue a substantial part of that evidence.[143] Where a party seeks to rely on a witness statement at trial as hearsay evidence and the other party applies for permission to cross-examine that person, then if the person does not attend it is open to the court to exclude that evidence.[144] Whilst in judicial review proceedings evidence is usually in writing, the court retains a power to direct that witnesses should attend for cross-examination on their witness statements and affidavits.[145]   **17.26**

It is not satisfactory to put a witness statement before the trial judge for his pre-reading, where it is not intended to call that person as a witness (and it is not intended to rely on it as hearsay).[146] Although it is desirable for a   **17.27**

---

[138] *Cole v Kibells (A Firm), The Times*, May 2, 1997, CA; *Mercer v Chief Constable of Lancashire* [1991] 2 All E.R. 504 at 507.
[139] *Mercer v Chief Constable of Lancashire* [1991] 2 All E.R. 504 at 507, CA.
[140] CPR, r.32.5(3) and (4).
[141] CPR, r.32.5(5); *Chancery Guide*, para.8.13; *The Admiralty and Commercial Courts Guide* (7th edn, 2006), para.H1.7(b); *Society of Lloyd's v Jaffray, The Times*, August 3, 2000; *The Green Opal* [2003] 1 Lloyd's Rep. 523.
[142] CPR, r.33.4(1); *Douglas v Hello! Ltd* [2003] EWCA Civ 332, [2003] E.M.L.R. 30, CA.
[143] *McPhilemy v Times Newspapers Ltd* [2000] 1 W.L.R. 1732, CA. Under RSC, Ord.38, r.2A(6) no other party was allowed to put the statement in evidence at trial if the party serving the statement elected not to call the witness.
[144] *Polansi v Condé Nast Publications* [2003] EWCA Civ 1573, [2004] 1 W.L.R. 387, CA. In the House of Lords it was stated that such an exclusionary order should not be made automatically: [2005] UKHL 10 and [2005] 1 W.L.R. 637 at [36, 67 and 79].
[145] *R. v Ealing BC, ex p. PG* [2002] EWHC 250 (Admin).
[146] *Jaffray v Society of Lloyd's* [2002] EWCA Civ 1101 at [406].

party to inform the judge that it may not call all the witnesses before he is asked to read their statements, the mere fact that the judge has read the statement of a witness who is ultimately is not called, does not make the trial unfair—Judges often have to put matters of which they were once aware out of their minds in resolving issues of fact.[147] The trial judge has no power requiring the party who served the statement to call the maker to give evidence as a witness.[148] However the judge may draw an adverse inference against a party in failing to call the witness to deal with certain evidence.[149]

17.28   A witness statement may be used only for the purpose of the proceedings in which it is served, unless either the witness or the court gives permission for some other use, or the witness statement has been put in evidence at a hearing held in public.[150] A witness statement which stands as evidence in chief is open to inspection unless the court otherwise directs during the course of the trial. Any person may ask for a direction that a witness statement is not open to inspection. However, the court will not make such a direction unless it is satisfied that a witness statement should not be open to inspection because of the interests of justice, the public interest, the nature of any expert medical evidence of the statement, the nature of any confidential information (including information relating to personal financial matters) in the statement, or the need to protect the interests of any child or patient. The court may exclude from inspection words or passages in the statement.[151] Even after a witness has given evidence, the court can still restrict inspection of a statement by redacting the names of persons referred to in the interests of justice.[152] The power to inspect a witness statement during the course of the trial does not extend to cover documents referred to in those statements.[153]

17.29   Where a witness is called to give evidence at trial he may be cross-examined on his witness statement, whether or not the statement or any part of it was referred to during the witness' evidence in chief.[154] The court has power to curtail the length of cross-examination,[155] but it should give the parties reasonable notice of an intention to do so.[156] The court may even limit the scope of cross-examination.[157] If in cross-examination the witness concedes that he no longer has any recollection of a matter set out in his

---

[147] *Jaffray v Society of Lloyd's* [2002] EWCA Civ 1101 at [561–569].
[148] *Jaffray v Society of Lloyd's* [2002] EWCA Civ 1101 at [567–568].
[149] *Jaffray v Society of Lloyd's* [2002] EWCA Civ 1101 at [406–407]; *Wisniewski v Central Manchester Health Authority* [1998] P.I.Q.R. 324.
[150] CPR, r.32.12.
[151] CPR, r.32.13.
[152] *Cox v Jones* [2004] EWHC 1006 (Ch.).
[153] *Gio Personal Investment Services Ltd v Liverpool and London Steamship Protection and Indemnity Association Ltd* [1999] 1 W.L.R. 984, CA.
[154] CPR, r.32.11.
[155] *Three Rivers District Council v Bank of England* [2005] EWCA Civ 889.
[156] *Hayes v Transco Plc* [2003] EWCA Civ 1261.
[157] *Watson v Chief Constable of Cleveland* [2001] EWCA Civ 1547.

witness statement, that does not automatically mean that the relevant part of his statement is no longer admissible.[158] In general, evidence at hearings other than trial is by witness statement.[159] Where, at a hearing other than the trial, evidence is given in writing, any party may apply to the court for permission to cross-examine the person giving the evidence. If the court gives permission but the person fails to attend, his evidence may not be used unless the court gives permission.[160]

It is imperative that legal advisors ensure that a witness fully understands **17.30** the importance of making a true and accurate witness statement. The primary responsibility to prevent abuse of the witness statement procedure must lie with each party's solicitors.[161] However, in many cases it will be impossible to determine at the trial whether the solicitors are in default, or the extent of default, both because that is not in issue at the trial (and the solicitors would generally not have given evidence at the trial) and because of client privilege.[162] Proceedings for contempt of court may be brought against a person if he makes, or causes to make, a false statement in a document verified by a statement of truth (thus including a witness statement) without honest belief in its truth. However, such proceedings may only be brought by the Attorney General or with the permission of the court.[163]

Other forms of written evidence

Instead of filing a witness statement, it is open to a party to serve an **17.31** affidavit. Whilst evidence at a hearing other than trial should normally be given by witness statement, a witness may give evidence by affidavit if he wishes to do so, but the party putting forward the affidavit may not recover the additional cost of making it from any other party unless the court orders otherwise. This costs penalty does not apply where the court, a provision contained in any other rule, a Practice Direction or any other enactment requires that the evidence must be given by affidavit.[164] The affidavit must comply with the requirements set out in the relevant Practice Direction.[165]

Where a person is unwilling to permit the party concerned to take a **17.32** sufficient witness statement beforehand, it may be impracticable to serve a

---

[158] *Nederlandse v Bacon & Woodrow* [1995] 2 Lloyd's Rep. 406.
[159] CPR, r.32.6.
[160] CPR, r.32.7. In practice orders for cross-examination prior to trial are not routinely made; for an example, see *Kensington International Limited v Republic of Congo* [2006] EWHC 1848 (Comm).
[161] *Chancery Guide*, Appendix 9, para.6.
[162] *ZYX Music GmbH v King* [1995] 3 All E.R. 1 at 11, 15.
[163] CPR, r.32.14.
[164] CPR, r.32.15.
[165] CPR, r.32.16; CPR, Pt 32, Practice Direction—Written Evidence, paras 1–10.

full witness statement. The only obligation of a witness served with a witness summons is to attend court to be examined; there is no obligation to co-operate with the calling party in advance. A party who is required to serve a witness statement for use at trial but is unable to obtain one, may apply, without notice for permission to serve a witness summary instead.[166] A witness summary is a summary of the evidence, if known, which would otherwise be included in a witness statement, or, if the evidence is not known, the matters about which the party serving the witness summary proposes to question the witness. Unless the court orders otherwise, a witness summary must include the name and address of the attended witness and the witness summary must be served within the period within which a witness statement would have had to be served.[167]

---

[166] CPR, r.32.9(1); *Harrison v Bloom Camillin*, unreported, March 30, 1999, May 4, 1999, Neuberger J.

[167] CPR, r.32.9. Where a party serves a witness summary, so far as practicable, rr.32.4, 32.5(3) and 32.8 apply to the summary: CPR, r.32.9(5).

CHAPTER 18

Experts' reports

CHAPTER 18

Experts' reports

A. GENERAL

It is not the function of this chapter to deal with all aspects of expert **18.01** evidence.[1] Instead it concentrates on the disclosure aspects of expert evidence. In relation to experts reports, a variety of sources need to be taken into consideration. In particular:

(1) CPR Pt 35 Experts and Assessors.
(2) CPR, Pt 35, Practice Direction—Experts and Assessors.
(3) Protocol for the Instruction of Experts to give Evidence in Civil Claims published by the Civil Justice Council (2005), annexed to CPR, Pt 35, Practice Direction. This is an extremely helpful piece of guidance which should be followed by experts and those instructing them.
(4) Relevant court guides issued by the respective divisions of the High Court.[2]
(5) Guidance issued by any relevant institute or professional body.[3]
(6) An increasing corpus of case law.

---

[1] For a more comprehensive discussion, see James, *Expert Evidence: Law and* Practice (2nd edn, 2006); *Phipson on Evidence* (16th edn, 2005), Ch.33.
[2] *Chancery Guide* (5th edn, 2005), paras 4.6–4.20; *Queen's Bench Guide*, para.7.9; *Admiralty and Commercial Courts Guide* (7th edn, 2006), para.H2 and Appendix 11; *Technology and Construction Court Guide* (2nd edn, 2005), para.13.
[3] *Peet v Mid-Kent Healthcare Trust (Practice Note)* [2002] 1 W.L.R. 210, CA. See, for example, *Code of Guidance for Experts and those instructing them*, published by the Academy of Experts (June 1, 2001 revision) and *Code of Guidance on Expert Evidence: A Guide for Experts and those instructing them for the purpose of Court proceedings*, published by the Expert Witness Institute (December 2001). These two codes were replaced in 2005 by the Protocol.

CPR, Pt 35 is directed at controlling the volume, cost, quality and impartiality of expert evidence and its application is subject to the overriding objective of dealing with cases justly. This general objective requires the court to have regard specifically to matters of proportionality, dealing with cases expeditiously, saving expense and ensuring that parties are on an equal footing.[4]

18.02   The High Court has long enjoyed power to limit the number of expert witnesses who may be called at trial,[5] but the High Court and the county court also have the power to regulate advance disclosure of expert evidence, in the form of experts' reports. These are a form of witness statement containing (expert) opinion evidence, although sometimes factual evidence as well. Indeed, there is authority for saying that an expert's report must provide the factual basis upon which the opinion evidence rests,[6] and this is good practice. They have been in use much longer than ordinary witness statements, and were brought within a comprehensive framework of rules of court in 1974, with the introduction of Pt IV (rr.35–44) of RSC, Ord.38. It was widely felt that under the former practice, expert evidence had considerably increased the cost and delay of litigation, with the resultant necessity for the court to have control over such evidence both before and at trial. Under the CPR it is now expressly provided in the rules that expert evidence should be restricted to that which is reasonably required to resolve the proceedings.[7] Under CPR, Pt 35 which now regulates expert evidence, a reference to an "expert" is a reference to an expert who has been instructed to give or prepare evidence for the purpose of court proceedings.[8] Permission of the court is required to rely on expert evidence. However, it is inappropriate in family proceedings involving children to instruct an expert witness without the knowledge of the court or other side's advisors. It is also contrary to good practice to seek to avoid obtaining the court's permission by providing information in an anonymous form to the expert.[9] Obviously parties are free to instruct experts (generally at their own cost) who are to assist them in litigation, without their being instructed to give or prepare evidence for the purpose of court proceedings.[10]

18.03   The main themes underpinning CPR Pt 35 are that expert evidence should only be deployed when it is relevant, necessary and proportionate. CPR, r.35.1 provides that the starting point is that "expert evidence should be restricted to that which is reasonably required to resolve the proceedings".

---

[4] CPR, r.1.1.

[5] Formerly RSC, Ord.38, r.4; C.C.R.—no equivalent.

[6] *Ollett v Bristol Aerojet Ltd* [1979] 1 W.L.R. 1197; *Re J* [1990] F.C.R. 193 (*sub nom. Re R.* [1991] 1 F.L.R. 291; *The Ikarian Reefer* [1993] 2 Lloyds' Rep. 68 at 81–82; see para.18.14, below.

[7] CPR, r.35.1; *Thermus v Aladdin Sales*, unreported, October 25, 1999, Jacob J. (expert evidence in registered design infringement held redundant).

[8] CPR, r.35.2.

[9] *Re A (Children: Expert Evidence)*, *The Times*, February 27, 2001, Fam. D. (Wall J.)

[10] Protocol, para.5.

The key question now in relation to expert evidence is the question as to what added value such evidence will provide to the court in its determination of a given case.[11] The experts duties are now quite onerous and the highest standards are now expected. The expert must be objective and impartial; his duty is to the court. As emphasised by the Court of Appeal in *Mutch v Allen*[12]:

> "This new regime is designed to ensure that experts no longer serve the exclusive interest of those who retain them, but rather contribute to a just disposal of disputes by making their expertise available to all. The overriding objective requires that the court be provided with all relevant matters in the most cost effective and expeditious way. This policy is exemplified by provisions such as rule 35.11 which allows one party to use an expert's report disclosed by the other party even if that other party has decided not to rely on it himself."

B. DIRECTION OF THE COURT

The primary rule under CPR, r.35.4 is that no party may call an expert or put in evidence an expert's report without the court's permission. Expert evidence includes expert evidence given by a party himself or his employees, as well as evidence from independent experts, and thus a party's own expert evidence is subject to the rules set out in Pt 35.[13] When a party applies for permission he must identify the field in which he wishes to rely on expert evidence and where practicable the expert in that field on whose evidence he wishes to rely.[14] If permission is granted it is in relation only to the expert named or in the field identified in the order.[15] In deciding whether or not to give permission for expert evidence, the court has to make a judgment on at least three matters[16]: **18.04**

(1) how cogent the proposed expert evidence will be;
(2) how helpful it will be in resolving any of the issues in the case; and
(3) how much it will cost and the relationship of that cost to the sums at stake.

---

[11] *Chancery Guide* (5th edn, 2005), para.4.6.
[12] [2001] 2 C.P.L.R. 200 at [24].
[13] *Shell Pensions Trust Ltd v Pell Frischmann & Partners* [1986] 2 All E.R. 911.
[14] *Queen's Bench Guide*, para.7.9.3.
[15] CPR, r.35.4(1)–(3). Small Claims, CPR, r.27.5. Pre-action protocols make specific provision for expert evidence without the need for a court order: see para.18.06, below.
[16] *Mann v Messrs Chetty & Patel* [2001] Lloyd's Rep. P.N. 38 at [17]. The court has power to exclude relevant evidence: *Grobbelaar v Sun Newspapers, The Times*, August 12, 1999, CA.

18.05   With claims on the small claims track permission should be sought at the directions stage. If there is a preliminary hearing permission should be sought then.[17] Where the court has given some directions and directed that it will consider further directions within 28 days, this gives another opportunity for a party to seek permission and this can be done by letter.[18] With small claims most of the provisions in CPR, Pt 35 do not apply.[19] In such cases no expert may give evidence without the permission of the court.[20] With cases on the fast track, when the court allocates a case to the fast track, the court will give directions for the management of the case and set a timetable including directions as to expert evidence.[21] The court can give directions as to expert evidence upon the filing of listing questionnaires.[22] With cases on the Multi-Track the court may give directions as to expert evidence upon allocation of the case to that track.[23] Generally expert evidence is dealt with at the case management conference on cases on the Multi-Track.[24] Similarly directions as to expert evidence can be sought in the listing questionnaire[25] or at the Pre-Trial Review if ordered.[26] In the Commercial Court any application for permission to call an expert witness, or serve an expert's report, should normally be made at the case management conference.[27] Late applications to adduce expert evidence are discouraged. The closer to trial the less likely the court will give permission to adduce expert evidence, and the court will refuse permission where it is sought very late in the day and would cause injustice to the opponent.[28] However where there is good reason for the late application, such as in the light of a report of a single joint expert, permission may be granted.[29] The court will refuse permission where a previous application has been refused and there has been no material change in circumstances.[30]

---

[17] CPR, r.27.6.

[18] CPR, r.27.4(1).

[19] CPR, r.27.2(1)(e)—those which apply to small claims are CPR, rr.35.1, 35.3 and 35.8.

[20] CPR, r.27.5. Recoverable fees for an experts report are limited to £200.

[21] CPR, r.28.3(1)(c).

[22] CPR, r.28.5; CPR, Pt 28, Practice Direction—The Fast Track, para.7.

[23] CPR, r.27.2(1).

[24] CPR, r.29.3; CPR, Pt 29, Practice Direction—The Multi-Track, para.5.3(4) and 5.5.

[25] CPR, r.29.6.

[26] CPR, r.29.7.

[27] *Admiralty and Commercial Court Guide*, (7th edn, 2006) para.H2.1. Similarly in the TCC, where expert evidence is dealt with at the first CMC and usually further considered at subsequent stages: *Technology and Construction Court Guide* (2nd edn, 2005), para.13.3.4.

[28] *Calenti v North Middlesex NHS Trust*, March 2, 2001 (unreported), Buckley J., Q.B.D. (permission refused weeks before trial where no excuse for not seeking permission earlier); *Dew Pitchmastic Plc v Birse Construction Ltd*, 78 Con.L.R. 162, Q.B.D. (TCC).

[29] *Holmes v SGB Services Plc* [2001] EWCA Civ 354, CA (permission to call further expert and trial adjoined in light of report of single joint expert); *Hanley v Stage and Catwalk Ltd* [2001] EWCA Civ 1739, CA (permission for both sides shortly before trial); *May v Smith* [2005] UKHL 7, [2005] 1 W.L.R. 581 at [29], [61], [62], HL (doubted judge correct in refusing permission to adduce late evidence).

[30] *Jameson v Smith* [2001] EWCA Civ 1264, [2001] 6 C.P.L.R. 489, CA.

In giving directions, the court will generally order that expert evidence is   **18.06**
to be given in a written report.[31] In cases on the Fast Track, the court will
not direct an expert to attend a hearing unless it is necessary to do so in the
interests of justice.[32] In most cases the court will order mutual exchange of
expert evidence, however in recent years the court has been more willing to
order sequential exchange of evidence,[33] particularly where that is likely to
reduce costs or one party's expert evidence is largely responsive to that of
another party. The pre-action protocol for personal injury actions promotes
the practice of the claimant obtaining a medical report, disclosing it to a
defendant who then asks questions and/or agrees it and does not obtain his
own report.[34] Particularly in the cases of clinical disputes, parties are
encouraged to be flexible as to whether reports should be exchanged
sequentially or a joint expert engaged.[35] In the case of road traffic accidents,
insurers are expected to send to the other side their engineers reports and
medical experts are usually jointly nominated.[36]

Once an order has been made for the service of an expert's report, this   **18.07**
does not mean that the party who has obtained a report is obliged to
produce the report to his opponent if he decides not to use it or call the
expert.[37] Where the order specifies the name of the expert and the party
desires to substitute him with another expert, the court may grant permission on condition that the original expert report be disclosed.[38] Where the
original order does not name the expert, then permission will not be
required to use a different expert of the same discipline provided for in the
order and the court cannot require him to produce the expert report of the
original expert.[39]

In giving directions the court will endeavour to ensure that the expert   **18.08**
evidence is truly appropriate and necessary,[40] and proportionate.[41] The
court should try to avoid the multiplicity of experts of the same discipline,[42]
but where there is good reason it may allow a party to call more than one

---

[31] CPR, r.35.5(1).

[32] CPR, r.35.5(2).

[33] *Rayment v Ministry of Defence*, *The Times*, July 6, 1998; *Admiralty and Commercial Courts Guide* (7th edn, 2006), para.H2.11; *Chancery Guide* (5th edn, 2005), para.4.14.

[34] *Pre-action Protocols for Personal Injury Claims*, paras 2.11, 3.14–3.21.

[35] *Pre-action Protocol for the Resolution of Clinical Disputes*, para.4.

[36] *Pre-action Protocol for Road Traffic Accidents*, paras 3.6 and 3.12.

[37] *Carlson v Townsend* [2001] 1 W.L.R. 2415, CA (party not obliged to disclose expert report to opponent even though his selection had not been opposed using the procedure in the Pre-Action Protocol for Personal Injury Claims, paras 3.14–3.21).

[38] *Beck v Ministry of Defence* [2003] EWCA Civ 1043, *The Times*, July 21, 2003.

[39] *Hajigeorgiou v Vassilcou* [2005] EWCA Civ 236.

[40] Protocol, para.6. *Thermus v Aladdin Sales*, unreported, October 25, 1999, Jacob J. (expert evidence in registered design infringement held redundant); *J.P. Morgan Chase Bank v Springwell Navigation* [2006] EWHC 2755 (Comm) at [19–23].

[41] *Technology and Construction Court Guide* (2nd edn, 2005), para.13.2.

[42] *Heywood v Plymouth Hospital NHS Trust* [2005] EWCA Civ 939, *The Times*, August 1, 2005, CA (parties limited to one consultant psychiatrist each as proportionate).

expert of the same discipline.[43] There is no absolute rule that each party must be allowed an equal number of experts on the basis of the equality of arms aspiration.[44] Nevertheless, in practice parties are usually allowed the same number of experts. The court may limit the amount of expert's fees and expenses that the party who wishes to rely on the expert may recover from the other party.[45] A party who fails to disclose an expert's report may not use the report at the trial or call the expert to give evidence orally unless the court gives permission.[46]

C. SINGLE JOINT EXPERTS

18.09   Under the RSC there was power for the court to appoint a court expert, but this was rarely exercised.[47] The current practice encourages the use of a single joint expert appointed pursuant to CPR, r.35.7. This has the advantages of reducing the cost of such evidence as well as removing any suspicion that an expert is merely a "hired gun" of one of the parties. Thus where two or more parties wish to submit expert evidence on a particular issue, the court may direct that the evidence on that issue is to be given by one expert only. It is not necessarily an objection to this that the parties have already chosen separate experts.[48] Joint experts are particularly suitable where a claim is small and it would be disproportionate to have a multiplicity of experts.[49] In areas where the expert view is likely to be not controversial then a single joint expert is often appropriate. However, where the area is controversial, such as in a developing field, or where it is known that there is more than one expert approach, it is often best to allow each party to call separate experts.[50] Cost is often the determining factor in the decision to permit or direct a joint expert.[51] Single joint experts are not usually appro-

---

[43] *Chesterfield v North Derbyshire Royal Hospital NHS Trust* [2004] Lloyd's Rep. Med. 90 (claimant permitted to call two consultant obstetricians to avoid inequality of arms as defendant was calling one such expert, but also two consultant obstetricians as witnesses of fact).

[44] *Kirman v Euro Exide Corporation (CMP Batteries Ltd)*, The Times, February 6, 2007, CA.

[45] CPR, r.35.4(4); *Queen's Bench Guide*, para.7.9.3.

[46] CPR, r.35.13; see *Baron v Lovell* [2000] P.I.Q.R. 20, CA (failure to disclose; permission refused).

[47] RSC, Ord.40; *Abbey National Mortgages Plc v Key Surveyors Ltd* [1996] 1 W.L.R. 1534, CA.

[48] *Queen's Bench Guide*, para.7.9.6; Chancery Guide (5th edn, 2005), para.4.12.

[49] *Field v Leeds City Council* [2001] 2 C.P.L.R. 129, CA. For a list of situations where a single joint expert can often be appropriate, see *Technology and Construction Court Guide* (2nd edn, 2005), para.13.4.3. See also Chancery Guide (5th edn, 2005), para.4.11.

[50] *Casey v Cartwright* [2006] EWCA Civ 1280 at [36], CA; *Oxley v Penwarden* [2001] C.P.L.R. 1, CA.

[51] *Kranidiotes v Paschali* [2001] C.P. Rep. 81, CA (judge entitled to substitute a cheaper expert in place of one originally appointed).

priate for the principal liability disputes in a large case, or in a case where considerable sums have been spent on an expert in the pre-action stage. They are generally inappropriate where the issue involves questions of risk assessment or professional competence.[52] Where the parties cannot agree who should be the expert the court may select the expert from a list prepared or identified by the instructing parties or direct that the expert be selected in such other manner as the court may direct.[53] Where a court has directed that there be a single joint expert, but there are a number of disciplines relevant to the issue, a leading expert in the dominant discipline should be identified as the single expert. He is responsible for incorporating or annexing the expert evidence of the experts in other disciplines.[54] There are specific provisions as to the instructions to a single expert which require the co-operation of the parties.[55] Where a joint expert has been appointed under the CPR, r.35.7, each party may give separate instructions to the expert, the court has no power to insist upon a single letter of instruction,[56] albeit this is generally desirable and is the usual course of action. It is inappropriate for him to meet with one party and discuss his evidence in the absence of the other party.[57]

Where there has been a report of a single joint expert, the court in its discretion may refuse to allow a party to call his own expert.[58] In a number of cases the court has permitted a party to call his own expert, where he has disagreed with the conclusions set out in a joint experts report.[59] The relevant principles on such an application may be summarised as follows[60]:

18.10

---

[52] *Technology and Construction Court Guide* (2nd edn, 2005), para.13.4.2.

[53] CPR, r.35.7. Practice Direction—Experts and Assessors, para.6: Protocol, para.17. In certain types of proceedings the usual practice is to have a joint expert: e.g. *Practice Direction: (Family Proceedings: Ancillary relief procedure), The Times*, July 4, 2000; *Re B (a Minor) (Sexual abuse: Expert's report), The Times*, March 29, 2000, CA. CPR, rr.35.7 (single joint expert), 35.8 (instructions to joint expert) and 35.9 (power to direct party to provide information) do not apply to committal applications: Sch.1 to CPR, RSC, Ord.52, Practice Direction—Committal Applications, para.6.

[54] CPR, Pt 35, Practice Direction, para.6. This can give rise to practical difficulties.

[55] CPR, r.35.8; *Queen's Bench Guide*, para.7.9.7; *Admiralty and Commercial Courts Guide* (7th edn, 2006), para.H2.3; *Technology and Construction Court Guide* (2nd edn, 2005), para.13.4; *Chancery Guide* (5th edn, 2005), para.4.13.

[56] CPR, r.35.8(1); *Yorke v Katra* [2003] EWCA Civ 867, CA.

[57] *Peet v Mid-Kent Healthcare Trust (Practice Note)* [2002] 1 W.L.R. 210, CA; *Sutton Smith v Stephens*, January 26, 2001 (unreported) (held claimant and his advisors not entitled to hold a consultation with joint experts in absence of defendant or his advisors).

[58] *Layland v Fairview New Homes* [2002] EWHC 1350 (Ch.), [2003] 1 C.P.L.R. 19 (claimant refused permission to call own expert, in face of single joint expert report concluding no loss suffered); *Popek v National Westminster Bank Plc* [2002] EWCA Civ 42, CA (late application for permission to call own expert refused).

[59] *Daniels v Walker* [2000] 1 W.L.R. 1382, CA; *Holmes v SGB Services Plc* [2001] EWCA Civ 354, CA; *cf. Stallwood v David* [2006] EWHC 2600 (Q.B.), [2007] 1 All E.R. 206, in context of seeking permission to call a further expert after meeting of experts.

[60] *Layland v Fairview New Homes* [2002] EWHC 1350 (Ch.), [2003] 1 C.P.L.R. 19 at [30], *per* Neuberger J.; see also *Cosgrove v Pattison* [2001] 2 C.P.L.R. 177.

(1) The court has a discretion whether or not to accede to the application.

(2) Whether or not it will accede to the application depends on all the circumstances, which will normally include the value of the claim involved and the grounds upon which the desire to challenge the single expert's view is based.

(3) Even where there may be ground for permitting the party to call his own expert, the court may well require further steps to be taken first.

(4) Subject to the above, the court will normally permit a party to call his own expert, if he has reasonable grounds for wishing to take that course.

In an appropriate case the court may allow the appointment of a second single joint expert where there is a valid objection to the first one.[61]

D. RULNG ON ADMISSIBILITY

18.11   Under the RSC, there had been authority that, prior to trial, the court could not rule on the admissibility of expert evidence.[62] Whatever the position may have been in the past, under the CPR, the court does have the power to rule on the admissibility and necessity of expert evidence both at the permission stage and at any other later stage up to and including trial. Even where the court has given permission for expert evidence, the court may rule on its admissibility after service of experts reports and before trial.[63] It clearly serves the purposes of effective case management that, as far as possible, issues relating to the admissibility of expert evidence be disposed of well before the trial starts so that significant costs can be saved.[64] The relevant principles as to the admissibility of expert evidence may be summarised as follows[65]:

(1) Expert evidence is admissible under s.3 of the Civil Evidence Act 1972 in any case where the court accepts that there exists a

---

[61] *Smolen v Solon Co-operative Housing Services Ltd* [2003] EWCA Civ 1240 (first expert had been instructed by defendant's solicitors many times before).

[62] *Sullivan v West Yorkshire Passenger Transport Executive* [1985] 2 All E.R. 134, CA; *The Scotch Whisky Association v Kella Distillers Ltd, The Times,* December 27, 1996; *cf. Bown v Gould & Swayne* [1996] P.N.L.R. 130, CA (ruling on admissibility at pre-trial review); *Woodford & Ackroyd v Burgess, The Times,* February 1, 1999, CA.

[63] *J.P. Morgan Chase Bank v Springwell* [2006] EWHC 2755 (Comm).

[64] *Barings Plc v Coopers & Lybrand* [2001] Lloyd's Rep. Bank 85 at [20], *per* Evans-Lombe J, Ch.D. However, in a different context it has been held that disputes about admissibility of evidence are usually best left to the judge at trial: *Beazer Homes Ltd v Stroude* [2005] EWCA Civ 265, *The Times,* April 28, 2005, CA.

[65] *Barings Plc v Coopers & Lybrand* [2001] Lloyd's Rep. Bank 85 at [45].

recognised expertise governed by recognised standards and rules of conduct capable of influencing the court's decision on any of the issues which it has to decide and the witness to be called must satisfy the court that he has a sufficient familiarity with and knowledge of the expertise in question to render his opinion potentially of value in resolving any of those issues.[66]

(2) Evidence meeting this test can still be excluded by the court if the court takes the view that calling it will not be helpful to the court in resolving any issue in the case justly.

(3) Such evidence will not be helpful where the issue to be decided is one of law or is otherwise one on which the court is able to come to a fully informed decision without hearing such evidence.

It is for the party seeking to call expert evidence to satisfy the court that expert evidence is available which would have a bearing on the issues which the court has to decide and would be helpful to the court in coming to a conclusion on those issues.[67]

E. DUTIES OF EXPERT

It is the duty of an expert to help the court on matters within his expertise **18.12** and this overrides any obligation to the person from whom he has received instructions or by whom he is paid.[68] Thus a contract whereby an expert has bound himself not to act as an expert for the other party is unenforceable as contrary to public policy.[69] Allegations of bias, incompetence, conflict of interest and even personal interest are sometimes raised. The courts have repeatedly emphasised the necessity for experts to be impartial and objective and to present their evidence in a manner which properly assists the court.[70] This does not necessarily mean that an employee of a party cannot give expert evidence so long as he appreciates that his primary duty is to the court.[71] Although in one case it was suggested that a party may not call a friend as an expert witness,[72] there is no such automatic exclusion.[73] As

---

[66] See the classic test of King C.J. in *R. v Bonython* [1984] S.A.S.R. 45 at 46.

[67] *Barings Plc v Coopers & Lybrand* [2001] Lloyd's Rep. Bank 85 at [20]; *Clarke v Marlborough Fine Arts (London) Limited* [2002] EWHC 11 (Ch.) at [5].

[68] CPR, r.35.3; CPR, Pt 35, Practice Direction, paras 1.1–1.6; Protocol, para.4.

[69] *Lilly Icos LLC v Pfizer Ltd* (2000) 23 (11) I.P.D. 23089, Ch.D.

[70] *The Ikarian Reefer* [1993] 2 Lloyd' Rep. 68 at 81–2, Cresswell J.; *Stevens v Gullis* [2000] 1 All E.R. 527, CA; *R. v Griffin* [2001] 3 N.Z.L.R. 577 at 603–604, N.Z.C.A., *per* Thomas J. (perceived lack of objectivity of experts).

[71] *Field v Leeds City Council* [2000] 17 E.G. 165, [2001] 2 C.P.L.R. 129, CA.

[72] *Liverpool Roman Catholic Archdiocesan Trust v Goldberg (No.3)* [2001] 1 W.L.R. 2337, ChD (evidence from a barrister in same chambers as party calling him disregarded).

[73] *Admiral Management Services Ltd v Para-Protect Ltd* [2002] 1 W.L.R. 2722 at [33]; *cf. Snolen v Solan Co-operative Housing* [2003] EWCA Civ 1240.

long as the judge is satisfied that the expert is fully aware of the primacy of his duty to the court, the effect that a relationship between the expert and a party may have on the suspicions of a reasonable observer does not of itself prevent such evidence being admissible.[74] An expert should not be remunerated on a conditional or contingency fee basis.[75] The current state of the law may be summarised by the following principles[76]:

(1) It is always desirable that an expert should have no actual or apparent interest in the outcome of the proceedings.

(2) The existence of such an interest, whether as an employee of one of the parties or otherwise, does not automatically render the evidence of the proposed expert inadmissible. It is the nature and extent of the interest or connection which matters, not the mere fact of the interest or connection.

(3) Where the expert has an interest of one kind or another in the outcome of the case, the question of whether he should be permitted to give evidence should be determined as soon as possible in the course of case management.

(4) The decision as to whether an expert should be permitted to give evidence in such circumstances is a matter of fact and degree. The test of apparent bias is not relevant to the question of whether an expert should be permitted to give evidence.

(5) The questions which have to be determined are whether:

(a) the person has relevant expertise; and

(b) he is aware of his primary duty to the court if he gives expert evidence, and is willing and able, despite the interest or connection with the litigation or a party thereto, to carry out that duty.

(6) The judge will have to weigh the alternative choices open if the expert's evidence is excluded, having regard to the overriding objective of the Civil Procedure Rules.

(7) If the expert has an interest which is not sufficient to preclude him from giving evidence the interest may nevertheless affect the weight of his evidence. A person cannot appear as an advocate and give evidence in the same case.[77]

---

[74] R. (Factortame Ltd) v Transport Secretary (No.8) [2003] Q.B. 381 at [70], CA. It is highly undesirable that the expert has a significant financial interest in the outcome of the case, such as under a contingency fee arrangement. See also Davis v Stena Line Ltd [2005] EWHC 420 (Q.B.)—payment of contingency fees impermissible.

[75] Protocol, para.7.6.

[76] Armchair Passenger Transport Ltd. v Helical Bar Plc [2003] EWHC 367 (Q.B.) at [29] per Nelson J.

[77] Franks v Towse [2001] EWCA Civ 9, CA (Lands Tribunal). Nor should an expert act like an advocate when giving evidence: Cairnstores v Aktiebolaget Hassle [2002] EWCA Civ 1504.

The expert witness must be careful to give his own evidence, and not **18.13** allow it to be distorted by lawyers or others.[78] Whilst an expert report may resemble a witness statement to some extent, there are specific rules as to the contents of the report. The report should be addressed to the court and not the party from whom the expert has received his instructions.[79] It should also comply with the protocol. The expert report must include a statement that the expert understands his duty to the court and he has complied with his duty and must also state the substance of all material instructions, on the basis of which the report was written.[80] With his report he should produce his curriculum vitae, which should give details of any employment or activity which raises a possible conflict of interest.[81]

It is important that the court should be informed of the matters of fact on **18.14** the basis of which the opinion is expressed.[82] The evidence should be intelligible. All too often reports are full of complex analyses and technical terms and are difficult to follow. It is also important to separate and identify the relevant opinion of the expert and the material on which the opinion is based.[83] The report should make it clear whether any question or issue falls outside the experts expertise or his conclusions are based on inadequate evidence.[84] The parties and expert should take care to ensure that the expert is provided with all the relevant material before he finalises his report. Thus in care proceedings, the experts should be provided with any relevant photographs before they issue their reports.[85] In addition disclosure should be provided of any relevant literature relied upon by an expert.[86] In the Commercial Court, it is specifically provided that unless they have already been provided on inspection of documents at the stage of disclosure, copies of any photographs, plans, analyses, measurements, survey reports or other similar documents relied on by an expert witness as well as copies of any unpublished sources must be provided to all parties at the same time as his

---

[78] *Whitehouse v Jordan* [1981] 1 W.L.R. 245 at 256.

[79] CPR, Pt 35, Practice Direction, para.2.1.

[80] CPR, r.35.10; CPR, Pt 35, Practice Direction—Experts and Assessors, para.2.2; *Admiralty and Commercial Court Guide* (7th edn, 2006), para.H2.6, App.11.

[81] *Toth v Jarman* [2006] EWCA Civ 1028, [2006] 4 All E.R. 1276, *The Times*, August 17, 2006, CA.

[82] *Admiralty and Commercial Courts Guide* (7th edn, 2006), para.H2.6; *Makita (Aust) Pty Ltd v Sprowles* (2001) 52 N.S.W.L.R. 705; *Re Doran Constructions* [2002] N.S.W.S.C. 215, (2002) 194 A.L.R. 101, Sup.Ct. N.S.W.; *ASIC v Rich* [2005] N.S.W.C.A. 152, (2005) 218 A.L.R. 764.

[83] *Evans Deakin Pty Ltd v Sebel Furniture Ltd* [2003] F.C.A. 171 at [668–680], Fed.Ct. Aus.

[84] CPR, Pt 35, Practice Direction, para.1.5; *Anglo Group Plc v Winther Browne and Co. Ltd* [2000] 1 W.L.R. 820; *Queen's Bench Guide*, para.7.9.2; *Chancery Guide* (5th edn, 2005), para.4.9.

[85] *Re T (Children) (Sexual Abuse: standard of proof)* [2004] EWCA Civ 558, *The Independent*, May 27, 2004.

[86] *Breeze v Ahmad* [2005] EWCA Civ 223; *Wardlaw v Farrar* [2004] Lloyd's Rep. Med. 98 at [23]; *DN v London Borough of Greenwich* [2005] EWCA Civ 1659.

report.[87] A party may inspect a document mentioned in an expert's report.[88] An experts report which is intended to be adduced into evidence should contain a statement of truth.[89] Any material change of view by an expert should be communicated in writing (through legal representatives) to the other parties without delay, and when appropriate to the court.[90]

18.15   The court may debar an expert from giving evidence if he fails to comply with Pt 35 or the relevant practice direction and Protocol.[91] Irrelevant expert evidence may be excluded and the expert may be the subject of judicial criticism for inappropriate expert evidence.[92] An expert who fails to comply with the CPR or court order or causes excessive delay, may find the party who instructed him penalised in costs and even his evidence excluded.[93] An expert witness who by his evidence in a civil case causes significant costs to be incurred through his evidence given in breach of his duties to the court, may be personally liable for costs.[94] Whilst he may not be sued in respect of any evidence he gives in court,[95] this does not mean he cannot be prosecuted for perjury if he gives untruthful evidence. Proceedings for contempt of court may be brought against a person if he makes, or causes to be made, without an honest belief in its truth, a false statement in an expert's report verified by a statement of truth.[96] He may also be subject to disciplinary proceedings before his own professional body.[97]

---

[87] *Admiralty and Commercial Courts Guide* (7th edn, 2006), para.H2.20.
[88] CPR, r.31.14(e) (subject to CPR, r.35.10(4)); *Admiralty and Commercial Courts Guide* (7th edn, 2006), para.H2.21; see Ch.9, paras 9.04–9.10, above.
[89] CPR, Pt 35, Practice Direction, paras 2.3–2.5.
[90] *Chancery Guide* (5th edn, 2005), para.4.9; CPR, Pt 35, Practice Direction, para.1.6.
[91] *Stevens v Gullis* [2000] 1 All E.R. 527, CA; see also *Baron v Lovell* [2000] P.I.Q.R. 20, CA (defendant debarred from calling medical expert where CCR automatic directions not complied with and report served four months after receipt).
[92] *Pozzolanic Lytag Ltc v Bryan Hobson Associates* [1999] B.L.R. 267 at 274–275 (criticism of inappropriate expert evidence); *McNeil v Commissioner of Taxation* [2003] F.C.A. 985, (2003) 202 A.L.R. 35, Fed. Ct. Aus. (exclusion of expert evidence as irrelevant).
[93] Protocol, para.4.7; *Balmoral Group Ltd v Borealis (UK) Ltd* [2006] EWHC 2531 (Comm)—indemnity costs awarded against party whose experts evidence was seriously deficient.
[94] *Phillips v Symes (A Bankrupt)* [2004] EWHC 2330 (Ch.), *The Times*, November 5, 2004.
[95] *X (Minors) v Bedfordshire County Council* [1995] 2 A.C. 633, HL.
[96] CPR, Pt 35, Practice Direction, para.2.5; *Admiralty and Commercial Courts Guide* (6th edn, 2002), para.H2.8; CPR, r.32.14.
[97] *General Medical Council v Meadow* [2006] EWCA Civ 1390, [2007] 1 All E.R. 1 (disciplinary proceedings not limited even where a judge has not referred an expert's conduct to his regulatory body for investigation); *Pearce v Ove Arup Partnership Ltd (Copying)* (2002) 25(2) I.P.D. 25011 (judge may refer to expert's conduct to his professional body); *Hussein v William Hill Group* [2004] EWHC 208 (Q.B.) (reference of General Medical Council).

F. PRIVILEGE

As with witness statements, the purpose of Pt 35 is not to destroy **18.16** litigation privilege generally in the preparation of material for trial,[98] but to advance the point at which a party must decide whether or not to give up that privilege: he must serve a report of the expert's evidence if he wishes to call him at trial.[99] Unlike a witness statement, however, the service of an expert's report, whilst it means that privilege goes, does not cause an obligation to arise to keep the contents confidential until trial.[100] Nor is there any property in an expert witness and he can be made the subject of a witness summons served by the other side to appear at trial if he is not called by his own client.[101] However it is inappropriate to use a witness summons and seek to compel an expert who had been instructed by another party but not called, into giving his opinion which had been based on privileged material provided to the expert in privileged circumstances.[102] An expert's report must state the substance of all material instructions, whether written or oral, on the basis of which the report was written.[103] Once an expert report has been served then privilege in the instructions given to that expert is in effect waived by virtue of CPR, r.35.10.[104] But, although such instructions are not privileged against disclosure, the court will not, in relation to those instructions order disclosure of any specific document or permit any questioning in court, other than by the party who instructed the expert, unless it is satisfied that there are reasonable grounds to consider that the statement of instructions given in the report is inaccurate or incomplete.[105] The material supplied by the instructing party to the expert as the basis on which the expert is asked to advise should be considered as part of the instructions.[106] It should be noted that the reference in CPR, r.35.10 is an actual expert's report, and hence does not override privilege in any earlier draft reports that there may be.[107] In some jurisdictions, in

---

[98] See, *Worral v Reich* [1954] 1 Q.B. 296.
[99] *Derby & Co. Ltd v Weldon, The Times*, November 9, 1990, CA; CPR, r.35.13.
[100] *Prudential Assurance Co. Ltd v Fountain Page Ltd* [1991] 1 W.L.R. 756.
[101] *Harmony Shipping Co. S.A. v Saudi Europe Line Ltd* [1979] 1 W.L.R. 1380, CA; *cf. Shaw v Skeet* [1996] 7 Med.L.R. 371; see also *Connolly v Dale* [1996] Q.B. 120, CA; and *Brown v Bennett, The Times*, November 2, 2000 (witness summons directed to own unwilling expert—unpaid—discharged).
[102] *R. v Davies* [2002] EWCA Crim. 85 at [28], *The Times*, March 4, 2002, CA.
[103] CPR, r.35.10(3).
[104] This rule, in abrogating privilege for instructions to an expert, is probably not *ultra vires* the Rules Committee (*cf.* r.48.7(3), and *General Mediterranean Holdings S.A. v Patel* [1999] 3 All E.R. 673), because under normal circumstances no party is *obliged* to adduce expert evidence and hence doing so pursuant to CPR, Pt 35, can be treated as a waiver of privilege in those instructions.
[105] CPR, r.35.10(4); CPR, Pt 35, Practice Direction—Experts and Assessors, para.4; *Salt v Consignia* [2002] C.L.Y. 420.
[106] *Lucas v Barking, Havering & Redbridge Hospitals NHS Trust* [2003] EWCA Civ 1102, [2004] 1 W.L.R. 220, CA.
[107] *Jackson v Marley Davenport Ltd* [2004] EWCA Civ 1225, [2004] 1 W.L.R. 2926, CA.

certain circumstances, experts reports may not be privileged in the first place.[108] An expert retained by a party may be liable for breach of confidence if he sends a copy of his report to a third party without the consent of his client.[109]

G. QUESTIONS FOR EXPERT

18.17   Once a report has been served, a party may put to an expert instructed by another party or the single joint expert written questions about his report. Such written questions may be put once only and within 28 days of the service of the expert's report and must be for the purpose only of clarification of the report, unless the court gives permission or the other party agrees an expert's answers to questions put are treated as part of the expert's report. Where a party has put a written question in accordance with the rules and the expert does not answer the question, the court may direct that the party who instructed the expert may not rely on the evidence of that expert or that the party may not recover the fees and expenses of that expert from any other party.[110] Not all experts reports are appropriate for questions[111] and questions should not relate to matters falling outside the scope of the report.[112] The court will be astute to ensure that the questions are not oppressive and are properly limited to seeking clarification of an expert's report. The expert's answers to questions may be adduced in evidence at trial.[113]

H. REQUEST FOR INFORMATION

18.18   Where a party has access to information which is not reasonably available to the other party, the court may direct the party who has access to the information to prepare and file a document recording the information and serve a copy of that document on the other party.[114] This provision may be particularly useful where the information is only reasonably available to one party, such as where it would be prohibitively expensive for the other party

---

[108] *Morrissey v Morrissey* (2000) 196 D.L.R. (4th) 94, Newfoundland (CA) (privilege in medical report overriden by r.34.04(2) of the Rules of the Supreme Court and litigation privilege had to give way to the importance of the facts being available).

[109] *De Taranto v Cornelius* [2002] E.M.L.R. 6, CA.

[110] CPR, r.35.6; CPR, Pt 35, Practice Direction—Experts and Assessors, para.5; Protocol, para.16; *Queen's Bench* Guide, para.7.9.9; *Chancery Guide*, (5th edn, 2005) para.4.18; *Admiralty and Commercial Courts Guide* (7th edn, 2006), para.H2.19.

[111] *MMR and MR Vaccine Litigation (No.4)* [2002] EWHC 1213 (Q.B.) (not suitable for report for interim hearing and not trial).

[112] *Mutch v Allen* [2001] 2 C.P.L.R. 200, CA.

[113] *Mutch v Allen* [2001] 2 C.P.L.R. 200, CA.

[114] CPR, r.35.9; CPR, Pt 35, Practice Direction—Experts and Assessors, para.3; Protocol, para.12.

to obtain the information himself. Documents referred to in an expert report should be made available for inspection by the other parties and in default an application may be made to the court.[115]

I. MEETINGS OF EXPERTS

Prior to trial, the Rules and Practice Directions encourage discussions and meetings between experts so as to limit the issues and reduce the necessity for oral evidence at trial. Meetings between experts pursuant to CPR, r.35.12, in the absence of the parties does not infringe Art.6 of the ECHR.[116] The court will usually direct that following a discussion between the experts they must prepare a statement for the court showing those issues on which they agree and those issues on which they disagree and a summary of their reasons for disagreeing.[117] The meetings are generally without prejudice. In most circumstances, once a joint statement has been agreed that statement is not without prejudice even where the court ordered one to be prepared with a potential mediation in mind.[118] In most cases a joint statement is not prepared until after experts' reports have been exchanged, although in the Technology and Construction Court experts sometimes draw up a joint statement at an earlier stage. There are dangers inherent in producing a joint statement prior to exchange of experts' reports. The danger is that one expert might express agreement with the other expert which, on taking full instructions from the client and after production of his report, the expert might wish to reside from.[119] In a rare case a party may be allowed to call a new expert, if his original expert has changed his views after the meeting of experts.[120]

18.19

J. EXPERT'S REQUEST FOR DIRECTIONS

An expert may file with the court a written request for directions to assist him in carrying out his function as an expert, but (unless the court orders otherwise) at least seven days before he does so he should provide a copy of his proposed request to the party instructing him and at least four days

18.20

---

[115] CPR, r.31.14(e); see para.18.14, above; cf. *Clough v Tameside and Glossop Health Authority* [1998] 2 All E.R. 971.

[116] *Hubbard v Lambeth, Southwark and Lewisham Health Authority, The Times,* October 8, 2001, CA.

[117] CPR, r.35.12; Protocol, para.18; *Technology and Construction Court Guide* (2nd edn, 2005), para.13.5–6. *Queen's Bench Guide,* para.7.9.8; *Admiralty and Commercial Courts Guide* (7th edn, 2006), paras H2.12–18; *Chancery Guide* (5th edn, 2005), para.4.15.

[118] *Aird v Prime Meridian Ltd* [2006] EWHC 2338 (TCC) (unusually statement found to be privileged).

[119] *Aird v Prime Meridian Ltd* [2006] EWCA Civ 1866 at [38] *The Times,* February 14, 2007, CA.

[120] *Stallwood v David* [2006] EWHC 2600 (Q.B.), [2007] 1 All E.R. 206.

before he does so he should provide a copy of his proposed request to all other parties.[121] The expert should guard against accidentally informing the court about, or about matters connected with, communications or potential communications between the parties that are without prejudice or privileged.[122] When giving directions the court may also direct the party be served with a copy of the directions and a copy of the request for directions.[123] This rule emphasises that the expert's duty is to the court. It enables the expert to obtain guidance as to his duties and the extent and nature of his evidence.

K. PROCEDURE AT TRIAL

18.21   Where a party has served an expert report, the party may call the expert and the report may be put in evidence as the expert's evidence in chief. A witness statement which stands as evidence in chief is open to inspection, unless the court orders otherwise.[124] In cases on the Fast Track, the expert may only give evidence at trial in respect of his report unless the court gives permission.[125] In practice the court usually takes all the experts together, after all the factual evidence has been given.[126] Before calling the expert, it is important to ensure that he is aware of new developments and all fresh material that may have an impact on his opinion.[127] Where a party has disclosed an expert's report, any party may use that expert's report as evidence at trial.[128] Where a party has consented to a medical examination by the other side's expert, he cannot prevent the other side from receiving and deploying the resultant expert report.[129] In most cases where there is a single joint expert's report, supplemented by written answers to questions from the parties, it is not necessary for the expert to be called.[130]

18.22   It is open to the judge at trial to shut out expert evidence, even where permission had been given to call such evidence.[131] What weight is given to

---

[121] CPR, r.35.14(1)–(2); Protocol, para.11; *Admiralty and Commercial Courts Guide* (7th edn, 2006), para.H2.10; *Chancery Guide* (5th edn, 2005), para.4.19.

[122] *Queen's Bench Guide*, para.7.9.10; *Chancery Guide* (5th edn, 2005), para.4.19.

[123] CPR, r.35.14.

[124] CPR, r.32.13.

[125] CPR, r.35.5(2).

[126] *Alpine Zurich Insurance v Bain Clarkson, The Times*, January 23, 1989; *Admiralty and Commercial Courts Guide* (7th edn, 2006), para.H2.22.

[127] *Re G (Minors) (Care Proceedings: wasted costs)* [2002] Fam.104; *Re T (Children) (Sexual abuse: standard of proof)* [2004] EWCA Civ 558, *The Independent*, May 27, 2004.

[128] CPR, r.35.11; *Gurny Consulting Engineers v Gleeds* [2006] EWHC 43 (TCC).

[129] *Kapadia v Lambeth London Borough Council, The Times*, July 4, 2000, CA.

[130] *Technology and Construction Court Guide* (2nd edn, 2005), para.13.4.7; Protocol, para.17.15.

[131] *National Bank of Egypt International Ltd v Oman Housing Bank SAOC* [2002] EWHC 1760 (Comm)—expert evidence on foreign law excluded as there was court authority directly in point, applying principles in *MCC Proceeds Inc v Bishopsgate Investments Trust Plc (No.4)* [1999] C.L.C. 418, CA.

expert evidence is generally a matter for the trial judge and depends on all the circumstances. Thus it is not necessarily the case that the evidence of the expert will be accepted at trial in preference to that of lay witnesses.[132] On appeal the appellate court should be very slow to interfere with a trial judge's views on the quality of the expert witnesses he has heard.[133] But there are cases where the Court of Appeal has overturned a trial judge's treatment of expert evidence. Thus in one case it was held that where medical reports had been filed, it was inappropriate to have dismissed an action on a no case to answer submission without hearing the experts who had expressed conflicting views in their reports.[134] In another case a judge was held to be wrong in rejecting the uncontested evidence of three expert witnesses on an application for a care order.[135] A judge should give reasons for preferring the evidence of one expert over another.[136]

L. ASSESSORS

In addition or in substitution of experts, it should be noted that the court has the power to appoint an assessor to assist it in dealing with matters in which the assessor has skill and experience. The court may direct the assessor to prepare a report and to attend the trial to advise the court on any matter. If the assessor prepares a report for the court before the trial the court will send a copy to each of the parties and the parties may use it at trial.[137] The court may appoint assessors to assist it in fixing the remuneration of provisional liquidators under s.70 of the Supreme Court Act 1981 and CPR, r.35.15.[138] In patent cases and appeals the court may appoint a scientific advisor, whose position is governed by CPR, r.35.15.[139] However

18.23

---

[132] *Armstrong & Connor v First York* [2005] EWCA Civ 277; *Fuller v Strum* [2002] 1 W.L.R. 1097 Ch.D., [2002] 2 All E.R. 87 at [23], CA (evidence of lay witness as to handwriting preferred to that of expert); *c.f. Re B (A Child)* [2000] 1 W.L.R. 790, CA (refusal to accept evidence of two lay witnesses in preference to uncontroverted expert medical evidence); *Coopers Payen Ltd v Southampton Container Terminal Ltd* [2003] EWCA Civ 1223 (where witness of fact evidence contradicted by single joint expert, it would be unusual to disregard the expert's evidence).

[133] *Wardlow v Farrar* [2003] EWCA Civ 1719, [2003] 4 All E.R. 1358, applying *Wilsher v Essex Area Health Authority* [1988] A.C. 1074 at 1091.

[134] *Yousif v Jordan* [2003] EWCA Civ 1852, *The Times*, January 22, 2004, CA.

[135] *Re M (Child: residence), The Times*, July 24, 2002.

[136] *Flannery v Halifax Estate Agencies* [2000] 1 W.L.R. 377; *Temple v South Manchester Health Authority* [2002] EWCA Civ 1406.

[137] CPR, r.35.15; CPR, Pt 35, Practice Direction—Experts and Assessors, para.7; *Queen's Bench Guide*, para.7.9.11; *Admiralty and Commercial Courts Guide* (7th edn, 2006), para.N14; CPR, r.61.13 (admiralty claims); *Chancery Guide* (5th edn, 2005), para.4.20.

[138] *In re Independent Insurance Company Ltd* [2002] EWHC 1577 (Ch.).

[139] *Halliburton Energy Services Inc v Smith International (North Sea) Ltd* [2006] EWCA Civ 1599.

CPR, r.35.15 does not apply to assessors appointed by virtue of s.67(4) of the Race Relations Act 1976.[140]

18.24 In the Admiralty jurisdiction the use of assessors is commonplace. They do not actually decide any issue. Instead they assist or advise the judge so as to enable the judge to reach a conclusion.[141] Fairness requires that where in an admiralty claim a judge seeks advice from nautical assessors, their advice should be disclosed to the parties counsel so as to afford them the opportunity of making representations as to whether the judge should accept the advice.[142]

18.25 The use that a judge makes of assessors is very much within his discretion. It will depend upon the type of case. It will depend on how far assessors are fulfilling an evidential role and how far they are simply assisting in the decision making process. A judge should have in mind what fairness to the parties requires.[143] When advising tribunals on issues of fact, experts and assessors should do so openly and in the presence of the parties who should have an opportunity to make submissions before the tribunal makes its decision.[144]

18.26 Where assessors are used, this may affect the extent and need for expert evidence. In the Admiralty Court it is well established that when the court is assisted by nautical assessors, expert evidence on matters of navigation and seamanship may not be adduced. This rule is subject to variation and exception in appropriate cases.[145] In patent cases, where a scientific advisor is appointed, the parties are entitled to call expert evidence.[146]

---

[140] *Ahmed v Governing Body of the University of Oxford* [2002] EWCA Civ 1907, [2003] 1 W.L.R. 995, CA.

[141] *The Aid* [1881] P.D. 84.

[142] *Owners of Bow Spring v Owners of Manzanillo II* [2004] EWCA Civ 1007, [2005] 1 W.L.R. 144, disapproving a dictum in *The Hannibal* (1867) L.R. 2 Ad. & E. 53 at 56, in light of Art.6 of ECHR. As to the procedure to be followed in relation to permitting the parties to comment on advice provided by nautical assessors, see *Global Mariner (Owner) v Atlantic Crusader (Owners)* [2005] EWHC 380 at [14] (Admiralty), [2005] 1 Lloyd's Rep. 699.

[143] *Owners of Bow Spring v Owners of Manzanillo II* [2004] EWCA Civ 1007, [2005] 1 W.L.R. 144, CA.

[144] *Watson v General Medical Council* [2005] EWHC 1896 (Admin), [2005] Lloyd's Rep. Med. 435, Q.B.

[145] *The Victory* [1996] 2 Lloyd's Rep. 482 at 492; *Eleftheria (Owners) v Hakki Deval (Owners)* [2006] EWHC 2809 (Comm.) at [12–21]; CPR, r.61.13; *Admiralty and Commercial Courts Guide* (7th edn, 2006), para.N14.1.

[146] *Halliburton Energy Services Inc. v Smith International* [2006] EWCA Civ 1599, at [20].

CHAPTER 19

Real evidence

CHAPTER 19

Disclosure of real evidence

INTRODUCTION

This chapter is concerned with the various ways in which information can **19.01** be obtained by a litigant about things in an opponent's or a third party's hands or about other people themselves, by inspection, examination or experiment, so as to produce direct, or "real", evidence. There are four main topics to cover:

    (a) inspection of property (immovable and movable);
    (b) sampling of property and the conducting of experiments;
    (c) physical or medical examinations of persons; and
    (d) plans, photographs and models.

Each will be dealt with in turn.

A. INSPECTION OF PROPERTY

Before substantive proceedings commenced

The court has power[1] to make an order providing for, *inter alia*, the **19.02** inspection and photographing of "property which appears to the court to be property which may become the subject-matter of subsequent proceedings in the [court], or as to which any question may arise in any such proceedings." The "subsequent proceedings" may be of any nature, except that the Crown is only bound by such an order if those proceedings will involve a

---

[1] Supreme Court Act 1981, s.33(1) (High Court); County Courts Act 1984, s.52(1) (county court); CPR, r.25.1(1)(i).

claim in respect of personal injuries to a person or in respect of a person's death.[2] Subject to the exception for the Crown, the jurisdiction has always been much wider than the equivalent pre-action *documentary* disclosure power,[3] discussed elsewhere,[4] although since 1998 the latter has become available in all kinds of action.[5] A written instrument or other object carrying information (e.g. a photograph, tape recording or computer disk) can be both "property" for the purposes of the one power and a "document" for the purposes of the other. Which it is in a particular case depends on whether the legal proceedings are concerned with the medium[6] (when it is "property") or the message[7] (when it is a "document"). If it is the latter, the court has no jurisdiction under the present power.[8]

19.03   An application under this provision is made by ordinary application, as if in an existing action,[9] supported, unless the court otherwise orders, by evidence[10] (a copy of which is filed with the court and served on the person against whom the order is sought together with the claim form[11]) showing that it is property which is or may become the subject-matter of subsequent proceedings or is relevant to the issues that will arise in relation to such proceedings, if practicable by reference to the statement of case or intended statement of case.[12] Formerly the rules expressly provided that any order made under these provisions might be conditional upon security being given for costs, or any other terms.[13] That has now gone, although the court under the CPR has the power to make any order subject to conditions,[14] and there is specific power to require security for costs.[15] Under the old rules, no order could be made if the court would refuse an application for inspection in the substantive proceedings themselves on the ground that "a secret

---

[2] Supreme Court Act 1981, s.35(4) (High Court); County Courts Act 1984, s.54(4) (county court). As to these expressions, see Ch.2, para.2.27, above.

[3] Supreme Court Act 1981, s.33(2) (High Court); County Courts Act 1984, s.52(2) (county court).

[4] See Ch.3, paras 3.28–3.39, above.

[5] See Ch.3, para.3.26, above.

[6] e.g. *Re Saxton* [1962] 1 W.L.R. 859 (alleged forged agreement), varied [1962] 1 W.L.R. 968; *Vowell v Shire of Hastings* [1970] V.R. 764; *Snow v Hawthorn* [1969] N.Z.L.R. 776; *cf. Nicholls v McLevy* (1971) 1 S.A.S.R. 442; *Athlete's Foot Australia Pty Ltd v Divergent Technologies Pty Ltd* (1997) 78 F.C.R. 283, Fed.Ct.Aus.

[7] e.g. *Huddleston v Control Risks Information Services Ltd* [1987] 1 W.L.R. 701 (alleged defamation).

[8] *Taylor v Anderton, The Times*, October 21, 1986; *Huddleston v Control Risks Information Services Ltd* [1987] 1 W.L.R. 701; *cf. Dun & Bradstreet Ltd v Typesetting Facilities Ltd* [1992] F.S.R. 320 at 322–323.

[9] CPR, r.25.4(2); under the old rules it had to be made by originating summons in the High Court (RSC, Ord.24 r.7A(1), or originating application in the county court (C.C.R., Ord.13, r.7(3)).

[10] CPR, r.25.3(2).

[11] CPR, r.25.5(3)(a).

[12] CPR, r.25.5(2).

[13] RSC, Ord.24, r.7A(5).

[14] CPR, r.3.1(3).

[15] CPR, rr.25.12–15.

process, discovery or invention not in issue in the proceedings" would thereby be disclosed.[16] The CPR contain no similar provision. A person against whom an order is sought is entitled to his costs of the application and of complying with any order made on that application, subject to the power of the court to make a different order having regard to all the circumstances.[17]

In addition to the specific power under the Rules, the court also has an **19.04** inherent power to order inspection and similar treatment of property before substantive proceedings are commenced under the search order (*Anton Piller*) jurisdiction, which has already been discussed in the context of documentary disclosure.[18] This jurisdiction is *in personam*, i.e. it involves an order addressed to a particular defendant that he permit the inspection required, and accordingly the court may make an order in respect of movable or immovable property outside the jurisdiction as well as inside. But it is essential, in a case involving property outside the jurisdiction, that the defendant be personally subject to the court's jurisdiction, for example, because he can be served here or because he has submitted to it.[19] The fact that the court gives leave to serve proceedings out of jurisdiction[20] is not enough, at least until an application has been made to set aside service.[21] If he is not so subject then the court cannot make the order.[22] "Interim relief" may be granted by the High Court in aid of proceedings within the scope of the Brussels Convention 1968 or the Lugano Convention 1988, commenced or to be commenced in a jurisdiction (not being England and Wales) covered by either of those Conventions, even though the High Court would otherwise have no jurisdiction.[23] It might be thought that search (*Anton Piller*) orders are excluded from the scope of this power, as constituting "provision for obtaining evidence."[24] But cases decided in the context of *Norwich Pharmacal* and similar orders suggest otherwise.[25] Although an order that a defendant disclose or deliver up property or documents to the claimant is subject to the defendant's privilege against self-incrimination[26] (in cases where statute has not removed such privilege[27]), it has been held that an order that the plaintiff be permitted to enter the defendant's premises and take note of what he may observe without the defendant's further assistance

---

[16] RSC, Ord.29, r.7A(6).
[17] CPR, rr.48.1(2), (3).
[18] See Ch.2, paras 2.20–2.28, above.
[19] *Cook Industries Inc. v Galliher* [1979] Ch. 439.
[20] Under CPR, Pt 6, s.III (formerly RSC, Ord.11).
[21] *Altertext Inc. v Advanced Data Communications Ltd* [1985] 1 W.L.R. 457.
[22] *Altertext Inc. v Advanced Data Communications Ltd* [1985] 1 W.L.R. 457; see also *Protector Alarms v Maxim Alarms* [1978] F.S.R. 442.
[23] Civil Jurisdiction and Judgments Act 1982, s.25 (as amended).
[24] *ibid.*, s.25(7)(b).
[25] See Ch.4, para.4.8, and cases there cited.
[26] See Ch.2, paras 2.23–2.28 above, and Ch.11, paras 11.104—11.120, above.
[27] See Ch.11, paras 11.103—11.117, above.

is not inconsistent with the privilege,[28] although this seems contrary to principle.

19.05   Finally, although it may be an unusual use of language to describe it as "inspection of property," it should be noted that generally certain persons have the right to be represented at the post-mortem examination of a deceased person directed by a coroner.[29]

After substantive proceedings commenced

19.06   Once substantive proceedings have been started, the scope for inspection of property is widened. First of all, the search order (*Anton Piller*) jurisdiction already referred to continues to be available.[30] Secondly, the court has power under the CPR to order the inspection of property the subject of a claim or as to which any question may arise on a claim,[31] and may for this purpose authorise any person to "enter any land or building" in the possession of a party to the proceedings.[32] Unlike a search (*Anton Piller*) order,[33] this appears to be a kind of "search warrant," and the inspecting party would seem (in theory) to have a right to force his way on to the land in question,[34] a conclusion reinforced by the fact that only a judge may grant such an authorisation.[35] An application for such an order is made by ordinary application in the action,[36] and must be supported by evidence, unless the court otherwise orders.[37] Normally the application will be on notice (formerly *inter partes*), but the court has power to grant relief on an application without notice (formerly *ex parte*) if it appears to the court that there are good reasons for not giving notice.[38] In the latter case, the evidence must say why notice has not been given.[39] A claimant may apply for an order at any time, including before proceedings have been started, and after judgment has been given.[40] (If proceedings have not yet been started, the court may only grant the relief sought if the matter is urgent or it is

---

[28] *Twentieth Century Film Corp. v Tryrare Ltd* [1991] F.S.R. 58; see Ch.2, para.2.24, above.

[29] Coroners Rules 1984, r.7(3); see *Jervis on Coroners*, 11th edn, 1993, paras 6.41–42.

[30] See para.19.04, above.

[31] CPR, r.25.1(1)(c)(ii), (2); formerly RSC, Ord.29, r.2(1), under which rule "inspection" included photography: *Lewis v Earl Londesborough* [1893] 2 Q.B. 191.

[32] CPR, r.25.1(1)(d), formerly RSC, Ord.29, r.2(2); no doubt the court would provide in its order for appropriate safeguards, as in exercising the search (*Anton Piller*) jurisdiction.

[33] See, *Z Ltd v A* [1982] Q.B. 558, CA.

[34] *cf. East India Company v Kynaston* (1821) 3 Bligh 153 at 163.

[35] CPR, Pt 2, Practice Direction—Allocation of Cases to Levels of Judiciary, para.2.1.

[36] See CPR, Pt 23.

[37] CPR, r.25.3(2).

[38] CPR, r.25.3(1).

[39] CPR, r.25.3(3).

[40] CPR, r.25.2(1); see *Unilever Plc v Pearce* [1985] F.S.R. 475 at 478; *cf. Smith-Myers Communications v Motorola Ltd* [1991] F.S.R. 262.

otherwise desirable to do so in the interests of justice.[41]) But, unless the court otherwise orders, a defendant may not apply before he files an acknowledgement of service or a defence in the proceedings.[42] Such an order may be made subject to conditions,[43] and there is specific power to require security for costs.[44] Information obtained upon an inspection ordered under the old rules was subject to the implied undertaking as to collateral use,[45] and there is nothing in the CPR to suggest otherwise for an inspection under the new ones.[46]

For the purposes of the former rule, "property" included any physical matter bona fide the subject-matter of the proceedings,[47] even a document if, for example, its authenticity (rather than its message[48]) was in question,[49] but did not include a manufacturing process.[50] However, an order might be made that facilities be provided for the making of a video film of an industrial process, in an appropriate case.[51] Under the RSC, an order could not be made under the former rule[52] for the inspection of property where the person having possession of that property was not a party.[53] Moreover, it was not proper to join that person to the proceedings solely for the purpose of facilitating such an order,[54] unless he fell within the *Norwich Pharmacal* exception.[55] The new rule refers simply to "relevant property", defined as that "which is the subject of a claim or as to which any question may arise on a claim",[56] and this may not necessarily be in the possession of a party. It is not clear from this wording whether the court is to have power under this rule to order inspection in such a case.[57] However, given the existence of the separate statutory jurisdiction to order disclosure and inspection of property against a non-party,[58] it is likely that the present rule is intended to be restricted to the case where the property concerned is indeed in the party's possession.

19.07

---

[41] CPR, r.25.2(2)(b).
[42] CPR, r.25.2(2)(c), formerly RSC, Ord.29, r.7(4).
[43] CPR, r.3.1(3)(a).
[44] CPR, rr.25.12–15.
[45] *Grapha Holding A.G. v Quebecor Printing (UK) Plc* [1996] F.S.R. 711; see Ch.15, para.15.11, above.
[46] *cf.* CPR, r.31.22, applying only to documents.
[47] *Scott v Mercantile Accident Insurance Co.* (1892) 8 T.L.R. 320.
[48] *cf. Huddleston v Control Risks Iformation Services Ltd* [1987] 1 W.L.R. 701.
[49] *Re Saxton* [1962] 1 W.L.R. 859.
[50] *Tudor Accumulator Co. Ltd v China Mutual Co.* [1931] W.N. 201, CA; *Unilever Plc v Pearce* [1985] F.S.R. 475.
[51] *Ash v Buxted Poultry Ltd, The Times,* November 29, 1989.
[52] i.e., RSC, Ord.29, r.2(2).
[53] *Reid v Powers* (1884) 28 S.J. 653; *Garrard v Edge* (1889) 37 W.R. 501.
[54] *Douiech v Findlay* [1990] 1 W.L.R. 269; *cf. Penfold v Pearlberg* [1955] 1 W.L.R. 1068.
[55] See Ch.3, paras 3.02–3.25, above.
[56] CPR, r.25.1(2).
[57] Note that r.25.1(1)(d), referring to property "in the possession of a party", is now separate from r.25.1(1)(c)(ii).
[58] See para.19.08, below.

19.08   In addition to the above powers to inspect the property of a party, the court also has statutory power to order the inspection of property neither belonging to nor in the possession of a party, but which is the subject-matter of the proceedings or as to which any question arises in the proceedings.[59] This is the counterpart of the jurisdiction, in an existing action, to order documentary disclosure from a third party, discussed elsewhere.[60] An application under this provision is made in the same way, and subject to the same rules, including as to terms of the order and costs, as an application for inspection before proceedings are commenced, previously discussed.[61] In addition to the person against whom the order is sought, an application under this provision must be served on every party to the proceedings other than the applicant.[62]

Admiralty proceedings

19.09   In Admiralty proceedings there was formerly an additional power to order inspection of property. Under an earlier version of the CPR,[63] replacing even older rules under the RSC,[64] the Admiralty Court[65] might, on the application of any interested persons or on its own initiative, make an order for the inspection by any person of any ship or other property, whether real or personal, the inspection of which might be necessary or desirable for the purpose of obtaining full information or evidence in connection with any issue in a claim or proposed claim whether *in rem* or *in personam*.[66] It was held under the RSC that an order would not be made when the facts required might be proved by evidence in the ordinary way.[67] In modern times such orders were commonly made, although the applicant was required to give an undertaking in damages against any loss suffered as a result of the order.[68] It was held under the RSC that the order was not an injunction however and hence might be made by the Admiralty Registrar or any Queen's Bench Division Master.[69] This seems also to have been the

---

[59] Supreme Court Act 1981, s.34(3); County Courts Act 1984, s.53(3); CPR, r.25.1(1)(j).
[60] See Ch.4, paras 4.48–3.60.
[61] See para.19.03, above.
[62] CPR, r.25.5(3)(b).
[63] CPR, Pt 49, Practice Direction—Admiralty, para.11.
[64] RSC, Ord.75, r.28.
[65] Then defined as the Admiralty Court of the High Court or any other court exercising Admiralty jurisdiction: see CPR, Pt 49, Practice Direction—Admiralty, para.1.4(a). See now CPR, r.61.1(2)(b), defining it as the Admiralty Court of the Queen's Bench Division of the High Court of Justice.
[66] For examples under the former rule, see *The Magnet* (1874) L.R. 4 A. & E. 417; *The Olympic and H.M.S. Hawke* [1913] P. 214; *The Cumberland Queen* (1921) 126 L.T. 679, CA.
[67] *The Victor Covacevich* (1885) 10 P.D. 40.
[68] *The Mare del Nord* [1990] 1 Lloyd's Rep. 40.
[69] *The Mare del Nord* [1990] 1 Lloyd's Rep. 40.

position under the CPR.[70] However, the latest version of the CPR relating to specialist Admiralty proceedings makes no equivalent provision.[71] Nonetheless, where those specialist rules are silent, the Commercial Court rules apply,[72] and those rules in turn refer on to the general rules of the CPR,[73] which do make provision for orders to be made for the inspection of property the subject of the claim.[74]

Patent cases

Although the general rule is that a process cannot be inspected,[75] there was formerly special provision made in patent proceedings in the High Court. On the summons for directions in such proceedings (but not before) the court had jurisdiction to order inspection of a manufacturing process[76] and even to order the reconstruction of a discontinued process to enable such inspection to be made.[77] The costs of such a reconstruction were usually left to the trial judge.[78] There is no similar provision expressly made under the CPR. However, the court has the general power to "take any other step or make any other order for the purpose of managing the case and furthering the overriding objective,"[79] and, since there is nothing in the CPR to forbid it,[80] if the court considered that it was appropriate to do so for case-management and to further the overriding objective, it could make a similar order under the new system. All Patents Court[81] business was formerly allocated to the multi-track,[82] and accordingly the court's direction for inspection would be made in accordance with the rules on multi-track case management.[83] But there is no longer an automatic allocation to the multi-track, because a "streamlined procedure" has been introduced in the Patents Courts, rather resembling the fast-track in ordinary litigation. This

19.10

---

[70] See CPR, r.2.4, and Pt 49, Practice Direction—Admiralty, para.16.3; *cf.* Pt 2, Practice Direction—Allocation of Cases to Levels of Judiciary, para.2.1.

[71] See now CPR, Pt 61 and Practice Direction; see also *The Admiralty and Commercial Courts Guide*, 7th edn, 2006.

[72] CPR, r.61.1(3), referring to CPR, Pt 58.

[73] CPR, r.58.3.

[74] CPR, r.25.1(1)(c)(ii); para.19.06 above.

[75] See para.19.07, above.

[76] RSC, Ord.104, r.14(2)(h); *Unilever Plc v Pearce* [1985] F.S.R. 475 at 479.

[77] *British Xylonite Co. Ltd v Fibrenyle Ltd* [1959] R.P.C. 252, CA; *Dow Chemical Co. v Monsanto Chemicals Ltd* [1969] F.S.R. 504.

[78] *ibid.*

[79] CPR, r.3.1(2)(m).

[80] Cf. CPR, r.3.1(2), beginning: "Except where these Rules otherwise provide . . . "

[81] This expression includes the Patents Court of the High Court and any county court designated as a Patents County Court: see CPR, r.63.1(2)(g).

[82] Formerly CPR, Pt 49, Practice Direction—Patents Etc., para.2.4.

[83] i.e., CPR, Pt 29, and the Practice Direction.

"streamlined procedure", available on application, has no disclosure or experiments unless specifically ordered.[84]

19.11 Under the old system, caselaw established that an order for inspection would not be made in the absence of evidence going beyond a mere suspicion of infringement.[85] On the other hand, although it would normally be made as of course if the plaintiff could establish a prima facie case of infringement,[86] it was not necessary for the plaintiff to go that far[87]: the court had merely to be satisfied that there really was a genuine and substantial issue to be tried.[88] Although the wording of the equivalent rule in the Patents County Court[89] was not identical to that in the High Court, it was in substance the same, and it was considered that that court had similar power, in an appropriate case, on the application for directions to order inspection of a process.

Judicial inspection

19.12 Under the former rules, the judge by whom a matter was tried might inspect any place or thing with respect to which any question arose in the proceedings,[90] and if he did so in a case being tried with a jury he might authorise the jury to do so as well.[91] The CPR make no specific provision for judicial inspections, but, as mentioned already, the court has the general power to "take any other step or make any other order for the purpose of managing the case and furthering the overriding objective,"[92] and, since there is nothing in the CPR to forbid it,[93] if the court considered that it was appropriate to do so for case-management and to further the overriding objective, it could make a similar order under the new system. The judge's decision whether or not to inspect is a matter of judicial discretion, and he may decide to inspect even if the parties do not wish him to do so.[94] The power to inspect applies to land or other property outside the jurisdiction as well as within it.[95]

---

[84] *The Patents Court Guide*, November 2003, para.10.
[85] *Wahl v Buhler-Miag (England) Ltd* [1979] F.S.R. 183.
[86] *British Thomson-Houston Co. Ltd v Durham Ltd* (1920) 37 R.P.C. 121; *British Xylonite Co. Ltd v Fibrenyle Ltd* [1959] R.P.C. 252, at 258, 263, CA.
[87] *British Xylonite Co. Ltd v Fibrenyle Ltd* [1959] R.P.C. 252 at 261, 263, CA; *Unilever Plc v Pearce* [1985] F.S.R. 475.
[88] *Unilever Plc v Pearce* [1985] F.S.R. 475.
[89] CCR, Ord.48A, r.8(5)(h).
[90] RSC, Ord.35, r.8(1); CCR, Ord.21, r.6(1); as to the words "with respect to which any question arises", see *Tito v Waddell* [1975] 1 W.L.R. 1303; *Phipson on Evidence*, 16th edn, 2005, paras 1–19—1–24.
[91] RSC, Ord.35, r.8(2); CCR, Ord.21, r.6(2).
[92] CPR, r.3.1(2)(m).
[93] *cf.* CPR, r.3.1(2), beginning: "Except where these Rules otherwise provide".
[94] *Tito v Waddell* [1975] 1 W.L.R. 1303; in some kinds of case (e.g. Technology and Construction Court business) judicial views are common.
[95] *Tito v Waddell* [1975] 1 W.L.R. 1303.

The inspection is evidence in itself, which the judge may rely on even in **19.13** preference to that of other witnesses.[96] Thus an application to the judge that he should inspect is in effect an application to adduce evidence and, except in cases where it is clear that a view would be a waste of time and money, the court should incline in favour of the inspection.[97] The parties must be given an opportunity to be present at an inspection,[98] and normally they both will be. It is undesirable, though not improper, for the judge to make an inspection in the parties' absence, because unknown to him the position may have changed before trial.[99] Where in one case the judge visited the site and took notes, but lost them and revisited to make another, less extensive set, the question was not whether one of the parties had lost confidence in him, but whether a just result had been reached.[100]

B. SAMPLES AND EXPERIMENTS

Before substantive proceedings commenced

As with the inspection of property,[101] the court has power to make an **19.14** order providing for the taking of samples of, or the carrying out of any experiment on or with, any "property which may become the subject-matter of subsequent proceedings in the [court], or as to which any question may arise in any such proceedings."[102] Again, the "subsequent proceedings" may be of any nature, except where the Crown is concerned.[103] The practice and procedure in applying for such an order is identical to that already set out above in relation to orders for the inspection of property.[104] In addition to the statutory procedure, there seems no reason why the court should not be able, in the exercise of its inherent jurisdiction,[105] to make orders for samples to be taken or experiments made, in appropriate cases, by analogy with the search order (*Anton Piller*) jurisdiction.[106]

---

[96] *Buckingham v Daily News Ltd* [1956] 2 Q.B. 534; *Tameshwar v R.* [1957] A.C. 476.
[97] *Tito v Waddell* [1975] 1 W.L.R. 1303.
[98] *Goold v Evans & Co.* [1951] 2 T.L.R. 1189 at 1191.
[99] *Salsbury v Woodland* [1970] 1 Q.B. 324; *Parry v Boyle* (1986) 83 Cr.App.R. 310; *R. v Ely Justices, ex p. Burgess, The Times,* August 21, 1992, D.C.
[100] *Memarian v Ghanadian,* unreported, June 23, 2000, CA (no misconduct; appeal dismissed).
[101] See paras 19.02–19.05, above.
[102] Supreme Court Act 1981, s.33(1); County Courts Act 1984, s.52(1); CPR, r.25.1(1) (i).
[103] Supreme Court Act 1981, s.35(4); County Courts Act 1984, s.54(4); see Ch.2, para.19.02, above.
[104] See para.19.03, above.
[105] See, e.g. *S v S; W v Official Solicitor* [1972] A.C. 24 at 46–47.
[106] See Ch.2, paras 2.20–2.28 above, and para.19.04, above.

After substantive proceedings commenced

19.15 The inherent jurisdiction of the court aside,[107] the court has power to order the taking of a sample of,[108] or for the carrying out of an experiment on or with,[109] any property (including land) which is the subject of a claim or as to which any question may arise on a claim.[110] The court may for the purpose of enabling such an order to be carried out authorise "any person to enter upon any land or building in the possession of any party to the proceedings."[111] However, only a judge may grant such an authorisation.[112] The procedure on an application for an order under this rule is similar to that for an order for inspection of property.[113] It should be noted that there is no express requirement that the property be in the possession of a party to the proceedings, although, given the existence of the power to order the taking of samples and the carrying out of experiments with, the property of third parties, discussed below, this seems to be implied.[114]

19.16 Finally, there is also statutory power, for the court to order the taking of samples, and the carrying out of any experiment on or with property neither belonging to nor in the possession of a party, but which is the subject-matter of the proceedings or as to which any question arises in the proceedings.[115] Formerly this was restricted to cases involving claims in respect of personal injuries or death,[116] but since 1998 the power has extended to all kinds of proceedings.[117] The procedure for obtaining such an order[118] is the same as that for an order for inspection of third party property, already discussed.[119]

Patent cases

19.17 It is frequently necessary in patent cases for a party, in the absence of admissions from his opponent, to resort to experiments in order to provide evidence to support his case. But it is highly desirable that, before experi-

---

[107] See para.19.14, above.
[108] CPR, r.25.1(1)(c)(iii).
[109] CPR, r.25.1(1)(c)(iv).
[110] CPR, r.25.1(2), formerly RSC, Ord.29, r.3(1), CCR, Ord.13, r.7(1)(e).
[111] CPR, r.25.1(1)(d), formerly RSC, Ord.29, r.3(2).
[112] CPR, Pt 2, Practice Direction—Allocation of Cases to Levels of Judiciary, para.2.1.
[113] See para.19.06, above.
[114] And s.34(3)(b) of the Supreme Court Act 1981 seems to assume the existence of such a requirement.
[115] Supreme Court Act 1981, s.34(3); County Courts Act 1984, s.53(3); CPR, r.25.1(1)(j).
[116] As to these expressions, see Ch.3, para.3.28, above.
[117] See Ch.3, para.3.26, above.
[118] CPR, rr.25.2, 25.3, 25.5, formerly RSC, Ord.29, r.7A(2)–(6).
[119] See para.19.08, above.

ments are embarked upon by a party, he should seek admissions from the other side as to the facts which he would hope such experiments to establish.[120] This is particularly important if the experiments are to be conducted before the court gives directions.[121] There used to be a formal procedure for serving a notice to admit facts specifically for use in patent cases.[122] This has now gone. But, where the specialist rules are silent, the general rules of the CPR apply,[123] and of course these provide for the service of notices to admit facts in ordinary litigation.[124] In any event, it is usual to conduct experiments only after directions have been given, and hence the costs of experiments beforehand will normally be disallowed on detailed assessment (formerly taxation), unless they were needed for the adequate framing of the statements of case (pleadings).[125]

Under the former rules,[126] a notice of proposed experiments, stating the facts intended to be established, had to be served by the proposer of the experiments upon his opponent within 21 days after service of lists of documents.[127] Within 21 days after service of such notice, the summons for directions was taken out,[128] and the party upon whom an experiments notice had been served had to serve notice on the other party stating in respect of each fact intended to be so established whether or not he admitted it.[129] Unless all such facts were admitted, at the directions hearing the proposer of the experiments might seek directions in respect of the proposed experiments.[130] The position is different under the CPR. First of all, where any fact which a party desires to establish by experimental proof is not admitted, he must, at least 21 days before the service of the notice of his application for directions, or within such other time as the court may direct at a hearing for further directions,[131] serve on the other party a notice stating the facts which he desires to establish and giving full particulars of the experiments proposed to establish them.[132] The other party must, within 21 days after service of that notice, serve upon the other party a notice stating in respect of each fact whether or not he admits it.[133] If the fact is not

19.18

---

[120] *Monsanto Co. v Stauffer Chemical Co.* [1985] F.S.R. 55.

[121] *Monsanto Co. v Stauffer Chemical Co.* [1985] F.S.R. 55, where the court refused to vary an interlocutory injunction to permit experiments to take place before summons for directions.

[122] CPR, Pt 49, Practice Direction—Patents Etc., para.8, formerly RSC, Ord.104, r.10.

[123] CPR, r.63.2.

[124] CPR, r.32.18.

[125] *Re Nossen's Patent* [1969] 1 W.L.R. 638; see also *Pall Corp. v Commercial Hydraulics (Bedford) Ltd* [1990] F.S.R. 329.

[126] RSC, Ord.104, r.12(1).

[127] Under RSC, Ord.104, r.11.

[128] RSC, Ord.104, r.14(1).

[129] RSC, Ord.104, r.12(2).

[130] RSC, Ord.104, r.12(3).

[131] Pursuant to CPR, Pt 49, Practice Direction–Patents Etc., para.2.5(4).

[132] CPR, Pt 63, Practice Direction—Patents Etc., para.9.1.

[133] CPR, Pt 63, Practice Direction—Patents Etc., para.9.2.

admitted, the first party must apply to the court for directions in respect of the experiments.[134]

19.19 Under the old rules, the notice procedure was held to be mandatory, and failure to comply with its requirements meant that it would be unfair on the opposing party to admit in evidence experiments so conducted.[135] The current procedure under the CPR, where the overriding objective of dealing with cases justly, is less universally prescriptive, and admits of more exceptions. Nevertheless, the court will take into account the previous practice, including the following, even if it is not binding. An order for experiments ought to include a direction requiring the experimenting party to give full particulars of the facts which it was claimed would be established.[136] The costs of unnecessary experiments might subsequently be disallowed,[137] so these particulars served a useful purpose. If that party discovered that the experiment established other facts as well, an application to amend was to be received with judicial sympathy.[138] In appropriate circumstances, the form of order for experiments might be subsequently varied.[139] Sometimes it was appropriate for a party to repeat an experiment for the benefit of the other party, and the court might apply sanctions (e.g. striking out the notice of experiments) for a wrongful failure to repeat.[140] Application for an order for experiments might be made after the order on directions, but late applications which might result in further delay and expense were likely to be refused.[141] There was a difference of opinion as to whether the court should infer that a party who abandoned experiments did so because the results were helpful to his opponent.[142] The better view was that it should not.

C. MEDICAL EXAMINATIONS

19.20 The disclosure rules of some jurisdictions confer a general power upon the court to order a physical or mental examination of a person party to (or in the custody of a person party to) litigation, where the condition of that

---

[134] CPR, Pt 63, Practice Direction—Patents Etc., para.9.3.
[135] *Electrolux Northern Ltd v Black & Decker,* unreported, April 25, 1996, Laddie J.
[136] *C. Van der Lely v Watveare Overseas Ltd* [1982] F.S.R. 122.
[137] *Pall Corp. v Commercial Hydraulics (Bedford) Ltd* [1990] F.S.R. 329.
[138] *Pall Corp. v Commercial Hydraulics (Bedford) Ltd* [1990] F.S.R. 329.
[139] *British Thomson-Houston Co. Ltd v Tungstalite Ltd* (1938) 55 R.P.C. 280; *Re White's Patent* [1957] R.P.C. 405.
[140] *American Cyanimid Co. v Ethicon Ltd* [1978] R.P.C. 667.
[141] *H & R Johnson Tiles Ltd v Candy Tiles Ltd* [1985] F.S.R. 253.
[142] *Honeywell Ltd v Appliance Components Ltd,* unreported, February 22, 1996, Jacob J. (Yes); *Electrolux Northern Ltd v Black & Decker,* unreported, April 25, 1996, Laddie J. (No); in *Mayne Pharma Pty Ltd v Debiopharm S.A.* [2006] EWHC 164 (Pat.), Pumphrey J. preferred the view of Jacob J. on another point.

person is in issue.[143] But in England there is no such general power. From early on the ecclesiastical courts ordered medical examinations in matrimonial causes where sexual incapacity was in issue[144] and even at common law the writ *de ventre inspiciendo* could be used to order a woman to be examined (by "matrons") to see if she was indeed pregnant, for how long she had been so and to have "matrons" view her daily and be present at the birth of her child.[145] The purpose of all this was, as Lord King L.C. put it, "for the security of the next heir, to guard him against fraudulent or suppositious births."[146] The court today still retains power, in proceedings for nullity on the ground of impotence or incapacity to consummate the marriage, to order a medical examination of the parties,[147] but the writ *de ventre inspiciendo* has no modern counterpart.[148] In addition there are a number of statutory powers to order medical examination, each of which carries with it an appropriate sanction for failure to comply. These include the Family Law Reform Act 1969, ss.20–23 (blood and other tests to determine paternity)[149]; the Social Security Administration Act 1992, ss.9 and 55 (medical examinations for claimants); and the Road Traffic Act 1988, ss.6 and 7 (breath tests). In cases involving children under the Children Act 1989 (e.g. child abuse)[150] or in wardship[151] the court may give leave for a medical examination of the child to take place.

However, there is still no general power for the court to order a medical examination in a case where the condition of a party is in issue.[152] Nevertheless, the common law has found a way, in its inherent jurisdiction to stay proceedings for good cause. Thus, where a defendant in a personal injuries case in light of further evidence sought a further medical examination of the plaintiff, but the plaintiff refused to submit voluntarily, the Court of Appeal **19.21**

---

[143] See, e.g. the US Federal Rules of Civil Procedure, R.35; Cairns, *Australian Civil Procedure*, 4th edn, 1996, at 422–423.

[144] e.g. *Briggs v Morgan* (1820) 2 Hag. Con. 324.

[145] *Willoughby's case* (1597) Cro. Eliz. 566; *Theaker's case* (1625) Cro. Jac. 686; *Ex p.Aiscough* (1730) 2 P. Wms 591; *ex p. Bellet* (1786) 1 Cox. 297; *Re Brown* (1792) 4 Bro. C.C. 91; Levine, *Discovery*, 1982, at 68–69.

[146] *ex p. Aiscough* (1730) 2 P. Wms 591 at 593.

[147] Family Proceedings Rules 1991, r.2.22; see Rayden and Jackson on *Divorce and Family Matters*, 17th edn, 1997, paras 12.12–12.20.

[148] Levine, *loc. cit.*, takes the view that it must still exist.

[149] See, *S v S, W v W* [1972] A.C. 24, HL; *T v T, The Times*, July 31, 1992, CA; *Re H (A Minor)* [1997] Fam. 89, CA; *Re T (A Child)* [2001] 2 F.L.R. 1190. The court's previously existing inherent jurisdiction to order a blood sample be taken from a child for testing was abrogated by the statute, and the statute gives to the person with care and control of the child the absolute right to refuse the sample to be taken: *Re O (A Minor) (Blood Tests: Constraint)* [2000] Fam. 139; *cf. Re R. (Blood Test: Constraint)* [1998] Fam. 66.

[150] Family Proceedings Rules 1991, r.4.18; *Re C (A Child) (HIV Testing)* [2000] Fam. 48, *per* Wilson J. (H.I.V. test ordered of child against wishes of parents); see Rayden and Jackson, *op. cit.*, para.38.18.

[151] *Re R. (PM) (an infant)* [1968] 1 W.L.R. 385; *Re S (infants)* [1967] 1 W.L.R. 396; *B(M) v B(R)* [1968] 1 W.L.R. 1182n., CA.

[152] Nor do the pre-action protocols on personal injury and clinical negligence claims require the claimant to submit to such an examination.

ordered a stay of the proceedings until the examination was completed.[153] The reason is that a claimant who sues for damages for personal injury must afford the defendant a reasonable opportunity to have him medically examined. By choosing to sue he forgoes his right to protest at the invasion of his privacy which a medical examination involves.[154] This reasoning does not apply to defendants, yet in at least one case the court has held that it could strike out the defence of a defendant who unreasonably refused to submit to a medical examination when his memory was in issue.[155] If a party does submit to an examination, he consents to the disclosure of the expert's report to those instructing the expert, and the expert is not entitled to refuse to disclose it on the basis that the claimant has not expressly consented to this.[156]

19.22   On such an application for a stay, the parties must put all available evidence in their possession before the court.[157] The onus is on the party seeking a stay to show that he cannot properly prepare his case without the examination sought[158]; in the absence of any concrete basis for requiring a medical examination, a stay will not be ordered.[159] In the ultimate analysis, the question is one of reasonableness: is the proposed examinee behaving unreasonably in refusing to submit to an examination.[160] Where the proposed examination is unpleasant, painful or risky, the court will be reluctant to order a stay unless the interests of justice imperatively require.[161] An alternative to a complete stay is to permit a claimant who declines to be examined to proceed only with those aspects of his claim which are unaffected by the expert evidence in question.[162] Although some proposed examinees undoubtedly would prefer to have their own doctor present at a medical examination conducted by their opponent's nominated doctor, the court has to have good and substantial reasons put before it before it is entitled to impose a condition that the examinee's doctor should be present at the examination.[163] Nor is the claimant entitled to impose, as a condition

---

[153] *Edmeades v Thames Board Mills Ltd*[1969] 2 Q.B. 67, CA; *S v S, W v W* [1972] A.C. 24, HL.

[154] *Hookham v Wiggins Teape Fine Papers Ltd* [1995] P.I.Q.R. 392, CA.

[155] *Lacey v Harrison, The Times*, April 22, 1992, Judge Dobry Q.C.

[156] *Kapadia v Lambeth London Borough Council* [2000] EWCA Civ. 81, at para.34, *The Times*, July 4, 2000, CA.

[157] *Starr v National Coal Board* [1977] 1 W.L.R. 63, CA.

[158] *Lane v Willis* [1972] 1 W.L.R. 326.

[159] *Baugh v Delta Fittings Ltd* [1971] 1 W.L.R. 1295.

[160] *Starr v National Coal Board* [1977] 1 W.L.R. 63, CA; *Aspinall v Sterling Mansell Ltd* [1981] 3 All E.R. 866; *Hookham v Wiggins Teape Fine Papers Ltd* [1995] P.I.Q.R. 392, CA.

[161] *Aspinall v Sterling Mansell Ltd* [1981] 3 All E.R. 866; *Prescott v Bulldog Tools Ltd* [1981] 3 All E.R. 869.

[162] *James v Baily Gibson & Co.* [2003] EWCA Civ 1690.

[163] *Hall v Avon Area Health Authority* [1980] 1 W.L.R. 481, CA; cf. *Shaw v Skeet* [1996] 7 Med.L.R. 371 (no right for claimant to insist on being present when his doctors were interviewed on defendants' behalf).

of submitting to an examination by the defendant's expert, the requirement that the ensuing report be disclosed to him.[164]

D. PLANS, PHOTOGRAPHS AND MODELS

Under the former rules, if plans, photographs or models were to be used at trial, the other parties had to have the opportunity, at least 10 days before trial, to inspect and agree them without further proof. If the other parties were not given this opportunity, the items concerned could not be admitted at trial without the leave of the court.[165] Caselaw built up on the admissibility of covert video and film evidence of the plaintiff in personal injury or medical negligence cases. Originally it was held that leave could be given in an alleged malingering case where the evidence had not been disclosed under the rules.[166] Subsequently, however, the courts took the view that, in light of various changes in practice,[167] the norm would be to refuse leave in such a case, i.e. the covert evidence would not be admitted where it had not been made available to the other party beforehand.[168]

19.23

Under the CPR, where a party wishes to adduce any non-oral evidence (such as a plan, photograph or model)[169] of which advance notice would not otherwise have to be given to the other parties under the rules,[170] he must give notice to the other parties before the hearing concerned.[171] If he fails to do so then, unless the court otherwise orders, the evidence is not receivable at the hearing,[172] and the judge will be wrong to admit it in evidence.[173] Notice must be given not later than the date for serving witness statements,[174] unless (a) it forms part of expert evidence, (b) there are not to

19.24

---

[164] *Hookham v Wiggins Teape Fine Papers Ltd* [1995] P.I.Q.R. 392, CA. But the court may impose a condition on a litigant of disclosing to his opponent an earlier (unserved) report of an expert in whom he had lost confidence as the price of allowing the litigant to instruct another expert: *Beck v Ministry of Defence* [2003] EWCA Civ. 1043, *The Times*, July 21, 2003, CA; see also *Hajigeorgiou v Vasiliou* [2005] EWCA Civ. 236; see Ch.21, para.21.07, above.

[165] RSC, Ord.38, r.5.

[166] *McGuinness v Kellogg Co. of Great Britain* [1988] 1 W.L.R. 913, CA.

[167] In particular the exchange of witness statements, automatic discovery in personal injury cases, and the "cards on the table" approach to litigation.

[168] *Digby v Essex County Council* [1994] P.I.Q.R. 53, CA; *Khan v Armaguard Ltd* [1994] 1 W.L.R. 1204, CA; *Crompton v Lancashire County Council, The Times*, November 24, 1994; *Libby-Mills v Metropolitan Police Commissioner* [1995] P.I.Q.R. 324, CA.

[169] Plainly this includes a video recording (e.g. *Rall v Hume* [2001] 3 All E.R. 248, CA), but presumably also a sound recording (*cf. R. (Ministry of Defence) v Wiltshire and Swindon Coroner* [2006] 1 W.L.R. 134).

[170] e.g. because contained in a witness statement, affidavit or expert's report, or because it is hearsay (as to which see CPR, r.33.2).

[171] CPR, r.33.6(1), (3); the rule applies to documents receivable in evidence without further proof under the Civil Evidence Act 1995, s.9: *ibid.*, r.33.6(2).

[172] CPR, r.33.6(3).

[173] *Orford v Rasmi Electronics* [2002] EWCA Civ. 1672, [2003] 3 C.P.L.R. 213, CA.

[174] CPR, r.33.6(4).

be any witness statements, (c) the evidence is to be put in solely to disprove an allegation made in a witness statement, or (d) it is to be produced to the court for any reason other than as part of factual or expert evidence. In case (a), notice must be given when the expert's report is served.[175] In cases (b), (c) and (d), it must be given at least 21 days before the hearing.[176] A party giving such notice must give the other parties opportunity to inspect the evidence and to agree to its admission without further proof.[177]

19.25   Far from the CPR having weakened the stance of the court under the former rules, it seems clear that they have, if anything, strengthened it. The requirement to notify opponents of non-oral evidence before the hearing has become more complex and hence more rigorous. In one case,[178] liability being admitted, the defendants made covert video recordings of the claimant between hearings on quantum. On judgment the claimant had failed to beat the payment in, but she was nonetheless awarded costs. The Court of Appeal held that where a party failed to provide necessary information to another party, that was a material matter for the court to take into account when considering what order for costs should be made. From this case it can be inferred that an application to admit covert video evidence without having given notice under the rules would fail in normal circumstances. Thus, where a party wishes to rely on a video, it is necessary in the interests of proper case management and the avoidance of wasted court time that the matter be ventilated with the judge managing the case at the first practicable opportunity once a decision had been made to rely upon it.[179] In one case, the Court of Appeal refused to exclude video evidence under CPR, r. 32.1 as having been obtained in breach of Art.8 of the European Convention on Human Rights, although the defendants were penalised in costs.[180] On the other hand, in an employment case the court held that it would be contrary to public policy at a employment tribunal hearing to admit sound recording evidence covertly obtained of the private deliberations of an employer's disciplinary tribunal.[181]

---

[175] CPR, r.33.6(6).
[176] CPR, r.33.6(5), (7).
[177] CPR, r.33.6(8).
[178] *Ford v GKR Construction Ltd* [2000] 1 W.L.R. 1397, CA.
[179] *Rall v Hume* [2001] 3 All E.R. 248, CA (for use of video in cross-examination)
[180] *Jones v University of Warwick* [2003] 1 W.L.R. 954, CA (secret filming in claimant's home on behalf of defendant's insurers).
[181] *Governors of Amwell View School v Dogherty*, [2006] U.K.E.A.T. 0243–06–1509, E.A.T.; cf. *R. v Mirza* [2004] 1 A.C. 1118, HL; *R. v Smith (No.2)* [2005] U.K.H.L. 12.

CHAPTER 20

Disclosure in other courts and tribunals

CHAPTER 20

Disclosure in other courts and tribunals

A. INTRODUCTION

Hitherto the question of disclosure has been considered from the stand- 20.01
point of the High Court and the county court. But many non-criminal
disputes in England and Wales are dealt with, not by the High Court or the
county courts, but by specialist courts and tribunals. Thus, for example,
unfair dismissal and many other employment related claims are dealt with
by employment (formerly industrial) tribunals, rating disputes by valuation
tribunals and the Lands Tribunal, ecclesiastical matters by the consistory
courts, and so on. In addition, many disputes are dealt with privately, by
arbitration or by mediation. Some of these courts and tribunals adopt all or
part of the disclosure procedures of the High Court or the county court;
others have their own procedures or none at all. In this chapter an overview
is given of the disclosure aspects of the various procedures of these courts
and tribunals.

B. AGRICULTURAL LAND TRIBUNALS[1]

These were established under the Agriculture Act 1947, s.73, to hear and 20.02
determine various matters concerning agricultural land. The procedure in all
cases, except those concerning succession to agricultural tenancies, is governed by the Agricultural Land Tribunals (Rules) Order 1978,[2] as amended,
and that in succession cases is governed by the Agricultural Land Tribunals
(Succession to Agricultural Tenancies) Order 1984.[3] However, the bulk of

---

[1] Muir Watt & Moss, *Agricultural Holdings*, 14th edn, 1998, Ch.16; Scammell and Den-
sham, *Law of Agricultural Holdings*, 8th edn, 1997, Ch.22.
[2] SI 1978/259.
[3] SI 1984/1301.

the disclosure rules of the former are specifically incorporated by reference in the latter so that, in this respect, the procedure is practically the same.

20.03   There are two main rules of significance. Rule 16 of the 1978 Rules[4] requires an applicant to provide, to the secretary to the tribunal, at the time of his application or reply, copies of any documents (including plans) which he intends to adduce in support of his case. Rule 20[5] requires a party to supply to the secretary to the tribunal, on his request, any document or other information which the tribunal may require and which that party can supply and also requires him to give other parties an opportunity to inspect any such document or a copy, and to take copies. There is a saving in r.20(2) for information protected by public interest immunity. An application for disclosure is made in writing to the secretary to the tribunal under r.19,[6] and the secretary notifies other parties. The County Court Rules as to witness summonses are specifically incorporated by r.29(4).[7] It must be assumed that this now means the CPR.

C. ARBITRATIONS[8]

20.04   The High Court formerly had power to order discovery of documents and interrogatories for the purposes of an arbitration,[9] but this power has now gone.[10] Similarly every arbitration agreement was formerly deemed, subject to contrary provision, to contain a discovery obligation,[11] but this has also now gone.[12] Now all matters of procedure and evidence, if not agreed by the parties, are for the arbitration tribunal[13] (and this includes disclosure of documents[14] and interrogatories[15]), or otherwise as provided for by the arbitration agreement[16] or any governing rules[17] or statute. That agreement

---

[4] Applied by rr.11(1) and 28 of the 1984 Rules.
[5] Applied by rr.14 and 30 of the 1984 Rules.
[6] Applied by rr.14 and 30 of the 1984 Rules.
[7] Applied by rr.20 and 33 of the 1984 Rules.
[8] See Merkin, *Arbitration Law,* 1991 (looseleaf), Ch.15; Cato, *Arbitration Practice and Procedure,* 3rd edn, 2002, Ch.13; Bernstein, *Handbook of Arbitration Practice,* 4th edn, 2003, paras 2.695–2.712; Redfern and Hunter, *Law and Practice of International Commercial Arbitration,* 4th edn, 2004, paras 6.61–6.103; Tweeddale & Tweeddale, *Arbitration of Commercial Disputes,* 2005, paras 9.19–9.32, 25.17–25.44.
[9] Arbitration Act 1950, s.12(6(b).
[10] Courts and Legal Services Act 1990, s.103.
[11] Arbitration Act 1950, s.12(1).
[12] Arbitration Act 1996, s.107(2), Sch.4.
[13] Arbitration Act 1996, s.34(1); see, e.g. *ABB A.G. v Hochtief Airport Gmbh* [2006] 2 Lloyd's Rep. 1. But Pt I of the Act does not apply to arbitration under the County Courts Act 1984, s.64: see s.92.
[14] Arbitration Act 1996, s.34(2)(d).
[15] Arbitration Act 1996, s.34(2)(e).
[16] See Mustill and Boyd, *Commercial Arbitration,* 2nd edn, 1989, at 324–326.
[17] e.g. L.C.I.A. Arbitration Rules, Art.22(1)(e) (power to order parties to produce documents in possession or power); I.C.S.I.D. Arbitration Rules, r.34(2), (3) (power to call upon parties to produce documents, if deemed necessary).

or statute will often limit or otherwise affect the scope of disclosure, for example by providing for assumed facts.[18] Unless otherwise agreed by the parties the arbitration tribunal may appoint experts or legal advisers to report to it and the parties, or assessors to assist it on technical matters.[19]

But by statute the arbitration tribunal also has power to give directions in relation to any property the subject of the proceedings owned by or in the possession of a party, including for the inspection or photographing of such property or taking samples from or observing it,[20] and for the preservation of evidence in a party's custody or control.[21] And the court retains the power to issue witness summonses for the purposes of an arbitration,[22] although the power is exercisable only if the witness is in the United Kingdom and the proceedings are being conducted in England and Wales[23] and then only with the permission of the tribunal or the agreement of all the parties.[24] It does not, however, extend to requiring the production of privileged material.[25] Nor does the court have power to order disclosure from a third party in respect of arbitration proceedings.[26]   **20.05**

The High Court has, unless otherwise agreed by the parties, certain statutory powers exercisable in support of arbitral proceedings.[27] These powers are to do the same things as the court might do in legal proceedings before it, in relation to (*inter alia*); (i) the taking of the evidence of witnesses[28]; (ii) the preservation of evidence[29]; and (iii) the inspection, photographing, sampling or experimenting upon any property the subject of, or as to which any question arises in, the proceedings.[30] As to (i), this must cover depositions[31] and letters of request.[32] As to (iii), the powers of the court to make such orders have already been discussed.[33] But these powers are only   **20.06**

---

[18] See Ch.4, para.4.27, above.

[19] Arbitration Act 1996, s.37; Redfern and Hunter, *op. cit.*, para.6.81.

[20] Arbitration Act 1996, s.38(4).

[21] Arbitration Act 1996, s.38(5).

[22] Under CPR, r.34.4; see *Bengalla Mining Co. Pty Ltd v Barclay Mowlem Construction* [2001] N.S.W.S.C. 93, Sup.Ct. N.S.W. (subpoena issued against opponent in arbitration).

[23] Arbitration Act 1996, s.43(3).

[24] Arbitration Act 1996, s.43(1), (2); CPR Pt 62, Practice Direction—Arbitration, para.7. This replaces the power to issue a *subpoena* in aid of an arbitration, under the Arbitration Act 1950, s.12(4); see, e.g. *The Lorenzo Halcoussi* [1988] 1 Lloyd's Rep. 180.

[25] Arbitration Act 1996, s.43(4).

[26] *BNP Paribas v Deloitte & Touche* [2004] 1 Lloyd's Rep. 233; *Assimina Maritimes Ltd v Pakistan Shipping Corp.* [2005] 1 Lloyd's Rep. 525.

[27] Arbitration Act 1996, s.44(1).

[28] Arbitration Act 1996, s.44(2)(a).

[29] Arbitration Act 1996, s.44(2)(b).

[30] Arbitration Act 1996, s.44(2)(c); *Hiscox Underwriting Ltd v Dickson Manchester & Co. Ltd* [2004] EWHC 479 (Comm). This replaces the power to order the inspection or sampling of any property in dispute or experiment which might be necessary or expedient, under the Arbitration Act 1950, s.12(6)(g); as to failure to comply, see *Richco International Ltd v Industrial Food Co.* [1989] 1 All E.R. 613.

[31] See Ch.17, paras 17.01–15.09, above.

[32] See Ch.17, paras 17.10–17.19, above.

[33] See Ch.19, paras 19.02–19.19, above.

available to the court to the extent that they are not available to the arbitration tribunal or other person given such power by the parties, or such tribunal or other person is unable to act effectively.[34]

20.07   On the other hand, the powers conferred on the court[35] are not confined to making orders in support of arbitrations in this jurisdiction. Thus, where appropriate, the court has jurisdiction to make an order for the examination of a witness in order to provide evidence in the form of a deposition for use in a foreign arbitral hearing.[36] And in the exercise of discretion it may be appropriate to make the order where the procedures of the foreign arbitration are similar to those in English law. However, disclosure of information by pre-trial depositions of witnesses, merely for the purpose of enabling an opponent to find out whether he has information which may assist him in advancing his case, is not a procedure known to English law.[37]

20.08   The procedure for obtaining disclosure will vary depending on the arbitration rules that have been incorporated into the agreement (or are otherwise agreed by the parties), any governing statute, and indeed on the identity of the arbitrator(s) and/or umpire.[38] But arbitrators will rarely, if ever, order disclosure without a request from one or both parties. Generally, the courts are reluctant to interfere with the exercise of the arbitrator's discretion in ordering disclosure[39] and the powers of the court are now even more circumscribed.[40] The question how far documents and information disclosed will be subject to an implied obligation of confidence has already been discussed.[41]

20.09   To the extent that the parties do not agree on the powers of the tribunal in case of a party's default, where a party fails to comply with the tribunal's order or directions, it may make a peremptory order to that effect.[42] Unless otherwise agreed by the parties, the court may make an order requiring a party to comply with such a peremptory order.[43] If a party fails to comply

---

[34] Arbitration Act 1996, s.44(5); see also s.44(6) (court order may be made to cease to be effective on order made by arbitration tribunal or other person).

[35] i.e. under s.44 of the Arbitration Act 1996.

[36] Where the requirements of s.44(5) are met

[37] *Commerce and Industry Co. of Canada and Certain Underwriters at Lloyd's of London* [2002] 1 W.L.R. 1323, Comm. Ct, *per Moore-Bick* J. (application refused).

[38] For guidelines, see Mustill and Boyd, *Commercial Arbitration*, 2nd edn, 1989, at 322–326 (but see also *Companion to 2nd edition*, 2001, 190–91, 307–09, 322–23); for international aspects, see Marriott (1989) 5 *Arbitration International*, 280; Raeschke-Kessler (2002) 18 Arbitration International 411; Redfern and Hunter, *The Law and Practice of International Commercial Arbitration*, 4th edn, 2004, paras 6.69–6.79; Craig, Park and Paulsson, *International Chamber of Commerce Arbitration*, 3rd edn, 2000, paras 8.09 and 27.05; Buhler & Webster, *Handbook of ICC Arbitration*, 2005, paras 20.1–20.83; Pietrowski (2006) 22 Arbitration International 373; see para.19.04 above.

[39] See, e.g. *Urban Small Spaces Ltd v Burford Investment Co.* [1990] 2 E.G.L.R. 120; *ABB A.G. v Hochtief Airport Gmbh* [2006] 2 Lloyd's Rep. 1 (refusal of arbitrators to order production of documents did not amount to serious irregularity).

[40] Arbitration Act 1996, s.1(c).

[41] See Ch.15, para.15.47, above.

[42] Arbitration Act 1996, s.41(5).

[43] Arbitration Act 1996, s.42(1); there are however limits on this power: s.42(3), (4).

with a peremptory order (other than one requiring security for costs[44]) the tribunal may (a) direct that that party may not rely on any allegation or material the subject of the order[45]; (b) draw averse inferences from the non-compliance[46]; (c) proceed to an award on the basis of existing material; or (d) make appropriate costs orders.[47] An innocent failure to disclose documents in an arbitration (as opposed to a deliberate withholding) is not a ground for the court to interfere with an award under s.68 of the Arbitration Act 1996.[48] The court may find that an arbitration award has been obtained by fraud if it can be shown that a party deliberately concealed a document ordered to be disclosed and as a consequence of that concealment has obtained an award in his favor.[49]

D. BARMOTE COURTS

The Great Barmote Courts and the Small Barmote Courts of the High **20.10** Peak are ancient courts with jurisdiction relating to lead-mining rights and civil pleas relating to such rights in the King's Field or King's Fee and other parts of the hundred of High Peak in Derbyshire.[50] The Barmote Courts of Wirksworth are similar to those of the High Peak.[51] The procedure of both the High Peak and Wirksworth Courts is regulated by statute,[52] in the former case as subsequently amended.[53] In neither case are there any provisions for interrogatories or disclosure of documents, though there are provisions for writs of *subpoena*[54] and the inspection of property.[55]

E. COMMITTEE OF PRIVILEGES OF THE HOUSE OF LORDS

Although only the Sovereign has jurisdiction to decide a claim to a **20.11** peerage, such claims are nowadays referred to the Committee for Privileges

---

[44] As to which see Arbitration Act 1996, s.41(6).
[45] See Ch.13, para.13.32.
[46] See Ch.13, para.13.34.
[47] Arbitration Act 1996, s.41(7).
[48] *Profilati v Paine Webber* [2001] 1 Lloyd's Rep. 715.
[49] *Elektrim S.A. v Vivendi Universal S.A.* [2007] EWHC 1 (Comm.).
[50] See the High Peak Mining Customs and Mineral Courts Act 1851.
[51] See the Derbyshire Mining Customs and Mineral Courts Act 1852.
[52] See the Schedules to the 1851 Act and the 1852 Act respectively.
[53] See the order of the Chancellor of the Duchy of Lancaster dated May 30, 1859, S. R. & O. Rev. 1948, Vol.X, p.1005.
[54] High Peak Mining Customs and Mineral Courts Act 1851, ss.31, 40.
[55] High Peak Mining Customs and Mineral Courts Act 1851, Sch.1, paras 22–25.

of the House of Lords.[56] In practice, therefore, it is this tribunal, infrequently called upon, but certainly not obsolete,[57] that adjudicates on claims to peerages. Such claims may be claims to call a peerage out of abeyance in favour of a particular claimant, or disputes between two or more persons as to which (if any) should succeed to a particular peerage. It is important to note that peerage decisions are in one sense *in rem* and bind the world, so that even when there is a disputed claim admissions by one party will not be accepted by the Committee unless properly proved. The procedure of the Committee,[58] which is governed by the Standing Orders of the House of Lords, does not include any provision for disclosure to be given, although there have occasionally been cases where voluntary disclosure of damaging evidence has been made against interest.[59] The abolition of the right of hereditary peers to sit as members of the House of Lords[60] has removed one of the reasons for disputes as to the holder of a title, but in itself has not altered any of the procedures involved in the resolution of that dispute.

F. COMMONS COMMISSIONERS[61]

20.12   These have certain judicial functions under the Commons Registration Act 1965, in connection with the registration of land as common land. Hearings before Commons Commissioners are now rare, but they are governed by statutory regulations.[62] They contain no power for disclosure (whether of documents or of facts) to be provided, although the Commissioner before whom the hearing is held has power by summons, upon the application of a person entitled to be heard at a hearing, to require a witness to attend the hearing and give oral evidence or to produce "any document in his possession or power."[63] However a witness must be provided with (or at least tendered) conduct money[64] and cannot be required to give any evidence or produce any document which he could not be required to give

---

[56] Courts of law have no jurisdiction in the matter (*Earl Cowley v Countess Cowley* [1901] A.C. 450) except in relation to Scottish titles, when the court of the Lord Lyon may have jurisdiction (see, e.g. *Douglas-Hamilton, Petitioner* 1996 S.L.T. (Lyon Ct.) 8).

[57] See, e.g. *The Ampthill Peerage* [1977] A.C. 547; *The Annandale and Hartfell Peerage Claim* [1986] A.C. 319; *Barony of Moynihan* [2000] 1 F.L.R. 113.

[58] See Gadd, *Peerage Law*, 1985, Ch.9.

[59] See, e.g. *Chandos Peerage Claim*, 1834, in Beltz, *A Review of the Chandos Peerage Case*, 1834.

[60] House of Lords Act 1999.

[61] See generally Gadsden, *The Law of Commons*, 1988; Oswald, *A Practitioner's Guide to Common Land and the Commons Registration Act 1965*, 1989; Ubhi and Denyer-Green, *Law of Commons and of Town and Village Greens*, 2nd edn, 2006, para.8.7.9.

[62] Commons Commissioners Regulations 1971, SI 1971/1727; see also Oswald, *op. cit.*, Ch.3.

[63] Commons Commissioners Regulations 1971, reg.23(1); note the absence of "custody".

[64] Commons Commissioners Regulations 1971, reg.23(3).

or produce on the trial of an action in the High Court.[65] When the provisions of the 1965 Act are replaced by those of the Commons Act 2006, Pt I,[66] the Commons Commissioners will cease to exercise their judicial functions.

G. COMPETITION COMMISSION APPEAL TRIBUNAL

This tribunal has jurisdiction to hear appeals under s.46 or 47 of the Competition Act 1998, concerned with decisions by the Director General of Fair Trading. The procedure is governed by statutory rules.[67] The notice of appeal by which the appeal must be made must not only state certain information about the applicant[68] and the case itself,[69] but must also annex copies of all documents on which the applicant relies, including written statements of witnesses of fact or expert witnesses.[70] These are all sent to the registrar, who forwards a copy to the respondent.[71] The respondent has six weeks from receipt of the appeal notice in which to send a defence to the registrar,[72] containing similar information about the respondent[73] and his case,[74] and also annexing copies of all documents on which he relies, including written statements of witnesses of fact or expert witnesses.[75] There is a procedure for advertisement, on the Tribunal's website[76] and elsewhere, to invite intervention by third parties in the proceedings,[77] with those granted permission to intervene[78] having to produce a statement of intervention,[79] to which are annexed copies of all documents on which he relies, including written statements of witnesses of fact or expert witnesses.[80]

20.13

There are provisions for the tribunal to give directions, including directions (*inter alia*):

20.14

(a) requiring persons to attend and give evidence or to produce documents[81];

---

[65] Commons Commissioners Regulations 1971, reg.23(2).
[66] From a date to be appointed under the 2006 Act.
[67] Competition Appeal Tribunal Rules 2003, SI 2003/1372.
[68] Competition Appeal Tribunal Rules 2003, r.8(3).
[69] Competition Appeal Tribunal Rules 2003, r.8(4).
[70] Competition Appeal Tribunal Rules 2003, r.8(6).
[71] Competition Appeal Tribunal Rules 2003, r.13(b).
[72] Competition Appeal Tribunal Rules 2003, r.14(1).
[73] Competition Appeal Tribunal Rules 2003, r.12(2).
[74] Competition Appeal Tribunal Rules 2003, r.14(3).
[75] Competition Appeal Tribunal Rules 2003, r.14(5).
[76] Competition Appeal Tribunal Rules 2003, r.6.
[77] Competition Appeal Tribunal Rules 2003, r.15.
[78] Competition Appeal Tribunal Rules 2003, r.16(1)–(6).
[79] Competition Appeal Tribunal Rules 2003, r.16(7).
[80] Competition Appeal Tribunal Rules 2003, r.16(9)(c).
[81] Competition Appeal Tribunal Rules 2003, r.19(2)(d).

(b) as to the submission in advance of witness statements or expert reports[82];

(c) for the disclosure between, or production by, the parties of documents or classes of documents.[83]

There is also express provision for the tribunal, of its own motion (*inter alia*);

(a) to ask the parties or third parties for information or particulars[84];

(b) to ask for documents or any papers relating to the case to be produced.[85]

If that were not enough, there is also power for the tribunal at any time, either of its own motion or on the request of any party, to issue a summons requiring any person in the United Kingdom to attend as a witness before the tribunal and answer questions or produce any documents or other material in his possession or under his control which relate to any matter in question in the proceedings.[86] But a request by a party for the issue of a summons must state with reasons the facts on which the witness is to be examined or the documents to be produced,[87] and the witness must have seven days' notice of the hearing and an allowance and expenses on the High Court scale.[88] Failure to comply with any directions may lead to the party concerned being debarred from further part in the proceedings.[89] Most of the tribunal's interlocutory orders may be made by the President (or the Chairman of a tribunal constituted to deal with those proceedings) acting alone.[90]

H. COPYRIGHT TRIBUNAL[91]

20.15   This tribunal hears and determines various applications and references under the Copyright, Designs and Patents Act 1988. In relation to references and applications with respect to licensing schemes, the chairman of the tribunal may give directions as to various matters, including the discovery

---

[82] Competition Appeal Tribunal Rules 2003, r.19(2)(f).
[83] Competition Appeal Tribunal Rules 2003, r.19(2)(k).
[84] Competition Appeal Tribunal Rules 2003, r.19(3)(c).
[85] Competition Appeal Tribunal Rules 2003, r.19(3)(d).
[86] Competition Appeal Tribunal Rules 2003, r.23(1).
[87] Competition Appeal Tribunal Rules 2003, r.23(2).
[88] Competition Appeal Tribunal Rules 2003, r.23(3).
[89] Competition Appeal Tribunal Rules 2003, r.24.
[90] Competition Appeal Tribunal Rules 2003, r.62.
[91] Copinger and Skone James, *Copyright*, 15th edn, 2005, esp. paras 29.93–29.171; Laddie, Prescott and Vitoria, *The Law of Copyright*, 3rd edn, 2000, Ch.26.

and inspection of documents.[92] This rule applies also to references and applications with respect to licensing by licensing bodies,[93] appeals under s.139 of the 1988 Act against orders made by the Secretary of State,[94] applications under s.142 of the Act to settle royalty or other sums payable,[95] applications under s.144 of the Act to settle terms of licence as of right,[96] applications under s.190 of the Act for the tribunal's consent on behalf of a performer,[97] applications under Sch.6, para.5 of the Act for the tribunal's determination of the royalty or other remuneration to be paid to the Hospital for Sick Children,[98] and to appeals to the High Court from decisions of the tribunal.[99]

In addition, the provisions of, *inter alia*, s.12 of the Arbitration Act 1950[100] "shall apply in the case of proceedings before the Tribunal in England and Wales."[101] The form of s.12 set out in Pt 1 of Sch.2 is the form before the repeal[102] of s.12(6)(b) of the provisions relating to discovery orders of the High Court. The remainder of s.12 has now been repealed.[103] It is not clear whether the version of s.12(6) incorporated in the Rules is that in force at the time the Rules were made, or that in force from time to time,[104] or whether the section is now completely gone in this context.[105]   **20.16**

I. CORONERS' COURTS[106]

Coroners make preliminary inquiries into certain deaths, and hold inquests on others, and also on cases of treasure trove.[107] In holding inquests (often with a jury), a coroner acts judicially and constitutes an inferior court of record.[108] But the proceedings are inquisitorial and not accusatorial, there are no "parties," and there is no disclosure process comparable to that in ordinary civil proceedings,[109] although non-statutory   **20.17**

---

[92] Copyright Tribunal Rules 1989, r.11(2)(v); see also the Copyright Tribunal 1995 Practice Direction (as amended), para.6(b).

[93] Copyright Tribunal Rules 1989, r.22(2).

[94] Copyright Tribunal Rules 1989, r.25(2).

[95] Copyright Tribunal Rules 1989, r.29(2).

[96] Copyright Tribunal Rules 1989, r.32(2).

[97] Copyright Tribunal Rules 1989, r.36(2).

[98] Copyright Tribunal Rules 1989, r.40(2).

[99] Copyright Tribunal Rules 1989, r.43(3).

[100] Set out in Pt 1 of Sch.2 to the 1988 Act.

[101] Copyright Tribunal Rules 1989, r.46.

[102] By the Courts and Legal Services Act 1990, s.103.

[103] By the Arbitration Act 1996, s.107(2) and Sch.4.

[104] See further, para.20.60, below.

[105] See also the Copyright Designs and Patents Act 1988, s.150(2), as substituted by the Arbitration Act 1996, Sch.3 para.50.

[106] See generally, *Jervis on Coroners*, 12th edn, 2002, with 3rd cumulative supplement 2006; Dorries, *Coroners' Courts*, 2nd edn, 2004.

[107] See, *Jervis on Coroners*, 12th edn, 2002, Ch.1, paras 1.08, 1.11.

[108] *ibid.* Ch.11, para.11.01.

[109] *ibid.* Ch.10, paras 10.42–10.48.

pre-inquest disclosure sometimes occurs in limited classes of case, such as inquests into deaths in custody.[110] Procedure in death cases is governed by statutory rules,[111] and in treasure trove cases by the common law, supplemented by statute[112] and a code of practice.[113]

20.18   Under the statutory rules the coroner has power by summons to require any person within his own jurisdiction (usually a county, but in Wales the whole country) to attend the hearing,[114] but it has been held that he cannot thereby require the witness to bring relevant or specified documents with him.[115] To secure the attendance of a witness outside his jurisdiction, or to obtain documents, the coroner formerly could apply for the issue of a Crown Office *subpoena* in aid of his court as an inferior court or tribunal,[116] although usually witnesses co-operated, and this was unnecessary. The CPR have made new provision for witness summonses to be issued in aid of inferior courts and tribunals,[117] instead of writs of *subpoena*, but there is an unfortunate drafting slip. The new rule, giving the High Court or county court the power to issue the witness summons, only applies in favour of a court or tribunal that does not have power to issue a witness summons in relation to proceedings before it.[118] But the coroner's court *does* have power to issue witness summonses; it is simply that they cannot be addressed to a person outside the particular coroner's jurisdiction. So on its face the new rule cannot apply to coroners' inquests. Probably, however, the provision will be construed as applying to any court or tribunal that does not have the power to issue *the witness summons in question*, rather than witness summonses in general.

20.19   Just because a person is entitled to examine witnesses at an inquest[119] does not automatically entitle him also to copies of witness statements prepared for the coroner or supplied to him for the inquest,[120] although the Home Office view is that the *witness* who made a statement may be given a copy of it at the coroner's discretion.[121] However, a coroner who has no good reason for refusing a request from a person is entitled to examine witnesses to see such documents may find that his refusal is judicially

---

[110] See Prison Service Protocol, April 1, 1999; Home Office Circular No.20 of 1999.

[111] Coroners Rules 1984, SI 1984/552, as amended.

[112] Treasure Act 1996, s.9.

[113] Issued by the Department of Culture, Media and Sport in 1997, and available on the world wide web at *http://www.britarch.ac.uk/cba/potant10.html*.

[114] Coroners Rules 1984, r.60, Sch.4, Form 8.

[115] *R. v Southwark Coroner, ex p. Hicks* [1987] 1 W.L.R. 1624 at 1629.

[116] *Jervis on Coroners*, 12th edn, 2002, Ch.10, paras 10.18–10.21.

[117] CPR, r.34.4; see generally, Ch.10, para.10.24, above.

[118] CPR, r.34.4(3).

[119] See the Coroners Rules 1984, r.20 (parents, spouses, children, personal representatives, insurer and beneficiary under life assurance, persons who may have been responsible for the death, the police, and certain others).

[120] *R. v Hammersmith Coroner, ex p. Peach* [1980] 2 W.L.R. 496 at 502–505; *R. v Lincoln Coroner, ex p. Hay* [2000] Lloyd's Rep. Medical 264, D.C.

[121] Home Office Circular No.82 of 1969, para.3.

reviewed.[122] In the special case where the coroner intends to admit documentary evidence at an inquest, it does entitle him to see a copy of the document before it is admitted.[123] And a coroner must on application and on payment of the prescribed fee supply to any "properly interested person" a copy of a post-mortem examination or special examination report, any notes of evidence or any document put in evidence at the inquest.[124] There is no definition of "properly interested person" for this purpose, although the better view seems to be that it means a person entitled to examine witnesses at the inquest.[125] This would exclude, for example, the media.

There is also the question whether documents supplied to a "properly interested person" are subject to an implied obligation to keep the information contained in them confidential so far as not already public, analogous to the CPR, r.31.22 obligation on disclosure.[126] This question has never been decided,[127] and the analogy is certainly inexact. Whether such an obligation can be implied into the right conferred by the rules[128] seems doubtful. The information is not being extorted from any third party by compulsion.[129] On the contrary, an inquest is a form of public inquiry, the purpose of which (unlike litigation) is to inquire into certain facts and make them known. However, the position may be different where the documents concerned have been produced only as the result of the issue and service of a witness summons, for then the information is being provided under compulsion.[130] On the other hand, if it is made public at the hearing, it is difficult to see how any confidentiality obligation can continue to attach.

20.20

J. COURT OF ADMIRALTY OF THE CINQUE PORTS

This ancient court may exercise, within the boundaries of the cinque ports,[131] the same inherent jurisdiction as the High Court of Admiralty possessed before 1875[132] and an additional statutory appellate jurisdiction as to salvage disputes within the same boundaries, concurrently with the Admiralty Court of the High Court,[133] from the Salvage Commissioners of

20.21

---

[122] See, e.g. *R. (Bentley) v Avon Coroner* (2002) 166 J.P. 297.
[123] Coroners Rules 1984, r.37.
[124] Coroners Rules 1984, r.57(1).
[125] Coroners Rules 1984, r.20(2).
[126] See Ch.15, above.
[127] *cf. Jervis on Coroners*, 12th edn, 2002, Ch.18, para.18.40.
[128] Coroners Rules 1984, r.57(1).
[129] *cf.* Ch.15, para.15.01, above.
[130] See Ch.15, para.15.11, above.
[131] As to which see the Cinque Ports Act 1821, s.18 (*cf.* the Local Government Act 1972, s.271(3)).
[132] Saved by the Merchant Shipping Act 1894, s.571, now the Merchant Shipping Act 1995, Sch.14 para.11.
[133] As to which see the Administration of Justice Act 1970, s.1(3), and the Supreme Court Act 1981, ss.6(1)(b), 20–24, 27 and 62(2).

the Cinque Ports.[134] The court has not sat for many years, but has never been abolished. Rules of procedure were last made specifically for this court on March 6, 1891, by the then Judge Official and Commissary.[135] They contained rules for interrogatories,[136] discovery and inspection of documents[137] and *subpoenas*[138] modelled on the then High Court Rules applicable to Admiralty jurisdiction. The special Admiralty rules of the CPR[139] only apply to "admiralty claims" before "the Admiralty Court of the Queen's Bench Division of the High Court of Justice".[140] Accordingly, in relation to this court, it appears that the 1891 Rules continue to apply.

K. COURT OF PROTECTION[141]

20.22   This is an office of the Supreme Court, constituted under Pt VII of the Mental Health Act 1983. The Master of the Court of Protection (with nominated judges of the Supreme Court) exercises jurisdiction over the affairs of the mentally incapable, as a successor to the jurisdiction in lunacy originally exercised by the King as *parens patriae* and subsequently by the Lord Chancellor and then the Lords Justices.[142] The procedure is governed by the statutory rules,[143] which contain no general disclosure provisions, though there is power to summon witnesses to produce documents,[144] to direct a medical examination of the mental patient concerned,[145] to inspect property of the patient,[146] and to direct the production of documents from third parties in making inquiries as to testamentary documents executed by the patient.[147] There is also provision for copies to be obtained of documents in court proceedings, if the court is satisfied that there is good reason for allowing it.[148] Subject to that, documents filed with the court may be inspected only with leave of the court, and leave will be given to any person

---

[134] Cinque Ports Act 1821, s.4.
[135] S. R. & O. Rev. 1904, Vol.II, *Cinque Ports*, p.1.
[136] Ord.XXVI, rr.1–11, 19–24.
[137] Ord.XXVI, rr.12–19, 21–24.
[138] Ord.XXX, rr.20–27.
[139] CPR, Pt 61.
[140] CPR, r.61.1(1), (2)(a),(b).
[141] See generally, Hine, *Court of Protection Practice*, 1997; Terrell, *The Court of Protection*, 2003; Haywood and Massey, *Court of Protection Practice*, 2006 (looseleaf).
[142] Story, *Equity Jurisprudence*, 2nd edn, 1839, Vol.II, Ch.XXXV; *Snell's Equity*, 2nd edn, 1872, Ch.VI; Holdsworth, *A History of English Law*, 7th edn, 1956, Vol.1, pp.473–476.
[143] Court of Protection Rules 2001, SI 2001/824.
[144] Court of Protection Rules 2001, r.48.
[145] Court of Protection Rules 2001, r.67.
[146] Court of Protection Rules 2001, r.68.
[147] Court of Protection Rules 2001, r.70.
[148] Court of Protection Rules 2001, r.75.

who can show a reasonable and proper purpose which does not harm the patient (if living), privilege in itself being no bar to inspection.[149]

L. ECCLESIASTICAL COURTS[150]

The principal ecclesiastical court is the Consistory Court,[151] which deals with applications for faculty, i.e. permission to do something in a church or connected with its fabric and also with ecclesiastical discipline.[152] Procedure in the former case[153] is governed by statutory rules.[154] These rules require the submission with the petition for a faculty of all "designs, plans, photographs and other documents giving particulars of the works or proposals for which the faculty is required" and of certain other documents.[155] The chancellor or registrar has the power to give directions to the parties for various purposes, including "to encourage the parties to co-operate with each other in the exchange of information and documents in preparation for a hearing".[156]   **20.23**

Procedure in ecclesiastical discipline cases is governed by further rules,[157] which inter alia confer power on the registrar on the application of a party before trial and on the court on application or of its own motion at trial or on appeal, to order: **20.24**

(a) a party to produce specified documents for inspection and for copying;

(b) a party or any other person to produce specified documents at the trial;

(c) any person to attend at the trial to give evidence.[158]

This power plainly enables the making of specific disclosure orders, but not of orders for general disclosure to be given by reference to issues in the proceedings.

---

[149] *Re Strachan* [1895] 1 Ch. 439, CA; *Re E* [1985] 1 W.L.R. 245, CA.

[150] For a historical survey, see *The Report on the Commission on Ecclesiastical Courts set up by the Archbishops of Canterbury and York in 1951*, 1954; on procedure, see Newsom, *Faculty Jurisdiction in the Church of England*, 2nd edn, 1993; Leeder, *Ecclesiastical Law Handbook*, 1997, Ch.11; Hill, *Ecclesiastical Law*, 2nd edn, 2001, Ch.7.

[151] Established under the Ecclesiastical Jurisdiction Measure 1963, s.1, as amended by the Care of Churches and Ecclesiastical Jurisdiction Measure 1991, Pt III.

[152] Other courts may also exercise an original jurisdiction in relation to discipline: see the Ecclesiastical Jurisdiction (Discipline) Rules 1964, para.19.23, below.

[153] See Newsom, *op. cit.*; Hill, *op. cit.*; Leeder, *op. cit.*

[154] Faculty Jurisdiction Rules 2000, SI 2000/2047.

[155] *ibid.*, r.4(1)(b) and Appendix C, Form 2.

[156] *ibid.* r.19(1), (2)(i).

[157] Ecclesiastical Jurisdiction (Discipline) Rules 1964, SI 1964/1755.

[158] *ibid.*, r.62.

20.25   However, the Measure which established the modern system of ecclesiastical courts provides that any court or commission established under the Measure and the Vicar-General's court of each of the provinces of Canterbury and York are to have "the same powers as the High Court in relation to the attendance and examination of witnesses and the production and inspection of documents."[159] It is not entirely clear whether the reference to production and inspection of documents is intended to bring in the whole of the High Court's pre-trial procedures for obtaining production for inspection under CPR, Pt 31,[160] or whether it is intended to be restricted to procedures for production at trial (such as the witness summons).[161] If it is intended to confer pre-trial powers, it is odd that the power to order general or specific disclosure was not included, since production for inspection is only a meaningful process once it is known what there is to produce. Perhaps the draftsman meant the words "production and inspection" to include disclosure as well, but this must be doubtful.

20.26   If, on the other hand, the intention was to restrict production to that at trial, why add "inspection" (a pre-trial process)? It is submitted that the better view is to construe these beneficial powers in a wide sense, to include pre-trial production, if not disclosure.[162] It is however clear that there is no power to permit information requests (formerly interrogatories).

M. EMPLOYMENT TRIBUNALS (FORMERLY INDUSTRIAL TRIBUNALS)[163]

20.27   These tribunals are concerned with a wide variety of disputes arising in the field of employment and industrial relations, especially claims for unfair dismissal. Procedure is governed by statutory rules[164] These rules confer power on the chairman of the tribunal, even acting on his own initiative, with or without hearing the parties[165]:

(a) to order that a party provide additional information[166];

---

[159] Ecclesiastical Jurisdiction Measure 1963, s.81(1) (as amended).

[160] See Ch.9, above.

[161] See Ch.10, paras 10.02–10.36.

[162] A similar problem arises in relation to the Transport Tribunal: see para.20.83, below.

[163] See generally, Harvey, *Industrial Relations and Employment Law*, T [453]–[551]; Slade, *Tolley's Employment Law Handbook*, 18th edn, 2004, Ch.10.

[164] Employment Tribunals (Constitution and Rules of Procedure) Regs 2004, SI 2004/1861, Schs 1 (ordinary claims), 2 (national security claims), 3 (levy appeals), 4 (improvement and prohibition notice appeals), 5 (non-discrimination notice appeals), 6 (equal value claims).

[165] Employment Tribunals (Constitution and Rules of Procedure) Regulations 2004, Sch.1, r.12.

[166] Employment Tribunals (Constitution and Rules of Procedure) Regulations 2004, Sch.1, r.10(2)(b).

   (b) to order any person in Great Britain to disclose documents or information to a party to allow a party to inspect such material as might be ordered by a county court[167];

   (c) to order the attendance of any person in Great Britain either to give evidence or to produce documents or information[168];

   (d) to require the provision of written answers to questions put by the tribunal or chairman[169];

   (e) to order that a witness statement be prepared or exchanged[170];

   (f) to make provision for the use of experts or interpreters in the proceedings.[171]

The power at (b) above is discussed further below.[172] The power at (c) above is exercisable by the tribunal on the basis of its decision whether the evidence which the witness could give is sufficiently relevant, and is challengeable only on *Wednesbury* grounds.[173] It goes further than the equivalent power in the CPR.[174] Prior to the introduction in 1993 of the predecessor of the power at (d) above, it was held that a tribunal had no power to order a party to create documents (other than particulars under (a) above) which did not then exist, and neither could it require answers to interrogatories.[175] But the power at (d) (and also that at (a) above) now largely performs that role. In cases involving national security, the powers at (b) and (c) are modified.[176] As to the power at (e), it is nowadays common for tribunals to give standard directions to the parties requiring such preparation and exchange, and also providing that such statements are to stand as evidence in chief.   **20.28**

There is no automatic disclosure in employment tribunals, although since 1993 they have had the express power to make a discovery order, a witness summons, or a written answer of their own motion.[177] Some tribunals nowadays give standard directions by letter to the parties, requiring them   **20.29**

---

[167] Employment Tribunals (Constitution and Rules of Procedure) Regulations 2004, Sch.1, r.10(2)(d).

[168] Employment Tribunals (Constitution and Rules of Procedure) Regulations 2004, Sch.1, r.10(2)(c); see *Clapson v British Airways Plc* [2001] I.R.L.R. 184, E.A.T. (tribunal order of its own motion requiring party to attend as a witness).

[169] Employment Tribunals (Constitution and Rules of Procedure) Regulations 2004, Sch.1, r.10(2)(f).

[170] Employment Tribunals (Constitution and Rules of Procedure) Regulations 2004, Sch.1, r.10(2)(s); see also *Eurobell (Holdings) Plc v Barker* [1998] I.C.R. 299, E.A.T.

[171] Employment Tribunals (Constitution and Rules of Procedure) Regulations 2004, Sch.1, r.10(2)(t).

[172] See para.19.29, below.

[173] *Noorani v Merseyside Tec Ltd* [1999] I.R.L.R. 184, CA.

[174] CPR, r.31.17; see Ch.3, para.3.48.

[175] *Carrington v Helix Lighting Ltd* [1990] I.C.R. 6, E.A.T.; *cf. West Midlands Passenger Transport Executive v Singh* [1988] I.C.R. 614, CA.

[176] Employment Tribunals (Constitution and Rules of Procedure) Regulations 2004, Sch.2, r.6.

[177] Employment Tribunals (Constitution and Rules of Procedure) Regulations 1993, Sch.1, r.4(1)–(3); *cf. Honeyrose Products Ltd v Joslin* [1981] I.C.R. 317, E.A.T.

(for example) "to disclose to each other all documents upon which either party wishes to rely[178] at the full merits hearing by exchange of documents within 21 days . . . " If either party wishes wider disclosure, and it is not volunteered by the other side,[179] it is usual to apply to the tribunal for it, whether general or specific, by letter. The application will be dealt with by the tribunal chairman,[180] usually without an oral hearing, and the decision is communicated to the parties by letter. In complex cases, the application may be made on notice (*inter partes*), or the chairman may call for an on notice (*inter partes*) hearing if he is otherwise minded to refuse the application. A request for an oral hearing of an interlocutory application ought not be refused without good cause.[181] Where (as often happens) the application is made and considered without notice, the other side may apply to vary it or set it aside.[182] The width of the disclosure sought, and ordered, will vary greatly according to the nature of the claim.[183] Tribunals are usually more generous (especially in breaching third party confidentiality) where the claim contains a discrimination element.[184]

20.30 Since the power of the tribunal to order disclosure is the same as the power of the county court to order disclosure, the tribunal must now look to the CPR, and the growing case law on those rules, in deciding whether or not to make an order. As under the CPR,[185] the duty to disclose is a continuing one, so that if an employer creates relevant documents during the course of the proceedings, they must also be disclosed.[186] A tribunal concerned to protect the confidentiality of documents to be disclosed should not restrict their disclosure to itself, but should direct disclosure to the party seeking them and make orders restricting or prohibiting further use.[187] But the tribunal can direct the editing of the documents to produce an anonymised or redacted form.[188] The ordinary rules as to privilege and other objections to production[189] apply in employment tribunal proceedings.[190] A failure to comply with an order for particulars, disclosure, or witness

---

[178] The ambiguity of this phrase is unfortunate.

[179] See para.19.30, below.

[180] Employment Tribunals (Constitution and Rules of Procedure) Regulations 2004, Sch.1, r.10(1).

[181] *Halford v Sharples* [1992] I.C.R. 146 at 151, E.A.T.

[182] Employment Tribunals (Constitution and Rules of Procedure) Regulations 2004, Sch.1, r.10(4).

[183] See e.g. *British Aerospace Plc v Green* [1995] I.R.L.R.433, CA; *FDR Ltd v Holloway* [1995] I.R.L.R.400, E.A.T.

[184] See, e.g. *Science Research Council v Nassé* [1980] A.C. 1028, HL; *Selvarajan v Inner London Education Authority* [1980] I.R.L.R. 313, E.A.T.

[185] CPR, r.31.11(1); see Ch.5, para.5.41.

[186] *Scott v I.R.C.* [2004] I.R.L.R. 713, CA.

[187] *Knight v Department of Social Security* [2002] I.R.L.R. 249, E.A.T.

[188] *Asda Stores Ltd v Thompson* [2002] I.R.L.R. 245, E.A.T.; *Asda Stores Ltd v Thompson (No.2)* [2004] I.R.L.R. 598, E.A.T.

[189] See Ch.11, above.

[190] See, e.g. *Science Research Council v Nasse* [1980] A.C. 1028, HL; *Halford v Sharples* [1992] I.C.R. 146, E.A.T.; *University of Southampton v Kelly*, unreported, November 14, 2005, E.A.T.

attendance is a criminal offence if committed without reasonable excuse, punishable by fine,[191] and in addition may lead to the striking out of the claim or the response,[192] although before taking such a step the party in default must be given an opportunity to be heard.[193] The principles to be applied are those applicable in the like situation in standard civil litigation.[194]

Notwithstanding that there is no disclosure obligation without order, it is common for parties to give voluntary disclosure, by preparing and serving on the other side either lists of the documents which are intended to be adduced at the hearing or bundles of copies of the documents themselves. If lists are served, however, they are not to be treated as if they were Lists of Documents prepared in performance of an obligation to give disclosure.[195] On the other hand, a party who chooses to make voluntary disclosure of any documents in his possession or power must not be unfairly selective in his disclosure. Once a party has voluntarily disclosed certain documents, it becomes his duty not to withhold from disclosure any further documents in his possession or power (regardless of whether they support his case or not) if there is any risk that the effect of withholding them might be to convey to his opponent or to the tribunal a false or misleading impression as to the true nature, purport or effect of any disclosed document.[196] This duty is to be interpreted broadly and enforced strictly.[197] Where a party discloses part only of a document, he must not only make this clear, but must offer the remainder if another party or the tribunal requires it.[198] One important disadvantage of voluntary disclosure is that there is no implied undertaking not to use the information for collateral purposes,[199] although it is open to the parties to agree appropriate restrictions on use. In certain kinds of claims where the burden of proof is reversed,[200] it will be in the interests of the employer to produce (if it can) the material needed to discharge that burden of proof.[201]

20.31

---

[191] Employment Tribunals Act 1996, s.7(4); *University of Southampton v Kelly*, unreported, November 14, 2005, E.A.T.

[192] Employment Tribunals (Constitution and Rules of Procedure) Regulations 2004, Sch.1, r.13.

[193] Employment Tribunals (Constitution and Rules of Procedure) Regulations 2004, Sch.1, r.19.

[194] *National Grid Co. Ltd v Virdee* [1992] I.R.L.R. 555, E.A.T.; see Ch.13, paras 13.07–13.17, above.

[195] *Birds Eye Walls Ltd v Harrison* [1985] I.R.L.R. 47, E.A.T.

[196] *Birds Eye Walls Ltd v Harrison* [1985] I.R.L.R. 47, E.A.T.

[197] *Birds Eye Walls Ltd v Harrison* [1985] I.R.L.R. 47, E.A.T.

[198] *C.J. O'Shea Construction Ltd v Bassi* [1998] I.C.R. 1130, at 1139, E.A.T.

[199] See Ch.15, para.15.12, above.

[200] See Sex Discrimination Act 1975, s.63A; Race Relations Act 1976, s.54A; Disability Discrimination Act 1995, s.17A(1C).

[201] *EB v BA* [2006] I.R.L.R. 471, CA.

N. EUROPEAN COURT OF JUSTICE AND THE EUROPEAN COURT OF FIRST INSTANCE[202]

20.32   The European Court of Justice ("E.C.J.") and the European Court of First Instance ("C.F.I.") differ from most of the other courts and tribunals referred to in this chapter in that neither is internal to the English legal system (or United Kingdom legal systems), but both play an important part in the legal systems of all European Union countries. In addition the E.C.J., in its role as a part of the English legal system,[203] is usually not a court of first instance but a court of appeal of a peculiar kind, hearing references from, and giving advice to, the national courts.[204] The procedure of both courts is heavily civilian in basis; that of the E.C.J. is governed by the statutes of the Court of Justice[205] and by the Rules of Procedure of June 19, 1991,[206] and that of the C.F.I.[207] is governed by the same Statutes and by the Rules of Procedure of May 2, 1991.[208] In each case there are broadly three phases:

(a) *The Written Procedure*,[209] broadly equivalent to pleadings in the English system.

(b) *A preparatory phase*,[210] dealing with various more or less "interlocutory" matters, including disclosure (but *including* the taking of evidence from witnesses and experts).

(c) *The Oral Procedure*,[211] equivalent to the *argument* part of the final hearing in the English system.

In the civilian systems, the role of the English "trial" is largely performed by a series of hearings at which evidence may be taken and argument made.[212] Thus, by the time of the final arguments, the evidence is already complete.

---

[202] See generally, Vaughan, *Law of the European Communities,* 1991, Pt 2; Lasok, *The European Court of Justice, Practice and Procedure,* 2nd edn, 1994, Ch.11; Brown and Jacobs, *The Court of Justice of the European Communities,* 5th edn, 2000; Anderson and Demetriou, *References to the European Court,* 2002, Ch.12; Barents, Von Halstein (eds.), *European Courts Procedure,* 2004; Lenaerts, Arts and Maselis, *Procedural Law of the European Union,* 2nd edn, 2006, Ch.24.

[203] European Communities Act 1972, s.3(1).

[204] See E.E.C. Treaty, Art.177; E.C.S.C. Treaty, Art.41; Euratom Treaty, Art.150; Dine, Douglas-Scott and Persaud, *Procedure and the European Court,* 1991, Ch.2; CPR, Sch.1, RSC, Ord.114; CPR, Sch.2, CCR Ord.19 r.15.

[205] Of which there are three: one for the E.C.S.C. cases, one for E.E.C. cases, and one for Euratom cases.

[206] O.J. 1991 L. 176/7.

[207] See also *Practice Note* [1999] All E.R. (E.C.) 641.

[208] O.J. 1991 L. 136/1, as amended in 1994 (O.J. 1994 L. 249/17), 1995 (O.J. 1995 L. 172/3) and 1997 (O.J. 1997 L. 103/6).

[209] Arts 37–44a (E.C.J.); Arts 43–54 (C.F.I.).

[210] Arts 45–54 (E.C.J.); Arts 64–76 (C.F.I.).

[211] Arts 55–62 (E.C.J.); Arts 55–63 (C.F.I.).

[212] *cf.* Ch.1, para.1.01, above.

It is necessary to distinguish the rules laid down in the Statutes of the **20.33** Court from the Rules of Procedure. The former confer power on either court to require the parties, Member States and institutions which are not parties "to produce all documents and to supply all information which the court considers desirable."[213] This is the appropriate procedure for disclosure of documents.[214] The only sanction for breach of an order under this power, however, is that "formal note" is taken, and adverse inferences may be drawn.[215] The E.C.S.C. Statute contains the sole example of "automatic" disclosure, in that an institution of the E.C.S.C. against whom proceedings are instituted is obliged to send "all the documents relating to the case" to the court.[216] Apart from that provision, there is no automatic duty to disclose relevant documents.

The disclosure aspects of the Rules of Procedure arise partly in the **20.34** Written Procedure, but mostly in the preparatory phase. In the former it is provided that a party must annex to his pleading a file of the documents relied on in support,[217] and where certain kinds of application are made, or defences to such applications are made, a party must state the nature of any evidence relied on or offered by him.[218] Similarly, where a reply or rejoinder is made, further evidence may be offered.[219] In the preparatory phase, there are specific provisions for what are called "Measures of Inquiry." These are prescribed by the court, after hearing the Advocate-General, and include requests for information and production of documents from parties and non-parties,[220] the commissioning of an expert's report,[221] and inspection of a place or thing in question.[222] The court must hear the parties before ordering the second and third of these,[223] but there is no requirement to do so for the first. It is also possible for the court to issue a letter of request where the witness is to be examined in the territory of a member State.[224]

In proceedings before the European Commission, the Commission has an **20.35** obligation to make available to undertakings involved all documents, whether in their favour or otherwise which it has obtained during the course of the investigation, save where the business secrets of other undertakings, the internal documents of the commission or other confidential information

---

[213] E.C.S.C. Statute, Art.24; E.E.C. Statute, Art.21; Euratom Statute, Art.22.
[214] *Case 121/86R, Epikhinseon Metalleftikon Viomikhanikon Kai Naftiliakon A.E. v E.C. Council and Commission* [1987] 1 C.M.L.R. 57, E.C.J.
[215] *cf.* Ch.1, para.1.24, n.102, above.
[216] E.C.S.C. Statute, Art.23; see *Case 2/54, Italy v High Authority* [1954–56] E.C.R. 37.
[217] Rules of Procedure (E.C.J.), Art.37, para.4; Rules of Procedure (C.F.I.), Art.43, para.4.
[218] Rules of Procedure (E.C.J.), Arts 38, para.1(e), 40, para.(d); Rules of Procedure (C.F.I.), Arts 44, para.1(e), 46(d).
[219] Rules of Procedure (E.C.J.), Art.42, para.1; Rules of Procedure (C.F.I.), Art.48, para.1.
[220] Rules of Procedure (E.C.J.), Art.45, para.2(b); Rules of Procedure (C.F.I.), Art.65(b).
[221] Rules of Procedure (E.C.J.), Arts 45, para.2(d), 49; Rules of Procedure (C.F.I.), Art.65(d), 68.
[222] Rules of Procedure (E.C.J.), Art.45, para.2(e); Rules of Procedure (C.F.I.), Art.65(e).
[223] Rules of Procedure (E.C.J.), Art.45, para.1; Rules of Procedure (C.F.I.), Art.66, para.1.
[224] Supplementary Rules, 4 December 1974, Arts 1–3.

are concerned.[225] But in proceedings before the European Court, the Commission may not use as evidence on a document not disclosed to the other party and not included in the files submitted to the court.[226] Moreover, access by parties to Council and Commission documents should only be refused where documents had been produced specifically for particular court proceedings, not only those subject to normal legal privilege but also correspondence about the case between the individual Directorate General and the relevant lawyer or legal office. Purely administrative documents, even if prejudicial to the Commission's case, should not be withheld.[227]

Interim measures

20.36   It is necessary to mention one other aspect of the procedure of the court and that relates to what are known as "interim measures," which can be ordered by the court under Art.186 of the EEC Treaty and Art.83 of the Rules of Procedure. Broadly this covers measures which are provisional or interlocutory, designed to preserve the status quo until the court can render a final judgment. But, in the absence of exceptional circumstances (e.g. a risk of destruction, concealment or falsification of relevant documents), an application for interim measures is not an appropriate procedure for obtaining the production of documents.[228]

Privilege

20.37   There are circumstances in which documents need not be produced in proceedings as set out above, but the rules governing such circumstances are less well developed than, and not to the same effect as, the English rules of privilege.[229] Protection is given to written communications between an independent (but not an "in-house") lawyer and his client made for the purposes and in the interests of the client's rights of defence,[230] to medical information about a patient, unless the patient consents to disclosure or the

---

[225] *Hercules Chemicals v E.C. Commission* [1992] 4 C.M.L.R. 84; *Cimenteries C.B.R. v E.C. Commission* [1993] 4 C.M.L.R. 259; *B.P.B. Industries Plc v E.C. Commission* [1997] 4 C.M.L.R. 238.

[226] *A.K.Z.O. Chemie B.V. v E.C. Commission* [1994] F.S.R. 25, E.C.J.

[227] *Interporc Im- und Export GmbH v Commission of the European Communities* [2000] 1 C.M.L.R. 181, C.F.I.

[228] *Case 129/86R, Re Anti-Dumping Documents: Greece v EC Council and Commission* [1988] 3 C.M.L.R. 728, [1987] E.C.R. 833; see also at [1987] 1 C.M.L.R. 57.

[229] As to which, see Ch.11, above.

[230] *Case 155/79, A.M. & S. Europe Ltd v Commission of the European Communities* [1983] Q.B. 878, E.C.J.

examination is carried out in an administrative recruitment procedure,[231] and to documents disclosure of which might threaten national security.[232] Protection may also be given to confidential information of a Community institution required for the proper functioning of that institution.[233]

O. FINANCIAL SERVICES AND MARKETS TRIBUNAL

This tribunal was set up to deal with various references and appeals made **20.38** to it under the Financial Services and Markets Act 2000.[234] It is one of four known as "the Finance and Tax Tribunals", which share a common head and administration and are based at the same address. Rules of procedure have been made by the Lord Chancellor.[235] In addition, however, there are also procedural provisions in the primary legislation itself.[236] Thus, for example, the tribunal may by summons require any person to attend, at a specified time and place, to give evidence or to produce any document in his custody or under his control which it considers it necessary to examine.[237] The Act contains wide-ranging information-gathering powers. For instance, the Inland Revenue may pass on Revenue information to the Financial Services Authority for the purposes of a s.168 investigation.[238]

Under the rules, the statement of case of the Financial Services Authority **20.39** must be accompanied by a list of the documents on which the Authority relies in support of the referred action and the further material which in the opinion of the Authority might undermine the decision to take that action.[239] The reply of the applicant must be accompanied by a list of all the documents on which the applicant relies in support of his case.[240] Within 14 days of service of the reply the Authority must file a further list of any further material which might be reasonably expected to assist the applicant's case as disclosed by the applicant's reply and which is not mentioned in the Authority's initial list.[241] A party who has provided a list must on request provide copies of documents or make them available for inspection

---

[231] *Case 155/78, M. v Commission of the European Communities* [1980] E.C.R. 1797, E.C.J.; *cf. Case 18/70, X v Council of the European Communities* [1972] E.C.R. 1205, E.C.J.
[232] E.E.C. Treaty, Art.223(1)(a).
[233] *Case 2/54, Italy v High Authority* [1954–56] E.C.R. 37 at 54–55; *Case 110/75, Mills v European Investment Bank* [1976] E.C.R. 1613, E.C.J.
[234] Financial Services and Markets Act 2000, s.132(1).
[235] Financial Services and Markets Tribunal Rules 2001, SI 2001/2476, made under the Financial Services and Markets Act 2000, s.132(3).
[236] Financial Services and Markets Act 2000, Sch.13 Pt IV.
[237] Financial Services and Markets Act 2000, Sch.13, para.11(1).
[238] Financial Services and Markets Act 2000, s.350.
[239] Financial Services and Markets Tribunal Rules 2001, r.5(3).
[240] Financial Services and Markets Tribunal Rules 2001, r.6(3).
[241] Financial Services and Markets Tribunal Rules 2001, r.7.

and inspection.[242] There are various exceptions to disclosure, and also provision for applications to the tribunal for authority not to disclose (e.g. on public interest grounds).[243] The tribunal may make directions for the provision of further information,[244] the filing of any document that is in the custody or the control of a party which the tribunal considers is or may be relevant to the determination of the reference,[245] and as to expert evidence.[246] Any documents or information sought must be relevant to the issues in the reference.[247] The tribunal has power to summon witnesses to give oral evidence or provide documents.[248] The tribunal has power to deal with failures to comply with the rules or a direction.[249]

P. HIGH COURT OF CHIVALRY[250]

20.40   This ancient civil-law[251] court has jurisdiction in questions of the right to arms, descent, precedence[252] and similar matters of honour, falling outside the jurisdiction of the old common law courts. However, it has no jurisdiction in relation to peerages, which in England are in practice dealt with by the Committee of Privileges of the House of Lords.[253] After not having sat for over 200 years and having been considered by Blackstone[254] to have fallen into contempt and disuse, but never having been formally abolished; the High Court of Chivalry sat again in 1955.[255] It appears that the practice and procedure of the court are civilian,[256] as were its practitioners and judges[257] and that it has never enjoyed the documentary disclosure procedures known to modern courts. But, as happened in other civilian courts,[258] evidence of witnesses was taken on commission, in advance of trial,[259] and

---

[242] Financial Services and Markets Tribunal Rules 2001, r.8(7).
[243] Financial Services and Markets Tribunal Rules 2001, r.8.
[244] Financial Services and Markets Tribunal Rules 2001, r.10(1)(f).
[245] Financial Services and Markets Tribunal Rules 2001, r.10(1)(g).
[246] Financial Services and Markets Tribunal Rules 2001, r.10(1)(l).
[247] *Davidson v Financial Services Authority* [2004] U.K.F.S.M. FSM011, at paras 40–42.
[248] Financial Services and Markets Tribunal Rules 2001, r.12.
[249] Financial Services and Markets Tribunal Rules 2001, r.27.
[250] See generally, Squibb, *The High Court of Chivalry*, 1959.
[251] i.e. based on Roman law rather than common law.
[252] However, see Squibb, *Precedence in England and Wales*, 1981, at 90–93.
[253] See para.20.11, above.
[254] 3 Bl. Comm. 105.
[255] *Manchester Corporation v Manchester Palace of Varieties Ltd* [1953] P. 133; see Squibb, *The High Court of Chivalry*, 1959, Ch.9.
[256] Squibb, *op. cit.*, Ch.13
[257] Squibb, *op. cit.*, Ch.10.
[258] e.g. the ecclesiastical courts until 1854: see Holdsworth, *A History of English Law*, 7th edn, 1956, Vol.XII, pp.678–685.
[259] Squibb, *op. cit.*, at 200–207.

invariably included interrogatories.[260] Interrogatories could also be applied to the parties, by means of separate letters commissory.[261]

Q. IMMIGRATION APPEALS[262]

There were formerly three tribunals involved with immigration appeals: the immigration adjudicator, the Immigration Appeals Tribunal, and the Special Immigration Appeals Commission (dealing with cases involving national security issues). The third continues to exist today. The first two have since April 2005 been amalgamated into the Asylum and Immigration Tribunal ("AIT").[263] There are two kinds of procedure for appeals to the AIT, normal and fast-track, each governed by statutory rules.[264] But most of the general rules of procedure in the normal system apply also to the fast track system.[265] Under the old rules it was held that there was nothing in either the Rules or the Immigration Act 1971 giving power to order general disclosure.[266] The ordinary rules of privilege applied to evidence to be given and documents to be produced.[267] If judicial review proceedings were subsequently instituted, then disclosure might be ordered in accordance with the rules governing such proceedings, but only for the purpose of those proceedings, and not for the purpose of retrying the original appeal.[268]

20.41

The new rules likewise contain no power to order general disclosure. But they provide for directions to be given (*inter alia*) concerning the preparation for a hearing,[269] including requiring witness statements to be filed in advance[270] (and served on the other parties), for summoning persons in the United Kingdom as witnesses, whether to give oral evidence or to produce documents in their custody or under their control relating to any matter in issue in the appeal,[271] and for the making available to all parties of evidence

20.42

---

[260] Squibb, *op. cit.*, at 203–205.

[261] Squibb, *op. cit.*, at 207–208.

[262] See generally, Jackson and Warr, *Immigration Law and Practice*, 3rd edn, 2001 (looseleaf), Chs 21–24; Macdonald & Webber, *Immigration Law & Practice*, 6th edn, 2005, Ch.18; Joint Council for Welfare of Immigrants, *Immigration, Nationality and Refugee Law Handbook*, 2006, s.10.

[263] Asylum and Immigration (Treatment of Claimants etc.) Act 2004, s.26(1), substituting a new s.81 into the Nationality, Immigration and Asylum Act 2002.

[264] Asylum and Immigration Tribunal (Procedure) Rules 2005, SI 2005/230; Asylum and Immigration Tribunal (Fast Track Procedure) Rules 2005, SI 2005/560;

[265] Asylum and Immigration Tribunal (Fast Track Procedure) Rules 2005, r.27, incorporating most of Pt 5 of the Asylum and Immigration Tribunal (Procedure) Rules 2005.

[266] *R. v Immigration Adjudicator, ex p. Home Secretary* [1989] Imm.A.R. 423, *The Times*, March 29, 1989.

[267] 1984 Rules, r.29(2); 1996 Rules, r.29(2).

[268] *R. v Home Secretary, ex p.Gardian* [1996] Imm.A.R. 6, CA.

[269] Asylum and Immigration Tribunal (Procedure) Rules 2005, r.45(1).

[270] Asylum and Immigration Tribunal (Procedure) Rules 2005, r.45(4)(e)(i).

[271] Asylum and Immigration Tribunal (Procedure) Rules 2005, r.50(1).

taken into account by the tribunal (with a public interest exception).[272] Evidence not complying with a direction setting time limits for filing and serving written evidence must not be considered by the tribunal unless it is satisfied that there are good reasons for doing so.[273] The ordinary rules of privilege apply to evidence to be given and documents to be produced.[274] Under the old rules, where the tribunal had documents which had not been seen by the applicants' representatives, there was a procedural irregularity, but it was always necessary to consider its effect. If on the facts there was no breach of natural justice and no possibility of a different decision (e.g. because the documents concerned were either irrelevant or helpful to the appellant taken as a whole), the decision would not be impugned.[275] Now there is an express rule that an error of procedure odes not invalidate the decision, but the tribunal has power to step any step to correct it.[276] There is no requirement of disclosure on the Home Secretary beyond the Rules themselves, so the fact that he decides to refuse asylum having taken into account information not made available to the special adjudicator is not a basis for judicial review of his decision.[277]

20.43   The Special Immigration Appeals Commission hears appeals against exclusion, deportation and removal from the United Kingdom in cases where there would normally be a right of appeal, but a "conducive to the public good" exception applies.[278] The procedure is governed by the Special Immigration Appeals Commission (Procedure) Rules 1998.[279] These Rules provide for directions to be given (*inter alia*) for the conduct of proceedings,[280] including requiring witness statements to be filed in advance[281] (and served on the other parties[282]), for summoning persons in the United Kingdom as witnesses, whether to give oral evidence or to produce documents in their custody or under their control relating to any matter in question in the appeal.[283] The ordinary rules of privilege apply to evidence to be given and documents to be produced.[284] There is no provision for general disclosure. Moreover, and unlike the case of appeals to the AIT,[285] there is no provision for the inspection by all parties of evidence taken into consideration by the

---

[272] Asylum and Immigration Tribunal (Procedure) Rules 2005, r.51(7).
[273] Asylum and Immigration Tribunal (Procedure) Rules 2005, r.51(4).
[274] Asylum and Immigration Tribunal (Procedure) Rules 2005, r.51(2).
[275] *R. v Secretary of State for the Home Department, ex p. Singh* [1992] Imm.A.R. 607; *R. v Secretary of State for the Home Department, ex p. Fulop* [1995] Imm.A.R. 323, CA.
[276] Asylum and Immigration Tribunal (Procedure) Rules 2005, r.59.
[277] *R. v Secretary of State for the Home Department, ex p. Abdi* [1995] C.O.D. 73, *The Times*, April 25, 1994, CA.
[278] Special Immigration Appeals Commission Act 1997, s.2.
[279] SI 1998/1881, as amended by SI 2000/1849.
[280] Special Immigration Appeals Commission (Procedure) Rules 1998, r.13(1).
[281] Special Immigration Appeals Commission (Procedure) Rules 1998, r.13(2)(c)(i).
[282] Special Immigration Appeals Commission (Procedure) Rules 1998, r.13(2)(c).
[283] Special Immigration Appeals Commission (Procedure) Rules 1998, r.21(1).
[284] Special Immigration Appeals Commission (Procedure) Rules 1998, r.20(4).
[285] Asylum and Immigration Tribunal (Procedure) Rules 2005, r.51(7); see para.19.40, above.

Commission. Indeed, the Commission is under a general duty to ensure that information is not disclosed contrary to the public interest.[286]

R. INFORMATION TRIBUNAL

The Information Tribunal (previously called Data Protection Tribunal) **20.44** was originally set up to hear appeals under the Data Protection Act 1984. It continued to hear appeals after the Data Protection Act 1998 came into effect, but later it also became responsible for hearing information appeals under the Freedom of Information Act 2000, after which it was renamed the Information Tribunal. Since then, it has acquired further jurisdiction under the Privacy and Electronic Communications Regulations 2003 and the Environmental Information Regulations 2004. Procedure is governed by the Information Tribunal (Enforcement Appeals) Rules 2005,[287] the Information Tribunal (National Security Appeals)(Telecommunications) Rules 2000,[288] and the Information Tribunal (National Security Appeals) Rules 2005.[289]

The Tribunal may give directions for disclosure to be given by list,[290] **20.45** followed by inspection,[291] and exchange of statements of evidence,[292] for supply to the Tribunal and other parties of documents and material in the party's power,[293] limits on expert witnesses,[294] and so on. There is the usual provision for privilege attaching to documents and other communications to be respected,[295] and it is made express that information supplied under compulsion of these rules or directions under them may only be used for the purposes of these proceedings.[296] A failure to comply with a direction may lead to a claim or defence being struck out.[297] The Tribunal has made a practice direction[298] relating to the maintenance of confidentiality of documents produced to it in connection with enforcement appeals. This is of particular importance in the Information Tribunal, where the Tribunal will often wish to see the information the subject of the appeal (being the "best evidence" for the respondent) before deciding the appeal.

The Tribunal also has power to order any occupier of land in the UK to **20.46** permit the Tribunal, accompanied by the parties, to enter their land and

---

[286] Special Immigration Appeals Commission (Procedure) Rules 1998, r.3; see also r.13(1).
[287] SI 2005/14 (hereafter "ITEAR").
[288] SI 2000/XX (hereafter "ITNSATR").
[289] SI 2005/XX (hereafter "ITNSAR").
[290] ITEAR, r.14(2)(b)(i); ITNSATR, r.15(4)(b)(i); ITNSAR, r.16(4)(b)(i).
[291] ITEAR, r.14(2)(b)(ii); ITNSATR, r.15(4)(b)(ii); ITNSAR, r.16(4)(b)(ii.
[292] ITEAR, r.14(2)(b)(iii); ITNSATR, r.15(4)(b)(iii); ITNSAR, r.16(4)(b)(iii).
[293] ITEAR, r.14(2)(d)(v); ITNSATR, r.15(4)(b)(v); ITNSAR, r.16(4)(b)(v).
[294] ITEAR, r.14(2)(f); ITNSATR, r.15(4)(e); ITNSAR, r.16(4)(e).
[295] ITEAR, r.14(5); ITNSATR, r.15(6); ITNSAR, r.16(6).
[296] ITEAR, r.14(6); ITNSATR, r.15(7); ITNSAR, r.16(7).
[297] ITEAR, r.14(9), (10); cf. ITNSATR, r.28(1)(c); ITNSAR, r.16(11).
[298] Practice Direction 1, March 2006.

inspect or test equipment on those premises connected with the processing of personal data or the storage or recording of other information, and to inspect or test any documents or other material on those premises similarly connected,[299] but again subject to privilege.[300] Finally, the Tribunal may by summons require any person in the UK to attend as a witness at a hearing of an appeal and to produce any documents in his custody or under his control which relate to any matter in question in the appeal.[301]

S. INTERNATIONAL TRIBUNALS

20.47 Some tribunals created to hear and determine international disputes between parties from different states may have power, under their constitutive treaties, to order disclosure of documents or other information. But usually there is no machinery for compelling compliance with such orders and the usual sanction for non-compliance is the drawing by the tribunal of adverse inferences on the facts.[302]

T. LAND REGISTRY[303]

20.48 The registrar has power, for the purposes of proceedings before him, to compel the production by any person of "a document".[304] He may exercise the power if he is satisfied that the document concerned is in the control of the document holder, may be relevant to the proceedings, and disclosure is necessary to dispose fairly of the proceedings or to save costs.[305] However, where disputes arise in relation to: (i) objections to applications[306]; (ii) appeals about access to the Land Registry network[307]; or (iii) claims to rectification or setting aside of certain documents,[308] these are referred to the Adjudicator to the Land Registry. There are statutory rules of procedure for the preparation and conduct of hearings in the exercise of that jurisdiction.[309] Like the CPR, these contain a statement of the "overriding objec-

---

[299] ITEAR, r.5(1).
[300] ITEAR, r.15(9).
[301] ITEAR, r.18(1); ITNSATR, r.20(2); ITNSAR, r.21(2).
[302] See, e.g. *I.N.A. Corporation v Iran* (1985) 8 Iran-US Claims Tribunals Reports 373, 382.
[303] See generally, Ruoff & Roper, *Law & Practice of Registered Land.*
[304] Land Registration Act 2002, s.75, Land Registration Rules 2003, r.201.
[305] Land Registration Rules 2003, r.201(7).
[306] Land Registration Act 2002, s.73(7),
[307] Land Registration Act 2002, Sch.5, para.4.
[308] Land Registration Act 2002, s.108(2).
[309] Adjudicator to Her Majesty's Land Registry (Practice and Procedure) Rules 2003, SI 2003/2171.

tive",[310] and make detailed provision for directions to be given,[311] including that a party produce any document or other material either to the adjudicator or to another party,[312] for further information to be supplied by either side,[313] for disclosure and inspection of specific documents,[314] witness statements,[315] for "requirement notices" (in effect witness summonses, both for evidence to be given, and for documents and material to be produced),[316] for site inspections,[317] for experts,[318] and for failure to comply with directions.[319] It is also provided that failure to follow a rule does not necessarily invildate steps taken in the proceedings, and may be corrected.[320]

U. LANDS TRIBUNAL[321]

The Lands Tribunal is a specialist tribunal[322] having jurisdiction over a number of matters concerned with valuing land (e.g. in relation to rating and compensation claims).[323] Procedure generally is governed by statutory rules.[324] Under these rules, the Tribunal or its registrar has power, either of its or his own motion or on application by a party, to order any party (*inter alia*):

20.49

    (a) to deliver to the registrar any document or information required by the tribunal and within his power to deliver, and to allow them to be inspected and copied by other parties[325];

    (b) to give "discovery"[326] by list or affidavit of specified documents or classes of documents now or in the past "in his possession, custody

---

[310] Adjudicator to Her Majesty's Land Registry (Practice and Procedure) Rules 2003, r.3.
[311] Adjudicator to Her Majesty's Land Registry (Practice and Procedure) Rules 2003, r.20.
[312] Adjudicator to Her Majesty's Land Registry (Practice and Procedure) Rules 2003, r.21(3).
[313] Adjudicator to Her Majesty's Land Registry (Practice and Procedure) Rules 2003, r.25.
[314] Adjudicator to Her Majesty's Land Registry (Practice and Procedure) Rules 2003, rr.27, 47.
[315] Adjudicator to Her Majesty's Land Registry (Practice and Procedure) Rules 2003, r.26.
[316] Adjudicator to Her Majesty's Land Registry (Practice and Procedure) Rules 2003, r.28.
[317] Adjudicator to Her Majesty's Land Registry (Practice and Procedure) Rules 2003, r.30.
[318] Adjudicator to Her Majesty's Land Registry (Practice and Procedure) Rules 2003, r.49.
[319] Adjudicator to Her Majesty's Land Registry (Practice and Procedure) Rules 2003, r.55.
[320] Adjudicator to Her Majesty's Land Registry (Practice and Procedure) Rules 2003, r.56.
[321] See generally, Preston and Newsom, *Restrictive Covenants Affecting Freehold Land*, 9th edn, 1998.
[322] Established under the Lands Tribunal Act 1949.
[323] See the Land Compensation Act 1961.
[324] Lands Tribunal Rules 1996, SI 1996/1022.
[325] Lands Tribunal Rules 1996, r.34(1)(a), (b).
[326] So stated in the heading to r.34, though the rule itself refers neither to discovery nor to disclosure.

or power", and (if in the past) stating when he parted with them[327];

(c) to answer interrogatories on affidavit as to any matter in issue between the parties concerned[328];

(d) to deliver to the registrar witness statements or proofs of evidence.[329]

20.50   However, the Rules do not empower the Tribunal to order a party to give general disclosure of documents (i.e. all documents relevant to the matters in issue).[330] It was formerly possible for application to be made to the High Court for an order for general discovery in Lands Tribunal proceedings, under the Arbitration Act 1950, s.12(6)(b),[331] but that provision was repealed in 1990,[332] and the Rules themselves are now different.[333] There is provision for site inspections by the Tribunal.[334] In the first instance, interlocutory applications are made to the registrar,[335] with a right of appeal to the President.[336] Curiously, there is no provision in the Rules for compelling the attendance of witnesses at the hearing, so the relevant provisions of the CPR will apply.[337]

20.51   Where a party is ordered to deliver any document to the registrar, the Tribunal or registrar may give directions as to the time for such delivery (being at least 14 days from the date of the direction).[338] This provision also refers to directions as to "the parties to whom copies of the document are to be sent", although nothing in the earlier part of the Rule[339] confers power to order that a party *send* copies to anyone else; instead it refers to affording others an opportunity to *inspect and take* copies.[340] It may be that when the previous Rules were replaced this wording was overlooked and not changed.[341]

20.52   The Rules make detailed provision for expert evidence applying in Lands Tribunal proceedings. Unless the Tribunal otherwise orders,[342] only one expert is allowed on each side,[343] except in mineral valuation or business

---

[327] Lands Tribunal Rules 1996, r.34(1)(c).
[328] Lands Tribunal Rules 1996, r.34(1)(e).
[329] Lands Tribunal Rules 1996, r.34(1)(g).
[330] *Kingsley v I.R.C.* [1987] 2 E.G.L.R. 217.
[331] Applied by virtue of the Lands Tribunal Rules 1975, r.38.
[332] Courts and Legal Services Act 1990, s.103.
[333] *cf.* Lands Tribunal Rules 1996, r.32 (as substituted by SI 1997/1965).
[334] Lands Tribunal Rules 1996, r.29.
[335] Lands Tribunal Rules 1996, r.38(1).
[336] Lands Tribunal Rules 1996, r.38(9).
[337] CPR, r.34.4(1); see Ch.10, paras 10.24, above.
[338] Lands Tribunal Rules 1996, r.34(2).
[339] i.e. r.34(1).
[340] See r.34(1)(b).
[341] *cf.* Lands Tribunal Rules 1975, r.40(2).
[342] Lands Tribunal Rules 1996, r.42(4).
[343] Lands Tribunal Rules 1996, r.42(2).

disturbance cases, when two are permitted on a side.[344] A party must within 28 days of receiving a request from the registrar send to him and to every other party a copy of (a) the expert's report (including plans and valuations) and (b) *either* details of all comparable properties and transactions intended to be referred to by the party at the hearing *or* a statement that there are none.

If a party fails to send a document as required under the Rules, the Tribunal may: **20.53**

(a) direct that a copy of the document be sent;
(b) adjourn the further hearing of the proceedings; and
(c) order the party at fault to pay any additional costs occasioned as a result.[345]

In addition, a failure to comply with any of the provisions of the Rules enables the registrar or the Tribunal, on the application of a party or of its own motion, after giving the parties an opportunity to be heard, to make

(a) an order that the proceedings be heard by the Tribunal; or
(b) an order that the proceedings be dismissed or that any party be debarred from taking any further part;
(c) such other order as may be appropriate for expediting or disposing of the proceedings, including an order for costs.[346]

V. LLOYD'S DISCIPLINARY COMMITTEE AND APPEAL TRIBUNAL

The Disciplinary Committee (Enforcement Committees) and Appeal Tri-   **20.54** bunal of Lloyd's are established, by subordinate legislation,[347] to deal with disciplinary proceedings against members, subscribers, brokers, agents and others and with appeals from such proceedings. The primary legislation does not provide for any general or specific disclosure procedures as between the parties to such proceedings. However, any such party may obtain witness summonses,[348] although no one can be thereby compelled to

---

[344] Lands Tribunal Rules 1996, r.42(3).
[345] Lands Tribunal Rules 1996, r.46(1).
[346] Lands Tribunal Rules 1996, r.46(2).
[347] i.e. byelaws under the Lloyd's Act 1982, s.7, and see in particular Enforcement Byelaw (2005).
[348] Lloyd's Act 1982, s.7(4).

produce any document which he could not be compelled to produce at the trial of an action.

W. MEDIATION[349]

20.55   Mediation is a form or alternative dispute resolution, by which the parties to a dispute engage a third party to facilitate their discussions and possible resolution of that dispute. Where it leads to a settlement, it saves significant legal costs. *Ex hypothesi* it occurs outside the framework of court proceedings, although the courts mostly encourage it,[350] and the CPR refer to it at various points.[351] Unreasonable failure to mediate may sound in costs.[352] Mediations can take place at any stage of a dispute, so in broad terms they can be any of three kinds: (i) mediation before any proceedings have been commenced; (ii) mediation after proceedings commenced but *before* disclosure and inspection have taken place; (iii) mediation after proceedings commenced and *after* disclosure and inspection have taken place. In considering the *scope* of disclosure of documents in litigation, the fact that a mediation may or will take place, and that documents may or will be relevant to that, is irrelevant.[353] Nor can the fact that the court has case-management powers, including to suggest (or even direct) mediation, have any impact on matters of privilege.[354]

20.56   Even where the mediation is not of type (iii) above, there is often some form of disclosure (almost always voluntary) beforehand, as parties are usually unhappy at settling without knowing what cards the other side holds. Sometimes such information is provided by a would-be claimant pursuant to a pre-action protocol[355]; sometimes it is sought by pro-active lawyers acting for the would-be defendant to whom a claim has been intimated. Sometimes a party discloses information where not to do so would or might amount to a misrepresentation, in order to preserve any resulting settlement from the risk of being avoided subsequently on that ground. Every mediation is consensual, and normally a contract is entered into between the parties and the mediator. Typically this will make clear that the fact of the mediation and any confidential disclosures of information made at it or for its purposes are "without prejudice" and not to be

---

[349] Boulle and Nesic, *Mediation*, 2001, Ch.12, esp. at 487–506.

[350] Though see *Yorkshire Electricity Distribution Plc v Telewest Plc* [2006] EWCA Civ 1418, para.47 (encouragement to parties to use expert determination in future, as mediation "carries too much potential for the leisurely ventilation of extensive issues").

[351] CPR, rr.1.4(2)(f), 26.4, 56.3(4)(a).

[352] See, e.g. *Halsey v Milton Keynes N.H.S. Trust* [2004] 1 W.L.R. 3002, CA.

[353] *Beneficial Finance Corporation Ltd v Price Waterhouse* (1996) 68 S.A.S.R. 19, Sup.Ct.S.A. (Full Ct.).

[354] *South Australia v Peat Marwick Mitchell* (1995) 65 S.A.S.R. 72, Sup.Ct.S.A.

[355] See CPR Practice Directions—Protocols.

disclosed or used in any proceedings.[356] Even without such agreement, the courts have so treated such information.[357] But without prejudice privilege has its limits, and the parties may wish to go further than these by express contract. So the agreement may also provide that the mediator is not to be asked to give evidence or give disclosure relating to the mediation in any legal proceedings thereafter. But this would not prevent the *court* or other tribunal doing so,[358] and if there were no contract to inhibit the parties one or other might apply for a witness summons against him. In that event he could not be required to reveal anything covered by "without prejudice" privilege, unless the parties together waived that privilege.[359] The court in subsequent litigation cannot take account of any without prejudice communication on the question of unreasonable failure to mediate unless it is "without prejudice save as to costs".[360]

It sometimes happens that documents subject to legal professional privilege are shown either to the mediator or to the other side during a mediation. Where a document is shown to the mediator in complete confidence (i.e. so that he may not pass on the contents or even the substance to the other side), privilege will be maintained.[361] Where, however, the mediator is authorised to confirm to the other side something limited about the document, say, that it is an opinion from leading counsel supporting his client's claim, the matter is not so clear, because the client has authorised a disclosure of an important aspect of the substance for the purpose of persuading the other side of the rightness of his cause. It is a question of fairness.[362] But, given that the disclosure occurred at a mediation, and mediation is to be encouraged, the court would probably be reluctant to hold that privilege is thereby waived. On the other hand, where the document is actually *shown* to the other side, whilst there is no clear authority, on principle it seems that it must lose its legal privilege.[363] Whether it could then be said to enjoy "without prejudice" privilege for the future seems difficult. The original document *ex hypothesi* was not brought into existence for the purpose

20.57

---

[356] See, e.g. Centre for Dispute Resolution, *Model Mediation Procedure*; City Disputes Panel, *Mediation Rules*; London Chamber of International Arbitration, *Mediation Procedure*.

[357] *AWA Ltd v Daniels* (1992) 7 A.C.S.R. 463; *Lukies v Ripley (No.2)* (1994) 35 N.S.W.L.R. 283; *Mercantile Mutual Custodians Pty Ltd v Village Nine Network Restaurants and Bars* [1999] Q.C.A. 276, Qld CA; *Re D (Minors)* [1993] Fam.231, CA; *Smiths Group Plc v Weiss*, March 22, 2002 (Ch.D. unreported); *Halsey v Milton Keynes N.H.S. Trust* [2004] 1 W.L.R. 3002, CA; *Hall v Pertemps Group Ltd, The Times*, December 23, 2005, Lewison J. (threats made during a mediation covered by privilege, unless waived by other action); *cf. Aird v Prime Meridian Ltd* [2006] EWCA Civ 1866 (joint statement by parties' experts under CPR r.35.12 but also used in mediation held not privileged).

[358] See, e.g. *Knight v Truss-Michaelis*, unreported, April 14, 1993, Queensland District Ct. (mediator's notes ordered to be made available in order to see if agreement come to).

[359] *Re D (Minors)* [1993] Fam.231, CA.

[360] *Reed Executive Plc v Reed Business Information Ltd* [2004] 1 W.L.R. 3026, CA.

[361] *cf. Leif Hoegh & Co. A/S v Petrolsea Inc.* [1993] 1 Lloyd's Rep. 363.

[362] See Ch.12, para.12.6.

[363] See Ch.12, para.12.7 above; though see *South Australia v Peat Marwick Mitchell* (1995) 65 S.A.S.R. 72, Sup.Ct. S.A.

of seeking to settle the dispute, even though a new photocopy made expressly for the purpose of showing the other side could be said to have been.

X. MENTAL HEALTH REVIEW TRIBUNALS[364]

20.58   These tribunals provide a forum for reviewing decisions and consequent action taken by medical authorities in relation to the state of mental health of patients who have been detained or are subject to guardianship under the Mental Health Act 1983. Their procedure is governed by the Mental Health Review Tribunal Rules 1983.[365] There is no power to order general "pre-trial" disclosure, but there are certain procedures for obtaining information prior to the hearing. Thus, unless the patient has been "conditionally discharged,"[366] within three weeks of an application having been made to the tribunal the "responsible authority" (the managers of the hospital or nursing home where the patient is detained, or the local authority social services department responsible for a patient subject to guardianship, as to the case may be) must provide the tribunal (and, in the case of a "restricted patient",[367] the Secretary of State for Health) with certain prescribed information and medical reports.[368] But if the patient is (or is to be) subject to after-care under supervision, the responsible authority shall send a statement of prescribed information to the tribunal alone.[369] Where the patient is a "restricted patient," the Secretary of State must do the same within three weeks of receiving the responsible authority's statement.[370] In the case of a conditionally discharged patient, the Secretary of State must send different prescribed information and reports to the tribunal within six weeks of the application having been made.[371]

20.59   In the first, third and fourth cases, the tribunal must upon receipt of the prescribed information and reports send copies to the applicant and to the patient (if he is not the applicant) excluding any information or report considered by the responsible authority or Secretary of State to be such that disclosure would adversely affect the health of the patient or others.[372] There is also a wider obligation on the tribunal to send, as soon as possible, copies of all the documents it receives which are relevant to the application

---

[364] Gostin, Rassaby and Buchan, *Mental Health: Tribunal Procedure*, 2nd edn, 1992; Hoggett, *Mental Health Law*, 4th edn, 1996, Ch.8; Eldergill, *Mental Health Review Tribunals Law and Practice*, 1997.

[365] SI 1983/942.

[366] See the Mental Health Act 1983, ss.42(2), 73 and 74.

[367] See the Mental Health Act 1983, s.79.

[368] Mental Health Review Tribunal Rules 1983, r.6(1).

[369] Mental Health Review Tribunal Rules 1983, r.6(3A) (inserted by SI 1996/314).

[370] Mental Health Review Tribunal Rules 1983, r.6(2).

[371] Mental Health Review Tribunal Rules 1983, r.6(3).

[372] Mental Health Review Tribunal Rules 1983, r.6(5).

to the applicant, the patient (if he is not the applicant), the responsible authority and (in the case of a restricted patient) the Secretary of State.[373] But where documents have been withheld from the applicant or the patient on the basis of the authority's or Secretary of State's opinion that disclosure would adversely affect the health of the patient or others, the tribunal must consider the matter afresh and, if it reaches the same conclusion, it must record its decision in writing.[374] However, the documents so withheld must nonetheless be disclosed to any authorised representative of the applicant or patient (being a lawyer, medical practitioner, or other suitable person), but expressly on the basis that no such information may be disclosed, directly or indirectly, to any other person (including the applicant or patient) without the tribunal's consent, or used otherwise than in connection with the application.[375]

In addition to the disclosure requirements outlined above, the tribunal **20.60** also had the power to *subpoena* any witness to appear before it or to produce documents, and the president of the tribunal might sue out a writ of *subpoena* (whether *ad testificandum* or *duces tecum*) as if he were a party to a reference under an arbitration agreement under the Arbitration Act 1950, s.12(4).[376] But s.12 of the 1950 Act has been repealed,[377] and though the replacement legislation contains a similar provision (referring to "court procedures" rather than writs of subpoena),[378] the CPR have also replaced the writ of subpoena with the witness summons.[379] Perhaps the unchanged rule will be construed now as a reference to obtaining a witness summons in aid of the tribunal. In any event, however, no one may be compelled to give any evidence or produce any document which could not be compelled at the trial of an action.[380]

Y. PENSIONS APPEAL TRIBUNALS

The procedure of this tribunal, which considers appeals relating to pen- **20.61** sions arising from government service, is governed by statutory rules.[381] On receipt of a notice of appeal,[382] the Secretary of State must prepare a "Statement of Case" containing all the relevant facts (including medical

---

[373] Mental Health Review Tribunal Rules 1983, r.12(1); see *R. v Oxford Mental Health Tribunal* [1986] 3 All E.R. 239, CA.
[374] Mental Health Review Tribunal Rules 1983, r.12(2).
[375] Mental Health Review Tribunal Rules 1983, r.12(3).
[376] Mental Health Review Tribunal Rules 1983, r.14(1).
[377] Arbitration Act 1996, s.107(2), Sch.4.
[378] *cf.* Arbitration Act 1996, s.43; para.20.05, above.
[379] See Ch.10, para.10.24, above.
[380] Mental Health Review Tribunal Rules 1983, r.14(1).
[381] Pensions Appeal Tribunals (England and Wales) Rules 1980, SI 1980/1120.
[382] Pensions Appeal Tribunals (England and Wales) Rules 1980, r.4.

history of the appellant).[383] Two copies must be sent to the appellant, who may then reply, disputing any of the facts alleged in the Statement of Facts and putting forward further relevant facts.[384] Where the appellant so disputes any of the facts, or puts forward further facts in reply, he must attach to his reply such documentary evidence in support as is in his possession or as he can reasonably obtain.[385]

20.62   Where for the purposes of his appeal an appellant seeks disclosure of any document (or part document) which he has reason to believe is in the possession of a government department, he may, not later than six weeks after the Statement of Case was sent to him, apply to the President of the tribunal for such disclosure.[386] If the President considers that the document (or part) is likely to be relevant to any issue to be determined on the appeal, he may require the department concerned (assuming possession) to give disclosure in such manner and upon such terms and conditions as he may think fit.[387] Disclosure of a certified true copy of a document is sufficient compliance with a disclosure order.[388] However, he cannot require disclosure of documents in the nature of departmental minutes or reports, or the name of a Crown servant who has given a report or medical certificate relevant to the case, and for this purpose the certificate of a government officer authorised by the minister that a specified document or name is within the exception is conclusive.[389]

20.63   In addition, the Minister may, on receipt of a disclosure direction from the President, certify to him either that it would be contrary to the public interest to disclose the document (or part) publicly, or that for reasons of security it ought not to be disclosed at all. In the former case, the President must give directions prohibiting or restricting the public disclosure of the document; in the latter case the President must direct the tribunal to consider whether the appellant's case will suffer without the disclosure and, if it will, they must adjourn the hearing of the appeal until the security problem no longer exists.[390] The tribunal must sit in private to the extent necessary to comply with the President's directions.[391]

20.64   At the hearing the appellant may apply to the tribunal for disclosure which he could have sought from the President, but the tribunal itself has no power to order such disclosure. Instead, if it appears to the tribunal that the document sought is likely to be relevant to any issue to be determined on the appeal, and that the appellant has a reasonable excuse for having failed to

---

[383] Pensions Appeal Tribunals (England and Wales) Rules 1980, r.5(1).
[384] Pensions Appeal Tribunals (England and Wales) Rules 1980, r.5(2).
[385] Pensions Appeal Tribunals (England and Wales) Rules 1980, r.5(3).
[386] Pensions Appeal Tribunals (England and Wales) Rules 1980, r.6(1); see *McGinley and Egan v UK* (1998) 4 EHRC 421.
[387] Pensions Appeal Tribunals (England and Wales) Rules 1980, r.6(1).
[388] Pensions Appeal Tribunals (England and Wales) Rules 1980, r.6(4).
[389] Pensions Appeal Tribunals (England and Wales) Rules 1980, r.6(3).
[390] Pensions Appeal Tribunals (England and Wales) Rules 1980, r.6(2).
[391] Pensions Appeal Tribunals (England and Wales) Rules 1980, r.35(2).

make an application to the President before the hearing, the tribunal may adjourn the case to enable the appellant to apply to the President.[392] Although the tribunal has power to summon "expert or other witnesses" before it,[393] there is no power expressly given to require persons to bring documents to the hearing. Accordingly, it would appear that the proper method of compelling the production of such documents should be by means of a witness summons, issued out of the High Court or any county court, in aid of the tribunal.[394] However, the new rule in the CPR, giving the court the power to issue a witness summons, only applies in favour of a court or tribunal that does not have power to issue a witness summons in relation to proceedings before it.[395] But the Pensions Appeal Tribunal *does* have power to summon witnesses[396]; what it apparently cannot do is to require the production of documents. So on its face the new rule cannot apply. Probably, however, the provision will be construed as applying to any court or tribunal that does not have the power to issue *the witness summons in question*, rather than witness summonses in general.

Z. PRIZE COURTS[397]

Prize courts administer the law of prize, that is, the law anciently relating to ships or goods captured by the maritime force of a belligerent at sea or seized in port, but now extended to cover aircraft and goods carried in aircraft, even where they are on or over land.[398] Prize courts determine whether a given ship, aircraft or goods is or are prize, and also questions relating to prize salvage (payable by the original owner on recapture of a prize from the enemy), and may even decide claims to civil salvage rendered to a ship or aircraft before seizure in prize. The prize courts are, broadly speaking, those courts exercising admiralty jurisdiction in Her Majesty's dominions.[399] In the United Kingdom,[400] this means the Admiralty Court of the High Court[401] and (theoretically) the Court of Admiralty of the Cinque Ports.[402] Appeals in prize causes lie to the Judicial Committee of the Privy

20.65

---

[392] Pensions Appeal Tribunals (England and Wales) Rules 1980, r.6(3).
[393] Pensions Appeal Tribunals (England and Wales) Rules 1980, r.12(4).
[394] CPR, r.34.4.
[395] CPR, r.34.4(3).
[396] Pensions Appeal Tribunals (England and Wales) Rules 1980, r.12(4).
[397] See generally, Colombos, *Law of Prize*, 3rd edn, 1949; Halsbury's *Laws of England*, 4th edn, Vol.34 (2004 Reissue), paras 1047 *et seq.*
[398] Prize Act 1939, s.1(1).
[399] Naval Prize Act 1864, s.3.
[400] i.e. including Scotland: see Court of Session Act 1825, s.57.
[401] Supreme Court Act 1981, ss.27, 61(1) and Sch.1 para.2(c), and 62(2). Admiralty county courts have no prize jurisdiction: County Courts Act 1984, s.27(8).
[402] See para.20.21, above.

Council.[403] The procedure of prize courts is governed, not by the CPR,[404] but by certain provisions of the Naval Prize Act 1864 and the Prize Court Rules 1939.[405] The procedure provides (*inter alia*) for delivery up to the court of ship/aircraft papers,[406] discovery by order (both specific[407] and general, although not automatic[408]) and inspection of documents,[409] interrogatories,[410] inspection of the prize by a party or the court's appointee,[411] depositions of witnesses[412] and the compulsory attendance of witnesses by means of writs of *subpoena*.[413] A prize court administers international law, and hence cannot be affected, in considering what disclosure should be given by a party, by any municipal law restricting the disclosures that may be made by that party.[414]

AA. PUBLIC INQUIRIES

20.66   This rather imprecise term covers different kinds of inquiry. First, there is the so-called "statutory inquiry," meaning an inquiry or hearing which is subject to the Tribunals and Inquiries Act 1992 and which is either held pursuant to a duty imposed by statute,[415] or is an inquiry or hearing at the discretion of a minister, being of a class designated by the Lord Chancellor.[416] Secondly, there is the inquiry or hearing required by a specific enactment but which is not subject to the Tribunals and Inquiries Act 1992. Thirdly, there is the inquiry, formerly known as the "non-statutory inquiry", but now held under the Inquiries Act 2005, at the instigation of a minister on the basis of "public concern" caused by the occurrence of particular events, or by the events themselves.[417] Like inquests,[418] public inquiries are not civil litigation to resolve disputes between two or more persons or bodies, or to apportion blame,[419] but instead inquisitorial procedures to

---

[403] Naval Prize Act 1864, s.5.
[404] CPR, r.2.1(2), Table, para.3.
[405] S. R. & O. 1939 No.1466.
[406] Naval Prize Act 1864, s.17, S. R. & O. 1939 No.1466, Ord.4.
[407] *The Consul Corfitzon* [1917] A.C. 550, P.C.
[408] S. R. & O. 1939 No.1466, Ord.IX, rr.1–3, Ord.XV, r.4.
[409] S. R. & O. 1939 No.1466, Ord.IX, rr.4–5, Ord.XV, r.4.
[410] S. R. & O. 1939 No.1466, Ord.XV, r.4.
[411] S. R. & O. 1939 No.1466, Ord.XI, r.11.
[412] S. R. & O. 1939 No.1466, Ord.XV, r.3, 11–14.
[413] S. R. & O. 1939 No.1466, Ord.XXIV, r.1–4.
[414] *The Baron Stjernblad* [1918] A.C. 173, P.C.; *The Kronpinzessin Victoria* [1919] A.C. 261, P.C.
[415] Particularly concerned with town and country planning or compulsory purchase of land.
[416] Tribunals and Inquiries Act 1992, s.16(1), (2); as to the designated classes, see the Tribunals and Inquiries (Discretionary Inquiries) Order 1967, SI 1967/451, treated as made under the 1992 Act.
[417] Inquiries Act 2005, s.1(1).
[418] See para.20.17, above.
[419] Inquiries Act 2005, s.2(1).

find facts or make recommendations for public purposes.[420] Accordingly, their procedures do not involve disclosure in the usual sense.

The Lord Chancellor has power under s.9 of the Tribunals and Inquiries   **20.67**
Act 1992[421] to make rules of procedure for many kinds of statutory inquiry.[422] These rules differ significantly from each other in the provision that they make for disclosure, and there is not space to set these out individually. The Inquiries Act 2005 provides that the procedure to be followed at an inquiry under that Act is to be as directed by the chairman,[423] and that he may by notice require a person to attend to give evidence or produce documents or any other thing in his custody or under his control that relate to a matter in question in the inquiry, or to provide a written statement.[424] But this is subject to a general exception for privileged information.[425] Rules have also been made for the procedure to be followed in the case of such inquiries,[426] but these do not include any disclosure provisions.

---

[420] B. *Johnson & Co. (Builders) Ltd v Minister of Health* [1947] 2 All E.R. 395 at 399, CA.
[421] Formerly s.11 of the Tribunals and Inquiries Act 1971.
[422] The Gas (Underground Storage) (Inquiries Procedure) Rules 1966, SI 1966/1375; The Electricity (Compulsory Wayleaves) (Hearings Procedure) Rules 1967, SI 1967/450; The Health and Safety Licensing Appeals (Inquiries Procedure) Rules 1974, SI 1974/2040; The Road Humps (Secretary of State) (Inquiries Procedure) Rules 1986, SI 1986/1957; The Medicines Act 1968 (Hearings by Persons Appointed) Rules 1986, SI 1986/1761; The Compulsory Purchase by Non-Ministerial Acquiring Authorities (Inquiries Procedure) Rules 1990, SI 1990/512; The Electricity Generating Stations and Overhead Lines (Inquiries Procedure) Rules 1990, SI 1990/528; The Public Libraries (Inquiries Procedure) Rules 1992, SI 1992/1627; The Highways (Inquiries Procedure) Rules 1994, SI 1994/3263; The Compulsory Purchase by Ministers (Inquiries Procedure) Rules 1994, SI 1994/3264; The Pipe-lines (Inquiries Procedure) Rules 1995, SI 1995/1239; The Town and Country Planning (Inquiries Procedure) (England) Rules 2000, SI 2000/1624; The Town and Country Planning Appeals (Determination by Inspectors) (Inquiries Procedure) (England) Rules 2000, SI 2000/1625; The Town and Country Planning (Hearings Procedure) (England) Rules 2000, SI 2000/1626; The Town and Country Planning (Major Infrastructure Project Inquiries Procedure) (England) Rules 2002, SI 2002/1223; The Town and Country Planning (Enforcement) (Hearings Procedure) (England) Rules 2002, SI 2002/2684; The Town and Country Planning (Enforcement) (Determination by Inspectors) (Inquiries Procedure) (England) Rules 2002, SI 2002/2685; The Town and Country Planning (Enforcement) (Inquiries Procedure) (England) Rules 2002, SI 2002/2686; The Town and Country Planning (Inquiries Procedure) (Wales) Rules 2003, SI 2003/1266; The Town and Country Planning Appeals (Determination by Inspectors) (Inquiries Procedure) (Wales) Rules 2003, SI 2003/1267; The Town and Country Planning (Enforcement) (Hearings Procedure) (Wales) Rules 2003, SI 2003/1268; The Town and Country Planning (Enforcement) (Inquiries Procedure) (Wales) Rules 2003, SI 2003/1269; The Town and Country Planning (Enforcement) (Determination by Inspectors) (Inquiries Procedure) (Wales) Rules 2003, SI 2003/1270; The Town and Country Planning (Hearings Procedure) (Wales) Rules 2003, SI 2003/1271; The Transport and Works (Inquiries Procedure) Rules 2004, SI 2004/2018; The Town and Country Planning (Major Infrastructure Project Inquiries Procedure) (England) Rules 2005, SI 2005/2115.
[423] Inquiries Act 2005, s.19.
[424] Inquiries Act 2005, s.21; it is an offence not to comply with a requirement under this section: s.35(1).
[425] Inquiries Act 2005, s.22.
[426] The Inquiry Rules 2006, SI 2006/1838.

20.68   Inquiries under the Local Government Act 1972 or other enactments relating to the functions of a local authority are governed by s.250 of the 1972 Act. This creates no real disclosure procedure, though it does confer power on the person appointed to hold the inquiry to require any person by summons to attend at a stated time and place to give evidence or to produce "any documents in his custody or under his control which relate to any matter in question at the inquiry." However, such a person must first be paid or tendered the necessary expenses of his attendance and he cannot be required to produce any title document of any land not owned by a local authority. Refusal or deliberate failure to comply with such a summons is a summary criminal offence. A challenge to a summons may be made by way of judicial review, e.g. because it is argued that the documents concerned are protected by public interest immunity.[427]

20.69   A question arises as to whether documents obtained at a public inquiry are subject to any implied obligation of confidentiality, similar to that obtaining in ordinary civil litigation.[428] Where documents are voluntarily submitted to an inquiry the submitter must be taken to waive confidence in them.[429] Where documents are obtained by compulsory procedures, the matter is more difficult. On the one hand, one could take the view that, to the extent that the documents have been obtained by compulsion, the invasion of privacy should be restricted so far as possible.[430] But it is necessary to be practical about this: these documents are not going to a limited number of litigants, but are perhaps being disseminated generally to the public. Moreover, like inquests, public inquiries are designed to bring facts out into the open, to enable decisions to be made thereafter. It is quite different from the purpose of litigation. Accordingly, it may be argued that documents obtained from public inquiries are not subject to any restrictions in the use that may be made of them in subsequent legal proceedings.

BB. RENT ASSESSMENT COMMITTEES

20.70   These tribunals carry out functions, connected with domestic landlord and tenant law, conferred upon them by a variety of statutes. As a result, their procedure is governed by different regulations depending on the function being exercised. The Rent Assessment Committees (England and Wales) Regulations 1971[431] deal with procedure in references under Pt IV of the Rent Act 1977 and under Pt I of the Housing Act 1988. The Rent Assessment Committees (England and Wales) (Rent Tribunal) Regulations

---

[427] Re Ashworth Special Hospital, unreported, December 1991, Schiemann J.
[428] See Ch.15, above.
[429] cf. Derby & Co. Ltd v Weldon, unreported, October 19, 1988, Browne-Wilkinson V.C.
[430] Taylor v Serious Fraud Office [1999] 2 A.C. 177 at 210; A v A, B v B [2000] 1 F.L.R. 701 at 715–716.
[431] SI 1971/1065.

1980[432] deal with procedure when the Committees are carrying out the functions conferred upon them by s.72 of the Housing Act 1980. Confusingly, such Committees are then known as "rent tribunals." Finally, the Leasehold Valuation Tribunal (Procedure) (England) Regulations 2003[433] govern procedure when the committees are acting under the Leasehold Reform Act 1967, the Landlord and Tenant Act 1985, the Landlord and Tenant Act 1987, the Housing, Leasehold Reform and Urban Development Act 1993, or the Commonhold and Leasehold Reform Act 2002. When they are so acting, the Committees are then known as "leasehold valuation tribunals."[434]

Although the 1971 Regulations distinguish between those cases where the **20.71** reference is to be subject to a hearing, and those where it is not (i.e. on documents alone), in neither case is provision made for disclosure. There is provision for each party to be supplied with copies of documents (or extracts) received from the rent officer or a party, and relevant to the proceedings, and also copies of documents embodying the results of enquiries made by or for the Committee for the purposes of the reference or containing relevant information in relation to rents or other terms in other cases.[435] There is also power for the Committee to inspect the dwelling-house which is the subject of the reference.[436] Parallel powers are provided for by the 2003 Regulations.[437] Even these very limited provisions do not find a place in the 1980 Regulations, which merely state that "the procedure at a hearing shall be such as the rent tribunal may determine . . . "[438]

CC. SOCIAL SECURITY ADJUDICATIONS AND APPEALS[439]

The decision-making and appeals processes in connection with social **20.72** security matters are governed by the Social Security Act 1998, as amended.[440] Unified appeals tribunals are constituted to hear appeals

---

[432] SI 1980/1700.

[433] SI 2003/2099; there are similar regulations for Wales: Leasehold Valuation Tribunal (Procedure) (Wales) Regulations 2004, SI 2004/681.

[434] Commonhold and Leasehold Reform Act 2002, s.173.

[435] Rent Assessment Committees (England and Wales) Regulations 1971, regs 5, 6.

[436] Rent Assessment Committees (England and Wales) Regulations 1971, reg.7.

[437] Leasehold Valuation Tribunal (Procedure) (England) Regulations 2003, regs 16, 17.

[438] Rent Assessment Committees (England and Wales) (Rent Tribunal) Regulations 1980, reg.7(1).

[439] See generally, Wilkeley, Ogus and Barendt, *The Law of Social Security*, 5th edn, 2002, Ch.6; Smith, Knipe, Tonge (eds), *Welfare Law*, 1994 (looseleaf), Div. H, Ch.4.

[440] Replacing the Social Security Administration Act 1992 and the Social Security Contributions Benefits Act 1992, themselves replacing provisions of the Family Income Supplements Act 1970, the Social Security Acts 1975–1986, the Industrial Injuries and Diseases (Old Cases) Act 1975, the Child Benefit Act 1975 and the Supplementary Benefits Act 1976. The 1998 Act has been amended notably by the Social Security Contributions (Transfer of Functions etc.) Act 1999.

against decisions, and further appeals lie to a Commissioner, and thence to the Court of Appeal on a point of law.[441] Notwithstanding the obvious importance of such decisions and appeals to those involved in them and despite the fact that those administering the social security system would have documents relevant to such proceedings in their possession or custody, there are virtually no provisions for disclosure in the procedural rules governing them. There are however provisions for claimants to undergo medical examination in certain cases,[442] with sanctions for failure to comply,[443] for claimants (not the Secretary of State) to provide information,[444] for *non*-disclosure of medical evidence to a party if in the opinion of the adjudicating body such disclosure would be harmful to him,[445] and for the summoning of witnesses to attend and give evidence or produce documents (subject to a privilege exception) at a hearing.[446]

DD. SPECIAL AND GENERAL COMMISSIONERS[447]

20.73   The Special and General Commissioners deal with a wide range of tax appeals concerning income tax, capital gains tax, corporation tax and (Special Commissioners only) inheritance tax. Whereas the General Commissioners are part-time, unpaid laymen and sit locally, rather like justices of the peace, the Special Commissioners are salaried professionals. They are one of the four tribunals grouped together with a common administration.[448] Some matters are reserved to the Special Commissioners, but otherwise it is a matter of choice by the taxpayer as to which tribunal deals with the appeal. Procedure before the Commissioners is governed by the primary statutory provisions in Pt V of the Taxes Management Act 1970, and by regulations made thereunder, one set for the Special Commissioners and one for the General.[449] In addition there are regulations applying only to capital

---

[441] Social Security Act 1998, ss.12–15, Schs 1–4.
[442] Social Security Act 1998, ss.19–20.
[443] Social Security Act 1998, ss.22–24.
[444] The Social Security and Child Support (Decisions and Appeals) Regulations 1999, SI 1999/991, reg.17.
[445] The Social Security and Child Support (Decisions and Appeals) Regulations 1999, SI 1999/991, reg.42; The Social Security Commissioners (Procedure) Regulations 1999, SI 1999/1495, reg.22.
[446] The Social Security and Child Support (Decisions and Appeals) Regulations 1999, SI 1999/991, reg.43; The Social Security Commissioners (Procedure) Regulations 1999, SI 1999/1495, reg.25.
[447] See generally *Tolley's Income Tax 2006–2007*, s.5; *Tolley's Inheritance Tax 2006–2007*, s.15
[448] Collectively known as the Finance and Tax Tribunals; the same individual is the formal head of each of the tribunals concerned, and they are based at the same address. See also the Financial Services and Markets Tribunal, para.20.38 above.
[449] Special Commissioners (Jurisdiction and Procedure) Regulations 1994, SI 1994/1811; General Commissioners (Jurisdiction and Procedure) Regulations 1994, SI 1994/1812

gains tax appeals,[450] but they do not contain any provisions for disclosure.

Commissioner powers

The regulations make provision for a single Special Commissioner, or the **20.74**
tribunal, to serve notice on any party other than the Revenue directing him
to make available for inspection (whether by the tribunal or the Revenue) all
such books, accounts or other documents in the party's possession or power,
containing or possibly containing (in the Commissioner or tribunal's opinion) information relating[451] to the subject matter of the proceedings, as may
be specified or described in the notice.[452] In the case of the Special Commissioners, the rule appears to contemplate that the notice will only be issued
at a hearing (preliminary or final),[453] at which the party receiving the notice
will have been present or represented.[454] But where the General Commissioners are concerned, the rule is differently worded,[455] and it may be that
no hearing at which the recipient is present or represented need take place
before the notice is issued.[456] Under the former rules, such a notice might be
challenged only by way of judicial review, and not, for instance, by originating summons[457] in the Chancery Division.[458] There are financial penalties
for non-compliance with a notice under the General Commissioners'
power,[459] but apparently not the Special Commissioners'.

In addition, a single Commissioner may issue witness summonses requir- **20.75**
ing the attendance at the hearing of any person (wherever he may be in the
United Kingdom) to give evidence or to produce any document in his
possession, custody or power relevant to the subject matter of the proceedings.[460] Unlike the provision just discussed,[461] the Revenue is not excluded
from the scope of this power. The witness must be given at least seven days'

---

[450] Capital Gains Tax Regulations 1967, SI 1967/149.

[451] "Relevant" in the General Regulations.

[452] Special Commissioners (Jurisdiction and Procedure) Regulations 1994, reg.10; General
Commissioners (Jurisdiction and Procedure) Regulations 1994, reg.10.

[453] Special Commissioners (Jurisdiction and Procedure) Regulations 1994, reg.10(1).

[454] Special Commissioners (Jurisdiction and Procedure) Regulations 1994, regs 9(2), 14.

[455] General Commissioners (Jurisdiction and Procedure) Regulations 1994, reg.10(1).

[456] cf. R. v I.R.C., ex p.Taylor (No.2) [1989] S.T.C. 600 at 606, dealing with the predecessor
provision, Taxes Management Act 1970, s.51.

[457] The equivalent would now be a claim under CPR, Pt 8.

[458] Parikh v Birmingham North General Commissioners [1976] S.T.C. 365.

[459] General Commissioners (Jurisdiction and Procedure) Regulations 1994, reg.10(3); see
Johnson v Blackpool General Commissioners [1997] S.T.C. 1202 (penalty upheld where
inspection offered at unreasonable time); Slater v General Commissioners [2002] S.T.C.
246, Ch.D.

[460] Special Commissioners (Jurisdiction and Procedure) Regulations 1994, reg.5(1); General
Commissioners (Jurisdiction and Procedure) Regulations 1994, reg.4(1); Tilbury Consulting Ltd v Gittins, unreported, August 15, 2003, Sp.C.

[461] i.e. Special Commissioners (Jurisdiction and Procedure) Regulations 1994, reg.10; General
Commissioners (Jurisdiction and Procedure) Regulations 1994, reg.10.

notice of the hearing and receive conduct money at the time of service. Moreover, he cannot be required to give evidence or produce a document which he could not be required to give or produce in a court of law,[462] and an auditor or tax adviser cannot be compelled to produce a document protected by their special statutory privilege.[463]

20.76   Those regulations also make specific provision for expert evidence. No such evidence may be adduced at the hearing unless it has been disclosed to the other parties in accordance with an agreement to do so in advance of the hearing or in accordance with a direction of the tribunal.[464] The Special Commissioners also have power to give such directions as they think fit, for the purpose of enabling the parties to prepare or assisting the tribunal to determine any of the issues.[465] But this provision does not permit disclosure more generally to be ordered between co-appellants, as there are no issues between them to which such disclosure could go,[466] and neither does it permit the disclosure of an expert's report to another party to be directed, as expert evidence is dealt with by a separate provision.[467] By parity of reasoning, the power to give directions cannot be used to require the Revenue to give disclosure, as the provision dealing with requiring such disclosure[468] specifically excludes the Revenue from its scope. The Special Commissioners may award the costs of proceedings where it is of opinion that a party has acted wholly unreasonably in connection with a hearing,[469] and that may include a failure to comply with directions for disclosure.[470]

Revenue powers

20.77   Other powers are conferred by statute to enable the Revenue to obtain information and documents, both from taxpayers and from those with whom taxpayers have dealings. Some of these powers are designed for use

---

[462] Special Commissioners (Jurisdiction and Procedure) Regulations 1994, reg.5(8); General Commissioners (Jurisdiction and Procedure) Regulations 1994, reg.4(8).

[463] Special Commissioners (Jurisdiction and Procedure) Regulations 1994, reg.5(9); General Commissioners (Jurisdiction and Procedure) Regulations 1994, reg.4(9). As to the privilege, see para.19.73, below.

[464] Special Commissioners (Jurisdiction and Procedure) Regulations 1994, reg.12; General Commissioners (Jurisdiction and Procedure) Regulations 1994, reg.9.

[465] Special Commissioners (Jurisdiction and Procedure) Regulations 1994, reg.4; see *Phillips v Burrows* [2000] S.T.C. (S.C.D.) 107, 112.

[466] *cf.* Ch.4, para.4.11, above.

[467] Unreported Special Commissioner decision (Mr D.A. Shirley), March 1996; see (1996) 5 P.T.P.R. 7.

[468] i.e. Special Commissioners (Jurisdiction and Procedure) Regulations 1994, reg.10; General Commissioners (Jurisdiction and Procedure) Regulations 1994, reg.10.

[469] 1994 Regulations, reg.21.

[470] *Phillips v Burrows* [2000] S.T.C. (S.C.D.) 107, 112.

in specific fact situations,[471] or in relation to specific events,[472] others are for general use in certain relationships.[473] However, the most general powers and the ones most commonly met in practice, are those in s.20 of the Taxes Management Act 1970. These permit an inspector[474] or the Board[475] to require the taxpayer to supply both: (i) documents in his "possession or power"[476] in their reasonable opinion containing or possibly containing information; and (ii) "particulars", in either case relevant to a tax liability of the taxpayer or to the amount of such liability. In this context, "particulars" means information,[477] or "points of information; a detailed account",[478] but probably does not require the taxpayer to carry out calculations or any researches to obtain the information sought.[479] On the other hand, the fact that providing the particulars would be costly does not of itself make the notice unreasonable.[480]

In addition, an inspector can require a third party to supply documents 20.78 relevant to the taxpayer's liability, but not particulars.[481] In certain circumstances, with the authority of the Board and the consent of a Special Commissioner, this power may be exercised without naming the taxpayer concerned,[482] and the giving of the Board's authority may be delegated,[483] even to an inspector.[484] The notice may seek documents whose existence is conjectural; it is for the Special Commissioner to consider whether the

---

[471] e.g. transfers of assets abroad (Income and Corporation Taxes Act 1988, s.745).
[472] e.g. making a tax return (Taxes Management Act 1970, ss.9A, 19A: see *Siwek v I.R.C.*, unreported, May 15, 2002, Sp.C.; *R.(Murat) v I.R.C.* [2005] S.T.C. 184; Finance Act 1998, Sch.18, para.27: *Meditor Capital Management Ltd v Feighan* [2004] S.T.C. (S.C.D.), Sp.C.; *Spring Salmon & Seafood Ltd v I.R.C.*, unreported, October 3, 2005, Sp.C.
[473] e.g. employer/employee (Taxes Management Act 1970, s.15), banker/customer (Taxes Management Act 1970, s.17).
[474] Taxes Management Act 1970, s.20(1).
[475] Taxes Management Act 1970, s.20(2).
[476] *cf.* Ch.5, paras 5.39–5.54, above.
[477] *Essex v I.R.C.* [1980] S.T.C. 378.
[478] *R. v Macdonald and I.R.C., ex p. Hutchinson & Co. Ltd* [1998] S.T.C. 680.
[479] *cf. Clinch v I.R.C.* [1970] S.T.C. 155; *R. v Macdonald and I.R.C., ex p. Hutchinson & Co. Ltd* [1998] S.T.C. 680 at 696.
[480] *Kempton v Special Commissioner* [1992] S.T.C. 823; *cf. R. v Macdonald and I.R.C., ex p. Hutchinson & Co. Ltd* [1998] S.T.C. 680 at 696–697.
[481] Taxes Management Act 1970, s.20(3).
[482] Taxes Management Act 1970, s.20(8A); for successful applications by H.M.R.C. for Special Commissioner consent to notices seeking information about *possible* taxpayers within wide classes (defined only by reference to being involved in certain kinds of transaction with the "target" financial institution), see *Re an application by H.M.R.C. to serve s.20 Notice* [2006] S.T.C. (S.C.D.) 71 (use of credit cards linked to offshore account), *Re an application by H.M.R.C. to serve s.20 Notice (No.2)* [2006] S.T.C. (S.C.D.) 360 (use of credit cards linked to offshore account), *Re an application by H.M.R.C. to serve s.20 Notice* [2006] S.T.C. (S.C.D.) 310 (share transactions via offshore company), *Re an application by H.M.R.C. to serve s.20 Notice (Note)* [2006] S.T.C. (S.C.D.) 376 (share transactions via offshore company).
[483] Under the Inland Revenue Regulation Act 1890, s.4A.
[484] *R. v Special Commissioner of Income Tax, ex p.I.R.C.* [2000] S.T.C. 537 (where authorisation was oral).

notice is in all the circumstances oppressive.[485] The inspector's powers are exercisable even once an appeal has been lodged, and the Revenue are not then obliged to resort to the Commissioners' power to serve a notice under the procedural rules, or even to weigh up the merits of using s.20 and the notice procedure before proceeding under s.20.[486] However, the inspector's powers are not exercisable in respect of documents or particulars "relating to the *conduct* of any pending appeal".[487]

20.79 The difference between the inspector's powers under s.20 and those of the Board is that an inspector must first obtain the consent of a General or Special Commissioner, who must first be satisfied that in all the circumstances the inspector is justified in proceeding under s.20.[488] This implies a duty on the inspector to put before the Commissioner all the information he has on the relevant circumstances, including information unfavourable to the Revenue's case.[489] The application to the Commissioner is without notice (*ex parte*),[490] and indeed it has been held that a taxpayer has no right to attend.[491] However, if the taxpayer has already recorded his objections to the inspector in writing, the inspector will in practice have to place these before the Commissioner.[492] The validity of a notice under s.20, whether issued by an inspector or by the Board, may be challenged by way of judicial review.[493] Notices to third parties cannot be challenged on the basis of breach of confidentiality and the right to privacy.[494] In appropriate cases a wide-ranging enquiry is justified, and is not oppressive.[495] The impact of privilege on s.20 notices is considered below.

20.80 Further invasive powers are available to the Board where a circuit judge, on information given on oath by one of the Board's officers, issues (a) an order for the delivery of documents by "any person",[496] or even (b) a

---

[485] *R. v I.R.C., ex p. Ulster Bank Ltd* [1997] S.T.C. 832, CA.

[486] *R. v I.R.C., ex p. Taylor (No. 2)* [1990] S.T.C. 379, CA.

[487] Taxes Management Act 1970, s.20B(2) (emphasis supplied).

[488] Taxes Management Act 1970, s.20(7).

[489] *R. v I.R.C., ex p. T.C. Coombs & Co.* [1991] 2 A.C. 283, HL; *R. v Macdonald and I.R.C., ex p. Hutchinson & Co. Ltd* [1998] S.T.C. 680; *R. v I.R.C., ex p. Lorimer* [2000] S.T.C. 751.

[490] *Taxpayer v Inspector of Taxes* [1996] S.T.C. (S.C.D.) 261; *R. v O'Kane and Clarke, ex p. Northern Bank Ltd* [1996] S.T.C. 1249 at 1265; *R. v I.R.C., ex p. Mohammed* [1999] S.T.C. 129; *cf. R. v City of London Magistrates, ex p. Asif* [1996] S.T.C. 611 (Value Added Tax Act 1994, Sch.11, para.11).

[491] *An Applicant v An Inspector of Taxes* [1999] S.T.C. (S.C.D.) 128; *cf. R. v Epsom Justices, ex p. Bell* [1989] S.T.C. 169.

[492] *R. v I.R.C., ex p. T.C. Coombs & Co.* [1991] 2 A.C. 283, HL; *R. v Macdonald and I.R.C., ex p.Hutchinson & Co. Ltd* [1998] S.T.C. 680.

[493] *R. v I.R.C., ex p. Goldberg* [1988] S.T.C. 524; *R. v I.R.C., ex p. T.C. Coombs & Co.* [1991] 2 A.C. 283, HL; *R. v I.R.C., ex p. Taylor (No.2)* [1990] S.T.C. 379, CA; *R. (Werner) v I.R.C.* [2002] S.T.C. 1213, CA.

[494] *R. v I.R.C., ex p. Banque Internationale à Luxembourg* [2000] S.T.C. 708; *cf. Niemitz v Germany* (1992) 16 E.H.R.R. 97, and Art.8(1) of the European Convention on Human Rights.

[495] *R. v Inland Revenue Commissioners, ex p. Archon Shipping Corp.* [1998] S.T.C. 1151; *Guyer v Walton* [2001] S.T.C. (S.C.D.) 75, Special Commissioners.

[496] Taxes Management Act 1970, s.20BA.

warrant for entry (by force if need be) to enter premises and search for and seize and remove documents and other "things",[497] which (in either case) may be required as evidence of serious fraud in relation to tax.[498] There is an exception for items subject to legal privilege (with a statutory definition of how far this extends) in relation to (b),[499] but there is no similar provision with respect to (a). However, the absence of any express protection does not take away such a fundamental right as legal professional privilege.[500]

Privilege

Finally there is the impact of privilege on s.20 notices.[501] So far as   **20.81** concerns legal professional privilege, it must first be noted that an inspector has no power to serve a s.20 notice on a barrister, advocate or solicitor[502]: only the Board may do that, although it may delegate its power,[503] even to an inspector.[504] If the Board does so, to require documents from the lawyer relating to his client's affairs, the lawyer is not obliged to disclose any document covered by legal professional privilege, without the client's consent.[505] It is not oppressive to require a small firm of lawyers to look at numerous documents relating to over 100 transactions during six years.[506] It might appear that, if the notice requires documents or information relating to the lawyer's *own* affairs, the lawyer can thereby be required to disclose privileged information or documents relating to his clients' affairs.[507] But legal professional privilege is a fundamental right, only to be taken away by clear statutory authority. Hence these provisions do not entitle the inspector of taxes to issue a notice requiring disclosure of material covered by legal professional privilege.[508]

---

[497] This includes computers: *R. (H) v I.R.C.* [2002] S.T.C. 1354.

[498] Taxes Management Act 1970, s.20C; in Australia, see *JMA Accounting Pty Ltd v Commissioner of Taxation* (2004) 211 A.L.R. 380, Fed.Ct.Aus.

[499] Taxes Management Act 1970, s.20C(4)–(4B); *R. v I.R.C., ex p. Tamosius & Partners (a firm)* [1999] S.T.C. 1077.

[500] *R. v I.R.C., ex p. Morgan Grenfell* [2003] 1 A.C. 563, HL.

[501] See generally Foster (1999) 7 P.T.P.R. 27.

[502] Taxes Management Act 1970, s.20B(3); the terms "barrister, advocate or solicitor" refer to those qualified under English, Scots or Northern Irish law only.

[503] Under the Inland Revenue Regulation Act 1890, s.4A.

[504] *R. v I.R.C., ex p. Davis Frankel & Mead* [2000] S.T.C. 595. See also *R. (Cooke) v H.M.R.C., The Times*, February 12, 2007. [2007] EWHC 81 (Admin).

[505] Taxes Management Act 1970, s.20B(8).

[506] *R. v I.R.C., ex p. Davis Frankel & Mead* [2000] S.T.C. 595; see also *R. v I.R.C., ex p. Archon Shipping Corp.* [1998] S.T.C. 1151.

[507] *R. v I.R.C., ex p. Lorimer* [2000] S.T.C. 751; cf. *R. v I.R.C., ex p. Taylor* [1988] S.T.C. 832.

[508] *R. v I.R.C., ex p. Morgan Grenfell* [2003] 1 A.C. 563; the reasoning in *R. v IRC, ex p. Taylor (No.2)* (1990) 62 T.C. 578 at 593–594 was too broad: Mr Taylor would have been entitled to refuse to produce documents in respect of which he personally was entitled to LPP (see *per* Lord Hoffmann at para.36).

20.82   A notice to deliver documents does not require the delivery of documents relating to the conduct of any pending appeal by the taxpayer.[509] This covers some of the ground covered by "litigation" privilege,[510] but goes both wider (documents relating to conduct of an appeal are not necessarily privileged), and narrower (documents may be privileged by relating to other legal proceedings). If a "third party" notice is served on an auditor or a "tax adviser" (as defined),[511] he is not obliged to disclose documents consisting of "relevant communications" (also as defined).[512] Lastly, if the notice, whether "taxpayer" or "third party," is served on one who is neither a (United Kingdom) qualified lawyer nor a tax adviser, he cannot resist disclosure of documents or information on the grounds of legal privilege. The conclusion on legal professional privilege is that there is no exception in terms for documents covered by that privilege. Such protection as exists is given by, and limited to, the express terms of the statute, already discussed.[513] Turning to the privilege against self-incrimination, it has been held that the powers to require documents and information under s.20 override that privilege.[514]

EE. TRANSPORT TRIBUNAL

20.83   This tribunal deals, *inter alia*, with applications under the Transport Act 1968, the Public Passenger Vehicles Act 1981 and the Transport Act 1985, mainly concerned with objections to and variations of transport operators' licences.[515] Procedure is governed in the main by the Transport Tribunal Rules 2000,[516] but also by the Transport Act 1985, Sch.4.[517] That Schedule provides that, as respects the attendance and examination of witnesses, the production and inspection of documents, the enforcement of their orders, the entry on and inspection of property and other matters necessary or proper for the due exercise of their jurisdiction, the tribunal is to have the same powers as the High Court.[518] That provision is similar to (though wider than) that made for ecclesiastical courts by the Ecclesiastical Jurisdiction Measure 1963, s.81, and the same question arises as to whether it extends to pre-hearing production and inspection.[519]

---

[509] Taxes Management Act 1970, s.20B(2).
[510] See Ch.11, paras 11.31–11.80, above.
[511] Taxes Management Act 1970, s.20B(9), (10).
[512] Taxes Management Act 1970, s.20B(10).
[513] *An Applicant v An Inspector of Taxes* [1999] S.T.C. (S.C.D.) 128; *R. v I.R.C., ex p. Lorimer* [2000] S.T.C. 751.
[514] *B. & S. Displays Ltd v Special Commissioners* [1978] S.T.C. 331.
[515] It also deals with disputes under the Postal Services Act 2000, s.94.
[516] SI 2000/3226.
[517] Paras 8–12.
[518] Transport Act 1985, Sch.4, para.8(2).
[519] See para.20.25, above.

The 2000 Rules also confer power on the tribunal to compel a party to **20.84** proceedings, or a traffic commissioner involved in them, to deliver to the tribunal any document within the power of such party or commissioner that the tribunal may require,[520] The tribunal must supply a copy of any document obtained in this way to all parties (except the original supplier), but the supply is on condition that it can only be used for the purposes of the proceedings.[521] The predecessor rules contained provision that the Tribunal could not require production of a document which could not be compelled on the trial of an action,[522] but this has not been carried over into the present rules. However, legal professional privilege is a fundamental right, and cannot be taken away except by clear statutory authority, so that the mere absence of words protecting it will make no difference.[523] Failure to comply with the rules does not render the proceedings void, but the Tribunal may take steps to cure the irregularity.[524]

FF. UNIVERSITY COURTS

The Court of the Chancellor of Oxford University[525] and the Court of the **20.85** Chancellor of Cambridge University[526] still exist, although most of their respective jurisdictions have been abolished,[527] and they are left merely with that which existed prior to October 17, 1977 under the statutes of each university. Practice and procedure in the Oxford Court are regulated by rules made by the Vice Chancellor on March 21, 1892,[528] as amended by rules of October 5, 1907[529] and February 3, 1919.[530] The rules provide for inspection by one party of documents in the hands of the other in which he has an interest and to production of which he is entitled,[531] and also for witness summonses to be issued requiring a person to attend and bring documents to the hearing,[532] but there are no other disclosure provisions. In the last half-century the court has sat only rarely.[533] The Cambridge Court has fallen into abeyance.

---

[520] Transport Tribunal Rules 2000, r.25(1).
[521] Transport Tribunal Rules 2000, r.25(2). See Ch.15, above.
[522] Transport Tribunal Rules 1986, r.18(2).
[523] *R. v I.R.C., ex p. Morgan Grenfell* [2003] 1 A.C. 563, HL.
[524] Transport Tribunal Rules 2000, r.37.
[525] Granted by charter (5 Edw. 3, October 16, 1331), and increased in jurisdiction by further charter (14 Hen. 8) (confirmed by the Oxford and Cambridge Act 1571); commonly called the Vice Chancellor's Court.
[526] Granted by charter of Elizabeth I, dated April 26, 1561, confirming an earlier grant (7 Ric. 2); see also the Cambridge Award Act 1856, s.18.
[527] Administration of Justice Act 1977, s.23(3).
[528] Under the Oxford University Act 1862.
[529] S. R. & O. 1927 No.756.
[530] S. R. & O. 1927 No.757.
[531] r.XII.
[532] r.XV.
[533] The last three occasions were in 1955, 1958, and 1968.

GG. VALUATION TRIBUNALS

20.86   The work of these tribunals is twofold: first, they deal with appeals against objections to proposals for the alteration of valuation lists for the purpose of business rates; second, they deal with appeals in connection with the system of council tax introduced into England and Wales in 1993. Their procedure in connection with the former is contained in the Non-Domestic Rating (Alteration of Lists and Appeals) Regulations 2005[534] and in connection with the latter in the Council Tax (Alteration of Lists and Appeals) Regulations 1993.[535] These regulations provide that: (a) certain information cannot be used by a listing or valuation officer in proceedings before the tribunals unless its existence has been disclosed to the other parties at least two weeks (for council tax) or three weeks (for non-domestic rating) beforehand and the other parties have had the opportunity to inspect the documents and take copies[536]; and (b) any of such other parties who wish to rely on comparable dwellings must be permitted on request to inspect and copy documents in the possession of the listing officer containing information relating to the comparable dwellings.[537] Subject to that, these regulations make no provision for disclosure.

HH. VAT AND DUTIES TRIBUNALS[538]

20.87   These tribunals deal with disputes between the H.M. Revenue and Customs in relation to VAT and other duties and the taxpayer. Although for administrative purposes they are grouped with other tribunals[539] such as the Special and General Commissioners,[540] they are legally separate from them, and their procedure is governed by the Value Added Tax Tribunals Rules 1986,[541] as amended. Compared with the Special and General Commissioners, the procedure of these tribunals includes much more developed disclosure processes, even if, in practice, they are rarely invoked.

20.88   The principal rule relating to disclosure is that each party should serve at the appropriate tribunal centre "a list of the documents in his possession, custody or power which he proposes to produce at the hearing of the appeal

---

[534] SI 2005/659.
[535] SI 1993/290.
[536] SI 2005/659, reg.31(3); SI 1993/290, reg.26(3).
[537] SI 2005/659, reg.31(4); SI 1993/290, reg.26(4).
[538] See generally, Potter and Prosser, *Tax Appeals*, 1991, Ch.14; *Tolley's V.A.T.*, 2006, s.5.
[539] Collectively known as the Finance and Tax Tribunals; the same individual is the formal head of each of the tribunals concerned, and they are based at the same address. See also the Financial Services and Markets Tribunal, para.20.38 above.
[540] See paras 20.73–20.82, above.
[541] SI 1986/590.

or application."[542] This is of course not general disclosure, i.e. by reference to relevance to issues, but one-sided and self-serving. By analogy with the position where employment tribunals are concerned, it may be that a party who gives such disclosure must not be unfairly selective and is under a duty to disclose further documents where not to do so might convey a false or misleading impression as to the nature or effect of any disclosed document.[543] However, a failure to include a document in the list which it is then sought to admit in evidence is not necessarily a procedural irregularity.[544] The time limit for service of this list is generally 30 days after giving notice of appeal,[545] which is also the time limit within which the Commissioners of Customs & Excise must serve their Statement of Case.[546] This means that if the taxpayer is unclear what is the Commissioners' case before the formal Statement of Case is served, he should apply for a direction extending his time for service of his List.[547]

In addition, the tribunal may, "where it appears necessary for disposing **20.89** fairly of the proceedings," direct a party to prepare and serve at the tribunal centre "a list of the documents or any class of documents which are or have been in his possession, custody or power relating to any question in issue in the appeal,"[548] and may also order him to verify such disclosure by affidavit.[549] The overriding test for disclosure and the admissibility of evidence before the Tribunal was that of relevance to the issues in dispute.[550] A claim to privilege from production in the appeal must be made in the List "with a sufficient statement of the grounds of privilege."[551] Once served at the tribunal centre, a copy of a List (whether the original "self-serving" List, or one directed by the tribunal) is sent to the other party, who then is entitled to inspect and take copies of such of the documents in the List as are in the possession, custody or power of the party and are not privileged from production.[552] Production for inspection takes place as and when agreed, or in default as directed by the tribunal.[553] Such documents must also be produced at the hearing when called for by the other party.[554] Failure to

---

[542] Value Added Tax Tribunals Rules 1986, r.20(1).
[543] See *Birds Eye Walls Ltd v Harrison* [1985] I.R.L.R. 47, E.A.T.; *cf.* para.20.31, above.
[544] *Koca v Customs & Excise Commissioners*, 1996 S.T.C. 58.
[545] Value Added Tax Tribunals Rules 1986, r.20(2).
[546] Value Added Tax Tribunals Rules 1986, r.8.
[547] Value Added Tax Tribunals Rules 1986, r.11; *Nene Packaging Ltd v Commissioners of Customs & Excise* [2002] S.T.I. 217, V.A.D.T.; *Moti Mahal* [1992] V.A.T.T.R. 188, V.A.D.T.
[548] i.e. general disclosure.
[549] Value Added Tax Tribunals Rules 1986, r.20(3); *MMO2 Plc v H.M.R.C.*, unreported, March 16, 2006, V.A.T. Trib.
[550] Value Added Tax Tribunals Rules 1986, r.20(4); *Nene Packaging Ltd v Commissioners of Customs & Excise* [2002] S.T.I. 217, V.A.D.T.; *Moti Mahal* [1992] V.A.T.T.R. 188, V.A.D.T.
[551] *Lai v Customs & Excise Commissioners*, unreported, July 1, 2002, V.A.D.T.
[552] Value Added Tax Tribunals Rules 1986, r.20(5).
[553] Value Added Tax Tribunals Rules 1986, r.20(5).
[554] Value Added Tax Tribunals Rules 1986, r.20(6).

comply with a direction to give disclosure may lead to a party's case being struck out, and the other side succeeding.[555]

20.90   In addition to the rules concerning disclosure, there are also rules:

(a) Permitting affidavits and depositions from other legal proceedings which are specified as such in the original "self-serving" list of documents to be rendered admissible evidence at the hearing of the appeal or application.[556]

(b) Providing for written witness statements to be served at the tribunal centre and rendered admissible evidence similarly.[557]

In each case provision is made for objections to admissibility to be made: in the former case there is a directions hearing for the objection to be adjudicated upon[558]; in the latter the objection is total and the statement cannot be read or admitted at the hearing (though the witness may of course give oral evidence).[559]

20.91   The position regarding third parties is interesting. First, there is power for a tribunal chairman or the Registrar, upon the application of a party, to issue a summons requiring the attendance of a witness to give oral evidence at the hearing or the production by him at the hearing of a document within his possession, custody or power and necessary for the purpose of that hearing, wherever such witness may be in the United Kingdom or the Isle of Man.[560] The territorial scope is accordingly wider than a witness summons under the CPR,[561] although no person may be compelled to attend to give evidence or provide a document which he could not be compelled to give or produce on the trial of an action,[562] and nor may he be so compelled unless he has been provided with sufficient conduct money.[563] As usual, a summons may be issued without notice, even without a hearing,[564] and any person may apply for such a summons to be set aside.[565]

20.92   The second aspect of the position regarding third parties is that the tribunal chairman or the Registrar has power on the application of a party to issue a summons directed to another person (whether party or non-party) in the United Kingdom or the Isle of Man, requiring that person to allow inspection of a document in his possession, custody or power and which is

---

[555] *Costello v Customs & Excise Commissioners*, unreported, June 9, 2000, VAT Tribunal.

[556] Value Added Tax Tribunals Rules 1986, r.21A.

[557] Value Added Tax Tribunals Rules 1986, r.21. Failure to comply does not necessarily render evidence inadmissible: *Wayne Farley Ltd v Customs & Excise Commissioners* [1986] S.T.C. 487.

[558] Value Added Tax Tribunals Rules 1986, r.21A(4).

[559] Value Added Tax Tribunals Rules 1986, r.21(4).

[560] Value Added Tax Tribunals Rules 1986, r.22(1).

[561] See Ch.10, para.10.09, above.

[562] Value Added Tax Tribunals Rules 1986, r.22(6).

[563] Value Added Tax Tribunals Rules 1986, r.22(7).

[564] Value Added Tax Tribunals Rules 1986, r.22(3).

[565] Value Added Tax Tribunals Rules 1986, r.22(8).

"necessary for the purpose of the hearing" of the appeal or application in question.[566] This power is plainly exercisable to permit pre-trial inspection of third-party documents. The summons will require either attendance of the document-holder at a specified time and place to produce the document for immediate inspection and copying, or the posting (by ordinary first class post) of the document by the document-holder to the party seeking to inspect it).[567] It is not entirely clear whether the option of personal attendance and production or posting is to be the option of the tribunal or of the document-holder, but the more sensible view is that it is the latter.[568]

---

[566] Value Added Tax Tribunals Rules 1986, r.22(2).
[567] Value Added Tax Tribunals Rules 1986, r.22(2).
[568] cf. Potter and Prosser, Tax Appeals, 1991, para.14–11, who appear to take a different view.

CHAPTER 21

The impact of the Human Rights Act 1998

CHAPTER 21

The Impact of the Human Rights Act 1998

A. INTRODUCTION

In this chapter, we deal with the Human Rights Act 1998, which came **21.01** fully into effect on October 2, 2000.[1] This is intended to give more direct effect than hitherto in domestic United Kingdom law to a number of rights guaranteed by the European Convention on Human Rights 1950[2] (the so called "Convention rights"[3]). Until the Act it had been necessary for those complaining that UK law infringes the Convention first to exhaust domestic remedies and then to apply to the Convention institutions to determine whether there had been a violation. The scope for UK judges to have regard to the Convention was limited.[4] But the scheme of the Act now empowers those judges to consider the compatibility of legislation with Convention rights, whilst maintaining the principle of parliamentary sovereignty.[5] These rights may bear not only on rules of substantive law, but also on rules of procedure, such as disclosure, and hence they are relevant to this

---

[1] SI 2000/1851, Art.2. As to the effect of the Act on events occurring before it came into force, see the Human Rights Act 1998, ss.3, 22(4); *Wilson v First County Trust (No.2)* [2004] 1 A.C. 816, HL; *Re McKerr* [2004] 1 W.L.R. 807, HL, *Metropolitan Police Commissioner v Hurst* [2005] 1 W.L.R. 3892, CA (under appeal to HL); *Atkin's Court Forms*, Vol.21—Human Rights, 2nd edn, 2006 issue, para.36.
[2] E.T.S. No.5, signed at Rome on November 4, 1950.
[3] 1998 Act, s.1(1); they are set out in Sch.I to the 1998 Act.
[4] See Hunt, *Using Human Rights Law in English Courts*, 1997.
[5] See Bingham (1998) 2 J.L.Rev. 257 at 262–263. A similar, though not identical, approach has been adopted in Ireland, under the European Convention on Human Rights Act 2003, which is clearly based on the 1998 Act: see Kilkelly (edn), *ECHR and Irish Law*, 2004.

work. However the Court of Appeal has warned against over-enthusiastic use of the Convention in case management situations, and has called on litigation lawyers to take a responsible attitude as to raising a Human Rights Act point.[6]

21.02   The Act works at a number of levels. First, it requires a domestic court or tribunal (of whatever level) in determining questions concerning Convention rights to take into account various sources of relevant information,[7] including jurisprudence of the European Court of Human Rights, and opinions and decisions of the European Commission on Human Rights.[8] Despite this obligation, however, English lower courts are bound by the reasoning of the superior courts which have examined and expressed a view on those sources,[9] even if the European Court of Human Rights has apparently expressed different views since.[10] Secondly, courts and tribunals (as "public authorities"[11]) must not develop, or apply, the common law, or award remedies, in a way which is incompatible with a Convention right.[12] So there may be a positive obligation on them to develop the common law in ways compatible with such rights.[13] Thirdly, primary and subordinate legislation must, so far as is possible, be read and given effect to in a way compatible with the Convention rights.[14] However, there may be cases where the legislation concerned cannot be read and given effect to in that way. The approach to be taken then differs for primary and subordinate legislation.

21.03   Incompatible subordinate legislation will be one of two kinds: (i) that where the relevant primary legislation prevents removal of the incompatibility; and (ii) that where it does not. In the latter case the action of making (or perhaps of failing to exercise a power to revoke[15]) the subordinate legislation will, if occurring after the commencement of the 1998 Act, have been unlawful,[16] with limited exceptions,[17] and hence in such a case the sub-

---

[6] *Walker v Daniels* [2000] U.K.H.R.R. 648, CA (party dissatisfied with jointly appointed expert); see also *Barclays Bank Plc v Ellis, The Times*, October 24, 2000, CA (citation of E.Ct.H.R. decisions).

[7] 1998 Act, s.2(1); *R. v Johnson, The Times*, July 25, 2000, CA; *D v East Berkshire Community N.H.S. Trust* [2004] Q.B. 558, at para.79, CA.

[8] The Commission and the court were merged into a single institution (the court) by the 11th Protocol, as from November 1, 1998.

[9] *Kaya v Haringey London Borough Council* [2001] EWCA Civ 677, [2002] H.L.R. 1, at paras 35–38; *R. (Bright) v Central Criminal Court* [2001] 1 W.L.R. 662, at 682, CA, referring to *R. v Hertfordshire City Council, ex p. Green Environmental Industries Ltd* [2000] A.C. 412, HL.

[10] *Kay v Lambeth London Borough Council* [2006] 4 All E.R. 128, HL.

[11] 1998 Act, s.6(3)(a).

[12] 1998, Act, s.6(1); Starmer, *European Human Rights Law,* 2000, para.1.42.

[13] Lester and Pannick, *Human Rights Law and Practice,* 2nd edn, 2004, paras 2.03(b), 2.04(c).

[14] 1998 Act, s.3; see, e.g., *Haig v Aitken* [2000] 3 All E.R. 80.

[15] *cf.* 1998 Act, s.3(2)(b).

[16] 1998 Act, s.6(1).

[17] 1998 Act, s.6(2).

ordinate legislation will be invalid or unenforceable,[18] apparently "on vires grounds in the ordinary way".[19] In the case of incompatible primary legislation, or incompatible subordinate legislation where the primary legislation prevents removal of the incompatibility, the courts may not strike it down, but the higher courts (including in England the High Court, the Court of Appeal and the House of Lords)[20] may make a "declaration of incompatibility".[21] However, lower courts and tribunals may not do this. Such a declaration does not affect the validity of the legislation, or the rights of the parties,[22] but may lead to "fast-track" amendment of the legislation to remove the incompatibility.[23]

Convention rights may be relevant to disclosure law in a number of areas, **21.04** and reference has been made throughout this work to Convention jurisprudence at appropriate points. In summary, however, the rights most likely to be raised in this context are:

(1) The right to a fair hearing (Art.6(1)).
(2) The right to respect for private life (Art.8(1)).
(3) The right to freedom of expression (Art.10(1)).
(4) The prohibition on discrimination (Art.14).

But other rights may also be relevant, such as the right to life,[24] as where publication of confidential information[25] or revelation of the identity of a person[26] may give rise to a serious risk to life. The text of the various rights is set out in Appendix 1. Because the United Kingdom, Ireland and Cyprus are the only states parties to the Convention with fully developed disclosure systems as part of the rules of civil procedure, there have been very few cases before the Convention institutions dealing with the subject. Nonetheless, a brief discussion of some of the available jurisprudence follows.[27]

---

[18] Lester and Pannick, *Human Rights Law and Practice*, 2nd edn, 2004, para.2.3.6; Starmer, *European Human Rights Law*, 2000, para.1.36; Grosz, Beatson, Duffy, *Human Rights*, 2000, para.3.42. The Act does not say this expressly (*cf.* s.10(4)), and the point is regrettably obscure; see Squires [2000] E.H.R.L.R. 116, esp. at 123–125, and also Hansard, H.C., June 3, 1998, col.426ff.

[19] *Per* the Lord Chancellor, H.L.Debs., November 18, 1997, col.544.

[20] 1998 Act, s.4(5).

[21] 1998 Act, s.4(l)–(4); the Crown may intervene in the proceedings: s.5.

[22] 1998 Act, s.4(6).

[23] 1998 Act, s.10.

[24] Art.2.

[25] e.g *Venables v News Group Newspapers* [2001] Fam.430, Fam.D.

[26] *Bennett v A and B* [2004] EWCA Civ 1439, [2004] Inq.L.R. 81, *The Times*, 11 November 2004 (coroner's inquest).

[27] For full treatments of the subject, see Lester & Pannick (eds), *Human Rights Law and Practice*, 2nd edn, 2004; Starmer, *European Human Rights Law*, 2000; Grosz, Beatson, Duffy, *Human Rights*, 2000; Amos, *Human Rights Law*, 2006; Simor (edn), *Human Rights Law*, 2006 (looseleaf); in Ireland, see Kilkelly (edn), *ECHR and Irish Law*, 2004. Most of the caselaw is available on the E.Ct.H.R. website, at *www.echr.coe.int*.

B. THE RIGHT TO A FAIR HEARING[28]

21.05   *Scope.* Article 6(1) confers upon a person the right "to a fair and public hearing" in the "determination of his civil rights and obligations or of any criminal charge against him".[29] It implies the right of access to the courts.[30] It has been said that Art.6 does no more than reflect the approach of the common law, and there is no difference between the right to a fair hearing and the overriding objective of the CPR.[31] It is not engaged until there are proceedings to determine those rights and obligations,[32] and so cannot apply (for example) to the collection of information for tax purposes,[33] to answers given by the registered keeper of a motor vehicle as to questions as to who was the driver on a particular occasion,[34] to the investigative functions of company inspectors under the Companies Act 1985, s.432(2),[35] or to those of local authorities under the Environmental Protection Act 1990, s.71(2),[36] or, for that matter, to those of coroners holding an inquest.[37] Nor can it apply in favour of a person who has no civil rights to be determined in the proceedings, or where, if he does, those rights cannot be determined in them.[38] On the other hand it *is* engaged where proceedings are taken in another, specialist tribunal whose decision may influence the outcome of other proceedings in the ordinary courts.[39] It has been held not

---

[28] See Lester & Pannick (eds), *Human Rights Law and Practice*, 2nd edn, 2004, 203–54; *Phipson on Evidence*, 16th edn, 2005, paras 1–56—1–61, 1–67—1–69.

[29] As to the meaning of "civil rights and obligations", see *R. (Hussain) v Asylum Support Adjudicator* [2001] EWHC 852 (Admin.), *The Times*, November 15, 2001; *Begum (Runa) v Tower Hamlets L.B.C.* [2003] 2 A.C. 430, HL; *Matthews v Ministry of Defence* [2003] 1 A.C. 1163, HL; note that the French version of the Convention uses the word "*contestation*" (dispute), which is not replicated in the English version.

[30] *Golder v UK* (1975) 1 E.H.R.R. 524, at para.40

[31] *Ebert v Venvil* [2000] Ch. 484, CA.

[32] *Powell v UK* (1990) 12 E.H.R.R. 355, para.36; *Masson v Netherlands* (1995) 22 E.H.R.R. 491, paras 50–52; *R. v Secretary of State for Health, ex p. C*, unreported, February 21, 2000, CA. cf. *Osman v UK* [1999] 1 F.L.R. 193, 5 B.H.R.C. 293, E.Ct.H.R., paras 133–140.

[33] *Abas v Netherlands* (1997) 88B D.R. 120, E.Cn.H.R.

[34] *Brown v Stott (Procurator Fiscal, Dunfermline)* [2003] 1 A.C. 681, P.C. (Road Traffic Act 1988, s.172(2)(a)); see also *D.P.P. v Wilson* [2002] R.T.R. 37, Admin. Ct. (Road Traffic Act 1988, s.172(2)(b)).

[35] *Fayed v UK* (1994) 18 E.H.R.R. 393; *Saunders v UK* (1997) 23 E.H.R.R. 313, para.67; see also *Tora Tolmas v Spain*, Appn. 23816/94, May 17, 1995, E.Cn.H.R. (penalty imposed for failure by car's registered owner to reveal identity of driver on particular occasion: no violation); cf. *Brown v Procurator Fiscal* [2000] S.C.C.R. 314.

[36] *R. v Hertfordshire County Council, ex p. Green Environmental Industries Ltd* [2000] 1 All E.R. 773, HL; see also *Elanay Contracts Ltd v The Vestry*, unreported, August 30, 2000, Judge Havery Q.C. (proceedings before adjudicator under Housing Grants, Construction and Regeneration Act 1996).

[37] cf. de Mello (edn), *Human Rights Act 1998, A Practical Guide*, 2000, para.3.13 (mistaking the nature and lack of admissibility of inquest findings).

[38] *McMichael v UK* (1995) 20 E.H.R.R. 205, at paras 76–77; *Hamer v France* (1996) 23 E.H.R.R. 313, paras 73–78.

[39] *Ruiz-Mateos v Spain* (1993) 16 E.H.R.R. 505, paras 31–32; *Sussmann v Germany* (1996) 25 E.H.R.R. 64, para.43–45; *Probstmeier v Germany*, unreported, July 1, 1997, paras

to apply to preliminary hearings concerning matters of procedure.[40] Articles 6(2) and (3) only apply where there is a criminal charge, to be determined by Convention rather than local law, and depend on: (a) the classification of the proceedings in local law; (b) the nature of the offence; and (c) the severity of the penalty imposed.[41] For this purpose it has been held that company director disqualification proceedings do not involve a criminal charge,[42] whereas prison disciplinary proceedings,[43] proceedings for penalties for tax evasion,[44] and committal for non-payment of community charge[45] or for contempt of court[46] have all been held to do so. Professional disciplinary proceedings have no sharp distinction between criminal and civil proceedings and the matter should be looked at in the round.[47]

Relevant rights. The principle of "equality of arms" underlying Art.6(1)[48] requires that the parties[49] must have the same access to records and documents of a case which play a part in the court's opinion,[50] and must have the opportunity to present their case under conditions not putting them at a disadvantage[51] and to know of and comment on the documents[52] or other

21.06

48–53; *Pammel v Germany* (1997) 26 E.H.R.R. 100, paras 53–57 (Constitutional Court ruling on validity of legislation).

[40] *X v UK* (1982) 5 E.H.R.R. 273 (appointment of new solicitors to represent defendant); *B v UK* (1984) 38 D.R. 213; *Hubbard v Lambeth, Southwark & Lewisham Health Authority* [2001] EWCA Civ 1455 (meeting of experts before trial).

[41] *Engel v Netherlands (No.1)* (A/22) (1980) 1 E.H.R.R. 647, para.82; *AP v Switzerland* (1997) 26 E.H.R.R. 541, E.Ct.H.R.; *R. (Al-Hasan) v Home Secretary* [2002] 1 W.L.R. 545, CA (prison disciplinary proceedings not categorised as criminal where award of additional days); *R. v Secretary of State for the Home Department, ex p. Singh Sunder*, unreported, April 5, 2001, (Admin. Ct.) (Arts 5 and 6 do not apply to decisions as to categorisation of prisoner serving mandatory life sentence).

[42] *EDC v UK* [1998] B.C.C. 370, E.Cn.H.R.; *DC v UK*, Appn. No.39031/97, September 14, 1999, E.Ct.H.R.; *Official Receiver v Stern* [2000] U.K.H.R.R. 332, CA.

[43] *Campbell v UK* (1984) 7 E.H.R.R. 165; *cf. R. v Board of Visitors of Hull Prison, ex p. St Germain (No.1)* [1979] Q.B. 425.

[44] *Bendenoun v France* (1994) 18 E.H.R.R. 54; *E.L. v Switzerland* [1997] H.R.C.D. 3/10, 668 E.Ct.H.R.; *Han v Commissioners of Customs & Excise* [2001] 1 W.L.R. 2253, CA; *Murrell v Commissioners of Customs and Excise* [2001] S.T.I. 256, V.A.D.T.; *Nene Packaging Ltd v Commissioners of Customs & Excise* [2002] S.T.I. 217, V.A.D.T.

[45] *Benham v UK* (1996) 22 E.H.R.R. 293.

[46] *Harman v UK* (1984) 38 D.R. 53; *R. v MacLeod* [2001] Crim.L.R. 589, CA.

[47] *Official Receiver v Stern* [2000] 1 W.L.R. 2230, CA; *R. (Fleurose) v Financial Services Authority*, [2002] 1 R.L.R. 297, CA (not criminal); see also *R.(Thompson) v Law Society* [2004] 1 W.L.R. 2522, CA.

[48] *Borgers v Belgium*, unreported, October 30, 1999, E.Ct.H.R.

[49] Or at any rate their lawyers: *Kamasinski v Austria* (1989) 13 E.H.R.R. 36. As to the use of special advocates in case of very sensitive material, see *Re McClean* [2005] U.K.H.R.R. 826, HL.

[50] *McMichael v UK* (1995) 20 E.H.R.R. 205, para.80; *Vermeulen v Belgium*, February 20, 1996, E.Ct.H.R.

[51] *Dombo Beheer v Netherlands* (1993) 18 E.H.R.R. 188, para.33 (rule prohibiting party from giving evidence held violation); *Bulut v Austria* (1996) 24 E.H.R.R. 84; *Ankerl v Switzerland*, unreported, 1996, E.Ct.H.R., para.38; *Helle v Finland* (1997) 26 E.H.R.R. 159; *Wildman v DPP* [2001] Crim.L.R. 563, CA.

[52] *Mantovanelli v France* (1997) 24 E.H.R.R. 370, paras 33–36 (court expert's report); *Re McClean* [2005] U.K.H.R.R. 826, HL (communication of *gist* of documents).

evidence produced or observations or arguments made by others (whether opponents,[53] independent counsel,[54] a legal assessor,[55] or a lower court[56]), or even obtained by the court of its own motion and not disclosed to anyone.[57] Being informed of the material orally during the hearing is not enough.[58] In some cases the principle requires that parties be able to cross-examine witnesses.[59] It may also require communications with lawyers to be protected.[60] In civil (as opposed to criminal[61]) cases Art.6(1) appears to confer no right to obtain disclosure from an opponent of relevant material in the opponent's possession not being produced to the court,[62] unless the opponent is the state itself (or an equivalent public authority).[63] Were it otherwise, the civilian systems of Europe would nearly all be in constant violation of Art.6(1).[64] Where a party chooses not to use a system of disclosure provided by the rules, he cannot complain of lack of disclosure as a breach of Art.6.[65] The duty to give continuing disclosure does not breach Art.6.[66] Meetings of experts pursuant to CPR, r.35.12[67] in the absence of the parties do not infringe Art.6(1).[68] The wasted costs order procedure does not involve a breach of Art.6(1), even though a respondent is not entitled to rely upon privileged communications between himself and his client in the absence of an express waiver by the client.[69]

21.07   The rules of evidence are for each state to determine,[70] and the court's only role in relation to them is to see if the proceedings as a whole were

---

[53] *Feldbrugge v Netherlands* (1986) 8 E.H.R.R. 425; *Ruiz-Mateos v Spain* (1993) 16 E.H.R.R. 505; *Kuopila v Finland,* unreported, April 27, 2000, E.Ct.H.R.; *cf. R. v Smith (Joe)* [2001] 1 W.L.R. 1031, CA: judge at criminal trial entitled to rely on PII material not disclosed to defence in finding there were reasonable grounds for suspicion.

[54] *Lobo Machado v Portugal* (1996) 23 E.H.R.R. 79; *Van Orhoven v Belgium* (1998) 26 E.H.R.R. 55, para.39.

[55] *Nwabueze v The General Medical Council* [2000] 1 W.L.R. 1760 at 1775, P.C.

[56] *Niderost-Huber v Switzerland* (1998) 25 E.H.R.R. 709.

[57] *Kerojavi v Finland* [1996] E.H.R.L.R. 66; *Krcmar v Czech Republic,* unreported, March 3, 2000, para.40.

[58] *Krcmar v Czech Republic,* unreported, March 3, 2000, paras 42–43.

[59] *X v Austria* (1972) 42 C.D. 145, E.Cn.H.R.; see also *Unterpetinger v Austria* (1986) 13 E.H.R.R. 175 (criminal case).

[60] *S v Switzerland* (1992) 14 E.H.R.R. 670, at para.48; *General Mediterranean Holdings v Patel* [1999] 3 All E.R. 673; *cf. Re L. (A Minor)* [1997] A.C. 16, HL.

[61] *Jespers v Belgium* (1981) 27 D.R. 61; *Bonisch v Austria* (1985) 9 E.H.R.R. 191; *Edwards v UK* (1992) 15 E.H.R.R. 417; *Foucher v France* (1997) 25 E.H.R.R. 234; *Cannon v UK,* unreported, January 17, 1997, E.Ct.H.R.; *Rowe and Davis v UK* (2000) 30 E.H.R.R. 1.

[62] *cf. McMichael v UK* (1995) 20 E.H.R.R. 205, para.80 ("vital documents" undisclosed to the other parties, but produced to the court).

[63] *McGinley and Egan v UK* (1998) 27 E.H.R.R. 1, 4 E.H.R.C. 421, para.86.

[64] See Ch.1, para.1.24, above.

[65] *McGinley and Egan v UK* (1998) 27 E.H.R.R. 1, 4 E.H.R.C. 421.

[66] *Vernon v UK,* unreported September 7, 1999, Appn. 38753/97, E.Cn.H.R.

[67] See Ch.18, para.18.19 above.

[68] *Hubbard v Lambeth, Southwark and Lewisham Health Authority* [2001] EWCA Civ 1455, CA.

[69] *Medcalf v Mardell* [2003] 1 A.C. 120, HL.

[70] *L v UK* [2000] F.L.R. 322, E.Ct.H.R.

fair.[71] So for example the burden or standard of proof is not regulated, except that it must not create an imbalance between the parties.[72] The privilege against self-incrimination is not expressly guaranteed by Art.6 of the Convention.[73] It is of course recognised in European Human Rights jurisprudence.[74] But it is an implied right, and not an absolute one. Limited qualification of Art.6 rights is acceptable if reasonably directed by national authorities towards a clear and proper public objective and if representing no greater qualification than the situation calls for.[75] The court must give reasons for its judgment,[76] though the degree of detail may vary according to the nature of the decision.[77] In criminal cases, the use of screens[78] or other methods to preserve the anonymity of witnesses is justified in some cases,[79] provided: (i) such methods are restricted to what is strictly neces-sary[80]; and (ii) there are "counterbalancing procedures" to enable the relia-bility of the evidence to be tested.[81] But it is harder to justify anonymity for police officer witnesses.[82] Where an *inquiry* is being held, however, Art.6 does not apply,[83] and risks to the safety of police officers, and considera-tions under Art.2, may more easily justify the grant of anonymity to them.[84]

---

[71] *Ludi v Switzerland* (1992) 15 E.H.R.R. 173, at para.43; *Miailhe v France (No.2)* (1996) 23 E.H.R.R. 491, para.43; *R. v Marylebone Magistrates Court, ex p. Clingham* (2001) 165 J.P. 322, D.C.

[72] *G. v France* (1988) 57 D.R. 100, 106.

[73] *R. (Bright) v Central Criminal Court* [2001] 1 W.L.R. 662 at 697, Div. Ct.

[74] *Funke v France* (1993) 16 E.H.R.R. 297; *Saunders v UK* (1996) 23 E.H.R.R. 313; *R. v Hertfordshire County Council, ex p. Green Environmental Industries Ltd* [2000] 2 A.C. 412, HL; *Allan v UK, The Times*, November 12, 2002, E.Ct.H.R.; *Kansal v UK* (2004) 39 E.H.R.R. 31, E.Ct.H.R.; *cf. Murray v UK* (1996) 22 E.H.R.R. 29 (adequate safeguards; no violation).

[75] *Brown v Stott (Procurator Fiscal, Dunfermline)* [2003] 1 A.C. 681, P.C. (*per* Lord Bing-ham); *R. v Kearns* [2002] 1 W.L.R. 2815, CA.

[76] *Van de Hurk v Netherlands* (1994) 18 E.H.R.R. 481, para.61; *Hiro Balani v Spain* (1995) 19 E.H.R.R. 566, para.27.

[77] *Ruiz Torija v Spain* (1994) 19 E.H.R.R. 553, para.29; *Georgiadis v Greece* (1997) 24 E.H.R.R. 606, paras 42–43; *Helle v Finland* (1997) 26 E.H.R.R. 159, paras 55–60; *Stefan v General Medical Council* [2000] 1 W.L.R. 1299, P.C.

[78] *X v UK* (1993) 15 E.H.R.R. C.D. 113.

[79] *Doorson v Netherlands* (1996) 22 E.H.R.R. 330.

[80] *Van Mechelen v Netherlands* (1998) 25 E.H.R.R. 647.

[81] *Kostovski v Netherlands* (1990) 12 E.H.R.R. 434.

[82] *Van Mechelen v Netherlands* (1998) 25 E.H.R.R. 647.

[83] *R. v Hertfordshire County Council, ex p. Green Environmental Industries Ltd* [2000] 2 A.C. 412, HL.

[84] *Bennett v A and B* [2004] EWCA Civ 1439 (coroner's inquest).

C. THE RIGHT TO RESPECT FOR PRIVATE LIFE[85]

21.08   *Scope.* Article 8 confers the right to respect[86] for a person's private and family life, home and correspondence,[87] subject to important exceptions, in the form of justification for prima facie infringements.[88] There is some doubt as to whether this right attaches to legal persons,[89] such as companies, but they can have rights of confidence in law, the law of privilege protects their communications and the Convention elsewhere extends to legal persons, so the better view is that Art.8 can do so to at least some extent (e.g. privacy of communications). States' obligations under this article are both negative[90] and positive.[91] A person claiming a violation of this article needs to show that he is a "victim",[92] although sometimes the threat of a violation has been sufficient for this.[93] The article does not however protect against the effects of a person's own conduct.[94] In the context of disclosure law, the most important aspects of the right are those concerning respect for the physical integrity of the "home", and for private communications and information. Other aspects include respect for private life and family life.

21.09   *Integrity of the "home".* The concept of the "home" for this purpose has been held to extend beyond an individual's place of permanent residence,[95] to a place intended to become so in the future,[96] to holiday homes[97] and

---

[85] See Lester & Pannick (eds), *Human Rights Law and Practice*, 2nd edn, 2004, 261–321; *Phipson on Evidence*, 16th edn, 2005, paras 1–62 — 1–64.

[86] Thus an interference is not automatically a violation: see further *Abdulaziz, Cabales, and Balkandali v UK* (1985) 7 E.H.R.R. 471, para.67, and *Sheffield and Horsham v UK* (1998) 27 E.H.R.R. 163, para.52.

[87] Art.8(1).

[88] Art.8(2) (accordance with the law, *and* necessity in a democratic society in certain national interests, or to protect others' rights: see para.21.12 below).

[89] *R. v Broadcasting Standards Commission, ex p. B.B.C.* [2000] U.K.H.R.R. 158 at 169 (no); *cf.* on appeal at [2000] 3 All E.R. 989, 999, 1001 (point left open); *Cantabrica Coach Holdings Ltd v Vehicle Inspectorate, The Times,* April 13, 2000, D.C. (point left open).

[90] *Belgian Linguistics Case (No.2)* (1968) 1 E.H.R.R. 252; *Lingens v Austria* (1986) 8 E.H.R.R. 407.

[91] *Marckx v Belgium* (1979) 2 E.H.R.R. 330; *X and Y v Netherlands* (1985) 8 E.H.R.R. 235, para.23; *Johnstone v Ireland* (1986) 9 E.H.R.R. 203, para.55; *Gaskill v UK* (1989) 12 E.H.R.R. 36, para.38; *Kroon v Netherlands* (1994) 19 E.H.R.R. 263, para.31; *Sheffield and Horsham v UK* (1998) 27 E.H.R.R. 163, para.52.

[92] *Campbell v UK* (1992) 15 E.H.R.R. 137, paras 32–33.

[93] *Klass v Germany* (1978) 2 E.H. R.R. 214; *Dudgeon v UK* (1981) 4 E.H.R.R. 149; *Leander v Sweden* (1987) 9 E.H.R.R. 433; *Norris v Ireland* (1988) 13 E.H.R.R. 186; *Modinos v Cyprus* (1993) 16 E.H.R.R. 485; *Douglas v Hello! Ltd* [2001] Q.B. 967, CA; *A. v B Plc* [2002] EWCA Civ 337, [2002] 3 W.L.R. 542, CA.

[94] *McFeely v UK* (1980) 20 D.R. 44, E.Cn.H.R. (prisoners' "dirty protest").

[95] *Murray v UK* (1994) 19 E.H.R.R. 193, paras 84–96.

[96] *Gillow v UK* (1986) 11 E.H.R.R. 335; *cf. Loizidou v Turkey* (1996) 23 E.H.R.R. 513, para.66 (property where intended to build in future).

[97] *Kanthak v Germany* (1988) 58 D.R. 94.

caravans,[98] and also to the businessman's or professional's office.[99] However the protection accorded to the last of these is in practice (i.e. considering the exceptions in Art.8(2)[100]) likely to be less than the others.[101] Nevertheless, there is a considerable overlap with the First Protocol, Art.1 (protection of property). Turning to substantive matters, search (*Anton Piller*) orders[102] and search warrants[103] constitute a prima facie infringement of Art.8(1), and have to be justified under Art.8(2).

Private communications and information. Article 8 refers to "correspondence",[104] but this includes telephone calls,[105] pager messages,[106] and no doubt other means of communication. Hence all state telephone tapping[107] and mail interception[108] is prima facie an infringement of Art.8(1). But in principle, so is requiring a person, whether a party to proceedings or a third party (or witness), to reveal confidential information to a court[109] or other state agency.[110] The communications intercepted may be from the person's business premises,[111] and need not be domestic in nature.[112] Indeed, they may even be criminal.[113] Similarly, the information required to be revealed

21.10

---

[98] *Buckley v UK* (1996) 23 E.H.R.R. 101, paras 52–55.
[99] *Niemietz v Germany* (1992) 16 E.H.R.R. 97, para.30; *Hildebrand v Germany*, unreported, April 16, 1998, E.Cn.H.R.; see also *Schnabel v Austria*, unreported, November 30, 1994, E.Cn.H.R. (out of time).
[100] para.21.12, below.
[101] *Niemietz v Germany* (1992) 16 E.H.R.R. 97, para.30.
[102] *Chappell v UK* (1990) 12 E.H.R.R. 1.
[103] *Niemietz v Germany* (1992) 16 E.H.R.R. 97; *Funke v France* (1993) 16 E.H.R.R. 97.
[104] This includes the medium as well as the message: *Haig v Aitken* [2001] Ch. 110 (trustee in bankruptcy has no right to sell personal letters).
[105] *Klass v Germany* (1978) 2 E.H.R.R. 214; *R. v P.* [2002] 1 A.C. 147, HL (justified within Art.8(2)).
[106] *Taylor-Sabori v UK*, Appn. 47114/99, October 22, 2002, E.Ct.H.R.
[107] *Klass v Germany* (1978) 2 E.H.R.R. 214; *Malone v UK* (1984) 7 E.H.R.R. 14; *Huvig v France* (1990) 12 E.H.R.R. 528; *Kruslin v France* (1990)12 E.H.R.R. 547; *A v France* (1994) 17 E.H.R.R. 462; *Halford v UK* (1997) 24 E.H.R.R. 523; *Kopp v Switzerland* (1998) 27 E.H.R.R. 91.
[108] *Silver v UK* (1983) 5 E.H.R.R. 347; *Campbell v UK* (1993) 15 E.H.R.R. 137; *Herczegfalvy v Austria* (1993) 15 E.H.R.R. 437; *Foxley v UK* (2000) 31 E.H.R.R. 25, E.Ct.H.R.
[109] *Z v Finland* (1998) 25 E.H.R.R. 371, 45 B.M.L.R. 107 (doctor required to give evidence of patient's medical condition); see also *R. v Home Secretary, ex p. Belgium*, unreported, February 15, 2000, D.C. (disclosure to other parties of medical reports relied on by Home Secretary).
[110] *X v Belgium* (1982) 31 D.R. 231, E.Cn.H.R. (taxpayer required to explain personal expenditure in detail); *Visser v Netherlands*, unreported, May 2, 1989, E.Cn.H.R. (disclosure by telephone service to tax authorities of telephone number); *MS v Sweden* (1997) 28 E.H.R.R. 313, 3 B.H.R.C., 45 B.M.L.R. 133 (disclosure of medical records to Social Insurance Office); *Cantabrica Coach Holdings Ltd v Vehicle Inspectorate* (2000) 164 J.P. 593, D.C. (transport business required to hand over tachograph records).
[111] *Halford v UK* (1997) 24 E.H.R.R. 523; *Cantabrica Coach Holdings Ltd v Vehicle Inspectorate*, 2000, D.C.; *Hewitson v UK*, Appn. 50015/99, My 27, 2003, E.Ct.H.R.
[112] *Huvig v France* (1990) 12 E.H.R.R. 538, paras 8, 25; *Kopp v Switzerland* (1998) 27 E.H.R.R. 91; *Cantabrica Coach Holdings Ltd v Vehicle Inspectorate* (2000) 164 J.P. 593, D.C.
[113] *A v France* (1993) 17 E.H.R.R. 462, paras 34–37.

may be of a commercial rather than domestic nature. The respect for private correspondence may involve positive obligations on the state.[114]

21.11 *Private and family life.* Police files[115] and local authority social services casefiles[116] relating to an individual relate to private and family life and hence access to those files falls under Art.8. But although Art.8 may give rise to positive duties,[117] there is no requirement for a general right of access. On the other hand, a system giving access to the person concerned conditionally on the consent of the various contributors to the files (given a confidentiality undertaking) must provide for an independent authority to decide whether access should be given in cases where a contributor fails to answer or improperly refuses consent.[118] Covert filming in a person's home is a breach of Art.8,[119] and it may also be a breach even in a public place, and even though there is no private element to the events filmed.[120] But media intrusion (in particular by photography) into the private life of a personality, even in public when she is going about her everyday affairs, can also amount to a violation.[121] On the other hand, Art.8 is not engaged in the case of covert sound recording of an employer's disciplinary tribunal deliberating in private.[122]

21.12 *Exceptions.* Article 8(2) allows significant exceptions to the basic rights in Art.8(1),[123] where: (i) the law permits it on a sufficiently precise basis to foresee when it will be applied,[124] *and*; (ii) it is necessary in a democratic society in the interests of national security, public safety or the economic well-being of the country, for the prevention of disorder or crime, for the protection of health or morals, or the protection of the rights or freedoms of others. The phrase "necessary in a democratic society" has been interpreted as implying the existence of a "pressing social need".[125] So, for

---

[114] *Boyle v UK* (1985) 41 D.R. 90, E.Cn.H.R.; *Grace v UK* (1988) 62 D.R. 22, E.Cn.H.R.; *cf.* *X v Germany* (1979) 17 D.R. 227, E.Cn.H.R. (no positive obligation to ensure perfectly functioning postal service).

[115] *Leander v Sweden* (1987) 9 E.H.R.R. 433.

[116] *Gaskin v UK* (1989) 12 E.H.R.R. 36, paras 36–37.

[117] See n.91, above.

[118] *Gaskin v UK* (1989) 12 E.H.R.R. 36, para.49.

[119] *Jones v University of Warwick* [2003] 1 W.L.R. 954, CA.

[120] *R. v Loveridge* [2001] 2 Cr.App.R. 591, CA; *R. v Broadcasting Standards Commission, ex p. B.B.C.* [2001] Q.B. 885, CA; see also *Campbell v M.G.N. Ltd.* [2004] 2 W.L.R. 1232, HL.

[121] *Von Hannover v Germany* [2004] E.M.L.R. 21, E.Ct.H.R. (Princess Caroline of Monaco).

[122] *Governors of Amwell View School v Dogherty*, unreported, September 15, 2006, E.A.T.

[123] *R. v Home Secretary, ex p. Daly* [2001] 2 A.C. 532, HL.

[124] *Silver v UK* (1983) 5 E.H.R.R. 347; *Huvig v France* (1990) 12 E.H.R.R. 538; *Amann v Switzerland*, unreported, February 16, 2000, E.Ct.H.R., para.56; *Foxley v UK*, (2000) 31 E.H.R.R.25, E.Ct.H.R., para.34; *Khan v UK*, (2000) 30 E.H.R.R. 1016, E.Ct.H.R.; *Taylor-Sabori v UK*, Appn. 47114/99, October 22, 2002, E.Ct.H.R.

[125] *Handyside v UK* (1976) 1 E.H.R.R. 737, para.48; *Dudgeon v UK* (1982) 4 E.H.R.R. 149.

example, it has been held that requiring a doctor to reveal his patient's medical history in criminal proceedings against her husband was proportionate measure taken in the interests of investigating and prosecuting crime, and hence justifiable,[126] and a search (*Anton Piller*) order was not a violation of Art.8, because the relevant law was accessible and sufficiently precise as to be foreseeable and there were sufficient safeguards against abuse.[127] Similar conclusions have been reached in relation to out of court disclosure.[128] And a police policy of normally retaining fingerprints and D.N.A. samples even following acquittal of suspects was held to be justified and proportionate, within Art.8(2), by reference to the need to protect the public from the consequences of crime.[129] Presumably witness summonses seeking the production of highly confidential documents or information will be justified, if at all, as in the interests of protecting the rights of others.[130]

Privilege. Communications protected by legal privilege[131] must be specially   **21.13**
mentioned. There is no specific regime for them in the Convention, but they are protected by Art.8 on the same basis as other confidential information. However, lawyer-client privilege may be given a higher degree of protection than other confidential information cases.[132] Indeed, legal professional privilege has been described as a fundamental human right which can be invaded only in exceptional circumstances.[133] Thus it is doubtful that the public interest in the collection of the revenue could provide the necessary

---

[126] *Z. v Finland* (1998) 25 E.H.R.R. 371, 45 B.M.L.R. 107; see also *Re B (A Child)* [2004] EWHC 411 (Fam.) (mother who claimed to be a victim of a miscarriage of justice in care proceedings brought by the local authority permitted to put material about the case into the public domain (through the media), but on condition of anonymity, and subject to orders protecting identities of the child and the experts involved).

[127] *Chappell v UK* (1990) 12 E.H.R.R. 1; *cf. Niemietz v Germany* (1992) 16 E.H.R.R. 97 (violation, where no safeguards, and interference with professional secrecy disproportionate), *Funke v France* (1993) 16 E.H.R.R. 97 (violation, where no judicial authorisation).

[128] *MS v Sweden* (1997) 28 E.H.R.R. 313, 3 B.H.R.C., 45 B.M.L.R. 133 (disclosure of medical records to Social Insurance Office to resolve claim made by patient held justifiable), *Cantabrica Coach Holdings Ltd v Vehicle Inspectorate* (2000) 164 J.P. 593, D.C. (disclosure of tachograph records necessary in interests of public safety), and *R. v Banque Internationale a Luxembourg* [2000] S.T.C. 708 (disclosure of client banking records to Inland Revenue held justifiable); *A Health Authority v X* [2001] 2 F.C.R. 634, Munby J., [2002] 2 All E.R. 780, CA (disclosure of medical records required by health authority for purposes of investigation into possible breach of its terms of service by medical practitioners); see also *Kent County Council, Re B (A Child) v The Mother* [2004] EWHC 411 (Fam.) (privacy of proceedings involving children).

[129] *R. (S) v Chief Constable of South Yorkshire Police* [2004] 1 W.L.R. 2196, HL.

[130] This was argued, but not decided, in *Z v Finland* (1998) 25 E.H.R.R. 371, 45 B.M.L.R. 107; see also *L. v UK*, Appn. 34222/96 (1999) (interference with rights to confidence justified by "protection of health and morals" and "protection of rights and freedoms" of third party).

[131] The privilege against self-incrimination falls under Art.6: see para.21.07, above.

[132] *Niemietz v Germany* (1993) 16 E.H.R.R. 97, para.37; see also para.21.06 above.

[133] *Foxley v United Kingdom* (2001) 31 E.H.R.R. 25.

justification.[134] But there may still be circumstances where interference with privileged communications is justified.[135] In the context of criminal proceedings the question of privilege overlaps with the right to a fair hearing under Art.6,[136] and is hence doubly protected. There are special considerations where the correspondence of convicted prisoners is concerned, but in particular their privileged communications should not be interfered with unless there is some basis for suspecting the integrity of the lawyer.[137] Thus, both a policy of requiring a prisoner's absence whenever privileged legal correspondence held by him in his cells was examined, by giving rise to the possibility that an officer might improperly read it and to the inhibiting effect such possibility would have on the prisoner's willingness to communicate freely with his legal advisor,[138] and also the use by the police of solicitors or their clerks as informants was a breach by solicitors and clerks of their duties to clients, and also by police of the rights of citizens,[139] amounted to an infringement of the prisoner's right to legal professional privilege and infringement with his right to respect for correspondence under Art.8(1) of the ECHR. But on the other hand a policy requiring prisoners to obtain authorisation prior to exchanging legal documents with visiting legal advisers was proportionate.[140] Although legal privilege may be waived, Convention jurisprudence holds that waiver must be unequivocal and must not violate any important public interest.[141] This is not necessarily compatible with the English rules on implied waiver.[142]

D. THE RIGHT TO FREEDOM OF EXPRESSION[143]

21.14   *Scope.* Article 10(1) confers the right to freedom of expression, to hold opinions and to receive and impart information without public interference. But it is subject to the limitations in Art.10(2), being those prescribed by

---

[134] *R. v I.R.C., ex p. Morgan Grenfell* [2002] UKHL 21 at [39], [2003] 1 A.C. 563, HL.

[135] *B.R. v Germany*, unreported, October 23, 1997; *Foxley v UK* (2001) 35 E.H.R.R. 637, at para.44; *R. v I.R.C., ex p. Banque Internationale a Luxembourg* [2000] S.T.C. 708 at 723, Ch.D. (notice requiring access to a bank's files for revenue purposes).

[136] *S v Switzerland* (1992) 14 E.H.R.R. 670, para.48; see para.21.07, above.

[137] *Campbell v UK* (1993) 15 E.H.R.R. 137: see also *Silver v UK* (1984) 5 E.H.R.R. 347; *R. v Home Secretary, ex p. Leach* [1994] Q.B. 198; *R. v Home Secretary, ex p. Simms* [1999] Q.B. 349.

[138] *R. (Daly) v Secretary of State for the Home Department* [2001] 2 A.C, 532, HL.

[139] *R. v Robinson, The Times*, November 13, 2002, CA.

[140] *R. (Cannan) v Governor of Full Sutton Prison, The Times*, January 30, 2003.

[141] *Deweer v Belgium* (1980) 2 E.H.R.R. 439; *Van Leuven v Belgium* (1981) 4 E.H.R.R. 1, para.43; *Hakansson v Sweden* (1990) 13 E.H.R.R. 1, para.66; *Pfeifer v Austria* (1992) 14 E.H.R.R. 692, para.37; *Bulut v Austria* (1996) 24 E.H.R.R. 84.

[142] See Ch.12, paras 12.03–12.06, above.

[143] See Lester & Pannick (eds), *Human Rights Law and Practice*, 2nd edn, 2004, 335–37.

law,[144] necessary in a democratic society, and in one of various public interests, or the protection of others' rights or *preventing* the disclosure of confidential information.[145] Moreover, it does not impose any duty on states to collect, disseminate or supply information.[146] But Art.10 covers nearly all[147] kinds of expression, including artistic[148] and commercial and professional,[149] and legal as well as natural persons may take advantage of it.[150] However, the margin of appreciation accorded to states has been greater in commercial than political matters.[151] The right not to be restricted in receiving information does not depend on what use will be made of it.[152] Article 10 can sometimes give rise to positive obligations on the part of states.[153] However, it imposes no obligation on a state to provide a forum in which a wider dissemination of views and information may be obtained.[154]

Relevant rights. An order that a journalist disclose sources[155] must be justified, if at all, under Art.10(2). Sometimes the public interest in protection of a journalist's source has been held to outweigh an employer's need for disclosure in order to identify a disloyal employee,[156] sometimes not.[157] **21.15**

---

[144] This includes common law: *Tolstoy Miloslavsky v UK* (1995) 20 E.H.R.R. 442, para.37; *Douglas v Hello! Ltd* [2005] 4 All E.R. 128, CA.

[145] See *A.G. v Punch Ltd* [2003] 1 A.C. 1046, HL; *Jockey Club v Buffham* [2003] Q.B. 462; *A. v B Plc* [2002] 3 W.L.R. 542, [2001] E.M.L.R. 371, CA; *H. v N (A Health Authority, The Times,* March 19, 2002, CA; *Prudential Assurance Co. Ltd v Prudential Insurance Co. of America,* [2002] EWHC 2809 (Ch.), Morritt V.C. ("without prejudice" privilege engaged ECHR, but justified by public interest), affd. [2003] EWCA Civ 1154, CA (where the point did not arise); *Douglas v Hello! Ltd* [2005] 4 All E.R. 128, CA.

[146] *Leander v Sweden* (1987) 9 E.H.R.R. 433; *Guerra v Italy* (1998) 26 E.H.R.R. 357, para.53.

[147] It does not cover physical expressions of feelings: *Case of X* (1977) 19 D.R. 66, E.Cn.H.R.

[148] *Muller v Switzerland* (1988) 13 E.H.R.R. 212; *Chorherr v Austria* (1993) 17 E.H.R.R. 358.

[149] *Markt Intern Verlag v Germany* (1989) 12 E.H.R.R. 161; *Open Door Counselling v Ireland* (1992) 15 E.H.R.R. 244; *Casado Coca v Spain* (1994) 18 E.H.R.R. 1; *Jacubowski v Germany* (1994) 19 E.H.R.R. 64.

[150] *Autronic A.G. v Switzerland* (1990) 12 E.H.R.R. 485; *The Observer Ltd v UK* (1991) 14 E.H.R.R. 153; *Open Door Counselling v Ireland* (1992) 15 E.H.R.R. 244.

[151] *Markt Intern Verlag v Germany* (1989) 12 E.H.R.R. 161; *Casado Coca v Spain* (1994) 18 E.H.R.R. 1; *Ashdown v Telegraph Group Ltd* [2002] Ch. 149, CA (intellectual property); *Imutran Ltd v Uncaged Campaigns Ltd.* [2002] F.S.R. 20, Ch.D.; *Gündem Özgür v Turkey* (2001) 31 E.H.R.R. 49, E.C.H.R.

[152] *Autronic A.G. v Switzerland* (1990) 12 E.H.R.R. 485.

[153] e.g. *Plattform Artze fur das Leben v Austria* (1988) 13 E.H.R.R. 204 (state's duty to take steps to prevent disruption of demonstration by mob).

[154] *R. (Pewsey) v Secretary of State for the Environment, Food and Rural Affairs* [2003] Q.B. 794.

[155] See Ch.4, paras 4.18–4.21, above.

[156] *Goodwin v UK* (1997) 22 E.H.R.R. 123; *Ashworth Hospital Authority v M.G.N. Ltd.* [2001] 1 W.L.R. 515, CA, [2002] 1 W.L.R. 2033, HL; *Mersey Care NHS Trust v Ackroyd,* [2003] EWCA Civ 663, [2003] E.M.L.R. 36, *The Times,* May 21, 2003, CA.

[157] *Camelot Group Ltd v Centaur Communications Ltd* [1999] Q.B. 124, CA; and see *Fressoz and Roire v France* [1999] E.H.R.L.R. 339.

Although reporting of court proceedings contributes to the achievement of a fair hearing,[158] by exposing judges to public scrutiny,[159] it is legitimate to restrict reporting which may prejudice pending proceedings, especially criminal proceedings,[160] or where this is required in the interests of protecting children.[161] But the restriction must be proportionate to the aim, whether of achieving a fair hearing,[162] or of protecting national security.[163] In considering what information is confidential for the purpose of restraining the media from revealing it, the court has to have regard to both Art.8 and Art.10 rights.[164] A complaint under Art.10 following the conviction of a journalist for reporting the confidential deliberations of a criminal jury has been dismissed.[165] Similarly, where a juror wrote to the mother of two convicted defendants in criminal proceedings about the jury's deliberations, in the belief that they were the victims of a miscarriage of justice, the subsequent contempt proceedings were not a violation of Art.10.[166] On the other hand, a conviction for breaching confidentiality of court proceedings was not justifiable where the material concerned was already public.[167] And a mother who claimed to be a victim of a miscarriage of justice in care proceedings brought by the local authority was permitted to put material about the case into the public domain (through the media), but on condition of anonymity, and subject to orders protecting identities of the child and the experts involved.[168]

---

[158] *Axen v Germany* (1984) 6 E.H.R.R. 195, para.25; *Worm v Austria* (1997) 25 E.H.R.R. 454, para.50.

[159] *Scott v Scott* [1913] A.C. 417, HL; see also *Axen v Germany* (1984) 6 E.H.R.R. 195, at para.25, E.Ct.H.R.; *Prager and Oberschlick v Austria* (1996) 21 E.H.R.R.1, at para.34, E.Ct.H.R.; *Worm v Austria* (1998) 25 E.H.R.R.454, at para 40, E.Ct.H.R.

[160] *Hodgson v UK* (1987) 51 D.R. 136; *C Ltd v UK* (1989) 61 D.R. 285; *cf. Worm v Austria* (1997) 25 E.H.R.R. 454, para.50.

[161] *B v UK* (2002) 34 E.H.R.R. 529, [2001] 2 F.L.R. 261, at para.38, E.Ct.H.R.; *Kent County Council, Re B (A Child) v The Mother* [2004] EWHC 411 (Fam.).

[162] *Sunday Times v UK* (1979) 2 E.H.R.R. 245, para.56.

[163] *The Observer Ltd v UK* (1991) 14 E.H.R.R. 153; *R. v Shaylor* [2003] 1 A.C. 247, HL (ban on disclosure of information by members and former members of the security services without lawful authority imposed by Official Secrets Act 1989 held to be a justified interference within Art.10(2)); *Gündem Özgür v Turkey* (2001) 31 E.H.R.R. 49, ECHR.

[164] *Campbell v M.G.N. Ltd.* [2003] Q.B. 633, CA, revsd [2004] 2 A.C. 457, HL in applying principle to facts; see also *Von Hannover v Germany* [2004] E.M.L.R. 21, E.Ct.H.R. (Princess Caroline of Monaco).

[165] *Associated Newspapers Ltd v UK*, unreported, November 30, 1994, E.Cn.H.R.

[166] *A.G. v Scotcher* [2005] 1 W.L.R. 637, HL.

[167] *Weber v Switzerland* (1990) 12 E.H.R.R. 508.

[168] *Kent County Council, Re B (A Child) v The Mother* [2004] EWHC 411 (Fam.).

E. OTHER MISCELLANEOUS RIGHTS

Forced labour.[169] Article 4 prohibits slavery (4(1)) and forced labour (4(2)),[170] subject to exceptions (4(3)). But the obligation imposed on employers to calculate and deduct tax from employees' salaries, and to account to the tax authorities for it,[171] or on the self-employed to create accounting documents such as balance sheets so that they can properly be assessed to income tax,[172] do not infringe Art.4(2), as they do not go beyond "normal civic obligations" (one of the exceptions in Art.4(3)). Similarly, compulsory fire service[173] and participation by gun licensees in anti-rabies activity[174] have been held within the same exception. Accordingly there is very little scope for arguing that complying with a witness summons or other court order, and producing documents or other information, infringes this article.

21.16

Right to liberty.[175] Article 5(1) confers the right to liberty, subject to six enumerated cases, and in all cases in accordance with a legally prescribed procedure.[176] The second case is that of lawful arrest or detention of a person: (i) for non-compliance with a lawful order of the court or; (ii) in order to secure the fulfilment of any obligation prescribed by law.[177] As to (i), this has been held to justify detention for (*inter alia*) failure to pay a fine,[178] or refusal to undergo a court-ordered blood test[179] or medical examination.[180] The alternative limb (ii) only justifies detention to secure the fulfilment of the obligation, not to punish the offender.[181] It has been held in particular to justify detention to secure the provision of information and documentation at border controls.[182]

21.17

---

[169] See Lester & Pannick (eds), *Human Rights Law and Practice*, 2nd edn, 2004, 153–59.

[170] *Van der Mussele v Belgium* (1983) 6 E.H.R.R. 163.

[171] *Companies W, X, Y, Z v Austria* (1976) 7 D.R. 148, E.Cn.H.R.; *Borghini v Italy*, unreported, November 29, 1995, E.Cn.H.R.

[172] *R. (Murat) v I.R.C.* [2005] S.T.C. 184, at paras 19–21; *Patrick v I.R.C.* [2002] EWCA Civ 1649.

[173] *Schmidt v Germany* (1994) 18 E.H.R.R. 513, para.22.

[174] *X v Germany* (1984) 39 D.R. 90, E.Cn.H.R.

[175] See Lester & Pannick (eds), *Human Rights Law and Practice*, 2nd edn, 2004, 161–202; *Phipson on Evidence*, 16th edn, 2005, para.1–55.

[176] See also Art.5(2)–(4), setting out procedural safeguards.

[177] Art.5(1)(b).

[178] *Airey v Ireland* (1977) 8 D.R. 42.

[179] *X v Austria* (1979) 18 D.R. 154.

[180] *X v Germany* (1975) 3 D.R. 92.

[181] *Engel v Netherlands* (1979) 1 E.H.R.R. 647; *Johansen v Norway* (1985) 44 D.R. 155; see also *Benham v UK* (1996) 22 E.H.R.R. 293; see also *Mubarek v Mubarek (No.1)* [2001] F.L.R. 698, CA (judgment summons).

[182] *McVeigh, O'Neill and Evans v UK* (1981) 25 D.R. 15.

21.18 *Prohibition of discrimination.*[183] Article 14 prohibits discrimination, but only "in the enjoyment of the rights and freedoms" set out in the Convention (and Protocols). So it is not a "free-standing" guarantee of equal treatment. A claim cannot be made unless the case falls within one of the articles conferring substantive rights.[184] Article 14 refers to "property", but it is not clear whether discrimination on financial grounds is covered.[185] A difference in treatment is discriminatory unless it has an "objective and reasonable justification",[186] which means showing the pursuit of a "legitimate aim" and proportionality.[187]

---

[183] See Lester & Pannick (eds), *Human Rights Law and Practice*, 2nd edn, 2004, 441–450. For examples of its application, see: *R. (Purja) v Ministry of Defence* [2004] 1 W.L.R. 289 (differences in pay and conditions between British soldiers and Gurkhas—no infringement); *Ghaidan v Godin-Mendoza* [2004] 2 A.C. 557 (distinctions between unmarried heterosexual and homosexual couples—Arts 1 and 14 infringed); *R. (S) v Chief Constable of South Yorkshire* [2004] 1 W.L.R. 1296 (samples on arrest—no infringement); *R. (Carson) v Secretary of State fro Work and Pensions* [2005] 2 W.L.R. 1369, HL.

[184] *Botta v Italy* (1998) 26 ECHR 241, paras 39–40.

[185] See *Airey v Ireland* (1979) 2 E.H.R.R. 305, para.30; *Johnstone v Ireland* (1987) 9 E.H.R.R. 203.

[186] *Belgian Linguistic Case (No.2)* (1979) 1 E.H.R.R. 252, para.32.

[187] *Darby v Sweden* (1991) 13 E.H.R.R. 774, para.31; *Petrovic v Austria* (1998) 5 B.H.R.C. 232, para.30.

APPENDIX 1

Statutes

Arbitration Act 1996, s.43

43.—Securing the attendance of witnesses

(1) A party to arbitral proceedings may use the same court procedures as are   **A.01**
available in relation to legal proceedings to secure the attendance before the tribunal
of a witness in order to give oral testimony or to produce documents or other
material evidence.

(2) This may only be done with the permission of the tribunal or the agreement of
the other parties.

(3) The court procedures may only be used if—
    (a) the witness is in the United Kingdom, and
    (b) the arbitral proceedings are being conducted in England and Wales or, as
        the case may be, Northern Ireland.

(4) A person shall not be compelled by virtue of this section to produce any
document or other material evidence which he could not be compelled to produce in
legal proceedings.

44.—Court powers exercisable in support of arbitral proceedings

(1) Unless otherwise agreed by the parties, the court has for the purposes of and   **A.02**
in relation to arbitral proceedings the same power of making orders about the
matters listed below as it has for the purposes of and in relation to legal proceedings.

(2) Those matters are—
    (a) the taking of the evidence of witnesses;
    (b) the preservation of evidence;
    (c) making orders relating to property which is the subject of the proceedings
        or as to which any question arises in the proceedings—
        (i) for the inspection, photographing, preservation, custody or detention
           of the property, or
       (ii) ordering that samples be taken from, or any observation be made of or
          experiment conducted upon, the property;
        and for that purpose authorising any person to enter any premises in the
        possession or control of a party to the arbitration;
    (d) the sale of any goods the subject of the proceedings;
    (e) the granting of an interim injunction or the appointment of a receiver.

(3) If the case is one of urgency, the court may, on the application of a party or proposed party to the arbitral proceedings, make such orders as it thinks necessary for the purpose of preserving evidence or assets.

(4) If the case is not one of urgency, the court shall act only on the application of a party to the arbitral proceedings (upon notice to the other parties and to the tribunal) made with the permission of the tribunal or the agreement in writing of the other parties.

(5) In any case the court shall act only if or to the extent that the arbitral tribunal, and any arbitral or other institution or person vested by the parties with power in that regard, has no power or is unable for the time being to act effectively.

(6) If the court so orders, an order made by it under this section shall cease to have effect in whole or in part on the order of the tribunal or of any such arbitral or other institution or person having power to act in relation to the subject-matter of the order.

(7) The leave of the court is required for any appeal from a decision of the court under this section.

Bankers' Books Evidence Act 1879

1. Short title

A.03   This Act may be cited as the Bankers' Books Evidence Act 1879.

2.[−]¹

3. Mode of proof of entries in bankers' books

A.04   Subject to the provisions of this Act, a copy of any entry in a banker's book shall in all legal proceedings be received as prima facie evidence of such entry, and of the matters, transactions, and accounts therein recorded.

4. Proof that book is a banker's book

A.05   [Where the proceedings concerned are proceedings before a magistrates' court inquiring into an offence as examining justices, this section shall have effect with the omission of the words "orally or".]² A copy of an entry in a banker's book shall not be received in evidence under this Act unless it be first proved that the book was at the time of the making of the entry one of the ordinary books of the bank, and that the entry was made in the usual and ordinary course of business, and that the book is in the custody or control of the bank.

Such proof may be given by a partner or officer of the bank, and may be given orally or by an affidavit sworn before any commissioner or person authorised to take affidavits.

5. Verification of copy

A.06   A copy of an entry in a banker's book shall not be received in evidence under this Act unless it be further proved that the copy has been examined with the original entry and is correct.

---

¹ Repealed by Statute Law Revision Act 1894 (c.56), Sch.1.
² Added by Criminal Procedure and Investigations Act (1996 c.25), Sch.1, Part II, para.15.

Such proof shall be given by some person who has examined the copy with the original entry, and may be given either orally or by an affidavit sworn before any commissioner or person authorised to take affidavits.[Where the proceedings concerned are proceedings before a magistrates' court inquiring into an offence as examining justices, this section shall have effect with the omission of the words "either orally or".][3]

6. Case in which banker, &c. not compellable to produce book, &c.

A banker or officer of a bank shall not, in any legal proceeding to which the bank is not a party, be compellable to produce any banker's book the contents of which can be proved under this Act,[4] or to appear as a witness to prove the matters, transactions, and accounts therein recorded, unless by order of a judge made for special cause.

A.07

7. Court or judge may order inspection, &c.

On the application of any party to a legal proceeding a court or judge may order that such party be at liberty to inspect and take copies of any entries in a banker's book for any of the purposes of such proceedings. An order under this section may be made either with or without summoning the bank or any other party, and shall be served on the bank three clear days before the same is to be obeyed, unless the court or judge otherwise directs.

A.08

8. Costs

The costs of any application to a court or judge under or for the purposes of this Act, and the costs of anything done or to be done under an order of a court or judge made under or for the purposes of this Act shall be in the discretion of the court or judge, who may order the same or any part thereof to be paid to any party by the bank where the same have been occasioned by any default or delay on the part of the bank. Any such order against a bank may be enforced as if the bank was a party to the proceeding.

A.09

9.—Interpretation of "bank" "banker", and "bankers' books"

  (1) In this Act the expressions "bank" and "banker" mean—
    [(a) a deposit-taker;][5]
    (b) [...][6]
    (c) the National Savings Bank;
    (d) [...][7]

A.10

---

[3] Added by Criminal Procedure and Investigations Act (1996 c.25), Sch.1, Part II, para.16.

[4] In relation to Scotland s.6 reads:
> "A banker or officer of a bank shall not, in any legal proceeding to which the bank is not a party, be compellable to produce any banker's book the contents of which can be proved under this Act, or under the Civil Evidence (Scotland) Act 1988[or Schedule 8 to the Criminal Procedure (Scotland) Act 1995] or Schedule 3 to the Prisoners and Criminal Proceedings (Scotland) Act 1993 or to appear as a witness to prove the matters, transactions, and accounts therein recorded, unless by order of a judge made for special cause."

[5] Substituted for paras (a) and (aa) by SI 2001/3649 (Financial Services and Markets Act 2000. (Consequential Amendments and Repeals) Order), Part 8, art.265(1), (2).

[6] Repealed by Trustee Savings Bank 1985, ss.4(3), 7(3), Sch.4.

[7] Repealed by SI 2001/1149 (Postal Services Act 2000 (Consequential Amendments No 1) Order), art.3(2), Sch.2.

[(1A) "Deposit taker" means—

    (a) a person who has permission under Part 4 of the Financial Services and Markets Act 2000 to accept deposits; or

    (b) an EEA firm of the kind mentioned in paragraph 5(b) of Schedule 3 to that Act which has permission under paragraph 15 of that Schedule (as a result of qualifying for authorisation under paragraph 12(1) of that Schedule) to accept deposits or other repayable funds from the public.

(1B) But a person is not a deposit-taker if he has permission to accept deposits only for the purpose of carrying on another regulated activity in accordance with that permission.

(1C) Subsections (1A) and (1B) must be read with—

    (a) section 22 of the Financial Services and Markets Act 2000;

    (b) any relevant order under that section; and

    (c) Schedule 2 to that Act.][8]

(2) Expressions in this Act relating to "bankers' books" include ledgers, day books, cash books, account books and other records used in the ordinary business of the bank, whether those records are in written form or are kept on microfilm, magnetic tape or any other form of mechanical or electronic data retrieval mechanism.

10. Interpretation of "legal proceeding,""court," "judge."

A.11   In this Act—

The expression "legal proceeding" means any civil or criminal proceeding or inquiry in which evidence is or may be given, and includes an

    (a) an arbitration;

    (b) an application to, or an inquiry or other proceeding before, the Solicitors Disciplinary Tribunal or any body exercising functions in relation to solicitors in Scotland or Northern Ireland corresponding to the functions of that Tribunal; and

    [(c) an investigation, consideration or determination of a complaint by a member of the panel of ombudsmen for the purposes of the ombudsman scheme within the meaning of the Financial Services and Markets Act 2000][9]

The expression "the court" means the court, judge, arbitrator, persons or person before whom a legal proceeding is held or taken;

The expression "a judge" means with respect to England a judge of the High Court, and with respect to Scotland a lord ordinary of the Outer House of the Court of Session, and with respect to Ireland a judge of the High Court in Northern Ireland;

The judge of a county court may with respect to any action in such court exercise the power of a judge under this Act.

11. Computation of time

A.12   Sunday, Christmas Day, Good Friday, and any bank holiday shall be excluded from the computation of time under this Act.

---

[8] Added by SI 2001/3649 (Financial Services and Markets Act 2000 (Consequential Amendments and Repeals) Order), Part 8, art.265(1), (3).

[9] Substituted by SI 2001/3649 (Financial Services and Markets Act 2000 (Consequential Amendments and Repeals) Order), Part 8, art.266.

Civil Evidence Act 1968, ss.14, 16 and 18

14.—Privilege against incrimination of self or spouse [or civil partner][10]

(1) The right of a person in any legal proceedings other than criminal proceedings **A.13**
to refuse to answer any question or produce any document or thing if to do so would
tend to expose that person to proceedings for an offence or for the recovery of a
penalty—
   (a)   shall apply only as regards criminal offence under the law of any part of the
         United Kingdom and penalties provided for by such law; and
   (b)   shall include a like right to refuse to answer any question or produce any
         document or thing if to do so would tend to expose the [spouse or civil
         partner][11] of that person to proceedings for any such criminal offence or
         for the recovery of any such penalty.

(2) In so far as any existing enactment conferring (in whatever words) powers of
inspection or investigation confers on a person (in whatever words) any right
otherwise than in criminal proceedings to refuse to answer any question or give any
evidence tending to incriminate that person, subsection (1) above shall apply to that
right as it applies to the right described in that subsection; and every such existing
enactment shall be construed accordingly.

(3) In so far as any existing enactment provides (in whatever words) that in any
proceedings other than criminal proceedings a person shall not be excused from
answering any question or giving any evidence on the ground that to do so may
incriminate that person, that enactment shall be construed as providing also that in
such proceedings a person shall not be excused from answering any question or
giving any evidence on the ground that to do so may incriminate the husband or wife
of that person.

(4) Where any existing enactment (however worded) that—
   (a)   confers powers of inspection or investigation; or
   (b)   provides as mentioned in subsection (3) above,
further provides (in whatever words) that any answer or evidence given by a person
shall not be admissible in evidence against that person in any proceedings or class of
proceedings (however described, and whether criminal or not), that enactment shall
be construed as providing also that any answer or evidence given by that person
shall not be admissible in evidence against the husband or wife of that person in the
proceedings or class of proceedings in question.

(5) In this section "existing enactment" means any enactment passed before this
Act; and the references to giving evidence are references to giving evidence in any
manner, whether by furnishing information, making discovery, producing documents or otherwise.

16.—Abolition of certain privileges

(1) The following rules of law are hereby abrogated except in relation to criminal **A.14**
proceedings, that is to say—
   (a)   the rule whereby, in any legal proceedings, a person cannot be compelled to
         answer any question or produce any document or thing if to do so would
         tend to expose him to a forfeiture; and
   (b)   the rule whereby, in any legal proceedings, a person other than a party to
         the proceedings cannot be compelled to produce any deed or other docu-
         ment relating to his title to any land.

---

[10] Added by Civil Partnership Act (2004) c.33), Sch.27, para.30(b).
[11] Words substituted by Civil Partnership Act (2004 c.33), Sch.27, para.30(a).

(2) The rule of law whereby, in any civil proceedings, a party to the proceedings cannot be compelled to produce any document relating solely to his own case and in no way tending to impeach that case or support the case of any opposing party is hereby abrogated.

(3)[—][12]

(4)[—][13]

(5) A witness in any proceedings instituted in consequence of adultery, whether a party to the proceedings or not, shall not be excused from answering any question by reason that it tends to show that he or she has been guilty of adultery; and accordingly the proviso to section 3 of the Evidence Further Amendment Act 1869 and, in section 43(2) of the Matrimonial Causes Act 1965, the words from "but" to the end of the subsection shall cease to have effect.

18.—General interpretation, and savings

A.15   (1) In this Act "civil proceedings" includes, in addition to civil proceedings in any of the ordinary courts of law—

      (a) civil proceedings before any other tribunal, being proceedings in relation to which the strict rules of evidence apply; and

      (b) an arbitration or reference, whether under an enactment or not,

but does not include civil proceedings in relation to which the strict rules of evidence do not apply.

    (2) In this Act—

      "court" does not include a court-martial, and, in relation to an arbitration or reference, means the arbitrator or umpire and, in relation to proceedings before a tribunal (not being one of the ordinary courts of law), means the tribunal;

      "legal proceedings" includes an arbitration or reference, whether under an enactment or not;

and for the avoidance of doubt it is hereby declared that in this Act, and in any amendment made by this Act in any other enactment, references to a person's husband or wife do not include references to a person who is no longer married to that person.

    (3) Any reference in this Act to any other enactment is a reference thereto as amended, and includes a reference thereto as applied, by or under any other enactment.

    (4) Nothing in this Act shall prejudice the operation of any enactment which provides (in whatever words) that any answer or evidence given by a person in specified circumstances shall not be admissible in evidence against him or some other person in any proceedings or class of proceedings (however described).

    In this subsection the reference to giving evidence is a reference to giving evidence in any manner, whether by furnishing information, making discovery, producing documents or otherwise.

    (5) Nothing in this Act shall prejudice—

      (a) any power of a court, in any legal proceedings, to exclude evidence (whether by preventing questions from being put or otherwise) at its discretion; or

      (b) the operation of any agreement (whenever made) between the parties to any legal proceedings as to the evidence which is to be admissible (whether generally or for any particular purpose) in those proceedings.

---

[12] Amends Evidence (Amendment) Act 1853 (c.83), s.3.

[13] Amends Matrimonial Causes Act 1965 (c.72), s.43(1).

(6) It is hereby declared that where, by reason of any defect of speech or hearing from which he is suffering, a person called as a witness in any legal proceedings gives his evidence in writing or by signs, that evidence is to be treated for the purposes of this Act as being given orally.

Civil Procedure Act 1997[14]

(1997 c.12)

1.—Civil Procedure Rules

(1) There are to be rules of court (to be called "Civil Procedure Rules") governing the practice and procedure to be followed in— **A.16**
    (a) the civil division of the Court of Appeal,
    (b) the High Court, and
    (c) county courts.
(2) Schedule 1 (which makes further provision about the extent of the power to make Civil Procedure Rules) is to have effect.
(3) The power to make Civil Procedure Rules is to be exercised with a view to securing that the civil justice system is accessible, fair and efficient.[15]

2.—Rule Committee

[(1) Civil Procedure Rules are to be made by a committee known as the Civil Procedure Rule Committee, which is to consist of the following persons— **A.17**
    (a) the Head of Civil Justice;
    (b) the Deputy Head of Civil Justice (if there is one);
    (c) the persons currently appointed in accordance with subsections (1A) and (1B).
(1A) The Lord Chief Justice must appoint the persons falling within paragraphs (a) to (d) of subsection (2).
(1B) The Lord Chancellor must appoint the persons falling within paragraphs (e) to (g) of subsection (2).][16]
(2) [The persons to be appointed in accordance with subsections (1A) and (1B) are][17]—
    [(a) either two or three judges of the Supreme Court[18],][19]
    (b) one Circuit judge,

---

[14] Note that this Act has been heavily amended subsequently, in some cases with immediate effect, but in many with merely prospective effect. Here the text shown is that considered to be current at the time of writing. Square brackets indicate changes that have taken effect. Where footnotes indicate a prospective amendment but there are no square brackets, this shows the old (ie current) text, not the new one.

[15] A new sub-s.(3) is prospectively substituted as from a date to be appointed, by Courts Act 2003, s.82.

[16] Substituted by Constitutional Reform Act (2005 c.4), s.15(1), Sch.4 Part I, paras 261, 263(1), (2).

[17] Substituted by Constitutional Reform Act (2005 c.4), s.15(1), Sch.4 Part 1, paras 261, 263(1), (3).

[18] The expression "Supreme Court", wherever it appears in this Act, is prospectively amended to "Senior Courts", by Constitutional Reform Act (2005 c.4), s.59(5), Sch.11 (This will also change the name of the Supreme Court Act 1981.)

[19] Substituted by Courts Act 2003, s.83(2).

(c) [either one or two district judges][20],

(d) one person who is a Master referred to in Part II of Schedule 2 to the Supreme Court Act 1981,

(e) three persons who have a Supreme Court qualification (within the meaning of section 71 of the Courts and Legal Services Act 1990), including at least one with particular experience of practice in county courts,

(f) three persons who have been granted by an authorised body, under Part II of that Act, the right to conduct litigation in relation to all proceedings in the Supreme Court, including at least one with particular experience of practice in county courts, [and

(g) two persons with experience in and knowledge of the lay advice sector or consumer affairs.][21]

[(3) Before appointing a person in accordance with subsection (1A), the Lord Chief Justice must consult the Lord Chancellor.][22]

(4) Before appointing a person [in accordance with subsection (1B), the Lord Chancellor must consult the Lord Chief Justice and, if the person falls within paragraph (e) or (f) of subsection (2), must also consult][23] any body which—

(a) has members who are eligible for appointment under that paragraph, and

(b) is an authorised body for the purposes of section 27 or 28 of the Courts and Legal Services Act 1990.

(5) The Lord Chancellor may reimburse the members of the Civil Procedure Rule Committee their travelling and out-of-pocket expenses.

(6) The Civil Procedure Rule Committee must, before making or amending Civil Procedure Rules—

(a) consult such persons as they consider appropriate, and

(b) meet (unless it is inexpedient to do so).[24]

(7) The Civil Procedure Rule Committee must, when making Civil Procedure Rules, try to make rules which are both simple and simply expressed.[25]

(8) Rules made by the Civil Procedure Rule Committee must be signed by at least eight members of the Committee and be submitted to the Lord Chancellor, who may allow or disallow them.[26]

[(9) If the Lord Chancellor disallows rules under subsection (8), he must give the Civil Procedure Rule Committee written reasons for doing so.][27]

[(9) The Lord Chief Justice may nominate a judicial office holder (as defined in section 109(4) of the Constitutional Reform Act 2005) to exercise his functions under this section.][28]

---

[20] Words substituted by SI 2006/1847 (Civil Procedure Act 1997 (Amendment) Order), art.2.

[21] Substituted by Courts Act 2003, s.83(3).

[22] Substituted by Constitutional Reform Act (2005 c.4), s.15(1), Sch.4, Part I, paras 261, 263(1), (4).

[23] Substituted by Constitutional Reform Act (2005 c.4), s.15(1), Sch.4, Part I, paras 261, 263(1), (5).

[24] Prospectively repealed by Courts Act 2003, s.85(1), 109(3), Sch.10, as from a date to be appointed. The substance of this provision will then appear in s.3(1) below.

[25] Prospectively repealed by Courts Act 2003, s.85(1), 109(3), Sch.10, as from a date to be appointed.

[26] Prospectively repealed by Courts Act 2003, s.85(1), 109(3), Sch.10, as from a date to be appointed. The substance of this provision will then appear in s.3(2), (3) below.

[27] Added by Constitutional Reform Act (2005 c.4), Sch.4, part 2, para.361, 385, until the coming into force of the Courts Act 2003, s.85(1) (which will repeal sub-s.(8)), when the substance of this provision will appear in s.3(4) below..

[28] Added by Constitutional Reform Act (2005 c.4), Sch.4, part 1, para.261(1), (6).

[2A Power to change certain requirements relating to Committee

(1) The Lord Chancellor may by order—

    [(a) amend section 2(2), (3) or (4), and][29]

    (b) make consequential amendments in any other provision of section 2.

[(2) The Lord Chancellor may make an order under this section only with the concurrence of the Lord Chief Justice.

(2A) Before making an order under this section the Lord Chancellor must consult the following persons—

    (a) the Head of Civil Justice;

    (b) the Deputy Head of Civil Justice (if there is one).

(2B) The Lord Chief Justice may nominate a judicial office holder (as defined in section 109(4) of the Constitutional Reform Act 2005) to exercise his functions under this section.][30]

(3) The power to make an order under this section is exercisable by statutory instrument.

(4) A statutory instrument containing such an order is subject to annulment in pursuance of a resolution of either House of Parliament.[31]

A.18

3.—Section 2: supplementary

(1) Rules made and allowed under section 2 are to—

    (a) come into force on such day as the Lord Chancellor may direct, and

    (b) be contained in a statutory instrument to which the Statutory Instruments Act 1946 is to apply as if it contained rules made by a Minister of the Crown.

(2) A statutory instrument containing Civil Procedure Rules shall be subject to annulment in pursuance of a resolution of either House of Parliament.[32]

A.19

[3A Rules to be made if required by Lord Chancellor

(1) This section applies if the Lord Chancellor gives the Civil Procedure Rules Committee written notice that he thinks it is expedient for Civil Procedure Rules to include provision that would achieve a purpose specified in the notice.

(2) The Committee must make such Rules as it considers necessary to achieve the specified purpose.

(3) Those rules must be—

    (a) made within a reasonable period after the Lord Chancellor gives notice to the Committee;

    (b) made in accordance with section 3.][33]

A.20

4.—Power to make consequential amendments

(1) The Lord Chancellor may [, after consulting the Lord Chief Justice,][34] by order amend, repeal or revoke any enactment to the extent he considers necessary or desirable in consequence of—

A.21

---

[29] Substituted by Constitutional Reform Act (2005 c.4), Sch.4, part 1, paras 261, 264(1), (2).

[30] Substituted by Constitutional Reform Act (2005 c.4), Sch.4 part 1, paras 261, 264(1), (3).

[31] Added by Courts Act 2003, s.84.

[32] Prospectively substituted by Courts Act 2003, s.85(2), as from a date to be appointed. The substance of the existing s.3 will then appear in sub-ss.((5) and (6) of the new s.3.

[33] Added by Constitutional Reform Act (2005 c.4), Sch.4, Part 1, para.266.

[34] Added by Constitutional Reform Act (2005 c.4), Sch.4, Part 1, paras 261, 267(1), (2).

(a) section 1 or 2, or

(b) Civil Procedure Rules.

(2) The Lord Chancellor may [, after consulting the Lord Chief Justice,]³⁵ by order amend, repeal or revoke any enactment passed or made before the commencement of this section to the extent he considers necessary or desirable in order to facilitate the making of Civil Procedure Rules.

(3) Any power to make an order under this section is exercisable by statutory instrument.

(4) A statutory instrument containing an order under subsection (1) shall be subject to annulment in pursuance of a resolution of either House of Parliament.

(5) No order may be made under subsection (2) unless a draft of it has been laid before and approved by resolution of each House of Parliament.

[(6) The Lord Chief Justice may nominate a judicial office holder (as defined in section 109(4) of the Constitutional Reform Act 2005) to exercise his functions under subsection (1) or (2).]³⁶

[5. Practice directions

A.22   (1) Practice directions may be given in accordance with Part 1 of Schedule 2 to the Constitutional Reform Act 2005.

(2) Practice directions given otherwise than under subsection (1) may not be given without the approval of—

(a) the Lord Chancellor, and

(b) the Lord Chief Justice.

(3) Practice directions (whether given under subsection (1) or otherwise) may provide for any matter which, by virtue of paragraph 3 of Schedule 1, may be provided for by Civil Procedure Rules.

(4) The power to give practice directions under subsection (1) includes power—

(a) to vary or revoke directions given by any person;

(b) to give directions containing different provision for different cases (including different areas);

(c) to give directions containing provision for a specific court, for specific proceedings or for a specific jurisdiction.

(5) Subsection (2)(a) does not apply to directions to the extent that they consist of guidance about any of the following—

(a) the application or interpretation of the law;

(b) the making of judicial decisions.

(6) Subsection (2)(a) does not apply to directions to the extent that they consist of criteria for determining which judges may be allocated to hear particular categories of case; but the directions may, to that extent, be given only—

(a) after consulting the Lord Chancellor, and

(b) with the approval of the Lord Chief Justice.]³⁷

6.—Civil Justice Council

A.23   (1) The Lord Chancellor is to establish and maintain an advisory body, to be known as the Civil Justice Council.

(2) The Council must include—

(a) members of the judiciary,

(b) members of the legal professions,

(c) civil servants concerned with the administration of the courts,

³⁵ Added by Constitutional Reform Act (2005 c.4), Sch.4, Part 1, paras 261, 267(1), (2).
³⁶ Added by Constitutional Reform Act (2005 c.4), Sch.4, Part 1, paras 261, 267(1), (3).
³⁷ Substituted by Constitutional Reform Act (2005 c.4), Sch.2, Part 2, para.6.

    (d) persons with experience in and knowledge of consumer affairs,

    (e) persons with experience in and knowledge of the lay advice sector, and

    (f) persons able to represent the interests of particular kinds of litigants (for example, businesses or employees).

[(2A) The Lord Chancellor must decide the following questions, after consulting the Lord Chief Justice —

    (a) how many members of the Council are to be drawn from each of the groups mentioned in subsection (2);

    (b) how many other members the Council is to have.

(2B) It is for —

    (a) the Lord Chief Justice to appoint members of the judiciary to the Council, after consulting the Lord Chancellor;

    (b) the Lord Chancellor to appoint other persons to the Council.][38]

(3) The functions of the Council are to include —

    (a) keeping the civil justice system under review,

    (b) considering how to make the civil justice system more accessible, fair and efficient,

    (c) advising the Lord Chancellor and the judiciary on the development of the civil justice system,

    (d) referring proposals for changes in the civil justice system to the Lord Chancellor and the Civil Procedure Rule Committee, and

    (e) making proposals for research.

(4) The Lord Chancellor may reimburse the members of the Council their travelling and out-of-pocket expenses.

[(5) The Lord Chief Justice may nominate a judicial office holder (as defined in section 109(4) of the Constitutional Reform Act 2005) to exercise his functions under this section.][39]

7.—Power of courts to make orders for preserving evidence, etc

(1) The court may make an order under this section for the purpose of securing, **A.24** in the case of any existing or proposed proceedings in the court —

    (a) the preservation of evidence which is or may be relevant, or

    (b) the preservation of property which is or may be the subject-matter of the proceedings or as to which any question arises or may arise in the proceedings.

(2) A person who is, or appears to the court likely to be, a party to proceedings in the court may make an application for such an order.

(3) Such an order may direct any person to permit any person described in the order, or secure that any person so described is permitted —

    (a) to enter premises in England and Wales, and

    (b) while on the premises, to take in accordance with the terms of the order any of the following steps.

(4) Those steps are —

    (a) to carry out a search for or inspection of anything described in the order, and

    (b) to make or obtain a copy, photograph, sample or other record of anything so described.

(5) The order may also direct the person concerned —

---

[38] Added by Constitutional Reform Act (2005 c.4), Sch.4, Part 1, paras 261, 268(1), (2).
[39] Added by Constitutional Reform Act (2005 c.4), Sch.4, Part 1, paras 261, 268(1), (3).

(a) to provide any person described in the order, or secure that any person so described is provided, with any information or article described in the order, and

(b) to allow any person described in the order, or secure that any person so described is allowed, to retain for safe keeping anything described in the order, and

(6) An order under this section is to have effect subject to such conditions as are specified in the order.

(7) This section does not affect any right of a person to refuse to do anything on the ground that to do so might tend to expose him or his spouse [or civil partner][40] to proceedings for an offence or for the recovery of a penalty.

(8) In this section—

"court" means the High Court, and

"premises" includes any vehicle;

and an order under this section may describe anything generally, whether by reference to a class or otherwise.

8.—Disclosure etc. of documents before action begun

A.25   (1) The Lord Chancellor may by order amend the provisions of section 33(2) of the Supreme Court Act 1981, or section 52(2) of the County Courts Act 1984 (power of court to order disclosure etc. of documents where claim may be made in respect of personal injury or death), so as to extend the provisions—

(a) to circumstances where other claims may be made, or

(b) generally.

(2) The power to make an order under this section is exercisable by statutory instrument which shall be subject to annulment in pursuance of a resolution of either House of Parliament.[41]

9.—Interpretation

A.26   (1) A court the practice and procedure of which is governed by Civil Procedure Rules is referred to in this Act as being "within the scope" of the rules; and references to a court outside the scope of the rules are to be read accordingly.

(2) In this Act—

"enactment" includes an enactment contained in subordinate legislation (within the meaning of the Interpretation Act 1978, and

"practice directions" means directions as to the practice and procedure of any court within the scope of Civil Procedure Rules.

10. Minor and consequential amendments

A.27   Schedule 2 (which makes minor and consequential amendments) is to have effect.

11.—Short title, commencement and extent

A.28   (1) This Act may be cited as the Civil Procedure Act 1997.

(2) Sections 1 to 10 are to come into force on such day as the Lord Chancellor may by order made by statutory instrument appoint, and different days may be appointed for different purposes.

(3) This Act extends to England and Wales only.

---

[40] Added by Civil Partnership Act (2004 c.33), Sch.27, para.154.
[41] Amended prospectively by Constitutional Reform Act (2005 c.4), Sch.11, Part 1, para.1(2).

SCHEDULE 1

CIVIL PROCEDURE RULES

Matters dealt with by the former rules

1. Among the matters which Civil Procedure Rules may be made about are any matters which were governed by the former Rules of the Supreme Court or the former county court rules (that is, the Rules of the Supreme Court (Revision) 1965 and the County Court Rules 1981. **A.29**

Exercise of jurisdiction

2. Civil Procedure Rules may provide for the exercise of the jurisdiction of any court within the scope of the rules by officers or other staff of the court. **A.30**

Removal of proceedings

3.— **A.31**
(1) Civil Procedure Rules may provide for the removal of proceedings at any stage—
  (a) within the High Court (for example, between different divisions or different district registries), or
  (b) between county courts.
(2) In sub-paragraph (1)—
  (a) "provide for the removal of proceedings" means—(i) provide for transfer of proceedings, or (ii) provide for any jurisdiction in any proceedings to be exercised (whether concurrently or not) elsewhere within the High Court or, as the case may be, by another county court without the proceedings being transferred, and
  (b) "proceedings" includes any part of proceedings.

Evidence

4. Civil Procedure Rules may modify the rules of evidence as they apply to proceedings in any court within the scope of the rules. **A.32**

Application of other rules

5.— **A.33**
(1) Civil Procedure Rules may apply any rules of court which relate to a court which is outside the scope of Civil Procedure Rules.
(2) Any rules of court, not made by the Civil Procedure Rule Committee, which apply to proceedings of a particular kind in a court within the scope of Civil Procedure Rules may be applied by Civil Procedure Rules to other proceedings in such a court.
(3) In this paragraph "rules of court" includes any provision governing the practice and procedure of a court which is made by or under an enactment.
(4) Where Civil Procedure Rules may be made by applying other rules, the other rules may be applied—
  (a) to any extent,
  (b) with or without modification, and
  (c) as amended from time to time.

Practice directions

6. Civil Procedure Rules may, instead of providing for any matter, refer to provision made or to be made about that matter by directions. **A.34**

Different provision for different cases etc

A.35   7. The power to make Civil Procedure Rules includes power to make different provision for different cases or different areas, including different provision—

(a) for a specific court or specific division of a court, or

(b) for specific proceedings, or a specific jurisdiction,

specified in the rules.

SCHEDULE 2

MINOR AND CONSEQUENTIAL AMENDMENTS

Supreme Court Act 1981 (c.54)

A.36   1.—

(1) The Supreme Court Act 1981 is amended as follows.

(2) [. . .][42]

(3) In section 68 (exercise of High Court jurisdiction otherwise than by judges)—

(a) in subsection (1), paragraph (c) and the word "or" immediately preceding it are omitted,

(b) in subsection (2)—

(i) paragraph (a) is omitted, and

(ii) in paragraph (b), for "any such person" there is substituted "a special referee",

(c) in subsection (3) for the words from "any" onwards there is substituted "a special referee or any officer or other staff of the court", and

(d) in subsection (4)—

(i) after "decision of" there is inserted "(a)", and

(ii) after "subsection (1)" there is inserted—

"or

(b) any officer or other staff of the court".

(4) In section 84 (power to make rules of court)—

(a) in subsection (1), for "Supreme Court" there is substituted "Crown Court and the criminal division of the Court of Appeal",

(b) subsection (4) is omitted,

(c) for subsections (5) and (6) there is substituted—

"(5) Special rules may apply—

(a) any rules made under this section, or

(b) Civil Procedure Rules,

to proceedings to which the special rules apply.

(5A) Rules made under this section may apply—

(a) any special rules, or

(b) Civil Procedure Rules,

to proceedings to which rules made under this section apply.

(6) Where rules may be applied under subsection (5) or (5A), they may be applied—

(a) to any extent,

(b) with or without modification, and

(c) as amended from time to time."

---

[42] Repealed by Access to Justice Act (1999 c.22), Sch.15, Part III.

, and
  (d) in subsection (9), for "Supreme Court Rule Committee" there is substituted "Civil Procedure Rule Committee".

(5) Section 85 (Supreme Court Rule Committee) is omitted.

(6) In section 87 (particular matters for which rules of court may provide)—
  (a) subsections (1) and (2) are omitted, and
  (b) in subsection (3), for "Supreme Court" there is substituted "Crown Court or the criminal division of the Court of Appeal".

(7) In section 151 (interpretation)—
  (a) in subsection (3), after the second "rules of court" there is inserted "in relation to the Supreme Court" and for "Supreme Court Rule Committee" there is substituted "Civil Procedure Rule Committee", and
  (b) in subsection (4), the definition of "Rules of the Supreme Court" is omitted.

County Courts Act 1984 (c.28)

2.—   **A.37**
(1) The County Courts Act 1984 is amended as follows.

(2) For "county court rules", wherever occurring, there is substituted "rules of court".

(3) For "rule committee", wherever occurring, there is substituted "Civil Procedure Rule Committee".

(4) In section 1 (county courts to be held for districts), in subsection (1), for the words from "throughout" to "the district" there is substituted "each court".

(5) In section 3 (places and times of sittings of courts), subsection (3) is omitted.

(6) Section 75 (county court rules) is omitted.

(7) In section 77(1), for "the rules of the Supreme Court" there is substituted "Civil Procedure Rules".

(8) In section 81(2), for "any rules of the Supreme Court" there is substituted "Civil Procedure Rules".

(9) In section 147(1), the definitions of "county court rules" and "the rule committee" are omitted.

Matrimonial and Family Proceedings Act 1984 (c.42)

3. In section 40 of the Matrimonial and Family Proceedings Act 1984 (family **A.38** proceedings rules)—
  (a) after subsection (3) there is inserted—

"(3A) Rules made under this section may make different provision for different cases or different areas, including different provision—
  (a) for a specific court, or
  (b) for specific proceedings, or a specific jurisdiction,
specified in the rules.",

and
  (b) in subsection (4) the words from the first "in" to "and may" are omitted.[43]

---

[43] Prospectively repealed by Courts Act 2003, s.109(3), Sch.10.

Courts and Legal Services Act 1990 (c.41)

A.39   4. In section 120 of the Courts and Legal Services Act 1990 (regulations and orders), in subsection (4), "1(1)" is omitted.

Copyright, Designs and Patents Act 1988

280.—Privilege for communications with patent agents

A.40   (1) This section applies to communications as to any matter relating to the protection of any invention, design, technical information[or trade mark][44], or as to any matter involving passing off.

(2) Any such communication—
  (a) between a person and his patent agent, or
  (b) for the purpose of obtaining, or in response to a request for, information which a person in seeking for the purpose of instructing his patent agent,

is privileged from disclosure in legal proceedings in England, Wales or Northern Ireland in the same way as a communication between a person and his solicitor or, as the case may be, a communication for the purpose of obtaining, or in response to a request for, information which a person seeks for the purpose of instructing his solicitor.

(3) In subsection (2) "patent agent" means—
  (a) a registered patent agent or a person who is on the European list,
  (b) a partnership entitled to describe itself as a firm of patent agents or as a firm carrying on the business of a European patent attorney, or
  (c) a body corporate entitled to describe itself as a patent agent or as a company carrying on the business of a European patent attorney.

(4) It is hereby declared that in Scotland the rules of law which confer privilege from disclosure in legal proceedings in respect of communications extend to such communications as are mentioned in this section.

County Courts Act 1984, ss.52–54 and 59

Discovery and related procedures

52.—Powers of court exercisable before commencement of action

A.41   (1) On the application of any person in accordance with [rules of court],[45] a county court shall, in such circumstances as may be prescribed, have power to make an order providing for any one or more of the following matters, that is to say—
  (a) the inspection, photographing, preservation, custody and detention of property which appears to the court to be property which may become the subject-matter of subsequent proceedings in the court, or as to which any question may arise in any such proceedings; and
  (b) the taking of samples of any such property as is mentioned in paragraph (a), and the carrying out of any experiment on or with any such property.

---

[44] Words substituted by Trade Marks Act (1994 c.26), Sch.4, para.8(3).
[45] Substituted by Civil Procedure Act 1997, Sch.2, para.2(2).

(2) On the application, in accordance with [rules of court],[46] of a person who appears to a county court to be likely to be a party to subsequent proceedings in that court[...][47] the county court shall, in such circumstances as may be prescribed, have power to order a person who appears to the court to be likely to be a party to the proceedings and to be likely to have or to have had in his possession, custody or power any documents which are relevant to an issue arising or likely to arise out of that claim —

(a) to disclose whether those documents are in his possession, custody or power; and

(b) to produce such of those documents as are in his possession, custody or power to the applicant or, on such conditions as may be specified in the order, —

(i) to the applicant's legal advisers; or

(ii) to the applicant's legal advisers and any medical or other professional adviser of the applicant; or

(iii) if the applicant has no legal adviser, to any medical or other professional adviser of the applicant.

[(3) This section is subject to any provision made under section 38.][48]

53.—Power of court to order disclosure of documents, inspection of property etc. in proceedings for personal injuries or death

(1) [...][49]
A.42

(2) On the application, in accordance with [rules of court],[50] of a party to any proceedings[...][51], a county court shall, in such circumstances as may be prescribed, have power to order a person who is not a party to the proceedings and who appears to the court to be likely to have in his possession, custody or power any documents which are relevant to an issue arising out of the said claim—

(a) to disclose whether those documents are in his possession, custody or power; and

(b) to produce such of those documents as are in his possession, custody or power to the applicant or, on such conditions as may be specified in the order, —

(i) to the applicant's legal advisers; or

(ii) to the applicant's legal advisers and any medical or other professional adviser of the applicant; or

(iii) if the applicant has no legal adviser, to any medical or other professional adviser of the applicant.

(3) On the application, in accordance with [rules of court][52], of a party to any proceedings[...][53], a county court shall, in such circumstances as may be prescribed, have power to make an order providing for any one or more of the following matters, that is to say—

---

[46] Substituted by Civil Procedure Act 1997, Sch.2, para.2(2).
[47] Words repealed by SI 1998/2940 (Civil Procedure (Modification of Enactments) Order), art.6(b).
[48] Added by Courts and Legal Services Act 1990, s.125(3), Sch.18, para.43.
[49] Repealed by SI 1998/2940 (Civil Procedure (Modification of Enactments) Order), art.6(c).
[50] Substituted by Civil Procedure Act 1997, Sch.2, para.2(2).
[51] Repealed by SI 1998/2940 (Civil Procedure (Modification of Enactments) Order), art.6(c)(ii).
[52] Substituted by Civil Procedure Act 1997, Sch.2, para.2(2).
[53] Repealed by SI 1998/2940 (Civil Procedure (Modification of Enactments) Order), art.6(c)(ii).

(a) the inspection, photographing, preservation, custody and detention of property which is not the property of, or in the possession of, any party to the proceedings but which is the subject-matter of the proceedings or as to which any question arises in the proceedings;

(b) the taking of samples of any such property as is mentioned in paragraph (a) and the carrying out of any experiment on or with any such property.

(4) The preceding provisions of this section are without prejudice to the exercise by a county court of any power to make orders which is exercisable apart from those provisions.

[(5) This section is subject to any provision made under section 38.][54]

54.—Provisions supplementary to sections 52 and 53

A.43

(1) A county court shall not make an order under section 52 or 53 if it considers that compliance with the order, if made, would be likely to be injurious to the public interest.

(2) Rules of court may make provision as to the circumstances in which an order under section 52 or 53 can be made; and any rules making such provision may include such incidental, supplementary and consequential provisions as the [Civil Procedure Rule Committee][55] may consider necessary or expedient.

(3) Without prejudice to the generality of subsection (2), rules of court shall be made for the purpose of ensuring that the costs of and incidental to proceedings for an order under section 52(2) or 53 incurred by the person against whom the order is sought shall be awarded to that person unless the court otherwise directs.

(4) Sections 52(2) and 53 and this section bind the Crown; and section 52(1) binds the Crown so far as it relates to property as to which it appears to the court that it may become the subject-matter of subsequent proceedings involving a claim in respect of personal injuries to a person or in respect of a person's death.

In this subsection references to the Crown do not include references to Her Majesty in Her private capacity or to Her Majesty in right of Her Duchy of Lancaster or to the Duke of Cornwall.

(5) In sections 52 and 53 and this section—

"property" includes any land, chattel or other corporeal property of any description;

"personal injuries" includes any disease and any impairment of a person's physical or mental condition.

[(6) This section is subject to any provision made under section 38.][56]

59.—Evidence in Admiralty proceedings

A.44

(1) In any Admiralty proceedings, evidence taken before a registrar of an Admiralty county court, in accordance with the directions of a judge or pursuant to [rules of court][57], may be received as evidence in any other Admiralty county court.

(2) The registrar of any Admiralty county court shall, for the purpose of the examination of any witness within the district assigned to that court for Admiralty purposes, have all the power of an examiner of the High Court, and evidence taken by him in that capacity may be received as evidence in the High Court.

---

[54] Added by Courts and Legal Services Act 1990, s.125(3), Sch.18, para.44.
[55] Substituted by Civil Procedure Act (1997 c.12), Sch.2, para.2(3).
[56] Added by Courts and Legal Services Act 1990, s.125(3), Sch.18, para.43.
[57] Substituted by Civil Procedure Act (1997 c.12), Sch.2, para.2(2).

Evidence (Proceedings in Other Jurisdictions) Act 1975

(1975 c.34)

Evidence for civil proceedings

1. Application to United Kingdom court for assistance in obtaining evidence for civil proceedings in other court

Where an application is made to the High Court, the Court of Session or the High **A.45**
Court of Justice in Northern Ireland for an order for evidence to be obtained in the
part of the United Kingdom in which it exercises jurisdiction, and the court is
satisfied—
- (a) that the application is made in pursuance of a request issued by or on
behalf of a court or tribunal ("the requesting court") exercising jurisdiction
in any other part of the United Kingdom or in a country or territory outside
the United Kingdom; and
- (b) that the evidence to which the application relates is to be obtained for the
purposes of civil proceedings which either have been instituted before the
requesting court or whose institution before that court is contemplated,
the High Court, Court of Session or High Court of Justice in Northern Ireland, as
the case may be, shall have the powers conferred on it by the following provisions
of this Act.

2.—Power of United Kingdom court to give effect to application for assistance

(1) Subject to the provisions of this section, the High Court, the Court of Session **A.46**
and the High Court of Justice in Northern Ireland shall each have power, on any
such application as is mentioned in section 1 above, by order to make such provision
for obtaining evidence in the part of the United Kingdom in which it exercises
jurisdiction as may appear to the court to be appropriate for the purpose of giving
effect to the request in pursuance of which the application is made; and any such
order may require a person specified therein to take such steps as the court may
consider appropriate for that purpose.

(2) Without prejudice to the generality of subsection (1) above but subject to the
provisions of this section, an order under this section may, in particular, make
provision—
- (a) for the examination of witnesses,either orally or in writing;
- (b) or the production of documents;
- (c) for the inspection, photographing, preservation, custody or detention of
any property;
- (d) for the taking of samples of any property and the carrying out of any
experiments on or with any property;
- (e) for the medical examination of any person;
- (f) without prejudice to paragraph (e) above, for the taking and testing of
samples of blood from any person.

(3) An order under this section shall not require any particular steps to be taken
unless they are steps which can be required to be taken by way of obtaining evidence
for the purposes of civil proceedings in the court making the order (whether or not
proceedings of the same description as those to which the application for the order
relates); but this subsection shall not preclude the making of an order requiring a
person to give testimony (either orally or in writing) otherwise than on oath where
this is asked for by the requesting court.

(4) An order under this section shall not require a person—

(a) to state what documents relevant to the proceedings to which the application for the order relates are or have been in his possession, custody or power; or

(b) to produce any documents other than particular documents specified in the order as being documents appearing to the court making the order to be, or to be likely to be, in his possession, custody or power.

(5) A person who, by virtue of an order under this section, is required to attend at any place shall be entitled to the like conduct money and payment for expenses and loss of time as on attendance as a witness in civil proceedings before the court making the order.

3.—Privilege of witnesses

A.47   (1) A person shall not be compelled by virtue of an order under section 2 above to give any evidence which he could not be compelled to give—

(a) in civil proceedings in the part of the United Kingdom in which the court that made the order exercises jurisdiction; or

(b) subject to subsection (2) below, in civil proceedings in the country or territory in which the requesting court exercises jurisdiction.

(2) Subsection (1)(b) above shall not apply unless the claim of the person in question to be exempt from giving the evidence is either—

(a) supported by a statement contained in the request (whether it is so supported unconditionally or subject to conditions that are fulfilled); or

(b) conceded by the applicant for the order;

and where such a claim made by any person is not supported or conceded as aforesaid he may (subject to the other provisions of this section) be required to give the evidence to which the claim relates but that evidence shall not be transmitted to the requesting court if that court, on the matter being referred to it, upholds the claim.

(3) Without prejudice to subsection (1) above, a person shall not be compelled by virtue of an order under section 2 above to give any evidence if his doing so would be prejudicial to the security of the United Kingdom; and a certificate signed by or on behalf of the Secretary of State to the effect that it would be so prejudicial for that person to do so shall be conclusive evidence of that fact.

(4) In this section references to giving evidence include references to answering any question and to producing any document and the reference in subsection (2) above to the transmission of evidence given by a person shall be construed accordingly.

4. Extension of powers of High Court etc. in relation to obtaining evidence for proceedings in that court

A.48   [The Attendance of Witnesses Act 1854 (which enables the Court of Session to order the issue of a warrant of citation in special form, enforceable throughout the United Kingdom, for the attendance of a witness at a trial) shall][58] have effect as if references to attendance at a trial included references to attendance before an examiner or commissioner appointed by the court or a judge thereof in any cause or matter in that court, including an examiner or commissioner appointed to take evidence outside the jurisdiction of the court.

Evidence for criminal proceedings

A.49   5. [. . .][59]

---

[58] Substituted by Supreme Court Act 1981 (c.54), s.152(4), Sch.5.
[59] Repealed by Criminal Justice (International Co-operation) Act (1990 c.5), Sch.5.

Evidence for international proceedings

6.—Power of United Kingdom court to assist in obtaining evidence for international proceedings

(1) Her Majesty may by Order in Council direct that, subject to such exceptions, **A.50** adaptations or modifications as may be specified in the Order, the provisions of sections 1 to 3 above shall have effect in relation to international proceedings of any description specified in the order.

(2) An Order in Council under this section may direct that section 1(4) of the Perjury Act 1911 or section 1(4) of the Perjury Act (Northern Ireland) 1946 shall have effect in relation to international proceedings to which the Order applies as it has effect in relation to a judicial proceedings in a tribunal of a foreign state.

(3) In this section "international proceedings" means proceedings before the International Court of Justice or any other court, tribunal, commission, body or authority (whether consisting of one or more persons) which, in pursuance of any international agreement or any resolution of the General Assembly of the United Nations, exercises any jurisdiction or performs any functions of a judicial nature or by way of arbitration, conciliation or inquiry or is appointed (whether permanently or temporarily) for the purpose of exercising any jurisdiction or performing any such functions.

Supplementary

7. Rules of court

[Civil Procedure Rules or rules of court under][60] section 7 of the Northern Ireland **A.51** Act 1962 may make provision

    (a) as to the manner in which any such application as is mentioned in section 1 above is to be made;

    (b) subject to the provisions of this Act, as to the circumstances in which an order can be made under section 2 above; and

    (c) as to the manner in which any such reference as is mentioned in section 3(2) above is to be made;

and any such rules may include such incidental, supplementary and consequential provision as the authority making the rules may consider necessary or expedient.

8.—Consequential amendments and repeals

(1) [*Provides for amendment of enactments specified in Sch.1*] **A.52**

(2) [*Repeals enactments specified in Sch.2.*]

(3) Nothing in this section shall affect—

    (a) any application to any court or judge which is pending at the commencement of this Act;

    (b) any certificate given for the purposes of any such application;

    (c) any power to make an order on such an application; or

    (d) the operation or enforcement of any order made on such an application.

(4) Subsection (3) above is without prejudice to section 38(2) of the Interpretation Act 1889 (effect of repeals).

9.—Interpretation

(1) In this Act— **A.53**

    "civil proceedings", in relation to the requesting court, means proceedings in any civil or commercial matter;

---

[60] Substituted by Courts Act (2003 c.39), Sch.8, para.177(a).

"requesting court" has the meaning given in section 1 above;

"property" includes any land, chattel or other corporeal property of any description;

"request" includes any commission, order or other process issued by or on behalf of the requesting court.

(2) In relation to any application made in pursuance of a request issued by the High Court under [section 56 of the County Courts Act 1984][61] or the High Court of Justice in Northern Ireland under section 58 of the County Courts Act (Northern Ireland) 1959, the reference in section 1(b) above to proceedings instituted before the requesting court shall be construed as a reference to the relevant proceedings in the county court.

(3) Any power conferred by this Act to make an Order in Council includes power to revoke or vary any such Order by a subsequent Order in Council.

(4) Nothing in this Act shall be construed as enabling any court to make an order that is binding on the Crown or on any person in his capacity as an officer or servant of the Crown.

(5) Except so far as the context otherwise requires, any reference in this Act to any enactment is a reference to that enactment as amended or extended by or under any other enactment.

10.—Short title, commencement and extent

A.54

(1) This Act may be cited as the Evidence (Proceedings in Other Jurisdictions) Act 1975.

(2) This Act shall come into operation on such day as Her Majesty may by Order in Council appoint.

(3) Her Majesty may by Order in Council make provision for extending any of the provisions of this Act (including section 6 or any Order in Council made thereunder), with such exceptions, adaptations or modifications as may be specified in the Order, to any of the Channel Islands, the Isle of Man, any colony (other than a colony for whose external relations a country other than the United Kingdom is responsible) or any country or territory outside Her Majesty's dominions in which Her Majesty has jurisdiction in right of Her Majesty's Government in the United Kingdom.

SCHEDULE 1

[*Inserts s.1A in Perjury Act 1911 (c.6); Amends False Oaths (Scotland) Act 1933 (c.20), s.2 and Administration of Justice (Scotland) Act 1933 (c.41), s.6(3)(f); Inserts s.1A.A in Perjury Act (Northern Ireland) 1946 (c.13); Amends Maintenance Orders (Reciprocal Enforcement) Act 1972 (c.18), s.44(2)*]

SCHEDULE 2

[*Specifies enactments repealed by s.8(2)*]

---

[61] Substituted by County Courts Act 1984 (c.28), s.148(1)(2), Sch.2, Pt V, para.53, Sch.3, para.9.

Human Rights Act 1998

1. The Convention Rights

(1) In this Act "the Convention rights" means the rights and fundamental free-   **A.55**
doms set out in—
  (a) Articles 2 to 12 and 14 of the Convention,
  (b) Articles 1 to 3 of the First Protocol, and
  (c) [Article 1 of the Thirteenth Protocol],[62]
as read with Articles 16 to 18 of the Convention.

(2) Those Articles are to have effect for the purposes of this Act subject to any
designated derogation or reservation (as to which see sections 14 and 15).

(3) The Articles are set out in Schedule 1.

(4) The Secretary of State may by order make such amendments to this Act as he
considers appropriate to reflect the effect, in relation to the United Kingdom, of a
protocol.

(5) In subsection (4) "protocol" means a protocol to the Convention—
  (a) which the United Kingdom has ratified; or
  (b) which the United Kingdom has signed with a view to ratification.

(6) No amendment may be made by an order under subsection (4) so as to come
into force before the protocol concerned is in force in relation to the United Kingdom.

2. Interpretation of Convention rights

(1) A court or tribunal determining a question which has arisen in connection with   **A.56**
a Convention right must take into account any—
  (a) judgment, decision, declaration or advisory opinion of the European Court
       of Human Rights,
  (b) opinion of the Commission given in a report adopted under Article 31 of
       the Convention,
  (c) decision of the Commission in connection with Article 26 or 27(2) of the
       Convention, or
  (d) decision of the Committee of Ministers taken under Article 46 of the
       Convention,
whenever made or given, so far as, in the opinion of the court or tribunal, it is
relevant to the proceedings in which that question has arisen.

(2) Evidence of any judgment, decision, declaration or opinion of which account
may have to be taken under this section is to be given in proceedings before any
court or tribunal in such manner as may be provided by rules.

(3) In this section "rules" means rules of court or, in the case of proceedings before
a tribunal, rules made for the purposes of this section—
  (a) by[the Lord Chancellor or][63] the Secretary of State, in relation to any
       proceedings outside Scotland;
  (b) by the Secretary of State, in relation to proceedings in Scotland; or
  (c) by a Northern Ireland department, in relation to proceedings before a
       tribunal in Northern Ireland—
       (i) which deals with transferred matters; and
       (ii) for which no rules made under paragraph (a) are in force.

---

[62] Substituted by SI 2004/1574 (Human Rights Act 1998 (Amendment) Order), art.2(1).
[63] Inserted by SI 2005/3429 (Transfer of Functions (Lord Chancellor and Secretary of State)
Order), Sch.1, para.3.

3. Interpretation of legislation

A.57   (1) So far as it is possible to do so, primary legislation and subordinate legislation must be read and given effect in a way which is compatible with the Convention rights.

(2) This section—

    (a) applies to primary legislation and subordinate legislation whenever enacted;

    (b) does not affect the validity, continuing operation or enforcement of any incompatible primary legislation; and

    (c) does not affect the validity, continuing operation or enforcement of any incompatible subordinate legislation if (disregarding any possibility of revocation) primary legislation prevents removal of the incompatibility.

6. Acts of public authorities

A.58   (1) It is unlawful for a public authority to act in a way which is incompatible with a Convention right.

(2) Subsection (1) does not apply to an act if—

    (a) as the result of one or more provisions of primary legislation, the authority could not have acted differently; or

    (b) in the case of one or more provisions of, or made under, primary legislation which cannot be read or given effect in a way which is compatible with the Convention rights, the authority was acting so as to give effect to or enforce those provisions.

(3) In this section "public authority" includes—

    (a) a court or tribunal, and

    (b) any person certain of whose functions are functions of a public nature,

but does not include either House of Parliament or a person exercising functions in connection with proceedings in Parliament.

(4) In subsection (3) "Parliament" does not include the House of Lords in its judicial capacity.

(5) In relation to a particular act, a person is not a public authority by virtue only of subsection (3)(b) if the nature of the act is private.

(6) "An act" includes a failure to act but does not include a failure to—

    (a) introduce in, or lay before, Parliament a proposal for legislation; or

    (b) make any primary legislation or remedial order.

SCHEDULE 1

THE ARTICLES

PART I THE CONVENTION RIGHTS AND FREEDOMS

Prohibition of slavery and forced labour

Article 4

A.59   1. No one shall be held in slavery or servitude.

2. No one shall be required to perform forced or compulsory labour.

3. For the purpose of this Article the term "forced or compulsory labour" shall not include:

    (a) any work required to be done in the ordinary course of detention imposed according to the provisions of Article 5 of this Convention or during conditional release from such detention;

   (b) any service of a military character or, in case of conscientious objectors in countries where they are recognised, service exacted instead of compulsory military service;

   (c) any service exacted in case of an emergency or calamity threatening the life or well-being of the community;

   (d) any work or service which forms part of normal civic obligations.

Right to a fair trial

Article 6

1. In the determination of his civil rights and obligations or of any criminal charge **A.60** against him, everyone is entitled to a fair and public hearing within a reasonable time by an independent and impartial tribunal established by law. Judgment shall be pronounced publicly but the press and public may be excluded from all or part of the trial in the interest of morals, public order or national security in a democratic society, where the interests of juveniles or the protection of the private life of the parties so require, or to the extent strictly necessary in the opinion of the court in special circumstances where publicity would prejudice the interests of justice.

2. Everyone charged with a criminal offence shall be presumed innocent until proved guilty according to law.

3. Everyone charged with a criminal offence has the following minimum rights:

   (a) to be informed promptly, in a language which he understands and in detail, of the nature and cause of the accusation against him;

   (b) to have adequate time and facilities for the preparation of his defence;

   (c) to defend himself in person or through legal assistance of his own choosing or, if he has not sufficient means to pay for legal assistance, to be given it free when the interests of justice so require;

   (d) to examine or have examined witnesses against him and to obtain the attendance and examination of witnesses on his behalf under the same conditions as witnesses against him;

   (e) to have the free assistance of an interpreter if he cannot understand or speak the language used in court.

Right to respect for private and family life

Article 8

1. Everyone has the right to respect for his private and family life, his home and **A.61** his correspondence.

2. There shall be no interference by a public authority with the exercise of this right except such as is in accordance with the law and is necessary in a democratic society in the interests of national security, public safety or the economic well-being of the country, for the prevention of disorder or crime, for the protection of health or morals, or for the protection of the rights and freedoms of others.

Freedom of expression

Article 10

1. Everyone has the right to freedom of expression. This right shall include **A.62** freedom to hold opinions and to receive and impart information and ideas without interference by public authority and regardless of frontiers. This Article shall not prevent States from requiring the licensing of broadcasting, television or cinema enterprises.

2. The exercise of these freedoms, since it carries with it duties and responsibilities, may be subject to such formalities, conditions, restrictions or penalties as are

prescribed by law and are necessary in a democratic society, in the interests of national security, territorial integrity or public safety, for the prevention of disorder or crime, for the protection of health or morals, for the protection of the reputation or rights of others, for preventing the disclosure of information received in confidence, or for maintaining the authority and impartiality of the judiciary.

Prohibition of discrimination

Article 14

A.63   The enjoyment of the rights and freedoms set forth in this Convention shall be secured without discrimination on any ground such as sex, race, colour, language, religion, political or other opinion, national or social origin, association with a national minority, property, birth or other status.

Prohibition of abuse of rights

Article 17

A.64   Nothing in this Convention may be interpreted as implying for any State, group or person any right to engage in any activity or perform any act aimed at the destruction of any of the rights and freedoms set forth herein or at their limitation to a greater extent than is provided for in the Convention.

Limitation on use of restrictions on rights

Article 18

A.65   The restrictions permitted under this Convention to the said rights and freedoms shall not be applied for any purpose other than those for which they have been prescribed.

Supreme Court Act 1981,[64] ss.33–35 and 72

33.—Powers of High Court exercisable before commencement of action

A.66   (1) On the application of any person in accordance with rules of court, the High Court shall, in such circumstances as may be specified in the rules, have power to make an order providing for any one or more of the following matters, that is to say—

   (a) the inspection, photocopying, preservation, custody and detention of property which appears to the court to be property which may become the subject-matter of subsequent proceedings in the High Court, or as to which any question may arise in any such proceedings; and

   (b) the taking of samples of any such property as is mentioned in paragraph (a), and the carrying out of any experiment on or with any such property.

(2) On the application, in accordance with rules of court, of a person who appears to the High Court to be likely to be a party to subsequent proceedings in that court [. . .][65] the High Court shall, in such circumstances as may be specified in the rules,

---

[64] The title "Supreme Court Act 1981" is prospectively amended to "Senior Courts Act 1981" by Constitutional Reform Act (2005 c.4), s.59(5), Sch.11.

[65] Repealed by SI 1998/2940 (Civil Procedure (Modification of Enactments) Order), art.5(a).

have power to order a person who appears to the court to be likely to be a party to the proceedings and to be likely to have or to have had in his possession , custody or power any documents which are relevant to an issue arising or likely to arise out of that claim—

    (a) to disclose whether those documents are in his possession, custody or power; and

    (b) to produce such of those documents as are in his possession, custody or power to the applicant or, on such conditions as may be specified in the order—

        (i) to the applicant's legal advisers; or

        (ii) to the applicant's legal advisers and any medical or other professional adviser of the applicant; or

        (iii) if the applicant has no legal adviser, to any medical or other professional adviser of the applicant.[66]

34.—Powers of High Court to order disclosure of documents, inspection of property etc. in proceedings for personal injuries or death

(1) [. . .][67]

A.67

(2) On the application, in accordance with rules of court, of a party to any proceedings [. . .],[68] the High Court shall, in such circumstances as may be specified in the rules, have power to order a person who is not a party to the proceedings and who appears to the court to be likely to have in his possession, custody or power any documents which are relevant to an issue arising out of the said claim—

    (a) to disclose whether those documents are in his possession, custody or power; and

    (b) to produce such of those documents as are in his possession, custody or power to the applicant or, on such conditions as may be specified in the order—

        (i) to the applicant's legal advisers; or

        (ii) to the applicant's legal advisers and any medical or other professional adviser of the applicant; or

        (iii) if the applicant has no legal adviser, to any medical or other professional adviser of the applicant.

(3) On the application, in accordance with rules of court, of a party to any proceedings [. . .],[69] the High Court shall, in such circumstances as may be specified in the rules, have power to make an order providing for any one or more of the following matters, that is to say—

    (a) the inspection, photographing, preservation, custody and detention of property which is not the property of, or in the possession of, any party to the proceedings or as to which any question arises in the proceedings;

    (b) the taking of samples of any such property as is mentioned in paragraph (a) and the carrying out of any experiment on or with any such property.

(4) The preceding provisions of this section are without prejudice to the exercise by the High Court of any power to make orders which is exercisable apart from those provisions.[70]

---

[66] In relation to county courts: s.33 is repealed.

[67] Repealed by SI 1998/2940 (Civil Procedure (Modification of Enactments) Order), art.5(b)(i).

[68] Repealed by SI 1998/2940 (Civil Procedure (Modification of Enactments) Order), art.5(b)(ii).

[69] Repealed by SI 1998/2940 (Civil Procedure (Modification of Enactments) Order), art.5(b)(iii).

[70] In relation to county courts: s.34 is repealed.

35.—Provisions supplementary to ss.33 and 34

A.68
(1) The High Court shall not make an order under section 33 or 34 if it considers that compliance with the order, if made, would be likely to be injurious to the public interest.

(2) Rules of court may make provision as to the circumstances in which an order under section 33 or 34 can be made; and any rules making such provision may include such incidental, supplementary and consequential provisions as the rule-making authority may consider necessary or expedient.

(3) Without prejudice to the generality of subsection (2), rules of court shall be made for the purpose of ensuring that the costs of and incidental to proceedings for an order under section 33(2) or 34 incurred by the person against whom the order is sought shall be awarded to that person unless the court otherwise directs.

(4) Sections 33(2) and 34 and this section bind the Crown so far as it relates to property as to which it appears to the court that it may become the subject-matter of subsequent proceedings involving a claim in respect of personal injuries to a person or in respect of a person's death.

In this subsection references to the Crown do not include references to Her Majesty in Her private capacity or to Her Majesty in right of Her Duchy of Lancaster or to the Duke of Cornwall.

(5) In sections [32A,][71] 33 and 34 and this section—
"property" includes any land, chattel or other corporeal property of any description;
"personal injuries" includes any disease and any impairment of a person's physical or mental condition.[[72]][73]

72.—Withdrawal of privilege against incrimination of self or spouse in certain proceedings

A.69
(1) In any proceedings to which this subsection applies a person shall not be excused, by reason that to do so would tend to expose that person, or his or her spouse [or civil partner],[74] to proceedings for a related offence or for the recovery of a related penalty—
(a) from answering any questions put to that person in the first-mentioned proceedings; or
(b) from complying with any order made in those proceedings.

(2) Subsection (1) applies to the following civil proceedings in the High Court, namely—
(a) proceedings for infringement of rights pertaining to any intellectual property or for passing off;
(b) proceedings brought to obtain disclosure of information relating to any infringement of such rights or to any passing off; and
(c) proceedings brought to prevent any apprehended infringement of such rights or any apprehended passing off.

(3) Subject to subsection (4), no statement or admission made by a person—
(a) in answering a question put to him in any proceedings to which subsection (1) applies; or
(b) in complying with any order made in any such proceedings,
shall, in proceedings for any related offence or for the recovery of any related penalty, be admissible in evidence against that person or (unless they [married or

---

[71] Added by Administration of Justice Act 1982, s.6(2).
[72] In relation to county courts: s.35 is repealed.
[73] Repealed by County Courts Act (1984 c.28), Sch.4.
[74] Added by Civil Partnership Act (2004) c.33), Sch.27, para.69.

became civil partners after the making of the statement or admission) against the spouse or civil partner]75 of that person.

(4) Nothing in subsection (3) shall render any statement or admission made by a person as there mentioned inadmissible in evidence against that person in proceedings for perjury or contempt of court.

(5) In this section—

"intellectual property" means any patent, trade mark, copyright, design right, registered design, technical or commercial information or other intellectual property;

"related offence", in relation to any proceedings to which subsection (1) applies, means—

(a) in the case of proceedings within subsection (2)(a) or (b)—

    (i) any offence committed by or in the course of the infringement or passing off to which those proceedings relate; or

    (ii) any offence not within sub-paragraph (i) committed in connection with that infringement or passing off, being an offence involving fraud or dishonesty;

(b) in the case of proceedings within subsection (2)(c), any offence revealed by the facts on which the plaintiff relies in those proceedings;

"related penalty", in relation to any proceedings to which subsection (1) applies means—

(a) in the case of proceedings within subsection (2)(a) or (b), any penalty incurred in respect of anything done or omitted in connection with the infringement or passing off to which those proceedings relate;

(b) in the case of proceedings within subsection (2)(c), any penalty incurred in respect of any act or omission revealed by the facts on which the plaintiff relies in those proceedings.

(6) Any reference in this section to civil proceedings in the High Court of any description includes a reference to proceedings on appeal arising out of civil proceedings in the High Court of that description.

Trade Marks Act 1994, s.87

87.—Privilege for communications with registered trade mark agents

(1) This section applies to communications as to any matter relating to the   **A.70** protection of any design or trade mark, or as to any matter involving passing off.

(2) Any such communication—

(a) between a person and his trade mark agent, or

(b) for the purpose of obtaining, or in response to a request for, information which a person is seeking for the purpose of instructing his trade mark agent,

is privileged from, or in Scotland protected against, disclosure in legal proceedings in the same way as a communication between a person and his solicitor or, as the case may be, a communication for the purpose of obtaining, or in response to a request for, information which a person is seeking for the purpose of instructing his solicitor.

(3) In subsection (2) "trade mark agent" means—

(a) a registered trade mark agent, or

---

75 Substituted by Civil Partnership Act (2004 c.33), Sch.27, para.69(3).

(b) a partnership entitled to describe itself as a firm of registered trade mark agents, or

(c) a body corporate entitled to describe itself as a registered trade mark agent

Theft Act 1968, s.31

31.—Effect on civil proceedings and rights

A.71   (1) A person shall not be excused, by reason that to do so may incriminate that person or the [spouse or civil partner][76] of that person of an offence under this Act—

(a) from answering any question put to that person in proceedings for the recovery or administration of any property, for the execution of any trust or for an account of any property or dealings with property; or

(b) from complying with any order made in any such proceedings;

but no statement or admission made by a person in answering a question put or complying with an order made as aforesaid shall, in proceedings for an offence under this Act, be admissible in evidence against that person or (unless they [married or became civil partners after the making of the statement or admission) against the spouse or civil partner][77] of that person.

(2) Notwithstanding any enactment to the contrary, where property has been stolen or obtained by fraud or other wrongful means, the title to that or any other property shall not be affected by reason only of the conviction of the offender.

[76] Added by Civil Partnership Act (2004) c.33), Sch.27, para.28.
[77] Substituted by Civil Partnership Act (2004 c.33), Sch.27, para.28(b).

APPENDIX 2

Rules of Court

The Civil Procedure Rules 1998, as amended, together with their relevant Practice Directions, can be found in *Civil Procedure 2000*, with updates on the Sweet & Maxwell website at *www.sweetandmaxwell.co.uk/online/whitebook/index.htm*. They can be found also on the website of the Lord Chancellor's Department, at *www.dca.gov.uk/civil/procrules_fin/index.htm*.

However, many readers will not have ready access at all times to the Rules and Practice Directions. For ease of reference, and also as a record of the state of the rules at the date of writing, there are reproduced in this Appendix the texts of the Parts of the CPR which are most relevant to this work, together with their Practice Directions, namely Parts 18, 31, 32, 34 and 35, and also the text of Rule 33.6.

PART 18

FURTHER INFORMATION

Contents

Obtaining further information

(1) The court may at any time order a party to—
    (a) clarify any matter which is in dispute in the proceedings; or
    (b) give additional information in relation to any such matter, whether or not the matter is contained or referred to in a statement of case.

(2) Paragraph (1) is subject to any rule of law to the contrary.

(3) Where the court makes an order under paragraph (1), the party against whom it is made must—
    (a) file his response; and
    (b) serve it on the other parties, within the time specified by the court.

(Part 22 requires a response to be verified by a statement of truth)

(Part 53 (defamation) restricts requirements for providing further information about sources of information in defamation claims)

Restriction on the use of further information

18.2 The court may direct that information provided by a party to another party (whether given voluntarily or following an order made under rule 18.1) must not be used for any purpose except for that of the proceedings in which it is given.
[Amended April 18, 2000, coming into force May 2, 2000.]

Practice direction—further information

This Practice Direction supplements CPR Part 18

Attention is also drawn to Part 22 (Statements of Truth).

Preliminary request for further information or clarification

B.02   **1.1** Before making an application to the court for an order under Part 18, the party seeking clarification or information (the first party) should first serve on the party from whom it is sought (the second party) a written request for that clarification or information (a Request) stating a date by which the response to the Request should be served. The date must allow the second party a reasonable time to respond.

1.2 A Request should be concise and strictly confined to matters which are reasonably necessary and proportionate to enable the first party to prepare his own case or to understand the case he has to meet.

1.3 Requests must be made as far as possible in a single comprehensive document and not piecemeal.

1.4 A Request may be made by letter if the text of the Request is brief and the reply is likely to be brief; otherwise the Request should be made in a separate document.

1.5 If a Request is made in a letter, the letter should, in order to distinguish it from any other that might routinely be written in the course of a case,

(1) state that it contains a Request made under Part 18, and

(2) deal with no matters other than the Request.

1.6—(1) A Request (whether made by letter or in a separate document) must—

    (a) be headed with the name of the court and the title and number of the claim,

    (b) in its heading state that it is a Request made under Part 18, identify the first party and the second party and state the date on which it is made,

    (c) set out in a separate numbered paragraph each request for information or clarification,

    (d) where a Request relates to a document, identify that document and (if relevant) the paragraph or words to which it relates,

    (e) state the date by which the first party expects a response to the Request,

  (2) (a) A Request which is not in the form of a letter may, if convenient, be prepared in such a way that the response may be given on the same document.

    (b) To do this the numbered paragraphs of the Request should appear on the left hand half of each sheet so that the paragraphs of the response may then appear on the right.

    (c) Where a Request is prepared in this form an extra copy should be served for the use of the second party.

1.7 Subject to the provisions of paragraphs 3.1 to 3.3 of the Practice Direction to Part 6, a request should be served by e-mail if reasonably practicable.

Responding to a request

2.1 A response to a Request must be in writing, dated and signed by the second party or his legal representative.

2.2—(1) Where the Request is made in a letter the second party may give his response in a letter or in a formal reply.

(2) Such a letter should identify itself as a response to the Request and deal with no other matters than the response.

2.3—(1) Unless the Request is in the format described in paragraph 1.6(2) and the second party uses the document supplied for the purpose, a response must:

- (a) be headed with the name of the court and the title and number of the claim,
- (b) in its heading identify itself as a response to that Request,
- (c) repeat the text of each separate paragraph of the Request and set out under each paragraph the response to it,
- (d) refer to and have attached to it a copy of any document not already in the possession of the first party which forms part of the response.

(2) A second or supplementary response to a Request must identify itself as such in its heading.

2.4 The second party must when he serves his response on the first party serve on every other party and file with the court a copy of the Request and of his response.

Statements of Truth

3. Attention is drawn to Part 22 and to the definition of a statement of case in Part 2 of the rules; a response should be verified by a statement of truth.

General matters

4.1—(1) If the second party objects to complying with the Request or part of it or is unable to do so at all or within the time stated in the Request he must inform the first party promptly and in any event within that time.

(2) He may do so in a letter or in a separate document (a formal response), but in either case he must give reasons and, where relevant, give a date by which he expects to be able to comply.

4.2—(1) There is no need for a second party to apply to the court if he objects to a Request or is unable to comply with it at all or within the stated time. He need only comply with paragraph 4.1(1) above.

(2) Where a second party considers that a Request can only be complied with at disproportionate expense and objects to comply for that reason he should say so in his reply and explain briefly why he has taken that view.

Applications for Orders under Part 18

5.1 Attention is drawn to Part 23 (Applications) and to the Practice Direction which supplements that Part.

5.2 An application notice for an order under Part 18 should set out or have attached to it the text of the order sought and in particular should specify the matter or matters in respect of which the clarification or information is sought.

5.3—(1) If a Request under paragraph 1 for the information or clarification has not been made, the application notice should, in addition, explain why not.

(2) If a Request for clarification or information has been made, the application notice or the evidence in support should describe the response, if any.

5.4 Both the first party and the second party should consider whether evidence in support of or in opposition to the application is required.

5.5 — (1) Where the second party has made no response to a Request served on him, the first party need not serve the application notice on the second party, and the court may deal with the application without a hearing.

(2) Sub-paragraph (1) above only applies if at least 14 days have passed since the Request was served and the time stated in it for a response has expired.

5.6 Unless paragraph 5.5. applies the application notice must be served on the second party and on all other parties to the claim.

5.7 An order made under Part 18 must be served on all parties to the claim.

5.8 Costs:

(1) Attention is drawn to the Costs Practice Direction and in particular the court's power to make a summary assessment of costs.

(2) Attention is also drawn to rule 43.5(5) which provides that if an order does not mention costs no party is entitled to costs relating to that order.

PART 31

DISCLOSURE AND INSPECTION OF DOCUMENTS

AMENDED SEPTEMBER 28, 2000, IN FORCE OCTOBER 2, 2000

Contents

[Inserted September 28, 2000, in force October 2, 2000]

Scope of this part

31.1 — (1) This Part sets out rules about the disclosure and inspection of documents.

(2) This Part applies to all claims except a claim on the small claims track.

Meaning of disclosure

31.2 A party discloses a document by stating that the document exists or has existed.

Right of inspection of a disclosed document

31.3—(1) A party to whom a document has been disclosed has a right to inspect that document except where—

   (a) the document is no longer in the control of the party who disclosed it;

   (b) the party disclosing the document has a right or a duty to withhold inspection of it; or

   (c) paragraph (2) applies.

(Rule 31.8 sets out when a document is in the control of a party)

(Rule 31.19 sets out the procedure for claiming a right or duty to withhold inspection)

(2) Where a party considers that it would be disproportionate to the issues in the case to permit inspection of documents within a category or class of document disclosed under rule 31.6(b)—

   (a) he is not required to permit inspection of documents within that category or class; but

   (b) he must state in his disclosure statement that inspection of those documents will not be permitted on the grounds that to do so would be disproportionate.

(Rule 31.6 provides for standard disclosure)

(Rule 31.10 makes provision for a disclosure statement)

(Rule 31.12 provides for a party to apply for an order for specific inspection of documents)

Meaning of document

31.4 In this Part—

"document" means anything in which information of any description is recorded; and

"copy", in relation to a document, means anything onto which information recorded in the document has been copied, by whatever means and whether directly or indirectly.

Disclosure limited to standard disclosure

31.5—(1) An order to give disclosure is an order to give standard disclosure unless the court directs otherwise.

(2) The court may dispense with or limit standard disclosure.

(3) The parties may agree in writing to dispense with or to limit standard disclosure.

(The court may make an order requiring standard disclosure under rule 28.3 which deals with directions in relation to cases on the fast track and under rule 29.2 which deals with case management in relation to cases on the multi-track)

Standard disclosure—what documents are to be disclosed

31.6 Standard disclosure requires a party to disclose only—

   (a) the documents on which he relies; and

   (b) the documents which—

      (i) adversely affect his own case;

     (ii) adversely affect another party's case; or

    (iii) support another party's case; and

(c) the documents which he is required to disclose by a relevant practice direction.

Duty of search

31.7—(1) When giving standard disclosure, a party is required to make a reasonable search for documents falling within rule 31.6(b) or (c).

(2) The factors relevant in deciding the reasonableness of a search include the following—

(a) the number of documents involved;

(b) the nature and complexity of the proceedings;

(c) the ease and expense of retrieval of any particular document; and

(d) the significance of any document which is likely to be located during the search.

(3) Where a party has not searched for a category or class of document on the grounds that to do so would be unreasonable, he must state this in his disclosure statement and identify the category or class of document.

(Rule 31.10 makes provision for a disclosure statement)

Duty of disclosure limited to documents which are or have been in a party's control

31.8—(1) A party's duty to disclose documents is limited to documents which are or have been in his control.

(2) For this purpose a party has or has had a document in his control if—

(a) it is or was in his physical possession;

(b) he has or has had a right to possession of it; or

(c) he has or has had a right to inspect or take copies of it.

Disclosure of copies

31.9—(1) A party need not disclose more than one copy of a document.

(2) A copy of a document that contains a modification, obliteration or other marking or feature—

(a) on which a party intends to rely; or

(b) which adversely affects his own case or another party's case or supports another party's case;

shall be treated as a separate document.

(Rule 31.4 sets out the meaning of a copy of a document)

Procedure for standard disclosure

31.10—(1) The procedure for standard disclosure is as follows.

(2) Each party must make and serve on every other party, a list of documents in the relevant practice form.

(3) The list must identify the documents in a convenient order and manner and as concisely as possible.

(4) The list must indicate—

(a) those documents in respect of which the party claims a right or duty to withhold inspection; and

(b) (i) those documents which are no longer in the party's control; and

(ii) what has happended to those documents.

(Rule 31.19(3) and (4) require a statement in the list of documents relating to any documents inspection of which a person claims he has a right or duty to withhold)

(5) The list must include a disclosure statement.

(6) A disclosure statement is a statement made by the party disclosing the documents—
- (a) setting out the extent of the search that has been made to locate documents which he is required to disclose;
- (b) certifying that he understands the duty to disclose documents; and
- (c) certifying that to the best of his knowledge he has carried out that duty.

(7) Where the party making the disclosure statement is a company, firm, association or other organisation, the statement must also—
- (a) identify the person making the statement; and
- (b) explain why he is considered an appropriate person to make the statement.

(8) The parties may agree in writing—
- (a) to disclose documents without making a list; and
- (b) to disclose documents without the disclosing party making a disclosure statement.

(9) A disclosure statement may be made by a person who is not a party where this is permitted by a relevant practice direction.

Duty of disclosure continues during proceedings

31.11—(1) Any duty of disclosure continues until the proceedings are concluded.

(2) If documents to which that duty extends come to a party's notice at any time during the proceedings, he must immediately notify every other party.

Specific disclosure or inspection

31.12—(1) The court may make an order for specific disclosure or specific inspection.

(2) An order for specific disclosure is an order that a party must do one or more of the following things—
- (a) disclose documents or classes of documents specified in the order;
- (b) carry out a search to the extent stated in the order;
- (c) disclose any documents located as a result of that search.

(3) An order for specific inspection is an order that a party permit inspection of a document referred to in rule 31.3(2).

(Rule 31.3(2) allows a party to state in his disclosure statement that he will not permit inspection of a document on the grounds that it would be disproportionate to do so)

Disclosure in stages

31.13 The parties may agree in writing, or the court may direct, that disclosure or inspection or both shall take place in stages.

Documents referred to in statements of case etc.

31.14—(1) A party may inspect a document mentioned in—
- (a) a statement of case;
- (b) a witness statement;
- (c) a witness summary;
- (d) an affidavit; or
- (e) [. . .]*

---

* Revoked by Civ Proc (Amdt No 5) Rules 2001 SI 2001/4015.

(2) Subject to rule 35.10(4), a party may apply for an order for inspection of any document mentioned in an expert's report which has not already been disclosed in the proceedings.
(Rule 35.10(4) makes provision in relation to instructions referred to in an expert's report)

Inspection and copying of documents

31.15 Where a party has a right to inspect a document—
  (a) that party must give the party who disclosed the document written notice of his wish to inspect it;
  (b) the party who disclosed the document must permit inspection not more than 7 days after the date on which he received the notice; and
  (c) that party may request a copy of the document and, if he also undertakes to pay reasonable copying costs, the party who disclosed the document must supply him with a copy not more than 7 days after the date on which he received the request.
(Rules 31.3 and 31.14 deal with the right of a party to inspect a document)

Disclosure before proceedings start

31.16—(1) This rule applies where an application is made to the court under any Act for disclosure before proceedings have started.[1]
(2) The application must be supported by evidence.
(3) The court may make an order under this rule only where—
  (a) the respondent is likely to be a party to subsequent proceedings;
  (b) the applicant is also likely to be a party to those proceedings;
  (c) if proceedings had started, the respondent's duty by way of standard disclosure, set out in rule 31.6, would extend to the documents or classes of documents of which the applicant seeks disclosure; and
  (d) disclosure before proceedings have started is desirable in order to—
    (i) dispose fairly of the anticipated proceedings;
    (ii) assist the dispute to be resolved without proceedings; or
    (iii) save costs.
(4) An order under this rule must—
  (a) specify the documents or the classes of documents which the responent must disclose; and
  (b) require him, when making disclosure, to specify any of those documents—
    (i) which are no longer in his control; or
    (ii) in respect of which he claims a right or duty to withhold inspection.
(5) Such an order may—
  (a) require the respondent to indicate what has happened to any document which are no longer in his control; and
  (b) specify the time and place for disclosure and inspection.

Orders for disclosure against a person not a party

31.17—(1) This rule applies where an application is made to the court under any Act for disclosure by a person who is not a party to the proceedings.[2]

---

[1] An application for disclosure before proceedings have started is permitted under section 33 of the Supreme Court Act 1981 (c.54) or section 52 of the County Courts Act 1984 (c. 28).
[2] An application for disclosure against a person who is not a party to proceedings is permitted under section 34 of the Supreme Court Act 1981 or section 53 of the County Courts Act 1984.

(2) The application must be supported by evidence.

(3) The court may make an order under this rule only where—

    (a) the documents of which disclosure is sought are likely to support the case of the applicant or adversely affect the case of one of the other parties to the proceedings; and

    (b) disclosure is necessary in order to dispose fairly of the claim or to save costs.

(4) An order under this rule must—

    (a) specify the documents or the classes of documents which the respondent must disclose; and

    (b) require the respondent, when making disclosure, to specify any of those documents—

        (i) which are no longer in his control; or

        (ii) in respect of which he claims a right or duty to withhold inspection.

(5) Such an order may—

    (a) require the respondent to indicate what has happened to any documents which are no longer in his control; and

    (b) specify the time and place for disclosure and inspection.

Rules not to limit other powers of the court to order disclosure

31.18 Rules 31.16 and 31.17 do not limit any other power which the court may have to order—

    (a) disclosure before proceedings have started; and

    (b) disclosure against a person who is not a party to proceedings.

Claim to withhold inspection or disclosure of a document

31.19—(1) A person may apply, without notice, for an order permitting him to withhold disclosure of a document on the ground that disclosure would damage the public interest.

(2) Unless the court orders otherwise, an order of the court under paragraph (1)—

    (a) must not be served on any other person; and

    (b) must not be open to inspection by any person.

(3) A person who wishes to claim that he has a right or a duty to withhold inspection of a document, or part of a document must state in writing—

    (a) that he has such a right or duty; and

    (b) the grounds on which he claims that right or duty.

(4) The statement referred to in paragraph (3) must be made—

    (a) in the list in which the document is disclosed; or

    (b) if there is no list, to the person wishing to inspect the document.

(5) A party may apply to the court to decide whether a claim made under paragraph (3) should be upheld.

(6) For the purpose of deciding an application under paragraph (1) (application to withhold disclosure) or paragraph (3) (claim to withhold inspection) the court may—

    (a) require the person seeking to withhold disclosure or inspection of a document to produce that document to the court; and

    (b) invite any person, whether or not a party, to make representations.

(7) An application under paragraph (1) or paragraph (5) must be supported by evidence.

(8) This Part does not affect any rule of law which permits or requires a document to be withheld from disclosure or inspection on the ground that its disclosure or inspection would damage the public interest.

Restriction on use of a privileged document inspection of which has been inadvertently allowed

31.20 Where a party inadvertently allows a privileged document to be inspected, the party who has inspected the document may use it or its contents only with the permission of the court.

Consequence of failure to disclose documents or permit inspection

31.21 A party may not rely on any document which he fails to disclose or in respect of which he fails to permit inspection unless the court gives permission.

Subsequent use of disclosed documents

31.22—(1) A party to whom a document has been disclosed may use the document only for the purpose of the proceedings in which it is disclosed, except where—
  (a) the document has been read to or by the court, or referred to, at a hearing which has been held in public;
  (b) the court gives permission; or
  (c) the party who disclosed the document and the person to whom the document belongs agree.

(2) The court may make an order restricting or prohibiting the use of a document which has been disclosed, even where the document has been read to or by the court, or referred to, at a hearing which has been held in public.

(3) An application for such an order may be made—
  (a) by a party; or
  (b) by any person to whom the document belongs.

[**False disclosure statements**

31.23—(1) Proceedings for contempt of court may be brought against a person if he makes, or causes to be made, a false disclosure statement, without an honest belief in its truth.

(2) Proceedings under this rule may be brought only—
  (a) by the Attorney General; or
  (b) with the permission of the court.][3]

Practice direction—disclosure and inspection

This Practice Direction supplements CPR Part 31

General

B.04   **1.1** The normal order for disclosure will be an order that the parties give standard disclosure

1.2 In order to give standard disclosure the disclosing party must make a reasonable search for documents falling within the paragraphs of rule 31.6.

1.3 Having made the search the disclosing party must (unless rule 31.10(8) applies) make a list of the documents of whose existence the party is aware that fall within those paragraphs and which are or have been in the party's control (see rule 31.8).

---

[3] Added by the Civil Procedure (Amendment) Rules 2000, r.16.

1.4 The obligations imposed by an order for standard disclosure may be dispensed with or limited either by the court or by written agreement between the parties. Any such written agreement should be lodged with the court.

The search

2. The extent of the search which must be made will depend upon the circumstances of the case including, in particular, the factors referred to in rule 31.7(2). The parties should bear in mind the overriding principle of proportionality (see rule 1.1(2)(c)). It may, for example, be reasonable to decide not to search for documents coming into existence before some particular date, or to limit the search to documents in some particular place or places, or to documents falling into particular categories.

Electronic disclosure

2A.1 Rule 31.4 contains a broad definition of a document. This extends to electronic documents, including e-mail and other electronic communications, word processed documents and databases. In addition to documents that are readily accessible from computer systems and other electronic devices and media, the definition covers those documents that are stored on servers and back-up systems and electronic documents that have been 'deleted'. It also extends to additional information stored and associated with electronic documents known as metadata.

2A.2 The parties should, prior to the first Case Management Conference, discuss any issues that may arise regarding searches for and the preservation of electronic documents. This may involve the parties providing information about the categories of electronic documents within their control, the computer systems, electronic devices and media on which any relevant documents may be held, the storage systems maintained by the parties and their document retention policies. In the case of difficulty or disagreement, the matter should be referred to a judge for directions at the earliest practical date, if possible at the first Case Management Conference.

2A.3 The parties should co-operate at an early stage as to the format in which electronic copy documents are to be provided on inspection. In the case of difficulty or disagreement, the matter should be referred to a Judge for directions at the earliest practical date, if possible at the first Case Management Conference.

2A.4 The existence of electronic documents impacts upon the extent of the reasonable search required by Rule 31.7 for the purposes of standard disclosure. The factors that may be relevant in deciding the reasonableness of a search for electronic documents include (but are not limited to) the following:—

- (a) The number of documents involved.
- (b) The nature and complexity of the proceedings.
- (c) The ease and expense of retrieval of any particular document. This includes:
  - (i) The accessibility of electronic documents or data including e-mail communications on computer systems, servers, back-up systems and other electronic devices or media that may contain such documents taking into account alterations or developments in hardware or software systems used by the disclosing party and/or available to enable access to such documents.
  - (ii) The location of relevant electronic documents, data, computer systems, servers, back-up systems and other electronic devices or media that may contain such documents.
  - (iii) The likelihood of locating relevant data.
  - (iv) The cost of recovering any electronic documents.

705

(v) The cost of disclosing and providing inspection of any relevant electronic documents.

(vi) The likelihood that electronic documents will be materially altered in the course of recovery, disclosure or inspection.

(d) The significance of any document which is likely to be located during the search.

2A.5 It may be reasonable to search some or all of the parties' electronic storage systems. In some circumstances, it may be reasonable to search for electronic documents by means of keyword searches (agreed as far as possible between the parties) even where a full review of each and every document would be unreasonable. There may be other forms of electronic search that may be appropriate in particular circumstances.

The List

3.1 The list should be in practice form N265.

3.2 In order to comply with rule 31.10(3) it will normally be necessary to list the documents in date order, to number them consecutively and to give each a concise description (e.g. letter, claimant to defendant). Where there is a large number of documents all falling into a particular category the disclosing party may list those documents as a category rather than individually e.g. 50 bank statements relating to account number   at   Bank,
19   to   19   ; or, 35 letters passing between   and   between   19   and   19   .

3.3 The obligations imposed by an order for disclosure will continue until the proceedings come to an end. If, after a list of documents has been prepared and served, the existence of further documents to which the order applies comes to the attention of the disclosing party, the party must prepare and serve a supplemental list.

Disclosure statement

4.1 A list of documents must (unless rule 31.10(8)(b) applies) contain a disclosure statement complying with rule 31.10. The form of disclosure statement is set out in the Annex to this practice direction.

4.2 The disclosure statement should:

(1) expressly state that the disclosing party believes the extent of the search to have been reasonable in all the circumstances, and

(2) in setting out the extent of the search (see rule 31.10(6)) draw attention to any particular limitations on the extent of the search which were adopted for proportionality reasons and give the reasons why the limitations were adopted e.g. the difficulty or expense that a search not subject to those limitations would have entailed or the marginal relevance of categories of documents omitted from the search.

4.3 Where rule 31.10(7) applies, the details given in the disclosure statement about the person making the statement must include his name and address and the office or position he holds in the disclosing party.

4.4 If the disclosing party has a legal representative acting for him, the legal representative must endeavour to ensure that the person making the disclosure statement (whether the disclosing party or, in a case to which rule 31.10(7) applies, some other person) understands the duty of disclosure under rule 31.

4.5 If the disclosing party wishes to claim that he has a right or duty to withhold a document, or part of a document, in his list of documents from inspection (see rule 31.19(3)), he must state in writing:

(1) that he has such a right or duty, and

(2) the grounds on which he claims that right or duty.

4.6 The statement referred to in paragraph 4.5 above should normally be included in the disclosure statement and must identify the document, or part of a document, to which the claim relates.

4.7 An insurer or the Motor Insurers' Bureau may sign a disclosure statement on behalf of a party where the insurer or the Motor Insurers' Bureau has a financial interest in the result of proceedings brought wholly or partially by or against that party. Rule 31.10(7) and paragraph 4.3 above shall apply to the insurer or the Motor Insurers' Bureau making such a statement.

Specific disclosure

5.1 If a party believes that the disclosure of documents given by a disclosing party is inadequate he may make an application for an order for specific disclosure (see rule 31.12).

5.2 The application notice must specify the order that the applicant intends to ask the court to make and must be supported by evidence (see rule 31.12(2) which describes the orders the court may make).

5.3 The grounds on which the order is sought may be set out in the application notice itself but if not there set out must be set out in evidence filed in support of the application.

5.4 In deciding whether or not to make an order for specific disclosure the court will take into account all the circumstances of the case and, in particular, the overriding objective described in Part 1. But if the court concludes that the party from whom specific disclosure is sought has failed adequately to comply with the obligations imposed by an order for disclosure (whether by failing to make a sufficient search for documents or otherwise) the court will usually make such order as is necessary to ensure that those obligations are properly complied with.

5.5 An order for specific disclosure may in an appropriate case direct a party to—

(1) carry out a search for any documents which it is reasonable to suppose may contain information which may—

    (a) enable the party applying for disclosure either to advance his own case or to damage that of the party giving disclosure; or

    (b) lead to a train of enquiry which has either of those consequences; and

(2) disclose any documents found as a result of that search.

Claims to withhold disclosure or inspection of a document

6.1 A claim to withhold inspection of a document, or part of a document, disclosed in a list of documents does not require an application to the court. Where such a claim has been made, a party who wishes to challenge it must apply to the court (see rule 31.19(5)).

6.2 Rule 31.19(1) and (6) provide a procedure enabling a party to apply for an order permitting disclosure of the existence of a document to be withheld.

Inspection of documents mentioned in expert's report (rule 31.14(2))

7.1 If a party wishes to inspect documents referred to in the expert report of another party, before issuing an application he should request inspection of the documents informally, and inspection should be provided by agreement unless the request is unreasonable.

7.2 Where an expert report refers to a large number or volume of documents and it would be burdensome to copy or collate them, the court will only order inspection of such documents if it is satisfied that it is necessary for the just disposal of the proceedings and the party cannot reasonably obtain the documents from another source.

False disclosure statement

8 Attention is drawn to rule 31.23 which sets out the consequences of making a false disclosure statement without an honest belief in its truth, and to the procedures set out in paragraphs 28.1–28.3 of the practice direction supplementing Part 32.

Annex

Disclosure statement

I, the above named claimant [or defendant] [if party making disclosure is a company, firm or other organisation identify here who the person making the disclosure statement is and why he is the appropriate person to make it] state that I have carried out a reasonable and proportionate search to locate all the documents which I am required to disclose under the order made by the court on   day of   . I did not search;

(1) for documents predating   ,

(2) for documents located elsewhere than   ,

(3) for documents in categories other than   .

(4) for electronic documents

I carried out a search for electronic documents contained on or created by the following: [list what was searched and extent of search]

I did not search for the following:

(1) documents created before,

(2) documents contained on or created by the Claimant's/Defendant's PCs/portable data storage media/databases/servers/back-up tapes/off-site storage/mobile phones/laptops/notebooks/handheld devices/PDA devices (delete as appropriate),

(3) documents contained on or created by the Claimant's/Defendant's mail files/ document files/calendar files/spreadsheet files/graphic and presentation files/web-based applications (delete as appropriate),

(4) documents other than by reference to the following keyword(s)/concepts (delete if your search was not confined to specific keywords or concepts).

I certify that I understand the duty of disclosure and to the best of my knowledge I have carried out that duty. I certify that the list above is a complete list of all documents which are or have been in my control and which I am obliged under the said order to disclose.

PART 32

EVIDENCE

Contents

708

Power of court to control evidence

32.1—(1) The court may control the evidence by giving directions as to—
  (a) the issues on which it requires evidence;
  (b) the nature of the evidence which it requires to decide those issues; and
  (c) the way in which the evidence is to be placed before the court.
(2) The court may use its power under this rule to exclude evidence that would otherwise be admissible.
(3) The court may limit cross-examination.

Evidence of witness—general rule

32.2—(1) The general rule is that any fact which needs to be proved by the evidence of witness is to be proved—
  (a) at trial, by their oral evidence given in public; and
  (b) at any other hearing, by their evidence in writing.
(2) This is subject—
  (a) to any provision to the contrary contained in these Rules or elsewhere; or
  (b) to any order of the court.

Evidence by video link or other means

32.3 The court may allow a witness to give evidence through a video link or by other means.

Requirement to serve witness statements for use at trial

32.4—(1) A witness statement is a written statement signed by a person which contains the evidence, and only that evidence, which that person would be allowed to give orally.
(2) The court will order a party to serve on the other parties any witness statement of the oral evidence which the party serving the statement intends to rely on in relation to any issues of fact to be decided at the trial.
(3) The court may give directions as to—
  (a) the order in which witness statements are to be served; and
  (b) whether or not the witness statements are to be filed.

Use at trial of witness statements which have been served

32.5—(1) If—
  (a) a party has served a witness statement; and
  (b) he wishes to rely at trial on the evidence of the witness who made the statement,

he must call the witness to give oral evidence unless the court orders otherwise or he puts in the statement as hearsay evidence.

(Part 33 contains provisions about hearsay evidence.)

(2) Where a witness is called to give oral evidence under paragraph (1), his witness statement shall stand as his evidence in chief unless the court orders otherwise.

(3) A witness giving oral evidence at trial may with the permission of the court—

(a) amplify his witness statement; and

(b) give evidence in relation to new matters which have arisen since the witness statement was served on the other parties.

(4) The court will give permission under paragraph (3) only if it considers that there is good reason not to confine the evidence of the witness to the contents of his witness statement.

(5) If a party who has served a witness statement does not—

(a) call the witness to give evidence at trial; or

(b) put in the witness statement as hearsay evidence,

any other party may put in the witness statement as hearsay evidence.

Evidence in proceedings other than at trial

32.6—(1) Subject to paragraph (2), the general rule is that evidence at hearings other than the trial is to be by witness statement unless the court, a practice direction or any other enactment requires otherwise.

(2) At hearings other than the trial, a party may [. . .]⁴, rely on the matters set out in—

(a) his statement of case; or

(b) his application,

if the statement of case or application is verified by, a statement of truth.

Order for cross-examination

32.7—(1) Where, at a hearing other than the trial, evidence is given in writing, any party may apply to the court for permission to cross-examine the person giving the evidence.

(2) If the court gives permission under paragraph (1) but the person in question does not attend as required by the order, his evidence may not be used unless the court gives permission.

Form of witness statement

32.8 A witness statement must comply with the requirements set out in the relevant practice direction.

(Part 22 requires a witness statement to be verified by a statement of truth.)

Witness summaries

32.9—(1) A party who—

(a) is required to serve a witness statement for use at trial; but

(b) is unable to obtain one,

may apply, without notice, for permission to serve a witness summary instead.

(2) A witness summary is a summary of—

(a) the evidence, if known, which would otherwise be included in a witness statement; or

---

⁴ Repealed by the Civil Procedure (Amendment) Rules 2000, r.17.

(b) if the evidence is not known, the matters about which the party serving the witness summary proposes to question the witness.

(3) Unless the court orders otherwise, a witness summary must include the name and address of the intended witness.

(4) Unless the court orders otherwise, a witness summary must be served within the period in which a witness statement would have had to be served.

(5) Where a party serves a witness summary, so far as practicable, rules 32.4 (requirement to serve witness statement for use at trial), 32.5(3) (amplifying witness statements), and 32.8 (form of witness statement) shall apply to the summary.

Consequence of failure to serve witness statement or summary

32.10 If a witness statement or a witness summary for use at trial is not served in respect of an intended witness within the time specified by the court, then the witness may not be called to give oral evidence unless the court gives permission.

Cross-examination on a witness statement

32.11 Where a witness is called to give evidence at trial, he may be cross-examined on his witness statement, whether or not the statement or any part of it was referred to during the witness's evidence in chief.

Use of witness statements for other purposes

32.12—(1) Except as provided by this rule, a witness statement may be used only for the purpose of the proceedings in which it is served.

(2) Paragraph (1) does not apply if and to the extent that—
    (a) the witness gives consent in writing to some other use of it;
    (b) the court gives permission for some other use; or
    (c) the witness statement has been put in evidence at a hearing held in public.

Availability of witness statements for inspection

32.13—(1) A witness statement which stands as evidence in chief is open to inspection [during the course of the trial unless the court otherwise directs].*

(2) Any person may ask for a direction that a witness statement is not open to inspection.

(3) The court will not make a direction under Paragraph (2) unless it is satisfied that a witness statement should not be open to inspection because of—
    (a) the interests of justice;
    (b) the public interest;
    (c) the nature of any expert medical evidence in the statement;
    (d) the nature of any confidential information (including information relating to personal financial matters) in the statement; or
    (e) the need to protect the interests of any child or patient.

(4) The court may exclude from inspection words or passages in the statement.

False statements

32.14—(1) Proceedings for contempt of court may be brought against a person if he makes, or causes to be made, a false statement in a document verified by a statement of truth without an honest belief in its truth.

---

* Substd by CP(A)R 2001/256.

(Part 22 makes provision for a statement of truth.)

(2) Proceedings under this rule may be brought only—

    (a) by the Attorney General; or

    (b) with the permission of the court.

Affidavit evidence

32.15—(1) Evidence must be given by affidavit(GL) instead of or in addition to a witness statement if this is required by the court, a provision contained in any other rule, a practice direction or any other enactment.

(2) Nothing in these Rules prevents a witness giving evidence by affidavit at a hearing other than the trial if he chooses to do so in a case where paragraph (1) does not apply, but the party putting forward the affidavit may not recover the additional cost of making it from any other party unless the court orders otherwise.

Form of affidavit

32.16 An affidavit must comply with the requirements set out in the relevant practice direction.

Affidavit made outside the jurisdiction

32.17 A person may make an affidavit outside the jurisdiction in accordance with—

    (a) this Part; or

    (b) the law of the place where he makes the affidavit.

Notice to admit facts

32.18—(1) A party may serve notice on another party requiring him to admit the facts, or the part of the case of the serving party, specified in the notice.

(2) A notice to admit facts must be served no later than 21 days before the trial.

(3) Where the other party makes any admission in response to the notice, the admission may be used against him only—

    (a) in the proceedings in which the notice to admit is served; and

    (b) by the party who served the notice.

(4) The court may allow a party to amend or withdraw any admission made by him on such terms as it thinks just.

Notice to admit or produce documents

32.19—(1) A party shall be deemed to admit the authenticity of a document disclosed to him under Part 31 (disclosure and inspection of documents) unless he serves notice that he wishes the document to be proved at trial.

(2) A notice to prove a document must be served—

    (a) by the latest date for serving witness statements; or

    (b) within 7 days of disclosure of the document,

whichever is later.

Notarial acts and instruments

32.20 A notarial act or instrument may be received in evidence without further proof as duly authenticated in accordance with the requirements of law unless the contrary is proved.

Practice direction—written evidence

This Practice Direction supplements CPR Part 32

Evidence in General

1.1 Rule 32.2 sets out how evidence is to be given and facts are to be proved.   **B.06**

1.2 Evidence at a hearing other than the trial should normally be given by witness statement[5] (see paragraph 17 onwards). However a witness may give evidence by affidavit if he wishes to do so[6] (and see paragraph 1.4 below).

1.3 Statements of case (see paragraph 26 onwards) and application notices[7] may also be used as evidence provided that their contents have been verified by a statement of truth.[8]

(For information regarding evidence by deposition see Part 34 and the practice direction which supplements it.)

1.4 Affidavits must be used as evidence in the following instances—

(1) where sworn evidence is required by an enactment,[9] Statutory Instrument, rule,[10] order or practice direction,

(2) in any application for a search order, a freezing injunction, or an order requiring an occupier to permit another to enter his land, and

(3) in any application for an order against anyone for alleged contempt of court.

1.5 If a party believes that sworn evidence is required by a court in another jurisdiction for any purpose connected with the proceedings, he may apply to the court for a direction that evidence shall be given only by affidavit on any pre-trial applications.

1.6 The court may give a direction under rule 32.15 that evidence shall be given by affidavit instead of or in addition to a witness statement or/statement of case—

(1) on its own initiative, or

(2) after any party has applied to the court for such a direction.

1.7 An affidavit, where referred to in the Civil Procedure Rules or a practice direction, also means an affirmation unless the context requires otherwise.

Affidavits

Deponent

2. A deponent is a person who gives evidence by affidavit or affirmation.

Heading

3.1 The affidavit should be headed with the title of the proceedings (see paragraph 4 of the practice direction supplementing Part 7 and paragraph 7 of the practice direction supplementing Part 20); where the proceedings are between several parties with the same status it is sufficient to identify the parties as follows:

---

[5] *See* rule 32.6(1).

[6] *See* rule 32.15(2).

[7] *See* Part 23 for information about making an application.

[8] Rule 32.6(2) and see Part 22 for information about the statement of truth.

[9] *See e.g.*, sec. 3(5)(a) of the Protection from Harassment Act 1997.

[10] *See e.g.*, RSC, O.115, rr.2B, 14 and others (Confiscation and Forfeiture in Connection with Criminal Proceedings) and RSC, O.110, r.(3) (Environmental Control Proceedings— injunctions "in rem" against unknown Defendant).

	Number
A.B. (and others)	Claimants/Applicants
C.D. (and others)	Defendants/Respondents
	(as appropriate)

3.2 At the top right hand corner of the first page (and on the backsheet) there should be clearly written—

(1) the party on whose behalf it is made,

(2) the initials and surname of the deponent,

(3) the number of the affidavit in relation to that deponent,

(4) the identifying initials and number of each exhibit referred to, and

(5) the date sworn.

Body of Affidavit

4.1 The affidavit must, if practicable, be in the deponent's own words, the affidavit should be expressed in the first person and the deponent should—

(1) commence "I *(full name)* of *(address)* state on oath . . . ",

(2) if giving evidence in his professional, business or other occupational capacity, give the address at which he works in (1) above, the position he holds and the name of this firm or employer,

(3) give his occupation or, if he has none, his description, and

(4) state if he is a party to the proceedings or employed by a party to the proceedings, if it be the case.

4.2 An affidavit must indicate—

(1) which of the statements in it are made from the deponent's own knowledge and which are matters of information or belief, and

(2) the source for any matters of information or belief.

4.3 Where a deponent—

(1) refers to an exhibit or exhibits, he should state "there is now shown to me marked ' . . . ' the *(description of exhibit)*", and

(2) makes more than one affidavit (to which there are exhibits) in the same proceedings, the numbering of the exhibits should run consecutively throughout and not start again with each affidavit.

Jurat

5.1 The jurat of an affidavit is a statement set out at the end of the document which authenticates the affidavit.

5.2 It must—

(1) be signed by all deponents,

(2) be completed and signed by the person before whom the affidavit was sworn whose name and qualification must be printed beneath his signature,

(3) contain the full address of the person before whom the affidavit was sworn, and

(4) follow immediately on from the text and not to be put on a separate page.

Format of Affidavits

6.1 An affidavit should—

(1) be produced on durable quality A.4 paper with a 3.5 cm margin,

(2) be fully legible and should normally be typed on one side of the paper only,

(3) where possible, be bound securely in a manner which would not hamper filing, or otherwise each page should be endorsed with the case number and should bear the initials of the deponent and of the person before whom it was sworn,

(4) have the pages numbered consecutively as a separate document (or as one of several documents contained in a file),

(5) be divided into numbered paragraphs,

(6) have all numbers, including dates, expressed in figures, and

(7) give in the margin the reference to any document or documents mentioned.

6.2 It is usually convenient for an affidavit to follow the chronological sequence of events or matters dealt with; each paragraph of an affidavit should as far as possible be confined to a distinct portion of the subject.

Inability of Deponent to read or sign Affidavit

7.1 Where an affidavit is sworn by a person who is unable to read or sign it, the person before whom the affidavit is sworn must certify in the jurat that—

(1) he read the affidavit to the deponent,

(2) the deponent appeared to understand it, and

(3) the deponent signed or made his mark, in is presence.

7.2 If that certificate is not included in the jurat, the affidavit may not be used in evidence unless the court is satisfied that it was read to the deponent and that he appeared to understand it. Two versions of the form of jurat with the certificate are set out in Annex 1 to this practice direction.

Alterations to Affidavits

8.1 Any alteration to an affidavit must be initialled by both the deponent and the person before whom the affidavit was sworn.

8.2 An affidavit which contains an alteration that has not been initialled may be filed or used in evidence only with the permission of the court.

Who may administer oaths and take Affidavits

9.1 Only the following may administer oaths and take affidavits;

(1) Commissioners for oaths[11];

(2) practising solicitors,[12]

(3) other persons specified by statute,[13]

(4) certain officials of the Supreme Court,[14]

(5) a circuit judge or district judge,[15]

(6) any justice of the peace,[16] and

(7) certain officials of any county court appointed by the judge of that court for the purpose.[17]

9.2 An affidavit must be sworn before a person independent of the parties or their representatives.

Filing of Affidavits

10.1 If the court directs that an affidavit is to be filed,[18] it must be filed in the court or Division, or Office or Registry of the court or Division where the action in which it was or is to be used, is proceeding or will proceed.

10.2 Where an affidavit is in a foreign language;

(1) the party wishing to rely on it

---

[11] Commissioner for Oaths Act 1889 and 1891.

[12] S.81 of the Solicitors Act 1984.

[13] S.65 of the Administration of Justice Act 1985 s.113 of the Courts and Legal Services Act 1990 and the Commissioners for Oaths (Prescribed Bodies) Regulations 1994 and 1995.

[14] S.2 of the Commissioners for Oaths Act 1889.

[15] S.58 of the County Courts Act 1984.

[16] S.58 as above.

[17] S.58 as above.

[18] Rules 52.1(3) and 32.4(3)(b).

(a) must have it translated, and

(b) must file the foreign language affidavit with the court, and

(2) the translator must make and file with the court an affidavit verifying the translation and exhibiting both the translation and a copy of the foreign language affidavit.

Exhibits

Manner of Exhibiting Documents

11.1 A document used in conjunction with an affidavit should be—

(1) produced to and verified by the deponent, and remain separate from the affidavit, and

(2) identified by a declaration of the person before whom the affidavit was sworn.

11.2 The declaration should be headed with the name of the proceedings in the same way as the affidavit.

11.3 The first page of each exhibit should be marked—

(1) as in paragraph 3.2 above, and

(2) with the exhibit mark referred to in the affidavit.

Letters

12.1 Copies of individual letters should be collected together and exhibited in a bundle or bundles. They should be arranged in chronological order with the earliest at the top, and firmly secured.

12.2 When a bundle of correspondence is exhibited, the exhibit should have a front page attached stating that the bundle consists of original letters and copies. They should be arranged and secured as above and numbered consecutively.

Other documents

13.1 Photocopies instead of original documents may be exhibited provided the originals are made available for inspection by the other parties before the hearing and by the judge at the hearing.

13.2 Court documents must not be exhibited (official copies of such documents prove themselves).

13.3 Where an exhibit contains more than one document, a front page should be attached setting out a list of the documents contained in the exhibit; the list should contain the dates of the documents.

Exhibits other than documents

14.1 Items other than documents should be clearly marked with an exhibit number or letter in such a manner that the mark cannot become detached from the exhibit.

14.2 Small items may be placed in a container and the container appropriately marked.

General provisions

15.1 Where an exhibit contains more than one document—

(1) the bundle should not be stapled but should be securely fastened in a way that does not hinder the reading of the documents, and

(2) the pages should be numbered consecutively at bottom centre.

15.2 Every page of an exhibit should be clearly legible; typed copies of illegible documents should be included, paginated with "a" numbers.

15.3 Where affidavits and exhibits have become numerous, they should be put into separate bundles and the pages numbered consecutively throughout.

15.4 Where on account of their bulk the service of exhibits or copies of exhibits on the other parties would be difficult or impracticable, the directions of the court should be sought as to arrangements for bringing the exhibits to the attention of the other parties and as to their custody pending trial.

Affirmations

16. All provisions in this or any other practice direction relating to affidavits apply to affirmations with the following exceptions—

(1) the deponent should commence "I (*name*) of (*address*) do solemnly and sincerely affirm . . . ", and

(2) in the Jurat the word "sworn" is replaced by the word "affirmed".

Witness Statements

Heading

17.1 The witness statement should be headed with the title of the proceedings (see paragraph 4 of the practice direction supplementing Part 7 and paragraph 7 of the practice direction supplementing Part 20); where the proceedings are between several parties with the same status it is sufficient to identify the parties as follows:

	Number
A.B. (and others)	Claimants/Applicants
C.D. (and others)	Defendants/Respondents
	(as appropriate)

17.2 At the top right hand corner of the first page there should be clearly written—

(1) the party on whose behalf it is made,

(2) the initials and surname of the witness,

(3) the number of the statement in relation to that witness,

(4) the identifying initials and number of each exhibit referred to, and

(5) the date the statement was made.

Body of Witness Statement

18.1 The witness statement must, if practicable, be in the intended witness's own words, the statement should be expressed in the first person and should also state—

(1) the full name of the witness,

(2) his place of residence or, if he is making the statement in his professional, business or other occupational capacity, the address at which he works, the position he holds and the name of his firm or employer,

(3) his occupation, or if he has none, his description, and

(4) the fact that he is a party to the proceedings or is the employee of such a party if it be the case.

18.2 A witness statement must indicate—

(1) which of the statements in it are made from the witness's own knowledge and which are matters of information or belief, and

(2) the source for any matters of information or belief.

18.3 An exhibit used in conjunction with a witness statement should be verified and identified by the witness and remain separate from the witness statement.

18.4 Where a witness refers to an exhibit or exhibits, he should state "I refer to the (*description of exhibit*) marked ' . . . ' ".

18.5 The provisions of paragraphs 11.3 to 15.4 (exhibits) apply similarly to witness statements as they do to affidavits.

18.6 Where a witness makes more than one witness statement to which there are exhibits, in the same proceedings, the numbering of the exhibits should run consecutively throughout and not start again with each witness statement.

Format of Witness Statement

19.1 A witness statement should—

(1) be produced on durable quality A.4 paper with a 3.5 cm margin,

(2) be fully legible and should normally be typed on one side of the paper only,

(3) where possible, be bound securely in a manner which would not hamper filing, or otherwise each page should be endorsed with the case number and should bear the initials of the witness,

(4) have the pages numbered consecutively as a separate statement (or as one of several statements contained in a file),

(5) be divided into numbered paragraphs,

(6) have all numbers, including dates, expressed in figures, and

(7) give in the margin the reference to any document or documents mentioned.

19.2 It is usually convenient for a witness statement to follow the chronological sequence of the events or matters dealt with, each paragraph of a witness statement should as far as possible be confined to a distinct portion of the subject.

Statement of Truth

20.1 A witness statement is the equivalent of the oral evidence which that witness would, if called, give in evidence; it must include a statement by the intended witness that he believes the facts in it are true.[19]

20.2 To verify a witness statement the statement of truth is as follows: "I believe that the facts stated in this witness statement are true."

20.3 Attention is drawn to rule 32.14 which sets out the consequences of verifying a witness statement containing a false statement without an honest belief in its truth.

Inability of Witness to read and sign Statement

[. . .]*

Alterations to Witness Statements

22.1 Any alteration to a witness statement must be initialled by the person making the statement or by the authorised person where appropriate (see paragraph 21).

22.2 A witness statement which contains an alteration that has not been initialled may be used in evidence only with the permission of the court.

Filing of Witness Statements

23.1 If the court directs that a witness statement is to be filed,[20] it must be filed in the Court or Division, or Office or Registry of the Court or Division where the action in which it was or is to be used, is proceeding or will proceed.

23.2 Where the court has directed that a witness statement in a foreign language is to be filed—

(1) the party wishing to rely on it must:

---

[19] See Part 22 for information about the statement of truth.

* Since omitted.

[20] Rule 32.4(3)(b).

(a) have it translated and

(b) file the foreign language witness statement with the court, and

(2) the translator must make and file with the court an affidavit verifying the translation and exhibiting both the translation and a copy of the foreign language witness statement.

Certificate of court officer

24.1 Where the court has ordered that a witness statement is not to be open to inspection by the public[21] or that words or passages in the statement are not to be open to inspection[22] the court officer will so certify on the statement and make any deletions directed by the court under rule 32.13(4).

Defects in affidavits, witness statements and exhibits

25.1 Where—

(1) an affidavit

(2) a witness statement, or

(3) an exhibit to either an affidavit or a witness statement does not comply with Part 32 or this practice direction in relation to its form, the court may refuse to admit it as evidence and may refuse to allow the costs arising from its preparation.

25.2 Permission to file a defective affidavit or witness statement or to use a defective exhibit may be obtained from a Judge[23] in the court where the case is proceeding.

Statement of Case

26.1 A statement of case may be used as evidence in an interim application provided it is verified by a statement of truth.[24]

26.2 To verify a statement of case the statement of truth should be set out as follows:

"[I believe] [the (party on whose behalf the statement of case is being signed) believes] that the facts stated in the statement of case are true."

26.3 Attention is drawn to rule 32.14 which sets out the consequences of verifying a witness statement containing a false statement without an honest belief in its truth.

(For information regarding statements of truth see Part 22 and the practice direction which supplements it.)

(Practice directions supplementing Parts 7, 9 and 17 provide further information concerning statements of case.)

Agreed bundles for hearings

27.1 The court may give directions requiring the parties to use their best endeavours to agree a bundle or bundles of documents for use at any hearing.

27.2 All documents contained in bundles which have been agreed for use at a hearing shall be admissible at that hearing as evidence of their contents, unless—

(1) the court orders otherwise; or

---

[21] Rule 32.13(2).

[22] Rule 32.13(4).

[23] Rule 2.3(1); definition of Judge.

[24] See rule 32.6(2)(a).

(2) a party gives written notice of objection to the admissibility of particular documents.

Penalty

28.1—(1) Where a party alleges that a statement of truth or a disclosure statement is false the party shall refer that allegation to the court dealing with the claim in which the statement of truth or disclosure statement has been made.

(2) the court may—
    (a) exercise any of its powers under the rules;
    (b) initiate steps to consider if there is a contempt of court and, where there is, to punish it;
        (The practice direction to RSC Order 52 (Schedule 1) and CCR Order 29 (Schedule 2) makes provision where committal to prison is a possibility if contempt is proved)
    (c) direct the party making the allegation to refer the matter to the Attorney General with a request to him to consider whether he wishes to bring proceedings for contempt of court.

28.2—(1) An application to the Attorney General should be made to his chambers at 9 Buckingham Gate London SW1E 6JP in writing. The Attorney General will initially require a copy of the order recording the direction of the judge referring the matter to him and information which—
    (a) identifies the statement said to be false; and
    (b) explains—
        (i) why it is false, and
        (ii) why the maker knew it to be false at the time he made it; and
    (c) explains why contempt proceedings would be appropriate in the light of the overriding objective in Part 1 of the Civil Procedure Rules.

(2) The practice of the Attorney General is to prefer an application that comes from the court, and so has received preliminary consideration by a judge, to one made direct to him by a party to the claim in which the alleged contempt occurred without prior consideration by the court. An application to the Attorney General is not a way of appealing against, or reviewing, the decision of the judge.

28.3 Where a party makes an application to the court for permission for that party to commence proceedings for contempt of court, it must be supported by written evidence containing the information specified in paragraph 28.2(1) and the result of the application to the Attorney General made by the applicant.

28.4 The rules do not change the law of contempt or introduce new categories of contempt. A person applying to commence such proceedings should consider whether the incident complained of does amount to contempt of court and whether such proceedings would further the overriding objective in Part 1 of the Civil Procedure Rules.

Annex 1

Certificate to be used where a deponent to an affidavit is unable to read or sign it

Sworn at ... this ... day of ... Before me, I having first read over the contents of this affidavit to the deponent [*if there are exhibits, add* "and explained the nature and effect of the exhibits referred to in it"] who appeared to understand it and approved its content as accurate, and made his mark on the affidavit in my presence.

Or, (after, *Before me*) the witness to the mark of the deponent having been first sworn that he had read over etc. (*as above*) and that he saw him make his mark on the affidavit. (*Witness must sign.*)

Certificate to be used where a deponent to an affirmation is unable to read or sign it

Affirmed at ... this ... day of ... Before me, I having first read over the contents of this affirmation to the deponent [*if there are exhibits, add* "and explained the nature and effect of the exhibits referred to in it"] who appeared to understand it and approved its content as accurate, and made his mark on the affirmation in my presence.

Or, (after, *Before me*) the witness to the mark of the deponent having been first sworn that he had read over etc. (*as above*) and that he saw him make his mark on the affirmation. (*Witness must sign.*)

Annex 2

Certificate to be used where a witness is unable to read or sign a witness statement

[...]*

PART 33

MISCELLANEOUS RULES ABOUT EVIDENCE

Use of plans, photographs and models as evidence

33.6—(1) This rule applies to evidence (such as a plan, photograph or model) which is not—   **B.07**
  (a) contained in a witness statement, affidavit or expert's report;
  (b) to be given orally at trial; or
  (c) evidence of which prior notice must be given under rule 33.2.
(2) This rule includes documents which may be received in evidence without further proof under section 9 of the Civil Evidence Act 1995.[25]
(3) Unless the court orders otherwise the evidence shall not be receivable at a trial unless the party intending to put it in evidence has given notice to the other parties in accordance with this rule.
(4) Where the party intends to use the evidence as evidence of any fact then, except where paragraph (6) applies, he must give notice not later than the latest date for serving witness statements.
(5) He must give notice at least 21 days before the hearing at which he proposes to put in the evidence, if—
  (a) there are not to be witness statements; or
  (b) he intends to put in the evidence solely in order to disprove an allegation made in a witness statement.
(6) Where the evidence forms part of expert evidence, he must give notice when the expert's report is served on the other party.
(7) Where the evidence is being produced to the court for any reason other than as part of factual or expert evidence, he must give notice at least 21 days before the hearing at which he proposes to put in the evidence.
(8) Where a party has given notice that he intends to put in the evidence, he must give every other party an opportunity to inspect it and to agree to its admission without further proof.

---

* Since omitted.
[25] Section 9 of the Civil Evidence Act 1995 provides that documents that form part of the records of a business or public authority, as defined in that section, may be received in evidence without further proof.

PART 34

DEPOSITIONS AND COURT ATTENDANCE BY WITNESSES

Contents

Scope of this Part

34.1—(1) This Part provides—
(a) for the circumstances in which a person may be required to attend court to give evidence or to produce a document; and
(b) for a party to obtain evidence before a hearing to be used at the hearing.
(2) In this Part, reference to a hearing includes a reference to the trial.

Witness summonses

34.2—(1) A witness summons is a document issued by the court requiring a witness to—
(a) attend court to give evidence; or
(b) produce documents to the court.
(2) A witness summons must be in the relevant practice form.
(3) There must be a separate witness summons for each witness.
(4) A witness summons may require a witness to produce documents to the court either—
(a) on the date fixed for a hearing; or
(b) on such date as the court may direct.
(5) The only documents that a summons under this rule can require a person to produce before a hearing are documents which that person could be required to produce at the hearing.

Issue of a witness summons

34.3—(1) A witness summons is issued on the date entered on the summons by the court.
(2) A party must obtain permission from the court where he wishes to—
(a) have a summons issued less than 7 days before the date of the trial;

    (b) have a summons issued for a witness to attend court to give evidence or to produce documents on any date except the date fixed for the trial; or

    (c) have a summons issued for a witness to attend court to give evidence or to produce documents at any hearing except the trial.

(3) A witness summons must be issued by—

    (a) the court where the case is proceeding; or

    (b) the court where the hearing in question will be held.

(4) The court may set aside or vary a witness summons issued under this rule.

Witness summons in aid of inferior court or of tribunal*

34.4—(1) The court may issue a witness summons in aid of an inferior court or of a tribunal.

(2) The court which issued the witness summons under this rule may set it aside.

(3) In this rule, "inferior court or tribunal" means any court or tribunal that does not have power to issue a witness summons in relation to proceedings before it.

Time for serving a witness summons*

34.5—(1) The general rule is that a witness summons is binding if it is served at least 7 days before the date on which the witness is required to attend before the court or tribunal.

(2) The court may direct that a witness summons shall be binding although it will be served less than 7 days before the date on which the witness is required to attend before the court or tribunal.

(3) A witness summons which is—

    (a) served in accordance with this rule; and

    (b) requires the witness to attend court to give evidence;

is binding until the conclusion of the hearing at which the attendance of the witness is required.

Who is to serve a witness summons*

34.6—(1) A witness summons is to be served by the court unless the party on whose behalf it is issued indicates, in writing, when he asks the court to issue the summons, that he wishes to serve it himself.

(2) Where the court is to serve the witness summons, the party on whose behalf it is issued must deposit, in the court office, the money to be paid or offered to the witness under rule 34.7.

Right of witness to travelling expenses and compensation for loss of time*

34.7 At the time of service of a witness summons the witness must be offered or paid—

    (a) a sum reasonably sufficient to cover his expenses in travelling to and from the court; and

    (b) such sum by way of compensation for loss of time as may be specified in the relevant practice direction.

Evidence by deposition*

34.8—(1) A party may apply for an order for a person to be examined before the hearing takes place.

---

* Amdd by CP(A)R 2002/2058.

(2) A person from whom evidence is to be obtained following an order under this rule is referred to as a "deponent" and the evidence is referred to as a "deposition".

(3) An order under this rule shall be for a deponent to be examined on oath before—

    (a) a judge;

    (b) an examiner of the court; or

    (c) such other person as the court appoints.

(Rule 34.15 makes provision for the appointment of examiners by the court.)

(4) The order may require the production of any document which the court considers is necessary for the purposes of the examination.

(5) The order must state the date, time and place of the examination.

(6) At the time of service of the order the deponent must be offered or paid—

    (a) a sum reasonably sufficient to cover his expenses in travelling to and from the place of examination; and

    (b) such sum by way of compensation for loss of time as may be specified in the relevant practice direction.

(7) Where the court makes an order for a deposition to be taken, it may also order the party who obtained the order to serve a witness statement or witness summary in relation to the evidence to be given by the person to be examined.

(Part 32 contains the general rules about witness statements and witness summaries.)

Conduct of examination*

34.9—(1) Subject to any directions contained in the order for examination, the examination must be conducted in the same way as if the witness were giving evidence at a trial.

(2) If all the parties are present, the examiner may conduct the examination of a person not named in the order for examination if all the parties and the person to be examined consent.

(3) The examiner may conduct the examination in private if he considers it appropriate to do so.

(4) The examiner must ensure that the evidence given by the witness is recorded in full.

(5) The examiner must send a copy of the deposition—

    (a) to the person who obtained the order for the examination of the witness; and

    (b) to the court where the case is proceeding.

(6) The party who obtained the order must send each of the other parties a copy of the deposition which he receives from the examiner.

Enforcing attendance of witness*

34.10—(1) If a person served with an order to attend before an examiner—

    (a) fails to attend; or

    (b) refuses to be sworn for the purpose of the examination or to answer any lawful question or produce any document at the examination,

a certificate of his failure or refusal, signed by the examiner, must be filed by the party requiring the deposition.

---

* Amdd by CP(A)R 2002/2058.

(2) On the certificate being filed, the party requiring the deposition may apply to the court for an order requiring that person to attend, or to be sworn or to answer any question or produce any document, as the case may be.

(3) An application for an order under this rule may be made without notice.

(4) The court may order the person against whom an order is made under this rule to pay any costs resulting from his failure or refusal.

Use of deposition at a hearing*

34.11—(1) A deposition ordered under rule 34.8 may be given in evidence at a hearing unless the court orders otherwise.

(2) A party intending to put in evidence a deposition at a hearing must serve notice of his intention to do so on every other party.

(3) He must serve the notice at least 21 days before the day fixed for the hearing.

(4) The court may require a deponent to attend the hearing and give evidence orally.

(5) Where a deposition is given in evidence at trial, it shall be treated as if it were a witness statement for the purposes of rule 32.13 (availability of witness statements for inspection).

Restrictions on subsequent use of deposition taken for the purpose of any hearing except the trial*

34.12—(1) Where the court orders a party to be examined about his or any other assets for the purpose of any hearing except the trial, the deposition may be used only for the purpose of the proceedings in which the order was made.

(2) However, it may be used for some other purpose—
    (a) by the party who was examined;
    (b) if the party who was examined agrees; or
    (c) if the court gives permission.

Where a person to be examined is out of the jurisdiction—letter of request*†

34.13—(1) Where a party wishes to take a deposition from a person outside the jurisdiction, the High Court may order the issue of a letter of request to the judicial authorities of the country in which the proposed deponent is.

(1A) The High Court may order the issue of a letter of request to the judicial authorities of the country in which the proposed deponent is.

(2) A letter of request is a request to a judicial authority to take the evidence of that person, or arrange for it to be taken.

(3) The High Court may make an order under this rule in relation to county court proceedings.

(4) If the government of a country allows a person appointed by the High Court to examine a person in that country, the High Court may make an order appointing a special examiner for that purpose.

(5) A person may be examined under this rule on oath or affirmation or in accordance with any procedure permitted in the country in which the examination is to take place.

(6) If the High Court makes an order for the issue of a letter of request, the party who sought the order must file—

* Amdd by CP(A)R 2002/2058.
† Amdd by CP(A No 4)R 2003/2113.

   (a) the following documents and, except where paragraph (7) applies, a translation of them —
     (i) a draft letter of request;
     (ii) a statement of the issues relevant to the proceedings;
     (iii) a list of questions or the subject matter of questions to be put to the person to be examined; and
   (b) an undertaking to be responsible for the Secretary of State's expenses.
  (7) There is no need to file a translation if —
   (a) English is one of the official languages of the country where the examination is to take place; or
   (b) a practice direction has specified that country as a country where no translation is necessary.

Letter of request — Proceeds of Crime Act 2002

34.13A — (1) This rule applies where a party to existing or contemplated proceedings in —
   (a) the High Court; or
   (b) a magistrates' court,
under Part 5 of the Proceeds of Crime Act 2002 (civil recovery of the proceeds etc. of unlawful conduct) wishes to take a deposition from a person who is out of the jurisdiction.

(2) The High Court may, on the application of such a party, order the issue of a letter of request to the judicial authorities of the country in which the proposed deponent is.

(3) Paragraphs (4) to (7) of rule 34.13 shall apply irrespective of where the proposed deponent is, and rule 34.23 shall not apply in cases where the proposed deponent is in a Regulation State within the meaning of Section III of this Part.

Fees and expenses of examiner of the court*

34.14 — (1) An examiner of the court may charge a fee for the examination.

(2) He need not send the deposition to the court unless the fee is paid.

(3) The examiner's fees and expenses must be paid by the party who obtained the order for examination.

(4) If the fees and expenses due to an examiner are not paid within a reasonable time, he may report that fact to the court.

(5) The court may order the party who obtained the order for examination to deposit in the court office a specified sum in respect of the examiner's fees and, where it does so, the examiner will not be asked to act until the sum has been deposited.

(6) An order under this rule does not affect any decision as to the party who is ultimately to bear the costs of the examination.

Examiners of the court*

34.15 — (1) The Lord Chancellor shall appoint persons to be examiners of the court.

(2) The persons appointed shall be barristers or solicitor-advocates who have been practising for a period of not less than three years.

(3) The Lord Chancellor may revoke an appointment at any time.

---

* Amdd by CP(A)R 2002/2058.

II Evidence for Foreign Courts

Scope and interpretation**

34.16—(1) This Section applies to an application for an order under the 1975 Act for evidence to be obtained, other than an application made as a result of a request by a court in another Regulation State.

(2) In this Section—

   (a) "the 1975 Act" means the Evidence (Proceedings in Other Jurisdictions) Act 1975; and

   (b) "Regulation State" has the same meaning as in Section III of this Part.

Application for order**

34.17 An application for an order under the 1975 Act for evidence to be obtained—

   (a) must be—

      (i) made to the High Court;

      (ii) supported by written evidence; and

      (iii) accompanied by the request as a result of which the application is made, and where appropriate, a translation of the request into English; and

   (b) may be made without notice.

Examination**

34.18—(1) The court may order an examination to be taken before—

   (a) any fit and proper person nominated by the person applying for the order;

   (b) an examiner of the court; or

   (c) any other person whom the court considers suitable.

(2) Unless the court orders otherwise—

   (a) the examination will be taken as provided by rule 34.9; and

   (b) rule 34.10 applies.

(3) The court may make an order under rule 34.14 for payment of the fees and expenses of the examination.

Dealing with deposition**

34.19—(1) The examiner must send the deposition of the witness to the Senior Master unless the court orders otherwise.

(2) The Senior Master will—

   (a) give a certificate sealed with the seal of the Supreme Court for use out of the jurisdiction identifying the following documents—

      (i) the request;

      (ii) the order of the court for examination; and

      (iii) the deposition of the witness; and

   (b) send the certificate and the documents referred to in paragraph (a) to—

      (i) the Secretary of State; or

      (ii) where the request was sent to the Senior Master by another person in accordance with a Civil Procedure Convention, to that other person, for transmission to the court or tribunal requesting the examination.

** Amdd by CP(A)R 2002 and CP(A No 4)R 2003.

Claim to privilege**

34.20—(1) This rule applies where—
(a) a witness claims to be exempt from giving evidence on the ground specified in section 3(1)(b) of the 1975 Act; and
(b) That claim is not supported or conceded as referred to in section 3(2) of that Act.

(2) The examiner may require the witness to give the evidence which he claims to be exempt from giving.

(3) Where the examiner does not require the witness to give that evidence, the court may order the witness to do so.

(4) An application for an order under paragraph (3) may be made by the person who obtained the order under section 2 of the 1975 Act.

(5) Where such evidence is taken—
(a) it must be contained in a document separate from the remainder of the deposition;
(b) the examiner will send to the Senior Master—
(i) the deposition; and
(ii) a signed statement setting out the claim to be exempt and the ground on which it was made;

(6) On receipt of the statement referred to in paragraph (5)(b)(ii), the Senior Master will—
(a) retain the document containing the part of the witness's evidence to which the claim to be exempt relates; and
(b) send the statement and a request to determine that claim to the foreign court or tribunal together with the documents referred to in rule 34.17.

(7) The Senior Master will—
(a) if the claim to be exempt is rejected by the foreign court or tribunal, send the document referred to in paragraph (5)(a) to that court or tribunal;
(b) if the claim is upheld, send the document to the witness; and
(c) in either case, notify the witness and person who obtained the order under section 2 of the foreign court or tribunal's decision.

Order under 1975 Act as applied by Patents Act 1977**

34.21 Where an order is made for the examination of witnesses under section 1 of the 1975 Act as applied by section 92 of the Patents Act 1977 the court may permit an officer of the European Patent Office to—
(a) attend the examination and examine the witnesses; or
(b) request the court or the examiner before whom the examination takes place to put specified questions to them.

III Taking of Evidence—Member States of the European Union

Interpretation**

34.22 In this Section—
(a) "designated court" has the meaning given in the relevant practice direction;
(b) "Regulation State" has the same meaning as "Member State" in the Taking of Evidence Regulation, that is all Member States except Denmark;
(c) "the Taking of Evidence Regulation" means Council Regulation (EC) No. 1206/2001 of 28 May 2001 on co-operation between the courts of the Member States in the taking of evidence in civil and commercial matters.

** Amdd by CP(A)R 2002 and CP(A No 4)R 2003.

Where a person to be examined is in another Regulation State**

34.23—(1) Subject to rule 34.13A, this rule applies where a party wishes to take a deposition from a person who is in another Regulation State—

    (a) outside the jurisdiction; and

    (b) in a Regulation State.

(2) The court may order the issue of a request to a designated court ("the requested court") in the Regulation State in which the proposed deponent is.

(3) If the court makes an order for the issue of a request, the party who sought the order must file—

    (a) a draft Form A as set out in the annex to the Taking of Evidence Regulation (request for the taking of evidence);

    (b) except where paragraph (4) applies, a translation of the form;

    (c) an undertaking to be responsible for costs sought by the requested court in relation to—

        (i) fees paid to experts and interpreters; and

        (ii) where requested by that party, the use of special procedures or communications technology; and

    (d) an undertaking to be responsible for the court's expenses.

(4) There is no need to file a translation if—

    (a) English is one of the official languages of the Regulation State where the examination is to take place; or

    (b) the Regulation State has indicated, in accordance with the Taking of Evidence Regulation, that English is a language which it will accept.

(5) Where article 17 of the Taking of Evidence Regulation (direct taking of evidence by the requested court) allows evidence to be taken directly in another Regulation State, the court may make an order for the submission of a request in accordance with that article.

(6) If the court makes an order for the submission of a request under paragraph (5), the party who sought the order must file—

    (a) a draft Form I as set out in the annex to the Taking of Evidence Regulation (request for direct taking of evidence);

    (b) except where paragraph (4) applies, a translation of the form; and

    (c) an undertaking to be responsible for the court's expenses.

Evidence for courts of other Regulation States**

34.24—(1) This rule applies where a court in another Regulation State ("the requesting court") issues a request for evidence to be taken from a person who is in the jurisdiction.

(2) An application for an order for evidence to be taken—

    (a) must be made to a designated court;

    (b) must be accompanied by—

        (i) the form of request for the taking of evidence as a result of which the application is made; and

        (ii) where appropriate, a translation of the form of request; and

    (c) may be made without notice.

(3) Rule 34.18(1) and (2) apply.

(4) The examiner must send—

    (a) the deposition to the court for transmission to the requesting court; and

    (b) a copy of the deposition to the person who obtained the order for evidence to be taken.

** Amdd by CP(A)R 2002 and CP(A No 4)R 2003.

Practice direction—depositions and court attendance by witnesses

This Practice Direction supplements CPR Part 34

Witness Summonses

Issue of Witness Summons

B.09   **1.1** A witness summons may require a witness to:
(1) attend court to give evidence,
(2) produce documents to the court, or
(3) both,
on either a date fixed for the hearing or such date as the court may direct.[26]

1.2 Two copies of the witness summons[27] should be filed with the court for sealing, one of which will be retained on the court file.

1.3 A mistake in the name or address of a person named in a witness summons may be corrected if the summons has not been served.

1.4 The corrected summons must be re-sealed by the court and marked "Amended and Re-Sealed".

Witness Summons issued in aid of an inferior court or tribunal

2.1 A witness summons may be issued in the High Court or a county court in aid of a court or tribunal which does not have the power to issue a witness summons in relation to the proceedings before it.[28]

2.2 A witness summons referred to in paragraph 2.1 may be set aside by the court which issued it.[29]

2.3 An application to set aside a witness summons referred to in paragraph 2.1 will be heard—
(1) in the High Court by a Master at the Royal Courts of Justice or by a District Judge in a District Registry, and
(2) in a county court by a District Judge.

2.4 Unless the court otherwise directs, the applicant must give at least 2 days notice to the party who issued the witness summons of the application, which will normally be dealt with at a hearing.

Travelling expenses and compensation for loss of time

3.1 When a witness is served with a witness summons he must be offered a sum to cover his travelling expenses to and from the court and compensation for his loss of time.[30]

3.2 If the witness summons is to be served by the court, the party issuing the summons must deposit with the court—
(1) a sum sufficient to pay for the witness's expenses in travelling to the court and in returning to his home or place of work, and
(2) a sum in respect of the period during which earnings or benefit are lost, or such lesser sum as it may be proved that the witness will lose as a result of his attendance at court in answer to the witness summons.

[26] Rule 34.2(4).
[27] In Practice form N20.
[28] Rule 34.4(1).
[29] Rule 34.4(2).
[30] Rule 34.7.

730

3.3 The sum referred to in 3.2(2) is to be based on the sums payable to witnesses attending the Crown Court.[31]

3.4 Where the party issuing the witness summons wishes to serve it himself,[32] he must—

(1) notify the court in writing that he wishes to do so, and

(2) at the time of service offer the witness the sums mentioned in paragraph 3.2 above.

Depositions

To be taken in England and Wales for use as evidence in proceedings in Courts in England and Wales

4.1 A party may apply for an order for a person to be examined on oath before—

(1) a judge,

(2) an examiner of the court, or

(3) such other person as the court may appoint.[33]

4.2 The party who obtains an order for the examination of a deponent[34] before an examiner of the court[35] must;

(1) apply to the Foreign Process Section of the Masters' Secretary's Department at the Royal Courts of Justice for the allocation of an examiner,

(2) when allocated, provide the examiner with copies of all documents in the proceedings necessary to inform the examiner of the issues, and

(3) pay the deponent a sum to cover his travelling expenses to and from the examination and compensation for his loss of time.[36]

4.3 In ensuring that the deponent's evidence is recorded in full, the court or the examiner may permit it to be recorded on audiotape or videotape, but the deposition[37] must always be recorded in writing by him or by a competent shorthand writer or stenographer.

4.4 If the deposition is not recorded word for word, it must contain, as nearly as may be, the statement of the deponent; the examiner may record word for word any particular questions and answers which appear to him to have special importance.

4.5 If a deponent objects to answering any question or where any objection is taken to any question, the examiner must—

(1) record in the deposition or a document attached to it:

    (a) the question,

    (b) the nature of and grounds for the objection, and

    (c) any answer given, and

(2) give his opinion as to the validity of the objection and must record it in the deposition or a document attached to it.

The court will decide as to the validity of the objection and any question of costs arising from it.

4.6 Documents and exhibits must—

(1) have an identifying number or letter marked on them by the examiner, and

---

[31] Fixed pursuant to the Prosecution of Offences Act 1985 and the Costs in Criminal Cases (General) Regulations 1986.

[32] Rule 34.6(1).

[33] Rule 34.8(3).

[34] *See* rule 34.8(2) for explanation of "deponent" and "deposition".

[35] Rule 34.8(6).

[36] Rule 34.8(6).

[37] *See* rule 34.8(2) for explanation of "deponent" and "deposition".

(2) be preserved by the party or his legal representative[38] who obtained the order for the examination, or as the court or the examiner may direct.

4.7 The examiner may put any question to the deponent as to—

(1) the meaning of any of his answers or

(2) any matter arising in the course of the examination.

4.8 Where a deponent—

(1) fails to attend the examination, or

(2) refuses to:

    (a) be sworn, or

    (b) answer any lawful question, or

    (c) produce any document,

the examiner will sign a certificate[39] of such failure or refusal and may include in his certificate any comment as to the conduct of the deponent or of any person attending the examination.

4.9 The party who obtained the order for the examination must file the certificate with the court and may apply for an order that the deponent attend for examination or as may be.[40] The application may be made without notice.[41]

4.10 The court will make such order on the application as it thinks fit including an order for the deponent to pay any costs resulting from his failure or refusal.[42]

4.11 A deponent who wilfully refuses to obey an order made against him under Part 34 may be proceeded against for contempt of court.

4.12 A deposition must—

(1) be signed by the examiner,

(2) have any amendments to it initialled by the examiner and the deponent,

(3) be endorsed by the examiner with:

    (a) a statement of the time occupied by the examination and

    (b) a record of any refusal by the deponent to sign the deposition and of his reasons for not doing so, and

(4) be sent by the examiner to the court where the proceedings are taking place for filing on the court file.

4.13 Rule 34.14 deals with the fees and expenses of an examiner.

Depositions to be taken abroad for use as evidence in proceedings before Courts in England and Wales

5.1 Where a party wishes to take a deposition from a person outside the jurisdiction, the High Court may order the issue of a letter of request to the judicial authorities of the country in which the proposed deponent is.[43]

5.2 An application for an order referred to in paragraph 5.1 should be made by application notice in accordance with Part 23.

5.3 The documents which a party applying for an order for the issue of a letter of request must file with his application notice are set out in rule 34.13(6). They are as follows—

(1) a draft letter of request in the form set out in Annex A to this practice direction,

(2) a statement of the issues relevant to the proceedings,

(3) a list of questions or the subject matter of questions to be put to the proposed deponent,

---

[38] For the definition of legal representative see rule 2.3.

[39] Rule 34.10.

[40] Rule 34.10(2) and (3).

[41] Rule 34.10(3).

[42] Rule 34.10(4).

[43] Rule 34.13(1).

(4) a translation of the documents in (1), (2) and (3) above unless the proposed deponent is in a country of which English is an official language, and

(5) an undertaking to be responsible for the expenses of the Secretary of State, and [words added to draft order]

5.4 The above documents should be filed with the Masters' Secretary in Room E214, Royal Courts of Justice, Strand, London WC2A 2LL.

5.5 The application will be dealt with by the Senior Master of the Queen's Bench Division of the High Court who will, if appropriate, sign the letter of request.

5.6 Attention is drawn to the provisions of rule 23.10 (application to vary or discharge an order made without notice).

5.7 If parties are in doubt as to whether a translation under paragraph 5.3(4) above is required, they should seek guidance from the Foreign Process Section of the Masters' Secretary's Department.

5.8 A special examiner appointed under rule 34.13(4) may be the British Consul or the Consul-General or his deputy in the country where the evidence is to be taken if;

(1) there is in respect of that country a Civil Procedure Convention providing for the taking of evidence in that country for the assistance of proceedings in the High Court or other court in this country, or

(2) with the consent of the Secretary of State.

5.9 The provisions of paragraphs 4.1 to 4.12 above apply to the depositions referred to in this paragraph.

Depositions to be taken in England and Wales for use as evidence in proceedings before courts abroad pursuant to letters of request

6.1 Section 11 of Part 34 relating to obtaining evidence for foreign courts applies to letters of request and should be read in conjunction with this part of the practice direction.

6.2 The Evidence (Proceedings in Other Jurisdictions) Act 1975 applies to these depositions.

6.3 The written evidence supporting an application under rule 34.17 (which should be made by application notice—see Part 23) must include or exhibit—

(1) a statement of the issues relevant to the proceedings;

(2) a list of questions or the subject matter of questions to be put to the proposed deponent;

(3) a draft order; and

(4) a translation of the documents in (1) and (2) into English, if necessary.

6.4—(1) The Senior Master will send to the Treasury Solicitor any request—

   (a) forwarded by the Secretary of State with a recommendation that effect should be given to the request without requiring an application to be made; or

   (b) received by him in pursuance of a Civil Procedure Convention providing for the taking of evidence of any person in England and Wales to assist a court or tribunal in a foreign country where no person is named in the document as the applicant.

(2) In relation to such a request, the Treasury Solicitor may, with the consent of the Treasury—

   (a) apply for an order under the 1975 Act; and

   (b) take such other steps as are necessary to give effect to the request.

6.5 The order for the deponent to attend and be examined together with the evidence upon which the order was made must be served on the deponent.

6.6 Attention is drawn to the provisions of rule 23.10 (application to vary or discharge an order made without notice).

6.7 Arrangements for the examination to take place at a specified time and place before an examiner of the court or such other person as the court may appoint shall be made by the applicant for the order (*i.e.* the agent referred to in paragraph 6.3 or the Treasury Solicitor) and approved by the Senior Master.

6.8 The provisions of paragraph 4.2 to 4.12 apply to the depositions referred to in this paragraph, except that the examiner must send the deposition to the Senior Master.

(For further information about evidence see Part 32 and the practice direction which supplements it.)

Taking of evidence between EU Member States

Taking of Evidence Regulation

7.1 Where evidence is to be taken—

    (a) from a person in another Member State of the European Union for use as evidence in proceedings before courts in England and Wales; or

    (b) from a person in England and Wales for use as evidence in proceedings before a court in another Member State, Council Regulation (EC) No 1206/2001 of 28 May 2001 on co-operation between the courts of the Member States in the taking of evidence in civil or commercial matters ("the Taking of Evidence Regulation") applies.

7.2 The Taking of Evidence Regulation is annexed to this practice direction as Annex B.

7.3 The Taking of Evidence Regulation does not apply to Denmark. In relation to Denmark, therefore, rule 34.13 and Section II of Part 34 will continue to apply.

(Article 21(1) of the Taking of Evidence Regulation provides that the Regulation prevails over other provisions contained in bilateral or multilateral agreements or arrangements concluded by the Member States and in particular the Hague Convention of 1 March 1954 on Civil Procedure and the Hague Convention of 18 March 1970 on the Taking of Evidence Abroad in Civil or Commercial Matters)

Originally published in the official languages of the European Community in the Official Journal of the European Communities by the Office for Official Publications of the European Communities.

Meaning of "designated court"

8.1 In accordance with the Taking of Evidence Regulation, each Regulation State has prepared a list of courts competent to take evidence in accordance with the Regulation indicating the territorial and, where appropriate, special jurisdiction of those courts.

8.2 Where Part 34, Section III refers to a "designated court" in relation to another Regulation State, the reference is to the court, referred to in the list of competent courts of that State, which is appropriate to the application in hand.

8.3 Where the reference is to the "designated court" in England and Wales, the reference is to the appropriate competent court in the jurisdiction. The designated courts for England and Wales are listed in Annex C to this practice direction.

Central Body

9.1 The Taking of Evidence Regulation stipulates that each Regulation State must nominate a Central Body responsible for—

    (a) supplying information to courts;

    (b) seeking solutions to any difficulties which may arise in respect of a request; and

(c) forwarding, in exceptional cases, at the request of a requesting court, a request to the competent court.

9.2 The United Kingdom has nominated the Senior Master, Queen's Bench Division, to be the Central Body for England and Wales.

9.3 The Senior Master, as Central Body, has been designated responsible for taking decisions on requests pursuant to Article 17 of the Regulation. Article 17 allows a court to submit a request to the Central Body or a designated competent authority in another Regulation State to take evidence directly in that State.

Evidence to be taken in another Regulation State for use in England and Wales

10.1 Where a person wishes to take a deposition from a person in another Regulation State, the court where the proceedings are taking place may order the issue of a request to the designated court in the Regulation State (Rule 34.23(2)). The form of request is prescribed as Form A in the Taking of Evidence Regulation.

10.2 An application to the court for an order under rule 34.23(2) should be made by application notice in accordance with Part 23.

10.3 Rule 34.23(3) provides that the party applying for the order must file a draft form of request in the prescribed form. Where completion of the form requires attachments or documents to accompany the form, these must also be filed.

10.4 If the court grants an order under rule 34.23 (2), it will send the form of request directly to the designated court.

10.5 Where the taking of evidence requires the use of an expert, the designated court may require a deposit in advance towards the costs of that expert. The party who obtained the order is responsible for the payment of any such deposit which should be deposited with the court for onward transmission. Under the provisions of the Taking of Evidence Regulation, the designated court is not required to execute the request until such payment is received.

10.6 Article 17 permits the court where proceedings are taking place to take evidence directly from a deponent in another Regulation State if the conditions of the article are satisfied. Direct taking of evidence can only take place if evidence is given voluntarily without the need for coercive measures. Rule 34.23(5) provides for the court to make an order for the submission of a request to take evidence directly. The form of request is Form I annexed to the Taking of Evidence Regulation and rule 34.23(6) makes provision for a draft of this form to be filed by the party seeking the order. An application for an order under rule 34.23(5) should be by application notice in accordance with Part 23.

10.7 Attention is drawn to the provisions of rule 23.10 (application to vary or discharge an order made without notice).

Evidence to be taken in England and Wales for use in another Regulation State

11.1 Where a designated court in England and Wales receives a request to take evidence from a court in a Regulation State, the court will send the request to the Treasury Solicitor.

11.2 On receipt of the request, the Treasury Solicitor may, with the consent of the Treasury, apply for an order under rule 34.24.

11.3 An application to the court for an order must be accompanied by the Form of request to take evidence and any accompanying documents, translated if required under paragraph 11.4.

11.4 The United Kingdom has indicated that, in addition to English, it will accept French as a language in which documents may be submitted. Where the form or request and any accompanying documents are received in French they will be translated into English by the Treasury Solicitor.

11.5 The order for the deponent to attend and be examined together with the evidence on which the order was made must be served on the deponent.

11.6 Arrangements for the examination to take place at a specified time and place shall be made by the Treasury Solicitor and approved by the court.

11.7 The court shall send details of the arrangements for the examination to such of

(a) the parties and, if any, their representatives; or

(b) the representatives of the foreign court,

who have indicated, in accordance with the Taking of Evidence Regulation, that they wish to be present at the examination.

11.8 The provisions of paragraph 4.3 to 4.12 apply to the depositions referred to in this paragraph.

Annex A

Draft Letter of Request

To the Competent Judicial Authority of   in the   of

I [*name*] Senior Master of the Queen's Bench Division of the Supreme Court of England and Wales respectfully request the assistance of your court with regard to the following matters.

1. A claim is now pending in the   Division of the High Court of Justice in England and Wales entitled as follows

   [*set out full title and claim number*]

   in which [*name*] of [*address*] is the claimant and [*name*] of [*address*] is the defendant.

2. The names and addresses of the representatives or agents of [*set out names and addresses of representatives of the parties*].

3. The claim by the claimant is for:

   (a) [*set out the nature of the claim*]

   (b) [*the relief sought, and*]

   (c) [*a summary of the facts.*]

4. It is necessary for the purposes of justice and for the due determination of the matters in dispute between the parties that you cause the following witnesses, who are resident within your jurisdiction, to be examined. The names and addresses of the witnesses are as follows:

5. The witnesses should be examined on oath or if that is not possible within your laws or is impossible of performance by reason of the internal practice and procedure of your court or by reason of practical difficulties, they should be examined in accordance with whatever procedure your laws provide for in these matters.

6. Either/

   The witnesses should be examined in accordance with the list of questions annexed hereto.

   Or/

   The witnesses should be examined regarding [*set out full details of evidence sought*]

   N.B. Where the witness is required to produce documents, these should be clearly identified.

7. I would ask that you cause me, or the agents of the parties (if appointed), to be informed of the date and place where the examination is to take place.

8. Finally, I request that you will cause the evidence of the said witnesses to be reduced into writing and all documents produced on such examinations to be

duly marked for identification and that you will further be pleased to authenticate such examinations by the seal of your court or in such other way as is in accordance with your procedure and return the written evidence and documents produced to me addressed to me as follows:

Senior Master of the Queen's Bench Division
Royal Courts of Justice
Strand
London WC2A 2LL
England

Practice direction—fees for examiners of the court

This Practice Direction supplements CPR Part 34

Scope

1.1 This practice direction sets out—   B.10
(1) how to calculate the fees an examiner of the court ("an examiner") may charge; and
(2) the expenses he may recover.
(CPR Rule 34.8(3)(b) provides that the court may make an order for evidence to be obtained by the examination of a witness before an examiner of the court.)
1.2 The party who obtained the order for the examination must pay the fees and expenses of the examiner.
(CPR rule 34.14 permits an examiner to charge a fee for the examination and contains other provisions about his fees and expenses, and rule 34.15 provides who may be appointed as an examiner of the court.)

The examination fee

2.1 An examiner may charge an hourly rate for each hour (or part of an hour) that he is engaged in examining the witness.
2.2 The hourly rate is to be calculated by reference to the formula set out in paragraph 3.
2.3 The examination fee will be the hourly rate multiplied by the number of hours the examination has taken. For example—

Examination fee = hourly rate × number of hours.

How to calculate the hourly rate—the formula

3.1 Divide the amount of the minimum annual salary of a post within Group 7 of the judicial salary structure as designated by the Review Body on Senior Salaries,[44] by 220 to give "x"; and then divide "x" by 6 to give the hourly rate.
For example—

$$\frac{\text{minimum annual salary}}{220} = x$$

$$\frac{x}{6} = \text{hourly rate}$$

---

[44] The Report of the Review Body on Senior Salaries is published annually by the Stationery Office.

Single fee chargeable on making the appointment for examination

4.1 An examiner of court is also entitled to charge a single fee of twice the hourly rate (calculated in accordance with paragraph 3 above) as "the appointment fee" when the appointment for the examination is made.

4.2 The examiner is entitled to retain the appointment fee where the witness fails to attend on the date and time arranged.

4.3 Where the examiner fails to attend on the date and time arranged he may not charge a further appointment fee for arranging a subsequent appointment.

(The examiner need not send the deposition to the court until his fees are paid—see CPR rule 34.14(2).)

Examiners' expenses

5.1 The examiner of court is also entitled to recover the following expenses—

(1) all reasonable travelling expenses;

(2) any other expenses reasonably incurred; and

(3) subject to paragraph 5.2, any reasonable charge for the room where the examination takes place.

5.2 No expenses may be recovered under sub-paragraph (3) above if the examination takes place at the examiner's usual business address.

(If the examiner's fees and expenses are not paid within a reasonable time he may report the fact to the court, see CPR Rule 34.14(4) and (5).)

PART 35

EXPERTS AND ASSESSORS

Contents

Duty to restrict expert evidence

35.1 Expert evidence should be restricted to that which is reasonably required to resolve the proceedings.

Interpretation

35.2 A reference to an "expert" in this Part is a reference to an expert who has been instructed to give or prepare evidence for the purpose of court proceedings.

Experts—overriding duty to the court

35.3—(1) It is the duty of an expert to help the court on the matters within his expertise.

(2) This duty overrides any obligation to the person from whom he has received instructions or by whom he is paid.

Court's power to restrict expert evidence

35.4—(1) No party may call an expert or put in evidence an expert's report without the court's permission.

(2) When a party applies for permission under this rule he must identify—
    (a) the field in which he wishes to rely on expert evidence; and
    (b) where practicable the expert in that field on whose evidence he wishes to rely.

(3) If permission is granted under this rule it shall be in relation only to the expert named or the field identified under paragraph (2).

(4) The court may limit the amount of the expert's fees and expenses that the party who wishes to rely on the expert may recover from any other party.

General requirement for expert evidence to be given in a written report

35.5—(1) Expert evidence is to be given in a written report unless the court directs otherwise.

(2) If a claim is on the fast track, the court will not direct an expert to attend a hearing unless it is necessary to do so in the interests of justice.

Written questions to experts

35.6—(1) A party may put to—
    (a) an expert instructed by another party; or
    (b) a single joint expert appointed under rule 35.7,
written questions about his report.

(2) Written questions under paragraph (1)—
    (a) may be put once only;
    (b) must be put within 28 days of service of the expert's report; and
    (c) must be for the purpose only of clarification of the report,
unless in any case—
      (i) the court gives permission; or
      (ii) the other party agrees.

(3) An expert's answers to questions put in accordance with paragraph (1) shall be treated as part of the expert's report.

(4) Where—
    (a) a party has put a written question to an expert instructed by another party in accordance with this rule; and
    (b) the expert does not answer that question,
the court may make one or both of the following orders in relation to the party who instructed the expert—
      (i) that the party may not rely on the evidence of that expert; or
      (ii) that the party may not recover the fees and expenses of that expert from any other party.

Court's power to direct that evidence is to be given by a single joint expert

35.7—(1) Where two or more parties wish to submit expert evidence on a particular issue, the court may direct that the evidence on that issue is to be given by one expert only.

(2) The parties wishing to submit the expert evidence are called "the instructing parties".

(3) Where the instructing parties cannot agree who should be the expert, the court may—

    (a) select the expert from a list prepared or identified by the instructing parties; or

    (b) direct that the expert be selected in such other manner as the court may direct.

Instructions to a single joint expert

35.8—(1) Where the court gives a direction under rule 35.7 for a single joint expert to be used, each instructing party may give instructions to the expert.

(2) When an instructing party gives instructions to the expert he must, at the same time, send a copy of the instructions to the other instructing parties.

(3) The court may give directions about—

    (a) the payment of the expert's fees and expenses; and

    (b) any inspection, examination or experiments which the expert wishes to carry out.

(4) The court may, before an expert is instructed—

    (a) limit the amount that can be paid by way of fees and expenses to the expert; and

    (b) direct that the instructing parties pay that amount into court.

(5) Unless the court otherwise directs, the instructing parties are jointly and severally liable for the payment of the expert's fees and expenses.

Power of court to direct a party to provide information

35.9 Where a party has access to information which is not reasonably available to the other party, the court may direct the party who has access to the information to—

    (a) prepare and file a document recording the information; and

    (b) serve a copy of that document on the other party.

Contents of report

35.10—(1) An expert's report must comply with the requirements set out in the relevant practice direction.

(2) At the end of an expert's report there must be a statement that—

    (a) the expert understands his duty to the court; and

    (b) he has complied with that duty.

(3) The expert's report must state the substance of all material instructions, whether written or oral, on the basis of which the report was written.

(4) The instructions referred to in paragraph (3) shall not be privileged against disclosure but the court will not, in relation to those instructions—

    (a) order disclosure of any specific document; or

    (b) permit any questioning in court, other than by the party who instructed the expert,

unless it is satisfied that there are reasonable grounds to consider the statement of instructions given under paragraph (3) to be inaccurate or incomplete.

Use by one party of expert's report disclosed by another

35.11 Where a party has disclosed an expert's report, any party may use that expert's report as evidence at the trial.

Discussions between experts*

35.12—(1) The court may, at any stage, direct a discussion between experts for the purpose of requiring the experts to—
    (a) identify the issues in the proceedings; and
    (b) where possible, reach agreement on an issue.
(2) The court may specify the issues which the experts must discuss.
(3) The court may direct that following a discussion between the experts they must prepare a statement for the court showing—
    (a) those issues on which they agree; and
    (b) those issues on which they disagree and a summary of their reasons for disagreeing.
(4) The content of the discussion between the experts shall not be referred to at the trial unless the parties agree.
(5) Where experts reach agreement on an issue during their discussions, the agreement shall not bind the parties unless the parties expressly agree to be bound by the agreement.

Consequence of failure to disclose expert's report

35.13 A party who fails to disclose an expert's report may not use the report at the trial or call the expert to give evidence orally unless the court gives permission.

Expert's right to ask court for directions*

35.14—(1) An expert may file a written request for directions to assist him in carrying out his function as an expert.
(2) [substd]
(3) The court, when it gives directions, may also direct that a party be served with a copy of the directions.

Assessors

35.15—(1) This rule applies where the court appoints one or more persons (an "assessor") under section 70 of the Supreme Court Act 1981[45] or section 63 of the County Courts Act 1984.[46]
(2) The assessor shall assist the court in dealing with a matter in which the assessor has skill and experience.
(3) An assessor shall take such part in the proceedings as the court may direct and in particular the court may—
    (a) direct the assessor to prepare a report for the court on any matter at issue in the proceedings; and
    (b) direct the assessor to attend the whole or any part of the trial to advise the court on any such matter.
(4) If the assessor prepares a report for the court before the trial has begun—
    (a) the court will send a copy to each of the parties; and
    (b) the parties may use it at trial.
(5) The remuneration to be paid to the assessor for his services shall be determined by the court and shall form part of the costs of the proceedings.
(6) The court may order any party to deposit in the court office a specified sum in respect of the assessor's fees and, where it does so, the assessor will not be asked to act until the sum has been deposited.

---

* Amdd by CP(A No 5)R 2001/4015.
[45] 1981 c. 54.
[46] 1984 c. 28 Section 63 was amended by S.I. 1998/2940.

(7) Paragraphs (5) and (6) shall not apply where the remuneration of the assessor is to be paid out of money provided by Parliament.

Practice direction—experts and assessors

This Practice Direction supplements CPR Part 35

Part 35 is intended to limit the use of oral expert evidence to that which is reasonably required. In addition, where possible, matters requiring expert evidence should be dealt with by a single expert. Permission of the court is always required either to call an expert or to put an expert's report in evidence. There is annexed to this Practice Direction a protocol for the instruction of experts to give evidence in civil claims. Experts and those instructing them are expected to have regard to the guidance contained in the protocol.

Expert Evidence—General Requirements

1.1 It is the duty of an expert to help the court on matters within his own expertise: rule 35.3(1). This duty is paramount and overrides any obligation to the person from whom the expert has received instructions or by whom he is paid: rule 35.3(2).

1.2 Expert evidence should be the independent product of the expert uninfluenced by the pressures of litigation.

1.3 An expert should assist the court by providing objective, unbiased opinion on matters within his expertise, and should not assume the role of an advocate.

1.4 An expert should consider all material facts, including those which might detract from his opinion.

1.5 An expert should make it clear:

    (a) when a question or issue falls outside his expertise; and

    (b) when he is not able to reach a definite opinion, for example because he has insufficient information.

1.6 If, after producing a report, an expert changes his view on any material matter, such change of view should be communicated to all the parties without delay, and when appropriate to the court.

Form and Content of Expert's Reports

2.1 An expert's report should be addressed to the court and not to the party from whom the expert has received his instructions.

2.2 An expert's report must:

(1) give details of the expert's qualifications;

(2) give details of any literature or other material which the expert has relied on in making the report;

(3) contain a statement setting out the substance of all facts and instructions given to the expert which are material to the opinions expressed in the report or upon which those opinions are based;

(4) make clear which of the facts stated in the report are within the expert's own knowledge;

(5) say who carried out any examination, measurement, test or experiment which the expert has used for the report, give the qualifications of that person, and say whether or not the test or experiment has been carried out under the expert's supervision;

(6) where there is a range of opinion on the matters dealt with in the report—

742

    (a) summarise the range of opinion, and

    (b) give reasons for his own opinion;

(7) contain a summary of the conclusions reached;

(8) if the expert is not able to give his opinion without qualification, state the qualification; and

(9) contain a statement that the expert understands his duty to the court, and has complied and will continue to comply with that duty.

2.3 An expert's report must be verified by a statement of truth as well as containing the statements required in paragraph 2.2(8) and (9) above.

2.4 The form of the statement of truth is as follows:

> "I confirm that insofar as the facts stated in my report are within my own knowledge I have made clear which they are and I believe them to be true, and that the opinions I have expressed represent my true and complete professional opinion."

2.5 Attention is drawn to rule 32.14 which sets out the consequences of verifying a document containing a false statement without an honest belief in its truth.

(For information about statements of truth see Part 22 and the practice direction which supplements it.)

Information

3 Under Rule 35.9 the court may direct a party with access to information which is not reasonably available to another party to serve on that other party a document which records the information. The document served must include sufficient details of all the facts, tests, experiments and assumptions which underlie any part of the information to enable the party on whom it is served to make, or to obtain, a proper interpretation of the information and an assessment of its significance.

Instructions

4 The instructions referred to in paragraph 2.2(3) will not be protected by privilege (see rule 35.10(4)). But cross-examination of the expert on the contents of his instructions will not be allowed unless the court permits it (or unless the party who gave the instructions consents to it). Before it gives permission the court must be satisfied that there are reasonable grounds to consider that the statement in the report of the substance of the instructions is inaccurate or incomplete. If the court is so satisfied, it will allow the cross-examination where it appears to be in the interests of justice to do so.

Questions to Experts

5.1 Questions asked for the purpose of clarifying the expert's report (see rule 35.6) should be put, in writing, to the expert not later than 28 days after receipt of the expert's report (see paragraphs 1.2 to 1.5 above as to verification).

5.2 Where a party sends a written question or questions direct to an expert, a copy of the questions should, at the same time, be sent to the other party or parties.

5.3 The party or parties instructing the expert must pay any fees charged by that expert for answering questions put under rule 35.6. This does not affect any decision of the court as to the party who is ultimately to bear the expert's costs.

Single Expert

6 Where the court has directed that the evidence on a particular issue is to be given by one expert only (rule 35.7) but there are a number of disciplines relevant to that issue, a leading expert in the dominant discipline should be identified as the single expert. He should prepare the general part of the report and be responsible for annexing or incorporating the contents of any reports from experts in other disciplines.

Orders

6A Where an order requires an act to be done by an expert, or otherwise affects an expert, the party instructing that expert must serve a copy of the order on the expert instructed by him. In the case of a jointly instructed expert, the claimant must serve the order.

Assessors

7.1 An assessor may be appointed to assist the court under rule 35.15. Not less than 21 days before making any such appointment, the court will notify each party in writing of the name of the proposed assessor, of the matter in respect of which the assistance of the assessor will be sought and of the qualifications of the assessor to give that assistance.

7.2 Where any person has been proposed for appointment as an assessor, objection to him, either personally or in respect of his qualification, may be taken by any party.

7.3 Any such objection must be made in writing and filed with the court within 7 days of receipt of the notification referred to in paragraph 6.1 and will be taken into account by the court in deciding whether or not to make the appointment (section 63(5) of the County Courts Act 1984).

7.4 Copies of any report prepared by the assessor will be sent to each of the parties but the assessor will not give oral evidence or be open to cross-examination or questioning.

Protocol for the Instruction of Experts to give evidence in civil claims

1. Introduction

B.12   Expert witnesses perform a vital role in civil litigation. It is essential that both those who instruct experts and experts themselves are given clear guidance as to what they are expected to do in civil proceedings. The purpose of this Protocol is to provide such guidance. It has been drafted by the Civil Justice Council and reflects the rules and practice directions current [in June 2005], replacing the Code of Guidance on Expert Evidence. The authors of the Protocol wish to acknowledge the valuable assistance they obtained by drawing on earlier documents produced by the Academy of Experts and the Expert Witness Institute, as well as suggestions made by the Clinical Dispute Forum. The Protocol has been approved by the Master of the Rolls.

2. Aims of Protocol

2.1 This Protocol offers guidance to experts and to those instructing them in the interpretation of and compliance with Part 35 of the Civil Procedure Rules (CPR 35) and its associated Practice Direction (PD 35) and to further the objectives of the Civil Procedure Rules in general. It is intended to assist in the interpretation of those provisions in the interests of good practice but it does not replace them. It sets out standards for the use of experts and the conduct of experts and those who instruct them. The existence of this Protocol does not remove the need for experts and those who instruct them to be familiar with CPR35 and PD35.

2.2 Experts and those who instruct them should also bear in mind para 1.4 of the Practice Direction on Protocols which contains the following objectives, namely to:

(a) encourage the exchange of early and full information about the expert issues involved in a prospective legal claim;

(b) enable the parties to avoid or reduce the scope of litigation by agreeing the whole or part of an expert issue before commencement of proceedings; and

(c) support the efficient management of proceedings where litigation cannot be avoided.

3. Application

3.1 This Protocol applies to any steps taken for the purpose of civil proceedings by experts or those who instruct them on or after 5th September 2005.

3.2 It applies to all experts who are, or who may be, governed by CPR Part 35 and to those who instruct them. Experts are governed by Part 35 if they are or have been instructed to give or prepare evidence for the purpose of civil proceedings in a court in England and Wales (CPR 35.2).

3.3 Experts, and those instructing them, should be aware that some cases may be "specialist proceedings" (CPR 49) where there are modifications to the Civil Procedure Rules. Proceedings may also be governed by other Protocols. Further, some courts have published their own Guides which supplement the Civil Procedure Rules for proceedings in those courts. They contain provisions affecting expert evidence. Expert witnesses and those instructing them should be familiar with them when they are relevant.

3.4 Courts may take into account any failure to comply with this Protocol when making orders in relation to costs, interest, time limits, the stay of proceedings and whether to order a party to pay a sum of money into court.

Limitation

3.5 If, as a result of complying with any part of this Protocol, claims would or might be time barred under any provision in the Limitation Act 1980, or any other legislation that imposes a time limit for the bringing an action, claimants may commence proceedings without complying with this Protocol. In such circumstances, claimants who commence proceedings without complying with all, or any part, of this Protocol must apply, giving notice to all other parties, to the court for directions as to the timetable and form of procedure to be adopted, at the same time as they request the court to issue proceedings. The court may consider whether to order a stay of the whole or part of the proceedings pending compliance with this Protocol and may make orders in relation to costs.

4. Duties of experts

4.1 Experts always owe a duty to exercise reasonable skill and care to those instructing them, and to comply with any relevant professional code of ethics. However when they are instructed to give or prepare evidence for the purpose of civil proceedings in England and Wales they have an overriding duty to help the court on matters within their expertise (CPR 35.3). This duty overrides any obligation to the person instructing or paying them. Experts must not serve the exclusive interest of those who retain them.

4.2 Experts should be aware of the overriding objective that courts deal with cases justly. This includes dealing with cases proportionately, expeditiously and fairly (CPR 1.1). Experts are under an obligation to assist the court so as to enable them to deal with cases in accordance with the overriding objective. However the overriding objective does not impose on experts any duty to act as mediators between the parties or require them to trespass on the role of the court in deciding facts.

4.3 Experts should provide opinions which are independent, regardless of the pressures of litigation. In this context, a useful test of 'independence' is that the expert would express the same opinion if given the same instructions by an opposing party. Experts should not take it upon themselves to promote the point of view of the party instructing them or engage in the role of advocates.

4.4 Experts should confine their opinions to matters which are material to the disputes between the parties and provide opinions only in relation to matters which lie within their expertise. Experts should indicate without delay where particular questions or issues fall outside their expertise.

4.5 Experts should take into account all material facts before them at the time that they give their opinion. Their reports should set out those facts and any literature or any other material on which they have relied in forming their opinions. They should indicate if an opinion is provisional, or qualified, or where they consider that further information is required or if, for any other reason, they are not satisfied that an opinion can be expressed finally and without qualification.

4.6 Experts should inform those instructing them without delay of any change in their opinions on any material matter and the reason for it.

4.7 Experts should be aware that any failure by them to comply with the Civil Procedure Rules or court orders or any excessive delay for which they are responsible may result in the parties who instructed them being penalised in costs and even, in extreme cases, being debarred from placing the experts' evidence before the court. In[47] *Phillips v Symes* Peter Smith J held that courts may also make orders for costs (under section 51 of the Supreme Court Act 1981) directly against expert witnesses who by their evidence cause significant expense to be incurred, and do so in flagrant and reckless disregard of their duties to the Court.

5. Conduct of Experts instructed only to advise

5.1 Part 35 only applies where experts are instructed to give opinions which are relied on for the purposes of court proceedings. Advice which the parties do not intend to adduce in litigation is likely to be confidential; the Protocol does not apply in these circumstances.[48,49]

5.2 The same applies where, after the commencement of proceedings, experts are instructed only to advise (e.g. to comment upon a single joint expert's report) and not to give or prepare evidence for use in the proceedings.

5.3 However this Protocol does apply if experts who were formerly instructed only to advise are later instructed to give or prepare evidence for the purpose of civil proceedings.

6. The Need for Experts

6.1 Those intending to instruct experts to give or prepare evidence for the purpose of civil proceedings should consider whether expert evidence is appropriate, taking account of the principles set out in CPR Parts 1 and 35, and in particular whether:

    (a) it is relevant to a matter which is in dispute between the parties.

    (b) it is reasonably required to resolve the proceedings (CPR 35.1);

    (c) the expert has expertise relevant to the issue on which an opinion is sought;

    (d) the expert has the experience, expertise and training appropriate to the value, complexity and importance of the case; and whether

---

[47] *Phillips v Symes* [2004] EWHC 2330 (Ch).
[48] *Carlson v Townsend* [2001] 1 W.L.R. 2415.
[49] *Jackson v Marley Davenport* [2004] 1 W.L.R. 2926.

(e) these objects can be achieved by the appointment of a single joint expert (see section 17 below).

6.2 Although the court's permission is not generally required to instruct an expert, the court's permission is required before experts can be called to give evidence or their evidence can be put in (CPR 35.4).

7. The appointment of experts

7.1 Before experts are formally instructed or the court's permission to appoint named experts is sought, the following should be established:

(a) that they have the appropriate expertise and experience;

(b) that they are familiar with the general duties of an expert;

(c) that they can produce a report, deal with questions and have discussions with other experts within a reasonable time and at a cost proportionate to the matters in issue;

(d) a description of the work required;

(e) whether they are available to attend the trial, if attendance is required; and

(f) there is no potential conflict of interest.

7.2 Terms of appointment should be agreed at the outset and should normally include:

(a) the capacity in which the expert is to be appointed (e.g. party appointed expert, single joint expert or expert advisor);

(b) the services required of the expert (e.g. provision of expert's report, answering questions in writing, attendance at meetings and attendance at court);

(c) time for delivery of the report;

(d) the basis of the expert's charges (either daily or hourly rates and an estimate of the time likely to be required, or a total fee for the services);

(e) travelling expenses and disbursements;

(f) cancellation charges;

(g) any fees for attending court;

(h) time for making the payment; and

(i) whether fees are to be paid by a third party;

(j) if a party is publicly funded, whether or not the expert's charges will be subject to assessment by a costs officer.

7.3 As to the appointment of single joint experts, see section 17 below.

7.4 When necessary, arrangements should be made for dealing with questions to experts and discussions between experts, including any directions given by the court, and provision should be made for the cost of this work.

7.5 Experts should be informed regularly about deadlines for all matters concerning them. Those instructing experts should promptly send them copies of all court orders and directions which may affect the preparation of their reports or any other matters concerning their obligations.

Conditional and Contingency Fees

7.6 Payments contingent upon the nature of the expert evidence given in legal proceedings, or upon the outcome of a case, must not be offered or accepted. To do so would contravene experts' overriding duty to the court and compromise their duty of independence.

7.7 Agreement to delay payment of experts' fees until after the conclusion of cases is permissible as long as the amount of the fee does not depend on the outcome of the case.

8. Instructions

8.1 Those instructing experts should ensure that they give clear instructions, including the following:

    (a) basic information, such as names, addresses, telephone numbers, dates of birth and dates of incidents;

    (b) the nature and extent of the expertise which is called for;

    (c) the purpose of requesting the advice or report, a description of the matter(s) to be investigated, the principal known issues and the identity of all parties;

    (d) the statement(s) of case (if any), those documents which form part of standard disclosure and witness statements which are relevant to the advice or report;

    (e) where proceedings have not been started, whether proceedings are being contemplated and, if so, whether the expert is asked only for advice;

    (f) an outline programme, consistent with good case management and the expert's availability, for the completion and delivery of each stage of the expert's work; and

    (g) where proceedings have been started, the dates of any hearings (including any Case Management Conferences and/or Pre-Trial Reviews), the name of the court, the claim number and the track to which the claim has been allocated.

8.2 Experts who do not receive clear instructions should request clarification and may indicate that they are not prepared to act unless and until such clear instructions are received.

8.3 As to the instruction of single joint experts, see section 17 below.

9. Experts' Acceptance of Instructions

9.1 Experts should confirm without delay whether or not they accept instructions. They should also inform those instructing them (whether on initial instruction or at any later stage) without delay if:

    (a) instructions are not acceptable because, for example, they require work that falls outside their expertise, impose unrealistic deadlines, or are insufficiently clear;

    (b) they consider that instructions are or have become insufficient to complete the work;

    (c) they become aware that they may not be able to fulfil any of the terms of appointment;

    (d) the instructions and/or work have, for any reason, placed them in conflict with their duties as an expert; or

    (e) they are not satisfied that they can comply with any orders that have been made.

9.2 Experts must neither express an opinion outside the scope of their field of expertise, nor accept any instructions to do so.

10. Withdrawal

10.1 Where experts' instructions remain incompatible with their duties, whether through incompleteness, a conflict between their duty to the court and their instructions, or for any other substantial and significant reason, they may consider withdrawing from the case. However, experts should not withdraw without first discussing the position fully with those who instruct them and considering carefully whether it would be more appropriate to make a written request for directions from the court. If experts do withdraw, they must give formal written notice to those instructing them.

11. Experts' Right to ask Court for Directions

11.1 Experts may request directions from the court to assist them in carrying out their functions as experts. Experts should normally discuss such matters with those who instruct them before making any such request. Unless the court otherwise orders, any proposed request for directions should be copied to the party instructing the expert at least seven days before filing any request to the court, and to all other parties at least four days before filing it. (CPR 35.14).

11.2 Requests to the court for directions should be made by letter, containing.

- (a) the title of the claim;
- (b) the claim number of the case;
- (c) the name of the expert;
- (d) full details of why directions are sought; and
- (e) copies of any relevant documentation.

12. Power of the Court to Direct a Party to Provide Information

12.1 If experts consider that those instructing them have not provided information which they require, they may, after discussion with those instructing them and giving notice, write to the court to seek directions (CPR 35.14).

12.2 Experts and those who instruct them should also be aware of CPR 35.9. This provides that where one party has access to information which is not readily available to the other party, the court may direct the party who has access to the information to prepare, file and copy to the other party a document recording the information. If experts require such information which has not been disclosed, they should discuss the position with those instructing them without delay, so that a request for the information can be made, and, if not forthcoming, an application can be made to the court. Unless a document appears to be essential, experts should assess the cost and time involved in the production of a document and whether its provision would be proportionate in the context of the case.

13. Contents of Experts' Reports

13.1 The content and extent of experts' reports should be governed by the scope of their instructions and general obligations, the contents of CPR 35 and PD35 and their overriding duty to the court.

13.2 In preparing reports, experts should maintain professional objectivity and impartiality at all times.

13.3 PD 35, para 2 provides that experts' reports should be addressed to the court and gives detailed directions about the form and content of such reports. All experts and those who instruct them should ensure that they are familiar with these requirements.

13.4 Model forms of Experts' Reports are available from bodies such as the Academy of Experts or the Expert Witness Institute.

13.5 Experts' reports must contain statements that they understand their duty to the court and have complied and will continue to comply with that duty (PD35 para 2.2(9)). They must also be verified by a statement of truth. The form of the statement of truth is as follows:

> "I confirm that insofar as the facts stated in my report are within my own knowledge I have made clear which they are and I believe them to be true, and that the opinions I have expressed represent my true and complete professional opinion."

This wording is mandatory and must not be modified.

Qualifications

13.6 The details of experts' qualifications to be given in reports should be commensurate with the nature and complexity of the case. It may be sufficient merely to state academic and professional qualifications. However, where highly specialised expertise is called for, experts should include the detail of particular training and/or experience that qualifies them to provide that highly specialised evidence.

Tests

13.7 Where tests of a scientific or technical nature have been carried out, experts should state:
  (a) the methodology used; and
  (b) by whom the tests were undertaken and under whose supervision, summarising their respective qualifications and experience.

Reliance on the work of others

13.8 Where experts rely in their reports on literature or other material and cite the opinions of others without having verified them, they must give details of those opinions relied on. It is likely to assist the court if the qualifications of the originator(s) are also stated.

Facts

13.9 When addressing questions of fact and opinion, experts should keep the two separate and discrete.

13.10 Experts must state those facts (whether assumed or otherwise) upon which their opinions are based. They must distinguish clearly between those facts which experts know to be true and those facts which they assume.

13.11 Where there are material facts in dispute experts should express separate opinions on each hypothesis put forward. They should not express a view in favour of one or other disputed version of the facts unless, as a result of particular expertise and experience, they consider one set of facts as being improbable or less probable, in which case they may express that view, and should give reasons for holding it.

Range of opinion

13.12 If the mandatory summary of the range of opinion is based on published sources, experts should explain those sources and, where appropriate, state the qualifications of the originator(s) of the opinions from which they differ, particularly if such opinions represent a well-established school of thought.

13.13 Where there is no available source for the range of opinion, experts may need to express opinions on what they believe to be the range which other experts would arrive at if asked. In those circumstances, experts should make it clear that the range that they summarise is based on their own judgement and explain the basis of that judgement.

Conclusions

13.14 A summary of conclusions is mandatory. The summary should be at the end of the report after all the reasoning. There may be cases, however, where the benefit to the court is heightened by placing a short summary at the beginning of the report whilst giving the full conclusions at the end. For example, it can assist with the comprehension of the analysis and with the absorption of the detailed facts if the court is told at the outset of the direction in which the report's logic will flow in cases

750

involving highly complex matters which fall outside the general knowledge of the court.

Basis of report: material instructions

13.15 The mandatory statement of the substance of all material instructions should not be incomplete or otherwise tend to mislead. The imperative is transparency. The term "instructions" includes all material which solicitors place in front of experts in order to gain advice. The omission from the statement of "off-the-record" oral instructions is not permitted. Courts may allow cross-examination about the instructions if there are reasonable grounds to consider that the statement may be inaccurate or incomplete.

14. After receipt of experts' reports

14.1 Following the receipt of experts' reports, those instructing them should advise the experts as soon as reasonably practicable whether, and if so when, the report will be disclosed to other parties; and, if so disclosed, the date of actual disclosure.

14.2 If experts' reports are to be relied upon, and if experts are to give oral evidence, those instructing them should give the experts the opportunity to consider and comment upon other reports within their area of expertise and which deal with relevant issues at the earliest opportunity.

14.3 Those instructing experts should keep experts informed of the progress of cases, including amendments to statements of case relevant to experts' opinion.

14.4 If those instructing experts become aware of material changes in circumstances or that relevant information within their control was not previously provided to experts, they should without delay instruct experts to review, and if necessary, update the contents of their reports.

15. Amendment of reports

15.1 It may become necessary for experts to amend their reports:
  (a) as a result of an exchange of questions and answers;
  (b) following agreements reached at meetings between experts; or
  (c) where further evidence or documentation is disclosed.

15.2 Experts should not be asked to, and should not, amend, expand or alter any parts of reports in a manner which distorts their true opinion, but may be invited to amend or expand reports to ensure accuracy, internal consistency, completeness and relevance to the issues and clarity. Although experts should generally follow the recommendations of solicitors with regard to the form of reports, they should form their own independent views as to the opinions and contents expressed in their reports and exclude any suggestions which do not accord with their views.

15.3 Where experts change their opinion following a meeting of experts, a simple signed and dated addendum or memorandum to that effect is generally sufficient. In some cases, however, the benefit to the court of having an amended report may justify the cost of making the amendment.

15.4 Where experts significantly alter their opinion, as a result of new evidence or because evidence on which they relied has become unreliable, or for any other reason, they should amend their reports to reflect that fact. Amended reports should include reasons for amendments. In such circumstances those instructing experts should inform other parties as soon as possible of any change of opinion.

15.5 When experts intend to amend their reports, they should inform those instructing them without delay and give reasons. They should provide the amended version (or an addendum or memorandum) clearly marked as such as quickly as possible.

16. Written Questions to Experts

16.1 The procedure for putting written questions to experts (CPR 35.6) is intended to facilitate the clarification of opinions and issues after experts' reports have been served. Experts have a duty to provide answers to questions properly put. Where they fail to do so, the court may impose sanctions against the party instructing the expert, and, if, there is continued non-compliance, debar a party from relying on the report. Experts should copy their answers to those instructing them.

16.2 Experts' answers to questions automatically become part of their reports. They are covered by the statement of truth and form part of the expert evidence.

16.3 Where experts believe that questions put are not properly directed to the clarification of the report, or are disproportionate, or have been asked out of time, they should discuss the questions with those instructing them and, if appropriate, those asking the questions. Attempts should be made to resolve such problems without the need for an application to the court for directions.

Written requests for directions in relation to questions

16.4 If those instructing experts do not apply to the court in respect of questions, but experts still believe that questions are improper or out of time, experts may file written requests with the court for directions to assist in carrying out their functions as experts (CPR 35.14). See Section 11 above.

17. Single Joint Experts

17.1 CPR 35 and PD35 deal extensively with the instruction and use of joint experts by the parties and the powers of the court to order their use (see CPR 35.7 and 35.8, PD35, para 5).

17.2 The Civil Procedure Rules encourage the use of joint experts. Wherever possible a joint report should be obtained. Consideration should therefore be given by all parties to the appointment of single joint experts in all cases where a court might direct such an appointment. Single joint experts are the norm in cases allocated to the small claims track and the fast track.

17.3 Where, in the early stages of a dispute, examinations, investigations, tests, site inspections, experiments, preparation of photographs, plans or other similar preliminary expert tasks are necessary, consideration should be given to the instruction of a single joint expert, especially where such matters are not, at that stage, expected to be contentious as between the parties. The objective of such an appointment should be to agree or to narrow issues.

17.4 Experts who have previously advised a party (whether in the same case or otherwise) should only be proposed as single joint experts if other parties are given all relevant information about the previous involvement.

17.5 The appointment of a single joint expert does not prevent parties from instructing their own experts to advise (but the costs of such expert advisers may not be recoverable in the case).

Joint instructions

17.6 The parties should try to agree joint instructions to single joint experts, but, in default of agreement, each party may give instructions. In particular, all parties should try to agree what documents should be included with instructions and what assumptions single joint experts should make.

17.7 Where the parties fail to agree joint instructions, they should try to agree where the areas of disagreement lie and their instructions should make this clear. If separate instructions are given, they should be copied at the same time to the other instructing parties.

17.8 Where experts are instructed by two or more parties, the terms of appointment should, unless the court has directed otherwise, or the parties have agreed otherwise, include:

    (a) a statement that all the instructing parties are jointly and severally liable to pay the experts' fees and, accordingly, that experts' invoices should be sent simultaneously to all instructing parties or their solicitors (as appropriate); and

    (b) a statement as to whether any order has been made limiting the amount of experts' fees and expenses (CPR 35.8(4)(a)).

17.9 Where instructions have not been received by the expert from one or more of the instructing parties the expert should give notice (normally at least 7 days) of a deadline to all instructing parties for the receipt by the expert of such instructions. Unless the instructions are received within the deadline the expert may begin work. In the event that instructions are received after the deadline but before the signing off of the report the expert should consider whether it is practicable to comply with those instructions without adversely affecting the timetable set for delivery of the report and in such a manner as to comply with the proportionality principle. An expert who decides to issue a report without taking into account instructions received after the deadline should inform the parties who may apply to the court for directions. In either event the report must show clearly that the expert did not receive instructions within the deadline, or, as the case may be, at all.

Conduct of the single joint expert

17.10 Single joint experts should keep all instructing parties informed of any material steps that they may be taking by, for example, copying all correspondence to those instructing them.

17.11 Single joint experts are Part 35 experts and so have an overriding duty to the court. They are the parties' appointed experts and therefore owe an equal duty to all parties. They should maintain independence, impartiality and transparency at all times.

17.12 Single joint experts should not attend any meeting or conference which is not a joint one, unless all the parties have agreed in writing or the court has directed that such a meeting may be held[50] and who is to pay the experts' fees for the meeting.

17.13 Single joint experts may request directions from the court—see Section 11 above.

17.14 Single joint experts should serve their reports simultaneously on all instructing parties. They should provide a single report even though they may have received instructions which contain areas of conflicting fact or allegation. If conflicting instructions lead to different opinions (for example, because the instructions require experts to make different assumptions of fact), reports may need to contain more than one set of opinions on any issue. It is for the court to determine the facts.

Cross-examination

17.15 Single joint experts do not normally give oral evidence at trial but if they do, all parties may cross-examine them. In general written questions (CPR 35.6) should be put to single joint experts before requests are made for them to attend court for the purpose of cross-examination.[51]

---

[50] *Peet v Mid Kent Area Healthcare NHS Trust* [2002] 1 W.L.R. 210.
[51] *Daniels v Walker* [2000] 1 W.L.R. 1382.

18. Discussions between Experts

18.1 The court has powers to direct discussions between experts for the purposes set out in the Rules (CPR 35.12). Parties may also agree that discussions take place between their experts.

18.2 Where single joint experts have been instructed but parties have, with the permission of the court, instructed their own additional Part 35 experts, there may, if the court so orders or the parties agree, be discussions between the single joint experts and the additional Part 35 experts. Such discussions should be confined to those matters within the remit of the additional Part 35 experts or as ordered by the court.

18.3 The purpose of discussions between experts should be, wherever possible, to:

    (a)   identify and discuss the expert issues in the proceedings:

    (b)   reach agreed opinions on those issues, and, if that is not possible, to narrow the issues in the case;

    (c)   identify those issues on which they agree and disagree and summarise their reasons for disagreement on any issue; and

    (d)   identify what action, if any, may be taken to resolve any of the outstanding issues between the parties.

Arrangements for discussions between experts

18.4 Arrangements for discussions between experts should be proportionate to the value of cases. In small claims and fast-track cases there should not normally be meetings between experts. Where discussion is justified in such cases, telephone discussion or an exchange of letters should, in the interests of proportionality, usually suffice. In multi-track cases, discussion may be face to face, but the practicalities or the proportionality principle may require discussions to be by telephone or video conference.

18.5 The parties, their lawyers and experts should co-operate to produce the agenda for any discussion between experts, although primary responsibility for preparation of the agenda should normally lie with the parties' solicitors.

18.6 The agenda should indicate what matters have been agreed and summarise concisely those which are in issue. It is often helpful for it to include questions to be answered by the experts. If agreement cannot be reached promptly or a party is unrepresented, the court may give directions for the drawing up of the agenda. The agenda should be circulated to experts and those instructing them to allow sufficient time for the experts to prepare for the discussion.

18.7 Those instructing experts must not instruct experts to avoid reaching agreement (or to defer doing so) on any matter within the experts' competence. Experts are not permitted to accept such instructions.

18.8 The parties' lawyers may only be present at discussions between experts if all the parties agree or the court so orders. If lawyers do attend, they should not normally intervene except to answer questions put to them by the experts or to advise about the law.[52]

18.9 The content of discussions between experts should not be referred to at trial unless the parties agree (CPR 35.12(4)). It is good practice for any such agreement to be in writing.

18.10 At the conclusion of any discussion between experts, a statement should be prepared setting out:

    (a)   a list of issues that have been agreed, including, in each instance, the basis of agreement;

---

[52] *Hubbard v Lambeth, Southwark and Lewisham HA* [2001] EWCA 1455.

   (b) a list of issues that have not been agreed, including, in each instance, the basis of disagreement;

   (c) a list of any further issues that have arisen that were not included in the original agenda for discussion;

   (d) a record of further action, if any, to be taken or recommended, including as appropriate the holding of further discussions between experts.

18.11 The statement should be agreed and signed by all the parties to the discussion as soon as may be practicable.

18.12 Agreements between experts during discussions do not bind the parties unless the parties expressly agree to be bound by the agreement (CPR 35.12(5)). However, in view of the overriding objective, parties should give careful consideration before refusing to be bound by such an agreement and be able to explain their refusal should it become relevant to the issue of costs.

19. Attendance of Experts at Court

19.1 Experts instructed in cases have an obligation to attend court if called upon to do so and accordingly should ensure that those instructing them are always aware of their dates to be avoided and take all reasonable steps to be available.

19.2 Those instructing experts should:

   (a) ascertain the availability of experts before trial dates are fixed;

   (b) keep experts updated with timetables (including the dates and times experts are to attend) and the location of the court;

   (c) give consideration, where appropriate, to experts giving evidence via a video-link.

   (d) inform experts immediately if trial dates are vacated.

19.3 Experts should normally attend court without the need for the service of witness summonses, but on occasion they may be served to require attendance (CPR 34). The use of witness summonses does not affect the contractual or other obligations of the parties to pay experts' fees.

APPENDIX 3

Forms

The CPR include a large number of prescribed forms, and in addition practice **C.01** forms have been produced by the different divisions and specialist courts of the High Court. Those most relevant to this work are listed below, and they are also set out in full text following the list.

Prescribed Forms

N20 Witness Summons
N21 Order for Examination of Deponent (before the hearing)
N244 Application Notice
N265 List of Documents: Standard Disclosure
N268 Notice to Prove Documents at Trial

High Court Prescribed Forms

No. 32 Order for examination within jurisdiction of witness before trial (rule 34.8) No. 33 Application for issue of letter of request to judicial authority out of jurisdiction (rule 34.8) No. 34 Order for issue of letter of request to judicial authority out of jurisdiction (rule 34.13) No. 35 Letter of request for examination of witness out of jurisdiction (rule 34.13) No. 37 Order for appointment of special examiner to take evidence of witness out of jurisdiction (rule 34.13(4) PD para 5)

High Court Practice Forms

PF56 Request for further information or clarification with provision for response
PF57 Application for further information or clarification
PF58 Order for further information or clarification
       Miscellaneous Forms: Freezing and Search Orders

Commercial Court Guide

Appendix 5 Draft Freezing Injunctions and Draft Search Order Draft
N265(CC)   List of Documents: Standard Disclosure

Patents Court Guide

Standard Form Minute of Order for Directions

Technology and Construction Court Practice Direction

Appendix 2 Case Management Conference Directions Form

C.02

Witness Summons

To

In the	
Claim No.	
Claimant (including ref)	
Defendant (including ref)	
Issued on	

You are summoned to attend at *(court address)*

on   of   at   (am)(pm)

(and each following day of the hearing until the court tells you that you are no longer required.)

☐ to give evidence in respect of the above claim

☐ to produce the following document(s) *(give details)*

The sum of £   is paid or offered to you with this summons. This is to cover your travelling expenses to and from court and includes an amount by way of compensation for loss of time.

This summons was issued on the application of the claimant (defendant) or the claimant's (defendant's) solicitor whose name, address and reference number is:

Do not ignore this summons

If you were offered money for travel expenses and compensation for loss of time, at the time it was served on you, you must –

- attend court on the date and time shown and/or produce documents as required by the summons; and

- take an oath or affirm as required for the purposes of answering questions about your evidence or the documents you have been asked to produce.

If you do not comply with this summons you will be liable, in county court proceedings, to a fine. In the High Court, disobedience of a witness summons is a contempt of court and you may be fined or imprisoned for contempt. You may also be liable to pay any wasted costs that arise because of your non-compliance.

If you wish to set aside or vary this witness summons, you may make an application to the court that issued it.

The court office at

is open between 10 am and 4 pm Monday to Friday. When corresponding with the court, please address forms or letters to the Court Manager and quote the claim number.

N20 Witness Summons (September 2002)   Crown Copyright. Reproduced by Sweet & Maxwell Ltd

Certificate of service

Claim No.	

I certify that the summons of which this is a true copy, was served by posting to _____

(the witness) on _____ at the address stated on the summons in accordance with the request

of the applicant or his solicitor.

I enclosed a P.O. for £   for the witness's expenses and compensation for loss of time.

Signed _____
Officer of the Court

C.03

Application Notice

	In the

You should provide this information for listing the application

1. How do you wish to have your application dealt with

a) at a hearing? ☐

b) at a telephone conference? ☐ } *complete all questions below*

c) without a hearing? ☐ *complete Qs 5 and 6 below*

Claim no.	
Warrant no. (If applicable)	
Claimant (including ref.)	

2. Give a time estimate for the hearing/conference
———(hours)———(mins)

3. Is this agreed by all parties? ☐ Yes ☐ No

4. Give dates of any trial period or fixed trial date ————

5. Level of judge

6. Parties to be served ————

Defendant(s) (including ref.)	
Date	

Note You must complete Parts A **and** B, **and** Part C if applicable. Send any relevant fee and the completed application to the court with any draft order, witness statement or other evidence; and sufficient copies for service on each respondent.

Part A

1. Enter your full name, or name of solicitor

I (We)[1]   (on behalf of)(the claimant)(the defendant)

2. State clearly what order you are seeking and if possible attach a draft

intend to apply for an order (a draft of which is attached) that[2]

3. Briefly set out why you are seeking the order. Include the material facts on which you rely, identifying any rule or statutory provision

because[3]

Part B

I (We) wish to rely on: *tick one box*

the attached (witness statement)(affidavit) ☐   my statement of case ☐

4. If you are not already a party to the proceedings, you must provide an address for service of documents

evidence in Part C in support of my application ☐

Signed [_____]

(Applicant)('s Solicitor)('s litigation friend)

Position or office held [_____]

(if signing on behalf of firm or company)

Address to which documents about this claim should be sent (including reference if appropriate)[4]

		if applicable
	fax no.	
	DX no.	
Tel.no. Postcode	e-mail	

The court office at

is open from 10am to 4pm Monday to Friday. When corresponding with the court please address forms or letters to the Court Manager and quote the claim number.

N244 Application Notice (April 2000)   Crown Copyright. Reproduced by Sweet & Maxwell Ltd

Part C   Claim No. [   ]

I (We) wish to rely on the following evidence in support of this application:

Statement of Truth

*(I believe) *(The applicant believes) that the facts stated in Part C are true

delete as appropriate

Signed [   ]   **Position or office held** [   ]

(Applicant)('s Solicitor)('s litigation friend)   (if signing on behalf of firm or company)

Date [   ]

C.04

List of documents: standard disclosure

Notes

- The rules relating to standard disclosure are contained in Part 31 of the Civil Procedure Rules.
- Documents to be included under standard disclosure are contained in Rule 31.6
- A document has or will have been in your control if you have or have had possession, or a right of possession, of it **or** a right to inspect or take copies of it.

In the	
Claim No.	
Claimant (including ref)	
Defendant (including ref)	
Date	

Disclosure Statement

I, the above named

☐ Claimant   ☐ Defendant

☐ **Party** (if party making disclosure is a company, firm or other organisation identify here who the person making the disclosure statement is and why he is the appropriate person to make it)

state that I have carried out a reasonable and proportionate search to locate all the documents which I am

required to disclose under the order made by the court on (date of order)

☐ I did not search for documents:-

☐ pre-dating

☐ located elsewhere than

☐ in categories other than

☐ for electronic documents

☐ I carried out a search for electronic documents contained on or created by the following: (list what was searched and extent of search)

N265 Standard disclosure (October 2005)

763

☐ I did not search for the following:-

☐ documents created before [   ]

documents contained on or created by the ☐ Claimant ☐ Defendant

☐ PCs   ☐ portable data storage media

☐ databases   ☐ servers

☐ back-up tapes   ☐ off-site storage

☐ mobile phones   ☐ laptops

☐ notebooks   ☐ handheld devices

☐ PDA devices

documents contained on or created by the ☐ Claimant ☐ Defendant

☐ mail files   ☐ document files

☐ calendar files   ☐ web-based applications

☐ spreadsheet files   ☐ graphic and presentation files

documents other than by reference to the following keyword(s)/concepts
(delete if your search was not confined to specific keywords or concepts)

[   ]

I certify that I understand the duty of disclosure and to the best of my knowledge I have carried out that duty. I further certify that the list of documents set out in or attached to this form, is a complete list of all documents which are or have been in my control and which I am obliged under the order to disclose.

I understand that I must inform the court and the other parties immediately if any further document required to be disclosed by Rule 31.6 comes into my control at any time before the conclusion of the case.

☐ I have not permitted inspection of documents within the category or class of documents (as set out below) required to be disclosed under Rule 31(6)(b)or (c) on the grounds that to do so would be disproportionate to the issues in the case.

[   ]

Signed [   ]   **Date** [   ]

(Claimant)(Defendant)('s litigation friend)

List and number here, in a convenient order, the documents (or bundles of documents if of the same nature, e.g. invoices) in your control, which you do not object to being inspected. Give a short description of each document or bundle so that it can be identified, and say if it is kept elsewhere i.e. with a bank or solicitor

I have control of the documents numbered and listed here. I do not object to you inspecting them/producing copies.

List and number here, as above, the documents in your control which you object to being inspected. (Rule 31.19)

I have control of the documents numbered and listed here, but I object to you inspecting them:

Say what your objections are

I object to you inspecting these documents because:

List and number here, the documents you once had in your control, but which you no longer have. For each document listed, say when it was last in your control and where it is now.

I have had the documents numbered and listed below, but they are no longer in my control.

C.05

Notice to prove documents at trial

In the	
Claim No.	
Claimant (include Ref.)	
Defendant (include Ref.)	

I (We) give notice that you are requested to prove the following documents disclosed under CPR Part 31 in this claim at the trial:

Signed

(Claimant)(Defendant)('s Solicitor)

Position or office held
(If signing on behalf of firm or company)

Date

The court office at

is open between 10 am and 4 pm Monday to Friday. Address all communication to the Court Manager quoting the claim number

N268 - W3 Notice to prove documents at trial (April 1999)   Crown Copyright. Reproduced by Sweet & Maxwell Ltd

No. 32

Order for examination within jurisdiction of witness before trial (rule 34.8)

IN THE HIGH COURT OF JUSTICE
[   ] **DIVISION**
[   ] **District Registry**

Claim No.

Before *(Judge/Master/District Judge)* [sitting in Private]

Claimant

Defendant

AN APPLICATION was made by [application notice/letter] dated *(date) or* by [Counsel][solicitor] for *(party)* and was attended by (   )

The Master [District Judge] read the written evidence filed

IT IS ORDERED that:

1.   *(name)* a witness on behalf of the *(party)* be examined orally on oath or affirmation before [a Judge][a Master][a District Judge][an examiner of the court][*(name)* whom the court hereby appoints].

2.   the *(party's)* solicitor is to give to the *(party's)* solicitor (   ) days notice in writing of the time and place where the examination is to take place *(or as ordered)*

3.   the depositions taken at the examination be filed in the Central Office of the Supreme Court *(or as appropriate- see note below)* and that official copies of them may be read and given in evidence at the trial of these proceedings, saving all just exceptions.

4.   the costs of this application are [summarily assessed in the sum of £   ] [to be the subject of a detailed assessment] and to be paid by *(party)*.

Dated

Note- the depositions should be filed in the court office where the claim is proceeding.

C.06
No. 33
Application for issue of letter of request to judicial authority out of jurisdiction (rule 34.13)

Parties should use form PF 244/N244 and add the following text:

" ... ... for an order that:

1. a letter of request be issued to the proper judicial authority of (*country*) for the examination of (*names of witnesses*) on the (*party*)'s behalf at (*address*) in (*country*).
2. the claim be stayed until the return of the letter of request and examination.
3. the costs of this application, letter of request and examination be assessed and paid to (*party*)."

No. 34
Order for issue of letter of request to judicial authority out of jurisdiction
(rule 34.13)

C.07

IN THE HIGH COURT OF JUSTICE
QUEEN'S BENCH DIVISION
[   ] **District Registry**

Claim No.

Before (*Master/District Judge*)

Claimant

Defendant

An Application was made by [application notice/letter] dated (*date*) *or* by [Counsel] [solicitor] for (*party*) and was attended by (   )

The Master [District Judge] read the written evidence filed

IT IS ORDERED that:

1. a letter of request be issued directed to the proper judicial authority of (*country*) for the examination of the following witnesses, namely:
    (*give names and addresses of witnesses*)

2. the depositions of those witnesses when received be filed in the Central Office of the Supreme Court (*or as appropriate- see note below*) and that official copies of them may be read and given in evidence at the trial of these proceedings, saving all just exceptions.

[3. the trial of these proceedings be stayed until the depositions are filed.]

4. the costs of and caused by this application and the letter of request and examination are [summarily assessed in the sum of £][to be the subject of a detailed assessment] and to be paid by (*party*).

Dated

Note- the depositions should be filed in the court office where the claim is proceeding.

769

C.08

No. 35
Letter of request for examination of witness out of jurisdiction
(rule 34.13)

To the Competent Judicial Authority of (*name of court*) in (*country*)

I (*name*) Senior Master of the Queen's Bench Division of the Supreme Court of England and Wales respectfully request the assistance of your court with regard to the following matters.

1. A claim is now pending in the [   ] Division of the High Court of Justice in England and Wales [County Court] entitled as follows:
   (*set out full title and claim number*)
   in which (*name*) of (*address*) is the claimant and (*name*) of (*address*) is the defendant.

2. The names and addresses of the representatives or agents of the parties are:
   (*set out names and addresses of representatives of the parties*).

3. The claim by the claimant is for:-
   (a) (*set out the nature of the claim*)
   (b) (*the relief sought*) and
   (c) (*a summary of the facts*).

4. It is necessary for the purposes of justice and for the due determination of the matters in dispute between the parties that you cause the following witnesses, who are resident within your jurisdiction, to be examined. The names and addresses of the witnesses are as follows:-

5. The witnesses should be examined on oath or if that is not possible within your laws or is impossible of performance by reason of the internal practice and procedure of your court or by reason of practical difficulties, they should be examined in accordance with whatever procedure your laws provide for in these matters.

6. *Either:*
   The witnesses should be examined in accordance with the list of questions annexed hereto.
   Or:
   The witnesses should be examined regarding (*set out full details of evidence sought*)
   (*N.B. Where the witness is required to produce documents, these should be clearly identified.*)

7. I would ask that you cause me, or the agents of the parties (if appointed), to be informed of the date and place where the examination is to take place.

8. Finally, I request that you will cause the evidence of the said witnesses to be reduced into writing and all documents produced on such examinations to be duly marked for identification and that you will further be pleased to

authenticate such examinations by the seal of your court or in such other way as is in accordance with your procedure and return the written evidence and documents produced to me addressed as follows:-

Senior Master of the Queen's Bench Division
Royal Courts of Justice
Strand
London WC2A 2LL
England

Dated

Signed:

Senior Master of the Queen's Bench Division

C.09

No. 37
Order for appointment of special examiner to take evidence of witness out of jurisdiction (rule 34.13(4) PD para. 5)

IN THE HIGH COURT OF JUSTICE
QUEEN'S BENCH DIVISION
[   ] District Registry

Claim No.

Before (*Master/District Judge*) [sitting in Private]

Claimant

Defendant

An Application was made by [application notice/letter] dated (*date*) *or* by [Counsel] [solicitor] for (*party*) and was attended by (   )

The Master [District Judge] read the written evidence filed

IT IS ORDERED that:

1.   the British Consul or his deputy at (*place*) is appointed as special examiner for the purpose of taking the examination, cross-examination and re-examination orally, on oath or affirmation, of (*names of witnesses*) on the part of (*party*) at (*place*) in (*country*). The examiner shall not exercise any compulsory powers but may invite the attendance of witnesses and the production of documents. Otherwise the examination shall be taken in accordance with the English procedure.

2.   the solicitors for the (*party*) give to the solicitors for the (*party*) [ ] days notice in writing of the date on which they propose to send out this order to (*country*) for execution, and that [ ] days after service of that notice the solicitors for the parties respectively exchange the names of their agents at (*place*) to whom notice relating to the examination of the witnesses may be sent.

3.   the agent of the party on whose behalf the witness is to be examined must give to the agent of the other party [ ] days notice (exclusive of Sundays) of the examination, before the examination of any witness under this order.

4.   the depositions when taken together with any documents referred to in them, or certified copies of those documents or of extracts from them be sent by the

examiner under seal to the Senior Master of the Supreme Court of England and Wales, Royal Courts of Justice, Strand, London WC2A 2LL (*or as appropriate- see note below*) to be filed in the Central Office (*or as appropriate- see note below*).

5.   either party has permission to read and give the depositions in evidence at the trial of these proceedings, saving all just exceptions.

[6.   the trial of these proceedings be stayed until the depositions are filed.]

7.   the costs of and caused by this application and the examination are [summarily assessed in the sum of £   ][to be the subject of a detailed assessment] and to be paid by (*party*).

Dated

Note- Where appropriate the depositions should be sent to the Admiralty Registrar at the Royal Courts of Justice, the District Judge of a District Registry of the High Court or the Senior District Judge of the Family Division, First Avenue House, Holborn, London. and should be filed in the appropriate court office.

C.10 # PF 56

Request for further information
(CPR Part 18 and Part 18 Practice Direction)

In the High Court of Justice
[   ] **Division**
[   ] **District Registry**
[   ] **County Court**

Claim No.

Claimant

Defendant

To [Claimant][Defendant]['s Solicitor]

You are requested to provide the following clarification or information under CPR Part 18 and the Part 18 Practice Direction by (*date*):-

Request:	Response:
1.*	1.*

* in numerical sequence

continued overleaf

Request:	Response:

Signed
    (Claimant)(Defendant)('s Solicitor)

Position or office held
(If signing on behalf of firm or company)

Date

Applicant's/applicant's solicitor's address, or DX or e-mail.	TO:- Respondent/Respondent's solicitor of (address)
Ref: Tel no: Fax no:	Ref: Tel no: Fax no:

The Statement of truth is to be completed by the Responding Party when responding on this form.

Statement of truth
*(I believe)(The [Claimant][Defendant] believes) that the facts contained in this Response are true.
* I am duly authorised by the [Claimant][Defendant] to sign this statement

Full
name _____

Name of [claimant][defendant]'s solicitor's firm _____

signed_____position or office held_____
*(Claimant)(Defendant)(Litigation friend)(solicitor)   (if signing on behalf of firm or company)
* delete as appropriate

C.11

PF 57
Application for clarification or further information
(Part 18; PD 18 para.5)

Parties should use form PF 244/N244 and include in Part A the following:

" ... ... for an order that the (*party*) give [clarification of][further information in relation to] the matter(s) set out [on the attached Request] [below]."

Parties should set out the matter(s) requiring clarification/further information using separate numbered paragraphs, and, where a request relates to a document, identify the document and (if relevant) the paragraph or words to which it relates.

Where a Request has been made, the Request together with any response to it, should be attached to the application notice.

If a Request for further information or clarification has not been made, the parties should state in Part B or C the reason why not.

If evidence is relied on in support of the application, it may be included in Part C.

PF 58
Order for clarification or further information (Rule 18.1)

C.12

IN THE HIGH COURT OF JUSTICE
[   ] DIVISION
[   ] District Registry

Claim No.

Before (*Master or District Judge*) [sitting in Private]

Claimant

Defendant

An Application was made by [application notice/letter] dated (*date*) *or* by [Counsel] [solicitor] for (*party*) and was attended by ( )

The Master [District Judge] read the written evidence filed

IT IS ORDERED that:

1.   the (*party*) provide by (*date*) the following [clarification] [further informa-
        tion] [as requested by (*party*) in the attached Request dated (*date*) initialled
        by the [Master][District Judge]] *or* [as set out below:]

2.   the costs of this application are [summarily assessed in the sum of £   ]
        [to be the subject of a detailed assessment] and to be paid by

        Dated

Forms of Freezing Injunction and Search Order
adapted for use in the Commercial Court

C.13

FREEZING INJUNCTION

IN THE HIGH COURT OF JUSTICE
QUEEN'S BENCH DIVISION
COMMERCIAL COURT

Before The Honourable Mr Justice [   ]

Claim No.

BETWEEN

Claimant(s)

–and–

Defendant(s)

Applicant(s)

Respondent(s)

PENAL NOTICE

If you [   ][1] disobey this order you may be held to be in contempt of court and may be imprisoned, fined or have your assets seized.

Any other person who knows of this order and does anything which helps or permits the Respondent to breach the terms of this order may also be held to be in contempt of court and may be imprisoned, fined or have their assets seized.

THIS ORDER

1. This is a Freezing Injunction made against [   ] ("the Respondent") on [   ] by Mr Justice [   ] on the application of [   ] ("the Applicant"). The Judge read the Affidavits listed in Schedule A and accepted the undertakings set out in Schedule B at the end of this Order.

2. This order was made at a hearing without notice to the Respondent. The Respondent has a right to apply to the court to vary or discharge the order—see paragraph 13 below.

3. There will be a further hearing in respect of this order on [   ] ("the return date").

---

[1] Insert name of Respondent(s).

778

4.   If there is more than one Respondent —

    (a)   unless otherwise stated, references in this order to "the Respondent" mean both or all of them; and

    (b)   this order is effective against any Respondent on whom it is served or who is given notice of it.

FREEZING INJUNCTION

[For injunction limited to assets in England and Wales]

5.   Until the return date or further order of the court, the Respondent must not remove from England and Wales or in any way dispose of, deal with or diminish the value of any of his assets which are in England and Wales up to the value of £   .

[For worldwide injunction]

5.   Until the return date or further order of the court, the Respondent must not —

    (1)   remove from England and Wales any of his assets which are in England and Wales up to the value of £   ; or

    (2)   in any way dispose of, deal with or diminish the value of any of his assets whether they are in or outside England and Wales up to the same value.

[For either form of injunction]

6.   Paragraph 5 applies to all the Respondent's assets whether or not they are in his own name and whether they are solely or jointly owned. For the purpose of this order the Respondent's assets include any asset which he has the power, directly or indirectly, to dispose of or deal with as if it were his own. The Respondent is to be regarded as having such power if a third party holds or controls the asset in accordance with his direct or indirect instructions.

7.   This prohibition includes the following assets in particular —

    (a)   the property known as *[title/address]* or the net sale money after payment of any mortgages if it has been sold;

    (b)   the property and assets of the Respondent's business [known as *[name]* [carried on at *[address]*]] or the sale money if any of them have been sold; and

    (c)   any money in the account numbered *[account number]* at *[title/address]*.

[For injunction limited to assets in England and Wales]

8. If the total value free of charges or other securities ("unencumbered value") of the Respondent's assets in England and Wales exceeds £ , the Respondent may remove any of those assets from England and Wales or may dispose of or deal with them so long as the total unencumbered value of his assets still in England and Wales remains above £ .

[For worldwide injunction]

8. (1) If the total value free of charges or other securities ("unencumbered value") of the Respondent's assets in England and Wales exceeds £ , the Respondent may remove any of those assets from England and Wales or may dispose of or deal with them so long as the total unencumbered value of the Respondent's assets still in England and Wales remains above £ .

    (2) If the total unencumbered value of the Respondent's assets in England and Wales does not exceed £ , the Respondent must not remove any of those assets from England and Wales and must not dispose of or deal with any of them. If the Respondent has other assets outside England and Wales, he may dispose of or deal with those assets outside England and Wales so long as the total unencumbered value of all his assets whether in or outside England and Wales remains above £ .

PROVISION OF INFORMATION

9. (1) Unless paragraph (2) applies, the Respondent must [immediately] [within hours of service of this order] and to the best of his ability inform the Applicant's solicitors of all his assets [in England and Wales] [worldwide] [exceeding £ in value] whether in his own name or not and whether solely or jointly owned, giving the value, location and details of all such assets.

    (2) If the provision of any of this information is likely to incriminate the Respondent, he may be entitled to refuse to provide it, but is recommended to take legal advice before refusing to provide the information. Wrongful refusal to provide the information is contempt of court and may render the Respondent liable to be imprisoned, fined or have his assets seized.

10. Within [ ] working days after being served with this order, the Respondent must swear and serve on the Applicant's solicitors an affidavit setting out the above information.

Exceptions to this Order

11. (1) This order does not prohibit the Respondent from spending £ a week towards his ordinary living expenses and also £ [*or* a reasonable sum] on legal advice and representation. [But

before spending any money the Respondent must tell the Applicant's legal representatives where the money is to come from.]

[(2) This order does not prohibit the Respondent from dealing with or disposing of any of his assets in the ordinary and proper course of business.]

(3) The Respondent may agree with the Applicant's legal representatives that the above spending limits should be increased or that this order should be varied in any other respect, but any agreement must be in writing.

(4) The order will cease to have effect if the Respondent—

    (a)   provides security by paying the sum of £   into court, to be held to the order of the court; or

    (b)   makes provision for security in that sum by another method agreed with the Applicant's legal representatives.

Costs

12.   The costs of this application are reserved to the judge hearing the application on the return date.

Variation or Discharge of this Order

13.   Anyone served with or notified of this order may apply to the court at any time to vary or discharge this order (or so much of it as affects that person), but they must first inform the Applicant's solicitors. If any evidence is to be relied upon in support of the application, the substance of it must be communicated in writing to the Applicant's solicitors in advance.

Interpretation of this Order

14.   A Respondent who is an individual who is ordered not to do something must not do it himself or in any other way. He must not do it through others acting on his behalf or on his instructions or with his encouragement.

15.   A Respondent which is not an individual which is ordered not to do something must not do it itself or by its directors, officers, partners, employees or agents or in any other way.

Parties other than the Applicant and Respondent

16.   Effect of this order

It is a contempt of court for any person notified of this order knowingly to assist in or permit a breach of this order. Any person doing so may be imprisoned, fined or have their assets seized.

17.   **Set off by banks**

This injunction does not prevent any bank from exercising any right of set off it may have in respect of any facility which it gave to the Respondent before it was notified of this order.

18.   **Withdrawals by the Respondent**

No bank need enquire as to the application or proposed application of any money withdrawn by the Respondent if the withdrawal appears to be permitted by this order.

[For worldwide injunction]

19.   **Persons outside England and Wales**

(1)   Except as provided in paragraph (2) below, the terms of this order do not affect or concern anyone outside the jurisdiction of this court.

(2)   The terms of this order will affect the following persons in a country or state outside the jurisdiction of this court—

   (a)   the Respondent or his officer or agent appointed by power of attorney;

   (b)   any person who—
      (i)   is subject to the jurisdiction of this court;
      (ii)   has been given written notice of this order at his residence or place of business within the jurisdiction of this court; and
      (iii) is able to prevent acts or omissions outside the jurisdiction of this court which constitute or assist in a breach of the terms of this order; and

   (c)   any other person, only to the extent that this order is declared enforceable by or is enforced by a court in that country or state.

[For worldwide injunction]

20.   **Assets located outside England and Wales**

Nothing in this order shall, in respect of assets located outside England and Wales, prevent any third party from complying with—

(1)   what it reasonably believes to be its obligations, contractual or otherwise, under the laws and obligations of the country or state in which those assets are situated or under the proper law of any contract between itself and the Respondent; and

(2)   any orders of the courts of that country or state, provided that reasonable notice of any application for such an order is given to the Applicant's solicitors.

Communications with the Court

All communications to the court about this order should be sent to Room EB09, Royal Courts of Justice, Strand, London WC2A 2LL quoting the case number. The telephone number is 020 7947 6826.

The offices are open between 10 a.m. and 4.30 p.m. Monday to Friday.

Schedule A

Affidavits

The Applicant relied on the following affidavits—

	[name]	[number of affidavit]	[date sworn]	[filed on behalf of]
(1)				
(2)				

Schedule B

Undertakings given to the Court by the Applicant

(1) If the court later finds that this order has caused loss to the Respondent, and decides that the Respondent should be compensated for that loss, the Applicant will comply with any order the court may make.

[(2) The Applicant will—

    (a) on or before *[date]* cause a written guarantee in the sum of £   to be issued from a bank with a place of business within England or Wales, in respect of any order the court may make pursuant to paragraph (1) above; and

    (b) immediately upon issue of the guarantee, cause a copy of it to be served on the Respondent.]

(3) As soon as practicable the Applicant will issue and serve a claim form [in the form of the draft produced to the court] [claiming the appropriate relief].

(4) The Applicant will [swear and file an affidavit] [cause an affidavit to be sworn and filed] [substantially in the terms of the draft affidavit produced to the court] [confirming the substance of what was said to the court by the Applicant's counsel/solicitors].

(5) The Applicant will serve upon the Respondent [together with this order] [as soon as practicable]—

    (i) copies of the affidavits and exhibits containing the evidence relied upon by the Applicant, and any other documents provided to the court on the making of the application;

(ii) the claim form; and
(iii) an application notice for continuation of the order.

[(6) Anyone notified of this order will be given a copy of it by the Applicant's legal representatives.]

(7) The Applicant will pay the reasonable costs of anyone other than the Respondent which have been incurred as a result of this order including the costs of finding out whether that person holds any of the Respondent's assets and if the court later finds that this order has caused such person loss, and decides that such person should be compensated for that loss, the Applicant will comply with any order the court may make.

(8) If this order ceases to have effect (for example, if the Respondent provides security or the Applicant does not provide a bank guarantee as provided for above) the Applicant will immediately take all reasonable steps to inform in writing anyone to whom he has given notice of this order, or who he has reasonable grounds for supposing may act upon this order, that it has ceased to have effect.

[(9) The Applicant will not without the permission of the court use any information obtained as a result of this order for the purpose of any civil or criminal proceedings, either in England and Wales or in any other jurisdiction, other than this claim.]

[(10) The Applicant will not without the permission of the court seek to enforce this order in any country outside England and Wales [or seek an order of a similar nature including orders conferring a charge or other security against the Respondent or the Respondent's assets].]

Name and Address of Applicant's Legal Representatives

The Applicant's legal representatives are—

[Name, address, reference, fax and telephone numbers both in and out of office hours and e-mail]

SEARCH ORDER

IN THE HIGH COURT OF JUSTICE
QUEEN'S BENCH DIVISION
COMMERCIAL COURT

Before The Honourable Mr Justice [   ]

Claim No.

BETWEEN

Claimant(s)

–and–

Defendant(s)

Applicant(s)

Respondent(s)

PENAL NOTICE

If you [   ]² disobey this order you may be held to be in contempt of court and may be imprisoned, fined or have your assets seized.

Any other person who knows of this Order and does anything which helps or permits the Respondent to breach the terms of this Order may also be held to be in contempt of court and may be imprisoned, fined or have their assets seized.

THIS ORDER

1.   This is a Search Order made against [   ] ("the Respondent") on [   ] by Mr Justice [   ] on the application of [   ] ("the Applicant"). The Judge read the Affidavits listed in Schedule F and accepted the undertakings set out in Schedules C, D and E at the end of this order.

2.   This order was made at a hearing without notice to the Respondent. The Respondent has a right to apply to the court to vary or discharge the order—see paragraph 27 below.

3.   There will be a further hearing in respect of this order on [   ] ("the return date").

---

² Insert name of Respondent.

4. If there is more than one Respondent—

    (a) unless otherwise stated, references in this order to "the Respondent" mean both or all of them; and

    (b) this order is effective against any Respondent on whom it is served or who is given notice of it.

5. This order must be complied with by—

    (a) the Respondent;

    (b) any director, officer, partner or responsible employee of the Respondent; and

    (c) if the Respondent is an individual, any other person having responsible control of the premises to be searched.

The Search

6. **The Respondent must permit the following persons[3]—**

    (a) [   ] ("the Supervising Solicitor);

    (b) [   ], a solicitor in the firm of [   ], the Applicant's solicitors; and

    (c) up to [   ] other persons[4] being [*their identity or capacity*] accompanying them,

    (together "the search party"), to enter the premises mentioned in Schedule A to this order and any other premises of the Respondent disclosed under paragraph 18 below and any vehicles under the Respondent's control on or around the premises ("the premises") so that they can search for, inspect, photograph or photocopy, and deliver into the safekeeping of the Applicant's solicitors all the documents and articles which are listed in Schedule B to this order ("the listed items").

7. Having permitted the search party to enter the premises, the Respondent must allow the search party to remain on the premises until the search is complete. In the event that it becomes necessary for any of those persons to leave the premises before the search is complete, the Respondent must allow them to re-enter the premises immediately upon their seeking re-entry on the same or the following day in order to complete the search.

---

[3] Where the premises are likely to be occupied by an unaccompanied woman and the Supervising Solicitor is a man, at least one of the persons accompanying him should be a woman.

[4] None of these persons should be people who could gain personally or commercially from anything they might read or see on the premises, unless their presence is essential.

Restrictions on Search

8.   This order may not be carried out at the same time as a police search warrant.

9.   Before the Respondent allows anybody onto the premises to carry out this order, he is entitled to have the Supervising Solicitor explain to him what it means in everyday language.

10. The Respondent is entitled to seek legal advice and to ask the court to vary or discharge this order. Whilst doing so, he may ask the Supervising Solicitor to delay starting the search for up to 2 hours or such other longer period as the Supervising Solicitor may permit. However, the Respondent must—

   (a) comply with the terms of paragraph 27 below;

   (b) not disturb or remove any listed items; and

   (c) permit the Supervising Solicitor to enter, but not start to search.

11. Before permitting entry to the premises by any person other than the Supervising Solicitor, the Respondent may, for a short time (not to exceed two hours, unless the Supervising Solicitor agrees to a longer period), gather together any documents he believes may be [incriminating or][5] privileged and hand them to the Supervising Solicitor for him to assess whether they are [incriminating or] privileged as claimed. If the Supervising Solicitor decides that any of the documents may be [incriminating or] privileged or is in any doubt as to their status, he will exclude them from the search and retain them in his possession pending further order of the court.

12. If the Respondent wishes to take legal advice and gather documents as permitted, he must first inform the Supervising Solicitor and keep him informed of the steps being taken.

13. No item may be removed from the premises until a list of the items to be removed has been prepared, and a copy of the list has been supplied to the Respondent, and he has been given a reasonable opportunity to check the list.

14. The premises must not be searched, and items must not be removed from them, except in the presence of the Respondent.

15. If the Supervising Solicitor is satisfied that full compliance with paragraphs 13 or 14 is not practicable, he may permit the search to proceed and items to be removed without fully complying with them.

---

[5] References to incriminating documents should be omitted from orders made in intellectual property proceedings, where the privilege against self-incrimination does not apply—see paragraph 8.4 of the practice direction.

Delivery up of Articles/Documents

16. The Respondent must immediately hand over to the Applicant's solicitors any of the listed items, which are in his possession or under his control, save for any computer or hard disk integral to any computer. Any items the subject of a dispute as to whether they are listed items must immediately be handed over to the Supervising Solicitor for safekeeping pending resolution of the dispute or further order of the court.

17. The Respondent must immediately give the search party effective access to the computers on the premises, with all necessary passwords, to enable the computers to be searched. If they contain any listed items the Respondent must cause the listed items to be displayed so that they can be read and copied.[6] The Respondent must provide the Applicant's Solicitors with copies of all listed items contained in the computers. All reasonable steps shall be taken by the Applicant and the Applicant's solicitors to ensure that no damage is done to any computer or data. The Applicant and his representatives may not themselves search the Respondent's computers unless they have sufficient expertise to do so without damaging the Respondent's system.

PROVISION OF INFORMATION

18. The Respondent must immediately inform the Applicant's Solicitors (in the presence of the Supervising Solicitor) so far as he is aware—

    (a) where all the listed items are;

    (b) the name and address of everyone who has supplied him, or offered to supply him, with listed items;

    (c) the name and address of everyone to whom he has supplied, or offered to supply, listed items; and

    (d) full details of the dates and quantities of every such supply and offer.

19. Within [   ] working days after being served with this order the Respondent must swear and serve an affidavit setting out the above information.[7]

---

[6] If it is envisaged that the Respondent's computers are to be imaged (i.e. the hard drives are to be copied wholesale, thereby reproducing listed items and other items indiscriminately), special provision needs to be made and independent computer specialists need to be appointed, who should be required to give undertakings to the court.

[7] The period should ordinarily be longer than the period in paragraph (2) of Schedule D, if any of the information is likely to be included in listed items taken away of which the Respondent does not have copies.

Prohibited Acts

20. Except for the purpose of obtaining legal advice, the Respondent must not directly or indirectly inform anyone of these proceedings or of the contents of this order, or warn anyone that proceedings have been or may be brought against him by the Applicant until 4.30 p.m. on the return date or further order of the court.

21. Until 4.30 p.m. on the return date the Respondent must not destroy, tamper with, cancel or part with possession, power, custody or control of the listed items otherwise than in accordance with the terms of this order.

22. [Insert any negative injunctions.]

23. [Insert any further order]

Costs

24. The costs of this application are reserved to the judge hearing the application on the return date.

Restrictions on Service

25. This order may only be served between [   ] a.m./p.m. and [   ] a.m./p.m. [and on a weekday].[8]

26. This order must be served by the Supervising Solicitor, and paragraph 6 of the order must be carried out in his presence and under his supervision.

Variation and Discharge of this Order

27. Anyone served with or notified of this order may apply to the court at any time to vary or discharge this order (or so much of it as affects that person), but they must first inform the Applicant's solicitors. If any evidence is to be relied upon in support of the application, the substance of it must be communicated in writing to the Applicant's solicitors in advance.

Interpretation of this Order

28. Any requirement that something shall be done to or in the presence of the Respondent means—

   (a) if there is more than one Respondent, to or in the presence of any one of them; and

---

[8] Normally, the order should be served in the morning (not before 9.30 a.m.) and on a weekday to enable the Respondent more readily to obtain legal advice.

(b)   if a Respondent is not an individual, to or in the presence of a director, officer, partner or responsible employee.

29.   A Respondent who is an individual who is ordered not to do something must not do it himself or in any other way. He must not do it through others acting on his behalf or on his instructions or with his encouragement.

30.   A Respondent which is not an individual which is ordered not to do something must not do it itself or by its directors, officers, partners, employees or agents or in any other way.

Communications with the Court

All communications to the court about this order should be sent to Room EB09, Royal Courts of Justice, Strand, London WC2A 2LL quoting the case number. The telephone number is 020 7947 6826.

The offices are open between 10 a.m. and 4.30 p.m. Monday to Friday.

Schedule A

The Premises

Schedule B

The Listed Items

Schedule C

Undertakings given to the Court by the Applicant

(1)   If the court later finds that this order or carrying it out has caused loss to the Respondent, and decides that the Respondent should be compensated for that loss, the Applicant will comply with any order the court may make. Further if the carrying out of this order has been in breach of the terms of this order or otherwise in a manner inconsistent with the Applicant's solicitors' duties as officers of the court, the Applicant will comply with any order for damages the court may make.

[(2)   As soon as practicable the Applicant will issue a claim form [in the form of the draft produced to the court] [claiming the appropriate relief].]

(3)   The Applicant will [swear and file an affidavit] [cause an affidavit to be sworn and filed] [substantially in the terms of the draft affidavit produced to the court] [confirming the substance of what was said to the court by the Applicant's counsel/solicitors].

(4)   The Applicant will not, without the permission of the court use any information or documents obtained as a result of carrying out this

order nor inform anyone else of these proceedings except for the purposes of these proceedings (including adding further Respondents) or commencing civil proceedings in relation to the same or related subject matter to these proceedings until after the return date.

[(5)   The Applicant will maintain pending further order the sum of £[   ] in an account controlled by the Applicant's solicitors.]

[(6)   The applicant will insure the items removed from the premises.]

Schedule D

Undertakings given by the Applicant's Solicitors

(1)   The Applicant's solicitors will provide to the Supervising Solicitor for service on the Respondent—

   (i)   a service copy of this order;

   (ii)   the claim form (with defendant's response pack) or, if not issued, the draft produced to the court;

   (iii)   an application for hearing on the return date;

   (iv)   copies of the affidavits *[or draft affidavits]* and exhibits capable of being copied containing the evidence relied upon by the applicant;

   (v)   a note of any allegation of fact made orally to the court where such allegation is not contained in the affidavits or draft affidavits read by the judge; and

   (vi)   a copy of the skeleton argument produced to the court by the Applicant's [counsel/solicitors].

(2)   The Applicants' solicitors will answer at once to the best of their ability any question whether a particular item is a listed item.

(3)   Subject as provided below the Applicant's solicitors will retain in their own safe keeping all items obtained as a result of this order until the court directs otherwise.

(4)   The Applicant's solicitors will return the originals of all documents obtained as a result of this order (except original documents which belong to the Applicant) as soon as possible and in any event within [two] working days of their removal.

Schedule E

Undertakings given by the Supervising Solicitor

(1)   The Supervising Solicitor will use his best endeavours to serve this order upon the Respondent and at the same time to serve upon the Respondent the other documents required to be served and referred to in paragraph (1) of Schedule D.

(2) The Supervising Solicitor will offer to explain to the person served with the order its meaning and effect fairly and in everyday language, and to inform him of his right to take legal advice (such advice to include an explanation that the Respondent may be entitled to avail himself of [the privilege against self-incrimination or] [legal professional privilege]) and to apply to vary or discharge this order as mentioned in paragraph 27 above.

(3) The Supervising Solicitor will retain in the safe keeping of his firm all items retained by him as a result of this order until the court directs otherwise.

(4) Within [48] hours of completion of the search the Supervising Solicitor will make and provide to the Applicant's solicitors, the Respondent or his solicitors and to the judge who made this order (for the purposes of the court file) a written report on the carrying out of the order.

Schedule F

Affidavits

The Applicant relied on the following affidavits—

      [name]   [number of affidavit]   [date sworn]
[filed on behalf of]

(1)
(2)

Name and Address of Applicant's Solicitors

The Applicant's solicitors are—
[Name, address, reference, fax and telephone numbers both in and out of office hours.]

List of documents:
standard disclosure

Notes:
- The rules relating to standard disclosure are contained in Part 31 of the Civil Procedure Rules and Section E of the Commercial Court Guide.
- Documents to be included under standard disclosure are contained in Rule 31.6
- A document has or will have been in your control if you have or have had possession, or a right of possession, of it **or** a right to inspect or take copies of it.

In the High Court of Justice Queen's Bench Division Commercial Court Royal Courts of Justice		C.14
Claim No.		
Claimant(s) (including ref)		
Defendant(s) (including ref)		
Date		
Party returning this form		

Disclosure Statement of (Claimant)(Defendant)

1. (I/We), (name(s)) state that (I/we) have carried out a reasonable search to locate all the documents which

   (I am *or* [   ] *here name the party* is)

   required to disclose under (the order made by the court *or* the agreement in writing made between the

   parties on) *(insert date)* [   ]

2. The extent of the search that (I/we) made to locate documents that

   (I am *or* [   ] *here name the party* is)

   required to disclose was as follows:

3. (I/We) limited the search in the following respects:-

☐ I did not search for documents:-

    ☐ pre-dating [   ]

    ☐ located elsewhere than

    [   ]

    ☐ in categories other than

    [   ]

    ☐ for electronic documents

☐ I carried out a search for electronic documents contained on or created by the following:
(list what was searched and extent of search)

[   ]

☐ I did not search for the following:-

    ☐ documents created before [   ]

    documents contained on or created by the ☐ Claimant   ☐ Defendant

☐ PCs	☐ portable data storage media
☐ databases	☐ servers
☐ back-up tapes	☐ off-site storage
☐ mobile phones	☐ laptops
☐ notebooks	☐ handheld devices
☐ PDA devices	

    documents contained on or created by the ☐ Claimant   ☐ Defendant

☐ mail files	☐ document files
☐ calendar files	☐ web-based applications
☐ spreadsheet files	☐ graphic and presentation files

    documents other than by reference to the following keyword(s)/concepts
(delete if your search was not confined to specific keywords or concepts)

[   ]

4. The facts considered in arriving at the decision that it was reasonable to limit the search in the respects identified above were as follows
(the facts must be set out in detail: see paragraph E3.6 of the Commercial Court Guide):

5. (I/We) certify that (I/we) understand the duty of disclosure and to the best of (my/our) knowledge (I have *or* _____ *here name the party* has) carried out that duty. (I/We) further certify that the list above is a complete list of all documents which are or have been in (my *or* _____ *here name the* party's) control which (I am *or here name the party* is) obliged under (the said order *or* the said agreement in writing) to disclose.

6. (I *or* _____ *here name the party*) understand(s) that (I *or* _____ *here name the party*) must inform the court and the other parties immediately if any further documents required to be disclosed by Rule 31.6 comes into (my *or* _____ *here name the party's*) control at any time before the conclusion of the case.

7. ((I *or* _____ *here name the party*) (have/has) not permitted inspection of documents within the category or class of documents (as set out below) required to be disclosed under Rule 31(6)(b) or (c) on the grounds that to do so would be disproportionate to the issues in the case.

Signed _____ **Date** _____

Name(s) _____

Position or office held _____

Please state why you are the appropriate person(s) to make the disclosure statement.

A. (I)(The claimant)(The defendant) (have/has) control of the documents numbered and listed here. (I)(the claimant)(the defendant) (do not)(does not) object to you inspecting them/producing copies.

List and number here, in a convenient order, the documents (or bundles of documents if of the same nature, e.g. invoices) in your/the claimant's/the defendant's control, which you/the claimant/ the defendant do/does not object to being inspected. Give a short description of each document or bundle so that it can be identified, and say if it is kept elsewhere i.e. with a bank or solicitor

B. (I)(The claimant)(The defendant) (have)(has) control of the documents numbered and listed here, but (I)(the claimant)(the defendant) (object)(objects) to you inspecting them:

List and number here, as above, the documents in the claimant's/the defendant's control which the claimant/the defendant objects to being inspected. (Rule 31.19)

Say what the claimant's/the defendant's objections are

(I)(The claimant)(The defendant) (object)(objects) to you inspecting these documents because:

C. (I)(The claimant)(The defendant) (have)(had) the documents numbered and listed below, but they are no longer in (my)(the claimant's)(the defendant's) control.

List and number here, the documents the claimant/the defendant once had in his/her/its control, but which the claimant/the defendant no longer has. For each document listed, say when it was last in the claimant's/the defendant's control and where it is now.

Patents Court

Standard form of order for directions

(*indicates a provision which may be necessary when a rule has not been complied with, for example, standard disclosure in accordance with the Practice Direction supplementing CPR Part 63.)   **C.15**

[Recitals as necessary]

Transfer

1. [This Action and Counterclaim be transferred to the Patents County Court.] (If this order is made, no other Order will generally be necessary, though it will generally be desirable for procedural orders to be made at this time to save the costs of a further conference in the County Court.)

Proof of Documents

2. Legible copies of the specification of the Patent in suit [and any patent specifications or other documents cited in the Particulars of Objections] may be used at the trial without further proof thereof or of their contents.

Amendments to Pleadings

3. The Claimants have leave to amend their Claim Form shown in red on the copy [annexed to the Application Notice/as signed by the solicitors for the parties/ annexed hereto] and [to re-serve the same on or before [date]/and that re-service be dispensed with] and that the Defendants have leave to serve a consequentially amended Defence within [number] days [thereafter/hereafter] and that the Claimants have leave to serve a consequentially amended Reply (if so advised) within [number] days thereafter.

4.(a) The Defendants have leave to amend their Defence [and Part 20 Claim and Grounds of Invalidity] as shown in red on the copy [annexed to the Application notice/as signed by the solicitors for the parties/annexed hereto] and [to reserve the same within [number] days/on or before [date]] [and that re-service be dispensed with] and that the Claimants have leave to serve a consequentially amended Reply (if so advised) within [number] days thereafter.

(b) The Claimants do on or before [date] elect whether they will discontinue this Claim and withdraw their Defence to Part 20 Claim and consent to an Order for the revocation of Patent No. ..... ("the patent in suit") AND IF the Claimants shall so elect and give notice thereof in the time aforesaid IT IS ORDERED THAT the patent in suit be revoked [and that it be referred to the Costs Judge to assess the costs of the Defendants and this Action and Grounds of Invalidity up to and including [date] being the date of service of the [amended] Grounds of Invalidity and Part 20 Claim to the date of this Order [except so far as the same have been increased by the failure of the Defendants originally to deliver the Defence and Grounds of Invalidity in its amended form], and to assess the costs of the Claimants in this Action and Part 20 Claim from [date] [insofar as they have been increased by the failure of the Defendants aforesaid] AND IT IS ORDERED that the said Costs Judge is set off the costs of the Defendants and of the Claimants when so assessed as aforesaid and to certify to which of them the balance after such set-off is due.][Order for payment of sums determined by the Court on a summary assessment].

797

Further Information and Clarification

5. (a) The [Claimants/Defendants] do on or before [date] serve on the [Defendants/Claimants] the Further Information or Clarification of the [specify Statement of case] as requested by the [Claimants/Defendants] by their Request served on the [Defendants/Claimants] on [date] [and/or]

(b) The [Claimants/Defendants] do on or before [date] serve on the [Defendants/Claimants] a response to their Request for Further Information or Clarification of the [identify statement of case] served on the [Defendants/Claimants] on [date].

Admissions*

6. The [Claimants/Defendants] do on or before [date] state in writing whether or not they admit the facts specified in the [Defendants'/Claimants'] Notice to Admit facts dated [date].

Security

7. The Claimants do provide security for the Defendants' costs in the sum of £ [state sum] by [specify manner in which security to be given] and that in the meantime all further proceedings be stayed.

Lists of Documents*

8. (a) The Claimants and the Defendants respectively do on or before [state date] make and serve on the other of them a list in accordance with form N265 of the documents in their control which they are required to disclose in accordance with the obligation of standard disclosure in accordance with CPR Part 31 as modified by paragraph 5 of the Practice Direction—Patents etc. supplementing CPR Part 63.

(b) In respect of those issues identified in Schedule [number] hereto disclosure shall be limited to those [documents/categories of documents] listed in Schedule [number].

Inspection*

9. If any party wishes to inspect or have copies of such documents as are in another party's control it shall give notice in writing that it wishes to do so and such inspection shall be allowed at all reasonable times upon reasonable notice and any copies shall be provided within [number] working days of the request upon the undertaking of the party requesting the copies to pay the reasonable copying charges.

Experiments*

10. (a) Where a party desires to establish any fact by experimental proof, including an experiment conducted for the purposes of litigation or otherwise not being an experiment conducted in the normal course of research, that party shall on or before [date] serve on all the other parties a notice stating the facts which it desires to establish and giving full particulars of the experiments proposed to establish them.

(b) A party upon whom a notice is served under the preceding sub-paragraph shall within [number] days, serve on the party serving the notice a notice stating in respect of each fact whether or not that party admits it.

(c) Where any fact which a party wishes to establish by experimental proof is not admitted that party shall apply to the Court for further directions in respect of such experiments.

[Or where paragraph 9 of the Practice Direction—Patents etc. supplementing CPR Part 63 has been complied with.]

11. (a) The Claimants/Defendants are to afford to the other parties an opportunity, if so requested, of inspecting a repetition of the experiments identified in paragraphs [specify them] of the Notice[s] of Experiments served on [date]. Any such inspection must be requested within [number] days of the date of this Order and shall take place within [number] days of the date of the request.

(b) If any party shall wish to establish any fact in reply to experimental proof that party shall on or before [date] serve on all the other parties a notice stating the facts which it desires to establish and giving full particulars of the experiments proposed to establish them.

(c) A party upon whom a notice is served under the preceding sub-paragraph shall within [number] days serve on the party serving the notice a notice stating in respect of each fact whether or not that party admits it.

(d) Where any fact which a party wishes to establish by experimental proof in reply is not admitted the party may apply to the Court for further directions in respect of such experiments.

Notice of Models, etc.

12. (a) If any party wishes to rely at the trial of this action upon any model, apparatus, drawing, photograph, cinematograph or video film whether or not the same is contained in a witness statement, affidavit or expert's report that party shall on or before [date] give notice thereof to all the other parties; shall afford the other parties an opportunity within [number] days of the service of such notice of inspecting the same and shall, if so requested, furnish the other party with copies of any such drawing or photograph and a sufficient drawing photograph or other illustration of any model or apparatus.

(b) If any party wishes to rely upon any such materials in reply to any matter of which notice was given under sub-paragraph (a) of this paragraph, that party shall within [number] days after the last inspection to be made in pursuance of the said sub-paragraph (a) give to the other parties a like notice, and if so requested within [number] days of delivery of such notice shall afford like opportunities of inspection which shall take place within [number] days of such request; and shall in like manner furnish copies of any drawing or photograph and illustration of any such model or apparatus.

(c) No further or other model apparatus drawing photograph cinematograph or video film shall be relied upon in evidence by either party save with consent or by leave of the Court.

Written Evidence

13. (a) Each party may call up to [number] expert witnesses in this Action and Part 20 Claim provided that the said party:

(i) supplies the name of such expert to the other parties and to the Court on or before [date]; and

(ii) no later than [date/[number days] before the date set for the hearing of this Action and Part 20 Claim] serve upon the other parties a report of each such expert comprising the evidence which that expert intends to give at trial.

(b) Each party shall on or before [date] serve on the other parties [signed] written statements of the oral evidence which the party intends to lead on any issues of fact to be decided at the trial, such statements to stand as the evidence in chief of the witness unless the Court otherwise directs;

(c) The parties shall [here insert the particular directions sought, e.g. within 21 days after service of the other party's expert reports and written statements state in writing the facts and matters in those reports and statements which are admitted].

Admissibility of Evidence

14. A party who objects to any statements of any witness being read by the Judge prior to the hearing of the trial, shall serve upon each other party a notice in writing to that effect setting out the grounds of the objection.

Non-Compliance

15. Where either party fails to comply with the directions relating to experiments and written evidence it shall not be entitled to adduce evidence to which such directions relate without the leave of the Court.

Trial Bundles

16. Each party shall no later than [number] days before the date fixed for the trial of this Action and Counterclaim serve upon the parties a list of all the documents to be included in the trial bundles. The Claimants shall no later than [number] days before the date fixed for trial serve upon the Defendants ...... sets of the bundles for use at trial.

Trial

17. The trial of these proceedings shall be before an Assigned Judge alone in [London], estimated length [number] days and a pre-reading estimate for the Judge of [number] days.

Liberty to Apply

18. The parties are to be at liberty on two days' notice to apply for further directions and generally.

Costs

19. The costs of this Application are to be costs in the Action and Part 20 Claim.

Technology and Construction Court

Case Management Directions Form

Action no   HT–.............   C.16

Delete or amend the following directions, as appropriate to the circumstances of the case.

1. Trial date .... For the purposes of payment of the trial fee, but for no other purposes, this date is provisional. This date will cease to be provisional and the trial fee will become payable on .... [usually be 2 months before the trial date].

2. Estimated length of trial ....

3. Directions, if appropriate, (a) for the trial of any preliminary issues or (b) for the trial to be divided into stages ....

4. This action is to be [consolidated] [managed and tried with] action no .... The lead action shall be .... All directions given in the lead action shall apply to both actions, unless otherwise stated.

5. Further statements of case shall be filed and served as follows:

- Defence and any counterclaim by 4 p.m. on ....
- Reply (if any) and defence to counterclaim (if any) by 4 p.m. on ....

6. Permission to make the following amendments ....

7. Disclosure of documents by 5 p.m. on .... [Standard disclosure dispensed with/limited/varied as follows ....]. Specific directions in respect of electronic disclosure ....

8. There shall be a Scott Schedule in respect of defects/items of damage/other ....

- The column headings shall be as follows ....
- Claimant/defendant to serve Scott Schedule by 5 p.m. on ....
- Defendant/claimant to respond to Scott Schedule by 5 p.m. on ....

9. Signed statements of witnesses of fact to be served by 5 p.m. on .... [Supplementary statements of witnesses of fact to be served by 5 p.m. on ....]

10. The parties have permission to call the following expert witnesses in respect of the following issues:

- ....
- ....
- ....

11. In respect of any expert evidence permitted under paragraph 10:

- Directions for carrying out inspections/taking samples/conducting experiments/performance of calculations shall be ....
- Experts in like fields to hold discussions in accordance with rule 35.12 by ....
- Experts' statements rule 35.12(3) to be prepared and filed by 5 p.m. on...
- Experts' reports to be served by 5 p.m. on ...

12. A single joint expert shall be appointed by the parties to report on the following issue(s) .... The following directions shall govern the appointment of the single joint expert:

- ....
- ....

13. The following documents shall be provided to the court electronically or in computer readable form, as well as in hard copy ....

14. A review case management conference shall be held on .... at .... a.m./p.m. Time allowed.................

15. The pre-trial review shall be held on .... at .... a.m./p.m. Time allowed ....

16. The above dates and time limits may be extended by agreement between the parties. Nevertheless:

- The dates and time limits specified in paragraphs .... may not be extended by more than .... days without the permission of the court.
- The dates specified in paragraph 1 (trial) and paragraph 15 (pre-trail review) cannot be varied without the permission of the court.

16. Liberty to restore.

17. Costs in the case.

18. Claimant's solicitors to draw up this order by .... [Delete if order is to be drawn up by the court.]

INDEX

LEGAL TAXONOMY
FROM SWEET & MAXWELL

This index has been prepared using Sweet and Maxwell's Legal Taxonomy. Main index entries conform to keywords provided by the Legal Taxonomy except where references to specific documents or non-standard terms (denoted by quotation marks) have been included. These keywords provide a means of identifying similar concepts in other Sweet & Maxwell publications and online services to which keywords from the Legal Taxonomy have been applied. Readers may find some minor differences between terms used in the text and those which appear in the index. Suggestions to *taxonomy@sweetandmaxwell.co.uk*.

(All references are to paragraph number)